GOVERNMENT ASSISTANCE ALMANAC
★2009★

GOVERNMENT ASSISTANCE ALMANAC
★2009★

The Guide to Federal Domestic Financial and Other Programs

Covering Grants, Loans, Insurance, Personal Payments and Benefits, Subsidies, Fellowships, Scholarships, Traineeships, Technical Information, Advisory Services, Investigation of Complaints, Sales and Donations of Federal Property — with Funding Summaries, over 4,000 Program Headquarters and Field Office Addresses and Phone Numbers, an Agency Index, and a Comprehensive Master Index

★21st EDITION★

Omnigraphics

PO Box 31-1640, Detroit, MI 48231
Phone (800) 234-1340 • Fax (800) 875-1340 • www.omnigraphics.com

GOVERNMENT ASSISTANCE ALMANAC 2009:
The Guide to Federal Domestic Financial and Other Programs Covering Grants, Loans, Insurance, Personal Payments and Benefits, Subsidies,Fellowships, Scholarships, Traineeships, Technical Information, Advisory Services, Investigation of Complaints, Sales and Donations of Federal Property — with Funding Summaries, Over 4,000 Program Headquarters and Field Office Addresses and Phone Numbers, and a Comprehensive Master Index

Co-published by:

Omnigraphics, Inc.
PO Box 31-1640
Detroit, Michigan 48231-1640

Co-published by:

Foggy Bottom Publications
P.O. Box N-7776
Nassau, Bahamas

Printed in the United States of America

The Library of Congress has assigned the following International Standard Serial Number:

ISSN 0883-8690

International Standard Book Number:

ISBN 978-0-7808-0702-0

CONTENTS

DISCLAIMER/INVITATION

We have attempted to compile and present the information in this book accurately and in the most helpful form possible. The information is intended to provide basic guidance concerning programs and benefits available from the federal agencies cited.

Federal program policies, regulations, funding levels, addresses, and phone numbers tend to change. There could be unintentional errors in the information, caused by changes in government programs or organization, inaccuracies in the source material, omissions, or typographical or other inadvertent mistakes. A great deal of care was taken to avoid such errors.

The information in this publication was compiled from the sources cited and from other sources considered reliable. While every possible effort has been made to ensure reliability, the publisher and the editor will not assume liability for damages caused by inaccuracies in the data, and make no warranty, express or implied, on the accuracy of the information contained herein.

Users of *GOVERNMENT ASSISTANCE ALMANAC* are invited to send their observations about the book, its form, and their experience in referring to the information, to the editor at the address below. Suggestions for improvements in any aspect of the book will be especially appreciated.

Editor
GOVERNMENT ASSISTANCE ALMANAC
c/o Omnigraphics, Inc
P.O. Box 31-1640
Detroit, MI 48231-1640

Abbreviations Used in This Book

ACF	Administration for Children and Families (HHS)
ADA	Americans with Disabilities Act
ADAA	Anti-Drug Abuse Act of 1988
AFDC	Aid to Families with Dependent Children
AIDS	acquired immunodeficiency syndrome
AMS	Agricultural Marketing Service (USDA)
AOA	Administration on Aging (HHS)
ARDA	Appalachian Regional Development Act of 1965
ARDRA	Appalachian Regional Development Reform Act of 1998
ARS	Agricultural Research Service (USDA)
ATEDPA	Anti-Terrorism and Effective Death Penalty Act of 1996
ATELS	Apprenticeship, Training, Employer and Labor Service (DOL)
ATF	Bureau of Alcohol, Tobacco and Firearms (DOJ)
AREERA	Agricultural Research, Extension, and Education Reform Act of 1998
BAT	Bureau of Apprenticeship and Training (DOL) *(Note: BAT functions now are in OATELS)*
BEA	Bureau of Export Administration (USDC) *(Note: BEA is now Bureau of Industry and Security*
BECA	Bureau of Educational and Cultural Affairs (Department of State)
BIA	Bureau of Indian Affairs (DOI)
BJA	Bureau of Justice Assistance (DOJ)
BLM	Bureau of Land Management (DOI)
BLS	Bureau of Labor Statistics (DOI)
BPRM	Bureau of Population, Refugees, and Migration (Department of State)
C of C	chamber of commerce
CAA	Clean Air Act
CARE	Comprehensive AIDS Resources Emergency
CBRNE	chemical, biological, radiological, nuclear, and explosive (devices)
CCC	Commodity Credit Corporation (USDA)
CDAPCA	Comprehensive Drug Abuse Prevention and Control Act of 1970
CDBG	Community Development Block Grant
CDCP	Centers for Disease Control and Prevention (HHS)
CDCU	Community Development Credit Union

CDPVTEA	Carl D. Perkins Vocational and Technical Education Act of 1998
CEPP	Chemical Emergency Preparedness and Prevention
CERCLA	Comprehensive Environmental Response, Compensation and Liability Act ("Superfund")
CERT	Council of Energy Resource Tribes
CFDA	Catalog of Federal Domestic Assistance
CFRDA	Consolidated Farm and Rural Development Act
CJAA	Children's Justice and Assistance Act of 1986
CMHS	Center for Mental Health Services (SAMHSA-DHS)
CMS	Centers for Medicare and Medicaid Services (HHS) *(formerly, HCFA)*
CNCS	Corporation for National and Community Service
COATES	Community Opportunities, Accountability, Training, and Educational Services Act of 1998
CODIS	Combined DNA Index System
COPS	Community Oriented Policing Services
CPD	Community Planning and Development (HUD)
CRA	Civil Rights Act of 1964
CRIPA	Civil Rights of Institutionalized Persons Act
CRP	Conservation Reserve Program
CRS	Community Relations Service (DOJ)
CSAP	Center for Substance Abuse Prevention (SAHMSA-HHS)
CSAT	Center for Substance Abuse Treatment (SAHMSA HHS)
CSBG	Community Services Block Grant
CSREES	Cooperative State Research, Education and Extension Service (USDA)
CWA	Clean Water Act
DC	District of Columbia
DEA	Drug Enforcement Administration (DOJ)
DHS	Department of Homeland Security
DIC	dependency and indemnity compensation
DOD	Department of Defense
DOE	Department of Energy
DOED	Department of Education
DOI	Department of the Interior
DOJ	Department of Justice
DOL	Department of Labor
DOT	Department of Transportation

DVA	Department of Veterans Affairs
EBS	Emergency Broadcast System
EBSA	Employee Benefits Security Administration (DOL)
ECOA	Equal Credit Opportunity Act
EDA	Economic Development Administration (USDC)
EEOC	Equal Employment Opportunity Commission
EFN	exceptional financial need
EHS	environmental health center
EIS	environmental impact statement
ELOA	Early Learning Opportunities Act of 2001
EMI	Emergency Management Institute (FEMA-DHS)
EMS	emergency medical services
EOC	emergency operating center
EPA	Environmental Protection Agency
ERDDIA	Educational Research, Development, Dissemination, and Improvement Act of 1994
ESA	Economics and Statistics Administration (USDA)
ESEA	Elementary and Secondary Education Act of 1965
ESL	English as a second language
EST	estimate
ETA	Employment and Training Administration (DOL)
FAA	Federal Aviation Administration (DOT)
FACE	Freedom of Access to Clinic Entrances Act
FACTA	Food, Agriculture, Conservation, and Trade Act of 1990
FAIRA	Federal Agriculture Improvement and Reform Act of 1996
FAS	Foreign Agricultural Service (USDA)
FCA	Flood Control Act
FCC	Federal Communications Commission
FCIC	Federal Crop Insurance Corporation (USDA)
FDA	Food and Drug Administration (HHS)
FEMA	Federal Emergency Management Agency (DHS)
FFB	Federal Financing Bank
FFP	federal financial participation
FHA	Federal Housing Administration (HUD)
FHAP	Fair Housing Assistance Program
FHIP	Fair Housing Initiatives Program
FHWA	Federal Highway Administration (DOT)
FIFRA	Federal Insecticide, Fungicide, and Rodenticide Act
FIP	Forestry Incentives Program
FLAS	foreign language and area studies
FMCS	Federal Mediation and Conciliation Service

FMCSA	Federal Motor Carrier Safety Administration (DOT)
FmHA	Farmers Home Administration (USDA) *(Note: FmHA functions now are within FSA and RHS)*
FNS	Food and Nutrition Service (USDA)
FRA	Fund for Rural America
FS	Forest Service (USDA)
FSRIA	Farm Security and Rural Investment Act of 2002
FSA	Farm Service Agency (USDA)
FTA	Federal Transit Administration (DOT)
FTC	Federal Trade Commission
FTZ	foreign trade zone
FY	Fiscal Year *(Federal fiscal year: October 1 through September 30)*
FWS	U.S. Fish and Wildlife Service (DOI)
GAA	Government Assistance Almanac
GPO	U.S. Government Printing Office
GSA	General Services Administration
HBCU	Historically Black College and University
HCFA	Health Care Financing Administration (HHS) *(Note: HCFA functions now are within CMS)*
HEA	Higher Education Act of 1965
HEAL	Health Education Assistance Loan
HHS	Department of Health and Human Services
HIP	Housing Improvement Program (BIA)
HIV	human immunodeficiency virus
HMO	health maintenance organization
HOPE	Housing Opportunities for People Everywhere
HPEPA	Health Professions Education Partnership Act of 1998
HQ	headquarters
HRSA	Health Resources and Services Administration (HHS)
HSA	health system agency
HUD	Department of Housing and Urban Development
IBDC	Indian business development center
ICE	Immigration and Customs Enforcement (DHS) (*formerly,*) INS)
IDEA	Individuals with Disabilities Education Act
IHE	institution of higher education
IHS	Indian Health Service (DHS)
IMLS	Institute of Museum and Library Services
INS	Immigration and Naturalization Service (DHS) (*Now, ICE*)

IRS	Internal Revenue Service
ISDEAA	Indian Self-Determination and Education Assistance Act
ITA	International Trade Administration (USDC)
JJDPA	Juvenile Justice and Delinquency Prevention Act
JTPA	Job Training Partnership Act of 1982
LC	Library of Congress
LEA	local education agency
LSCA	Library Services and Construction Act
MARC	minority access to research careers
MB&IA	minority business and industry association
MBDA	Minority Business Development Agency (USDC)
MBDC	minority business development center
MBE	minority business enterprise
MECEA	Mutual Educational and Cultural Exchange Act of 1961
MFB	marine and freshwater biology
MIA	missing in action
MIP	mortgage insurance premium
MMA	Medicare Modernization Act (i.e. , Medicare Prescription Drug, Improvement and Modernization Act of 2003)
MMA	Merchant Marine Act
MPRSA	Marine Protection, Research, and Sanctuaries Act
MRA	Migration and Refugee Assistance Act of 1962
MSA	Metropolitan Statistical Area
MSLA	Museum and Library Services Act of 1996
MVHAA	McKinney-Vento Homeless Assistance Act
N.A.	not available, or not applicable
NAFSA	National Association of Foreign Student Advising Associations
NAHASDA	Native American Housing Assistance and Self-Determination Act of 1996
NARETPA	National Agricultural Research, Extension, and Teaching Policy Act of 1977
NASA	National Aeronautics and Space Administration
NASS	National Agricultural Statistics Service (USDA)
NBS	National Bureau of Standards (USDC) (*Note: as of 1988, NBS became NIST)*
NBSOA	National Bureau of Standards Organic Act
NCIC	National Crime Information Center
NCRR	National Center for Research Resources(HHS)
NCSA	National Community Service Act

NCSCI	National Center for Standards and Certification Information
NCUA	National Credit Union Administration
NEA	National Endowment for the Arts
NEH	National Endowment for the Humanities
NEIC	National Energy Information Center
NESDIS	National Environmental Satellite, Data, and Information Service
NFAHA	National Foundation on the Arts and Humanities Act of 1965
NFIP	National Flood Insurance Program
NHA	National Housing Act of 1934
NHSC	National Health Service Corps (HHS)
NIAAA	National Institute on Alcohol and Abuse and Alcoholism (HHS)
NIDA	National Institute on Drug Abuse (HHS)
NIEHS	National Institute of Environmental Health Sciences (HHS)
NIH	National Institutes of Health (HHS)
NIMH	National Institute of Mental Health (HHS)
NINDS	National Institute of Neurological Disorders and Stroke (HHS)
NIOSH	National Institute for Occupational Safety and Health (HHS)
NIS	New Independent States (of the former Soviet Union)
NIST	National Institute for Standards and Technology (USDC)
NLRB	National Labor Relations Board
NMFS	National Marine Fisheries Service (USDC)
NOAA	National Oceanic and Atmospheric Administration (USDC)
NOS	National Ocean Service (USDC)
NPS	National Park Service (DOI)
NRC	Nuclear Regulatory Commission
NRCS	Natural Resources Conservation Service (USDA)
NRSA	National Research Service Award
NSA	National Security Agency (DOD)
NSEP	National Security Education Program
NSF	National Science Foundation
NSFA	National Science Foundation Act of 1950
NSRDS	National Standard Reference Data System

NTIA	National Telecommunications and Information Administration (USDC)
NTIS	National Technical Information Service (USDC)
NWS	National Weather Service (NOAA-USDC)
OAA	Older Americans Act of 1965
OAR	Office of Air and Radiation (EPA)
OATELS	Office of Apprenticeship, Training, Employer and Labor Service (DOL)
OCCSSA	Omnibus Crime Control and Safe Streets Act
OCSE	Office of Child Support Enforcement
OEA	Office of Export Administration (USDC)
OECA	Office of Enforcement and Compliance Assurance (EPA)
OEERE	Office of Energy Efficiency and Renewable Energy (DOE)
OERI	Office of Educational Research and Improvement (DOED)
OESE	Office of Elementary and Secondary Education (DOED)
OFCCP	Office of Federal Contract Compliance Programs
OFHEO	Office of Fair Housing and Equal Opportunity (HUD)
OFSA	Office of Federal Student Aid (DOED)
OJJDP	Office of Juvenile Justice and Delinquency Prevention (DOJ)
OJP	Office of Justice Programs (DOJ)
OMB	Office of Management and Budget
OPDR	Office of Policy Development and Research (HUD)
OPE	Office of Postsecondary Education (DOED)
OPIC	Overseas Private Investment Corporation
OPM	Office of Personnel Management
OPPPTS	Office of Pollution Prevention, Pesticides, and Toxic Substances (EPA)
OS	Office of the Secretary
OSERS	Office of Special Education and Rehabilitative Services (DOED)
OSHA	Occupational Safety and Health Administration (DOL)
OSTI	Office of Scientific and Technical Information (USDC)
OSWER	Office of Solid Waste and Emergency Response (EPA)
OTAA	Office of Trade Adjustment Assistance
OVAE	Office of Vocational and Adult Education (DOED)
OW	Office of Water (EPA)
OWOW	Office of Wetlands, Oceans, and Watersheds (EPA)
PACA	Perishable Agricultural Commodities Act
PD&R	Office of Policy Development and Research (HUD)

PHPEPA	Public Health Professions Education Partnership Act of 1998
PHS	Public Health Service (HHS)
PHSA	Public Health Service Act
PIK	payment-in-kind
PL	Public Law
PR	Puerto Rico
PRM	Population, Refugees, and Migration *(Bureau of)* (Department of State)
PRNS	projects of regional and national significance
PRWORA	Personal Responsibility and Work Opportunity Reconciliation Act of 1996
PWBA	Pension and Welfare Benefits Administration (DOL) *(Note: PWBA is now EBSA)*
PWEDA	Public Works and Economic Development Act of 1965
R&D	research and development
RBCS	Rural Business-Cooperative Service (USDA)
RC&D	resource conservation and development
RCRA	Resource Conservation and Recovery Act
REA	Rural Electrification Act of 1936
REA	Rural Electrification Administration (USDA) *(Note: REA functions now are within RUS)*
REACH	Racial and Ethnic Approaches to Community Health
RHA	River and Harbor Act
RHS	Rural Housing Service (USDA)
RLUIPA	Religious Land Use and Institutionalized Persons Act
RMA	Research and Marketing Act of 1946
RMA	Risk Management Agency (USDA)
RSVP	Retired and Senior Volunteer Program
RUS	Rural Utilities Service (USDA)
SAMHSA	Substance Abuse and Mental Health Services Administration (HHS)
SARA	Superfund Amendments and Reauthorization Act
SBA	Small Business Administration
SBIC	Small Business Investment Center
SBIR	small business innovation research
SBIRPRA	Small Business Innovation Research Program Reauthorization Act of 1992
SBMHAA	Stewart B. McKinney Homeless Assistance Act of 1987
SBRDEA	Small Business Research and Development Enhancement Act of 1992

SCORE	Service Corps of Retired Executives (SBA)
SCS	Soil Conservation Service (USDA) *(Note: SCS functions now are within NRCS)*
SDWA	Safe Drinking Water Act
SEA	state education agency
SEOG	supplemental educational opportunity grant
SEPA	Science Education Partnership Award
SERCA	Special Emphasis Research Center Award
SESA	state employment security agency
SIG	shared instrumentation grant
SMSA	Standard Metropolitan Statistical Area
SPRANS	special projects of regional and national significance
SRM	Standard Reference Materials
SRO	single room occupancy
SSA	Social Security Act of 1935
SSA	Social Security Administration
SSBG	Social Services Block Grant
SSBIC	Specialized Small Business Investment Center
SSI	Supplemental Security Income
STORET	storage and retrieval
STTR	Small Business Technology Transfer
SWDA	Solid Waste Disposal Act
TANF	Temporary Assistance to Needy Families
TDD	telecommunications devices for the deaf
TDHE	Tribally-Designated Housing Authority
TERO	Tribal Employment Rights Office
TRIO	three—i.e. , not an abbreviation *(Per DOED, when the "TRIO" programs began in the Division of Student Services, Office of Postsecondary Education, three programs were established; the original nomenclature has remained.)*
TSA	Transportation Security Administration (DHS)
TSCA	Toxic Substances Control Act
TVA	Tennessee Valley Authority *(Note: TVA programs were deleted from the CFDA in 2001)*
USAID	United States Agency for International Development
USAPA	U.S.A. Patriot Act of 2001 (*officially,* Uniting and Strengthening America by Providing Appropriate Tools Required to Intercept and Obstruct Terrorism Act of 2001)
U.S.C.	United States Code

USCG	U.S. Coast Guard (DHS)
USDA	U.S. Department of Agriculture
USDC	U.S. Department of Commerce
USDOD	U.S. Department of Defense
USFS	U.S. Forest Service (USDA)
USGPO	U.S. Government Printing Office
USGS	U.S. Geological Survey (DOI)
USIA	U.S. Information Agency *(Note: USIA no longer exists; its functions now are in BECA)*
USIP	U.S. Institute of Peace
USIS	U.S. Information Service
VA	Veterans Administration *(Note: as of 1989, VA became DVA)*
VAWA	Violence Against Women Act of 2000
VCCLEA	Violent Crime Control and Law Enforcement Act
VI	Virgin Islands (U.S.)
VISTA	Volunteers in Service to America
VOCA	Victims of Crime Act
VTVPA	Victims of Trafficking and Violence Prevention Act of 2000
WIA	Workforce Investment Act of 1998
WIC	Women, Infants, and Children
WIN	Work Incentive Program
WMD	weapons of mass destruction *(including nuclear, biological, chemical, and explosive)*

PART I

Obtaining Federal Assistance

What This Book Gives You

GOVERNMENT ASSISTANCE ALMANAC has two purposes: (1) to provide information enabling users to identify *all domestic programs offering financial or nonfinancial assistance available from federal agencies*; (2) to help users reach the point of obtaining assistance.

This twenty-first edition describes 1,796 federal programs, 227 of which were added since the last edition. The information presented is based on data in the *Catalog of Federal Domestic Assistance* ("CFDA"), maintained by the General Services Administration pursuant to federal statute.

The *ALMANAC* reduces the information in the CFDA's approximately 2,500 pages to the essentials needed by most persons seeking federal assistance. Modifications in the presentation of the information, especially the *ALMANAC*'s indexes, enable users to identify available programs and their features more efficiently.

PART I provides *basic guidance on using this book* to identify and obtain available assistance. The guidelines are intended for newcomers to federal programs; more experienced users of similar information may find some helpful reminders.

PART II outlines *domestic financial and other assistance programs available per the CFDA as of June 30, 2008*. For each program the following is provided:

- federal program number and title; popular title when applicable;
- types of assistance available;
- description of objectives, permitted uses of funds, and project examples when they clarify program purposes; enacting legislation is noted to help define program purposes;
- eligibility factors concerning both applicants and beneficiaries;
- range and average amounts awarded through programs providing financial assistance;

- summary of recent activity;
- mailing address, phone number, and web site for program headquarters, and other referrals when applicable; generic e-mail addresses appearing in the CFDA.

PART III provides tables showing *funding levels for all programs and administering agencies* for the last four fiscal years. To our knowledge such comprehensive tables showing allocations specifically for federal domestic programs are exclusive to the *ALMANAC*. Table 1 also serves as a *listing of the programs in the numerical sequence* in which they appear in PART II. The *fifty largest and smallest programs* are also identified.

PART IV provides *addresses and phone numbers for more than 3,000 field offices*, organized to correspond with the program numbers within their purview. This system was established specifically for users of the *ALMANAC*; like the tables, this system exists nowhere else.

The **AGENCY INDEX** provides an *alphabetical listing of federal administrative units and sub-units*, including the program numbers within their purview. (The CFDA does not provide an alphabetical listing.) While administrative units also are incorporated within the MASTER INDEX, the AGENCY INDEX may expedite user searches specifically for these entities.

ALMANAC users will find the **MASTER INDEX** unique and exhaustive, particularly its subject headings, references, and cross-references. This index identifies all available federal domestic assistance programs. It also includes: administrative units and cross-references to sub-units; official and popular program titles; abbreviated program, agency, and other titles and terms; many enabling laws and their section and title numbers; and, general program references not found in other indexes of government assistance. The format enables users to distinguish programs providing financial assistance from those that do not, through the use of italicized program numbers. The copyright for *GOVERNMENT ASSISTANCE ALMANAC* makes its index an exclusive feature.

The list of **Abbreviations Used in This Book** preceding this section does not appear in the CFDA.

By definition, "domestic programs" do not necessarily include assistance available through ongoing government activities—e.g., operation of federal facilities and services, public information activities, enforcement of many federal laws and regulations, or products or services obtained through contractors, etc. The section entitled "Types of Federal Assistance Available," beginning below, explains what assistance is and is not covered.

Encountering the information in this book for the first time, some will be surprised by the scope of available federal assistance, which may seem very broad or rather meager in many areas. The assistance is available subject to program eligibility criteria, discussed under "Who May Obtain Federal Assistance?"

Timeliness of the Information

The twentieth edition of the *ALMANAC* (2006-07), based on CFDA-2005, identified 1,636 federal programs. Since the publication of that edition 227 programs were added and 67 were deleted, producing the present total of 1,796 as of June 30, 2008; this twenty-first edition incorporates the new programs, as well as many program changes.

Federal programs rarely are terminated unless similar assistance is available through another program; this book helps identify those other programs. The accompanying table shows an almost steady increase in the total number of domestic programs since the mid-1980s.

Currently some 56 departments, commissions, agencies, bureaus, and other federal entities administer the assistance programs. They manage the programs either through their main offices, through 175 "administrative sub-units," or through approximately 3,000 field offices.

Regarding the reliability of addresses and phone numbers, generally, ten to twelve percent of phone numbers and five to seven percent of office addresses change in the course of a year, based on federal directories studied. It can reasonably be expected that few changes in program contact information will be encountered.

Changes are inevitable in program application requirements, governmental organization, and addresses and phone numbers. Keeping abreast of all changes would require a daily compilation, such as is provided in the *Federal Register*. However, most substantive program changes affect the details of regulations, seldom affecting the factors included in the *ALMANAC*'s program entries; in pursuing programs with federal officials, inquirers will be advised of major changes.

Types of Federal Assistance Available

Fifteen types of federal domestic assistance are available through existing programs, providing financial or nonfinancial resources.
Programs that provide *financial assistance* are classified as:

DOMESTIC ASSISTANCE PROGRAM TOTALS 1984 THROUGH 2008

(Per GOVERNMENT ASSISTANCE ALMANAC, 1st-21st editions.)

GAA 1985-86	—	989 programs in 1984
	—	1,013 programs in 1985
GAA 1988	—	1,025 programs in 1987
	—	1,052 programs in 1988
GAA 1989-90	—	1,117 programs in 1989
GAA 1990-91	—	1,157 programs in 1990
GAA 1991-92	—	1,183 programs in 1991
GAA 1992-93	—	1,246 programs in 1992
GAA 1993-94	—	1,288 programs in 1993
GAA 1994-95	—	1,335 programs in 1994
GAA 1995-96	—	1,370 programs in 1995
GAA 1996-97	—	1,392 programs in 1996
GAA 1997-98	—	1,327 programs in 1997
GAA 1998-99	—	1,368 programs in 1998
GAA 1999-00	—	1,386 programs in 1999
GAA 2000-01	—	1,424 programs in 2000
GAA 2001-02	—	1,454 programs in 2001
GAA 2002-03	—	1,479 programs in 2002
GAA 2003-04	—	1,499 programs in 2003
GAA 2004-05	—	1,557 programs in 2004
GAA 2005-06	—	1,613 programs in 2005
GAA 2006-07	—	1,636 programs in 2006
GAA 2009	—	1,796 programs in 2008

Direct loans—offering the loan of federal funds for a specific term, with or without interest, with repayment expected. Example: FSA's "Emergency Loans" program provides USDA loans directly to farmers and others (see **10.404**).

Direct payments/specified use—providing funds for a specified purpose, with no repayment expected. Example: "Payments for Essential Air Services" to air carriers by DOT (see **20.901**).

Direct payments/unrestricted use—providing federal funds for use at will by the recipient, with no repayment expected. Example: "Social Security—

Retirement Insurance," administered by SSA (see **96.002**). Programs in this classification may be known as "entitlements."

Formula grants—through which federal funds are distributed to states or other recipients according to a formula (often based on population), for continuing activities not confined to a specific project. No repayment is expected. Example: DOED's "Adult Education—State Grant Program" (see **84.002**). Programs in this classification also may be known as "entitlements."

Guaranteed/insured loans—offering private or public lending institutions a guarantee or insurance against loan defaults, covering all or a portion of the amount borrowed. Example: HUD's "Mortgage Insurance—Homes" program (see **14.117**).

Insurance—assuring reimbursement for losses under specified conditions. Insurance coverage may be provided directly by a federal agency or through a private company, depending on specific program provisions. Example: "Foreign Investment Insurance," administered by OPIC (see **70.003**). Some programs also provide for federal payment of a portion of insurance premiums. Example: USDA's "Crop Insurance" program (see **10.450**).

Project grants—awarding federal funds for specific projects, services, products, or other activities such as scholarships, construction, research, planning, technical assistance. Some project grants cover cooperative agreement arrangements with state governments or other organizations to assist the federal granting agency in the performance of a certain function. No repayment is expected. Project grants do not necessarily cover 100 percent of project costs. Example: NSF's "Geosciences" program (see **47.050**).

The classifications of programs providing *nonfinancial assistance* are:

Advisory services/counseling—through which federal specialists provide consultation, advice, or other assistance—delivered through conferences, workshops, personal contacts, or published information. Example: USDA-NRCS's "Soil and Water Conservation" program (see **10.902**).

Federal employment—offering jobs with the federal government through the activities of OPM in recruiting and hiring civilian personnel. Example: "Federal Summer Employment" (see **27.006**). Note that only OPM programs provide federal employment as structured programs; the ongoing recruitment activities of other federal agencies are not classified as "domestic programs."

Investigation of complaints—through which federal agencies examine or investigate claims of violations of federal laws, policies, or regulatory procedures. The claim must originate outside the federal government. Example: "Shipping—Investigation of Complaints," conducted by the Federal Maritime Commission (see **33.001**).

Sale, exchange, or donation of property and goods—featuring the transfer of federally-owned real estate or personal property, commodities, and other goods including equipment, food, drugs, or supplies. Example: "Disposal of Federal Surplus Real Property," administered by GSA (**39.002**).

Specialized services—providing federal personnel to perform certain services for communities, individuals, or others. Example: "Planning Assistance to States," administered by the DOD-Corps of Engineers (**12.110**). *(Note that several Corps of Engineers programs provide specialized services involving construction activities; however, these programs are not classified as providing financial assistance, and a portion of total costs for such projects usually must be matched locally.)*

Technical information—through which technical information is prepared, published, and distributed—often through clearinghouses, libraries, centers, or through electronic media. Example: USDC-NIST's "Standard Reference Materials" (see **11.604**).

Training—offering federal agency instruction to persons not employed by the federal government. Example: DHS-FEMA's "Emergency Management Institute (EMI)—Resident Educational Program" (see **97.028**).

Use of property, facilities, and equipment—providing for the temporary use of or access to federally-owned resources, with or without charge to the user. Example: "National Gallery of Art Extension Service" (see **68.001**).

Not included as a classification, but reflected in the list and included, are "block grants" which may be used for a range of related activities. Block grants usually are awarded as "formula grants" or "project grants." Their permitted uses generally are more flexible than other types of programs. Such programs are cited in the index under the subject heading "Block grant programs."

Many programs offer more than one type of assistance; for example, the second program listed in PART II, **10.025**, offers project grants as well as specialized services, advisory services/counseling, technical information, and training.

The following types of government activities are not defined as domestic programs; they are *not included*:

- *Procurement contracts* for the purchase of goods and services by the federal government. For instance, basic DOD contracting activities do not meet the definition of domestic programs; however, DOD administers several programs classified as providing "domestic assistance." Programs offering assistance to firms wanting to do business with the federal government through its procurement contracts *are included.*

- *U.S. government foreign activities* without a direct benefit in the domestic economy. For instance, most Department of State activities are not classified as domestic programs; however, the state department also administers several domestic programs; and, the federal government sponsors several programs pertaining to importing and exporting—which *are included.*

- *Employee recruitment programs* of individual federal departments and agencies.

- *Programs benefiting only current or retired military personnel or federal employees.* However, all DVA benefit programs *are included*—although many DVA programs are not classified as providing financial assistance.

- *Ongoing public information services* of federal entities.

- *Basic domestic functions of the federal government* such as operation and maintenance of services and facilities, collection of taxes, enforcement of federal laws and regulations, judicial processes, etc.

Also not included are various tax incentives offered through the Internal Revenue Code, which are not classified as federal programs. These include so-called tax shelters, tax credits, writeoffs, and the like. Such government benefits to private taxpayers have stimulated activity in the domestic economy in recent years. Their features are the subject of other books dealing with taxes, finance, investment, etc.

Frequently, however, such "non-programs" relate directly to certain structured domestic programs which *are included* in this book. Examples: program **15.904**, "Historic Preservation Fund Grants-in-Aid," can be used to obtain accelerated depreciation of the value of improvements for tax purposes; program **20.812**, "Construction Reserve Fund," relating to merchant vessels, offers tax incentives to participants.

Resources for the Resourceful

GOVERNMENT ASSISTANCE ALMANAC may reveal previously unknown resources available to various types of users—farmers, students, small businesses, investors, entrepreneurs, homemakers, scientists, the elderly, parents, journalists, civic and social organizations, health professionals, guidance counselors, scholars, state and municipal governments, educators, artists and arts sponsors, members of minority groups, veterans and their dependents, community improvement groups, researchers, and others including those interested in the needs of the foregoing groups, as well as persons planning to enter those fields. They may find programs that offer technical information, services, training, or other types of assistance that they did not know existed.

The simplest assistance programs are those meeting a single purpose. For instance, someone seeking resources for an elderly person whose home needs repairs will find that the index cites a number of programs that could provide help. Selecting the most appropriate of the available programs is a matter of finding the programs in the index, carefully reading the program entries in PART II, and pursuing the most promising. The section entitled "Obtaining Federal Assistance: How to Use PART II," beginning on page 14, provides guidance along these lines.

Frequently, assistance will be found for elderly persons with several needs. For instance, in addition to programs providing loan or grant funds to repair property, subsidies are available to help pay fuel bills—even the cost of air conditioning under certain conditions. Also available are programs through which older persons might obtain part-time employment, or meals, or help with home management tasks; dependents of deceased veterans may be entitled to pensions, health care, and burial expenses and grave markers for the deceased veteran.

Seeking federal assistance becomes more challenging when two or more programs are combined to meet more complex needs. For instance, someone interested in obtaining mortgage insurance on a loan covering a multi-unit housing structure in an older declining area through **14.123** may decide to also pursue the rental subsidies available to tenants through **14.871**.

Resourcefulness often is the key to obtaining federal assistance. The successful outcome of use of available assistance is illustrated across the country, in virtually all fields—from child care to environmental enhancement to job creation to the performing arts to scientific research.

Often, those who have successfully applied public resources are eager to show what they did and how they went about it. Their experience could save prospective applicants countless hours of trial and error. Federal officials also may provide guidance in learning how to use federal programs effectively; their perspective can be unique, an important resource to tap.

The challenge may increase when federal assistance is channeled through a state, municipal, or private organization. The next section, "Who May Obtain Federal Assistance?" addresses the situation. In such instances, the application *process* is usually similar to making federal office contacts. However, the competition for funds help could be stiffer. The award process could be more complicated, requiring a good deal of groundwork at the community level to obtain the assistance. An applicant's resourcefulness usually pays off, just as with federal contacts.

Who May Obtain Federal Assistance?

Eligibility depends on the specific program.

Assistance through many programs is available to the general public—e.g., use of the national libraries, technical information, and similar facilities and services.

Some programs, because of laws or regulations governing their administration, offer assistance only to certain categories of *applicants*—e.g., farmers, states, small businesses, native Americans. Only specified categories of prospective recipients may *apply.*

Other programs may directly *benefit* only certain industries—e.g., shipbuilding or agriculture, or certain population groups such as the elderly, or teenagers, or immigrants from specific countries.

Under still other federal programs, eligible applicants and beneficiaries are the same. Examples include certain veterans, small business, and student programs.

The distinction between programs offering assistance specifically to eligible applicants, eligible beneficiaries, and eligible applicants/beneficiaries is clear in the program entries presented in PART II.

The point to be understood is that the distinction between eligible applicants and eligible beneficiaries is very important to those seeking assistance. Many deserving persons have not obtained assistance to which they were entitled because this distinction was not understood. Being ineligible to *apply* to a federal agency for assistance under certain programs does not necessarily mean that one cannot *benefit* from those programs. The following actual example illustrates the point.

"The Case of the Muffin Machine"

Several years ago, a baker in a small city used his savings to establish a franchised doughnut business. The city was economically depressed; it managed to obtain relatively large sums of federal money for economic development from several federal agencies.

In a relatively short time after starting, the business did well enough for the owner to meet expenses while employing eleven persons, mostly waiters and waitresses for its 24-hour operation.

The owner was notified by the franchise company of a new product, muffins, that was boosting other franchise owners' sales and profits substantially in market test areas. The franchise company offered an $11,000 package that would include the necessary equipment to begin making and selling muffins. The owner's assets were tied up in the business and in keeping it solvent. So, he applied to a bank for an $11,000 loan to finance purchase of the package. The bank told the owner that it would lend him only $5,500 toward the purchase. The owner did not have the $5,500 balance that he needed, nor would any other bank lend him more because his assets were heavily mortgaged.

Meanwhile, the city's success in obtaining federal funds to help in the creation of new jobs was publicized in the local media. The owner phoned the Department of Housing and Urban Development's nearest office for information about obtaining the funds, because he had heard that HUD was the source of much of the money received by the city. Unfortunately, whoever answered the phone at HUD told the owner that only the city could receive that type of funds from HUD.

Several weeks passed before the owner "badmouthed" the HUD program to the right customer. The customer happened to be another small business owner who had obtained some of the HUD funds to finance the expansion of his business. The customer told the owner whom to contact *locally* to apply for funds. Following a short meeting with an official in the city's economic development organization, the baker-owner had an entirely different attitude toward the program he had been complaining about.

Three weeks later, financing had been arranged to purchase the "muffin machine." The bank loaned the small businessman $5,500 at its commercial interest rate. From the city's funds received from HUD, he obtained $4,400 at 5 percent interest. And, he scraped up the remaining $1,100, or 10 percent of the total investment, on his own. One full-time job and two part-time jobs resulted from this loan.

In this particular program (**14.228**) only small cities may *apply* for the available project grants, which may be used for quite a broad range of activities, including revolving loan funds with interest rates established locally. However, as an *eligible beneficiary* of the program the small business owner was able to obtain the assistance; the city accomplished its objectives of creating jobs and "leveraging" private funds through its economic development efforts; and, most important perhaps, three persons received jobs generated by the program.

The importance of this example to persons seeking federal assistance is the distinction between eligible *applicants* and eligible *beneficiaries*. If only certain types of applicants may apply for a program and you are not eligible, but you are eligible to *benefit*—say, under a training program—find out who has obtained funds and apply there for the training. If it cannot be established who has received funds by contacting organizations at the community level, contact the appropriate federal field office listed in PART IV of this book; if there is no field office, contact the program headquarters listed in PART II.

Organization of the Federal Programs in This Book

PART II of *GOVERNMENT ASSISTANCE ALMANAC* uses the same numerical system of listing federal programs followed in the CFDA. The system is not totally logical, in that the programs are not listed alphabetically, functionally, or by type of assistance. They are organized according to their administering department or agency; this makes this book's MASTER INDEX especially useful in identifying available assistance.

Each program is identified by a five-digit number. The first two digits identify the administrative entity responsible for the program. The last three digits identify the administrative sub-unit, if any, and the program. For example, the programs described in PART II, beginning on page 29, illustrate the numerical system:

DEPARTMENT OF COMMERCE

This administrative entity has responsibility for all programs that begin with the digits "11."

BUREAU OF THE CENSUS

This administrative sub-unit of the Department of Commerce has management responsibility for the programs outlined. **11.001** through **11.006** are the numbers identifying programs managed by the Bureau of the Census.

All programs with "**12**" as their first two digits, beginning on page 158, are administered by the Department of Defense. The system continues throughout PART II and PART III, as well as PART IV which provides field contact information.

PART III. Program Funding Levels—Summary Tables lists the departments, agencies, commissions, and other governmental entities in the order in which they are presented in PART II.

Note, however, that PARTS II and III provide headings for administrative sub-units only when the sub-unit's program series is uninterrupted in the CFDA. The *ALMANAC*'s AGENCY INDEX lists all administrative units and sub-units alphabetically, and it includes the program numbers within their respective purviews.

(The numerical system originated in the 1960s when the first edition of the *Catalog of Federal Domestic Assistance* was published. It was organized alphabetically by the name of the administering agency. Many numbers were not used, to allow for inclusion of new programs. Through the years, new agencies and programs were established and existing ones were terminated. The new agencies were added to the end of the list, to avoid changing the numerical sequence within the numbering system. Program numbers for terminated agencies or programs were removed altogether, and reserved in case they are reinstated eventually.)

Red Tape—Should You Hire a Consultant?

Federal laws, regulations, statutory provisions, policies, forms, criteria, procedures, processes, standards, deadlines, audits, certifications, documentation, appeals, authorizations, records, credentials, formulas, obligations, guidelines—these terms and many others signify the "red tape" of federal programs.

The terms form an important part of the language used in administering federal programs. Expect to encounter the language in seeking federal assistance. Depending on the program pursued, none, some, or all of the terms may be encountered.

The following general principles concerning "red tape" are understood by persons experienced in applying for federal assistance.

1. *Programs involving financial benefits in any form involve more red tape than other types of assistance.*

2. *The more persons served by a given program, the less red tape to the beneficiaries.* For example, applicants for basic Social Security benefits must produce certain information to enable federal officials to

verify their eligibility and to calculate their benefits. Because millions of persons participate in the Social Security program, red tape has been minimized and usually is simple enough to overcome.

3. *Programs providing for one-on-one contacts between federal officials and applicants usually involve less red tape.* Examples: persons applying for some types of farming assistance or fellowships, training, veterans benefits, and similar assistance. In such cases, the applicant/beneficiary usually can easily arrange to provide the required information.

4. *Programs with relatively few participants nationwide and with large benefit amounts involve extensive lengths of red tape.* Examples: programs addressing the problem of toxic waste; multi-year intensive research projects; financial assistance programs based on the recipient's promise to perform certain tasks, such as construction projects involving federal mortgage insurance.

5. *Programs with several parties to an application for assistance involve increased red tape.* For example, a housing developer applying for a mortgage guaranty on apartments to receive rental subsidies will be required to produce documents from a lender, attorneys, architects, housing management experts, local housing officials, and others—with each party needing to satisfy various requirements. Such applications must be "packaged" into a single application. Moreover, the approval process requires "sign-off" (i.e., approval) by several officials both outside and within the administering federal agency.

6. *Programs that provide federal assistance to beneficiaries through nonfederal offices may or may not have added red tape.* The five preceding principles apply. Examples: information about drug abuse might be obtained easily through a federally-funded state agency, but obtaining federal funds through the same state agency to establish a local drug abuse program could be more difficult than dealing with a federal office because of complex state requirements *in addition to* federal requirements; a student applying to a college financial aid office for federal educational assistance could have to meet federal, state, *and* the institution's requirements.

For most programs, paid consultants are not needed to apply for federal assistance. Generally, the official receiving the application will guide applicants in meeting requirements. Many programs require that applications be submitted through public administering agencies, private organizations, banks, or similar entities. Personnel in these organizations might well be considered the "consultant" or advocate for the application.

Programs involving complicated applications may require expert assistance to assure favorable action by the funding agency. Applicants without the time or patience to learn about and fulfill all requirements may find it advantageous to hire an experienced consultant.

In selecting a consultant, verify his or her credentials, experience, and record in obtaining federal assistance *of the type to be sought*. Check with the consultant's other clients and with federal offices to confirm that the qualifications are pertinent to the specific program. A consultant's impressive background in one field or with one federal agency is not necessarily a recommendation in another field or with a different federal agency. Most federal offices will provide advice about the need for a consultant's help in applying for given programs.

Keep the red tape in perspective. Try to understand its necessity. Federal requirements are intended to assure the proper use of federal funds. Virtually everyone agrees that many federal programs involve excessive red tape. Separate complaints and constructive recommendations about program requirements from the application process.

Obtaining Federal Assistance: How to Use PART II

Identifying and obtaining federal assistance is a reasonably straightforward process when one proceeds carefully and resourcefully. The previous section commented generally on the most complicated part of the process: the requirements that must be met to obtain assistance from the federal government. Complications can be minimal if a few basic steps are followed.

STEP ONE: USE THE MASTER INDEX

Thumb through the MASTER INDEX at the end of this book. Each program appears in the index an average of ten times. Together with the cross-references, the index assures that users will be able to identify *all* available assistance programs. Become familiar with the types of headings, sub-headings, and cross references. The index presents:

- subjects (shown in bold face);
- official program titles (in capital letters); bracketed agency identifiers are added to program titles to clarify the federal agency involved in cases where the program title alone is indistinct;
- popular titles of programs;
- miscellaneous (abbreviations, agency names, names of Acts, etc.)

The numbers following the headings refer to the program numbers in PART II where they appear in the left column. *Indexed programs that offer financial assistance are italicized, distinguishing them from programs that do not,* to further assist users in quickly identifying programs most pertinent to their needs.

Finding programs by title, popular name, abbreviation, or administrative entity is a simple procedure of looking in the index alphabetically, and then turning to PART II where the program descriptions are presented in numerical order. The introductory notes preceding the MASTER INDEX may prove useful.

Finding programs by subject involves looking for a main term and then scanning the indented entries under it. Generally, programs *intended* for the benefit of certain groups of people, such as women, youth, Indians, the disadvantaged, the disabled or handicapped, etc., are indexed directly under the common name of the group. Many programs are available to group members even though not targeted primarily for them. For example, programs relating to housing for Indians will be found under "Indian housing;" however, programs listed under the more general headings beginning with "Housing"—such as "Housing, rental" or "Housing, construction"—may also be applicable. To ascertain that every possible available program has been identified, both approaches should be followed.

The MASTER INDEX also includes section and title numbers of certain Acts, as well as the names of the Acts themselves. So if an *ALMANAC* user is interested in "section 109," for example, but does not know or cannot remember the exact name of the Act, in looking under "Section" numerous section numbers will be found with their corresponding program numbers.

Finding programs by administrative entity, such as "Department of Labor," can be done through the MASTER INDEX for all agencies. Or, the AGENCY INDEX might be consulted instead. The AGENCY INDEX also shows programs administered by sub-units. "PART III. Program Funding Levels—Summary Tables" gives the names of all the agencies, arranged by government department, in the order in which the programs are presented in PARTS II and IV.

For other programs, the recommended procedure is to check first under the specific term, and then under more general terms. "*See*" and "*see also*" references have been used liberally to direct searches. For example, under "Aquaculture" a "*see also*" reference suggests looking under such other headings as "Farm, nonfarm enterprises," "Fish," and "Fisheries industry" for more entries of possible interest.

Or, if a scholarship to attend podiatry school is sought, users should look first under "Podiatry" where one or more programs will be found; but the *see also* reference directs users to "Health professions" where more general programs will be found that may be of interest; users also will be referred to "Fellowships, scholarships, traineeships" for still other related programs.

The index includes some terms indicating permitted uses of programs, which may not be mentioned in the program entry. These terms are included in the index for programs where it is known that program funds possibly may be used for activities embodied in the indexed term. "Block grant" programs frequently are indexed in this manner.

Often, more than one program will be found providing assistance under a given heading. Read all program entries in PART II carefully, and pursue the most pertinent.

After perusing the index, if no reference is found to a program providing assistance for a specific purpose, it is almost certain that such federal assistance is unavailable. There is one more step that might be taken: contact the federal office most apt to know about assistance available for specific purposes. Many programs can be "stretched" to cover activities that are not found in the program entry or in the index.

STEP TWO: "READ" A FEDERAL PROGRAM

PART II provides outlines of all available domestic programs. Properly "reading" the information on a given program—that is, understanding the program entry—will facilitate decisions on whether to pursue the available assistance. The following explanation of the program entries explains how to "read" the entries to greatest advantage. Program **14.239** on page 199 serves as the example.

① COMMUNITY PLANNING AND DEVELOPMENT

② 14.239 HOME INVESTMENT PARTNERSHIPS PROGRAM
③ ("HOME Program")

④ **Assistance:** formula grants. (67-75 percent/2-5 years).

⑤ **Purposes:** pursuant to the National Affordable Housing Act as amended, to support partnerships among all levels of government and the private sector, including profit and nonprofit organizations, in the production and operation of affordable housing, particularly rental housing for low- and very-low-income families. Funds may be used for: planning; development of model projects; technical assistance; housing rehabilitation; tenant-based rental assistance; assistance to homebuyers; new construction of housing; site acquisition and improvements including improved energy efficiency, demolition, relocation. As of FY 03, the American Dream Downpayment Initiative (ADDI) may provide funds for low-income families to make down payments on or to rehabilitate suitable housing. Ineligible funds uses include: public housing modernization; matching funds for other federal programs; rental housing operating subsidies; activities under the Low Income Housing Preservation Act, except for priority purchasers.

⑥ **Eligible applicants:** formula allocations—states, cities, urban counties, or consortia of general local government units; Insular Areas. Technical Assistance—nonprofit and profit firms; public purpose organizations; nonprofit national and regional HOME organizations; community development organizations (CHDOs).

⑦ **Eligible beneficiaries:** rental housing—90 percent of funds for families with incomes at 60 percent of area median, and the remainder for families below 80 percent. Homeownership assistance—families with incomes below 80 percent of the area median.

⑧ **Range:** $287,780 to $129,144,702. **Average:** $3,088,433.

⑨ **Activity:** cumulatively through FY 05, 632,998 were completed; 131,327 tenants received rental assistance.

⑩ **HQ:** Director, Office of Affordable Housing Programs, CPD-HUD, 451 Seventh St. SW - Rm.7164, Washington, DC 20410. Phone: (202) 708-2470.

Internet: www.hud.gov/offices/cpd/affordablehousing/index.cfm.

---

① *Administrative sub-unit* with management responsibility for all programs under the heading.

② *Program number,* and *official program title.*

③ *Popular title.*

Many program titles in PART II are followed by one or more *popular titles*, shown within parentheses and quotation marks as in this illustration. Field office officials and others may refer to programs only by their popular titles.

④ *Classification of assistance* available through the program. (The fifteen "Types of Federal Assistance Available" are defined beginning on page 3.)

Many programs provide more than one type of assistance. When financial assistance is provided this line indicates the percentage of assistance provided by the federal agency, as well as the usual project term *when the term is other than for one year*. For some programs, the percentage and project term are clarified under "⑤ **Purposes**."

Project grants usually are awarded either through competitions or solicitations of proposals by the sponsoring federal agency; however, authorizing statutes for some programs allocate funds on the basis of a formula, as in the "HOME Program," in which case the federal administrative agency notifies eligible applicants of the availability of funds. It is necessary for prospective applicants for competitive, solicited, or unsolicited proposals to remain aware of available programs.

Although the percentage of federal assistance may say "100 percent," most programs have maintenance of effort ("MOE") or "non-supplementation" requirements—meaning that federal funds may not supplant existing non-federal funding allocated to the effort for which federal funds are sought. Also, some level of cost sharing by the applicant almost always is required, if only through the provision of administrative space and services supporting project activities; such contributions by applicants are known as "in-kind" contributions. *Frequently, the level of "MOE" or of cost sharing by applicants will influence the approval of applications.*

⑤ Description of the *basic objectives* and *permitted uses* of the program, as well as *restrictions* on the use of funds. Examples of funded projects also are included when they help to explain the types of activities that are eligible.

The information on the purposes of program **14.239** should be sufficient to permit a decision on whether to pursue it. Note that many programs include more than a single program purpose. Other program features also are included in program descriptions.

⑥ *Who may apply* for the available assistance.

⑦ *Who may benefit* from the program.

Thus, the headings setting forth the eligibility for program **14.239** indicate that only states, cities, urban counties, or consortia or general local government units, and Insular Areas may apply directly for available formula grants; however, other types of applicants are eligible to apply for technical assistance funding. And, when program assistance is sought for rental housing, 90 percent of approved funds must benefit families with incomes at 60 percent of area median, and the remainder for families below 80 percent; when assistance is approved for homeownership projects, families with incomes below 80 percent of the area median may benefit.

It follows that someone interested in participating in this program, if not an eligible applicant, should contact appropriate state or local officials to learn more about it. Contact the state or city public information office to find out whom to contact for details; if that fails, contact the nearest HUD Community Planning and Development field office listed in PART IV.

Frequently, there is no distinction between eligible applicants and eligible beneficiaries, because they are one and the same. Many program descriptions name the intended beneficiaries; those beneficiaries need not apply because services will (or should) be provided to them by the applicants—for instance, programs intended to benefit elderly persons, children and youth, substance abusers, and other general categories of beneficiaries. Such programs have the following eligibility heading:

Eligible applicants/beneficiaries:

Review the section beginning on page 9 entitled "Who May Obtain Federal Assistance?" for a discussion and example of the significance of eligible applicants vs. eligible beneficiaries.

Occasionally a notation in this heading will indicate "same as for" another program. In "reading" program entries, take such a notation to mean that the two programs probably have related purposes—suggesting that, if the one being considered does not meet certain needs, perhaps the other will.

⑧ Indicates the *range and average amounts* provided to applicants or, sometimes, to beneficiaries for programs that provide financial assistance

Knowing range and average amounts helps in assessing the chances of obtaining a certain sum. Often, applying for a sum that is outside the range shown is pointless, whether the sum sought is below or above the range.

Complementing the "Range" heading are the tables in PART III. *Used together*, the amounts provide a perspective of the funding available nationally for a given activity, and how much an applicant or a beneficiary might expect to obtain through that program.

In "reading" the tables, remember that the U.S. government's fiscal year begins on October 1 and ends on September 30. Fiscal years are expressed in the ending date; thus, FY 08 ends September 30, 2008. Table 1 shows the following funding available for program **14.239**:

(FY 05) $1,858,016,000; (FY 06) $1,757,250,000; (FY 07) $1,757,250,000 e; (FY 08) $1,966,640,000 e

Note that amounts are rounded to the nearest $1,000 in Tables 1, 2, and 3 (but not in the line above).

The information on funding for the four years: (1) indicates the amount available nationally; (2) shows whether, from year to year, a program's funding level remains relatively consistent or if it is increasing or decreasing.

"*" following an amount indicates that the amount is a "credit" rather than an actual outlay of funds. For purposes of the tables, amounts loaned or insured by the government were classified as credits. Program **14.239** provides formula grants and, therefore, is classified as an outlay.

"e" next to an amount indicates that it is *estimated*. In the example, the amounts shown are actual for FY 05 and FY 06; the FY 07 and FY 08 amounts are estimated.

Estimated amounts could mean that Congress had not approved a specific amount when the information was compiled, or that the amount obligated for a program fluctuates depending on demands for the funds.

Estimates of "$0" also may indicate that the program has been proposed for termination.

Amounts shown in the tables must meet demands nationwide. The total often is allocated geographically by government agencies to regions, states, districts, or areas, according to legislative or administrative policy. Therefore, it could be useful to learn the amount available in a given geographical area, from the officials contacted concerning a specific program—for an indication of the extent of competition to be expected.

The tables offer a perspective of government support for agencies and programs, in relation to one another and to other federal domestic activities.

The introduction to the tables further discusses their usefulness in "reading" federal programs.

⑨ *Activity within the program* in the most recent period reported by the administering entity, including such information as the number of assistance awards or of persons benefiting. It is also noted when the program is new, with or without reported activity.

In combination with the information provided under *Range/Average* and in the Tables, "reading" the level of activity provides an indication of the participation nationally in given programs.

⑩ *Program headquarters address, phone number, and web sites* of the administering agency. FAX numbers and generic e-mail addresses are included when provided in the source material.

THE FIRST CONTACT WITH A FEDERAL AGENCY ABOUT A PROGRAM SHOULD ALWAYS BE WITH THE FIELD OFFICE IF ONE EXISTS. The "HQ" entry always indicates when there are no field offices for a given program with "(Note: no field offices for this program.)" following the HQ address. If the notation does not appear, field office contact information is provided in PART IV.

Contacting field offices has advantages for both applicants and federal officials: the nearer a federal office is to applicants, the more probable it is that the officials will be able to provide pertinent information; field office personnel usually are more aware of needs in the area they serve; contacts with them add to this awareness.

Also, they are more apt to know who else in a given area has similar interests; they could provide leads to others experienced with the program. It is important for the field offices to know the extent of interest in the programs that they manage. Generally, headquarters personnel are more involved with "big picture" matters than with handling individual contacts from throughout the country.

PART IV provides contact information for regional, state, and area or district offices. The hierarchy should be followed upwards when deciding which office to contact—that is, if there is a district, branch, or area office, it should be contacted before state or regional offices; state offices should be contacted before regional offices.

When contacting a field office, address the "Director" unless the entry in PART IV suggests otherwise. Include the full name of the agency. For example, correspondence with HUD's Chicago state office, concerning program **14.239**, should be addressed as follows:

Director, State Office
Community Planning and Development
Department of Housing and Urban Development
Metcalfe Federal Bldg.
77 W. Jackson Blvd.
Chicago, IL 60604-3507

PART IV also provides contact information for specialized field service offices such as research centers, laboratories, and testing stations.

STEP THREE: ASK THE RIGHT QUESTIONS

"STEP ONE" and "STEP TWO" involve the selection of programs to pursue. The process of obtaining federal assistance begins when those steps are completed. Hundreds of programs involve very little red tape. They require little or no additional "homework", especially those involving nonfinancial assistance. For nonfinancial programs, one or two contacts with the right federal official usually will bring the desired assistance.

This "step" is meant for newcomers to federal programs, deciding to pursue the more complicated programs involving awards of funds. All the points discussed will not be pertinent to all the programs, obviously.

Before formally applying for financial assistance under all but the least complicated programs, a preliminary contact with the responsible federal office is always advisable; indeed, some programs *require* a preapplication conference. An appointment with the responsible official should be requested; when making this request, the eligibility criteria for the program being pursued should be discussed generally. At this first meeting at least the following should be accomplished:

1. *Verify the eligibility of the applicant*—whether as an individual or as an organization. This should have been done verbally when the appointment was made. If the official mentioned credentials required to document eligibility, these should be shown at the meeting. The required credentials could include documents such as a birth certificate, academic certificates, a financial statement, endorsements, a copy of the organization's charter or license, etc. If the required credentials are not ready, evidence that they be can produced should be

shown—e.g., publications, sample products, leaflets describing the organization, a good resume.

2. *Explain the applicant's specific need for the assistance in very basic terms.* Prior to the meeting an outline for using the assistance should be prepared, and it should be shown to the official. This will open a discussion of the program, its objectives, the permitted uses of funds, program restrictions, etc. All possible questions about the program should be posed, including the availability of funding. The official should be allowed to do most of the talking—the purpose of the meeting is for the applicant to obtain information, not give it. On the other hand, prospective applicants should answer all questions honestly to reveal potential problems early in the process; if problems do surface, the official's advice should be sought on how to resolve them. *Written* notes should be made, both during and immediately after the meeting.

3. *Obtain all available written information pertaining to the program.* The following could be useful in preparing a thorough application:

- a copy of the law establishing the program;
- policy statements;
- procedural guidelines and instructions to applicants;
- regulations governing the program, including those published in the *Federal Register* and those pertaining mainly to the processing requirements that federal agencies themselves must fulfill—the latter often provide instructions for "scoring" the merits of applications, giving insights into what those reviewing an application will look for;
- statements of application deadlines, if any;
- general literature describing the program and the experiences of others that have obtained funds under the same or similar programs;
- a copy of a sample successful application;
- most important, copies of any pertinent circulars governing the program issued by the Office of Management and Budget, as well as Executive Orders or other regulations issued by federal or state agencies that will coordinate or review applications—e.g., the Environmental Protection Agency;
- lists of requirements for records to be kept and reports to be filed if the application is approved—including copies of pertinent accounting procedures;
- a description of the "appeal process," in case the application is not approved and the decision is appealed.

4. *If the program requires cost sharing or a matching contribution* by the applicant, it should be determined whether any portion of this sum can be provided through "in-kind" services, use of facilities or equipment, or other noncash contributions. Review the explanation of the program description entry heading "Assistance" on page 18 for insights on cost sharing.

5. *Ask to be placed on the office's mailing list* to receive announcements, news releases, notifications of invitations to apply or of awards, changes in regulations or deadlines, and the like.

6. *Keep the meeting as brief as possible.*

STEP FOUR: COMPLETE YOUR HOMEWORK

Examine carefully all the material obtained in "STEP THREE." Make a list of the most important points. Note especially items that are not readily understood, and follow through on each of them. Follow all instructions carefully. In your application, projecting an ability to adhere carefully and fully to instructions and regulations is all-important. "Dot every i, cross every t."

At this point, the "grantsmanship" process begins. Grantsmanship is a term often used inaccurately to describe *obtaining* federal assistance. Successful grantsmanship necessitates thorough familiarity with program and project planning, development, and operations. A good application will reflect complete understanding of program purposes and requirements, *as well as sound project management capability*. The grantsmanship process is both an art and a science; its productive outcome requires extensive research, discipline, precise work, sound psychology, effective presentation, a good sense of business, and persistence.

The *ALMANAC*'s author/editor and publisher wish users success in their quest, trusting that this book points them in the right direction.

Finding More Information

Several sources might be checked for more information on obtaining federal assistance.

1. The principal source providing additional details about the programs outlined in the *ALMANAC* is the *Catalog of Federal Domestic Assistance* ("CFDA"), subscriptions to which may be ordered from:

   Superintendent of Documents
   U.S. Government Printing Office
   Washington, DC 20402

The "Catalog" is published every year, pursuant to federal statute; it contains some 2,500 pages and is mailed unbound for filing in a loose-leaf binder. Subscriptions no longer include the "Update to the Catalog of Federal Domestic Assistance," formerly published in December and numbering several hundred additional pages; the General Services Administration, which maintains the data base for the CFDA, discontinued preparation of a printed version of the Update in 2001. GSA also no longer offers the CFDA on CD-ROM.

GSA recommends now that interested parties use its "on-line version" of the CFDA to obtain updated information, which may be accessed through the following web site: "http://www.cfda.gov".

It should be noted that the CFDA web site provides most of the information presented in the ALMANAC *only in printer definition file ("PDF") format, including the CFDA's several indexes; the CFDA on-line version provides ongoing updates only for individual programs—i.e., the version in PDF format has been updated only annually in recent years.*

The catalog contains a brief section with "Suggestions for Proposal Writing and Following Grant Application Procedures," which could be helpful to newcomers to federal programs.

Until 2003 GSA distributed free copies of the CFDA to the entities listed below; however, this policy was changed, requiring the recipients to purchase subscriptions; presumably, many of them did so and would have copies available for examination:

Members of Congress
Congressional staff
All federal Depository Libraries (see program **40.002**)
Federal offices
Governors
State coordinators of federal-state relations
Directors of state departments of administration
Directors of state agricultural extension services
Directors of state departments of community affairs
Directors of state planning agencies
State budget offices
State municipal leagues
State associations of counties
Chief state school officers

State employment security agencies
Mayors
County chairmen
Chairmen of boards of commissioners
City planners
Some other state and local government agencies and officials

Federal Information Centers and *Federal Regional Councils* also may have copies available for examination.

2. *The United States Government Manual* is a useful reference source for persons wanting to better understand the federal government. The manual describes the basic functions and operations of all government agencies, including the judicial, legislative, and executive branches. Most libraries have copies available for reference. The current manual may be purchased from the Government Printing Office.

3. *The Federal Register,* published daily, provides the public with federal agency regulations and other legal documents covering government activities, including *proposed* changes in regulations. Newly authorized programs and the availability of funding also are announced in *The Federal Register.*

The Federal Register Index, published monthly, consolidates entries appearing in the basic publication, with broad references to the contents.

Additional *Federal Register* resources include "Weekly Compilation of Presidential Documents" and "The Federal Register: What It Is and How to Use It."

The *Code of Federal Regulations* ("CFR") codifies the general and permanent rules published in the *The Federal Register* by federal executive departments and agencies. The CFR includes all statutory regulations; it is updated by *The Federal Register.*

The foregoing publications are available for examination in federal depository libraries and major libraries, or for purchase from the Government Printing Office.

4. *Libraries* are obvious places to look for additional information about government programs, "grantsmanship," proposal writing, and similar topics. Larger or more specialized libraries also will have available directories of trade or professional associations and of commercial

publishers specializing in information on various government activities, which might provide assistance or guidance concerning certain federal assistance programs. Directories of consultants and consulting organizations also are available.

5. *Government Phone Book USA—A Comprehensive Guide to Federal, State, County, and Local Government Offices in the United States*, provides standard and e-mail addresses, as well as web sites, and phone and FAX numbers, totaling some 164,000 listings. Published annually by Omnigraphics, Inc., this comprehensive reference should be available at libraries.

6. *Congressional offices* may or may not be able to provide help in obtaining additional information or actual assistance. Some senators and representatives are more anxious to do so than others, depending on the capacity, interest, and capabilities of their staffs.

Many elected officials respond more quickly to requests for assistance from other elected officials, or from campaign supporters. Keep this in mind when deciding to seek a congressman's intercession. The first contact should be with district or state offices. The Washington addresses for offices of Members of Congress are:

United States Senate	House of Representatives
Washington, DC 20510	Washington, DC 20515

The best source of more information about given programs and obtaining the assistance they provide usually is someone experienced in those programs or similar ones.

PART II

Program Information

DEPARTMENT OF AGRICULTURE

10.001 AGRICULTURAL RESEARCH—BASIC AND APPLIED RESEARCH ("Extramural Research")

Assistance: project grants (100 percent).

Purposes: for agricultural discovery research; to provide scientific technical information. Most projects are conducted with in-house staff; limited discretionary research funds are available.

Eligible applicants/beneficiaries: nonprofit IHEs and other research organizations.

Range: $1,000 to $25,000. **Average:** $3,000.

Activity: N.A.

HQ: Administrator, Agriculture Research Service (ARS)-USDA, Washington, DC 20250. Phone: (202) 720-3656; Extramural Agreements Division, (301) 504-1147.

Internet: www.ars.usda.gov.

10.025 PLANT AND ANIMAL DISEASE, PEST CONTROL, AND ANIMAL CARE

Assistance: project grants (cost sharing).

Purposes: pursuant to the Plant Protection Act, Farm Security and Rural Investment Act of 2002 (FSRIA), and Animal Welfare Act as amended, for surveys, demonstration projects, and inspections to detect, appraise, eradicate, and control plant and animal diseases and pests injurious to agriculture, including brucellosis and tuberculosis; to ensure the safety and potency of veterinary biologics. Emphasis is on prevention of interstate spread of infestations and diseases.

Eligible applicants: foreign, state, local, and territorial government agencies; nonprofit IHEs and other organizations.

Eligible beneficiaries: in addition to applicants: farmers, ranchers, agricultural producers.

Range/Average: N.A.

Activity: FY 06 estimate, 50 states brucellosis-free, 47 tuberculosis-free.

HQ: Agreement Services Center, Marketing and Regulatory Programs, Animal and Plant Health Inspection Service-USDA, USDA Center, 4700 River Rd. - Unit 55, Riverdale, MD 20737. Phone: (301) 734-8792.

Internet: www.aphis.usda.gov.

10.028 WILDLIFE SERVICES

Assistance: project grants (cost sharing).

Purposes: pursuant to the Animal Damage Control Act of 1931 as amended, to reduce damage caused by nuisance mammals and birds, including those carrying zoonotic diseases. Project examples: predator control programs in the western states, including coyote, mountain lion, and bear; aerial blackbird hazing program protecting the sunflower crop; control of beaver, deer, and cormorants against damage to aquaculture in the eastern and southern states. Most direct technical assistance is provided through state fish and game, agriculture, and health departments.

Eligible applicants/beneficiaries: state, local, territorial, and tribal governments; public or private nonprofit organizations; nonprofit IHEs; individuals.

Range/Average: N.A.

Activity: FY 03 estimate, 88,000 projects.

HQ: Agreement Services Center, Marketing and Regulatory Programs, Animal and Plant Health Inspection Service-USDA, USDA Center, 4700 River Rd. - Unit 55, Riverdale, MD 20737. Phone: (301) 734-8792.

Internet: www.aphis.usda.gov.

10.029 AVIAN INFLUENZA INDEMNITY PROGRAM ("AII")

Assistance: direct payments/unrestricted use.

Purposes: to provide indemnity payments to owners of animals required to be destroyed because of foot-and-mouth disease, pleuropneumonia, rinderpest, exotic Newcastle disease, highly pathogenic avian influenza, infectious salmon anemia, or any other communicable disease of livestock or poultry that constitutes an emergency and threatens the U.S. livestock or poultry population. Payment for animals destroyed is based on fair market value.

Eligible applicants/beneficiaries: poultry owners and contract growers.

Range/Average: 100 percent of eligible losses, up to the eligible amount before grower compensation is deducted.

Activity: N.A.

HQ: Animal and Plant Health Inspection Service-USDA, 1400 Independence Ave. SW, Washington, DC 20250. Phone: (no number provided)

Internet: www.fsa.usda.gov.

10.051 COMMODITY LOANS AND LOAN DEFICIENCY PAYMENTS ("Price Supports")

Assistance: direct payments/unrestricted use; direct loans (to 9 months).

Purposes: pursuant to the Agricultural Adjustment Act of 1938, Commodity Credit Corporation Charter Act, Food, Agriculture, Conservation, and Trade Act of 1990 (FACTA), Federal Agriculture Improvement and Reform Act of 1996 (FAIRA), Agricultural Risk Protection Act of 2000, amendments, and other acts, to help growers stabilize their income from commodities through a system of price supports involving loans and purchases by the CCC. Producers may receive nonrecourse loans against the support price established for crops serving as loan collateral; if market prices exceed the support price, farmers may market the commodity and repay the loan principal plus interest; if market prices are low, the loan is repaid through forfeiture of the collateral to the CCC in return for a loan deficiency payment (LDP) for the difference between the support and the market prices. Commodities eligible for loans include feed grains, wheat, rice, peanuts, tobacco, upland cotton, extra-long staple cotton, sugar, soybeans, canola, flaxseed, mustard seed, rapeseed, safflower, and sunflower seed. LDPs are offered for feed grains, wheat, upland cotton, rice, soybeans, canola, flaxseed, mustard seed, rapeseed, safflower, and sunflower seed. If the loan repayment rates are less than the established loan levels, producers may forego the loan and elect to receive LDPs which are equal to the amount by which the loan rate exceeds the loan repayment rate in effect on the delivery date. Recourse loans may be made for low quality grain or unginned seed cotton; such loans require repayment at maturity.

Eligible applicants/beneficiaries: owners, landlords, tenants, or sharecroppers on farms producing eligible commodities; for sugar, processors or refiners meeting USDA program requirements.

Range: loans, $162 to $1,006,400; purchases, N.A. **Average:** $22,959. Note: maximum total LDP and any gain from repaying a loan at a level lower than the original loan per "person", $75,000 ($150,000 in for 1999 crops).

Activity: FY 02, $14,299,113,000 total commodity loans and loan deficiency payments.

HQ: Price Support Division, FSA-USDA, 1400 Independence Ave. SW, Washington, DC 20250-0512. Phone: (202) 720-7901.

Internet: www.fsa.usda.gov.

10.053 DAIRY INDEMNITY PROGRAM

Assistance: direct payments/unrestricted use (100 percent).

Purposes: pursuant to the Agricultural Act of 1970, Agriculture and Consumer Protection Act of 1973, FACTA, amendments, and other acts, to indemnify dairy farmers and dairy product manufacturers against losses when their milk or dairy products are contaminated by pesticides, chemicals, toxic substances, or nuclear radiation or fallout, if the cause was outside their control; in such cases CCC pays the fair market value of the product.

Eligible applicants/beneficiaries: dairy farmers and manufacturers with products removed from the market by a public agency. Available also in PR.

Range: $88 to $95,000. **Average:** $40,000.

Activity: N.A.

HQ: FSA-USDA, 1400 Independence Ave. SW, Washington, DC 20250-0512. Phone: (202) 720-7641.

Internet: www.fsa.usda.gov.

10.054 EMERGENCY CONSERVATION PROGRAM ("ECP")

Assistance: direct payments/specified use.

Purposes: pursuant to the Agricultural Credit Act of 1978 as amended, for emergency conservation measures to control wind erosion; to rehabilitate farmlands damaged by wind, floods, or other natural disasters; to take water enhancing or conservation measures during drought. Assistance is limited basically to new conservation problems created by natural disasters. Cost-sharing payment rates vary.

Eligible applicants/beneficiaries: owners, landlords, tenants, or sharecroppers on farms or ranches, including associated groups. Available also in Guam, Northern Marianas, PR, and VI.

Range: $50 to $64,000. **Average:** $2,681.

Activity: FY 03 estimate, $82,000,000 in cost-share and technical assistance.

HQ: FSA-USDA (CEPD), 1400 Independence Ave. SW, Washington, DC 20250-0513. Phone: (202) 720-6221.

Internet: www.fsa.usda.gov.

10.055 DIRECT AND COUNTER-CYCLICAL PAYMENTS PROGRAM ("DCP")

Assistance: direct payments/specified use.

Purposes: pursuant to the FSRIA, to provide CCC income support to producers of covered commodities. Contract payments equal the contract payment rate, times 85 percent of the contract acreage, times the farm program payment yield. Participants must: share the risk of producing a crop on base acres and be entitled to share in the crop available for marketing from the base acres; comply with conservation, wetland, and similar requirements; comply with planting flexibility requirements; use the base acres for agricultural or related activities.

Eligible applicants/beneficiaries: owners, operators, landlords, tenants, or sharecroppers on producing farms—enrolled in DCP for the 2002-2007 crop years. FSA offices should be consulted for specifics.

Range/Average: N.A.

Activity: N.A., new program.

HQ: Compliance Branch, Production Emergencies and Compliance Division, FSA-USDA, 1400 Independence Ave. SW, Washington, DC 20250-0514. Phone: (202) 720-9882.

Internet: www.fsa.usda.gov.

10.056 FARM STORAGE FACILITY LOANS

Assistance: direct loans. (85 percent/7 years).

Purposes: for new, remodeled, or refinanced farm grain storage structures and drying equipment; to meet handling requirements for genetically enhanced production.

Eligible applicants/beneficiaries: owner, landlord, tenant, or sharecropper producing one or more of the CCC-approved commodities, participating in the Federal Crop Insurance program, and producing proof of flood insurance.

Range: $1,000 to $100,000.

Activity: FY 01, 1500 loans out of 2200 applications.

HQ: FSA, Director, Price Support Division, 14th and Independence Ave. SW, Washington, DC 20250. Phone: (202) 720-7935.

Internet: http://www.fsa.usda.gov.

10.066 LIVESTOCK ASSISTANCE PROGRAM ("LAP")

Assistance: direct payments/unrestricted use.

Purposes: for cash payments to livestock producers that suffered grazing losses of at least 40 percent during calendar year 2000 because of disease, insect infestation, natural disasters, droughts, or other emergencies.

Eligible applicants/beneficiaries: in counties with a declared severe natural disaster—U.S. citizens or legal resident aliens, farm cooperatives, private domestic corporations or partnerships or joint operations, or Indian tribes or tribal organizations, that: are actively engaged in farming; do not have gross annual income exceeding $2,500,000; receive at least 10 percent of their total gross income from livestock production.

Range: $10 to $40,000. **Average:** $875.

Activity: N.A.

HQ: Emergency Preparedness and Program Branch, Production Emergencies and Compliance Division, FSA-USDA, 1400 Independence Ave. SW, Washington, DC 20250-0517. Phone: (202) 720-7641.

Internet: www.fsa.usda.gov.

10.069 CONSERVATION RESERVE PROGRAM ("CRP")

Assistance: direct payments/specified use (10-15 years).

Purposes: pursuant to the Food Security Act of 1985 as amended, FACTA, and FAIRA, to convert highly erodible or environmentally sensitive cropland to less intensive uses such as grasses, legumes, shrubs, trees. Basic program objectives include reducing soil erosion or sedimentation, and improving water quality and wildlife habitat. Participants must institute approved conservation plans and reduce the aggregate total of acreage bases, allotments, and quotas for the contract period.

Eligible applicants/beneficiaries: individuals, partnerships, associations, tribal ventures corporations, estates, trusts, other businesses and legal entities; states and their political subdivisions.

Range: $50 to $50,000. **Average:** $4,000; contracts, rental rate, $45.95/acre.

Activity: 33,500,000 acres under active contracts; average of 74 acres/contract.

HQ: FSA-USDA (CEPD), 1400 Independence Ave. SW, Washington, DC 20250-0513. Phone: (202) 720-6221.

Internet: www.fsa.usda.gov.

10.070 COLORADO RIVER BASIN SALINITY CONTROL PROGRAM ("CRBSCP")

Assistance: direct payments/specified use. (to 70 percent/3-10 years).

Purposes: pursuant to the Colorado River Basin Salinity Control Act of 1974 as amended, for salinity control activities in the Colorado River basin, toward the improvement of water quality in the U.S. and Mexico. Assistance may be financial or technical, to: identify salt source areas; employ conservation practices to reduce salt loads; conduct research, education, and demonstration projects.

Eligible applicants/beneficiaries: owners, landlords, operators, or tenants of eligible lands; individuals, tribes, partnerships, firms, associations, corporations, joint stock companies, conservation or irrigation districts, estates, trusts, states, local public or nonpublic entities.

Range: N.A. **Average:** $20,000.

Activity: operated in 6 project areas in Colorado, Utah, and Wyoming.

HQ: Natural Resources Conservation Service (NRCS)-USDA, P.O. Box 2890, Washington, DC 20013. Phone: (202) 720-1873.

Internet: www.nrcs.usda.gov.

10.072 WETLANDS RESERVE PROGRAM ("WRP")

Assistance: direct payments/specified use. (to 100 percent/5-30 years).

Purposes: pursuant to the Food Security Act of 1985 as amended, FACTA, FAIRA, and other acts, to install restoration practices needed to protect farmed or converted wetlands, certain riparian areas, and buffer areas. Landowners must: place the wetlands under permanent or long-term easement with USDA; provide an access road to the land to enable easement management and monitoring. Landowners receive payments based on the fair agricultural market value of the land or 75 percent of such value. Permitted land uses after installing restoration or protective practices include haying, grazing, and buffer areas.

Eligible applicants/beneficiaries: individual landowners, partnerships, associations, corporations, estates, trusts; other businesses or legal entities; states and their political subdivisions.

Range/Average: N.A.

Activity: None.

HQ: Watersheds and Wetlands Division, NRCS-USDA, P.O. Box 2890, Washington, DC 20013. Phone: (202) 690-0848.

Internet: www.nrcs.usda.gov.

10.073 CROP DISASTER PROGRAM ("CDP")

Assistance: direct payments/unrestricted use.

Purposes: for producers that suffered crop losses greater than 35 percent during the 2000 crop year, because of adverse weather, disaster conditions, drought, insect infestation, or similar causes—preventing planting, or reducing production, or resulting in value loss crops, including in nursery and aquaculture. Crops eligible for federal crop insurance are covered regardless of whether insurance was purchased.

Eligible applicants/beneficiaries: producers meeting FSA requirements. "Persons" with gross annual revenues exceeding $2,500,000 for the 2000 tax year are ineligible for 2000 CDP benefits.

Range: to $80,000 per "person".

Activity: N.A.

HQ: Compliance Branch, Production Emergencies and Compliance Division, FSA-USDA, 1400 Independence Ave. SW, Washington, DC 20250-0514. Phone: (202) 720-9882.

Internet: www.fsa.usda.gov.

10.077 LIVESTOCK COMPENSATION PROGRAM ("LCP")

Assistance: direct payments/unrestricted use.

Purposes: pursuant to the Act of August 24, 1935 as amended by the Agricultural Assistance Act of 2003, to provide immediate assistance to livestock producers in counties that have received primary disaster designation due to drought in 2001 and/or 2002.

Eligible applicants/beneficiaries: producers of cattle, sheep, goats, buffalo, and catfish in designated counties—subject to a gross revenue limitation of $2,500,000 during the preceding tax year, with payments limited to $40,000 "per person.".

Range/Average: payments vary according to the type of livestock or feed lost—ranging from $4.50 per head for sheep and goats born prior to 1 June 2002 to $31.50 per head for adult dairy cattle, and $34.00 per ton for catfish feed.

Activity: new program listing in 2003.

HQ: Production Emergencies and Compliance Division, FSA-USDA, Washington, DC 20250. Phone: (no number provided).

Internet: www.fsa.usda.gov.

10.078 BIOENERGY PROGRAM ("BIO")

Assistance: direct payments/specified use.

Purposes: pursuant to FSRIA, to encourage increased purchases of eligible commodities toward expansion of bioenergy (fuel grade ethanol and biodiesel) through conversion of crops grown in the U.S. and its territories. Eligible commodities include barley, corn, grain sorghum, oats, rice, wheat, soybeans, sunflower seed, canola, crambe, rapeseed, safflower, sesame seed, flaxseed, mustard seed, and cellulosic crops such as switchgrass and short rotation trees grown on farms for the purpose of producing ethanol and/or biodiesel or any other commodity or commodity by-product approved by the CCC.

Eligible applicants/beneficiaries: all bioenergy producers that can provide evidence of increased production, purchase, and utilization to meet program purposes. Producers with less than 65,000,000 gallons annual production capacity are favored.

Range/Average: based on rate of increased production, reimbursements at 50 percent of the rate.

Activity: N.A.

HQ: Kansas City Commodity Office, FSA-USDA, Kansas City, MO 64141-6205. Phone: (816) 926-6525.

Internet: www.fsa.usda.gov/daco/bio_daco.htm. (Note: the field office serves as headquarters.)

10.079 BILL EMERSON HUMANITARIAN TRUST ("EHT")

Assistance: direct payments/unrestricted use.

Purposes: pursuant to the Agricultural Act of 1980 as amended, to provide a trust solely to meet emergency humanitarian food needs in developing countries—consisting of a trust stock of wheat, rice, corn, or sorghum, or any combination, and totaling not more than 4,000,000 metric tons. Commodities may be released when domestic supplies are insufficient to meet availability criteria or in instances when unanticipated needs cannot be met in a timely manner under normal means.

Eligible applicants/beneficiaries: developing countries that suffer from natural disasters, prolonged war or diseases, and/or acute hunger.

Range/Average: N.A.

Activity: new program listing in 2003. (Note: program was originally authorized as the Food Security Wheat Reserve, and was renamed in 1998.)

HQ: Kansas City Commodity Office, FSA-USDA, 6501 Beacon Dr., Kansas City, MO 64131-4676. Phone: (816) 926-6715.

Internet: www.fsa.usda.gov/daco/default.htm. (Note: the field office serves as headquarters.)

10.080 MILK INCOME LOSS CONTRACT PROGRAM ("MIL")

Assistance: direct payments/unrestricted use.

Purposes: pursuant to FSRIA, to provide payments to milk producers for milk produced and marketed between 1 December 2001 and 30 September 2005—when the prices under milk marketing orders fall below $16.94 per cwt.

Eligible applicants/beneficiaries: U.S. dairy producers with MIL contracts; foreign producers with a working U.S. visa or other valid taxpayer identification number.

Range/Average: N.A.

Activity: None, new program listing in 2004.

HQ: Price Support Division, FSA-USDA, 1400 Independence Ave. SW, Washington, DC 20250-0517. Phone: (202) 720-1919.

Internet: www.fsa.usda.gov/dafp/psd/MILC.htm.

10.081 LAMB MEAT ADJUSTMENT ASSISTANCE PROGRAM ("LMA")

Assistance: direct payments/unrestricted use.

Purposes: pursuant to the Act of August 24, 1935 as amended, for sheep and lamb producers to: in Year 1 of the program, purchase eligible rams for breeding and enroll herds in a sheep improvement program; improve production facilities; in Years 2-4, market eligible slaughtered lambs, feeder lambs or ewe lambs.

Eligible applicants/beneficiaries: producers of eligible sheep and lambs, with 1999 gross annual revenue of $2,500,000 or less, and that marketed their products between 1 August 2001 and 31 July 2003.

Range/Average: varies (consult FSA for details).

Activity: FY 00- FY 03, $30,000,000 paid to producers.

HQ: Price Support Division, FSA-USDA, 1400 Independence Ave. SW, Washington, DC 20250-0517. Phone: (202) 720-1919.

Internet: www.fsa.usda.gov/dafp/psd/lamb.htm.

10.082 TREE ASSISTANCE PROGRAM ("TAP")

Assistance: direct payments/unrestricted use.

Purposes: pursuant to FSRIA, for payments to tree, bush, and vine owners that lost crops due to natural disasters. Payments are restricted to owners that produce annual crops from trees for commercial purposes and that actually replant or rehabilitate eligible crops within 12 months of application approval. Payments may not exceed 75 percent of eligible costs—i.e., that loss over and above the calculated 15 percent mortality.

Eligible applicants/beneficiaries: private stand owners with gross annual revenue not exceeding $2,500,000 for the previous tax year.

Range: to $75,000 per program year for planting up to 500 acres.

Activity: None, new program in FY 04.

HQ: Production, Emergencies, and Compliance Division, FSA-USDA, 1400 Independence Ave. SW, Washington, DC 20250-0517. Phone: (202) 720-7641.

Internet: www.fsa.usda.gov.

10.084 DAIRY MARKET LOSS ASSISTANCE PROGRAM ("DMLA III")

Assistance: direct payments/unrestricted use.

Purposes: pursuant to the Military Construction Appropriations and Emergency Hurricane Supplemental Appropriations Act of 2005, to provide financial assistance to dairy operations affected by a declared hurricane disaster in 2004, in connection with normal milk production sold on the commercial market.

Eligible applicants/beneficiaries: dairy producers that were paid under DMLA II and new producers that began production in calendar 2000.

Range: to $25,225. **Average:** $8,300.

Activity: new program in FY 05.

HQ: Price Support Division, FSA-USDA, 1400 Independence Ave. SW, Washington, DC 20250-0517. Phone: (202) 720-1919.

Internet: www.fsa.usda.gov/dafp/psd/dairy.htm.

10.085 TOBACCO TRANSITION PAYMENT PROGRAM ("TTPP")

Assistance: direct payments/unrestricted use (years beginning 2005, ending 2014).

Purposes: pursuant to the Fair and Equitable Tobacco Reform Act of 2004 (FETRA) which repeals the federal tobacco price support control program, to compensate tobacco quota owners for the elimination of their government-created asset—i.e., quota—through a system of transition payments by the CCC.

Eligible applicants/beneficiaries: tobacco producers owning, controlling, or growing eligible tobacco on farms with an established marketing quota or allotment for the 2004 marketing year, or their assignees.

Range/Average: according to formula based on the FSA-established basic quota.

Activity: None, new program in FY 05.

HQ: Tobacco Branch, FSA-USDA, 1400 Independence Ave. SW, Washington, DC 20250-0540. Phone: (202) 720-2715.

Internet: www.fsa.usda.gov/tobacco; www.fsa.usda.gov/pas/publications/facts/html/ttpp05.htm.

10.153 MARKET NEWS

Assistance: technical information.

Purposes: pursuant to the Agricultural Marketing Act of 1946, Food Security Act of 1985, amendments, and other acts, to provide reports on prices, demand, movement, volume, and quality of all major U.S. agricultural commodities. Information is disseminated through news media and through printed reports, bulletin boards, phone, facsimile machines, data networks, and telegraph.

Eligible applicants/beneficiaries: anyone may subscribe.

Range/Average: N.A.

Activity: None.

HQ: Associate Administrator, AMS-USDA, Washington, DC 20250. Phone: (202) 720-4276.

Internet: www.ams.usda.gov.

10.155 MARKETING AGREEMENTS AND ORDERS

Assistance: specialized services; advisory services/counseling.

Purposes: pursuant to the Agricultural Marketing Agreement Act of 1937 as amended, Agriculture and Food Act of 1981, and other acts, to help maintain adequate prices to producers of agricultural products by issuing federal marketing orders or agreements relating to marketing and economic problems of the commodity or area covered by the federal actions. Marketing orders are issued by USDA only after a public hearing where milk, fruit, and vegetable producers, marketers, and consumers testify, and after farmers vote approval through a referendum.

Eligible applicants/beneficiaries: generally, growers of certain fruits, vegetables, and specialty crops (e.g., nuts, raisins, olives, hops); dairy farmers.

Range/Average: N.A.

Activity: FY 06 estimate, $24.9 billion in marketing.

HQ: Associate Administrator, AMS-USDA, Washington, DC 20250. Phone: (202) 720-4276. (Note: no field offices for this program.)

Internet: www.ams.usda.gov.

10.156 FEDERAL-STATE MARKETING IMPROVEMENT PROGRAM

Assistance: project grants (50 percent).

Purposes: pursuant to the Agricultural Marketing Act of 1946, for state pilot marketing service projects to improve the marketability of agricultural products, expand export markets, and improve economic and physical marketing efficiency and competitive trading.

Eligible applicants: state agencies.

Eligible beneficiaries: producers, processors, marketing agencies, and general public.

Range: $21,000 to $135,000. **Average:** $51,385.

Activity: FY 06 estimate, 25 projects funded.

HQ: Staff Officer, Federal-State Marketing Improvement Program, AMS-USDA, Washington, DC 20250. Phone: (202) 720-2704.

Internet: www.ams.usda.gov/tmd/fsmip.htm. (Note: no field offices for this program.)

10.162 INSPECTION GRADING AND STANDARDIZATION ("Agricultural Fair Practices Act")

Assistance: specialized services.

Purposes: pursuant to the Agricultural Marketing Act of 1946, Food Security Act of 1985, amendments, and other acts, to develop and apply standards of quality and condition for agricultural commodities, for use by owners and dealers; to help develop international standards; to conduct quarterly inspections of egg handlers and hatcheries.

Eligible applicants: agricultural commodity owners or dealers with a financial interest in the commodity to be graded; egg hatcheries and shell egg handlers with an annual production from 3,000 or more hens, packing for the retail consumer—located within the U.S. or its territories.

Eligible beneficiaries: buyers and sellers of agricultural commodities, shell handlers with annual production of 3,000 or more hens, and located in the U.S. or its Territories.

Range/Average: N.A.

Activity: FY 06 estimates, 17,726,000 bales of cotton classed; 0 tobacco auctions and 60,000,000 pounds of imported and domestic tobacco inspected; 13,102 million pounds of poultry products graded; 40,500 million pounds of meat graded; 2,750 million dozen shell eggs graded; 20,500 million pounds of processed fruit and vegetables graded; 70,000 million pounds of fresh fruit and vegetables graded; 40 million pounds of livestock graded; 1,570 million pounds of dairy products graded.

HQ: Associate Administrator, AMS-USDA, Washington, DC 20250. Phone: (202) 720-4276.

Internet: www.ams.usda.gov.

10.163 MARKET PROTECTION AND PROMOTION

Assistance: specialized services; advisory services/counseling; training.

Purposes: pursuant to the Agricultural Marketing Act of 1946, Agricultural Fair Practices Act, amendments, and other acts, to assure a fair and open marketing distribution system for agricultural products, through the prevention and elimination of deceptive, unfair, or fraudulent trade practices. Various activities fall under the national dairy promotion research and nutrition education program, the Federal Seed Program, the Plant Variety Protection Program, the Research and Promotion Program, and the Pesticide Data Program.

Eligible applicants/beneficiaries: any state government, public or private organization, business, or individual.

Range/Average: N.A.

Activity: FY 06 estimates, 2,000 seed samples tested, 325 plant variety certificates of protection issued, 11,000 pesticide data samples collected.

HQ: Associate Administrator, AMS-USDA, Washington, DC 20250. Phone: (202) 720-4276.

Internet: www.ams.usda.gov.

10.164 WHOLESALE FARMERS AND ALTERNATIVE MARKET DEVELOPMENT

Assistance: advisory services/counseling; training.

Purposes: pursuant to the Agricultural Marketing Act of 1946, to provide marketing assistance to food producers through studies on wholesaling, conducted in cooperation with other government agencies and private industry. Project examples: central refrigeration systems in modern food centers; wholesale and farmers markets for distributing produce.

Eligible applicants: government agencies and private industry. Cooperative agreements—states, trade associations, universities, and other nonprofit organizations.

Eligible beneficiaries: producers, processors, marketing agencies, and consumers.

Range/Average: N.A.

Activity: FY 06 estimate, 12 projects and studies.

HQ: (Note: no field offices for this program.)

Internet: www.ams.usda.gov. (Note: no field offices for this program.)

10.165 PERISHABLE AGRICULTURAL COMMODITIES ACT ("PACA")

Assistance: investigation of complaints.

Purposes: pursuant to the Act of 1930 as amended and Produce Agency Act, to suppress unfair and fraudulent practices in the marketing of perishable agricultural commodities in interstate and foreign commerce, such as dumping or destruction of farm produce.

Eligible applicants/beneficiaries: businesses or individuals may apply for a PACA license.

Range/Average: N.A.

Activity: FY 03 estimate, 57,850 license actions completed.

HQ: Associate Administrator, AMS-USDA, Washington, DC 20250. Phone: (202) 720-4276.

Internet: www.ams.usda.gov.

10.167 TRANSPORTATION SERVICES

Assistance: advisory services/counseling; training.

Purposes: pursuant to the Agricultural Adjustment Act of 1938, Agricultural Marketing Act of 1946, Rural Development Act of 1972, and other acts, for the development and promotion of efficient agricultural transportation policies and systems, toward improved farm income and expanded exports. Assistance is provided in cases of significant regional impact or with broad policy implications.

Eligible applicants/beneficiaries: any state government, public or private organization, business or industry, individual.

Range/Average: N.A.

Activity: FY 06 estimate, 12 research projects, 12 publications, 25 workshops to be completed.

HQ: Deputy Administrator, Transportation and Marketing Programs, AMS-USDA, Washington, DC 20250. Phone: (202) 690-1305.(Note: no field offices for this program.)

Internet: www.ams.usda.gov.

10.168 FARMERS' MARKET PROMOTION PROGRAM ("FMPP")

Assistance: project grants. (100 percent/to 18 months).

Purposes: pursuant to FSRIA, to improve or expand existing or develop new domestic farmers markets, roadside stands, community-supported agriculture programs, and other direct producer-to-consumer market opportunities—through innovative approaches to market operations and management, improving access to pertinent marketing and financial opportunities, and consumer-based education and market access. Funds may not be used for routine operational expenses such as salaries, utility charges, insurance premiums, nor for any real estate-related costs.

Eligible applicants: agricultural cooperatives; local and tribal governments; nonprofit, public benefit, and economic development corporations; regional farmers market authorities; projects located within 50 states or District of Columbia.

Eligible beneficiaries: direct marketing operations that include two or more farm vendors; consumers.

Range: to $75,000.

Activity: N.A.

HQ: FMPP, Marketing Services Branch, AMS-USDA - Rm.2646-South, 1400 Independence Ave. SW, Washington, DC 20250-0269. Phone: (202) 720-8317.

Internet: www.www.ams.usda.gov/tmd/MSB/index.ht. (Note: no field offices for this program.)

10.169 SPECIALTY CROP BLOCK GRANT PROGRAM

Assistance: project grants. (100 percent/to 3 years).

Purposes: pursuant to Specialty Crops Competitiveness Act of 2004, to increase fruit, vegetable, and nut consumption—enhancing the competitiveness of crop producers.

Eligible applicants/beneficiaries: state agriculture departments, agencies, or commissions.

Range: from $100,000 per state, plus additional formula-based amount.

Activity: new program, 2006.

HQ: Project Manager, Specialty Crop Block Grant Program, AMS-USDA - Rm.2086-South, 1400 Independence Ave. SW, Washington, DC 20250. Phone: (202) 690-4942; FAX (202) 690-0102.

Internet: N.A. (Note: no field offices for this program.)

10.200 GRANTS FOR AGRICULTURAL RESEARCH, SPECIAL RESEARCH GRANTS ("Special Research Grants")

Assistance: project grants (1-3 years).

Purposes: for applied research, extension, and education projects toward breakthroughs in the food and agricultural sciences, and for ongoing state-federal programs. Current priority areas include integrated pest management and pest management alternatives. Project examples: small fruit crops research; arid rangelands.

Eligible applicants/beneficiaries: state agricultural experiment stations; U.S. IHEs, federal agencies, private organizations and corporations, individuals.

Range: $56,664 to $9,549,325. **Average:** $46,183.

Activity: not quantified specifically.

HQ: Proposal Services Unit, Competitive Programs, CSREES-USDA, 1400 Independence Ave. SW, Washington, DC 20250-2245. Phone: (202) 401-5048.

Internet: www.reeusda.gov. (Note: no field offices for this program.)

10.202 COOPERATIVE FORESTRY RESEARCH ("McIntire-Stennis Act")

Assistance: formula grants.

Purposes: pursuant to the Cooperative Forestry Research Act of 1962 and other acts, for forestry research and research training at state forestry schools, in such categories as reforestation, forest and watershed management, rangeland management, production of wildlife and domestic livestock forage, forest pest control, outdoor recreation, wood products development, and protection against fire, insects, and diseases.

Eligible applicants/beneficiaries: governor-designated state institutions; territories and possessions.

Range: $30,281 to $694,074. **Average:** $322,889.

Activity: not quantified specifically.

HQ: Deputy Administrator/Natural Resources and Environment, CSREES-USDA, Washington, DC. 20250. Phone: (202) 720-4318.

Internet: www.reeusda.gov. (Note: no field offices for this program.)

10.203 PAYMENTS TO AGRICULTURAL EXPERIMENT STATIONS UNDER THE HATCH ACT ("Hatch Act")

Assistance: formula grants (50 percent).

Purposes: pursuant to the Hatch Act of 1887 as amended and other acts, for basic and applied research in broad subject areas at state agricultural experiment stations—to promote efficient production, marketing, distribution, and use of farm products. Funds also may be used to pay for administrative planning and direction, and for such purposes as purchasing or renting land and acquiring or constructing or repairing buildings used for research. The stations may contract with agencies and individuals for research projects.

Eligible applicants/beneficiaries: state agricultural experiment stations; territories and possessions.

Range: $611,608 to $5,831,557. **Average:** $2,796,141.

Activity: not quantified specifically.

HQ: Deputy Administrator/Partnerships, CSREES-USDA, Washington, DC 20250-2201. Phone: (202) 720-5623.

Internet: www.reeusda.gov. (Note: no field offices for this program.)

10.205 PAYMENTS TO 1890 LAND-GRANT COLLEGES AND TUSKEGEE UNIVERSITY

Assistance: formula grants (50 percent).

Purposes: pursuant to the National Agricultural Research, Extension, and Teaching Policy Act of 1977 as amended (NARETPA) and other acts, for continuing agricultural research and research training, toward the promotion of efficient production, marketing, distribution, and utilization of farm products, and toward sound agriculture and rural life. Funds may be used to pay for developmental costs, retirement programs, administrative planning and direction, and for such purposes as purchasing or renting land and acquiring or constructing or repairing buildings used for research. Recipients may contract with agencies and individuals.

Eligible applicants/beneficiaries: Tuskegee University and the "1890" land grant colleges in Alabama, Arkansas, Delaware, Florida, Georgia, Kentucky, Louisiana, Maryland, Mississippi, Missouri, North Carolina, Oklahoma, South Carolina, Tennessee, Texas, Virginia, and West Virginia.

Range: $518,078 to $1,539,502. **Average:** $1,571,245.

Activity: not quantified specifically.

HQ: National Program Leader, Multicultural Alliances, CSREES- USDA, 1400 Independence Ave. SW, Washington, DC 20250-2251. Phone: (202) 720-3511.

Internet: www.reeusda.gov. (Note: no field offices for this program.)

10.206 GRANTS FOR AGRICULTURAL RESEARCH—COMPETITIVE RESEARCH GRANTS ("National Research Initiative Competitive Grants Program")

Assistance: project grants. (100 percent/to 4 years).

Purposes: for research, education and extension grants in food, agriculture, and related areas. Priority areas for funding include agricultural security, plant science and plant pathology, animal science, entomology and nematology, nanotechnology, nutrition/obesity, food quality and health, natural resources and environment, nutrition, rural development, and new products and processes.

Eligible applicants/beneficiaries: state agricultural experiment stations; U.S. IHEs, federal agencies, private organizations and corporations, individuals.

Range: $4,000 to $5,000,000. **Average:** $183,607.

Activity: not quantified specifically.

HQ: Chief Scientist, National Research Initiative Competitive Grants Program, CSREES-USDA, 14th & Independence Ave. SW, Washington, DC 20250-2241. Phone: (202) 401-5022.

Internet: www.reeusda.gov. (Note: no field offices for this program.)

10.207 ANIMAL HEALTH AND DISEASE RESEARCH

Assistance: formula grants (50 percent matching above base amount).

Purposes: pursuant to NARETPA, amendments, and other acts, for research on health and disease of food animals and horses. Focus is on: infectious diseases; internal and external parasites; noninfectious diseases, toxins, poisons, transportation losses, predators, and other hazards; diseases and parasites of wildlife and other animals transmissible to food animals, horses, or humans.

Eligible applicants/beneficiaries: public nonprofit schools and colleges of veterinary medicine; state agricultural experiment stations.

Range: $1,586 to $408,854. **Average:** $65,515.

Activity: not quantified specifically.

HQ: Deputy Administrator/Plant and Animal Science, CSREES-USDA, Washington, DC. 20250. Phone: (202) 401-4329.

Internet: www.reeusda.gov. (Note: no field offices for this program.)

10.210 FOOD AND AGRICULTURAL SCIENCES NATIONAL NEEDS GRADUATE FELLOWSHIP GRANTS

Assistance: project grants. (100 percent/to five years).

Purposes: pursuant to NARETPA as amended, to support graduate degree candidates and professionals in the food and agricultural sciences. Fellowships are awarded to outstanding students pursuing graduate degrees in fields for which there is a national need for the development of scientific expertise. Doctoral and masters fellows may receive three and two years of support, respectively. The targeted national need areas include: animal, plant biotechnology; food science; human nutrition; food, forest product, or agricultural engineering; water science; agribusiness marketing or management.

Eligible applicants: U.S. public and private nonprofit IHEs.

Eligible beneficiaries: graduate students.

Range/Average: N.A.

Activity: not quantified specifically.

HQ: National Program Leader, Higher Education Programs, CSREES-USDA, 1400 Independence Ave. SW, Washington, DC 20250-2251. Phone: (202) 720-7854.

Internet: www.reeusda.gov. (Note: no field offices for this program.)

10.212 SMALL BUSINESS INNOVATION RESEARCH ("SBIR Program")

Assistance: project grants. (100 percent/phase I, to 6 months; phase II, to 2 years).

Purposes: pursuant to the Small Business Innovation Development Act of 1982 as amended, for research by small businesses to stimulate technological innovation, mainly in the areas of: forests and related resources; plant, animal production and protection; air, water, and soils; food science and nutrition; rural and community development; industrial applications; aquaculture; industrial applications; marketing and trade. Previous phase I grants have ranged up to $65,000 for six months of activity; phase II, to $300,000 for up to two years; phase III covers pursuit of commercialization of research products, and receives no federal funding. An objective of SBIR programs is to foster and encourage participation by women-owned and socially disadvantaged firms.

Eligible applicants/beneficiaries: small, U.S. for-profit businesses.

Range: $46,000 to $300,000. **Average:** $94,990.

Activity: not quantified specifically.

HQ: SBIR Director, CSREES-USDA, 14th & Independence Ave. SW, Washington, DC 20250-2243. Phone: (202) 401-4002.

Internet: www.reeusda.gov. (Note: no field offices for this program.)

10.215 SUSTAINABLE AGRICULTURE RESEARCH AND EDUCATION

Assistance: project grants. (100 percent/1-5 years).

Purposes: pursuant to NARETPA and FACTA, for scientific investigations and education to: reduce the use of chemical pesticides, fertilizers, and toxic materials; improve management of farm resources to enhance productivity and competitiveness; promote crop, livestock, and enterprise diversification; facilitate research projects designed to study agricultural production systems located in areas with various soil, climatic, and physical characteristics; study farms that are managed using production practices optimizing on-farm resources and conservation practices. Funds may not be used to pay indirect costs or tuition.

Eligible applicants/beneficiaries: land grant colleges or universities, other universities, state agricultural experiment and cooperative extension stations, nonprofit organizations, individuals, federal or state government entities.

Range: $8,000 to $1,752,250. **Average:** $855,540.

Activity: not quantified specifically.

HQ: Deputy Administrator/Economic and Community Systems, CSREES-USDA, Washington, DC. 20250. Phone: (202) 720-7948.

Internet: www.reeusda.gov. (Note: no field offices for this program.)

10.216 1890 INSTITUTION CAPACITY BUILDING GRANTS

Assistance: project grants. (100 percent/1-5 years).

Purposes: pursuant to NARETPA as amended, to build research and teaching capacities at "1890" land grants institutions and Tuskegee University. Teaching grants may support: curricula design and materials development; faculty development; instruction delivery systems; scientific instrumentation; student recruitment and retention; student experiential learning. Research grants may support studies and experimentation in food and agricultural sciences, centralized research support systems, and technology delivery systems. CSREES encourages cost-sharing by grant recipients.

Eligible applicants/beneficiaries: "1890" land grant institutions, Tuskegee University.

Range: teaching grants, $88,470 to $225,000; research, $107,574 to $349,793. **Average:** teaching, $171,443; research, $242,524.

Activity: not quantified specifically.

HQ: National Program Leader, Higher Education Programs, CSREES-USDA, 1400 Independence Ave. SW, Washington, DC 20250-2251. Phone: (202) 720-2186.

Internet: www.reeusda.gov. (Note: no field offices for this program.)

10.217 HIGHER EDUCATION CHALLENGE GRANTS

Assistance: project grants. (50 percent/1-5 years).

Purposes: pursuant to NARETPA as amended, to increase institutional capacity to respond to state, regional, national, or international educational needs in food and agricultural sciences. Funds may be used for curriculum design and materials development, faculty development, instruction delivery systems, scientific instrumentation, student recruitment and retention.

Eligible applicants/beneficiaries: U.S. colleges and universities.

Range: $47,936 to $152,000. **Average:** $89,479.

Activity: not quantified specifically.

HQ: National Program Leader/Higher Education Challenge Grants, Higher Education Programs, CSREES-USDA, 1400 Independence Ave. SW, Washington, DC 20250-2251. Phone: (202) 720-1973, FAX (202) 720-2030.

Internet: www.reeusda.gov/1700/funding/ourfund.htm. (Note: no field offices for this program.)

10.219 BIOTECHNOLOGY RISK ASSESSMENT RESEARCH

Assistance: project grant. (100 percent/1-5 years).

Purposes: for research focusing on environmental effects of agricultural biotechnology. Project examples: gene crop flow and introgression into natural populations; hazard of pest evolution.

Eligible applicants/beneficiaries: any public or private research or educational institution or organization.

Range: $50,220 to $223,269. **Average:** $147,583.

Activity: not quantified specifically.

HQ: Deputy Administrator, Competitive Programs, CSREES-USDA, Washington, DC 20250. Phone: (202) 401-1761.

Internet: www.reeusda.gov.

10.220 HIGHER EDUCATION MULTICULTURAL SCHOLARS PROGRAM ("Minority Scholars Program")

Assistance: project grants. (75 percent/5 years).

Purposes: pursuant to NARETPA as amended and the Food and Agriculture Act of 1977, for four-year undergraduate scholarships supporting minority students pursuing baccalaureate degrees in the food and agricultural sciences, including natural resources, forestry, veterinary medicine, home economics, and closely allied disciplines.

Eligible applicants: all U.S. colleges and universities with appropriate baccalaureate or higher degree programs and with significant minority enrollments.

Eligible beneficiaries: full-time students from groups traditionally underrepresented in the fields of study in which funds are awarded.

Range: $20,000 to $80,000. **Average:** $52,004.

Activity: not quantified specifically.

HQ: National Program Leader, Higher Education Programs, CSREES-USDA, 1400 Independence Ave. SW, Washington, DC 20250-2251. Phone:(202) 720-1973.

Internet: www.reeusda.gov (Note: no field offices for this program.)

10.221 TRIBAL COLLEGES EDUCATION EQUITY GRANTS

Assistance: formula grants (1-2 years).

Purposes: pursuant to the Equity in Educational Land-Grant Status Act of 1994 as amended, to enhance educational opportunities at the 30 tribal colleges designated as the "1994 Land-Grant Institutions" by strengthening their teaching programs in the food and agricultural sciences in targeted need areas. Funds may support: curricula design and instructional materials development; faculty development; instruction delivery systems; scientific instrumentation; student experiential learning; student recruitment and retention.

Eligible applicants/beneficiaries: the 30 tribal colleges designated as 1994 Land-Grant Institutions.

Range/Average: $50,000 to each institution.

Activity: N.A.

HQ: Science and Education Resources Development, Higher Education Programs, CSREES-USDA, 800 Ninth St. SW - Rm.3901, Washington, DC 20250-2251. Phone: (202) 720-1973.

Internet: www.reeusda.gov.

10.222 TRIBAL COLLEGES ENDOWMENT PROGRAM

Assistance: formula grants (100 percent).

Purposes: pursuant to the Equity in Educational Land-Grant Status Act of 1994, to enhance educational opportunities at the 30 tribal colleges designated as the "1994 Land-Grant Institutions" by strengthening their teaching programs in the food and agricultural sciences in targeted need areas. Funds may be used to establish an endowment supporting activities described in **10.221**.

Eligible applicants/beneficiaries: the 30 tribal colleges designated as 1994 Land-Grant Institutions.

Range: $7,932 to $40,191. **Average:** $14,943.

Activity: N.A.

HQ: Science and Education Resources Development, Higher Education Programs, CSREES-USDA, 800 Ninth St. SW - Rm.3901, Washington, DC 20250-2251. Phone: (202) 720-1973.

Internet: www.reeusda.gov (Note: no field offices for this program.)

10.223 HISPANIC SERVING INSTITUTIONS EDUCATION GRANTS

Assistance: project grants. (some matching/1-3 years).

Purposes: pursuant to NARETPA as amended, to support activities by a consortium of Hispanic serving institutions to enhance educational equity for under-represented students, by strengthening their capacities to respond to identified state, regional, national, or international needs in the food and agricultural sciences. Funds may support cooperative initiatives between two or more institutions and units of state government or the private sector, for activities such as: student mentoring beginning at the high school level and continuing with the provision of financial support for students through graduate training; library resources; curricula design and materials development; faculty development; instruction delivery systems; scientific instrumentation; student experiential learning; student recruitment and retention.

Eligible applicants/beneficiaries: Hispanic-serving IHEs with an enrollment of at least 25 percent Hispanic students, and providing postsecondary programs for which a two-year associate, baccalaureate, or higher degree is awarded.

Range: $25,000 to $75,000. **Average:** N.A.

Activity: N.A.

HQ: Multicultural Alliances, Science and Education Resources Development, Higher Education Programs, CSREES-USDA, Waterfront Center - Rm.3240, Washington, DC 20250-2251. Phone: (202) 720- 1254.

Internet: www.reeusda.gov.

10.224 FUND FOR RURAL AMERICA—RESEARCH, EDUCATION, AND EXTENSION ACTIVITIES ("Fund for Rural America")

Assistance: project grants. (50 percent/6 months-4 years).

Purposes: pursuant to FAIRA, for research, education, and extension projects to aid farmers, ranchers, and rural communities in addressing changes resulting from fundamental reforms to federal farm programs. Funded projects are expected to: increase international competitiveness, efficiency, and farm profitability; reduce economic and health risk; conserve and enhance natural resources; develop new crops, crop uses, and agricultural applications of biotechnology; enhance animal agricultural resources; preserve plant and animal germplasm; increase economic opportunities in farming and rural communities; and, expand locally-owned, value-added processing. Funds may support: applied, developmental, and adaptive research; technology transfer; extension and related activities; and, education—with emphasis on biological, physical, and social sciences to address systems-based problems; planning costs toward development of Fund for Rural America (FRA) Centers.

Eligible applicants: federal research agencies; national laboratories; IHEs and their research foundations; private research organizations.

Eligible beneficiaries: producers, commodity groups, environmental interests, rural communities, others.

Range: $25,000 to $600,000. **Average:** standard grants, $271,000; center planning grants, $25,000.

Activity: N.A.

HQ: Deputy Administrator, Competitive Programs, CSREES-USDA, Washington, DC 20250. Phone: (202) 401-1761.

Internet: www.reeusda.gov (Note: no field offices for this program.)

10.225 COMMUNITY FOOD PROJECTS

Assistance: project grants. (50 percent/1-3 years).

Purposes: pursuant to the Food Stamp Act of 1977 as amended and FAIRA, for community food projects designed to provide food to low-income persons; to increase self-reliance in communities; to promote comprehensive responses to local food, farm, and nutrition issues. Funds may support: improving access to affordable food by low-income households; local food systems such as urban gardening and obtaining food from local farms; expanding economic opportunities for community residents through local businesses or other economic development, job training, youth apprenticeships, school-to-work transitions. Projects should link the food sector to community development, economic opportunity, and environmental enhancement.

Eligible applicants: experienced private nonprofit entities and partnerships thereof.

Eligible beneficiaries: low income people.

Range: $10,000 to $250,000. **Average:** N.A.

Activity: 2001, 16 grants.

HQ: Deputy Administrator, Competitive Programs, CSREES-USDA, Washington, DC 20250. Phone: (202) 401-1761.

Internet: www.reeusda.gov (Note: no field offices for this program.)

10.226 SECONDARY AND TWO-YEAR POSTSECONDARY AGRICULTURE EDUCATION CHALLENGE GRANTS

Assistance: project grants. (50 percent/1-5 years).

Purposes: pursuant to FAIRA as amended, to promote excellence in agriscience and agribusiness education, and to encourage increased pursuit of undergraduate and higher degrees in the food and agricultural sciences. Funds may be used for such targeted areas as curricula design and materials development, promotion of teaching competency, student experiential learning, increasing the diversity of students enrolling.

Eligible applicants/beneficiaries: public secondary schools; public or private nonprofit junior and community colleges.

Range: $15,000 to $40,000. **Average:** $20,900.

Activity: not quantified specifically.

HQ: National Program Leader/Secondary and Two-Year Postsecondary Agriculture Education Challenge Grants, Higher Education Programs, 1400 Independence Ave. SW, Washington, D.C. 20250-2251. Phone: (202) 720-1973. FAX (202) 720-2030. (Note: no field offices for this program.)

Internet: www.reeusda.gov/1700/funding/ourfund.htm (Note: no field offices for this program.)

10.227 1994 INSTITUTIONS RESEARCH PROGRAM

Assistance: project grants. (100 percent/to 3 years).

Purposes: pursuant to the Equity in Educational Land-Grant Status Act of 1994 as amended, for competitive research grants to the 30 institutions designated as "1994 Institutions," to conduct agricultural research addressing high priority concerns of tribal, national, or multi-state significance.

Eligible applicants/beneficiaries: the 30 institutions designated as "1994 Institutions" (i.e., specified Indian colleges and institutions).

Range: $40,963 to $150,000. **Average:** $66,221.

Activity: not quantified specifically.

HQ: Administrator, CSREES-USDA, 14th & Independence Ave. SW, Washington, DC. 20250-2201. Phone: (202) 720-4423.

Internet: www.reeusda.gov (Note: no field offices for this program.)

10.228 ALASKA NATIVE SERVING AND NATIVE HAWAIIAN SERVING INSTITUTIONS EDUCATION GRANTS

Assistance: project grants. (100 percent/1-3 years).

Purposes: to recruit, support, and educate under-represented scientists and professionals, and to advance the educational capacity of Alaska native- and Hawaii native-serving institutions in the food, agricultural, and natural resource systems and careers. Funds may support: curriculum, faculty and library development; scientific instrumentation; instruction delivery systems; student recruitment and retention; and, cooperative initiatives between institutions, state governments, the private sector.

Eligible applicants/beneficiaries: Alaska native- and Hawaii native-serving IHEs.

Range: $100,000 to $150,000. **Average:** N.A.

Activity: N.A., newly funded program.

HQ: Multicultural Alliances, Science and Education Resources Development, CSREES-USDA, Waterfront Center - Rm.3901, 1400 Independence Ave. SW, Washington, DC 20250-2251. Phone: (202) 720- 1973.

Internet: www.reeusda.gov.

10.250 AGRICULTURAL AND RURAL ECONOMIC RESEARCH

Assistance: technical information.

Purposes: to provide economic and other social science information and analysis related to U.S. and world agriculture, food, natural resources, and rural America. Reports are prepared by USDA staff, and are available in printed or electronic form. Fees may be charged.

Eligible applicants/beneficiaries: anyone in the U.S. and territories.

Range/Average: N.A.

Activity: FY 06, 224 active projects; FY 06 estimate, responses to 50,000 requests for information; 170 reports published.

HQ: Director, Extramural Agreement Division, Economic Research Service-USDA, Sunnyside Ave. - ARS Rm.5601, Beltsville, MD 20705-5110. Phone: (301) 504-1147; *sales through NTIS,* (800) 999- 6779.

Internet: www.ers.usda.gov. (Note: no field offices for this program.)

10.253 FOOD ASSISTANCE AND NUTRITION RESEARCH PROGRAMS ("FANRP")

Assistance: technical information.

Purposes: pursuant to FY 2006 Agricultural, Rural Development, Food and Drug Administration, and Related Agencies Appropriation Act, to provide economic and other social science information and analysis related to U.S. and world agriculture, food, natural resources, and rural America. Reports are available in printed or in electronic form on the ERS web site. There are no restrictions on use of ERS- produced information, although a fee may be charged.

Eligible applicants/beneficiaries: anyone in the U.S. and territories.

Range/Average: N.A.

Activity: FY 06, 224 active projects; FY 06, responses to 50,000 requests for information; 170 reports published.

HQ: Director, Extramural Agreement Division, Economic Research Service-USDA, Sunnyside Ave. - ARS, Rm. 5601, Beltsville, MD 20705-5110. Phone: (301) 504-1147. *sales through NTIS,* (800) 999- 6779.

Internet: www.ers.usda.gov. (Note: no field offices for this program.)

10.254 PROGRAM OF RESEARCH ON THE ECONOMIC OF INVASIVE SPECIES MANAGEMENT ("PREISM")

Assistance: technical information.

Purposes: pursuant to FY 2006 Agricultural, Rural Development, Food and Drug Administration, and Related Agencies Appropriation Act, to provide economic and other social science information and analysis related to U.S. and world agriculture, food, natural resources, and rural America. Reports are available in printed or in electronic form on the ERS web site. There are no restrictions on use of ERS- produced information, although a fee may be charged.

Eligible applicants/beneficiaries: anyone in the U.S. and territories.

Range/Average: N.A.

Activity: FY 06, 224 active projects; FY 06, responses to 50,000 requests for information; 170 reports published.

HQ: Director, Extramural Agreement Division, Economic Research Service-USDA, Sunnyside Ave. - ARS, Rm. 5601, Beltsville, MD 20705-5110. Phone: (301) 504-1147. *sales through NTIS,* (800) 999- 6779.

Internet: www.ers.usda.gov. (Note: no field offices for this program.)

10.255 RESEARCH INNOVATION AND DEVELOPMENT GRANTS IN ECONOMIC ("RIDGE")

Assistance: technical information.

Purposes: pursuant to FY 2006 Agricultural, Rural Development, Food and Drug Administration, and Related Agencies Appropriation Act, to provide economic and other social science information and analysis related to U.S. and world agriculture, food, natural resources, and rural America. Reports are available in printed or in electronic form on the ERS web site. There are no restrictions on use of ERS- produced information, although a fee may be charged.

Eligible applicants/beneficiaries: anyone in the U.S. and territories.

Range/Average: N.A.

Activity: FY 06, 224 active projects; FY 06, responses to 50,000 requests for information; 170 reports published.

HQ: Director, Extramural Agreement Division, Economic Research Service-USDA, Sunnyside Ave. - ARS, Rm. 5601, Beltsville, MD 20705-5110. Phone: (301) 504-1147. *sales through NTIS,* (800) 999- 6779.

Internet: www.ers.usda.gov. (Note: no field offices for this program.)

10.256 CONSUMER DATA INITIATIVE ("CDI")

Assistance: technical information.

Purposes: pursuant to FY 2006 Agricultural, Rural Development, Food and Drug Administration, and Related Agencies Appropriation Act, to provide economic and other social science information and analysis related to U.S. and world agriculture, food, natural resources, and rural America. Reports are available in printed or in electronic form on the ERS web site. There are no restrictions on use of ERS- produced information, although a fee may be charged.

Eligible applicants/beneficiaries: anyone in the U.S. and territories.

Range/Average: N.A.

Activity: FY 06, 224 active projects; estimated publications and requests for information, 50,000.

HQ: Director, Extramural Agreement Division, Economic Research Service-USDA, Sunnyside Ave. - ARS, Rm. 5601, Beltsville, MD 20705-5110. Phone: (301) 504-1147. *sales through NTIS,* (800) 999- 6779.

Internet: www.ers.usda.gov. (Note: no field offices for this program.)

10.290 AGRICULTURAL MARKET AND ECONOMIC RESEARCH

Assistance: project grants.

Purposes: to conduct research in cooperation with the Office of the Chief Economist's in-house research and analysis programs. Projects may cover such areas as: nation's agricultural commodity markets; risk and cost-benefit analyses related to international food and agriculture; sustainable development; energy issues related to agricultural economy; agricultural labor and global climate change.

Eligible applicants/beneficiaries: nonprofit institutions of higher education; nonprofit scientific or economic research organizations.

Range: $20,000 to $1,948,384. **Average:** $245,102.

Activity: N.A.

HQ: Chief Economist, Department of Agriculture, Washington, DC 20250. Phone: (202) 720-4164. Information Officer, Phone: (202) 720-5447.

Internet: www.ers.usda.gov/oce. (Note: no field offices for this program.)

10.303 INTEGRATED PROGRAMS

Assistance: project grants. (100 percent/to 3 years).

Purposes: pursuant to the Food Stamp Act of 1977, for competitive integrated and multi-functional research, education, and extension projects addressing priorities in U.S. agriculture.

Eligible applicants/beneficiaries: state agricultural experiment stations; U.S. IHEs, federal agencies, private organizations and corporations, individuals.

Range: $20,000 to $2,080,000. **Average:** $499,050.

Activity: not quantified specifically.

HQ: Administrator, CSREES-USDA, 14th & Independence Ave. SW, Washington, DC. 20250-2201. Phone: (202) 720-4423.

Internet: www.reeusda.gov (Note: no field offices for this program.)

10.304 HOMELAND SECURITY—AGRICULTURAL ("Homeland Security Program")

Assistance: project grants (100 percent/1-3 years).

Purposes: pursuant to NARETPA as amended, to protect the food supply and agricultural production; to protect USDA facilities and other agricultural infrastructure; and to protect USDA staff and manage emergency preparedness. Project examples: establishment of two diagnostic networks-one each for plant and animal diseases and pests. Research projects may not be funded.

Eligible applicants/beneficiaries: recipients eligible under Section 1472(c) of NARETPA.

Range: $250,000 to $2,000,000.

Activity: new program listing in 2003.

HQ: Office of the Administrator, CSREES-USDA, 1400 Independence Ave. SW - Rm.305-A, Washington, DC. 20250-2201. Phone: (no number provided).

Internet: www.reeusda.gov (Note: no field offices for this program.)

10.305 INTERNATIONAL SCIENCE AND EDUCATION GRANTS

Assistance: project grants (1-4 years).

Purposes: pursuant to NARETPA as amended, to strengthen the global competence of students, faculty, and staff in agriculture and related areas, and to enhance business performance in international agriculture and related sectors—through extension, research, and teaching programs. Projects should be designed to: enhance the international content of curricula; enable U.S. faculty to work beyond the U.S. and bring back lessons learned; promote international partnerships; enhance the use of foreign technologies in the U.S.; strengthen the role of IHEs in maintaining U.S. competitiveness.

Eligible applicants/beneficiaries: accredited public or other nonprofit U.S. IHEs that award bachelor's or higher degrees.

Range/Average: N.A.

Activity: new program listing in 2005 (CFDA on-line version).

HQ: International Programs, CSREES-USDA, 1400 Independence Ave. SW, Washington, DC. 20250-2203. Phone: (202) 720-3801.

Internet: www.csrees.usda.gov. (Note: no field offices for this program.)

10.306 BIODIESEL

Assistance: project grants. (100 percent/5 years).

Purposes: to educate governmental and private entities that operate vehicle fleets, as well as the general public, about the benefits of biodiesel fuel use—through education and outreach activities.

Eligible applicants/beneficiaries: nonprofit organizations or IHEs.

Range: $190,000 to $770,000.

Activity: new program listing in 2005 (CFDA on-line version).

HQ: Plant and Animal Systems, CSREES-USDA, 1400 Independence Ave. SW, Washington, DC. 20250-2220. Phone: (202) 401-5877.

Internet: www.csrees.usda.gov (Note: no field offices for this program.)

10.307 ORGANIC AGRICULTURE RESEARCH AND EXTENSION INITIATIVE

Assistance: project grants (50-100 percent).

Purposes: pursuant to FSRIA as amended and FACTA, for projects emphasizing research and outreach activities that assist farmers and ranchers with whole farm planning and ecosystem integration. Field work for both program areas must be done on certified organic land or land in transition to certification. Projects should: facilitate the development of organic agriculture production, breeding, and processing methods; explore both barriers to and opportunities for marketing, both domestically and abroad; be designed to study and apply most related aspects of organic agriculture.

Eligible applicants/beneficiaries: state agricultural experiment stations, IHEs, other research institutions and organizations, federal agencies, national laboratories, private organizations and corporations, individuals.

Range/Average: N.A.

Activity: new program listing in 2005 (CFDA on-line version).

HQ: Plant and Animal Systems, CSREES-USDA, 1400 Independence Ave. SW, Washington, DC. 20250-2220. Phone: (202) 401-3356. (Note: no field offices for this program.)

Internet: www.csrees.usda.gov (Note: no field offices for this program.)

10.308 RESIDENT INSTRUCTION GRANTS FOR INSULAR AREA ACTIVITIES

Assistance: project grants (100 percent).

Purposes: pursuant to FSRIA, to enhance teaching programs in extension programs in U.S. insular areas, including PR, VI, Guam, Samoa, Northern Marianas, Micronesia, Marshall Islands, and Palau. Funded activities should be similar to those funded under **10.228**, and they facilitate cooperative initiatives between two or more insular area institutions and organizations.

Eligible applicants/beneficiaries: institutions with demonstrated commitment to higher education in the food and agricultural sciences.

Range/Average: N.A.

Activity: new program in FY 05.

HQ: Science and Education Resources Development, CSREES-USDA, 1400 Independence Ave. SW, Washington, DC 20250-2250. Phone: (no number provided).

Internet: www.csrees.usda.gov (Note: no field offices for this program.)

10.309 SPECIALTY CROP RESEARCH INITIATIVE

Assistance: project grants (matching/to 10 years).

Purposes: pursuant to the Agricultural Research, Extension, and Education Reform Act of 1998, as amended to address the critical needs of the specialty crop industry by developing and disseminating science-based tools. Funds shall not be used for the construction of a new building or facility or the acquisition, expansion, remodeling, or alteration of an existing building or facility (including site grading and improvement, and architect fees).

Eligible applicants/beneficiaries: federal agencies, national laboratories, colleges and universities, research and private institutions or organizations, state agricultural experiment stations, individuals, or groups consisting of two or more of these entities.

Range/Average: N.A.

Activity: N.A. New program in FY 08.

HQ: National Program Leader, Plant and Animal Systems, CSREES-USDA, 1400 Independence Ave. SW - MS 2220, Washington, DC 20250-2220. Phone: (202) 401-3356.

Internet: www.csrees.usda.gov/index.html. (Note: no field offices for this program.)

10.350 TECHNICAL ASSISTANCE TO COOPERATIVES

Assistance: specialized services; advisory services/counseling; training; technical information.

Purposes: pursuant to the Cooperative Marketing Act of 1926 and Agricultural Marketing Act of 1946, to develop and administer research, technical assistance, and educational programs on the financial, organization, management, legal, social, and economic aspects of rural cooperatives. Assistance may include publications, workshops, audiovisual materials, computer systems.

Eligible applicants/beneficiaries: farmer cooperatives and groups of rural residents, Native Americans, farmers, ranchers, agricultural producers, including in the territories.

Range/Average: N.A.

Activity: not quantified specifically.

HQ: Deputy Administrator/Cooperative Services, RBCS-USDA, Washington, DC 20250-3250. Phone: (202) 720-7558, FAX (202) 720- 4641.

Internet: www.rurdev.usda.gov/rbs/coops/csdir.htm.

10.352 VALUE-ADDED PRODUCER GRANTS ("VAPG")

Assistance: project grants (50 percent).

Purposes: pursuant to Agricultural Risk Protection Act of 2000 as amended and FSRIA, to refine agricultural commodity product values and enhance returns to producers. Grants may cover either: planning activities to prepare feasibility studies, and business plans; or, working capital for operating expenses of ventures.

Eligible applicants/beneficiaries: independent agricultural commodity producers and producer groups, farmer and rancher cooperatives, and majority-controlled, producer-based business ventures.

Range: planning, to $100,000; working capital, to $300,000.

Activity: FY 05, 172 awards.

HQ: Deputy Administrator/Cooperative Services, RBCS-USDA, Washington, DC 20250-3250. Phone: (202) 720-7558.

Internet: www.rurdev.usda.gov/rbs/.

10.404 EMERGENCY LOANS

Assistance: direct loans. (80-100 percent/15-40 years).

Purposes: pursuant to the Consolidated Farm and Rural Development Act of 1987 (CFRDA) and other acts, to repair, restore, or replace damaged or destroyed farm property, required as a result of declared natural disasters;

for farm operating expenses and other costs necessary to return disaster victims' farming operations to financially sound condition, including debt refinancing. Loans at 3.75 percent interest may cover: 100 percent of the cost of physical loss for up to 40 years; 80 percent of actual production loss for up to 15 years.

Eligible applicants/beneficiaries: established family farmers, ranchers, or aquaculture operators (tenant- or owner-operator) conducting a farming operation at the time of the disaster, as proprietors, partnerships, cooperatives, corporations, or joint operations—and that: are U.S. citizens or legal resident aliens, or entities operated by citizens owning over a 50 percent interest; are unable to obtain necessary credit from other sources to qualify for subsidized loss loans; are capable of managing the operation; have county committee eligibility certification; provide suitable collateral to secure the loan; have crop insurance if available for affected crops; have not caused a loss to FSA, nor received FSA debt forgiveness on more than one occasion, after 4 April 1996. Available also in most territories when those areas are designated. Prospective applicants should contact FSA county offices immediately after sustaining the loss.

Range: $500 to $500,000. **Average:** $58,000.

Activity: FY 01, 2,451 loans obligated.

HQ: Director, Loan Making Division, FSA-USDA, Washington, DC 20250-0522. Phone: (202) 720-1632.

Internet: www.fsa.usda.gov.

10.405 FARM LABOR HOUSING LOANS AND GRANTS ("Labor Housing - Sections 514 and 516")

Assistance: project grants; guaranteed/insured loans. (to 90 percent/1 percent/to 33 years).

Purposes: pursuant to the Housing Act of 1949 as amended, to construct, repair, or purchase basic year-round or seasonal housing and related support facilities for domestic farm laborers. Funds may be used for land acquisition, recreation areas, central cooking and dining facilities, small infirmaries, laundry facilities, day care centers. Grants are available only when there is a pressing need and when facilities could not be developed otherwise.

Eligible applicants: loans—farmers, family farm partnerships or corporations, associations of farmers. Loans and grants—states and their political subdivisions, PR, VI, broad-based public or private nonprofit organizations, tribes, and nonprofit corporations of farm workers.

Eligible beneficiaries: domestic farm laborers that are U.S. citizens or legal permanent residents.

Range: initial grants, $48,270 to $5,412,973; initial loans, $196,400 to $300,000,000. **Average:** grants, $2,365,805; loans $1,297,028.

Activity: FY 05, 818 new, 1,222 rehabilitated units provided.

HQ: Multifamily Housing Processing Division, RHS-USDA, Washington, DC 20250. Phone: (202) 720-1604.

Internet: www.rurdev.usda.gov.

10.406 FARM OPERATING LOANS

Assistance: direct loans; guaranteed/insured loans (7-22 years).

Purposes: pursuant to CFRDA and other acts, to enable family farm operators to: purchase livestock, poultry, fur-bearing and other farm animals, fish, and bees; purchase farm, forestry, recreation, or nonfarm enterprise equipment and provide operating funds for such enterprises; meet family subsistence needs; purchase essential home equipment; refinance certain secured and unsecured debts; pay property taxes and property insurance premiums; finance youth projects. The interest rate on guaranteed loans may be subsidized at 4 percent; direct loans are awarded at one percent interest above the federal borrowing rate.

Eligible applicants/beneficiaries: U.S. citizens or permanent residents with: experience or training to operate a farm; an acceptable credit history; legal capacity to incur a loan obligation; inability to obtain a reasonable loan elsewhere; and, who will become owners or tenants operating family farms through the program; except for youth projects, no history of causing a loss to FSA, nor of receiving FSA debt forgiveness more than three times after 4 April 1996. Certain corporations, cooperatives, partnerships, and joint operations conducting family farms. Available also in most territories.

Range: direct loans, to $200,000; guaranteed, to $731,000. **Average:** direct, $47,365; guaranteed, $157,339.

Activity: FY 01, 14,023, direct, 11,444 guaranteed loans.

HQ: Director, Loan Making Division, FSA-USDA, Washington, DC 20250-0522. Phone: (202) 720-1632.

Internet: www.fsa.usda.gov.

10.407 FARM OWNERSHIP LOANS

Assistance: direct loans; guaranteed/insured loans (to 40 years).

Purposes: pursuant to CFRDA and other acts, to: purchase, enlarge, and improve family farms; provide necessary water and water facilities; take necessary basic soil treatment and land conservation measures; construct, repair, or improve buildings needed in farm operations; provide facilities to produce fish under controlled conditions.

Eligible applicants/beneficiaries: U.S. citizens or permanent residents with: experience or training to operate a farm; an acceptable credit history; legal capacity to incur a loan obligation; inability to obtain a reasonable loan elsewhere; and, who will become owners or tenants operating family farms through the program; except for youth projects, no history of causing a loss to FSA, nor of receiving FSA debt forgiveness more than three times after 4 April 1996. Certain corporations, cooperatives, partnerships, and joint operations conducting family farms. Available also in most territories. If an individual, not have a combined farm ownership loan, soil and water loan, and recreation loan indebtedness to FSA of more than $200,000 for direct loans, and $717,000 for guaranteed loans, or a total indebtedness against the property securing the loan of more than the market value of the security, whichever is the lesser amount.

Range: direct, to $200,000; guaranteed, to $731,000. **Average:** direct, $112,762; guaranteed, $250,421.

Activity: FY 01, 2,085 direct, 3,488 guaranteed loans.

HQ: Director, Loan Making Division, FSA-USDA, Washington, DC 20250-0522. Phone: (202) 720-1632.

Internet: www.fsa.usda.gov.

10.410 VERY LOW TO MODERATE INCOME HOUSING LOANS ("Section 502 Rural Housing Loans")

Assistance: direct loans; guaranteed/insured loans (guaranteed, to 30 years; direct, to 38 years).

Purposes: pursuant to the Housing Act of 1949 and CFRDA as amended and other acts, for below-market-rate loan financing to lower-income rural families to: purchase, construct, improve, or repair housing to be used as a permanent residence; to finance the cost of sewage disposal, water supply facilities, weatherization, and essential household equipment; and, under certain conditions, to refinance housing debts, finance the purchase of manufactured homes and sites for their location. Loans can be subsidized through interest credits to as low as an effective rate of one percent, depending on the loan amount and applicant income and family size; interest subsidies are subject to recapture if property is liquidated.

Eligible applicants/beneficiaries: applicants determined to be very low income (below 50 percent of area median), low income (between 50 and 80 percent or area median), or moderate income (below 115 percent of area median)—with adequate and dependable available income to meet operating and family living expenses, including taxes, insurance, maintenance, and repayments on debts including the proposed loan, and without sufficient resources to obtain the necessary housing or related facilities. For direct loans, applicants must be eligible for interest credit, with income not above established limits. Available in territories and possessions.

Range: $1,000 to $105,000. **Average:** direct loans, $73,350; guaranteed, $98,000—more in high-cost areas.

Activity: N.A.

HQ: Director, Single Family Housing Direct Loan Division *or* Director, Single Family Housing Guaranteed Loan Division, RHS-USDA, Washington, DC 20250. Phone: *direct loans,* (202) 720-1474; *guaranteed loans,* (202) 720-1452.

Internet: www.rurdev.usda.gov.

10.411 RURAL HOUSING SITE LOANS AND SELF-HELP HOUSING LAND DEVELOPMENT LOANS ("Section 523 and 524 Site Loans")

Assistance: direct loans (2 years).

Purposes: pursuant to the Housing Act of 1949 as amended, to buy land for housing sites and to install improvements thereon—to be sold to low- or very-low-income households. Loans also may cover the costs of water and sewer facilities, walks, driveways, parking areas, landscaping, engineering and legal fees, and closing costs.

Eligible applicants: private or public nonprofit organizations that will provide the developed sites to qualified borrowers without profit, in open country or towns of 10,000 population or less, or in places up to 25,000 population under certain conditions. Available also in PR, VI, Guam, and the Northern Marianas.

Eligible beneficiaries: Section 524—low- and very-low-income families, nonprofit organizations, public agencies, cooperatives. Sites developed under Section 523 must be used for housing built under the self-help method.

Range: to $200,000 (except with RHS approval). **Average:** Section 523, $573,750.; Section 524, $450,000.

Activity: FY 05, 4 Section 523, 1 Section 524 loans.

HQ: Director, Single-Family Housing Processing Division, RHS- USDA, Washington, DC 20250. Phone (202) 720-1474.

Internet: www.rurdev.usda.gov.

10.415 RURAL RENTAL HOUSING LOANS ("Sections 515 and 521")

Assistance: direct loans; project grants (loans, 30 years).

Purposes: pursuant to the Housing Act of 1949 as amended, for the purchase, construction, or substantial rehabilitation of rural rental or cooperative housing with two or more family units, including manufactured housing, and certain related uses including recreational and service facilities. Loans may be made in communities with up to 10,000 population, and up to 20,000 under certain conditions. Tenants pay basic rent or 30 percent of adjusted income, whichever is greater; RHS rental assistance subsidies can be used to limit rental payments to 30 percent of income (see **10.427**). Loans may not cover nursing, special care, or institutional homes.

Eligible applicants: individuals, cooperatives, nonprofit organizations, state or local public agencies, profit corporations, trusts, partnerships, limited partnerships and, except for state or local public agencies, unable to finance the housing either with their own resources or with credit obtained from private sources. Available also in territories.

Eligible beneficiaries: very-low-, low-, and moderate-income households, elderly, and handicapped or disabled persons.

Range: to $1,000,000 per application; to $2,500,000 per state.

Activity: FY 05, 783 new, 5,077 rehabilitated units provided.

HQ: Director, Multifamily Housing Processing Division, RHS-USDA, Washington, DC 20250. Phone: (202) 720-1604.

Internet: www.rurdev.usda.gov.

10.417 VERY LOW-INCOME HOUSING REPAIR LOANS AND GRANTS ("Section 504 Rural Housing Loans and Grants")

Assistance: direct loans; project grants (direct, 1 percent interest/direct, to 20 years).

Purposes: pursuant to the Housing Act of 1949 as amended, to provide loans of up to $20,000 to very low-income rural owner-occupants and/or grants of up to $7,500 to eligible elderly persons—to repair or modernize their existing homes, including weatherization, and to upgrade water and waste disposal systems.

Eligible applicants/beneficiaries: owner-occupants of rural homes, with sufficient income to repay loans, and that are U.S. citizens or legal residents or on indefinite parole. Applicant's income may not exceed very-low-income limits set forth in USDA instructions. Grant recipients must be at least age 62 and unable to repay the part of the assistance received as a grant. Available also in territories.

Range/Average: loans, $5,971; grants, $5,241.

Activity: FY 05, 5,971 loans, 6,029 grants.

HQ: Director, Single-Family Housing Processing Division, RHS- USDA, Washington, DC 20250. Phone (202) 720-1474.

Internet: www.rurdev.usda.gov.

10.420 RURAL SELF-HELP HOUSING TECHNICAL ASSISTANCE ("Section 523 Technical Assistance")

Assistance: project grants. (100 percent/2 years).

Purposes: pursuant to the Housing Act of 1949 as amended, for the organizational, administrative, and basic costs of carrying out mutual self-help housing programs in rural areas. Grant funds may be used to pay the costs of training self-help group members and of purchasing tools and equipment—but not to hire construction personnel, nor to buy real estate or building materials.

Eligible applicants: states or political subdivisions, public or private nonprofit corporations. Available also in PR, VI, Guam, Northern Marianas.

Eligible beneficiaries: very-low- and low-income rural families, usually in groups of 6 to 10 families.

Average: $375,897.

Activity: FY 05, 99 grants.

HQ: Director, Single-Family Housing Processing Division, RHS- USDA, Washington, DC 20250. Phone (202) 720-1474.

Internet: www.rurdev.usda.gov.

10.421 INDIAN TRIBES AND TRIBAL CORPORATION LOANS

Assistance: direct loans. (100 percent/to 40 years).

Purposes: pursuant to the Loans to Indian Tribes and Tribal Corporations Act, to buy land within tribal reservations and Alaskan communities. Loan funds may be used to acquire land and for related costs, for such purposes as rounding out farming or ranching units or to eliminate fractional heir ships. Loan funds may not be used for development, improvements, or operating costs.

Eligible applicants/beneficiaries: recognized tribes and tribal corporations or Alaska communities.

Range: $450,000 to $2,000,000. **Average:** $224,000.

Activity: FY 02 estimate, 1 loan.

HQ: Director, Loan Servicing and Property Management Division, FSA-USDA, Ag Box 0523, Washington, DC 20250. Phone: (202) 720-4572.

Internet: www.fsa.usda.gov.

10.427 RURAL RENTAL ASSISTANCE PAYMENTS ("Rental Assistance - Section 521")

Assistance: direct payments/specified use (5 years).

Purposes: pursuant to the Housing Act of 1949 as amended, to subsidize rents paid by low-income senior citizens, families, and domestic farm laborers occupying eligible RHS-assisted units, and whose rents exceed 30 percent of an adjusted annual income figure established for each state.

Eligible applicants: basically, state and local agencies and nonprofit or limited-profit sponsors of certain rural rental housing projects financed by RHS. (New construction and rehabilitation projects receiving Section 8 assistance from HUD are ineligible.)

Eligible beneficiaries: low- or very-low-income families and handicapped or senior citizens occupying eligible rural rental, cooperative, or farm labor housing.

Range: N.A.

Activity: FY 05 estimate, 45,428 households to be assisted.

HQ: Director, Multifamily Housing Portfolio Management Division, RHS-USDA, Washington, DC 20250. Phone: (202) 720-1615.

Internet: www.rurdev.usda.gov.

10.433 RURAL HOUSING PRESERVATION GRANTS ("HPG - Section 533")

Assistance: project grants.

Purposes: pursuant to the Housing Act of 1949 as amended, to assist low- and very-low-income rural homeowners, rental property owners, and cooperatives to repair or rehabilitate their housing. Generally, assistance is used in conjunction with other federal funding, such as HUD's CDBG or HHS's weatherization programs, or with programs sponsored by states. Revolving loan funds may be established. Applicants may use up 20 percent of funds for project operating costs, including training of project personnel; the remaining 80 percent must be used as loans or grants for housing improvements.

Eligible applicants/beneficiaries: authorized public or private nonprofit organizations; city and county agencies, state governments; tribes; consortia of eligible entities—in communities with up to 10,000 population, or up to 20,000 under certain conditions. Available also in territories and possessions.

Range/Average: N.A.

Activity: FY 05, 164 grants obligated to provide assistance for 2,108 units.

HQ: Multifamily Housing Processing Division, RHS-USDA, Washington, DC 20250. Phone: (202) 720-1604.

Internet: www.rurdev.usda.gov.

10.435 STATE MEDIATION GRANTS

Assistance: project grants (70 percent).

Purposes: pursuant to the Agricultural Credit Act of 1987, FACTA, Agricultural Credit Improvement Act of 1992, Federal Crop Insurance Reform and Department of Agriculture Reorganization Act of 1994, and United States Grain Standards Act of 2000, to cover state operating and administrative costs in connection with certified agricultural loan mediation programs for producers, creditors, and others affected by USDA actions.

Eligible applicants: state governments.

Eligible beneficiaries: agricultural producers and their creditors; others directly affected by USDA actions.

Range: $5,000 to $391,880.

Activity: FY 02 estimate, 26 states certified.

HQ: FSA-USDA (Stop 0539), Washington, DC 20250. Phone: (202) 720-1471, FAX (202) 690-0644.

Internet: www.fsa.usda.gov (Note: no field offices for this program.)

10.437 INTEREST ASSISTANCE PROGRAM

Assistance: guaranteed/insured loans. (to 90 percent/ to 10 years).

Purposes: pursuant to CFRDA as amended, for interest rate buy-downs on behalf of family farms indebted to conventional lenders. Essentially, FSA pays up to four percent of a farm-borrower's interest costs on loans taken for operations including livestock, farm and home equipment, family living expenses, water system development, and similar costs.

Eligible applicants/beneficiaries: individuals, partnerships, joint operations, legal resident aliens, corporations, and cooperatives. Loans may be obtained through lender.

Range: to $731,000. **Average:** $158,000.

Activity: FY 01, 4,646 farmers assisted.

HQ: Director, Loan Making Division, FSA-USDA, Washington, DC 20250-0522. Phone: (202) 720-1632.

Internet: www.fsa.usda.gov.

10.438 SECTION 538 RURAL RENTAL HOUSING GUARANTEED LOANS

Assistance: guaranteed/insured loans.

Purposes: pursuant to the Housing Act of 1949 as amended, for partnerships between RHS and major lenders including state and local housing finance agencies and bond insurers, resulting in an increased supply of new, affordable, multifamily, rural housing consisting of two or more family units. Projects must provide new forms of credit enhancements for housing development. Nursing, special care, and industrial type housing are ineligible.

Eligible applicants: lenders approved by the Federal National Mortgage Association, Federal Home Loan Mortgage Corporation, HUD, or state housing finance agencies.

Eligible beneficiaries: rural households with income not exceeding 115 percent of the median.

Range/Average: N.A.

Activity: FY 05, awards to provide 3,300 units.

HQ: Director, Multifamily Housing Processing Division, RHS-USDA, Washington, DC 20250. Phone: (202) 720-1604.

Internet: www.rurdev.usda.gov.

10.441 TECHNICAL AND SUPERVISORY ASSISTANCE GRANTS ("Section 525(a)")

Assistance: project grants. (100 percent/1-2 years).

Purposes: pursuant to the Housing Act of 1949 as amended, for housing delivery and counseling projects to assist low-income rural persons obtain adequate rental housing, homeownership, or continued occupancy in existing housing—through technical and supervisory assistance provided by grantees. Project funds may cover such costs as staff salaries, travel, administrative and office expenses, training. Grant funds may not be used for real estate acquisition or improvement, vehicles, equipment, or for financial assistance to families participating in the projects.

Eligible applicants/beneficiaries: public or private nonprofit corporations, organizations, agencies, institutions, tribal governments, and other associations; sponsored organizations including community development, model cities, and community action agencies; IHEs, hospitals.

Range/Average: N.A.

Activity: N.A.

HQ: Housing Programs, RHS-USDA, 14th & Independence Ave. SW, Washington, DC 20250. Phone: (202) 720-1474.

Internet: www.rurdev.usda.gov.

10.442 HOUSING APPLICATION PACKAGING GRANTS ("Section 509 Grants")

Assistance: project grants.

Purposes: pursuant to the Housing Act of 1949 as amended, to package applications for single-family housing for very-low- and low-income rural residents wishing to buy, build, or repair houses for their own use—in colonias and designated counties; to package applications for organizations developing rental units for lower-income families. Funds may cover operating, administrative, and coordinating costs.

Eligible applicants/beneficiaries: states, state and local agencies, local government units, private nonprofit housing organizations.

Range/Average: up to $500 for each loan/grant (includes Sec. 502, Single Family Housing; Sec. 504, Repairs; Sec. 514, Farm Labor Housing; all others refer to Exhibit B of RD Instruction 1944-B.

Activity: N.A.

HQ: Director, Single-Family Housing Processing Division, RHS- USDA, Washington, DC 20250. Phone (202) 720-1474.

Internet: www.rurdev.usda.gov.

10.443 OUTREACH AND ASSISTANCE FOR SOCIALLY DISADVANTAGED FARMERS AND RANCHERS

Assistance: project grants. (100 percent/1-5 years).

Purposes: pursuant to FACTA, to provide outreach, training, and technical assistance socially disadvantaged farmers and ranchers—toward their ownership and operation of farms and their participation in farm programs.

Eligible applicants: experienced "1890" land-grant colleges and Tuskegee University; tribal community colleges and Alaska native cooperative colleges, Hispanic-serving and other postsecondary educational institutions, and community-based organizations.

Eligible beneficiaries: socially disadvantaged farmers or ranchers including Blacks, women, American Indians, Alaska natives, Hispanics, Asians, and Pacific Islanders.

Range: $66,437 to $276,822. **Average:** $200,000.

Activity: cumulatively, 27 awards assisting 8,686 farmers, outreach to 107,566 constituents.

HQ: Office of Outreach (1710), USDA, 1400 Independence Ave. SW, Washington, DC 20250. Phone: (202) 720-6350, FAX (202) 720-7489.

Internet: www.usda.gov/agency/outreach.

10.444 DIRECT HOUSING—NATURAL DISASTER LOANS AND GRANTS ("Section 504 Rural Housing Loans and Grants")

Assistance: direct loans; project grants (grants, 100 percent).

Purposes: pursuant to the Housing Act of 1949 as amended, to meet emergency housing assistance needs of very-low-income owner-occupants, resulting from natural disasters. Funds may be used to repair or replace damaged property, only to the extent that funds are not provided by FEMA.

Eligible applicants/beneficiaries: loans—very-low income owner-occupants with sufficient income to repay the loans. Grants—owner-occupants at least age 62 and unable to repay loans.

Range/Average: loans, $6,167; grants, $5,241.

Activity: FY 05, 1,322 houses improved.

HQ: Director, Single-Family Housing Processing Division, RHP-USDA, Washington, DC 20250. Phone (202) 720-1474.

Internet: www.rurdev.usda.gov.

10.445 DIRECT HOUSING—NATURAL DISASTER ("Section 502 Very Low and Low Income Loans")

Assistance: direct loans.

Purposes: pursuant to the Housing Act of 1949 and CFRDA as amended and other acts, to meet emergency housing assistance needs of lower-income families, resulting from natural disasters. Funds may be used to buy, build, rehabilitate, or improve dwellings in rural areas. Subsidies may be available to eligible low- and very-low-income applicants, in the form of payment assistance or interest credits, to effectively reduce interest payments to as low as one percent—and are subject to recapture if the borrower transfers title or ceases to occupy the property. Funds are available only to the extent that funds are not provided by FEMA.

Eligible applicants/beneficiaries: households without adequate resources to obtain housing or related facilities, and unable to secure credit from other sources.

Range/Average: loans, $0.

Activity: None for FY 05; no funding provided for FY 06.

HQ: Director, Single-Family Housing Processing Division, RHP-USDA, Washington, DC 20250. Phone (202) 720-1474.

Internet: www.rurdev.usda.gov.

10.446 RURAL COMMUNITY DEVELOPMENT INITIATIVE

Assistance: project grants. (50 percent/3 years).

Purposes: for capacity building toward the improvement of rural housing, community facilities, and community and economic development projects. Grant funds may be used to train and provide technical assistance to subgrantees in such areas as: conducting homeownership education and minority entrepreneurial programs, and developing child care facilities; strategic planning, obtaining alternative funding, fundraising, board training. Funds may also be used to develop training tools including videos, workbooks, and reference guides.

Eligible applicants/beneficiaries: private, public, or tribal organizations with three years of pertinent rural experience, including in territories and possessions.

Range: $50,000 to $500,000. **Average:** $250,000.

Activity: FY 05, 31 grants.

HQ: Deputy Administrator/Community Programs, RHS-USDA, Washington, DC 20250-3222. Phone: (202) 720-1490.

Internet: www.rurdev.usda.gov/rhs/rcdi/index.htm.

10.447 THE RURAL DEVELOPMENT (RD) MULTI-FAMILY HOUSING REVITALIZATION DEMONSTRATION PROGRAM ("Restructuring Program")

Assistance: debt deferral; grants; loans (to 50 years).

Purposes: pursuant to the Housing Act of 1949, as amended, Section 515, and The Agriculture, Rural Development, Food and Drug Administration, and Related Agencies Appropriation Act of 2007, to preserve and revitalize existing rural rental projects financed by RHS under Section 515 of the Housing Act of 1949 and to ensure continued safe and affordable housing for low-income residents.

Eligible applicants: owners or buyers of financially viable Section 515 financed rental properties.

Eligible beneficiaries: low-income rural renters.

Range: bullet loan, to $5,000 per unit; revitalization grant, to $5,000 per unit; total grant and loan assistance, to $10,000 per unit; Section 515 one percent loan, to $20,000 per unit. **Average:** N.A.

Activity: FY 06: 78 properties received assistance.

HQ: Director, Office of Rental Housing Preservation, Rural Development, Department of Agriculture, Washington, DC 20250. Telephone: (202) 720-1611.

Internet: www.rurdev.usda.gov.

10.449 BOLL WEEVIL ERADICATION LOAN PROGRAM

Assistance: direct loans. (100 percent/1-7 years).

Purposes: to eradicate boll weevils from the U.S. Loan funds may be used to: purchase or lease supplies and equipment; pay operating expenses, salaries, and benefits—but not for lobbying, public relations, or similar activities.

Eligible applicants/beneficiaries: nonprofit entities authorized under appropriate state law.

Range: $1,000,000 to $46,000,000. **Average:** $7,000,000.

Activity: FY 02, 13 loans.

HQ: Director, Loan Making Division, FSA-USDA, 1400 Independence Ave. SW, Washington, DC 20250-0522. Phone: (202) 720-1632.

Internet: www.fsa.usda.gov (Note: no field offices for this program.)

10.450 CROP INSURANCE

Assistance: insurance.

Purposes: pursuant to the Federal Crop Insurance Act, Agricultural Adjustment Act of 1938, Federal Crop Insurance Reform Act of 1994, FAIRA, AREERA, Agriculture Risk Protection Act of 2000, amendments, and other acts, to insure farmers against losses resulting from unavoidable causes and uncontrollable events. Producers must obtain at least the catastrophic level of coverage to be eligible under the price support or production adjustment programs, the Conservation Reserve Program, or farm credit programs. The premium is fully subsidized on catastrophic crop insurance, except for a processing fee. Coverage compensates producers for yield losses exceeding 50 percent, at a price equal to 55 percent of maximum price. Additional protection at higher levels of coverage is also offered. The program provides for ongoing research to devise and establish crop insurance protection programs, as well as risk management education for producers including futures and options trading. Pilot insurance programs currently are being tested for various crops. Various insurance programs in certain areas cover specific crops; regulations concerning crops and insurance coverage may be obtained from USDA regional offices or private industry crop insurance agents.

Eligible applicants/beneficiaries: owners or operators of farmland, with an insurable interest in a crop in a county where insurance is offered on that crop. The Noninsured Assistance Program is available in other areas (see **10.451**). Note: applications are to be submitted to companies reinsured by FCIC.

Range/Average: N.A.

Activity: crop year 2003 estimate, 207,900,000 acres covered, with protection of $34.3 billion.

HQ: Administrator, RMA-USDA, Ag Box 0801, Washington, DC 20250. Phone: (202) 690-2803.

Internet: www.rma.usda.gov.

10.451 NONINSURED ASSISTANCE ("NAP")

Assistance: direct payments/unrestricted use.

Purposes: pursuant to FAIRA as amended, to provide producers with protection comparable to the catastrophic risk protection plan of crop insurance (see **10.450**) and to help reduce production risks faced by crop producers for which federal insurance is not available under the Federal Crop Insurance Act; to reduce financial losses that occur when natural disasters cause catastrophic loss of production or prevent planting of an eligible crop. Payment eligibility is based on an expected yield for the area and the producer's approved yield based on actual production history, or a transitional yield if sufficient records are unavailable. Yields must fall below specified percentages to be eligible for payment. Eligible areas may be located within or outside the continental U.S., as determined by USDA; generally, areas within the continental U.S. are eligible if they have suffered a greater than 35 percent loss of eligible production because of damaging weather or of an adverse natural occurrence. Eligible crops include any commercial agricultural crop (excluding livestock and their by-products, tobacco, and trees grown for wood, paper, or pulp), commodity, or acreage of a commodity grown for food or fiber for which catastrophic coverage is unavailable; included also are floriculture, ornamental nursery, Christmas tree crops, turfgrass sod, seed crops, aquaculture including ornamental fish, and industrial crops.

Eligible applicants/beneficiaries: producers including owners, landlords, tenants, or sharecroppers with total annual gross revenue less than $2,000,000 for the preceding tax year.

Range/Average: N.A.

Activity: N.A.

HQ: Noninsured Assistance Program Branch (0517), Production, Emergency, and Compliance Division, FSA-USDA, 1400 Independence Ave. SW, Washington, DC 20250-0526. Phone: (202) 720-5172.

Internet: ww.fsa.usda.gov.

10.452 DISASTER RESERVE ASSISTANCE ("DRAP")

Assistance: direct payments/specified use.

Purposes: pursuant to the Agricultural Act of 1970 as amended, to provide emergency assistance to livestock owners in USDA-approved areas where livestock emergencies exist because of disease, insect infestation, flood, drought, fire, hurricane, earthquake, hail storm, hot or cold weather, freeze, snow, ice, winterkill, or other natural disaster. Assistance may be provided for losses of feed grain crops, forage, and grazing. Direct payments are for unrestricted use; feed obtained must be fed to the producer's livestock, may not be resold, and must be used during the established feeding period.

Eligible applicants/beneficiaries: U.S. citizens or legal resident aliens, cooperatives, private domestic corporations, partnerships, or joint operations, tribal organizations that: (1) do not have total annual gross revenue in excess of $2,500,000; (2) are actively engaged in farming with at least 10 percent of gross revenue derived from producing grain or livestock; (3) have suffered a 40 percent or greater loss of normal feed production; (4) have insufficient feed for eligible livestock for the duration of the emergency. Applicants must choose whether to receive disaster assistance program benefits or benefits under another USDA program for the same crop loss (applicants are not eligible for both).

Range/Average: N.A.

Activity: not quantified specifically.

HQ: Emergency and Noninsured Assistance Program Division, FSA-USDA, 1400 Independence Ave. SW, Washington, DC 20250-0526. Phone: (202) 720-3168.

Internet: www.fsa.usda.gov.

10.454 DAIRY OPTIONS PILOT PROGRAM ("DOPP")

Assistance: direct payments/specified use (80 percent).

Purposes: pursuant to FAIRA, Agricultural Market Transition Act, and Agricultural Risk Protection Act of 2000, to educate and assist dairy producers in certain regions in managing their price risk by purchasing options on milk futures. Payments, including some fee costs, are made to commodities brokers for options contracts purchased by participants.

Eligible applicants/beneficiaries: dairy farmers producing at least 100,000 pounds of milk during the consecutive six-month period preceding application—including individuals, entities, or joint operations, owners, operators, landlords, tenants, or sharecroppers.

Range: the farmer pays 20 percent of the premium and broker fees exceeding $30 per contract.

Activity: Round III, 790 producers bought 2,816 milk put options.

HQ: RMA-USDA, 1400 Independence Ave. SW, Washington, DC 20250-0808. Phone: (202) 690-0520, FAX (202) 690-3605.

Internet: www.rma.usda.gov; e-mail, rma.options@wdc.usda.gov. (Note: no field offices for this program.)

10.455 COMMUNITY OUTREACH AND ASSISTANCE PARTNERSHIP PROGRAM

Assistance: project grants.

Purposes: pursuant to the Federal Crop Insurance Act as amended, for partnerships to develop and implement community outreach programs for women, limited-resource, socially disadvantaged, and other traditionally underserved producers of priority commodities—providing them with information and training necessary to use financial management, crop insurance, marketing contracts and other existing and emerging risk management tools to mitigate risks associated with farming.

Eligible applicants: educational institutions, community-based organizations, and associations of farmers, ranchers, and other nonprofit organizations.

Eligible beneficiaries: women, limited resource, traditionally underserved and socially disadvantaged producers of priority commodities.

Range: $5,000 to $300,000. **Average:** $75,000.

Activity: new program listing in 2004. FY 04 estimate, 30,000 producers assisted.

HQ: Community Outreach and Assistance Partnership Program, RMA-USDA (Stop 0805), 1400 Independence Ave. SW, Washington, DC 20250. Phone: (202) 690-2686.

Internet: www.rma.usda.gov.

10.456 PARTNERSHIP AGREEMENTS TO DEVELOP NON-INSURANCE RISK MANAGEMENT TOOLS FOR PRODUCERS (FARMERS)

Assistance: project grants (100 percent/to 3 years).

Purposes: pursuant to the Federal Crop Insurance Act and Agricultural Market Transition Act, for research partnerships to develop noninsurance risk management tools for agricultural producers, emphasizing producers of specialty crops, livestock, rangeland, and underserved commodities.

Eligible applicants/beneficiaries: public and private entities including: IHEs; federal, state, and local government agencies; tribal organizations; nonprofit and profit organizations or corporations; other qualified entities.

Range: $99,338 to $1,023,038. **Average:** $411,912.

Activity: new program listing in 2004. FY 05, 20 partnerships funded.

HQ: Research and Evaluation Division (0813), RMA-USDA, 6501 Beacon Dr., Kansas City, MO 64133-4676. Phone: (816) 926-6343, FAX, 926-7343.

Internet: www.rma.usda.gov; e-mail, applications@rma.usda.gov. (Note: the field office serves as headquarters.)

10.457 COMMODITY PARTNERSHIPS FOR RISK MANAGEMENT EDUCATION

Assistance: project grants (100 percent).

Purposes: pursuant to the Federal Crop Insurance Act as amended, for programs delivering training and information in the management of production, marketing, and financial risk to agricultural producers and agribusiness professionals—with priority for producers of crops not insurable by RMA, specialty crops, and underserved commodities. Funds may be used for planning, instructional materials development, outreach, and educational activities.

Eligible applicants: state departments of agriculture, universities, nonprofit agricultural organizations, other public and private organizations.

Eligible beneficiaries: agricultural producers, especially those with crops not insurable by Federal crop insurance, specialty crops, and undeserved commodities.

Range: $49,360 to $150,000. **Average:** $130,942.

Activity: new program listing in 2004. FY 05, 30,000 producers assisted.

HQ: Risk Management Education Division, RMA-USDA, 1400 Independence Ave. SW, Washington, DC 20250- 0808. Phone: (202) 720-5265.

Internet: www.rma.usda.gov; e-mail, rma.risk- ed@usda.gov.

10.458 CROP INSURANCE EDUCATION IN TARGETED STATES ("Targeted States")

Assistance: project grants.

Purposes: pursuant to the Federal Crop Insurance Act as amended, to deliver crop insurance education and information to agricultural producers in designated states historically underserved by crop insurance—including specifically Connecticut, Delaware, Maine, Maryland, Massachusetts, Nevada, New Hampshire, New Jersey, New York, Pennsylvania, Rhode Island, Utah, Vermont, West Virginia, and Wyoming.

Eligible applicants/beneficiaries: state departments of agriculture, universities, nonprofit agricultural organizations, other public and private organizations, agricultural producers, individuals.

Range: $157,000 to $754,000. **Average:** $393,400.

Activity: new program listing in 2004. FY 05 estimate, training provided to 15,000 producers.

HQ: Risk Management Education Division, RMA-USDA, 1400 Independence Ave. SW, Washington, DC 20250- 0808. Phone: (202) 720-5265.

Internet: www.rma.usda.gov; e-mail, rma.risk- ed@usda.gov.

10.459 COMMODITY PARTNERSHIPS FOR SMALL AGRICULTURAL RISK MANAGEMENT EDUCATION SESSIONS ("Commodity Partnerships Small Sessions Program")

Assistance: project grants (100 percent).

Purposes: pursuant to the Federal Crop Insurance Act as amended, to deliver training and information during small sessions in the management, production, marketing, and financial risk to U.S. agricultural producers, with priority to producers of crops not insurable with federal crop insurance, specialty crops, and underserved commodities. Funding is through cooperative agreements, covering such costs as program planning, development of instructional materials, awareness promotion, educational activities, and project documentation.

Eligible applicants: state departments of agriculture, universities, nonprofit agricultural organizations, other public and private organizations.

Eligible beneficiaries: agricultural producers, especially those with crops not insurable by Federal crop insurance, specialty crops, and undeserved commodities.

Range: $8,979 to $10,000. **Average:** $9,879.

Activity: new program in FY 05; some 3,000 producers estimated to be trained in FY 05.

HQ: Risk Management Education Division, RMA-USDA, 1400 Independence Ave. SW, Washington, DC 20250- 0808. Phone: (202) 720-5265.

Internet: www.rma.usda.gov; e-mail, rma.risk-ed@usda.gov.

10.475 COOPERATIVE AGREEMENTS WITH STATES FOR INTRASTATE MEAT AND POULTRY INSPECTION ("Meat and Poultry Inspection State Programs")

Assistance: project grants (to 50 percent).

Purposes: pursuant to the Federal Meat Inspection Act, Federal-State Cooperative Act ("Talmadge-Aiken"), and Poultry Products Inspection Act, to cover cooperating states' costs of meat and poultry inspection programs.

Eligible applicants/beneficiaries: state or territorial agencies administering meat or poultry inspection programs under applicable laws equivalent to federal acts.

Range: $204,000 to $5,356,000. **Average:** $1,622,000.

Activity: FY 05 estimate, 28 states participating under the Federal Meat Inspection Act, 25 under the Poultry Products Inspection Act; 500,000,000 pounds of products inspected.

HQ: Director, Federal-State Relations Staff, Field Operations, FSIS-USDA, Congressional Quarterly Bldg. - Rm.329, Washington, DC 20250-3700. (202) 418-8897.

Internet: www.fsis.usda.gov.

10.477 MEAT, POULTRY, AND EGG PRODUCTS INSPECTION

Assistance: specialized services.

Purposes: pursuant to the Federal Meat Inspection Act, Poultry Products Inspection Act, and other acts, to provide inspection by USDA personnel of the slaughtering, processing, and labeling of meat, poultry, and egg products shipped in commerce. All U.S. plants are required to be under continuous USDA inspection, including in the territories.

Eligible applicants/beneficiaries: any meat or poultry plant engaging in slaughtering or processing meat, poultry, and all egg products processing—for shipment in commerce.

Range/Average: N.A.

Activity: FY 04, some 100.4 billion pounds of products inspected at some 6,300 establishments. FY 05 and FY 06 estimated same.

HQ: Assistant Administrator/Field Operations, FSIS-USDA, Washington, DC 20250. Phone: (202) 720-8803.

Internet: www.fsis.usda.gov.

10.479 FOOD SAFETY COOPERATIVE AGREEMENTS

Assistance: project grants (100 percent).

Purposes: to reduce the incidence of foodborne illnesses associated with meat, poultry, and egg products. Funds are available for educational programs or special studies, and to further develop the Food Emergency Response Network, consisting of federal, state, and, local laboratories that provide the analytic capabilities and capacity to cope with agents threatening the national food supply.

Eligible applicants/beneficiaries: state, local, and tribal government agencies; academic institutions; nonprofit organizations.

Range: $12,000 to $100,000. **Average:** $52,000.

Activity: new program listing in 2006 (CFDA on-line); not quantified specifically.

HQ: Strategic Initiatives, Partnerships and Outreach Staff, FSIS- USDA, Aerospace Bldg (MC 405), Washington, DC 20250. Phone: (202) 690-6520.

Internet: www.fsis.usda.gov/about_FSIS/Cooperative_Agreements/. (Note: no field offices for this program.)

10.500 COOPERATIVE EXTENSION SERVICE

Assistance: formula grants; project grants (50 percent).

Purposes: pursuant to the Smith-Lever Act, Food and Agriculture Act of 1977, FACTA, FAIRA, AREERA, FSRIA, amendments, and other acts, for land grant institutions to operate state and county agricultural extension service programs providing educational and technical assistance to: farmers, producers, and marketing firms in applying technical developments ensuing from research; community organizations to develop natural, economic, and human resources; homemakers and youth regarding food and nutrition, home economics, child development, and parent education; 4-H youth programs. "1890" institutions may receive funds to construct, renovate, plan, and develop new facilities and to purchase equipment.

Eligible applicants/beneficiaries: designated state land grant institutions including in the territories; "1890" and "1994" institutions, and Tuskegee extension programs.

Range: $890,000 to $19,962,000. **Average:** $7,210,000.

Activity: not quantified specifically.

HQ: Deputy Administrator/Planning and Accountability, CSREES-USDA, 1400 Independence Ave. SW, Washington DC 20250 Phone: (202) 720-5623.

Internet: http://www.reeusda.gov (Note: no field offices for this program.)

10.551 FOOD STAMPS

Assistance: direct payments/specified use (100 percent).

Purposes: pursuant to the Food Stamp Act of 1977 as amended, to enable low-income households to purchase food. Eligible recipients receive a coupon allotment, varying according to household size and income, to be used to buy food or seeds and plants to produce food for their personal consumption. Coupons may also be used to purchase meals by special categories of recipients, including the elderly, handicapped, homeless persons living in authorized shelters, alcoholics and drug addicts participating in rehabilitation programs, disabled or blind, specific categories of noncitizens, and residents of shelters for battered women and children.

Eligible applicants: state or territorial agencies.

Eligible beneficiaries: households receiving welfare assistance in some form, or unemployed, part-time employed, working for low wages, receiving limited pensions. Able-bodied adults must meet a work requirement.

Average: FY 05, $92.69 per person per month.

Activity: FY 05 monthly participation average, 25,680,000 persons.

HQ: Deputy Administrator/Food Stamp Program, FNS-USDA, Alexandria, VA 22302. Phone: (703) 305-2026.

Internet: www.fns.usda.gov.

10.553 SCHOOL BREAKFAST PROGRAM

Assistance: formula grants.

Purposes: pursuant to the Child Nutrition Act of 1966 as amended, to reimburse participating entities for the cost of providing breakfasts to eligible public and private nonprofit school children through the high school grades, through cash grants and food donations. Breakfasts are served free or at a reduced price to children determined by local school authorities to be unable to pay the full price, based on income eligibility guidelines. Reimbursements rates are based on the "Food Away From Home" series of the Consumer Price Index. The maximum reduced price charged for breakfast is 30 cents.

Eligible applicants: state and territorial agencies; public and nonprofit private schools and residential child care institutions except Job Corps Centers; residential summer camps that participate in the Summer Food Service Program.

Eligible beneficiaries: all children attending schools where the breakfast program is operating may participate.

Range: FY 05, per meal reimbursement range of 23 cents to $1.48.

Activity: FY 05, 1.6 billion breakfasts served.

HQ: Director, Child Nutrition Division, FNS-USDA, Alexandria, VA 22302. Phone: (703) 305-2590.

Internet: www.fns.usda.gov/cnd.

10.555 NATIONAL SCHOOL LUNCH PROGRAM ("School Lunch Program")

Assistance: formula grants (70 percent).

Purposes: pursuant to the National School Lunch Act as amended, to reimburse participating entities for the cost of providing school lunches to public and private nonprofit school children through the high school grades, through cash grants and food donations. Eligible schools also may be reimbursed for snacks served to children in after-school-hour care programs. Meals are served free or at a reduced price to children determined by local school authorities to be unable to pay the full price, based on income eligibility guidelines. Reimbursement rates are based on the "Food Away from Home" series of the Consumer Price Index. The maximum reduced price charge for lunch is 40 cents.

Eligible applicants: state and territorial agencies; public and nonprofit private schools and residential child care institutions except Job Corps Centers; residential summer camps that participate in the Summer Food Service Program.

Eligible beneficiaries: All children attending schools where the breakfast program is operating may participate.

Range: FY 05, 5 cents for snacks to 274 cents per meal. **Average:** FY 05, 142 cents.

Activity: FY 05, 4.9 billion lunches served; FY06 estimate, increase of 70 million lunches.

HQ: Director, Child Nutrition Division, FNS-USDA, Alexandria, VA 22302. Phone: (703) 305-2590.

Internet: www.fns.usda.gov.

10.556 SPECIAL MILK PROGRAM FOR CHILDREN

Assistance: formula grants.

Purposes: pursuant to the Child Nutrition Act of 1966 as amended, to reimburse the cost of milk served to primary and secondary pupils in public and private nonprofit schools and institutions. A portion of the cost of the milk is subsidized for non-needy children; milk is free to students meeting certain income guidelines. Nonprofit schools with split-session kindergartens and pre-kindergartens that do not have access to the meal service program operating in the school may receive milk subsidies. States bear the costs in excess of the federal reimbursement.

Eligible applicants: state or territorial agencies; public or private nonprofit schools or child care institutions of high school grade or under, including nursery schools, child-care centers, settlement houses, summer camps, and similar institutions devoted to the care and training of children, except Job Core Centers— provided they do not participate in a meal service program authorized under the National School Lunch Act or Child Nutrition Act of 1966.

Eligible beneficiaries: All children attending schools where the Special Milk Program is in operation may participate.

Average: FY 05 reimbursements, 15.5 cents per subsidized half-pint served free.

Activity: FY 05, 99.5 million half-pints served.

HQ: Director, Child Nutrition Division, FNS-USDA, Alexandria, VA 22302. Phone: (703) 305-2590.

Internet: www.fns.usda.gov/cnd.

10.557 SPECIAL SUPPLEMENTAL NUTRITION PROGRAM FOR WOMEN, INFANTS, AND CHILDREN ("WIC Program")

Assistance: formula grants (100 percent).

Purposes: pursuant to the Child Nutrition Act of 1966 as amended, to supply supplemental foods, nutrition education, and health care referrals at no cost to low-income pregnant, postpartum, and breast-feeding women, infants, and children under age five, identified as at nutritional risk. Grants are awarded to state health or comparable agencies and certain tribes or Indian groups; in turn, funds and food are distributed through local public or nonprofit agencies.

Eligible applicants: local public or private nonprofit health or human service agencies. Applications must be submitted to the responsible state or territorial agency.

Eligible beneficiaries: pregnant, postpartum, or breast-feeding women, infants and children to age five—determined to be in need of supplemental foods, meeting an income standard or receiving benefits under the Food Stamp, Medicaid, or Temporary Assistance for Needy Families Programs. Must also reside in the state in which benefits are received.

Range: $72,937 to $876,411,882. **Average:** FY 05: $57,984,539; cost, $37.42 per person per month.

Activity: FY 05, participation by 89 state, territorial, and Indian agencies; monthly average, 8,022,615 participants.

HQ: Director, Supplemental Food Programs Division, FNS-USDA, Alexandria, VA 22302. Phone: (703) 305-2746.

Internet: www.fns.usda.gov.

10.558 CHILD AND ADULT CARE FOOD PROGRAM

Assistance: formula grants.

Purposes: pursuant to the National School Lunch Act as amended, to provide funding and commodity foods to institutional food service programs that serve meals to eligible children, including in emergency shelters, or to elderly or impaired adults receiving care in nonresidential day care facilities.

Eligible applicants: state and territorial agencies. In Virginia where the state does not administer the program, institutions may receive funds directly from USDA.

Eligible beneficiaries: public and private nonprofit organizations, including day care centers, outside-school-hour centers, settlement houses, recreation centers, family and group day care home programs, Head Start programs, institutions providing day care services to children with disabilities; certain licensed private for-profit centers that receive compensation under Title XX for at least 25 percent of the children, or under Title XIX or XX for at least 25 percent of the adults, enrolled in nonresidential day care services.

Range: state grants, $48,726 to $241,324,362.

Activity: FY 05, 1,828,400,000 meals served.

HQ: Director, Child Nutrition Division, FNS-USDA, Alexandria, VA 22302. Phone: (703) 305-2590.

Internet: www.fns.usda.gov/cnd.

10.559 SUMMER FOOD SERVICE PROGRAM FOR CHILDREN

Assistance: formula grants.

Purposes: pursuant to the National School Lunch Act as amended, to provide funding and other donations to nonprofit food service programs for needy children age 18 and under and for disabled persons, when schools are closed for summer vacation or for periods of 15 days or more during the regular school year. Funds are available to institutions conducting regularly scheduled programs for children in areas where at least 50 percent of the children meet the family income eligibility criteria for free and reduced-price lunches. Disbursements equal the full cost of food service operations, but cannot exceed per meal rates.

Eligible applicants: state and territorial agencies. Where states do not administer the program, beneficiary agencies may apply directly.

Eligible beneficiaries: public and private nonprofit school food authorities, residential summer camps serving eligible children, and IHEs operating the National Youth Sports Program; units of local, municipal, county, or state government. Other organizations may participate under certain conditions.

Range: state grants, $279,251 to $36,713,705.

Activity: FY 05, 117,000,000 meals served.

HQ: Director, Child Nutrition Division, FNS-USDA, Alexandria, VA 22302. Phone: (703) 305-2590.

Internet: www.fns.usda.gov/cnd.

10.560 STATE ADMINISTRATIVE EXPENSES FOR CHILD NUTRITION

Assistance: formula grants.

Purposes: pursuant to the Child Nutrition Act of 1966 as amended, for the costs of administering various child nutrition programs, including technical assistance to operating agencies. Program funds may be used to purchase supplies, equipment, and services.

Eligible applicants/beneficiaries: state and territorial agencies administering child nutrition programs, and agencies distributing USDA donated commodities to schools.

Range: $306,620 to $18,688,202. **Average:** $2,898,109.

Activity: not quantified specifically.

HQ: Director, Child Nutrition Division, FNS-USDA, Alexandria, VA 22302. Phone: (703) 305-2590.

Internet: www.fns.usda.gov/cnd.

10.561 STATE ADMINISTRATIVE MATCHING GRANTS FOR FOOD STAMP PROGRAM

Assistance: formula grants (from 50-60 percent).

Purposes: pursuant to the Food Stamp Act of 1977 as amended, for the administrative costs of operating the food stamp program, including for fraud investigations and for developing computer systems. States also conduct an employment and training program requiring no state matching funds. Reimbursements are made to participants for up to 50 percent their dependent care costs, not exceeding $25 monthly per participant; states also receive 50 percent of case management costs.

Eligible applicants/beneficiaries: state and territorial cooperators.

Range: $2.6 million to $352.4 million. **Average:** FY 05, $45.1 million.

Activity: not quantified specifically.

HQ: Deputy Administrator/Food Stamp Program, FNS-USDA, Alexandria, VA 22302. Phone: (703) 305-2026.

Internet: www.fns.usda.gov.

10.565 COMMODITY SUPPLEMENTAL FOOD PROGRAM

Assistance: sale, exchange, or donation of property and goods; formula grants.

Purposes: pursuant to the Agriculture and Consumer Protection Act of 1973 and Food and Agriculture Act of 1977 as amended, for the donation of supplemental foods to low-income persons. Grant funds may be used only for administrative costs incurred in making the donated goods and nutrition education services available to beneficiaries.

Eligible applicants: state agencies; recognized tribes, bands, or groups—which distribute funds to local public or nonprofit agencies.

Eligible beneficiaries: infants or children to age 6; pregnant, postpartum, or breast-feeding women; or, elderly persons age 60 or older—certified as income-eligible for benefits under existing federal, state, or local food, health, or welfare program.

Range: $5,937 to $4,672,000 per state.

Activity: FY 05, 54,477, infants, and children and 459,780 elderly persons participated monthly.

HQ: Director, Food Distribution Division, FNS-USDA, Alexandria, VA 22302. Phone: (703) 305-2680.

Internet: www.fns.usda.gov/fdd/programs/csfp.

10.566 NUTRITION ASSISTANCE FOR PUERTO RICO ("NAP")

Assistance: direct payments/specified use (benefits, 100 percent; administrative, 50 percent).

Purposes: for low-income Puerto Ricans to purchase food—as an alternative to Food Stamps.

Eligible applicants: only the Commonwealth of PR.

Eligible beneficiaries: low-income Puerto Rican individuals and families.

Average: $105.97/person/month.

Activity: FY 05, 1,490,000 persons assisted monthly.

HQ: Deputy Administrator/Food Stamp Program, FNS-USDA, Alexandria, VA 22302. Phone: (703) 305-2026.

Internet: www.fns.usda.gov.

10.567 FOOD DISTRIBUTION PROGRAM ON INDIAN RESERVATIONS

Assistance: project grants; sale, exchange, or donation of property and goods (75 percent).

Purposes: pursuant to the Agricultural Act of 1949, Food and Agriculture Act of 1963, Food Stamp Act of 1977, amendments, and other legislation, to provide food to needy persons living on or near Indian reservations, and funds for the administrative costs incurred by organizations operating the program. Donated foods may be acquired under USDA's surplus removal or price support operations.

Eligible applicants: state agencies; tribal organizations.

Eligible beneficiaries: households living on Indian reservations; Indian households living near an Indian reservation (or, for Oklahoma, living in Indian country)—certified by local authorities as having inadequate income and resources. Upper limits of allowable income vary with family size.

Range: $79,031 to $4,937,577.

Activity: FY 05, 99,011 persons participating monthly; 97 tribal organizations and 5 states administering the program for 247 participating tribes.

HQ: Director, Food Distribution Division, FNS-USDA, Alexandria, VA 22302. Phone: (703) 305-2680.

Internet: www.fns.usda.gov/fdd/programs.

10.568 EMERGENCY FOOD ASSISTANCE PROGRAM (ADMINISTRATIVE COSTS)

Assistance: formula grants.

Purposes: pursuant to the Emergency Food Assistance Act of 1983 as amended and other acts, to cover state and local costs of processing, storage, and distribution of food used to feed needy persons.

Eligible applicants: state agencies.

Eligible beneficiaries: public or private non-profit organizations that operate USDA food programs.

Range: $9,202 to $5,717,291. **Average:** $821,715.

Activity: not quantified specifically.

HQ: Director, Food Distribution Division, FNS-USDA, Room 500, 3101 Park Center Dr., Alexandria, VA 22302. Phone: (703) 305-2680.

Internet: www.fns.usda.gov/fdd/programs/tefap.

10.569 EMERGENCY FOOD ASSISTANCE PROGRAM (FOOD COMMODITIES)

Assistance: formula grants (100 percent).

Purposes: pursuant to the Emergency Food Assistance Act of 1983 and Hunger Prevention Act of 1988, to make food commodities available to needy persons, including for meals served at congregate meal sites.

Eligible applicants: designated state food commodity distributing agencies.

Eligible beneficiaries: needy persons including the unemployed, homeless, welfare recipients, and the low-income.

Range: FY 05: $23,000 to $16,710,000. **Average:** $2,593,000.

Activity: not quantified specifically.

HQ: Director, Food Distribution Division, FNS-USDA, Room 500, 3101 Park Center Dr., Alexandria, VA 22302. Phone: (703) 305-2680.

Internet: www.fns.usda.gov/fncs/.

10.572 WIC FARMERS' MARKET NUTRITION PROGRAM ("FMNP")

Assistance: formula grants (70 percent; tribal organizations, 70- 90 percent).

Purposes: pursuant to the WIC Farmers' Market Nutrition Act of 1992 and Child Nutrition Act of 1966 as amended, to provide fresh and nutritious unprepared foods (such as fruits and vegetables) from farmers' markets to low-income women, infants, and children at nutritional risk—through the use of FMNP coupons; to expand awareness and use of farmers' markets. States may meet matching fund requirements through state contributions to similar programs.

Eligible applicants: state health, agriculture, and other agencies; recognized Indian organizations.

Eligible beneficiaries: WIC program participants (i.e., pregnant, postpartum, or breast-feeding women, infants over age 4 months, children to age 5). At the discretion of the states, WIC program applicants may also participate.

Range: $6,337 to $4,452,384. **Average:** $621,155.

Activity: FY 06, 45 programs.

HQ: Branch Chief, Supplemental Food Programs Division, FCS-USDA, 3101 Park Center Dr. - Rm. 540, Alexandria, VA 22302. Phone: (703) 305-2746.

Internet: www.fns.usda.gov/wic/.

10.574 TEAM NUTRITION GRANTS ("TN Training Grants")

Assistance: project grants. (100 percent/2 years).

Purposes: pursuant to the National School Lunch Act and amendments, to establish and enhance nutrition training and technical assistance programs to school food service professionals, as well as to children and parents. The program provides start-up money for projects, and may include a cafeteria-classroom link to support nutrition education and healthy food choices. States may use funds to provide comprehensive, action-oriented delivery of training programs for schools.

Eligible applicants: state agencies—applying individually or as coalitions.

Eligible beneficiaries: school and child care decision makers, service staff, and caregivers; children, parents, and teachers/educators.

Range: $50,197 to $200,000. **Average:** $182,094.

Activity: FY 05, 32 applicants, 21 grants; total funding, $3,823,979.

HQ: Grants Management Division, FNS-USDA, Alexandria, VA 22302. Phone: (703) 305-2867.

Internet: www.teamnutrition.usda.gov/grants.html.

10.576 SENIOR FARMERS MARKET NUTRITION PROGRAM ("SFMNP")

Assistance: project grants.

Purposes: pursuant to FSRIA, to expand, develop, or aid domestic farmers markets, roadside stands, and community-supported agriculture programs serving low-income seniors. Grants are competitive, and may support costs of food only.

Eligible applicants: states, territories, and tribal governments, which may make subgrants to local governments and nonprofit organizations.

Eligible beneficiaries: low-income seniors, generally defined as individuals at least age 60 with household income not exceeding 185 percent of federal poverty guidelines.

Range/Average: N.A.

Activity: new program listing in 2004. FY 04, 802,000 seniors served; FY 06, 46 state agencies and tribal governments operated programs.

HQ: Grant Officer, Grants Management Division, FNS-USDA, Alexandria, VA 22302. Phone: (703) 305-2760.

Internet: www.fns.usda.gov/fns.

10.578 WIC GRANTS TO STATES ("WGS")

Assistance: project grants. (100 percent/ 1-3 years).

Purposes: pursuant to the Child Nutrition Act of 1966 as amended, to provide funding to WIC state agencies for Electronic Benefit Transfer Projects (EBT) and pilots exploring the technical and financial feasibility of providing WIC benefits electronically; for WIC state agencies and tribal governments to fund, implement, and evaluate innovative projects that improve WIC services provisions and impact the nutrition and health of WIC participants. Grants are competitive. Special projects examples: motivational interviewing in nutrition education; increasing breastfeeding among Indians.

Eligible applicants/beneficiaries: state WIC program agencies; state coalitions.

Range: EBT, $262,138 to $2,300,000; discretionary grants, $20,000 to $1,076,125. **Average:** EBT, $907,394; discretionary, $474,777.

Activity: new program listing in 2004; as of FY 01, 42 awards granted.

HQ: Grants Management Division, FNS-USDA, Alexandria, VA 22302. Phone: (no number provided).

Internet: www.fns.usda.gov.

10.579 CHILD NUTRITION DISCRETIONARY GRANTS LIMITED AVAILABILITY

Assistance: project grants (100 percent).

Purposes: pursuant to National School Lunch Act, Child Nutrition Act of 1966 and amendments, to assist states through cash and food donations in making food and milk service programs available, by providing school breakfasts and lunches—and through nutrition programs for children, the elderly, and impaired adults in nonresidential day care facilities and child emergency shelters. Program emphasis is on the school breakfast program.

Eligible applicants/beneficiaries: determined legislatively.

Range/Average: N.A.; determined legislatively.

Activity: N.A.; new program listing in 2004.

HQ: Chief, Grants Management Division, FNS-USDA, Alexandria, VA 22302. Phone: (703) 305-2854.

Internet: www.fns.usda.gov.

10.580 FOOD STAMP PROGRAM OUTREACH/PARTICIPATION PROGRAM

Assistance: project grants (100 percent).

Purposes: pursuant to the Food Stamp Act of 1977, for research into food stamp outreach activities, methods, or technologies, directed to targeted groups that are eligible but that traditionally under-use food stamp benefits—involving new technology and partnerships to educate eligible beneficiaries about the nutrition benefits of the program and about how to apply.

Eligible applicants: non-food stamp governmental authorities, nonprofit organizations.

Eligible beneficiaries: persons potentially eligible for food stamps (low-income individuals or families).

Average: N.A.

Activity: N.A.; new program listing in 2004.

HQ: Grants Management Division, FNS-USDA, Alexandria, VA 22302. Phone: (703) 305-2867.

Internet: www.fns.usda.gov.

10.582 FRESH FRUIT AND VEGETABLE PROGRAM ("FFVP")

Assistance: project grants (100 percent).

Purposes: pursuant to the National School Lunch Act as amended, to reimburse states providing free fresh fruits and vegetables to school children of high school grade and under in designated public and private schools.

Eligible applicants: state agencies specified in Section 18(g) of the National School Lunch Act or selected by USDA, including Indian tribal organizations and public and private schools participating in the National School Lunch Program or School Breakfast Program and selected by their State agencies to participate in the FFVP. States must ensure that the majority of schools have 50 percent or more students eligible for free or reduced price meals, with priority to schools with partnerships with nonfederal resources, except for schools previously participating in the Fresh Fruit and Vegetable Pilot Program prior to 1 May 2004.

Eligible beneficiaries: All children enrolled in schools participating in the Fresh Fruit and Vegetable Program.

Range/Average: N.A.

Activity: N.A.; new program in FY 05.

HQ: Director, Child Nutrition Division, FNS-USDA, Alexandria, VA 22302. Phone: (703) 305-2590. *And:* Director, Grants Management Division, Special Nutrition Programs, FNS-USDA, Alexandria, VA 22302. Phone: (703) 305-2161.

Internet: www.fns.usda.gov/cnd (Note: no field offices for this program.)

10.600 FOREIGN MARKET DEVELOPMENT COOPERATOR PROGRAM

Assistance: direct payments/specified use. (50 percent/ 1-3 years).

Purposes: pursuant to the Agricultural Trade Act of 1978, for CCC projects abroad to develop, expand, and maintain long-term export markets for U.S. agricultural products, usually conducted by U.S. nonprofit trade associations ("Cooperators"). Funded activities may include trade servicing, market research, and technical assistance to actual or potential foreign purchasers. (FAS administers the program for the CCC.)

Eligible applicants/beneficiaries: U.S. nonprofit nationwide or industry-wide agricultural trade groups.

Range: $11,000 to $7,000,000. **Average:** $1,243,000.

Activity: FY 05, 22 cooperator programs in 100 foreign countries.

HQ: Deputy Administrator, Commodity and Marketing Programs, FAS-USDA, Washington, DC 20250. Phone: (202) 720-4761.

Internet: www.fas.usda.gov/mos/programs/fmd.html. (Note: no field offices for this program.)

10.601 MARKET ACCESS PROGRAM ("MAP")

Assistance: direct payments/specified use. (50-90 percent/ 1-3 years).

Purposes: pursuant to the Agricultural Trade Act of 1978 as amended, to develop, expand, and maintain export markets for U.S. agricultural commodities. Projects may involve generic (90 percent funding) or brand-specific (50 percent) promotions. Activities may include consumer advertising, point-of-sale demonstrations, public relations, trade fairs, exhibits, market research, or technical assistance. Funding is through CCC reimbursements for authorized activities.

Eligible applicants/beneficiaries: U.S. nonprofit agricultural trade organizations, state regional trade groups, agricultural cooperatives, state agencies, small private entities.

Range: $22,000 to $9,611,000. **Average:** $1,375,000.

Activity: 2005, allocations to 68 groups.

HQ: Deputy Administrator, Commodity and Marketing Programs, FAS-USDA, Washington, DC 20250. Phone: (202) 720-4761.

Internet: www.fas.usda.gov/mos/programs/mapprog.html. (Note: no field offices for this program.)

10.603 EMERGING MARKETS PROGRAM ("EMP")

Assistance: direct payments/specified use.

Purposes: pursuant to FACTA as amended and FAIRA, to promote, enhance, or expand U.S. agricultural commodity exports to emerging markets abroad. Project funds may finance feasibility studies, market research, sector assessments, orientation visits, specialized training, business workshops, and similar activities. Funding is provided through the Commodity Credit Corporation. Implementers contribute a share of project costs.

Eligible applicants/beneficiaries: U.S. agricultural or agribusiness organizations, nonprofit trade associations, universities, state departments of agriculture, certain consultant groups.

Range: $5,000 to $500,000.

Activity: FY 05, allocations to 71 organizations.

HQ: Director, Marketing Operations Staff, FAS-USDA, Washington, DC 20250. Phone: (202) 720-4327.

Internet: www.fas.usda.gov/mos/em-markets/em-markets.html. (Note: no field offices for this program.)

10.604 TECHNICAL ASSISTANCE FOR SPECIALTY CROPS PROGRAM ("TASC")

Assistance: direct payments/specified use.

Purposes: pursuant to FSRIA, for projects addressing sanitary, phytosanitary, and technical barriers that prohibit or threaten the export of U.S. specialty crops. Activities eligible for funding include initial preclearance programs, export protocol and work plan support, seminars and workshops, study tours, field surveys, pest lists development, pest and disease research, data base development, logistical and administrative support, and travel costs. Costs are reimbursed by CCC.

Eligible applicants/beneficiaries: federal and state government agencies; U.S. nonprofit trade associations, universities, agricultural cooperatives, private companies, and other organizations.

Range: to $250,000 per year for projects.

Activity: new program listing in 2004; 24 organizations funded in 2005.

HQ: Director, Marketing Operations Staff, FAS-USDA, Washington, DC 20250. Phone: (202) 720-4327.

Internet: www.fas.usda.gov/mos/tasc/tasc.asp. (Note: no field offices for this program.)

10.605 QUALITY SAMPLES PROGRAM ("QSP")

Assistance: direct payments/specified use.

Purposes: pursuant to the CCC Charter Act, to develop and expand export markets for U.S. agricultural commodities by assisting U.S. entities in providing commodity samples to potential foreign importers. Costs of purchasing and transporting the samples may be reimbursed by the CCC; technical assistance costs may not.

Eligible applicants/beneficiaries: U.S. entities.

Range: to $75,000 for projects.

Activity: new program listing in 2004; 20 organizations assisted in 2005.

HQ: Director, Marketing Operations Staff, FAS-USDA, Washington, DC 20250. Phone: (202) 720-4327.

Internet: www.fas.usda.gov/mos/programs/qspfact.html. (Note: no field offices for this program.)

10.606 FOOD FOR PROGRESS

Assistance: project grants. (100 percent/1-3 years).

Purposes: pursuant to the Food for Progress Act of 1985, to provide agricultural commodities to developing countries and emerging democracies committed to introducing and expanding free enterprise in the agricultural sector.

Eligible applicants/beneficiaries: "Cooperating Sponsors" including: foreign governments; entities registered with USAID; entities demonstrating satisfactory experience and other qualifications to the CCC.

Range/Average: N.A.

Activity: N.A.; new program listing in 2003.

HQ: Director, Programming Division, FAS-USDA, 1400 Independence Ave. SW, Washington, DC 20250-1034. Phone: (202) 720-4221.

Internet: www.fas.usda.gov/. (Note: no field offices for this program.)

10.607 SECTION 416(B)

Assistance: project grants. (100 percent/1-3 years).

Purposes: pursuant to the Agricultural Act of 1949, to provide agricultural commodities to developing countries and emerging democracies committed to introducing and expanding free enterprise in the agricultural sector. Essentially same as **10.606**.

Eligible applicants/beneficiaries: "Cooperating Sponsors" including: foreign governments; entities registered with USAID; entities demonstrating satisfactory experience and other qualifications to the CCC.

Range/Average: N.A.

Activity: N.A.; new program listing in 2003.

HQ: Director, Programming Division, FAS-USDA, 1400 Independence Ave. SW, Washington, DC 20250-1034. Phone: (202) 720-4221.

Internet: www.fas.usda.gov/. (Note: no field offices for this program.)

10.608 FOOD FOR EDUCATION ("FFE")

Assistance: project grants. (100 percent/1-3 years).

Purposes: pursuant to the FSRIA, to reduce hunger and improve literacy and primary education, especially for girls, with a focus on developing countries. Projects may provide for such activities as school meals, teacher training, and related support including nutrition programs for pregnant women, nursing mothers, and pre-school youngsters.

Eligible applicants/beneficiaries: "Cooperating Sponsors" including: foreign governments; entities registered with USAID; entities demonstrating satisfactory experience and other qualifications to the CCC.

Range/Average: N.A.

Activity: N.A.

HQ: Director, Programming Division, FAS-USDA, 1400 Independence Ave. SW, Washington, DC 20250-1034. Phone: (202) 720-4221.

Internet: www.fas.usda.gov (Note: no field offices for this program.)

10.609 TRADE ADJUSTMENT ASSISTANCE ("TAA")

Assistance: direct payments/unrestricted use.

Purposes: pursuant to the Trade Act of 1974 as amended by the Trade Act of 2002, to provide technical assistance and cash benefits to farmers, ranchers, fish farmers, and fishermen competing with imported aquaculture products, if increased imports have contributed to a price decline of at least 20 percent. Technical assistance may be provided by CSREES in cooperation with county Extension Services, in helping producers respond proactively to import competition through training, cash benefits, and employment services.

Eligible applicants/beneficiaries: producers of raw commodities that: are owners, operators, landlords, tenants, or sharecroppers—sharing in production risk and entitled to share in the crop availability; have been adversely affected by import competition; are covered by a certification of eligibility.

Range: to $10,000 per year.

Activity: N.A.; new program listing in 2004.

HQ: Trade Adjustment Assistance, FAS-USDA, 1400 Independence Ave. SW, Washington, DC 20250-1021. Phone: (202) 720-2916.

Internet: www.fas.usda.gov/itp/taa/taaindex.htm.

10.652 FORESTRY RESEARCH ("Research Grants & Agreements")

Assistance: project grants (1-5 years).

Purposes: pursuant to the Forest and Rangeland Renewable Resources Research Act of 1978, for fundamental research in: management of forests, watersheds, forest ranges, wildlife habitat; recreation; fire protection; insect and disease protection and control; forest products utilization; forest engineering; forest production economics and marketing; forest surveying; urban forestry; and social/cultural influences.

Eligible applicants/beneficiaries: state agricultural experiment stations, IHEs, state and local governments, territories; profit, nonprofit, and international organizations; individuals.

Range: $2,000 to $300,000. **Average:** $35,000.

Activity: FY 01, 425 grants awarded.

HQ: Deputy Chief/Research and Development, Forest Service-USDA, Washington, DC 20090-6090. Phone: (202) 205-1075.

Internet: www.fs.fed.us/links/research.html.

10.664 COOPERATIVE FORESTRY ASSISTANCE

Assistance: formula grants; project grants (50-80 percent).

Purposes: pursuant to the Cooperative Forestry Assistance Act of 1978 and FACTA as amended, for state forest stewardship programs on private, local, state, and other nonfederal forest and rural lands. Programs may include: timber production: insect and disease control; processing of wood products; producing and distributing tree seeds and seedlings, urban forestry; conversion of wood to energy; improvement and maintenance of fish and wildlife habitat; financial and technical assistance for rural firefighting; organizational improvement; technology transfer; acquisition and loan of federal surplus property.

Eligible applicants: states, tribes, municipalities, territories and possessions, nonprofit organizations.

Eligible beneficiaries: owners of nonfederal lands; rural community firefighting forces; urban and municipal governmental and other state, local, and private agencies acting through state foresters or equivalent state officials.

Range: $25,000 to $6,000,000. **Average:** $1,000,000.

Activity: estimated 2003 activities (representative): 37,000 landowners enrolled, covering 3,914,000 acres.

HQ: Deputy Chief, State and Private Forestry, Forest Service- USDA, Washington, DC 20090-6090. Phone: (202) 205-1657.

Internet: www.fs.fed.us/spf/coop.

10.665 SCHOOLS AND ROADS—GRANTS TO STATES ("25 Percent Payments to States")

Assistance: formula grants.

Purposes: to return 25 percent of revenues from the national forests to states and U.S. territories, for the benefit of public schools and public roads of the counties in which the forests are located.

Eligible applicants/beneficiaries: states or territories with national forest land.

Range: $35 to $161,888,715.

Activity: N.A.

HQ: Acquisitions Management, Grants and Agreements, Forest Service-USDA, RPE - Rm.706, Washington, DC 20090-6090. Phone: (703) 605-4776.

Internet: www.fs.fed.us.

10.666 SCHOOLS AND ROADS—GRANTS TO COUNTIES ("Payments to Counties")

Assistance: formula grants.

Purposes: to return 25 percent of revenues from national grasslands and land utilization projects, for the benefit of public schools and roads of the counties in which they are located.

Eligible applicants/beneficiaries: U.S. counties with national grasslands or land utilization projects.

Range: $5 to $1,707,000. **Average:** $69,000.

Activity: N.A.

HQ: Director/Procurement and Property, Acquisitions Management, Grants and Agreements, Forest Service-USDA, RPE - Rm.706, Washington, DC 20090-6090. Phone: (202) 605-4662.

Internet: www.fs.fed.us.

10.670 NATIONAL FOREST—DEPENDENT RURAL COMMUNITIES ("Economic Recovery")

Assistance: project grants; use of property, facilities, and equipment; training (80 percent).

Purposes: pursuant to the National Forest Dependent Rural Communities Economic Diversification Act of 1990 as amended, to provide accelerated assistance to rural communities with acute economic problems associated with federal, state, or private sector forest management policies. Assistance is coordinated with other USDA agencies and may be provided through a community action team to identify and develop opportunities to promote economic improvement, diversification, and revitalization. Funds may support costs of technical assistance, planning, and community training related to the upgrading of existing industries, and development of new economic activities in industries unrelated to the forests.

Eligible applicants/beneficiaries: general purpose local governments or tribes represented by state-authorized nonprofit corporations, with not more than 10,000 population; counties not within metropolitan statistical areas—located inside or within 100 miles of the national forest, and whose economies are strongly related to activities within the forest.

Range: $1,000 to $30,000.

Activity: FY 01, 800 communities receiving assistance.

HQ: Deputy Chief, State and Private Forestry, Forest Service- USDA, Washington, DC 20090-6090. Phone: (202) 205-1657.

Internet: www.fs.fed.us/spf.

10.671 SOUTHEAST ALASKA ECONOMIC DISASTER FUND

Assistance: direct payments/specified use.

Purposes: to counter the effects of the declining timber program of the Tongass National Forest. Funds may be used to employ former timber workers and for related community development projects. Note: this program is scheduled to end with the expenditure of FY 03 payments.

Eligible applicants/beneficiaries: local communities/boroughs named in PL 104-134.

Range: $500,000 to $4,000,000.

Activity: N.A.

HQ: Forest Service-USDA, 3301 C St. - Ste.522, Anchorage, AK 99503-3956. Phone: (907) 271-2519.

Internet: www.fs.fed.us (Note: the field office serves as headquarters.)

10.672 RURAL DEVELOPMENT, FORESTRY, AND COMMUNITIES ("Rural Development Through Forestry")

Assistance: project grants (to 5 years).

Purposes: for projects to analyze and assess forest resource opportunities, maximize local economic potential through market development and expansion, and diversify the community economic base. Funds may support costs such as for technical assistance, training and education, equipment, marketing, and related expenses.

Eligible applicants/beneficiaries: state foresters; tribal, state, and federal agencies; local governments, nonprofit organizations; others.

Range: $1,000 to $50,000.

Activity: N.A.

HQ: Forest Service-USDA, Washington, DC 20090. Phone: (202) 205-1657.

Internet: www.fs.fed.us/spf/coop/programs/eap.shtml.

10.673 WOOD IN TRANSPORTATION PROGRAM ("WIT")

Assistance: project grants (50 percent).

Purposes: pursuant to FACTA, to construct demonstration modern timber bridges and related technology transfer projects for structures to be built on public lands—toward the development and commercialization of new technologies that incorporate under- utilized timber and related resources.

Eligible applicants/beneficiaries: nonfederal agencies, state and local governments, nonprofit organizations, tribal nations.

Range: commercialization projects, to $150,000; single vehicle bridges, to 50,000; pedestrian bridges, to $20,000; special projects, $30,000.

Activity: FY 02, 42 projects (latest data reported in CFDA).

HQ: Forest Service-USDA, 180 Canfield St., Morgantown, WV 26505. Phone: (304) 285-1591, FAX (304) 285-1587.

Internet: www.fs.fed.us/na/wit; e-mail, na-wit@fs.us. (Note: the field office serves as headquarters.)

10.674 FOREST PRODUCTS LAB: TECHNOLOGY MARKETING UNIT (TMU) ("TMU Biomass Grant/Assistance Program")

Assistance: project grants. (80 percent/to 3 years).

Purposes: to turn small diameter and under-utilized wood species into marketable forest products, including biomass energy. Programs may include: technical assistance for processing and manufacturing; prototype development of potential new products; demonstration projects showcasing innovative uses; economic feasibility and market assessments. Land treatment must be adjacent to national forest system lands, and may include other lands as part of treatment activities.

Eligible applicants/beneficiaries: nonprofit organizations; local, state, and tribal, governments; special purpose districts; profit businesses.

Range: $50,000 to $250,000.

Activity: N.A.; new program listing in 2003.

HQ: Technology Marketing Unit, State and Private Forestry, Forest Service-USDA, 1 Gifford Pinchot Dr., Madison, WI 53276-2398. Phone: (608) 231-9200.

Internet: www.fpl.fs.fed.us/tmu. (Note: the field office serves as headquarters.)

10.675 URBAN AND COMMUNITY FORESTRY PROGRAM ("UCF")

Assistance: project grants (50 percent).

Purposes: pursuant to the Cooperative Forestry Assistance Act of 1978 as amended, to improve urban livability through projects to: plan, establish, and protect trees, forests, green spaces, and related resources in and adjacent to cities and towns; link governmental, private, and grass-roots organizations and resources to address environmental issues at the local, regional, and national levels; engage people in citizen-based, grass-roots volunteer efforts to assist in retaining and protecting their natural environment to provide a balance between quality of life and land consumption associated with urban sprawl; improve the ecological function and social and economic stability of cities and communities.

Eligible applicants/beneficiaries: state forestry or equivalent state agencies; interested members of the public; private nonprofit organizations, tribes and others. Available also in territories and possessions.

Range/Average: N.A.

Activity: new program listing in 2003. FY 04 estimate, 10,500 communities assisted.

HQ: Deputy Chief, State and Private Forestry, Forest Service- USDA, 1400 Independence Ave. SW, Washington, DC 20090-1123. Phone:(202) 205-1657.

Internet: www.fs.fed.us/ucf/.

10.676 FOREST LEGACY PROGRAM ("FLP")

Assistance: project grants. (75 percent/2 years).

Purposes: pursuant to Cooperative Forestry Assistance Act of 1978 FACTA. FAIRA, and amendments, to protect and conserve environmentally important forest areas threatened by conversion to nonforest uses, through conservation easements and other mechanisms. Projects must be conducted on a strictly voluntary basis—i.e., without eminent domain or other legal compulsions.

Eligible applicants: state lead agencies in consultation with state forest stewardship coordinating committees, including in territories and possessions.

Eligible beneficiaries: state agencies, private forest landowners and land trust organizations.

Range/Average: N.A.

Activity: new program listing in 2003. As of April 2005, more than 1,000,000 acres protected.

HQ: Cooperative Forestry (1123), State and Private Forestry, Forest Service-USDA, 1400 Independence Ave. SW Washington, DC 20250. Phone: (202) 205-1389.

Internet: www.fs.fed.us/spf/coop/programs/loa/flp.shtml.

10.677 FOREST LAND ENHANCEMENT PROGRAM ("FLEP")

Assistance: project grants (100 percent).

Purposes: pursuant to FSRIA, for sustainable forest management of nonindustrial private forest and other suitable rural lands. Funds may be used for: technical and educational assistance; practices such as management plan development, tree planting, forest stand improvement, agro-forestry implementation, water quality improvement and watershed protection, fish and wildlife habitat improvement, forest health protection, invasive species control, wildfire and catastrophic protection, and approved special practices. Landowners and managers may not receive grants exceeding 75 percent of project costs.

Eligible applicants: state forestry or equivalent agencies in the states, territories, and possessions; municipalities; nonprofits.

Eligible beneficiaries: owners of nonfederal lands, nonprofit organizations, universities, other state and local private organizations and agencies acting through states.

Range: $1,100 to $832,000.

Activity: 7,800 owners of 610,000 acres to benefit.

HQ: none.

Internet: www.fs.fed.us/contactus/regions.shtml; www.stateforesters.org (Note: all contacts are with field offices.)

10.678 FOREST STEWARDSHIP PROGRAM ("FSP")

Assistance: project grants (12-18 months).

Purposes: pursuant to the Cooperative Forestry Assistance Act of 1978 and FACTA as amended, to provide financial, technical, educational, and related assistance to promote and enable the long-term active management of nonindustrial private and other nonfederal forest land.

Eligible applicants: state forestry or equivalent agencies in the states, territories, and possessions; municipalities; nonprofits; tribes.

Eligible beneficiaries: owners of nonfederal lands, nonprofit organizations, tribes, other state and local private organizations and agencies acting through states.

Range: $25,000 to $2,000,000. **Average:** $450,000.

Activity: FY 02, 186,000 landowners assisted, 18,000 plans completed, 1,640,000 acres encompassed (latest data reported in CFDA).

HQ: Forest Stewardship Program Manager, State & Private/Cooperative Forestry, Forest Service-USDA, Washington, DC 20090-6090. Phone: (202) 205-6206.

Internet: www.na.fs.fed.us/spfo/stewardship/index.htm.

10.679 COLLABORATIVE FOREST RESTORATION ("CFRP")

Assistance: project grants. (80 percent/to 4 years).

Purposes: pursuant to Secure Rural Schools and Community Self- Determination Act of 2000, to promote healthy watersheds and to reduce high intensity wildfires, insect infestation, and diseases in federal, tribal, state, county, and municipal forest lands in New Mexico; to improve the forests' ecosystems functioning and enhance plant and wildlife biodiversity by reducing the high number and density of small diameter trees; to improve communication and joint problem-solving among interested groups. Funds may support costs of technical assistance, training and education, equipment, marketing, and related services.

Eligible applicants/beneficiaries: local and tribal governments, educational institutions, landowners, conservation associations, and other public and private entities that include a diverse and balanced group of stakeholders, including public officials.

Range: $66,000 to $360,000.

Activity: new program listing in 2005. 2001-04, 62 proposals recommended for funding.

HQ: Cooperative and International Forestry Staff, Southwestern Region, Forest Service-USDA, 333 Broadway SE, Albuquerque, NM 87122. Phone: (505) 842-3289.

Internet: www.fs.fed.us/r3/spf/cfrp. (Note: the field office serves as headquarters.)

10.680 FOREST HEALTH PROTECTION ("FHP")

Assistance: formula grants; project grants (50-100 percent).

Purposes: pursuant to the Cooperative Forestry Assistance Act of 1978 and FACTA as amended, to protect nonfederal forest and tree resources from damaging insects, disease-causing agents, and invasive plants; to develop or improve forest health protection technologies. Project funds may be used for project planning, surveys, assessments, monitoring, technical assistance, technology and applied methods development.

Eligible applicants/beneficiaries: state forestry, agriculture, and equivalent agencies, including in territories; municipalities; profit and nonprofit organizations in all states, possessions and territories; Alaska native corporations, tribal governments.

Range: $25,000 to $6,000,000. **Average:** $1,000,000.

Activity: new program listing in 2005; 2001-03, all applications for base funding approved; FY 03, 1,500,000 acres of forest insect/disease surveyed and suppressed.

HQ: Deputy Chief, State and Private Forestry, Forest Service- USDA, Washington, DC 20090-6090. Phone: (202) 205-1657.

Internet: www.fs.fed.us/spf/coop.

10.681 WOOD EDUCATION AND RESOURCE CENTER ("WERC")

Assistance: project grants (50 percent/18 months).

Purposes: pursuant to the Cooperative Forestry Assistance Act of 1978 and the Forest and Rangeland Renewable Resources Act of 1978, as amended, to provide funds, on a cost-share basis, for projects that focus on enhancing opportunities for sustained forest products production for primary and secondary hardwood industries located in the eastern hardwood forest region. Projects should compliment existing activities and/or focus on niches that are not being met by either industry or service providers and to clearly document industry support and involvement.

Eligible applicants: non-federal agencies, including public, private, state, local and tribal agencies or governments; institutions of higher education;

non-profit and for-profit organizations ; corporations, businesses and others.

Eligible beneficiaries: non-federal agencies, including public, private, state, local and tribal agencies or governments; institutions of higher education; non-profit and for-profit organizations; corporations, businesses and others located in the 35 states of the eastern hardwood forest region (AL, AR, CT, DE, FL, GA, IL, IN, IA, KS, KY, LA, ME, MD, MA, MI, MN, MS, MO, NE, NH, NJ, NY, NC, OH, OK, PA, RI, SC TN, TX, VT, VA, WV, WI).

Range: $10,000 to $20,0000. **Average:** $63,000.

Activity: N.A.

HQ: USDA Forest Service, Wood Education and Resource Center, 301 Hardwood Lane, Princeton, WV 24740. Phone: (304) 487-1510, FAX: (304) 487-6661.

Internet: www.na.fs.fed.us/werc.

10.684 INTERNATIONAL FORESTRY PROGRAMS

Assistance: project grants (to 5 years).

Purposes: pursuant to the International Forestry Cooperation Act of 1990, to extend Forest Service efforts to improve forest policies and practices internationally, conserve and protect critical global forest environments and resources, and improve the lives of forest-dependent peoples by awarding grants to and entering into cooperative agreements with nonprofit organizations, multilateral organizations, and other individuals, organizations, institutions, and governments engaged in forest conservation and management. Eligible applicant cost share may consist of: funds, donations, in-kind contributions, direct costs, indirect costs, and other as determined by the Forest Service.

Eligible applicants: U.S. and international organizations sanctioned by the State Department, educational institutions, government entities, and individuals.

Eligible beneficiaries: host-country forest management agencies, non-profit organizations, forest landowners, forest-dependent communities and peoples in target countries, and U.S. landowners and organizations.

Range/Average: N.A.

Activity: FY 05 to 07, approximately 50 grants.

HQ: Outreach & Partnerships Unit, International Programs, FS-USDA, 1099 14th Street, NW, Ste. 5500W, Washington DC, 20005. Phone: (202) 273-4695; FAX: (202) 273-4750.

Internet: www.fs.fed.us/global. (Note: no field offices for this program.)

10.700 NATIONAL AGRICULTURAL LIBRARY

Assistance: technical information.

Purposes: to provide agricultural information products and services through traditional library functions and through electronic distribution. Publications are available through interlibrary loan or photo-reproduction.

Eligible applicants/beneficiaries: general public.

Range/Average: N.A.

Activity: 3,300,000 items available.

HQ: Office of the Director, National Agricultural Library, ARS- USDA, Beltsville, MD 20705-2351. Phone: (301) 504-6780.

Internet: www.nal.usda.gov. (Note: no field offices for this program.)

10.760 WATER AND WASTE DISPOSAL SYSTEMS FOR RURAL COMMUNITIES

Assistance: project grants; direct loans, guaranteed/insured loans. (grants, 45-75 percent/loans, 40 years).

Purposes: pursuant to CFRDA as amended, to install, repair, improve, or expand rural water facilities and waste disposal systems including the collection and treatment of sanitary, storm, and solid wastes. Funds may be used to pay for distribution lines, well-pumping facilities, and their related costs. Loans have varying interest rates beginning as low as 4.5 percent, depending on area median income. Grants are made only when necessary to reduce the average annual benefited user charges to a reasonable level, with the matching percentage based on the applicant area's median income. Grant funds may not be used to pay loan interest, operation and maintenance costs, nor to acquire or refinance existing systems. Grants funding for this program includes **10.761** and **10.770**.

Eligible applicants: municipalities, counties, state political subdivisions such as districts and authorities; associations, cooperatives, and nonprofit corporations; tribes on federal and state reservations and other federally recognized tribes; also authorized in territories.

Eligible beneficiaries: farmers, ranchers, rural residents and businesses; other users in eligible applicant areas.

Range: direct loans, $3,400 to $9,999,900; grants, $600 to $8,090,000. **Average:** loans, $1,064,000; grants, $619,000.

Activity: FY 06 estimate, 900 direct, 2 guaranteed loans; 800 grants.

HQ: Assistant Administrator, Water and Environmental Programs, RUS-USDA, Washington, DC 20250. Phone: (202) 690-2670.

Internet: www.rurdev.usda.gov.

10.761 TECHNICAL ASSISTANCE AND TRAINING GRANTS

Assistance: project grants (100 percent).

Purposes: pursuant to CFRDA as amended, to identify and evaluate solutions to rural water problems relating to source, storage, treatment, and waste disposal; to provide training to improve the management, operation, and maintenance of water and waste disposal facilities. Funding for this program is included in **10.760**.

Eligible applicants: tax-exempt nonprofit organizations.

Eligible beneficiaries: state political subdivisions such as counties, municipalities, districts, and authorities; tribes; cooperatives; nonprofit corporations.

Range: $40,000 to $5,555,200. **Average:** $2,264.

Activity: FY 05, 8 grants.

HQ: Assistant Administrator, Water and Environmental Programs, RUS-USDA, Washington, DC 20250 Phone: (202) 690-2670.

Internet: www.rurdev.usda.gov.

10.762 SOLID WASTE MANAGEMENT GRANTS

Assistance: project grants (100 percent).

Purposes: pursuant to CFRDA as amended, to evaluate landfill conditions to determine threats to water resources in rural areas; to provide technical assistance and training in the operation of landfills, and to reduce the solid waste stream; to provide planning assistance for closing landfill sites and for future uses of such sites. Funds may not be used to pay for capital assets.

Eligible applicants/beneficiaries: tax-exempt nonprofit organizations; public bodies including local government-based multijurisdictional organizations.

Range: $5,000 to $720,000. **Average:** $75,000.

Activity: FY 05, 45 grants awarded.

HQ: Assistant Administrator, Water and Environmental Programs, RUS-USDA, Washington, DC 20250 Phone: (202) 690-2670.

Internet: www.rurdev.usda.gov.

10.763 EMERGENCY COMMUNITY WATER ASSISTANCE GRANTS

Assistance: project grants (100 percent).

Purposes: pursuant to CFRDA and FACTA, to assist rural areas experiencing a significant decline in quality or quantity of water, in complying with the Safe Drinking Water Act. Funds may be used to: extend or repair water lines on existing systems; construct new lines, new wells, reservoirs, transmission lines, treatment plants, storage tanks; and, for similar projects and related activities and costs.

Eligible applicants/beneficiaries: public bodies, private nonprofit corporations, state political subdivisions, tribes—in communities with populations not above 10,000, with household income below the statewide nonmetropolitan median.

Range: $4,100 to $500,000. **Average:** $297,000.

Activity: FY 05, 36 grants.

HQ: Assistant Administrator, Water and Environmental Programs, RUS-USDA, Washington, DC 20250. Phone: (202) 690-2670.

Internet: www.rurdev.usda.gov.

10.766 COMMUNITY FACILITIES LOANS AND GRANTS

Assistance: direct loans; guaranteed loans; project grants.

Purposes: pursuant to CFRDA as amended, to construct, enlarge, extend, or improve public facilities serving rural residents, including child care, food recovery and distribution, assisted living, group homes, mental health clinics, shelters, fire and rescue services, industrial park sites, transportation, access ways, utility extensions, educational facilities.

Eligible applicants: state agencies, counties, cities, state political and quasi-political subdivisions, tribes, associations including nonprofit corporations—in communities with populations under 20,000. Available also in territories.

Eligible beneficiaries: farmers, ranchers, rural residents, rural businesses, and other users of such public facilities in eligible applicant areas.

Range: direct loans, $3,000 to $11,000,000; guaranteed, $20,000 to $17,000,000; grants, $570 to $120,750. **Average:** direct, $847,971; guaranteed, $2,377,243; grants $36,753.

Activity: FY 05, 503 direct; 82 guaranteed loans; 542 grants.

HQ: Deputy Administrator/Community Programs, RHS-USDA, Washington, DC 20250-0788. Phone: (202) 720-1490.

Internet: www.rurdev.usda.gov.

10.767 INTERMEDIARY RELENDING PROGRAM

Assistance: direct loans. (75 percent at 1 percent interest/to 30 years).

Purposes: pursuant to the Health and Human Services Act of 1986, Food Security Act of 1985, and Community Economic Development Act of 1981, and amendments, for business facilities and community development in rural areas with under 25,000 population. Successful applicants become intermediary lenders that may make loans to ultimate recipients to finance up to 75 percent of project costs, but not more than $250,000 to any one ultimate recipient.

Eligible applicants: private nonprofit organizations, state or local governments, recognized tribes, cooperatives.

Eligible beneficiaries: individuals, public and private profit or nonprofit organizations.

Range: $150,000 to $1,000,000. **Average:** $595,427.

Activity: estimate FY 06, 69 loan approvals.

HQ: RBCS-USDA, South Agriculture Bldg. - Rm.6867, Washington, DC 20250-3225. Phone: (202) 690-4100.

Internet: www.rurdev.usda.gov.

10.768 BUSINESS AND INDUSTRY LOANS

Assistance: guaranteed/insured loans (to 80-90 percent).

Purposes: pursuant to CFRDA as amended, for the development or improvement of rural businesses, industry, and employment. Loan funds may cover such costs as business and industrial acquisition, construction, conversion, enlargement, repair, modernization, equipment, machinery, supplies, pollution control and abatement—for 30 years for real estate, up to 15 years for machinery and equipment, and 7 years for working capital. Assistance is unavailable for community antenna TV services or facilities, charitable and educational institutions, hotels and tourist facilities, large businesses, or uses other than those that will protect or create jobs, improve existing business and industry, and provide economic stability to rural areas. Project examples: agri-business expansion; radio station start-up; catfish farm operating loan; printing company expansion.

Eligible applicants/beneficiaries: cooperatives, corporations, partnerships, trusts, or other for-profit enterprises; certain nonprofit entities; tribes, municipalities, counties, or other state political subdivisions; individuals. Applicants must be U.S. citizens or legal permanent residents; if corporations, 51 percent ownership must be held by U.S. citizens. Available also in some territories. Projects must be in rural jurisdiction under 50,000 population, with preference to those under 25,000.

Range: guaranteed loans, $35,000 to $17,500,000. **Average:** $2,000,000.

Activity: FY 07, 495 guaranteed loans. (Note: no funds have been available for direct loans since FY 01.)

HQ: Administrator, RBCS-USDA, Washington, DC 20250-3201. Phone: (202) 690-4730, FAX (202) 690-4737.

Internet: www.rurdev.usda.gov.

10.769 RURAL BUSINESS ENTERPRISE GRANTS ("RBEG")

Assistance: project grants.

Purposes: pursuant to CFRDA as amended, to facilitate the development of small and emerging private business, industry, and related employment—toward economic improvement of rural areas. Grants may be used to: create, expand, or operate distance learning networks or programs providing educational or job training instruction; to establish revolving loan funds, provide operating capital, and finance industrial sites—including land acquisition; construction, conversion, enlargement, repair, or modernization of buildings, plants, machinery, equipment; access streets and roads, parking areas, transportation serving the site; utility extensions; water supply and waste disposal facilities, pollution control and abatement; technical assistance, fees, and refinancing. Television demonstration grants (TDG) may be used for programming demonstrating the effectiveness of providing information on agriculture and other issues of importance to farmers and other rural residents.

Eligible applicants: RBEG—public bodies and nonprofit corporations serving rural areas, such as states, counties, cities, townships, and incorporated towns and villages, boroughs, authorities, districts, and tribes on federal and state reservations serving rural areas. TDG—statewide nonprofit public television systems whose coverage is predominantly rural. For this program, "rural area" is defined as city, town, or unincorporated area with a population of 50,000 or less. Priority is accorded to projects: in areas with a large number of low-income persons; designed to save existing or to create new jobs; in areas with high unemployment.

Eligible beneficiaries: private businesses that will employ 50 or fewer new employees, and with under $1,000,000 in projected revenue.

Range: $25,000 to $500,000. **Average:** $96,668.

Activity: FY 06 estimate, 427 grants.

HQ: Director, Specialty Lenders Division, RBCS-USDA, Washington, DC 20250-3222. Phone: (202) 720-1400.

Internet: www.rurdev.usda.gov.

10.770 WATER AND WASTE DISPOSAL LOANS AND GRANTS ("Section 306C")

Assistance: project grants; direct loans (100 percent).

Purposes: pursuant to CFRDA as amended and FACTA, to develop water and waste disposal facilities and services for rural low- income communities facing significant health risks. Funds may be used to: construct, enlarge, extend, or improve community water or sewer systems; connect residences to community systems; enable individuals to install plumbing and related fixtures and to construct bathrooms within their dwellings. Funded projects must primarily serve residents of counties with per capita incomes not more than 70 percent of the national average, and with unemployment not less than 125 percent of the national average rate. Grant funds for this program are included in **10.760**, and may be used only in colonias.

Eligible applicants/beneficiaries: local governments, tribes, nonprofit associations, cooperatives—including territories and possessions.

Average: colonias, $757,600; tribal, $586,900.

Activity: FY 05: colonias, 33 infrastructure projects, 242 individual connections funded; tribal, 29 grants.

HQ: Assistant Administrator, Water and Environmental Programs, RUS-USDA, Washington, DC 20250-3200. Phone: (202) 690-2670.

Internet: www.rurdev.usda.gov.

10.771 RURAL COOPERATIVE DEVELOPMENT GRANTS ("RCDG")

Assistance: project grants (75 percent).

Purposes: pursuant to the FACTA, CFRDA, and FAIRA, to establish and operate centers for rural cooperative development to improve economic conditions by promoting development of new cooperatives, or to improve existing cooperatives. Funds may be used for basic feasibility studies, technical assistance, advisory services, and research or technical support for individuals, small businesses, cooperatives, or rural industries.

Eligible applicants: nonprofit corporations and IHEs serving rural areas not within the outer boundary of any city having a population of 50,000 or more according to latest U.S. decennial census.

Eligible beneficiaries: rural residents.

Range: $85,000 to $300,000. **Average:** $264,000.

Activity: FY 04, 24 grants.

HQ: Assistant Deputy Administrator/Cooperative Services, RBCS- USDA, Washington, DC 20250. Phone: (202) 720-8460.

Internet: www.rurdev.usda.gov.

10.772 EMPOWERMENT ZONES PROGRAM ("Empowerment Zones and Enterprise Communities")

Assistance: project grants. (100 percent/to 10 years).

Purposes: pursuant to the Taxpayer Relief Acts of 1997 and 2000 and other acts, to establish job creation zones in rural areas toward the revitalization of economically distressed areas for the benefit of the disadvantaged and long-term unemployed. Through national competitions among applicants demonstrating a certain level of distress, designated rural Empowerment Zones and Enterprise Communities became eligible for private activity tax exempt bonding authority to finance qualifying enterprises and facilities. Some Round I Empowerment Zones designated in 1994 are eligible for: employer wage credits; accelerated IRS Section 179 expensing for eligible property; priority funding or special consideration under other federal programs; empowerment zone/enterprise community social service block grants (EZ/EC- SSBG) from HHS, based on activities identified in strategic plans. Round II designations were made in late 1998; provisions changed slightly. (Urban area programs are described under **14.244**.)

Eligible applicants/beneficiaries: generally, rural areas with pervasive poverty, unemployment, general distress, and with a maximum population of 30,000, no larger than 1,000 square miles, located entirely within no more than three contiguous states, and not including any portion of an Indian reservation. No new designations are authorized currently; additional details should be obtained from RDA state offices.

Range: $500,000 to $40,000,000.

Activity: cumulatively, 57 rural areas designated as EZs and ECs.

HQ: Deputy Administrator, Office of Community Development-USDA, Reporters Bldg. - Rm.266, 300 Seventh St. SW, Washington, DC 20024. Phone: (202) 619-7980;.

Internet: www.ezec.gov, *and* www.rurdev.usda.gov.

10.773 RURAL BUSINESS OPPORTUNITY GRANTS ("RBOG")

Assistance: project grants (2 years).

Purposes: pursuant to FAIRA, to promote sustainable economic development in rural communities with exceptional needs. Grants may support technical assistance, training, and planning costs.

Eligible applicants/beneficiaries: public bodies, nonprofit corporations, tribes, cooperatives.

Range: $12,000 to $344,750. **Average:** $78,846.

Activity: FY 05, 39 grants.

HQ: Specialty Lenders Division, RBCS-USDA, 1400 Independence Ave. SW - Rm.6767, Washington, DC 20250-1521. Phone: (202) 720-1400.

Internet: www.rurdev.usda.gov.

10.774 NATIONAL SHEEP INDUSTRY IMPROVEMENT CENTER ("Rural Development")

Assistance: direct loans; guaranteed/insured loans; direct payments/specified use; project grants. (guaranteed, 80 percent; direct payment, 50 percent/guaranteed, to 40 years).

Purposes: pursuant to FAIRA, for the sheep and goat industries to strengthen and enhance production and marketing. Funds may support such activities as making capital available to increase production or improve efficiency, coordination of marketing systems, and public communication programs. An appropriated revolving fund supports this program.

Eligible applicants/beneficiaries: public, private, cooperative, and nonprofit organizations; tribes; public and quasi-public agencies.

Range: loans, to $1,000,000.

Activity: not quantified specifically.

HQ: NSIIC-USDA, 1400 Independence Ave. SW - Rm.2117, Washington, DC 20250. Phone: (202) 690-0632, FAX (207) 236-6576.

Internet: www.rurdev.usda.gov/rbs/coops/cssheep.htm. (Note: no field offices for this program.)

10.775 RENEWABLE ENERGY SYSTEMS AND ENERGY EFFICIENCY IMPROVEMENTS PROGRAM ("RES and EEI")

Assistance: project grants; guaranteed loans and direct loans (project grants, 25 percent; loans, 50 percent).

Purposes: pursuant to the FSRIA, for farmers, ranchers, and small rural businesses to purchase renewable energy systems or energy efficiency improvements. Projects combining grant and loan funds may not receive more than 50 percent federal funding.

Eligible applicants/beneficiaries: agricultural producers and small rural businesses that are U.S. citizens or legally admitted permanent residents.

Range: $2,500 to $500,000. **Average:** $125,000.

Activity: FY 05, 156 projects.

HQ: RBCS-USDA, 1400 Independence Ave. SW, Washington, DC 20013. Phone: (202) 720-1400.

Internet: www.rurdev.usda.gov/rbs.

10.778 RESEARCH ON THE ECONOMIC IMPACT OF COOPERATIVES ("REIC")

Assistance: direct payments/specified use (100 percent/to 2 years).

Purposes: for research on the national economic impact or value of all types of cooperatives in the U.S.

Eligible applicants/beneficiaries: IHEs including consortia of academic institutions, IHE research foundations and IHE private nonprofit organizations.

Range: single award, $495,000.

Activity: new program in 2006 (CFDA on-line); single award anticipated.

HQ: Cooperative Programs, RBCS-USDA, 1400 Independence Ave. SW, Washington, DC 20250-3252. Phone: (202) 690-0368; FAX (202) 690-2723.

Internet: www.rurdev.usda.gov/rbs/coops/reic.htm; e-mail, cpgrants@wdc.usda.gov. (Note: no field offices for this program.)

10.850 RURAL ELECTRIFICATION LOANS AND LOAN GUARANTEES ("RUS")

Assistance: direct loans. (70-90 percent/to 35 years).

Purposes: pursuant to the Rural Electrification Act of 1936 (REA) as amended, to supply or improve central station electric services in rural areas—i.e., any farm or nonfarm area not within the boundaries of an urban area. RUS also guarantees loans used primarily for generation and transmission projects.

Eligible applicants/beneficiaries: rural electric cooperatives, public utility districts, power companies, municipalities, and other qualified power suppliers, including in territories.

Range: direct loans, $772,000 to $1,000,000,000; FFB guarantees, $334,600 to $82,448,000. **Average:** direct, $23,664,000; FFB, $12,924,000.

Activity: FY 04, 173 direct, 48 guaranteed loans.

HQ: Administrator, RUS-USDA, Washington, DC 20250-1500. Phone: (202) 720-9540.

Internet: www.rurdev.usda.gov (Note: no field offices for this program.)

10.851 RURAL TELEPHONE LOANS AND LOAN GUARANTEES

Assistance: direct loans; guaranteed/insured loans.

Purposes: pursuant to REA as amended, to improve, expand, construct, acquire, and operate telecommunications systems in rural areas—i.e., any area of the U.S. not within the boundaries of a city, village, or borough with over 5,000 population. Average loan term, 18 years.

Eligible applicants/beneficiaries: telephone companies or cooperatives; nonprofit, limited dividend, or mutual associations; public bodies—including in territories.

Range: direct loans, $56,000 to $65,377,000; guaranteed, $149,000 to $35,535,750. **Average:** direct, $7,705,882; guaranteed, $7,352,941.

Activity: FY 04, 65 loans.

HQ: Assistant Administrator, Telecommunications Program, RUS-USDA, 1400 Independence Ave, SW-Room 5151, Washington, DC 20250-1590. Phone: (202) 720-9554, FAX (202) 720-0810.

Internet: www.usda.gov/rus (Note: no field offices for this program.)

10.854 RURAL ECONOMIC DEVELOPMENT LOANS AND GRANTS

Assistance: direct loans; project grants. (loans, 80 percent; grants, 80 percent/loans, no interest/10 years).

Purposes: pursuant to REA as amended, for rural economic and job development projects, including the costs of feasibility studies, project start-up, and other reasonable expenses. Project examples: business incubators; establishment or expansion of factories or businesses; revolving loan funds.

Eligible applicants: electric and telephone utilities with current RUS loans.

Eligible beneficiaries: rural/general public.

Range: loans, $450,000 to $740,000; grants, $120,000 to $300,000. **Average:** loans, $467,353; grants, $261,935.

Activity: FY 05, 83 projects funded.

HQ: Specialty Lenders Division, RBCS-USDA, 1400 Independence Ave. SW, Washington, DC 20250. Phone: (202) 720-1400.

Internet: www.rurdev.usda.gov.

10.855 DISTANCE LEARNING AND TELEMEDICINE LOANS AND GRANTS

Assistance: project grants; direct loans. (grants, 85 percent; loans, 100 percent/grants and loans, 3 years).

Purposes: pursuant to FAIRA, for telecommunications, computer networks, and related technologies in rural areas, providing educational and/or medical benefits to students, teachers, medical professionals, and rural residents—through distance learning and telemedicine projects.

Eligible applicants/beneficiaries: legally organized corporations, partnerships; tribes and tribal organizations; state and local governments; schools, libraries, hospitals, medical centers, and similar organizations.

Range: from $50,000.

Activity:FY 06, 103 grants to 38 states.

HQ: Assistant Administrator, Telecommunications Program, RUS-USDA, 1400 Independence Ave, SW-Room 5151, Washington, DC 20250-1590. Phone: (202) 720-9554, FAX (202) 720-0810.

Internet: www.usda.gov/rus/telecom/dit/dlt.htm. (Note: no field offices for this program.)

10.856 1890 LAND GRANT INSTITUTIONS RURAL ENTREPRENEURIAL OUTREACH PROGRAM ("1890 REOD Initiative")

Assistance: direct payments/specified use (75 percent).

Purposes: pursuant to the Rural Development Act of 1972 as amended by FAIRA, to promote rural development programs; to provide outreach and technical assistance, advisory services, training, counseling, and disseminate technical information; to develop programs to develop future entrepreneurs and businesses in rural America—in communities with the greatest economic need. Project activities may include assistance in: business start-up; best practices in community economic development; computer technology outreach and network systems.

Eligible applicants: 1890 land grant institutions, Tuskegee University.

Eligible beneficiaries: rural residents in areas with economic need and in Empowerment Zones, Enterprise Communities, Champion Communities; tribal groups.

Range: $75,000 to $150,000. **Average:** $136,000.

Activity: new program listing in 2004. FY 03, 15 cooperative agreements awarded.

HQ: RBS Land Grant Outreach Manager, Cooperative Services, RBCS-USDA, 1400 Independence Ave. SW, Washington, DC 20250-3252. Phone: (202) 690-3407.

Internet: www.rurdev.usda.gov/rbs/oa/1890.htm.

10.857 STATE BULK FUEL REVOLVING FUND GRANTS ("RUS")

Assistance: project grants. (100 percent/3 years).

Purposes: pursuant to REA as amended, for states to establish revolving funds to enable cost-effective fuel purchases for communities where fuel cannot be shipped by surface transportation.

Eligible applicants/beneficiaries: state entities in existence as of 9 November 2000, including in territories and possessions.

Average: FY 01, $5,000,000; FY 05, $350,000 (two single competitive grants).

Activity: 2 grants.

HQ: Assistant Administrator, Electric Program, RUS-USDA, Washington, DC 20250-1560. Phone: (202) 720-9540.

Internet: www.usda.gov/rus/electric/hecgp/index.htm. (Note: no field offices for this program.)

10.858 DENALI COMMMISSION GRANTS AND LOANS

Assistance: project grants; direct loans (project grants, from 3 years).

Purposes: pursuant to REA as amended, for the Denali Commission to finance facilities serving several rural communities in Alaska where average residential energy expenditures are at least 275 percent of the national average—in coordination with state rural development initiatives. Project examples: improvements in bulk fuel storage and handling facilities; electric distribution system improvements.

Eligible applicants: Denali Commission only.

Eligible beneficiaries: Alaska rural residents.

Range: $10,000,000 to $18,500,000 (single grant). **Average:** $10,000,000 to $18,500,000.

Activity: more than 100 Alaskan communities have benefited from RUS grants.

HQ: Administrator, RUS-USDA, Washington, DC 20250-1500. Phone: (202) 720-9540.

Internet: www.rurdev.usda.gov (Note: no field offices for this program.)

10.859 ASSISTANCE TO HIGH ENERGY COST—RURAL COMMUNITIES ("RUS High Energy Cost Grants")

Assistance: project grants; direct loans.

Purposes: pursuant to REA as amended, for projects in rural communities with high energy costs to acquire, construct, extend, upgrade, and improve energy generation, transmission, or distribution facilities—where the average residential home energy expenditure is at least 275 percent of the national average.

Eligible applicants/beneficiaries: states, state political subdivisions, and state entities including profit and nonprofit businesses, partnerships, associations, cooperatives, public bodies, tribal entities, and individuals—including in territories and possessions.

Range: $75,000 to $5,000,000. **Average:** N.A.

Activity: FY 05 estimate, 60 applications submitted; 12 to 15 projects funded.

HQ: Assistant Administrator, Electric Program, RUS-USDA, Washington, DC 20250-1560. Phone: (202) 720-9545.

Internet: www.usda,gov/rus/electric/hecgp/index.htm (Note: no field offices for this program.)

10.860 RURAL BUSINESS INVESTMENT PROGRAM ("RBIP")

Assistance: guaranteed/insured loans; project grants (loans, to 10 years; grants, 5 years).

Purposes: pursuant to CFRDA as amended, to promote economic development and create wealth and job opportunities in rural areas. USDA licenses newly formed Rural Business Investment Companies (RBICs), and guarantees their debentures to fund their investments in rural areas; in turn, RBICs use the proceeds to make equity capital investments in mostly smaller enterprises. The program also provides operational assistance grants to RBICs, enabling them to provide operational and technical assistance to the enterprises in which they invest.

Eligible applicants: RBICs—newly formed, for-profit entities or their subsidiaries with appropriate community development or venture capital financing expertise, and with at least $10,000,000 in private equity capital.

Eligible beneficiaries: rural individual businesses, enterprises, or tribal groups that are public, private, or cooperative profit or nonprofit organizations; other persons or entities.

Average: debentures, $20,000,000; grants, $1,000,000.

Activity: new program listing in 2005 (CFDA on-line version).

HQ: Administrator, RBCS-USDA, Washington, DC, 20250-3201. Phone: (202) 690-4730.

Internet: www.sba.gov/INV/RBIP.

10.861 PUBLIC TELEVISION STATION DIGITAL TRANSITION GRANT PROGRAM

Assistance: project grants. (100 percent/3-4 years).

Purposes: to convert rural analog public television broadcasting to digital signals, pursuant to FCC regulations. Project funds may be used to cover such costs as digital transmitters and translators, transmitting antennas, towers and tower improvement, and some production and management equipment.

Eligible applicants/beneficiaries: public television stations serving rural areas, or consortia, eligible to be licensed as noncommercial educational broadcast stations owned and operated by public agencies or nonprofit private foundations, corporations, associations, or municipalities.

Range: individual stations, to $2,000,000; consortia, to $2,000,000 for the first station and $1,000,000 for each additional station to a maximum of $5,000,000. **Average:** $851,000.

Activity: new program listing in 2005. FY 04, 34 grants awarded.

HQ: Assistant Administrator, Telecommunications Program, RUS- USDA, 1400 Independence Ave. SW-Room 5151, Washington, DC 20250-1590. Phone: (202) 720-9554, FAX (202) 720-0810.

Internet: www.usda.gov/rus/telecom/index.htm. (Note: no field offices for this program.)

10.862 HOUSEHOLD WATER WELL SYSTEM GRANT PROGRAM ("HWWS Program")

Assistance: project grants.

Purposes: pursuant to CFRDA as amended, to establish and maintain revolving loan funds to make loans, in turn, to eligible rural homeowners to construct, refurbish, and service individually owned household water well systems.

Eligible applicants: experienced private nonprofit corporations.

Eligible beneficiaries: households with a combined income not exceeding 100 percent of the nonmetropolitan median for the area.

Average: $500,000.

Activity: new program listing in 2005 (CFDA on-line version); FY 04 estimate, 2 grants.

HQ: Assistant Administrator, Water and Environmental Programs, RUS-USDA, Washington, DC 20250-3200. Phone: (202) 690-2670.

Internet: www.rurdev.usda.gov.

10.863 COMMUNITY CONNECT GRANT PROGRAM

Assistance: project grants. (to 85 percent/3 years).

Purposes: to deploy broadband transmission services to critical rural community facilities such as schools, education centers, libraries, hospitals, health care providers, law enforcement agencies, public safety organizations, fire and rescue services, and residents and businesses that will operate a community center providing free and open access to area residents. Funds may cover costs of construction, acquisition, expansion, and operation of centers for at least 2 years.

Eligible applicants/beneficiaries: incorporated profit or nonprofit organizations; tribes and tribal organizations, state or local governments.

Range: from $50,000.

Activity: new program listing in 2004; FY 05, 35 grants approved.

HQ: Assistant Administrator, Telecommunications Program, RUS- USDA, 1400 Independence Ave. SW-Room 5151, Washington, DC 20250-1590. Phone: (202) 720-9554, FAX (202) 720-0810.

Internet: www.usda.gov/rus/telecom/commconnect.htm. (Note: no field offices for this program.)

10.864 GRANT PROGRAM TO ESTABLISH A FUND FOR FINANCING WATER AND WASTEWATER PROJECTS

Assistance: project grants (80 percent).

Purposes: pursuant to CFRDA as amended, to establish and maintain a revolving loan fund to finance small and short-term predevelopment costs of proposed or existing water and wastewater projects or systems, including costs of replacement equipment and small-scale extension of services—in rural communities with populations not higher 10,000.

Eligible applicants: private nonprofit organization.

Eligible beneficiaries: municipalities, counties, other state political subdivisions including districts and authorities; associations, cooperatives, nonprofit corporations; tribes.

Average: $497,000 (single grant).

Activity: new program listing in 2005. Single grant.

HQ: Assistant Administrator, Water and Environmental Programs, RUS-USDA, Washington, DC 20250. Phone: (202) 690-2670.

Internet: None given.

10.886 RURAL BROADBAND ACCESS LOANS AND LOAN GUARANTEES

Assistance: direct loans; guaranteed/insured loans. (direct loans, 4 percent/guaranteed/insured loans, 5 years).

Purposes: pursuant to REA as amended, for rural communities to finance the construction, improvement, and acquisition of telecommunications facilities and equipment to provide broadband service comparable in reliability and quality to the rest of the nation.

Eligible applicants/beneficiaries: cooperative, nonprofit, limited dividend, or mutual associations; limited liability companies; commercial organizations; tribes and tribal organizations; state and local governments; territories and possessions—serving communities with population not exceeding more than 20,000.

Range: $100,000 to $168,406,000. **Average:** $18,271,000.

Activity: new program listing in 2005; FY 04, 34 loans approved.

HQ: Assistant Administrator, Telecommunications Program, RUS- USDA, 1400 Independence Ave. SW-Room 5151, Washington, DC 20250-1590. Phone: (202) 720-9554, FAX (202) 720-0810.

Internet: www.usda.gov/rus/telecom/broadband.htm. (Note: no field offices for this program.)

10.901 RESOURCE CONSERVATION AND DEVELOPMENT ("RC&D")

Assistance: advisory services/counseling.

Purposes: to encourage and improve capabilities to plan, develop, and execute programs for resource conservation and development, in approved RC&D areas. Assistance is available for approved measures for land conservation, water management, community development, and environmental enhancement. Project examples include: promotion of economic development, cluster zoning, land conservation easements, historic preservation; formation of water quality associations; use of low-grade timber for housing development; fertilizer development from composting.

Eligible applicants/beneficiaries: state and local governments and nonprofit organizations in multi-jurisdictional areas. Available also in PR, VI, Guam, Northern Marianas.

Range/Average: N.A.

Activity: 52,241 completed projects as of FY 02 (latest data reported).

HQ: Deputy Chief/Programs, Resource Conservation and Community Development Division, Natural Resources Conservation Service (NRCS)-USDA, P.O. Box 2890, Washington, DC 20013. Phone: (202) 720-2847.

Internet: www.nrcs.usda.gov.

10.902 SOIL AND WATER CONSERVATION

Assistance: advisory services/counseling.

Purposes: pursuant to the Soil Conservation and Domestic Allotment Act of 1936 as amended, to assist in planning and applying soil and water conservation practices, systems, and treatment; to provide technical natural resource conservation information.

Eligible applicants/beneficiaries: land users and owners, community organizations, state and local governments. Available also in PR, VI, and Western Pacific Trust Territories.

Range/Average: N.A.

Activity: FY 00, 34,000,000 acres covered by NRCS services to landowners and users (latest data reported).

HQ: Deputy Chief/Programs, Resource Conservation and Community Development Division, Natural Resources Conservation Service (NRCS)-USDA, P.O. Box 2890, Washington, DC 20013. Phone: (202) 720-4527.

Internet: www.nrcs.usda.gov.

10.903 SOIL SURVEY

Assistance: technical information.

Purposes: to produce and maintain current published soil surveys and related data bases of counties and areas of comparable size for use by environmentalists, engineers, planners, zoning and tax commissions, homeowners, farmers, ranchers, land developers, and others—in selecting and implementing appropriate use and treatment of the soils surveyed.

Eligible applicants/beneficiaries: anyone needing soil surveys.

Range/Average: N.A.

Activity: FY 03-04 estimate, 22,000,000 acres surveyed.

HQ: Deputy Chief/Soil Survey and Resource Assessment, Natural Resources Conservation Service (NRCS)-USDA, P.O. Box 2890, Washington, DC 20013. Phone: (202) 690-4616.

Internet: www.nrcs.usda.gov.

10.904 WATERSHED PROTECTION AND FLOOD PREVENTION ("Small Watershed Program - PL-566 Operations Phase")

Assistance: project grants; advisory services/counseling (project grants, 50-100 percent).

Purposes: pursuant to the Watershed Protection and Flood Prevention Act as amended and other acts, to plan and execute projects to protect, develop, and utilize land and water resources in small watersheds (250,000 acres or less). Funds may support watershed protection measures, flood prevention, irrigation, drainage, agricultural water management, sedimentation control, and public water-based fish, wildlife, and recreation resources; also, to extend long-term credit to help local interests with their share of costs. Single structure capacity is limited to 25,000 acre-feet of total capacity and 12,500 acre-feet of flood-water detention capacity.

Eligible applicants/beneficiaries: any authorized state agency, county or groups of counties, municipality, town or township, soil and water conservation district, flood prevention or flood control district, tribe or tribal organization, or nonprofit agency. Available also in territories.

Range: to $2,164,000. **Average:** $650,000.

Activity: FY 02 estimate, 8 projects approved for operations; 512 projects under construction; 931 projects completed.

HQ: Watersheds and Wetlands Division, Natural Resources Conservation Service (NRCS)-USDA, P.O. Box 2890, Washington, DC 20013. Phone: (202) 720-3534.

Internet: www.nrcs.usda.gov.

10.905 PLANT MATERIALS FOR CONSERVATION

Assistance: specialized services.

Purposes: pursuant to the Soil Conservation and Domestic Allotment Act of 1936 as amended, to assemble, evaluate, select, release, and introduce into commerce the use of new and improved plant materials such as grasses, legumes, forbs, shrubs, and trees for soil, water, and related resource conservation and environmental improvement programs—including erosion control, roadside and stream bank protection, surface-mined land reclamation, and wildlife food and cover. Plant materials are produced only for field testing and to provide commercial producers with breeder and foundation quality seed or propagules. Free plants or seed are not provided to the general public under this program.

Eligible applicants/beneficiaries: cooperating state and federal agencies and cooperators of conservation districts; commercial seed growers and nurseries interested in the production of selected plant materials, including in PR and VI.

Range/Average: N.A.

Activity: to date, over 450 releases for commercial increase.

HQ: Deputy Chief/Science and Technology, Natural Resources Conservation Service (NRCS)-USDA, P.O. Box 2890, Washington, DC 20013. Phone: (202) 720-4630.

Internet: www.nrcs.usda.gov.

10.906 WATERSHED SURVEYS AND PLANNING ("Small Watershed Program - PL-566")

Assistance: specialized services; advisory services/counseling.

Purposes: pursuant to the Watershed Protection and Flood Prevention Act as amended and other acts, to assist in the planning and development of coordinated water and related land resource programs in watersheds and river basins to help solve such problems as those involving upstream rural community flooding, agricultural nonpoint source pollution, wetlands preservation, and drought management—through such disciplines as engineering, economics, social sciences, landscape architecture, agronomy, range management, forestry, biology, waste management, hydrology, archaeology. The program emphasizes assisting communities wishing to adopt floodplain management regulations meeting National Flood Insurance Program requirements, and to assist states in developing a strategic water resource plan.

Eligible applicants/beneficiaries: any local or state water resource agency or federal agency concerned with water and related land resource development. Available also in territories.

Range/Average: N.A.

Activity: since 1954 program inception, 1,660 watershed plans, 550 flood insurance studies, 602 flood plain management studies, 461 river basin studies, 171 resource plans completed.

HQ: Watersheds and Wetlands Division, Natural Resources Conservation Service (NRCS)-USDA, P.O. Box 2890, Washington, DC 20013. Phone: (202) 720-3534.

Internet: www.nrcs.usda.gov.

10.907 SNOW SURVEY AND WATER SUPPLY FORECASTING ("Snow Surveys")

Assistance: technical information.

Purposes: pursuant to the Soil Conservation and Domestic Allotment Act of 1936 as amended, to provide information on forthcoming seasonal water supplies from streams that derive most of their runoff from snowmelt in the mountain states and the far west—assisting farm operators, rural communities, municipalities, and others in planning for and managing water resources. Data are used in the regulation of small and large reservoirs for irrigation, flood control, power generation, recreation, industry, and municipal supplies.

Eligible applicants/beneficiaries: general public, including in the territories.

Range/Average: N.A.

Activity: daily snow and precipitation data gathered from 670 automated snow telemetry sites and 1,100 manual snow courses in the U.S. and Alaska; 11,000 forecasts of seasonal volume streamflows at 575 stream gaging points provided to water users.

HQ: Deputy Chief/Science and Technology, Natural Resources Conservation Service (NRCS)-USDA, P.O. Box 2890, Washington, DC 20013. Phone: (202) 720-4630.

Internet: www.nrcs.usda.gov.

10.910 RURAL ABANDONED MINE PROGRAM ("RAMP")

Assistance: direct payments/specified use. (25-100 percent/5-10 years).

Purposes: pursuant to the Surface Mining Control and Reclamation Act of 1977, Abandoned Mine Reclamation Act of 1990, and Energy Policy Act of 1992, for conservation practices needed for the reclamation, conservation, and development of abandoned rural coal mine land or lands and waters affected by coal mining activities. Up to 320 acres per owner may be assisted.

Eligible applicants/beneficiaries: individuals, groups, or units of government that own or control the surface or water rights of abandoned coal land or lands and water affected by coal mining practices before August 3, 1977. (These areas are ineligible if: (1) reclamation responsibility on the part of the mine operator or the state is continuing; (2) the lands are in federal ownership; and (3) surface rights are under easement or lease to be remined.)

Range/Average: N.A.

Activity: as of FY 01, 20 active projects.

HQ: Deputy Chief/Programs, Resource Conservation and Community Development Division, Natural Resources Conservation Service (NRCS)-USDA, P.O. Box 2890, Washington, DC 20013. Phone: (202) 720-1873.

Internet: www.nrcs.usda.gov.

10.912 ENVIRONMENTAL QUALITY INCENTIVES PROGRAM ("EQIP")

Assistance: direct payments/specified use. (to 75 percent/5-10 years).

Purposes: pursuant to FSRIA, FAIRA, and Food Security Act of 1985, to assist farmers and ranchers in complying with environmental laws and to encourage environmental enhancement by providing technical, educational, and financial assistance to implement structural, vegetative, and land management practices that address soil, water, and related natural resource concerns. Program is funded through the CCC. Fifty percent of available funding must be targeted at practices relating to livestock production.

Eligible applicants/beneficiaries: agricultural producers including owners, landlords, operators, or tenants of eligible lands—with special encouragement to apply to limited resource producers, small-scale producers, and minority groups, tribal governments, Alaskan natives and Pacific Islanders.

Range: to $10,000 per person per year; to $50,000 for life of contract. **Average:** $15,000.

Activity: since FY 98 program inception, 655 priority areas approved, 20,000 long-term contracts.

HQ: Deputy Chief/Programs, Natural Resources Conservation Service (NRCS)-USDA, P.O. Box 2890, Washington, DC 20013. Phone: (202) 720-1845, FAX (202) 720-4265.

Internet: www.nrcs.usda.gov.

10.913 FARM AND RANCH LANDS PROTECTION PROGRAM

Assistance: direct payments/specified use (50 percent).

Purposes: pursuant to Food Security Act of 1985, to purchase conservation easements or other interests in lands to limit nonagricultural uses of farm land with prime, unique, or other productive soils—with a minimum 30-year duration.

Eligible applicants/beneficiaries: local or state agencies, counties, municipalities, towns, local government units, tribes, soil and water conservation districts—with a farmland protection program. Available also in territories.

Range: $2,700 to $1,000,000 per landowner. **Average:** $97,000.

Activity: FY 02, 89 cooperative agreements to protect over 71,000 acres.

HQ: Farmland Protection and Community Planning Staff, NRCS-USDA, P.O. Box 2890, Washington, DC 20013. Phone: (202) 720-9476, FAX (202) 720-0745.

Internet: www.nrcs.usda.gov.

10.914 WILDLIFE HABITAT INCENTIVE PROGRAM ("WHIP")

Assistance: direct payments/specified use. (to 75 percent/ 5-10 years minimum).

Purposes: pursuant to FAIRA, to develop habitats for upland and wetland wildlife, threatened and endangered species, and fish. Technical assistance is provided to prepare a Wildlife Habitat Development Plan.

Eligible applicants/beneficiaries: owners, landlords, operators, tenants of eligible lands. Limited resource producers, small- scale producers, and minority groups, tribal governments, Alaska natives, and Pacific Islanders are encouraged to apply.

Average: $4,500.

Activity: since FY 98, 1,400,000 acres enrolled, with average agreement covering 165 acres.

HQ: Director, Watersheds and Wetlands Division, NRCS-USDA, P.O. Box 2890, Washington, DC 20013. Phone: (202) 720-3534, (202) 720- 7157, FAX (202) 720-2143.

Internet: www.nrcs.usda.gov.

10.916 WATERSHED REHABILITATION PROGRAM ("PL-566 Watershed Program")

Assistance: project grants; advisory services/counseling (grants, 65-100 percent).

Purposes: pursuant to the Watershed Protection and Flood Prevention Act and other acts, to plan, design, and implement watershed rehabilitation and improvement projects involving dams originally constructed with USDA assistance. Projects may include reconstruction or decommissioning of dams and relocation or flood proofing of downstream property.

Eligible applicants/beneficiaries: state agencies, counties or groups of counties, towns or townships, soil and water conservation districts, flood prevention or flood control districts, tribes or tribal organizations, other state-authorized nonprofit organizations.

Range: to $6,451,000 per state. **Average:** $770,000.

Activity: new program listing in 2003; FY 03, 3 projects completed, 6 under construction, 14 in design.

HQ: Watersheds and Wetlands Division, NRCS-USDA, P.O. Box 2890, Washington, DC 20013. Phone: (202) 720-3534.

Internet: www.nrcs.usda.gov.

10.917 AGRICULTURAL MANAGEMENT ASSISTANCE

Assistance: direct payments/specified use. (75 percent/3-10 years).

Purposes: pursuant to the Agricultural Risk Protection Act of 2000, for producers on private lands to: construct or improve water management or irrigation structures; plant trees for windbreaks or to improve water quality; mitigate financial risk through production or marketing diversification or resource conservation practices including soil erosion control, integrated pest management, or transition to organic farming.

Eligible applicants/beneficiaries: applicants with control of the land during the contract period—i.e., 3-10 years—only in Connecticut, Delaware, Maine, Maryland, Massachusetts, Nevada, New Hampshire, New Jersey, New York, Pennsylvania, Rhode Island, Utah, Vermont, West Virginia, and Wyoming.

Range: to $50,000 per year; to $150,000 per contract period.

Activity: new program listing in 2004; as of FY 03, 1,176 active contracts covering 287,000 acres in all 15 states.

HQ: Conservation Operations Division, NRCS-USDA, P.O. Box 2890, Washington, DC 20013. Phone: (202) 720-1873, FAX (202) 720-4265.

Internet: www.nrcs.usda.gov.

10.918 GROUND AND SURFACE WATER CONSERVATION—ENVIRONMENTAL QUALITY INCENTIVES PROGRAM ("EQIP-G&SW")

Assistance: direct payments/specified use. (75-90 percent/to 10 years).

Purposes: pursuant to the Food Security Act of 1985, FAIRA, and FSRIA, to help farmers and ranchers achieve net savings of water usage on their agricultural lands in an environmentally beneficial and cost-effective manner, through: technical assistance in conservation planning; incentive payments to install structural and land management practices that comply with federal, state, and tribal environmental laws. Limited-resource producers and beginning farmers may receive up to 90 percent of project costs. Funding is through the CCC.

Eligible applicants/beneficiaries: owners, landlords, operators, tenants of eligible lands. Limited resource producers, small- scale producers, and minority groups, tribal governments, Alaska natives, and Pacific Islanders are encouraged to apply. (Program may not be available in all states.)

Range: to $450,000 per entity for 10-year contract period.

Activity: FY 02, 20,000 applications funded (latest data reported).

HQ: Deputy Chief/Programs, Natural Resources Conservation Programs (NRCS)-USDA, P.O. Box 2890, Washington, DC 20013. Phone: (202) 720-1845, FAX (202) 720-4265.

Internet: www.nrcs.usda.gov.

10.919 KLAMATH BASIN—ENVIRONMENTAL QUALITY INCENTIVES PROGRAM ("EQIP-KB")

Assistance: direct payments/specified use. (75-90 percent/to 10 years).

Purposes: pursuant to the Food Security Act of 1985, FAIRA, and FSRIA, to help farmers and ranchers achieve net savings of water usage on their agricultural lands in an environmentally beneficial and cost-effective manner, through: technical assistance in conservation planning; incentive payments to install structural and land management practices that comply with federal, state, and tribal environmental laws. Limited-resource producers and beginning farmers may receive up to 90 percent of project costs. Funding is through the CCC.

Eligible applicants/beneficiaries: owners, landlords, operators, tenants of eligible lands. Limited resource producers, small- scale producers, and minority groups, tribal governments, Alaska natives, and Pacific Islanders are encouraged to apply. Program available only in the Klamath Basin area of California and Oregon.

Range: to $450,000 per entity for 10-year contract period.

Activity: new program listing in 2004. Activity included in report for **10.918**. FY 02, 20,000 applications funded.

HQ: Deputy Chief/Programs, Natural Resources Conservation Programs (NRCS)-USDA, P.O. Box 2890, Washington, DC 20013. Phone: (202) 720-1845, FAX (202) 720-4265.

Internet: www.nrcs.usda.gov.

10.920 GRASSLAND RESERVE PROGRAM ("GRP")

Assistance: project grants.

Purposes: to restore and protect eligible grasslands and certain other lands through rental agreements and easements that: permit controlled grazing; permit controlled haying, mowing, or harvesting for seed production; allow for fire rehabilitation and construction of firebreaks, fencing, water facilities; prohibit production of row crops, fruit trees, vineyards, and the like.

Eligible applicants/beneficiaries: easements—owners of eligible lands; rental agreements—entities with sufficient control of land.

Average: easements, $382 per acre; rental agreements, $134 per acre.

Activity: new program listing in 2004. FY 03, 240,000 acres enrolled.

HQ: Deputy Chief/Programs, Natural Resources Conservation Programs (NRCS)-USDA, P.O. Box 2890, Washington, DC 20013 Phone: (202) 720-4527; NRCS program manager, (202) 720-0242; FSA program manager, (202) 720- 9562.

Internet: www.nrcs.usda.gov.

10.921 CONSERVATION SECURITY PROGRAM ("CSP")

Assistance: direct payments/specified use (5-10 years).

Purposes: pursuant to the Food Security Act of 1985 and FSRIA, for the conservation and improvement through approved appropriate stewardship of soil, water, air, energy, and plant and animal life on tribal and working lands—including cropland, grassland, prairie land, improved pasture, and rangeland, as well as forested land incidental to an agricultural operation. Funding is provided through the CCC.

Eligible applicants/beneficiaries: individual producers, partnerships, associations, corporations, estates, trusts, and other business entities enrolling eligible lands.

Range/Average: N.A.

Activity: new program listing in 2004. FY 04 estimate, 3,000 to 5,000 contracts.

HQ: Financial Assistance Programs Division, NRCS-USDA, P.O. Box 2890, Washington, DC 20013. Phone: (202) 690-0848.

Internet: www.nrcs.usda.gov.

10.922 HEALTHY FORESTS RESERVE PROGRAM ("HFRP")

Assistance: direct payments/specified use; technical assistance (restoration, 10 years; easement, 30 or 99 years).

Purposes: pursuant to Title V of the Healthy Forest Restoration Act of 2003, to assist landowners in restoring and enhancing forest ecosystems in order to promote the recovery of threatened and endangered species, improve biodiversity, and enhance carbon sequestration. Restoration agreements and easements are designed for working agricultural lands and landowners, their heirs, successors and assigns shall enter into contract with the United States through the NRCS. Lump sum or annual easement payments made in no more than 10 annual payments of equal or unequal size to landowner in agreement with NRCS.

Eligible applicants/beneficiaries: landowners of eligible private land as determined by the NRCS.

Range: FY 06, $2.3 million for three states. **Average:** easement acquisition: $1,048 per acre, estimated.

Activity: FY 06, 496,000 acres enrolled in Arkansas, Maine, and Mississippi; FY07, 196,000 acres enrolled in the same states.

HQ: Deputy Chief for Programs, NRCS-USDA, 14th and Independence Ave, SW-Rm. 5109-S, Washington, DC 20250. Phone: (202) 720-4527; NRCS Director, Easements Program Division, (202) 720-1875; NCRS Program Manager, Healthy Forest Reserves, (202) 720-1836.

Internet: www.nrcs.usda.gov.

10.923 EMERGENCY WATERSHED PROTECTION PROGRAM ("EWP")

Assistance: project grants (75-90 percent/until all recovery measures installed).

Purposes: pursuant to FCA of 1950, FAIRA, and the Agricultural Credit Act of 1978, as amended, to assist in the implementation of emergency recovery measures to a watershed impaired as the result of a natural disaster. All work must reduce threats to life and property and be environmentally, economically, socially, and technically sound.

Eligible applicants/beneficiaries: public and private landowners represented by state, local, or tribal government or agency with a legal interest or responsibility for values threatened by a watershed emergency and capable of carrying out operation and maintenance responsibilities and furnishing local cost share. Work can be done through federal or local contracts and is authorized in all U.S. states and territories.

Range: FY06, $22,211 to $6,047,723. **Average:** $955,410.

Activity: N.A.

HQ: Conservation Planning and Technical Assistance Division, USDA, P.O. Box 2890, Washington, DC 20013. Phone: (202) 690-0793.

Internet: www.nrcs.usda.gov/programs/ewp.

10.950 AGRICULTURAL STATISTICS REPORTS ("Agricultural Estimates")

Assistance: technical information.

Purposes: to collect and publish statistics related to agriculture, resources, and rural communities. Reports cover crops, agricultural chemical usage, livestock and poultry estimates, prices received by farmers, prices for commodities and services, data on farm employment and wage rates.

Eligible applicants/beneficiaries: farmers and agricultural producers, marketing and processing groups, transportation and handler groups, consumers, state governments, educational institutions, and the general public, including in the territories.

Range/Average: N.A.

Activity: annually, estimates on some 120 crops and 45 livestock items, published in 400 reports.

HQ: Administrator, National Agricultural Statistics Service-USDA, Washington, DC 20250. Phone: (202) 720-2707.

Internet: www.usda.gov/nass. (Note: no field offices for this program.)

10.960 TECHNICAL AGRICULTURAL ASSISTANCE

Assistance: project grants (100 percent).

Purposes: pursuant to NARETPA and Food Security Act of 1985 as amended, for technical research and assistance projects dealing with international agricultural problems in developing countries. Program is conducted in cooperation with the State Department's Agency for International Development.

Eligible applicants/beneficiaries: U.S. IHEs, public and private nonprofit scientific research organizations—including in territories.

Range: $30,000 to $600,000. **Average:** $160,000.

Activity: not quantified specifically.

HQ: Development Resources Division, Office of International Cooperation and Development, FAS-USDA, Washington, DC 20250-1089. Phone: (202) 690-1924.

Internet: www.fas.usda.gov (Note: no field offices for this program.)

10.961 SCIENTIFIC COOPERATION AND RESEARCH ("International Collaborative Research and Scientific Exchanges" - "Scientific Cooperation Program")

Assistance: project grants (cost sharing); direct payments/specified use.

Purposes: pursuant to NARETPA and Food Security Act of 1985 as amended, for research on international agriculture and the environment in collaboration with foreign scientists—through short- (2-4 weeks) and long-term (1-3 years) exchanges.

Eligible applicants/beneficiaries: U.S. IHEs, public and private nonprofit scientific research organizations—including in territories—and federal or state agencies; designated international agricultural research centers.

Range: long-term, to $45,000. **Average:** $20,000.

Activity: 356 projects ongoing in 85 countries.

HQ: Director, Research and Scientific Exchanges Division, Office of International Cooperation and Development, FAS-USDA, Washington, DC 20250-1084. Phone: (202) 690-4872.

Internet: www.fas.usda.gov/icd/grants/scrp.htm. (Note: no field offices for this program.)

10.962 COCHRAN FELLOWSHIP PROGRAM—INTERNATIONAL TRAINING—FOREIGN PARTICIPANT

Assistance: project grants (100 percent).

Purposes: pursuant to NARETPA and Food Security Act of 1985 as amended, for international research training and extension in food, agricultural, and related subjects, including in the areas of course development and evaluation. Funding currently supports projects involving short-term agricultural and trade-related training and orientation for senior and mid-level officials, including marketing and production of forestry and wood products, soybean utilization, rice processing, food safety, and dairy production and livestock management.

Eligible applicants/beneficiaries: U.S. IHEs or nonprofit organizations.

Range: $10,000 to $40,000 Average. **Average:** $19,000.

Activity: not quantified specifically.

HQ: Food Industries Division, Office of International Cooperation and Development, FAS-USDA, Washington, DC 20250-1086. Phone: (202) 690-1339.

Internet: www.fas.usda.gov (Note: no field offices for this program.)

10.994 PEANUT QUOTA BUYOUT PROGRAM ("PQB")

Assistance: direct payment/unrestricted use (5 years).

Purposes: pursuant to FSRIA, to terminate the marketing quota program for peanuts and offer compensation to peanut quota holders for losses in quota asset value.

Eligible applicants/beneficiaries: peanut producers that owned a farm and were eligible for a permanent peanut quota for the 2002- 2006 crop years.

Average: $0.11 per pound or $220 per ton, based on producer's eligible quota.

Activity: new program listing in 2005.

HQ: Production Emergency and Compliance Division, FSA-USDA, 1400 Independence Ave. SW. Washington, DC 20250-0512. Phone: (no number provided).

Internet: www.fsa.usda.gov.

10.995 HARD WHITE WHEAT INCENTIVE PROGRAM ("HWW")

Assistance: direct payment/unrestricted use.

Purposes: pursuant to the Agricultural Assistance Act of 2002, to increase the production of both spring and winter varieties of hard white wheat during the 2003 through 2005 crop years.

Eligible applicants/beneficiaries: hard white wheat producers with an interested buyer that will use the wheat for all purposes except for feed.

Average: $0.20 per bushel; planting incentive, $2.00 per acre—within stipulated program maximum.

Activity: new program listing in 2005.

HQ: Production Emergency and Compliance Division, FSA-USDA, 1400 Independence Ave. SW. Washington, DC 20250-0512. Phone: (202) 720-7641.

Internet: www.fsa.usda.gov.

10.999 LONG TERM STANDING AGREEMENTS FOR STORAGE, TRANSPORTATION AND LEASE ("Farm Service Agency")

Assistance: direct payment/specified use.

Purposes: to provide payments for the storage, transportation, and leasing for wheat, grain and other commodities during the designated CCC price support period of activity. Payments may go to private entities in addition to State and local government's for STO/CTY lease agreements.

Eligible applicants: approved, certified crop storage facilities, transportation companies, state and local governments, and private entities that participate in STO/CTY lease agreements.

Eligible beneficiaries: farmers and producers whose crops meet CCC price support eligibility requirements. For storage and lease agreements: state, county and local governments.

Range/Average: N.A

Activity: N.A. New program in FY 08.

HQ: Farm Service Agency, USDA, 1400 Independence Ave. SW, Washington, DC 20250-0540.

Internet: www.fsa.usda.gov.

DEPARTMENT OF COMMERCE

BUREAU OF THE CENSUS

11.001 CENSUS BUREAU DATA PRODUCTS

Assistance: technical information.

Purposes: pursuant to the Act of August 31, 1954, to provide statistical results of censuses, surveys, and other programs. Data cover population, housing, American Community Survey, retail and wholesale trade, service and construction industries, transportation, communications, utilities, manufacturing, mineral industries, governments, foreign trade statistics, and financial, insurance, real estate industries. Certain estimates, projections, and boundary and code maps covering various types of geographic areas also are available. Reports include statistical compendia, directories, indexes, catalogues, and guides—distributed both in print form and on computer disks and tapes, CD-ROMs, DVDs, online, and other media.

Eligible applicants/beneficiaries: anyone may purchase Census products.

Range/Average: N.A.

Activity: not quantified specifically.

HQ: Customer Services Center, Marketing Services Office, Bureau of the Census-USDC, Washington, DC 20233. Phone: (301) 763-4636.

Internet: www.census.gov.

11.002 CENSUS CUSTOMER SERVICES

Assistance: advisory services/counseling; technical information; training.

Purposes: pursuant to the Act of August 31, 1954, to assist census data users in the access to and use of census data—through newsletters, on-line catalogues, conferences, training courses, and related activities including development of informational and data products to meet specific user needs. Staff are available to participate in conferences and workshops on the censuses and other Census Bureau programs.

Eligible applicants/beneficiaries: materials and consultation at the Census Bureau—anyone. User training—officials of federal, state, and local governments, universities, community organizations, the private sector; nominal fees may be charged.

Range/Average: N.A.

Activity: not quantified specifically.

HQ: Customer Services Center, Marketing Services Office, Bureau of the Census-USDC, Washington, DC 20233. Phone: (301) 763-4636. Phone: *training opportunities,* (301) 763-4094.

Internet: www.census.gov.

11.003 CENSUS GEOGRAPHY ("Census Mapping and Statistical Areas")

Assistance: specialized services; technical information.

Purposes: pursuant to the Act of August 31, 1954, to prepare computer-generated maps for use in conducting censuses and surveys, and to show their results geographically; to determine names and current boundaries of selected statistical areas; to develop geographic code systems; to provide maps and area reports for states and local areas throughout the U.S. including territories and possessions; to develop computer files of area measurements, geographic boundaries, and map features with address ranges. The "TIGER" (Topologically Integrated Geographic Encoding and Referencing) system, an automated cartographic data base developed in cooperation with the U.S. Geological Survey, covers the entire U.S. and its possessions; the system generates maps and other geographic products; geographic base files, called TIGER/Line files, are available on computer tape, CD-ROM, and online. Published maps are sold by GPO; unpublished maps are sold directly by the Census Bureau.

Eligible applicants/beneficiaries: anyone.

Range/Average: N.A.

Activity: publications.

HQ: Geography Division, Bureau of the Census-USDC, Washington, DC 20233-7400. Phone: (301) 457-1128. Customer Services, Phone: (301) 763-3646.

Internet: www.census.gov ; *and,* e-mail, geography@geo.census.gov.

11.004 CENSUS INTERGOVERNMENTAL SERVICES ("Intergovernmental Services Program")

Assistance: advisory services/counseling; technical information; training.

Purposes: pursuant to the Act of August 31, 1954, to provide technical assistance and information on methods of making population estimates and projections. Consultation services are available to local officials to plan and conduct special surveys. Special surveys are taken on a cost reimbursement basis. Assistance is provided to states in establishing and operating State Data Centers and Business and Industry Data Centers (BIDC).

Eligible applicants/beneficiaries: federal, state, local government officials; community organizations.

Range/Average: N.A.

Activity: currently, all states, DC, and PR participating in Federal-State Cooperative Program for the preparation of county population estimates; all states participating in the State Data Center Program, along with DC, Guam, Northern Marianas, PR, and VI; over 1,800 government agencies, universities and other organizations affiliated with programs.

HQ: Bureau of the Census-USDC, Washington, DC 20233. Phone: *special censuses*, Office of Special Censuses, (301) 457- 1429; *population estimates and projections*, Population Division, (301) 763-2422; *State*

Data Center and BIDC Programs, Customer Liaison Office Staff, (301) 763-1305.

Internet: www.census.gov.

11.005 CENSUS SPECIAL TABULATIONS AND SERVICES

Assistance: technical information; specialized services.

Purposes: pursuant to the Act of August 31, 1954, to provide customized census tabulations in a variety of output forms to meet user needs and to conduct statistical surveys, on a reimbursable basis.

Eligible applicants/beneficiaries: federal, state, local government officials; community and private organizations; individuals.

Range/Average: N.A.

Activity: not quantified specifically.

HQ: Director, Bureau of the Census-USDC, Washington, DC 20233. Phone: *demographic and household special surveys*, Chief, Demographic Surveys Division, (301) 763-3773; Office of Special Censuses, (301) 763-1429; *special economic surveys*, Chief, Economic Planning and Coordination Division, (301) 763-2558; *special tabulations-demographic*, Population Division, (301) 763-2429; *special tabulations-housing*, Chief, Survey Processing Branch, (310) 763-3204.

Internet: www.census.gov.

11.006 PERSONAL CENSUS SEARCH ("Age Search")

Assistance: specialized services.

Purposes: pursuant to the Act of August 31, 1954, to provide data for proof of age, family relationship, or citizenship, for such purposes as qualifying for: government program benefits (e.g., Medicare, Social Security, pensions); certain types of employment; inheritances, annuities, and other rights or benefits. A $65 fee is charged for searches, whether or not the applicant's record is found.

Eligible applicants/beneficiaries: personal information from census records is confidential and may be furnished only upon written request by the person to whom it relates, or, for a proper purpose, to a legal representative of an estate. Information regarding a child not of legal age may be obtained upon written request by either parent. For records of a deceased person, application must be signed by either: (1) a blood relative in the immediate family; (2) the surviving spouse; (3) a beneficiary; or, (4) the administrator or executor of the estate. Appropriate certifications are required.

Range/Average: N.A.

Activity: FY 05, 3,300 requests processed.

HQ: Chief, Survey Coding Section, Technical Services Supervisor, Personal Census Search Unit, Bureau of the Census-USDC, P.O. Box 1545, Jeffersonville, IN 47131 Phone (812) 218-3046.

Internet: www.census.gov/genealogy (Note: the field office serves as headquarters.)

ECONOMICS AND STATISTICS ADMINISTRATION

11.025 MEASURES AND ANALYSES OF THE U.S. ECONOMY

Assistance: technical information.

Purposes: to produce measures and analyses of national economic accounts statistics, as well as a series of related economic data analyses, used to formulate and execute fiscal, financial, international, and other policies. The principal analyses include: gross domestic product; corporate profits; personal income by state and region; U.S. balance of payments; international trade; gross domestic product by industry. Regular and special reports are produced, including the monthly "Survey of Current Business," available by subscription through GPO. On-line services and CD-ROMs are available.

Eligible applicants/beneficiaries: general public.

Range/Average: N.A.

Activity: publications.

HQ: Public Information Office, Bureau of Economic Analysis (BE- 53), Economics and Statistics Administration-USDC, 1441 L St. NW, Washington, DC 20230. Phone: (202) 606-9900; TDD (202) 606-5335; Order Desk, (800) 704-0415, (202) 606-9666.

Internet: www.bea.doc.gov; e-mail, webmaster@bea.gov. (Note: no field offices for this program.)

11.026 STAT-USA: KEY BUSINESS, ECONOMIC, AND INTERNATIONAL TRADE INFORMATION

Assistance: technical information.

Purposes: pursuant to the Omnibus Trade and Competitiveness Act of 1988, to provide the public with access to key business, economic, and international trade information in an easy to use "one-stop shop" format. STAT-USA/Internet offers a single point of access and consists of two main databases: 1) State of the Nation (SOTN), which tracks the direction of the U.S. economy and provides a repository for statistical releases of economic indicators from a number of federal agencies; and 2) Global Business Opportunities (GLOBUS) and the National Trade Data Bank (NTDB), offering daily trade leads, exchange rates, extensive market and country research, and contact databases. STAT-USA publishes over 100,000 documents, which are updated daily, weekly, monthly, quarterly, and annually. Funding for this program is derived from revolving fund proceeds from product sales.

Eligible applicants/beneficiaries: subscriptions available to the general public.

Range/Average: N.A.

Activity: currently, over 120 program titles including market research, country profiles, export and import statistics, and export "how-to" guides.

HQ: Director, STAT-USA, ESA-USDC, HCHB - Rm.4885, Washington, DC 20230 Phone: (202) 482-3429; *subscriptions,* (202) 482-1986,Toll Free (800) STAT-USA, FAX (202) 482-2164.

Internet: www.stat-usa.gov; e- mail (*subscriptions,*) statmail@esa.doc.gov (Note: no field offices for this program.)

INTERNATIONAL TRADE ADMINISTRATION

11.106 REMEDIES FOR UNFAIR FOREIGN TRADE PRACTICES—ANTIDUMPING AND COUNTERVAILING DUTY INVESTIGATIONS

Assistance: specialized services; investigation of complaints.

Purposes: pursuant to the Tariff Act of 1930 as amended, Trade Agreements Act of 1979, Trade and Tariff Act of 1984, and Uruguay Round Agreements Act, to protect U.S. industries against economic injury from the sale of foreign merchandise at less than fair value and by unfair subsidies provided by foreign governments. Import duties are assessed against such merchandise if "dumping" or countervailing subsidies are found to occur, which may be revoked five years after violations of the act have ceased.

Eligible applicants/beneficiaries: any interested party may file a complaint on behalf of an affected U.S. industry.

Range/Average: N.A.

Activity: not quantified specifically.

HQ: Office of Policy, Import Administration, ITA-USDC, 14th & Constitution Ave. NW, Washington, DC 20230. Phone: (202) 482-1255.

Internet: www.ia.ita.doc.gov. (Note: no field offices for this program.)

11.108 COMMERCIAL SERVICE

Assistance: advisory services/counseling.

Purposes: pursuant to the Omnibus Trade and Competitiveness Act of 1988, to expand export markets by providing information and guidance on overseas trade markets and opportunities to U.S. firms, through: nonfinancial assistance in export promotion with displays, trade and industrial exhibits, trade missions, catalog shows, and foreign buyer shows; information on trade statistics, foreign tariffs, customs regulations and procedures; overseas government-to-government advocacy and representation; assistance on sources of export finance available from the U.S. Export- Import Bank, SBA, and USAID—in U.S. Export Assistance Centers.

Eligible applicants/beneficiaries: any U.S. citizen, firm, organization or branch of government.

Range/Average: N.A.

Activity: not quantified specifically.

HQ: none; all contacts are with USDC Export Assistance Centers listed in Part IV.

Internet: www.ita.doc.gov.

11.110 MANUFACTURING AND SERVICES

Assistance: advisory services/counseling.

Purposes: to provide a central federal source of industry- specific expertise, negotiation and enforcement of bilateral and multilateral trade agreements, and industry and trade competitiveness analysis. Principal services include regular statistical reports, forecasts of industry/sector outputs and cost trends, information on technological developments, and other foreign market information.

Eligible applicants/beneficiaries: anyone.

Range/Average: N.A.

Activity: not quantified specifically.

HQ: ITA-USDC, 14th & Constitution Ave. NW, Washington, DC 20230. Phone: *manufacturing*, (202) 482-1872; *aerospace, automotive affairs,* (202) 482-0554; *energy, environment, materials*, (202) 482-5225; *health, consumer goods,* (202) 482.

Internet: www.export.gov.

11.111 FOREIGN-TRADE ZONES IN THE UNITED STATES

Assistance: specialized services.

Purposes: pursuant to the Foreign Trade Zones Act of 1934 as amended, to stimulate domestic production of export goods by encouraging domestic warehousing, manufacturing, and processing activity in foreign trade zones (FTZs). States and local communities establish FTZs that are operated by local public or quasi-public corporations. The FTZs function like public utilities, subject to U.S. Customs and other requirements, providing access to businesses and manufacturers.

Eligible applicants/beneficiaries: public and private corporations in states with enabling legislation.

Range/Average: N.A.

Activity: annually, 60-80 FTZ orders issued, covering zones, sub- zones, and expansions.

HQ: Executive Secretary, Foreign-Trade Zones Board, ITA-USDC, 1401 Constitution Ave. NW - Rm.FCB-4100W, Washington, DC 20230. Phone: (202) 482-2862.

Internet: www.trade.gov.

11.112 MARKET DEVELOPMENT COOPERATOR PROGRAM ("MDCP")

Assistance: project grants (33 percent/to 3 years).

Purposes: pursuant to the Omnibus Trade and Competitiveness Act of 1988, to develop, maintain, and expand foreign markets for nonagricultural goods and services produced in the U.S. "Cooperators" conduct activities abroad to promote certain industries, including outreach campaigns, conferences, consultative services, exhibitions, training, market research. Project funds support direct costs only.

Eligible applicants/beneficiaries: nonprofit industry organizations, trade associations, state departments of trade and their regional associations, and, if approved, private industry firms or groups of firms.

Range: $10,000 to $400,000. **Average:** $298,000.

Activity: not quantified specifically.

HQ: MDCP Manager, Trade Development, Management and Planning Division, Office of Planning, Coordination and Management, ITA- USDC, HCHB - Rm.3215, Washington, DC 20230. Phone: (202) 482-2969, FAX (202) 482-5828.

Internet: www.export.gov/mdcp. (Note: no field offices for this program.)

11.113 ITA SPECIAL PROJECTS

Assistance: project grants (100 percent).

Purposes: to assist organizations identified by Congress to provide information and conduct research and development activities assisting small- and medium-sized businesses in expanding exports.

Eligible applicants/beneficiaries: organizations or individuals specifically identified by Congress.

Range: $500,000 to $10,000,000.

Activity: not quantified specifically.

HQ: Trade Development, Management and Planning Division, Office of Planning, Coordination and Management, ITA- USDC, HCHB - Rm. 3215, Washington, DC 20230. Phone: (202) 482-3197, FAX (202) 482-4462.

Internet: (none). (Note: no field offices for this program.)

BUREAU OF EXPORT ADMINISTRATION

11.150 EXPORT LICENSING SERVICE AND INFORMATION ("Export Control - Exporter Assistance Program")

Assistance: advisory services/counseling.

Purposes: pursuant to the Export Administration Act of 1979 as amended and extended under the International Emergency Economic Powers Act, to provide information, training, seminars, and other assistance on export licensing requirements, regulations, and policies; to expedite export applications when priority action is warranted.

Eligible applicants/beneficiaries: anyone.

Range/Average: N.A.

Activity: FY 06 estimate, 3,200 exporters counseled; 45 export licensing seminars.

HQ: Outreach and Educational Services Division, Office of Exporter Services, Bureau of Industry and Security-USDC, Rm.1099, P.O. Box 273, Washington, DC 20044. Phone: (202) 482-4811.

Internet: www.bis.doc.gov.

ECONOMIC DEVELOPMENT ADMINISTRATION

11.300 INVESTMENTS FOR PUBLIC WORKS AND ECONOMIC DEVELOPMENT FACILITIES

Assistance: project grants (50-100 percent).

Purposes: pursuant to the Public Works and Economic Development Act of 1965 (PWEDA) as amended, to construct or improve public works and economic development facilities to create or retain permanent jobs in the private sector in areas experiencing substantial economic distress. Projects may involve water and sewer systems, railroad spurs, industrial parks, access roads, other business infrastructure, port facilities, tourism facilities, vocational schools, renovation and recycling of old industrial buildings, business incubator facilities, technology infrastructure, projects enabling telecommunications, redevelopment of brownfields. Projects must be consistent with approved Comprehensive Economic Development Strategies. Grants cover 50 percent of costs; severely depressed areas may receive 80 percent; designated tribes receive 100 percent; projects in redevelopment areas supporting Economic Development Districts may receive 80 percent and a 10 percent bonus for public works projects.

Eligible applicants/beneficiaries: states, cities, counties, other political subdivisions; IHEs; consortia; tribes; private or public nonprofit organizations or associations; territories and possessions.

Range: FY 05, public work investments: $69,000 to $4,046,270. **Average:** $1,265,590.

Activity: FY 05, 140 projects approved.

HQ: no address/phone provided; contact regional offices listed in Part IV.

Internet: www.eda.gov.

11.302 ECONOMIC DEVELOPMENT—SUPPORT FOR PLANNING ORGANIZATIONS ("Section 203 Grants for Planning and Administrative Expenses")

Assistance: project grants. (grants, from 50 percent; tribes, to 100 percent/to 3 years).

Purposes: pursuant to PWEDA as amended, for economic development planning and to formulate and establish comprehensive economic development, process, and strategies to reduce unemployment and increase incomes. Funds may be used to pay administrative expenses.

Eligible applicants/beneficiaries: economic development districts, tribes, states, cities, IHEs, public or private nonprofit organizations.

Range: $10,000 to $450,000. **Average:** $61,626; economic development districts, $58,691; Indian tribes, $48,826; states/others, $82,081.

Activity: FY 05, 417 grantees funded.

HQ: no address/phone provided; contact regional offices listed in Part IV.

Internet: www.eda.gov.

11.303 ECONOMIC DEVELOPMENT—TECHNICAL ASSISTANCE ("National, University Center and Local Technical Assistance")

Assistance: project grants (from 50 percent/to 3 years).

Purposes: pursuant to PWEDA as amended, to provide technical assistance in developing data and expertise in evaluating and planning specific economic development projects and programs in depressed areas. Technical assistance is provided through: university economic development centers; innovative projects; information dissemination and studies of issues of national significance; feasibility studies and other projects leading to local economic development.

Eligible applicants/beneficiaries: public or private nonprofit organizations, educational institutions; tribal, state, municipal, county, and territorial governments.

Range: $17,544 to $473,000. **Average:** university programs, $100,404; national technical assistance projects, $274,436; local projects, $33,883.

Activity: FY 05, 88 projects funded.

HQ: *university and local projects,* no address/phone provided; contact regional offices listed in Part IV. *National grants,* Office of External Affairs and Communication, EDA-USDC, HCHB - Rm.7816, 1401 Constitution Ave, NW, Washington, DC 20230. Phone: (202) 482-4208.

Internet: www.eda.gov.

11.307 ECONOMIC ADJUSTMENT ASSISTANCE

Assistance: project grants (50-100 percent).

Purposes: pursuant to PWEDA as amended, to design and implement strategies to address problems stemming from serious structural deterioration of local economies, such as result from corporate or industrial restructuring, new requirements in federal laws, reduction in defense expenditures, natural disasters, or depletion of natural resources. Strategy Investments may be used for plan development resulting in a Comprehensive Economic Development Strategy. Implementation Investments may be used for development of organizational capacity, business development and financing including through the capitalization of revolving loan funds, infrastructure improvement, and market or industry research and analysis.

Eligible applicants/beneficiaries: economic development districts, tribes, states, cities, IHEs, public or private nonprofit organizations.

Range: $20,000 to $4,000,000. **Average:** economic adjustment assistance, $609,305; disaster assistance, $829,705; regular assistance projects, $602,489.

Activity: FY 05, 100 projects funded.

HQ: no address/phone provided; contact regional offices listed in Part IV.

Internet: www.eda.gov.

11.312 RESEARCH AND EVALUATION PROGRAM

Assistance: project grants (50-100 percent).

Purposes: pursuant to PWEDA as amended, for research, evaluative and otherwise, and technical assistance programs to promote competitiveness and innovation in urban and rural regions throughout the U.S. and territories.

Eligible applicants/beneficiaries: economic development districts, tribes, states, cities, IHEs, public or private nonprofit organizations.

Average: $222,550.

Activity: FY 05, 2 projects funded.

HQ: Office of External Affairs and Communication, EDA-USDC, HCHB. - Rm.7816, Washington, DC 20230. Phone: (202) 482-4208.

Internet: www.eda.gov (Note: no field offices for this program.)

11.313 TRADE ADJUSTMENT ASSISTANCE FOR FIRMS ("TAA")

Assistance: project grants (50-100 percent).

Purposes: pursuant to the Trade Act of 1974 as amended, for trade adjustment assistance to firms and industries adversely affected by increased imports, in the form of technical assistance for which participants must share the expense. Assistance may consist of such detailed aid as industrial engineering, marketing studies, product diversification, and the like. To receive Trade Act certification, firms must demonstrate that increased imports of articles like or directly competitive with those that they produce contribute significantly to declines in sales or production, and to separation or threat of separation of their workers. Firms must submit an acceptable adjustment proposal to be eligible to apply. Industry associations or other organizations must submit evidence demonstrating import competition, and that the industry includes a substantial number of Trade Act-certified firms or workers.

Eligible applicants: intermediary organizations including Trade Adjustment Assistance Centers or industry groups that can demonstrate injury from imports.

Eligible beneficiaries: private firms with Trade Act certification.

Range: $951,173 to $1,428,834. **Average:** $1,091,455.

Activity: FY 05, 171 firms certified; 132 adjustment proposals accepted.

HQ: Office of Strategic Initiatives, EDA-USDC, HCHB Rm.7005, 1401 Constitution Ave. NW, Washington, DC 20230. Phone: (202) 482- 4687.

Internet: www.eda.gov ; *and,* www.taacenters.org.

NATIONAL OCEANIC AND ATMOSPHERIC ADMINISTRATION

11.400 GEODETIC SURVEYS AND SERVICES ("Geodesy and Applications of the National Geodetic Reference System")

Assistance: project grants. (cost sharing/1-5 years).

Purposes: pursuant to the Coast and Geodetic Survey Act, to assist in the development and implementation of Multipurpose Land Information Systems/Geographic Information Systems (MPLIS/GIS) into areas inadequately covered by the national networks. The networks consist of horizontal and vertical geodetic reference monuments at various specified intervals, providing scale, orientation, coordinated positions, and elevations of specific points—for use in surveying, boundary delineation and demarcation, mapping, planning, and development. The system provides the standards of reference which provide the basis for state plane coordinate systems, land and public utility records, and boundary delineations—and from which restricted coastal and other boundaries are marked. This program also provides funding to the University of New Hampshire for research and other programs at the Joint Hydrographic Center (JHC).

Eligible applicants/beneficiaries: state, local, municipal, or regional agencies and universities. JHC funding, University of New Hampshire only.

Range/Average: N.A.

Activity: estimated FY 06, 8 continuation, 1 new project.

HQ: Grant Program Office, Geodetic Service Division, National Ocean Service, NOAA-USDC, Silver Spring, MD 20910. Phone: (301) 713-3228.

Internet: www.ngs.noaa.gov; JHC, http://chartmaker.ncd.noaa.gov (Note: no field offices for this program.)

11.405 ANADROMOUS FISH CONSERVATION ACT PROGRAM

Assistance: project grants (50-90 percent).

Purposes: pursuant to the 1965 act as amended, for the conservation, development, and enhancement of anadromous fish stocks and fish in the Great Lakes and Lake Champlain that ascend streams to spawn; to control sea lamprey. Permissible uses of funds include: spawning area improvement; fishways installation; construction of fish protection devices and hatcheries; research to improve anadromous fish resources.

Eligible applicants/beneficiaries: interested persons or organizations, in coordination with state fishery agencies.

Range: $2,000 to $400,000. **Average:** $40,000.

Activity: not quantified specifically.

HQ: Director, Office of Sustainable Fisheries, NMFS-NOAA-USDC, 1315 East-West Hwy., Silver Spring, MD 20910. Phone: (301) 713- 2334, FAX (301) 713-0596.

Internet: www.nmfs.noaa.gov/sfa/state_federal/state_federal.htm.

11.407 INTERJURISDICTIONAL FISHERIES ACT OF 1986

Assistance: formula grants (75-90 percent).

Purposes: pursuant to the act of 1986 as amended, to manage interjurisdictional fisheries resources. Permissible uses of funds include research, management planning, enforcement, restoration of resources damaged by natural disasters.

Eligible applicants/beneficiaries: state agencies; the Pacific, Atlantic, and Gulf Interstate Marine Fisheries Commissions.

Range: $12,000 to $250,000. **Average:** $63,000.

Activity: not quantified specifically.

HQ: Director, Office of Sustainable Fisheries, NMFS-NOAA-USDC, 1315 East-West Hwy., Silver Spring, MD 20910. Phone: (301) 713- 2334, FAX (301) 713-0596.

Internet: www.nmfs.noaa.gov/sfa/state_federal/state_federal.htm.

11.408 FISHERMEN'S CONTINGENCY FUND ("Title IV")

Assistance: direct payments/unrestricted use.

Purposes: pursuant to the Outer Continental Shelf Lands Act Amendments of 1978, to compensate U.S. commercial fishermen for damage to or loss of fishing gear, and 50 percent of resulting financial loss caused by oil- and gas-related activities in Outer Continental Shelf areas.

Eligible applicants/beneficiaries: U.S. commercial fishermen.

Range: $500 to $54,000. **Average:** $6,000.

Activity: FY 05, 17 claims paid.

HQ: Chief, Financial Services Division, NMFS-NOAA-USDC, 1315 East-West Hwy., Silver Spring, MD 20910. Phone: (301) 713-2396, FAX (301) 713-1306.

Internet: www.nmfs.noaa.gov.

11.413 FISHERY PRODUCTS INSPECTION AND CERTIFICATION ("Inspection and Grading of Fishery Products")

Assistance: specialized services.

Purposes: pursuant to the Agricultural Marketing Act of 1946 and Fish and Wildlife Act of 1956 as amended, to provide voluntary inspection, grading, and certification of seafood harvesting and processing operations to ensure adherence to minimum public health requirements, as well as product identity, condition, quality, and quantity. Fees are charged for the service, in support of program costs.

Eligible applicants/beneficiaries: individuals; federal, state, county, or municipal agencies; carriers with a financial interest in the commodity.

Range/Average: N.A.

Activity: 2004, contract inspections at 325 plants, 175 establishments participating voluntarily.

HQ: Inspection Services Division, NMFS-NOAA-USDC, 1315 East-West Hwy., Silver Spring, MD 20910. Phone: (301) 713-2355, (800) 422- 2750.

Internet: www.seafood.nmfs.noaa.gov. (Note: no field offices for this program.)

11.415 FISHERIES FINANCE PROGRAM

Assistance: direct loans. (to 80 percent/to 25 years).

Purposes: for certain fisheries costs including: purchase or reconstruction of used vessels; refinancing of existing debt; financing or refinancing of shoreside fishery and aquaculture facilities; financing of Individual Fishing Quota (IFQ) for first-time purchasers and small vessel operators in the Halibut Sablefish industries and to Community Development Quota (CDQ) groups fisheries investments in the Bering Sea Aleutian Islands Pollock fishery; long-term fishery buyback financing to retire fishing permits or fishing vessels in overcapitalized fisheries. Funds may not be used for loans that add to fishing capacity or that over-capitalize the industry.

Eligible applicants/beneficiaries: commercial fishermen, fishery products processors or distributors.

Range: $10,000 to $100,000,000. **Average:** $1,000,000.

Activity: 31 direct, 27 quota share.

HQ: Chief, Financial Services Division, NMFS-NOAA-USDC, 1315 East-West Hwy., Silver Spring, MD 20910. Phone: (301) 713-2390. FAX: (301713-1306).

Internet: www.nmfs.noaa.gov.

11.417 SEA GRANT SUPPORT

Assistance: project grants (67-100 percent).

Purposes: pursuant to the Sea Grant College Program Improvement Act of 1976 as amended, for marine resources research, education, training, and advisory services. Some institutions may obtain coherent area, institutional, or Sea Grant College support. Project examples: cardiovascular, anti-cancer, and central nervous system drugs from marine organisms; marine fouling and corrosion in seawater; marine finfish and shellfish aquaculture; seafood quality and safety; coastal erosion. Funds may not be used to purchase or construct ships or facilities.

Eligible applicants/beneficiaries: IHEs, junior colleges, technical schools, institutes, laboratories; public or private corporations, partnerships, or other associations or entities; states or political subdivisions or agencies; individuals.

Range: $5,000 to $3,900,000.

Activity: FY 04, 800 projects funded.

HQ: Director, National Sea Grant College Program, NOAA-USDC, 1315 East-West Hwy., Silver Spring, MD 20910. Phone: (301) 713-2448.

Internet: www.noaa.gov (Note: no field offices for this program.)

11.419 COASTAL ZONE MANAGEMENT ADMINISTRATION AWARDS

Assistance: formula grants; project grants (cost sharing/18 months).

Purposes: pursuant to the Coastal Zone Management Act of 1972 and amendments, to administer various elements of approved Coastal Zone Management programs, including such activities as management and protection of coastal wetlands, natural hazards management, public access improvements, reduction of marine debris, ocean resource planning, siting of coastal energy facilities.

Eligible applicants/beneficiaries: coastal states including those bordering the Great Lakes; territories and possessions.

Range: $300,000 to $2,000,000. **Average:** Average: $1,300,000.

Activity: 34 coastal states and U.S. island territories participating.

HQ: Chief, Coastal Programs Division, Office of Ocean and Coastal Resource Management, NOS-NOAA-USDC, 1305 East-West Hwy.- 11th floor, Silver Spring, MD 20910. Phone: (301) 713-3155.

Internet: www.coastalmanagement.nos.noaa.gov/czm/. (Note: no field offices for this program.)

11.420 COASTAL ZONE MANAGEMENT ESTUARINE RESEARCH RESERVES

Assistance: project grants (to 50 percent/from 18 months).

Purposes: pursuant to the Coastal Zone Management Act of 1972 and amendments, to acquire, monitor, develop, and operate national estuarine research reserves; for data gathering, research, and educational purposes.

Eligible applicants/beneficiaries: acquisition, development, construction operating grants—coastal states including those bordering the Great Lakes; territories. Research or monitoring grants—qualified scientists, educators, students, and entities.

Range: $20,000 to $6,000,000. **Average:** $300,000.

Activity: FY 05, 26 designated reserves.

HQ: Chief, Estuarine Reserves Division, Office of Ocean and Coastal Resource Management, same address/phone as **11.419**. NOS-NOAA-USDC, 1305 East-West Hwy., N/ORM5- 10th floor, Silver Spring, MD 20910. Phone: (301) 713-3155.

Internet: www.nerrs.nos.noaa.gov/. (Note: no field offices for this program.)

11.426 FINANCIAL ASSISTANCE FOR NATIONAL CENTERS FOR COASTAL OCEAN SCIENCE

Assistance: project grants (100 percent/to 5 years).

Purposes: pursuant to the Marine Protection, Research, and Sanctuaries Act of 1972 and National Ocean Pollution Planning Act of 1978, for research to determine the long-term consequences of human activities affecting the coastal and marine environment; to assess the ecological, economic, and social impacts of these activities upon human, physical, and biotic environments; to define and evaluate management alternatives that minimize adverse consequences of human use of marine environments and resources. Project examples: analyses of estuarine and marine contaminants, habitats, and natural resources; data set of characteristics of coasts and oceans including erosion rates, coastal vulnerability indices, and coastal hazards for incorporation into a geographic information system.

Eligible applicants/beneficiaries: IHEs, junior colleges, technical schools, institutes, laboratories, public or private profit or nonprofit entities, state and local government agencies, individuals.

Range: $20,000 to $550,000. **Average:** Average : $250,000.

Activity: not quantified specifically.

HQ: National Centers for Coastal Ocean Science (N/SCI), NOS-NOAA-USDC, 1305 East-West Hwy., Silver Spring, MD 20910. Phone: (no number provided).

Internet: www.nccos.noaa.gov. (Note: no field offices for this program.)

11.427 FISHERIES DEVELOPMENT AND UTILIZATION RESEARCH AND DEVELOPMENT GRANTS AND COOPERATIVE AGREEMENTS PROGRAM

Assistance: project grants. (50-90 percent/2 years).

Purposes: pursuant to the Saltonstall-Kennedy Act as amended, for research to develop and strengthen the U.S. fishing industry. Project examples: risk management of a new oyster disease threat; engineering design and analysis for more secure salmon net pen systems.

Eligible applicants/beneficiaries: U.S. citizens or nationals including in the territories and possessions; state and local governments. Federal and Regional Fishery Management Council employees are ineligible.

Range/Average: N.A.

Activity: N.A.

HQ: Financial Services Division, State/Federal Liaison Branch, NMFS-NOAA-USDC, 1315 East-West Highway, Rm. 13134, Silver Spring, MD 20910. Phone: (301) 713-2358, FAX (301) 713-1306.

Internet: www.nmfs.noaa.gov/sfweb/skhome.html.

11.429 MARINE SANCTUARY PROGRAM

Assistance: project grants (100 percent).

Purposes: pursuant to the Marine Protection, Research, and Sanctuaries Act of 1972 and amendments, for research and educational programs in the marine sanctuary system; for enforcement activities at sanctuary sites; for projects enhancing public awareness, appreciation, and wise use of the marine environment. Scholarships are available for masters and doctorate level studies, particularly by women and minorities pursuing degrees in marine biology, maritime archaeology, and oceanography.

Eligible applicants/beneficiaries: project grants—states, local, and tribal governments; regional and interstate agencies, K-12 public and independent schools and school systems; IHEs; commercial and nonprofit organizations; other persons. Agreements to solicit private donation—nonprofit organizations. Scholarships—U.S. citizens, particularly women and minorities with financial needs.

Range: cooperative agreements, $200,000 to $3,940,000; competitive awards, $10,000 to $50,000. **Average:** agreements, $1,695,000; scholarships, $32,000.

Activity: currently, 13 designated sanctuaries, management plan reviews under way at 7 sites.

HQ: Director, National Marine Sanctuary Program, NOS-NOAA-USDC, 1305 East-West Hwy., Silver Spring, MD 20910. Phone: (301) 713- 3125, ext. 2731; scholarships, (301) 713-4204; Monterey Bay program, (831) 647-4204.

Internet: www.sanctuaries.nos.noaa.gov/; *scholarships,* www.fosterscholars.noaa.gov.

11.430 UNDERSEA RESEARCH

Assistance: project grants (100 percent).

Purposes: pursuant to the Coast and Geodetic Act, for undersea research and development projects. Funds may be used to acquire necessary technology. Examples: Nutrient Cycling and Primary Productivity of Marine Ecosystems; diving safety and physiology research; submarine venting of liquids and gases.

Eligible applicants/beneficiaries: IHEs, junior colleges, technical schools, institutes, laboratories; states, political subdivisions, agencies; individuals.

Range: $15,000 to $2,225,000.

Activity: FY 03, 13 grants awarded.

HQ: Director, Office of Undersea Research, NOAA-USDC, 1315 East- West Hwy., Silver Spring, MD 20910. Phone: (301) 713-2427.

Internet: www.nurp.noaa.gov. (Note: no field offices for this program.)

11.431 CLIMATE AND ATMOSPHERIC RESEARCH

Assistance: project grants. (95-100 percent/1-5 years).

Purposes: pursuant to the Federal Aviation Act and National Climate Program Act as amended, and Weather Service Organic Act, for research and development, advisory services, and operational systems designed to establish a predictive capability for short- and long-term climate fluctuations and trends. Projects funded to date have ranged from some with a global scope to specific activities in the Indian Ocean and the S.W. Tropical Pacific Ocean.

Eligible applicants/beneficiaries: IHEs and other nonprofits, commercial and international organizations; state, local, tribal governments.

Range: $50,000 to $200,000. **Average:** $85,000.

Activity: FY 05, 65 new grants awarded.

HQ: Director, Climate Program Office, NOAA-USDC, 1100 Wayne Ave., Silver Spring, MD 20910. Phone: (301) 427-2089.

Internet: www.nurp.noaa.gov. (Note: no field offices for this program.)

11.432 OFFICE OF OCEANIC AND ATMOSPHERIC RESEARCH (OAR) JOINT AND COOPERATIVE INSTITUTES ("OAR Cooperative Institutes")

Assistance: project grants (cost sharing/5 years).

Purposes: for research and development, education, training, advisory services, and operational systems as they relate to specific programs in the environmental sciences. Projects involve research in oceanography, atmospherics, limnology, and the solar, Arctic, near-space environments.

Eligible applicants/beneficiaries: universities or nonprofit research institutions, usually located near NOAA environmental research laboratories or facilities.

Range: cooperative institutes, $74,000 to $20,000,000. **Average:** $8,700,000.

Activity: FY 06 estimate, 13 cooperative agreements.

HQ: Program Manager, OAR (R/OSSX5), NOAA-USDC, 1315 East-West Hwy., Silver Spring, MD 20910. Phone: (301) 713-9397, ext. 206.

Internet: www.oarhq.noaa.gov/OSS_Jl.html. (Note: no field offices for this program.)

11.433 MARINE FISHERIES INITIATIVE ("MARFIN")

Assistance: project grants (cooperative grants). (100 percent/to 3 years).

Purposes: pursuant to the Fish and Wildlife Act of 1956, Magnuson Fishery Conservation and Management Act, and Saltonstall-Kennedy Act, for fisheries research and development projects involving harvest methods, economic analyses, processing methods, and fish stock assessment and enhancement in the Gulf of Mexico, South Atlantic, and New England fisheries.

Eligible applicants/beneficiaries: state or local governments, IHEs, profit and nonprofit entities, U.S. citizens.

Range: $21,000 to $374,000. **Average:** $64,000.

Activity: not quantified specifically.

HQ: State/Federal Liaison Office, NMFS-NOAA-USDC, 263 13th Ave. South, St. Petersburg, FL 33701. Phone: (727) 824-5324. *Or*: Northeast Regional Office, NMFS-NOAA-USDC, One Blackburn Drive, Gloucester, MA 01930. Phone: (978) 281-9267.

Internet: e-mail, grants.information@noaa.gov. (Note: the field offices serve as headquarters.)

11.434 COOPERATIVE FISHERY STATISTICS

Assistance: project grants (100 percent/to 5 years).

Purposes: pursuant to the Fish and Wildlife Act of 1956, for cooperative state-federal programs to collect, analyze, and distribute statistics on commercial and recreational fishing in the States' Territorial Sea and the U.S. Exclusive Economic Zone—supporting the Magnuson-Stevens Fishery Conservation and Management Act.

Eligible applicants/beneficiaries: fisheries conservation agencies in the southeast and Gulf states, and PR and VI; Gulf States Marine Fisheries Commission.

Range: $59,000 to $124,000—not including award of $3,305,000 to Gulf States Marine Fisheries Commission.

Activity: not quantified specifically.

HQ: Fisheries Statistics and Economics Division, Office of Science and Technology (SSMC3), NMFS-NOAA-USDC, 1315 East-West Hwy, -

Rm.12441, Silver Spring, MD 20910. Phone: (301) 713-2328; FAX (301) 713-4137.

Internet: www.st.nmfs.gov/st1/; http://caldera.sero.nmfs.gov/grants/programs/csp.htm.

11.435 SOUTHEAST AREA MONITORING AND ASSESSMENT PROGRAM ("SEAMAP")

Assistance: project grants (100 percent/to 5 years).

Purposes: pursuant to the Fish and Wildlife Act of 1956, to collect, manage, and disseminate independent information on marine fisheries, and to participate in inter-jurisdictional fisheries management programs, exclusively in the Gulf of Mexico, South Atlantic, and U.S. Caribbean—supporting the Magnuson- Stevens Fishery Conservation and Management Act.

Eligible applicants/beneficiaries: fisheries conservation agencies in the southeast and Gulf states, and PR and VI; Gulf States Marine Fisheries Commission.

Range: $25,000 to $299,000. **Average:** $111,000.

Activity: not quantified specifically.

HQ: State/Federal Liaison Office, NMFS-NOAA/USDC, 263 13th Ave. South, St. Petersburg, FL 33701. Phone: (727) 824-5324. FAX (727) 824-5324.

Internet: http://caldera.sero.nmfs.gov/grants/programs/seamap.htm. (Note: the field office serves as headquarters.)

11.436 COLUMBIA RIVER FISHERIES DEVELOPMENT PROGRAM

Assistance: project grants (100 percent).

Purposes: pursuant to the Mitchell Act, to develop measures to protect and enhance salmon and steelhead resources in the Columbia River Basin, using the facilities and personnel of state fisheries agencies.

Eligible applicants/beneficiaries: state governments, quasi- public nonprofit organizations.

Range: $57,000 to $4,912,000. **Average:** $1,991,000.

Activity: not quantified specifically.

HQ: Director, Columbia River Fisheries Development Program, Hatcheries and Inland Fisheries Branch, Salmon Recovery Division, NMFS-NOAA-USDC, 1201 NE Lloyd Blvd., Portland, OR 97232-1274. Phone: (503) 231-2009, FAX (503) 872-2737.

Internet: www.noaa.gov (Note: the field offices serve as headquarters.)

11.437 PACIFIC FISHERIES DATA PROGRAM

Assistance: project grants (100 percent).

Purposes: pursuant to the Magnuson-Stevens Fishery Conservation and Management Act as amended, to enhance state fishery data collection and analysis systems to respond to Pacific coastwide and insular fisheries management needs, including projects providing catch, effort, and economic and biological data on federally managed species.

Eligible applicants/beneficiaries: state governments, quasi- public non-profit organizations, and Guam, Samoa, and Northern Marianas.

Range: $36,000 to $7,694,000. **Average:** $3,775,000.

Activity: not quantified specifically.

HQ: Fisheries Statistics and Economics Division, Office of Science and Technology (SSMC3), NMFS-NOAA-USDC, 1315 East-West Hwy, - Rm.12441, Silver Spring, MD 20910. Phone: (301) 713-2328; FAX (301) 713-4137.

Internet: www.st.nmfs.gov/st1/.

11.438 PACIFIC COAST SALMON RECOVERY—PACIFIC SALMON TREATY PROGRAM

Assistance: project grants (75-100 percent).

Purposes: pursuant to the Pacific Coast Salmon Treaty Act, to fund state fishery agencies assisting the U.S. in fulfilling its administrative and management responsibilities for salmon recovery.

Eligible applicants/beneficiaries: state governments, treaty tribes.

Range: $58,000 to $17,850,000. **Average:** $8,954,000.

Activity: not quantified specifically.

HQ: program administered by field offices; see Part IV.

Internet: Alaska office, www.fakr.noaa.gov.

11.439 MARINE MAMMAL DATA PROGRAM

Assistance: project grants. (75-100 percent/to 3 years).

Purposes: pursuant to the Marine Mammal Act of 1972 and Marine Mammal Rescue Assistance Act of 2000, to collect and analyze information on the abundance and distribution of marine mammals and their interactions with fisheries and other marine resources, toward the conservation of such mammals. Funds may be available for related research projects.

Eligible applicants/beneficiaries: state governments, quasi- public non-profit organizations; U.S. Marine Mammal Stranding Network participants including state and local governments, academia, aquaria, nonprofits, individuals, and organizations.

Range: $50,000 to $2,807,000. **Average:** $531,000.

Activity: FY 05 estimate, 41 awards.

HQ: Office of Protected Resources, NMFS-NOAA-USDC, 1315 East-West Hwy., Silver Spring, MD 20910. Phone: (301) 713-2322, ext. 178.

Internet: www.nmfs.noaa.gov/prot_res/PR2/.

11.440 ENVIRONMENTAL SCIENCES, APPLICATIONS, DATA, AND EDUCATION

Assistance: project grants (100 percent/1-5 years).

Purposes: for applied research, data assimilation and management, technology development, and education in environmental science. Funds also may support advisory services and long-term partnerships between the federal government and research institutions and IHEs for cooperative science and education.

Eligible applicants/beneficiaries: any state IHE, institute, laboratory; any public or private nonprofit institution or consortium.

Range: projects, to $200,000; cooperative agreements, $250,000 to $5,000,000.

Activity: FY 05, 20 continuation grants, some additional awards.

HQ: Office of Research and Applications, NESDIS-NOAA-USDC, 5200 Auth Rd. - Rm.701, Camp Springs, MD 20746-4304. Phone: (301) 763-8127, FAX (301) 763-8108.

Internet: www.noaa.gov; *and,* ORA, http://orbit-net.nesdis.noaa.gov/ora/; grant applications, www.ofa.noaa.gov/%eago/index.html. (Note: no field offices for this program.)

11.441 REGIONAL FISHERY MANAGEMENT COUNCILS

Assistance: project grants (100 percent/to 5 years).

Purposes: pursuant to the Magnuson-Stevens Fishery Conservation and Management Act as amended, for the eight regional fishery management councils to prepare, monitor, and revise fishery management plans and data collection programs for domestic and foreign fishing within the 200-mile U.S. Exclusive Economic Zone.

Eligible applicants/beneficiaries: Regional Fishery Management Councils (New England, Mid-Atlantic, South Atlantic, Gulf of Mexico, Caribbean, Pacific, North Pacific, and Western Pacific).

Range: $891,000 to $2,035,000. **Average:** $1,638,000.

Activity: 2002, 1 new fishery management plan, 8 amendments.

HQ: Financial Services Division, State/Federal Liaison Branch, NMFS-NOAA-USDC, 1315 East-West Highway, Rm. 13134, Silver Spring, MD 20910. Phone: (301) 713-2358, FAX (301) 713-1306.

Internet: www.nmfs.noaa.gov/sfa/domes_fish/index/index.htm.

11.443 SHORT TERM CLIMATE FLUCTUATIONS

Assistance: project grants (95 percent).

Purposes: for studies relevant to the diagnosis and prediction of short-term climate fluctuations.

Eligible applicants/beneficiaries: public and private educational institutions; qualified institutional personnel.

Range/Average: N.A.

Activity: FY 01, 1 renewal grant.

HQ: Climate Prediction Center, National Centers for Environmental Prediction, National Weather Service, NOAA-USDC, World Weather Bldg., 5200 Auth Rd., Camp Springs, MD 20746. Phone: (301) 763- 8000, ext. 7512.

Internet: www.noaa.gov (Note: no field offices for this program.)

11.444 HAWAII SUSTAINABLE FISHERIES DEVELOPMENT (AQUACULTURE PROGRAM)

Assistance: project grants (100 percent).

Purposes: to develop commercially feasible technology for high- value marine finfish in the U.S., to increase availability for aquaculture and stock enhancement in the U.S.—through the Hawaiian Fisheries Development Project.

Eligible applicants/beneficiaries: Oceanic Institute.

Range: $440,000 to $869,000. **Average:** $654,000.

Activity: funding restricted to one applicant.

HQ: Pacific Islands Fisheries Science Center, NMFS-NOAA-USDC, 2570 Dole St., Honolulu, HI 96822. Phone: (808) 983-5374, FAX (808) 983-2902.

Internet: www.pifsc.noaa.gov. (Note: the field office serves as headquarters.)

11.445 HAWAII STOCK MANAGEMENT PROGRAM ("SEMFISH")

Assistance: project grants (100 percent).

Purposes: pursuant to the Magnuson Fishery Conservation and Management Act, to develop and test the technology of a marine stock enhancement program in Hawaii, as a management option to protect and enhance depleted near-shore fishery resources.

Eligible applicants: private nonprofit institutions.

Eligible beneficiaries: general public.

Range: $439,000 to $475,000. **Average:** $457,000.

Activity: funding to date restricted to one applicant.

HQ: Pacific Islands Fisheries Science Center, NMFS-NOAA-USDC, 2570 Dole St., Honolulu, HI 96822. Phone: (808) 983-5374, FAX (808) 983-2902.

Internet: www.pifsc.noaa.gov. (Note: the field office serves as headquarters.)

11.449 INDEPENDENT EDUCATION AND SCIENCE PROJECTS AND PROGRAMS

Assistance: project grants (100 percent).

Purposes: to increase minority high school student enrollment in college and majoring in math, science, and engineering, and to recruit scientists and engineers to serve as volunteer tutors primarily for high school girls and minority students. Funds are used for: student stipends, tutoring, and field trips to government facilities; advisors training.

Eligible applicants: Colorado Minority Engineering Achievement Association/Mathematics, Engineering, Science Achievement (CMEA/MESA).

Eligible beneficiaries: teachers who are MESA advisors and students with a GPA of 3.0 who are interested in pursuing careers related to mathematics, engineering or science.

Range: grants, $5,000 to $10,000; cooperative agreements, $45,000 to $172,000.

Activity: funding suspended in FY 04 for two years or until budget stabilizes.

HQ: Program Officer, Office of Atmospheric Research, NOAA-USDC, Bldg. 22, 325 Broadway, Boulder, CO 80303. Phone: (303) 497-6731.

Internet: www.noaa.gov (Note: the field office serves as headquarters.)

11.450 AUTOMATED FLOOD WARNING SYSTEMS ("AFWS")

Assistance: project grants. (to 100 percent/to 2 years).

Purposes: to improve flood warning capabilities. Program funds are used for initial costs of acquiring equipment, software development, personnel training, developing technical procedures, and implementation personnel.

Eligible applicants: states, counties, municipalities, educational institutions, nonprofit organizations.

Eligible beneficiaries: general public.

Range: $5,000 to $100,000. **Average:** $55,000.

Activity: not quantified specifically.

HQ: AFWS Program Office, Hydrologic Services Division, National Weather Service (W/OS3), NOAA-USDC, 1325 East-West Hwy., Silver Spring, MD 20910. Phone: (301) 713-0006, ext. 154.

Internet: http://ofa.noaa.gov/-grants/index.html.

11.452 UNALLIED INDUSTRY PROJECTS

Assistance: project grants (to 100 percent).

Purposes: pursuant to the Fish and Wildlife Coordination Act of 1956 and the Saltonstall-Kennedy Act, for biological, economic, sociological, public policy, and other research and administration projects benefiting the U.S. fisheries; to develop innovative approaches and methods to ensure the safety, quality, and integrity of fishery products; to develop, test, and apply new technology in molecular biology for use in the management of commercial and recreational marine fisheries, emphasizing the development of molecular genetics techniques. Project funds may support research and management activities for high-priority marine and estuarine resources, especially for species and habitats currently under or proposed for federal or interjurisdictional management.

Eligible applicants/beneficiaries: state and local governments, IHEs, territorial agencies, tribal governments, private profit and nonprofit research and conservation organizations, individuals.

Range: $50,000 to $150,000. **Average:** $100,000.

Activity: not quantified specifically.

HQ: Management and Administration Division, NMFS-NOAA-USDC, 1315 East-West Hwy., Silver Spring, MD 20910. Phone: (301) 713-1364, FAX (301) 713-2258.

Internet: www.noaa.gov.

11.454 UNALLIED MANAGEMENT PROJECTS

Assistance: project grants (to 100 percent).

Purposes: pursuant to the Fish and Wildlife Coordination Act of 1956 and the Magnuson Fishery Conservation and Management Act, for fisheries management and conservation activities by providing economic, sociological, public policy, and other information relating to fishery resources and protected species and their environments—in federal, state, and territorial waters. Activities are intended to benefit high-priority marine and estuarine resources, especially for species and habitats currently under or proposed for federal or interjurisdictional management.

Eligible applicants/beneficiaries: state and local governments, IHEs, territorial agencies, tribal governments, private profit and nonprofit research and conservation organizations, individuals.

Range: $147,000 to $1,225,000. **Average:** $539,000.

Activity: not quantified specifically.

HQ: Management and Administration Division, NMFS-NOAA-USDC, 1315 East-West Hwy., Silver Spring, MD 20910. Phone: (301) 713-1364, FAX (301) 713-2258.

Internet: www.noaa.gov.

11.455 COOPERATIVE SCIENCE AND EDUCATION PROGRAM

Assistance: project grants (to 100 percent).

Purposes: pursuant to the Fish and Wildlife Coordination Act of 1956 and Fish and Wildlife Act, to support partnerships with NMFS for cooperative science and education on marine issues, especially living marine resources and their habitat, confronting local, regional, and national resources managers; to develop innovative approaches and methods for marine and estuarine science and education—through programs including: Cooperative Marine Education and Research Programs (CMER); Joint Institute for Marine Observation (JIMO); Cooperative Unit of Fisheries Education and Research (CUFER); Cooperative Institute of Fishery Oceanography (CIFO); Cooperative Education and Research Program (CERP); Cooperative Institute Agreement (CIA); Cooperative Institute for Marine Resources Studies (CIMRS); Cooperative Institute for Marine and Atmospheric Studies (CIMAS); Cooperative Institute for Arctic Research (CIFAR); Joint Institute for the Study of the Atmosphere and Oceans (JISAO).

Eligible applicants/beneficiaries: state, territorial, and private IHEs; private and public research organizations affiliated with IHEs; national and international organizations.

Range: $33,000 to $1,777,000. **Average:** $136,000.

Activity: not quantified specifically.

HQ: contact regional NMFS science and research directors (addresses in Part IV).

Internet: www.noaa.gov.

11.457 CHESAPEAKE BAY STUDIES

Assistance: project grants (to 100 percent/to 3 years).

Purposes: pursuant to the Fish and Wildlife Act of 1956 and NOAA Authorization Act of 1992, for research and development projects providing information for the living marine resources of Chesapeake Bay; for the Chesapeake Bay Watershed Education and Training Initiative, providing environment-based education to students, teachers, and communities.

Eligible applicants/beneficiaries: IHEs, hospitals, other nonprofits, commercial organizations; state, local, and tribal governments; international organizations; foreign governments and their jurisdictional entities.

Range: $8,000 to $350,000. **Average:** $85,000.

Activity: not quantified specifically.

HQ: Chesapeake Bay Office, NOAA-USDC, 410 Severn Ave. Ste.107A, Annapolis, MD 21403. Phone: (410) 267-5660, FAX (410) 267-5666.

Internet: www.noaa.chesapeakebay.net/. (Note: the field office serves as headquarters.)

11.459 WEATHER AND AIR QUALITY RESEARCH

Assistance: project grants (100 percent).

Purposes: pursuant to the Federal Aviation Act, Weather Service Organic Act, and National Climate Program Act as amended, and Clean Air Act Amendments of 1990, for research and development, science assessments, advisory services, and operational systems to establish a predictive capability for short- and long-term climate and air quality fluctuations and trends.

Eligible applicants/beneficiaries: IHEs, technical schools, institutions, laboratories; states, political subdivisions, agencies; individuals.

Range: (funds no longer available).

Activity: 1-3 contracts per year.

HQ: Director, Office of Weather and Air Quality, Office of Oceanic and Atmospheric Research, NOAA-USDC, 1315 East-West Hwy., Silver Spring, MD 20910. Phone: (301) 713-9397, -9121.

Internet: www.noaa.gov (Note: no field offices for this program.)

11.460 SPECIAL OCEANIC AND ATMOSPHERIC PROJECTS

Assistance: project grants (100 percent).

Purposes: pursuant to the National Weather Service and Related Agencies Authorization Act of 1999 as amended, for research and development, education and training, advisory services, and operational systems relating to oceanic and atmospheric resources.

Eligible applicants/beneficiaries: organizations and individuals specified in NOAA special announcements.

Average: N.A.

Activity: not quantified specifically.

HQ: Director, Planning and Evaluation, OAR-NOAA-USDC, 1315 East-West Hwy., Silver Spring, MD 20910. Phone: (301) 713-2465, ext. 119.

Internet: www.noaa.gov.

11.462 HYDROLOGIC RESEARCH

Assistance: project grants (to 100 percent).

Purposes: pursuant to the Weather Service Organic Act, for research and development on issues relating to the forecasting of surface hydrologic conditions. Project examples: automated calibration of hydrologic models; flash flood guidance procedures and models.

Eligible applicants/beneficiaries: IHEs, state and local government agencies, quasi-public institutions such as water supply or power companies, and hydrologic consultants and companies.

Range: $5,000 to $100,000. **Average:** $25,000.

Activity: not quantified specifically.

HQ: Chief, Hydrology Laboratory, National Weather Service (W/OHD- 1), NOAA-USDC, 1325 East-West Hwy., Silver Spring, MD 20910. Phone: (301) 713-0640.

Internet: www.noaa.gov. (Note: no field offices for this program.)

11.463 HABITAT CONSERVATION

Assistance: project grants (50-100 percent/to 2 years).

Purposes: pursuant to the Fish and Wildlife Coordination Act of 1956 and Coral Reef Conservation Act, for biological, economic, sociological, public policy, and other research, and for administration, public education, and construction activities relating to marine and estuarine habitats, especially for species currently under or proposed for federal or interjurisdictional management.

Eligible applicants/beneficiaries: state and local governments, IHEs, territorial agencies, tribal governments, private profit and nonprofit research and conservation organizations, individuals.

Range: $15,000 to $10,000,000; typical award, $35,000 to $200,000.

Activity: not quantified specifically.

HQ: Office of Habitat Conservation, NMFS-NOAA-USDC, 1315 East-West Hwy., Silver Spring, MD 20910. Phone: Community-based Restoration Program, (301) 713-0174, FAX (301) 713-0184; General Coral Reef Conservation Grant Program, (301) 713-3159, FAX (301) 713-159.

Internet: www.nmfs.noaa.gov/habitat/ecosystem/index.htm.

11.467 METEOROLOGIC AND HYDROLOGIC MODERNIZATION DEVELOPMENT ("Hydrometeorological Development")

Assistance: project grants; direct payments/specified use; direct payments/unrestricted use; technical information; training (grants, to 100 percent).

Purposes: pursuant to the Weather Service Organic Act, to maintain a cooperative university-federal partnership to conduct meteorological training, education, professional development, and research and development on hydrometeorological issues. Funding supports the Cooperative Program for Operational Meteorology, Education and Training (COMET) and outreach.

Eligible applicants/beneficiaries: IHEs and consortia; state or local government agencies including school systems, quasi-public institutions; consultants, companies.

Range: $15,000 to $4,000,000. **Average:** small projects, $8,500; collaborative projects, $35,000.

Activity: FY 02, 27 projects funded.

HQ: Chief, Training Division, National Weather Service (OS6), NOAA-USDC, 1325 East-West Hwy., Silver Spring, MD 20910. Phone: (301) 713-0280, FAX (301) 713-1598.

Internet: www.noaa.gov (Note: no field offices for this program.)

11.468 APPLIED METEOROLOGICAL RESEARCH

Assistance: project grants (to 100 percent/1-3 years).

Purposes: for the Collaborative Science, Technology, and Applied Research (CSTAR) program, designed to create a cost-effective transition from basic and applied research to operations and services. Project examples include: operational system for probalistic quantitative precipitation forecasts to improve prediction of warm- and cold-season heavy precipitation events; forecasts of topographically-forced weather systems; improving operational radar algorithms.

Eligible applicants/beneficiaries: U.S. IHEs.

Range: $100,000 to $3,700,000. **Average:** $460,000.

Activity: not quantified specifically.

HQ: CSTAR Program Manager (SSMC2 - W/OST12), National Weather Service, NOAA-USDC, 1325 East-West Hwy. - Rm.15326, Silver Spring, MD 20910. Phone: (301) 713-5570, ext. 150.

Internet: www.noaa.nws.gov. (Note: no field offices for this program.)

11.469 CONGRESSIONALLY IDENTIFIED AWARDS AND PROJECTS

Assistance: project grants (to 100 percent).

Purposes: to facilitate education, research, and development in the atmospheric and marine sciences; for related construction of facilities.

Eligible applicants/beneficiaries: state and local governments, IHEs, tribal governments, private profit and nonprofit research and conservation organizations, individuals.

Range: $140,000 to $28,500,000.

Activity: not quantified specifically.

HQ: Chief, Grants Management Division, (OFA62 - SSMC2), NOAA- USDC, 1325 East-West Hwy., Silver Spring, MD 20910. Phone: (301) 713-0926.

Internet: www.noaa.gov (Note: no field offices for this program.)

11.472 UNALLIED SCIENCE PROGRAM

Assistance: project grants (to 100 percent).

Purposes: pursuant to the Fish and Wildlife Coordination Act of 1956 and Fish and Wildlife Act, for biological, socio-economic, and physical science research on the stocks of U.S. fishery and protected resources and their environment, contributing to their optimal management; to develop innovative approaches and methods for marine and estuarine science.

Eligible applicants/beneficiaries: state and local governments, U.S. territories, IHEs, tribal governments, private profit and nonprofit research and conservation organizations, individuals.

Range: $25,000 to $2,455,000. **Average:** $546,000.

Activity: not quantified specifically.

HQ: Management and Administration Division, NMFS-NOAA-USDC, 1315 East-West Hwy., Silver Spring, MD 20910. Phone: (301) 713-1364, FAX (301) 713-2258.

Internet: Alaska: www.fakr.noaa.gov; Region: www.caldera.sero.nmfs.gov.

11.473 COASTAL SERVICES CENTER ("CSC")

Assistance: project grants (100 percent/1-3 years).

Purposes: to develop a science-based, multi-dimensional approach allowing for the maintenance or improvement of environmental quality while allowing for economic growth. Funds may be used for such activities as: outreach; coastal fellowships and apprenticeships; training materials development and information dissemination; development of geographic information system and tabular and spatial data bases; to generate, archive, interpret, and validate aircraft, satellite, and other remotely sensed data and derived products; related purposes.

Eligible applicants/beneficiaries: IHEs, hospitals, other nonprofits, commercial organizations; state, local, and tribal governments; international organizations; foreign governments and their jurisdictional entities.

Range: competitive grants, $55,000 to $378,000; congressional directed grants (non-competitive), $380,000 to $2,811,000.

Activity: not quantified specifically.

HQ: Assistant Administrator, Coastal Services Center, NOS-NOAA- USDC, 1305 East-West Hwy., Silver Spring, MD 20910. Phone: (301) 713-3074.

Internet: www.csc.noaa.gov.

11.474 ATLANTIC COASTAL FISHERIES COOPERATIVE MANAGEMENT ACT

Assistance: project grants (to 100 percent).

Purposes: pursuant to the act, to develop, implement, and enforce interstate conservation and management plans pertaining to Atlantic Coastal fishery resources, and for activities required by such plans including: collection, management, and analysis of fishery data; law enforcement; habitat conservation; fishery research and management planning.

Eligible applicants/beneficiaries: Atlantic States Marine Fisheries Commission; Atlantic Coast state governments; Potomac River Fisheries Commission; DC.

Range: $14,000 to $1,926,000. **Average:** $150,000.

Activity: not quantified specifically.

HQ: Director, Office of Sustainable Fisheries, NMFS-NOAA-USDC, 1315 East-West Hwy., Silver Spring, MD 20910. Phone: (301) 713- 2334. FAX (301) 713-0596.

Internet: www.nmfs.noaa.gov/sfa/state_federal/state_federal.htm.

11.477 FISHERIES DISASTER RELIEF

Assistance: project grants (75 percent).

Purposes: pursuant to the Magnuson-Stevens Fishery Conservation and Management Act of 1966, to assess the effects of commercial fishery failures caused by natural or man-made disasters; to restore fisheries or prevent future failures; to assist communities affected by the failures. Funded activities may not expand assisted commercial fishery failures.

Eligible applicants/beneficiaries: state agencies; fishing communities including vessel owners, operators, crew; U.S. fish processors.

Range: $344,000 to $7,000,000. **Average:** $2,781,000.

Activity: not quantified specifically.

HQ: Financial Services Division, State/Federal Liaison Branch, NMFS-NOAA-USDC, 1315 East-West Highway, Rm. 13134, Silver Spring, MD 20910. Phone: (301) 713-2358, FAX (301) 713-1306.

Internet: www.nmfs.noaa.gov.

11.478 CENTER FOR SPONSORED COASTAL OCEAN RESEARCH—COASTAL OCEAN PROGRAM ("CSCOR/COP")

Assistance: project grants (100 percent/1-5 years).

Purposes: to provide a predictive capability for managing coastal ecosystems, including in Great Lakes areas. Funds support research and interagency initiatives in coastal ecosystem oceanography, cumulative coastal impacts, and forecasting coastal and natural hazards.

Eligible applicants/beneficiaries: IHEs; nonprofit institutions; state, local, and tribal governments; federal agencies.

Range: $25,000 to $1,000,000.

Activity: currently, 68 projects funded.

HQ: Coastal Ocean Program, Center for Sponsored Coastal Ocean Research, NOAA, 1305 East-West Hwy.-Room 8243, Silver Spring, MD 20910. Phone: (301) 713-3338.

Internet: www.cop.noaa.gov.

11.480 NATIONAL OCEAN SERVICE INTERN PROGRAM ("NOS Intern Program")

Assistance: project grants (100 percent/5 years).

Purposes: to establish internship programs providing opportunities for cooperative study, research and development—to increase the number and diversity of skilled engineers, scientists, and managers in the environmental arena, in the techniques and technologies used by the National Ocean Service. Funds may support: recruitment and evaluation of candidates; stipends for a maximum of two years.

Eligible applicants: nonprofit organizations.

Eligible beneficiaries: recent college graduates.

Range: $40,000 to $1,800,000/year to support 1-50 interns.

Activity: currently, 30 internships; grant closed in FY06.

HQ: Office of Coast Survey, National Ocean Service, NOAA-USDC, 1305 East-West Hwy. - 6th floor, Silver Spring, MD 20910. Phone: (301) 713-2780, ext. 137.

Internet: (none). (Note: no field offices for this program.)

11.481 EDUCATIONAL PARTNERSHIP PROGRAM

Assistance: project grants (100 percent/1-5 years).

Purposes: to develop programs to increase research and educational partnerships between NOAA and minority-serving institutions, by establishing: new cooperative science centers in atmospheric, oceanic, environmental sciences, and remote sensing (AOES); an environmental entrepreneurship program supporting restoration projects in environmentally depleted zones and program development in AOES. Funds may support a distinguished professor, research and development programs, and students undertaking NOAA-related sciences course work and/or research.

Eligible applicants/beneficiaries: DOED-approved minority serving institutions with AOES graduate programs; non-minority institutions in partnerships with minority-serving institutions.

Range: $20,000 to $2,500,000 per year.

Activity: 4 centers funded; 79 Ph.D., 100 MS, and 223 BS students in training at the funded centers.

HQ: Education Partnership Program (SSMC 3), Office of Oceanic and Atmospheric Research, NOAA-USDC, 1315 East-West Hwy. - Rm.10600, Silver Spring, MD 20910. Phone: (301) 713-9437.

Internet: www.epp.noaa.gov (Note: no field offices for this program.)

NATIONAL TELECOMMUNICATIONS AND INFORMATION ADMINISTRATION

11.550 PUBLIC TELECOMMUNICATIONS FACILITIES PLANNING AND CONSTRUCTION ("PTFP")

Assistance: project grants. (75-100 percent/to 2 years).

Purposes: pursuant to the Communications Act of 1934 as amended, to plan, acquire, install, or modernize public telecommunications facilities including conversion to digital broadcasting. Planning grants may cover 100 percent of costs. Construction grant funds, requiring a 25 percent match, may be applied against costs of apparatus needed for production, dissemination, interconnection, and reception of noncommercial educational and cultural radio and television programs. Real estate, operating, or indirect expenses are ineligible.

Eligible applicants/beneficiaries: public or noncommercial educational broadcast stations, entities, or systems; nonprofit foundations, corporations, institutions, or associations organized primarily for educational or cultural purposes; state, local, tribal governmental agencies. Applications for facilities involving ownership, operation, and participation by minorities and women receive special consideration.

Range: $9,255 to $927,937. **Average:** $175,000.

Activity: FY 05, 124 grants awarded.

HQ: Director, Public Telecommunications Facilities Program, Office of Telecommunications and Information Applications, NTIA- USDC, 1401 Constitution Ave. NW - Rm.4096, Washington, DC 20230. Phone: (202) 482-5802.

Internet: http://www.ntia.doc.gov/ptfp. (Note: no field offices for this program.)

11.554 LOW-POWER TELEVISION AND TRANSLATOR DIGITAL-TO-ANALOG CONVERSION

Assistance: project grants (ninety days).

Purposes: to provide compensation toward digital-to-analog conversion device. Priority given to eligible television stations for which the license is held by nonprofit corporations and low-power stations that serve rural areas of fewer than 10,000 viewers.

Eligible applicants: low-power, Class A, translator, or booster televisions stations broadcasting exclusively in analog format that have not purchased a digital-to-analog conversion device before February 8, 2006.

Eligible beneficiaries: general public.

Range/Average: $1,000.

Activity: N.A.

HQ: Director, Broadcast Division, Office of Telecommunications and Information Applications, NTIA-USDC, 1401 Constitution Ave., NW-Room 4812, Washington, DC 20230. Phone: (202) 482-5802.

Internet: www.ntia.doc.gov/lptv. (Note: no field offices for this program.)

11.555 PUBLIC SAFETY INTEROPERABLE COMMUNICATIONS GRANT PROGRAM ("PSIC")

Assistance: project grants (90 days).

Purposes: pursuant to the Deficit Reduction Act of 2005 as amended, and the Call Home Act of 2006, to assist public safety agencies with the planning and coordination associated with acquisition and deployment of and training in the use of interoperable communications systems, software, and equipment that utilize reallocated public safety spectrum for radio communication.

Eligible applicants: the State Administrative Agency designated by each state's or territory's governor.

Eligible beneficiaries: public safety agencies.

Range/Average: Part I: states, DC and PR: minimum $3,000,000; territories: $500,000; Part II: remaining 80% of funds allocated using formula based on three variables—threat, vulnerability and consequence.

Activity: $968,385,000 awarded to fund projects in 56 states and territories.

HQ: Program Specialist, Office of Telecommunications and Information Applications, NTIA-USDC, 1401 Constitution Ave., NW-Room 4812, Washington, DC 20230. Phone: (202) 482-5802.

Internet: www.ntia.doc.gov/psic. (Note: no field offices for this program.)

11.556 TV CONVERTER BOX COUPON PROGRAM

Assistance: coupons for dollars-off purchase made by recipient (100 percent/coupon expires 90 days after mailing).

Purposes: pursuant to the Communications Act of 1934, as amended and Title III of the Deficit Reduction Act of 2005, to provide financial assistance offsetting the cost of a certified digital-to-analog converter box by providing two free $40 coupons to each applicant. Coupon dispersal is in response to the February 17, 2009 deadline requiring TV channels to broadcast only in digital. Supplies are limited and consumers must request coupons on or before March 31, 2009.

Eligible applicants: consumers in U.S. states and territories are eligible for the first 22.25 million coupons, with 11.25 million additional coupons available to only those households who rely on over-the-air broadcasts.

Eligible beneficiaries: general public.

Range/Average: $40 - $80.

Activity: N.A. New program.

HQ: Consumer Education Director, Office of Telecommunications and Information Applications, NTIA-USDC, 1401 Constitution Ave., NW-Room 4812, Washington, DC 20230. Phone: (202) 482-2048.

Internet: www.dtv2009.gov. (Note: no field offices for this program.)

NATIONAL INSTITUTE FOR STANDARDS AND TECHNOLOGY

11.601 CALIBRATION PROGRAM

Assistance: specialized services.

Purposes: pursuant to the National Bureau of Standards Organic Act (NBSOA) as amended, to provide a national consistent system of physical measurements used for assurance of interchangeability and uniformity of manufactured items, for process control, for informational and scientific purposes, and for fairness and objectivity in commerce and regulation. Fees are charged for tests and calibrations.

Eligible applicants/beneficiaries: state and local governments, academic institutions, laboratories, industrial firms, corporations, individuals.

Range/Average: N.A.

Activity: FY 05, 12,849 tests conducted.

HQ: Calibration Program, NIST-USDC, 100 Bureau Drive, Gaithersburg, MD 20899-2330. Phone: (301) 975-2092, FAX (301) 869- 3548.

Internet: http://ts.nist.gov/ts/htdocs/230/233/calibration; e- mail, calibrations @nist.gov. (Note: no field offices for this program.)

11.603 NATIONAL STANDARD REFERENCE DATA SYSTEM ("NSRDS")

Assistance: sale, exchange, or donation of property and goods.

Purposes: pursuant to the Standard Reference Data Act and NBSOA as amended, to provide evaluated scientific and technical data on the chemical, physical, and other properties of substances and systems. Publications, data bases, and online services may be purchased, subject to copyright restrictions.

Eligible applicants/beneficiaries: federal agencies, firms, corporations, universities, industrial laboratories, research establishments, general public.

Range/Average: N.A.

Activity: annually, some 20 publications and 5-10 computerized data bases issued.

HQ: Standard Reference Data Group, NIST-USDC, 100 Bureau Drive, Gaithersburg, MD 20899-2320. Phone: (301) 975-2208, FAX (301) 926-0416.

Internet: www.nist.gov/srd.

11.604 STANDARD REFERENCE MATERIALS ("SRM")

Assistance: sale, exchange, or donation of property and goods.

Purposes: pursuant to NBSOA as amended, to develop accurate methods of analysis and to calibrate measurement systems, through the certification and dissemination of reference materials used to: facilitate the exchange of goods; institute quality control; determine material performance characteristics; measure materials at state-of-the-art limits; assure the long-term adequacy and integrity of measurement quality assurance programs. SRMs are used as primary reference measurement standards for such purposes as: clinical laboratories testing; monitoring of air, water, and low-level radioactive pollution; quality control in the production of basic materials such as steel, rubber, cement, and plastics. Materials may be purchased from NIST.

Eligible applicants/beneficiaries: federal agencies, state and local governments, societies, institutions, firms, corporations, individuals.

Range/Average: N.A.

Activity: FY 05, sales of 32,163 units.

HQ: SRM Program, NIST-USDC, Bldg. 820 - Rm.113, 100 Bureau Dr., Gaithersburg, MD 20899-2322. Phone: (301) 975-6776, FAX (301) 948-3730.

Internet: www.nist.gov/srm; e-mail, srminfo@nist.gov.

11.606 WEIGHTS AND MEASURES SERVICE

Assistance: advisory services/counseling; specialized services; technical information; training.

Purposes: pursuant to NBSOA as amended, to provide education, technical and other assistance, and training to states, users and manufacturers of weights and measures devices, and other devices users—concerning: weights and measures operations development of model laws and regulations; upgrading of state laboratories; administration of device evaluation; promotion of a uniform national weights and measures system; harmonization of national and international legal metrology standards; transition to the metric system.

Eligible applicants/beneficiaries: states, political subdivisions, private industry, general public.

Range/Average: N.A.

Activity: not quantified specifically.

HQ: Chief, Weights and Measures Division, NIST-USDC, 100 Bureau Drive, Gaithersburg, MD 20899-2600. Phone: (301) 975-4004.

Internet: http://ts.nist.gov/ts/htdocs/230/235/ownhome.htm. (Note: no field offices for this program.)

11.609 MEASUREMENT AND ENGINEERING RESEARCH AND STANDARDS

Assistance: project grants (100 percent/1-3 years).

Purposes: pursuant to NBSOA as amended, for scientific research and technology transfer for measurement and engineering research and standards, in such areas as fire prevention, building construction, precision measurement, automation manufacturing, materials science, chemistry, physics, biotechnology, electronics, optical technologies, mathematics, communications and information.

Eligible applicants/beneficiaries: IHEs, professional institutes and associations, nonprofit and commercial organizations, state and local governments.

Range/Average: N.A.

Activity: FY 06-07 estimate, 329 grant, cooperative agreement, and amendment awards.

HQ: NIST-USDC, Bldg. 411 - Rm.A120, 100 Bureau Drive, Gaithersburg, MD 20899-3580. Phone: (301) 975-6328.

Internet: www.nist.gov. (Note: no field offices for this program.)

11.610 NATIONAL CENTER FOR STANDARDS AND CERTIFICATION INFORMATION ("NCSCI")

Assistance: technical information.

Purposes: pursuant to NBSOA as amended and the Trade Agreements Act of 1979, to serve as an information center and referral service—maintaining a reference collection of standards and specifications, regulations, certification rules, directories, reference books, special publications, copyrights, lending restrictions, and similar data; information relating to foreign trade. NCSCI does not analyze, evaluate, translate, or interpret standards. Published directories, indexes, and bibliographies are available from GPO, NTIS, and NCSCI.

Eligible applicants/beneficiaries: state and local governments; private, public, profit and nonprofit organizations; individuals.

Range/Average: N.A.

Activity: N.A.

HQ: Global Standards and Information Group, NIST-USDC, 100 Bureau Dr., Gaithersburg, MD 20899-2100. Phone: (301) 975-4040, FAX (301) 926-1559; Standards Information Program, (301) 975-2573.

Internet: http://ts.nist.gov/ncsci; e-mail, ncsci@nist.gov. (Note: no field offices for this program.)

11.611 MANUFACTURING EXTENSION PARTNERSHIP

Assistance: project grants; technical information. (project grants, 50 percent/project grants, to 2 years).

Purposes: pursuant to the Omnibus Trade and Competitiveness Act of 1988, American Technology Preeminence Act of 1991, and Technology Administration Act of 1998, to establish and maintain extension centers and services for the transfer of appropriate manufacturing technology to smaller U.S. manufacturing firms. Funding may support: demonstrations and technology deployment especially to firms with fewer than 500 employees; statewide planning and pilot testing projects.

Eligible applicants/beneficiaries: extension services—U.S. nonprofit organizations. Planning and pilot services grants—state and local governments, state-affiliated nonprofit organizations, consortia.

Range: extension planning, testing, \$25,000 to \$100,000; extension centers, \$200,000 to \$6,500,000.

Activity: not quantified specifically.

HQ: Director, Manufacturing Extension Partnership, NIST-USDC, 100 Bureau Drive, Gaithersburg, MD 20899-4800. Phone: (301) 975-5020.

Internet: www.mep.nist.gov. (Note: no field offices for this program.)

11.612 ADVANCED TECHNOLOGY PROGRAM ("ATP")

Assistance: project grants (from 40 percent/3-5 years).

Purposes: pursuant to the Omnibus Trade and Competitiveness Act of 1988 and American Technology Preeminence Act of 1991, to foster development and broad dissemination of high-risk technologies offering potential for significant, broad-based, national economic benefits. Project examples: printed wiring board; flat panel display manufacturing; magnetoresistive random access memories; deep ultraviolet lasers; high temperature superconducting material processes.

Eligible applicants/beneficiaries: U.S. businesses, joint research and development ventures, certain foreign-owned businesses. IHEs, governmental entities, and nonprofit independent research organizations may participate in joint ventures that include at least two profit companies.

Range: $434,000 to $31,000,000. **Average:** $2,900,000.

Activity: since 1990 program inception, 768 awards.

HQ: ATP, NIST-USDC, 100 Bureau Drive, Gaithersburg, MD 20899- 4701. Phone: (301) 975-4447, FAX (301) 869-1150; *application kit*, (800) ATP-FUND.

Internet: www.atp.nist.gov; *application kit*, e-mail, atp@nist.gov. (Note: no field offices for this program.)

11.617 CONGRESSIONALLY-IDENTIFIED PROJECTS

Assistance: project grants.

Purposes: to assist organizations identified by Congress to achieve objectives specified by Congress. Project examples: windstorm mitigation initiative; biocommodity engineering initiative.

Eligible applicants/beneficiaries: organizations specifically identified by Congress.

Range: $500,000 to $20,000,000.

Activity: N.A.; new program listing in 2003.

HQ: Office of the Director (MS 1001), NIST-USDC, Bldg. 101 - Rm.A1126, 100 Bureau Drive, Gaithersburg, MD 20899. Phone: (301) 975-2397, FAX (301) 869-8972.

Internet: http://www.nist.gov. (Note: no field offices for this program.)

NATIONAL TECHNICAL INFORMATION SERVICE

11.650 NATIONAL TECHNICAL INFORMATION SERVICE ("NTIS")

Assistance: technical information.

Purposes: pursuant to the Research and Technical Services Act, Omnibus Trade and Competitiveness Act of 1988, National Institute of Standards and Technology Authorization Act, National Technical Information Act of 1988, and American Technology Preeminence Act of 1991, to serve as the principal source for the sale of federally-sponsored technical information products, related business information, register of research in progress, machine-processed data files, and computer software. NTIS operates the National Audiovisual Center which distributes videotapes, slide sets, and multimedia kits—covering subjects ranging from foreign languages and history to law enforcement and natural resources. NTIS recently established the Homeland Security Information Center, directing users to information products on homeland security. Fees are charged, supporting a revolving fund.

Eligible applicants/beneficiaries: any U.S. and most foreign organizations; individuals.

Range/Average: N.A.

Activity: not quantified specifically.

HQ: Director, NTIS-USDC, Sills - Rm.1014, 5285 Port Royal Rd., Springfield, VA 22161. Phone: (703) 605-6400; Sales Division, (800) 553-6847.

Internet: http://www.ntis.gov; Homeland Security Information Center, http://www.ntis.gov/hs; Sales Division, e-mail, info@ntis.gov. (Note: no field offices for this program.)

OFFICE OF THE SECRETARY

11.702 INTERNSHIP PROGRAM FOR POSTSECONDARY STUDENTS ("Postsecondary Internship Program")

Assistance: project grants (100 percent/3 years).

Purposes: to aid and promote experiential training activities through internships fostering future employment at USDC or the federal government in general—primarily in the Washington, DC area.

Eligible applicants: 2- and 4-year IHEs including graduate and law schools, nonprofit organizations.

Eligible beneficiaries: postsecondary students.

Range: $196,000 to $514,000. **Average:** $289,000.

Activity: FY 05, 110 internships.

HQ: Office of Human Resources Management, OS-USDC, Washington, DC 20230. Phone: (202) 482-1445.

Internet: www.ohrm.doc.gov/internwebsite/htm. (Note: no field offices for this program.)

MINORITY BUSINESS DEVELOPMENT AGENCY

11.800 MINORITY BUSINESS ENTERPRISE CENTERS ("MBDC")

Assistance: project grants (85 percent/1-3 years).

Purposes: for the operation of electronic MBDCs—i.e., organizations offering electronic and one-on-one business development services and technical assistance in all phases of business development and management by existing or proposed minority firms. No loans are offered to businesses. Client service fees may be charged.

Eligible applicants/beneficiaries: state and local governments, tribes, educational institutions, nonprofit and profit organizations, individuals.

Range: $155,000 to $400,000.

Activity: FY 05 estimate, 26 MBDCs funded.

HQ: Office of Business Development, MBDA-USDC, 14th & Constitution Ave. NW, Washington, DC 20230. Phone: (202) 482-1940.

Internet: http://www.mbda.gov.

11.801 NATIVE AMERICAN BUSINESS ENTERPRISE CENTERS ("NABEC")

Assistance: project grants (100 percent/1-3 years).

Purposes: for eight designated Native American Business Development Centers (NABDCs) to provide electronic and one-on-one business development and technical assistance of all types to new or existing American Indian businesses. No loans or grants are awarded to individual businesses under this program; however, businesses may be helped in obtaining financial assistance for their operations.

Eligible applicants/beneficiaries: state and local governments, tribes, educational institutions, nonprofit and profit organizations, individuals.

Range: $155,000 to $288,000.

Activity: estimate FY 06/07, 1229 clients with $117,776,442 in financings and contracts.

HQ: Office of Business Development, MBDA-USDC, 14th & Constitution Ave. NW, Washington, DC 20230. Phone: (202) 482-1940.

Internet: www.mbda.gov.

11.803 MINORITY BUSINESS OPPORTUNITY CENTER ("MBOC")

Assistance: project grants (from 50 percent/1-2 years).

Purposes: for MBOCs to provide minority businesses and individuals with enhanced access to markets by identifying and facilitating procurement and contract awards, marketing and sales opportunities, financing resources, potential joint venture partners, timely market leads, and other business information.

Eligible applicants/beneficiaries: federal, state, local government or quasi-governmental entities; tribes, IHEs, and nonprofit and profit organizations.

Range: $150,000 to $300,000.

Activity: FY 05, $366,200,000 in financial transactions generated.

HQ: Office of Business Development, MBDA-USDC, 14th & Constitution Ave. NW, Washington, DC 20230. Phone: (202) 482-1940.

Internet: www.mbda.gov.

PATENT AND TRADEMARK OFFICE

11.900 PATENT AND TRADEMARK TECHNICAL INFORMATION DISSEMINATION

Assistance: technical information.

Purposes: to support the growth of American commerce and technology through the utilization and dissemination of technical information available through patents and trademarks, and for the maintenance of public search centers. The office examines patent and trademark applications, and grants patents and approves trademarks when legal requirements are met. Fees are charged for services.

Eligible applicants/beneficiaries: general public.

Range/Average: N.A.

Activity: annually (representative), processing of more than 839,000 customer requests for general patent and trademark information served through a network of 83 Patent and Trademark Depository Libraries.

HQ: General Information Services, U.S. Patent and Trademark Office-USDC, Alexandria, VA 20313-1450. Phone: General Information Services, (703) 308-4357, (800) 786-9199.

Internet: http://www.uspto.gov.

DEPARTMENT OF DEFENSE

DEFENSE LOGISTICS AGENCY

12.002 PROCUREMENT TECHNICAL ASSISTANCE FOR BUSINESS FIRMS ("PTA Cooperative Agreement Program")

Assistance: project grants (50-75 percent).

Purposes: to establish and operate new or existing procurement technical assistance programs to assist business firms in selling their goods and services to DOD, other federal agencies, and state and local governments.

Eligible applicants/beneficiaries: state and local governments, private nonprofit organizations, tribal organizations, profit or nonprofit Indian economic enterprises.

Range: $30,000 to $300,000. **Average:** $160,000.

Activity: FY 02 estimate, 66 cooperative agreements.

HQ: Office of Small and Disadvantaged Business Utilization (DDAS), Defense Logistics Agency-DOD, 8725 John J. Kingman Rd. - Ste.2533, Ft. Belvoir, VA 22060-6221. Phone: (703) 767-1650.

Internet: www.d/a.mil/ddas. (Note: no field offices for this program.)

DEPARTMENT OF THE ARMY, OFFICE OF THE CHIEF OF ENGINEERS

12.100 AQUATIC PLANT CONTROL

Assistance: specialized services; technical information.

Purposes: pursuant to the River and Harbor Act of 1958 as amended, to assist in controlling and eradicating obnoxious aquatic plants in rivers, harbors, and allied waters. Localities must provide 50 percent matching funds.

Eligible applicants/beneficiaries: states, political subdivisions, instrumentalities.

Range/Average: N.A.

Activity: N.A.

HQ: Commander, U.S. Army Corps of Engineers - Attn: CECW-ON, DOD, Washington, DC 20314-1000. Phone: (202) 272-0247.

Internet: http://www.usace.army.mil/business.html.

12.101 BEACH EROSION CONTROL PROJECTS ("Small Beach Erosion Control Projects")

Assistance: specialized services; technical information.

Purposes: pursuant to the River and Harbor Act of 1962 as amended, to design and construct beach and shore erosion control projects not specifically authorized by Congress. The Corps funds the first $100,000 in planning costs, and 50 percent of additional study costs; localities must provide the balance. Cost-sharing is required for construction, with a $2,000,000 maximum federal share.

Eligible applicants/beneficiaries: states, political subdivisions, other authorized local agencies.

Range/Average: N.A.

Activity: N.A.

HQ: U.S. Army Corps of Engineers - Attn: CECW-PM, DOD, Washington, DC 20314-1000. Phone: (202) 761-1975.

Internet: http://www.usace.army.mil/business.html.

12.102 EMERGENCY REHABILITATION OF FLOOD CONTROL WORKS OR FEDERALLY AUTHORIZED COASTAL PROTECTION WORKS ("Public Law 84-99, Code 300 Program")

Assistance: specialized services.

Purposes: pursuant to the Flood Control Act of 1941 as amended, to assist in the emergency repair or rehabilitation of flood control works damaged by flood, or federally authorized hurricane flood and shore protection works damaged by extraordinary wind, wave, or water action. Nonfederal sources must provide 20 percent of project costs.

Eligible applicants/beneficiaries: owners of damaged flood protective works, or state and local public entities responsible for their maintenance, repair, and operation.

Range/Average: N.A.

Activity: 200 individual projects since 1993 Midwest flood (latest available data).

HQ: Commander, U.S. Army Corps of Engineers - Attn: CECW-OE, DOD, Washington, DC 20314-1000. Phone: (202) 272-0251.

Internet: http://www.usace.army.mil/business.html.

12.103 EMERGENCY OPERATIONS FLOOD RESPONSE AND POST FLOOD RESPONSE ("Public Law 84-99, Code 200 Program")

Assistance: specialized services.

Purposes: pursuant to the Flood Control Act of 1941 as amended, to provide emergency assistance in all phases of flood fighting, and post-flood response and rescue operations in times of flood or coastal storm.

Eligible applicants/beneficiaries: state or local public agencies.

Range/Average: N.A.

Activity: annually, 50 to 250 operations.

HQ: Commander, U.S. Army Corps of Engineers - Attn: CECW-OE, DOD, Washington, DC 20314-1000. Phone: (202) 272-0251.

Internet: http://www.usace.army.mil/business.html.

12.104 FLOOD PLAIN MANAGEMENT SERVICES ("FPMS")

Assistance: advisory services/counseling; technical information.

Purposes: pursuant to the Flood Control Act of 1960 as amended, to promote recognition of flood hazards in land and water use planning and development, by providing and interpreting historical data maintained by the Corps on floods and flood plains areas subject to flooding and flood losses from streams, lakes, and oceans. Services are available to states and local governments on a reimbursable basis; fees are charged to private parties.

Eligible applicants/beneficiaries: states, political subdivisions, general public.

Range/Average: N.A.

Activity: N.A.

HQ: U.S. Army Corps of Engineers - Attn: CECW-PF, DOD, Washington, DC 20314-1000. Phone: (202) 761-0169.

Internet: http://www.usace.army.mil/business.html.

12.105 PROTECTION OF ESSENTIAL HIGHWAYS, HIGHWAY BRIDGE APPROACHES, AND PUBLIC WORKS ("Emergency Bank Protection")

Assistance: specialized services.

Purposes: pursuant to the Flood Control Act of 1946 as amended, to design and construct projects protecting highways, highway bridges, essential public works, churches, hospitals, schools, and other nonprofit public services endangered by flood-caused erosion. Federal costs are limited to $1,000,000 per project; localities are responsible for costs in excess.

Eligible applicants/beneficiaries: states, political subdivisions, other authorized local agencies.

Range/Average: N.A.

Activity: N.A.

HQ: U.S. Army Corps of Engineers - Attn: CECW-PM, DOD, Washington, DC 20314-1000. Phone: (202) 761-1975.

Internet: http://www.usace.army.mil/business.html.

12.106 FLOOD CONTROL PROJECTS ("Small Flood Control Projects")

Assistance: specialized services.

Purposes: pursuant to the Flood Control Act of 1948 as amended, to design and construct flood control projects not specifically authorized by Congress. The Corps funds the first $100,000 in planning costs, and 50 percent of additional study costs; localities must provide the balance. Cost-sharing is required for construction, with a $7,000,000 maximum federal share.

Eligible applicants/beneficiaries: states, political subdivisions, other authorized local agencies.

Range/Average: N.A.

Activity: N.A.

HQ: U.S. Army Corps of Engineers - Attn: CECW-PM, DOD, Washington, DC 20314-1000. Phone: (202) 761-1975.

Internet: http://www.usace.army.mil/business.html.

12.107 NAVIGATION PROJECTS ("Small Navigation Projects")

Assistance: specialized services.

Purposes: pursuant to the River and Harbor Act of 1960 as amended, to design and construct small general navigation projects not specifically authorized by Congress. The federal cost limit is $4,000,000 per project; localities must provide a share of study costs, and pay construction costs exceeding the federal maximum.

Eligible applicants/beneficiaries: states, political subdivisions, other authorized local agencies.

Range/Average: N.A.

Activity: N.A.

HQ: U.S. Army Corps of Engineers - Attn: CECW-PM, DOD, Washington, DC 20314-1000. Phone: (202) 761-1975.

Internet: http://www.usace.army.mil/business.html.

12.108 SNAGGING AND CLEARING FOR FLOOD CONTROL ("Section 208")

Assistance: specialized services.

Purposes: pursuant to the Flood Control Act of 1937 as amended, to design and construct snagging and clearing projects for flood control. The federal cost limit is $500,000 per project; localities must share in construction costs.

Eligible applicants/beneficiaries: states, political subdivisions, other authorized local agencies.

Range/Average: N.A.

Activity: N.A.

HQ: U.S. Army Corps of Engineers - Attn: CECW-PM, DOD, Washington, DC 20314-1000. Phone: (202) 761-1975.

Internet: http://www.usace.army.mil/business.html.

12.109 PROTECTION, CLEARING AND STRAIGHTENING CHANNELS ("Section 3 Emergency Dredging Projects")

Assistance: specialized services.

Purposes: pursuant to the River and Harbor Act of 1945 as amended, for the emergency protection, clearing, and straightening of navigation channels in rivers, harbors, and other waterways, including for flood control purposes. Localities must provide maintenance.

Eligible applicants/beneficiaries: states, political subdivisions, other authorized local agencies.

Range/Average: N.A.

Activity: no current projects.

HQ: Commander, U.S. Army Corps of Engineers - Attn: CECW-OD, DOD, Washington, DC 20314-1000. Phone: (202) 272-8835.

Internet: http://www.usace.army.mil/business.html.

12.110 PLANNING ASSISTANCE TO STATES ("Section 22")

Assistance: specialized services.

Purposes: pursuant to the Water Resources Development Act of 1974 as amended, to assist states in preparing comprehensive plans for the development, utilization, or conservation of water and related land resources of drainage basins. No state may receive more than $500,000 in assistance in any one year; 50 percent cost sharing is required.

Eligible applicants/beneficiaries: states, tribes, territories.

Range/Average: N.A.

Activity: N.A.

HQ: U.S. Army Corps of Engineers - Attn: CECW-PF, DOD, Washington, DC 20314-1000. Phone: (202) 272-0169.

Internet: http://www.usace.army.mil/business.html.

12.111 EMERGENCY ADVANCE MEASURES FOR FLOOD PREVENTION ("Public Law 84-99, Code 500 Program")

Assistance: specialized services.

Purposes: pursuant to the Flood Control Act of 1941 as amended, to provide assistance when there is an immediate threat of unusual flooding, including such work as removal of waterway obstructions, dam failure prevention, and work necessary to prepare for abnormal snowmelt.

Eligible applicants/beneficiaries: state governors.

Range/Average: N.A.

Activity: N.A.

HQ: Commander, U.S. Army Corps of Engineers - Attn: CECW-OE, DOD, Washington, DC 20314-1000. Phone: (202) 272-0251.

Internet: http://www.usace.army.mil/business.html.

12.112 PAYMENTS TO STATES IN LIEU OF REAL ESTATE TAXES

Assistance: formula grants (100 percent).

Purposes: pursuant to the Flood Control Acts of 1941, 1946, and 1954 as amended, to compensate local taxing units for loss of real estate taxes lost as the result of federal acquisition of land for flood control, navigation, hydroelectric power projects, and allied purposes. Funds are derived from federal receipts from leases covering such lands, 75 percent of which are distributed through this program.

Eligible applicants: state governments.

Eligible beneficiaries: state, county governments.

Range/Average: N.A.

Activity: N.A.

HQ: Headquarters - Attn: CERM-FC, U.S. Army Corps of Engineers, DOD, 20 Massachusetts Ave. NW, Washington, DC 20314-1000. Phone: (202) 272-1931.

Internet: http://www.usace.army.mil/business.html. (Note: no field offices for this program.)

12.113 STATE MEMORANDUM OF AGREEMENT PROGRAM FOR THE REIMBURSEMENT OF TECHNICAL SERVICES ("DSMOA")

Assistance: project grants (100 percent/2 years).

Purposes: pursuant to CERCLA as amended and Superfund amendments, to reimburse states for costs incurred to provide technical services in support of the DOD Environmental Restoration Program, in cleaning up DOD hazardous wastes sites.

Eligible applicants: state, territorial governments.

Eligible beneficiaries: state, local, territorial governments; public, private, nonprofit and profit organizations.

Range: $104,000 to $11,400,000.

Activity: to date, 4 territories and 38 states entered into the program; 27 awards have been made.

HQ: Corps of Engineers, CEMP-RI, DOD, 20 Massachusetts Ave. NW, Washington, DC 20314. Phone: (202) 504-4950.

Internet: http://www.usace.army.mil/business.html. (Note: no field offices for this program.)

12.114 COLLABORATIVE RESEARCH AND DEVELOPMENT ("Construction Productivity Advanced Research Program" - "CPAR")

Assistance: project grants (50 percent).

Purposes: pursuant to the Water Resources Development Act of 1988, to improve construction productivity through research and development and application of advanced technologies involving collaborative projects, field demonstrations, licensing agreements, and other means of commercialization and technology transfer. Corps laboratories must perform a significant portion of projects.

Eligible applicants/beneficiaries: U.S. private firms including corporations, partnerships, and industrial development organizations; public and private foundations; nonprofit organizations; units of state or local government; academic institutions; other.

Range: $200,000 to $900,000. **Average:** $400,000.

Activity: 76 projects to date.

HQ: Headquarters - Attn: CERD-C, U.S. Army Corps of Engineers, DOD, 20 Massachusetts Ave. NW, Washington, DC 20314-1000. Phone: (202) 272-1846.

Internet: http://www.usace.army.mil/business.html.

12.116 DEPARTMENT OF DEFENSE APPROPRIATION ACT OF 2003 ("Section 8044")

Assistance: specialized services.

Purposes: pursuant to the Act, to develop a system for prioritization of environmental impacts mitigation and costs to complete estimates for mitigation on Indian lands resulting from DOD activities, including: training and technical assistance to tribes; related administrative support; information gathering; documenting environmental damage.

Eligible applicants/beneficiaries: states, tribes, territories and possessions.

Range/Average: N.A.

Activity: new program listing in FY 03.

HQ: U.S. Army Corps of Engineers - Attn: CEMP-RF, DOD, Washington, DC 20314-1000. Phone: (202) 761-5145.

Internet: none.

DEPARTMENT OF THE NAVY, OFFICE OF THE CHIEF OF NAVAL RESEARCH

12.300 BASIC AND APPLIED SCIENTIFIC RESEARCH

Assistance: project grants (100 percent).

Purposes: for basic and applied research and training in the physical, mathematical, environmental, engineering, and life sciences, leading to the improvement of naval operations; for programs encouraging careers in those disciplines by supporting outstanding graduate, undergraduate, and high school students; to increase the number of graduates from under-represented minority groups; to assist universities in buying major high-cost research equipment; for symposia.

Eligible applicants/beneficiaries: nonprofit private and public IHEs and other research organizations.

Range: $1,000 to $15,000,000. **Average:** $111,000.

Activity: FY 02 estimate, 1,200 new grants (latest data available).

HQ: Office of Naval Research (ONR 22), Department of the Navy- DOD, 800 N. Quincy St., Arlington, VA 22217-5000. Phone: (703) 696-2570.

Internet: http://www.onr.navy.mil. (Note: no field offices for this program.)

12.350 DEPARTMENT OF DEFENSE HIV/AIDS PREVENTION PROGRAM

Assistance: project grants.

Purposes: to train and assist select foreign militaries with establishing and implementing HIV/AIDS prevention, care and treatment programs for their military personnel and dependents.

Eligible applicants/beneficiaries: anyone, especially U.S. non-governmental organizations and educational institutions. Individuals may not apply.

Range: $50,000 to $1,500,000.

Activity: N.A.

HQ: Department of Defense HIV/AIDS Prevention Program, Naval Health Research Center, PO Box 85122, San Diego, CA 92186-5122 Phone: (619) 553-8528.

Internet: www.nhrc.navy.mil/programs/dhapp/index.html (Note: no field offices for this program.)

12.351 BASIC SCIENTIFIC RESEARCH - COMBATING WEAPONS OF MASS DESTRUCTION

Assistance: project grants.

Purposes: to support and stimulate basic, applied, and advanced scientific research and technology at accredited educational or research institutions, nonprofit organizations, and commercial firms with an emphasis on innovative methods for combating or countering WMDs.

Eligible applicants/beneficiaries: in general, private and public nonprofit accredited institutions of higher learning that carry out research or education in science and/or engineering. Some awards are available for nonprofit, commercial or federal laboratories for basic research. No awards made to individuals.

Range/Average: $450,000.

Activity: FY 07, 33 grants awarded to 27 universities.

HQ: Defense Threat Reduction Agency BE-BC, 8725 John J. Kingman Rd., MS 6201, Ft. Belvoir, VA 22060-6201. Phone: (703) 767-5870, FAX: (703) 767-4450, Toll-free: (800) 701-5096.

Internet: www.dtra.mil/be/business_opp/procurement/acq_procopp.cfm. (Note: no field offices for this program.)

12.352 SCIENTIFIC RESEARCH - COMBATING WEAPONS OF MASS DESTRUCTION

Assistance: project grants (50-100 percent).

Purposes: to support and stimulate basic, applied, and advanced scientific research and technology at accredited educational or research institutions, nonprofit organizations, and commercial firms with an emphasis on innovative methods for combating or countering WMDs.

Eligible applicants/beneficiaries: any domestic or foreign industrial/commercial concerns including small business; accredited degree-granting institutions of higher learning; nonprofit organizations; and certain DoD and DOE-sponsored Federally Funded Research and Development Centers (FFRDCs). No awards are made to U.S. government agencies and organizations, individuals and federal academic institutions or laboratories not specifically identified in DFARS 235-071-1.

Range/Average: N.A.

Activity: N.A.

HQ: Defense Threat Reduction Agency, 8725 John J. Kingman Rd., MS 6201, Ft. Belvoir, VA 22060-6201. Phone: (703) 767-5870, FAX: (703) 767-4450, Toll-free: (800) 701-5096.

Internet: www.dtra.mil. (Note: no field offices for this program.)

12.360 RESEARCH ON CHEMICAL AND BIOLOGICAL DEFENSE

Assistance: project grants (100 percent/to 5 years).

Purposes: to further the capability to prevent, detect, diagnose, and treat the effects of chemical, radiological, and biological warfare agents.

Eligible applicants: public or private educational institutions, nonprofit organizations operated for public interest, and commercial firms.

Eligible beneficiaries: independent investigators associated with an applicant organization.

Range/Average: N.A.

Activity: N.A.

HQ: Chemical and Biological Medical Systems, 64 Thomas Johnson Dr., Frederick, MD 21702. Phone: (302) 619-2895.

Internet: www.jpeocbd.osd.mil. (Note: no field offices for this program.)

NATIONAL GUARD BUREAU

12.400 MILITARY CONSTRUCTION, NATIONAL GUARD

Assistance: project grants (75-100 percent).

Purposes: to provide facilities for training and administering Army and Air Force National Guard units. Funds may be used for armories or to provide offices, storage, assembly areas, rifle ranges, and classrooms. For non-armories, funds may provide for maintenance, supply, training, and other logistical and administrative expenses.

Eligible applicants/beneficiaries: states, DC, territories and possessions.

Range: from $300,000.

Activity: FY 02 estimate, 5 armory, 23 non-armory projects (latest available data).

HQ: Chief of Installations (NGB-ARI), National Guard Bureau, Department of the Army-DOD, ARNG Readiness Center, DOD, 111 S. George Mason Drive, Arlington, VA 22204-1382. Phone: (703) 607- 7900.

Internet: http://www.ngb.dtic.mil/indexshtm/. (Note: no field offices for this program.)

12.401 NATIONAL GUARD MILITARY OPERATIONS AND MAINTENANCE (O&M) PROJECTS

Assistance: project grants (75-100 percent).

Purposes: for services provided by states for such National Guard activities as real property maintenance and repair, environmental resources management and services, security guard services, electronic security systems, telecommunications services, air traffic control, automated target systems, recruitment, fire protection, and related activities.

Eligible applicants/beneficiaries: states, DC, PR, VI, Guam.

Range: from $100,000.

Activity: not quantified specifically.

HQ: *National Guard Bureaus*—Army National Guard Bureau, Department of the Army-DOD, ARNG Readiness Center, 111 S. George Mason Drive, Arlington, VA 22204-1382. Phone: Real Property O&M Projects, (703) 607-7922; Environmental Resources Management,.

Internet: http://www.ngb.dtic.mil/indexshtm/. (Note: no field offices for this program.)

12.404 NATIONAL GUARD CIVILIAN YOUTH OPPORTUNITIES ("National Guard ChalleNGe Program")

Assistance: formula grants (60 percent).

Purposes: to use the National Guard to provide military-based training to civilian youth that have graduated from secondary school, including supervised work experience in community service and conservation projects—to improve their life skills and employment potential. Funds may support civilian personnel hired to conduct the program.

Eligible applicants/beneficiaries: states and territories.

Range/Average: N.A.

Activity: 25 states participating; 22,000 graduates to date.

HQ: Youth Programs Division (NGB/NGB-YP), National Guard Bureau, Department of the Army-DOD, 1411 Jefferson Davis Hwy (JP1), Arlington, VA 22202-3221. Phone: (703) 607-5975.

Internet: http://www.ngb.dtic.mil/indexshtm/. (Note: no field offices for this program.)

U.S. ARMY MEDICAL COMMAND

12.420 MILITARY MEDICAL RESEARCH AND DEVELOPMENT

Assistance: project grants. (100 percent/to 5 years).

Purposes: for fundamental basic and applied medical research projects that expand the technology base or understanding of biological-medical processes. Project examples: analysis of investigational drugs in biological fluids; altered response to infection induced by severe injury; conferences and symposia.

Eligible applicants/beneficiaries: public, quasi-public, or private nonprofit institutions and organizations; specialized groups.

Range: $100,000 to $5,000,000. **Average:** $650,000.

Activity: not quantified specifically.

HQ: U.S. Army Medical Research and Material Command-DOD (ATTN: MCMR-ACQ-BA), Fort Detrick, Frederick, MD 21702-5012. Phone: (301) 619-7216; Army Medical Research Acquisition Activity (ATTN: SGRD-RMA-RC), (301) 619-2036.

Internet: http://mrmc-www.army.mil; http://cdmrp.army.mil. (Note: the field office serves as headquarters for this program.)

U.S. ARMY MATERIEL COMMAND

12.431 BASIC SCIENTIFIC RESEARCH

Assistance: project grants (100 percent/3-5 years).

Purposes: for basic research in the mathematical, physical, engineering, biological, and geosciences related to the improvement of Army programs or operations. Funds may support: programs encouraging careers for outstanding graduate, undergraduate, and high school students; increases in the number of graduates from under-represented minority groups; symposia; purchases of major high-cost research equipment.

Eligible applicants/beneficiaries: educational institutions, nonprofit scientific research organizations.

Range: $25,000 to $1,000,000.

Activity: N.A.

HQ: U.S. Army Research Office-DOD (ATTN: AMXRO-RT), Research Triangle Park, NC 27709-2211. Phone: (919) 549-4204.

Internet: http://www.amc.army.mil. (Note: no field offices for this program.)

ASSISTANT SECRETARY (STRATEGY AND REQUIREMENTS)

12.550 NATIONAL FLAGSHIP LANGUAGE PROGRAM GRANTS TO U.S. INSTITUTIONS OF HIGHER EDUCATION ("National Security Education Program - NSEP")

Assistance: project grants. (to 75 percent/1-2 years).

Purposes: to develop and strengthen IHE capabilities in critical language education, area studies, and international fields. International exchanges are ineligible for funding. The National Security Education Trust Fund supports this program.

Eligible applicants/beneficiaries: U.S. IHEs. Others may be included in proposals, but may not receive direct grants.

Range: $150,00 to $1,000,000 annually, for multi-year projects.

Activity: N.A.

HQ: NSEP, Under Secretary of Defense/Policy, Assistant Secretary/Strategy and Requirements, DOD, 1101 Wilson Blvd. - Ste.1210, Arlington, VA 22209-2248. Phone: (703) 696-1991.

Internet: www.ndu.edu/nsep. (Note: no field offices for this program.)

12.551 NATIONAL SECURITY EDUCATION—SCHOLARSHIPS

Assistance: project grants. (100 percent/2 academic terms per year).

Purposes: for undergraduate scholarships in critical languages and world area studies. Recipients must agree to work in a federal organization or in higher education for a time equal to the award period. Studies may be conducted abroad. International exchanges are ineligible for funding. The National Security Education Trust Fund supports this program.

Eligible applicants/beneficiaries: U.S. citizens enrolled in public or private two- or four-year IHEs. Students in federal government schools are ineligible.

Range: to $8,000/academic term.

Activity: since 1993 program inception, 800 awards in all 50 states.

HQ: NSEP, Under Secretary of Defense/Policy, Assistant Secretary/Strategy and Requirements, DOD, 1101 Wilson Blvd. - Ste.1210, Arlington, VA 22209-2248. Phone: (703) 696-1991.

Internet: www.ndu.edu/nsep (Note: no field offices for this program.)

12.552 NATIONAL SECURITY EDUCATION PROGRAM DAVID L. BOREN FELLOWSHIPS

Assistance: project grants (100 percent/one semester to 2 years).

Purposes: for graduate fellowships in critical languages and world area studies. All Boren Fellowship recipients must agree to work in a federal organization for a time equal to the award period but not less than one year. Studies may be conducted abroad.

Eligible applicants/beneficiaries: U.S. citizens enrolled in graduate programs in public or private U.S. IHEs. Students in federal government schools are ineligible.

Range: overseas study, to $24,000; domestic study, to $12,000; maximum to $30,000. **Average:** $20,000 per fellow.

Activity: since 1996, over 1100 fellowships awarded in all 50 states and DC.

HQ: NSEP, DOD, 1101 Wilson Blvd. - Ste.1210, Arlington, VA 22209-2248 Phone: (703) 696-1991; Or, Institute of International Education, NSEP

David L. Boren Fellowship Program, 1400 K Street, NW, Washington, DC 20005-2403 Phone: (800) 618-6737.

Internet: www.iie.org/programs/nsep/graduate; e-mail, nsepo@ndu.edu *or* nsep@iie.org (Note: no field offices for this program.)

12.553 NATIONAL FLAGSHIP LANGUAGE PROGRAM FELLOWSHIPS

Assistance: project grants (100 percent/to 2 years).

Purposes: for fellowships to address the urgent and growing need for Americans with professional levels of competency in languages critical to national security. All Flagship Fellowship recipients must agree to work in a federal organization for a time equal to the award period but not less than one year. Studies may be conducted abroad.

Eligible applicants/beneficiaries: U.S. citizens with superior level proficiency in English and minimum proficiency in the appropriate foreign language, possessing an undergraduate degree at the time of beginning NFLP Fellowship, and not currently employed by U.S. government. Past recipients of NSEP Boren scholarships or fellowships are eligible and encouraged to apply.

Range: $30,000 to $60,000 covers all program costs for 1 to 2 academic years. **Average:** $38,000 per fellow.

Activity: since 2003, 100 Flagship Fellowships awarded.

HQ: NSEP, DOD, 1101 Wilson Blvd. - Ste.1210, Arlington, VA 22209-2248 Phone: (703) 696-1991; Or, Institute of International Education, National Flagship Language Program, 1400 K Street, NW, Washington, DC 20005-2403 Phone: (800) 618-6737.

Internet: www.iie.org/programs/nsep/flagship; e-mail, nsepo@ndu.edu *or* flagship@iie.org (Note: no field offices for this program.)

12.554 ENGLISH FOR HERITAGE LANGUAGE SPEAKERS GRANTS TO U.S. INSTITUTIONS OF HIGHER EDUCATION

Assistance: project grants (100 percent).

Purposes: to provide intensive English language instruction for U.S. citizens who are native speakers of critical languages, with the goal of enabling participants to reach professional working proficiency in English in order to build a critical base of future leaders in government service and the broader professional community.

Eligible applicants/beneficiaries: U.S. private and public 2 and 4 year colleges and universities. Other organizations, agencies, associations, and foreign institutions may be included in proposals, but may not be direct recipients of a grant.

Range: $250,000 to $400,000. **Average:** $300,000.

Activity: new program 2006 (CFDA on-line version).

HQ: National Security Education Department, National Defense University, DOD, 1101 Wilson Blvd. - Ste.1210, Arlington, VA 22209-2248 Phone: (703) 696-1991 Or: Center for Applied Linguistics, 4646 40th St NW, Washington, DC 20016 Phone: (202) 355-1572.

Internet: www.cal.org/ehls (Note: no field offices for this program.)

12.555 ENGLISH FOR HERITAGE LANGUAGE SPEAKERS SCHOLARSHIPS

Assistance: project grants. (100 percent/6 months).

Purposes: to provide intensive English language instruction for U.S. citizens who are native speakers of critical languages, with the goal of enabling participants to reach professional working proficiency in English in order to build a critical base of future leaders in government service and the broader professional community.

Eligible applicants/beneficiaries: U.S. citizens with superior level proficiency in their native language and a minimum proficiency in English, possessing an undergraduate degree at the time of application, and not currently employed by U.S. government. Eligible native languages of interest are updated annually and available on the program web site.

Average: $24,000 per 6 month program.

Activity: new program 2006 (CFDA on-line version).

HQ: National Security Education Department, National Defense University, DOD, 1101 Wilson Blvd. - Ste.1210, Arlington, VA 22209-2248 Phone: (703) 696-1991 Or: Institute for International Education, English for Heritage Language Program, 1400 K St, NW, Washington, DC 20005-2403 Phone: (800) 618-6737.

Internet: www.cal.org/ehls (Note: no field offices for this program.)

OFFICE OF ECONOMIC ADJUSTMENT

12.607 COMMUNITY ECONOMIC ADJUSTMENT ASSISTANCE FOR ESTABLISHMENT, EXPANSION, REALIGNMENT, OR CLOSURE OF A MILITARY INSTALLATION ("Community Planning Assistance")

Assistance: project grants (75 percent).

Purposes: for community economic adjustment planning activities in coordination with communities, concerning military installation closures or realignment. Funds may be used for staffing, operating and administrative costs, studies.

Eligible applicants/beneficiaries: in DOD-approved areas—local governments or states on their behalf; regional organizations; tribes, DC, PR, Guam.

Range: $36,000 to $226,000. **Average:** $100,000.

Activity: 1990-2002, 73 communities reporting creation of 87,000 new jobs replacing 130,000 lost jobs.

HQ: Director, Office of Economic Adjustment, DOD, 400 Army-Navy Dr. - Ste.200, Arlington, VA 22202-4704. Phone: (703) 604-6020.

Internet: www.oea.gov; e-mail, oeafeedback@osd.gov.

12.610 COMMUNITY ECONOMIC ADJUSTMENT PLANNING ASSISTANCE FOR JOINT LAND USE STUDIES

Assistance: project grants (75 percent).

Purposes: pursuant to the Defense Authorization Act, to prepare joint military/community comprehensive land use plans concerning public or private land development around military installation, to assure that land uses are compatible with both military operations and plans of nonmilitary jurisdictions; in certain cases, to carry out the recommendations of such a study.

Eligible applicants/beneficiaries: in DOD-approved areas—local governments or states on their behalf; regional organizations; tribes, DC, PR, Guam.

Range: $45,000 to $90,000. **Average:** $70,000.

Activity: not quantified specifically.

HQ: Director, Office of Economic Adjustment, DOD, 400 Army-Navy Dr. - Ste.200, Arlington, VA 22202-4704. Phone: (703) 604-6020.

Internet: www.oea.gov; e-mail, oeafeedback@osd.gov.

12.611 COMMUNITY ECONOMIC ADJUSTMENT PLANNING ASSISTANCE FOR REDUCTIONS IN DEFENSE INDUSTRY EMPLOYMENT

Assistance: project grants (75 percent).

Purposes: for communities to undertake economic adjustment planning activities to respond to major reductions in defense industry employment resulting from the cancellation, termination, or failure to proceed with DOD spending under a previously approved program. Funds may be used for planning expenses including staffing, operating and administrative costs, studies.

Eligible applicants/beneficiaries: states on behalf of local governments, local governments, tribes, DC, PR, Guam—if the spending reduction involves the loss of at least: 2,500 full-time contractor employee jobs in a metropolitan statistical area; or1,000 jobs outside a metropolitan statistical area; or one percent of the total number of jobs in that area.

Range: $100,000 to $200,000. **Average:** $150,000.

Activity: not quantified specifically.

HQ: Director, Office of Economic Adjustment, DOD, 400 Army-Navy Dr. - Ste.200, Arlington, VA 22202-4704. Phone: (703) 604-6020.

Internet: www.oea.gov; e-mail, oeafeedback@osd.gov.

12.614 COMMUNITY ECONOMIC ADJUSTMENT DIVERSIFICATION PLANNING

Assistance: project grants (90 percent).

Purposes: for community economic adjustment planning activities to lessen dependence on military base-related defense spending; to prepare strategies and schematic plans for the potential reuse of redevelopment of active bases.

Eligible applicants/beneficiaries: states; local governments or states on their behalf; regional governmental organizations.

Range: to $175,000.

Activity: new program listing in 2005. Not quantified specifically.

HQ: Deputy Director, Office of Economic Adjustment, DOD, 400 Army-Navy Dr. - Ste.200, Arlington, VA 22202-4704. Phone: (703) 604-4828.

Internet: www.oea.gov.

OFFICE OF THE SECRETARY OF DEFENSE

12.630 BASIC, APPLIED, AND ADVANCED RESEARCH IN SCIENCE AND ENGINEERING

Assistance: project grants.

Purposes: for research in areas that cut across traditional academic disciplines, in mathematical, physical, engineering, environmental, life sciences, and other fields—with long-term potential for contributing to technology for DOD missions; for fellowships and research traineeships for graduate education.

Eligible applicants: private and public educational institutions.

Eligible beneficiaries: graduate and undergraduate students in science and engineering disciplines important to DOD.

Range: $1,000 to $3,000,000. **Average:** $120,000.

Activity: not quantified specifically.

HQ: contact the executive agents listed under "HQ" for programs **12.300**, **12.431**, **12.800**, or **12.910**.

Internet: http://www.usace.army.mil/business.html. (Note: no field offices for this program.)

SECRETARIES OF MILITARY DEPARTMENTS

12.700 DONATIONS/LOANS OF OBSOLETE DOD PROPERTY

Assistance: use of property, facilities, and equipment.

Purposes: to donate or lend obsolete combat material and other specified items for historical, ceremonial, or display purposes—including books, manuscripts, models, vessels. Recipients must pay packing and handling costs.

Eligible applicants/beneficiaries: veterans' organizations recognized by the Office of the Deputy Under Secretary of Defense (LIMDM); libraries, historical societies, educational institutions, and tax-exempt museums operated and maintained only for education purposes; municipalities, states, territories, and possessions.

Range/Average: N.A.

Activity: none.

HQ: appropriate military department, DOD, Pentagon, Washington, DC 20301.

Internet: http://www.usace.army.mil/business.html.

DEPARTMENT OF THE AIR FORCE, MATERIEL COMMAND

12.800 AIR FORCE DEFENSE RESEARCH SCIENCES PROGRAM

Assistance: project grants (1-3 years).

Purposes: for research to maintain technological superiority in scientific areas relevant to Air Force needs; to prevent technology surprise to the nation and to create it for adversaries; to maintain a strong research infrastructure composed of Air Force laboratories, industry, and universities; to complement the national research effort. Projects may be in such areas as the aerospace, engineering, chemistry and materials, and life, environmental, mathematical, and computer sciences.

Eligible applicants/beneficiaries: private and public educational institutions; private and public nonprofit organizations; commercial concerns.

Range: $50,000 to $5,000,000. **Average:** $500,000.

Activity: N.A.

HQ: HQ-Air Force Materiel Command/PKT, DOD, 4375 Childlaw Rd. - Ste.6, Wright-Patterson AFB, OH 45433-5006. Phone: (513) 257-8934.

Internet: http://www.usace.army.mil/business.html.

NATIONAL SECURITY AGENCY

12.900 LANGUAGE GRANT PROGRAM

Assistance: project grants (100 percent).

Purposes: to foster foreign language training of Americans. Funded projects have included documentation of low density languages, foreign language reference works, and research in training methods and computer-assisted instruction technologies.

Eligible applicants/beneficiaries: employees of U.S. private or public IHEs and nonprofit organizations operated primarily for language training.

Range: $5,000 to $500,000.

Activity: not quantified specifically.

HQ: Chief, Language Training, National Security Agency (ATTN: E41), DOD, Fort George Meade, MD 20755-6000. Phone: (410) 859- 6087.

Internet: http://www.darpa.mil/cmo. (Note: no field offices for this program.)

12.901 MATHEMATICAL SCIENCES GRANTS PROGRAM

Assistance: project grants. (100 percent/to 2 years).

Purposes: pursuant to the National Security Act of 1959, to stimulate developments and promote careers in areas of mathematics identified with cryptography, including number theory, discrete mathematics, statistics, probability. Funds may support summer salary (one month maximum), professional travel, publishing costs, graduate or postgraduate student support, conferences.

Eligible applicants/beneficiaries: employees and graduate students at U.S. IHEs, that are U.S. citizens, permanent residents, or intending to apply for citizenship.

Range: $5,000 to $60,000. **Average:** $15,000.

Activity: none.

HQ: National Security Agency (ATTN: R51A), DOD, Fort George Meade, MD 20755-6000. Phone: (301) 688-0400.

Internet: http://www.darpa.mil/cmo. (Note: no field offices for this program.)

12.902 INFORMATION SECURITY GRANT PROGRAM ("Information Security University Research Program - URP")

Assistance: project grants. (100 percent/1-2 years).

Purposes: for research to design, build, and maintain secure computing systems involving unclassified information; to develop and train computer science graduates to be recruited by NSA. Project examples: "Multilevel Secure Distributed Systems Security;" "Computer Misuse and Anomaly Detection." Funds may support summer salary (two months maximum), professional travel, publishing costs, graduate and postdoctoral student support, conferences.

Eligible applicants/beneficiaries: employees and graduate students at U.S. IHEs, that are U.S. citizens, permanent residents, or intending to apply for citizenship.

Range: $50,000 to $100,000. **Average:** $80,000.

Activity: 2002, 45 proposals received (latest data available).

HQ: Program Director, INFOSEC University Research Program, National Security Agency (ATTN: R23), DOD, 9840 O'Brien Rd., Fort George Meade, MD 20755-6000. Phone: (301) 688-0847, FAX (301) 688- 0255.

Internet: http://www.darpa.mil/cmo; e-mail, urp@tycho.ncsc.mil. (Note: no field offices for this program.)

ADVANCED RESEARCH PROJECTS AGENCY

12.910 RESEARCH AND TECHNOLOGY DEVELOPMENT

Assistance: project grants (50 percent/3-5 years).

Purposes: for basic and applied research and development in science and technology; for projects advancing the state of the art or resulting in fundamental changes in technology—in areas that may have military or dual-use applications. Funds may also support: symposia and conferences; programs encouraging careers in science, technology, and engineering, and an increase in the number of graduates from under-represented minority groups; university research instrumentation.

Eligible applicants/beneficiaries: grants—public and private educational institutions and nonprofit organizations. Cooperative agreements—educational institutions, nonprofit organizations, commercial firms.

Range: $100,000 to $100,000,000. **Average:** $1,150,000.

Activity: FY 02 estimate, 30 grant awards and 20 "other transactions.".

HQ: Director, Contract Management Office (CMO), Defense Advanced Research Projects Agency, DOD, 3701 N. Fairfax Drive, Arlington, VA 22203. Phone: (703) 696-2399.

Internet: http://www.darpa.mil/cmo. (Note: no field offices for this program.)fi214103-6.ws.

DEPARTMENT OF HOUSING AND URBAN DEVELOPMENT

NOTE: *For most HUD mortgage insurance programs, applications should be submitted to HUD-approved lenders authorized to act on mortgages covering single-family housing. Multifamily project proposals generally require HUD approval of prospective sponsors; pre-application conferences are held with HUD field offices to determine project feasibility, particularly if housing subsidies are sought.*

14.103 INTEREST REDUCTION PAYMENTS—RENTAL AND COOPERATIVE HOUSING FOR LOWER INCOME FAMILIES ("Section 236")

Assistance: direct payments/specified use; guaranteed/insured loans (loans, 40 years).

Purposes: pursuant to the National Housing Act (NHA) as amended, to subsidize interest costs for mortgages on rental or cooperative housing developed for the low- and moderate-income. Subsidies are paid directly to lenders during the term of the mortgage; payments are adjusted to equal the difference between market rate interest costs and as low as one percent, depending on the incomes of tenants who must pay at least 30 percent of their adjusted gross incomes toward rent. The program now is inactive except for commitments to existing projects; no new projects have been insured since 1992.

Eligible applicants: nonprofit, cooperative, builder-seller, investor-sponsor, and limited-distribution sponsors. Public bodies were ineligible.

Eligible beneficiaries: within certain locally determined income limits, families and individuals including the elderly or handicapped or those displaced by government action or natural disaster. Families with incomes exceeding eligibility for subsidies may occupy apartments, but with no benefit from subsidy payments.

Range/Average: N.A.

Activity: FY 92 status, 378,000 rental units insured, valued at $6.5 billion; program now inactive, no new applications accepted.

HQ: Director, Office of Multifamily Housing Management, Housing- HUD, Washington, DC 20410. Phone: (202) 708-3730.

Internet: www.hud.gov/offices/hsg//mfh/progdesc.cfm.

14.108 REHABILITATION MORTGAGE INSURANCE ("Section 203(k)")

Assistance: guaranteed/insured loans (30 years).

Purposes: pursuant to NHA as amended, to insure loans for rehabilitation, acquisition and rehabilitation, acquisition and relocation from another site, and rehabilitation, or rehabilitation and debt refinancing—for existing one- to four-unit residential buildings. Rehabilitation cost must be at least $5,000. Certain application fees must be paid by purchasers.

Eligible applicants/beneficiaries: individual purchasers (*see NOTE preceding* **14.103**).

Range: $172,632 maximum insurable loans for single-family units, $220,992 for two-family housing, $267,120 for three-family, $312,895 for four-family—which may be increased in high-cost areas (details available from HUD area offices).

Activity: FY 06, 2,928 loans insured.

HQ: (no address provided). Phone: (202) 708-2121.

Internet: www.hud.gov/offices/hsg/sfh/ins/singlefamily.cfm.

14.110 MANUFACTURED HOME LOAN INSURANCE—FINANCING PURCHASE OF MANUFACTURED HOMES AS PRINCIPAL RESIDENCES OF BORROWERS ("Title I")

Assistance: guaranteed/insured loans. (to 90 percent/15-25 years).

Purposes: pursuant to NHA as amended, to insure loans to manufactured home purchasers when the unit will be used as the principal residence. 5 percent down payments and fees must be provided by purchasers. Funding for this program includes **14.162**.

Eligible applicants/beneficiaries: anyone (*see NOTE preceding* **14.103**).

Range: to $48,600 (whether single or multiple modules).

Activity: FY 06 estimate, 4,067 loans.

HQ: Chief, Home Mortgage Insurance Division, Housing-HUD, 451 7th St. SW - Rm. 9272, Washington, DC 20410. Phone: (202) 708-2121.

Internet: www.hud.gov/progdesc/manuf14.cfm. (Note: no field offices for this program.)

14.112 MORTGAGE INSURANCE FOR CONSTRUCTION OR SUBSTANTIAL REHABILITATION OF CONDOMINIUM PROJECTS ("Section 234(d) Condominiums")

Assistance: guaranteed/insured loans. (to 90 percent/to 40 years).

Purposes: pursuant to NHA and Housing Act of 1964 as amended, to insure for the construction or substantial rehabilitation of multifamily housing structures by sponsors intending to sell individual units as condominiums; in turn, purchasers may obtain mortgage insurance through **14.133**. Funding for this program is included in **14.135**.

Eligible applicants/beneficiaries: private profit-motivated developers, public bodies, certain other sponsors (*see NOTE preceding* **14.103**).

Average: to 90 percent of replacement cost within statutory limits.

Activity: no loans insured in recent years.

HQ: Office of Multifamily Development, Housing-HUD, 451 Seventh St. SW, Washington, DC 20410. Phone: (202) 708-1142.

Internet: www.hud.gov/offices/hsg/hsgmulti.cfm.

14.117 MORTGAGE INSURANCE—HOMES ("Section 203(b)")

Assistance: guaranteed/insured loans (to 30 years).

Purposes: pursuant to NHA as amended, to insure loans to purchasers acquiring existing or newly constructed one- to four- unit housing. Mortgage indebtedness on existing housing owned by applicants may also be refinanced. Small down payments, certain closing costs, and other expenses must be covered by purchasers. Funding for this program includes **14.119**, **14.126**, **14.159**, **14.163**, **14.172**, and **14.175**.

Eligible applicants/beneficiaries: purchasers that will occupy insured units (*see NOTE preceding* **14.103**).

Range: $200,160 maximum insurable loans for single-family units, $256,248 for two-family housing, $309,744 for three-family, $384,936 for four-family—which may be increased in high-cost areas (details available from HUD area offices).

Activity: FY 05, 479,160 loans insured.

HQ: none; all contacts are with Homeownership Centers at field offices listed in Part IV.

Internet: www.hud.gov/offices/hsg/sfh/ins/sfh203b.cfm.

14.119 MORTGAGE INSURANCE—HOMES FOR DISASTER VICTIMS ("Section 203(h)")

Assistance: guaranteed/insured loans. (100 percent/to 30-35 years).

Purposes: pursuant to NHA as amended, to insure loans to enable disaster victims to acquire new or reconstructed existing single- family housing. Certain fees must be paid by purchasers. Funding for this program is included in **14.117**.

Eligible applicants/beneficiaries: victims of major disasters that will occupy acquired housing as their principal residence (*see NOTE preceding* **14.103**).

Range: to 100 per cent of the maximum limits: $200,160 maximum insurable loans for single-family units, $256,248 for two-family housing, $309,744 for three-family, $384,936 for four-family—which may be increased in high-cost areas (details available from HUD area offices).

Activity: FY 05, 96 loans insured.

HQ: none; all contacts are with Homeownership Centers at field offices listed in Part IV.

Internet: www.hud.gov80/progdesc/203h-dft.cfm.

14.122 MORTGAGE INSURANCE—HOMES IN URBAN RENEWAL AREAS ("Section 220 Homes")

Assistance: guaranteed/insured loans (to 30-35 years).

Purposes: pursuant to the Housing Act of 1954, to insure loans for new, existing, or rehabilitated, owner-occupied one- to 11- unit housing acquired or rehabilitated in approved urban renewal or code enforcement areas. Small down payments and fees must be paid by purchasers. Funding for this program is included in **14.133**.

Eligible applicants/beneficiaries: all families (*see NOTE preceding* **14.103**).

Range: $200,160 maximum insurable loans for single-family units, $256,248 for two-family housing, $309,744 for three-family, $384,936 for four-family, plus $9,165 for each unit over four.

Activity: FY 05, no mortgage endorsements.

HQ: none; all contacts are with Homeownership Centers at field offices listed in Part IV.

Internet: www.hud.gov/fha/sfh/sf_home.html.

14.123 MORTGAGE INSURANCE—HOUSING IN OLDER, DECLINING AREAS ("Section 223(e)")

Assistance: guaranteed/insured loans.

Purposes: pursuant to NHA as amended, for purchasers of existing, new, or rehabilitated single-family or multifamily housing in older declining areas where conditions are such that certain normal eligibility requirements for mortgage insurance cannot be met. HUD insures loans made under other programs (e.g., **14.135**); claims are paid from the Special Risk Insurance Fund. Small down payments and insurance fees may be required of beneficiaries. Funding for this program is included in **14.133**.

Eligible applicants: HUD-approved mortgagees.

Eligible beneficiaries: single-family houses—individuals or families. Multifamily sponsorship eligibility is determined by applicable program requirements.

Range: varies according to program under which mortgage is insured.

Activity: FY 05, 4 projects with 609 units insured; FY 06, no activity anticipated for this program.

HQ: none; all contacts are with field offices listed in Part IV.

Internet: www.hud.gov/fha/sfh/sf_home.html.

14.126 MORTGAGE INSURANCE—COOPERATIVE PROJECTS ("Section 213 Cooperatives")

Assistance: guaranteed/insured loans. (90-98 percent/to 40 years).

Purposes: pursuant to NHA as amended, Housing Acts of 1950 and 1956, and other acts, to insure loans for existing, new, or rehabilitated cooperative housing consisting of detached, semi- detached, row, walk-up, or elevator structures, with five units minimum. Certain fees must be paid by purchasers. Maximum mortgage term: "management-type" projects, 40 years; "sales-type," 35 years. Funding for this program is included in **14.117**.

Eligible applicants: nonprofit cooperatives, ownership housing corporations, or trusts that may sponsor projects directly, sell individual units to cooperative members, or purchase projects from investor-sponsors (*see NOTE preceding* **14.103**).

Eligible beneficiaries: members of cooperatives.

Range: $1,321,000 to $11,039,000; maximum mortgage to investor- sponsor, 90 percent of replacement cost; cooperative member, 98 percent—within statutory maximums for individual units under program **14.117**. **Average:** $6,300,000.

Activity: project sizes, from 24 to 119 units; average, 71 units.

HQ: Office of Multifamily Development, Housing-HUD, 451 Seventh St. SW, Washington, DC 20410. Phone: (202) 708-1142.

Internet: www.hud.gov/offices/hsg/hsgmulti.cfm.

14.127 MORTGAGE INSURANCE—MANUFACTURED HOME PARKS ("Section 207 Manufactured Home Parks")

Assistance: guaranteed/insured loans. (90 percent/to 40 years).

Purposes: pursuant to NHA as amended, to insure loans for manufactured home park development, new or rehabilitated, with five or more spaces. Funding for this program is included in **14.135**.

Eligible applicants: investors, builders, developers, others (*see NOTE preceding* **14.103**).

Eligible beneficiaries: families or individuals owning manufactured houses and leasing spaces.

Range: loans, $1,890,000 to $7,830,000. **Average:** $4,500,000.

Activity: FY 05, 1 manufactured home park with 173 spaces insured; estimated FY 06, no mortgages insured.

HQ: Office of Multifamily Development, Housing-HUD, 451 Seventh St. SW, Washington, DC 20410. Phone: (202) 708-1142.

Internet: www.hud.gov/offices/hsg/hsgmulti.cfm.

14.128 MORTGAGE INSURANCE—HOSPITALS ("Section 242 Hospitals")

Assistance: guaranteed/insured loans. (to 90 percent/to 25 years).

Purposes: pursuant to NHA as amended, to insure loans for acute care hospital construction, rehabilitation, or refinancing, including the costs of major movable equipment—including facilities designated as "Critical Access Hospitals.".

Eligible applicants/beneficiaries: profit or nonprofit hospitals licensed or regulated by the state, municipality, or other political subdivision.

Range: $10,000,000 to $94,020,000. **Average:** $40,698,000.

Activity: estimated FY 06, 8 mortgages.

HQ: Office of Insured Health Care Facilities, Housing-HUD, 451 Seventh St. SW - Rm.9224, Washington, DC 20410. Phone: (202) 708- 0599. *Or*: Division of Facilities Loans, HHS, Bethesda, MD 20814. Phone: (301) 443-5317.

Internet: www.hud.gov/groups/healthcare.cfm. (Note: no field offices for this program.)

14.129 MORTGAGE INSURANCE—NURSING HOMES, INTERMEDIATE CARE FACILITIES, BOARD AND CARE HOMES AND ASSISTED LIVING FACILITIES ("Section 232 Nursing Homes")

Assistance: guaranteed/insured loans.

Purposes: pursuant to NHA and Housing Act of 1959 as amended, and Housing and Urban Development Act of 1969, to insure loans for the purchase, construction, rehabilitation, or refinancing of nursing homes providing skilled nursing care or intermediate care facilities accommodating 20 or more patients, or board and care homes and assisted living facilities with five or more accommodations or units, or a combination of the foregoing types of facilities. Loans also may cover the cost of fire safety equipment and major equipment.

Eligible applicants/beneficiaries: investors, builders, developers, public entities, nursing homes, and private nonprofit corporations or associations (*see NOTE preceding* **14.103**).

Range: 40-year mortgage insurance on 90 percent loans for new or substantially rehabilitated facilities (95 percent for nonprofit sponsors); 35 years on 85 percent loans for refinanced existing HUD-insured facilities not requiring substantial rehabilitation (to 90 percent for nonprofit sponsors).

Activity: FY 05, 201 loans insured, with 23,278 beds total.

HQ: Office of Multifamily Development, Housing-HUD, 451 Seventh St. SW, Washington, DC 20412. Phone: (202) 708-1142.

Internet: www.hud.gov/offices/hsg/hsgmulti.cfm.

14.132 MORTGAGE INSURANCE—PURCHASE OF SALES-TYPE COOPERATIVE HOUSING UNITS ("Section 213 Sales")

Assistance: guaranteed/insured loans (30-35 years).

Purposes: pursuant to NHA as amended and Housing Act of 1950, to insure loans for purchases of new dwelling units by members of cooperatives in projects with at least five units. Small down payments are required. Funding for this program is included in **14.135**.

Eligible applicants: members of nonprofit cooperative ownership housing corporations or trusts (*see NOTE preceding* **14.103**).

Eligible beneficiaries: individual/families and nonprofit organizations.

Range: $200,160 maximum insurable loans for single-family units, $256,248 for two-family housing, $309,744 for three-family, $384,936 for four-family—which may be increased in high-cost areas (details available from HUD area offices).

Activity: included in report for **14.117**.

HQ: none; all contacts are with Homeownership Centers at field offices listed in Part IV.

Internet: www.hud.gov/progdesc/coops213.cfm.

14.133 MORTGAGE INSURANCE—PURCHASE OF UNITS IN CONDOMINIUMS ("Section 234(c)")

Assistance: guaranteed/insured loans (to 30-35 years).

Purposes: pursuant to NHA as amended, to insure loans to purchase new or existing individual units in condominium projects containing four or more dwellings. Units converted from rental to condominiums are insurable, provided: the conversion occurred more than one year prior to the application for insurance; mortgagor occupied the rental housing; conversion was sponsored by an approved tenants organization. Small down payments and fees must be paid by purchasers. Funding for this program includes **14.122**, **14.123**, **14.165**, **14.183**, and **14.184**.

Eligible applicants/beneficiaries: condominium purchasers (*see NOTE preceding* **14.103**).

Range: $200,160 maximum insurable loans for single-family units, $256,248 for two-family housing, $309,744 for three-family, $384,936 for four-family—which may be increased in high-cost areas (details available from HUD area offices).

Activity: FY 05, 30,224 loans insured.

HQ: none; all contacts are with Homeownership Centers at field offices listed in Part IV.

Internet: www.hud.gov/progdesc/234c-df.cfm.

14.134 MORTGAGE INSURANCE—RENTAL HOUSING ("Section 207")

Assistance: guaranteed/insured loans. (90 percent/to 40 years).

Purposes: pursuant to NHA as amended, to insure loans for the construction or rehabilitation of middle-income rental housing in detached, semidetached, row, walk-up, or elevator structures, with five units minimum. Funding for this program is included in **14.135**.

Eligible applicants/beneficiaries: investors, builders, developers, others (*see NOTE preceding* **14.103**).

Range: to 90 percent of value.

Activity: FY 05, 38 projects insured.

HQ: Office of Multifamily Development, Housing-HUD, 451 Seventh St. SW, Washington, DC 20412. Phone: (202) 708-1142.

Internet: www.hud.gov/offices/hsg/hsgmulti.cfm.

14.135 MORTGAGE INSURANCE—RENTAL AND COOPERATIVE HOUSING FOR MODERATE INCOME FAMILIES AND ELDERLY, MARKET INTEREST RATE ("Section 221(d)(3) and (4) Multifamily - Market Rate Housing")

Assistance: guaranteed/insured loans. (90-100 percent/to 40 years).

Purposes: pursuant to NHA as amended, to insure loans to sponsors of new or rehabilitated market-rate rental or cooperative housing developed for moderate-income families, the elderly, and the handicapped, including for "single-room occupancy" (**14.184**). Units may be in detached, semi-detached, row, walk-up, or elevator structures containing five units minimum. Funding for this program includes **14.112**, **14.127**, **14.132**, **14.134**, **14.138**, and **14.139**.

Eligible applicants: public, profit-motivated, limited- distribution, nonprofit, cooperative, builder-seller, investor, and general sponsors (*see NOTE preceding* **14.103**).

Eligible beneficiaries: all households regardless of income.

Range: Section 221(d)(3), to 90 percent of replacement cost for profit-motivated or limited-distribution sponsors; to 100 percent for public, cooperative, or nonprofit sponsors. Section 221(d)(4), to 90 percent of replacement cost—within statutory maximums; loans, $675,000 to $45,000,000. **Average:** $12,100,000.

Activity: FY 05, 452 projects with 55,344 units insured.

HQ: Office of Multifamily Development, Housing-HUD, 451 Seventh St. SW, Washington, DC 20412. Phone: (202) 708-1142.

Internet: www.hud.gov/offices/hsg/hsgmulti.cfm.

14.138 MORTGAGE INSURANCE—RENTAL HOUSING FOR THE ELDERLY ("Section 231")

Assistance: guaranteed/insured loans. (90-100 percent/to 40 years).

Purposes: pursuant to NHA as amended, to insure loans for rental housing for elderly or handicapped persons—in new or rehabilitated detached, semi-detached, walk-up, or elevator structures with a minimum of five units. Funding for this program is included in **14.135**.

Eligible applicants/beneficiaries: private profit-motivated investors, nonprofit sponsors (*see NOTE preceding* **14.103**).

Range: within statutory maximum per unit costs—nonprofit and public sponsors, 100 percent of replacement cost; other sponsors, 90 percent.

Activity: FY 05, 7 mortgages with 891 units.

HQ: Office of Multifamily Development, Housing-HUD, 451 Seventh St. SW, Washington, DC 20412. Phone: (202) 708-1142.

Internet: www.hud.gov/offices/hsg/hsgmulti.cfm.

14.139 MORTGAGE INSURANCE—RENTAL HOUSING IN URBAN RENEWAL AREAS ("Section 220 Multifamily")

Assistance: guaranteed/insured loans. (90 percent/40 years).

Purposes: pursuant to NHA as amended, to insure loans for new or rehabilitated rental housing located in urban renewal, code enforcement, or other approved public program areas including disaster areas; loans may also cover existing properties rehabilitated by a local public agency. Projects must include a minimum of two units, and may involve detached, semi-detached, walk-up, or elevator structures. Funding for this program is included in **14.135**.

Eligible applicants: private profit entities, public bodies, others (*see NOTE preceding* **14.103**).

Eligible beneficiaries: all families.

Range: to 90 percent of replacement cost; loans, $1,366,000 to $45,495,000. **Average:** $17,900,000.

Activity: FY 05, 14 projects insured with 1,398 total units.

HQ: Office of Multifamily Development, Housing-HUD, 451 Seventh St. SW, Washington, DC 20412. Phone: (202) 708-1142.

Internet: www.hud.gov/offices/hsg/hsgmulti.cfm.

14.142 PROPERTY IMPROVEMENT LOAN INSURANCE FOR IMPROVING ALL EXISTING STRUCTURES AND BUILDING OF NEW NONRESIDENTIAL STRUCTURES ("Title I")

Assistance: guaranteed/insured loans. (90 percent/20-30 years).

Purposes: pursuant to NHA as amended, to insure loans for property improvement for existing housing, including the cost of erecting new nonresidential structures that substantially protect or improve the livability or utility of the properties.

Eligible applicants/beneficiaries: owners of properties to be improved; lessees with a lease extending at least six months beyond loan maturity; purchasers under a land installment contract (*see NOTE preceding* **14.103**).

Range: $25,000 maximum for one-family dwelling or nonresidential structure; $12,000 maximum per unit for multifamily structures, not to exceed $60,000.

Activity: FY 05, 9,874 loans insured.

HQ: none; all contacts are with Homeownership Centers at field offices listed in Part IV.

Internet: www.hud.gov/offices/hsg/sfh/titlei_home.cfm.

14.149 RENT SUPPLEMENTS—RENTAL HOUSING FOR LOWER INCOME FAMILIES

Assistance: direct payments/specified use (to 40 years).

Purposes: pursuant to the Housing and Urban Development Act of 1965, to subsidize rents paid by lower-income tenants of certain HUD-insured and other housing. Assistance covers the difference between the rent paid by the tenant and up to 70 percent of the market rent, with the tenant paying between 25 and 30 percent of monthly adjusted income. This program is inactive except for commitments to existing projects.

Eligible applicants: eligible sponsors included nonprofit, cooperative, builder-seller, investor-sponsor, and limited- distribution mortgagors.

families with income within the limits for admission to Section 8 housing (see 14.856). Families may continue in occupancy if 30 percent of adjusted monthly income exceeds market rents, but subsidy may be adjusted downward or eliminated.

Range/Average: N.A.

Activity: N.A.; no new project commitments under this program.

HQ: Director, Office of Multifamily Housing Management, Housing- HUD, Washington, DC 20410. Phone: (202) 708-3730.

Internet: wwwhud.gov/offices/hsg/mfh/progdesc.

14.151 SUPPLEMENTAL LOAN INSURANCE—MULTIFAMILY RENTAL HOUSING ("Section 241(a)")

Assistance: guaranteed/insured loans. (90 percent/varying term).

Purposes: pursuant to NHA as amended, to insure loans for expansion or improvement of existing multifamily housing and health care facilities, including hospitals, group practice facilities, or nursing homes, already covered by HUD mortgage insurance—including energy conservation and purchase of major movable equipment for health facilities.

Eligible applicants/beneficiaries: owners of multifamily projects or facilities subject to a HUD-insured mortgage (*see NOTE preceding* **14.103**).

Range: to 90 percent of the value of the improvements; loans, $755,000 to $1,153,000. **Average:** $954,000.

Activity: FY 05, 15 mortgages insured, with 3,705 units/beds.

HQ: Office of Multifamily Development, Housing-HUD, 451 Seventh St. SW, Washington, DC 20411. Phone: (202) 708-2556.

Internet: www.hud.gov/offices/hsg/hsgmulti.cfm.

14.155 MORTGAGE INSURANCE FOR THE PURCHASE OR REFINANCING OF EXISTING MULTIFAMILY HOUSING PROJECTS ("Sections 223(f) and 207")

Assistance: guaranteed/insured loans. (85 percent/10-35 years).

Purposes: pursuant to NHA and Housing and Community Development Act of 1974 as amended, to insure loans for the purchase or refinancing existing rental multifamily housing not requiring substantial rehabilitation. The property must have five or more living units; three years must have elapsed from the later of completion of project construction or substantial rehabilitation, or beginning of occupancy to date of application for mortgage insurance; the remaining economic life must be long enough to permit at least a ten-year mortgage term.

Eligible applicants/beneficiaries: private or public mortgagors (*see NOTE preceding* **14.103**).

Range: repairs, maximum of 15 percent of estimated value after repairs or $6,500 per unit—more in high-cost areas; loans, $425,000 to $31,750,000. **Average:** $5,500,000.

Activity: FY 05, 197 projects with 23,174 total units insured.

HQ: Office of Multifamily Development, Housing-HUD, 451 Seventh St. SW, Washington, DC 20411. Phone: (202) 708-1142.

Internet: www.hud.gov/offices/hsg/hsgmulti.cfm.

14.157 SUPPORTIVE HOUSING FOR THE ELDERLY ("Section 202")

Assistance: direct payments/specified use.

Purposes: pursuant to the Housing Act of 1959 as amended, Housing and Community Development Act of 1992, and American Homeownership and Economic Opportunity Act of 2000, for the acquisition, construction, or substantial rehabilitation of rental or cooperative housing with supportive services and related facilities (e.g., central dining) for the very low-income elderly. Capital advances are provided by HUD to meet development costs; these advances need not be repaid, provided the project is available to the very-low-income elderly for 40 years. HUD project rental assistance payments may cover the difference between per-unit operating cost and the rent amount paid by tenants, under five-year contracts with project sponsors. Funding for this program includes **14.191**, **14.314**, and **14.315**.

Eligible applicants/beneficiaries: private nonprofit organizations and consumer cooperatives. Also, profit-motivated limited partnerships may participate in projects with mixed financing.

Range: $424,000 to $13,830,000. **Average:** $4,349,00.

Activity: FY 05, 4,719 units assisted.

HQ: Office of Housing Assistance and Grants Administration, Housing-HUD, Washington, DC 20410. Phone: (202) 708-3000.

Internet: www.hud.gov/offices/hsg/mfh/progrdesc/eld202.cfm.

14.159 SECTION 245 GRADUATED PAYMENT MORTGAGE PROGRAM

Assistance: guaranteed/insured loans (30 years).

Purposes: pursuant to NHA, Housing and Community Development Acts of 1974 and 1979, and amendments, to insure loans for existing or new single-family housing, and condominiums financed with graduated payment mortgages—allowing smaller monthly payments initially, and with increased amounts over time as the borrower's income increases. Small down payments are required, and mortgagors must pay certain closing costs. Funding for this program is included in **14.117**.

Eligible applicants/beneficiaries: prospective owner-occupants (*see NOTE preceding* **14.103**).

Range: basically, 97 percent of appraised value and closing costs minus deferred interest during graduated term.

Activity: FY 05 estimate, 1 loan insured.

HQ: none; all contacts are with Homeownership Centers at field offices listed in Part IV.

Internet: www.hud.gov/progdesc/245-dft.cfm.

14.162 MORTGAGE INSURANCE—COMBINATION AND MANUFACTURED HOME LOT LOANS ("Title I")

Assistance: guaranteed/insured loans. (90 percent/15-25 years).

Purposes: pursuant to NHA as amended, to insure loans to purchase manufactured homes and lots. The maximum term is 20 years for a single module and lot, 25 years for a double module, and 15 years for a lot only. Funding for this program is included in **14.110**.

Eligible applicants/beneficiaries: purchasers intending to use property as their principal place of residence (*see NOTE preceding* **14.103**).

Range: to $64,800 for a manufactured home and lot; to $16,200 for a developed lot only—more in high-cost areas.

Activity: FY 05, 4,067 loans insured.

HQ: Chief, Home Mortgage Insurance Division, Housing-HUD, 451 7th St. SW - Rm. 9272, Washington, DC 20410. Phone: (202) 708-2121; *and,* general information, phone: (800) 767-7468.

Internet: www.hud.gov/progdesc/manuf14.cfm. (Note: no field offices for this program.)

14.163 MORTGAGE INSURANCE—SINGLE FAMILY COOPERATIVE HOUSING ("Section 203(n)")

Assistance: guaranteed/insured loans (to 30 years).

Purposes: pursuant to NHA as amended and the Emergency Home Purchase Assistance Act of 1974, to insure loans to purchase the Corporate Certificate and Occupancy Certificate for a unit in a HUD-insured cooperative housing project covered by a blanket mortgage, giving purchasers the right to occupy the unit. Funding for this program is included in **14.117**.

Eligible applicants/beneficiaries: potential owner-occupant mortgagors (*see NOTE preceding* **14.103**).

Range: to maximums stipulated for **14.117**.

Activity: included in report for **14.117**.

HQ: none; all contacts are with Homeownership Centers at field offices listed in Part IV.

Internet: www.hud.gov80/progdesc/203n-df.cfm.

14.164 OPERATING ASSISTANCE FOR TROUBLED MULTIFAMILY HOUSING PROJECTS ("Flexible Subsidy Fund - Troubled Projects")

Assistance: direct payments/specified use (75-100 percent).

Purposes: pursuant to the Housing and Community Development Amendments of 1978 as amended, to restore or maintain the physical and financial soundness of HUD-assisted (i.e., subsidized) low- and moderate-income multifamily rental projects—through repairs, augmentation of replacement reserves, or funding of operating deficits. Owners, except nonprofits, must contribute at least 25 percent of the total needed.

Eligible applicants/beneficiaries: nonprofit owners with existing assisted housing program loans. Public bodies are ineligible. Field offices recommend projects to be assisted.

Range/Average: N.A.

Activity: FY 06, no activity anticipated.

HQ: Office of Housing Assistance and Grants Administration, Housing-HUD, Washington, DC 20420. Phone: (202) 708-2866.

Internet: www.hud.gov/offices//hsg/mfh/progdesc/progdesc.cfm.

14.165 MORTGAGE INSURANCE—HOMES—MILITARY IMPACTED AREAS ("Section 238(c)")

Assistance: guaranteed/insured loans (30-35 years).

Purposes: pursuant to NHA as amended, to insure loans for the purchase of existing, new, or to refinance one- to four-unit structures in areas impacted by military facilities. Small down payments are required, and mortgagors must pay certain closing costs. Funding for this program is included in **14.133**.

Eligible applicants/beneficiaries: purchasers in approved areas, intending to occupy the housing (*see NOTE preceding* **14.103**).

Range: $200,160 maximum insurable loans for single-family units, $256,248 for two-family housing, $309,744 for three-family, $384,936 for four-family—which may be increased in high-cost areas (details available from HUD area offices).

Activity: FY 05, no activity.

HQ: none; all contacts are with Homeownership Centers at field offices listed in Part IV.

Internet: www.hud.gov80/progdesc/snglindx.cfm.

14.167 MORTGAGE INSURANCE—TWO YEAR OPERATING LOSS LOANS, SECTION 223(D) ("Two Year Operating Loss Loans")

Assistance: guaranteed/insured loans.

Purposes: pursuant to NHA as amended, to insure loans covering operating losses incurred during the first two years of occupancy of HUD-insured multifamily projects, and/or for any other two- year period within 10 years of project completion. Such loans may extend for the unexpired term of the original mortgage.

Eligible applicants/beneficiaries: owners of multifamily projects or facilities subject to a HUD-insured mortgage (*see NOTE preceding* **14.103**).

Range: 2-year loans, essentially to the maximum loss amount supported by debt service limitations; 10-year loans, 80 percent of unreimbursed funds invested; $721,000 to $3,098,700. **Average:** $1,900,000.

Activity: FY 05, 2 loans.

HQ: Office of Multifamily Development, Housing-HUD, 451 Seventh St. SW, Washington, DC 20411. Phone: (202) 708-1142.

Internet: www.hud.gov/offices/hsg/hsgmulti.cfm.

14.168 LAND SALES—CERTAIN SUBDIVIDED LAND ("Interstate Land Sales Registration Program")

Assistance: technical information; investigation of complaints.

Purposes: pursuant to the Interstate Land Sales Full Disclosure Act as amended, to provide consumer protection in subdivision lot sales through enforcement of fraud prohibitions and full disclosure requirements. The law requires developers that engage in interstate land sales consisting of 100 or more nonexempt lots to register with HUD; prospective purchasers must be given a property report with pertinent facts about the development and the developer. Anti-fraud provisions of the act apply to subdivisions of 25 lots or more. Affected land developers are required to submit a filing in compliance with registration requirements. Lot purchasers are entitled to certain rights and remedies.

Eligible applicants/beneficiaries: lot purchasers.

Range/Average: N.A.

Activity: FY 05 (representative), 724 filings processed, 514 annual reports, 13 exemption requests.

HQ: Office of RESPA and Interstate Land Sales, Housing-HUD, 451 Seventh St. SW - Rm.9154, Washington, DC 20410. Phone: (202) 708- 0502.

Internet: www.hud.gov/offices/hsg/sfh/ils/ilshome.cfm. (Note: no field offices for this program.)

14.169 HOUSING COUNSELING ASSISTANCE PROGRAM

Assistance: project grants.

Purposes: pursuant to the Housing and Urban Development Act of 1968 as amended, to provide counseling services to homeowners, homebuyers, and prospective tenants in HUD-assisted or -insured housing and other housing—toward the prevention and reduction of mortgage or rental delinquencies, defaults, and foreclosures.

Eligible applicants/beneficiaries: HUD-approved national, regional, multistate, or state agencies.

Range: $15,000 to local agencies to $4,000,000 to intermediaries. **Average:** $40,000 to local agencies, $1,200,000 to intermediaries.

Activity: grant activity not quantified specifically.

HQ: Program Support Division, Office of Insured Single Family Housing, Housing-HUD, 451 Seventh St. SW, Washington, DC 20410. Phone: (202) 708-0317.

Internet: www.hud.gov/offices/hsg/sfh/hcc/hcc_home.cfm.

14.171 MANUFACTURED HOME CONSTRUCTION AND SAFETY STANDARDS ("Manufactured Housing")

Assistance: technical information; investigation of complaints.

Purposes: pursuant to the National Manufactured Housing Construction and Safety Standards Act as amended, to provide consumer protection for manufactured homes purchasers and residents, by enforcing standards covering safety, quality, durability, and installation—through certifications, testing, in-plant inspections, design review, and investigations of complaints against manufacturers or dealers. Siting and other local activity are considered to be under state or local jurisdiction, and are not covered by the program; however, model siting standards are under development; in the interim such work must meet at least minimum standards established by HUD.

Eligible applicants/beneficiaries: purchasers of manufactured homes built since June 15, 1976.

Range/Average: N.A.

Activity: annually, 200,000 homes produced.

HQ: Office Manufactured Housing Programs, Office of Regulatory Affairs and Manufactured Housing, Housing-HUD - Rm.9164, Washington, DC 20410-8000. Phone: (202) 708-6409, consumer hotline, (800) 927-2891 (messages only), FAX (202) 708-4213.

Internet: www.hud.gov/offices/hsg/sfh/mhs/mhshome.cfm; e-mail, mhs@hud.gov. (Note: no field offices for this program.)

14.172 MORTGAGE INSURANCE—GROWING EQUITY MORTGAGES ("GEMs - Section 245(a)")

Assistance: guaranteed/insured loans (varying term).

Purposes: pursuant to NHA as amended, to insure loans to purchase existing, new, or refinanced single-family housing including condominiums, with growing equity mortgages providing for a rapid principal reduction and shorter mortgage terms, by gradually increasing monthly payments over a 10-year period. Small down payments are required, and mortgagors must pay certain closing costs. Funding for this program is included in **14.117**.

Eligible applicants/beneficiaries: prospective purchasers (*see NOTE preceding* **14.103**).

Range: $200,160 maximum insurable loans for single-family units, $256,248 for two-family housing, $309,744 for three-family, $384,936 for four-family—which may be increased in high-cost areas (details available from HUD area offices).

Activity: FY 02-05 estimate, no loans insured.

HQ: none; all contacts are with Homeownership Centers at field offices listed in Part IV.

Internet: www.hud.gov/progdesc/245a-df.cfm.

14.175 ADJUSTABLE RATE MORTGAGES ("ARMs - Section 251")

Assistance: guaranteed/insured loans (30 years).

Purposes: pursuant to NHA as amended and Housing and Urban-Rural Recovery Act of 1983, to insure loans with adjustable rate mortgages financing the purchase of new, existing, or refinanced one- to four-family housing including condominiums—offering lenders more assurance of long-term profitability than fixed rate mortgages. Interest rates may not increase more than one percent per year or five percent over the mortgage term. Small down payments are required, and mortgagors must pay certain closing costs. Funding for this program is included in **14.117**.

Eligible applicants/beneficiaries: prospective owner-occupants (*see NOTE preceding* **14.103**).

Range: $200,160 maximum insurable loans for single-family units, $256,248 for two-family housing, $309,744 for three-family, $384,936 for four-family—which may be increased in high-cost areas (details available from HUD area offices).

Activity: FY 05, 52,486 loans insured.

HQ: none; all contacts are with Homeownership Centers at field offices listed in Part IV.

Internet: www.hud.gov/progdesc/251-df.cfm.

14.181 SUPPORTIVE HOUSING FOR PERSONS WITH DISABILITIES ("Section 811")

Assistance: direct payments/specified use (100 percent).

Purposes: pursuant to the National Affordable Housing Act and American Homeownership and Economic Opportunity Act of 2000, to provide capital advances to construct, acquire, or rehabilitate supportive housing for persons with disabilities, including group homes, for 40-year projects. Project Rental Assistance Contract payments may be obtained for 5-year periods (renewable), and may cover operating costs not met from project income; payments cover the difference between approved operating costs and tenant rental contributions of 30 percent of adjusted income.

Eligible applicants: "501(c)(3)" nonprofit corporations. Also, profit-motivated limited dividend organizations may participate in projects with mixed financing.

Eligible beneficiaries: very-low-income physically or developmentally disabled or chronically mentally ill persons, age 18 or older.

Range: $288,000 to $3,221,000. **Average:** $990,000.

Activity: FY 05, 1,173 units receiving rental assistance.

HQ: Office of Housing Assistance and Grants Administration, Housing-HUD, Washington, DC 20410. Phone: (202) 708-3000.

Internet: www.hud.gov/progdesc/811main.cfm.

14.183 HOME EQUITY CONVERSION MORTGAGES ("Section 255")

Assistance: guaranteed/insured loans.

Purposes: pursuant to NHA as amended and Housing and Community Development Act of 1987, to insure "reverse mortgage" loans obtained by elderly homeowners to convert equity in their homes to monthly streams of income or (except in Texas) lines of credit. Eligible properties are one- to four-unit dwellings including condominiums and manufactured homes. Borrowers must pay loan origination charges and other fees. Funding for this program is included in **14.133**.

Eligible applicants/beneficiaries: homeowners at least age 62 (*see NOTE preceding* **14.103**).

Range: determined by calculating the limit of the principal, established by using a factor corresponding to the age of the borrower, the interest rate, and the value of the property.

Activity: FY 05, 43,082 units insured.

HQ: Director, Insured Family Development Division, Office of Single Family Housing, Housing-HUD, Washington, DC 20410. Phone: (202) 708-2121.

Internet: www.hud.gov/progdesc/hecm- df.cfm.

14.184 MORTGAGE INSURANCE FOR SINGLE ROOM OCCUPANCY (SRO) PROJECTS ("Section 221(d) Single Room Occupancy")

Assistance: guaranteed/insured loans. (90-100 percent/to 40 years).

Purposes: pursuant to NHA as amended, to insure loans for the construction or substantial rehabilitation of multifamily properties with at least five single-room occupancy residential units—intended to provide housing for tenants with income insufficient to enable them to rent a standard apartment. Projects may have no more than 10 percent of total gross floor space dedicated to commercial use (20 percent for substantial rehabilitation). Funding for this program is included in **14.133**.

Eligible applicants: nonprofit entities; builder-sellers with a nonprofit purchaser; limited-distribution, private profit, or public sponsors (*see NOTE preceding* **14.103**).

Eligible beneficiaries: anyone, subject to normal tenant selection procedures.

Range: 100 percent of replacement cost financing for nonprofits, 90 percent for others.

Activity: FY 05, no loans insured; no activity expected in FY 06.

HQ: Office of Multifamily Development, Housing-HUD, 451 Seventh St. SW, Washington, DC 20411. Phone: (202) 708-1142.

Internet: www.hud.gov/offices/hsg/hsgmulti.cfm.

14.188 HOUSING FINANCE AGENCIES (HFA) RISK SHARING ("Section 542(c) Risk Sharing Program")

Assistance: guaranteed/insured loans.

Purposes: pursuant to the Housing and Community Development Act of 1992 as amended, to provide HUD mortgage insurance to state and local housing finance agencies on affordable multifamily projects for which they share in the insurance risk. The program provides for HUD and HFAs to share between 10 and 90 percent of the financial risk.

Eligible applicants: state and local housing finance agencies.

Eligible beneficiaries: investors, builders, developers, public entities, private nonprofit corporations or associations. Applications are submitted to qualified housing finance agencies.

Range: $465,000 to $24,052,000 (for projects with 33 to 745 units). **Average:** 136 units.

Activity: FY 05, 90 projects with 11,097 total units insured.

HQ: Office of Multifamily Development, Housing-HUD, 451 Seventh St. SW, Washington, DC 20411. Phone: (202) 708-1142.

Internet: www.hud.gov/offices/hsg/hsgmulti.cfm.

14.189 QUALIFIED PARTICIPATING ENTITIES (QPE) RISK SHARING ("Section 542(b) Risk Sharing Program")

Assistance: guaranteed/insured loans (50 percent).

Purposes: pursuant to the Housing and Community Development Act of 1992 as amended, for projects in which HUD provides reinsurance on multifamily housing projects whose loans covering affordable housing are originated, underwritten, serviced, and disposed of by QPEs or approved lenders. In the event of default, the QPE will pay all costs associated with loan disposition, 50 percent of which may be reimbursed by HUD.

Eligible applicants/beneficiaries: HUD-approved lenders and QPEs. Investors, builders, developers, public entities, private nonprofit corporations or associations submit applications to the lender.

Range: $1,800,000 to $6,600,000 (for projects with 64-133 units). **Average:** $3,500,000 (98 units).

Activity: FY 05, 26 loans insured with 3,112 total units.

HQ: Office of Multifamily Development, Housing-HUD, 451 Seventh St. SW, Washington, DC 20411. Phone: (202) 708-1142.

Internet: www.hud.gov/offices/hsg/hsgmulti.cfm.

14.191 MULTIFAMILY HOUSING SERVICE COORDINATORS

Assistance: project grants (100 percent).

Purposes: pursuant to the National Affordable Housing Act and Housing and Community Development Act of 1992 as amended and American Homeownership and Economic Opportunity Act of 2000, to hire multifamily housing service coordinators—to link elderly, especially the frail and disabled, or disabled non- elderly, assisted-housing residents to community supportive or medical services; to prevent premature and unnecessary institutionalization; and, to assess individual service needs, determine eligibility for public services, and make resource allocation decisions enabling residents to remain in the community longer. Coordinators are social service staff persons providing such services as: formal case management; resident and management education; monitoring of services; and, resident advocacy. Project funds may not be used to pay coordinators to serve as recreational or activities director, nor to provide supportive services directly or perform administrative duties. Funding for this program is included in **14.157**.

Eligible applicants: owners of HUD-assisted housing projects, including in rural areas, that are under management and current in mortgage payments. Congregate Housing Service Programs, Section 202 Capital Advance, or Section 811 projects are ineligible.

Eligible beneficiaries: residents of approved projects, at least age 62 and frail (unable to perform at least three activities of daily living), disabled, or *at risk* (i.e., deficient in one or two activities of daily living).

Range: $27,000 to $381,000. **Average:** $155,000.

Activity: FY 05, 92 grants awarded to serve 13,500 units.

HQ: Office of Housing Assistance and Grants Administration, Housing-HUD, Washington, DC 20410. Phone: (202) 708-3000.

Internet: www.hud.gov/offices/hsg/mfh/scp/schome.cfm; e-mail, sercoor@hud.com.

14.195 SECTION 8 HOUSING ASSISTANCE PAYMENTS PROGRAM—SPECIAL ALLOCATIONS ("Project-based Section 8")

Assistance: direct payments/specified use (to 20 years).

Purposes: pursuant to the U.S. Housing Act of 1937, to reduce claims on HUD's insurance fund by aiding insured or Secretary- held projects mortgages with immediate or potentially serious financial difficulties. HUD makes payments to owners of assisted housing on behalf of tenants, representing the difference between the contract and tenant rent. Assistance is available only on a renewable basis; current projects receive a one-year renewal upon expiration of a Section 8 contract.

Eligible applicants/beneficiaries: only Section 8 project owners of record, with an expiring Section 8 contract. No funding is available to new applicants.

Average: tenants pay no more than 30 percent or their adjusted monthly income for rent.

Activity: FY 05, 1,200,000 families assisted.

HQ: Office of Housing Assistance and Grants Administration, Housing-HUD, Washington, DC 20410. Phone: (202) 708-3000.

Internet: www.hud.gov/fha/mfh/mfhsec8.html.

14.197 MULTIFAMILY ASSISTED HOUSING REFORM AND AFFORDABILITY ACT ("Market-to-Market")

Assistance: direct payments/specified use.

Purposes: pursuant to the Multifamily Assisted Housing and Affordability Act of 1997 as amended and Market-to-Market Extension Act of 2001, to retain affordable housing resources represented by existing FHA-insured Section 8 assisted housing, maintain such housing in good physical and financial condition, and reduce ongoing federal subsidies. HUD assists participating owners in restructuring their mortgages, and works with willing owners and lenders to reduce the Section 8 rents and operating expenses to true market levels, while providing for the project's capital improvement needs. Participating owners must commit to maintaining project affordability for 30 years.

Eligible applicants/beneficiaries: owners of FHA-insured project mortgages supported by Section 8 contracts, with rent levels exceeding comparable market rents.

Range: to the amount of the unpaid principal mortgage balance.

Activity: FY 05, assistance to 326 projects with 27,610 total units.

HQ: Director, Office of Affordable Housing Preservation, HUD, 451 7th St, SW - Ste.6230, Washington, DC 20410. Phone: (202) 708-0001.

Internet: www.hud.gov/offices/omhar; e-mail, m2minfo@hud.gov.

14.198 GOOD NEIGHBOR NEXT DOOR SALES PROGRAM

Assistance: sale, exchange, donation of property and goods.

Purposes: to improve security in HUD-designated revitalization areas, by providing 50 percent discounts to law enforcement officers purchasing homes in those neighborhoods. Officers must agree to occupy the homes as their sole residence for at least 3 years; if they do not, a proportion of the discount must be returned to HUD. Available homes are listed on the Internet; purchasers are selected by lottery when more than one officer indicates an interest in a property.

Eligible applicants/beneficiaries: federal, state, county, municipal, and academic institution law enforcement officers possessing general arrest powers.

Range: to 50 percent discount off list price.

Activity: as of end of FY 06, over 13,000 properties sold.

HQ: Asset Management and Disposition Division, Housing-HUD, 451 Seventh St. SW, Washington, DC 20410. Phone: (202) 708-1672.

Internet: www.hud.gov/offices/hsg/sfh/reo/ond.ond.cfm.

14.199 MULTIFAMILY PROPERTY DISPOSITION

Assistance: sale, exchange, donation of property and goods.

Purposes: pursuant to the National Housing Act and subsequent legislation, to provide for the sales of multifamily properties owned or held by HUD to new owners, with Section 8 contracts remaining in place. Properties may be: purchased by governmental entities or nonprofits without competition, or sold to others through bidding procedures; sold with tenant-based Section 8 vouchers (**14.871**) allowing tenants to remain on-site or to relocate; sold with up-front rehabilitation grants of the lesser of 50 percent of development costs or $40,000 per unit, provided the housing remains affordable for at least 20 years.

Eligible applicants/beneficiaries: governmental entities, private individuals, corporations, nonprofit organizations.

Range/Average: N.A.

Activity: annually, 50-125 HUD-owned projects sold.

HQ: Multifamily Housing Programs, Office of Asset Management, Housing-HUD, 451 Seventh St. SW, Washington, DC 20410. Phone: (202) 708-3730.

Internet: www.hud.gov/offices/hsg/mfh/progdesc/progdesc.cfm.

14.218 COMMUNITY DEVELOPMENT BLOCK GRANTS/ENTITLEMENT GRANTS ("CDBG")

Assistance: formula grants (100 percent).

Purposes: pursuant to the Housing and Community Development Act of 1974 as amended, for a broad range of activities designed to result in decent housing and suitable living environments, neighborhood revitalization, economic development, and improved community facilities and services. Program policy requires that the "principal benefit" of projects be to low- and moderate-income persons—i.e., at least 70 percent of the grant allocation. Projects may be operated by the locality or through subgrantees, including public or nonprofit agencies, neighborhood-based organizations, local development corporations, small business investment companies, and other groups. Permitted uses of funds include: virtually any aspect of residential or nonresidential rehabilitation, including historic preservation and energy conservation; energy development; grants or loans to businesses; revolving loan funds for rehabilitation or for economic development purposes; real property acquisition; relocation of households or businesses; demolition; redevelopment site clearance and preparation for re-use; improvement or installation of public works; certain public service programs; housing code enforcement; meeting urgent community needs that present an immediate threat to health or welfare; city planning and related studies. Ineligible uses include: facilities for the general conduct of government; community-wide facilities; new housing construction; housing subsidies paid directly to occupants; income maintenance payments. Cities must: include citizen participation in program planning; have an approved comprehensive housing assistance plan. For "entitlement" communities CDBG grant amounts are based on a statutory formula.

Eligible applicants: cities in metropolitan areas with populations over 50,000; qualified urban counties of at least 200,000 (excluding the population in entitlement cities); and cities with populations under 50,000 that are central cities in Metropolitan Statistical Areas. NOTE: small cities obtain CDBG funds under **14.228**.

Eligible beneficiaries: low- and moderate-income residents, including those benefiting from projects sponsored by CDBG subgrantees or others awarded CDBG funds.

Range/Average: N.A.

Activity: FY 05, 1,100 eligible local government units.

HQ: Entitlement Communities Division, Office of Block Grant Assistance, CPD-HUD, 451 Seventh St. SW, Washington, DC 20410. Phone: (202) 708-1577.

Internet: www.hud.gov/offices/cpd/indx.cfm.

14.225 COMMUNITY DEVELOPMENT BLOCK GRANTS/SPECIAL PURPOSE GRANTS/INSULAR AREAS

Assistance: project grants (formula based, 100 percent).

Purposes: pursuant to the Housing and Community Development Act of 1974 as amended, to provide community development assistance to the Pacific Islands of American Samoa, Guam, the Northern Marianas and the Virgin Islands in the Caribbean. Basically the same as for pogram **14.218**.

Eligible applicants/beneficiaries: Samoa, Guam, Northern Marianas, VI.

Range: FY 04, $1,022,000 (Samoa) to $2,764,000 (Guam).

Activity: N.A.

HQ: Office of Block Grant Assistance, CPD-HUD, 451 Seventh St. SW, Washington, DC 20410. Phone: (202) 708-1322.

Internet: www.hud.gov/offices/cpd/aboutcpd_programs.cfm/.

14.227 COMMUNITY DEVELOPMENT BLOCK GRANTS/TECHNICAL ASSISTANCE PROGRAM

Assistance: project grants (100 percent/100 percent).

Purposes: pursuant to the Housing and Community Development Act of 1974 as amended, for technical assistance and training in planning and administering CDBG programs—through publications, training sessions, and consultations.

Eligible applicants/beneficiaries: states, general local government units, area-wide planning organizations, educational institutions; certain national or regional nonprofit organizations; profit and nonprofit professional and technical services companies or firms.

Range: $10,000 to $369,000. **Average:** $60,000.

Activity: no funding FY 99-03; FY 04, assistance to 50 states and 986 CDBG entitlement communities. No funds appropriated FY 06.

HQ: Technical Assistance Division, CPD-HUD, 451 Seventh St. SW, Washington, DC 20410. Phone: (202) 708-3176.

Internet: www.hud.gov/offices/cpd/communitydevelopment/programs/index.cfm.

14.228 COMMUNITY DEVELOPMENT BLOCK GRANTS/STATE'S PROGRAM AND NON-ENTITLEMENT GRANTS IN HAWAII

Assistance: formula grants (100 percent).

Purposes: pursuant to the Housing and Community Development Act of 1974 as amended, to provide funding to states—to be granted, in turn, to small cities for uses permitted in program **14.218**.

Eligible applicants: forty-nine state governments and the Commonwealth of Puerto Rico receive funds from HUD under this program. The state of Hawaii does not participate and HUD allocates the state's share of funds to the three Hawaii non-entitled counties. Funds are allocated to each state based on a statutory formula and states must distribute the funds to units of general local government in nonentitlement areas.

Eligible beneficiaries: residents with low- and moderate-income, generally defined as 80 percent of state, county or metropolitan-area median income, adjusted for family size.

Range: FY 08, $1,982,003 to $71,779,088 **Average:** $21,414,231.

Activity: FY 07, 17,492 total housing benefits; 27,487 jobs created.

HQ: State and Small Cities Division, Office of Block Grant Assistance, CPD-HUD, 451 Seventh St. SW, Washington, DC 20410. Phone: (202) 708-1322.

Internet: www.hud.gov/offices/cpd/about/cpd_programs.cfm/.

14.231 EMERGENCY SHELTER GRANTS PROGRAM ("ESG")

Assistance: formula grants. (50 percent/to 2 years).

Purposes: pursuant to the McKinney-Vento Homeless Assistance Act of 1987 (MVHAA) as amended, to improve existing or to develop additional emergency shelters, transitional housing, and homeless assistance programs. Funds may be used for: renovation, major rehabilitation, or conversion of existing buildings; essential social services; certain maintenance and operating costs; activities to prevent homelessness.

Eligible applicants/beneficiaries: states, metropolitan cities, urban counties, territories. Other local government units and nonprofit organizations apply to states for funds rather than to HUD. Grantees may, in turn, subcontract with nonprofit entities to conduct program activities.

Range: $879,358 to $7,969,319. **Average:** $435,165.

Activity: FY 06 estimate, 364 grants.

HQ: Office of Special Needs Assistance Programs, CPD-HUD, 451 Seventh St. SW - Rm.7262, Washington, DC 20410. Phone: (202) 708-1226.

Internet: www.hud.gov/offices/cpd/homeless/programs/esg/index.cfm.

14.235 SUPPORTIVE HOUSING PROGRAM

Assistance: project grants; direct payments/specified use. (from 50 percent/to 3 years).

Purposes: pursuant to MVHAA as amended, to develop transitional housing and supportive services to assist homeless persons in the transition from homelessness and to enable them to live as independently as possible. Funds support the following categories of projects: Transitional Housing, for a 24-month period and up to six months of follow-up services; Permanent Housing for Homeless Persons with Disabilities, to maximize participants' ability to live as independently as possible; Innovative Supportive Housing, to develop alternative methods of meeting the immediate and long-term needs of homeless individuals and families; Supportive Services for Homeless Persons Not in Conjunction with Supportive Housing; and, Safe Havens, for homeless persons with serious mental illness. Projects may include facilities acquisition and rehabilitation, limited new construction, operating costs and supportive services.

Eligible applicants/beneficiaries: state, local, and other governmental entities; private nonprofit organizations; public community mental health associations.

Range: acquisition/rehabilitation, to $200,000 ($400,000 in high- cost areas); new construction, to $400,000; to 75 percent of operating costs; leasing costs, to three years.

Activity: FY 05, 5,334 applications received.

HQ: Office of Special Needs Assistance Programs, CPD-HUD, 451 Seventh St. SW, Washington, DC 20410. Phone: (202) 708-2140.

Internet: www.hud.gov/offices/cpd/homeless/programs/shp/index.cfm.

14.238 SHELTER PLUS CARE

Assistance: project grants. (50 percent/5-10 years).

Purposes: pursuant to MVHAA as amended, to provide rental assistance in connection with supportive services available through other programs, to homeless persons with disabilities and their families—primarily those with serious mental illness, with substance addictions, or AIDS and related diseases. Four program components include: Tenant-based Rental Assistance (TRA); Sponsor-based Rental Assistance (SRA); Project-based Rental Assistance (PRA); Single Room Occupancy for Homeless Individuals (SRO). Grant funds must be matched by supportive services equal in value to the grant amount.

Eligible applicants/beneficiaries: states, local government units, public housing agencies.

Range: $14,000 to $6,340,320. **Average:** $363,879.

Activity: FY 05, 174 new, 663 renewal grants awarded.

HQ: Office of Special Needs Assistance Programs, CPD-HUD, 451 Seventh St. SW, Washington, DC 20410. Phone: (202) 708-1234.

Internet: www.hud.gov/offices/cpd/homeless/index.cfm.

14.239 HOME INVESTMENT PARTNERSHIPS PROGRAM ("HOME Program")

Assistance: formula grants. (67-75 percent/2-5 years).

Purposes: pursuant to the National Affordable Housing Act as amended, to support partnerships among all levels of government and the private sector, including profit and nonprofit organizations, in the production and operation of affordable housing, particularly rental housing for low- and very-low-income families. Funds may be used for: planning; development of model projects; technical assistance; housing rehabilitation; tenant-based rental assistance; assistance to homebuyers; new construction of housing; site acquisition and improvements including improved energy efficiency, demolition, relocation. As of FY 03, the American Dream Downpayment Initiative (ADDI) may provide funds for low-income families to make down payments on or to rehabilitate suitable housing. Ineligible funds uses include: public housing modernization; matching funds for other federal programs; rental housing operating subsidies; activities under the Low Income Housing Preservation Act, except for priority purchasers.

Eligible applicants: formula allocations—states, cities, urban counties, or consortia of general local government units; Insular Areas. Technical Assistance—nonprofit and profit firms; public purpose organizations; nonprofit national and regional HOME organizations; community development organizations (CHDOs).

Eligible beneficiaries: rental housing—90 percent of funds for families with incomes at 60 percent of area median, and the remainder for families below 80 percent. Homeownership assistance—families with incomes below 80 percent of the area median.

Range: $287,780 to $129,144,702. **Average:** $3,088,433.

Activity: cumulatively through FY 05, 632,998 were completed; 131,327 tenants received rental assistance.

HQ: Director, Office of Affordable Housing Programs, CPD-HUD, 451 Seventh St. SW - Rm.7164, Washington, DC 20410. Phone: (202) 708- 2470.

Internet: www.hud.gov/offices/cpd/affordablehousing/index.cfm.

14.241 HOUSING OPPORTUNITIES FOR PERSONS WITH AIDS ("HOPWA")

Assistance: formula grants; project grants (to 3 years).

Purposes: pursuant to the AIDS Housing Opportunity Act, to develop long-term comprehensive strategies to meet the housing needs of low-income persons with AIDS or related diseases, and their families. Eligible funds uses include: resource identification to establish, coordinate, and develop housing assistance; information services including counseling and referral; acquisition, rehabilitation, conversion, lease, and repair of facilities to provide housing and services; new construction of single-room occupancy and community residences; project- or tenant-based rental assistance including for shared housing arrangements; short-term rent, mortgage, and utility payments to prevent the homelessness of a tenant or mortgagor; supportive services including health, mental health, assessment, permanent housing placement, alcohol and drug abuse treatment and counseling, nutritional services, day care, intensive care; housing operating costs; training; technical assistance. Resident rent payments are required.

Eligible applicants/beneficiaries: entitlement (formula) grants—states and eligible metropolitan areas with the largest number of AIDS cases; communities in metropolitan areas must designate one unit of local government to serve as the applicant/grantee for the area. Competitive project grants—states, local governments, and nonprofit organizations for projects of national significance; states and localities not qualifying for formula grants.

Range: FY 06 formula grants, $112,000 to $56,610,000; FY 05 competitive, $281,326 to $1,430,000. **Average:** FY 06 formula, $13,769,913; FY 05 competitive, $1,071,459.

Activity: FY 05 estimate, housing assistance to 74,000 households, 35 recipient organizations; FY 06 estimate, 123 recipient communities.

HQ: Director, Office of HIV/AIDS Housing, CPD-HUD, 451 Seventh St. SW - Rm.7212, Washington, D.C. 20410. Phone: (202) 708-1934, TTY (800) 877-8339. *Technical assistance,* AIDS Housing of Washington, 2014 E. Madison. - Ste.200, Seattle, WA 98122. Phone: (206) 322-9444.

Internet: www.hud.gov/offices/cpd/aidshousing.

14.244 EMPOWERMENT ZONES PROGRAM ("Empowerment Zones and Enterprise Communities")

Assistance: project grants; direct payments/specified use (100 percent).

Purposes: pursuant to the Community Renewal Tax Relief Act of 2000, Taxpayer Relief Act of 1997, and other acts, to establish Empowerment Zones, Enterprise Communities, and Renewal Communities in urban and rural areas—to stimulate the creation of new jobs particularly for the disadvantaged and long- term unemployed and to promote revitalization of distressed areas. Areas designated in Round I receive Social Services Block Grant funds from HHS, special tax benefits to employers, and special consideration in obtaining funds under other federal programs; Round III communities and Renewal Communities receive tax incentives only.

Eligible applicants/beneficiaries: urban zones—basically, areas, including noncontiguous parcels meeting certain criteria, with 200,000 maximum population or the greater of 50,000 or 10 percent of the population of the most populous city, with pervasive poverty, unemployment, and general distress. Renewal Community criteria may differ slightly. Rural zones are defined by USDA (see **10.772**).

Range: FY 05 Round II Empowerment Zones, $661,000 each.

Activity: FY 02, 8 new urban Round III Empowerment Zones, 40 Renewal Communities, and 2 Rural Empowerment Zones designated.

HQ: RC/EZ/EC Office, CPD-HUD, Washington, DC 20410. Phone: (202) 708-6339; *general information*, (800) 998-9999.

Internet: www.hud.gov/cr.

14.246 COMMUNITY DEVELOPMENT BLOCK GRANTS/BROWNFIELDS ECONOMIC DEVELOPMENT INITIATIVE ("Section 108 - BEDI")

Assistance: project grants (to 5 years).

Purposes: pursuant to the Housing and Community Development Act of 1974 as amended, to enhance the security of loans or improve the viability of projects financed under the Section 108 loan guarantee program (**14.248**), including: commercial, industrial, and economic development revolving loan funds; qualified "brownfields" projects. Activities must be consistent with local CDBG plans and meet citizen participation requirements.

Eligible applicants/beneficiaries: local government units eligible under the Section 108 loan guarantee program.

Range: $347,500 to $2,000,000.

Activity: FY 05, 11 brownfields grants.

HQ: Economic Development Specialist, Office of Economic Development, CPD-HUD, 451 Seventh St. SW, Washington, DC 20410. Phone: (202) 708-3484, ext.4612.

Internet: www.hud.gov/offices/cpd/economicdevelopment/programs/.

14.247 SELF-HELP HOMEOWNERSHIP OPPORTUNITY PROGRAM ("SHOP")

Assistance: project grants (2-3 years).

Purposes: pursuant to the Housing Opportunity Extension Act of 1996 as amended, for innovative projects enabling low-income families to become homeowners under the self-help concept, by contributing "sweat equity" toward the construction of dwellings. Program funds may be used for land acquisition and infrastructure improvements, with a maximum of 20 percent of grants for administrative costs.

Eligible applicants/beneficiaries: nonprofit national or regional organizations or consortia.

Range: $527,000 to $10,773,000; to $15,000 maximum per dwelling on average. **Average:** $6,220,000.

Activity: FY 05, 2,098 units completed, 3,050 under development.

HQ: Office of Affordable Housing Programs, CPD-HUD, 451 Seventh St. SW, Washington, DC 20410. Phone: (202) 708-2684.

Internet: www.hud.gov/progdesc/cpdindx.html. (Note: no field offices for this program.)

14.248 COMMUNITY DEVELOPMENT BLOCK GRANTS—SECTION 108 LOAN GUARANTEES ("Section 108")

Assistance: guaranteed/insured loans (to 20 years).

Purposes: pursuant to the Housing and Community Development Act of 1974 as amended, to provide communities with a source of financing for economic development, housing rehabilitation, public facilities, and large-scale physical development projects—provided the "principal benefit" of such projects: is to low- or moderate-income persons; aids in the elimination or prevention of slums and blight; or, meets urgent community needs. Maximum approvable loan amounts generally are five times the latest CDBG amount received by the public entity, minus any outstanding Section 108 commitment or principal balances.

Eligible applicants/beneficiaries: CDBG recipients. The public entity may be the borrower, or it may designate a public agency.

Range: $159,000 to $76,000,000. **Average:** $6,600,000.

Activity: FY 06 estimate, 52 loan commitments, generating some 11,000 jobs.

HQ: Financial Management Division, CPD-HUD, 451 Seventh St. SW - Rm.7180, Washington, DC 20410. Phone: (no number provided).

Internet: www.hud.gov/offices/cpd/communitydevelopment/programs/.

14.249 SECTION 8 MODERATE REHABILITATION SINGLE ROOM OCCUPANCY

Assistance: project grants. (100 percent/11-year contracts).

Purposes: pursuant to MVHAA as amended, to provide rental assistance for homeless individuals to occupy single-room dwelling units rehabilitated under this program.

Eligible applicants/beneficiaries: local public housing agencies; private nonprofit organizations under contract with public housing agencies (PHAs).

Range: $72,600 to $6,432,000. **Average:** $1,063,234.

Activity: cumulatively FY 98-05, 456 grants.

HQ: Office of Special Needs Assistance Programs, CPD-HUD, 451 Seventh St. SW, Washington, DC 20410. Phone: (202) 708-1234.

Internet: www.hud.gov/offices/cpd/homeless/programs/sro/index.cfm.

14.250 RURAL HOUSING AND ECONOMIC DEVELOPMENT

Assistance: project grants. (100 percent/3 years).

Purposes: to build capacity to expand the supply of affordable housing and access to economic opportunities in rural areas. Funds may support capacity building and innovative housing and economic development activities.

Eligible applicants/beneficiaries: local rural nonprofit organizations; community development corporations; tribes; state housing finance, community, and economic development agencies.

Range: N.A. **Average:** $300,000.

Activity: FY 03 - FY 05, 3,736 jobs created, 7,891 persons trained, 602 new businesses assisted, 1,348 existing businesses assisted, 1,203 new housing units constructed, 1,292 existing housing units rehabilitated.

HQ: Office of Rural Housing and Economic Development, CPD-HUD, 451 Seventh St. SW - Rm.7137, Washington, D.C. 20410. Phone: (202) 708-2290.

Internet: www.hud.gov/offices/cpd/economicdevelopment/programs/.

14.251 ECONOMIC DEVELOPMENT INITIATIVE—SPECIAL PROJECT, NEIGHBORHOOD INITIATIVE AND MISCELLANEOUS GRANTS ("Congressional Grants")

Assistance: project grants (5-8 years).

Purposes: pursuant to the Transportation, Treasury, Housing and Urban Development, the Judiciary, the District of Columbia, and Independent Agencies Appropriations Act of 2006, for eligible activities as set forth in each grant enacted by Congress as well as in the appropriation of EDI-SP, NI and Miscellaneous grant funds.

Eligible applicants/beneficiaries: units of state or local government, Indian tribes or nonprofit organizations as specified by Congress.

Range: $10,000 to $30,000,000. **Average:** EDI-SP grant, $272,557; NI grant, $990,000.

Activity: N.A.

HQ: Director, Congressional Grants Division, Housing-HUD, 451 7th St. SW - Rm. 7149, Washington, DC 20410 Phone: (202) 708-3773.

Internet: www.hud.gov/progdesc/cpindex.cfm (Note: no field offices for this program.)

14.252 SECTION 4 CAPACITY BUILDING FOR AFFORDABLE HOUSING AND COMMUNITY DEVELOPMENT GRANTS

Assistance: project grants. (25 percent/to 5 years).

Purposes: pursuant to Section 4, HUD Demonstration Act of 1993, as amended, to improve the capacity of community organizations to develop affordable housing and other community development projects. Grants may used to assist community development corporations (CDCs) and community housing development organizations (CHDOs) to carry out community development and affordable housing activities that benefit low-income families and persons, including: training, education, support, advice, loans, grants, development assistance, predevelopment assistance, or other financial assistance.

Eligible applicants: per authorizing legislation, only four organizations are eligible: Enterprise Community Partners, Inc. (formerly The Enterprise Foundation), Local Initiatives Support Corporation, Habitat for Humanity, and YouthBuild USA.

Eligible beneficiaries: CDCs, CHDOs and other nonprofit community based organizations that develop affordable housing and community development projects and programs.

Range: $990,000 to $10,617,500. **Average:** $5,115,000.

Activity: FY 06: 13,014 homes renovated, preserved or built; 259 trainings provided to CDCs and CHDOs.

HQ: Office of Policy Development and Coordination, Community Planning and Development, HUD, 451 7th Street, SW., Washington, DC 20410. Phone: (202) 402-5552.

Internet: www.hud.gov (Note: no field offices for this program.)

14.311 SINGLE FAMILY PROPERTY DISPOSITION ("Good Neighbor Initiative")

Assistance: sale, exchange, donation of property and goods.

Purposes: pursuant to NHA as amended, to reduce the inventory of HUD-acquired properties, expand homeownership opportunities, and strengthen neighborhoods and communities, especially in revitalization areas established in consultation with local governments and nonprofit organizations, in urban or rural areas. Discounts of 30 percent off the list price are granted to sponsors in designated areas—and ten percent outside such areas. Ultimate eligible purchasers acquire and occupy one- to four-unit properties with low down payments, under the FHA Section 203(b) or 203(k) programs, and agree to rehabilitate the properties according to specified standards with funds included in the mortgage amount; generally, such loans include up to $5,000 placed in escrow, to improve the property to minimum standards. In addition, FHA may sell such homes to HUD contractors that, in turn, offer them to the general public. The collective "Good Neighbor Initiative" includes **14.198** and the "Discount Sales to Nonprofits and Local Governments" and "$ HOME to Local Governments Sales" (**14.313**) programs. Funding for this program includes **14.313**.

Eligible applicants: local governments and nonprofit organizations; others on a competitive basis.

Eligible beneficiaries: purchasers meeting FHA requirements.

Range: local governments and nonprofit organizations, 10 to 30 percent discounts off list price.

Activity: FY 05, 57,977 homes sold.

HQ: Asset Management and Disposition Division, Housing-HUD, 451 Seventh St. SW, Washington, DC 20410. Phone: (202) 708-1672.

Internet: www.hud.gov/offices/hsg/sfh/reo/reo_home.cfm.

14.313 DOLLAR HOME SALES

Assistance: sale, exchange, or donation of property and goods.

Purposes: to expand HUD's partnership with local governments to foster housing opportunities for low- to moderate-income families. Under the program, FHA-foreclosed single-family homes, remaining unsold for at least six months, may be sold to local governments for $1.00 plus closing costs—and then sold or rented to low- to moderate-income families, first-time homebuyers, or groups that will use the homes to provide such services as child care, shelters, or job training centers. Funding for this program is included in **14.311**.

Eligible applicants: local governments.

Eligible beneficiaries: low- to moderate- income families and communities.

Average: $50,000 in market value per home.

Activity: FY 05, 217 home sales.

HQ: Asset Management and Disposition Division, Housing-HUD, 451 Seventh St. SW, Washington, DC 20410. Phone: (202) 708-1672.

Internet: www.hud.gov/offices/hsg/sfh/reo/goodn/dhmaabout.cfm.

14.314 ASSISTED LIVING CONVERSION FOR ELIGIBLE MULTIFAMILY HOUSING PROJECTS ("ALCP")

Assistance: project grants.

Purposes: pursuant to the HUD Reform Act of 1989 and Housing Act of 1959 as amended, to enable owners of eligible elderly housing developments to convert some or all units in such facilities into Assisted Living Facilities (ALFs) serving frail elderly and disabled persons, designed to accommodate persons able to live independently but needing assistance with activities of daily living. ALFs must provide support services such as personal care, transportation, meals, housekeeping, and laundry. Funds may be used: for physical reconfiguration of individual units; to develop common, services, and administrative spaces, including central kitchens and dining areas, lounges, and recreation spaces; for necessary remodeling. Funding for the supportive services must be provided by the owners or borrowers, either directly or through a third party. Funding for this program is included in **14.157**.

Eligible applicants/beneficiaries: private nonprofit owners of certain unused or under-utilized commercial structures.

Range: $606,257 to $4,825,000. **Average:** $1,696,609.

Activity: FY 05, 218 units funded.

HQ: Office of Grant Policy and Management, Housing-HUD, 451 Seventh St. SW - Rm.6138, Washington, DC 20410. Phone: (202) 708- 3000.

Internet: www.hud.gov/offices/hsg/mfh/progdesc/alcp.html.

14.315 EMERGENCY CAPITAL REPAIR GRANTS FOR MULTIFAMILY HOUSING PROJECTS DESIGNATED FOR OCCUPANCY ("ECRP")

Assistance: project grants.

Purposes: pursuant to Housing Act of 1959 as amended, for emergency capital repairs to eligible nonprofit multifamily housing projects designated for occupancy by elderly tenants—to correct situations presenting an immediate threat to the life, health, and safety. Approved grant funds, along with funds from other sources, must remove the emergency conditions. Funding for this program is included in **14.157**.

Eligible applicants/beneficiaries: private nonprofit owners of eligible "assisted" elderly housing—i.e., receiving federal subsidies under HUD or USDA-RHS programs. Projects must have had closing on or before 1 January 1999.

Range: $37,000 to $500,000. **Average:** $235,000.

Activity: new program listing in 2006 (CFDA on-line). FY 05, 35 projects funded.

HQ: Director, Grant and Housing Assistance Field Support Division, Office of Multifamily Housing, Housing-HUD, Washington, DC 20410. Phone: (202) 708-3000.

Internet: www.hud.gov/offices/hsg/mfh/progrdesc/ecrp.cfm.

14.316 HOUSING COUNSELING TRAINING PROGRAM

Assistance: project grants (100 percent).

Purposes: pursuant to Housing and Urban Development Act of 1968, as amended, to support the training of counselors of HUD-approved housing counseling agencies.

Eligible applicants: public or private nonprofit organizations with at least 2 years nationwide housing-counseling training. Although the program has no matching requirements, applicants are required to demonstrate funding from other sources.

Eligible beneficiaries: housing counselors from HUD-approved counseling agencies.

Range/Average: N.A.

Activity: FY 05, 1,659 HUD-approved housing counselors trained; FY 06, one award anticipated.

HQ: Program Support Division, Office of Insured Single Family Housing, Housing-HUD, 451 Seventh St. SW, Washington, DC 20410 Phone: (202) 708-0317.

Internet: www.hud.gov/offices/hsg/sfh/hcc/hcchome.cfm (Note: no field offices for this program.)

14.400 EQUAL OPPORTUNITY IN HOUSING ("Fair Housing")

Assistance: investigation of complaints.

Purposes: pursuant to the Fair Housing Act, to enforce the protection of the right to choose housing suited to one's needs and financial ability, in areas where one chooses to live, without discrimination because of race, color, religion, sex, family status, handicap, or national origin, in the sale, lease, advertising, financing, or appraisal—including multifamily housing occupied after 13 March 1991, which must comply with accessibility guidelines. Complaints are investigated and conciliated; if discrimination is established and conciliation is unsuccessful, complainants receive legal representation in taking further legal action. Suits may be filed in a federal court, seeking injunctive relief and actual or punitive damages together with court costs and reasonable attorney fees. Litigation may be initiated by the individual, by HUD on behalf of the individual, or, under certain conditions, by the Attorney General. Technical assistance is available to attorneys, developers, real estate brokers, and the general public.

Eligible applicants/beneficiaries: aggrieved persons may file a complaint with HUD or with a HUD-approved state or local fair housing agency.

Range/Average: N.A.

Activity: FY 05, 2,227 cases filed by HUD, 7,034 by state and local agencies; $11,955,000 in monetary relief obtained.

HQ: OFHEO-HUD, 451 Seventh St. SW - Rm.5226, Washington, DC 20410. Phone: (202) 708-0836; *complaint lines*, (800) 669- 9777, TTY (800) 927-9275.

Internet: www.hud.gov/complaints/housediscrm.cfm.

14.401 FAIR HOUSING ASSISTANCE PROGRAM—STATE AND LOCAL ("FHAP")

Assistance: project grants (100 percent).

Purposes: pursuant to the Fair Housing Act, for state and local complaint processing, technical assistance, training, education, outreach, data and information systems, special enforcement efforts, and for the National Fair Housing Training Academy—to handle complaints regarding violations of fair housing laws.

Eligible applicants/beneficiaries: state and local enforcement agencies administering state and local fair housing laws and ordinances certified by

HUD as providing substantially equivalent rights and remedies as those provided by the Fair Housing Act.

Average: capacity building, $120,000.

Activity: 103 jurisdictions funded.

HQ: Director, FHAP Support Division, OFHEO-HUD, 451 Seventh Street SW - Rm.5221, Washington, DC 20410. Phone: (202) 708-2288, ext.7044.

Internet: www.hud.gov/offices/fheo/partners/FHAP/index.cfm.

14.402 NON-DISCRIMINATION IN FEDERALLY-ASSISTED PROGRAMS (ON THE BASIS OF AGE)

Assistance: investigation of complaints.

Purposes: pursuant to the Age Discrimination Act of 1975 as amended, to enforce the act prohibiting discrimination on the basis of age, in programs or activities receiving HUD financial assistance. Complaints are referred to FMCS; investigations are conducted by HUD if complaints cannot be mediated successfully.

Eligible applicants/beneficiaries: aggrieved persons may file a complaint with HUD. Complainants may file civil actions following exhaustion of administrative remedies.

Range/Average: N.A.

Activity: FY 05, 2 complaints received.

HQ: OFHEO-HUD, 451 Seventh St. SW - Rm.5240, Washington, DC 20410. Phone: (202) 708-2333, ext.7057.

Internet: www.hud.gov/prodesc/fheoindx.html.

14.404 NON-DISCRIMINATION IN FEDERALLY ASSISTED AND CONDUCTED PROGRAMS (ON THE BASIS OF DISABILITY) ("Section 504")

Assistance: investigation of complaints.

Purposes: pursuant Section 504 of the Rehabilitation Act of 1973 as amended, to enforce provisions of the act as it pertains to discrimination against persons with disabilities, in HUD programs except contracts of insurance and guaranty.

Eligible applicants/beneficiaries: aggrieved persons.

Range/Average: N.A.

Activity: FY 05, 696 Section 504 complaints received, 187 compliance reviews initiated.

HQ: OFHEO-HUD, 451 Seventh St. SW - Rm.5240, Washington, DC 20410. Phone: (202) 708-2333, ext.7057.

Internet: www.hud.gov/prodesc/fheoindx.html.

14.405 NON-DISCRIMINATION IN FEDERALLY ASSISTED PROGRAMS (ON THE BASIS OF RACE, COLOR, OR NATIONAL ORIGIN) ("Title VI")

Assistance: investigation of complaints.

Purposes: pursuant to Title VI of CRA as amended, to enforce provisions prohibiting discrimination on the basis race, color, or national origin, as it pertains to HUD assistance programs except contracts of insurance and guaranty.

Eligible applicants/beneficiaries: aggrieved persons.

Range/Average: N.A.

Activity: FY 05, 403 complaints received, 60 compliance reviews initiated.

HQ: OFHEO-HUD, 451 Seventh St. SW - Rm.5214, Washington, DC 20410. Phone: (202) 619-8041, ext.6995.

Internet: www.hud.gov/prodesc/fheoindx.html.

14.406 NON-DISCRIMINATION IN THE COMMUNITY DEVELOPMENT BLOCK GRANT PROGRAM (ON THE BASIS OF RACE, COLOR, NATIONAL ORIGIN, RELIGION, OR SEX) ("Section 109")

Assistance: investigation of complaints.

Purposes: pursuant to Title I of the Housing and Community Development Act of 1974 as amended, to enforce all nondiscrimination provisions of the CDBG program, including employment, on the basis of race, color, national origin, religion, or sex.

Eligible applicants/beneficiaries: aggrieved persons.

Range/Average: N.A.

Activity: FY 05, 31 complaints received, 7 compliance reviews initiated.

HQ: OFHEO-HUD, 451 Seventh St. SW - Rm.5214, Washington, DC 20410. Phone: (202) 619-8041, ext.6995.

Internet: www.hud.gov/prodesc/fheoindx.html.

14.407 ARCHITECTURAL BARRIERS ACT ENFORCEMENT ("Section 502 Architectural Barriers Act")

Assistance: investigation of complaints.

Purposes: pursuant to the Architectural Barriers Act of 1968 as amended, to assure that facilities assisted by the federal government are accessible to physically disabled persons, in programs involving HUD including its leased or owned facilities such as public housing.

Eligible applicants/beneficiaries: aggrieved persons. Complaints may be sent to HUD or to the Architectural and Transportation Barriers Compliance Board.

Range/Average: N.A.

Activity: FY 05, no complaints received.

HQ: OFHEO-HUD, 451 Seventh St. SW - Rm.5240, Washington, DC 20410. Phone: (202) 708-2333, ext.7057.

Internet: www.hud.gov/sec8.html. (Note: no field offices for this program.)

14.408 FAIR HOUSING INITIATIVES PROGRAM ("FHIP")

Assistance: project grants. (100 percent/to 5 years).

Purposes: pursuant to the Housing and Community Development Acts of 1987 and 1992 as amended, to develop, execute, or coordinate specialized programs or activities designed to obtain enforcement of the Fair Housing Act or state or local laws certified by HUD as providing substantially equivalent rights and remedies for discriminatory housing practices.

Eligible applicants/beneficiaries: experienced state and local fair housing agencies.

Range/Average: N.A.

Activity: FY 04, 106 grants to 42 states, DC, PR, and 93 cities.

HQ: Director, FIP/FHAP Support Division, OFHEO-HUD, 451 Seventh Street SW - Rm.5224, Washington, DC 20410. Phone: (202) 708-2288, ext.7095.

Internet: www.hud.gov/offices/fheo/partners/FHIP/fhip.cfm.

14.412 EMPLOYMENT OPPORTUNITIES FOR LOWER INCOME PERSONS AND BUSINESSES ("Section 3")

Assistance: investigation of complaints.

Purposes: pursuant to the Housing and Urban Development Act of 1968, to enforce provisions requiring development of opportunities for job training and employment to lower-income residents in connection with HUD-funded projects in their neighborhoods—as well as for contract opportunities to local businesses. Section 3 also applies to financial assistance in the form of insurance or guaranty, or assistance to tenant-based organizations.

Eligible applicants/beneficiaries: aggrieved lower-income persons residing, or businesses located, in or substantially owned by persons residing in Section 3 areas.

Range/Average: N.A.

Activity: FY 05, 21 complaints closed.

HQ: OFHEO-HUD, 451 Seventh Street SW - Rm.5222, Washington, DC 20410. Phone: (202) 708-2288.

Internet: www.hud.gov/offices/fheo/section3/section3.cfm.

14.414 NON-DISCRIMINATION ON THE BASIS OF DISABILITY BY PUBLIC ENTITIES ("Title II of the ADA")

Assistance: investigation of complaints.

Purposes: to enforce the provisions of Title II of the Americans with Disabilities Act of 1990, prohibiting discrimination against persons with disabilities, in all programs, services, and regulatory activities relating to state and local government, public housing, and housing assistance and referral.

Eligible applicants/beneficiaries: aggrieved persons.

Range/Average: N.A.

Activity: FY 04, 160 complaints received, 11 compliance reviews conducted.

HQ: OFHEO-HUD, 451 Seventh St. SW - Rm.5240, Washington, DC 20410. Phone: (202) 708-2333, ext.7057.

Internet: www.hud.gov/sec8.html.

14.415 NON-DISCRIMINATION ON THE BASIS OF SEX IN EDUCATION PROGRAMS AND ACTIVITIES RECEIVING FEDERAL FINANCIAL ASSISTANCE

Assistance: investigation of complaints.

Purposes: pursuant to Title IX of the Education Amendments Act of 1972 as amended, to investigate discrimination complaints on the basis of sex in HUD's education programs, including academic, research, training, employment, and related activities.

Eligible applicants/beneficiaries: aggrieved persons. Complaints may be filed on behalf of specific groups or individuals.

Range/Average: N.A.

Activity: FY 05, no complaints received.

HQ: OFHEO-HUD, 451 Seventh St. SW - Rm.5214, Washington, DC 20410. Phone: (202) 619-8041, ext.6995.

Internet: www.hud.gov/prodesc/fheoindx.html.

14.506 GENERAL RESEARCH AND TECHNOLOGY ACTIVITY

Assistance: project grants.

Purposes: pursuant to the Housing Act of 1970 as amended, for research, demonstration, and program evaluation and monitoring, in such HUD program-related areas as national housing needs, advancing technology, government-sponsored enterprises, international activities, and urban economic development.

Eligible applicants/beneficiaries: researchers, research organizations, state and local governments, academic institutions, public and private profit and nonprofit organizations.

Range: $13,000 to $1,400,000.

Activity: not quantified specifically.

HQ: Budget, Contracts, and Program Control Division, OPDR-HUD, 451 Seventh St. SW, Washington, DC 20410. Phone: (202) 708-1796.

Internet: www.huduser.org. (Note: no field offices for this program.)

14.511 COMMUNITY OUTREACH PARTNERSHIP CENTER PROGRAM

Assistance: project grants. (outreach, 75 percent; research, 50 percent/3-5 years).

Purposes: pursuant to the Community Outreach Partnership Act of 1992 and Housing and Community Development Act of 1992, for partnerships among IHEs and communities to address urban problems through research, outreach, and exchange of information. Projects must focus on housing, economic development, neighborhood revitalization, infrastructure, health care, job training, education, crime prevention, planning, community organizing, and similar areas.

Eligible applicants/beneficiaries: IHEs.

Range: $200,000 to $400,000.

Activity: FY 05, 13 new grants, 6 renewals.

HQ: Office of University Partnerships, OPDR-HUD, 451 Seventh St. SW, Washington, DC 20410. Phone: (202) 708-3061, ext.7495.

Internet: www.hud.gov; www.oup.org. (Note: no field offices for this program.)

14.514 HISPANIC-SERVING INSTITUTIONS ASSISTING COMMUNITIES

Assistance: project grants. (100 percent/to 3 years).

Purposes: for Hispanic-serving IHEs to expand their activities in addressing community development needs in their localities, including neighborhood revitalization, housing, and economic development consistent with the purposes Title I of the Housing and Community Development Act of 1974.

Eligible applicants/beneficiaries: nonprofit IHEs meeting statutory requirements.

Average: $600,000 per grantee.

Activity: FY 05, 121 grants.

HQ: Office of University Partnerships, OPDR-HUD, 451 Seventh St. SW, Washington, DC 20410. Phone: (202) 708-3061, ext.5939.

Internet: www.hud.gov/grants or www.oup.org. (Note: no field offices for this program.)

14.515 ALASKA NATIVE/NATIVE HAWAIIAN INSTITUTIONS ASSISTING COMMUNITIES

Assistance: project grants. (100 percent/to 3 years).

Purposes: for Alaska and Hawaii native IHEs to enhance their ability to address community development needs including neighborhood revitalization, housing, and economic development, consistent with Housing and Community Development Act of 1974 purposes.

Eligible applicants/beneficiaries: nonprofit Alaska and Hawaii native IHEs meeting statutory requirements.

Average: $800,000 per grantee.

Activity: 27 grants awarded since 2001.

HQ: Office of University Partnerships, OPDR-HUD, 451 Seventh St. SW, Washington, DC 20410. Phone: (202) 708-3061, ext.4200.

Internet: www.hud.gov/grants or www.oup.org. (Note: no field offices for this program.)

14.516 DOCTORAL DISSERTATION RESEARCH GRANTS

Assistance: project grants (2 years).

Purposes: pursuant to the Housing and Community Development Act of 1970, to assist Ph.D. candidates in completing their research and dissertations on housing and urban development issues. Funds may be used for stipends, software, data purchases, travel, compensation for interviews—but not for tuition, computer hardware, or meals.

Eligible applicants/beneficiaries: graduate students with approved dissertation proposals, whose institutions provide support.

Range: to $25,000.

Activity: annually, 16 candidates assisted.

HQ: Office of University Partnerships, OPDR-HUD, 451 Seventh St. SW, Washington, DC 20410. Phone: (202) 708-3061, ext.3852.

Internet: www.hud.gov/grants or www.oup.org. (Note: no field offices for this program.)

14.517 EARLY DOCTORAL STUDENT RESEARCH GRANTS

Assistance: project grants. (100 percent/1 year).

Purposes: pursuant to the Housing and Community Development Act of 1970, to assist doctoral students in completing their research manuscripts on housing and urban development issues. Funds may be used for stipends, software, data purchases, travel, compensation for interviews—but not for tuition, computer hardware, or meals.

Eligible applicants/beneficiaries: doctoral candidates with: at least two completed graduate semesters or three terms; approved dissertation proposals; and, whose institutions provide support.

Range: to $15,000.

Activity: annually, 10 students assisted.

HQ: Office of University Partnerships, OPDR-HUD, 451 Seventh St. SW, Washington, DC 20410. Phone: (202) 708-3061, ext.3852.

Internet: www.hud.gov/grants or www.oup.org. (Note: no field offices for this program.)

14.519 TRIBAL COLLEGES AND UNIVERSITIES PROGRAM

Assistance: project grants. (100 percent/3 years).

Purposes: for tribal colleges and universities to build, expand, renovate, and equip their facilities.

Eligible applicants/beneficiaries: tribal IHEs.

Average: $600,000.

Activity: not quantified specifically.

HQ: Office of University Partnerships, OPDR-HUD, 451 Seventh St. SW, Washington, DC 20410. Phone: (202) 708-3061, ext.4200.

Internet: www.hud.gov/grants or www.oup.org. (Note: no field offices for this program.)

14.520 HISTORICALLY BLACK COLLEGES AND UNIVERSITIES PROGRAM

Assistance: project grants. (100 percent/to 3 years).

Purposes: pursuant to the Housing and Community Development Act of 1974 as amended, to assist HBCUs in addressing community needs, including neighborhood revitalization, housing, and economic development.

Eligible applicants/beneficiaries: HBCUs.

Range: to $2,000,000, Category I; to $600,000, Category II.

Activity: FY 05, 13 HBCUs received grants.

HQ: Office of University Partnerships, OPDR-HUD, 451 Seventh St. SW, Washington, DC 20410. Phone: (202) 708-3061, ext.4390.

Internet: www.hud.gov/grants or www.oup.org.

14.850 PUBLIC AND INDIAN HOUSING

Assistance: direct payments/specified use.

Purposes: pursuant to the Housing Act of 1937 as amended, to support lower-income housing projects operated by local public housing agencies. For projects approved prior to 1 October 1986, HUD may award payments for up to 30 years (to 20 years for modernization) to meet debt service requirements that cannot be paid with rental revenue; for contracts executed after 1 October 1986, for up to 40 years. Operating subsidies may be used to achieve and maintain adequate operating and maintenance services and reserves. Localities make contributions through forgiveness of property taxes or payments in lieu of taxes (PILOTs). Note: development and reconstruction projects now are financed through **14.866**.

Eligible applicants: public housing agencies. (Note: per the Native American Housing Assistance and Self-Determination Act of 1996 (NAHASDA), Indian housing authorities now are ineligible.)

Eligible beneficiaries: lower-income families including families with or without children, the elderly and near-elderly, remaining members of a tenant family, certain single persons, the handicapped, and the displaced.

Average: N.A.

Activity: FY 05, subsidies provided for 1,176,766 public housing units.

HQ: Assistant Secretary/Public and Indian Housing-HUD, Washington, DC 20410. Phone: (202) 708-0950.

Internet: www.hud.gov/progdesc/pihindx.html.

14.856 LOWER INCOME HOUSING ASSISTANCE PROGRAM—SECTION 8 MODERATE REHABILITATION

("Section 8 Housing Assistance Payments Program for Very Low Income Families - Moderate Rehabilitation")

Assistance: direct payments/specified use.

Purposes: pursuant to the Housing Act of 1937, Housing and Urban- Rural Recovery Act of 1983, Department of Housing and Urban Development Reform Act of 1989, Housing Opportunity Program Extension Act of 1996, Multifamily Assisted Housing Reform and Affordability Act of 1997, and other housing acts and amendments, to pay rent subsidies to property owners, covering the difference between very-low-income renters' adjusted family income and the market rent for moderately rehabilitated housing. Payments to owners may be made for up to 180 days, and extended for 12 months at a time. Families must pay toward the rent the highest of: 30 percent of their adjusted monthly family income; ten percent of gross monthly family income; or, the portion of welfare assistance designated for their monthly housing cost. The program is inactive; no new projects are being approved.

Eligible applicants/beneficiaries: state, county, municipal, or other authorized public housing agencies. Housing owners coordinate with HUD and/or local agencies to obtain the subsidies for their tenants.

Range/Average: N.A.

Activity: approximately 32,000 units available for occupancy or receiving subsidies under this program.

HQ: Housing Voucher Management and Operations Division, Housing and Voucher Programs, Public and Indian Housing-HUD, Washington, DC 20410. Phone: (202) 708-0477.

Internet: www.hud.gov/progdesc/pihindx.html.

14.862 INDIAN COMMUNITY DEVELOPMENT BLOCK GRANT PROGRAM

Assistance: project grants. (100 percent/to 2 years).

Purposes: pursuant to the Housing and Community Development Act of 1974 as amended, to provide assistance to Indian tribes and Alaska Native villages in the development of viable Indian communities using a broad range of activities designed to result in decent housing and suitable living environments, neighborhood revitalization, economic development, and improved community facilities and services. Program policy requires that the "principal benefit" of projects be to low- and moderate-income persons—i.e., at least 70 percent of the grant allocation. Projects may be operated by the locality or through subgrantees, including public or nonprofit agencies, neighborhood-based organizations, local development corporations, small business investment companies, and other groups. Permitted uses of funds include: virtually any aspect of residential or nonresidential rehabilitation, including historic preservation and energy conservation; energy development; grants or loans to businesses; revolving loan funds for rehabilitation or for economic development purposes; real property acquisition; relocation of households or businesses; demolition; redevelopment site clearance and preparation for re-use; improvement or installation of public works; certain public service programs; housing code enforcement; meeting urgent community needs that present an immediate threat to health or welfare; city planning and related studies. Ineligible uses include: facilities for the general conduct of government; community-wide facilities; new housing construction; housing subsidies paid directly to occupants; income maintenance payments. Cities must: include citizen participation in program planning; have an approved comprehensive housing assistance plan. For "entitlement" communities CDBG grant amounts are based on a statutory formula.

Eligible applicants/beneficiaries: any tribe, band, group, or nation, including Alaska Indians, Aleuts, and Eskimos, and any Alaskan native village eligible for assistance under the Indian Self-Determination and Education

Assistance Act or, previously, under the Local Fiscal Assistance Act of 1972.

Range: $177,000 to $4,951,000 (FY 03 amounts; latest data provided). **Average:** $600,000.

Activity: not quantified specifically.

HQ: Office of Native American Programs, Public and Indian Housing-HUD, Public and Indian Housing-HUD, 451 Seventh St. SW - Rm.4126, Washington, DC 20410. Phone: (202) 401-7914.

Internet: www.hud.gov/offices/pih/ih/grants/icbdg.cfm.

14.865 PUBLIC AND INDIAN HOUSING—INDIAN LOAN GUARANTEE PROGRAM ("Loan Guarantees for Indian Housing")

Assistance: guaranteed/insured loans (to 30 years).

Purposes: pursuant to the Housing and Community Development Act of 1992 as amended, for Native Americans and tribal organizations to acquire new, existing, or rehabilitated homes in Indian areas—using guaranteed mortgage loans available through private financial institutions. Such homes may be sold or rented to families. Individual applicant's total debts should not exceed 41 percent of income, including amount of loan.

Eligible applicants/beneficiaries: native Americans including Alaska natives, or tribes, TDHEs, and Indian housing authorities (*see NOTE preceding* **14.103**).

Range: to 97.75 percent of appraised value if over $50,000; to 98.75 percent if under $50,000. **Average:** $121,089.

Activity: cumulatively 1995-March 2006, 3,017 loans guaranteed.

HQ: Director, Office of Loan Guaranty, Office of Native American Programs, Public and Indian Housing-HUD, 451 Seventh St. SW - Rm.4126, Washington, DC 20410. Phone: (202) 401-7914 (ext.4978).

Internet: www.codetalk.fed.us/loan184.html. (Note: no field offices for this program.)

14.866 DEMOLITION AND REVITALIZATION OF SEVERELY DISTRESSED PUBLIC HOUSING ("HOPE VI")

Assistance: project grants (95 percent).

Purposes: pursuant to the U.S. Housing Act of 1937 as amended by the HOPE VI Program Reauthorization and Small Community Mainstreet Revitalization Housing Act of 2003, to revitalize severely distressed public housing through: demolition of obsolete projects or portions thereof; where appropriate, revitalization of demolition sites by reducing concentrations of very-low-income families. Grant funds may be used for community and supportive services programs, including: relocation of affected residents; disposition activities; rehabilitation of existing public housing units and community facilities. HOPE VI "Mainstreet" funds may be used to develop affordable housing in so-designated rejuvenation areas.

Eligible applicants/beneficiaries: public housing agencies that operate housing projects, not including agencies that administer only Section 8 programs.

Range: revitalization, $16,900,000 to $20,000,000; Main Street grant awards, total $2,459,509. **Average:** revitalization, $19,600,000; Main Street, $492,000.

Activity: FY 05 (cumulative totals), 35 planning, 235 revitalization, 287 demolition-only grants, 5 Main Street awards.

HQ: Office of Urban Revitalization, Deputy Assistant Secretary/Public Housing Investments, Public and Indian Housing- HUD, Washington, DC 20410. Phone: (202) 401-8812.

Internet: www.hud.gov/offices/pih/programs/ph/hope6/.

14.867 INDIAN HOUSING BLOCK GRANTS

Assistance: formula grants. (100 percent/2 years).

Purposes: pursuant to NAHASDA as amended, for affordable housing activities such as: Indian housing assistance; development; housing management services; crime prevention and safety; model activities.

Eligible applicants/beneficiaries: tribes or TDHEs.

Range: $25,000 to $86,112,736. **Average:** $1,668,862.

Activity: N.A.

HQ: Office of Native American Programs, Public and Indian Housing-HUD, Public and Indian Housing-HUD, 451 Seventh St. SW - Rm.4126, Washington, DC 20410. Phone: (202) 401-7914.

Internet: www.hud.gov/progdesc/ihbg1208.cfm.

14.869 TITLE VI FEDERAL GUARANTEES FOR FINANCING TRIBAL HOUSING ACTIVITIES

Assistance: guaranteed/insured loans (from 20 years).

Purposes: pursuant to NAHASDA, to assist tribes or TDHEs to obtain financing for affordable housing where an obligation cannot be completed without such guaranty. Assistance is limited to eligible affordable housing activities listed in Section 202 of the Act, including housing assistance, development, services, crime prevention and safety activities, model activities.

Eligible applicants/beneficiaries: federally recognized Indian tribe or TDHE— approved recipients of Indian Housing Block Grants (IHBG) funds.

Range: to five times the amount of IHGB funds received (program **14.867**).

Activity: N.A.

HQ: Director, Economic Development Access Center, Office of Native American Programs, Public and Indian Housing-HUD, 451 Seventh St. SW - Rm.4126, Washington, DC 20410. Phone: (202) 708- 0614.

Internet: www.hud.gov/codetalk. (Note: no field offices for this program.)

14.870 RESIDENT OPPORTUNITY AND SUPPORTIVE SERVICES—SERVICE COORDINATORS ("ROSS")

Assistance: project grants. (some matching/3 years).

Purposes: pursuant to the U.S. Housing Act of 1937, to assist public housing residents through employment development and supportive services activities, including the employment of service coordinators or case managers. The primary focus is on a spectrum of services for families leading to homeownership and to promote independent living for the elderly and disabled.

Eligible applicants/beneficiaries: public and Indian housing agencies, TDHEs, resident management corporations; resident councils or organizations in partnerships to leverage resources.

Range: $125,000 to $1,000,000.

Activity: approximately 300 grants awarded annually.

HQ: Director, HOPE VI Community and Supportive Services, Office of Public and Voucher Programs, Public and Indian Housing-HUD, 451 Seventh St. SW - Rm.4204, Washington, DC 20410. Phone: (202) 401-8812 ext. 4258; TDD (202) 708-0850.

Internet: www.hud.gov/progdesc/pihindx.html.

14.871 SECTION 8 HOUSING CHOICE VOUCHERS

Assistance: direct payments/specified use.

Purposes: pursuant to the Housing Act of 1937 as amended, Quality Housing and Work Responsibility Act of 1998, and other acts, to consolidate previous Section 8 rental assistance programs into a market-driven program, making tenant-based rental assistance available to low-income families and increasing their housing choices. Payments are made to participating owners, representing the difference between the local standard rent and 30 percent of the family's adjusted income.

Eligible applicants: entities qualifying as public housing agencies including certain public and nonprofit entities that administer Section 8 voucher programs.

Eligible beneficiaries: very low income families—i.e., with income not exceeding 50 percent of the area median); lower income families—i.e., with income not exceeding 80 percent of the area median. Criteria are adjusted for smaller or larger families. For Welfare-to Work vouchers, families must also meet special Welfare-to-Work criteria.

Range: amount necessary to make housing assistance payments and cover related administrative expenses.

Activity: approximately 1,947,000 families receive voucher program assistance.

HQ: Housing Voucher Management and Operations Division, Housing and Voucher Programs, HUD, Washington, DC 20410. Phone: (202) 708-0477.

Internet: www.hud.gov/offices/pih/programs/hcv/index.html.

14.872 PUBLIC HOUSING CAPITAL FUND ("CFP")

Assistance: formula grants. (100 percent/to 4 years).

Purposes: pursuant to the U.S. Housing Act of 1937 as amended and Quality Housing and Work Responsibility Act of 1998, for public housing agencies to pay for their capital and management activities including public housing modernization and development.

Eligible applicants/beneficiaries: public housing agencies.

Range: \$668 to \$367,400,000. **Average:** \$704,000.

Activity: not quantified.

HQ: Assistant Secretary/Public and Indian Housing-HUD, Washington, DC 20410. Phone: (202) 708-0950.

Internet: www.hud.gov/offices/pih/programs/ph/capfund/index.cfm.

14.873 NATIVE HAWAIIAN HOUSING BLOCK GRANTS

Assistance: project grants.

Purposes: pursuant to the Hawaiian Homelands Homeownership Act of 2000, to provide housing assistance to native Hawaiian families. Grants may support development, housing services, crime prevention and safety activities, and model activities.

Eligible applicants: Hawaii Department of Native Hawaiian Home Lands.

Eligible beneficiaries: native Hawaiian families eligible to reside on the Hawaiian Home Lands.

Average: \$9,000,000 per year.

Activity: new program listing in 2003; FY 05, 72 new homes for Native Hawaiian families.

HQ: Office of Native American Programs, Public and Indian Housing-HUD, 500 Ala Moana Blvd. - Ste. 3A, Honolulu, HI 96813. Phone: (808) 522-8175, ext.223.

Internet: www.hud.gov/codetalk. (Note: no other field offices for this program.)

14.874 LOAN GUARANTEES FOR NATIVE HAWAIIAN HOUSING ("Section 184A")

Assistance: guaranteed/insured loans (to 30 years).

Purposes: pursuant to the Hawaiian Homelands Homeownership Act of 2000 and Housing and Community Act of 1992, for Hawaii natives to construct, purchase, or rehabilitate one- to four-family housing located on Hawaiian Home Lands. Small down payments are required.

Eligible applicants/beneficiaries: native Hawaiian families; Department of Hawaiian Homes Lands; Office of Hawaiian Affairs; experienced private nonprofit organizations (*see NOTE preceding* **14.103**).

Range/Average: N.A.

Activity: new program in 2004; 11 homes financed.

HQ: Office of Native American Programs, Public and Indian Housing-HUD, 500 Ala Moana Blvd. - Ste. 3A, Honolulu, HI 96813. Phone: (808) 522-8175, ext.223.

Internet: www.hud.gov/codetalk. (Note: no other field offices for this program.)

14.875 PUBLIC HOUSING NEIGHBORHOOD NETWORK GRANTS

Assistance: project grant. (75 percent/3 years).

Purposes: pursuant U.S. Housing Act of 1937, Section 9(d)(1)(E), for public housing authorities to establish community technology centers to provide internet access, job training, and other supportive services to public housing residents.

Eligible applicants/beneficiaries: public housing authorities.

Range: $100,000 to $550,000.

Activity: new program listing in 2005. FY 06 estimate, 20 awards from100 applicants.

HQ: Director, HOPE VI Community and Supportive Services, Public and Indian Housing-HUD, Washington, DC 20410. Phone: (202) 401- 8812, ext.4258.

Internet: www.hud.gov/pih/programs/ph/ross/aboutnn.cfm. (Note: no field offices for this program.)

14.876 RESIDENT OPPORTUNITY AND SUPPORTIVE SERVICES—ELDERLY AND PERSONS WITH DISABILITIES ("ROSS Elderly and Persons with Disabilities")

Assistance: project grants. (matching/3 years).

Purposes: for programs addressing the needs of public housing residents by providing supportive services, resident empowerment activities, and assisting residents in becoming economically self-sufficient—with a focus on independent living and "aging in place." Funds may be used to employ project coordinators and direct services staff.

Eligible applicants/beneficiaries: public housing authorities; tribes and TDHEs; resident councils, organizations, and nonprofit entities. Applicants must establish partnerships to leverage resources with other federal and nonfederal entities.

Range: $125,000 to $1,000,000.

Activity: new program listing in 2006 (CFDA on-line); approximately 300 grants awarded annually for all ROSS programs available 2001-2004.

HQ: Director, HOPE VI Community and Supportive Services, Public and Indian Housing-HUD, Washington, DC 20410. Phone: (202) 401- 8812, ext.4258.

Internet: www.hud.gov/pih/progdesc/phindxn.html.

14.877 PUBLIC HOUSING FAMILY SELF-SUFFICIENCY UNDER RESIDENT OPPORTUNITY AND SUPPORTIVE SERVICES ("PH FSS")

Assistance: project grants (100 percent).

Purposes: to develop local strategies to coordinate assistance available under the public housing program with public and private resources, to enable participating families to achieve economic independence and housing self-sufficiency. Funds may support the hiring of a program coordinator.

Eligible applicants/beneficiaries: public housing authorities; tribes and TDHEs.

Range: $63,500 to $65,000.

Activity: new program listing in 2006 (CFDA on-line); FY 01-04, 300 grants awarded.

HQ: Director, HOPE VI Community and Supportive Services, Public and Indian Housing-HUD, Washington, DC 20410. Phone: (202) 401- 8812, ext.4258.

Internet: www.hud.gov/pih/progdesc/phindxn.html.

14.878 AFFORDABLE HOUSING DEVELOPMENT IN MAIN STREET REJUVENATION PROJECTS ("Main Street")

Assistance: project grants. (95 percent/30 months).

Purposes: pursuant to the Consolidated Appropriations Act of 2006, HUD Appropriations Act of 2006, and others, to assist small communities in the rejuvenation of historic or traditional central business districts or "Main Street Areas" by replacing unused commercial space with affordable housing units.

Eligible applicants/beneficiaries: units of local government, whose jurisdiction contains a population of no more than 50,000 and have either no Public Housing Agency (PHA) or a PHA that administers less than 101 public housing units.

Range: $500,000 to $1,000,000. **Average:** $493,000.

Activity: new program listing in 2006 (CFDA on-line).

HQ: Office of Public Housing Investments, Office of Urban Revitalization, HUD, Washington, DC 20410 Phone: (202) 401-8812.

Internet: www.hud.gov/offices/pih/programs/ph/hope6.

14.879 MAINSTREAM VOUCHERS

Assistance: direct payments/specified use. (100 percent/5 years).

Purposes: pursuant to the Cranston Gonzalez National Affordable Housing Act, to provide housing assistance payments to participating owners on behalf of eligible tenants with the goal of providing safe, decent, affordable, and sanitary housing for persons with disabilities and Welfare-to-Work families meeting special criteria. Housing assistance payments are the difference between the local payment standard and 30 percent of the family's adjusted income.

Eligible applicants: authorized Public Housing Agencies (PHAs).

Eligible beneficiaries: disabled families who meet income eligibility requirements and are on the Housing Choice Voucher waiting list.

Activity: new program listing in 2006 (CFDA on-line); 12,529 families receive voucher program assistance.

HQ: Office of Public Housing and Voucher Programs, Housing Voucher Management and Operation Division, HUD, Washington, DC 20410 Phone: (202) 708-0477.

Internet: www.hud.gov/offices/pih/programs/hcv/about/fact_sheet.cfm.

14.900 LEAD-BASED PAINT HAZARD CONTROL IN PRIVATELY-OWNED HOUSING

Assistance: project grants. (90 percent/3 years).

Purposes: pursuant to the Housing and Community Development Act of 1992, for programs to identify and control lead-based paint hazards in housing owned by or rented to by low- or very-low- income families, and to prevent childhood lead poisoning caused by lead-based paint. Program objectives include: capacity building; integrating comprehensive community approaches; establishing public registries of lead-safe housing; promoting related job training and employment for low-income area residents. Projects must be conducted by certified contractors and inspectors.

Eligible applicants/beneficiaries: states, cities, or local general government units and tribes with a current, approved "Consolidated Plan.".

Range: $1,000,000 to $3,000,000.

Activity: FY 06 estimate, 32-40 grants; since program inception, 284,280 units tested, 75,000 units made lead-safe.

HQ: Director, Program Management and Assistance Division, Office of Lead Hazard Control-HUD, 451 Seventh St. SW - Rm.P-3206, Washington, DC 20410. Phone: *control grants,* (202) 755- 1785, ext.126; TTY (800) -877-8339.

Internet: www.hud.gov/offices/lead/. (Note: no field offices for this program.)

14.901 HEALTHY HOMES DEMONSTRATION GRANTS

Assistance: project grants. (100 percent/to 3 years).

Purposes: pursuant to the Housing and Urban Development Act of 1970, to develop, demonstrate, and promote cost-effective preventive measures to correct multiple safety and health hazards particularly in low-income home environments, with special focus on children, through: (1) demonstration projects implementing housing assessment, maintenance, renovation, and construction techniques to identify and correct housing-related illness and injury risk factors; (2) outreach and education activities.

Eligible applicants/beneficiaries: nonprofit institutions, profit firms (operating without profit), state and local governments, tribes.

Range: to $1,000,000. **Average:** $959,000.

Activity: FY 06 estimate, 4 to 6 grants.

HQ: Director, Program Management and Assistance Division, Office of Lead Hazard Control-HUD, 451 Seventh St. SW - Rm.P-3206, Washington, DC 20410. Phone: (336) 547-4002, ext.2067; TTY, (800) 877-8339.

Internet: www.hud.gov/offices/lead/. (Note: no field offices for this program.)

14.902 LEAD TECHNICAL STUDIES GRANTS

Assistance: project grants (100 percent/3-4 years).

Purposes: pursuant to the Housing and Community Development Act of 1992, to improve methods for detecting and controlling lead- based paint and other residential health and safety hazards. Project examples: measuring lead in soil using portable X-ray fluorescence analyzers.

Eligible applicants/beneficiaries: nonprofit institutions, profit firms (operating without profit), state and local governments, tribes.

Range: $200,000 to $1,000,000.

Activity: new program listing in 2003. FY 06 estimate, 2-10 awards.

HQ: Office of Healthy Homes and Lead Hazard Control-HUD, 451 Seventh St. SW - Rm.P-3206, Washington, DC 20410. Phone: (202) 755-1785, ext.7687; TTY (800) -877-8339.

Internet: www.hud.gov/offices/lead/techstudies/index.cfm. (Note: no field offices for this program.)

14.903 OPERATION LEAD ELIMINATION ACTION PROGRAM ("LEAP")

Assistance: project grants. (3 years/100 percent).

Purposes: pursuant to the Housing and Community Development Act of 1992, to provide seed money to leverage private sector resources to eliminate lead poisoning as a major public health threat to young children, on both a preventive and remedial basis. Funds have been awarded to such organizations as the National Safety Council, Neighborhood Improvement Development Corporation, and Energy Program Consortium.

Eligible applicants/beneficiaries: tax exempt ("501(c)(3)"), other nonprofit or profit entities or firms, including IHEs. State and local governments are ineligible.

Range: to $2,000,000.

Activity: new program listing in 2003. 23 grants awarded to date per CFDA (on-line) 2006.

HQ: Director, Program Management and Assurance Division, Office of Healthy Homes and Lead Hazard Control-HUD, 451 Seventh St. SW, Washington, DC 20410-3000. Phone: (202) 755-1785, ext. 126; TTY, (800) 877-8339.

Internet: www.hud.gov/offices/lead (Note: no field offices for this program.)

14.904 LEAD OUTREACH GRANTS

Assistance: project grants. (90 percent/to 2 years).

Purposes: pursuant to the Housing and Community Development Act of 1992, to increase enrollment of low-income housing units for treatment via the HUD lead hazard control grant program or another lead treatment program; to develop and distribute outreach and educational materials to raise public awareness of childhood lead poisoning, its prevention and proper lead hazard identification and control methods among at-risk communities and populations of children and workers in the housing maintenance or rehabilitation fields; and, to encourage occupants to identify potential lead-based paint hazards and report them to property managers, and public health and/or housing officials, as appropriate. Funding for FY 07 reported under program **14.902**.

Eligible applicants/beneficiaries: non-profit community-based organizations; academic, for-profit firms, tribes, and certain state and local government units.

Range: $200,000 to $500,000.

Activity: 4-10 grants anticipated.

HQ: Director, Program Management and Assistance Division, Office of Healthy Homes and Lead Hazard Control-HUD, 451 Seventh St. SW, Washington, DC 20410-3000. Phone: (202) 755-1785, est. 7593; TTY, (800) 877-8339.

Internet: www.hud.gov/offices/lead (Note: no field offices for this program.)

14.905 LEAD HAZARD REDUCTION DEMONSTRATION GRANT PROGRAM

Assistance: project grants. (75 percent/3-4 years).

Purposes: pursuant to the Housing and Community Development Act of 1992, for areas with the highest lead paint abatement needs to undertake programs for abatement, inspections, risk assessments, temporary relocations, and interim control of lead-based hazards in eligible private-owned units and multifamily buildings that are occupied by low-income families. Projects must be conducted using certified contractors and inspectors, as well as workers trained through EPA authorized programs.

Eligible applicants/beneficiaries: states, local government units, tribes with approved Consolidated Plan; consortia.

Range: $1,000,000 to $4,000,000.

Activity: FY 06, 10 to 12 grants anticipated.

HQ: Director, Program Management and Assistance Division, Office of Healthy Homes and Lead Hazard Control-HUD, 451 Seventh St. SW, Washington, DC 20410. Phone: (202) 755-1785, ext. 126; FAX (202) 755-1000. TTY, (800) 877-8339.

Internet: www.hud.gov/offices/lead (Note: no field offices for this program.)

14.906 HEALTHY HOMES TECHNICAL STUDIES GRANTS

Assistance: project grants. (100 percent/3-4 years).

Purposes: pursuant to the Housing and Urban Development Act of 1970, for technical studies to improve methods for detecting and controlling housing-related health and safety hazards. Funding for FY 07 reported under program **14.902**.

Eligible applicants/beneficiaries: U.S. academic, nonprofit and profit (operating without profit) institutions; state, local governments; tribes.

Range: $200,000 to $1,000,000.

Activity: new program listing in 2004; 2-8 awards anticipated.

HQ: Office of Healthy Homes and Lead Hazard Control-HUD, 451 Seventh St. SW - Rm.P-3206, Washington, DC 20410. Phone: (202) 755-1785, ext.7595; TTY (800) -877-8339.

Internet: www.hud.gov/offices/lead. (Note: no field offices for this program.)

DEPARTMENT OF THE INTERIOR

BUREAU OF INDIAN AFFAIRS

15.020 AID TO TRIBAL GOVERNMENTS

Assistance: direct payments/specified use.

Purposes: pursuant to the Indian Self-Determination and Education Assistance Act (ISDEAA) as amended, for general tribal government operations, to maintain up-to-date tribal enrollment records, to conduct tribal elections, and to develop tribal policies, legislation, and regulations.

Eligible applicants/beneficiaries: recognized tribal governments.

Range: $10,000 to $700,000. **Average:** $80,000.

Activity: not quantified specifically.

HQ: Deputy Director, Office of Tribal Services (MS-320 SIB), BIA- DOI, 1849 C St. NW, Washington, DC 20240. Phone: (202) 513-7640.

Internet: www.doi.gov/bia/tribegovserv/tribegov.htm; www.doi.gov/bureau-indian-affairs.html.

15.021 CONSOLIDATED TRIBAL GOVERNMENT PROGRAM

Assistance: direct payments/specified use.

Purposes: pursuant to ISDEAA as amended, to combine funding for certain ongoing programs into a single agreement, thus allowing greater flexibility in planning programs and lowering costs of administration—such as scholarships, adult education, job placement, and training.

Eligible applicants/beneficiaries: recognized tribal governments.

Range: $1,300 to $2,400,000. **Average:** $500,000.

Activity: not quantified specifically.

HQ: Deputy Director, Office of Tribal Services (MS-320 SIB), BIA- DOI, 1849 C St. NW, Washington, DC 20240. Phone: (202) 513-7640.

Internet: www.doi.gov/bia/tribegovserv/tribegov.htm; www.doi.gov/bureau-indian-affairs.html.

15.022 TRIBAL SELF-GOVERNANCE

Assistance: direct payments/specified use.

Purposes: pursuant to ISDEAA as amended, for tribal law enforcement, social services, scholarships, welfare payments, housing improvement, road maintenance, and other programs previously administered by DOI—but not for the operation of educational institutions.

Eligible applicants/beneficiaries: recognized tribal governments and consortia.

Range: $330,000 to $9,000,000. **Average:** $6,000,000.

Activity: FY 06, 91 agreements covering 231 tribes.

HQ: Office of Self-Governance (MS-4618 MIB), BIA-OS-DOI, 1849 C St. NW, Washington, DC 20240. Phone: (202) 219-0240.

Internet: www.doi.gov/bureau-indian-affairs.html.

15.024 INDIAN SELF-DETERMINATION CONTRACT SUPPORT ("Contract Support")

Assistance: direct payments/specified use.

Purposes: pursuant to ISDEAA as amended, to cover indirect costs incurred in administering federal programs.

Eligible applicants/beneficiaries: recognized tribal governments and authorized organization.

Range: $10,000 to $8,000,000. **Average:** $190,000.

Activity: annually, 500 tribal governments and organizations funded.

HQ: Deputy Director, Office of Tribal Services (MS-320 SIB), BIA- DOI, 1849 C St. NW, Washington, DC 20240. Phone: (202) 513-7640.

Internet: www.doi.gov/bia/tribegovserv/tribegov.htm; www.doi.gov/bureau-indian-affairs.html.

15.025 SERVICES TO INDIAN CHILDREN, ELDERLY AND FAMILIES ("Social Services")

Assistance: direct payments/specified use.

Purposes: pursuant to the Snyder Act of 1921 and ISDEAA as amended, to administer welfare assistance programs for adults and children including foster care placement; to reduce substance abuse. Funds may support caseworkers and counselors, staffing and operation of emergency shelters, and similar costs.

Eligible applicants/beneficiaries: recognized tribal governments.

Range: $10,000 to $4,800,000. **Average:** $100,000.

Activity: not quantified specifically.

HQ: Chief, Division of Human Services (MS-320 SIB), BIA-DOI, 1849 C St. NW, Washington, DC 20240. Phone: (202) 513-7642.

Internet: www.doi.gov/bia/childw-2.htm; www.doi.gov/bureau-indian-affairs.html.

15.026 INDIAN ADULT EDUCATION

Assistance: direct payments/specified use.

Purposes: pursuant to the Snyder Act of 1921 and ISDEAA as amended, to provide Indian adult education courses, programs, and related activities promoting opportunities for productive employment.

Eligible applicants/beneficiaries: recognized tribal governments.

Range: $100 to $629,000. **Average:** $25,000.

Activity: annually, 140 tribes funded.

HQ: Office of Indian Education Programs (MS-3609 MIB), BIA-DOI, 1849 C St. NW, Washington, DC 20240. Phone: (202) 208-4397.

Internet: www.oeip.bia.edu/contact.htm; www.doi.gov/bureau-indian-affairs.html.

15.027 ASSISTANCE TO TRIBALLY CONTROLLED COMMUNITY COLLEGES AND UNIVERSITIES

Assistance: project grants (100 percent).

Purposes: pursuant to the Tribally Controlled Community College Assistance Act, to operate and improve tribally controlled community colleges, including expansion of their physical resources.

Eligible applicants/beneficiaries: nonprofit, nonsectarian colleges sponsored by recognized tribal governments and organizations, offering certificates or associate, baccalaureate, or graduate degrees.

Range: $213,000 to $11,118,000 (based on enrollment). **Average:** $2,080,000.

Activity: annually, 20,000 Indian students enrolled; 1,000 graduates.

HQ: Office of Indian Education Programs (MS-3609 MIB), BIA-DOI, 1849 C St. NW, Washington, DC 20240. Phone: (202) 208-4397.

Internet: www.oeip.bia.edu/contact.htm; www.doi.gov/bureau-indian-affairs.html.

15.028 TRIBALLY CONTROLLED COMMUNITY COLLEGE ENDOWMENTS

Assistance: project grants (50 percent).

Purposes: pursuant to the Tribally Controlled College Assistance Act, to establish endowments for tribally controlled community colleges. Interest earned may be used to defray college operating costs, but not to benefit private persons.

Eligible applicants/beneficiaries: colleges chartered by recognized tribes, offering certificates or associate, baccalaureate, or graduate degrees.

Range: $10,000 to $64,000. **Average:** $47,000.

Activity: annually, 25 colleges receive grants.

HQ: Office of Indian Education Programs (MS-3609 MIB), BIA-DOI, 1849 C St. NW, Washington, DC 20240. Phone: (202) 208-4397.

Internet: www.oeip.bia.edu/contact.htm; www.doi.gov/bureau-indian-affairs.html.

15.029 TRIBAL COURTS

Assistance: direct payments/specified use.

Purposes: pursuant to ISDEAA as amended, to operate judicial systems. Funds may support salaries and related expenses of judges, prosecutors, defenders, clerks, probation and juvenile officers, and other court personnel.

Eligible applicants/beneficiaries: recognized tribal governments.

Range: $15,000 to $800,000. **Average:** $50,000.

Activity: annually, 250 tribal systems and Courts of Indian Offenses funded, serving 40 tribes.

HQ: Deputy Director, Office of Tribal Services (MS-320 SIB), BIA- DOI, 1849 C St. NW, Washington, DC 20240. Phone: (202) 513-7640.

Internet: www.doi.gov/bia/ots/otshome.htm;www.doi.gov/bureau-indian-affairs.html.

15.030 INDIAN LAW ENFORCEMENT ("Law Enforcement")

Assistance: direct payments/specified use.

Purposes: pursuant to ISDEAA as amended and Indian Law Enforcement Reform Act, to operate tribal police departments and detention facilities. Funds may be used for salaries and related expenses of criminal investigators, uniformed officers, detention personnel, radio dispatchers, administrative costs.

Eligible applicants/beneficiaries: recognized tribal governments.

Range: $20,000 to $20,000,000. **Average:** $200,000.

Activity: annually, 210 tribes funded; 80 detention facilities operated.

HQ: Deputy Director, Law Enforcement Services, (MS-2429 MIB), BIA-DOI, 1849 C St. NW, Washington, DC 20240. Phone: (202) 208- 5787.

Internet: www.bialaw.fedworld.gov/;www.doi.gov/bureau-indian-affairs.html.

15.031 INDIAN COMMUNITY FIRE PROTECTION ("Community Fire Protection")

Assistance: direct payments/specified use.

Purposes: pursuant to ISDEAA as amended, for fire protection services when tribal governments do not receive support for such services from state or local governments. Funds may cover costs of staff, volunteer firefighters training, equipment purchases and repairs, and to purchase smoke detectors, fire extinguishers, fire escapes, and emergency lighting for public buildings.

Eligible applicants/beneficiaries: recognized tribal governments.

Range: $200 to $138,000. **Average:** $10,000.

Activity: annually, 40 tribal fire protection programs on reservations.

HQ: Deputy Director, Office of Tribal Services (MS-320 SIB), BIA- DOI, 1849 C St. NW, Washington, DC 20240. Phone: (202) 513-7640.

Internet: www.doi.gov/bia/ots/otshome.htm;www.doi.gov/bureau-indian-affairs.html.

15.032 INDIAN ECONOMIC DEVELOPMENT

Assistance: direct payments/specified use.

Purposes: pursuant to the Snyder Act of 1921, ISDEAA as amended, and other acts, to administer revolving loan and loan guaranty programs, including assistance to Indian-owned businesses in obtaining private financing—toward improvement of tribal economies. Administered programs may include BIA's Loan Guaranty and Insurance Fund, Indian Business Development Program, and Community and Economic Development Program.

Eligible applicants/beneficiaries: recognized tribal governments.

Range: $5,000 to $300,000. **Average:** $215,000.

Activity: not quantified specifically.

HQ: Deputy Assistant Secretary/Policy and Economic Development (MS-4071 MIB), BIA-DOI, 1849 C St. NW, Washington, DC 20240. Phone: (202) 219-0005.

Internet: www.doi.gov/bia/ecodev/index.htm; www.doi.gov/bureau-indian-affairs.html.

15.033 ROAD MAINTENANCE—INDIAN ROADS

Assistance: direct payments/specified use.

Purposes: pursuant to the Federal Highway Act of 1921 and ISDEAA as amended, for limited routine maintenance of roads, bridges, and airstrips serving Indian reservations, emphasizing school bus routes and arterial highways.

Eligible applicants/beneficiaries: recognized tribal governments and authorized organizations.

Range: $300 to $500,000. **Average:** $100,000.

Activity: annually, maintenance of 50,000 miles of roads, 745 bridges, and numerous airstrips, and operation of a ferry.

HQ: Division of Transportation, Office of Trust Responsibilities (MS-4058 MIB), BIA-DOI, 1849 C St. NW, Washington, DC 20240. Phone: (202) 208-4359.

Internet: www.doi.gov/bia/otrhome.htm.

15.034 AGRICULTURE ON INDIAN LANDS

Assistance: direct payments/specified use; advisory services/counseling; specialized services.

Purposes: pursuant to ISDEAA as amended and American Indian Agriculture Resource Management Act, to protect and restore agronomic and rangeland resources on trust lands; to facilitate the development of renewable agricultural resources. Noxious weed eradication requires 50 percent local matching funds.

Eligible applicants/beneficiaries: recognized tribal governments and authorized organizations.

Range: $200 to $575,000; noxious weed eradication, $500 to $300,000. **Average:** $50,000; weed eradication, $20,000.

Activity: annually, 30,000 farmers, ranchers, and landowners assisted; 50 noxious weed eradication awards, treating 80,000 acres.

HQ: Branch of Agriculture and Range, Division of Water and Land Resources, Office of Trust Responsibilities (MS-4513 MIB), BIA- DOI, 1849 C St. NW, Washington, DC 20240. Phone: (202) 208-3598.

Internet: www.doi.gov/bia/otrhome.htm.

15.035 FORESTRY ON INDIAN LANDS

Assistance: direct payments/specified use; advisory services/counseling; specialized services.

Purposes: pursuant to the Snyder Act of 1921, ISDEAA as amended, and other acts, to maintain, protect, enhance, and develop Indian forest resources. Funds may be used for reforestation, commercial stand improvement, timber sales management, forest planning, and protection activities.

Eligible applicants/beneficiaries: recognized tribal governments and authorized organizations.

Range: $10,000 to $1,000,000. **Average:** $100,000.

Activity: to date, 105 management plans developed for activities on 15,000,000 acres.

HQ: Division of Forestry, Office of Trust Responsibilities (MS- 4513 MIB), BIA-DOI, 1849 C St. NW, Washington, DC 20240. Phone: (202) 208-4837.

Internet: www.doi.gov/bia/otrhome.htm#Forests.

15.036 INDIAN RIGHTS PROTECTION

Assistance: direct payments/specified use.

Purposes: pursuant to ISDEAA as amended and other acts, to protect Indian rights guaranteed through treaty or statute, by obtaining the services or information needed by the federal government to litigate challenges to these rights. Project examples include research and data collection concerning water and land title disputes, hunting and fishing rights, environmental problems.

Eligible applicants/beneficiaries: recognized tribal governments and authorized organizations.

Range: $1,000 to $100,000. **Average:** $25,000.

Activity: not quantified specifically.

HQ: Office of Trust Responsibilities (MS-4510 MIB), BIA-DOI, 1849 C St. NW, Washington, DC 20240. Phone: (202) 208-7737.

Internet: www.doi.gov/bia/Rightsprot.htm.

15.037 WATER RESOURCES ON INDIAN LANDS

Assistance: direct payments/specified use; advisory services/counseling; specialized services.

Purposes: pursuant to the Snyder Act of 1921 and ISDEAA as amended, to assist tribes in the management, planning, and development of their water and related land resources. Water Management, Planning, and Development funds are awarded competitively. Project examples: geographic, hydrologic quantitative and qualitative analysis of water, ground, surface water monitoring; aquifer classification and stream gauging.

Eligible applicants/beneficiaries: recognized tribal governments and authorized organizations.

Range: $50,000 to $1,000,000. **Average:** $50,000.

Activity: annually, 70 litigation and negotiation activities.

HQ: Division of Water and Land Resources, Office of Trust Responsibilities (MS-4513 MIB), BIA-DOI, 1849 C St. NW, Washington, DC 20240. Phone: (202) 208-6042.

Internet: www.doi.gov/bia/otrhome.htm.

15.038 MINERALS AND MINING ON INDIAN LANDS

Assistance: direct payments/specified use; specialized services; technical information.

Purposes: pursuant to the Snyder Act of 1921, ISDEAA as amended, and other acts, to assist and support the inventory and development of energy and minerals on Indian lands. Funds may be used to inventory, develop, and produce nonrenewable resources. Mineral Assessment funds, awarded competitively, may be used for inventory programs and to develop baseline data. Project examples: feasibility studies; lease compliance; environmental reviews; training; seismic explorations; mapping systems.

Eligible applicants/beneficiaries: recognized tribal governments and authorized organizations.

Range: assessments, $25,000 to $150,000. **Average:** $75,000.

Activity: annually, 10-15 assessment projects funded.

HQ: Division of Energy and Minerals, Office of Trust Responsibilities, BIA-DOI, 12136 W. Bayaud Ave. - Ste.300, Lakewood, CO 80228. Phone: (303) 969-5270, ext.222.

Internet: www.doi.gov/bia/otrhome.htm#Energy. (Note: this field office serves as headquarters for this program.)

15.039 FISH, WILDLIFE, AND PARKS PROGRAMS ON INDIAN LANDS ("Wildlife and Parks")

Assistance: direct payments/specified use.

Purposes: pursuant to the Snyder Act of 1921 and ISDEAA as amended, to promote the conservation, development, and utilization of fish, wildlife, and recreational resources for sustenance, cultural enrichment, economic support, and maximum benefit of Indians. Tribes participate in resource planning and management with their state and federal counterparts. The program supports continuing activities; generally, no new projects are funded.

Eligible applicants/beneficiaries: recognized tribal governments and authorized organizations.

Range: $5,000 to $800,000; fish hatchery maintenance, $1,500 to $22,000; also, approximately $1,150,000 for bison restoration support to 50 tribes. **Average:** hatcheries, $12,000.

Activity: annually, awards to 8 intertribal fish and wildlife commissions and authorities, 11 fish-producing tribes, 100 tribal fish hatcheries, 32 individual fish and wildlife resource tribes, 6 tribal fish and wildlife organizations.

HQ: Branch of Fish, Wildlife, and Recreation, Division of Water and Land Resources, Office of Trust Responsibilities (MS-3061 MIB), BIA-DOI, 1849 C St. NW, Washington, DC 20240. Phone: (202) 208-4088.

Internet: www.doi.gov/bia/otrhome.htm#Fish.

15.040 REAL ESTATE PROGRAMS—INDIAN LANDS

Assistance: direct payments/specified use.

Purposes: pursuant to ISDEAA as amended, Indian Land Consolidation Act, and other acts, to provide real property management, counseling, and land use planning services to individual Indian allottees and tribal and Alaska native entities owning an interest in the almost 56,000,000 acres of trust land; to provide appraisal services required in processing land transactions; to protect and enhance the Indian leasehold estate by providing individual landowners and tribes with lease compliance activities.

Eligible applicants/beneficiaries: recognized tribal governments and authorized organizations; individual American Indians.

Range: services, $1,000 to $500,000; appraisals, $500 to $2,500; lease compliance, $250 to $30,000. **Average:** lease compliance, to $5,000.

Activity: cumulatively, 12,000 surface leases approved; 7,800 acquisitions, 4,000 land sales processed; 20,000 appraisals; 25,000 inspections completed on 100,000 leases.

HQ: Division of Real Estate Services, Office of Trust Responsibilities (MS-4510 MIB), BIA-DOI, 1849 C St. NW, Washington, DC 20240. Phone: (202) 208-7737.

Internet: www.doi.gov/bia/otrhome.htm#Land.

15.041 ENVIRONMENTAL MANAGEMENT—INDIAN PROGRAMS

Assistance: direct payments/specified use.

Purposes: pursuant to ISDEAA as amended, CERCLA, SWDA, RCRA, and other acts, to determine environmental impacts of federal projects on Indian lands and to identify hazardous waste sites—to determine compliance with the National Environmental Policy Act; to prepare Environmental Assessments; to obtain information for compliance with the National Historic Preservation Act and the Archeological Resources Protection Act.

Eligible applicants/beneficiaries: recognized tribal governments and authorized organizations.

Range: $5,000 to $250,000. **Average:** $25,000.

Activity: annually, 3,000 compliance issues addressed, 50 emergency responses.

HQ: Division of Environmental and Cultural Resources Management, Office of Trust Responsibilities (MS-4513 MIB), BIA-DOI, 1849 C St. NW, Washington, DC 20240. Phone: (202) 208-5696.

Internet: www.doi.gov/bureau-indian-affairs.html.

15.042 INDIAN SCHOOL EQUALIZATION PROGRAM ("ISEP")

Assistance: direct payments/specified use.

Purposes: pursuant to ISDEAA as amended, Indian Education Amendments of 1978, and Tribally Controlled Schools Act, for primary and secondary education including residential programs for Indian students not served by public or sectarian schools.

Eligible applicants/beneficiaries: recognized tribes or tribal organizations currently served by a BIA-funded school.

Range: $120,000 to $7,091,000. **Average:** $1,700,000 per school.

Activity: annually, 30,000 students served by 122 tribally operated schools.

HQ: Office of Indian Education Programs (MS-3609 MIB), BIA-DOI, 1849 C St. NW, Washington, DC 20240. Phone: (202) 208-7658.

Internet: www.oiep.bia.edu.

15.043 INDIAN CHILD AND FAMILY EDUCATION ("Family and Child Education - FACE")

Assistance: project grants; training (100 percent).

Purposes: pursuant to the Indian Education Amendments of 1978, to conduct early childhood education, adult education, and parenting skills programs. Funds may not be used for administration costs.

Eligible applicants/beneficiaries: recognized tribes or tribal organizations currently served by a BIA-funded school.

Average: $250,000 per site.

Activity: annually, 1,800 children, 1,800 adults, and 1,700 families receive services.

HQ: Center for School Improvement, Office of Indian Education Programs, BIA-DOI, 1011 Indian School Rd, NW, 3rd Floor, Ste. 332, Albuquerque, NM 87104. Phone: (505) 563-5258.

Internet: www.oeip.bia.edu/sirc.htm. (Note: this field office serves as headquarters for this program.)

15.044 INDIAN SCHOOLS—STUDENT TRANSPORTATION

Assistance: direct payments/specified use.

Purposes: pursuant to ISDEAA as amended, Indian Education Amendments of 1978, and Tribally Controlled Schools Act, to provide round-trip transportation of students between home and schools.

Eligible applicants: recognized tribes or tribal organizations currently served by a BIA-funded school.

Eligible beneficiaries: Indian children age 5 to 21, enrolled in schools eligible for assistance under **15.042**.

Range: $2,000 to $1,133,000. **Average:** $204,000.

Activity: annually, 20,000 students served.

HQ: Office of Indian Education Programs (MS-3609 MIB), BIA-DOI, 1849 C St. NW, Washington, DC 20240. Phone: (202) 208-7658.

Internet: www.oiep.bia.edu.

15.045 ASSISTANCE FOR INDIAN CHILDREN WITH SEVERE DISABILITIES ("Institutionalized Handicapped")

Assistance: direct payments/specified use.

Purposes: pursuant to ISDEAA as amended, Indian Education Amendments of 1978, and IDEA, for special education and related services to Indian children with severe disabilities, including: physical, occupational, and speech therapy; counseling; direct academic services; administration and staff development.

Eligible applicants/beneficiaries: members or direct descendants of members of recognized tribes, age 5 to 21, enrolled in BIA- funded schools, and determined to need specialized services available only in residential settings.

Range: $140 to $300 per day.

Activity: annually, institutional services to 170 students requiring 24-hours/day attention.

HQ: Center for School Improvement, Office of Indian Education Programs, BIA-DOI, 500 Gold Ave, SW, 7th Floor. P.O. Box 1088, Albuquerque, NM 87103-1088. Phone: (505) 248-6942.

Internet: www.oeip.bia.edu/sped.htm. (Note: field office serves as headquarters for this program.)

15.046 ADMINISTRATIVE COST GRANTS FOR INDIAN SCHOOLS ("Institutionalized Handicapped")

Assistance: project grants (100 percent).

Purposes: pursuant to ISDEAA as amended, Indian Education Amendments of 1978, and Tribally Controlled Schools Act, to pay school operating costs including administration, property and procurement management, insurance, safety, and related expenses.

Eligible applicants/beneficiaries: recognized tribes or tribal organizations operating BIA-funded schools.

Range: $49,000 to $1,785,000. **Average:** $363,000.

Activity: annually, funding for 122 tribally operated schools.

HQ: Office of Indian Education Programs (MS-3609 MIB), BIA-DOI, 1849 C St. NW, Washington, DC 20240. Phone: (202) 208-7658.

Internet: www.oeip.bia.edu/administration.htm.

15.047 INDIAN EDUCATION FACILITIES, OPERATIONS, AND MAINTENANCE

Assistance: direct payments/specified use.

Purposes: pursuant to ISDEAA as amended, Indian Education Amendments of 1978, and Tribally Controlled Schools Act, to pay facilities operations and maintenance costs including personnel, utilities, minor repairs, equipment, and similar costs.

Eligible applicants/beneficiaries: recognized tribal governments or organizations currently served by BIA-funded elementary or secondary schools or peripheral dormitories.

Range: $9,600 to $1,326,000. **Average:** $360,000.

Activity: annually, 100 schools funded.

HQ: Office of Indian Education Programs (MS-3609 MIB), BIA-DOI, 1849 C St. NW, Washington, DC 20240. Phone: (202) 208-7658.

Internet: www.oiep.bia.edu.

15.048 BUREAU OF INDIAN AFFAIRS FACILITIES—OPERATIONS AND MAINTENANCE

Assistance: direct payments/specified use.

Purposes: pursuant to ISDEAA as amended, for basic operating and maintenance services provided to BIA-owned or -operated noneducation facilities, including expenses incurred for personnel, supplies, planning, utility costs, telecommunications equipment, and similar costs.

Eligible applicants/beneficiaries: recognized tribal governments with BIA-owned or -operated facilities on their reservations.

Range/Average: N.A.

Activity: annually, funding for 1,263 buildings, excluding quarters.

HQ: Director, Office of Facilities Management and Construction, BIA-DOI, 201 Third St. NW - Ste.500, P.O. Box 1248, Albuquerque, NM 87103. Phone: (505) 346-6522.

Internet: www.doi.gov/bia/ofmc/om/htm. (Note: field office serves as headquarters for this program.)

15.049 IRRIGATION OPERATIONS AND MAINTENANCE ON INDIAN LANDS ("Irrigation O and M")

Assistance: direct payments/specified use; specialized services; use of property, facilities, and equipment.

Purposes: pursuant to ISDEAA as amended, American Indian Agriculture Resource Management Act, Indian Dams Safety Act of 1994, and other acts, to operate and maintain existing Indian irrigation projects and the Indian Dams Safety Maintenance Program.

Eligible applicants/beneficiaries: recognized tribal governments and authorized organizations.

Range: $8,000 to $3,000,000.

Activity: not quantified specifically.

HQ: Branch of Irrigation, Power, and Safety of Dams, Division of Water and Land Resources, Office of Trust Responsibilities (MS-4513 MIB), BIA-DOI, 1849 C St. NW, Washington, DC 20240. Phone: (202) 208-5480.

Internet: www.doi.gov/bureau-indian-affairs.html.

15.050 UNRESOLVED INDIAN HUNTING AND FISHING RIGHTS

Assistance: direct payments/specified use.

Purposes: pursuant to the Snyder Act of 1921 and ISDEAA as amended, to assist tribes in negotiations with other fish and wildlife resource management authorities in clarifying and defining their off-reservation hunting, fishing, and gathering rights.

Eligible applicants/beneficiaries: recognized tribal governments and authorized organizations.

Range: $50,000 to $320,000.

Activity: generally, only 1 competitive award annually, supporting 20 tribes.

HQ: Division of Water and Land Resources, Branch of Fish, Wildlife and Recreation, Office of Trust Responsibilities (MS-3061 MIB), BIA-DOI, 1849 C St. NW, Washington, DC 20240. Phone: (202) 208-4088.

Internet: www.doi.gov/bureau-indian-affairs.html.

15.051 ENDANGERED SPECIES ON INDIAN LANDS

Assistance: direct payments/specified use; technical information; advisory services/counseling.

Purposes: pursuant to the Snyder Act of 1921, ISDEAA as amended, and the Endangered Species Act, to enable compliance with the Endangered Species Act, the Northern Spotted Owl Recovery Plan, and to implement the Cheyenne River Prairie Management Plan on Indian lands. Project examples: water impoundments, cross fencing and vegetative management; owl and habitat surveys.

Eligible applicants/beneficiaries: recognized tribal governments and authorized organizations whose reservations are inhabited by specific endangered species.

Range: $20,000 to $1,000,000. **Average:** $500,000.

Activity: annually, 12 tribes funded.

HQ: Branch of Environmental and Cultural Resources Management, Division of Water and Land Resources, Office of Trust Responsibilities (MS-4513 MIB), BIA-DOI, 1849 C St. NW, Washington, DC 20240. Phone: (202) 208-5037.

Internet: www.doi.gov/bia/otrhome.htm.

15.052 LITIGATION SUPPORT FOR INDIAN RIGHTS

Assistance: direct payments/specified use.

Purposes: pursuant to ISDEAA as amended, Indian Claims Limitation Act of 1982, and other acts, to establish or defend Indian property or treaty rights through judicial, administrative, or settlement actions. Funds may be used to pay for expert witnesses, research, data collection, technical support, and other evidence-gathering activities required to defend such rights issues as: hunting, fishing, and gathering; trespass; titles; allotment claims; mineral entry; Equal Access to Justice Act settlements.

Eligible applicants/beneficiaries: recognized tribal governments and authorized organizations.

Range: $2,000 to $220,000. **Average:** $76,000.

Activity: annually, 20-25 requests funded.

HQ: Office of Trust Responsibilities, BIA-DOI, (MS-4510 MIB), 1849 C St. NW, Washington, DC 20240. Phone: (202) 208-5831.

Internet: www.doi.gov/bia/otrhome.htm.

15.053 ATTORNEY FEES—INDIAN RIGHTS

Assistance: direct payments/specified use.

Purposes: pursuant to the Indian Claims Limitation Act of 1982 and other acts, to support tribes in protecting their treaty rights and other rights established through executive order or court action, by providing assistance in obtaining legal representation. Project examples: environmental damage claims; water rights negotiation or litigation; boundary disputes.

Eligible applicants/beneficiaries: recognized tribal governments.

Range: $20,000 to $237,000. **Average:** $60,000.

Activity: N.A.

HQ: Office of Trust Responsibilities, BIA-DOI, (MS-4510 MIB), 1849 C St. NW, Washington, DC 20240. Phone: (202) 208-5831.

Internet: www.doi.gov/bia/otrhome.htm.

15.055 ALASKAN INDIAN ALLOTMENTS AND SUBSISTENCE PREFERENCE—ALASKA NATIONAL INTEREST LANDS CONSERVATION ACT ("ANILCA")

Assistance: direct payments/specified use.

Purposes: pursuant to the Indian Claims Limitation Act of 1982, Alaska National Interest Lands Conservation Act of 1980, ISDEAA as amended, and other acts, to assist Alaska natives in acquiring title to lands they occupy; to study past subsistence uses and conduct population studies on subsistence resources.

Eligible applicants/beneficiaries: recognized tribal governments in Alaska and authorized organizations; individual Alaska natives.

Range: allotments, $12,000 to $221,000; subsistence preferences, $15,000 to $40,000.

Activity: cumulatively, 9,000 parcels finalized, 2,800 parcels awaiting final action.

HQ: Office of Trust Responsibilities, BIA-DOI, (MS-4510 MIB), 1849 C St. NW, Washington, DC 20240. Phone: (202) 208-5831.

Internet: www.doi.gov/bia/otrhome.htm.

15.057 NAVAJO-HOPI INDIAN SETTLEMENT PROGRAM

Assistance: direct payments/specified use.

Purposes: pursuant to the Navajo-Hopi Settlement Act and ISDEAA as amended, to restore the grazing potential of rangeland within the former Navajo/Hopi Joint Use Area, including: livestock monitoring; issuance of grazing permits; implementation of range management plans and grazing control methods; establishment of range units and grazing capacity; removal of trespass livestock on the Hopi Partitioned Lands; initiation of grazing control on the Navajo Partitioned Lands; natural resources restoration.

Eligible applicants/beneficiaries: recognized tribal governments of the Navajo and Hopi tribes and organizations authorized by either tribe.

Range: $5,000 to $150,000. **Average:** $75,000.

Activity: activities are ongoing; restoration of 910,021 acres, maintenance of 630 miles of fencing and 123 stock water facilities.

HQ: Office of Trust Responsibilities (MS-3061 MIB), BIA-DOI, 1849 C St. NW, Washington, DC 20240. Phone: (202) 208-6464.

Internet: www.doi.gov/bureau-indian-affairs.html.

15.058 INDIAN POST SECONDARY SCHOOLS ("Haskell Indian Nations University and Southwestern Indian Polytechnic Institute - SIPI")

Assistance: training.

Purposes: pursuant to the Snyder Act of 1921, to enable American Indian students to attend either of the BIA-operated postsecondary schools with minimal charge for tuition or room and board: Haskell Indian Nations University and Southwestern Indian Polytechnic Institute (SIPI).

Eligible applicants/beneficiaries: members of recognized tribes.

Range/Average: N.A.

Activity: annually, 900 students enrolled at Haskell, 174 graduates; 600 students enrolled at SIPI, 100 graduates.

HQ: Haskell Indian Nations University, 155 Indian Ave., Lawrence, KS 66046. Phone: (913) 749-8454. *Or,* SIPI, 9169 Coors Rd. NW, Albuquerque, NM 81774. Phone: (505) 346-2348.

Internet: same as **15.027** ; *and,* www.oiep.bia.edu; www.Haskell.edu.

15.059 INDIAN GRADUATE STUDENT SCHOLARSHIPS ("Special Higher Education Scholarships")

Assistance: project grants.

Purposes: pursuant to the Snyder Act of 1921, to provide financial aid to Indian students, enabling them to obtain advanced degrees.

Eligible applicants/beneficiaries: Indian students that are members of recognized tribal governments, admitted to a graduate program.

Range: $250 to $4,000 annually. **Average:** $3,200.

Activity: annually, 325 students assisted.

HQ: American Indian Graduate Center, BIA-DOI, 4520 Montgomery Blvd. - Ste.1-B, Albuquerque, NM 87109. Phone: (505) 881-4584.

Internet: www.oiep.bia.edu/contact.htm. (Note: no other field offices for this program.)

15.060 INDIAN VOCATIONAL TRAINING—UNITED TRIBES TECHNICAL COLLEGE

Assistance: training; direct payments/unrestricted use.

Purposes: pursuant to the Snyder Act of 1921, ISDEAA as amended, and Indian Adult Vocational Training Act of 1956, to provide vocational training to American Indians through the United Tribes Technical College in Bismarck, North Dakota.

Eligible applicants: the United Tribes Technical College.

Eligible beneficiaries: members of recognized tribes, residing on or near reservations under BIA jurisdiction and needing financial assistance.

Range: $500 to $3,000. **Average:** $2,500.

Activity: annually, 160 students admitted; 23 vocational certificates/degrees offered.

HQ: Division of Job Placement and Training, Office of Self- Governance and Self-Determination (MS-2542 MIB), BIA-DOI, 1849 C St. NW, Washington, DC 20240. Phone: (202) 219-5270.

Internet: www.united-tribes.tec.nd.us/.

15.061 INDIAN JOB PLACEMENT—UNITED SIOUX TRIBES DEVELOPMENT CORPORATION ("United Sioux Tribes")

Assistance: direct payments/specified use; advisory services/counseling.

Purposes: pursuant to the Snyder Act of 1921, ISDEAA as amended, and Indian Adult Vocational Training Act of 1956, to assist Indians in finding permanent employment through job development programs, counseling, and referrals to job training programs—through the United Sioux Tribes Development Corporation in Pierre, South Dakota. Participants receive stipends.

Eligible applicants: Eligible applicants: United Sioux Tribes Development Corporation.

Eligible beneficiaries: members of federally recognized tribes, residing on or near reservations under BIA jurisdiction.

Range: $500 to $1,200. **Average:** $1,000.

Activity: not quantified specifically.

HQ: Division of Job Placement and Training, Office of Economic Development (MS-2412 MIB), BIA-DOI, 1849 C St. NW, Washington, DC 20240. Phone: (202) 219-5270.

Internet: www.doi.gov.

15.062 REPLACEMENT AND REPAIR OF INDIAN SCHOOLS

Assistance: direct payments/specified use.

Purposes: pursuant to ISDEAA and Tribally Controlled Schools Act of 1988 as amended, and Tribal Self-Governance Act of 1994, for advanced planning, design, and construction of major expansion or replacement projects or improvement and repair projects—involving BIA-owned or -funded education facilities for the direct support of primary and secondary schools and dormitories.

Eligible applicants/beneficiaries: recognized tribal governments and organizations, including school boards.

Range: expansion/replacement, $6,000,000 to $25,000,000; improvement/ repair, to $7,000,000.

Activity: not quantified specifically.

HQ: Director, Office of Facilities Management and Construction, BIA-DOI, 201 Third St. NW - Ste.500, P.O. Box 1248, Albuquerque, NM 87103. Phone: (505) 346-6522.

Internet: www.doi.gov/bia/ofmc/om/htm.

15.063 IMPROVEMENT AND REPAIR OF INDIAN DETENTION FACILITIES

Assistance: direct payments/specified use.

Purposes: pursuant to ISDEAA as amended and Tribal Self- Governance Act of 1994, for advanced planning, design, and construction, and improvements, repair, additions to, BIA adult or juvenile detention facilities.

Eligible applicants/beneficiaries: recognized tribal governments.

Range: to $1,000,000.

Activity: not quantified specifically.

HQ: Director, Office of Law Enforcement Services, P.O. Box 66, Albuquerque, NM 87103. Phone: (505) 248-7937. *Or* Director, Office of Facilities Management and Construction, BIA-DOI, 201 Third St. NW - Ste.500, P.O. Box 1248, Albuquerque, NM 87103. Phone: (505) 346-6522.

Internet: www.doi.gov/bia/ofmc/cm/htm#3.

15.064 STRUCTURAL FIRE PROTECTION—BUREAU OF INDIAN AFFAIRS FACILITIES ("Fire Protection")

Assistance: direct payments/specified use.

Purposes: pursuant to ISDEAA and Tribally Controlled Schools Act of 1988 as amended, and the Tribal Self-Governance Act of 1994, to install fire protection and varied prevention equipment in schools, dormitories, detention centers, and other BIA facilities. Funds also may be used for personnel training, to conduct inventories, and to retrofit equipment.

Eligible applicants/beneficiaries: recognized tribal governments and organizations, including school boards.

Range: $5,000 to $250,000. **Average:** $120,000.

Activity: not quantified specifically.

HQ: Structural Fire Protection Program Manager, Office of Facilities Management and Construction, BIA-DOI, 201 Third St. NW - Ste.500, P.O. Box 1248, Albuquerque, NM 87103. Phone: (505) 346-6522.

Internet: www.doi.gov/bia/ofmc/sp/htm.

15.065 SAFETY OF DAMS ON INDIAN LANDS

Assistance: direct payments/specified use. (100 percent/1-5 years).

Purposes: pursuant to the Snyder Act of 1921, ISDEAA as amended, and Indian Dams Safety Act of 1994, to improve the structural integrity of the 116 dams on Indian lands, for which BIA has responsibility, including inspection, hazard classification, and modification construction.

Eligible applicants/beneficiaries: recognized tribal governments and authorized organizations.

Range: conception design, $100,000 to $300,000; final design, $300,000 to $1,000,000; construction, $1,000,000 to $17,000,000.

Activity: FY 03, 4 final design completions; FY 04, 1 appropriation request for construction phase.

HQ: Branch of Irrigation, Power, and Safety of Dams, Division of Water and Land Resources, Office of Trust Responsibilities (MS-4513 MIB), BIA-DOI, 1849 C St. NW, Washington, DC 20240. Phone: (202) 208-5480.

Internet: www.doi.gov/bia/otrhome.htm.

15.108 INDIAN EMPLOYMENT ASSISTANCE

Assistance: direct payments/specified use.

Purposes: pursuant to the Snyder Act of 1921, ISDEAA, Indian Adult Vocational Training Act, amendments, and other acts, for American Indians to obtain vocational training and employment opportunities. Funds may be used for subsistence, tuition, and related training costs. Payments may extend for up to two years—three years for registered nurses training.

Eligible applicants: federally recognized tribal governments and authorized organizations.

Eligible beneficiaries: unemployed or under-employed members of recognized tribes, residing on or near an Indian reservation under BIA jurisdiction.

Range: tribal awards, $7,000 to $350,000; individuals, $200 to $10,000 per year. **Average:** tribal, $46,000; individuals, $5,100.

Activity: annually, 175 tribal awards assisting 1,500 persons.

HQ: Division of Job Placement and Training, Office of Economic Development (MS-2412 MIB), BIA-DOI, 1849 C St. NW, Washington, DC 20240. Phone: (202) 219-5270.

Internet: www.doi.gov/bia/ecodev/index.htm.

15.113 INDIAN SOCIAL SERVICES—WELFARE ASSISTANCE

Assistance: direct payments/specified use.

Purposes: pursuant to the Snyder Act of 1921, for cash payments to needy Indians to pay for: food, clothing, shelter, etc.; adult nonmedical institutional or custodial care; foster home care; burial expenses; emergency assistance—when such assistance is unavailable from state or local public agencies. Extra benefits are provided when recipients are receiving general assistance and work under the Tribal Work Experience Program.

Eligible applicants/beneficiaries: needy members of recognized tribes, living on or near reservations.

Range: to several hundred dollars monthly.

Activity: monthly average of 41,000 persons receiving general assistance payments, 3,000 children receiving Indian Child Welfare Assistance, 1,100 disabled adults receiving nonmedical institutional or custodial care.

HQ: Deputy Director, Office of Tribal Services (MS-320 SIB), BIA- DOI, 1849 C St. NW, Washington, DC 20245. Phone: (202) 513-7642.

Internet: www.doi.gov/bia/childw~2.htm.

15.114 INDIAN EDUCATION—HIGHER EDUCATION GRANT PROGRAM

Assistance: project grants. (100 percent/to 5 years).

Purposes: pursuant to the Snyder Act of 1921, to provide financial assistance to Indian undergraduate college students, supplementing aid packages awarded by colleges.

Eligible applicants/beneficiaries: recognized tribal governments and authorized organizations; members of tribes in financial need, enrolled in or accepted by an accredited college.

Range: $300 to $5,000. **Average:** $3,000.

Activity: annually, 9,800 students assisted.

HQ: Office of Indian Education Programs (MS-3609 MIB), BIA-DOI, 1849 C St. NW, Washington, DC 20240. Phone: (202) 208-4397.

Internet: www.oeip.bia.edu/scholarships.htm.

15.124 INDIAN LOANS—ECONOMIC DEVELOPMENT ("Loan Guaranty Program")

Assistance: guaranteed/insured loans. (to 90 percent/to 30 years).

Purposes: pursuant to the Snyder Act of 1921, ISDEAA as amended, and other acts, for economic development on or near federal Indian reservations, through projects on or near reservations, involving business, industry, or agriculture. Borrowers must have 20 percent equity in businesses being financed.

Eligible applicants/beneficiaries: recognized tribal governments and authorized organizations; individual American Indians.

Range: individuals and tribal enterprises, $50,000 to $500,000; tribes, $500,000 to $12,000,000. **Average:** individuals and tribal enterprises, $200,000; tribes, $3,000,000.

Activity: cumulatively, $714,000,000 in guaranteed loans awarded.

HQ: Assistant Secretary Indian Affairs, Office of Indian Energy and Economic Development, (MS 20 SIB), BIA-DOI, 1951 Constitution Ave. NW, Washington, DC 20240. Phone: (202) 513-7681.

Internet: www.doi.gov/bia/ecodev/loanpgm.html.

15.130 INDIAN EDUCATION—ASSISTANCE TO SCHOOLS ("Johnson-O'Malley")

Assistance: direct payments/specified use.

Purposes: pursuant to the Johnson-O'Malley Act of 1934 as amended and ISDEAA, for supplemental education programs for Indians in public schools. Project examples: home-school coordinators; remedial tutoring; educational field trips; cultural programs.

Eligible applicants: tribal organizations, Indian corporations, school districts, or states with eligible Indian Education Committees.

Eligible beneficiaries: children age 3 through grade 12, of one- fourth or more degree of Indian blood and descendants of members of recognized tribes—with priority to those residing on or near reservations.

Range: $700 to $4,359,000. **Average:** $72,000.

Activity: annually, 272,000 students in 33 states served.

HQ: Office of Indian Education Programs (MS-3609 MIB), BIA-DOI, 1849 C St. NW, Washington, DC 20240. Phone: (202) 208-4397.

Internet: www.oeip.bia/edu/jom.htm.

15.141 INDIAN HOUSING ASSISTANCE

Assistance: project grants; technical information (grants, 100 percent).

Purposes: pursuant to ISDEAA as amended, for home improvements, for housing construction in certain situations, and for technical assistance in establishing housing plans. The HHS Indian Health Service may supplement this program by funding water and sanitary systems. Program is restricted to use within reservations and approved tribal service areas.

Eligible applicants/beneficiaries: recognized tribal governments and organizations; Indians needing Housing Improvement Program assistance.

Range: repairs/renovations, to $35,000; interim improvements, $2,500. **Average:** repairs, $17,500; new housing, $55,000.

Activity: annually, 500 families receive assistance.

HQ: Deputy Director, Office of Tribal Services (MS-320 SIB), BIA- DOI, 1849 C St. NW, Washington, DC 20245. Phone: (202) 513-7640.

Internet: www.doi.gov/bia/tservices/hip/housing.htm.

15.144 INDIAN CHILD WELFARE ACT—TITLE II GRANTS

Assistance: project grants (100 percent).

Purposes: pursuant to the Indian Child Welfare Act, for the operation and maintenance of counseling programs and facilities related to child and family services, including: family assistance; protective day and after-school care; recreational activities; respite care; foster care subsidies; preparation and administration of child welfare codes, including legal representation; education and training; related services and programs.

Eligible applicants/beneficiaries: recognized tribal governments.

Range: $26,000 to $750,000. **Average:** $60,000.

Activity: annually, 27,000 referrals to 500 child abuse and neglect investigation programs.

HQ: Deputy Director, Office of Tribal Services (MS-320 SIB), BIA- DOI, 1849 C St. NW, Washington, DC 20245. Phone: (202) 513-7640.

Internet: www.doi.gov/bia/ots/otshome.htm.

15.146 IRONWORKER TRAINING PROGRAM

Assistance: project grants. (100 percent/to 12 weeks).

Purposes: pursuant to the Snyder Act of 1921 and the Indian Adult Vocational Training Act of 1956 as amended, to pay stipends to native Americans to permit them to obtain vocational training and apprenticeships as ironworkers at the National Ironworker Training Program in Broadview, Illinois, and to provide job placement assistance.

Eligible applicants/beneficiaries: American Indian members of recognized tribes, at least age 20, with a high school diploma or equivalent certificate, residing on or near an Indian reservation under BIA jurisdiction, and in good physical health.

Average: $185/week plus work clothes and tools.

Activity: cumulatively, 120 participants; over 80 have completed training; 60 subsequently employed.

HQ: Division of Job Placement and Training, Office of Economic Development (MS-2412 MIB), BIA-DOI, 1849 C St. NW, Washington, DC 20240. Phone: (202) 219-5270.

Internet: www.doi.gov/bia/ecodev/index.htm.

15.147 TRIBAL COURTS—TRUST REFORM INITIATIVE

Assistance: project grants (formula-based).

Purposes: pursuant to ISDEAA as amended and the American Indian Trust Fund Management Reform Act of 1994, to supplement funds available to tribal governments assuming specific increased responsibilities such as: appointing guardians; determining competency; awarding child support from Indian Individual Money (IIM) accounts; determining paternity; sanctioning adoptions, marriages, and divorces; making presumptions of death; adjudicating claims involving trust assets. Funds may not be used for general operating costs.

Eligible applicants/beneficiaries: federally-recognized tribal governments.

Range: $3,000 to $216,000. **Average:** $50,000.

Activity: N.A.; new program listing in 2003.

HQ: Office of Tribal Government Services (MS-320 SIB), BIA-DOI, 1849 C St. NW, Washington, DC 20240. Phone: (202) 513-7641.

Internet: www.doi.gov/bia/ots/otshome.htm.

BUREAU OF LAND MANAGEMENT

15.214 NON-SALE DISPOSALS OF MINERAL MATERIAL ("Free Use of Mineral Material")

Assistance: sale, exchange, or donation of property and goods.

Purposes: pursuant to the Materials Act of 1947 as amended, to grant free use permits to extract mineral material from BLM lands for use in public projects. Such material may not be bartered or sold.

Eligible applicants/beneficiaries: federal or state agencies, municipalities; nonprofit entities.

Range/Average: N.A.

Activity: N.A.

HQ: Team Leader, Use Authorization Team, BLM-DOI, Washington, DC 20240. Phone: (202) 452-0350.

Internet: www.blm.gov/nhp/index.htm.

15.222 COOPERATIVE INSPECTION AGREEMENTS WITH STATES AND TRIBES ("Section 202 Agreements")

Assistance: project grants (to 100 percent).

Purposes: pursuant to the Federal Oil and Gas Royalty Act of 1982, for inspections of oil and gas leases on Indian lands, by tribal inspectors.

Eligible applicants/beneficiaries: tribes with producing oil and gas leases on Indian lands for which the federal government has trust responsibility; states with tribal permission.

Range: $664 to $260,000. **Average:** $68,000.

Activity: to date, 655 inspections, 394 violations detected.

HQ: Assistant Director, Resource Use and Protection (300), BLM- DOI, Washington, DC 20240. Phone: (202) 208-4201.

Internet: www.blm.gov/nhp/index.htm.

15.224 CULTURAL RESOURCE MANAGEMENT

Assistance: project grants; sale, exchange, donation, of property or goods; use of property, facilities, and equipment; specialized services; advisory services/counseling; technical information; training; investigation of complaints.

Purposes: pursuant to the Federal Land Policy and Management Act, Archaeological Resources Protection Act, and National Historic Preservation Act of 1966 as amended, to manage and protect cultural resources on BLM lands, and to increase public awareness of the resources, mainly in western states and Alaska. Project example: universities conducting management-focused archaeological field schools and scholarly research.

Eligible applicants/beneficiaries: anyone.

Range/Average: N.A.

Activity: 20 field schools participating; 7,000 new cultural properties identified; interpretive signing for 300 properties.

HQ: Group Administrator, Cultural and Recreation Group (WO 340), BLM-DOI, 1849 C St. NW, Washington, DC 20240. Phone: (202) 452- 0330.

Internet: www.blm.gov.

15.225 RECREATION RESOURCE MANAGEMENT

Assistance: project grants; use of property, facilities, and equipment; specialized services; advisory services/counseling; technical information; training (grants, cost sharing).

Purposes: pursuant to the Federal Land Policy and Management Act, to manage and upgrade recreational resources and related facilities on BLM lands, mainly in western states and Alaska; for related public education. Project examples: promotion of effective cave management; Back Country Byways program; "watchable" wildlife and recreational fishing programs.

Eligible applicants/beneficiaries: anyone.

Range: $500 to $250,000. **Average:** to $10,000.

Activity: not quantified specifically.

HQ: Manager, Recreation Group (WO 250), BLM-DOI, 1849 C St. NW - 302LS, Washington, DC 20240-9998. Phone: (202) 452-5041.

Internet: www.blm.gov/nhp/index.htm.

15.226 PAYMENTS IN LIEU OF TAXES ("PILT")

Assistance: direct payments/unrestricted use; direct payments/restricted use.

Purposes: to compensate local governmental taxing units for the loss of taxes from federal lands. Funds may be used for any governmental purpose.

Eligible applicants/beneficiaries: local government units with eligible lands.

Range/Average: N.A.

Activity: N.A.

HQ: PILT Specialist, Office of Budget, BLM-DOI, 1849 C St. NW - Rm.4012, Washington, DC 20240. Phone: (202) 208-3157.

Internet: www.blm.gov/budget/pilt. (Note: no field offices for this program.)

15.227 DISTRIBUTION OF RECEIPTS TO STATE AND LOCAL GOVERNMENTS ("Revenue Sharing, Public Lands and Resources")

Assistance: direct payments/specified use; direct payments/unrestricted use.

Purposes: pursuant to the Mineral Lands Leasing Act, Outer Continental Shelf Lands Act, Federal Land Policy and Management Act of 1976, Mineral Revenue Payments Clarification Act of 2000, amendments, and other acts, to share federal revenues from fees charged for sale or use of public lands, minerals, and vegetation. Payments are formula-based.

Eligible applicants/beneficiaries: local government units with eligible lands.

Average: N.A.

Activity: N.A.

HQ: Distribution of Receipts Specialist (BC-621), BLM-DOI, Bldg. 50, Denver Federal Center, Denver, CO 80225. Phone: (303) 236- 7135.

Internet: www.blm.gov (Note: no other field offices for this program.)

15.228 NATIONAL FIRE PLAN—WILDLAND URBAN INTERFACE COMMUNITY FIRE ASSISTANCE

Assistance: project grants (matching); use of property, facilities, and equipment; specialized services; advisory services/counseling; technical information; training (grants, matching).

Purposes: to implement the National Fire Plan and assist communities at risk from catastrophic wildland fires affecting BLM-managed lands, through community capability building including: assessment, planning, and mitigation activities; community and homeowner education and action; planning and implementation of hazardous fuels reduction including training, monitoring or maintenance; increasing the effectiveness of rural fire district protection; purchase of protective clothing and equipment.

Eligible applicants/beneficiaries: state and local governments, tribes, public and private education institutions, nonprofit organizations, rural fire departments serving communities under 10,000 population in the wildland/urban interface.

Range: $1,000 to $50,000.

Activity: N.A.

HQ: Chief, Community Protection and Assistance, Planning- Resources Group, National Interagency Fire Center (FA-130), BLM- DOI, 3833 S. Development Ave., Boise, ID 83705. Phone: (208) 387- 5150.

Internet: www.blm.gov/nhp/index.htm; www.nifc.gov. (Note: the field office serves as headquarters.)

15.229 WILD HORSE AND BURRO RESOURCE MANAGEMENT

Assistance: project grants; use of property facilities, and equipment; advisory services/counseling; technical information; training (grants, to 100 percent).

Purposes: pursuant to Wild Free-Roaming Horse and Burros Act of 1971 and Federal Land Policy and Management Act, to manage and protect wild free-roaming horses and burros, toward achievement and maintenance of natural ecological balance on public lands. Funds may be used in research activities for improved census techniques and fertility control methods, and for adopting excess animals removed from the range. Project example: development of the National Wild Horse and Burro Foundation and its pertinent activities.

Eligible applicants/beneficiaries: anyone.

Range: partnership projects, $10,000 to $400,000. **Average:** to $60,000.

Activity: new program listing in 2005 (CFDA on-line version).

HQ: Group Manager, Wild Horses and Burros Group (WO260), BLM, 1848 C St. NW - 402 LS, Washington, DC 20240-9998. Phone: (202) 452-5073.

Internet: www.wildhorseandborro.blm.gov.

15.231 FISH, WILDLIFE AND PLANT CONSERVATION RESOURCE MANAGEMENT

Assistance: project grants; use of property facilities, and equipment; advisory services/counseling; technical information; training (grants, to 100 percent).

Purposes: Federal Land Policy and Management Act of 1976, Endangered Species Act of 1973, Sikes Act, Fish and Wildlife Conservation and Water Resources Development Coordination Act, Oceans Act of 1992, Wyden Amendment, and other amendments, to manage fish, wildlife, and plant conservation resources on the public lands administered by BLM, and on certain other public or private lands. Funds may be used for activities involving protection, restoration, enhancement, and conservation, and to provide related public contact and education opportunities. Most projects are conducted by BLM staff; however, management partnerships are supported through challenge grants. No regular discretionary funding is available.

Eligible applicants/beneficiaries: anyone.

Range: $1,000 to $100,000. **Average:** to $10,000.

Activity: new program listing in 2005 (CFDA on-line version).

HQ: Manager, Fish, Wildlife and Botany Group, (WO230), BLM, 1848 C St. NW - LSB 204, Washington, DC 20240-9998. Phone: (202) 452- 5133.

Internet: www.blm.gov/nhp/index.htm.

15.242 NATIONAL FIRE PLAN—RURAL FIRE ASSISTANCE

Assistance: project grants; use of property, facilities, and equipment; specialized services; advisory services/counseling; technical information; training (grants, matching).

Purposes: to implement the National Fire Plan by increasing firefighter safety and enhancing the knowledge and fire protection capability of rural fire departments near BLM-managed lands, through: education and training, protective clothing and equipment purchases, public education.

Eligible applicants/beneficiaries: state and local governments, tribes, public and private education institutions, nonprofit organizations, rural fire departments serving communities under 10,000 population in the wildland/urban interface.

Range: $1,000 to $20,000. **Average:** $6,000.

Activity: new program listing in 2005. Annually, 1,200 rural fire departments assisted.

HQ: Chief, Community Protection and Assistance, Planning- Resources Group, National Interagency Fire Center (FA-130), BLM- DOI, 3833 S. Development Ave., Boise, ID 83705 Phone: National Interagency Fire Center, (208) 387-5169; Assistant Director, BIA Fire Operations, (208) 387-5372; Fire Management Specialist, Fish and Wildlife Service, (208) 387-5976; National Fire Operations Program Leader, National Park Service, (208) 387-5226.

Internet: www.nifc.gov/rfa/index.html.

OFFICE OF SURFACE MINING RECLAMATION AND ENFORCEMENT

15.250 REGULATION OF SURFACE COAL MINING AND SURFACE EFFECTS OF UNDERGROUND COAL MINING

Assistance: project grants; direct payments/specified use. (50-100 percent/to 3 years).

Purposes: pursuant to the Surface Mining Control and Reclamation Act of 1977, for regulatory activities to control surface impacts of coal mining. Grants may be used to develop state legislation, programs, and regulations, as well as for enforcement activities; also, to provide hydrologic and geologic data for small coal operators.

Eligible applicants/beneficiaries: state governors. Small coal mine operators (annual production under 300,000 tons) may apply for assistance in meeting technical permit application requirements.

Range: \$29,387 to \$11,992,212. **Average:** \$2,087,605.

Activity: currently, 24 states receive grants.

HQ: Chief, Division of Regulatory Support, Office of Surface Mining Reclamation and Enforcement, DOI, 1951 Constitution Ave. NW, Washington, DC 20240. Phone: (202) 208-2788.

Internet: www.osmre.gov/.

15.252 ABANDONED MINE LAND RECLAMATION (AMLR) PROGRAM

Assistance: formula grants; project grants. (100 percent/to 3 years).

Purposes: pursuant to the Surface Mining Control and Reclamation Act of 1977, for reclamation projects to correct environmental damage caused or affected by coal and other mining and related processes on eligible lands and waters—occurring prior to 3 August 1977, and certain post-1977 lands and waters beginning 1 October 1991. Subsidence insurance grants, limited to \$3,000,000, are also available to states to insure private property against damages caused by underground coal mining.

Eligible applicants/beneficiaries: states and tribes with eligible lands and coal mining operations, and paying reclamation fees.

Range: \$94,141 to \$29,469,486. **Average:** \$5,590,484.

Activity: 23 states, 3 tribes with approved programs.

HQ: Chief, Division of Reclamation Support, Office of Surface Mining Reclamation and Enforcement, DOI, 1951 Constitution Ave. NW, Washington, DC 20240. Phone: (202) 208-2788.

Internet: www.osmre.gov/.

15.253 NOT-FOR-PROFIT AMD RECLAMATION ("Acid Mining Drainage" - "AMD")

Assistance: project grants (100 percent/2 years).

Purposes: pursuant to the Surface Mining Control and Reclamation Act of 1977, for local acid mine drainage reclamation projects, especially in watershed areas, where lands and water were impacted by coal mining activities. Eligibility is limited to areas where mining and related damage occurred prior to 3 August 1977, and where there is no continuing state or federal legal responsibility.

Eligible applicants/beneficiaries: existing nonprofit organizations.

Range: $34,200 to $100,000.

Activity: not quantified specifically.

HQ: Office of Surface Mining Reclamation and Enforcement, DOI, 1951 Constitution Ave. NW, Washington, DC 20240. Phone: (202) 208-2788.

Internet: www.osmre.gov/.

15.254 SUMMER WATERSHED INTERN

Assistance: direct payments/specified use (12-24 weeks).

Purposes: pursuant to the Surface Mining Control and Reclamation Act of 1977, to hire summer interns to work on specified watershed projects toward the remediation of acid mine drainage. Funds may cover stipends and project expenses.

Eligible applicants: private and public nonprofit organizations and established watershed organizations in Alabama, Illinois, Indiana, Iowa, Kentucky, Maryland, Missouri, Ohio, Oklahoma, Pennsylvania, Tennessee, Virginia, West Virginia.

Eligible beneficiaries: undergraduate and graduate students.

Average: $2,000 stipend per 12-week full-time internship, plus $500 for related expenses (part-time hires may extend award to 24 weeks).

Activity: FY 05, 22 interns placed in 8 states.

HQ: Office of Surface Mining Reclamation and Enforcement, DOI, 1951 Constitution Ave. NW, Washington, DC 20240. Phone: (202) 208-2585.

Internet: www.osmre.gov.acsi/internindex.htm.

15.255 APPLIED SCIENCE PROGRAM COOPERATIVE AGREEMENTS RELATED TO COAL MINING AND RECLAMATION

Assistance: project grants (75-100 percent).

Purposes: pursuant to Surface Mining Control and Reclamation Act of 1977 (SMCRA), to support projects which focus on issues related to mining in the USA and its territories, including: development and demonstration of improved technologies to address public safety and environmental issues; encouragement of efforts to collect, preserve and convert into digital format, maps of underground mines that provide valuable information regarding protection of public and miner safety, mine pool evaluation, and mine subsidence investigation for previously mined areas. Funding will be limited to projects that can be completed without additional funding from the Office of Surface Mining (OSM) beyond those funds awarded in the current fiscal year. Cost sharing by applicants is not required but strongly encouraged.

Eligible applicants/beneficiaries: public, private, nonprofit, state, local or Tribal governments, colleges, and universities located in the USA. Mine Mapping: any US state or Indian Tribal agency or US Territory.

Range: Applied Science Project Award, to $100,000. **Average:** N.A.

Activity: not quantified specifically.

HQ: Chief, Division of Reclamation Support, Office of Surface Mining Reclamation and Enforcement, DOI, 1951 Constitution Ave., NW, Washington, DC 20240. Phone: (202) 208-2788.

Internet: www.grants.gov; www.mcrcc.osmre.gov.

15.421 ALASKA COASTAL MARINE INSTITUTE ("Alaska CMI")

Assistance: project grants (50 percent/1-4 years).

Purposes: to use highly qualified scientific expertise at local levels to collect and disseminate environmental information needed for Outer Continental Shelf oil, gas and marine minerals decisions; address local and regional environmental and resource issues of mutual interest; strengthen Mineral Management Service-State partnership in addressing OCS information needs. Funds may also be used for alternate energy development projects, national conference attendance, and dissemination of project results, but not for capitalization.

Eligible applicants/beneficiaries: University of Alaska named principal investigator; non-UA scientists may collaborate with a UA principal investigator.

Range: $97,400 to $250,000. **Average:** $169,000.

Activity: to date, over 30 ongoing research projects funded.

HQ: Minerals Management Service, 381 Elden St, MS-4041, Herndon, VA 20170, Phone: (703) 787-1721, FAX (703) 787-1053.

Internet: www.mms.gov/eppd/sciences/esp/profiles/partners/cmi/index.htm.

15.422 LOUISIANA STATE UNIVERSITY (LSU) COASTAL MARINE INSTITUTE (CMI) ("LSU CMI")

Assistance: project grants (50 percent/1-4 years).

Purposes: to use highly qualified scientific expertise at local levels to collect and disseminate environmental information needed for Outer Continental Shelf oil, gas and marine minerals decisions; address local and regional environmental and resource issues of mutual interest; strengthen Mineral Management Service-State partnership in addressing OCS information needs. Funds may also be used for national conference attendance, alternate energy development projects, and dissemination of project results, but not for capitalization.

Eligible applicants/beneficiaries: Louisiana State University named principal investigator; non-LSU scientists may collaborate with a LSU principal investigator.

Range: $32,000 to $500,000. **Average:** $190,000.

Activity: to date, over 50 research projects funded.

HQ: Minerals Management Service, 381 Elden St, MS-4041, Herndon, VA 20170, Phone: (703) 787-1727, FAX (703) 787-1053.

Internet: www.mms.gov/eppd/sciences/esp/profiles/partners/cmi/index.htm.

15.423 MINERALS MANAGEMENT SERVICE (MMS) ENVIRONMENTAL STUDIES PROGRAM (ESP) ("ESP")

Assistance: project grants (from 50 percent/1-8 years).

Purposes: to obtain information needed for assessment and management of environmental impacts; to predict impacts on marine biota; to monitor human, marine, and coastal environments in order to provide time series and data trend information. Funds may also be used for alternate energy development projects, national conference attendance, and dissemination of project results, but not for capitalization. Matched funding is strongly encouraged.

Eligible applicants/beneficiaries: state agencies and public IHEs; institutions may apply collaboratively.

Range: $100,000 to $700,000. **Average:** $300,000.

Activity: to date, over 12 ongoing research projects funded.

HQ: Minerals Management Service, 381 Elden St, MS-4041, Herndon, VA 20170, Phone: (703) 787-1727, FAX (703) 787-1053.

Internet: www.mms.gov/eppd/sciences/esp/index.htm (Note: no field offices for this program.)

15.424 MARINE MINERALS ACTIVITIES ("Marine Minerals Activities")

Assistance: project grants (50 percent).

Purposes: pursuant to the Outer Continental Shelf Lands Act, to evaluate OCS sand deposits for beach nourishment projects and to foster good working relationships with coastal states regarding OCS mineral issues.

Eligible applicants/beneficiaries: coastal states in need of coastal restoration.

Range: $30,000 to $100,000.

Activity: offshore cooperative sand programs with 14 states.

HQ: Minerals Management Service, 381 Elden St, MS-4021, Herndon, VA 20170, Phone: (no number provided).

Internet: www.mms.gov/sandandgravel.

15.425 OFFSHORE RESEARCH TECHNOLOGY CENTER (OTRC) TEXAS ENGINEERING EXPERIMENT STATION (TEES) ("OTRC, TEES")

Assistance: project grants.

Purposes: pursuant to the Outer Continental Shelf Lands Act, to ensure oil and gas activities on the OCS conserve resources, operate safely, and protect the coastal and marine environment. The OTRC uses funding given to the Technology Assessment and Research (TA&R) program by Congress in order to perform research through MMS on issues including oil spill response and clean-up capabilities.

Range: $20,000 to $200,000. **Average:** $50,000.

Activity: not specifically qualified.

HQ: Minerals Management Service, 381 Elden St, MS-4021, Herndon, VA 20170, Phone: (no number provided).

Internet: www.mms.gov/tarphome.

15.426 COASTAL IMPACT ASSISTANCE PROGRAM ("CIAP")

Assistance: formula grants.

Purposes: pursuant to Outer Continental Shelf (OCS) Lands Act, as amended, to conserve, protect, or restore coastal areas including wetlands; mitigation of damage to fish, wildlife, or natural resources; planning assistance and the administrative costs of complying with these objectives; implementation of a federally-approved marine, coastal, or comprehensive conservation management plan; and, mitigation of the impact of outer Continental Shelf activities through funding of onshore infrastructure projects and public service needs. In accordance with the language of the Act, no State will receive less than 1 percent of the $250 million to be disbursed per year. Of the percentage received by a State, 65 percent remains with the State, and 35 percent is awarded to the coastal political subdivisions (CPS).

Eligible applicants/beneficiaries: States eligible to receive funding are: Alabama, Alaska, California, Louisiana, Mississippi, and Texas and their 67 coastal political subdivisions.

Range/Average: N.A.

Activity: new program listing, FY 07.

HQ: National CIAP Coordinator, MMS, DOI, 381 Elden Street, MS 4040, Herndon, Virginia 20170. Phone: (703) 787-1011.

Internet: www.mms.gov.

15.427 FEDERAL OIL AND GAS ROYALTY MANAGEMENT ("FOGRMA")

Assistance: project grants (100 percent).

Purposes: pursuant to Federal Oil and Gas Royalty Management Act of 1982, to ensure that all oil, gas, and solid minerals originated on public lands and the Outer Continental Shelf are properly accounted for.

Eligible applicants/beneficiaries: state and tribal governments only.

Range: $40,000 to $1,800,000. **Average:** $500,000.

Activity: FY 06, 18 awards.

HQ: Associate Director, Minerals Revenue Management, MMS, 1849 C St, NW, Mail Stop 4230, Washington, DC 20240 Phone: (202) 208-3415.

Internet: www.mms.gov.

BUREAU OF RECLAMATION

15.504 WATER RECLAMATION AND REUSE PROGRAM

Assistance: formula grants (25 to 50 percent).

Purposes: pursuant to the Reclamation Wastewater and Groundwater Study and Facilities Act as amended other acts, for appraisals and feasibility studies (50 percent federal funding) on water reclamation and re-use projects, mainly in the western states; for research and demonstration programs and for construction of re-use projects (25 percent federal funding).

Eligible applicants/beneficiaries: projects—legally organized nonfederal entities such as irrigation districts, municipalities. Research—IHEs; architectural and engineering firms.

Range: to $20,000,000.

Activity: not quantified specifically.

HQ: Office of the Commissioner (D-5000), Bureau of Reclamation- DOI, Denver Federal Center, P.O. Box 25007, Denver, CO 80225. Phone: (303) 445-3710.

Internet: www.usbr.gov/pmts/writing/guidelines/. (Note: the field office serves as headquarters.)

15.506 WATER DESALINATION RESEARCH AND DEVELOPMENT PROGRAM ("Desal R & D Program")

Assistance: project grants (to 50 percent).

Purposes: pursuant to the Water Desalination Act of 1966, for water desalination studies, research, demonstrations, development projects, and related activities—to develop more cost- effective, technologically efficient, and implementable methods of producing usable water from saline or otherwise contaminated water.

Eligible applicants/beneficiaries: individuals, academic institutions, commercial and industrial organizations; other profit, nonprofit and public entities including state, local, and tribal governments.

Range: $20,000 to $150,000. **Average:** $85,000.

Activity: FY 02, 6 awards (latest data available).

HQ: Water Treatment Engineering and Research Group, Bureau of Reclamation-DOI, Federal Center (D-8230), P.O. Box 25007, Denver, CO 80225. Phone: *technical information (MC D-8230),* (303) 445-2260, FAX (303) 445-6329; *solicitation documents,* Acquisitions Operations Group (MCD-7810), (303) 445-2432, FAX (303) 445-6345.

Internet: www.usbr.gov/water/desal.html. (Note: no other field offices for this program.)

15.507 WATER 2025 ("Water 2025 Challenge Grant Program")

Assistance: project grants (50-100 percent/from 2 years).

Purposes: to prevent crisis and conflict over water in western United States through projects (50 percent funding) that will conserve water, increase water use efficiency, or enhance water management—using advanced technology, improvements to existing facilities, and water banks and markets. Up to 100 percent funding may be available for water use efficiency research.

Eligible applicants/beneficiaries: projects—irrigation or water districts in the western U.S. Research grants—IHEs and nonprofit institutions.

Range: challenge grants, $19,000 to $300,000. **Average:** $140,000; research, $1,000,000.

Activity: new program listing in 2005 (CFDA on-line version); FY 05, 49 awards.

HQ: Office of Program & Policy Services (D-5500), Bureau of Reclamation-DOI, Federal Center, P.O. Box 25007, Denver, CO 80225. Phone: (303) 445-2906, FAX (720) 544-4207.

Internet: www.doi.gov/water2025/. (Note: no other field offices for this program.)

15.508 PROVIDING WATER TO AT-RISK NATURAL DESERT TERMINAL LAKES ("Desert Terminal Lakes")

Assistance: project grants (100 percent).

Purposes: pursuant to FSRIA and appropriations acts, for activities to provide water only to Walker Lake, Pyramid Lake, and Summit Lake in Nevada.

Eligible applicants/beneficiaries: state and local public agencies, tribes, nonprofit organizations, individuals.

Range/Average: N.A.

Activity: new program listing in 2005 (CFDA on-line version). FY 05, 2 awards, totaling $1.5 million.

HQ: *technical program information,* Lahontan Basin Area Office, Bureau of Reclamation-DOI, 705 N. Plaza St. - Rm.320, Carson City, NV 89701-4015. Phone: (775) 882-3436, FAX (775) 882-7592 *Acquisition services,* Mid-Pacific Regional Office, Bureau of Reclamation, 2800 Cottage Way, Rm. E-1815, Sacramento, CA 95825-1898. Phone: (916) 978-5130, FAX (916) 978-5175/5182.

Internet: www.usbr.gov. (Note: field office serves as headquarters for this program.)

15.509 COLORADO RIVER BASIN SALINITY CONTROL PROGRAM

Assistance: project grants (100 percent/1-5 years).

Purposes: pursuant to Colorado River Basin Salinity Control Act, as amended, and other laws, to provide financial and technical assistance which help decrease salinity levels in the Colorado River and enhance water quality in the U.S. and Mexico.

Eligible applicants/beneficiaries: eligible owners or operators in approved project area.

Range: FY 05, $12,916 to $2,570,000. **Average:** $923,552.

Activity: since program inception, 570,000 tons of salt prevented from entering the Colorado River.

HQ: Technical Contact, Upper Colorado Region, Bureau of Reclamation, 125 South State Street, Salt Lake City, UT 84138. Phone: (801) 524-3753; FAX: (801) 524-5499 or Technical Contact, Lower Colorado Region, Bureau of Reclamation, 500 Fir St, Boulder City, NV 89005, Phone: (702) 293-8592; FAX: (702) 293-8042.

Internet: www.usbr.gov (Note: two field offices serve as headquarters for this program.)

15.510 COLORADO UTE INDIAN WATER RIGHTS SETTLEMENT ACT ("Colorado Ute Settlement Act/Animas La Plata")

Assistance: direct payments/specified use; project grants (100 percent/to 5 years).

Purposes: pursuant to Colorado River Basin Project Act, Colorado Ute Indian Water Rights Settlement Act of 1988, as amended, Colorado Ute Settlement Act Amendments of 2000, and others, to complete construction of, operate and maintain, a reconfigured Animas-La Plata Project, consisting of facilities to divert and store water from the Animas River. This water is for municipal and industrial water supply only, provided to the Ute Mountain Ute and Southern Ute Indian Tribes, and other tribal and non-tribal entities in the Four Corners Region of the United States.

Eligible applicants/beneficiaries: Federally Recognized Indian Tribal Government - Projects shall be subject to the provisions of the Indian Self-Determination and Education Assistance Act (ii Stat. 2203; 25 U.S.C. 450 et seq.) to the same extent as if such functions were performed by the Bureau of Indian Affairs; and for projects not awarded subject to Public Law 93-638: state, local, Federally recognized Indian Tribal governments, small businesses, individuals, and profit organizations.

Range: FY 05, $210 - $84,851,143; FY 06 $600 - $2,229,810. **Average:** FY 05, $200,000; FY 06, $20,000.

Activity: not quantified specifically.

HQ: Construction Engineer, ALP 100, Western Colorado Area Office, Bureau of Reclamation, DOI, 835 East 2nd Avenue, Suite 300 Durango, Colorado 8130. Phone: (970) 259-1110 ext. 1004; FAX: (970) 259-0059.

Internet: www.usbr.gov (Note: field office serves as headquarters.)

15.511 CULTURAL RESOURCES MANAGEMENT

Assistance: project grants (100 percent/to 5 years).

Purposes: pursuant to Archaeological Resources Protection Act of 1979, National Historic Preservation Act of 1966, and other laws, as amended, to manage, protect, and provide curation for cultural resources on Reclamation land. Cooperative agreements are used for providing long-term care of Reclamation-owned heritage assets; project grants for heritage education services.

Eligible applicants/beneficiaries: interstate, intrastate, state, local, sponsored organizations, public, private and quasi-public nonprofit or for-profit institutions/organizations, Federally-recognized Indian Tribal governments, minority groups, specialized groups, small businesses, and Native American Organizations.

Range: Heritage education agreements: one $15,000 grant annually; Curation projects: $5,000 - $190,000. **Average:** approximately $50,000.

Activity: not quantified specifically.

HQ: Federal Preservation Officer, Bureau of Reclamation, DOI, P.O. Box 25007 (Mail Code: 84-53000), Denver, Colorado 80225-0007. Phone: (303) 445-3311.

Internet: www.usbr.gov/cultural; www.usbr.gov/museumproperty (Note: field office serves as headquarters.)

15.512 CENTRAL VALLEY PROJECT IMPROVEMENT ACT, TITLE XXXIV ("Lower Rio Grande Valley Irrigation Projects")

Assistance: project grants (50 percent).

Purposes: pursuant to Lower Rio Grande Valley Water Resources Conservation and Improvement Act of 2000 and Lower Rio Grande Valley Water Resources Conservation and Improvement Act of 2002, as amended, to improve the supply of water in the program area known as Region M (Texas counties in the Rio Grande Regional Water Planning Area). Cost ceiling for conservation and improvements (section 3(g)) is $8,000,000; $47,000,000 for construction (section 4(c)). A substantial portion of this program is directed toward funding 19 construction projects specifically identified in the Lower Rio Grande Valley Water Resources Act, as amended.

Eligible applicants/beneficiaries: State of Texas, water users in the program area, specified irrigation districts, and other nonfederal entities.

Range: N.A. **Average:** $1,460,000.

Activity: not quantified specifically.

HQ: Tribal and Financial Assistance Officer, Bureau of Reclamation, DOI, P.O. Box 36900, 316 North 26th Street, Billings MT 59101. Phone: (406) 247-7710; FAX: (406) 247-7695.

Internet: www.usbr.gov (Note: field office serves as headquarters.)

15.513 DUTCH JOHN FEDERAL PROPERTY AND DISPOSITION ASSISTANCE ACT

Assistance: project grants. (100 percent/15 years).

Purposes: pursuant to Dutch John Federal Property Disposition and Assistance Act of 1998, to privatize lands in and around Dutch John, Utah; to improve and achieve efficient operation of Flaming Gorge National Recreation Area; and to help defray the cost of basic governmental services. For the purpose of defraying costs of transition in administration and provision of basic community services, an annual payment of $300,000 (as adjusted for changes in the Consumer Price Index) shall be provided from the Upper Colorado River Basin Fund to Daggett County, Utah, for a period not to exceed 15 years. Presently, no new awards are being made. Funds are only available for continuation of the existing grant with Daggett County.

Eligible applicants/beneficiaries: Daggett County, Utah.

Range: $345,668 to $373,874. **Average:** $359,679.

Activity: to date, 1810 acres have been transferred to Daggett County.

HQ: Acting Manager, Bureau of Reclamation, DOI, P.O. Box 278

Dutch John, UT 84023-0278. Phone: (435) 885-3238, FAX (435) 885-3224.

Internet: www.usbr.gov (Note: field office serves as headquarters.)

15.514 RECLAMATION STATES EMERGENCY DROUGHT RELIEF ("Emergency Drought Relief and Drought Contingency Planning")

Assistance: project grants; specialized services; advisory services/counseling (generally, 6 months).

Purposes: pursuant to Reclamation States Emergency Drought Relief Act of 1991, as amended and the Hawaii Water Resources Act of 2000, for planning assistance that would minimize and mitigate losses and damages resulting from drought conditions.

Eligible applicants/beneficiaries: state and local entities and Federally Recognized Indian Tribal Governments within the following 17 Western U.S. States: Arizona, California, Colorado, Idaho, Kansas, Montana, Nebraska, Nevada, New Mexico, North Dakota, Oklahoma, Oregon, South Dakota, Texas, Wyoming, Utah, and Washington) and Hawaii. All 50 U.S. States and most U.S. territories are eligible for technical assistance.

Range/Average: N.A.

Activity: not quantified specifically.

HQ: Reclamation Drought Coordinator, Bureau of Reclamation, DOI, Mail Code 84-52000, P.O. Box 25007, Denver, CO 80225-0007. Phone: (303) 445-2889.

Internet: www.usbr.gov (Note: field office serves as headquarters.)

15.515 FEDERAL RESOURCE PROTECTION

Assistance: project grants (100 percent).

Purposes: to enforce state and local laws and ordinances within DOI water resource development projects. Payment for recipient expenses limited to reimbursement method.

Eligible applicants: regulatory and law enforcement agencies of U.S. state or local governments.

Eligible beneficiaries: general public.

Range: $5,276 - $800,000. **Average:** $69,655.

Activity: N.A.

HQ: Chief of Law Enforcement, Regional Office-Bureau of Reclamation, Denver Federal Center, 6th & Kipling, Bldg 67, Denver, CO 80225. Phone: (303) 445-3245.

Internet: www.usbr.gov. (Note: field office serves as headquarters.)

15.516 FORT PECK RESERVATION RURAL WATER SYSTEM ("Fort Peck Water Supply Project")

Assistance: project grants (76-100 percent/10 years).

Purposes: pursuant to Fort Peck Reservation Rural Water System Act of 2000, to ensure a safe and adequate municipal, rural, and industrial water supply for residents of Fort Peck Indian Reservation in the State of Montana and portions of Roosevelt, Sheridan, Daniels, and Valley Counties that are outside Fort Peck Indian Reservation. Presently, no new project awards are being made under this authority. Funds only available for continuation of existing agreements.

Eligible applicants/beneficiaries: The Fort Peck Tribal Executive Board, Dry Prairie Rural Water Association Incorporated (or any successor non-Federal entity).

Average: FY 04 - FY 06, $10,167,000.

Activity: not quantified specifically.

HQ: Tribal and Financial Assistance Officer, Bureau of Reclamation, DOI, P.O. Box 36900, 316 North 26th Street, Billings, MT 59101. Phone: (406) 247-7710, FAX: (406) 247-7695.

Internet: www.nemontel.net/~dprw (Note: field office serves as headquarters.)

15.517 FISH AND WILDLIFE COORDINATION ACT ("FWCA")

Assistance: project grants (100 percent/1 to 5 years).

Purposes: pursuant to Fish and Wildlife Coordination Act of 1934, Public Law 85-624, as amended and limited by the Secretary of the Interior delegation of authority at 255 DM 14, to provide financial assistance to public or private organizations for the improvement of fish and wildlife habitats associated with water systems or water supplies affected by Bureau of Reclamation projects.

Eligible applicants/beneficiaries: state and local governments, public, private, nonprofit and for-profit organizations and institutions, Federally recognized Indian Tribal governments, individuals, small businesses, and Native American organizations.

Range: FY 05, $5,000 to $3,123,390.

Activity: not quantified specifically.

HQ: none provided.

Internet: www.usbr.gov.

15.518 GARRISON DIVERSION UNIT ("Garrison Diversion Unit Project")

Assistance: project grants.

Purposes: pursuant to Garrison Diversion Unit, Missouri River Basin Project, Public Law 89-108, Energy and Water Development Appropriation Act of 1985, and The Dakota Water Resources Act of 2000, as amended, to plan and construct a multi-purpose water resource development project within the State of North Dakota for; irrigation; municipal, rural, and industrial water; fish, wildlife, and other natural resource conservation and development; recreation; flood control; augmented stream flows; ground water recharge; and other project purposes.

Eligible applicants/beneficiaries: the State of North Dakota, the Garrison Conservancy District, the Standing Rock Sioux, the Three Affiliated Tribes, the Spirit Lake Nation, and the Turtle Mountain Band of Chippewa.

Range: FY 05, $2,000 to $1,427,500. **Average:** FY 05, $320,000.

Activity: not quantified specifically.

HQ: Tribal and Financial Assistance Officer, Bureau of Reclamation, DOI, P.O. Box 36900, 316 North 26th Street, Billings, MT 59101. Phone: (406) 247-7710, FAX: (406) 247-7695.

Internet: www.usbr.gov/gp (Note: field office serves as headquarters.)

15.519 INDIAN TRIBAL WATER RESOURCES DEVELOPMENT, MANAGEMENT, AND PROTECTION ("Indian Tribal Water Resources")

Assistance: project grants (100 percent/1 to 2 years).

Purposes: pursuant to Consolidated Appropriations Resolution, 2003, Division D - Energy and Water Development Appropriations, Title II, Section 201, Public Law 108-7, to increase opportunities for Indian tribes to develop, manage, and protect their water resources. Examples of funded projects include: well closures, drought relief, aquifer studies, water quality monitoring.

Eligible applicants/beneficiaries: Federally recognized Indian tribes, institutions of higher education, national Indian organizations, and tribal organizations located in the 17 western States identified in the Act of June 17, 1902, as amended; specifically, Arizona, California, Colorado, Idaho, Kansas, Montana, Nebraska, Nevada, New Mexico, North Dakota, Oklahoma, Oregon, South Dakota, Texas, Utah, Washington, and Wyoming.

Range: FY 05 $4,000 to $800,000, average $110,000. **Average:** FY 05 $4,000 to $800,000, average $110,000.

Activity: not quantified specifically.

HQ: none provided, see listing of field offices.

Internet: http://www.usbr.gov/native.

15.520 LEWIS AND CLARK RURAL WATER SYSTEM ("Lewis and Clark Project")

Assistance: project grants. (50-80 percent/until funds are expended).

Purposes: pursuant to Lewis and Clark Rural Water System, Public Law 106-246, and others, to plan and construct a bulk water supply system which will provide safe and adequate municipal, rural, and industrial water supplies, mitigation of wetland areas and water conservation for the Lewis and Clark Rural Water System member entities located in southeastern South Dakota, southwestern Minnesota, and northwestern Iowa. Presently, no new awards are being made. Funds are only available for continuation of existing agreements.

Eligible applicants/beneficiaries: Lewis and Clark Rural Water Supply System, Inc., and member entities (rural water systems in the following counties: Lake, McCook, Minnehaha, Turner, Lincoln, Clay, and Union, in southeastern South Dakota; Rock and Nobles, in Southwestern Minnesota; and Lyon, Sioux, Osceola, O'Brien Dickinson, and Clay, in northwestern Iowa).

Range: N.A. **Average:** FY 04 - FY 06, $17,500,000.

Activity: not quantified specifically.

HQ: Tribal and Financial Assistance Officer, Bureau of Reclamation, DOI, P.O. Box 36900, 316 North 26th Street, Billings, MT 59101. Phone: (406) 247-7710, FAX: (406) 247-7695.

Internet: www.lcrws.org.

15.521 LOWER RIO GRANDE VALLEY WATER RESOURCES CONSERVATION AND IMPROVEMENT ("Lower Rio Grande Valley Irrigation Projects")

Assistance: project grants (50 percent).

Purposes: pursuant to Lower Rio Grande Valley Water Resources Conservation and Improvement Act of 2000, and Lower Rio Grande Valley Water Resources Conservation and Improvement Act of 2002, as amended, to improve the supply of water in the program area identified as Region M (Texas counties in Rio Grande Regional Water Planning Area). Cost ceiling for conservation is $8,000,000; for improvements, $47,000,000.

Eligible applicants/beneficiaries: The State of Texas, water users in the program area, specified irrigation districts, and other non-Federal entities.

Range: N.A. **Average:** $1,460,000.

Activity: not quantified specifically.

HQ: Tribal and Financial Assistance Officer, Bureau of Reclamation, DOI, P.O. Box 36900, 316 North 26th Street, Billings MT 59101. Phone: (406) 247-7710; FAX: (406) 247-7695.

Internet: http://www.usbr.gov/gp (Note: field office serves as headquarters.)

15.522 MNI WICONI RURAL WATER SUPPLY PROJECT ("Mni Wiconi Project")

Assistance: project grants (80-100 percent).

Purposes: pursuant to Mni Wiconi Rural Project Act of 1988, as amended; Yavapai-Prescott Indian Tribe Water Rights Settlement Act of 1994, Title VIII, and Mni Wiconi Act Amendments of 1994, to ensure a safe and adequate municipal, rural, and industrial water supply for the residents of the Pine Ridge Indian, Rosebud Indian, and Lower Brule Indian Reservations and certain other counties located in South Dakota. Cooperative agreements are limited to planning, designing, constructing, operating, maintaining, and replacing the Oglala Sioux, the Rosebud, and the Lower Brule Sioux Rural Water Supply Systems; for planning and construction of the West River/Lyman-Jones Rural Water System. Presently, funds are only available for continuation of existing agreements; no new project awards are being made.

Eligible applicants: West River/Lyman-Jones Water Systems and the Oglala, Rosebud, and Lower Brule Sioux tribes.

Eligible beneficiaries: citizens of the southwest quarter of the State of South Dakota, including the Oglala, Rosebud, and Lower Brule Indian Reservations.

Average: $29,564,000.

Activity: not quantified specifically.

HQ: Tribal and Financial Assistance Officer, Bureau of Reclamation, DOI, P.O. Box 36900, 316 North 26th Street, Billings, MT 59101. Phone: (406) 247-7710; FAX: (406) 247-7695.

Internet: www.usbr.gov/gp; www.wrlj.com (Note: field office serves as headquarters.)

15.523 PERKINS COUNTY RURAL WATER SYSTEM ("Perkins County Water Project")

Assistance: project grants (75 percent).

Purposes: pursuant to Perkins County Rural Water System Act of 1999, to ensure functionality of new water supply system that will serve members of the Perkins County Rural Water System, Inc. in Perkins County, South Dakota. Presently, no new awards are being made; funds only available for continuation of existing agreements.

Eligible applicants/beneficiaries: Perkins County Rural Water System, Inc., Perkins County, South Dakota.

Average: $2,381,000.

Activity: not quantified specifically.

HQ: Tribal and Financial Assistance Officer, Bureau of Reclamation, DOI, P.O. Box 36900, 316 North 26th Street, Billings, MT 59101. Phone: (406) 247-7710; Fax: (406) 247-7695.

Internet: http://www.usbr.gov/gp (Note: field office serves as headquarters.)

15.524 RECREATION RESOURCES MANAGEMENT

Assistance: project grants (50-75 percent/to 5 years).

Purposes: pursuant to Federal Water Projects Recreation Act of 1965, and Reclamation Recreation Act of 1992, as amended, to provide opportunities for public recreation at Bureau of Reclamation or other publicly-owned water projects. Cost sharing agreements may be used by state, county, and local government for planning, construction and other facets of improving recreation access and assets at these project areas.

Eligible applicants/beneficiaries: state and local government entities willing to manage/maintain publicly-owned recreation facilities and assets.

Range: $5,000 to $6,000,000. **Average:** $272,000.

HQ: Bureau of Reclamation, DOI, P.O. Box 25007 (84-53000), Denver, Colorado 80225-0007. Phone: (303) 445-2913; FAX: (303) 445-6690.

Internet: www.usbr.gov/pmts/planning (Note: field office serves as headquarters.)

15.525 ROCKY BOY'S/NORTH CENTRAL MONTANA REGIONAL WATER SYSTEM

Assistance: project grants (80-100 percent/until funds are expended).

Purposes: pursuant to Indian Financing Amendments Act of 2002, Title IX and Rocky Boy's/North Central Montana Regional Water System Act of 2002, to develop safe and adequate rural, municipal, and industrial water supplies via construction of a rural water supply system that will serve the Chippewa-Cree of the Rocky Boy's Indian reservation and the surrounding, off-reservation communities in north central Montana. Presently, no new awards are being made; funds are only available for continuation of existing agreements.

Eligible applicants/beneficiaries: Chippewa-Cree of the Rocky Boy's Indian Reservation and the North Central Montana Regional Water Authority.

Range/Average: N.A.

Activity: new program listing, FY 06.

HQ: Tribal and Financial Assistance Officer, Bureau of Reclamation, DOI, P.O. Box 36900, 316 North 26th Street, Billings, MT 59101. Phone: (406) 247-7710; FAX: (406) 247-7695.

Internet: http://northcentralmontanawater.org (Note: field office serves as headquarters.)

15.526 SAN GABRIEL BASIN RESTORATION PROJECT

Assistance: project grants. (65 percent/to 10 years).

Purposes: pursuant to San Gabriel Basin Restoration Project and Energy and Water Development Appropriations Act, 2002, as amended, and other laws, to design, construct, operate, and maintain water quality projects within the San Gabriel Basin, Los Angeles County, California. Agreements for planning and construction projects are generally awarded for up to 5 years. Funds for operation and maintenance provided for a period not to exceed 10 years following the initial date of operation of the project, or until the project funding ceiling has been reached, whichever occurs first.

Eligible applicants/beneficiaries: San Gabriel Basin Water Quality Authority (or its successor agency) and/or the Central Basin Municipal Water District.

Range: $2,600,000 to $28,700,000. **Average:** $14,600,000.

Activity: since program inception, 5 grants awarded.

HQ: Area Engineer, Southern California Area Office, Bureau of Reclamation, DOI, 27708 Jefferson Ave., Ste. 202

Temecula, CA 92590. Phone: (951) 695-5310; FAX: (951) 695-5319.

Internet: http://www.usbr.gov/lc/socal (Note: no headquarters provided; field office contact only.)

15.527 SAN LUIS UNIT, CENTRAL VALLEY PROJECT

Assistance: project grants (cost sharing encouraged).

Purposes: pursuant to San Luis Unit, Central Valley Project Act of June 3, 1960, to be used for projects that will result in construction and operation of drainage facilities in the San Luis Unit and adjacent areas.

Eligible applicants/beneficiaries: any responsible source, including irrigation and/or water districts, State and local entities, public, private, and quasi-public nonprofit and for-profit institutions/organizations, Federally recognized Indian Tribal Governments, and small businesses.

Range: $16,345 to $1,650,000. **Average:** $246,770.

Activity: water treatment/drainage for approximately 90,000 acres.

HQ: South-Central California Area Office, Bureau of Reclamation, DOI, 1243 N Street, Fresno, CA, 93727. Phone: (559) 487-5039; FAX: (559) 487-5130.

Internet: www.mp.usbr.gov (Note: field office serves as headquarters for this program.)

15.528 ST. MARY STORAGE UNIT FACILITIES REHABILITATION PROJECT ("St. Mary Rehabilitation Project")

Assistance: project grants.

Purposes: pursuant to Energy and Water Development Appropriations Act, 2006, to fund the collection of technical and environmental data for use in evaluating potential rehabilitation of the St. Mary Storage Unit facilities, Milk River Project, Montana. Cost ceiling for project is $500,000.

Eligible applicants/beneficiaries: State of Montana and the Blackfeet Tribe of Montana.

Average: $250,000.

Activity: not quantified specifically.

HQ: Tribal and Financial Assistance Officer, Bureau of Reclamation, DOI, P.O. Box 36900, 316 North 26th Street, Billings, MT 59101. Phone: (406) 247-7710; FAX: (406) 247-7695.

Internet: http://www.usbr.gov/gp (Note: field office serves as headquarters.)

15.529 UPPER COLORADO AND SAN JUAN RIVER BASINS ENDANGERED FISH RECOVERY PROGRAMS ("Upper Colorado and San Juan River Recovery Implementation Program")

Assistance: project grants (cost sharing/1-5 years).

Purposes: pursuant to Upper Colorado and San Juan River Basins Endangered Fish Recovery Programs and Upper Colorado and San Juan River Basins Endangered Fish Recovery Programs Extension, as amended, to assist in the implementation of programs for endangered fish recovery in the Upper Colorado and San Juan River Basins. Periodically, the Bureau of Reclamation will have discretionary funding available to make awards for certain types of projects. As they become available, funding opportunity announcements will be posted to www.grants.gov.

Eligible applicants/beneficiaries: Federal, Interstate, Intrastate, State, and Local governments; Public Institution/Organizations, and Federally Recognized Indian Tribal Governments.

Range: $16,080 to $289,394. **Average:** $136,808.

Activity: not quantified specifically.

HQ: Western Colorado Area Office, Bureau of Reclamation, DOI, 2764 Compass Drive, Grand Junction, Colorado 81506. Phone: (970) 248-0641.

Internet: www.usbr.gov/uc/wcao; www.fws.gov/southwest/sjrip/index.html (Note: field office serves as headquarters.)

15.530 WATER CONSERVATION FIELD SERVICES PROGRAM (WCFSP) ("WCFSP")

Assistance: project grants (to 50 percent/2-5 years).

Purposes: pursuant to Soil and Moisture Conservation Act of 1935, Fish and Wildlife Coordination Act, Reclamation Projects Authorization And Adjustment Act of 1992, and Energy and Water Development Appropriations Act, 2006, and other public laws, to actively encourage water conservation and efficient use of water supplies on Federal Reclamation projects, assist water districts with their responsibility to develop and implement water conservation plans, and complement and support State and other conservation programs.

Eligible applicants/beneficiaries: Depending on the authorizing legislation, agricultural and/or municipal/industrial water districts, irrigation districts, water districts or entities, communities, state or local water agencies, water-related non-profit organizations, small entities (public or private) that have contracts for water with Reclamation under the Warren Act, Native American Tribes, universities or educational institutions proposing to conduct water conservation activities within Reclamation boundaries.

Range: to $25,000. **Average:** N.A.

Activity: not quantified specifically.

HQ: none provided, see listing of field offices.

Internet: http://www.usbr.gov/waterconservation.

15.531 YAKIMA RIVER BASIN WATER ENHANCEMENT PROJECT (YRBWEP)

Assistance: project grants (grants/cooperative agreements/1 to 5 years).

Purposes: pursuant to Yavapai-Prescott Indian Tribe Water Rights Settlement Act of 1994, within the Yakima River Basin: to protect, mitigate, and enhance fish and wildlife through improved water management; to improve instream flows, and water quality; and to protect, create and enhance wetlands; to improve the reliability of water supply for irrigation; to authorize a Yakima River basin water conservation program; to realize sufficient water savings from the program so that not less than 40,000 acre-feet of water savings per year are achieved by the end of the fourth year of the Basin Conservation Program; to encourage voluntary transactions among public and private entities which result in the implementation of water conservation measures, practices and facilities; and to provide for the implementation by the Yakima Indian Nation at its sole discretion of (A) an irrigation demonstration project on the Yakima Indian Reservation using water savings from system improvements to the Wapato Irrigation Project, and (B) a Toppenish Creek corridor enhancement project integrating agricultural, fish, wildlife, and cultural resources.

Eligible applicants: State of Washington, and Federally Recognized Indian Tribal Governments, water and irrigation districts, and water rights owners located within the project area.

Eligible beneficiaries: anyone/general public, Intrastate, Local, Individual/Family, and Federally Recognized Indian Tribal Governments within the project area.

Range: $5,000 to $21,000,000.

Activity: not quantified specifically.

HQ: YRBWEP Manager, Bureau of Reclamation, DOI, 1917 Marsh Rd., Yakima, WA 98901. Phone: (509) 575-5848 ext. 267; Fax: (509) 454-5611.

Internet: http://www.usbr.gov/pn (Note: field office serves as headquarters.)

15.532 CENTRAL VALLEY PROJECT, TRINITY RIVER DIVISION, TRINITY RIVER FISH AND WILDLIFE MANAGEMENT

Assistance: project grants (cost sharing encouraged).

Purposes: pursuant to the Central Valley Project Improvement Act (CVPIA) of 1992, to identify and address impacts of the Central Valley Project on fish and wildlife, and protect, restore and enhance associated habitats in California's Trinity River basin.

Eligible applicants: any responsible source, including irrigation and/or water districts, State and local entities, public, private, and quasi-public nonprofit and for-profit institutions/organizations, Federally recognized Indian Tribal Governments, and small businesses.

Eligible beneficiaries: general public.

Range: $24,000 to $550,000. **Average:** $170,000.

Activity: FY 07, 8 to 10 projects anticipated.

HQ: Trinity River Restoration Program, Bureau of Reclamation, DOI, P.O. Box 1300, Weaverville, CA 96093. Phone: (530) 623-1800, FAX: (530) 623-5944.

Internet: www.usbr.gov/mp/ncao. (Note: field office serves as headquarters.)

15.533 CALIFORNIA WATER SECURITY AND ENVIRONMENTAL ENHANCEMENT ("CALFED")

Assistance: project grants (50 percent or more/to 2 years).

Purposes: pursuant to Title I of the Water Supply, Reliability, and Environmental Enhancement Act, to expand and protect water supplies; to improve water quality and the health of the Bay-Delta system through restoration and protection of native species and habitats; and to improve levees for flood protection and ecosystem benefits.

Eligible applicants: agencies of the state of California.

Eligible beneficiaries: general public in and around the California Bay-Delta area.

Range: $35,000 to $1,650,000. **Average:** $281,663.

Activity: FY 06, $6.5 million invested in enhancing water management in CALFED focus area.

HQ: Special Projects Office (MP-120), Mid-Pacific Region, Bureau of Reclamation, DOI, 2800 Cottage Way, Sacramento, CA 95825. Phone: (916) 978-5022; FAX: (916) 978-5528.

Internet: www.mp.usbr.gov. (Note: field office serves as headquarters.)

U.S. FISH AND WILDLIFE SERVICE

15.602 CONSERVATION LAW ENFORCEMENT TRAINING ASSISTANCE

Assistance: training.

Purposes: pursuant to the Fish and Wildlife Coordination Act of 1958 and Fish and Wildlife Improvement Act of 1978, for state conservation officer training in criminal law and in principles, techniques, and procedures of wildlife law enforcement.

Eligible applicants/beneficiaries: state agencies.

Range/Average: N.A.

Activity: not quantified specifically.

HQ: Assistant Director, Office of Law Enforcement, FWS-DOI, 4401 N. Fairfax Dr. - Rm.520, Arlington, VA 22203. Phone: (703) 358- 1949.

Internet: www.le.fws.gov.

15.605 SPORT FISH RESTORATION PROGRAM ("Dingell-Johnson Program - D-J Program")

Assistance: formula grants. (to 75 percent/2 years).

Purposes: pursuant to the Federal Aid in Sport Fish Restoration Act of 1950 as amended, to restore, conserve, manage, or enhance sport fish populations for the preservation and improvement of sport fishing and related uses of fisheries resources. Funds may be used for acquisition of boating access to public waters, fresh water fish habitat improvement, lake and stream rehabilitation, research, operations and maintenance, similar uses.

Eligible applicants/beneficiaries: fish and wildlife agencies in states with laws prohibiting diversion of revenues from fishing licenses to uses other than administration of the agency; territories.

Range: $900,000 to $14,700,000. **Average:** $5,200,000.

Activity: not quantified specifically.

HQ: Sport Fish Restoration Program Coordinator, Division of Federal Aid (MS MBSP-4020), FWS-DOI, 4401 N. Fairfax Dr., Arlington, VA 22203. Phone: (703) 358-2156, FAX (703) 358-1837.

Internet: www.fa.r9.fws.gov.

15.608 FISH AND WILDLIFE MANAGEMENT ASSISTANCE

Assistance: specialized services.

Purposes: pursuant to the Fish and Wildlife Act of 1956 and Sikes Act of 1974 as amended, Fish and Wildlife Coordination Act of 1958, and other acts, for: conservation and management of fish and wildlife resources, based on biological, chemical, and physical examinations of land and waters; stocking of fishes from national fish hatcheries; co-management by Alaska natives of marine mammals for subsistence use. Services are provided on a cost recoverable basis.

Eligible applicants/beneficiaries: state agencies, local governments, native American organizations, public nonprofit and other organizations, federal agencies.

Range/Average: N.A.

Activity: assistance to 100 native American tribes, 254 national wildlife refuges, 150 DOD installations.

HQ: Chief, Division of Fish and Wildlife Management and Habitat Restoration, FWS-DOI, ARLSQ - Rm.840, Washington, DC 20240. Phone: (703) 358-1718.

Internet: www.fisheries.fws.gov.

15.611 WILDLIFE RESTORATION ("Pittman-Robertson Program - P-R Program")

Assistance: formula grants. (to 75 percent/2 years).

Purposes: pursuant to the Federal Aid in Wildlife Restoration Act of 1937 as amended, to restore or manage wildlife populations and to provide facilities and services for hunter safety programs. Funds may be used for land acquisition, development, research, and coordination.

Eligible applicants/beneficiaries: fish and wildlife agencies in states with laws prohibiting diversion of hunting license revenues to uses other than administration of the agency; territories.

Range: $268,000 to $7,187,000. **Average:** $2,750,000.

Activity: not quantified specifically.

HQ: Chief, Division of Federal Aid, FWS-DOI, (MS MBSP-4020), 4401 N. Fairfax Dr., Arlington, VA 22203. Phone: (703) 358-2156, FAX (703) 358-1837.

Internet: www.federalasst.fws.gov.

15.614 COASTAL WETLANDS PLANNING, PROTECTION AND RESTORATION ACT ("National Coastal Wetlands Conservation Grants")

Assistance: project grants (50-75 percent).

Purposes: pursuant to the act, for coastal wetlands conservation projects. Funds may be used to acquire interests in lands or waters, and for restoration, enhancement, or management of coastal wetlands ecosystems, including conservation of fish and wildlife.

Eligible applicants/beneficiaries: states bordering the Atlantic, Pacific, Great Lakes, or Gulf coasts (except Louisiana); territories and possessions.

Range: $75,000 to $1,000,000. **Average:** $753,000.

Activity: FY 04 estimate, 18,000 acres acquired or restored.

HQ: Program Coordinator, Sport Fish Restoration Program Coordinator, Division of Federal Aid (MS MBSP-4020), FWS-DOI, 4401 N. Fairfax Dr., Arlington, VA 22203. Phone: (703) 358-2156, FAX (703) 358-1837.*or*Chief, Division of Fish and Wildlife Management and Habitat Restoration, Phone: (703) 358-1718.

Internet: www.federalasst.fws.gov; www.fws.gov/coastal/CoastalGrants.

15.615 COOPERATIVE ENDANGERED SPECIES CONSERVATION FUND

Assistance: project grants (75-90 percent).

Purposes: pursuant to the Endangered Species Act of 1973 as amended, for programs for the conservation of endangered and threatened species of animals and plants. Funds may cover the costs of habitat surveys, research, planning, monitoring, management, land acquisition, habitat protection, and public education.

Eligible applicants/beneficiaries: states and territories with cooperative agreements with DOI.

Range: $500 to $10,000,000.

Activity: FY 05, 61 projects funded.

HQ: Chief, Endangered Species, Division of Consultation, Habitat Conservation, Planning, and Recovery (MS-420 ARLSQ), FWS-DOI, 1849 C St. NW, Washington, DC 20240. Phone: (703) 358-2171, FAX (703) 358-1735.

Internet: www.endangered.fws.gov/grants/section6/index.html.

15.616 CLEAN VESSEL ACT ("Clean Vessel Act Pumpout Grant Program")

Assistance: project grants (75 percent).

Purposes: pursuant to the 1992 act, for surveys and plans for installing pumpout/dump stations to protect sensitive areas in the coastal zone from recreational boat sewage; for station construction; for related public education programs.

Eligible applicants/beneficiaries: states bordering the Atlantic, Pacific, or Gulf coasts, or the Great Lakes; territories and possessions.

Range: $10,000 to $1,500,000. **Average:** $394,000.

Activity: FY 93-03, 3,000 pumpout and 1,900 dump stations constructed in 49 states.

HQ: Chief, Division of Federal Aid, FWS-DOI, (MS MBSP-4020), 4401 N. Fairfax Dr., Arlington, VA 22203. Phone: (703) 358-2156, FAX (703) 358-1837.

Internet: www.federalasst.fws.gov.

15.619 RHINOCEROS AND TIGER CONSERVATION FUND

Assistance: project grants (some matching).

Purposes: pursuant to the Rhinoceros and Tiger Conservation Act of 1994 as amended by the Rhino and Tiger Product Labeling Act of 1998, for rhinoceros and tiger conservation projects including: surveys and monitoring; conservation training and education; wildlife inspection, law enforcement, and forensic skills; research; protected area management; sustainable development in buffer zones surrounding rhinoceros and tiger habitat; management of human behavior and livestock to decrease conflicts; use of substitutes for tiger and rhinoceros products in oriental medicine.

Eligible applicants/beneficiaries: appropriate government agencies; experienced organizations and individuals.

Average: generally, to $50,000.

Activity: FY 04, 40 grants in 15 countries.

HQ: Chief, Division of International Conservation, FWS-DOI, ARLSQ 730, 4401 N. Fairfax Dr., Arlington, VA 22203. Phone: (703) 358- 1754, FAX (703) 358-2849.

Internet: www.fws.gov/international/grants/grants.html. (Note: no field offices for this program.)

15.620 AFRICAN ELEPHANT CONSERVATION FUND

Assistance: project grants (some matching).

Purposes: pursuant to the African Elephant Conservation Act, for African elephant conservation projects including research, management, and protection activities. Project examples: meritorious service awards program for game wardens in Africa; training in elephant biology and ecology; providing anti-poaching equipment.

Eligible applicants/beneficiaries: African government agencies; experienced organizations and individuals.

Range: generally, to $50,000.

Activity: FY 04, 26 grants in 12 countries.

HQ: Chief, Division of International Conservation, FWS-DOI, ARLSQ 730, 4401 N. Fairfax Dr., Arlington, VA 22203. Phone: (703) 358-1754, FAX (703) 358-2849.

Internet: www.fws.gov/international/grants/grants.html. (Note: no field offices for this program.)

15.621 ASIAN ELEPHANT CONSERVATION FUND

Assistance: project grants (some matching).

Purposes: pursuant to the Asian African Elephant Conservation Act, for Asian elephant conservation projects including research, management, and protection activities.

Eligible applicants/beneficiaries: Asian government agencies; experienced organizations and individuals.

Range: generally, to $50,000.

Activity: FY 04, 33 grants awarded in 10 countries.

HQ: Chief, Division of International Conservation, FWS-DOI, ARLSQ 730, 4401 N. Fairfax Dr., Arlington, VA 22203. Phone: (703) 358-1754, FAX (703) 358-2849.

Internet: www.fws.gov/international/grants/grants.html. (Note: no field offices for this program.)

15.622 SPORTFISHING AND BOATING SAFETY ACT ("Boating Infrastructure Grant Program")

Assistance: project grants (75 percent).

Purposes: pursuant to the act, to construct, renovate, or maintain tie-up facilities for transient, nontrailerable recreational vessels.

Eligible applicants/beneficiaries: states, possessions and territories.

Range: Tier 2 grants, $100,000 to $1,500,000. **Average:** Tier 1 grants, $100,000; Tier 2 grants, $500,000.

Activity: not quantified specifically.

HQ: Boating Infrastructure Grant Program Coordinator, Division of Federal Aid (MS MBSP-4020), FWS-DOI, 4401 N. Fairfax Dr., Arlington, VA 22203. Phone: (703) 358-2156, FAX (703) 358-1837.

Internet: www.federalasst.fws.gov.

15.623 NORTH AMERICAN WETLANDS CONSERVATION FUND ("NAWCF")

Assistance: project grants. (50 percent/2 years).

Purposes: pursuant to the North American Wetlands Conservation Act, for wetlands conservation projects in the U.S., Canada, and Mexico, including: acquisition of interests in lands or waters for fish and wildlife protection; restoration, management, or enhancement of wetland ecosystems and habitats—only in coastal wetlands ecosystems in coastal states.

Eligible applicants/beneficiaries: entities and individuals recommended by the North American Wetlands Conservation Council and approved by the Migratory Bird Conservation Commission.

Range: small grants, to $75,000; standard grants, $75,000 to $1,000,000. **Average:** small grants, $42,000; standard, $710,000.

Activity: FY 05, 122 new projects.

HQ: Chief, Division of Bird Habitat Conservation (MBSP 4075), FWS-DOI, 4401 N. Fairfax Dr., Arlington, VA 22203. Phone: (703) 358-1784, FAX (703) 358-2282.

Internet: www.birdhabitat.fws.gov/NAWCA/grants.htm.

15.625 WILDLIFE CONSERVATION AND RESTORATION

Assistance: formula grants (to 75 percent).

Purposes: pursuant to the Department of Transportation and Related Agencies (i.e. Commerce, Justice, State) Appropriations Act of 2001, to plan and implement projects encouraging a diverse array of wildlife and associated habitats, including species that are not hunted or fished and to provide wildlife education and recreation activities. State, Commonwealth or Territory must have an approved Comprehensive Wildlife Conservation Plan on file to receive grant funds.

Eligible applicants: state, commonwealth, or territorial fish and wildlife agencies with lead management responsibility for fish and wildlife resources.

Eligible beneficiaries: general public.

Range: $121,000 to $2,425,000. **Average:** $904,000.

Activity: funding for FY 02 only; with similar program **15.634**, contributed $380 million toward restoring and protecting severely threatened species.

HQ: Wildlife and Sport Fish Restoration Programs-Policy and Programs, FWS-DOI, 4401 N. Fairfax Dr.- FA-4020, Arlington, VA 22203. Phone: (703) 358-2156.

Internet: www.wsfprograms.fws.gov.

15.626 HUNTER EDUCATION AND SAFETY PROGRAM

Assistance: formula grants (75 percent).

Purposes: pursuant to the Federal Aid in Wildlife Restoration Act of 1937 as amended, to enhance hunter, bow, and archery education programs, and to construct firearm shooting and archery ranges.

Eligible applicants/beneficiaries: fish and wildlife agencies in states with laws prohibiting diversion of hunting license revenues to uses other than administration of the agency; territories.

Range: $13,300 to $240,000. **Average:** $145,000.

Activity: not quantified specifically.

HQ: Chief, Division of Federal Aid, FWS-DOI, (MS MBSP-4020), 4401 N. Fairfax Dr., Arlington, VA 22203. Phone: (703) 358-2156, FAX (703) 358-1837.

Internet: www.federalasst.fws.gov.

15.628 MULTI-STATE CONSERVATION GRANT PROGRAM

Assistance: project grants. (100 percent/to 3 years).

Purposes: pursuant to the Wildlife and Sport Fish Restoration Act of 2000 as amended and other acts, for sport fish and wildlife restoration projects identified by the International Association of Fish and Wildlife Agencies. Funds may be used for research, boating access development, hunter safety, aquatic education, habitat improvements, and similar purposes.

Eligible applicants/beneficiaries: states or groups of states; nongovernmental organizations.

Range: $25,000 to $500,000. **Average:** $140,000.

Activity: annually, 10-20 grants.

HQ: Multistate Conservation Grant Program Coordinator, Division of Federal Assistance, FWS-DOI, 4401 N. Fairfax Dr.- Rm.4020, Arlington, VA 22203. Phone: (703) 358-2156.

Internet: http://federalasst.fws.gov.

15.629 GREAT APES CONSERVATION FUND

Assistance: project grants (matching) (matching).

Purposes: pursuant to the Great Ape Conservation Act of 2000, for great apes research, conservation, management, and protection programs and projects in countries within their range.

Eligible applicants/beneficiaries: appropriate government agencies; experienced organizations and individuals.

Range: generally, to $50,000.

Activity: FY 04, 35 grants in 15 countries.

HQ: Chief, Division of International Conservation, FWS-DOI, ARLSQ 730, 4401 N. Fairfax Dr., Arlington, VA 22203. Phone: (703) 358-1754, FAX (703) 358-2849.

Internet: www.fws.gov/international/grants/grants.html. (Note: no field offices for this program.)

15.630 COASTAL PROGRAM

Assistance: project grants.

Purposes: pursuant to the Fish and Wildlife Act of 1956 and Fish and Wildlife Coordination Act of 1958, to provide financial and technical assistance via partnerships to identify, protect, and restore habitats in priority coastal areas. Funds may be used for assessments and acquisition of private or public lands.

Eligible applicants/beneficiaries: federal, state, interstate, and intrastate agencies; local and tribal governments; sponsored organizations; public nonprofit institutes and organizations such as watershed councils, land trusts, schools and IHEs; territories and possessions; private landowners including individuals and businesses.

Range: $5,000 to $50,000.

Activity: FY 05, 236 partnership agreements; protection of 70,138 acres of coastal wetlands, 309,206 acres of uplands, 69 miles of streams/shoreline; restoration of 13,830 acres of wetlands, 5,749 acres of uplands, 186 miles of streams/shoreline; remove 22 barriers to fish passage.

HQ: Chief, Branch of Habitat Restoration, FWS-DOI, 4401 N. Fairfax Dr. - Rm.400, Arlington, VA 22203. Phone: (703) 358-2201, FAX (703) 358-2232.

Internet: www.fws.gov/cep/coastweb.html.

15.631 PARTNERS FOR FISH AND WILDLIFE

Assistance: direct payments/specified use (50 percent).

Purposes: pursuant to the Fish and Wildlife Act of 1956 as amended and Fish and Wildlife Coordination Act of 1958, to provide financial and technical assistance to private landowners and tribes to voluntarily restore or improve native fish and wildlife habitats. Landowners must enter into 10-year cooperative agreements.

Eligible applicants/beneficiaries: private landowners, local governments, tribal organizations, educational institutions.

Range: $200 to $25,000. **Average:** $5,400.

Activity: FY 05, 2,700 landowner agreements completed.

HQ: Chief, Branch of Habitat Restoration, FWS-DOI, 4401 N. Fairfax Dr. - Rm.400, Arlington, VA 22203. Phone: (703) 358-2201, FAX (703) 358-2232.

Internet: www.partners.fws.gov.

15.632 CONSERVATION GRANTS PRIVATE STEWARDSHIP FOR IMPERILED SPECIES
("Private Stewardship Grants Program" - "PSGP")

Assistance: project grants (90 percent).

Purposes: pursuant to the Endangered Species Act of 1973 as amended, for the voluntary restoration, management, or enhancement of habitat on private lands—for endangered, threatened, proposed, or other at-risk species.

Eligible applicants/beneficiaries: sponsored organizations, individuals, families, specialized groups, public or private nonprofit organizations, small businesses.

Range: $12,000 to $300,000.

Activity: FY 05, 72 awards in 38 states.

HQ: Chief, Endangered Species, Division of Consultation, Habitat Conservation, Planning, and Recovery (MS-420 ARLSQ), FWS-DOI, 1849 C St. NW, Washington, DC 20240. Phone: (703) 358-2171, FAX (703) 358-1735.

Internet: www.endangered.fws.gov.

15.633 LANDOWNER INCENTIVE PROGRAM

Assistance: project grants (75 percent).

Purposes: pursuant to the Land and Water Conservation Fund Act of 1965, to establish new or supplement existing landowner incentive programs providing technical or financial assistance for habitat protection, restoration, and management—to benefit federally listed, proposed, or at-risk species on private lands; to encourage states to enhance private landowner conservation efforts.

Eligible applicants/beneficiaries: fish and wildlife agencies of the states, tribes, territories, and possessions.

Range: "Tier 2" grants, $204,900 to $767,000. **Average:** "Tier 2," $508,000; "Tier 1" grants, $180,000.

Activity: not quantified specifically.

HQ: Land Owner Incentive Program Coordinator, Division of Federal Aid, FWS-DOI, (MS MBSP-4020), 4401 N. Fairfax Dr., Arlington, VA 22203. Phone: (703) 358-2156, FAX (703) 358-1837.

Internet: www.federalasst.fws.gov.

15.634 STATE WILDLIFE GRANTS ("SWG")

Assistance: formula grants. (planning, 75 percent; implementation, 50 percent/2 years).

Purposes: to develop and implement programs for the benefit of wildlife and their habitat, including species that are not hunted or fished.

Eligible applicants/beneficiaries: fish and wildlife agencies of the states, tribes, territories, and possessions.

Average: N.A.

Activity: FY 05, 281 grants.

HQ: State Wildlife Program Coordinator, Division of Federal Assistance, FWS-DOI, 4401 N. Fairfax Dr.- Rm.4020, Arlington, VA 22203. Phone: (703) 358-2156.

Internet: http://federalasst.fws.gov.

15.635 NEOTROPICAL MIGRATORY BIRD CONSERVATION

Assistance: project grants. (25 percent/to 2 years).

Purposes: pursuant to the Neotropical Migratory Bird Conservation Act of 2000, for projects that: enhance the conservation of neotropical bird species in the U.S., Latin America, or the Caribbean; ensure adequate local public participation in project development and implementation; are conducted in consultation with relevant wildlife management authorities and other appropriate government officials; are sensitive to local historic and cultural resources and comply with applicable laws; and, promote sustainable effective, long-term programs. 75 percent of available funds must be expended outside the U.S.

Eligible applicants/beneficiaries: individuals, corporations, partnerships, trusts, or other private entities; officers, employees, agents, departments, or instrumentalities of any state, municipality, or political subdivision of state, or of any foreign government; entities subject to the jurisdiction of the U.S. or any foreign government; international organizations with an interest in neotropical migratory bird conservation.

Range: $2,000 to $250,000. **Average:** $88,000.

Activity: new program listing in 2003. FY 02-05, 144 awards to entities in 34 countries.

HQ: Chief, Division of Bird Habitat Conservation (MBSP 4075), FWS-DOI, 4401 N. Fairfax Dr., Arlington, VA 22203. Phone: (703) 358-1784, FAX (703) 358-2282.

Internet: www.birdhabitat.fws.gov/. (Note: no field offices for this program.)

15.636 ALASKA SUBSISTENCE MANAGEMENT

Assistance: project grants (100 percent).

Purposes: pursuant to the Alaska National Interest Lands Conservation Act of 1980, for approved fish and wildlife subsistence management, fisheries monitoring, and traditional ecological knowledge projects—involving partnerships within the ranges of designated fish and wildlife species. Project examples include tagging, studies, harvest surveys.

Eligible applicants/beneficiaries: individuals, families, profit and nonprofit organizations, federal and Alaska state employees and agents or instrumentalities, tribal governments.

Range: $3,000 to $513,000.

Activity: new program listing in 2004.

HQ: Administrative Specialist, Office of Subsistence Management, Fisheries Information Service Division, FWS-DOI, 3501 C St. - Ste.1030, Anchorage, AK 99503. Phone: (907) 786-3387.

Internet: www.alaska.fws.gov/asm/home.html. (Note: the field office serves as headquarters.)

15.637 MIGRATORY BIRD JOINT VENTURES

Assistance: direct payments/specified use; project grants (100 percent/1-5 years).

Purposes: pursuant to the Fish and Wildlife Act of 1956, Fish and Wildlife Coordination Act of 1958, Fish and Wildlife Conservation Act, Migratory Bird Treaty Act, and amendments, to protect, restore, and enhance wetland and upland ecosystems for the conservation of migratory birds. Project funds must be matched by joint ventures and may be used for costs of administration, coordination, bird habitat landscape planning, monitoring, evaluation, applied research, training, communications and outreach, and project implementation.

Eligible applicants/beneficiaries: federal, state, local, and tribal governments; public, private, profit, and nonprofit organizations; inter- and intrastate entities; individuals or families owning lands.

Range: $250 to $900,000. **Average:** $12,000.

Activity: new program listing in 2004. As of 2006, 17 joint ventures focusing on regions with critical habitats, 3 focused on individual species—in the U.S., Canada, and Mexico.

HQ: Joint Venture Liaison Officer, Division of Bird Habitat Conservation (MS 4075), FWS-DOI, 4401 N. Fairfax Dr., Arlington, VA 22203. Phone: (703) 358-1784, FAX (703) 358-2282.

Internet: www.birdhabitat.fws.gov/NAWMP/jv.htm.

15.638 TRIBAL LANDOWNER INCENTIVE PROGRAM ("TLIP")

Assistance: project grants (75 percent).

Purposes: pursuant to the Land and Water Conservation Fund Act of 1965, to establish new or supplement existing programs providing technical or financial assistance to tribal governments for habitat protection and management, to benefit federally listed, proposed, or candidate species or other at-risk species—whether on tribal trust or private lands.

Eligible applicants/beneficiaries: tribal governments.

Range: to $150,000.

Activity: new program in FY 04. FY 03, 23 proposals selected for funding.

HQ: Native American Liaison, Division of External Affairs (MS- 3251), FWS-DOI, 1849 C St. NW, Washington, DC 20240. Phone: (202) 208-4133, FAX (202) 501-3524.

Internet: http://grants.fws.gov/tribal.html.

15.639 TRIBAL WILDLIFE GRANTS PROGRAM ("TWG")

Assistance: project grants (to 100 percent).

Purposes: pursuant to the Land and Water Conservation Fund Act of 1965, to develop and implement programs for the benefit of wildlife and their habitat, including species that are not hunted or fished—whether on tribal trust or private lands.

Eligible applicants/beneficiaries: tribal governments.

Range: to $250,000.

Activity: new program listing in 2004. FY 04 estimate, 24 proposals selected for funding.

HQ: Native American Liaison, Division of External Affairs (MS- 3251), FWS-DOI, 1849 C St. NW, Washington, DC 20240. Phone: (202) 208-4133, FAX (202) 501-3524.

Internet: http://grants.fws.gov/tribal.html.

15.640 WILDLIFE WITHOUT BORDERS—LATIN AMERICA AND THE CARIBBEAN

Assistance: project grants (cost sharing).

Purposes: pursuant to the Endangered Species Act of 1973 as amended, for the management of fish, plant, and wildlife resources in the Western

Hemisphere. Priority is accorded to projects to strengthen capacity to conserve and use sustainable biological resources, and result in specific measurable on-the- ground management actions in agreement with the Convention on Nature Protection and Wildlife Preservation in the Western Hemisphere ("Western Hemisphere Convention, 1940"). Activities should be conducted on-site, and may include work such as: academic and technical training; applied research; community- level education; technology transfer and information exchange; promotion of networks, partnerships, and coalitions.

Eligible applicants/beneficiaries: federal, state, and local governments; nonprofit, nongovernmental organizations; public and private IHEs.

Average: preference to projects requesting less than $50,000.

Activity: new program listing in 2004. FY 04, 34 awards for projects in 18 countries.

HQ: Chief, Division of International Conservation, FWS-DOI, ARLSQ 730, 4401 N. Fairfax Dr., Arlington, VA 22203. Phone: (703) 358-1754, FAX (703) 358-2849.

Internet: www.fws.gov/international/grants/grants.html. (Note: no field offices for this program.)

15.641 WILDLIFE WITHOUT BORDERS—MEXICO

Assistance: project grants (cost sharing).

Purposes: pursuant to the Endangered Species Act of 1973 as amended, for the conservation and sustainable use of Mexico's wildlife and plant resources through projects that strengthen Mexico's capacity. Activities should be conducted in Mexico, and may include work such as: academic and technical training; applied research; community-level education; technology transfer and information exchange; promotion of networks, partnerships, and coalitions.

Eligible applicants/beneficiaries: federal, state, and local governments; nonprofit, nongovernmental organizations; public and private IHEs.

Average: preference to projects requesting less than $50,000.

Activity: new program listing in 2004. FY 04, 14 awards.

HQ: Chief, Division of International Conservation, FWS-DOI, ARLSQ 730, 4401 N. Fairfax Dr., Arlington, VA 22203. Phone: (703) 358-1754, FAX (703) 358-2849.

Internet: www.fws.gov/international/grants/grants.html. (Note: no field offices for this program.)

15.642 CHALLENGE COST SHARE ("CCS")

Assistance: project grants (50 percent).

Purposes: to encourage partnerships to support the mission of the U.S. Fish and Wildlife Service through projects involving conservation, protection, and enhancement of fish, wildlife, and plants, including recreational and educational activities—whether on or off FWS lands.

Eligible applicants/beneficiaries: individuals, families, and virtually any organization, whether public or private, profit or nonprofit—including territories and possessions.

Range: $300 to $25,000. **Average:** $7,800.

Activity: new program listing in 2004. FY 03, 1,400 approved partners provided $10,500,000 in matching funds.

HQ: Assistant Director, National Wildlife Refuge System, FWS-DOI, 4401 N. Fairfax Dr. - Ste.670, Arlington, VA 22203. Phone: (703) 358-1744, FAX (703) 358-2248.

Internet: www.fws.gov.

15.643 ALASKA MIGRATORY BIRD CO-MANAGEMENT COUNCIL ("AMBCC")

Assistance: project grants (100 percent).

Purposes: pursuant to the Fish and Wildlife Coordination Act of 1958 and Migratory Bird Treaty Act, to facilitate and administer programs to involve subsistence hunters of migratory birds in the management and regulation of migratory birds.

Eligible applicants/beneficiaries: native American and public nonprofit organizations, other public institutions, tribal and local governments.

Range: $14,000 to $26,500.

Activity: new program listing in 2005 (CFDA on-line version); 11 regional management bodies established.

HQ: Office of the Alaska Migratory Bird Co-Management Council (201), FWS-DOI, 1011 E. Tudor Rd., Anchorage, AK 99503. Phone: (907) 786-3499, FAX (907) 786-3641.

Internet: http://Alaska.fws/ambcc/index.htm.

15.644 FEDERAL JUNIOR DUCK STAMP CONSERVATION AND DESIGN ("Junior Duck Stamp Contest")

Assistance: direct payments/specified use; sale, exchange, or donation of property and goods.

Purposes: pursuant to the reauthorized Junior Duck Stamp Conservation and Design Program Act of 1994, for a nationwide design contest to teach K-12 students environmental science, wildlife management, wetlands ecology, and the importance of habitat conservation. Assistance may be used to: provide awards and scholarships to student-winners in state-territory contest rounds; provide awards to schools and other participants; pay costs of outreach and marketing. Cash awards are provided for scholarships to national round winners.

Eligible applicants/beneficiaries: U.S. and territorial K-12 students attending public, private, or home schools.

Range: state-territorial level, to $2,350; national level, $200 to $5,000.

Activity: new program listing in 2005 (CFDA on-line version). Program in existence since 1994. Annually, 26,500 participants from all states, DC, Samoa, and VI.

HQ: National Program Coordinator, Federal Duck Stamp Office (MBSP-4070), FWS-DOI, 4401 N. Fairfax Dr., Arlington, VA 22203. Phone: (703) 358-2000, FAX (703) 358-2009.

Internet: http://duckstamps.fws.gov; e-mail, duckstamps@fws.gov.

15.645 MARINE TURTLE CONSERVATION FUND

Assistance: project grants (to 100 percent).

Purposes: pursuant to the Marine Turtle Conservation Act of 2004, for foreign countries to conduct projects to conserve marine turtles and their nesting habitats; to address other threats to marine turtle survival. Applied research projects should address specific management needs and activities.

Eligible applicants/beneficiaries: appropriate responsible government agencies; other qualified organizations and individuals.

Range: preference to projects requesting less than $25,000.

Activity: new program in FY 05.

HQ: Chief, Division of International Conservation, FWS-DOI, ARLSQ 730, 4401 N. Fairfax Dr., Arlington, VA 22203. Phone: (703) 358-1754, FAX (703) 358-2849.

Internet: www.fws.gov/international/grants/grants.html.

15.647 MIGRATORY BIRD CONSERVATION

Assistance: project grants; direct payments/specified use (grants, 1-5 years).

Purposes: pursuant to the Fish and Wildlife Act of 1956, Fish and Wildlife Coordination Act of 1958, Fish and Wildlife Conservation Act, Migratory Bird Treaty Act, and amendments, to maintain and enhance populations and habitats of migratory bird species found in the Upper Midwest, including Illinois, Indiana, Iowa, Michigan, Minnesota, Missouri, Ohio, and Wisconsin. Funds may be used for population surveys and monitoring, applied research, compilation of technical information.

Eligible applicants/beneficiaries: federal, state, local, and tribal governments; public, private, profit, and nonprofit organizations.

Range: $1,500 to $50,000. **Average:** $11,000.

Activity: new program listing in 2005; FY 05, 12 proposals funded.

HQ: Division of Migratory Birds, FWS-DOI, 1 Federal Drive, Fort Snelling, MN 55111-4056. Phone: (612) 713-5473, -5470, FAX (612) 713-5393.

Internet: www.fws.gov/midwest/midwestbird (Note: no other field offices for this program.)

15.648 CENTRAL VALLEY PROJECT IMPROVEMENT (CVPI) ANADROMOUS FISH RESTORATION PROGRAM (AFRP) ("CVPI, AFRP")

Assistance: project grants (1-5 years).

Purposes: pursuant to the Central Valley Improvement Act-Title 34 and the Federal Grant and Cooperative Agreement Act, to protect, restore, and enhance fish, wildlife, and associated habitats in the California Central

Valley and Trinity River basins; to address environmental impact, improve operational flexibility, increase water-related benefits, and achieve a reasonable balance among competing demands for water use of the Central Valley Project. Funds may be used for research to improve management and increase Anadromous fish resources; spawning area improvement; installation of fish passages; construction of fish protection devices, and data collection.

Eligible applicants/beneficiaries: state, local governments; native American, public or private nonprofit organizations.

Average: $152,335.

Activity: not quantified specifically.

HQ: CNO-California Nevada Office, 2800 Cottage Way, Room W-2606, Sacramento, CA 95825.

Internet: www.delta.dfg.ca.gov/afrp/title34.asp#top.

15.649 SERVICE TRAINING AND TECHNICAL ASSISTANCE (GENERIC TRAINING)

Assistance: project grants; direct payments/specified use (cost sharing encouraged).

Purposes: pursuant to Fish and Wildlife Act of 1956, Fish and Wildlife Coordination Act, Fish and Wildlife Improvement Act of 1978, as amended, to assist in conservation of the Nation's natural resources by providing financial support for training, meetings, workshops and conferences for the promotion of public conservation awareness.

Eligible applicants/beneficiaries: Federal, state and local government agencies; Federally-recognized Tribal governments; private and public nonprofit institutions/organizations.

Range: $1000 to $500,000. **Average:** $10,000 to $50,000.

Activity: FY 04: 2,527 awards, totaling $149,000,000.

HQ: Chief, Division of Contracting and Facilities Management, Washington Office, 4401 North Fairfax Drive, Mail Stop 7118-43, Arlington, Virginia 22203. Phone: (703) 358-1901.

Internet: http://www.fws.gov.

15.650 RESEARCH GRANTS (GENERIC)

Assistance: project grants; direct payments/specified use (cost sharing encouraged).

Purposes: pursuant to Fish and Wildlife Improvement Act of 1978, Land and Water Conservation Fund Act of 1965, Endangered Species Act of 1973, as amended, to assist in the conservation of the Nation's natural resources through land management, research, and data collection/analysis in order to further the preservation and management of natural resources.

Eligible applicants/beneficiaries: Federal, State and local government agencies; Federally-recognized Tribal governments; private nonprofit institutions/organizations; public nonprofit institutions/organizations.

Range: $1,000 to $500,000. **Average:** $10,000 to $50,000.

Activity: FY 04: 2,527 awards, totaling $149,000,000.

HQ: Chief, Division of Contracting and Facilities Management, Washington Office 4401, North /Fairfax Drive, Mail Stop 7118-43, Arlington, Virginia 22203. Phone: (703) 358-1901.

Internet: http://www.fws.gov.

15.651 WILDLIFE WITHOUT BORDERS-AFRICA PROGRAM

Assistance: project grants (cost sharing encouraged).

Purposes: pursuant to the Endangered Species Act of 1973 as amended, to strengthen the ability of African institutions to manage and conserve species, habitats, and ecological process for the benefit of African people and the world. Some projects of particular interest are ones that would provide training to increase human and institutional capacity to: mitigate the impact of industry, human/wildlife conflict, climate change, illegal trade in bushmeat; provide community outreach and education, human resource and financial management, conflict resolution, and coalition building. Projects should take place in Africa or facilitate protected area conservation and management within Africa.

Eligible applicants: federal, state, and local government agencies; public and private institutions of higher education, nonprofit, nongovernmental organizations, or any of these entities acting on behalf of an eligible individual.

Eligible beneficiaries: federal, state, and local government agencies; public and private institutions of higher education, nonprofit, nongovernmental organizations. All recipients, both individual and institutional, must have a bank account and the ability to receive funds directly.

Range: usually to $50,000.

Activity: N.A. New program, funding to begin in FY 08.

HQ: Chief, Division of International Conservation, FWS-DOI, 4401 N. Fairfax Drive-Rm. 100, Arlington, Virginia 22203-1622. Phone: (703) 358-1754, FAX: (703) 358-2115.

Internet: http://www.fws.gov/international/dicprograms/africa_program.html.

15.653 NATIONAL OUTREACH AND COMMUNICATION PROGRAM ("NOC")

Assistance: project grants (matching encouraged).

Purposes: pursuant to the Transportation Equity Act for the 21st Century of 1998 and the Sportfishing and Boating Safety Act of 1998, to improve communications with the general public regarding angling and boating opportunities, sound practices, and water safety; to educate and encourage conservation and responsible use of the nations' aquatic resources.

Eligible applicants: anyone with the expertise to conduct work within the scope of the Strategic Plan for the Outreach and Communication Program as required by the Sportfishing and Boating Safety Act of 1998.

Eligible beneficiaries: general public.

Average: $12,000,000.

Activity: not quantified specifically.

HQ: Recreational Boating and Fishing Liaison, FWS-DOI, 4401 N. Fairfax Drive, MS 3103-AEA, Arlington, Virginia 22203. Phone: (703) 358-2435.

Internet: www.fws.gov/conservationpartnerships. (Note: no field offices for this program.)

15.654 VISITOR FACILITY ENHANCEMENTS - VEHICLE PULLOUTS, INTERPRETIVE TRAILS, AND KIOSKS ("Turnout Program")

Assistance: project grants (cost sharing encouraged/1-5 years).

Purposes: pursuant to the Fish and Wildlife Coordination Act of 1958, National Wildlife Refuge System Administration Act, and Fish and Wildlife Act of 1956 as amended, to encourage partnerships with interested parties to enhance wildlife viewing opportunities for the public. Projects must conserve, protect and enhance fish, wildlife, and plants and may include trails, scenic overlooks, interpretive pullouts, signs, and kiosks.

Eligible applicants/beneficiaries: any U.S. government, organization or individual supporting the mission of the FWS project.

Average: $102,000.

Activity: not quantified specifically.

HQ: Assistant Director, National Wildlife Refuge System, FWS-DOI, 4401 N. Fairfax Drive, Suite 670, Arlington, Virginia 22203. Phone: (703) 358-1744, FAX: (703) 358-2248.

Internet: www.fws.gov. (Note: no field offices for this program.)

15.655 MIGRATORY BIRD MONITORING, ASSESSMENT AND CONSERVATION ("Migratory Bird")

Assistance: project grants; direct payments/specified use (100 percent).

Purposes: pursuant to the Fish and Wildlife Coordination Act of 1958, Fish and Wildlife Conservation Act, Migratory Bird Treaty Act, and Fish and Wildlife Act of 1956 as amended, to maintain, enhance, and deepen understanding of the ecology and habitats of migratory bird species. Special emphasis will be placed on bird species listed in USFWS conservation and management priorities documents (e.g. USFWS Birds of Conservation Concern 2002, Focal Species list). Projects related to the priorities identified in the following plans will receive the greatest funding consideration: Implementing national, regional, flyway Bird Conservation Region, and state-level bird conservation plans (e.g., Partners in Flight North American Landbird Conservation (http://www.partnersinflight.org); U.S. Shorebird Conservation Plan (http://shorebirdplan.fws.gov); and North American Waterbird Conservation Plan (http://birdhabitat.fws.gov/NAWMP/nawmphp.htm).

Eligible applicants/beneficiaries: any individual or group in the U.S. or territories.

Range/Average: $500 to $1,000,000.

Activity: not quantified specifically.

HQ: Chief, Division of Migratory Bird Management, FWS-DOI, Arlington Square, 4107 N. Fairfax Drive - MS MBSP, Arlington, VA 22203. Phone: (703) 358-1966, FAX (703) 358-2272, 2217.

Internet: www.fws.gov/migratorybirds.

U.S. GEOLOGICAL SURVEY

15.805 ASSISTANCE TO STATE WATER RESOURCES RESEARCH INSTITUTES ("Water Research Institute Program")

Assistance: formula grants; project grants (formula, 33 percent; project, 50 percent).

Purposes: pursuant to the Water Resources Research Act of 1984 as amended, for basic or applied research, conferences, studies, student training, and related activities concerning regional, state, or local water problems. Project funds may not support formal instructional activities, general education, or costs of permanent buildings.

Eligible applicants/beneficiaries: university water research institutes in states and territories. Other IHEs may participate in cooperation with the designated state institute.

Range: $92,000 to $265,000. **Average:** $113,388.

Activity: FY 05, 54 formula grants, 8 competitive awards.

HQ: Chief, Office of External Research, USGS-DOI, 424 National Center, Reston, VA 20192. Phone: (703) 648-6800, FAX (703) 648- 5070.

Internet: www.water/usgs.gov/wrri. (Note: no field offices for this program.)

15.807 EARTHQUAKE HAZARDS REDUCTION PROGRAM

Assistance: project grants (cost sharing/to 2 years).

Purposes: for mitigation of earthquake losses. Projects may include providing earth science data and assessments, land use planning, engineering design, emergency preparedness systems.

Eligible applicants/beneficiaries: IHEs, profit and nonprofit organizations, state and local governments.

Range: $6,000 to $1,100,000. **Average:** $70,000.

Activity: FY 05, 140 awards.

HQ: External Research Program Manager, Earthquakes Hazards Program Office, Geologic Division, USGS-DOI, 905A National Center, Reston, VA 20192. Phone: (703) 648-6722, FAX (703) 648-6642.

Internet: http://erp-web.er.usgs.gov/; e-mail, gd-erp-coordinator@usgs.gov. (Note: no field offices for this program.)

15.808 U.S. GEOLOGICAL SURVEY—RESEARCH AND DATA ACQUISITION

Assistance: project grants (from 50 percent).

Purposes: pursuant to the Organic Act of 1879, for scientific research complementing USGS programs in classification of the public lands and examination of the geological structure, water, mineral, and biological resources and products of the national domain. Most funded research involves enhancing existing, long- term collaborative projects, including coastal and marine geology studies, volcano monitoring, and earth science research facilities.

Eligible applicants/beneficiaries: profit and nonprofit organizations; state and local governments. Note: funding for external projects is limited; applicants are urged to consult USGS prior to submitting proposals.

Range: $1,000 to $582,000. **Average:** $50,000.

Activity: FY 05, 288 grants and cooperative agreements.

HQ: none; all contacts are with field offices listed in Part IV.

Internet: www.usgs.gov/contracts.

15.809 NATIONAL SPATIAL DATA INFRASTRUCTURE COOPERATIVE AGREEMENTS PROGRAM

Assistance: project grants (from 50 percent).

Purposes: pursuant to the Organic Act of 1879, for collaborative projects to improve the discovery, access, transfer, and use of geospatial data, through the National Geospatial Data Clearinghouse to further development and implementation of the National Spatial Data Infrastructure (NSDI). Project funds may be used: to develop and promulgate the use of standards in data collection, documentation, transfer, and search and query; for educational outreach programs.

Eligible applicants/beneficiaries: collaborations of federal, state, and local government agencies; educational institutions; private firms and foundations; nonprofit organizations; recognized tribes or native American groups.

Range: $20,000 to $75,000. **Average:** $29,000.

Activity: FY 06, 50 awards.

HQ: Federal Geographic Data Committee Secretariat (MS 590), USGS-DOI, 12201 Sunrise Valley Dr., Reston, VA 20192. Phone: (703) 648-5514, FAX (703) 648-5755.

Internet: www.fgdc.gov/funding/cap2002.html; e-mail, gdc@usgs.gov. (Note: no field offices for this program.)

15.810 NATIONAL COOPERATIVE GEOLOGIC MAPPING PROGRAM ("STATEMAP - EDMAP")

Assistance: project grants. (50 percent/1-2 years).

Purposes: pursuant to the National Geologic Mapping Reauthorization Act of 1997, to produce geologic maps of areas important to the economic, social, or scientific welfare of individual states. "STATEMAP" supports projects: (1) producing new geologic maps with attendant explanatory information; (2) compiling existing geologic data in a digital form at a scale of 1 to 100,000 for inclusion in the National Digital Geologic Map Database. "EDMAP provides funding: (1) for graduate students in academic research programs involving geologic mapping and scientific data analysis as major components; (2) to expand research and educational capacity of graduate programs; (3) for publication and distribution of geologic maps generated in field-based graduate academic research programs.

Eligible applicants/beneficiaries: state geological surveys. State IHEs may apply on behalf of the state survey.

Range: STATEMAP, $27,381 to $227,531; EDMAP, $5,086 to $13,000 per student; maximum award, $15,000 per student. **Average:** STATEMAP, $128,514; EDMAP, $7,328.

Activity: FY 06, 47 STATEMAP awards, 65 EDMAP students funded at 39 institutions.

HQ: Coordinator, National Cooperative Geologic Mapping Program, USGS-DOI, 908 National Center, 12201 Sunrise Valley Dr., Reston, VA 20192. Phone: (no number provided).

Internet: www.ncgmp.usgs.gov. (Note: no field offices for this program.)

15.811 GAP ANALYSIS PROGRAM ("GAP")

Assistance: project grants.

Purposes: pursuant to the Endangered Species Act of 1973, Fish and Wildlife Act of 1956, and Fish and Wildlife Conservation Act, for studies where native animal species and natural plant communities occur—to identify gaps in their representation in support of the conservation of biodiversity. Studies are used by federal, state, and other governmental organizations to develop land use or acquisition plans that incorporate information about the presence and distribution of biodiversity.

Eligible applicants/beneficiaries: profit organizations, public and private nonprofit organizations, state and local governments.

Range: $33,000 to $370,000. **Average:** $122,277.

Activity: new program listing in 2003; FY 05, 14 cooperative agreements.

HQ: Coordinator, National GAP Program, USGS-DOI, 530 S. Asbury - Ste.1, Moscow, ID 83843. Phone: (no number provided).

Internet: www.gapanalysis.nbii.gov. (Note: no other field offices.)

15.812 COOPERATIVE RESEARCH UNITS PROGRAM ("CRUP")

Assistance: project grants (to 5 years).

Purposes: pursuant to the Cooperative Research Units Act as amended by the Fish and Wildlife Improvement Act of 1978, for research, technical assistance, and education projects addressing the information needs of local, state, and federal fish, wildlife, and natural resource agencies. Project examples: gopher tortoise relocation; Caspian terns in San Francisco Bay; black bear genetics; fish community response to pump-storage; Great Lakes colonial waterbirds.

Eligible applicants/beneficiaries: universities hosting CRUPs.

Range: $5,000 to $700,000. **Average:** $47,000.

Activity: new program listing in 2003; FY 05, 484 research work orders.

HQ: Cooperative Research Units, USGS-DOI, Sunrise Valley Dr., Reston, VA 20192. Phone: (703) 648-4261, -4262, FAX (703) 648-4269.

Internet: www.coopunits.org. (Note: no field offices for this program.)

15.813 COOPERATIVE RESEARCH UNITS TRAINING PROGRAM ("CRUTP")

Assistance: project grants (100 percent/to 5 years).

Purposes: pursuant to Organic Act of 1879, to provide financial support to Minority Serving Institutions to introduce a culturally diverse group of students, primarily undergraduates, to the fields of freshwater fisheries and aquatic sciences and train them for careers in the natural resource professions.

Eligible applicants: accredited four-year Historically Black College and Universities (HBCUs) under Title III of the higher Education Act of 1965 as amended, with program studies in freshwater fisheries or aquatic sciences.

Eligible beneficiaries: undergraduate, graduate or professional students of HBCUs who maintain satisfactory academic progress with grantee institution.

Range: $100,000 to $180,000 **Average:** $150,000

Activity: N.A.

HQ: Deputy Chief, Cooperative Research Units, USGS-DOI, 12201 Sunrise Valley Dr. - MS-303, Reston, VA 20192. Phone: (703) 648-4062.

Internet: www.usgs.gov. (Note: no field offices for this program.)

15.814 NATIONAL GEOLOGICAL AND GEOPHYSICAL DATA PRESERVATION PROGRAM

Assistance: project grants (50 percent).

Purposes: pursuant to the Federal Energy Policy Act of 2005, to preserve and provide access to geological, geophysical, and engineering samples (and related data) extracted from the earth.

Eligible applicants: state geological surveys or state universities affiliated with a geological survey.

Eligible beneficiaries: research scientists, engineers, and general public.

Range: FY 08, $5,000 to $60,000 **Average:** FY 07, $5,000

Activity: FY 07, 36 states received funds to inventory their collections.

HQ: Program Coordinator, Office of the Chief, USGS-DOI, National Center, 12201 Sunrise Valley Drive-MS-911, Reston, VA 20192. Phone: (703) 648-4000.

Internet: www.usgs.gov. (Note: no field offices for this program.)

INDIAN ARTS AND CRAFTS BOARD

15.850 INDIAN ARTS AND CRAFTS DEVELOPMENT

Assistance: use of property, facilities, and equipment; advisory services/counseling; investigation of complaints.

Purposes: pursuant to the Act to Promote the Development of Indian Arts and Crafts as amended, Indian Arts and Crafts Act of 1990, and Indian Arts and Crafts Enforcement Act of 2000, to provide program planning assistance in promoting the development of American Indian and native Alaskan arts and crafts. Assistance is nonfinancial including: development of innovative educational, promotional, production, and economic concepts related to native culture; investigations of misrepresentation of handicrafts. No financial assistance is provided through this program.

Eligible applicants/beneficiaries: American Indian and Alaska native individuals and organizations; recognized tribal governments; state and local governments; nonprofit organizations.

Range/Average: N.A.

Activity: annually, 6,500 native artists and craftsmen served. Also, operation of the Sioux Indian Museum in Rapid City, South Dakota, the Museum of the Plains Indian in Browning, Montana, and the Southern Plains Indian Museum in Anadarko, Oklahoma.

HQ: Director, Indian Arts and Crafts Board, DOI, Main Interior Bldg. - Rm.4004, Washington, DC 20240. Phone: (202) 208-3773.

Internet: www.iacb.doi.gov. (Note: no field offices for this program.)

OFFICE OF INSULAR AFFAIRS

15.875 ECONOMIC, SOCIAL, AND POLITICAL DEVELOPMENT OF THE TERRITORIES

Assistance: project grants (100 percent).

Purposes: pursuant to the Act of February 20, 1929 and other acts, to promote the economic, social, and political development of the U.S. territories and freely associated states, toward their self-government and self-sufficiency. Operational costs and capital improvements may be funded, such as the construction of water systems, roads, schools, hospitals, and power and sewer facilities. A small percentage of funding may be available for discretionary grants.

Eligible applicants/beneficiaries: Guam, VI, American Samoa, Northern Mariana Islands.

Range/Average: N.A.

Activity: not quantified specifically.

HQ: Director, Financial Management Division, Office of Insular Affairs-DOI, Washington, DC 20240. Phone: (202) 208-6971, FAX (202) 208-7585.

Internet: www.doi.gov/oia. (Note: no field offices for this program.)

NATIONAL PARK SERVICE

15.904 HISTORIC PRESERVATION FUND GRANTS-IN-AID

Assistance: formula grants; project grants. (project, 60 percent; territories, 100 percent/project grants, to 2 years).

Purposes: pursuant to the National Historic Preservation Act of 1966 as amended, to provide matching grants for the identification, evaluation, and protection of historic properties listed or eligible for listing in the National Register of Historic Places (see **15.914**). Historic properties may include districts, sites, buildings, structures, and objects significant in American history, architecture, archaeology, engineering, and culture at national, state, and local levels. Grants may finance studies and reports, preservation plans, state staff salaries, equipment, materials, necessary travel, acquisition, or repair. Development projects must involve preservation, restoration, rehabilitation, or nonmajor reconstruction. Certain tax incentives are available to owners of listed properties.

Eligible applicants/beneficiaries: states and territories operating programs administered by a state historic preservation officer, which may subgrant to public and private parties including local governments, profit and nonprofit organizations, or individuals to accomplish program objectives. Tribal Grant Program—tribal governments, Alaska or Hawaii native corporations.

Range: $197,000 to $1,194,000. **Average:** $661,000.

Activity: FY 03, 59 state grants and, in turn, 850 subgrants; 3,400 tax credit applications reviewed.

HQ: Associate Director, Cultural Resource Stewardship and Partnerships, NPS-DOI, Washington, DC 20240. Phone: (202) 354- 2054.

Internet: www.family.info.gov.cfda.index.htm; *State Historic Preservation Offices,* www.2cr.nps.gov.

15.910 NATIONAL NATURAL LANDMARKS PROGRAM

Assistance: specialized services; technical information.

Purposes: pursuant to the Historic Sites Act of 1935, General Authorities Act of 1970, and Mining in National Parks Act of 1976, to identify and recognize nationally significant natural areas and to encourage their preservation. Designation of natural landmarks renders them eligible for registration on the National Registry of Natural Landmarks. Technical assistance is available to landmark owners and administrators. No financial assistance is provided.

Eligible applicants/beneficiaries: anyone may suggest an area for inclusion.

Range/Average: N.A.

Activity: cumulatively as of 2004, 587 natural landmarks designated.

HQ: Natural Landmarks Program, Natural Systems Management Office (2320), NPS-DOI, Washington, DC 20240. Phone: (202) 513-7166.

Internet: www.family.info.gov/cfda/index.htm.

15.912 NATIONAL HISTORIC LANDMARK

Assistance: advisory services/counseling.

Purposes: pursuant to the Historic Sites Act of 1935, National Historic Preservation Act of 1966, and amendments, to study, identify, and encourage preservation of nationally-significant historic properties. Designation of historic landmarks and registration on the National Register of Historic Places (see **15.914**) renders them eligible for federal protection, some grants-in-aid programs, and certain tax benefits. Properties of only state or local significance do not qualify.

Eligible applicants/beneficiaries: anyone may suggest properties for inclusion. Property owners may be individuals, governments, or corporate bodies.

Range/Average: N.A.

Activity: cumulatively as of April 2004, 2,365 National Historic Landmarks designated.

HQ: National Historic Landmarks Survey (MS 2280), NRHE-NPS-DOI, 1849 C St. NW, Washington, DC 20240. Phone: (202) 354-2210.

Internet: www.cr.nps.gov/nhl.

15.914 NATIONAL REGISTER OF HISTORIC PLACES ("National Register")

Assistance: advisory services/counseling.

Purposes: pursuant to the Historic Preservation Act of 1966 and Amendments of 1980 and 1992, Economic Recovery Tax Act of 1981, Tax Reform Act of 1986, and other acts, to expand and maintain the National Register of Historic Places which serves as a planning tool and source of information on sites, buildings, districts, structures, and objects of historical, architectural, engineering, archaeological, and/or cultural significance. Designation of historic landmarks and registration on the National Register renders them eligible for federal protection, some grants-in-aid and loan programs, and certain tax benefits. Federal agencies are required to consider and nominate historic properties within their jurisdiction.

Eligible applicants/beneficiaries: states and territories operating programs administered by state historic preservation officers; tribal preservation officers; federal agencies. Applicants eligible for federal tax benefits include owners of individually listed properties and properties certified by NPS as historic and in a district certified as historic.

Range/Average: N.A.

Activity: cumulatively as of FY 04, 77,000 properties listed in the National Register, with some 125 entries added monthly; 31,000 projects representing $31 billion in rehabilitation work had received Tax Reform Act certifications.

HQ: Keeper of the National Register of Historic Places, NRHE-NPS-DOI, 1849 C St. NW (MS 2280),, Washington, DC 20240. Phone: (202) 345-2213.

Internet: www.cr.nps.gov/nr.

15.915 TECHNICAL PRESERVATION SERVICES

Assistance: advisory services/counseling; specialized services; technical information.

Purposes: pursuant to the Federal Property and Administrative Services Act of 1949 and National Historic Preservation Act of 1966, amendments, Mining in National Parks Act of 1976, Tax Reform Act of 1986, and other acts, to offer technical information pertaining to the treatment and maintenance of historic properties. The program provides for the development of policies and standards and for distribution of publications on the technical and design aspects of preservation and rehabilitation, as well as for monitoring acquisition and development grant awards under **15.904** ; the service also includes general technical assistance concerning preservation efforts, including certification for eligibility for tax credits.

Eligible applicants/beneficiaries: federal agencies, state and local governments, and individual owners.

Range/Average: N.A.

Activity: estimate FY 04, 31,000 building rehabilitations approved.

HQ: Chief, Heritage Preservation Services Program (ORG 2255), NPS-DOI, 1849 C St. NW, Washington, DC 20240. Phone: (202) 513- 7270.

Internet: www.cr.nps.gov.

15.916 OUTDOOR RECREATION—ACQUISITION, DEVELOPMENT AND PLANNING ("Land and Water Conservation Fund Grants")

Assistance: project grants. (50 percent/to 3 years).

Purposes: pursuant to the Land and Water Conservation Fund Act of 1965 as amended and other acts, to plan, acquire, and develop public outdoor recreation areas and facilities, including picnic areas, inner city parks, campgrounds, tennis courts, boat launching ramps, bike trails, outdoor swimming pools, roads, water supply, etc.; for studies, surveys, and data collection and analysis related to refinement and improvement of Statewide Comprehensive Outdoor Recreation Plans (SCORPs). Grant funds are not available to cover operating and maintenance costs.

Eligible applicants/beneficiaries: planning grants—only state agencies and territories. Acquisition and development grants—state agencies may apply for direct assistance, or on behalf of other state agencies or political subdivisions, such as cities, counties, and park districts; tribes functioning as general purpose units of government.

Range: $150 to $5,450,000. **Average:** $68,000.

Activity: not quantified specifically.

HQ: Chief, Recreation Programs (2225), NPS-DOI, 1849 C St. NW, Washington, DC 20240. Phone: (202) 354-6900, FAX (202) 371-5179.

Internet: www.ncrc.nps.gov/lwcf.

15.918 DISPOSAL OF FEDERAL SURPLUS REAL PROPERTY FOR PARKS, RECREATION, AND HISTORIC MONUMENTS ("Surplus Property Program - Federal Land-to-Parks Program - Historic Surplus Property Program")

Assistance: use of property, facilities, and equipment.

Purposes: pursuant to the Federal Property and Administrative Services Act of 1949 as amended and Federal Lands for Parks and Recreation Act, to transfer surplus federal real property for public park and recreation use, or for use as historic real property. Recipients must agree to manage the property in the public interest and for public use. Only properties listed on the National Register or so eligible may be transferred through the Historic Surplus Property Program. Examples of new uses include nature study areas, wildlife conservation areas, youth and senior citizen areas; arts and crafts centers.

Eligible applicants/beneficiaries: only states or local government units.

Range/Average: N.A.

Activity: since 1949, 1,400 properties transferred for park and recreation uses, comprising over 156,000 acres; 130 properties for historic purposes. FY 04, 25 properties transferred.

HQ: Historic Surplus Property Program, Heritage Preservation Services (ORG 2255), NPS-DOI, 1849 C St. NW, Washington, DC. Phone: (202) 354-2044. Federal Land-to-Parks Program, Recreation Programs Division, NPS-DOI, same address. Phone: (202) 354-6915.

Internet: Historic Surplus Property Program, www.cr.nps.gov/tps/hspp_p.htm; Federal Land-to-Parks Program, www.cr.nps.gov/flp.

15.921 RIVERS, TRAILS AND CONSERVATION ASSISTANCE ("RTCA")

Assistance: advisory services/counseling.

Purposes: pursuant to the Wild and Scenic Rivers Act of 1968 and National Trails System Act as amended, Outdoor Recreation Act of 1963, and the Federal Power Act, to support activities between government and citizens to conserve rivers, preserve open space, and develop trails and greenways.

Eligible applicants/beneficiaries: private nonprofit organizations; federal, state, and local government agencies.

Range/Average: N.A.

Activity: not quantified specifically.

HQ: Chief, Rivers, Trails and Conservation Assistance (ORG 2235), NPS-DOI, 1849 C St. NW, Washington, DC 20240. Phone: (202) 354- 6900.

Internet: www.nps.gov/rtca.

15.922 NATIVE AMERICAN GRAVES PROTECTION AND REPATRIATION ACT ("NAGPRA")

Assistance: project grants. (100 percent/to 18 months).

Purposes: pursuant to the act of 1990, for the documentation, inventory, and repatriation of native American human remains and cultural items including sacred objects, objects of cultural patrimony, funerary objects. Funds may be used: to involve specialists including lineal descendants, traditional religious leaders, and other officials; for staff training; for travel costs; to construct appropriate containers to transport finds. Ineligible uses of funds include documentation or repatriation of items from the Smithsonian Institution, care and curation of repatriated items, facilities construction or renovation, or real estate purchases.

Eligible applicants/beneficiaries: museum documentation—any institution or state or local government agency including IHEs with possession of, or control over, native American human remains or cultural items. Tribal documentation and repatriation—recognized tribes, Alaska native villages or corporations, native Hawaiian organizations.

Range: documentation, $5,000 to $75,000; repatriation, $5,000 to $15,000. **Average:** documentation, $60,107; repatriation, $8,635.

Activity: FY 03, 418 grants awarded.

HQ: National Center for Cultural Resources, NPS-DOI, 1849 C St. NW - Rm.NC-340, Washington, DC 20240. Phone: (202) 343-8161, FAX (202) 343-5260.

Internet: www.cr.nps.gov/nagpra/grants; e-mail, NAGPRA.grants@nps.gov. (Note: no field offices for this program.)

15.923 NATIONAL CENTER FOR PRESERVATION TECHNOLOGY AND TRAINING

Assistance: project grants (100 percent).

Purposes: pursuant to the National Historic Preservation Act Amendments of 1992, to develop and distribute preservation and conservation skills and technologies for the identification, evaluation, conservation, and interpretation of prehistoric and historic resources; to develop and facilitate training of federal, state, and local professional, managerial, maintenance, and other personnel; and for international cooperation efforts. Funds may support projects involving: information management; training and education in such disciplines as archeology, historic architecture, historic landscapes, object and materials conservation and interpretation; applied and fundamental research; pollutant research and treatment; analytical facilities; conferences; publications. Ineligible projects include: those focused on specific sites, structures, objects, or collections; internships and fellowships when integrated into funded projects; current projects.

Eligible applicants/beneficiaries: IHEs; nonprofit and quasi- public organizations; federal, state, local, and tribal preservation offices; profit organizations.

Range: $7,856 to $50,000. **Average:** $36,000.

Activity: FY 04, 9 awards.

HQ: Grants Administrator, Heritage Preservation Services Program, National Center for Cultural Resource Stewardship and Partnership (MS 2255), NPS-DOI, 1849 C St. NW, Washington, DC 20240. Phone: (202) 354-2088.

Internet: http://family.info.gov/cfda/index.htm.

15.925 NATIONAL MARITIME HERITAGE GRANTS

Assistance: project grants. (50 percent/to 2 years).

Purposes: pursuant to the National Maritime Heritage Act of 1994, to preserve historic maritime resources and increase public awareness and appreciation for the maritime heritage of the U.S. Eligible preservation activities include: acquisition; planning; documentation; protection and stabilization; preservation, restoration, or rehabilitation; maintenance of properties; reporting and publicity projects. Eligible education activities include: enhancement of public access, use, and appreciation for maritime heritage collections; activities focusing on heritage trails and corridors; field programs; preservation of traditional maritime skills; minor construction projects to improve access, use, and appreciation of educational and exhibit spaces; reconstruction or reproduction of well-documented properties. Generally, costs of staff training or professional development are ineligible.

Eligible applicants/beneficiaries: state and local governments, private nonprofit organizations.

Range: $2,500 to $50,000.

Activity: not quantified specifically.

HQ: National Maritime Initiative, NPS-DOI, Washington, DC 20240. Phone: (no number provided).

Internet: www.cr.nps.gov/maritime/grants.htm. (Note: no field offices for this program.)

15.926 AMERICAN BATTLEFIELD PROTECTION

Assistance: project grants (100 percent).

Purposes: pursuant to the Omnibus Parks and Public Lands Management Act of 1996 and American Battlefield Protection Act of 1996, for the protection and preservation of battlefield lands on American soil by supporting nonacquisition preservation methods such as planning, education, and survey and inventory. Project examples: preparation of Vision and Protection Plan; preparation of National Register nomination; archeological survey. Funds may not be used for such activities as battlefield reenactments, any construction, permanent staff positions, curation, or other ongoing activities.

Eligible applicants/beneficiaries: federal, intrastate, interstate, state, and local agencies; public and private nonprofit organizations; recognized tribal governments and organizations; territories and possessions; public and private IHEs. Multi-organizational applications are encouraged.

Range: $1,000 to $75,000. **Average:** $25,000.

Activity: FY 92-01 (latest data reported), 260 projects funded.

HQ: American Battlefield Protection Program (MS 2255), NPS-DOI, 1849 C St. NW, Washington, DC 20240. Phone: (202) 354-2037, -2023, FAX (202) 371-1616.

Internet: www.zcr.nps.gov/abpp/; www.cr.nps.gov/abpp. (Note: no field offices for this program.)

15.927 HYDROPOWER RECREATION ASSISTANCE ("Rivers and Trails, Hydropower Licensing")

Assistance: advisory services/counseling.

Purposes: pursuant to the Federal Power Act, Wild and Scenic Rivers Act of 1968 as amended, and Outdoor Recreation Act of 1963, to serve as a national technical resource to support government, industry, and nonprofit partnerships, concerning applications for hydropower licensing; to meet present and future outdoor recreation needs; to maintain and enhance a project's riparian areas.

Eligible applicants/beneficiaries: private nonprofit organizations; federal, state, and local government agencies; hydropower licensing applicants.

Range/Average: N.A.

Activity: not quantified specifically.

HQ: Rivers and Hydro Leader, Rivers, Trails, and Conservation Assistance (2220), NPS-DOI, 1849 C St. NW, Washington, DC 20240. Phone: (202) 354-6900.

Internet: www.nps.gov/hydro.

15.928 CIVIL WAR BATTLEFIELD LAND ACQUISITION GRANTS

Assistance: project grants (50 percent).

Purposes: pursuant to the American Battlefield Protection Act of 1996, to help states and communities acquire and preserve threatened Civil War battlefields. Grants may cover costs of fee simple acquisition of land and protective interests in land at Civil War Battlefields listed in the Civil War Sites Advisory Commission's 1993 report on the Nation's Civil War Battlefields. Administrative costs are ineligible.

Eligible applicants/beneficiaries: state and local governments, which may subgrant funds to private nonprofit organizations that convey perpetual protective easements to the state historic preservation officer or other agency acceptable to NPS.

Range: $47,000 to $540,000. **Average:** $287,000.

Activity: new program listing in 2003; FY 02, funds obligated to protect 590 acres at 5 battlefields.

HQ: American Battlefield Protection Program (2255), NPS-DOI, 1849 C St. NW, Washington, DC 20240-0001. Phone: (202) 354-2023, FAX (202) 371-1794.

Internet: www2.cr.nps.gov/abpp/; *interim guidelines,* www2.cr.nps.gov/abpp/lwcf2002.htm. (Note: no field offices for this program.)

15.929 SAVE AMERICA'S TREASURES

Assistance: project grants. (50 percent/2 years).

Purposes: pursuant to the Omnibus Parks and Lands Management Act of 1996 and National Historic Preservation Act of 1966 as amended, for preservation and conservation work on nationally significant intellectual and cultural artifacts, as well as historic structures and sites listed on the National Register. Funds may not be used for costs of acquisition or rent.

Eligible applicants/beneficiaries: federal, intrastate, interstate, state, and local agencies; public or private nonprofit organizations and IHEs; tribes.

Range: $50,000 to $500,000. **Average:** $200,000.

Activity: new program listing in 2004; FY 03, 60 projects funded.

HQ: Save America's Treasures Program, NPS-DOI, 1849 C St. NW, Washington, DC 20240. Phone: (202) 513-7270, ext,6, FAX (202) 371- 1794.

Internet: www2.cr.nps.gov/treasures. (Note: no field offices for this program.)

15.930 CHESAPEAKE BAY GATEWAYS NETWORK ("Chesapeake Bay Gateways")

Assistance: project grants (to 50 percent/to 18 months).

Purposes: pursuant to the Chesapeake Bay Initiative Act of 1993, to aid state and local governments, communities, nonprofit organizations and the private sector in conserving, restoring and interpreting historical, cultural, recreational and natural resources within the Chesapeake Bay Gateways and watershed network.

Eligible applicants: currently designated Gateways, their managing organizations or partners, including state and local governments and nonprofit organizations.

Eligible beneficiaries: general public.

Range: $5,000 to $150,000. **Average:** FY 06 $60,346.

Activity: from 2000 to 2006, 71% of grant requests funded.

HQ: Acting Regional Director, Northeast Region, NPS-DOI, 200 Chestnut St., Philadelphia, PA 19106. Phone: (215) 597-7013, FAX: (215) 597-0815.

Internet: www.baygateways.net.

15.931 CONSERVATION ACTIVITIES BY YOUTH SERVICE ORGANIZATIONS

Assistance: project grants (2 to 3 months).

Purposes: pursuant to the Omnibus Consolidated Appropriations Act of 1997, Omnibus Parks and Public Lands Management Act of 1996, Youth Conservation Corps Act of 1970 and other laws as amended, to utilize qualified youth or conservation groups to carry out appropriate conservation projects.

Eligible applicants: organizations that support youth training and development in resource management, conservation, and cultural resources, including: private and quasi-public nonprofit institutions and organizations, state and local government agencies.

Eligible beneficiaries: young people and general public.

Range: to $5,600,000. **Average:** $25,000.

Activity: FY 06, 277 Land Corp projects completed; 78 programs for HS students; conservation projects at more than 200 park sites.

HQ: WASO Youth Program Coordinator, NPS-DOI, 1201 I Street NW, Washington, DC 20005. Phone: (202) 513-7146, FAX: (202) 371-2263.

Internet: www.nps.gov/youthprograms/index.html.

15.978 UPPER MISSISSIPPI RIVER SYSTEM LONG TERM RESOURCE MONITORING PROGRAM ("LTRMP")

Assistance: project grants (100 percent).

Purposes: pursuant to the Upper Mississippi River Management Act of 1986, to maintain the Upper Mississippi River System as a sustainable large river ecosystem—through monitoring of trends and effects related to resources, and through research as specified in the LTRMP Operations Plan.

Eligible applicants/beneficiaries: states, local governments, intra- and interstate agencies, sponsored organizations, private nonprofit organizations.

Range: $303,042 to $607,450. **Average:** $326,644.

Activity: FY 04, 6 awards.

HQ: Upper Midwest Environmental Sciences Technical Center, USGS-DOI, 2630 Fanta Reed Rd. LaCrosse, WI 54603. Phone: Center Director, (608) 781-6221; Management Analyst, (608) 781-6229, FAX (608) 783-6066.

Internet: www.usgs.gov/trmp.html; (Note: no other field offices for this program.)

DEPARTMENT OF JUSTICE

16.001 LAW ENFORCEMENT ASSISTANCE—NARCOTICS AND DANGEROUS DRUGS—LABORATORY ANALYSIS

Assistance: specialized services; advisory services/counseling; technical information.

Purposes: pursuant to the Comprehensive Drug Abuse Prevention and Control Act of 1970 (CDAPCA), to provide drug evidence analysis, expert court testimony, and technical assistance to law enforcement agencies concerning narcotics and other abused drugs.

Eligible applicants/beneficiaries: state and local governments, law enforcement officials, forensic laboratories.

Range/Average: N.A.

Activity: FY 04, 5,889 drug samples analyzed.

HQ: Deputy Assistant Administrator, Office of Forensic Sciences, DEA-DOJ, Washington, DC 20537. Phone: (202) 307-8866.

Internet: www.usdoj.gov.

16.003 LAW ENFORCEMENT ASSISTANCE—NARCOTICS AND DANGEROUS DRUGS TECHNICAL LABORATORY PUBLICATIONS ("Microgram")

Assistance: technical information.

Purposes: pursuant to CDAPCA, to disseminate scientific information on the detection and analysis of narcotics and dangerous drugs, published monthly in "Microgram.".

Eligible applicants/beneficiaries: forensic laboratories; scientists working for law enforcement agencies.

Range/Average: N.A.

Activity: mail-subscription services; distribution via the internet.

HQ: Deputy Assistant Administrator, Office of Forensic Sciences, DEA-DOJ, Washington, DC 20537. Phone: (202) 307-8866.

Internet: www.usdoj.govl. (Note: no field offices for this program.)

16.004 LAW ENFORCEMENT ASSISTANCE—NARCOTICS AND DANGEROUS DRUGS TRAINING

Assistance: training.

Purposes: pursuant to CDAPCA, for DEA training of accredited professional and enforcement personnel in: drug investigations techniques; physical security aspects of legitimate drug distribution; evidence analysis; pharmacology, socio-psychology of drug abuse, and drug education; management and supervisory training of drug unit commanders.

Eligible applicants/beneficiaries: state, local, military, and other federal law enforcement and regulatory officials; crime laboratory technicians and forensic chemists.

Range/Average: N.A.

Activity: FY 05 estimate, 37,000 participants.

HQ: Office of Training, DEA-DOJ, Quantico, VA 22134-1475. Phone: (703) 632-5141.

Internet: www.usdoj.gov.

16.005 PUBLIC EDUCATION ON DRUG ABUSE—INFORMATION

Assistance: specialized services; training; technical information.

Purposes: pursuant to CDAPCA, to coordinate and facilitate the involvement of law enforcement and communities in drug abuse prevention and public education, through DEA field offices. No financial assistance is provided.

Eligible applicants/beneficiaries: anyone. Law enforcement agencies and community anti-drug coalitions receive priority.

Range/Average: N.A.

Activity: annually, 50 states and several foreign countries assisted.

HQ: Demand Reduction Section, Congressional and Public Affairs Staff, DEA-DOJ, Washington, DC 20537. Phone: (202) 307-7936, FAX (202) 307-4559.

Internet: www.dea.gov.

16.012 ALCOHOL, TOBACCO, AND FIREARMS—TRAINING ASSISTANCE

Assistance: training.

Purposes: pursuant to OCCSSA as amended, Gun Control Act of 1968, and Organized Crime Control Act of 1970, to provide training in the enforcement of laws relating to alcohol, tobacco, firearms, arson, explosives, and organized crime. Programs include identification of firearms problems, laboratory capability, undercover, interviewing, investigation techniques, case management.

Eligible applicants/beneficiaries: state, county, and local law enforcement agencies. Participation is limited to nonuniformed police personnel.

Range/Average: N.A.

Activity: annually, 600 officers participate.

HQ: Chief, Local and International Training Division, Bureau of Alcohol, Tobacco and Firearms-DOJ, 800 Seventh St. NW - Rm.600, Washington, DC 20226. Phone: (202) 927-3160.

Internet: www.atf.gov. (Note: no field offices for this program.)

16.013 VIOLENCE AGAINST WOMEN ACT COURT TRAINING AND IMPROVEMENT GRANTS

Assistance: project grants (to 100 percent).

Purposes: pursuant to Title I, Violence Against Women and Department of Justice Reauthorization Act of 2005, to improve court responses to adult and youth domestic violence, dating violence, sexual assault, and stalking.

Eligible applicants: federal, state, tribal, territorial, local courts or court-based programs; national, state, tribal, territorial, or local private, nonprofit organizations with demonstrated expertise in developing and providing judicial education about domestic violence, dating violence, sexual assault, or stalking.

Eligible beneficiaries: courts and nonprofit organizations.

Range/Average: N.A.

Activity: N.A. New program in FY 08.

HQ: Office on Violence Against Women, DOJ, 800 K Street, NW, Washington, DC 20530. Phone: (202) 307-6026.

Internet: www.ovw.usdoj.gov. (Note: no field offices for this program.)

16.014 ENGAGING MEN AND YOUTH IN PREVENTING DOMESTIC VIOLENCE, DATING VIOLENCE, SEXUAL ASSAULT, AND STALKING

Assistance: project grants (to 100 percent/2 years).

Purposes: pursuant to Title I, Violence Against Women and Department of Justice Reauthorization Act of 2005, to develop or enhance community-based programs which help men and youth develop mutually respectful, nonviolent relationships and prevent domestic and dating violence, sexual assault, and stalking.

Eligible applicants: first statutory purpose area: nonprofit, nongovernmental domestic violence, dating violence, sexual assault, or stalking victim service providers or coalitions; community-based child or youth services organizations with demonstrated experience and expertise in addressing the needs and concerns of young people; state, territorial, tribal, or unit of local governmental that is partnered with an organization described above; or program that provides culturally specific services. Second statutory purpose (public education campaigns and community organizing): nonprofit, nongovernmental organizations or coalitions that have a documented history of creating and administering effective public education campaigns addressing the prevention of domestic violence, dating violence, sexual assault or stalking.

Eligible beneficiaries: other nonprofit, nongovernmental organizations including community and faith-based organizations.

Range/Average: N.A.

Activity: N.A. New program in FY 08.

HQ: Office on Violence Against Women, DOJ, 800 K Street, NW, Washington, DC 20530. Phone: (202) 307-6026.

Internet: www.ovw.usdoj.gov. (Note: no field offices for this program.)

16.016 CULTURALLY AND LINGUISTICALLY SPECIFIC SERVICES PROGRAM

Assistance: project grants (to 100 percent/2 years).

Purposes: pursuant to Title I, Violence Against Women and Department of Justice Reauthorization Act of 2005, to enhance culturally and linguistically specific services for victims of domestic and dating violence, sexual assault, and stalking.

Eligible applicants/beneficiaries: community-based programs whose primary purpose is providing culturally and linguistically specific services to victims of domestic violence, dating violence, sexual assault, and stalking who can partner with a program having demonstrated expertise in serving such victims.

Range/Average: N.A.

Activity: N.A. New program in FY 08.

HQ: Office on Violence Against Women, DOJ, 800 K Street, NW, Washington, DC 20530. Phone: (202) 307-6026.

Internet: www.ovw.usdoj.gov. (Note: no field offices for this program.)

16.017 SEXUAL ASSAULT SERVICES PROGRAM

Assistance: project grants (one year or more).

Purposes: pursuant to Violence Against Women and Department of Justice Reauthorization Act of 2005, to increase intervention, advocacy, accompaniment, support services, and related assistance for adult, youth, and child victims of sexual assault and their families and household members.

Eligible applicants: states and territories.

Eligible beneficiaries: rape crisis centers and other nonprofit, nongovernmental organizations, including community and faith-based organizations.

Range/Average: N.A.

Activity: N.A. New program in FY 08.

HQ: Office on Violence Against Women, DOJ, 800 K Street, NW, Washington, DC 20530. Phone: (202) 307-6026.

Internet: www.ovw.usdoj.gov. (Note: no field offices for this program.)

16.100 DESEGREGATION OF PUBLIC EDUCATION

Assistance: specialized services.

Purposes: pursuant to Title IV of the Civil Rights Act of 1964 (CRA), Equal Educational Opportunities Act of 1974, and amendments, to secure equal educational opportunities in public schools and colleges, for all persons regardless of their race, color, religion, sex, or national origin. DOJ may: seek court orders to desegregate pubic schools or colleges; intervene in cases in which plaintiffs allege discriminatory practices; litigate referrals from DOED involving such discrimination, as well as on the basis of disability pursuant to the Rehabilitation Act of 1973; seek court orders to ensure that local school districts take steps to overcome language barriers in their instructional programs.

Eligible applicants/beneficiaries: public school parents or groups of parents; public college students or their parents.

Range/Average: N.A.

Activity: annually (sampling), compliance monitoring of school districts covered by desegregation orders; responses to routine citizen inquiries, Congressional referrals.

HQ: Educational Opportunities Litigation Section, Civil Rights Division-DOJ, Washington, DC 20530. Phone: (202) 514-4092; Office of Public Affairs, (202) 514-2007, TDD (202) 514-1888.

Internet: www.usdoj.gov/crt/edo/index.html. (Note: no field offices for this program.)

16.101 EQUAL EMPLOYMENT OPPORTUNITY

Assistance: specialized services.

Purposes: pursuant to Title VII of CRA as amended, to initiate legal processes enforcing the Act's provisions and regulations concerning equal employment opportunities, including authorized affirmative action programs—for all persons, regardless of their race, religion, national origin, or sex. Discrimination is forbidden by employers, labor organizations, employment agencies, state and local governments, public agencies, and government contractors and subcontractors.

Eligible applicants/beneficiaries: all persons.

Range/Average: N.A.

Activity: FY 05, 12 complaints filed; 15 court cases settled.

HQ: Employment Litigation Section, Civil Rights Division-DOJ, Washington, DC 20530. Phone: (202) 514-3831, TDD (800) 578-5404; Office of Public Affairs, (202) 514-2007, TDD (202) 514-1888.

Internet: www.usdoj.gov/crt/emp/index.html. (Note: no field offices for this program.)

16.103 FAIR HOUSING AND EQUAL CREDIT OPPORTUNITY

Assistance: specialized services.

Purposes: pursuant to the Acts cited below, to initiate legal processes assuring enforcement of the provisions of: Title VIII of the Civil Rights Act of 1968 as amended by the Fair Housing Amendments Act of 1988—assuring equal housing opportunities for all in the sale, rental, financing, and related housing activities—regardless of race, color, religion, sex, national origin, family status, or handicap (HUD investigates and attempts conciliation of fair housing cases; if unsuccessful, HUD may file administrative charges; DOJ brings suit in federal court); the Equal Credit Opportunity Act (ECOA) which prohibits discrimination in credit transactions on the basis of race, color, religion, sex, national origin, marital status, or age—because any part of the applicant's income is derived from public assistance, or because the applicant has in good faith exercised a right under the Consumer Credit Protection Act; Title II of CRA, prohibiting discrimination in places of public accommodation including hotels, motels, restaurants, gas stations, and places of entertainment; and, Section 2 of the Religious Land Use and Institutionalized Persons Act of 2000 prohibiting local governments from significantly burdening the exercise of religion or discriminating against religious institutions in their land use and zoning decisions.

Eligible applicants/beneficiaries: all persons.

Range/Average: N.A.

Activity: FY 05 (sampling), 22 pattern or practice cases filed and 24 cases resolved; enforcement of "New Freedom Initiative.".

HQ: Housing and Civil Enforcement Section, Civil Rights Division- DOJ, Washington, DC 20530. Phone: (202) 514-4713; Office of Public Affairs, (202) 514-2007, TDD (202) 514-1888.

Internet: www.usdoj.gov/crt/housing/hcehome.html. (Note: no field offices for this program.)

16.104 PROTECTION OF VOTING RIGHTS

Assistance: specialized services.

Purposes: pursuant to the Voting Rights Act of 1965, amendments, and related laws, to enforce the provisions of the Act regarding voter registration and voting in local, state, and federal elections. The laws protect the rights of all persons to register and vote, without discrimination based on race, color, membership in a language minority group, age, handicap, literacy, or residence overseas.

Eligible applicants/beneficiaries: all U.S. citizens of voting age.

Range/Average: N.A.

Activity: (sampling) participation in redistricting challenges, changes in voting practices and procedures, polling place monitoring.

HQ: Voting Section, Civil Rights Division-DOJ, Washington, DC 20530. Phone: (202) 307-3143, (800) 253-3931; Office of Public Affairs, (202) 514-2007, TDD (202) 514-1888.

Internet: www.usdoj.gov/crt/voting/index.htm. (Note: no field offices for this program.)

16.105 CIVIL RIGHTS OF INSTITUTIONALIZED PERSONS ("Equal Enjoyment of Rights in Public Facilities - Protection of Rights to Reproductive Health Services")

Assistance: specialized services.

Purposes: pursuant to the Civil Rights of Institutionalized Persons Act (CRIPA), RLUIPA, Freedom of Access to Clinic Entrances Act (FACE), VCCLEA, OCCSSA, and related laws, to enforce the provisions of the Acts. CRIPA assures the right of equal utilization of any public facility owned or operated by any state or subdivision thereof, without regard to race, religion, or national origin—including facilities for the mentally ill or for the retarded or chronically ill, prisons, jails, pretrial detention facilities, juvenile facilities, and homes for the elderly. FACE authorizes the Attorney General to investigate and, where appropriate, to initiate actions for relief from certain violent, threatening, obstructive, and destructive actions intended to injure, intimidate, or interfere with persons seeking reproductive health services, or deny religious freedom or destruction of property at places of religious worship. RLUIPA prohibits government entities from imposing a substantial burden on the religious exercise of a person residing in or confined to a publicly operated institution.

Eligible applicants/beneficiaries: anyone.

Range/Average: N.A.

Activity: (sampling), CRIPA compliance monitoring; police misconduct investigations initiated; since FY 03, 400 on-site inspections of institutions.

HQ: Special Litigation Section, Civil Rights Division-DOJ, Washington, DC 20530. Phone: (202) 514-6255; Office of Public Affairs, (202) 514-2007, TDD (202) 514-1888.

Internet: www.usdoj.gov/crt/split/index.html. (Note: no field offices for this program.)

16.108 AMERICANS WITH DISABILITIES ACT TECHNICAL ASSISTANCE PROGRAM ("ADA")

Assistance: project grants; technical information; training; investigation of complaints (100 percent).

Purposes: pursuant to the Americans with Disabilities Act (ADA), to ensure that public accommodations and commercial facilities and state and local governments learn and understand the requirements of the ADA. Publications, conferences, seminars, training, and other educational services and materials are developed and disseminated through technical assistance grants and contracts.

Eligible applicants/beneficiaries: nonprofit organizations including trade and professional associations; state and local government agencies; national and state organizations representing the disabled; individuals.

Range/Average: N.A.

Activity: (sampling), services through the ADA telephone information line; publications distribution through libraries; maintenance of ADA web site.

HQ: Disability Rights Section, Civil Rights Division-DOJ, Washington, DC 20530. Phone: (800) 514-0301, TDD (800) 514-0383; Office of Public Affairs, (202) 514-2007, TDD (202) 514-1888.

Internet: www.ada.gov. (Note: no field offices for this program.)

16.109 CIVIL RIGHTS PROSECUTION ("Criminal Section")

Assistance: investigation of complaints.

Purposes: to prosecute cases of national significance involving the deprivation of personal liberties that cannot be or are not sufficiently addressed by state or local authorities. The Criminal Section's jurisdiction includes: acts of racial violence; misconduct by local, state, or federal law enforcement officers; violations of the peonage and involuntary servitude statutes protecting migrant workers and others held in bondage; violations of the FACE Act.

Eligible applicants/beneficiaries: all persons.

Range/Average: N.A.

Activity: FY 05, 83 cases filed charging 167 defendants; 109 defendants successfully prosecuted.

HQ: Criminal Section, Civil Rights Division-DOJ, Washington, DC 20530. Phone: (202) 514-3204; Office of Public Affairs, (202) 514-2007, TDD (202) 514-1888;.

Internet: www.usdoj.gov/crt/crim/index.html.

16.110 EDUCATION AND ENFORCEMENT OF THE ANTIDISCRIMINATION PROVISION OF THE IMMIGRATION AND NATIONALITY ACT

Assistance: project grants; specialized services; investigation of complaints (grants,100 percent).

Purposes: pursuant to the Immigration and Nationality Act, to educate employers and workers about their rights and responsibilities under the Act, to prevent employment discrimination based on citizenship status or national origin, and unfair documentary practices with respect to verification or employment eligibility. Eligible funded project activities include outreach and education to workers and employers, and to immigrant service providers. For charges relating to national origin, the Office of the Special Counsel has jurisdiction only over employers with four to fourteen employees—with respect to the hiring, firing, recruiting, or referral for a fee of protected individuals and aliens authorized to work in the U.S.; employers with 15 or more employees are under the jurisdiction of the Equal Employment Opportunity Commission.

Eligible applicants/beneficiaries: local, regional, or national ethnic and immigrants' rights advocacy organizations; labor organizations; trade associations; industry groups; professional organizations; state and local government agencies; employer organizations; others including profit entities—providing information services to employers or potential victims of discrimination.

Range: $35,000 to $100,000.

Activity: FY 05 (sampling), staff participation in 395 outreach presentations; 21,000 calls handled; resolved 182 investigated matters.

HQ: Office of Special Counsel/Immigration-Related Unfair Employment Practices, Civil Rights Division-DOJ, Washington, DC 20530. Phone: (202) 616-5594, (800) 225-7688; TDD (202) 616-5525, (800) 237-2515.

Internet: www.usdoj.gov/crt/osc/index.html. (Note: no field offices for this program.)

16.200 COMMUNITY RELATIONS SERVICE ("CRS")

Assistance: specialized services.

Purposes: pursuant to CRA as amended, Title X, to provide conciliation, mediation, training, and technical services to communities in resolving community tensions, conflicts, and civil disorders perceived to be based on race, ethnicity, or national origin. Technical assistance, resource materials, and publications are available. No funds are provided.

Eligible applicants/beneficiaries: representatives of groups, communities; federal, state, or local governmental units.

Range/Average: N.A.

Activity: annually, 1,200 cases.

HQ: Community Relations Service-DOJ, 600 E St. NW - Ste.6000, Washington, DC 20530. Phone: (202) 305-2935.

Internet: www.usdoj.gov/crs.

16.202 PRISONER REENTRY INITIATIVE DEMONSTRATION (OFFENDER REENTRY)

Assistance: project grants (100 percent/2-3 years).

Purposes: to assist jurisdictions in facing challenges presented by the return of offenders from prison to the community, through enhanced surveillance and monitoring, strengthened individual and community support systems, and repairing harm to victims. The goal of the combined federal initiative supports delivery of pre-release assessments and services; develops transition plans with other justice and community-based agencies and providers.

Eligible applicants/beneficiaries: partnerships that include state and local corrections or juvenile justice and mental health and substance abuse agencies, and Workforce Investment Boards. Private, community, and religious organizations may be included.

Average: N.A.

Activity: N.A.

HQ: Policy Advisor, BJA- OJP-DOJ, 810 Seventh St. NW, Washington, DC 20531. Phone: (202) 616-6500. TF: 1-866-859-2687.

Internet: www.ojp.usdoj.gov/bja. (Note: no field offices for this program.)

16.203 COMPREHENSIVE APPROACHES TO SEX OFFENDER MANAGEMENT DISCRETIONARY GRANT ("CASOM")

Assistance: project grants (75 percent/to 2 years).

Purposes: pursuant VCCLEA, to implement comprehensive approaches to the effective management of juvenile and adult sex offenders, or to enhance existing programs. Projects must focus on the continuum of activities and services targeted to community reintegration and management of offenders released from incarceration, rather than on institutional services.

Eligible applicants/beneficiaries: state, local, or tribal units of government, including possessions and territories.

Range/Average: N.A.

Activity: N.A.

HQ: Policy Advisor, BJA- OJP-DOJ, 810 Seventh St. NW, Washington, DC 20531. Phone: (202) 616-6500. TF: 1-866-859-2687.

Internet: www.ojp.usdoj.gov/bja (Note: no field offices for this program.)

16.300 LAW ENFORCEMENT ASSISTANCE—FBI ADVANCED POLICE TRAINING ("FBI Academy, Advanced Specialized Courses")

Assistance: training (1-11 weeks).

Purposes: pursuant to the OCCSSA as amended, Crime Control Act of 1973, Comprehensive Crime Control Act of 1984, and VCCLEA, to provide advanced training at the FBI Academy in such topics as criminal law and investigations, behavioral science, forensic science, education, management, and fitness and health—emphasizing development of managers and administrators. Specialized advanced courses and seminars include firearms administration, white-collar and computer related crimes, latent fingerprint examination, police legal issues, hostage negotiations, executive development, technology, laboratory matters, budgeting, scientific technical analysis, death investigations, bombing and arson investigations, violent crimes against the elderly, sexual exploitation of children. Participants may be reimbursed for round-trip travel costs to Washington, DC; housing, food, laundry and dry cleaning are furnished to students at FBI Academy, Quantico, VA.

Eligible applicants/beneficiaries: regular full-time personnel of municipal, county, or state criminal justice agencies; qualified representatives of federal agencies—meeting age, experience, education, physical, and character requirements.

Range/Average: N.A.

Activity: FY 05, 2,011 participants.

HQ: Director, FBI-DOJ, Washington, DC 20535. Phone: (202) 324- 3000.

Internet: www.fbi.gov.

16.301 LAW ENFORCEMENT ASSISTANCE—FBI CRIME LABORATORY SUPPORT ("FBI Laboratory")

Assistance: specialized services; training.

Purposes: pursuant to OCCSSA as amended, to provide FBI Laboratory facilities and forensic assistance in examining evidence in criminal matters, technology transfer and access to information and forensic data bases, surveillance capabilities, related expert testimony, and specialized training in forensic disciplines.

Eligible applicants/beneficiaries: state and local law enforcement agencies in the U.S. or possessions.

Range/Average: N.A.

Activity: FY 05, 24,820 nonfederal scientific examinations.

HQ: Director, FBI-DOJ, Washington, DC 20535. Phone: (202) 324- 3000.

Internet: www.fbi.gov.

16.302 LAW ENFORCEMENT ASSISTANCE—FBI FIELD POLICE TRAINING ("FBI Field Police Training")

Assistance: training.

Purposes: pursuant to the OCCSSA as amended, Crime Control Act of 1973, Comprehensive Crime Control Act of 1984, and VCCLEA, to provide training courses by FBI instructors for criminal justice personnel, covering such areas as fingerprinting, legal topics, police-community relations, hostage negotiation, white collar crime, organized crime, computer fraud, management techniques, investigative support.

Eligible applicants/beneficiaries: municipal, county, local, and state criminal justice personnel.

Range/Average: N.A.

Activity: FY 05, 92,500 personnel attending.

HQ: Director, FBI-DOJ, Washington, DC 20535. Phone: (202) 324- 3000.

Internet: www.fbi.gov.

16.303 LAW ENFORCEMENT ASSISTANCE—FBI FINGERPRINT IDENTIFICATION ("FBI Criminal Justice Information Services Division")

Assistance: specialized services.

Purposes: to provide FBI fingerprint and arrest-record services. Besides criminal identification, services include locating missing persons and identifying unknown living or deceased persons and victims of major disasters.

Eligible applicants/beneficiaries: criminal justice agencies, federal government, and other authorized governmental and nongovernmental entities.

Range/Average: N.A.

Activity: FY 05, 20,629,099 fingerprint cards processed.

HQ: Assistant Director, Criminal Justice Information Services Division, FBI-DOJ, 1000 Custer Hollow Rd., Clarksburg, WV 26306. Phone: (304) 625-2222.

Internet: wwww.fbi.gov.

16.304 LAW ENFORCEMENT ASSISTANCE—NATIONAL CRIME INFORMATION CENTER ("NCIC")

Assistance: specialized services.

Purposes: to operate the FBI NCIC, complementing the development of similar metropolitan and statewide criminal justice information systems. Located in Washington, D.C., NCIC is a computerized index of crimes and criminals of nationwide interest, serving as a nucleus of a high-speed communications network that includes criminal justice agencies throughout the U.S., Canada, and some territories and possessions. The service can also be used to locate wanted or missing persons and stolen property. Technical assistance, consultant services, and training are provided to state agencies.

Eligible applicants/beneficiaries: local, state, and federal criminal justice agencies may participate through their individual control terminal agency.

Range/Average: N.A.

Activity: FY 05, 1.639,554,366 transactions.

HQ: Director, FBI-DOJ, Washington, DC 20535. Phone: (202) 324- 3000.

Internet: www.fbi.gov (Note: no field offices for this program.)

16.305 LAW ENFORCEMENT ASSISTANCE—UNIFORM CRIME REPORTS

Assistance: technical information.

Purposes: to collect, analyze, and publish nationwide crime statistics providing such information as crime trends, offenses known to police, demographic characteristics of arrested persons, police disposition of juveniles arrested, police employee information.

Eligible applicants/beneficiaries: all participating law enforcement agencies including state and local governments receive the annual publication and semiannual releases. Limited copies of semiannual releases are available to any interested individual; the annual publication may be purchased from GPO.

Range/Average: N.A.

Activity: annually, 25,000 copies of "Crime in the United States" distributed, plus 2,500 CD-ROM copies; beginning FY 06, internet publication only.

HQ: Assistant Director, Criminal Justice Information Services Division, FBI-DOJ, 1000 Custer Hollow Rd., Clarksburg, WV 26306. Phone: (304) 625-2000.

Internet: www.fbi.gov (Note: no field offices for this program.)

16.307 COMBINED DNA INDEX SYSTEM ("CODIS")

Assistance: project grants.

Purposes: pursuant to the DNA Identification Act of 1994, to develop and maintain a national data base containing DNA records from convicted offenders, unsolved crime scenes, and missing persons. CODIS software allows storage and matching of DNA records; installation, training, and user support are provided. The FBI administers the Forensic Laboratory Improvement grant program jointly with the DOJ National Institute of Justice, providing funds for required equipment, supplies, and contractual services.

Eligible applicants/beneficiaries: software and technical assistance—publicly funded state or local forensic science laboratories performing DNA analysis, or private laboratories under contract. DNA grants—publicly funded state or local forensic laboratories.

Range/Average: N.A.

Activity: as of March 2005, 17 state and local laboratories; CODIS installed in 50 states, PR, and U.S. Army Crime Laboratory.

HQ: *FBI CODIS Program,* Director, FBI-DOJ, Washington, DC 20535. Phone: (no number provided). *DNA grants program,* Director, Forensic Science Systems Unit, Laboratory Division, National Institute of Justice-DOJ, Washington, DC 20531. Phone: (202) 324-9440.

Internet: www.fbi.gov (Note: no field offices for this program.)

16.308 INDIAN COUNTRY INVESTIGATIONS

Assistance: training.

Purposes: pursuant to VCCLEA, to train BIA and tribal law enforcement officers in conducting investigations in Indian country, in coordination with the Federal Law Enforcement Training Center (FLETC) and the BIA—including in death investigations, child sexual/physical abuse, gaming, evidence recovery, supervision and management, street officer safety.

Eligible applicants/beneficiaries: BIA investigators, tribal and other law enforcement officers.

Range/Average: N.A.

Activity: FY 05, 916 students trained; cumulatively, 5,500 students trained.

HQ: FBI-DOJ, 935 Pennsylvania Ave. NW, Washington, DC 20535. Phone: (202) 324-3336.

Internet: www.fbi.gov. (Note: no field offices for this program.)

16.309 LAW ENFORCEMENT ASSISTANCE—NATIONAL INSTANT CRIMINAL BACKGROUND CHECK SYSTEM ("NICS")

Assistance: specialized services.

Purposes: pursuant to the Gun Control Act and National Firearms Act, to provide a system through which federal firearm licensees may obtain information on whether prospective buyers would violate federal or state laws, by telephone or other electronic means. Background checks are conducted by the NICS Operations Center; also provided are technical and operational support to users and State Points of Contacts.

Eligible applicants/beneficiaries: firearms licensees and purchasers.

Range/Average: N.A.

Activity: FY 04, 1,515,134,229 transactions handled.

HQ: Assistant Director, Criminal Justice Information Services Division, FBI-DOJ, 1000 Custer Hollow Rd., Clarksburg, WV 26306. Phone: (304) 625-2222.

Internet: www.fbi.gov (Note: no other field offices for this program.)

16.320 SERVICES FOR TRAFFICKING VICTIMS

Assistance: project grants; direct payments/specified use. (75 percent/1-3 years).

Purposes: pursuant to the Victims of Trafficking and Violence Prevention Act of 2000 (VTVPA), to provide assistance to victims of severe forms of trafficking, primarily to meet victims' pre- certifications needs as victims, through: comprehensive services awards to support the creation or enhancement of collaborative networks within given regions or communities, providing or coordinating services including shelter and sustenance, general health and mental health care, legal assistance, job skills training, cultural support, and educational services; and, supplemental and specialized services awards to support discrete, rapid response whenever and wherever trafficking victims are identified. Limited funding also is available for training, technical assistance, and research and evaluation projects.

Eligible applicants: state and local governments; tribes; nonprofit, nongovernmental victims services organizations.

Eligible beneficiaries: victims of severe forms of trafficking without regard to the victim's immigration status. ("Trafficking" is defined by DOJ as: sex trafficking in which a commercial sex act is induced by force, fraud, or coercion, or in which the person induced to perform such act is under age 18; or, the recruitment, harboring, transportation, provision, or obtaining of a person for labor or services through the use of force, fraud, or coercion for the purpose of subjection to involuntary servitude, peonage, debt bondage, or slavery.)

Range: services, $200,000 to $500,000.

Activity: since program inception, 25 direct service projects, 1 building shelter project, 1 technical assistance grant awarded; 1,184 victims pre-certified assisted; 51,000 personnel trained.

HQ: Office for Victims of Crime, OJP-DOJ, 810 Seventh St. NW, Washington, DC 20531. Phone: (202) 307-5983; Program Development and Dissemination Division, (202) 305-1715.

Internet: www.ovc.gov. (Note: no field offices for this program.)

16.321 ANTITERRORISM EMERGENCY RESERVE

Assistance: project grants; direct payments/specified use. (100 percent/to 3 years).

Purposes: pursuant to VOCA, ATEDPA, VTVPA, and USA Patriot Act of 2001, to provide assistance for victims of mass violence and terrorism occurring within and outside the United States, and a compensation program for victims of international terrorism—through: (1) Antiterrorism and Emergency Assistance Program (AEAP), providing assistance and compensation benefits for victims of domestic and international terrorism, mass violence, including emergency relief, crisis response efforts, training and technical assistance; (2) International Terrorism Victim Expense Reimbursement Program (ITVERP), to compensate victims for expenses associated with acts occurring outside the U.S. Victims all may receive appropriate support services and compensation specifically for medical, mental health, funeral and burial, lost wages, and loss of support.

Eligible applicants: AEAP—victim services organizations; federal, state, and local governments; nongovernmental organizations and similar organizations.

Eligible beneficiaries: ITVERP—generally, victims, family members, and dependents that are U.S. nationals or U.S. government officers or employees as of the date on which the international terrorism act occurred—on or after 21 December 1988, with respect to which an investigation or prosecution was ongoing after 24 April 1996. (Final regulations are still being developed.)

Range/Average: N.A.

Activity: assistance provided to victims such as of the Oklahoma City bombing, "9/11," U.S. Embassy bombings, and other terrorism incidents.

HQ: Office for Victims of Crime, OJP-DOJ, 810 Seventh St. NW, Washington, DC 2053 Phone: (202) 307-5983; Program Development and Dissemination Division, (202) 305-1715.

Internet: www.ovc.gov (Note: no field offices for this program.)

16.523 JUVENILE ACCOUNTABILITY BLOCK GRANTS ("JABG")

Assistance: formula grants; project grants (formula, 90 percent; project, 100 percent/formula, 3 years; project, 1-3 years).

Purposes: to develop programs promoting greater accountability in the juvenile justice system. Formula grant funds may be used for such purposes as: building, expanding, renovating, or operating temporary or permanent juvenile correction or detention facilities, including personnel training; to develop and administer accountability-based sanctions for juvenile offenders; to hire additional judges, probation officers, court-appointed defenders, and prosecutors; to enable prosecutors to address drug, gang, and youth violence problems more effectively; to acquire related technology, equipment, and training; to establish juvenile "gun courts" and "drug courts;" to establish and maintain interagency information-sharing programs involving the juvenile and criminal justice systems, schools, and social services agencies; for programs to protect students and school personnel from drug, gang, and youth violence; to implement a policy of controlled substance testing for appropriate categories of juveniles. Discretionary project grants may be awarded for pertinent research, demonstrations, evaluations, and training and technical assistance.

Eligible applicants/beneficiaries: formula grants—states, territories and possessions (except Palau), and local government units. Discretionary grants—public or private agencies, organizations, individuals.

Range/Average: N.A.

Activity: not quantified specifically.

HQ: OJJDP, OJP-DOJ, 810 Seventh St. NW, Washington, DC 20531. Phone: State Relations and Assistance Division, (202) 307-5924, (202) 514-9292; Demonstration Programs Division, (202) 616- 3646.

Internet: www.usdoj.gov (Note: no field offices for this program.)

16.524 LEGAL ASSISTANCE FOR VICTIMS

Assistance: project grants (100 percent/to 2 years).

Purposes: pursuant to the Violence Against Women Act of 2000 (VAWA), to increase direct legal services available to victims of domestic violence, sexual assault, and stalking—through innovative collaborative programs and services within the civil legal system, promoting victim safety and increased victim economic autonomy, including representation in such matters as protection orders, family law, or housing matters. Funded activities also may include training, technical assistance, and data collection.

Eligible applicants/beneficiaries: private nonprofit entities, tribal governments, publicly funded organizations not acting in their governmental capacity.

Range: $116,000 to $850,000. **Average:** $400,000.

Activity: 2006, 85 awards.

HQ: Office on Violence Against Women, OJP-DOJ, 800 K St. NW, Washington, DC 20530. Phone: (202) 307-6026.

Internet: www.usdoj.gov/ovw. (Note: no field offices for this program.)

16.525 GRANTS TO COMBAT DOMESTIC VIOLENCE, DATING VIOLENCE, SEXUAL ASSAULT, AND STALKING ON CAMPUS

Assistance: project grants. (100 percent/to 3 years).

Purposes: pursuant to VAWA and Department of Justice Reauthorization Act of 2005, to develop and strengthen security and investigation strategies to combat violent crimes against women on campuses, including domestic and dating violence, sexual assault, and stalking; for victim services programs. Funds may support such costs as: apprehension, investigation, and adjudication; personnel training; public education for prevention; lighting and communications systems; coordination with local law enforcement. Grant recipients must meet strict crime reporting requirements.

Eligible applicants/beneficiaries: IHEs or IHE consortia Range; $143,000 to $550,000.

Range: $200,000 to $400,000. **Average:** $225,000.

Activity: 2006, 39 awards.

HQ: Office on Violence Against Women, OJP-DOJ, 800 K St. NW, Washington, DC 20530 Phone: (202) 307-6026.

Internet: www.usdoj.gov/ovw (Note: no field offices for this program.)

16.526 OVW TECHNICAL ASSISTANCE INITIATIVE

Assistance: project grants (100 percent/to 2 years).

Purposes: pursuant to VAWA, to provide expertise and support to communities in: responding to violent crimes against women, including domestic violence, sexual assault, or stalking; increasing victim safety; and, bolstering offender accountability. Grantees participate in educational initiatives, conferences, peer-to-peer consultations, and targeted assistance from experts. Program aim also is to build the capacity of national criminal justice and victim advocacy organizations.

Eligible applicants/beneficiaries: public or private nonprofit victim advocacy and national criminal justice constituency organizations, judicial organizations and related agencies.

Range: $100,000 to $3,000,000. **Average:** $262,000.

Activity: N.A.

HQ: Office on Violence Against Women, OJP-DOJ, 800 K St. NW, Washington, DC 20530 Phone: (202) 307-6026.

Internet: www.usdoj.gov/ovw (Note: no field offices for this program.)

16.527 SUPERVISED VISITATION, SAFE HAVENS FOR CHILDREN

Assistance: project grants. (100 percent/to 2 years).

Purposes: pursuant to VTVPA, for projects enabling supervised visitation and safe exchange of children by and between parents, in situations involving domestic violence, child abuse, sexual assault, or stalking. Projects should involve collaborative relationships among courts, local victim coalitions and shelters, and related entities.

Eligible applicants/beneficiaries: states, tribal governments, local government units.

Range: $120,000 to $200,000. **Average:** $149,000.

Activity: 2006, 31 awards.

HQ: Office on Violence Against Women, OJP-DOJ, 800 K St. NW, Washington, DC 20530 Phone: (202) 307-6026.

Internet: www.usdoj.gov/ovw (Note: no field offices for this program.)

16.528 ENHANCED TRAINING AND SERVICES TO END VIOLENCE AND ABUSE OF WOMEN LATER IN LIFE ("Elder Abuse, Neglect, and Exploitation")

Assistance: project grants (100 percent/to 2 years).

Purposes: pursuant to VTVPA, to train law enforcement officers, prosecutors, and court personnel to recognize, address, investigate, and prosecute cases of elder abuse, neglect, financial exploitation, and violence against individuals with disabilities—including domestic violence and sexual assault. Projects must include coordination among appropriate services agencies and organizations.

Eligible applicants/beneficiaries: states, tribes, local government units; state or local government agencies; private nonprofit victim advocacy organizations; public or private nonprofit service organizations for older persons or the disabled; national criminal justice constituency or judicial organizations.

Range/Average: FY 05 total, $4,132,000.

Activity: only 4 non-competitive grants awarded to technical assistance providers in FY 05, to help revamp program.

HQ: Office on Violence Against Women, OJP-DOJ, 800 K St. NW, Washington, DC 20530 Phone: (202) 307-6026.

Internet: www.usdoj.gov/ovw (Note: no field offices for this program.)

16.529 EDUCATION, TRAINING, AND ENHANCED SERVICES TO END VIOLENCE AGAINST WOMEN WITH DISABILITIES ("Disability Grant Program")

Assistance: project grants. (100 percent/to 3 years).

Purposes: pursuant to VTVPA, to provide education, training, consultation, and information to organizations and programs that provide services to individuals with disabilities that are victims of domestic violence, stalking, or sexual assault—including independent living centers and disability- related service organizations. Funds may support outreach activities and cost-effective ways that shelters and victim services may accommodate the needs of the disabled. Projects must include coordination among appropriate services agencies and organizations.

Eligible applicants/beneficiaries: states, local government units, tribal governments, private nongovernmental entities serving disabled individuals.

Range/Average: FY 05, one award totalling $3,491,000.

Activity: 2006, 8-10 awards.

HQ: Office on Violence Against Women, OJP-DOJ, 800 K St. NW, Washington, DC 20530 Phone: (202) 307-6026.

Internet: www.usdoj.gov/ovw (Note: no field offices for this program.)

16.540 JUVENILE JUSTICE AND DELINQUENCY PREVENTION— ALLOCATION TO STATES ("State Formula Grants")

Assistance: formula grants; project grants. (50-100 percent/to 3 years).

Purposes: pursuant to JJDPA as amended, for state and local programs to prevent juvenile delinquency and improve the juvenile justice system, including: deinstitutionalization of status offenders; separation of adults and juveniles in secure custody; removal of juveniles from adult jails and lockups; community- based services such as group homes and halfway houses; personnel education and training; monitoring and evaluation; elimination of disproportionate contact of minority juveniles. Applicants must have three-year comprehensive plans for meeting program purposes. States must distribute two-thirds of formula funds to local governments, private nonprofit agencies, and tribes performing law enforcement functions.

Eligible applicants/beneficiaries: formula grants—designated state and territorial agencies. Technical assistance contracts—experienced organizations, agencies, and individuals.

Range: formula minimum—territories, $100,000; states, $600,000.

Activity: FY 01, 54 formula grant awards (latest data reported).

HQ: OJJDP-DOJ, Washington, DC 2053 Phone: (202) 307-5924.

Internet: www.usdoj.gov (Note: no field offices for this program.)

16.541 PART E - DEVELOPING, TESTING AND DEMONSTRATING PROMISING NEW PROGRAMS

Assistance: project grants; specialized services. (100 percent/to 3 years).

Purposes: pursuant to JJDPA as amended, for programs to design, test, and demonstrate approaches, techniques, and methods of preventing and controlling juvenile delinquency, such as: community-based alternatives to institutional confinement; diverting juveniles from the traditional justice and correctional system; advocacy activities; programs to strengthen the family unit; prevention and treatment programs for juveniles that commit serious crimes; hate crimes, gun and gang violence prevention programs; after-care and reintegration programs.

Eligible applicants/beneficiaries: public and private nonprofit agencies and organizations; individuals; state, local, and tribal government units or combinations thereof.

Range/Average: N.A.

Activity: not quantified specifically.

HQ: OJJDP-DOJ, Washington, DC 2053 Phone: (202) 307-5914.

Internet: www.usdoj.gov (Note: no field offices for this program.)

16.543 MISSING CHILDREN'S ASSISTANCE

Assistance: project grants (100 percent/1-3 years).

Purposes: pursuant to JJDPA as amended, to coordinate federal programs related to missing and exploited children and to establish and operate a national resource center and clearinghouse to: provide technical assistance and training in locating and recovering missing children; provide a toll-free hotline; disseminate information about innovative and model programs, services, and legislation; conduct national incidence studies. Research, demonstration, or service program contracts may be awarded for public education programs, services to missing children and their families, location and return of adults with Alzheimer's or related diseases, statewide clearinghouses, and related purposes.

Eligible applicants/beneficiaries: state and local governments, public and private nonprofit organizations; individuals.

Range/Average: N.A.

Activity: FY 04 (sampling), 10 new awards to state and local agencies; support for the National Center for Missing and Exploited Children and the Cyber Tipline; 150,000 calls received on the toll-free hotline; 500 law enforcement and prosecutors trained.

HQ: OJJDP-DOJ, Washington, DC 20531 Phone: (202) 307-5911.

Internet: www.usdoj.gov (Note: no field offices for this program.)

16.547 VICTIMS OF CHILD ABUSE ("Judicial Child Abuse Training - Investigation and Prosecution of Child Abuse Through the Criminal Justice System - Court Appointed Special Advocates (CASA) - Children's Advocacy Centers (CACs)")

Assistance: project grants. (100 percent/1-3 years).

Purposes: pursuant to the Victims of Child Abuse Act of 1990, to develop model technical assistance and training programs to improve court handling of child abuse and neglect cases; to facilitate the adoption of laws to protect child abuse victims against the potential "second assault" of courtroom proceedings; to address situations in which states have laws and procedures that outpace federal law, leaving children entering the federal system inadequately protected; to address inconsistencies and disparities among pertinent state laws; to train criminal justice system personnel on the latest investigative and prosecuting techniques; to promote a multidisciplinary approach to coordinating the investigation and prosecution of cases, by limiting the number of pre-trial interviews of child victims and better assuring interview accuracy; to provide technical assistance, information, and support to local CASA programs, and to assist communities in developing new programs; and, for similar projects and programs.

Eligible applicants/beneficiaries: per congressional designations—National Court Appointed Special Advocates (100 W. Harrison St. - Ste.500, Seattle, WA 98119-4123); National Children's Alliance (1612 K St. NW - Ste.500, Washington, DC 20006). Local nonprofit agencies, organizations, and children advocacy centers may apply to the national organizations.

Range/Average: N.A.

Activity: FY 04 (sampling), technical assistance to 910 local CASA and all state organizations; 81 training events; 75,260 volunteers providing services to 302,880 children.

HQ: Director, Child Protection Division, OJJDP-DOJ, Washington, DC 20531 Phone: (202) 616-3637.

Internet: www.usdoj.gov (Note: no field offices for this program.)

16.548 TITLE V—DELINQUENCY PREVENTION PROGRAM

Assistance: formula grants. (50 percent/3 years).

Purposes: pursuant to Incentive Grants for Local Delinquency Prevention Program Act of 2002, to increase the capacity of state and local governments to support more effective programs in the prevention of juvenile delinquency through risk and protective factor programming approaches—including such activities as mentoring, tutoring, after-school programs, gang prevention outreach, community team training.

Eligible applicants/beneficiaries: designated state and territorial agencies—for transmittal to local government units.

Range/Average: N.A.

Activity: FY 02, 55 states and territories participated. FY 03 (sampling), 63 communities received team orientation training, 54 received data collection and analysis training, 40 received program and plan development training.

HQ: OJJDP-DOJ, Washington, DC 20531 Phone: (202) 307-5924.

Internet: www.ojjdp.ncjrs.org/titleV (Note: no field offices for this program.)

16.550 STATE JUSTICE STATISTICS PROGRAM FOR STATISTICAL ANALYSIS CENTERS ("SACs")

Assistance: project grants (100 percent).

Purposes: pursuant to OCCSSA as amended, to establish and operate Statistical Analysis Centers for the collection, analysis, and dissemination of statistics pertaining to crime and criminal justice.

Eligible applicants/beneficiaries: state agencies.

Average: $50,000.

Activity: FY 05, 33 cooperative agreement awards.

HQ: Bureau of Justice Statistics (BJA), DOJ, Washington, DC 20531 Phone: (202) 514-9012.

Internet: www.ojp.usdoj.gov/bjs. (Note: no field offices for this program.)

16.554 NATIONAL CRIMINAL HISTORY IMPROVEMENT PROGRAM ("NCHIP")

Assistance: project grants (80 percent).

Purposes: pursuant to OCCSSA, for states to: establish or improve computerized criminal history record systems; to collect data on stalking and domestic violence; to improve data accessibility and transmission to the National Instant Criminal Background Check System (NICS). Projects are to permit immediate identification of persons prohibited from purchasing firearms, or subject to domestic violence protective orders, or ineligible to hold positions of responsibility involving children, the elderly, or the disabled. Funds may support participation in the Interstate Automated Identification System and the FBI's Sex Offender Registry.

Eligible applicants/beneficiaries: designated state agencies, which may allocate funds to other state or local agencies or courts. Private organizations may receive contracts.

Range/Average: N.A.

Activity: N.A.

HQ: Administrative Officer, Bureau of Justice Statistics-DOJ, Washington, DC 20531 Phone: (202) 307-0765.

Internet: www.ojp.usdoj.gov. (Note: no field offices for this program.)

16.556 GRANTS TO STATE SEXUAL ASSAULT AND DOMESTIC VIOLENCE COALITIONS

Assistance: formula grants. (75-100 percent/to 1 year).

Purposes: pursuant to OCCSSA and VAWA, to coordinate state victim services activities and collaborate and coordinate with federal, state, and local entities engaged in violence against women activities. Required matching funds may be provided through in- kind services.

Eligible applicants/beneficiaries: state domestic violence coalitions as determined by HHS under the Family Violence Prevention and Services Act; state sexual assault coalitions as determined by the CDCP's Center for Injury Prevention and Control under PHSA.

Range: $83,000 to $166,000. **Average:** $101,000.

Activity: new program listing in 2006 (CFDA on-line). Annually, 92 awards.

HQ: Office on Violence Against Women, OJP-DOJ, 800 K St. NW, Washington, DC 20530 Phone: (202) 307-6026.

Internet: www.usdoj.gov/ovw. (Note: no field offices for this program.)

16.557 TRIBAL DOMESTIC VIOLENCE AND SEXUAL ASSAULT COALITIONS PROGRAM

Assistance: project grants (75-100 percent/to 2 years).

Purposes: pursuant to OCCSSA and VAWA, to increase awareness of domestic violence and sexual assault against American Indian and Alaska native women; to enhance responses to such violence at the tribal, federal, and state levels; to identify and provide technical assistance to coalition membership and tribal communities to enhance victim access to essential services. Required matching funds may be provided through in-kind services.

Eligible applicants/beneficiaries: established nonprofit, nongovernmental tribal coalitions; individuals or organizations proposing to incorporate as nonprofit, nongovernmental coalitions.

Range: $150,000 to $400,000. **Average:** $302,000.

Activity: new program listing in 2006 (CFDA on-line). FY 05, 10 awards.

HQ: Office on Violence Against Women, OJP-DOJ, 800 K St. NW, Washington, DC 20530 Phone: (202) 307-6026.

Internet: www.usdoj.gov/ovw. (Note: no field offices for this program.)

16.560 NATIONAL INSTITUTE OF JUSTICE RESEARCH, EVALUATION, AND DEVELOPMENT PROJECT GRANTS

Assistance: project grants; technical information. (100 percent/to 2 years).

Purposes: pursuant to OCCSSA as amended and Anti-Drug Abuse Act of 1988 (ADAA), for research, development, and evaluation projects relating to the causes and correlates of crime and violence and the improvement of the criminal justice system. Priorities include violent crime, alcohol- and drug-related crime, community crime prevention, criminal justice system improvement, forensic science research, and technology development.

Eligible applicants/beneficiaries: state, local, and tribal governments; profit and nonprofit organizations; IHEs; qualified individuals—including in the territories.

Range/Average: N.A.

Activity: FY 06 estimate, 80 awards.

HQ: National Institute of Justice, OJP-DOJ, 810 Seventh St. NW, Washington, DC 20531 Phone: (202) 307-2942, FAX (202) 307-6394.

Internet: www.usdoj.gov/nij. (Note: no field offices for this program.)

16.562 CRIMINAL JUSTICE RESEARCH AND DEVELOPMENT—GRADUATE RESEARCH FELLOWSHIPS

Assistance: project grants. (100 percent/6-18 months).

Purposes: pursuant to the OCCSSA as amended and ADAA, for fellowships to doctoral candidates to conduct research related to law enforcement, crime, or criminal justice—covering stipends, project costs, and certain university fees.

Eligible applicants/beneficiaries: IHEs.

Range: to $15,000.

Activity: FY 03, 5 awards.

HQ: National Institute of Justice, OJP-DOJ, 810 Seventh St. NW, Washington, DC 20531 Phone: (202) 307-2942.

Internet: www.usdoj.gov/nij. (Note: no field offices for this program.)

16.566 NATIONAL INSTITUTE OF JUSTICE W.E.B. DUBOIS FELLOWSHIP PROGRAM

Assistance: project grants. (100 percent/6-12 months).

Purposes: pursuant to OCCSSA as amended and ADAA, for research fellowships concerning justice system administration, delinquency prevention, violence reduction, and related topics. Studies are conducted at the National Institute of Justice.

Eligible applicants/beneficiaries: individuals or their parent agencies or organizations on their behalf. Candidates must have a doctoral-level or legal degree of J.D. or higher.

Range/Average: N.A.

Activity: N.A.

HQ: National Institute of Justice, OJP-DOJ, 810 Seventh St. NW, Washington, DC 20531 Phone: (202) 307-2942.

Internet: www.usdoj.gov (Note: no field offices for this program.)

16.571 PUBLIC SAFETY OFFICERS' BENEFITS PROGRAM

Assistance: direct payments/unrestricted use.

Purposes: pursuant to OCCSSA as amended, to pay disability benefits to officers disabled in the line of duty, or death benefits to survivors of federal, state, or local public safety officers whose death results from a personal injury sustained in the line of duty.

Eligible applicants/beneficiaries: totally and permanently disabled officers or their surviving spouses and children (or their parents if there is no spouse or children). Public safety officers, including law enforcement officers, firefighters and public rescue squad or ambulance crew members, both paid and volunteer; law enforcement officers, including police, corrections, probation, parole, and judicial officers; FEMA personnel; state, local, and tribal emergency management and civil defense personnel. Available also in territories and possessions. (Note: eligibility by category of recipient varies by date of incident; a proportional distribution formula applies in instances of multiple beneficiaries. Details are available from the program headquarters.)

Range: FY 05, $275,658 death or disability benefit.

Activity: not quantified specifically.

HQ: Benefits Office, Public Safety Officers' Benefits Program, BJA-OJP-DOJ, Washington, DC 20531 Phone: (202) 616-6500; (888) 744-6513.

Internet: www.usdoj.gov/bja/psob. (Note: no field offices for this program.)

16.575 CRIME VICTIM ASSISTANCE

Assistance: formula grants (to 4 years).

Purposes: pursuant to VOCA and Children's Justice and Assistance Act of 1986 (CJAA) as amended, VCCLEA, ADAA, ATEDPA, VTVPA, USA Patriot Act of 2001 (USAPA), and other acts, for crime victim assistance programs. Primary program purposes include: to stimulate state participation and support for victim direct services programs; to promote victim cooperation with law enforcement; to provide direct compensation and services to victims of violent crimes, sexual assault, spousal abuse, or child abuse, or other crimes. Project examples: domestic violence shelter services; rape crisis programs; support groups for survivors of homicide victims and DUI/DWI crash victims.

Eligible applicants: states, all territories and possessions. Funds are subgranted to public agencies and nonprofit organizations.

Eligible beneficiaries: crime victims or their survivors.

Range: base amounts—states, $500,000 minimum; territories, possessions, $200,000 minimum. Additional amounts are based on population.

Activity: not quantified specifically.

HQ: Director, State Compensation and Assistance Division, Office for Victims of Crime, OJP-DOJ, 810 Seventh St. NW, Washington, DC 20531 Phone: (202) 616-3579.

Internet: www.usdoj.gov/ovc. (Note: no field offices for this program.)

16.576 CRIME VICTIM COMPENSATION

Assistance: formula grants (to 4 years).

Purposes: pursuant to VOCA and CJAA as amended, VCCLEA, ADAA, ATEDPA, VTVPA, USAPA, and other acts, for awards by states to crime victims (other than for property damage excluding damage to prosthetic devices, eyeglasses or corrective lenses, or dental devices); to support victim compensation programs, including for survivors of terrorism, drunk driving, and domestic violence. Compensation may be made for such expenses as medical costs including mental health counseling and care, loss of wages, funeral expenses, costs incurred by nonresidents of the jurisdictions with operating programs.

Eligible applicants: states, territories, and possessions with established crime victim compensation programs.

Eligible beneficiaries: victims of crime resulting in death or physical or personal injury.

Range: states receive 60 percent of their prior year payout from state funds.

Activity: not quantified specifically.

HQ: Director, State Compensation and Assistance Division, Office for Victims of Crime, OJP-DOJ, 810 Seventh St. NW, Washington, DC 20531 Phone: (202) 616-3579.

Internet: www.usdoj.gov. (Note: no field offices for this program.)

16.578 FEDERAL SURPLUS PROPERTY TRANSFER PROGRAM

Assistance: sale, exchange, or donation of property and goods.

Purposes: pursuant to the Comprehensive Crime Control Act of 1984, Surplus Federal Property Amendments of 1984, and other acts, to transfer or convey surplus federal real or other property for use in correctional or law enforcement programs and projects involving the care or rehabilitation of criminal offenders.

Eligible applicants/beneficiaries: state, local, and territorial governments; political subdivisions.

Range/Average: N.A.

Activity: 27 properties conveyed to date.

HQ: Manager, Special Projects, BJA-OJP-DOJ, 810 Seventh St. NW - 4th floor, Washington, DC 20531 Phone: (202) 353-2392; (866) 859-2687.

Internet: www.ojp.usdoj.gov/bja.

16.579 EDWARD BYRNE MEMORIAL FORMULA GRANT PROGRAM

Assistance: formula grants. (base amount plus 75 percent; tribes, 100 percent/4 years).

Purposes: pursuant to OCCSSA as amended, to reduce and prevent illegal drug activity, crime, and violence, and to improve the functioning of the criminal justice system. Funds may support costs of: additional personnel; equipment; facilities including upgraded and additional corrections and law enforcement crime laboratories; personnel training—to increase the apprehension, prosecution, and adjudication of persons that violate state and local laws relating to the production, possession, and transfer of controlled substances.

Eligible applicants/beneficiaries: states, territories, possessions.

Range: base amount to each participant state, whichever is greater: $500,000 or 25 percent of available amount.

Activity: not quantified specifically.

HQ: Manager, Special Projects, BJA-OJP-DOJ, 810 Seventh St. NW - 4th floor, Washington, DC 20531 Phone: (202) 616-6500; (866) 859-2687.

Internet: www.ojp.usdoj.gov/bja.

16.580 EDWARD BYRNE MEMORIAL STATE AND LOCAL LAW ENFORCEMENT ASSISTANCE DISCRETIONARY GRANTS PROGRAM ("Byrne Discretionary Program")

Assistance: project grants (to 100 percent/12-18 months).

Purposes: pursuant to OCCSSA as amended and Crime Control Act of 1990, to control the use and availability of illegal drugs and to improve the functioning of the criminal justice system, emphasizing violent crime and serious offenders. Funds may be used for: replicable demonstration programs that develop new concepts or strategies, national or multi-jurisdictional in scope; personnel education and training.

Eligible applicants/beneficiaries: state and local government agencies, public and private nonprofit organizations, tribal governments.

Range: $25,000 to $16,000,000.

Activity: annually, 200 awards.

HQ: Associate Director, Manager, Special Projects, BJA-OJP-DOJ, 810 Seventh St. NW - 4th floor, Washington, DC 20531 Phone: (202) 616-6500; (866) 859-2687.

Internet: www.ojp.usdoj.gov/bja. (Note: no field offices for this program.)

16.582 CRIME VICTIM ASSISTANCE/DISCRETIONARY GRANTS

Assistance: project grants; direct payments/specified use. (grants, 75-90 percent/grants, 6 months to 2 years).

Purposes: pursuant to VOCA and CJAA as amended, VCCLEA, ADAA, ATEDPA, VTVPA, USAPA, and other acts, for programs to improve the overall quality of services delivered to crime victims including victims of terrorism domestically and abroad, through: demonstration projects and technical assistance to and training of services providers; support of victims services programs including direct compensation benefits. Project focus examples: religious organizations' response to crime victims; victims of crimes in urban and rural areas and in Indian country (requiring 10 percent local matching share); working with grass roots organizations to identify and replicate promising practices; practitioners training; special populations programs.

Eligible applicants/beneficiaries: states, U.S. Attorneys offices, university sites and colleges, victim service agencies, private nonprofit agencies; tribes and tribal organizations.

Range: Federal Crime Victims Division, $40,000 to $305,000; Program Development and Dissemination Division (PDDD), $25,000 to $1,000,000. **Average:** PDDD, $150,000.

Activity: not quantified specifically.

HQ: Office for Victims of Crime, OJP-DOJ, 810 Seventh St. NW, Washington, DC 20531 Phone: (202) 307-5983.

Internet: www.ovc.gov (Note: no field offices for this program.)

16.583 CHILDREN'S JUSTICE ACT PARTNERSHIPS FOR INDIAN COMMUNITIES

Assistance: project grants; direct payments/specified use. (90 percent/1-3 years).

Purposes: pursuant to VOCA and CJAA as amended, VCCLEA, ADAA, ATEDPA, VTVPA, and other acts, for Indian tribes to develop, establish, and operate programs to improve the handling of child abuse cases, particularly cases of sexual abuse, and to improve the investigation and prosecution of such cases.

Eligible applicants/beneficiaries: tribal governments, nonprofit Indian organizations.

Range/Average: N.A.

Activity: 75 programs funded.

HQ: Director, Federal Assistance Division, Office for Victims of Crime, OJP-DOJ, 810 Seventh St. NW, Washington, DC 20531 Phone: (202) 616-9559; Program Manager, (202) 616-3218.

Internet: www.usdoj.gov (Note: no field offices for this program.)

16.585 DRUG COURT DISCRETIONARY GRANT PROGRAM

Assistance: project grants. (75 percent/2-3 years).

Purposes: pursuant to OCCSSA, to establish and develop drug courts to handle cases involving nonviolent adult and juvenile offenders. Program funds may support projects providing early and continuous judicial supervision and integrated administration of sanctions and services, including: mandatory periodic testing for controlled or addictive substance use during any period of supervised release or probation; treatment; diversion, probation, or other supervised release; offender management and aftercare services.

Eligible applicants/beneficiaries: states, local government units, state and local courts, tribal governments; joint applicants.

Range: implementation, to $500,000 for 3 years; enhancements, to $300,000.

Activity: not quantified specifically.

HQ: Associate Deputy Director, BJA-OJP-DOJ, Washington, DC 20531 Phone: (202) 616-6500; (866) 859-2687.

Internet: www.ojp.usdoj.gov/bja (Note: no field offices for this program.)

16.586 VIOLENT OFFENDER INCARCERATION AND TRUTH IN SENTENCING INCENTIVE GRANTS ("Prison Grants")

Assistance: formula grants. (90 percent/to 5 years).

Purposes: pursuant to VCCLEA as amended, to build, renovate, or expand: adult or juvenile correctional facilities for violent offenders; temporary or permanent correctional facilities, including on military bases, prison barges, and "boot camps," for confinement of nonviolent offenders; jails. As of FY 99, ten percent of funds may be used for approved drug testing programs.

Eligible applicants/beneficiaries: states; multi-state compacts; territories and possessions. Subgrants may be awarded to local government units.

Range/Average: N.A.

Activity: N.A.

HQ: Associate Deputy Director, BJA-OJP-DOJ, 810 Seventh St. NW, Washington, DC 20531 Phone: (202) 616-6500; (866) 859-2687.

Internet: www.ojp.usdoj.gov/bja/grant/voitis.html. (Note: no field offices for this program.)

16.587 VIOLENCE AGAINST WOMEN DISCRETIONARY GRANTS FOR INDIAN TRIBAL GOVERNMENTS

Assistance: project grants (90 percent).

Purposes: pursuant to VCCLEA and OCCSSA as amended and VAWA, to develop and strengthen law enforcement and prosecution strategies to combat violent crimes against women, and to augment victim services. Funding may be used to pay costs of personnel, training, technical assistance, data collection, equipment, and victim services. (Note: Beginning in 2007, 10 percent of STOP, Arrest, LAV, Transitional Housing, Rural, and Safe Haven is set aside for the Tribal Program.)

Eligible applicants/beneficiaries: tribal governments.

Range: $94,000 to $575,000. **Average:** $181,000.

Activity: 36 awards.

HQ: Office on Violence Against Women, OJP-DOJ, 800 K St. NW, Washington, DC 20530 Phone: (202) 307-6026.

Internet: www.usdoj.gov/ovw (Note: no field offices for this program.)

16.588 VIOLENCE AGAINST WOMEN FORMULA GRANTS

Assistance: formula grants (75 percent).

Purposes: pursuant to VCCLEA and OCCSSA as amended and VAWA, to develop and strengthen law enforcement and prosecution strategies to combat violent crimes against women, and to augment victim services. Grants may support costs of personnel, training, technical assistance, data collection and other equipment for apprehension, prosecution, and adjudication, and victim services.

Eligible applicants/beneficiaries: states, territories, and possessions. Subgrants will be awarded to local government units, nonprofit nongovernmental victim services programs, and tribal governments.

Range: $600,000 to $6,407,000. **Average:** $2,152,000.

Activity: 56 awards.

HQ: Office on Violence Against Women, OJP-DOJ, 800 K St. NW, Washington, DC 20530 Phone: (202) 307-6026.

Internet: www.usdoj.gov/ovw (Note: no field offices for this program.)

16.589 RURAL DOMESTIC VIOLENCE, DATING VIOLENCE, SEXUAL ASSAULT, AND STALKING GRANT PROGRAM

Assistance: project grants. (100 percent/to 2 years).

Purposes: pursuant to VCCLEA as amended and VAWA, for rural states to implement, expand, and establish cooperative efforts and projects among law enforcement officers, prosecutors, victim advocacy groups, and others—to: investigate and prosecute incidents of domestic violence, dating violence, and child victimization, including in immigration matters; provide treatment and counseling to victims; develop community education and prevention strategies.

Eligible applicants/beneficiaries: state agencies; local governments, tribal governments, and public and private entities in rural states—i.e., those with a population density of 52 or fewer persons per square mile, or in which the largest county's population is less than 150,000, including Alaska, Arkansas, Arizona, Colorado, Idaho, Iowa, Kansas, Maine, Montana, Nebraska, Nevada, New Mexico, North Dakota, Oklahoma, Oregon, South Dakota, Utah, Vermont, and Wyoming.

Range: $500,000 to $900,000. **Average:** $550,000.

Activity: 64 awards.

HQ: Office on Violence Against Women, OJP-DOJ, 800 K St. NW, Washington, DC 20530 Phone: (202) 307-6026.

Internet: www.usdoj.gov/ovw (Note: no field offices for this program.)

16.590 GRANTS TO ENCOURAGE ARREST POLICIES AND ENFORCEMENT OF PROTECTION ORDERS

Assistance: project grants. (100 percent/to 2 years).

Purposes: pursuant to VCCLEA as amended and VAWA, to implement mandatory arrest or pro-arrest programs and policies in police departments in cases of domestic violence including for protection order violations, dating violence, and assaults against older persons and the disabled; to develop related educational and training programs; to improve tracking of cases; to centralize and coordinate police enforcement in groups or units of police, probation, and parole officers, prosecutors, or judges; to coordinate computer tracking systems; to strengthen legal advocacy service programs for victims; to improve judicial handling or such cases.

Eligible applicants/beneficiaries: states, local government units, state or local courts, and tribal governments.

Range: $85,000 to $1,500,000. **Average:** $520,000.

Activity: FY 06, 96 awards.

HQ: Office on Violence Against Women, OJP-DOJ, 800 K St. NW, Washington, DC 20530 Phone: (202) 307-6026.

Internet: www.usdoj.gov/ovw (Note: no field offices for this program.)

16.593 RESIDENTIAL SUBSTANCE ABUSE TREATMENT FOR STATE PRISONERS ("RSAT")

Assistance: formula grants. (75 percent/to 3 years).

Purposes: pursuant to OCCSSA as amended, to develop and implement residential substance abuse treatment programs within state and local correctional facilities, including individual and group programs to develop cognitive, behavioral, social, vocational, and other skills—and lasting six to twelve months.

Eligible applicants/beneficiaries: states, possessions, territories. Subgrants may be awarded to state and local government units.

Range: $259,000 (Northern Marianas) to $6,802,000 (California).

Activity: N.A.

HQ: Associate Deputy Director, BJA-OJP-DOJ, 810 Seventh St. NW, Washington, DC 20531 Phone: (202) 616-6500.

Internet: www.ojp.usdoj.gov/bja (Note: no field offices for this program.)

16.595 COMMUNITY CAPACITY DEVELOPMENT OFFICE

Assistance: project grants; specialized services. (75 percent/to 5 years).

Purposes: in cooperation with several other federal departments and agencies, to implement "Operation Weed and Seed"—a comprehensive, multidisciplinary approach to combat violent crime, drug use, and gang activity in high-crime neighborhoods. The goal is to identify drug activity and then to "seed" the sites with an array of crime and drug prevention programs, along with human service resources to prevent crime from reoccurring. The strategy is to bring together federal, state, and local government, the community, and the private sector in a partnership.

Eligible applicants/beneficiaries: coalitions of community residents and local, county, state, and federal agencies, and the private sector.

Range: initial award, $175,000; continuation awards, $100,000 to $225,000.

Activity: not quantified specifically.

HQ: Community Capacity Development Office, OJP-DOJ, 810 Seventh St. NW, Washington, DC 20531 Phone: (202) 616-1152, FAX (202) 616-1159.

Internet: www.usdoj.gov/ccdo (Note: no field offices for this program.)

16.596 CORRECTIONAL GRANT PROGRAM FOR INDIAN TRIBES

Assistance: project grants. (90 percent/2 years).

Purposes: pursuant to VCCLEA as amended, to construct or expand jails on tribal lands for the incarceration of adult or juvenile offenders subject to tribal jurisdiction.

Eligible applicants/beneficiaries: tribes—defined as any Indian or Alaska native tribe, band, nation, pueblo, village, or community recognized by DOI.

Range/Average: N.A.

Activity: N.A.

HQ: Senior Policy Advisor, BJA-OJP-DOJ, 810 Seventh St. NW, Washington, DC 20531 Phone: (202) 616-6500.

Internet: www.ojp.usdoj.gov/bja (Note: no field offices for this program.)

16.597 MOTOR VEHICLE THEFT PROTECTION ACT PROGRAM ("Watch Your Car")

Assistance: project grants (100 percent/to 24 months).

Purposes: pursuant to VCCLEA and Motor Vehicle Theft Protection Act of 1994, to develop a national voluntary motor vehicle theft prevention program as a cooperative initiative among states, local governments, and DOJ. The Watch Your Car program allows owners to voluntarily display decals or devices alerting police that the vehicle normally is not driven between 1:00 a.m. and 5:00 a.m., nor across or in proximity of international borders or ports. Grant funds may be used: to print, purchase, and distribute decals and registration and consent forms; for public information campaigns; for law enforcement personnel training and overtime costs; for computer database upgrading; related costs.

Eligible applicants/beneficiaries: states; local government units (when states do not apply).

Range/Average: N.A.

Activity: 16 states with active programs.

HQ: Deputy Director, BJA-DOJ, 810 Seventh St. NW, Washington, DC 20531 Phone: (202) 616-6500; Department of Justice Response Center, Phone: (202) 307-1480; (800) -421-670.

Internet: www.usdoj.gov/bja (Note: no field offices for this program.)

16.601 CORRECTIONS—TRAINING AND STAFF DEVELOPMENT

Assistance: project grants; specialized services; technical information; training (100 percent).

Purposes: pursuant to JJDPA as amended, to upgrade operation of state and local correctional programs through training seminars, workshops, or other programs for law enforcement officers, judges and judicial personnel, probation and parole personnel, corrections personnel, welfare workers, lay ex-offenders, and paraprofessionals—involved in the treatment and rehabilitation of criminal and juvenile offenders; to develop technical training teams.

Eligible applicants/beneficiaries: states, local government units, public and private agencies, educational institutions, organizations, and individuals.

Range: $1,500 to $300,000. **Average:** $100,000.

Activity: FY 05, 66,000 participants, including through video conference and "E-Learning".

HQ: National Institute of Corrections-DOJ, 320 First St. NW - Rm.5007, Washington, DC 20534 Phone: (202) 307-3106, (800) 995- 6423, FAX (202) 307-3361; TDD (202) 307-3156.

Internet: www.usdoj.gov.

16.602 CORRECTIONS—RESEARCH AND EVALUATION AND POLICY FORMULATION

Assistance: project grants; specialized services; technical information (100 percent).

Purposes: pursuant to JJDPA as amended, for research and evaluation projects on the corrections system, including the causes, prevention, diagnosis, and treatment of criminal offenders. Project examples: classification systems and methods; community corrections options; communications audits.

Eligible applicants/beneficiaries: states, local government units, public and private agencies, educational institutions, organizations, and individuals.

Range: $1,500 to $200,000. **Average:** $75,000.

Activity: not quantified specifically.

HQ: National Institute of Corrections-DOJ, 320 First St. NW - Rm.5007, Washington, DC 20534 Phone: (202) 307-3106, (800) 995- 6423, FAX (202) 307-3361; TDD (202) 307-3156.

Internet: www.usdoj.gov.

16.603 CORRECTIONS—TECHNICAL ASSISTANCE/CLEARINGHOUSE

Assistance: project grants; specialized services; technical information (100 percent).

Purposes: pursuant to JJDPA as amended, to upgrade the operation of state and local correctional facilities, programs, and services for criminal and juvenile offenders; to provide consultation to federal, state, and local courts, departments, and agencies. Examples of funded projects: improved programs for female offenders; evaluation of offender classification systems; development of community sanctions.

Eligible applicants/beneficiaries: states, local government units, public and private agencies, educational institutions, organizations, and individuals.

Range: $1,500 to $50,000. **Average:** $7,500.

Activity: FY 05, technical assistance responding to 388 requests from correctional agencies in 50 states and DC.

HQ: Technical Assistance Coordinator/Prisons-Community Corrections, National Institute of Corrections-DOJ, 320 First St. NW - Rm.5007, Washington, DC 20534 Phone: (202) 307-3106, (800) 995- 6423, FAX (202) 307-3361; TDD (202) 307-3156.

Internet: www.usdoj.gov.

16.606 STATE CRIMINAL ALIEN ASSISTANCE PROGRAM ("SCAAP")

Assistance: direct payments/unrestricted use (100 percent).

Purposes: pursuant to the Immigration and Nationality Act as amended and VCCLEA, to reimburse states and localities for costs incurred to imprison undocumented aliens convicted of felonies or of two or more misdemeanors; to expedite the transfer of illegal aliens to federal custody for deportation.

Eligible applicants/beneficiaries: states, DC, PR, Guam, VI; authorized localities and local jurisdictions.

Range/Average: N.A.

Activity: cumulative 9-year reimbursement of $4-billion to 660 jurisdictions.

HQ: SCAAP, BJA-OJP-DOJ, 810 Seventh St. NW, Washington, DC 20531 Phone: (202) 616-6500.

Internet: www.usdoj.gov/bja/grant/scaap.html (Note: no field offices for this program.)

16.607 BULLETPROOF VEST PARTNERSHIP PROGRAM

Assistance: direct payments/specified use. (50 percent/to 4 years).

Purposes: pursuant to the Bulletproof Vest Partnership Grant Act of 1998 and Bulletproof Vest Program Act of 2000, to purchase armored vests for law enforcement officers, including costs of vest carriers, attachments, inserts, essential covers, and fitting, shipping, handling, and tax charges.

Eligible applicants/beneficiaries: chief executives of states, local governments units, recognized tribes, territories, possessions.

Range/Average: N.A.

Activity: 4-year cumulative estimate, 5,129 applications approved covering the purchase of 190,000 vests.

HQ: BJA-OJP-DOJ, 810 Seventh St. NW - 4th floor, Washington, DC 20531 Phone: (202) 616-6500, FAX (202) 616-0314; Justice Response Center, (800) 421-6770; Vest Technical Support Help Desk, (877) 758-3787.

Internet: www.usdoj.gov/bja *and* http://vests.ojp.gov; e-mail, askbja@ojp.usdoj.gov/bja. (Note: no field offices for this program.)

16.608 TRIBAL COURT ASSISTANCE PROGRAM

Assistance: project grants. (100 percent/to 18 months).

Purposes: to develop, enhance, and operate tribal courts, including intertribal systems.

Eligible applicants/beneficiaries: tribal governments.

Range/Average: N.A.

Activity: not quantified specifically.

HQ: Senior Policy Advisor, BJA-OJP-DOJ, 810 Seventh St. NW, Washington, DC 20531 Phone: (202) 616-6500.

Internet: www.ojp.usdoj.gov/bja (Note: no field offices for this program.)

16.609 COMMUNITY PROSECUTION AND PROJECT SAFE NEIGHBORHOODS ("Community Prosecution Program")

Assistance: project grants. (100 percent/to 18 months).

Purposes: pursuant to OCCSSA as amended and the Crime Control Act of 1990, to enable community leaders and residents to work with prosecutors and other justice officials in the identification of local priorities, problem solving, and strategic planning for public safety—through "Community Gun Violence Prosecution" projects. "Project Safe Neighborhoods" is designed to remove gun-wielding criminals from local neighborhoods. Funds may be used: to hire additional prosecutors to work on cases of firearm-related violent crime; for investigations; for training; for outreach efforts.

Eligible applicants/beneficiaries: state, county, city, and tribal public prosecutor offices.

Range: $50,000 to $480,000, depending on population.

Activity: as of FY 01, 34 awards (latest reported data).

HQ: Associate Deputy Director, BJA-OJP-DOJ, 810 Seventh St. NW, Washington, DC 20531 Phone: (202) 616-6500.

Internet: www.usdoj.gov/bja (Note: no field offices for this program.)

16.610 REGIONAL INFORMATION SHARING SYSTEMS ("RISS")

Assistance: project grants (100 percent).

Purposes: pursuant to OCCSSA, to enhance the ability of state and local criminal justice agencies to identify, target, and remove criminal conspiracies and activities that span interjurisdictional boundaries—by exchanging and sharing information among federal, state, and local law enforcement agencies, pertaining to known or suspected criminals or criminal activity; to provide technical resources, specialized equipment, and training.

Eligible applicants/beneficiaries: Middle Atlantic-Great Lakes Organized Crime Law Enforcement Center, Mid-States Organized Crime Information Center, New England State Police Information Network, Regional Organized Crime Information Center, Rocky Mountain Information Network, and the Western States Information Network.

Range: FY 05, $25,000,000 divided among six RISS projects (amount may fluctuate yearly).

Activity: information sharing to 6,000 law enforcement agencies nationwide; FY 01 (sampling), 3,000 arrests, $100,000,000 in illegal controlled substances, property, and currency seized or recovered, 125,000 match hits (latest data reported).

HQ: Associate Deputy Director, BJA-OJP-DOJ, 810 Seventh St. NW, Washington, DC 20531 Phone: (202) 616-6500.

Internet: www.usdoj.gov/bja (Note: no field offices for this program.)

16.611 CLOSED-CIRCUIT TELEVISING OF CHILD VICTIMS OF ABUSE ("CCTV")

Assistance: project grants (75 percent).

Purposes: pursuant to the Victims of Child Abuse Act as amended, to purchase equipment and provide personnel training for the closed-circuit televising and videotaping of the testimony of children in criminal proceedings for the violation of laws relating to the abuse of children.

Eligible applicants/beneficiaries: state or local units of government with enabling laws in effect.

Range: FY 05, $50,000 to $100,000 (amount may fluctuate yearly).

Activity: 10 to 15 grants.

HQ: Deputy Director, BJA-OJP-DOJ, 810 Seventh St. NW, Washington, DC 20531 Phone: (202) 616-6500.

Internet: www.usdoj.gov/bja (Note: no field offices for this program.)

16.612 NATIONAL WHITE COLLAR CRIME CENTER ("NWCCC")

Assistance: project grants (100 percent).

Purposes: pursuant to OCCSSA as amended, to support the NWCCC, a nationwide support system for the prevention, investigation, and prosecution of economic crime—through research, training, and investigative support services including the Internet Fraud Complaint Center (IFCC).

Eligible applicants/beneficiaries: state and local law enforcement authorities.

Range: FY 05, $7,000,000 to $10,000,000 (amount may fluctuate yearly).

Activity: 1,300 personnel trained.

HQ: Program Development Division, BJA-OJP-DOJ, 810 Seventh St. NW, Washington, DC 20531 Phone: (202) 616-6500; Justice Response Center, (800) 421-6770.

Internet: www.usdoj.gov/bja (Note: no field offices for this program.)

16.613 SCAMS TARGETING THE ELDERLY

Assistance: project grants (100 percent/12-18 months).

Purposes: pursuant to VCCLEA, to assist law enforcement in preventing and stopping marketing scams against senior citizens, through: training and technical assistance including a telemarketing fraud task force; state and local demonstration programs; public awareness initiatives and assistance through the National Fraud Information Center.

Eligible applicants/beneficiaries: public and private nonprofit organizations operating programs that are national in scope.

Range: $70,000 to $1,000,000.

Activity: not quantified specifically.

HQ: Associate Deputy Director, BJA-OJP-DOJ, 810 Seventh St. NW, Washington, DC 20531 Phone: (202) 616-6500.

Internet: www.usdoj.gov/bja (Note: no field offices for this program.)

16.614 STATE AND LOCAL ANTI-TERRORISM TRAINING ("SLATT")

Assistance: training; technical information; advisory services/counseling.

Purposes: pursuant to ATEDPA, to provide specialized multi-agency anti-terrorism preparedness training, covering both domestic and international threats and incidents. Training focus includes crisis and consequence management, anti-terrorist research, operational issues development, and technical assistance and support.

Eligible applicants/beneficiaries: state and local law enforcement and prosecution authorities.

Range/Average: N.A.

Activity: 50 workshop and training sessions with 7,600 line officers and 586 law enforcement officers participating.

HQ: Senior Policy Advisor, BJA-OJP-DOJ, 810 Seventh St. NW, Washington, DC 20531 Phone: (202) 616-6500.

Internet: www.usdoj.gov/bja (Note: no field offices for this program.)

16.615 PUBLIC SAFETY OFFICERS' EDUCATIONAL ASSISTANCE ("PSOEA")

Assistance: direct payments/unrestricted use. (100 percent/45 months).

Purposes: to provide financial assistance for higher education to dependents of public safety officers killed or totally disabled in the line of duty.

Eligible applicants/beneficiaries: spouses and surviving children under age 27—of federal, state, or local public safety officers including those who served public agencies with or without compensation in law enforcement, firefighting, or as members of public rescue squads or ambulance crews; effective November 1, 2000, FEMA personnel and state, local, and tribal emergency management and civil defense employees also became eligible. Categorical eligibility dates vary with service of victim; contact BJA for details.

Average: $170 monthly for less than half-time students to $600 monthly for full-time.

Activity: FY 02, 233 dependents received assistance (latest data reported).

HQ: Benefits Specialist, BJA-OJP-DOJ, 810 Seventh St. NW, Washington, DC 20531 Phone: (202) 616-6500; (888) 744-6513.

Internet: www.ojp.usdoj.gov/bja/topics/psobprogram.html. (Note: no field offices for this program.)

16.616 INDIAN COUNTRY ALCOHOL DRUG PREVENTION

Assistance: project grants. (100 percent/18 months).

Purposes: to assist tribal governments in the development and implementation of programs to reduce alcohol abuse and crime.

Eligible applicants/beneficiaries: tribal governments.

Range/Average: N.A.

Activity: N.A.

HQ: Senior Policy Advisor, BJA-OJP-DOJ, 810 Seventh St. NW, Washington, DC 20531 Phone: (202) 616-6500.

Internet: www.ojp.gov/bja. (Note: no field offices for this program.)

16.710 PUBLIC SAFETY PARTNERSHIP AND COMMUNITY POLICING GRANTS ("'COPS' Grants")

Assistance: project grants. (75-100 percent/3 years).

Purposes: pursuant to OCCSSA as amended and VCCLEA, to increase police presence in communities, to expand and improve cooperation between law enforcement agencies and communities in addressing problems of crime and disorder, and to enhance public safety. Funds may be used to hire or rehire career law enforcement officers and to procure equipment, technology, or support systems. Grants may also cover costs of programs or projects to: increase the number of officers interacting with community members on proactive crime control and prevention; train officers to increase their skills in conflict resolution, mediation, problem solving; increase participation in multidisciplinary early intervention teams; develop new technologies; support similar activities including innovative approaches to fulfilling the duties of police officers.

Eligible applicants/beneficiaries: states, local government units, tribal governments, other public and private entities, multijurisdictional or regional consortia. Available also in territories and possessions.

Range: $2,000 to $6,000,000. **Average:** $367,745.

Activity: FY 05, 886 awards.

HQ: Office of Community Oriented Policing Services, DOJ, 1100 Vermont Ave. NW, Washington, DC 20530 Phone: (202) 307-1480; DOJ Response Center, (800) 421-6770.

Internet: www.usdoj.gov/cops. (Note: no field offices for this program.)

16.726 JUVENILE MENTORING PROGRAM ("JUMP")

Assistance: project grants. (100 percent/3 years).

Purposes: pursuant to JJDPA as amended, to develop, implement, and pilot-test mentoring strategies and programs for youth in the juvenile justice system, re-entry youth, and those in foster care.

Eligible applicants/beneficiaries: states, territories, and possessions in partnership with mentoring and other public or private nonprofit organizations.

Range: $650,000 for 5 project sites, and $350,000 for training and technical assistance supporting the sites; evaluation, $400,000.

Activity: not quantified specifically.

HQ: Office of Juvenile Justice and Delinquency Prevention, OJP-DOJ, 810 Seventh St. NW, Washington, DC 20531 Phone: (202) 307-5914.

Internet: www.usdoj.gov (Note: no field offices for this program.)

16.727 ENFORCING UNDERAGE DRINKING LAWS PROGRAM

Assistance: project grants (1-3 years).

Purposes: to enforce state laws prohibiting alcohol purchase, possession, and use by minors—through projects conducted by partnerships among state and local governments, organizations, and agencies, including for training and technical assistance.

Eligible applicants/beneficiaries: states, DC.

Range: from $360,000.

Activity: all states and DC funded.

HQ: Office of Juvenile Justice and Delinquency Prevention, OJP-DOJ, 810 Seventh St. NW, Washington, DC 20531 Phone: (202) 307-5924.

Internet: www.ojjdp.ncjrs.org (Note: no field offices for this program.)

16.730 REDUCTION AND PREVENTION OF CHILDREN'S EXPOSURE TO VIOLENCE ("Safe Start")

Assistance: project grants (100 percent/1-5 years).

Purposes: for a demonstration initiative to prevent and reduce the impact of family and community violence on young children, primarily from birth to age 6, by expanding existing community partnerships between service providers such as law enforcement, mental health, early childhood education agencies and others. Funds may be used to: establish or enhance a broad range of local intervention and treatment services; develop multi-agency protocols; develop community-wide systems.

Eligible applicants/beneficiaries: public agencies applying on behalf of collaboratives including private agencies and organizations.

Range/Average: N.A.

Activity: FY 05 estimate, 14 sites to be awarded funds.

HQ: Child Protection Division, OJJDP, Office of Justice Programs- DOJ, 810 Seventh St. NW, Washington, DC 20531 Phone: (202) 616- 7323.

Internet: www.usdoj.gov (Note: no field offices for this program.)

16.731 TRIBAL YOUTH PROGRAM ("TYP")

Assistance: project grants (100 percent/3 years).

Purposes: to reduce, control, and prevent crime by or against native American youth; to provide interventions for court- involved tribal youth; to improve tribal juvenile justice systems; to provide prevention programs focusing on alcohol and drugs.

Eligible applicants/beneficiaries: tribes and Alaska native villages, including partnerships.

Range: $300,000 to $500,000.

Activity: FY 04, 3,929 tribal communities funded.

HQ: Program Manager, State and Tribal Assistance Division, Office of Juvenile Justice and Delinquency Prevention, OJP-DOJ, 810 Seventh St. NW, Washington, DC 20531 Phone: (202) 307-5924.

Internet: www.ojp.usdoj.gov (Note: no field offices for this program.)

16.734 SPECIAL DATA COLLECTIONS AND STATISTICAL STUDIES ("Statistics")

Assistance: project grants.

Purposes: pursuant to OCCSSA, to produce official national statistics on crime and the administration of justice to guide federal, state, and local policy-making; to improve the quality of and access to the information. Projects may involve: data collection and processing activities; statistical and methodological research; technical assistance to state, local, and tribal governments; dissemination and clearinghouse services.

Eligible applicants/beneficiaries: state, local, and tribal governments; private and public nonprofit and profit organizations, IHEs, and qualified individuals—including in territories.

Range: $50,000 to $600,000.

Activity: new program listing in 2003.

HQ: Bureau of Justice Statistics (BJA), DOJ, Washington, DC 20531 Phone: (202) 616-3561.

Internet: www.ojp.usdoj.gov (Note: no field offices for this program.)

16.735 PROTECTING INMATES AND SAFEGUARDING COMMUNITIES DISCRETIONARY GRANT PROGRAM ("Prison Rape Elimination")

Assistance: project grants (100 percent/2 years).

Purposes: pursuant to the Prison Rape Elimination Act of 2003, to protect male and female inmates in adult and juvenile facilities from prison rape; to safeguard communities to which inmates return. Funds may be used for such costs as: under the Protecting Inmates component—personnel, training, technical assistance, data collection, victim service and treatment, and equipment necessary for the proper prevention, investigation, and prosecution; Safeguarding Communities component—training and technical assistance to states on moderating the growth of prison populations, education of state and local governments on the risks of inmate reentry, developing state and local government collaborative efforts, programs reducing rates of parole and probation revocation.

Eligible applicants/beneficiaries: states—in coordination with stakeholders.

Range: to $1,000,000.

Activity: new program in FY 04.

HQ: Deputy Director, BJA-OJP-DOJ, 810 Seventh St. NW, Washington, DC 20531 Phone: (202) 616-6500.

Internet: www.ojp.usdoj.gov (Note: no field offices for this program.)

16.736 TRANSITIONAL HOUSING ASSISTANCE FOR VICTIMS OF DOMESTIC VIOLENCE, STALKING, OR SEXUAL ASSAULT ("Transitional Housing")

Assistance: project grants. (100 percent/to 3 years).

Purposes: pursuant to the Prosecutorial Remedies and Other Tools to End the Exploitation of Children Today Act of 2003 (PROTECT Act), for transitional housing assistance and related support services to minors, adults, and the dependents that are homeless or in need of such assistance as a result of fleeing from domestic violence, or for whom emergency shelter or other crisis intervention services are unavailable or insufficient. Funds may be used to pay for short-term rental or utilities and related expenses, and for transportation, counseling, child care, case management, employment counseling, and other assistance.

Eligible applicants/beneficiaries: states, local and tribal governments, other organizations.

Range: $175,000 to $350,000. **Average:** $300,000.

Activity: new program in FY 04; FY 05, 115 awards.

HQ: Office on Violence Against Women, OJP-DOJ, 800 K St. NW, Washington, DC 20530 Phone: (202) 307-6026.

Internet: www.usdoj.gov/ovw (Note: no field offices for this program.)

16.737 GANG RESISTANCE EDUCATION AND TRAINING ("GREAT")

Assistance: project grants. (100 percent/to 18 months).

Purposes: to help prevent youth crime, violence, and gang association, while developing positive relationships among law enforcement, families, and young persons. Funds may support personnel training and purchase of program materials and supplies.

Eligible applicants/beneficiaries: state, county, tribal, and municipal law enforcement agencies—including in territories; other special purpose law enforcement agencies (i.e., independent school districts).

Range: $3,500 to $500,000.

Activity: as of mid-2004 (sampling), 7,027 officers from 5,485 agencies funded; 3,900,000 youth trained.

HQ: Policy Office, BJA-OJP-DOJ, 810 Seventh St. NW -4th Floor, Washington, DC 20531 Phone: (202) 616-6500.

Internet: www.ojp.usdoj.gov/bja/great.htm.

16.738 EDWARD BYRNE MEMORIAL JUSTICE ASSISTANCE GRANT PROGRAM

Assistance: formula grants; project grants (4 years).

Purposes: to acquire additional personnel, equipment, supplies, contractual support, training, technical assistance, and information systems—related to programs of law enforcement, prosecution and courts, prevention and education, corrections, drug treatment, planning, evaluation.

Eligible applicants/beneficiaries: state, territorial, and local government units.

Range: $10,000 to $37,000,000.

Activity: new program in FY 05.

HQ: Programs Office, BJA-OJP-DOJ, 810 Seventh St. NW - 4th floor, Washington, DC 20531. Phone: (202) 616-6500.

Internet: www.ojp.usdoj.gov/bja (Note: no field offices for this program.)

16.739 NATIONAL PRISON RAPE STATISTICS PROGRAM

Assistance: project grants (100 percent/12-18 months).

Purposes: pursuant to OCCSA as amended and Prison Rape Elimination Act, to collect and analyze data on the incidence of sexual assault among individuals held in federal and state prisons, local jails, and juvenile facilities, as well as on former inmates.

Eligible applicants/beneficiaries: state and local governments, private and public nonprofit and profit organizations, IHEs, individuals.

Range: $1,000,000 to $3,500,000.

Activity: new program listing in 2005; 2,730 of 8,663 facilities surveyed.

HQ: Bureau of Justice Statistics (BJA), DOJ, Washington, DC 20531 Phone: (202) 616-3561.

Internet: www.ojp.usdoj.gov (Note: no field offices for this program.)

16.740 STATEWIDE AUTOMATED VICTIM INFORMATION NOTIFICATION (SAVIN) PROGRAM ("SAVIN")

Assistance: project grants; technical information. (50 percent/2 years).

Purposes: for states to build, implement, or improve their statewide automated victim notification systems, enabling them to provide critical information to victims in near-real time and to build a nationwide information sharing capability. Funding may support program staffing, facilities, communication infrastructure, and equipment.

Eligible applicants/beneficiaries: designated state agencies, including tribal governments and territories.

Range/Average: N.A.

Activity: new program in FY 05.

HQ: Senior Policy Advisor, BJA-OJP-DOJ, 810 Seventh St. NW- 4th floor, Washington, DC 20531 Phone: (202) 616-7829.

Internet: www.ojp.usdoj.gov/BJA (Note: no field offices for this program.)

16.741 FORENSIC DNA CAPACITY ENHANCEMENT PROGRAM

Assistance: formula grants (75 percent/12-18 months).

Purposes: to improve the infrastructure and analysis capacity of existing crime laboratories. Eligible project costs include: upgrading, replacing, and purchasing equipment, instrumentation, and computer hardware and software; supplies such as offender- related evidence collection kits; certain contracted services; facilities renovation; accreditation; personnel training and continuing education.

Eligible applicants/beneficiaries: state and local government units with existing crime labs complying with DOJ requirements.

Range/Average: N.A.

Activity: new program in FY 05 (CFDA on-line version).

HQ: National Institute of Justice, OJP-DOJ, 810 Seventh St. NW, Washington, DC 20531 Phone: (202) 307-3942.

Internet: www.usdoj.gov/nij (Note: no field offices for this program.)

16.742 PAUL COVERDELL FORENSIC SCIENCES IMPROVEMENT GRANT PROGRAM

Assistance: formula grants.

Purposes: pursuant to the Paul Coverdell National Forensic Sciences Improvement Act of 2000, to improve the capacity of state and local forensic science and medical examiner services, including elimination of analysis backlogs by training and employing additional personnel. Funds may be used for personnel, computerization, laboratory equipment, supplies, accreditation, education, training, and certification.

Eligible applicants/beneficiaries: state administering agencies and local government units with approved plans.

Range/Average: N.A.

Activity: new program listing in 2005 (CFDA on-line version).

HQ: National Institute of Justice, OJP-DOJ, 810 Seventh St. NW, Washington, DC 20531 Phone: (202) 307-2942.

Internet: www.usdoj.gov/nij (Note: no field offices for this program.)

16.743 FORENSIC CASEWORK DNA BACKLOG REDUCTION PROGRAM

Assistance: formula grants. (75-100 percent/12-18 months).

Purposes: to provide funds to state and local units of government with existing crime laboratories to identify and test backlogged forensic DNA casework samples and for post-conviction testing. Funds may be used to hire new directly associated project personnel, as well as certain directly related project costs including overtime pay to current laboratory and law enforcement staff.

Eligible applicants/beneficiaries: state and local government units with existing crime labs that conduct DNA analysis whether in accredited government-owned labs or through accredited fee-for-service vendors.

Range/Average: N.A.

Activity: new program listing 2005 in (CFDA on-line version).

HQ: National Institute of Justice, OJP-DOJ, 810 Seventh St. NW, Washington, DC 20531 Phone: (202) 307-2942.

Internet: www.usdoj.gov/nij (Note: no field offices for this program.)

16.744 ANTI-GANG INITIATVE

Assistance: project grants (100 percent/to 3 years).

Purposes: for new and expanded anti-gang enforcement and prevention activities under the "Project Safe Neighborhood Initiative." Funds may be used for such purposes as providing additional personnel and equipment for widespread prevention, apprehension, prosecution, and adjudication of violators of related federal, state, and local laws.

Eligible applicants/beneficiaries: states, local government units; educational institutions; community religious and other organizations; private nonprofit organizations—certified by the appropriate U.S. Attorney's Office.

Range: formula-based amounts.

Activity: new program in FY 06 (CFDA on-line).

HQ: BJA-OJP-DOJ, Washington, DC 20531 Phone: (202) 514-2350.

Internet: www.ojp.usdoj.gov/bja.

16.745 CRIMINAL AND JUVENILE JUSTICE AND MENTAL HEALTH COLLABORATION PROGRAM

Assistance: project grants (80 percent).

Purposes: pursuant to Mentally Ill Offender Treatment and Crime Reduction Act, to facilitate collaboration among the criminal justice, juvenile justice, mental health treatment, and substance abuse systems to increase access to treatment of mentally ill offenders. Project funds may be used: to develop comprehensive plans targeting preliminarily qualified offenders; to implement such activities as establishing or expanding mental health courts and diversion/alternative prosecution and sentencing programs including crisis intervention teams and treatment accountability services; for special related training; to provide such services as special housing, in-jail, and transitional services.

Eligible applicants/beneficiaries: joint applicants including mental health agencies and states, local government units, tribes and tribal organizations—responsible for criminal justice activities.

Range/Average: N.A.

Activity: new program in FY 06 (CFDA on-line).

HQ: BJA-OJP-DOJ, 810 Seventh St. NW - 4th floor, Washington, DC 20531 Phone: (202) 616-6500.

Internet: www.ojp.usdoj.gov/BJA (Note: no field offices for this program.)

16.746 CAPITAL CASE LITIGATION

Assistance: project grants (to 18 months).

Purposes: to provide attorneys and judges who litigate death penalty cases with specialized legal training and technical assistance regarding death penalty issues, in an effort to improve the quality of representation, produce reliable jury verdicts, and minimize post conviction litigation.

Eligible applicants/beneficiaries: state-based agencies/organizations and units of local government serving defense counsel, prosecutors and judges located in states that currently enforce death penalty statutes.

Range: to $50,000.

Activity: defenders, 34-36 participants per training; judges, 30 participants per training; prosecutors, 53 students trained in Florida, 39 trained in Arkansas.

HQ: Senior Policy Advisor, BJA-OJP-DOJ, 810 Seventh St. NW, Washington, DC 20531 Phone: (202) 616-6500 Toll-Free: (866) 859-2687.

Internet: www.ojp.usdoj.gov/BJA/grant; e-mail, AskBJA@usdoj.gov (Note: no field offices for this program.)

16.747 CRIME VICTIMS' RIGHTS ACT

Assistance: project grants.

Purposes: to support the enforcement of victims' rights at the federal level by enhancing and establishing crime victim legal clinics in Arizona, Maryland and South Carolina. National Crime Victim Law Institute (NCVLI) will award subgrant funding to the legal clinics and provide intensive technical assistance, training, support and also, undertake efforts to educate and train criminal justice professionals on the Crime Victims' Rights Act.

Eligible applicants/beneficiaries: funded by line item appropriation for National Crime Victim Law Institute.

Range: one award of $1,974,456.

Activity: new program in 2006 (CFDA on-line); FY 06 estimate, one award.

HQ: Office for Victims of Crime, OJP-DOJ, 810 Seventh St. NW, Washington, DC 20531 Phone: (202) 307-5983.

Internet: www.udoj.gov/ovc (Note: no field offices for this program.)

16.748 CONVICTED OFFENDER AND/OR ARRESTEE DNA BACKLOG REDUCTION PROGRAM (IN-HOUSE ANALYSIS AND DATA REVIEW)

Assistance: formula grants (100 percent).

Purposes: pursuant to Science, State, Justice, Commerce, and Related Agencies Appropriations Act, 2006, Public Law 109-108, to accelerate the analysis of convicted offender and/or arrestee DNA samples collected by States pursuant to applicable law for database purposes ("DNA database samples"), in order to provide timely Combined DNA Index System (CODIS)- compatible data for all 13 CODIS core STR locations for state and national DNA databases. All profiles obtained from DNA database samples using program funds must be entered in the Combined DNA Index System (CODIS) within 90 days of completion of analysis and uploaded to the National DNA Index System (NDIS).

Eligible applicants/beneficiaries: eligible applicants are States with a designated existing crime laboratory that conducts analysis of DNA database samples, and meets accreditation criteria.

Range/Average: N.A.

Activity: FY 05-06, 30 awards were made.

HQ: National Institute of Justice, DOJ, 810 7th Street, NW., Washington, DC 20531. Phone: (202) 307-2942.

Internet: www.ojp.usdoj.gov/nij (Note: no field offices for this program.)

16.749 RADIATION EXPOSURE COMPENSATION PROGRAM

Assistance: project grants (100 percent).

Purposes: pursuant to The Radiation Exposure Compensation Act as amended, to offer apology and monetary compensation to individuals who, due to exposure to above-ground nuclear testing (Nevada Test Site) or employment in the uranium production industry, contracted certain cancers and other serious diseases.

Eligible applicants/beneficiaries: There are five different categories of claimants under the Radiation Exposure Compensation Program: uranium miners, uranium millers, ore transporters, onsite participants, and downwinders. Uranium miners, millers and ore transporters who were involved in the mining, milling or transport of uranium for at least one year in certain states any time between January 1, 1942 and December 31, 1971 and have been diagnosed with a specified compensable disease are eligible for a payment of $100,000. Individuals who participated onsite in a test involving atmospheric detonation of a nuclear device in certain locations or individuals who were physically present in one of the affected areas downwind of the Nevada Test Site during a period of atmospheric nuclear testing and who have been diagnosed with a specified compensable disease are eligible for a payment of $75,000 and $50,000 respectively. If an eligible individual dies before filing a claim or receiving payment, an eligible surviving beneficiary may file a claim or receive payment.

Range: lump sum payments of $50,000, $75,000, or $100,000. **Average:** FY 06, $73,077; FY 07, $68,002.

Activity: FY 06: 2,260 claims received and $129.2 million awarded to 1,768 individuals; FY 07: 1,845 claims received, $154.5 million awarded to 2,272 individuals; FY 08 estimate: 1,302 claims received and $79.3 million awarded to 1,130 individuals.

HQ: Radiation Exposure Compensation Program, DOJ, P.O. Box 146, Ben Franklin Station, Washington, DC 20044-0146. Phone: (800) 729-7327.

Internet: www.usdoj.gov/civil/torts/const/reca/index.htm. (Note: no field offices for this program.)

16.750 SUPPORT FOR ADAM WALSH ACT IMPLEMENTATION GRANT PROGRAM ("Adam Walsh Act")

Assistance: project grants (to 75 percent/12 to 18 months).

Purposes: pursuant to the Adam Walsh Child Protection and Safety Act of 2006, to assist state, local, and tribal jurisdictions with developing and/or enhancing sex offender registration and tracking programs designed to implement requirements of the Sex Offender Registration and Notification Act (SORNA) under AWA.

Eligible applicants: state, local and tribal government agencies who have the intention of substantially implementing the requirements of SORNA are eligible to apply.

Eligible beneficiaries: state, local and tribal government agencies that have sex offender registry and tracking responsibilities and public as well as private organizations participating in collaborative endeavors with such agencies.

Range: to $300,000.

Activity: N.A.

HQ: SMART Office, Office of Justice Programs, DOJ, 810 7th St. NW, Washington, DC 20531. Phone: (202) 514-4689.

Internet: www.ojp.usdoj.gov/smart. (Note: no field offices for this program.)

16.751 EDWARD BYRNE MEMORIAL COMPETITIVE GRANT PROGRAM ("Byrne Competitive Program")

Assistance: project grants (to 100 percent/12 to 18 months).

Purposes: pursuant to the Consolidated Appropriations Act of 2008, to improve the capacity and function of the criminal justice system and provide for national support efforts such as training and technical assistance projects to strategically address needs, including crime prevention, control, and reduction.

Eligible applicants: state, regional, and local and tribal governments, public and private organizations, including for-profit (commercial) and nonprofit organizations, faith-based and community organizations, and institutions of higher education.

Eligible beneficiaries: state and local governments, public and private organizations, tribal governments and individuals.

Range/Average: N.A.

Activity: not quantified specifically.

HQ: Office of Justice Programs, Bureau of Justice Assistance, DOJ, 810 7th Street , NW., Washington, DC 20531. Phone: (202) 616-6500; (866) 859-2687.

Internet: www.ojp.usdoj.gov/BJA. (Note: no field offices for this program.)

16.752 ECONOMIC HIGH-TECH AND CYBER CRIME PREVENTION

Assistance: project grants (to 100 percent/12 to 18 months).

Purposes: pursuant to the Consolidated Appropriations Act of 2008, to provide a nationwide support system for agencies involved in the prevention, investigation, and prosecution of economic electronic and cyber crimes and to support and partner with other appropriate entities in addressing related homeland security initiatives. Grants provide training, technical assistance, and/or resources to state, local and tribal law enforcement, prosecutor, and other agencies on how to prevent, combat, investigate and prosecute electronic and cyber crimes.

Eligible applicants: state, local, and tribal government agencies and public and private nonprofit organizations including faith-based and community organizations.

Eligible beneficiaries: state, local, and tribal governments and public and private organizations.

Range/Average: N.A.

Activity: not quantified specifically.

HQ: Office of Justice Programs, Bureau of Justice Assistance, DOJ, 810 7th St. NW, Washington, DC 20531. Phone: (202) 616-6500; (866) 859-2687.

Internet: www.ojp.usdoj.gov/BJA. (Note: no field offices for this program.)

16.753 CONGRESSIONALLY RECOMMENDED AWARDS ("Congressionally Recommended")

Assistance: project grants (to 100 percent/12 to 18 months).

Purposes: pursuant to the Consolidated Appropriations Act of 2008, to provide leadership and direction in improving the functioning of the criminal justice system.

Eligible applicants/beneficiaries: state, local, and federally-recognized Indian Tribal governments and agencies; public, private nonprofit, faith-based and community organizations.

Range/Average: N.A.

Activity: not quantified specifically.

HQ: Office of Justice Programs, Bureau of Justice Assistance, DOJ, 810 7th St. NW, Washington, DC 20531. Phone: (202) 616-6500; (866) 859-2687.

Internet: www.ojp.usdoj.gov/bja/index.html. (Note: no field offices for this program.)

DEPARTMENT OF LABOR

BUREAU OF LABOR STATISTICS

17.002 LABOR FORCE STATISTICS

Assistance: project grants; technical information (100 percent).

Purposes: to provide statistical data on and analyses of labor force activities—e.g., employment and unemployment, wages, occupations, layoffs, plant closings. Quarterly and monthly reports are produced, providing national, state, and local analyses. The data and analyses appear in BLS publications such as "Monthly Labor Review," "Unemployment in States and Local Areas," and "Handbook of Labor Statistics" published by BLS.

Eligible applicants/beneficiaries: cooperative agreement grants—State Workforce Agencies (SWAs) or alternate agencies. Information—anyone (from SWAs and BLS).

Range: $45,062 (Guam) to $8,088,832 (California). **Average:** $1,582,915.

Activity: monthly (sampling), labor force survey of 60,000; 400,000 establishments reporting on employment, hours, and earnings; 7,200 labor areas covered by reports on state and local employment statistics.

HQ: Office of Employment and Unemployment Statistics, BLS-DOL, Washington, DC 20212 Phone: (202) 691-6400.

Internet: www.bls.gov.

17.003 PRICES AND COST OF LIVING DATA

Assistance: technical information.

Purposes: to provide statistical data for use in evaluating consumer, producer, export, and import prices and price changes, and consumer expenditures. Data are published periodically in the "Consumer Price Index," "Producer Price Index," international price indexes, and "Consumer Expenditure Surveys," as well as in other research and study reports.

Eligible applicants/beneficiaries: general public.

Range/Average: N.A.

Activity: BLS indexes and analyses refined continuously.

HQ: Office of Prices and Living Conditions, BLS-DOL, Washington, DC 20212 Phone: (202) 606-6960.

Internet: www.bls.gov.

17.004 PRODUCTIVITY AND TECHNOLOGY DATA

Assistance: technical information.

Purposes: to provide and analyze data and trends on productivity and technology in major sectors of the U.S. economy and specific industries, and in selected countries. Pertinent reports are published, found in "Major Programs-Bureau of Labor Statistics." Also produced periodically are: consumer price indexes in foreign countries; international comparisons of productivity, labor costs, and the labor force and unemployment.

Eligible applicants/beneficiaries: general public.

Range/Average: N.A.

Activity: FY 06 estimate, 29 reports, studies, and articles completed, 3,002 individual statistical series updated.

HQ: Office of Productivity and Technology, BLS-DOL, 2 Massachusetts Ave. NE, Washington, DC 20212 Phone: (202) 691- 5600.

Internet: www.bls.gov.

17.005 COMPENSATION AND WORKING CONDITIONS

Assistance: project grants (cooperative grants); technical information (50 percent).

Purposes: to develop and publish data on levels and trends in wages, employee benefits, compensation, occupational safety and health, and work stoppages.

Eligible applicants/beneficiaries: cooperative agreements—state and local governments to operate statistical programs concerning occupational health and safety. Technical information—general public.

Range: $4,100 (Idaho) to $637,300 (California). **Average:** $111,902.

Activity: annually, 125 bulletins, reports, studies, and research articles.

HQ: none; all contacts are with field offices listed in Part IV.

Internet: www.bls.gov.

EMPLOYEE BENEFITS SECURITY ADMINISTRATION

17.150 EMPLOYEE BENEFITS SECURITY ADMINISTRATION ("EBSA")

Assistance: technical information.

Purposes: pursuant to the Employee Retirement Income Security Act of 1974 as amended (ERISA), to protect the pension, health care, and other employee benefit plans of workers and their families, by: requiring reporting and disclosure of plan and financial information; developing and enforcing fiduciary standards; providing technical assistance, advisory and informational services, workshops and conferences; deterring and correcting violations of statutes through education, voluntary compliance, and civil and criminal enforcement actions. More than $4.8 trillion in assets are under control of ERISA, covering some 6,700,000 benefit plans with 150,000,000 participants.

Eligible applicants/beneficiaries: plan administrators, trustees, participants, beneficiaries.

Range/Average: N.A.

Activity: annually, 150,000 participants, employers, and plan administrators assisted; FY 05, $1,700,000 in monetary recoveries.

HQ: EBSA-DOL, 200 Constitution Ave. NW - Rm.N5656, Washington, DC 20210 Phone: (202) 693-8666; *publications hotline,* (866) 444-3272.

Internet: www.dol.gov/dol/ebsa.

EMPLOYMENT AND TRAINING ADMINISTRATION

17.201 REGISTERED APPRENTICESHIP AND OTHER TRAINING

Assistance: advisory services/counseling; project grants.

Purposes: pursuant to the National Apprenticeship Act of 1937 as amended, to assist industry in developing, expanding, and improving apprenticeship and other training programs; to register apprentices and programs; to provide technical assistance to state apprenticeship councils; to ensure equal employment opportunities in registered apprenticeship and other training programs. (Apprentice wage rates are exempt from prevailing wages requirements of the Davis-Bacon Act and the Service Contract Act when federal and state programs are registered.)

Eligible applicants: employers, groups or associations of employers, and individual employers—with or without union participation; for grants: community- and faith- based organizations.

Eligible beneficiaries: individuals at least age 16 with sufficient ability, aptitude, and education to master the rudiments of the trade or occupation and to satisfactorily complete required theoretical instruction.

Range/Average: N.A.

Activity: FY 05, 409,000 apprentices (including in the military) trained in 28,800 registered programs; 150,700 new apprentices registered.

HQ: Administrator, Office of Apprenticeship Training, Employer and Labor Services (OATELS), ETA-DOL, 200 Constitution Ave. NW - Rm.N-5311, Washington, DC 20210 Phone: (202) 693-2796; FAX (202) 693-2808.

Internet: www.doleta.gov/atels_bat.

17.207 EMPLOYMENT SERVICE/WAGNER-PEYSER FUNDED ACTIVITIES

Assistance: formula grants; project grants. (100 percent/formula grants, to 3 years).

Purposes: pursuant to the Wagner-Peyser Act of 1933 as amended and Workforce Investment Act of 1998 (WIA), for states to provide "One-Stop" job finding, counseling, recruitment, referral, re-employment, and placement services, including a computerized interstate listing of hard-to-fill openings, and testing services for job seekers and employers seeking qualified workers—in cooperation with the DOL's U.S. Employment Service nationwide network of public employment offices. Specialized services may be provided for groups such as veterans, migrant and seasonal farm workers, ex-offenders, and the disabled, disadvantaged, youth, minorities, and older workers.

Eligible applicants: states, DC, VI, PR, Guam.

Eligible beneficiaries: employers seeking workers; persons seeking employment; associated groups. Veterans receive priority, with handicapped veterans receiving preferential treatment.

Range/Average: N.A.

Activity: formula based on average state civilian labor force and unemployment.

HQ: Administrator, Office of Workforce Security, U.S. Employment Service, ETA-DOL, Washington, DC 20210 Phone: (202) 693-3580.

Internet: www.doleta.gov.

17.225 UNEMPLOYMENT INSURANCE

Assistance: formula grants; direct payments/unrestricted use.

Purposes: pursuant to SSA, Trade Act of 1974, Federal Unemployment Tax Act, Federal Employees and Ex-Service Members Act, Robert T. Stafford Disaster Relief and Emergency Assistance Act, and amendments, to administer state programs providing unemployment compensation, trade adjustment and disaster unemployment assistance, and unemployment compensation for eligible workers, federal employees, and ex-service members.

State unemployment insurance tax collections fund benefit payments; federal unemployment insurance tax collections fund state administrative costs, and reimburse states for one-half the costs of extended benefits paid under SSA and the Federal Unemployment Tax Act; benefits to former federal civilian employees and ex-service members are paid out of the Federal Employees Compensation Account in the Unemployment Trust Fund, and reimbursed by the former employing agency; Trade Adjustment Assistance payments and training costs are paid out of the Federal Unemployment Benefits and Allowance Appropriation account in the Unemployment Trust Fund; Disaster Unemployment Assistance is paid by FEMA.

Eligible applicants: state workforce agencies, including in DC, PR, and VI.

Eligible beneficiaries: workers with wages subject to state unemployment laws, federal civilian employees, ex-servicemembers, workers whose unemployment resulted from trade imports, workers whose unemployment resulted from a Presidentially declared disaster—all are eligible if they are involuntarily unemployed, able to and available for work, and meet state eligibility and qualifying requirements. Individual state eligibility requirements are available from local "One Stop" career centers.

Range: grants, $3,000,000 to $360,000,000. **Average:** $48,200,000.

Activity: not quantified specifically.

HQ: Administrator, Office of Workforce Security, ETA-DOL, 200 Constitution Ave. NW, Washington, DC 20210 Phone: (202) 693-3029.

Internet: www.workforcesecurity.doleta.gov/.

17.235 SENIOR COMMUNITY SERVICE EMPLOYMENT PROGRAM ("SCSEP - Older Worker Program")

Assistance: formula grants; project grants (90 percent).

Purposes: pursuant to the Older Americans Act of 1965 as amended, to provide, foster, and promote useful part-time (usually 20 hours weekly) training and work opportunities for unemployed persons age 55 or over—in community service activities such as schools, hospitals, day care centers, park systems, public housing projects, weatherization and nutrition programs, libraries, etc. Training, counseling, and other supportive services may be provided. The program also assists and promotes the transition of enrollees into unsubsidized employment.

Eligible applicants: states; national public and private nonprofit agencies and organizations other than political parties; tribal organizations.

Eligible beneficiaries: adults age 55 or older, with family income at or below 125 percent of the HHS poverty level.

Range: $330,000 to $86,000,000.

Activity: 2004 estimate, 103,000 part-time positions supported; 75 grant awards annually.

HQ: Division of Adult Services, Office of Workforce Investment, ETA-DOL, 200 Constitution Ave. NW - Rm.S4209, Washington, DC 20210 Phone: (202) 693-3842; FAX (202) 693-3817.

Internet: http://doleta.gov/seniors/ (Note: no field offices for this program.)

17.245 TRADE ADJUSTMENT ASSISTANCE

Assistance: direct payments/unrestricted use; formula grants (to 78 weeks).

Purposes: pursuant to the Trade Act of 1974 as amended, Omnibus Trade and Competitiveness Act of 1988, North American Free Trade Agreement Implementation Act, and other acts, to provide "adjustment assistance" payments to and assistance for workers adversely affected by increased imports—including relocation allowances, job testing, counseling, training, and placement services. Payments may be made only after state unemployment compensation benefits have been exhausted. The maximum number of weeks of state unemployment compensation, extended benefits, and trade readjustment allowances may not exceed 52—except that benefits may be paid for an additional 26 weeks to workers participating in approved training.

Eligible applicants: groups of three of more workers, or their union or authorized representative, working with designated state agencies.

Eligible beneficiaries: unemployed workers certified by DOL as eligible to apply for adjustment assistance, and meeting specific other requirements.

Range: same as weekly amount of state unemployment benefits.

Activity: cumulatively 1975-2004, 32,545 certifications covering 4,120,180 workers.

HQ: Director, Division of Trade Adjustment Assistance, ETA-DOL, 200 Constitution Ave. NW - Rm.C-5311, Washington, DC 20210 Phone: (202) 693-3560.

Internet: www.doleta.gov.

17.258 WIA ADULT PROGRAM

Assistance: formula grants. (100 percent/to 3 years).

Purposes: pursuant to WIA, for workforce investment activities that increase the unsubsidized employment, retention and earnings, and occupational skill attainment of participants, through One Stop Career Centers providing three levels of services: (1) "core," including outreach, job search and placement assistance, and labor market information; (2) "intensive," with comprehensive assessments, individual employment plans, counseling, and career planning; (3) "training," including occupation and basic skills, linked to job opportunities. Such supportive services as transportation and child care may also be provided.

Eligible applicants: states, DC, PR, and outlying areas, which allocate funds to Workforce Investment Boards.

Eligible beneficiaries: adults age 18 or older, with priority to public assistance recipients and other low-income individuals.

Range/Average: N.A.

Activity: 2006 estimate, 330,000 participants.

HQ: Office of Workforce Investments, ETA-DOL, 200 Constitution Ave. NW - Rm.C-4510, Washington, DC 20210 Phone: (202) 693-3937.

Internet: www.doleta.gov.

17.259 WIA YOUTH ACTIVITIES ("WIA Formula Youth")

Assistance: formula grants (to 3 years).

Purposes: pursuant to WIA, to help low-income youth acquire the educational and occupational skills, training, and support needed to achieve academic and employment success and make the transition to successful careers and productive adulthood. Funds may be used by local workforce investment boards for: employment and training activities; mentoring; supportive services; and, to develop opportunities for leadership development, citizenship, and community service.

Eligible applicants: state governors.

Eligible beneficiaries: individuals age 14-21 whose total family income does not exceed the higher of the poverty line or 70 percent of the lower living standard income, and are deficient in basic literacy skills, or school dropouts, homeless, runaways, foster children, pregnant or parents, offenders or require additional assistance to complete their education or secure and hold employment.

Range/Average: N.A.

Activity: FY 04, 348,401 youth enrolled.

HQ: Division of Youth Services, Office of Workforce Investment, ETA-DOL, 200 Constitution Ave. NW, Washington, DC 20210 Phone: (202) 693-3608; FAX (202) 693-3532.

Internet: www.doleta.gov.

17.260 WIA DISLOCATED WORKERS

Assistance: formula grants; project grants. (100 percent/formula, 3 years).

Purposes: pursuant to WIA, to assist dislocated workers in obtaining the services that increase the unsubsidized employment, retention and earnings, and occupational skill attainment of participants, through One Stop Career Centers providing three levels of services: (1) "core," including outreach, job search and placement assistance, and labor market information; (2) "intensive," with comprehensive assessments, individual employment plans, counseling, and career planning; (3) "training," including occupation and basic skills, linked to job opportunities. Such supportive services as transportation and child care may also be provided. National Emergency Grant funds also are available under this program (see eligibility factors below).

Eligible applicants: states, DC, PR, and outlying areas, including for National Emergency Grant funds.

Eligible beneficiaries: workers that have lost their jobs, including those dislocated because of plant closings or mass layoffs, and unlikely to return to their previous industry or occupations; formerly self-employed individuals; displaced, dependent homemakers no longer supported by the other's income. National Emergency Grant Funds—same eligibility; also includes certain military defense employees and individuals affected by mass layoffs, natural disasters, federal government actions, and other specified circumstances.

Range/Average: N.A.

Activity: estimate FY 06, 292,000 participants.

HQ: Office of Workforce Investments, ETA-DOL, 200 Constitution Ave. NW - Rm.C-4510, Washington, DC 20210 Phone: (202) 693-3937.

Internet: www.doleta.gov.

17.261 WIA PILOTS, DEMONSTRATIONS, AND RESEARCH PROJECTS

Assistance: project grants. (to 100 percent/1-2 years).

Purposes: pursuant to WIA, for pilot and demonstration projects with interstate validity, addressing national employment and training problems. Projects must include direct services to individuals to enhance employment opportunities, and an evaluation component. Eligible activities include: establishing advanced manufacturing technology skill centers involving local partnerships; training to upgrade the skills of employed workers or to increase employment of out-of-school youth residing in enterprise communities or empowerment zones; joint programs with DOD to develop training programs using innovative learning technology; distance learning projects; partnerships with national organizations experienced in employment and training programs; assistance to public housing authorities providing resident job training; local project evaluation.

Eligible applicants/beneficiaries: state and local governments, federal agencies, private nonprofit and profit organizations including religious and community-based, and educational institutions.

Range: $100,000 to $1,750,000.

Activity: FY 05, 50 new projects approved.

HQ: Division of Pilots, Demonstrations and Research, Office of Policy and Research, ETA-DOL, 200 Constitution Ave. NW - Rm. N- 4470, Washington, DC 20210 Phone: (202) 693-3676.

Internet: www.doleta.gov.

17.264 NATIONAL FARMWORKER JOBS PROGRAM

Assistance: formula grants; project grants. (100 percent/1-4 years).

Purposes: pursuant to WIA, for individual employability development assistance and related services to migrant and seasonal farm workers and their dependents suffering chronic unemployment and under-employment. Services may include initial assessment, "One-Stop" Center services, job placement, eligibility determination, intensive case management, basic education, drop-out prevention assistance, allowance payments, training including classroom and on-the-job, and emergency and other supportive services.

Eligible applicants: public agencies and state and local government units; private nonprofit organizations.

Eligible beneficiaries: individuals who, during any consecutive 12 months in the prior 24-month period, were seasonal or migrant farm workers, and are legally available for work in compliance with Selective Service Act requirements.

Range: $100,000 to $7,000,000.

Activity: FY 05, 53 grants awarded.

HQ: Division of Adult Services, Office of Workforce Investment, ETA-DOL, 200 Constitution Ave. NW - Rm.S-4206, Washington, DC 20210 Phone: (202) 693-3843; FAX (202) 693-3945.

Internet: http://wdsc.doleta.gov/msfw/. (Note: no field offices for this program.)

17.265 NATIVE AMERICAN EMPLOYMENT AND TRAINING ("Section 166 Program - Indian Program")

Assistance: project grants. (100 percent/1-3 years).

Purposes: pursuant to WIA, for employment and training activities for native Americans, including classroom and on-the-job training, work experience, youth employment programs. Grant funds may be used to pay for such services as day care, health care, job search, relocation and transportation allowances.

Eligible applicants/beneficiaries: tribes, bands, or groups; Alaska native villages or groups; Hawaiian native communities; consortia of the foregoing groups.

Range: $13,898 to $6,011,664. **Average:** $291,834.

Activity: 2004, 17,883 participants.

HQ: Indian and Native American Programs, Division of Adult Services, Office of Workforce Investment, ETA-DOL, 200 Constitution Ave. NW - Rm.S-4206, Washington, DC 20210 Phone: (202) 693-3737; FAX (202) 693-3818.

Internet: http://wdsc.doleta.gov/dinap (Note: no field offices for this program.)

17.266 WORK INCENTIVE GRANTS

Assistance: project grants. (100 percent/2 years).

Purposes: pursuant to WIA and the Wagner-Peyser Act, to develop a "One-Stop" system infrastructure toward the achievement of model seamless and comprehensive services for the disabled, increasing their employability, job retention, earning capacity, and occupational skill attainment. Funds support expanding the capacity within the One-Stop system through "Disability Program Navigator" (DPN) positions to better coordinate employment services available to the handicapped; DOL program activities are coordinated with SSA.

Eligible applicants/beneficiaries: states and tribal entities capable of launching DPN initiatives; consortia.

Range: $400,000 to $2,000,000.

Activity: 267 DPN positions funded in 17 participating states.

HQ: Older Workers and Disability Unit, Office of Workforce Investment, ETA-DOL, 200 Constitution Ave. NW, Washington, DC 20210 Phone: (202) 693-3844; FAX (202) 693-3818; TTY (202) 693-2871.

Internet: www.doleta.gov/disability.

17.267 INCENTIVE GRANTS - WIA SECTION 503

Assistance: formula grants; project grants. (100 percent/to 3 years).

Purposes: pursuant to WIA and the Carl D. Perkins Vocational and Applied Technology Education Amendments of 1998, for innovative programs furthering the purposes of the authorizing acts—including services and activities beyond those provided with regular WIA funding. Applicants should plan activities promoting cooperation and collaboration among administering agencies.

Eligible applicants/beneficiaries: states, DC, VI, PR, Guam—provided their performance under WIA exceeds expected outcome levels.

Range: $750,000 to $3,000,000; (may fluctuate based on available award money).

Activity: new program listing in 2003.

HQ: Chief, Division of System Accomplishments and Accountability, Office of Performance and Technology, ETA-DOL, 200 Constitution Ave. NW - Rm.S5206, Washington, DC 20210 Phone: (202) 693-3031.

Internet: www.doleta.gov/performance (Note: no field offices for this program.)

17.268 H-1B JOB TRAINING GRANTS

Assistance: project grants. (from 50 percent/1-3 years).

Purposes: pursuant to the American Competitiveness and Workforce Improvement Act of 1998, to engage business, educational and the workforce investment system to work together to develop solutions to the workforce challenges facing high growth industries. The ETA has identified 14 sectors that are projected to add substantial numbers of jobs to the economy or are existing or emerging businesses being transformed by technology or innovation and require new skills for workers: Advanced Manufacturing, Aerospace, Automotive, Biotechnology, Construction, Energy, Financial Services, Geospatial Technology, Health Care, Homeland Security, Hospitality, Information Technology, Retail, and Transportation.

Eligible applicants/beneficiaries: generally, public and private for-profit and non-profit organizations, including businesses, trade associations, Workforce Investment Boards, One-Stop Career Centers, units of state and local government, economic development agencies, education and training providers including community colleges and other faith-based organizations.

Range: High Growth Job Training Initiative, $750,000 to $1,500,000; WIRED Initiative, to $5,000,000.

Activity: as of March, 2006: High Growth Job Training, 131 grants; WIRED Initiative, 13 regional awards.

HQ: Business Relations Group, Office of Workforce Investment, ETA-DOL, 200 Constitution Ave. NW - Room N-4643, Washington, DC 20210 Phone: (202) 693-3949.

Internet: www.doleta.gov; e-mail, businessrelations@dol.gov.

17.269 COMMUNITY BASED JOB TRAINING GRANTS

Assistance: project grants. (to 100 percent/2-3 years).

Purposes: pursuant to WIA, for capacity building by community colleges to train workers to develop the skills required to succeed in: local industries and occupations expected to experience high growth; industries where demand for qualified workers is outstripping the supply. Funding supports capacity building and training activities. Grants are competitive, building on DOL-ETA's High Growth Job Training Initiative, a national model for demand-driven workforce development implemented by strategic partnerships.

Eligible applicants: first round—only approved community colleges including tribally-controlled IHEs. Subsequent funding rounds—aforementioned community colleges, community college districts, state community college systems, One-Stop Career Centers who meet criteria.

Eligible beneficiaries: dislocated and incumbent workers, new workforce entrants; untapped labor force pools including immigrant workers, workers with disabilities, veterans, older workers, youth, etc.

Range: $500,000 to $2,000,000.

Activity: new program listing in 2006 (CFDA on-line); FY 06, 70 community colleges funded in 40 states.

HQ: Office of Workforce Investment, ETA-DOL, 200 Constitution Ave. NW - Rm.-N-4643, Washington, DC 20210 Phone: (202) 693-3949.

Internet: www.doleta.gov; e-mail, busiinessrelations@dol.gov.

17.270 REINTEGRATION OF EX-OFFENDERS

Assistance: project grants. (100 percent/1-3 years).

Purposes: pursuant to WIA, to reduce prisoner recidivism by helping inmates find work when they return to their communities through employment-centered programs that incorporate mentoring, job training and placement, and other comprehensive transitional services.

Eligible applicants: religious and other community organizations located or with a staff presence in the urban community being served, and with the capacity to serve as the lead project agencies.

Eligible beneficiaries: individuals age 18 or older that have been convicted as an adult and imprisoned pursuant to an Act of Congress or state law, and that have never been convicted of a violent or sex-related offense—including those residing in a halfway house.

Average: $660,000.

Activity: new program listing in 2006 (CFDA on-line); FY 06, 30 grants awarded.

HQ: Division of Youth Services, Office of Workforce Investment, ETA-DOL, 200 Constitution Ave. NW - Rm.N-4511, Washington, DC 20210 Phone: (202) 693-3934.

Internet: www.doleta.gov.

17.271 WORK OPPORTUNITY TAX CREDIT PROGRAM

Assistance: formula grants (100 percent).

Purposes: pursuant to Small Business Job Protection Act of 1996, Taxpayer relief Act of 1997 and Working Families Tax Relief Act of 2004, as amended, to assist individuals from 10 target groups who face significant barriers to employment move from economic dependency to self-sufficiency by encouraging employment by private-sector businesses in the form of a tax credit against the wages paid to new hires during the first year of employment.

Eligible applicants: states, DC, VI, PR; individuals may not apply.

Eligible beneficiaries: employers seeking WOTC and/or WTWTC target group workers and target group workers seeking employment. Workers must be verified by state workforce agencies before certification will be issued to employer.

Range/Average: N.A.

Activity: not quantified specifically.

HQ: Office of Workforce Investment, ETA-DOL, 200 Constitution Ave. NW, Room C-4510, Washington, DC 20210 Phone: (202) 693-3937.

Internet: www.doleta.gov; www.ows.doleta.gov/employ/tax/asp.

17.272 PERMANENT LABOR CERTIFICATION FOR FOREIGN WORKERS

Assistance: specialized services.

Purposes: pursuant to Immigration and Nationality Act of 1952, as amended, to assist employers by supplementing the U.S. workforce with needed skills and assure that the jobs, wages, and working conditions of American workers will not be adversely affected by the admission of foreign workers.

Eligible applicants/beneficiaries: any employer who is unable to find qualified U.S. workers and who seeks to employ foreign workers in employment categories listed in DOL Schedule A (Part 656.10, Title 20, Code of Regulations).

Range/Average: N.A.

Activity: FY 05, 51,476 new permanent applications received.

HQ: Administrator, Office of Foreign Labor Certification, DOL, 200 Constitution Ave. NW, Room C-4312, Washington, DC 20210 Phone: (202) 693-3010.

Internet: www.foreignlaborcert.doleta.gov.

17.273 TEMPORARY LABOR CERTIFICATION FOR FOREIGN WORKERS

Assistance: formula grants; specialized services.

Purposes: pursuant to Immigration and Nationality Act of 1952, Immigration Act of 1990, and Immigration Reform and Control Act of 1986, as amended, to provide greater protection for U.S. and foreign workers without interfering with an employer's right to obtain temporary foreign workers to work in specialty occupations; to enable agricultural employers to obtain temporary seasonal employees when domestic workers are not available; to protect domestic workers against unfair competition from foreign workers; and to assure adequate working and living conditions for all workers.

Eligible applicants/beneficiaries: individual employers, partnership, corporation, association of agricultural producers, and other authorized agents may file on behalf of their employers or members. Grants related to H-2A and H-2B programs: State Workforce Agencies.

Range/Average: N.A.

Activity: 2005, 317,714 determinations issued; 6,598 employers certified for 48,337 workers.

HQ: Administrator, Office of Foreign Labor Certification, DOL, 200 Constitution Ave. NW, Room C-4312, Washington, DC 20210 Phone: (202) 693-3010.

Internet: www.foreignlaborcert.doleta.gov.

17.274 YOUTHBUILD

Assistance: project grants. (100 percent/2-3 years).

Purposes: pursuant to Workforce Investment Act (WIA) of 1998, Title I, Subtitle D, Section 173A, and other laws, to provide disadvantaged youth with: the education and employment skills necessary to achieve economic self sufficiency in occupations in high demand and postsecondary education and training opportunities; opportunities for meaningful work and service to their communities; and opportunities to develop employment and leadership skills and a commitment to community development among youth in low-income communities.

Eligible applicants: public or private nonprofit agency/organization (including a consortium of such agencies or organizations), including: community-based or faith-based organizations; an entity carrying out activities under this WIA, such as a local workforce investment board or One-Stop Career Center; a community action agency; a State or local housing development agency; an Indian tribe or other agency primarily serving Indians; a community development corporation; a State or local youth service conservation corps; or any other public or private non-profit entity that provides education or employment training and can meet the required elements of the grant.

Eligible beneficiaries: individuals who are between the ages of 16 and 24 on the date of enrollment, a member of a disadvantaged youth population (such as a member of a low-income family, or in foster care), a youth offender, an individual with a disability, a child of an incarcerated parent, a migrant youth and a school dropout. Up to 25 percent of the participants in the program may be youth who do not meet the education and disadvantaged criteria above but who are: basic skills deficient, despite attainment of a secondary school diploma, General Education Development (GED) credential, or other State-recognized equivalent; or have been referred by a local secondary school for participation in a YouthBuild program leading to the attainment of a secondary school diploma.

Range: $350,000 - $550,000. **Average:** $500,000.

Activity: new program listing, FY 06, (formerly administered by HUD, now DOL program).

HQ: Division of Youth Services, Office of Workforce Investment, Employment and Training Administration, DOL, 200 Constitution Ave., NW., Room N-4511 Washington, D.C. 20210. Phone: (202 693-3377.

Internet: http://www.doleta.gov; e-mail youthbuild@dol.gov.

EMPLOYMENT STANDARDS ADMINISTRATION

17.301 NON-DISCRIMINATION AND AFFIRMATIVE ACTION BY FEDERAL CONTRACTORS AND FEDERALLY ASSISTED CONSTRUCTION CONTRACTORS ("Office of Federal Contract Compliance Programs - OFCCP")

Assistance: investigation of complaints.

Purposes: pursuant to the Rehabilitation Act of 1973, Vietnam Era Readjustment Assistance Act of 1974, Veterans Codification Act of 1991, ADA, Immigration Reform and Control Act of 1986, and amendments, to enforce nondiscrimination and affirmative action regulations covering employment by federal contractors including subcontractors and those involved in federally-assisted construction. Complaints alleging employment discrimination on the basis of race, sex, religion, color, national origin, disability, or covered veteran status may be filed with OFCCP. Technical advice and assistance are available to employers.

Eligible applicants/beneficiaries: employment applicants, employees, and former employees of federal contractors or federally involved contractors performing work in the U.S., Panama Canal Zone, and possessions and territories—including those recruited in the U.S. to perform work abroad.

Range/Average: N.A.

Activity: FY 05, $45,000,000 in financial remedies to minority, female, and handicapped workers; completed 2,734 compliance evaluations covering over 3 million workers.

HQ: Deputy Assistant Secretary, OFCCP, Employment Standards Administration-DOL, Washington, DC 20210 Phone: (202) 693-0101.

Internet: www.dol.gov.

17.302 LONGSHORE AND HARBOR WORKERS' COMPENSATION

Assistance: direct payments/unrestricted use.

Purposes: pursuant to the Longshore and Harbor Workers Compensation Act as extended, to replace and supplement income to compensate for permanent disability or death resulting from injury, including occupational disease; to provide benefits for certain medical expenses including hospital care, and funeral expenses up to $3,000. Benefits are paid by private insurers or self-insured employers; federal funds are available in certain cases of permanent total disability and death.

Eligible applicants/beneficiaries: longshore and harbor workers; certain maritime employees working on U.S. navigable waters and in pier and dock areas; employees working on the Outer Continental Shelf, of nonappropriated fund instrumentalities, of private employers working in DC within specified periods or abroad under U.S. government contracts; survivors. PR is not covered.

Range: disability—two-thirds of average weekly wage; death benefits - 50 percent of average wages of deceased, to widow or widower, plus 16.7 percent for each surviving child with a 66.7 percent limit. Benefits are limited to 200 percent of national average weekly wage. Payments are made for the period of total or partial disability, with no monetary limit; death benefits are paid to the spouse until death or remarriage, and to children until age 18—or 23 if qualified as a student.

Activity: annually, 20,000 new lost-time injury claims.

HQ: Division of Longshore and Harbor Workers' Compensation, Office of Workers' Compensation Programs, Employment Standards Administration-DOL, Washington, DC 20210 Phone: (202) 693-0038.

Internet: www.dol.gov.

17.303 WAGE AND HOUR STANDARDS ("Federal Wage-Hour Laws")

Assistance: advisory services/counseling; investigation of complaints.

Purposes: pursuant to the Fair Labor Standards Act, Walsh-Healy Public Contracts Act, Davis-Bacon Act, Immigration and Nationality Acts, Family and Medical Leave Act of 1993, amendments, and other acts, to provide and enforce standards protecting wages and working conditions of working persons with respect to minimum rate of pay, overtime pay, prevailing hourly wage rates, fringe benefits, child labor, and family and medical leave including for adoptive parents; to enforce wage payment standards for professional performers and related professional employees, as well as for students, nonimmigrant agricultural and certain nonagricultural workers and employees, seasonal workers, handicapped workers, apprentices, and other employment categories; to curtail employer use of lie detector tests. Generally, federal wage and hour standards apply to employees engaged in interstate or foreign commerce, or in the production of goods for such commerce, and to government employees at all levels. Funding for this program includes **17.306** and **17.308**.

Eligible applicants/beneficiaries: any covered employee in the U.S., territories, possessions, and Outer Continental Shelf lands. Family and medical leave provisions apply to all public employers and private employers with 50 or more employees within 75-mile radius of work site.

Range/Average: N.A.

Activity: FY 04, $196,000,000 in back wages recovered.

HQ: Administrator, Wage and Hour Division, Employment Standards Administration-DOL, Washington, DC 20210. Phone: (202) 693-0051.

Internet: www.dol.gov.

17.306 CONSUMER CREDIT PROTECTION ("Federal Wage Garnishment Law")

Assistance: advisory services/counseling; investigation of complaints.

Purposes: pursuant to the Consumer Credit Protection Act as amended, to enforce federal restrictions on the amount of a person's earnings that may be garnisheed, and prohibiting employers from discharging employees by reason of garnishment for any one indebtedness. Earnings are defined as compensation paid or payable for personal services, whether as wages, salary, commission, bonuses, including periodic payments under a pension or retirement program. Funding for this program is included in **17.303**.

Eligible applicants/beneficiaries: persons with earnings subjected to garnishment—in the U.S., territories, and possessions.

Range/Average: N.A.

Activity: not quantified specifically.

HQ: Administrator, Wage and Hour Division, Employment Standards Administration-DOL, Washington, DC 20210 Phone: (202) 693-0051.

Internet: www.dol.gov.

17.307 COAL MINE WORKERS' COMPENSATION ("Black Lung")

Assistance: direct payments/unrestricted use.

Purposes: pursuant to the Federal Mine Safety and Health Amendments Act of 1977 as amended, to pay monthly cash benefits to coal miners totally disabled with black lung disease, and to their surviving dependents.

Eligible applicants/beneficiaries: disabled coal miners; widows, and other surviving dependents. Included are some workers involved in coal transportation in and around mines, and in coal mine construction. Beneficiaries must have become "totally disabled" from coal workers' pneumoconiosis, as defined in the Act. Applicants may work in areas other than coal mines and remain eligible for benefits. Benefits may be reduced in cases of excess earnings.

Range: effective January 2006, $574 monthly for claimant only, to $1,149 for three or more dependents (not including medical services).

Activity: FY 05, over 102,000 beneficiaries, 18,000 dependents received benefits.

HQ: Director, Division of Coal Mine Workers' Compensation, Office of Workers' Compensation Programs, Employment Standards Administration-DOL, Washington, DC 20210 Phone: (202) 693-0046.

Internet: www.dol.gov/esa/regs/compliance/owcp/bltable.htm.

17.308 FARM LABOR CONTRACTOR REGISTRATION ("Crew Leader")

Assistance: advisory services/counseling; investigation of complaints.

Purposes: pursuant to the Migrant and Seasonal Agricultural Worker Protection Act as amended, to enforce regulations covering farm labor contractors, agricultural employers, and agricultural associations regarding such factors as wages, records, transportation, health, safety, liability insurance, and housing provided for migrant and seasonal agricultural workers. Funding for this program is included in **17.303**.

Eligible applicants/beneficiaries: contractors and their full- time or regular employees that recruit, solicit, hire, furnish, or transport migrant or seasonal agricultural workers for employment for a fee in any form must register with DOL.

Range/Average: N.A.

Activity: FY 04, $1,194,000 in back pay collected for 3,700 agricultural workers.

HQ: Administrator, Wage and Hour Division, Employment Standards Administration-DOL, Washington, DC 20210 Phone: (202) 693-0051.

Internet: www.dol.gov.

17.309 LABOR ORGANIZATION REPORTS ("Landrum- Griffin Act")

Assistance: advisory services/counseling; technical information; investigation of complaints.

Purposes: pursuant to the Labor-Management Reporting and Disclosure Act of 1959 as amended, to provide for reporting and disclosure of financial transactions and administrative practices of labor organizations, employers, labor consultants, and others required to report under the Landrum-Griffin Act; to provide standards for the election of union officers, administration of trusteeships, fiduciary responsibilities of union officers, and rights of union members; for court enforcement of safeguards pertaining to union organizations.

Eligible applicants/beneficiaries: union officers, members, organizations. All required reports are available for disclosure to the general public.

Range/Average: N.A.

Activity: FY 05, 42,830 reports received and processed; 525 investigations; 619 compliance audits; 35 elections supervised.

HQ: Office of Labor-Management Standards-DOL, 200 Constitution Ave. NW, Washington, DC 20210 Phone: (202) 693-0123; *Public Disclosure Room (N-5608)*, (202) 693-0125.

Internet: www.dol.gov; e-mail, OLMS-Public@dol.gov.

17.310 ENERGY EMPLOYEES OCCUPATIONAL ILLNESS COMPENSATION

Assistance: direct payments/unrestricted use.

Purposes: pursuant to Energy Employees Occupational Illness Compensation Program Act of 2000 as amended, to provide lump-sum payments and medical benefits to: covered DOE employees and their survivors; certain DOE vendors, contractors, and subcontractors; individuals and survivors found eligible by DOJ under the Radiation Exposure Compensation Act, as well as eligible uranium miners, millers, and ore transporters. Benefits are variable, reflecting degree of impairment and years of qualifying wage- loss.

Eligible applicants/beneficiaries: employees and survivors, as applicable, of DOE others (as cited under "Purposes").

Range: lump-sum payments: Part B, $150,000; Part E, $250,000; medical coverage, no limitation.

Activity: new program listing in 2006 (CFDA on-line). Annually, 20,000 new claims.

HQ: Division of Energy Employees Occupational Illness Compensation, Office of Workers' Compensation Programs, Employment Standards Administration-DOL, Washington, DC 20210 Phone: (202) 693-0081.

Internet: www.dol.gov.

OCCUPATIONAL SAFETY AND HEALTH ADMINISTRATION

17.502 OCCUPATIONAL SAFETY AND HEALTH—SUSAN HARWOOD TRAINING GRANTS

Assistance: project grants.

Purposes: pursuant to the Occupational Safety and Health Act, to provide occupational safety and health training and education to employees and employers, particularly in the recognition, avoidance, and abatement of workplace hazards.

Eligible applicants/beneficiaries: nonprofit organizations.

Range: $56,000 to $999,000.

Activity: FY 05, 38 grants.

HQ: Assistant Secretary, OSHA-DOL, Washington, DC 20210 Phone: (202) 693-2000; (847) 297-4810.

Internet: www.osha.gov.

17.503 OCCUPATIONAL SAFETY AND HEALTH—STATE PROGRAM

Assistance: project grants (50 percent).

Purposes: pursuant to the Occupational Safety and Health Act, for state administration and enforcement of approved occupational safety and health programs.

Eligible applicants/beneficiaries: designated state agencies.

Range: $201,000 to $22,942,000.

Activity: FY 06 estimate, 55,000 state enforcement inspections.

HQ: Assistant Secretary, OSHA-DOL, Washington, DC 20210 Phone: (202) 693-1919.

Internet: www.osha.gov.

17.504 CONSULTATION AGREEMENTS

Assistance: project grants (90 percent).

Purposes: pursuant to the Occupational Safety and Health Act, for consultative workplace safety and health services by states to smaller employers, primarily those with hazardous operations.

Eligible applicants: designated state agencies.

Eligible beneficiaries: any private employer.

Range: $199,000 to $5,161,000.

Activity: FY 06 estimate, 32,250 consultation visits.

HQ: Assistant Secretary, OSHA-DOL, Washington, DC 20210 Phone: (202) 693-1919.

Internet: www.osha.gov.

17.505 OSHA DATA INITIATIVE

Assistance: project grants (100 percent).

Purposes: pursuant to the Occupational Safety and Health Act, for cooperative agreements for the collection of injury and illness data from employers in specified industries—for OSHA use in targeting interventions.

Eligible applicants/beneficiaries: designated state agencies.

Range: $5,750 to $186,000.

Activity: new program listing in 2004. FY 06 estimate, 80,000 employer samples collected.

HQ: Assistant Secretary, OSHA-DOL, Washington, DC 20210 Phone: (202) 693-1919.

Internet: www.osha.gov.

MINE SAFETY AND HEALTH ADMINISTRATION

17.600 MINE HEALTH AND SAFETY GRANTS

Assistance: project grants (80 percent).

Purposes: pursuant to the Federal Mine Safety and Health Amendments Act of 1977 as amended, to develop and enforce state laws and regulations related to the health and safety of miners; to improve workmen's compensation and occupational disease laws and programs; for miner training.

Eligible applicants/beneficiaries: any mining state.

Range: $3,700 to $597,000. **Average:** $156,000.

Activity: not quantified specifically.

HQ: Assistant Secretary/Mine Safety and Health, Mine Safety and Health Administration-DOL, 1100 Wilson Blvd., Arlington, VA 22209 Phone: (202) 693-9572, -9580.

Internet: www.msha.gov (Note: no field offices for this program.)

17.601 MINE HEALTH AND SAFETY COUNSELING AND TECHNICAL ASSISTANCE

Assistance: advisory services/counseling; technical information.

Purposes: pursuant to the Federal Mine Safety and Health Amendments Act of 1977 as amended, to establish or improve health and safety conditions in and around coal, metal, and nonmetallic mines and mineral facilities—through special studies, technical assistance, investigations, equipment testing.

Eligible applicants/beneficiaries: states, organizations, or individuals.

Range/Average: N.A.

Activity: not quantified specifically.

HQ: Assistant Secretary/Mine Safety and Health, Mine Safety and Health Administration-DOL, 1100 Wilson Blvd., Arlington, VA 22209 Phone: (202) 693-9472, -9478.

Internet: www.msha.gov.

17.602 MINE HEALTH AND SAFETY EDUCATION AND TRAINING

Assistance: training.

Purposes: pursuant to the Federal Mine Safety and Health Amendments Act of 1977 as amended, to provide initial and advanced technical mine safety and health training of federal mine inspectors, miners, and others. Curriculum materials and audiovisual programs are available.

Eligible applicants/beneficiaries: mine operators, miners, or their agents.

Range/Average: N.A.

Activity: 1,241 course days of federal employee training; mining industry, 208 days; distribution of 6,323,651 mine safety publications.

HQ: Director, Educational Policy and Development, Mine Safety and Health, Mine Safety and Health Administration-DOL, 1100 Wilson Blvd., Arlington, VA 22209 Phone: (202) 693-9572, (304) 256-3201.

Internet: www.msha.gov.

17.603 BROOKWOOD-SAGO GRANT

Assistance: project grants (100 percent).

Purposes: pursuant to the Mine Improvement and New Emergency Response Act of 2006 (Miner Act), to provide training and other educational programs or develop training materials for employers and miners concerning safety and health topics in priority areas designated by MSHA.

Eligible applicants: any mining state of the United States and nonprofit public and private organizations.

Eligible beneficiaries: miner-training program recipients, miners, any organization employing these individuals, and mine operators.

Range/Average: at least $50,000.

Activity: FY 07, 7 grants: PA, $135,000; IN, $50,000; WV, $50,000; CO, $53,000; VI, $85,000; UT, $ 54,000; and the United Mine Worker of America, $73,000.

HQ: Director, Educational Policy and Development, Mine Safety and Health, Mine Safety and Health Administration-DOL, 1100 Wilson Blvd. - Rm. 2102, Arlington, VA 22209-3909. Phone: (202) 693-9570.

Internet: www.msha.gov. (Note: no field offices for this program.)

WOMEN'S BUREAU, OFFICE OF THE SECRETARY

17.700 WOMEN'S BUREAU

Assistance: advisory services/counseling.

Purposes: to develop training and employment policies and programs affecting the employment of women and their retirement security; to expand employment opportunities for women and promote their entry into better paying jobs, especially in new technology and nontraditional occupations. Project examples: online newsletter; apprenticeship programs; Work and Family projects; planning for employer-sponsored child care; Girls 'E-Mentoring in Science, Engineering & Technology, and in nursing.

Eligible applicants/beneficiaries: any individual or group, including in territories.

Range/Average: N.A.

Activity: not quantified specifically.

HQ: Director, Women's Bureau, OS-DOL, Washington, DC 20210 Phone: (202) 693-6710; Office of Information and Support Services (Rm.S3305), (202) 693-6727.

Internet: www.dol.gov.

OFFICE OF DISABILITY EMPLOYMENT POLICY

17.720 DISABILITY EMPLOYMENT POLICY DEVELOPMENT

Assistance: project grants.

Purposes: to promote employment opportunities for persons with disabilities by providing disability employment policy leadership to DOL and other federal agencies, through: research and dissemination activities; outreach initiatives; coordination with such other initiatives as Workforce Investment Act projects and programs; technical information about the provisions of the ADA to business leaders, organized labor, and others; and, a range of related activities.

Eligible applicants/beneficiaries: varies according to grant.

Range: $15,000 to $1,500,000.

Activity: new program listing in 2002 (replacing former program **53.001**, operated by the President's Committee on Employment of People with Disabilities).

HQ: Office of Disability Employment Policy, DOL, 200 Constitution Ave. NW - Rm.S1303, Washington, DC 20210 Phone: (202) 693-7881; TTY (202) 693-7888; FAX (202) 693-7888.

Internet: www.dol.gov/odep; e-mail, infoodep@dol.gov (Note: no field offices for this program.)

OFFICE OF THE ASSISTANT SECRETARY FOR VETERANS' EMPLOYMENT AND TRAINING

17.801 DISABLED VETERANS' OUTREACH PROGRAM ("DVOP")

Assistance: formula grants (100 percent).

Purposes: pursuant to the Veterans' Rehabilitation and Education Amendments of 1980, to pay the salaries and expenses of DVOP specialists assigned to meet the employment needs of eligible veterans, with emphasis on those that are economically or educationally disadvantaged including the homeless and those with barriers to employment.

Eligible applicants/beneficiaries: state employment security agencies.

Range: $106,000 to $11,900,000. **Average:** $1,543,000.

Activity: FY 04, 220,689 veterans and other eligible entered employment, including 25,506 disabled veterans.

HQ: Assistant Secretary/Veterans' Employment and Training-DOL, 200 Constitution Ave. NW - Rm.S-1312, Washington, DC 20210 Phone: (202) 693-4708.

Internet: www.dol.gov/dol/vets.

17.802 VETERANS' EMPLOYMENT PROGRAM ("Veterans' Workforce Investment Program - VWIP")

Assistance: project grants (to 100 percent).

Purposes: pursuant to WIA, to enhance services to veterans in employment and training programs and related services; to provide innovative employment and training services and projects; for outreach and public information programs.

Eligible applicants: governors, state and local Workforce Investment Boards, public agencies, private nonprofit and community-based organizations.

Eligible beneficiaries: service-connected disabled veterans, veterans with significant employment barriers, and those recently separated from military service (48 months).

Range: 17 new grants totaling $3,800.000; 9 extensions totaling $3,100,000; $500,000 to support Chronic Homelessness Initiative.

Activity: 2004, 2,561 veterans of 3,728 enrolled entered employment.

HQ: Assistant Secretary/Veterans' Employment and Training-DOL, 200 Constitution Ave. NW - Rm.S-1312, Washington, DC 20210 Phone: (202) 693-4708.

Internet: www.dol.gov/dol/vets.

17.803 UNIFORMED SERVICES EMPLOYMENT AND REEMPLOYMENT RIGHTS

Assistance: advisory services/counseling; technical information; investigation of complaints.

Purposes: to assist in the employment and reemployment of non- career veterans or candidates for the uniformed services. (Discrimination in employment and acts of reprisal by employers are prohibited—against persons because of their obligation in the uniformed services, filing a claim, seeking assistance concerning an alleged violation, testifying in a proceeding, or otherwise participating in an investigation.) Unresolved complaints are referred to DOJ or to the DOL Office of Special Counsel for representation in federal district courts.

Eligible applicants/beneficiaries: persons that have served voluntarily or involuntarily on active duty, active duty for training, or training duty with the uniformed services, including reservists and National Guard members. Entitlement ceases upon termination of service with a bad conduct or dishonorable discharge, or upon separation under other then honorable conditions.

Range/Average: N.A.

Activity: FY 04, 895 new complaint cases processed, 1,440 cases closed; responses to 187,000 public inquiries.

HQ: Office of Veterans' Employment and Training-DOL, 200 Constitution Ave. NW - Rm.S-1312, Washington, DC 20210 Phone: (202) 693-4701.

Internet: www.dol.gov/dol/vets.

17.804 LOCAL VETERANS' EMPLOYMENT REPRESENTATIVE PROGRAM ("LVER Program")

Assistance: formula grants (100 percent).

Purposes: pursuant to the Servicemen's Readjustment Act of 1944, to fund salaries and expenses of Local Veterans' Employment Representatives assigned to conduct outreach to employers concerning employment, training, and job placement services and opportunities for veterans.

Eligible applicants/beneficiaries: state employment agencies.

Range: $57,000 to $6,881,000. **Average:** $1,455,057.

Activity: FY 04, 217,218 entered employment through the LVER program, including 21,641 disabled veterans.

HQ: Assistant Secretary/Veterans' Employment and Training-DOL, 200 Constitution Ave. NW - Rm.S-1312, Washington, DC 20210 Phone: (202) 693-4708.

Internet: www.dol.gov/dol/vets.

17.805 HOMELESS VETERANS REINTEGRATION PROJECT

Assistance: project grants (100 percent).

Purposes: pursuant to the SBMHAA as amended, for projects to reintegrate homeless veterans into the labor force—through activities including employment and training services, support services, linkages with other service providers, and outreach performed by formerly homeless veterans.

Eligible applicants/beneficiaries: state and local Workforce Investment Boards and public agencies, private nonprofit and profit organizations and entities.

Range: $100,000 to $300,000.

Activity: FY 05, 8,191 homeless veterans of 13,060 enrolled entered employment.

HQ: Assistant Secretary/Veterans' Employment and Training-DOL, 200 Constitution Ave. NW - Rm.S-1312, Washington, DC 20210 Phone: (202) 693-4708.

Internet: www.dol.gov/dol/vets.

17.806 VETERAN'S PREFERENCE IN FEDERAL EMPLOYMENT

Assistance: federal employment.

Purposes: pursuant to the Veterans Preference Act of 1944, to assist persons who perform services in the uniformed services to secure federal employment and to ensure a higher retention standing in the event of reduction-in-force; to assist veterans, employers, labor organizations, and others concerned with such preference; to investigate related complaints. A point system accords levels of preference to eligible veterans, based on such factors as when they served, receipt of the Purple Heart medal, disability if any, conditions of discharge. Details are available from federal agencies.

Eligible applicants/beneficiaries: veterans and certain of their dependents and survivors. Applicants should indicate their level of preference on job application forms.

Range/Average: N.A.

Activity: FY 04, 351 veterans preference cases processed.

HQ: Assistant Secretary/Veterans' Employment and Training-DOL, 200 Constitution Ave. NW - Rm.S-1312, Washington, DC 20210 Phone: (202) 693-4700.

Internet: www.dol.gov/dol/vets/public/programs/programs/preference/main.htm.

17.807 TRANSITION ASSISTANCE PROGRAM

Assistance: training.

Purposes: pursuant to the Defense Reauthorization Act of 1991, to provide employment instruction, information, and assistance to separating military personnel ad their spouses by offering job search and related services such as resume preparation and service benefits—through TAP workshops at military installations worldwide. Funding is not appropriated separately, and is derived from other funded accounts.

Eligible applicants: state employment agencies; contractors.

Eligible beneficiaries: service members within two years of retirement or one year of separation.

Average: N.A. (Project funds are used to purchase training manuals.)

Activity: new program listing in 2005. FY 05, 140,000 individuals participated; FY 06 estimate, 149,000 participants.

HQ: Assistant Secretary/Veterans' Employment and Training-DOL, 200 Constitution Ave. NW - Rm. S-1312, Washington, DC 20210 Phone: (202) 693-4708.

Internet: www.dol.gov/dol/vets.

DEPARTMENT OF STATE

BUREAU OF OCEANS AND INTERNATIONAL ENVIRONMENTAL A

19.204 FISHERMEN'S GUARANTY FUND ("Section 7")

Assistance: insurance.

Purposes: pursuant to the Fishermen's Protective Act of 1967 as amended and other acts, to reimburse U.S. commercial fishing vessel owners for losses resulting from the seizure of the vessel by a foreign country on the basis of rights or claims in territorial waters or on the high seas, not recognized by the U.S. (Effective 28 November 1990, the U.S. acknowledges the authority of coastal states to manage highly migratory species, reducing the basis for claims.)

Eligible applicants/beneficiaries: U.S. citizen-owners or -charterers of a documented or certified fishing vessel. Claimants must have paid a premium for the year in which the seizure occurs, if required.

Range: limited to the market value of fish caught before seizure, to the market value of the confiscated vessel or gear, and up to 50 percent of gross income lost as a result of seizure.

Activity: FY 05, no agreements; FY 06 estimate, 10 guaranty agreements.

HQ: Office of Marine Conservation, Bureau of Oceans and International Environmental and Scientific Affairs, Department of State, Rm.5806, Washington, DC 20520-7818 Phone: (202) 647-3941; FAX (202) 736-7350.

Internet: www.state.gov (Note: no field offices for this program.)

BUREAU OF INTELLIGENCE AND RESEARCH

19.300 PROGRAM FOR STUDY OF EASTERN EUROPE AND THE INDEPENDENT STATES OF THE FORMER SOVIET UNION ("Title VIII")

Assistance: project grants. (100 percent/to 3 years).

Purposes: pursuant to the Research and Training for Eastern Europe and the Independent States of the Former Soviet Union Act of 1983 as amended, for advanced research, graduate training, language training, and related activities—toward the development of American expertise on the countries of the former Soviet Union and Southeast Europe. Funds may support short-term research projects, fellowships, conferences, travel, and publication costs.

Eligible applicants: nonprofit organizations, IHEs.

Eligible beneficiaries: graduate students, scholars.

Range: $100,000 to $1,107,000. **Average:** $568,750.

Activity: not quantified specifically.

HQ: Executive Director *or* Program Officer, Program for Study of Eastern Europe and the Independent States of the Former Soviet Union (INR/RES), Department of State, 2201 C St. - Rm.2251, Washington, DC 20520-6510 Phone: (202) 736-4572; FAX (202) 736-4851.

Internet: www.state.gov/inr/grants (Note: no field offices for this program.)

BUREAU OF EDUCATIONAL AND CULTURAL AFFAIRS

19.400 EDUCATIONAL EXCHANGE—GRADUATE STUDENTS ("Fulbright Program")

Assistance: project grants. (100 percent/from 1 year).

Purposes: pursuant to the Mutual Educational and Cultural Exchange Act of 1961 (MECEA) as amended, for one-year scholarships to graduate students for one year of academic studies abroad, in the humanities and social sciences—covering costs of tuition, maintenance, transportation, books, insurance. Travel grants may supplement awards obtained from others.

Eligible applicants/beneficiaries: U.S. citizens with: B.A. degree or equivalent, with certain exceptions; no doctoral degree; the majority of their high school and undergraduate college education received at U.S. institutions; language proficiency; good health.

Range: $2,500 to $45,400. **Average:** $18,906.

Activity: FY 05, 1,200 grants.

HQ: Institute of International Education, 809 United Nations Plaza, New York, NY 10017 Phone: (no number provided).

Internet: http://exchanges.state.gov.

19.401 EDUCATIONAL EXCHANGE—UNIVERSITY LECTURERS (PROFESSORS) AND RESEARCH SCHOLARS ("Fulbright-Hays Program")

Assistance: project grants. (100 percent/3 months to 1 year).

Purposes: pursuant to MECEA as amended, for lectureships for university lecturers to serve as visiting professors abroad, and for research grants for scholars for postdoctoral work abroad—covering costs of travel for the grantee (and, in some cases, dependents), maintenance, books, and services.

Eligible applicants/beneficiaries: U.S. citizens with foreign language proficiency and, for lecturing, college or university teaching experience. Research grants—doctoral degree or, in some fields, recognized professional standing as demonstrated by faculty rank, publications, compositions, exhibition record, concerts, etc.

Range: $3,500 to $80,000. **Average:** $28,000.

Activity: FY 05, 820 grants.

HQ: Council for International Exchange of Scholars, 3007 Tilden St. NW - Ste.5M, Washington, DC 20008. Phone: (202) 686-4000.

Internet: http://exchanges.state.gov (Note: no field offices for this program.)

19.402 INTERNATIONAL VISITORS PROGRAM ("Fulbright- Hays Program")

Assistance: project grants (cost sharing).

Purposes: pursuant to MECEA as amended, to plan and conduct programs of travel, observation, consultation, study, and practical experience for foreign visitors selected and assigned by the Department of State upon recommendations from U.S. embassies—to bring visitors into contact with influential Americans and representative organizations and institutions, and increase communication and mutual understanding between the foreign and domestic parties.

Eligible applicants/beneficiaries: incorporated U.S. nonprofit organizations with at least four years experience.

Range: $137,000 to $4,690,000. **Average:** $142,000.

Activity: N.A.

HQ: Community Relations Branch, Office of International Visitors, BECA-Department of State, 301 Fourth St. SW - Rm.255, Washington, DC 20547 Phone: (202) 452-8624.

Internet: www.exchanges.state.gov.education (Note: no field offices for this program.)

19.403 AMERICAN COUNCIL OF YOUNG POLITICAL LEADERS ("ACYPL")

Assistance: project grants (50 percent).

Purposes: pursuant to MECEA as amended, to enable two-way exchanges with emerging U.S. and foreign political leaders, enabling them to experience firsthand the cultural and political dynamics of the countries visited, usually for two-week programs. Grants cover costs of travel, insurance, program activities, and orientation.

Eligible applicants: ACYPL (1612 K St. NW - Ste.300, Washington, DC 20006. Phone: (202) 857-0999).

Eligible beneficiaries: generally, state and local elected officials, staff and party activists—to age 41, and selected by a Delegate Selection Committee with Democratic and Republican co-chairs.

Range/Average: N.A.

Activity: 1 grant per year; FY 04, 30 countries involved, with 270 participants.

HQ: Youth Programs Division (ECA/PE/C/PY), Office of Citizen Exchanges, BECA-Department of State, 301 Fourth St. SW, Washington, DC 20547 Phone: (202) 203-7507; FAX (202) 203-7529.

Internet: www.exchanges.state.gov.education (Note: no field offices for this program.)

19.408 EDUCATIONAL EXCHANGE—TEACHERS FROM SECONDARY AND POSTSECONDARY LEVELS AND SCHOOL ADMINISTRATORS ("Fulbright Program Teacher and Administrator Program")

Assistance: project grants. (100 percent/2 weeks to 1 year).

Purposes: pursuant to MECEA as amended, to enable U.S. and foreign educators to live and teach in a foreign country. Participants from primary, secondary, or junior/community colleges exchange classroom assignments for six weeks, one semester, or one academic year. Generally, participants receive leave with pay and benefits from their respective employers; grants support transportation, maintenance, accident and health insurance.

Eligible applicants/beneficiaries: teachers and administrators with at least a B.A., 3 years full-time experience, English and foreign language proficiency, and U.S. citizenship (for U.S. participants).

Range: $2,000 to $27,000.

Activity: FY 05-06 estimate, 566 individual, 8 institutional grants.

HQ: Fulbright Teacher and Administrator Exchange Branch (ECA/A/S/X), BECA (SA-44), Department of State, 301 Fourth St. SW, Washington, DC 20547 Phone: (202) 453-8645; FAX (202) 453-8890 *Application booklet,* Fulbright Teacher Exchange Program, USDA.

Internet: www.fulbrightexchanges.org; e-mail, fulbright@grad.usda.gov (Note: no field offices for this program.)

19.409 ARTS EXCHANGES ON INTERNATIONAL ISSUES

Assistance: project grants. (70 percent/1-3 years).

Purposes: pursuant to MECEA as amended, for cooperative international group projects that introduce American and foreign participants to each other's cultural and artistic life and traditions—including composers, choreographers, playwrights, theater designers, writers, poets, filmmakers, visual artists, and arts administrators. Ineligible projects include those focused on youth, speaking tours, research, amateurs or semi- professionals, community-level presentations, or vocational and technical long-term academic study.

Eligible applicants: public or private "501(c)(3)" nonprofit organizations with four years experience.

Eligible beneficiaries: professional artists and arts administrators over age 25.

Range: $60,000 to $300,000.

Activity: FY 05 estimate, 8 grants.

HQ: Creative Arts Exchanges Program, Office of Citizen Exchanges, BECA-Department of State, 301 Fourth St. SW, Washington, DC 20547 Phone: (202) 203-7500.

Internet: www.exchanges.state.gov (Note: no field offices for this program.)

19.410 EDUCATIONAL EXCHANGE—CONGRESS-BUNDESTAG YOUTH EXCHANGE ("CBYX")

Assistance: projects grants. (to 100 percent/18 months).

Purposes: pursuant to MECEA as amended, to foster interaction between young people from the U.S. and Germany to promote mutual understanding through reciprocal exchanges of groups of high school students and practical trainees. Grants support costs of travel, insurance, orientation, selection, and administration. (The German government conducts a reciprocal counterpart program.)

Eligible applicants: nonprofit organizations with at least four years experience and with a German partner.

Eligible beneficiaries: generally, high school students and young professionals demonstrating language ability, social skills, academic achievement.

Range/Average: N.A.

Activity: 2005-06, 350 U.S. and 400 German participants.

HQ: Youth Programs Division (ECA/PE/C/PY), Office of Citizen Exchanges, BECA-Department of State, 301 Fourth St. SW, Washington, DC 20547 Phone: (202) 203-7507; FAX (202) 203-7529.

Internet: http://usagermanyscholarships.org (Note: no field offices for this program.)

19.415 PROFESSIONAL EXCHANGES—ANNUAL OPEN GRANT ("Office of Citizen Exchanges")

Assistance: project grants (cost sharing).

Purposes: pursuant to MECEA as amended, to foster, improve, and strengthen U.S. international relations by promoting mutual understanding among the peoples of the world through educational and professional exchanges. Grant funds should support: development of lasting institutional links; establishment of consortia, associations, and information networks; information transfer; development of internships.

Eligible applicants: public and private nonprofit organizations meeting the provisions of IRS regulation 26CFR1.501(c).

Eligible beneficiaries: U.S. citizens and foreign nationals.

Range: to $150,000; developing organizations, to $60,000.

Activity: FY 06 estimate, 20 grants.

HQ: Office of Citizen Exchanges, BECA-Department of State, 301 Fourth St. SW - Rm.220, Washington, DC 20547 Phone: (202) 453- 8181; FAX (202) 453-8168.

Internet: http://exchanges.state.gov/education/citizens/ (Note: no field offices for this program.)

19.418 EDUCATIONAL EXCHANGE, AMERICAN STUDIES INSTITUTE ("Study of the U.S. Program - Office of Academic Exchange Programs")

Assistance: project grants. (to 100 percent/6-8 months).

Purposes: pursuant to MECEA as amended, to provide foreign educators with a deeper understanding of American society, culture, and institutions to improve courses and teaching about the U.S. abroad. Participants attend an integrated series of lectures, readings, interactive discussions, research and independent study, faculty mentoring, and site visits. Grant recipients are responsible for institute design and implementation, as well as all logistical program aspects.

Eligible applicants: IHEs or consortia, other nonprofit academic organizations—with four years of pertinent experience.

Eligible beneficiaries: foreign university faculty nominated by a U.S. embassy, consulate, or Fulbright Commission.

Range: $260,000 to $385,000. **Average:** $322,500.

Activity: FY 05, 14 institutional cooperative agreements, hosting 200 foreign participants.

HQ: Study of the U.S. Branch (ECA/A/E/USS), BECA-Department of State, Rm.252 State Annex 44, 301 Fourth St. SW, Washington, DC 20547 Phone: (202) 453-8536; FAX (202) 4538533.

Internet: http://exchanges.state.gov/education/amstudy (Note: no field offices for this program.)

19.421 EXCHANGE—ENGLISH LANGUAGE FELLOW PROGRAM ("English Language Programs")

Assistance: project grants. (100 percent/to 1 year).

Purposes: pursuant to MECEA as amended, to provide highly qualified ESL/EFL teachers abroad to offer professional expertise in current English language methods and theory to host institutions; to provide specially designed courses for targeted high level groups, such as members and staffs of parliaments, and judicial, finance, and business officials; to develop communication skills among teachers and students that they need to participate in the global economy, to improve their access to diverse perspectives on a broad variety of issues, and to better understand America and its values and institutions. Grants support costs of participant travel, medical insurance, related living and project expenses, and a basic stipend.

Eligible applicants/beneficiaries: U.S. citizens with an M.A. or Ph.D. in TESL/TEFL, applied linguistics, or closely related field, and with specific teacher training experience.

Range: $55,000 to $75,000.

Activity: FY 05 estimate, 100 grants to teach in 63 countries.

HQ: Georgetown University, Center for Intercultural Education and Development, P.O. Box 579400, Washington, DC 20057-9400 Phone: (202) 687-6339.

Internet: http://exchanges.state.gov/education/engteaching/fellows.htm (Note: no field offices for this program.)

19.423 EXCHANGE—ENGLISH LANGUAGE SPECIALIST/SPEAKER PROGRAM

Assistance: project grants. (100 percent/2-6 weeks).

Purposes: pursuant to MECEA as amended, for short-term projects to improve the teaching and learning of English abroad, through curriculum development, teacher training seminars, textbook development, program evaluation, and "English for Specific Purposes" programs. Grants cover travel, living, materials, and related costs, and a $200/day honorarium.

Eligible applicants/beneficiaries: U.S. citizens with an M.A. or Ph.D. in TESL/TEFL, applied linguistics, or closely related field, and with specific teacher training experience.

Range: $1,500 to $9,000. **Average:** $5,500.

Activity: FY 05, 137 specialists assigned to 67 countries.

HQ: Programs Officer, Office of English Language Programs, BECA-Department of State, 301 Fourth St. SW, Washington, DC 20547 Phone: (202) 205-3636; FAX (202) 401-1250.

Internet: http://exchanges.state.gov/education/engteaching/specialists.htm (Note: no field offices for this program.)

19.425 BENJAMIN GILMAN INTERNATIONAL SCHOLARSHIP

Assistance: project grants (100 percent).

Purposes: pursuant to MECEA as amended, for scholarships to financially needy U.S. undergraduates to pursue study abroad for one semester or one academic year.

Eligible applicants/beneficiaries: U.S. citizens enrolled as undergraduates and receiving federal financial aid for schooling.

Average: $4,000.

Activity: FY 05, 351 scholarships awarded to recipients from 50 states, studying in 63 foreign countries.

HQ: Educational Information and Resources (ECA/A/S/A), BECA- Department of State, 301 Fourth St. SW (SA-44), Washington, DC 20547 Phone: (202) 453-8887; FAX (202) 453-8890.

Internet: http://exchanges.state.gov.

19.430 INTERNATIONAL EDUCATION TRAINING AND RESEARCH

Assistance: project grants.

Purposes: pursuant to MECEA as amended, for training of international education professionals on U.S. campuses; for research on specified international exchange programs.

Eligible applicants/beneficiaries: experienced incorporated U.S. nonprofit organizations.

Average: research, $190,000; training, $535,000; student advising training, $900,000.

Activity: new program listing in 2005. FY 05, 150 trainees.

HQ: Educational Information and Resources (ECA/A/S/A), BECA- Department of State, 301 Fourth St. SW (SA-44), Washington, DC 20547 Phone: (202) 453-8872; FAX (202) 453-8890.

Internet: http://exchanges.state.gov; http://www.nafsa.org; http://www.iie.org.

19.431 EDUCATIONAL EXCHANGE—SCHOLAR-IN-RESIDENCE (U.S. INSTITUTIONS OF HIGHER EDUCATION HOST LECTURING FACULTY FROM ABROAD)

Assistance: project grants. (cost sharing/to 10 months).

Purposes: pursuant to MECEA as amended, for U.S. IHEs to host scholars-in-residence to teach on global issues at the undergraduate level, as well as to participate in other internal institutional and community outreach activities. Project funds are paid to the scholar, not to the host institution.

Eligible applicants/beneficiaries: U.S. IHEs—with preference to those traditionally less involved in international exchange programs, and with priority to HBCUs, Hispanic-serving institutions, tribal IHEs, small liberal arts colleges, and community colleges.

Range: $16,000 to $40,000. **Average:** $27,000.

Activity: new program listing in 2005; FY 05 estimate, 36 grants.

HQ: Council for International Exchange of Scholars, 3007 Tilden St. NW - Ste.5M, Washington, DC 20008 Phone: (202) 686-4000.

Internet: www.cies.org/sir/sir.htm (Note: no field offices for this program.)

19.432 OVERSEAS EDUCATIONAL ADVISING

Assistance: project grants.

Purposes: pursuant to MECEA as amended, to establish an overseas network of "Education USA" educational advising and information centers, to ensure that prospective students in specific locations abroad receive unbiased, ethical, and current information on U.S. higher education. Project funds support program implementation including adviser orientation and training.

Eligible applicants/beneficiaries: experienced incorporated U.S. nonprofit organizations.

Range: $60,000 to $450,000. **Average:** $200,000.

Activity: new program listing in 2005; FY 05, over 20 million queries from overseas field offices.

HQ: Educational Information and Resources (ECA/A/S/A), BECA- Department of State, 301 Fourth St. SW (SA-44), Washington, DC 20547 Phone: (202) 453-8872; FAX (202) 453-8890.

Internet: www.educationusa.state.gov (Note: no field offices for this program.)

BUREAU OF NEAR EASTERN AFFAIRS

19.500 MIDDLE EAST PARTNERSHIP INITIATIVE ("MEPI")

Assistance: project grants.

Purposes: pursuant to the Foreign Assistance Act of 1961 as amended, to support economic, political, and educational reform efforts in the Middle East and North Africa, promoting opportunity especially for women and youth. Projects usually involve partnerships to provide training programs and projects involving local nongovernmental organizations (NGOs) and government officials. Some cost sharing is expected.

Eligible applicants: experienced nonprofit and profit organizations, state and local governments.

Eligible beneficiaries: ccountries covered by State Department's Bureau of Near Eastern Affairs, not currently subject to foreign assistance restrictions, such as: Morocco, Algeria, Tunisia, Egypt, West Bank/Gaza, Jordan, Lebanon, Kuwait, Iraq, Saudi Arabia, Qatar, Bahrain, UAE, Oman, and Yemen.

Range/Average: N.A.

Activity: new program listing in 2004; 350 programs funded.

HQ: Office of MEPI, Bureau of Near Eastern Affairs, Department of State, 2201 C St. NW - Rm.5253A, Washington, DC 20520 Phone: (no number provide).

Internet: www.mepi.state.gov (Note: no field offices for this program.)

BUREAU OF POPULATION, REFUGEES, AND MIGRATION

19.510 U.S. REFUGEE ADMISSIONS PROGRAM

Assistance: project grants.

Purposes: pursuant to the Immigration and Nationality Act and Migration and Refugee Assistance Act of 1962 as amended (MRA), to provide initial reception and placement services for refugees approved for admission in the U.S., including: resettlement activities; providing basic necessities and core services for a 90-day period; employment services coordinated with publicly sponsored assistance programs. The program provides a fixed $800 reimbursement per resettled refugee; sponsors are expected to contribute private funds toward actual costs.

Eligible applicants/beneficiaries: state governments, private nonprofit organizations.

Range: $20,000 to $2,873,000. **Average:** $1,021,000.

Activity: new program listing in 2004. FY 06, 53,813 refugees resettled through 9 private organizations, 1 state government.

HQ: Office of Refugee Admissions, Bureau of Population, Refugees, and Migration, Department of State, SA-1 - Ste.L505, Washington, DC 20522-0105 Phone: (202) 663-1056; Comptroller, (202) 663-1022.

Internet: www.state.gov/g/prm (Note: no field offices for this program.)

19.511 OVERSEAS REFUGEE ASSISTANCE PROGRAMS FOR EAST ASIA

Assistance: project grants.

Purposes: pursuant to MRA, for humanitarian activities and services for refugees in East Asia—particularly in Thailand along the Burmese border. Projects must be complementary to and coordinated with United Nations programs, as well as other organizations.

Eligible applicants/beneficiaries: United Nations; international and non-governmental organizations.

Range: NGOs, $1,150,000 to $4,544,776; international organizations, $970,000 to $8,000,000. **Average:** NGOs, $2,847,388.

Activity: new program listing in 2005.

HQ: Bureau of Population, Refugees, and Migration, Department of State, SA-1 - Ste.L505, Washington, DC 20522-0105 Phone: (202) 663-1056; Phone: Director, (202) 663-1063; Deputy Director, (202) 663-1065; Southeast Asia, (202) 663-3715; Northeast Asia, (202) 663-1950; Comptroller, (202) 663-1022.

Internet: www.state.gov/g/prm (Note: no field offices for this program.)

19.517 OVERSEAS REFUGEE ASSISTANCE PROGRAMS FOR AFRICA

Assistance: project grants.

Purposes: pursuant to MRA, for humanitarian activities and services for refugees across the African continent. Project must be complementary to and coordinated with United Nations programs.

Eligible applicants/beneficiaries: United Nations; international and non-governmental organizations.

Range: NGOs, $99,000 to $2,200,000. **Average:** NGOs, $2,100,000.

Activity: new program listing in 2005.

HQ: Bureau of Population, Refugees, and Migration, Department of State, SA-1 - Ste.L505, Washington, DC 20522-0105 Phone: Comptroller, (202) 663-1022; Phone: Director, (202) 663-1027; Deputy Director/Sahel, North Africa, Southern Africa, Horn of Africa,(202) 663-1014; Coastal West Africa, (202) 663-1031; Great Lakes-Central Africa, (202) 663-1476; Chad (Sudanese Refugees), (202) 663-1029.

Internet: www.state.gov/g/prm (Note: no field offices for this program.)

19.518 OVERSEAS REFUGEE ASSISTANCE PROGRAMS FOR WESTERN HEMISPHERE

Assistance: project grants.

Purposes: pursuant to MRA, for humanitarian activities and services for refugees in the Western Hemisphere—particularly in Columbia. Projects must be complementary to and coordinated with United Nations programs, as well as other organizations.

Eligible applicants/beneficiaries: United Nations; international and non-governmental organizations.

Range: NGOs, $356,500 to $1,287,858. **Average:** $979,667.

Activity: new program listing in 2005; assistance to 5 NGOs.

HQ: Bureau of Population, Refugees, and Migration, Department of State, SA-1 - Ste.L505, Washington, DC 20522-0105 Phone: Director, (202) 663-1062; FAX (202) 663-1530 Phone: Comptroller, (202) 663-1022.

Internet: www.state.gov/g/prm; e-mail, prm-eca@state.gov (Note: no field offices for this program.)

19.519 OVERSEAS REFUGEE ASSISTANCE PROGRAM FOR NEAR EAST AND SOUTH ASIA

Assistance: project grants.

Purposes: pursuant to MRA, for humanitarian activities and services for refugees in the Near East and South Asia—including those in and from Afghanistan, India, Iran, Iraq, Palestine, and Tibet. Projects must be complementary to and coordinated with United Nations programs.

Eligible applicants/beneficiaries: United Nations; international and non-governmental organizations.

Range: IOs, $142,800,000 total; NGOs, $55,481 to $2,000,000. **Average:** NGOs, $938,861.

Activity: new program listing in 2005; assistance to 4 IOs, 16 NGOs.

HQ: Bureau of Population, Refugees, and Migration, Department of State, SA-1 - Ste. L505, Washington, DC 20522-0105 Phone: Director, (202) 663-1063; Deputy Director/Iraq Team, (202) 663-1065; Afghan Team, (202) 663- 3717, -3442; South/Northeast Asia, Pacific, (202) 663-1950; Near East/UNRWA, (202) 663-1531; Iraq Team, (202) 663-3442; Comptroller, (202) 663-1022.

Internet: www.state.gov/g/prm (Note: no field offices for this program.)

19.520 OVERSEAS REFUGEE ASSISTANCE PROGRAMS FOR EUROPE

Assistance: project grants.

Purposes: pursuant to MRA, for humanitarian activities and services for refugees in Europe and Central Asia, including Armenia, Azerbaijan, the Balkans, the North and South Caucasus, Chechnya, Georgia, Kosovo, Macedonia, Serbia-Montenegro. Projects must be complementary to and coordinated with United Nations programs, as well as other organizations.

Eligible applicants/beneficiaries: United Nations; international and non-governmental organizations.

Range: total to IOs, $41,100,000; NGOs, $115,264 to $1,797,419. **Average:** NGOs, $803,176.

Activity: new program listing in 2005; assistance to 6 IOs, 10 NGOs.

HQ: Office of Assistance to Europe, Central Asia and the Americas, Bureau of Population, Refugees, and Migration, Department of State, SA-1 - Ste. L505, Washington, DC 20522-0105 Phone: Director, (202) 663-1062; FAX, (202) 663-1530; Comptroller, (202) 663-1022.

Internet: www.state.gov/g/prm (Note: no field offices for this program.)

19.522 OVERSEAS REFUGEE ASSISTANCE PROGRAMS FOR STRATEGIC GLOBAL PRIORITIES

Assistance: project grants.

Purposes: pursuant to MRA, for humanitarian activities and services promoting PRM's initiatives in areas that are cross- cutting, core priorities—including refugee women and children, prevention and response to gender-based violence, enhancing refugee protection and health including HIV/AIDS protection. Projects must be complementary to and coordinated with United Nations programs, as well as other organizations. (Most funding under this program is allocated to the United Nations High Commissioner for Refugees and the International Committee of the Red Cross.)

Eligible applicants/beneficiaries: United Nations; international and non-governmental organizations.

Range: total to IOs, $55,300,000; NGOs, $27,375 to $390,515. **Average:** NGOs, $382,506.

Activity: new program listing in 2005; assistance to 4 IOs, 9 NGOs.

HQ: Bureau of Population, Refugees, and Migration, Department of State, SA-1 - Ste. L505, Washington, DC 20522-0105 Phone: Director, (202) 663-1075; Refugee Children, (202) 663-1713; Refugee Women, GBV/NGO Liaison, (202) 663-1481; Office Director, (202) 663-3954; Policy Office, (202) 663-3881, -3104; Comptroller, (202) 663-1022.

Internet: www.state.gov/g/prm (Note: no field offices for this program.)

DEPARTMENT OF TRANSPORTATION

FEDERAL AVIATION ADMINISTRATION

20.100 AVIATION EDUCATION

Assistance: advisory services/counseling.

Purposes: pursuant to the Airport and Airway Development Act of 1970 as amended, for a broad range of public civil aviation education, career awareness, and related programs, from the elementary through college levels in all regions of the country. Also for: clearinghouse, data gathering and dissemination, communications, teacher training activities; conferences; and, publications on aviation including aviation mathematics, science, technology, computer literacy; Internet services.

Eligible applicants/beneficiaries: aviation and education administrators, IHE officials, officers of civil organizations, domestic and international governments, aviation industry, education organizations.

Range/Average: N.A.

Activity: 2006, 1 counselor workshop; estimate 2007, 6 workshops.

HQ: Assistant Administrator/Region and Center Operations, FAA- DOT, 800 Independence Ave. SW, Washington, DC 20590. Phone: (no number provided) *National HQ office for program implementation,* Regional Administrator, FAA-DOT, 12 New England Executive Park, Burlington, MA 01803 Phone: (no number provided).

Internet: www.faa.dot.gov/education.

20.106 AIRPORT IMPROVEMENT PROGRAM ("AIP")

Assistance: project grants; advisory services/counseling (75-95 percent).

Purposes: for planning, construction, or rehabilitation of public-use airports and related facilities and equipment, including for commercial passenger and cargo service, heliports, and seaplane landing bases. Eligible expenditures include airport master planning, land acquisition, site preparation, runway and related construction and improvement, noise reduction programs, weather reporting equipment, security and snow-removal equipment, firefighting and rescue equipment, lighting, and projects to comply with the ADA, Clean Air Act, and Federal Water Pollution Control. Ineligible uses of funds include hangar and most automobile parking facilities, buildings unrelated to safety, landscaping or artwork, routine maintenance and repair.

Eligible applicants/beneficiaries: development grants for airports listed in the National Plan of Integrated Airport Systems (NPIAS)—states, counties, municipalities, territories and possessions, and other public agencies including tribes or pueblos; private owners of public-use reliever airports or airports enplaning over 2,500 passengers annually. Noise compatibility grants—certain government units.

Range: $10,925 to $38,826,223. **Average:** $1,710,580.

Activity: FY 05, 2,099 grant agreements.

HQ: Financial Assistance Division (APP-500), Office of Airport Planning and Programming, FAA-DOT, 800 Independence Ave. SW, Washington, DC 20591 Phone: (202) 267-3831.

Internet: www.faa.gov/airports_airtraffic/AIP.

20.108 AVIATION RESEARCH GRANTS

Assistance: project grants; use of property, facilities, and equipment. (to 100 percent/6 month minimum).

Purposes: pursuant to the Federal Aviation Administration Research, Engineering and Development Authorization and the Aviation Security Improvement Act of 1990, for advanced applied research and development projects in: Capacity and Air Traffic Management Technology; Communications, Navigation, and Surveillance; Aviation Weather; Airport Technology; Aircraft Safety Technology; System Security Technology; Human Factors and Aviation Medicine; Environment and Energy; Systems Science and Operations Research; Commercial Space Transportation.

Eligible applicants/beneficiaries: IHEs, nonprofit institutions.

Range: $25,000 to $5,000,000 (multi-year). **Average:** $50,000 to $150,000.

Activity: not quantified specifically.

HQ: Aviation Research Grants Program (ACT-50), FAA-DOT, Hughes Technical Center, Atlantic City International Airport, NJ 08405 Phone: (609) 485-4781, FAX (609) 485-6509.

Internet: www.its.tc.faa.gov/logistics/grants (Note: no other field offices for this program.)

20.109 AIR TRANSPORTATION CENTERS OF EXCELLENCE ("FAA Centers of Excellence")

Assistance: project grants; use of property, facilities, and equipment; specialized services. (50 percent/to 10 years).

Purposes: pursuant to the Federal Aviation Administration Research, Engineering and Development Authorization Act of 1990, for centers conducting long-term continuing research in such areas as catastrophic failure of aircraft, airspace and airport planning and design, airport capacity enhancement techniques, human performance, aviation safety and security, air transportation personnel training.

Eligible applicants/beneficiaries: IHEs, which may partner with industry affiliates and other government laboratories.

Average: from $500,000 per year per center.

Activity: not quantified specifically.

HQ: Director, Centers of Excellence Program (AAR-400), Office of Aviation Research, Technical Center, Atlantic City International Airport, NJ 08405 Phone: (609) 485-5043, FAX (609) 485-9430.

Internet: www.coe.faa.gov (Note: no other field offices for this program.)

FEDERAL HIGHWAY ADMINISTRATION

20.200 HIGHWAY RESEARCH AND DEVELOPMENT PROGRAM

Assistance: project grants.

Purposes: pursuant to Safe, Accountable, Flexible, Efficient, Transportation Equity Act-a Legacy for Users (SAFETEA-LU), to conduct research needed to maintain and expand our vital transportation infrastructure and address challenges facing the transportation system such as, improving safety and efficiency in freight movement, reducing traffic congestion, increasing intermodal connectivity, and protecting the environment. Funding for this program is included in **20.205**.

Eligible applicants/beneficiaries: teams of state transportation, local government, and/or Canadian provinces who represent a Region (e.g. at least two states or a state and Canadian province).

Range/Average: N.A.

Activity: new program in 2006.

HQ: Office of Acquisition Management (HAAM), FHWA-DOT, 400 Seventh St. SW - Room 4410, Washington, DC 20590 Phone: (no number provided).

Internet: www.fhwa.dot.gov.

20.205 HIGHWAY PLANNING AND CONSTRUCTION ("Federal-Aid Highway Program")

Assistance: formula grants; project grants. (80-100 percent/to 4 years).

Purposes: for highway and related projects in the interstate and national highway systems, and for bridge and safety improvements on nonfederal-aid roads and within federal lands. Eligible fund uses include costs of planning, design, right-of-way acquisition, relocation assistance, construction, reconstruction, repair (but not maintenance), improvement of interstate and primary and secondary highways, bridge repairs, roads, and streets in urban systems, congestion mitigation and air quality improvement, and research. Related projects may involve railroad grade crossings, roadside beautification, bridges, bicycle paths, pedestrian walkways, carpool projects, fringe and corridor parking, wetland mitigation, forest highways, rest areas, scenic and historic highway improvements. In some cases, funds may be used for public mass transit improvements. Funding is derived from the Highway Trust Fund. Funding for this program includes **20.215** and **20.219**.

Eligible applicants/beneficiaries: state transportation agencies; territories, possessions. Projects related to Indian reservations, parkways and park roads, and public lands highways, certain projects in urban areas or off the state highway systems—tribal governments, counties, other political subdivisions or agencies and federal agencies applying through state agencies.

Range: $110,730,468 to $2,302,859,917. **Average:** $620,666,497.

Activity: not quantified specifically.

HQ: Director, Office of Program Administration, FHWA-DOT, 400 Seventh St. SW, Washington, DC 20590-0001 Phone: (202) 366-0494; *forest highways, Indian reservation roads, park roads and parkways,* Federal Lands Highways, (202) 366-9494.

Internet: www.fhwa.dot.gov.

20.215 HIGHWAY TRAINING AND EDUCATION

Assistance: project grants; training. (80-100 percent/3 months to 5 years).

Purposes: pursuant to the Transportation Equity Act for the 21st Century, to develop and administer training, educational, and technical assistance programs related to federal-aid highway work. Faculty, graduate, research, and minority fellowships may be awarded under the Dwight David Eisenhower Transportation Fellowship Program. Courses and study programs may be obtained from IHEs, government agencies, private entities, or the National Highway Institute. Funding for this program is included in **20.205**.

Eligible applicants/beneficiaries: training—state and local transportation agency employees. Fellowships—persons matriculating at U.S. IHEs in transportation-related disciplines.

Range/Average: N.A.

Activity: 1992-2005, 2,000 fellowships awarded.

HQ: Director, National Highway Institute, FHWA-DOT, 4600 N. Fairfax Dr. - Ste.800, Arlington, VA 22203-1553 Phone: (703) 235- 0500; Program Manager, University and Grants Program, Phone: (703) 235-0538.

Internet: www.nhi.fhwa.dot.gov.

20.218 NATIONAL MOTOR CARRIER SAFETY ("MCSAP")

Assistance: formula grants (to 80-100 percent).

Purposes: pursuant to the Surface Transportation Assistance Act of 1982, Motor Carrier Safety Act of 1991, and Transportation Equity Act for the 21st Century, for programs involving the development and enforcement of uniform rules, regulations, and standards concerning inter- and intrastate commercial motor vehicle safety, and of state hazardous materials regulations compatible with federal standards.

Eligible applicants/beneficiaries: states; territories and possessions (100 percent funding).

Range/Average: N.A.

Activity: FY 05, 10,000 state personnel supported; 13,000 trained.

HQ: State Programs Division (MC-ESS), FMCSA-DOT, 400 Seventh St. SW, Washington, DC 20590 Phone: (202) 366-9579.

Internet: www.fmcsa.dot.gov.

20.219 RECREATIONAL TRAILS PROGRAM

Assistance: formula grants; project grants. (80-95 percent/to 4 years).

Purposes: to provide new and maintain existing recreational trails and related facilities for motorized and nonmotorized uses. Project funds may be used to: maintain and restore existing trails; construct new trails; develop trail-side and trail-head facilities and trail linkages; acquire easements identified in state trail plans; acquire fee simple title from willing sellers; pay limited administrative and public education costs. Funds may not be used for property condemnation, nor to provide access by motorized users to trails used mainly by nonmotorized users. Funding for this program is included in **20.205**.

Eligible applicants/beneficiaries: state agencies, which may accept applications from private organizations, or city, county, or other governmental organizations including federal agencies. States must have an advisory committee representing both motorized and nonmotorized users.

Range: $482,843 to $3,327,065. **Average:** $965,686.

Activity: not quantified specifically.

HQ: Office of Planning and Environment (HEPN-50), FHWA-DOT, 400 Seventh St. SW - Rm.3240, Washington, DC 20590 Phone: (202) 366-5013, FAX (202) 366-3409.

Internet: www.fhwa.dot.gov/environment/rectrails.html.

20.223 TRANSPORTATION INFRASTRUCTURE FINANCE AND INNOVATION ACT (TIFIA) PROGRAM ("TIFIA Credit Program")

Assistance: direct loans; guaranteed loans; lines of credit (to 35 years).

Purposes: pursuant to legislation codified within sections 601 through 609 of title 23 of the United States Code (23 U.S.C. 601-609), and others, to finance projects of national or regional significance by filling market gaps and leveraging substantial non-Federal and private co-investment. TIFIA credit assistance is intended to facilitate financing of projects that would otherwise be significantly delayed because of funding limitations or difficulties accessing capital markets. Through TIFIA, the DOT provides Federal credit assistance to eligible highway, transit, rail, and intermodal freight projects, including access to seaports. All projects receiving TIFIA assistance must comply with generally applicable Federal laws and regulations, including title VI of the Civil Rights Act of 1964, the National Environmental Policy Act of 1969, and the Uniform Relocation Assistance and Real Property Acquisition Policies Act of 1970. Principal amount of requested credit assistance must not exceed 33 percent of eligible project costs.

Eligible applicants/beneficiaries: Public or private entities seeking to finance, design, construct, own, or operate an eligible surface transportation project may apply for TIFIA assistance, such as state departments of transportation; local governments; transit agencies; special authorities; special districts; railroad companies; and private firms or consortia that may include companies specializing in engineering, construction, materials, and/or the operation of transportation facilities.

Range: $42,000,000 to $917,000,000.

Activity: as of 3/31/07, one loan for $516,000,000.

HQ: TIFIA Joint Program Office (HCFT-1), Federal Highway Administration, DOT, 1200 New Jersey Avenue Room E-64-302, Washington, DC 20590. Phone:(202) 366-5785; FAX:(202) 366-2908.

Internet: http://tifia.fhwa.dot.gov (Note: no field offices for this program.)

20.231 PERFORMANCE AND REGISTRATION INFORMATION SYSTEMS MANAGEMENT ("PRISM")

Assistance: project grants (100 percent/to 2 years).

Purposes: pursuant to Motor Carrier Safety Act of 1991, Transportation Equity Act for the 21st Century, and Flexible, Efficient Transportation Act of 2006, to identify motor carriers responsible for the safety of commercial motor vehicles, and to monitor their safety fitness—by linking the vehicle registration process to safety performance monitoring and enforcement, which records the DOT vehicle number to the motor carrier. Funds may cover training, outreach, and development of system requirements.

Eligible applicants/beneficiaries: states, DC.

Average: $500,000 per state.

Activity: new program listing in 2006 (CFDA on-line). FY 05, 5 states funded; FY 06 estimate, 3 awards.

HQ: Office of Enforcement and Compliance (MC-ECE), FMCSA-DOT, 400 Seventh St. SW, Washington, DC 20590 Phone: (202) 366-9699.

Internet: www.fhwa.dot.gov.

20.232 COMMERCIAL DRIVER LICENSE STATE PROGRAMS

Assistance: project grants (100 percent).

Purposes: to prevent truck and bus accidents, fatalities, and injuries through programs requiring drivers to have a single commercial motor vehicle license, and by disqualifying drivers that operate commercial motor vehicles in an unsafe manner. Project examples: Social Security online verification; covert operations for third-party tester.

Eligible applicants/beneficiaries: states, DC.

Range/Average: N.A.

Activity: new program listing in 2005. FY 03, 6 states funded; 44 states using on-line verification system.

HQ: State Programs Division (CDL Team-MC-ESL), FMCSA-DOT, 400 Seventh St. SW, Washington, DC 20590 Phone: (202) 366-2964.

Internet: www.fmcsa.dot.gov.

20.233 BORDER ENFORCEMENT GRANTS

Assistance: project grants (100 percent/2 years).

Purposes: pursuant to the Safe, Accessible, Feasible, and Efficient Equity Act, to ensure that commercial motor carriers entering the U.S. from foreign country comply with U.S. commercial vehicle safety and financial standards, regulations, and requirements, and that their drivers are qualified and properly licensed; for enforcement activities and projects.

Eligible applicants/beneficiaries: entities and states sharing a land border with a foreign country.

Range/Average: N.A.

Activity: new program in FY 06.

HQ: Borders Division, (MC-ESB), FMCSA-DOT, 400 Seventh St. SW, Washington, DC 20590 Phone: (202) 366-4049.

Internet: www.fmcsa.dot.gov.

20.234 SAFETY DATA IMPROVEMENT PROGRAM

Assistance: project grants (80 percent).

Purposes: pursuant to Safe, Accountable, Flexible, Efficient, Transportation Equity Act: A Legacy for Users (SAFETEA-LU), to improve the overall data quality in the collection and analysis of truck and bus crash and inspection data. Funds may be used to: meet staffing requirements; train law enforcement officers; develop and acquire appropriate software.

Eligible applicants/beneficiaries: states, DC.

Range: $5,000 to $2,000,000. **Average:** $250,000.

Activity: new program listing in 2006 (CFDA on-line).

HQ: Analysis Division, Office of Research and Analysis (MC-RRA), FMCSA-DOT, 400 Seventh St. SW - Rm.8214, Washington, DC 20590 Phone: (202) 366-4134.

Internet: www.fmcsa.dot.gov (Note: no field offices for this program.)

20.235 COMMERCIAL MOTOR VEHICLE OPERATOR TRAINING GRANTS ("Federal Motor Carrier Safety Administration (FMCSA), Department of Transportation")

Assistance: project grants (80 percent/to 2 years).

Purposes: pursuant to SAFETEA-LU, to train present and future operators of commercial motor vehicles.

Eligible applicants/beneficiaries: state and local governments, public or private IHEs, vocational-technical schools, truck driver training schools.

Average: $1,000,000 (single award).

Activity: new program listing in 2006 (CFDA on-line). FY 05, one award (to the state of Florida).

HQ: State Programs Division (MC-ESS), FMCSA-DOT, 400 Seventh St. SW, Washington, DC 20590 Phone: (202) 366-9579.

Internet: www.fmcsa.dot.gov.

20.236 THERMAL IMAGING INSPECTION SYSTEM DEMONSTRATION PROJECT ("TIIS Demonstration Project")

Assistance: project grants (80 percent/2 years).

Purposes: pursuant to SAFETEA-LU, for a field demonstration project using a thermal imaging inspection system that leverages state-of-the-art technology integrated with signature recognition software—to provide the capability for real-time identification of faults and failures in tires, brakes, and bearings mounted on commercial vehicles. Project is to be conducted at multiple sites, including FMCSA's Roadside Test Lab in Tennessee with the state's Department of Safety.

Eligible applicants/beneficiaries: public and private nonprofit organizations including IHEs, profit organizations, federal agencies.

Average: $1,412,000 (single award).

Activity: new program listing in 2006 (CFDA on-line).

HQ: Technology Division, Office of Research and Analysis (MC- RRT), FMCSA-DOT, 400 Virginia Ave. SW - Ste.600, Washington, DC 20024 Phone: (202) 385-2363; FAX (202) 385-2422.

Internet: www.fmcsa.dot.gov (Note: no field offices for this program.)

20.237 COMMERCIAL VEHICLE INFORMATION SYSTEMS & NETWORKS ("CVISN")

Assistance: project grants (to 80 percent).

Purposes: pursuant to SAFETEA-LU, to focus state commercial vehicle safety enforcement on high-risk operators, to enable more effective HAZ-MAT safety compliance and enforcement, and to incorporate homeland security safeguards, through programs that: integrate data systems that improve the accuracy, integrity, and verifiability of credentials; improve electronic screening of commercial vehicles; and, enable on-line application for and issuance of credentials.

Eligible applicants/beneficiaries: states, DC meeting strict DOT requirements and criteria.

Range: $100,000 to $750,000.

Activity: new program listing in 2006 (CFDA on-line); FY 06 estimate, 45 awards.

HQ: Office of Research and Analysis (MC- RRT), FMCSA-DOT, 400 Virginia Ave. SW - Ste.600, Washington, DC 20024 Phone: (202) 385-2367, -2389; FAX (202) 385-2422.

Internet: www.fmcsa.dot.gov.

20.238 COMMERCIAL DRIVERS LICENSE INFORMATION SYSTEM ("CDLIS")

Assistance: project grants (to 80 percent).

Purposes: to modernize the Commercial Driver's License Information System in order for CDLIS to: comply with applicable Federal information technology security standards; provide for electronic exchange of all information including the posting of convictions; contain self-auditing features to ensure correct and consistent posting of data by States; and integrate the commercial driver's license and the medical certificate.

Eligible applicants/beneficiaries: qualified states and the District of Columbia; organizations representing agencies and officials of a state.

Range/Average: N.A.

Activity: N.A.

HQ: State Programs-CDL Division, MC-ESL, FMCSA, DOT, 400 Seventh Street SW, Washington DC 20590. Phone: (202) 366-2964.

Internet: http://www.fmcsa.gov.

20.240 FUEL TAX EVASION-INTERGOVERNMENTAL ENFORCEMENT EFFORT

Assistance: project grants (to 2 years).

Purposes: pursuant to Safe, Accountable, Flexible, Efficient, Transportation Equity Act: A Legacy for Users (SAFETEA-LU), to increase intergovernmental activities and enforcement efforts among public agencies to reduce Federal fuel tax evasion. Funds my be used only to expand or enhance efforts to increase motor fuel tax enforcement and payments, examinations and criminal investigations, and increase research and training in the area of Federal fuel tax evasion.

Eligible applicants/beneficiaries: states, DC, U.S. territories and possessions, other public agencies, including tribal or pueblo, republics of Marshall Islands and Palau, and the Federated States of Micronesia.

Range: $10,000 to $250,000.

Activity: N.A.

HQ: Program Manager, Office of Transportation Policy Studies (HTPS), FHWA-DOT, 400 Seventh St. SW, Washington, DC 20590-0001, Phone: (202) 366-9234.

Internet: www.fhwa.dot.gov/policy/otps/fueltax.htm (Note: no field offices for this program.)

FEDERAL RAILROAD ADMINISTRATION

20.301 RAILROAD SAFETY

Assistance: investigation of complaints.

Purposes: pursuant to Department of Transportation Act of 1966 and Federal Railroad Safety Act of 1970, as amended, to reduce railroad-related casualties and accidents through investigation of safety-related complaints and evaluations of petitions requesting waivers from standards, rules, and regulations.

Eligible applicants/beneficiaries: anyone concerned with railroad safety.

Range/Average: N.A.

Activity: not quantified specifically.

HQ: Associate Administrator for Safety, Federal Railroad Administration-DOT, 1120 Vermont Ave, NW - MS25, Washington, DC 20590 Phone: (202) 493-6304.

Internet: www.fra.gov/o/safety.

20.303 GRANTS-IN-AID FOR RAILROAD SAFETY—STATE PARTICIPATION ("State Participation in Railroad Safety")

Assistance: project grants (50 percent).

Purposes: pursuant to the Federal Railroad Safety Act of 1970 as amended and Hazardous Materials Transportation Uniform Safety Act of 1990, to subsidize costs of personnel, equipment, and activities related to enforcement of railroad safety standards, including the inspection of equipment, operating practices, signal and train control, and hazardous materials transport. Classroom training costs for state inspectors are reimbursed at 100 percent.

Eligible applicants/beneficiaries: states.

Range: $2,000 to $16,000 per inspector in FY 88 (no funds available since). **Average:** $9,000.

Activity: FY 04, 30 states participating with 153 inspectors.

HQ: Associate Administrator/Safety (MS 25), Federal Railroad Administration-DOT, 1120 Vermont Ave. NW, Washington, DC 20590 Phone: (202) 493-6300.

Internet: www.fra.dot.gov.

20.312 HIGH SPEED GROUND TRANSPORTATION—NEXT GENERATION HIGH SPEED RAIL PROGRAM ("HSGT")

Assistance: project grants.

Purposes: pursuant to the Transportation Equity Act for the 21st Century, to implement high speed passenger rail systems. Projects must benefit research, development, design, or operation of incremental high speed passenger rail systems. Project examples: high speed, high acceleration fossil-fueled locomotives; highway- rail grade crossing sensor and warning systems.

Eligible applicants/beneficiaries: any U.S. private business, educational institution, state or local government or public authority, or federal agency.

Range: $100,000 to $7,000,000. **Average:** $250,000.

Activity: not quantified specifically.

HQ: Office of Railroad Development (RDV-13), Federal Railroad Administration-DOT, 1120 Vermont Ave. NW, Washington, DC 20590 Phone: (no number provided).

Internet: ww.fra.dot.gov (Note: no field offices for this program.)

20.313 RAILROAD RESEARCH AND DEVELOPMENT

Assistance: project grants.

Purposes: for research advancing rail safety, by university organizations.

Eligible applicants/beneficiaries: academic research institutions with at least five years relevant experience.

Range: $50,000 to $250,000. **Average:** $100,000.

Activity: N.A.; new program.

HQ: Office of Research and Development (RDV-31), Federal Railroad Administration-DOT, 1120 Vermont Ave. NW, Washington, DC 20590 Phone: (no number provided).

Internet: www.fra.dot.gov/o/hsgt/index.htm (Note: no field offices for this program.)

20.314 RAILROAD DEVELOPMENT

Assistance: project grants.

Purposes: pursuant to SAFETEA-LU, to provide financial assistance for planning and developing railroad corridors (including environmental studies); rail line relocation and improvement; construction projects that improve rail lines, enhance service, and add capacity to the national rail system; capital construction, rehabilitation, and improvements benefiting train operations.

Eligible applicants/beneficiaries: state, regional, and local governments; for-profit organizations, such as railroads.

Range: $50,000 to over $700,000,000.

Activity: FY 06, 1 grant.

HQ: Passenger Rail Programs, Office of Railroad Development (RDV-13), Federal Railroad Administration-DOT, 1120 Vermont Ave. NW, Washington, DC 20005 Phone: (202) 493-6393, FAX (202) 493-6330.

Internet: www.fra.dot.gov.

20.315 NATIONAL RAILROAD PASSENGER CORPORATION GRANTS ("Amtrak Grants")

Assistance: project grants.

Purposes: to support the operation of and capital investment in U.S. intercity passenger rail service. Funds may be used for operating expenses, capital investment activities, and/or payment of debt service obligations.

Eligible applicants/beneficiaries: National Railroad Passenger Corporation, as authorized by appropriating statute.

Range: $10,000,000 to $700,000,000.

Activity: new program listing in 2006 (CFDA on-line). Amtrak operates rail passenger service in 46 states and DC.

HQ: Passenger Programs Division (RDV-13), Office of Railroad Development, Federal Railroad Administration-DOT, 1120 Vermont Ave, NW, Washington, DC 20590 Phone: (no number provided).

Internet: www.fra.gov.

20.316 RAILROAD REHABILITATION AND IMPROVEMENT FINANCING PROGRAM ("RRIF Loan Program")

Assistance: direct loans (25 years).

Purposes: pursuant to the Railroad Revitalization and Regulatory Reform Act of 1976, to provide direct loans and loan guarantees in order to: acquire, improve, or rehabilitate intermodal, rail freight or passenger equipment or facilities, including track, components of track, bridges, yards, buildings and shops; to develop or establish new intermodal or railroad facilities; and to refinance outstanding debt incurred for described purposes. The maximum loan amount will be based on the remaining available funds under the Program's authorization. The interest rate on direct loans will be equal to the rate on Treasury securities of a similar term.

Eligible applicants/beneficiaries: state and local governments, government-sponsored authorities and corporations, railroads, and joint ventures that include at least one railroad.

Range: FY 07, $48,000,000 to $59,000,000. **Average:** FY 07, $53,500,000.

Activity: since 2002, $800 million in direct loans. Currently, nine applications have been approved for a total of $248 million.

HQ: Office of Freight Programs, Federal Railroad Administration-DOT, 1120 Vermont Ave. NW, Washington, DC 20590 Phone: (202) 493-6381, FAX: (202) 493-6330.

Internet: www.fra.dot.gov. (Note: no field offices for this program.)

20.317 CAPITAL ASSISTANCE TO STATES - INTERCITY PASSENGER RAIL SERVICE

Assistance: project grants/matching (50 percent).

Purposes: pursuant to the Transportation, Housing and Urban Development, and Related Agencies Appropriations Act of 2008, to provide financial assistance to fund capital improvements and related planning activities necessary to support improved or new intercity passenger rail service. Only proposed planning projects which lead to a programmatic Environmental Impact Statement for the purpose of route selection and/or a corridor transportation plan prepared in accordance with the methodologies set forth in FRA's publication, entitled "Railroad Corridor Transportation Plans: A Guidance Manual," will be considered for possible funding.

Eligible applicants: state departments of transportation (including DC) that include intercity passenger rail service as an integral part of statewide transportation planning as required under section 135 of Title 23, United States Code.

Eligible beneficiaries: general public, both users and non-users of intercity passenger rail service; state departments of transportation and other public agencies; private transportation companies that participate through contractual arrangements with a state DOT.

Range/Average: N.A.

Activity: N.A. New program in FY 08.

HQ: Office of Railroad Development, 1200 New Jersey Ave. SE, Washington, DC 20590 Phone: (202) 493-6360, FAX: (202) 493-6333.

Internet: www.fra.dot.gov.

FEDERAL TRANSIT ADMINISTRATION

20.500 FEDERAL TRANSIT—CAPITAL INVESTMENT GRANTS

Assistance: formula grants; project grants (80-90 percent).

Purposes: for public transportation project costs in the following categories: fixed guideway modernization formula grants; bus and bus facilities discretionary grants and "New Starts" discretionary grants covering new systems and extensions, if specifically designated by Congress. Eligible costs include: acquisition, construction, reconstruction, and improvement of facilities and equipment; purchases of land, buses or other rolling stock; planning and engineering; new technological methods and techniques; park-and-ride lots; projects to meet the needs of the elderly and the disabled; certain projects enhancing urban economic development.

Eligible applicants/beneficiaries: public agencies including states, municipalities, and other state subdivisions; public agencies and instrumentalities of one or more states; public corporations, boards, and commissions established under state law. Private transportation companies may participate through contracts.

Range: fixed guideway modernization, $32,173 to $388,971,544; bus/bus facilities, $9,518 to $11,137,500; New Starts, $392,040 to $333,234,000. **Average:** fixed guideway modernization, $22,313,621; bus/bus facilities, $865,268; New Starts, $22,319,550.

Activity: not quantified specifically.

HQ: Office of Transit Programs, FTA-DOT, 400 Seventh St. SW, Washington, DC 20590. Phone: (202) 366-2053.

Internet: www.fta.dot.gov.

20.505 FEDERAL TRANSIT—METROPOLITAN PLANNING GRANTS ("Metropolitan Planning")

Assistance: formula grants. (80 percent/3 years).

Purposes: to develop transportation improvement projects, long- range transportation plans, and other technical studies related to management systems, capital requirements, and economic feasibility.

Eligible applicants/beneficiaries: states (for distribution to metropolitan planning organizations).

Range: $20,000 to $5,000,000.

Activity: not quantified specifically.

HQ: Office of Planning and Environment (TPE-11), FTA-DOT, 400 Seventh St. SW, Washington, DC 20590 Phone: (202) 366-1648.

Internet: www.fta.dot.gov.

20.507 FEDERAL TRANSIT—FORMULA GRANTS ("Urbanized Area Formula Program")

Assistance: formula grants. (50-90 percent/3 years).

Purposes: to plan, acquire, construct or reconstruct, improve, and maintain transit facilities and equipment. Transit projects may involve bringing equipment into compliance with the ADA and the Clean Air Act; also, they may involve bicycles (90 percent funding). Grants subsidizing operating costs may not exceed 50 percent.

Eligible applicants/beneficiaries: urbanized areas of 200,000 or more population—public entities jointly designated by the governor, responsible local officials, and publicly-owned operators of mass transportation services. Urbanized areas of 50,000 to 200,000 population—governors or their designees.

Range/Average: N.A.

Activity: not quantified specifically.

HQ: Director, Office of Resource Management and State Programs, Office of Program Management, FTA-DOT, 400 Seventh St. SW, Washington, DC 20590 Phone: (202) 366-1659.

Internet: www.fta.dot.gov.

20.509 FORMULA GRANTS FOR OTHER THAN URBANIZED AREAS ("Nonurbanized Area Formula Program")

Assistance: formula grants. (50-90 percent/2 years).

Purposes: for public transportation systems in nonurbanized areas—i.e., rural and small areas under 50,000 population, for uses similar to **20.507**.

Eligible applicants/beneficiaries: designated state agencies. Sub-grants may be awarded to state agencies, local public bodies and agencies, nonprofit organizations, tribes, and operators of public transportation services, including intercity bus service—in rural and small urban areas. Private operators may receive subcontracts.

Range/Average: N.A.

Activity: since 1979, assistance to over 1,300 rural/small urban transportation providers.

HQ: Office of Capital and Formula Assistance, Office of Program Management, FTA-DOT, 400 Seventh St. SW, Washington, DC 20590 Phone: (202) 366-0893.

Internet: www.fta.dot.gov.

20.513 CAPITAL ASSISTANCE PROGRAM FOR ELDERLY PERSONS AND PERSONS WITH DISABILITIES

Assistance: formula grants. (80 percent/3 years).

Purposes: to cover capital costs of providing specialized transportation services for elderly and handicapped persons. Specially designed vehicles may be purchased with grant funds. Awards favor projects involving private profit operators.

Eligible applicants/beneficiaries: designated states. Subgrants may be awarded to private nonprofit organizations or public bodies.

Range: $62,456 to $11,687,113.

Activity: cumulatively since 1975 program inception, funds to 1,000 organizations to purchase vehicles, involving some 4,000 subrecipients.

HQ: Program Coordinator, Office of Resource Management and State Programs, Office of Program Management, FTA-DOT, 400 Seventh St. SW, Washington, DC 20590 Phone: (202) 366-1655.

Internet: www.fta.dot.gov.

20.514 PUBLIC TRANSPORTATION RESEARCH ("National Planning and Research Programs")

Assistance: project grants; technical information; training (to 100 percent).

Purposes: for research on mobility management, transit operational efficiency, safety and emergency preparedness, transit capacity building, energy independence and environmental protection, infrastructure and equipment protection and innovation, and strategic program planning. Projects may involve research, development, demonstrations, training, planning studies, and human resource programs.

Eligible applicants/beneficiaries: public bodies, state and local agencies, nonprofit institutions, universities, profit organizations, and operators of public transportation services.

Range/Average: N.A.

Activity: not quantified specifically.

HQ: Associate Administrator/Research, Demonstration and Innovation (TRI-1), FTA-DOT, 400 Seventh St. SW - Rm.9401, Washington, DC 20590 Phone: (202) 366-4052, -4209.

Internet: www.fta.dot.gov/research (Note: no field offices for this program.)

20.515 STATE PLANNING AND RESEARCH

Assistance: formula grants (80 percent).

Purposes: to develop cost-effective multimodal transportation improvement programs, including the planning, engineering, and design of federal transit projects and other technical studies and training, within a unified or officially coordinated state- wide transportation system. States may authorize use of funds to supplement metropolitan planning funds. This program operates as a block grant program, for projects identified by states to accomplish planning and research objectives.

Eligible applicants/beneficiaries: states.

Range: $45,000 to $1,000,000 (plus per-state formula allocations).

Activity: not quantified specifically.

HQ: Office of Planning and Environment (TPE-11), FTA-DOT, 400 Seventh St. SW, Washington, DC 20590 Phone: (202) 366-1648.

Internet: www.fta.dot.gov.

20.516 JOB ACCESS—REVERSE COMMUTE

Assistance: project grants (50-80 percent/to 4 years).

Purposes: pursuant to the Transportation Equity Act for the 21st Century, to develop transportation services to connect welfare recipients and low-income persons to employment and support services. Funds may be used: for capital projects; to finance equipment, facilities, and associated support costs related to providing access to jobs—associated with adding reverse commute bus, train, carpool or service from urban areas, urbanized areas, and other areas to suburban work places.

Eligible applicants/beneficiaries: state and local government agencies, nonprofit agencies, transit providers.

Range: $24,000 to $1,500,000. **Average:** $356,000.

Activity: cumulatively, 450 grants in 45 states and DC.

HQ: Office of Program Management, FTA-DOT, 400 Seventh St. SW - Rm.9315, Washington, DC 20590 Phone: (202) 366-2053, -1622; Office of Research and Innovation (Rm.9407), (202) 366-1666.

Internet: www.fta.dot.gov.

20.518 CAPITAL AND TRAINING ASSISTANCE PROGRAM FOR OVER- THE-ROAD BUS ACCESSIBILITY

Assistance: project grants. (to 90 percent/3 years).

Purposes: pursuant to the Transportation Equity Act for the 21st Century, for private operators of over-the-road buses to finance the incremental capital and training costs of complying with DOT's "Transportation for Individuals with Disabilities" rule. Project costs may cover: adding wheelchair lifts and other accessibility components to new vehicle purchases; retrofitting existing vehicles; training in equipment operation and maintenance, boarding assistance, handling, and storage.

Eligible applicants/beneficiaries: certain private operators of over-the-road buses.

Range: $20,000 to $180,000. **Average:** $20,000.

Activity: FY 05, 93 companies funded, 194 vehicles made wheelchair-accessible.

HQ: Program Manager, Office of Program Management, FTA-DOT, 400 Seventh St. SW - Rm.9315, Washington, DC 20590 Phone: (202) 366-6053.

Internet: www.fta.dot.gov.

20.519 CLEAN FUELS

Assistance: project grants (80-90 percent).

Purposes: for the acquisition of approved "clean fuel buses" and related facilities by agencies providing public transportation in urbanized areas designated as non-attainment or maintenance area for ozone or carbon monoxide.

Eligible applicants/beneficiaries: public agencies including states and municipalities; public corporations, boards, and commissions established under state laws. States are applicants in urbanized areas of under 200,000 population.

Range: $160,000 to $5,250,000. **Average:** $1,112,000.

Activity: new program in FY 06 (CFDA on-line).

HQ: Office of Program Management, FTA-DOT, 400 Seventh St. SW, Washington, DC 20590 Phone: (202) 366-4020.

Internet: www.fta.dot.gov.

20.521 NEW FREEDOM PROGRAM

Assistance: formula grants (50-100 percent).

Purposes: pursuant to SAFETEA-LU, for new public transportation services or alternatives available to persons with disabilities, beyond ADA requirements. Funds may cover capital and operating expenses within certain limits.

Eligible applicants/beneficiaries: governor-designated recipients. Eligible subrecipients include public and nonprofit agencies, public transportation providers, human services transportation providers.

Range: $35,000 to $5,700,000.

Activity: new program in FY 06 (CFDA on-line).

HQ: Office of Program Management, FTA-DOT, 400 Seventh St. SW, Washington, DC 20590 Phone: (202) 366-2053.

Internet: www.fta.dot.gov.

20.522 ALTERNATIVES ANALYSIS

Assistance: project grants (80 percent).

Purposes: to conduct analyses of modal and multimodal alternatives and general alignment options for identified transportation needs in particular, broadly defined travel corridors, as part of the early planning for capital projects for new or extensions of existing fixed guideway systems.

Eligible applicants/beneficiaries: public agencies including states and municipalities; public corporations, boards, and commissions established under state laws.

Range: $300,000 to $2,500,000. **Average:** $139,000.

Activity: new program in FY 06 (CFDA on-line); estimated alternatives analysis support for over 18 fixed guideway transit systems.

HQ: Office of Program Management, FTA-DOT, 400 Seventh St. SW, Washington, DC 20590 Phone: (202) 366-2053.

Internet: www.fta.dot.gov.

NATIONAL HIGHWAY TRAFFIC SAFETY ADMINISTRATION

20.600 STATE AND COMMUNITY HIGHWAY SAFETY

Assistance: formula grants (80 percent).

Purposes: pursuant to the Highway Safety Act of 1966 as amended, for highway traffic safety enforcement program costs, such as police equipment purchases, training, and overtime pay; emergency medical services training and equipment purchases; public education projects. Program priority areas include alcohol and other drug countermeasures, police traffic services, occupant protection, traffic records, emergency medical services, motorcycle safety, pedestrian/bicycle safety, speed control, roadway safety, pupil transportation safety.

Eligible applicants/beneficiaries: states, tribes, territories, possessions.

Range: $340,000 to $13,000,000. **Average:** $2,200,000.

Activity: not quantified specifically.

HQ: Associate Administrator/Injury Control Operations and Resources, National Highway Traffic Safety Administration-DOT, Washington, DC 20590 Phone: (202) 366-2121 *Or*: Transportation Specialist, Safety Technology Division, Office of Highway Safety, Federal Highway Administration, Washington, DC 20590 Phone: (202) 366-2161.

Internet: www.nhtsa.whatsup.fedassist/index.html.

20.601 ALCOHOL TRAFFIC SAFETY AND DRUNK DRIVING PREVENTION INCENTIVE GRANTS

Assistance: project grants (50-75 percent).

Purposes: pursuant to the Highway Safety Act of 1998 as amended, for state programs to reduce crashes resulting from persons driving under the influence of alcohol and other controlled substances. Grant amounts are based on apportionments by states. Funds may be used: to purchase breath testing devices; to train law enforcement personnel; for public education; to pay for overtime by police personnel.

Eligible applicants/beneficiaries: states, DC, territories, possessions.

Average: $258,000 to $9,770,407.

Activity: N.A.

HQ: Associate Administrator/Injury Control Operations and Resources, National Highway Traffic Safety Administration-DOT, Washington, DC 20590 Phone: (202) 366-2121.

Internet: www.nhtsa.dot.gov.

20.602 OCCUPANT PROTECTION ("Section 405")

Assistance: project grants. (25-100 percent/to 6 years).

Purposes: pursuant to the Highway Safety Act of 1998 as amended, for states to implement and enforce automobile occupant protection programs.

Eligible applicants/beneficiaries: states, DC, PR, VI, Samoa, Northern Marianas, Guam, BIA.

Range: $77,758 to $2,989,991. **Average:** $603,659.

Activity: FY 06 estimate, 41 awards.

HQ: Associate Administrator/Injury Control Operations and Resources, National Highway Traffic Safety Administration-DOT, Washington, DC 20590 Phone: (202) 366-2121.

Internet: www.nhtsa.dot.gov.

20.605 SAFETY INCENTIVES TO PREVENT OPERATION OF MOTOR VEHICLES BY INTOXICATED PERSONS

Assistance: project grants (100 percent).

Purposes: Highway Safety Act of 1998 as amended, to encourage states to establish an 0.08 percent blood alcohol concentration as the legal limit for drunk driving.

Eligible applicants: states, DC, territories and Bureau of Indian Affairs.

Eligible beneficiaries: state highway safety agencies.

Range: $1,000,000 to $4,000,000. **Average:** $1,850,000.

Activity: N.A.

HQ: Associate Administrator/Injury Control Operations and Resources, National Highway Traffic Safety Administration-DOT, Washington, DC 20590. Phone: (202) 366-2121.

Internet: http://www.nhtsa/whatsup/fedassist/index.html.

20.607 ALCOHOL OPEN CONTAINER REQUIREMENTS

Assistance: project grants (to 6 years).

Purposes: pursuant to the Highway Safety Act of 1998 as amended, to encourage states to enact and enforce alcohol open container laws. Funding is based on the calculated annual savings in medical costs to the federal government, including in the Medicare and Medicaid programs.

Eligible applicants/beneficiaries: states, DC, and PR—provided they have no Repeat Intoxicated Driver Laws in effect.

Range: $2,500,000 to $13,700,000. **Average:** $5,500,000.

Activity: new program listing in 2004.

HQ: *program information,* Office of Injury Control Operations and Resources, NHTSA-DOT (NTI-200), 400 Seventh St. SW - Rm.5130, Washington, DC 20590. Phone: (202) 366-2121. *Legal issues,* Office of Chief Counsel, NHTSA-DOT (NCC-113), 400 Seventh St., SW-Room 5219, Washington, DC, 20590 Phone: (202) 366-1834.

Internet: www.nhtsa/whatsup/fedassist/index.html.

20.608 MINIMUM PENALTIES FOR REPEAT OFFENDERS FOR DRIVING WHILE INTOXICATED

Assistance: project grants (to 6 years).

Purposes: pursuant to the Highway Safety Act of 1998 as amended, to encourage states to enact Repeat Intoxicated Driver Laws. Program funding is based on the calculated annual savings in medical costs to the federal government, including in the Medicare and Medicaid programs.

Eligible applicants/beneficiaries: states, DC, and PR—provided they have no Repeat Intoxicated Driver Laws in effect.

Range: $2,400,000 to $47,500,000. **Average:** $7,000,000.

Activity: new program listing in 2004.

HQ: Office of Injury Control Operations and Resources, National Highway Traffic Safety Administration-DOT, Washington, DC 20590 Phone: (202) 366-2121.

Internet: www.nhsta/whatsup/fedassist/index.html.

20.609 SAFETY BELT PERFORMANCE GRANTS ("Section 406")

Assistance: project grants (100 percent).

Purposes: pursuant to SAFETEA-LU, Section 406, for states to adopt and implement programs improving the efficiency, completeness, uniformity, in-state, interstate, and national compatibility, integration, and accessibility of state data on trends—enabling observation and analysis of national trends in crash occurrences, rates, outcomes, and circumstances; for evaluations. Project examples include such activities as: highly visible enforcement of impaired driving and safety belt violations; paid and earned media campaigns supporting mobilizations and crackdowns; motorcycle rider education; pedestrian safety; speed management; DWI courts; technical training of law enforcement officers, prosecutors, and state highway safety officials.

Eligible applicants/beneficiaries: states, DC, PR, VI, Samoa, Northern Marianas, Guam.

Range: $300,000 to $35,000,000.

Activity: new program listing in 2006 (CFDA on-line). FY 06 estimate, 6-8 awards to "New Primary Law" states; 24 awards to "Pre-2003 Primary Law" states and territories.

HQ: *program information,* Office of Injury Control Operations and Resources, NHTSA-DOT (NTI-200), 400 Seventh St. SW - Rm.5130, Washington, DC 20590. Phone: (202) 366-2121. *Legal issues,* Office of Chief Counsel, NHTSA-DOT (NCC-113), 400 Seventh St., SW-Room 5219, Washington, DC, 20590 Phone: (202) 366-1834.

Internet: www.nhtsa.dot.gov.

20.610 STATE TRAFFIC SAFETY INFORMATION SYSTEM IMPROVEMENT GRANTS ("Section 406")

Assistance: project grants (to 4 years).

Purposes: pursuant to SAFETEA-LU, to encourage sates to adopt and implement effective programs to improve the timelines, accuracy, completeness, uniformity, integration, and accessibility of state data; to link state data systems with other systems within the state, and with other state and national data systems and improve compatibility between systems; to enhance the ability to observe and analyze trends in crash occurrences, rates, outcomes, and circumstances. Funds may be used only to implement data improvement programs.

Eligible applicants/beneficiaries: states, DC, PR, VI, Guam, American Samoa, Northern Mariana Islands, tribes. Applicants must meet certain NHTSA criteria.

Range: $300,000 to $2,255,376.

Activity: FY 06 estimate, 18 awards.

HQ: *program information,* Office of Injury Control Operations and Resources, NHTSA-DOT (NTI-200), 400 Seventh St. SW - Rm.5130, Washington, DC 20590 Phone: (202) 366-2121 *Legal issues,* Office of Chief Counsel, NHTSA-DOT (NCC-113), 400 Seventh St., SW-Room 5219, Washington, DC, 20590 Phone: (202) 366-1834.

Internet: http://webster.nhtsa.dot.gov.

20.611 INCENTIVE GRANT PROGRAM TO PROHIBIT RACIAL PROFILING ("Section 1906")

Assistance: project grants. (80 percent/to 2 years).

Purposes: pursuant to SAFETEA-LU, Section 1906, for states to enact and enforce laws prohibiting racial profiling in the enforcement of laws on federal-aid highways, and to maintain and allow public inspection of statistics on motor vehicle stops by officers in the enforcement of state laws. "Law states" may use funds to; collect, maintain, and evaluate pertinent data; develop and implement programs to reduce racial profiling, including training of law enforcement officers. "Assurances states" may use funds for: activities to prohibit racial profiling in the enforcement of state laws regulating the use of federal-aid highways; activities permitted to "law states;" providing public access to traffic stop data and evaluating the results of such data.

Eligible applicants/beneficiaries: states, DC, PR, VI, Samoa, Northern Marianas, Guam.

Range: $36,000 to $644,000. **Average:** $230,000.

Activity: new program in FY 06 (CFDA on-line). FY 06 estimate, 40 awards.

HQ: *program information,* Office of Injury Control Operations and Resources, NHTSA-DOT (NTI-122), 400 Seventh St. SW - Rm.5130, Washington, DC 20590 Phone: (202) 366-0543 *Legal issues,* Office of Chief Counsel, NHTSA-DOT (NCC-113), 400 Seventh St., SW-Room 5219, Washington, DC, 20590 Phone: (202) 366-1834.

Internet: www.webster.nhtsa.dot.gov.

20.612 INCENTIVE GRANT PROGRAM TO INCREASE MOTORCYCLIST SAFETY ("Section 2010")

Assistance: project grants (100 percent).

Purposes: pursuant to SAFETEA-LU, Section 2010, for states to adopt and implement programs to reduce the number of single and multi-vehicle crashes involving motorcyclists. Funds may be used for safety training and motorcyclist awareness programs including: improving training curricula and program delivery in urban and rural areas; acquiring practice motorcycles and suitable training facilities; instruction materials; mobile training units; recruitment and retention of instructors; public service announcements and other outreach methods. States may sub- allocate funds to nonprofit organizations.

Eligible applicants/beneficiaries: states, DC, PR.

Range: $100,000 to $464,000. **Average:** $120,000.

Activity: new program listing in 2006 (CFDA on-line). FY 06 estimate, 40 awards anticipated.

HQ: *program information,* Office of Injury Control Operations and Resources, NHTSA-DOT (NTI-122), 400 Seventh St. SW - Rm.5130, Washington, DC 20590 Phone: (202) 366-0543 *Legal issues,* Office of

Chief Counsel, NHTSA-DOT (NCC-113), 400 Seventh St., SW-Room 5219, Washington, DC, 20590 Phone: (202) 366-1834.

Internet: www.webster.nhtsa.dot.gov.

20.613 CHILD SAFETY AND CHILD BOOSTER SEATS INCENTIVE GRANTS ("Section 2011")

Assistance: project grants (50-75 percent).

Purposes: pursuant to SAFETEA-LU, Section 2010, for states to enact and enforce child restraint laws requiring children under age 8 and weighing up to 65 pounds to be properly restrained, unless they are 4'9" tall. No more than 50 percent of grant amounts may be used to purchase and distribute child safety seats and restraints to low-income families; remaining amounts may be used for program costs including: enforcement; training passenger safety personnel, educators, and parents; public education.

Eligible applicants/beneficiaries: states, DC, PR.

Range: $31,000 to $587,000. **Average:** $115,000.

Activity: new program listing in 2006 (CFDA on-line); FY 06 estimate, 15 awards.

HQ: *program information,* Office of Injury Control Operations and Resources, NHTSA-DOT (NTI-122), 400 Seventh St. SW - Rm.5130, Washington, DC 20590 Phone: (202) 366-0543 *Legal issues,* Office of Chief Counsel, NHTSA-DOT (NCC-113), 400 Seventh St., SW-Room 5219, Washington, DC, 20590 Phone: (202) 366-1834.

Internet: www.nhtsa.dot.gov.

20.614 NATIONAL HIGHWAY TRANSPORTATION SAFETY ADMINISTRATION (NHTSA) DISCRETIONARY SAFETY GRANTS ("Highway Safety Research and Development")

Assistance: project grants.

Purposes: pursuant to Highway Safety Act of 1966, as amended, to provide funds to conduct research and development on transportation safety and related issues, specifically projects identified in DOT's Annual Appropriation Legislation.

Eligible applicants/beneficiaries: grantee application eligibility will be developed on an individual grant or cooperative agreement basis by NHTSA Purchase Team.

Range/Average: N.A.

Activity: new program listing in 2006 (CFDA on-line).

HQ: Office of Acquisition Management, NHTSA-DOT, 400 Seventh St. SW - Rm.5301, Washington, DC 20590 Phone: (202) 366-9564, FAX (202) 366-9555.

Internet: www.nhsta.dot.gov (Note: no field offices for this program.)

PIPELINE AND HAZARDOUS MATERIALS SAFETY ADMINISTRATION

20.700 PIPELINE SAFETY PROGRAM BASE GRANTS

Assistance: formula grants (to 50 percent).

Purposes: pursuant to the Natural Gas Pipeline Safety Act of 1968 as amended and related acts, to pay personnel, inspection, equipment, training, and research costs related to natural gas, liquefied natural gas, and hazardous liquids pipeline safety programs.

Eligible applicants/beneficiaries: state agencies.

Range: $1,511 to $1,396,400.

Activity: FY 01, 49 grants (latest data reported).

HQ: Pipelines and Hazardous Materials Safety Administration-DOT, 400 Seventh St. SW, Washington, DC 20590 Phone: (202) 366-4595.

Internet: www.phmsa.dot.gov.

20.701 UNIVERSITY TRANSPORTATION CENTERS PROGRAM

Assistance: project grants. (50 percent/3 to 5 years).

Purposes: to provide assistance to nonprofit IHEs for the purpose of establishing and operating university transportation centers that conduct research, education, and technology transfer programs addressing regional and national transportation issues.

Eligible applicants/beneficiaries: public and private nonprofit IHEs; to apply for competitive grant, IHEs must have established transportation research programs.

Range: $300,000 to $3,500,000 per center, per fiscal year.

Activity: new program in 2006; FY 06, 20 grants anticipated.

HQ: Office of Innovation, Research, and Education (RDT-30), Research and Innovative Technology Administration (RITA)-DOT, 400 Seventh St. SW - Rm.2440, Washington, DC 20590 Phone: (202) 366-4434.

Internet: www.utc.dot.gov.

20.703 INTERAGENCY HAZARDOUS MATERIALS PUBLIC SECTOR TRAINING AND PLANNING GRANTS ("Hazardous Materials Emergency Preparedness Training and Planning Grants" - "HMEP")

Assistance: project grants. (80 percent/to 6 years).

Purposes: pursuant to the Federal Hazardous Materials Transportation Act, for the development, improvement, and implementation of emergency response plans to handle hazardous materials accidents and incidents; to enhance implementation of the Emergency Planning and Community Right-to-Know Act of 1986 (EPCRA); for related training of public sector employees.

Eligible applicants/beneficiaries: states, tribes, territories.

Range: $4,000 to $968,000. **Average:** $180,000.

Activity: all states, territories, and 41 tribes funded since program inception.

HQ: HMEP Grants Manager (PHM-64), Research and Special Programs Administration-DOT, 400 Seventh St. SW, Washington, DC 20590 Phone: (202) 366-0001.

Internet: www.phmsa.dot.gov (Note: no field offices for this program.)

20.704 RITA HYDROGEN ("SAFETEA-LU Hydrogen R&D")

Assistance: project grants. (80 percent/4 years).

Purposes: for national transportation-related research, education, and technology transfer programs in propulsion technology and alternative fuels.

Eligible applicants/beneficiaries: nonprofit IHEs earmarked in authorizing legislation.

Range: $750,000 to $2,500,000 per year.

Activity: new program listing in 2006 (CFDA on-line). Note: no new grants to be awarded.

HQ: Research Development and Technology (RDT), Research and Innovative Technology Administration (RITA)-DOT, 400 Seventh St. SW - Rm.2438, Washington, DC 20590. Phone: (202) 366-4999.

Internet: www.hydrogen.dot.gov (Note: no field offices for this program.)

20.720 STATE DAMAGE PREVENTION PROGRAM GRANTS ("SDPP Grants")

Assistance: project grants.

Purposes: to improve State Damage prevention programs, which are intended to protect underground facilities from excavation damage. Grant funds may not be used for lobbying or in direct support of litigation.

Eligible applicants: any state, territory, or possession authority designated by the Governor with appropriate US DOT Pipeline and Hazardous Materials Safety Administration (PHMSA) certification or agreement.

Eligible beneficiaries: states, territories and possessions.

Range/Average: $0 to $100,000.

Activity: N.A.

HQ: Pipelines and Hazardous Materials Safety Administration-DOT, Room E-22-103, 1200 New Jersey Ave. SE, Washington, DC 20590. Phone: (202) 366-6942.

Internet: www.phmsa.dot.gov. (Note: no field offices for this program.)

20.721 PHMSA PIPELINE SAFETY PROGRAM ONE CALL GRANT

Assistance: project grants (100 percent).

Purposes: pursuant to the Pipeline Safety Act of 1979, Pipeline Safety Reauthorization Act of 1988, Pipeline Safety Act of 1992, Accountable Pipeline Safety and Partnership Act of 1996, and Natural Gas Pipeline

Safety Act of 1968 as amended, to provide funding to state agencies in promoting damage prevention, including changes with theirs state underground damage prevention laws, related compliance activities, and training and public education. State agencies who participate in the pipeline safety program are eligible to apply for One Call grant funding on an annual basis. This optional grant program has a maximum amount request of $50,000 per state and supports initiatives to further promote efforts specifically for damage prevention, including one-call legislation, related compliance activities, training and public education.

Eligible applicants: states that have a certification or agreement with US DOT Pipeline and Hazardous Materials Safety Administration (PHMSA) to do pipeline safety inspections.

Eligible beneficiaries: state agencies.

Range/Average: $3,666 to $35,400.

Activity: FY 07, $1,021,000 to 37 state agencies for One Call grant fund.

HQ: State Program Director, Pipelines and Hazardous Materials Safety Administration-DOT, 1200 New Jersey Ave. SE, Washington, DC 20590. Phone: (202) 366-4595.

Internet: www.phmsa.dot.gov.

20.760 UNIVERSITY TRANSPORTATION CENTERS

Assistance: project grants (50 percent/3, 4, or 5 years as designated).

Purposes: to provide grants to nonprofit institutions of higher learning for the purpose of establishing and operating university transportation centers that conduct research, education, and technology transfer programs addressing regional and national transportation issues, both long-range and immediate.

Eligible applicants/beneficiaries: public and private nonprofit institutions of higher learning. For competitive grants, institutions must have established transportation research programs.

Range/Average: $300,000 and $3,500,000 per center, per fiscal year.

Activity: not quantified specifically.

HQ: Research Development and Technology (RDT), Research and Research and Innovative Technology Administration, (RITA)-DOT, 400 Seventh St. SW - Rm.2440, Washington, DC 20590. Phone: (202) 366-4934.

Internet: www.utc.dot.gov. (Note: no field offices for this program.)

20.761 BIOBASED TRANSPORTATION RESEARCH ("Biobased R & D")

Assistance: project grants (50 percent/4 years).

Purposes: pursuant to SAFTEA- LU, to carry out biobased research of national importance at the National Biodiesel Board and at research centers identified in section 9011 of the Farm Security and Rural Investment Act of 2002. No new grants will be awarded during the program's remaining authorization (through 2009).

Eligible applicants: applicants as designated in SAFTEA- LU.

Eligible beneficiaries: public and private nonprofit institutions of higher learning and industry trade groups.

Range/Average: $12,500,000/year.

Activity: N.A. New program in FY 08.

HQ: Research and Research and Innovative Technology Administration, Research Development and Technology (RDT)-DOT, 400 Seventh St. SW - Rm. 2448, Washington, DC 20590. Phone: (202) 366-4999.

Internet: www.rita.dot.gov. (Note: no field offices for this program.)

20.762 RESEARCH GRANTS

Assistance: project grants. (80 percent/1-4 years).

Purposes: grants awarded to three institutions/organizations: to develop a research facility in Lewiston, Montana for basic and applies research and testing on surface transportation issues facing rural and cold regions; to carry out the Rural Transportation Research Initiative in at North Dakota State University; and to conduct a feasibility study for the creation of a system of inland ports and distributions centers in Appalachia.

Eligible applicants/beneficiaries: legislated grants in SAFETEA-LU, Section 5513(d)(g) (i), to the following institutions: Western Montana Transportation Institute, Upper Great Plains Transportation Institute, and Appalachian Regional Commission.

Range: $300,000 to $707,000 per center.

Activity: new program in 2006.

HQ: Office of Intermodalism, Research and Innovative Technology Administration (RITA)-DOT, 400 Seventh St. SW - Rm.2420, Washington, DC 20590 Phone: (no number provided).

Internet: (none provided) (Note: no field offices for this program.)

20.763 RESEARCH AND INNOVATIVE TECHNOLOGY (RIT) HYDROGEN ALTERNATIVE FUEL LIFE CYCLE ("RIT H2 Life Cycle")

Assistance: project grants.

Purposes: to conduct research evaluating Hydrogen and Alternative Fuel Life Cycle, according to provisions provided in SAFETEA-LU.

Eligible applicants/beneficiaries: recipients earmarked in authorizing legislation.

Range: $1,000,000.

Activity: new program listing in 2006.

HQ: Office of Research, Development and Technology, (RITA)-DOT, 400 Seventh St. SW - Rm.2438, Washington, DC 20590 Phone: (202) 366-4999.

Internet: no web site address provided (Note: no field offices for this program.)

20.764 HYDROGEN STORAGE RESEARCH AND DEVELOPMENT ("RIT H2 Life Cycle")

Assistance: project grants (20 percent).

Purposes: pursuant to SAFTEA- LU, to conduct research to develop hydrogen storage technologies. No new grants will be awarded during the program's remaining authorization (through 2009).

Eligible applicants: recipients designated in SAFTEA-LU (Public Law 109-59, August. 10, 2005 119 Stat. 1406.) number 3891.

Eligible beneficiaries: public and private nonprofit institutions of higher learning and industry trade groups.

Range: $400,000/year. **Average:** N.A.

Activity: N.A.

HQ: Research and Innovative Technology Administration, Research Development and Technology (RDT), DOT, 400 Seventh Street, SW., Rm 2438, Washington, DC 20590. Phone: (202) 366-4999.

Internet: no internet address provided (Note: no field offices for this program.)

MARITIME ADMINISTRATION

20.801 DEVELOPMENT AND PROMOTION OF PORTS AND INTERMODAL TRANSPORTATION ("Ports and Domestic Shipping and Intermodal Development")

Assistance: advisory services/counseling; technical information.

Purposes: pursuant to Merchant Marine Acts, Defense Production Act of 1950, and amendments, to make federal personnel available to help promote and plan for the development and utilization of domestic waterways, ports, port facilities, and intermodal transportation systems by conducting studies in cooperation with port authorities and others—toward the enhancement of related economic development, as well as national security under national mobilization conditions. No grants are awarded under this program.

Eligible applicants/beneficiaries: state and local government agencies, metropolitan planning organizations, public port and intermodal authorities, trade associations, private terminal and intermodal operators.

Range/Average: N.A.

Activity: not quantified specifically.

HQ: Director, Office of Ports and Domestic Shipping, Maritime Administration-DOT, Washington, DC 20590 Phone: (202) 366-4357, FAX (202) 366-6988; Director, Office of Intermodal Development, (202) 366-8888, FAX (202) 366-6988.

Internet: www.marad.dot.gov.

20.802 FEDERAL SHIP FINANCING GUARANTEES ("Title XI")

Assistance: guaranteed/insured loans. (87.5 percent/to 25 years).

Purposes: pursuant to the Merchant Marine Act of 1936 as amended, to finance or refinance: construction, reconstruction, reconditioning, or refinancing of ships built in U.S. shipyards, used in foreign or domestic commerce, in research, or as ocean thermal energy conversion facilities—in coast-wide or intercostal trade, on the Great Lakes or on bays, sounds, rivers, harbors, inland lakes, or as floating dry-docks; for advanced shipbuilding technology of general shipyard facilities. Vessels must be larger than five net tons—other than towboats, barges, scows, lighters, car floats, canal boats, or tank vessels of less than 25 gross tons.

Eligible applicants/beneficiaries: qualified individuals, U.S. shipyards, U.S. and foreign ship owners.

Range: from less than $1,000,000 to several hundred million.

Activity: as of March, 2006, 10 applications pending, no approvals.

HQ: Associate Administrator/Shipbuilding, Office of Ship Financing, Maritime Administration-DOT, Washington, DC 20590 Phone: (202) 366-5744.

Internet: www.marad.dot.gov.

20.803 MARITIME WAR RISK INSURANCE ("Title XII, MMA, 1936")

Assistance: insurance.

Purposes: pursuant to the Merchant Marine Act of 1936 as amended, to provide war risk insurance binders or policies on vessels in operation or under construction. Insurance is available at nominal cost in peacetime.

Eligible applicants/beneficiaries: owners of U.S. flag vessels and certain foreign flag vessels.

Range/Average: N.A.

Activity: as of FY 04, 350 vessels covered.

HQ: Director, Office of Insurance and Shipping Analysis, Maritime Administration-DOT, 400 Seventh St. SW, Washington, DC 20590 Phone: (202) 366-2400.

Internet: www.marad.dot.gov.

20.806 STATE MARITIME SCHOOLS

Assistance: direct payments/specified use; use of property, facilities, and equipment (50 percent).

Purposes: for the operation and maintenance of state maritime schools; for loans to the schools of training vessels by the federal government, as well as their maintenance and repair; for incentive payments to selected cadets. States must admit out-of- state students.

Eligible applicants/beneficiaries: states (limited to one academy per state).

Range: states, $200,000 annually; student stipends, $4,000 per academic year for up to four years.

Activity: FY 04, 406 licensed mariners graduated; incentive payments to 45 cadets graduating as officers.

HQ: Director, Office of Policy and Plans, Maritime Administration-DOT, Washington, DC 20590 Phone: (202) 366-4468.

Internet: www.marad.dot.gov.

20.807 U.S. MERCHANT MARINE ACADEMY ("Kings Point")

Assistance: training.

Purposes: for the operation and maintenance of the federal maritime academy, including subsistence payments to students training to become merchant marine officers—as well as their quarters, medical care, program travel, and other expenses.

Eligible applicants/beneficiaries: U.S. citizens that are high school graduates; eligible international students.

Range: allowance prescribed for all personnel for uniforms and textbooks. (During the sea year a midshipman will earn $700 monthly from his/her steamship company employer.)

Activity: 2005, 221 graduates.

HQ: Director, Office of Policy and Plans, Maritime Administration-DOT, Washington, DC 20590 Phone: (202) 366-4468.

Internet: www.marad.dot.gov.

20.808 CAPITAL CONSTRUCTION FUND ("CCF")

Assistance: direct payments/specified use.

Purposes: pursuant to the Merchant Marine Act of 1936 as amended, to provide tax deferment incentives to shipbuilders to acquire, construct, or reconstruct vessels built in the U.S. for use in the U.S. foreign, Great Lakes, or noncontiguous domestic trades.

Eligible applicants/beneficiaries: U.S. citizens that own or lease one or more eligible vessels, with appropriate plans and financial capabilities.

Range/Average: N.A.

Activity: as of March 2005, 132 active agreements; cumulatively since program inception, over $2.7 billion in tax deferments. FY 04, 2 applications approved.

HQ: Associate Administrator/Shipbuilding, Office of Ship Financing, Maritime Administration-DOT, Washington, DC 20590 Phone: (202) 366-5744.

Internet: www.marad.dot.gov.

20.810 SUPPLEMENTARY TRAINING

Assistance: training.

Purposes: pursuant to the Merchant Marine Act of 1936 as amended, to train seafarers in shipboard firefighting, intermodal freight transportation, maritime defense, and safety-related subjects. Training is provided on a fee-paid basis.

Eligible applicants/beneficiaries: qualified U.S. merchant seafarers; operators of inland waterway, offshore drilling, and mining vessels; maritime academy students; NOAA, USCG, U.S. Army Corps of Engineers, and Naval Reserve personnel; qualified representatives of marine industry; state and local governments.

Range/Average: N.A.

Activity: FY 05, 418 firefighting training, 30 intermodal freight transportation, 45 national sealift training participants.

HQ: Associate Administrator/Policy and International Trade, Maritime Administration-DOT, Washington, DC 20590 Phone: (202) 366-5755.

Internet: www.marad.dot.gov.

20.812 CONSTRUCTION RESERVE FUND ("CRF")

Assistance: direct payments/specified use.

Purposes: pursuant to the Merchant Marine Act of 1936 as amended, to provide tax deferment incentives to shipbuilders to construct, reconstruct, recondition, or acquire vessels necessary for national defense or U.S. commerce.

Eligible applicants/beneficiaries: U.S. citizens that own in whole or in part one or more vessels operating in the foreign or domestic commerce of the U.S. or in the fisheries; citizens operating such vessel or vessels owned by another individual.

Range/Average: N.A.

Activity: as of March 2006, 22 active contracts with deposits totaling $100,000,000.

HQ: Associate Administrator/Shipbuilding, Office of Ship Financing, Maritime Administration-DOT, Washington, DC 20590 Phone: (202) 366-5744.

Internet: www.marad.dot.gov.

20.813 MARITIME SECURITY FLEET PROGRAM

Assistance: direct payments/specified use.

Purposes: pursuant to the Merchant Marine Act of 1936 as amended and Maritime Security Act of 2003, to maintain a U.S. flag merchant fleet crewed by U.S. citizens to serve both commercial and national security needs, including container ships, lighter- aboard ships, and roll-on/roll-off vessels.

Eligible applicants/beneficiaries: U.S. citizens and operators of U.S. flag vessels.

Average: FY 06-08, $2,600,000 per vessel per year.

Activity: as of January, 2006, 60 vessels enrolled.

HQ: Director, Office of Sealift Support, Maritime Administration- DOT, 400 Seventh St. SW, Washington, DC 20590 Phone: (202) 366- 2323, FAX (202) 366-3128.

Internet: www.marad.dot.gov (Note: no field offices for this program.)

20.814 ASSISTANCE TO SMALL SHIPYARDS ("Small Shipyard Grants")

Assistance: direct payments/specified use (75 percent).

Purposes: to award grants for capital and related infrastructure improvements at qualified shipyards that will facilitate the efficiency, cost effectiveness, and quality of domestic ship construction for commercial and Federal Government use. Federal funds can only exceed 75 percent of project cost if the cost is less than $26,075, or if a determination is made that project merits support and requires additional assistance.

Eligible applicants: shipyard; state or local government on behalf of a shipyard. The shipyard must be located in or near a maritime community, in a single geographical location and must be: a small business concern (section 3 of the Small Business Act) that has 600 or less production employees.

Eligible beneficiaries: shipyards.

Range/Average: to $10,000,000 (if matching requirement waived).

Activity: FY 08, 15 applications and 10 awards anticipated.

HQ: Associate Administrator/Business and Workforce Development, Maritime Administration-DOT, 1200 New Jersey Ave. SE-Room W21-318, Washington, DC 20590 Phone: (202) 366-5737, FAX: (202) 366-6988.

Internet: www.marad.dot.gov. (Note: no field offices for this program.)

OFFICE OF THE SECRETARY

20.900 TRANSPORTATION—CONSUMER AFFAIRS

Assistance: investigation of complaints.

Purposes: pursuant to the Federal Aviation Act of 1958 as amended, to provide assistance and information to consumers with complaints of all types against domestic and foreign air carriers, travel agents, and tour operators; to investigate alleged violations of airline passengers' civil rights.

Eligible applicants/beneficiaries: all users of air transportation.

Range/Average: N.A.

Activity: 2005, 11,716 complaints and information requests received.

HQ: Aviation Consumer Protection Division (C-75), DOT, 400 Seventh St. SW - Rm.4107, Washington, DC 20590 Phone: (202) 366- 5957 Consumer Complaints (Airline Service), Phone: (202) 366-2220; TTY (202) 366-0511 Toll Free Hotline for Airline Disability Problems, Phone: (800) 778-4838; TTY, (800) 455-9880.

Internet: http://airconsumer.ost.dot.gov.

20.901 PAYMENTS FOR ESSENTIAL AIR SERVICES

Assistance: direct payments/specified use.

Purposes: to subsidize air carriers providing commuter services to unserved communities, covering operating losses and a profit element.

Eligible applicants/beneficiaries: carriers selected by DOT.

Range: for continental U.S., $247,122 to 1,733,997. **Average:** $636,161 annually per point.

Activity: currently, some 154 affected communities receiving subsidies.

HQ: Director, Office of Aviation Analysis (X-50), DOT, 400 Seventh St. SW, Washington, DC 20590 Phone: (202) 366-5903.

Internet: www.ost.dot.gov (Note: no field offices for this program.)

20.904 BONDING ASSISTANCE PROGRAM

Assistance: insurance.

Purposes: to enhance opportunities for Small Disadvantaged Business Enterprises (SDBEs) to obtain bid, performance and payment bonds for transportation-related contracts emanating from DOT, its grantees, recipients, their contractors and subcontractors.

Eligible applicants/beneficiaries: certified minority, women-owned and disadvantaged business enterprises.

Average: $330,000.

Activity: 70 performance and payments bonds issued annually.

HQ: Bonding Manager, Office of Small and Disadvantaged Business Utilization (S- 40), Office of the Secretary-DOT, 400 Seventh St. SW, Washington, DC 20590 Phone: (202) 366-2852, (800) 532-1169.

Internet: http://osdbuweb.dot.gov (Note: no field offices for this program.)

20.905 DISADVANTAGED BUSINESS ENTERPRISES—SHORT TERM LENDING PROGRAM

Assistance: direct loans (1 year).

Purposes: to provide lines of credit to disadvantaged business enterprises to obtain accounts receivable financing for the performance of transportation-related contracts from DOT, its grantees, and recipients, and their contractors and subcontractors—including for maintenance, rehabilitation, restructuring, improvement, or revitalization of any mode of transportation with any public or commercial provider of transportation or any federal, state, or local transportation agency.

Eligible applicants/beneficiaries: certified disadvantaged business enterprises, minority- and women-owned enterprises; all SBA "Section 8(a)" firms; HUBZONE Empowerment-eligible and disabled veterans. Applicant must be in business for 2 -3 years; not for start-up business.

Range: to $500,000.

Activity: FY 05, 18 approvals.

HQ: Office of Small and Disadvantaged Business Utilization (S- 40), Office of the Secretary-DOT, 400 Seventh St. SW, Washington, DC 20590 Phone: (202) 366-2852, (800) 532-1169.

Internet: www.osdbuweb.dot.gov (Note: no field offices for this program.)

20.910 ASSISTANCE TO SMALL AND DISADVANTAGED BUSINESSES ("OSDBU's Small Business Transportation Resource Centers")

Assistance: project grants (100 percent).

Purposes: DOT's Office of Small and Disadvantaged Business Utilization (OSDBU) was established in accordance with Public Law 95-507, an amendment to the Small Business Act and the Small Business Investment Act of 1958. OSDBU ensures that small and disadvantaged business policies and goals of the Secretary of Transportation are developed and implemented in a fair, efficient and effective manner to serve small and disadvantaged businesses throughout DOT and the country. The DOT Short Term Lending Program provides assistance to enable small businesses to participate in transportation-related contracts and subcontracts funded by DOT, its grantees and recipients. Financial assistance provides lines of credit to finance accounts receivable arising from transportation-related contracts.

Eligible applicants: established 501 C(6) tax-exempt Chambers of Commerce, Trade Associations and 501 C(3) non-profit organizations, community colleges, minority educational institutions, tribal colleges and universities that have documented experience and capacity necessary to successfully operate and administer a coordinated, Small Business Transportation Resource Center (SBTRC) within their regions.

Eligible beneficiaries: small businesses, businesses owned and operated by socially/economically disadvantaged persons, and businesses owned and operated by women.

Range: N.A. **Average:** $150,000.

Activity: N.A.

HQ: Office of Small and Disadvantaged Business Utilization, S-40, Office of the Secretary, DOT, 400 Seventh Street, S.W., Washington, DC 20590. Phone:(202) 366-1930; TF(800) 532-1169.

Internet: http://www.dot.gov (Note: no field offices for this program.)

20.930 PAYMENTS FOR SMALL COMMUNITY AIR SERVICE DEVELOPMENT

Assistance: project grants. (to 100 percent/to 3 years).

Purposes: pursuant to the Wendell H. Ford Aviation Investment and Reform Act for the 21st Century and Vision 100-Century in Aviation Reauthorization Act, for smaller communities to enhance their air service and increase access to the national transportation system—through such activities as: marketing, advertising, and promotion; air service deficiency studies, measuring traffic loss or diversion to other communities; providing financial incentives including subsidies or revenue guarantees to cover air carrier's prospective operating losses or to ground service access providers.

Eligible applicants/beneficiaries: communities or consortia with airports not larger than a small hub airport, including in territories and possessions.

Range: $40,000 to $1,000,000. **Average:** $500,000.

Activity: new program in 2004; 30 communities participating.

HQ: Associate Director/Small Community Air Service Development Program, Office of Aviation Analysis (X-50), OS-DOT, 400 Seventh St. SW, Washington, DC 20590 Phone: (202) 366-5903, FAX (202) 366- 7638.

Internet: http://ostpxweb.dot.aviation/index.html (Note: no field offices for this program.)

20.931 TRANSPORTATION PLANNING, RESEARCH AND EDUCATION ("Transportation Planning, Research and Development")

Assistance: project grants.

Purposes: pursuant to DOT's FY 06 Appropriation Bill, to provide funds to conduct research and development on transportation, inter-modal systems and related issues. Examples of funded projects include: Evaluation of Shipper Requirement and Rail Services; Infrastructure and Transportations Support; Agriculture Transportation Pilot Project; and Eastern Seaboard Intermodal Transportation Study.

Eligible applicants/beneficiaries: mandated by Congress; only organizations identified in legislation may apply.

Range/Average: N.A.

Activity: new program; FY 06, 10 new grants.

HQ: Acquisition Services, OST-DOT, 400 Seventh St. SW-Room 5106, Washington, DC 20590 Phone: (202) 366-4968, FAX (202) 366-9848.

Internet: (none provided) (Note: no field offices for this program.)

DEPARTMENT OF THE TREASURY

INTERNAL REVENUE SERVICE

21.003 TAXPAYER SERVICE

Assistance: advisory services/counseling.

Purposes: to provide information and guidance on income tax matters, including taxpayer obligations and rights. Besides toll- free phone and Internet services and information offices, IRS sponsors volunteer programs, and offers films, seminars, and other services. Special educational programs are available to assist small businesses, secondary school teachers, adult education classes, colleges, and the elderly. Special procedures become effective for victims of natural disasters.

Eligible applicants/beneficiaries: individuals, groups.

Range/Average: N.A.

Activity: annually, 30,000,000 additional taxpayer contacts through partnership programs.

HQ: Commissioner, IRS, 1111 Constitution Ave. NW - Rm.3000IR, Washington, DC 20224 Phone: *general inquiries,* (800) 829-1040; National Taxpayer Advocate's Help Line, (877) 777-4778; TDD (800) 829-4059.

Internet: www.irs.gov.

21.004 EXCHANGE OF FEDERAL TAX INFORMATION WITH STATE TAX AGENCIES ("Agreement on Coordination of Tax Administration")

Assistance: specialized services.

Purposes: to increase taxpayer compliance and to reduce duplication of resources—through the confidential exchange of tax data, models, and extracts with states and municipalities for tax administration purposes.

Eligible applicants/beneficiaries: states, territories, and municipalities with over 250,000 population that impose taxes on income or wages.

Range/Average: N.A.

Activity: 50 state and several municipal and territorial agencies participating.

HQ: Director, Governmental Liaison and Disclosure, IRS, 1111 Constitution Ave. NW - Rm.1603, Washington, DC 20224 Phone: (202) 622-6200.

Internet: www.irs.gov/foia.

21.006 TAX COUNSELING FOR THE ELDERLY

Assistance: project grants.

Purposes: pursuant to the Revenue Act of 1978, to reimburse volunteers for their out-of-pocket expenses in receiving training and in providing tax counseling to elderly taxpayers.

Eligible applicants/beneficiaries: experienced private or public nonprofit organizations. Governmental agencies are ineligible.

Range/Average: N.A.

Activity: annually, 60 sponsors funded; 2,000,000 taxpayers assisted.

HQ: Program Analyst, Tax Counseling for the Elderly, IRS, 5000 Ellin Rd., Lanham, MD 20706 Phone: (202) 283-0189.

Internet: www.irs.gov (Note: no field offices for this program.)

21.008 LOW-INCOME TAXPAYER CLINICS

Assistance: project grants. (50 percent/to 3 years).

Purposes: to enable organizations to represent low-income taxpayers in controversies with the IRS, or to inform individuals with limited English language abilities of their tax rights and responsibilities.

Eligible applicants/beneficiaries: private nonprofit organizations; educational institutions with accredited law, business, or accounting schools.

Range/Average: N.A.

Activity: FY 05, 153 organizations funded.

HQ: Taxpayer Advocate Service, IRS, 1111 Constitution Ave, NW, Room 1034, Washington, DC 20224 Phone: (no number provided).

Internet: www.irs.gov/advocate; e-mail, LITCProgramOffice@irs.gov (Note: no field offices for this program.)

UNDER SECRETARY FOR DOMESTIC FINANCE

21.020 COMMUNITY DEVELOPMENT FINANCIAL INSTITUTIONS PROGRAM ("CDFI")

Assistance: project grants. (50 percent/to 3 years).

Purposes: to provide financial and technical assistance through CDFIs, promoting economic revitalization and community development, including for: CDFI staff training; acquiring products and services including technology; consulting services.

Eligible applicants/beneficiaries: private nonprofit institutions and organizations, and profit organizations that are or seek to become CDFIs. Governmental entities are ineligible.

Range: $50,000 to $2,000,000. **Average:** $800,000.

Activity: FY 05, 89 awards.

HQ: Program Manager, CDFI Fund, Department of the Treasury, 601 13th St. NW - Ste.200-S, Washington, DC 20005 Phone: (202) 622- 6355, FAX (202) 622-7754.

Internet: www.cdfifund.gov (Note: no field offices for this program.)

21.021 BANK ENTERPRISE AWARD PROGRAM ("BEA")

Assistance: project grants (100 percent).

Purposes: to encourage insured depository institutions to increase their level of community development activities in the form of loans, investments, services, and technical assistance within distressed communities; to provide assistance to community development financial institutions through grants, stock purchases, loans, deposits, and other forms of financial and technical assistance. Award amounts are based on a percentage of increases by the institutions in qualifying activities. Project example: multifamily housing financing.

Eligible applicants/beneficiaries: Federal Deposit Insurance Corporation-insured depository institutions.

Range: $1,100 to $500,000. **Average:** $186,000.

Activity: FY 05, 53 awards.

HQ: Program Manager, CDFI Fund, Department of the Treasury, 601 13th St. NW - Ste.200-S, Washington, DC 20005 Phone: (202) 622-6355, FAX (202) 622-7754.

Internet: www.cdfifund.gov (Note: no field offices for this program.)

APPALACHIAN REGIONAL COMMISSION

23.001 APPALACHIAN REGIONAL DEVELOPMENT (SEE INDIVIDUAL APPALACHIAN PROGRAMS) ("Appalachian Program")

Assistance: project grants.

Purposes: pursuant to the Appalachian Regional Development Act of 1965 (ARDA) and amendments, for programs and projects to stimulate public investments in public services, facilities, and institutions in the Appalachian region, through federal-state- local efforts. Priorities are established by the Appalachian Regional Commission, comprising the 13 state governors within the region or their alternates. All proposed projects must meet the requirements of the state Appalachian plan and the annual state investment program, both of which must be approved annually by the commission. (See individual Appalachian program descriptions). Funding is through the commission's various programs (**23.002 - 23.011**).

Eligible applicants/beneficiaries: only in the Appalachian region—states and, through the states, public bodies and private nonprofit organizations.

Average: see individual programs.

Activity: see individual programs.

HQ: Executive Director, Appalachian Regional Commission, 1666 Connecticut Ave. NW, Washington, DC 20009 Phone: (202) 884-7700.

Internet: www.arc.gov.

23.002 APPALACHIAN AREA DEVELOPMENT ("Supplemental and Direct Grants")

Assistance: project grants (10-80 percent).

Purposes: pursuant to ARDA and amendments, to supplement other federal project funding supporting self-sustaining development in the region's most distressed counties. Projects must hold high priority in the state's Appalachian development plan. Examples include water and sewer systems, industrial parks, entrepreneurship, export promotion, training, vocational education, health care, child development, revolving loan funds, and business incubator projects—in conjunction with private sector commitments.

Eligible applicants/beneficiaries: (Appalachia only) states, state subdivisions and instrumentalities, private nonprofit agencies.

Range: $1,000 to $1,225,000. **Average:** $163,000.

Activity: FY 05, 469 projects funded.

HQ: Executive Director, Appalachian Regional Commission, 1666 Connecticut Ave. NW, Washington, DC 20009 Phone: (202) 884-7700.

Internet: www.arc.gov.

23.003 APPALACHIAN DEVELOPMENT HIGHWAY SYSTEM ("Appalachian Corridors")

Assistance: project grants (80 percent).

Purposes: pursuant to ARDA as amended, to develop a highway system within the Appalachian region where commerce and communication have been inhibited by inadequate access. Grants may cover preliminary engineering, right-of-way acquisition, and construction costs. Additional funding for this program may be provided from the DOT Highway Trust Fund.

Eligible applicants/beneficiaries: (Appalachia only) state governments.

Range/Average: N.A.

Activity: cumulatively through FY 05, 2,632 miles completed or under construction.

HQ: Executive Director, Appalachian Regional Commission, 1666 Connecticut Ave. NW, Washington, DC 20009 Phone: (202) 884-7700.

Internet: www.arc.gov.

23.009 APPALACHIAN LOCAL DEVELOPMENT DISTRICT ASSISTANCE ("LDD")

Assistance: project grants (50-75 percent).

Purposes: pursuant to ARDA and amendments, for development planning and activities relating to local economic development. Funds may be used for: administrative expenses including technical services of local development districts; with ARC approval, real estate and vehicle purchases, construction and space improvement.

Eligible applicants/beneficiaries: (Appalachia only) multicounty organizations certified by the state.

Range: $10,131 to $384,000. **Average:** $83,457.

Activity: FY 05, 72 planning districts assisted.

HQ: Executive Director, Appalachian Regional Commission, 1666 Connecticut Ave. NW, Washington, DC 20009 Phone: (202) 884-7700.

Internet: www.arc.gov.

23.011 APPALACHIAN RESEARCH, TECHNICAL ASSISTANCE, AND DEMONSTRATION PROJECTS ("State Research")

Assistance: project grants.

Purposes: pursuant to ARDA and amendments, for research, planning, demonstration, and technical assistance projects relating to concerted economic and community development. Priority is on technical assistance projects leading to job creation.

Eligible applicants/beneficiaries: Appalachian states, state consortia; local public bodies; state instrumentalities.

Range: $7,500 to $202,253. **Average:** $68,244.

Activity: not quantified specifically.

HQ: Executive Director, Appalachian Regional Commission, 1666 Connecticut Ave. NW, Washington, DC 20009 Phone: (202) 884-7700.

Internet: www.arc.gov.

OFFICE OF PERSONNEL MANAGEMENT

27.001 FEDERAL CIVIL SERVICE EMPLOYMENT

Assistance: federal employment.

Purposes: pursuant to the Civil Service Reform Act of 1978, to fill federal job vacancies, usually through competitive exams and without discrimination on any nonmerit basis. Veterans receive preference. Special programs help place the physically handicapped, the mentally retarded or mentally restored, and the disadvantaged.

Eligible applicants/beneficiaries: U.S. citizens age 18 or older (age 16 in certain cases).

Range/Average: N.A.

Activity: FY 01, 10,212,000 inquiries answered (latest data reported).

HQ: Office of Personnel Management (no address provided) Phone: (202) 606-2700; *nation-wide,* (912) 757-3000, TTD (912) 744- 2299; Federal Job Opportunities Bulletin Board (FJOB), (912) 757- 3100.

Internet: USA JOBS site, www.usajobs.opm.gov; OPM, www.opm.gov.

27.002 FEDERAL EMPLOYMENT ASSISTANCE FOR VETERANS

Assistance: federal employment.

Purposes: pursuant to the Veterans Preference Act of 1944, to assist veterans in obtaining federal employment, with preferences according to their discharge status.

Eligible applicants/beneficiaries: nondisabled and disabled veterans, and certain spouses, widows, widowers, and mothers of veterans.

Range/Average: N.A.

Activity: as of FY 02, 480,000 veterans assisted, constituting 26.9 percent of non-postal federal workers (latest data available).

HQ: *Disabled Veterans Affirmative Action Programs,* Office of Diversity, Employment Service, OPM, 1900 E St. NW - Rm.2445, Washington, DC 20415. Phone: (202) 606-1059; *veterans preference and special hiring* *programs,* Office of Staffing Reinvention, Employment Service Phone: (202) 606-0830.

Internet: www.opm.gov (Note: no field offices for this program.)

27.003 FEDERAL STUDENT TEMPORARY EMPLOYMENT PROGRAM

Assistance: federal employment (to 1 year).

Purposes: to provide temporary federal employment for youth during school terms (full-time during extended vacation periods). OPM coordinates this program, but it is carried out by other participating federal agencies.

Eligible applicants/beneficiaries: students accepted for or enrolled at least half-time in a secondary, vocational, or technical school or IHE through the graduate level.

Range/Average: N.A.

Activity: FY 01, 32,000 participants (latest data reported).

HQ: *information available from personnel offices of the agencies of interest. For inquiries on policy issues,* Staffing Reinvention Office, Employment Service, OPM, 1900 E St. NW, Washington, DC 20415 Phone: (202) 606-0830.

Internet: www.opm.gov (Note: no field offices for this program.)

27.005 FEDERAL EMPLOYMENT FOR INDIVIDUALS WITH DISABILITIES ("Selective Placement Program")

Assistance: federal employment.

Purposes: pursuant to the Rehabilitation Act of 1973 as amended, to provide special OPM assistance to federal agencies to assist persons with disabilities, including veterans, in obtaining or retaining federal employment. Federal agencies have coordinators responsible for expanding employment opportunities under this program, to work with state vocational rehabilitation agencies, DVA facilities, and other public and private agencies. Funding is by the accounts of individual agencies.

Eligible applicants/beneficiaries: persons with physical, cognitive, or mental disabilities.

Range/Average: N.A.

Activity: as of FY 02, 127,000 federal employees with targeted and nontargeted disabilities; 12,000 full-time position hires (latest data reported).

HQ: information available from personnel offices of the agencies of interest. For inquiries on policy issues, Staffing Reinvention Office, Employment Service, OPM, 1900 E St. NW, Washington, DC 20415 Phone: (202) 606-0830.

Internet: www.opm.gov (Note: no field offices for this program.)

27.006 FEDERAL SUMMER EMPLOYMENT ("Summer Jobs in Federal Agencies")

Assistance: federal employment.

Purposes: pursuant to the Civil Service Reform Act of 1978, to provide summer employment primarily for college and high school students, in clerical, craft or trade, administrative, and subprofessional jobs. Summer jobs are filled through agency staffing plans, with funding by the participating agencies.

Eligible applicants/beneficiaries: any U.S. citizen at least age 16 at time of appointment.

Range/Average: N.A.

Activity: N.A.

HQ: Office of Personnel Management (no address provided) Phone: (202) 606-2700; *nation-wide,* (912) 757-3000, TTD (912) 744- 2299; Federal Job Opportunities Bulletin Board (FJOB), (912) 757- 3100.

Internet: USA JOBS site, www.usajobs.opm.gov; OPM, www.opm.gov.

27.011 INTERGOVERNMENTAL PERSONNEL ACT (IPA) MOBILITY PROGRAM

Assistance: specialized services; advisory services/counseling (to 4 years).

Purposes: pursuant to the Act of 1970 as amended and ISDEAA, to enable temporary assignments of professional, administrative, or technical personnel back and forth between federal, state, local, and tribal governments, IHEs, and other organizations. Assignments may be for up to two years, with one two-year extension. Upon completion of assignments, assigned federal employees must serve in the Civil Service for a period equal to that of the assignment. Cost sharing is negotiable.

Eligible applicants/beneficiaries: federal agencies; state, local, and tribal governments; IHEs. Other organizations include: national, regional, statewide, areawide, or metropolitan organizations of state or local governments; associations of state or local public officials; nonprofit organizations offering professional advisory, research, educational, or developmental services, or related services to governments or universities concerned with public management.

Range/Average: N.A.

Activity: annually, 1,400 mobility assignments with participation by all states, PR, VI, Samoa, Guam, Northern Marianas, DC, 519 local governments, 512 universities, 106 tribal governments, and 161 other organizations.

HQ: Office of Merit Systems Oversight and Effectiveness, OPM, 1900 E St. NW - Rm.7463, Washington, DC 20415-0001 Phone: (202) 606-1181.

Internet: www.opm.gov.

27.013 PRESIDENTIAL MANAGEMENT INTERN PROGRAM

Assistance: federal employment; training; specialized services.

Purposes: to attract graduate students of exceptional potential to the federal service. Two-year internships may be awarded for work in federal agencies (exceptionally, for three years). Awardees may be assigned to work temporarily for state or local governments. Nominations for awards are submitted by deans of graduate level programs. Participating entities reimburse OPM for certain program costs through a revolving loan fund.

Eligible applicants/beneficiaries: federal agencies; state, local, and tribal governments; IHEs. Other organizations include: national, regional, statewide, areawide, or metropolitan organizations of state or local governments; associations of state or local public officials; nonprofit organizations offering professional advisory, research, educational, or developmental services, or related services to governments or universities concerned with public management.

Range/Average: N.A.

Activity: FY 01, 350 interns hired (latest data reported).

HQ: Presidential Management Intern Program, Philadelphia Service Center, OPM, 600 Arch St., Philadelphia, PA 19106 Phone: (215) 597-7136, (215) 597-1920.

Internet: www.opm.gov (Note: no field offices for this program.)

COMMISSION ON CIVIL RIGHTS

29.001 CLEARINGHOUSE SERVICES, CIVIL RIGHTS DISCRIMINATION COMPLAINTS

Assistance: technical information.

Purposes: pursuant to the Civil Rights Commission Reauthorization Act of 1991, to serve as a national clearinghouse concerning the civil rights of individuals, entitling them to equal protection of the laws regardless of their race, color, religion, sex, age, handicap, or national origin; to provide related research, liaison, publications, and public information services to private and public groups and the media; and to process complaints for referral to appropriate federal agencies.

Eligible applicants/beneficiaries: anyone may seek information.

Range/Average: N.A.

Activity: FY 02-03 estimate (both years), 10,000 complaints processed, 12 publications completed.

HQ: Commission on Civil Rights, 624 Ninth St. NW, Washington, DC 20425 Phone: (202) 376-8177, TDD (202) 376-8116; *complaints,* (202) 376-8582, (800) 552-6843.

Internet: www.opm.gov.

EQUAL EMPLOYMENT OPPORTUNITY COMMISSION

30.001 EMPLOYMENT DISCRIMINATION—TITLE VII OF THE CIVIL RIGHTS ACT OF 1964

Assistance: advisory services/counseling; investigation of complaints.

Purposes: pursuant to the Acts of 1964 and 1991 and amendments, to provide for education, technical assistance, and enforcement of federal prohibitions against employment discrimination in the public and private sectors, based on race, sex, color national origin, or religion. Complaints are investigated and, if reasonable cause is found, mediation is offered; if mediation is not used or successful, charges are conciliated; if unsuccessful, civil action may be brought against named respondents. If conciliation fails on a charge against a state or local government, EEOC may refer the case to DOJ for further action. Funding for this program includes **30.008**, **30.010**, and **30.011**.

Eligible applicants/beneficiaries: any individual or any labor union, association, legal representative, or organization filing on behalf of an individual with reason to believe that an unlawful employment practice has been committed by an employer with 15 or more employees, an employment agency, a labor organization, or a joint labor-management committee controlling apprenticeship or other training activities.

Range/Average: N.A.

Activity: FY 05 (including **30.008**, **30.010**, and **30.011** for litigation and systemic data), 45,846 charges received to process, 46,885 cases resolved with $145,976,264 in benefits to 11,548 persons; 417 suits filed, 370 resolved; 31 appellate briefs filed.

HQ: Communications Staff, Office of Communications and Legislative Affairs, EEOC, 1801 L St. NW, Washington, DC 20507 Phone: (202) 663-4900, TTY (202) 663-4494.

Internet: www.eeoc.gov.

30.002 EMPLOYMENT DISCRIMINATION—STATE AND LOCAL FAIR EMPLOYMENT PRACTICES AGENCY CONTRACTS

Assistance: direct payments/specified use. (100 percent/1-3 years).

Purposes: pursuant to the Civil Rights Acts of 1964 and 1991, Age Discrimination in Employment Act of 1967, amendments, and ADA, for state and local fair employment practices agencies to assist in the enforcement and resolution of charges of violation of civil rights laws prohibiting discrimination in employment, based on race, color, national origin, sex, religion, disability, or age. Funding for this program includes **30.009**.

Eligible applicants: state and local government agencies designated as fair employment practices agencies.

Eligible beneficiaries: covered applicants, employees, and former employees.

Range: $6,500 to $2,354,000.

Activity: FY 05, 94 agencies funded to resolve 59,000 charges. FY 06 estimate, 96 agencies funded to resolve 56,000 charges.

HQ: Director, State and Local Programs, Office of Field Programs, EEOC, 1801 L St. NW - Rm.8030, Washington, DC 20507 Phone: (202) 663-4702.

Internet: www.eeoc.gov.

30.005 EMPLOYMENT DISCRIMINATION—PRIVATE BAR PROGRAM

Assistance: specialized services.

Purposes: pursuant to the Civil Rights Acts of 1964 and 1991 and amendments, to assist aggrieved individuals in locating lawyers to represent them in suits involving employment discrimination under provisions of Title VII of the Civil Rights Act of 1964, the Equal Pay Act, the Age Discrimination in Employment Act, or the ADA; to provide technical assistance to aggrieved parties and their attorneys.

Eligible applicants/beneficiaries: individuals filing charges.

Range/Average: N.A.

Activity: N.A.

HQ: Office of General Counsel, EEOC, 1801 L St. NW, Washington, DC 20507 Phone: (202) 663-4702.

Internet: www.eeoc.gov.

30.008 EMPLOYMENT DISCRIMINATION—AGE DISCRIMINATION IN EMPLOYMENT

Assistance: advisory services/counseling; investigation of complaints.

Purposes: pursuant to the Age Discrimination in Employment Act of 1967, amendments, and Civil Rights Act of 1991, to enforce regulations concerning arbitrary employment discrimination on the basis of age; to promote the employment of older workers. Individuals age 40 or older are protected from discrimination by: private commercial employers with 20 or more employees; federal, state, local governments; employment agencies; labor organizations. Funding for this program is included in **30.001**.

Eligible applicants/beneficiaries: persons age 40 or over.

Range/Average: N.A.

Activity: FY 05, 13,776 charges received; 14,076 charges resolved with $77,680,803 in benefits to 2,218 persons. (Information on systemic charges and suits filed is included under **30.001**.)

HQ: Communications Staff, Office of Communications and Legislative Affairs, EEOC, 1801 L St. NW, Washington, DC 20507 Phone: (202) 663-4900, TTY (202) 663-4494.

Internet: www.eeoc.gov.

30.009 EMPLOYMENT DISCRIMINATION PROJECT CONTRACTS—INDIAN TRIBES

Assistance: direct payments/specified use.

Purposes: pursuant to the Civil Rights Acts of 1964 and 1991 and amendments, for Tribal Employment Rights Offices (TEROs) to protect the employment rights of Indians working or seeking work on or near reservations. Funding for this program is included in **30.002**.

Eligible applicants/beneficiaries: land-based tribes with approved TEROs.

Average: $26,000 to each tribe.

Activity: FY 05, 63 offices funded.

HQ: Director, State and Local Programs, Office of Field Programs, EEOC, 1801 L St. NW - Rm.8030, Washington, DC 20507 Phone: (202) 663-4944.

Internet: http://www.eeoc.gov.

30.010 EMPLOYMENT DISCRIMINATION EQUAL PAY ACT

Assistance: advisory services/counseling; investigation of complaints.

Purposes: pursuant to the Equal Pay Act of 1963 as amended and Fair Labor Standards Act Amendment of 1974, to enforce laws prohibiting discrimination on the basis of sex in the payment of wages to men and women performing equal work in the same establishment, which is illegal for: employers engaged in commerce or in the production of goods; federal, state, and local governments. Also, labor organizations are prohibited from causing or attempting to cause employers to violate the law. Exceptions are permitted only where payments are based on systems recognizing seniority, merit, quantity or quality of production, or differentials based on factors other than sex. Funding for this program is included in **30.001**.

Eligible applicants/beneficiaries: employees believing that they or others have been or are being paid in violation of the Act, in any state, territory, or possession.

Range/Average: N.A.

Activity: FY 05, 774 complaints received, 889 complaints resolved with $3,072,871 in benefits to 161 persons. (Information on systemic charges and suits filed is included under **30.001**.)

HQ: Communications Staff, Office of Communications and Legislative Affairs, EEOC, 1801 L St. NW, Washington, DC 20507 Phone: (202) 663-4900, TTY (202) 663-4494.

Internet: www.eeoc.gov.

30.011 EMPLOYMENT DISCRIMINATION—TITLE I OF THE AMERICANS WITH DISABILITIES ACT

Assistance: advisory services/counseling; investigation of complaints.

Purposes: to enforce the ADA as amended, prohibiting employment discrimination by private employers and state and local governments against qualified individuals with disabilities. The commission investigates complaints and, if reasonable cause is found, mediation is offered; if mediation is not used or successful, charges are conciliated; if unsuccessful, legal action may be taken by DOJ against private respondents. If conciliation fails on a charge against a state or local government, EEOC refers the case to DOJ for further action. Funding for this program is included in **30.001**.

Eligible applicants/beneficiaries: any individual or any labor union, association, legal representative, or organization filing on behalf of an individual with reason to believe that an unlawful employment practice has been committed by an employer with 15 or more employees, an employment agency, a labor organization, or a joint labor-management committee controlling apprenticeship or other training activities.

Range/Average: N.A.

Activity: FY 05, 14,922 charges received, 15,357 charges resolved with $44,843,117 in benefits to 2,352 persons. (Information on systemic charges and suits filed is included under **30.001**.)

HQ: Communications Staff, Office of Communications and Legislative Affairs, EEOC, 1801 L St. NW, Washington, DC 20507 Phone: (202) 663-4900, TTY (202) 663-4494.

Internet: http://www.eeoc.gov.

FEDERAL COMMUNICATIONS COMMISSION

32.001 COMMUNICATIONS INFORMATION AND ASSISTANCE AND INVESTIGATION OF COMPLAINTS

Assistance: technical information; investigation of complaints.

Purposes: pursuant to the Communications Act of 1934 as amended, for public information, education, and investigation of complaints concerning public communications systems. FCC services relate to rates, broadcast signal interference, equal time for political candidates, and the presentation of issues.

Eligible applicants/beneficiaries: anyone.

Range/Average: N.A.

Activity: FY 01, received 23,000 broadcast and cable, 32,000 common carrier, and 30,000 interference complaints; 3,098 comments and information requests received (latest data reported).

HQ: Public Service Division, Federal Communications Commission, 1919 M St. NW - Rm.244, Washington, DC 20554 Phone: *Fees,* (202) 418-0220; *Cable,* (202) 418-0190.

Internet: www.fcc.gov.

FEDERAL MARITIME COMMISSION

33.001 SHIPPING—DISPUTE RESOLUTION AND INVESTIGATION OF COMPLAINTS

Assistance: investigation of complaints.

Purposes: pursuant to the Shipping Act of 1984 as amended, to provide a forum for settling disputes between carriers, shippers concerning maritime shipping and ocean transportation, including: cruise passengers seeking reimbursement of deposits when a cruise is canceled; complaints about unlawful rates or practices. Reparations may be awarded for violations.

Eligible applicants/beneficiaries: anyone.

Range/Average: N.A.

Activity: FY 05, responses to 3,500 informal inquiries and complaints.

HQ: Director, Office of Consumer Complaints, Federal Maritime Commission, 800 N. Capitol St. NW, Washington, DC 20573. Phone: (202) 523-5807, FAX (202) 275-0059; Dispute Resolution Specialist, (202) 523-5787, FAX (202) 523-5830.

Internet: (no web site) E-mail, Office of Consumer Complaints, COMPLAINTS@fmc.gov; Dispute Resolution Specialist, ADR@fmc.gov.

FEDERAL MEDIATION AND CONCILIATION SERVICE

34.001 LABOR MEDIATION AND CONCILIATION

Assistance: specialized services; advisory services/counseling.

Purposes: pursuant to the Labor-Management Relations Act of 1947 as amended and other acts, to prevent or minimize work stoppages caused by disputes between labor and management in industries affecting commerce, including federal labor disputes—through mediation of collective bargaining disputes, arbitration assistance, public education, conciliation.

Eligible applicants/beneficiaries: employers involved in interstate commerce, related labor organizations, federal agencies.

Range/Average: N.A.

Activity: FY 05 estimate, 18,000 arbitration panels handled.

HQ: FMCS, 2100 K St. NW, Washington, DC 20427 Phone: (202) 606-8100; Public Affairs Specialist, (202) 606-8091.

Internet: www.fmcs.gov.

34.002 LABOR-MANAGEMENT COOPERATION

Assistance: project grants (12-18 months).

Purposes: pursuant to the Labor-Management Cooperation Act of 1978, to establish, expand, and operate joint labor-management committees in the public or private sectors at the work-site, area, and industry-wide levels—to improve labor-management relations and productivity.

Eligible applicants/beneficiaries: private nonprofit labor- management committees; labor organizations and private companies or public agencies applying jointly; private nonprofit entities.

Range: work-site, $65,000; others, to $125,000.

Activity: annually, approximately 12 grants.

HQ: Grants Program Office, Labor Management Cooperation Program, FMCS, 2100 K St. NW, Washington, DC 20427 Phone: (202) 606-8181.

Internet: www.fmcs.gov (Note: no field offices for this program.)

FEDERAL TRADE COMMISSION

36.001 FAIR COMPETITION COUNSELING AND INVESTIGATION OF COMPLAINTS

Assistance: advisory services/counseling; investigation of complaints.

Purposes: pursuant to the Federal Trade Commission Act of 1914, amendments, and related acts, to prevent and eliminate anticompetitive, deceptive, and other practices adversely affecting consumers. The FTC's concerns include price-fixing, boycotts, price discrimination, illegal mergers and acquisitions, false and misleading advertising, consumer credit transactions and reporting, debt collection practices, food and drug advertising, and other practices affecting the consuming public.

Eligible applicants/beneficiaries: anyone.

Range/Average: N.A.

Activity: FY 05, 465 formal investigations initiated, 420 closed; 34 orders to cease and desist issued; 4 trade regulations promulgated or amended.

HQ: Federal Trade Commission, 600 Pennsylvania Ave. NW, Washington, DC 20580 Phone: Director, Bureau of Consumer Protection, (202) 326-3240; Director, Bureau of Competition, (202) 326-3175.

Internet: www.ftc.gov.

GENERAL SERVICES ADMINISTRATION

39.002 DISPOSAL OF FEDERAL SURPLUS REAL PROPERTY

Assistance: sale, exchange, or donation of property and goods.

Purposes: pursuant to the Federal Property and Administrative Services Act of 1949, Surplus Property Act of 1944, SBMHAA, and amendments, to dispose of surplus federal real and related personal property for public purposes, at discounts of up to 100 percent, through leases, permits, sale, exchange, or donation. Applicants for property coordinate with appropriate other federal agencies. Surplus property not deeded to public bodies is generally offered for sale to the public on a competitive bid basis.

Eligible applicants/beneficiaries: surplus real property for park, recreation, correctional facility, historic monument, public airport uses, for health, educational, or homeless programs, and for replacement housing and general public purposes—state and local government agencies. Property for wildlife conservation use—states. Property for health education and homeless program uses—tax-supported and nonprofit medical and educational institutions exempt from taxation under IRS Section 501(c)(3).

Range/Average: N.A.

Activity: FY 05, value of $1,805.1 million for 444 property disposals.

HQ: Assistant Commissioner, Office of Property Disposal, Public Building Service, GSA, Washington, DC 20405 Phone: (202) 501- 0084.

Internet: www.propertydisposal.gsa.gov/property.

39.003 DONATION OF FEDERAL SURPLUS PERSONAL PROPERTY

Assistance: sale, exchange, or donation of property and goods.

Purposes: pursuant to the Federal Property and Administrative Services Act of 1949, Surplus Property Act of 1944, Older Americans Act of 1965, and amendments, to donate surplus federal personal property to state and local public agencies for public purposes, to qualifying nonprofit entities for tax-exempt activities, or for educational and research activities. Examples of surplus property include office machines and supplies, furniture, hardware, textiles, special purpose motor vehicles, boats, airplanes, construction equipment. Participation requires prior GSA approval of state plans for distribution to eligible recipients. Items not donated are made available for sale to the general public (see **39.007**).

Eligible applicants/beneficiaries: state and local agencies, departments, instrumentalities, economic development districts, instrumentalities; multijurisdictional substate districts; tribes, bands, groups, pueblos; nonprofit, tax-exempt organizations such as schools, colleges, universities, public libraries, schools for the handicapped, educational radio or TV stations, child care centers, museums, hospitals, health centers, clinics, programs for the elderly or homeless; public airports; private service and educational organizations.

Range/Average: N.A.

Activity: FY 05, $411.5 million in original acquisition cost of property donated.

HQ: Director, Property Management Division, Office of Transportation and Property Management, Federal Supply Service, GSA, Washington, DC 20406 Phone: (703) 605-5610 *Service educational activities information,* Deputy Under Secretary of Defense/Production and Logistics, The Pentagon, Washington, DC, 20301.

Internet: www.gsa.gov/property.

39.007 SALE OF FEDERAL SURPLUS PERSONAL PROPERTY ("Sales Program")

Assistance: sale, exchange, or donation of property and goods.

Purposes: pursuant to the Federal Property and Administrative Services Act of 1949 as amended, to sell surplus federal personal property on behalf of most federal civil agencies—including vehicles, aircraft, hardware, electronic and electrical equipment, office supplies and equipment, scrap goods. Disposal is by competitive bid.

Eligible applicants/beneficiaries: general public.

Range/Average: N.A.

Activity: FY 05, $89.2 million in proceeds from sales.

HQ: Director, Property Management Division, Office of Transportation and Property Management, Federal Supply Service, GSA, Washington, DC 20406 Phone: (703) 605-5610.

Internet: www.gsa.gov; *GSA auctions,* www.gsaauctions.gov.

39.009 FEDERAL CITIZEN INFORMATION CENTER

Assistance: technical information.

Purposes: to assist federal agencies in releasing information of interest to consumers through: toll-free phone services, publications including a quarterly catalog of consumer-oriented publications, and several web sites including those cited under "HQ," below. Fees are charged for some products. A revolving fund partially supports the program.

Eligible applicants/beneficiaries: general public.

Range/Average: N.A.

Activity: FY 05, 231,000,000 public contacts.

HQ: Director, Federal Citizen Information Center, GSA, 1800 F St, Washington, DC 20405 Phone: (202) 501-1794; Federal Citizen Information Center, (800) 333-4636.

Internet: www.FirstGov.gov; *www.pueblo.gsa.gov*; *www.consumeraction.gov*; www.kids.gov; *www.espanol.gov*. (Note: no field offices for this program.)

GOVERNMENT PRINTING OFFICE

40.001 DEPOSITORY LIBRARIES FOR GOVERNMENT PUBLICATIONS

Assistance: technical information.

Purposes: to provide government publications and other information products, including electronic products, for public reference in 1,270 depository libraries in the U.S. and its possessions.

Eligible applicants: libraries designated by members of Congress (two Representative designations in each congressional district, four Senatorial designations in each state). By law, all state, highest state appellate court, land-grant college, and law school libraries are also eligible for designation.

Eligible beneficiaries: general public.

Range/Average: N.A.

Activity: FY 05, 10,301 titles distributed in paper, microfiche, and CD-ROM; 301,633 on-line titles on GPO servers; as of March, 2006, 1,266 Federal Depository Libraries.

HQ: Information Dissemination Department, Superintendent of Documents, GPO, 732 N. Capitol St., Washington, DC 20402. Phone: (202) 512-1114; GPO Contact Center, Phone: (202) 512-1800, FAX (202) 512-2104; Toll-Free (866) 512-1800.

Internet: www.access.gpo.gov/su_docs/fdlp/librpro.html.

40.002 GOVERNMENT PUBLICATIONS SALES AND DISTRIBUTION ("The Government Bookstore")

Assistance: sale, exchange, or donation of property and goods; technical information.

Purposes: to make available government publications, including 233 subscription services, for sale to the general public. Discounts are available to dealers and other purchasers of large quantities. A revolving fund supports this program.

Eligible applicants/beneficiaries: general public.

Range/Average: N.A.

Activity: FY 05, 186,000 mail orders processed; over 2,000,000 tangible products sold.

HQ: Superintendent of Documents, GPO, 732 N. Capitol St., Washington, DC 20402 Phone: Order Desk, (202) 512-1800, FAX (202) 512-2250; *toll-free*, (866) 512-2104.

Internet: www.bookstore.gpo.gov; e-mail, orders@gpo.gov *or* "gpo@cuthelp.com.

LIBRARY OF CONGRESS

42.001 BOOKS FOR THE BLIND AND PHYSICALLY HANDICAPPED

Assistance: use of property, facilities, and equipment.

Purposes: to provide library services to blind and physically handicapped persons—consisting of books on cassette, music scores, discs, and instructional materials in braille, large type, and on recorded formats, in 57 regional and 77 subregional libraries.

Eligible applicants/beneficiaries: U.S. residents and citizens living abroad, providing a certificate of inability to read or manipulate conventional printed material, from a competent authority.

Range/Average: N.A.

Activity: FY 05, 799,718 blind and physically handicapped readers served, from a collection of 423,000 titles.

HQ: Director, National Library Service for the Blind and Physically Handicapped, LC, 1291 Taylor St. NW, Washington, DC 20542 Phone: (202) 707-5100.

Internet: www.loc.gov/nls; e-mail, nls@loc.gov.

42.002 COPYRIGHT SERVICE

Assistance: technical information.

Purposes: to administer the U.S. Copyright Law, including: processing of applications, renewals, transfers, searches, and distribution of regulations; processing of compulsory licenses for satellite carriers and cable systems, and digital audio recording products, and collection and distribution of royalties; to administer the Copyright Arbitration Royalty Panels. Fees are charged for certain services. Funding for this program also supports **42.008**.

Eligible applicants/beneficiaries: anyone. Registration may be made by authors, their assignees, or their exclusive licensees, and others designated by law, or by their agents.

Range/Average: N.A.

Activity: FY 05 (sampling), 531,720 registrations.

HQ: Register of Copyrights, Copyright Office, LC, 101 Independence Ave. SE, Washington, DC 20559-6000 Phone: (202) 707- 3000.

Internet: www.gov/copyright (Note: no field offices for this program.)

42.008 SEMICONDUCTOR CHIP PROTECTION SERVICE

Assistance: technical information.

Purposes: to administer the provisions of the Semiconductor Chip Protection Act of 1984. The Copyright Office staff: examines and decides on the acceptability of applications and identifying materials for registration of claims of protection; records and publishes legal facts or data pertaining to registered works; furnishes pertinent information to the public; and, records transfer documents. Fees are charged for some services. Program operating costs are absorbed in the budget of the Copyright Office; fees collected are returned to the U.S. Treasury to offset program costs.

Eligible applicants: general public.

Eligible beneficiaries: owners of qualified mask works.

Range/Average: N.A.

Activity: FY 05, 506 mask work registrations.

HQ: Register of Copyrights, Copyright Office, LC, 101 Independence Ave. SE, Washington, DC 20559-6000 Phone: (202) 707-1497.

Internet: www.copyright.gov (Note: no field offices for this program.)

42.009 VESSEL HULL DESIGN PROTECTION SERVICE

Assistance: technical information.

Purposes: to administer the Vessel Hull Design Protection Act of 1998. The LC Copyright Office: examines and decides the acceptability of applications and identifying material for registration of claims; records and publishes legal facts or data pertaining to registered works. Fees are charged for services. Program operating costs are absorbed in the budget of the Copyright Office; fees collected are returned to the U.S. Treasury to offset program costs.

Eligible applicants/beneficiaries: registration may be made by owners of qualified vessel hull designs, or their agents. Information is available to anyone.

Range/Average: N.A.

Activity: new program listing in 2004; FY 05, 55 registrations.

HQ: Register of Copyrights, Copyright Office, LC, 101 Independence Ave. SE, Washington, DC 20559-6000 Phone: (202) 707-1497.

Internet: www.copyright.gov (Note: no field offices for this program.)

NATIONAL AERONAUTICS AND SPACE ADMINISTRATION

43.001 AEROSPACE EDUCATION SERVICES PROGRAM ("Spacemobile")

Assistance: technical information.

Purposes: pursuant to the National Aeronautics and Space Act of 1958 as amended, to support instruction and to initiate systemic change in mathematics, science, and technology education, using NASA specialists to provide inservice and preservice workshops for K-12 teachers, lectures, classroom demonstrations, and media broadcasts.

Eligible applicants/beneficiaries: schools, teacher training institutions, IHEs, civic groups, museums, planetaria.

Range/Average: N.A.

Activity: FY 05 (sampling), visited 1,609 schools in all 50 states and 2 territories; 4,913 assemblies to a total of 244,371 students.

HQ: Office of Education, NASA, Washington, DC 20546 Phone: (202) 358-1110.

Internet: www.nasa.gov.

43.002 TECHNOLOGY TRANSFER

Assistance: technical information.

Purposes: pursuant to the National Aeronautics and Space Act of 1958 as amended, to disseminate information about government- sponsored civilian aerospace research and development, including inventions, discoveries, innovations, and other improvements—through: NASA's "TechTracs" data system, via the Internet; publications including "Tech Briefs;" Regional Technology Transfer Centers; commercial technology field center offices.

Eligible applicants/beneficiaries: Tech Briefs subscriptions (no charge)—engineers, domestic enterprise managers, professionals, and others involved in technology transfer. Technical information search and retrieval services and computer programs/documentation—domestic organizations (fees charged for services beyond those available on the Internet); Technology Transfer Projects—those demonstrating a national public need.

Range/Average: N.A.

Activity: annually, information to 200,000 persons and firms.

HQ: Innovative Partnerships Program, Office of Exploration Systems, NASA, Washington, DC 20546-0001 Phone: (202) 358-2560.

Internet: www.nctn.hq.nasa.gov.

NATIONAL CREDIT UNION ADMINISTRATION

44.001 CREDIT UNION CHARTER, EXAMINATION, SUPERVISION, AND INSURANCE

Assistance: insurance; specialized services; advisory services/counseling.

Purposes: pursuant to the Federal Credit Union Act as amended, to assist in establishing and operating chartered federal credit unions; to provide $100,000 deposit insurance on individual accounts. Approval of applications is based on a combination of interests by group, economic feasibility, and other factors. Fees and insurance premiums support this program.

Eligible applicants/beneficiaries: generally, associations, employee groups, and communities with 500 or more potential members. State-chartered credit unions may apply for depositor insurance.

Range/Average: N.A.

Activity: 2005, 5 new charters granted. As of 2005, 5,393 federal credit unions operating, 3,302 state credit unions insured.

HQ: Board Chairman, NCUA, 1775 Duke St., Alexandria, VA 22314- 3428 Phone: (703) 518-6300.

Internet: www.ncua.gov.

44.002 COMMUNITY DEVELOPMENT REVOLVING LOAN FUND PROGRAM FOR CREDIT UNIONS ("CDCU")

Assistance: direct loans. (50-67 percent/1 to 3 percent interest/to 5 years).

Purposes: to stimulate economic development activities by: increasing income, business ownership, and employment opportunities among the low-income; providing basic financial and related services to community residents, such as financial counseling, membership and participation drives. Loans can also involve housing, including cooperatives and self-help. Funding is derived from a revolving loan fund.

Eligible applicants/beneficiaries: established state- and federally-chartered credit unions serving low-income communities. Available also in territories and possessions.

Range: $25,000 to $300,000.

Activity: FY 05, $1,700,000 in new loans.

HQ: Community Development Revolving Loan Program for Credit Unions, NCUA, 1775 Duke St., Alexandria, VA 22314-3428 Phone: (703) 518-6610.

Internet: www.ncua.gov (Note: no field offices for this program.)

NATIONAL FOUNDATION ON THE ARTS AND THE HUMANITIES

NATIONAL ENDOWMENT FOR THE ARTS

45.024 PROMOTION OF THE ARTS—GRANTS TO ORGANIZATIONS AND INDIVIDUALS

Assistance: project grants. (organizations,50 percent; individuals, 100 percent/both, to 2 years).

Purposes: pursuant to the National Foundation on the Arts and the Humanities Act of 1965 (NFAHA) as amended, to foster and preserve excellence in the arts, provide public access to the arts, and advance arts education for children and youth. Funds support national, regional, and field-wide organizations in the visual, literary, media, design, and performing arts—in projects involving one of more aspects of: creativity; organizational capacity including technology; heritage and preservation; access; arts learning; international exchanges; and, for national arts programs for television or radio. Also, to support published writers through fellowships for creative writing (fiction and nonfiction), poetry, and literary translations.

Eligible applicants/beneficiaries: organizations—nonprofit tax-exempt entities such as arts institutions and arts service organizations, local arts agencies, state and local governments, tribal organizations; consortia. Individuals—U.S. citizens or permanent residents with exceptional talent; currently, only published creative writers are eligible.

Range: organizations, $5,000 to $500,000. **Average:** to $25,000.

Activity: FY 05, 2,161 grants.

HQ: NEA, 1100 Pennsylvania Ave. NW, Washington, DC 20056-0001 Phone: (202) 682-5400, TTY (202) 682-5496; *audio recordings of guidelines*, (202) 682-5532.

Internet: www.arts.gov (Note: no field offices for this program.)

45.025 PROMOTION OF THE ARTS—PARTNERSHIP AGREEMENTS

Assistance: formula grants, project grants; advisory services/counseling (project grants, 50 percent).

Purposes: pursuant to NFAHA as amended, for development of basic state arts plans; for elements of state plans addressing arts learning and fostering arts in underserved areas; to provide basic support through Partnership Agreements for regional arts planning and for presenting and touring. Limited partnership funds are available for national services provided by membership organizations of state and regional arts organizations.

Eligible applicants/beneficiaries: state arts agencies in the states and in six special U.S. jurisdictions; regional and national arts organizations.

Range: states, \$241,300 to \$1,071,500; regions, \$907,200 to \$1,389,700. **Average:** states, \$619,345; regions, \$1,158,133.

Activity: FY 06, 64 partnership awards, supporting 24,000 projects in 5,300 communities.

HQ: State and Regional Director, NEA, 1100 Pennsylvania Ave. NW, Washington, DC 20056-0001 Phone: (202) 692-5429; voice/TT (202) 682-5496; *audio recordings of guidelines*, (202) 682- 5532.

Internet: www.arts.gov (Note: no field offices for this program.)

NATIONAL ENDOWMENT FOR THE HUMANITIES

45.129 PROMOTION OF THE HUMANITIES—FEDERAL/STATE PARTNERSHIP

Assistance: project grants (50 percent/3 years).

Purposes: pursuant to NFAHA as amended, for humanities councils for regranting to local groups and individuals to conduct local, statewide, and regional projects. Project examples: youth partnership programs with Boy and Girl Scouts of America, Boys and Girls Clubs, YMCA-YWCA; traveling exhibits; scholar-led seminars; elder reading initiative.

Eligible applicants: state and territorial nonprofit citizen councils. If the state matches a certain percentage of the federal grant, the governor may designate the existing council as a state agency.

Eligible beneficiaries: state and local governments, sponsored organizations, public and private nonprofit organizations, tribal governments, native American organizations, territories, minority organizations and other specialized groups, quasi-public nonprofit institutions.

Range: \$238,600 to \$1,644,700. **Average:** \$686,270.

Activity: annually, grants to 56 nonprofit organizations.

HQ: Federal/State Partnership, NEH (Rm.603), Washington, DC 20506 Phone: (202) 606-8254, FAX (202) 606-8365.

Internet: www.neh.gov; e-mail, fedstate@neh.gov (Note: no field offices for this program.)

45.130 PROMOTION OF THE HUMANITIES—CHALLENGE GRANTS

Assistance: project grants. (20-25 percent/1-4 years).

Purposes: pursuant to NFAHA as amended, for educational and cultural institutions and organizations to increase their financial stability and to sustain or improve humanities programs, services, or resources. Principally, project funds are used to establish endowments; also, for library acquisitions, technological enhancement, construction and renovation, or debt retirement. Grants may not fund general operating costs, projects eligible for other NEH support, or undergraduate scholarships or prizes.

Eligible applicants/beneficiaries: public or private nonprofit organizations including: two- and four-year IHEs; museums; historical or professional societies; research or public libraries; advanced study centers; university presses; media organizations; other similar and related organizations. States, local governments, and territories may apply on their own behalf or on behalf of organizations within their jurisdictions. Individuals and public and private elementary and secondary schools are ineligible.

Range: $63,000 to $1,000,000. **Average:** $400,000.

Activity: FY 05, 36 grants.

HQ: Office of Challenge Grants, NEH (Rm.420), Washington, DC 20506 Phone: (202) 606-8309.

Internet: www.neh.gov (Note: no field offices for this program.)

45.149 PROMOTION OF THE HUMANITIES—DIVISION OF PRESERVATION AND ACCESS

Assistance: project grants. (cost sharing/to 5 years).

Purposes: pursuant to NFAHA as amended, for the preservation of and activities to provide intellectual access to library, museum, archival, and other humanities collections, including still and moving images and recorded sound collections; for preservation practices and activities including microfilming, archival surveys, cataloguing; for a national program to catalog and preserve U.S. newspapers; for training; for research; for related uses.

Eligible applicants/beneficiaries: state and local governments, sponsored organizations, public and private nonprofit organizations, tribal governments, native American organizations, territories, minority organizations and other specialized groups, quasi-public nonprofit institutions.

Range: $5,000 to $700,000. **Average:** $120,487.

Activity: FY 05, 174 awards.

HQ: Division of Preservation and Access, NEH (Rm.411), Washington, DC 20506 Phone: (202) 606-8570, FAX (202) 606-8639.

Internet: www.neh.gov; e-mail, PRESERVATION@NEH.GOV (Note: no field offices for this program.)

45.160 PROMOTION OF THE HUMANITIES—FELLOWSHIPS AND STIPENDS

Assistance: project grants. (100 percent/2 months to 2 years).

Purposes: pursuant to NFAHA as amended, for six- to twelve-month fellowships and two-month summer stipends to scholars to undertake full-time independent research and writing in the humanities. Two-year faculty research awards are available to historically black, Hispanic-serving, and tribal IHEs.

Eligible applicants/beneficiaries: college, university, and other institutional faculty and staff, and independent scholars and writers that have completed their professional training. Degree candidates are ineligible. All applicants must be U.S. citizens or nationals, or foreign nationals with at least three years of U.S. legal residence.

Range: fellowships, research, to $40,000 for 9-12 months, $24,000 for 6-8 months; summer stipends, $5,000; faculty research, to $40,000.

Activity: FY 05, 338 awards.

HQ: Division of Research Programs, NEH (Rm.318), Washington, DC 20506 Phone: (202) 606-8200.

Internet: wwww.neh.gov (Note: no field offices for this program.)

45.161 PROMOTION OF THE HUMANITIES—RESEARCH

Assistance: project grants. (cost sharing/to 3 years).

Purposes: pursuant to NFAHA as amended, to support collaboration by scholars, and postdoctoral fellowship programs at independent humanities research centers. Grants may cover the costs of salaries, travel, supplies, and appropriate research assistance and consultation.

Eligible applicants: collaborative research, scholarly editions—U.S. IHEs, nonprofit professional associations, scholarly societies, other nonprofit organizations. Fellowships—U.S. independent research centers, scholarly societies, and international research organizations with existing fellowship programs.

Eligible beneficiaries: U.S. citizens and residents, state and local governments, sponsored organizations, public and private nonprofit organizations, tribal governments, native American organizations, territories, minority organizations and other specialized groups, quasi-public nonprofit institutions.

Range: $18,000 to $280,000. **Average:** $112,000.

Activity: FY 05 estimate, 54 awards.

HQ: Division of Research and Education, NEH (Rm.318), Washington, DC 20506 Phone: (202) 606-8200.

Internet: wwww.neh.gov (Note: no field offices for this program.)

45.162 PROMOTION OF THE HUMANITIES—TEACHING AND LEARNING RESOURCES AND CURRICULUM DEVELOPMENT

Assistance: project grants (to 3 years).

Purposes: pursuant to NFAHA as amended, to fund curriculum and materials development projects to create durable tools for teachers at all educational levels, to engage their students in substantive study in the humanities. Institutional grants are available to historically black, Hispanic-serving, and tribal IHEs, for faculty study programs, institutional planning, construction, acquisition of library and advanced technology resources.

Eligible applicants/beneficiaries: state and local governments, sponsored organizations, public and private nonprofit organizations, tribal governments, native American organizations, territories, minority organizations and other specialized groups, quasi-public nonprofit institutions. Institutional grants—historically black, Hispanic-serving, and tribal IHEs designated by the White House.

Range: curriculum and materials development, to $200,000; institutional grants, to $25,000.

Activity: FY 05, 24 awards.

HQ: Teaching and Learning Resources and Curriculum Development Program, NEH (Rm.302), Washington, DC 20506 Phone: (202) 606- 8380; *institutional grants,* (202) 606-8463.

Internet: www.neh.gov (Note: no field offices for this program.)

45.163 PROMOTION OF THE HUMANITIES—PROFESSIONAL DEVELOPMENT

Assistance: project grants (to 18 months).

Purposes: pursuant to NFAHA as amended, to promote better teaching and research in the humanities through summer seminars and national institutes, as well Landmarks of American History workshops. Grants may support salaries, participant stipends, travel, and related direct costs. Projects dealing with pedagogical theory or intended to improve writing and speaking normally are not supported.

Eligible applicants: distinguished humanities scholars and teachers applying through sponsoring institutions to direct a program for teachers. Landmarks of American History and Faculty Humanities workshops—state and local governments, sponsored organizations, public and private nonprofit organizations, tribal governments, Native American organizations, territories, minority organizations and other specialized groups, quasi-public nonprofit institutions.

Eligible beneficiaries: teachers in grades K-12 or colleges.

Range: N.A.

Activity: FY 05, 85 grants.

HQ: Professional Development, Division of Education Programs, NEH, Washington, DC 20506 Phone: (202) 606-8463; Faculty Humanities Workshops, (202) 606-8380.

Internet: www.neh.gov (Note: no field offices for this program.)

45.164 PROMOTION OF THE HUMANITIES—PUBLIC PROGRAMS

Assistance: project grants (6-24 months).

Purposes: pursuant to NFAHA as amended, for planning and implementation costs of humanities programs in museums, historical organizations, libraries, community centers, as well as on public television and radio.

Eligible applicants/beneficiaries: state and local governments, sponsored organizations, public and private nonprofit organizations, tribal governments, native American organizations, territories, minority organizations and other specialized groups, quasi-public nonprofit institutions.

Range: $10,000 to $800,000. **Average:** $137,000.

Activity: FY 05, 139 grants.

HQ: Division of Public Programs, NEH (Rm.426), Washington, DC 20506 Phone: (202) 606-8267.

Internet: www.neh.gov (Note: no field offices for this program.)

45.168 PROMOTION OF THE HUMANITIES—WE THE PEOPLE

Assistance: project grants; direct payments/unrestricted use.

Purposes: pursuant to NFAHA as amended, for scholarly, educational, preservation, and public projects that explore events and themes in U.S. history and culture and that advance principles defining America. Eligible activities include: Idea of America Essay Contest for U.S. high school juniors; We the People Bookshelf for community programs by libraries, conducted in collaboration with the American Library Association; Landmarks of American History projects; school teacher workshops; challenge grants.

Eligible applicants/beneficiaries: public libraries; K-12 school libraries including public, private, parochial, and charter schools—including in the territories.

Range: essay, $5,000 grand prize, $1,000 to finalist.

Activity: new program listing in 2004; FY 05, 6 awards.

HQ: Office of Public Information, NEH (Rm.402), Washington, DC 20506 Phone: (202) 606-8400; *challenge grants,* (202) 606- 8309; *education programs,* (202) 606-8463; *"Bookshelf,"* (202) 606-8589, American Library Association, (800) 545-2433, ext. 5045.

Internet: www.neh.gov; e-mail, info@neh.gov. (Note: no field offices for this program.)

45.169 PROMOTION OF THE HUMANITIES—OFFICE OF DIGITAL HUMANITIES

Assistance: project grants. (to 100 percent/to 18 months).

Purposes: pursuant to National Foundations for the Arts and Humanities Act of 1965, as amended, to support projects that utilize or study the impact of digital technology, including those that deploy digital technologies and methods to enhance our understanding of a topic or issue, or the humanities; those that explore the ways in which digital technology changes how we read, write, think, and learn; those that support increasing the public's ability to search and access humanities information.

Eligible applicants/beneficiaries: U.S. nonprofit organizations/institutions; state, local and tribal governments; U.S. citizens or foreign nationals with at least three years residency.

Range: to $30,000.

Activity: new program in 2006.

HQ: Office of Public Information, NEH (Rm.402), Washington, DC 20506 Phone: (202) 606-8400.

Internet: www.neh.gov.

FEDERAL COUNCIL ON THE ARTS AND THE HUMANITIES

45.201 ARTS AND ARTIFACTS INDEMNITY

Assistance: insurance.

Purposes: pursuant to NFAHA as amended, to provide indemnification against loss or damage to eligible art works, artifacts, and objects exhibited abroad or borrowed from abroad for display in the U.S. Deductibles and maximum amounts apply.

Eligible applicants/beneficiaries: federal, state, and local government entities; nonprofit agencies, institutions; individuals.

Range/Average: N.A.

Activity: FY 05, 30 indemnity certificates issued.

HQ: Indemnity Administrator, Museum Program, NEA, Washington, DC 20506-0001 Phone: (202) 682-5574.

Internet: www.arts.gov (Note: no field offices for this program.)

INSTITUTE OF MUSEUM AND LIBRARY SERVICES

45.301 MUSEUMS FOR AMERICA

Assistance: project grants; direct payments/unrestricted use. (50 percent/to 3 years).

Purposes: pursuant to the Museum and Library Services Act of 1996 (MSLA), for museums to conserve the nation's historic, scientific, and cultural heritage; to maintain and expand the educational roles of museums and libraries in their educational role. Funds may be used for projects to: sustain cultural heritage; support lifelong learning; or serve as centers of community.

Eligible applicants/beneficiaries: generally, museums in the states, territories, and possessions that have provided museum services for at least two years. Public or private nonprofit agencies, such as a municipality, college, or university responsible for operating a museum, may apply on behalf of museums. Under the IMS definition, a museum is a public or private nonprofit institution organized on a permanent basis for educational or aesthetic purposes, and which: owns or uses and cares for tangible objects, whether animate or inanimate; exhibits them to the general public on a regular basis. "Museums" includes aquariums and zoological parks, botanical gardens and arboreta, and nature centers; art, history (including historic buildings and sites), natural history, children's general, and specialized museums; science and technology centers; and planetariums. Federal museums are ineligible.

Range: $5,000 to $150,000.

Activity: FY 05, 169 grants.

HQ: IMLS, 1800 M St. NW - 9th fl., Washington, DC 20036-5802 Phone: (202) 653-4674, -4689, -4702.

Internet: www.imls.gov; e-mail, imlsinfo@imls.gov (Note: no field offices for this program.)

45.302 MUSEUM ASSESSMENT PROGRAM ("MAP")

Assistance: project grants; direct payments/specified use.

Purposes: pursuant to MSLA, for assessments of various aspects of museum collections and operations, including institutional, public dimensions, and governance.

Eligible applicants/beneficiaries: generally, museums in the states, territories, and possessions that have provided museum services for at least two years. Public or private nonprofit agencies, such as a municipality, college, or university responsible for operating a museum, may apply on behalf of museums. Under the IMS definition, a museum is a public or private nonprofit institution organized on a permanent basis for educational or aesthetic purposes, and which: owns or uses and cares for tangible objects, whether animate or inanimate; exhibits them to the general public on a regular basis. "Museums" includes aquariums and zoological parks, botanical gardens and arboreta, and nature centers; art, history (including historic buildings and sites), natural history, children's general, and specialized museums; science and technology centers; and planetariums. Federal museums are ineligible. (NOTE: applicants must complete a self-study questionnaire provided by the American Association of Museums, 1575 Eye St. NW - Ste.400, Washington, DC 20005. Phone: 202-289-9118.)

Average: $2,325 to $3,820.

Activity: FY 05, 160 awards.

HQ: IMLS, 1800 M St, NW-9th fl., Washington, DC 20036-5802 Assistant Director, Museum Assessment Program, American Association of Museums, 1575 Eye St., NW, Suite 400, Washington, DC 20005 Phone: (202) 289-9118.

Internet: www.imls.gov (Note: no field offices for this program.)

45.303 CONSERVATION PROJECT SUPPORT ("CPS")

Assistance: project grants. (50 percent/to 3 years).

Purposes: pursuant to MSLA, for projects involving the safekeeping of living and nonliving museum and library collections, including: surveys of collections and environmental conditions; collections treatment; research; staff training.

Eligible applicants/beneficiaries: generally, museums in the states, territories, and possessions that have provided museum services for at least two years. Public or private nonprofit agencies, such as a municipality, college, or university responsible for operating a museum, may apply on behalf of museums. Under the IMS definition, a museum is a public or private nonprofit institution organized on a permanent basis for educational or aesthetic purposes, and which: owns or uses and cares for tangible objects, whether animate or inanimate; exhibits them to the general public on a regular basis. "Museums" includes aquariums and zoological parks, botanical gardens and arboreta, and nature centers; art, history (including historic buildings and sites), natural history, children's general, and specialized museums; science and technology centers; and planetariums. Federal museums are ineligible.

Range: $1,706 to $250,000.

Activity: FY 06, 40 awards.

HQ: IMLS, 1800 M St. NW - 9th fl., Washington, DC 20036-5802 Phone: (202) 653-4641.

Internet: www.imls.gov; e-mail, imlsinfo@imls.gov (Note: no field offices for this program.)

45.304 CONSERVATION ASSESSMENT PROGRAM ("CAP")

Assistance: direct payments/specified use (cost sharing).

Purposes: pursuant to MSLA, for overall assessments of the conditions of museum environments and collections to identify their conservation needs and priorities.

Eligible applicants/beneficiaries: generally, museums in the states, territories, and possessions that have provided museum services for at least two years. Public or private nonprofit agencies, such as a municipality, college, or university responsible for operating a museum, may apply on behalf of museums. Under the IMS definition, a museum is a public or private nonprofit institution organized on a permanent basis for educational or aesthetic purposes, and which: owns or uses and cares for tangible objects, whether animate or inanimate; exhibits them to the general public on a regular basis. "Museums" includes aquariums and zoological parks, botanical gardens and arboreta, and nature centers; art, history (including historic buildings and sites), natural history, children's general, and specialized museums; science and technology centers; and planetariums. Federal museums are ineligible.

Average: $6,000.

Activity: FY 04, 119 awards.

HQ: IMLS, 1100 Pennsylvania Ave., NW-Room 510, Washington, DC 20506 Phone: (202) 606-4641; Public Affairs, (202) 606-8339; *general library programs information,* (202) 606-5226; *museum programs,* (202) 606-8539; TDD, (202) 6606-8636.

Internet: www.imls.gov; e-mail, imlsinfo@imls.gov (Note: no field offices for this program.)

45.307 21ST CENTURY MUSEUM PROFESSIONALS

Assistance: project grants (50 percent/to 3 years).

Purposes: for professional training projects in all areas of museum operations and in personnel and leadership development; for related assessment and information collection and dissemination, including through workshops, seminars, and courses or indirect communication through publications and web sites. Projects should reflect community needs and address issues facing museums of similar size and type.

Eligible applicants/beneficiaries: generally, museums in the states, territories, and possessions that have provided museum services for at least two years. Public or private nonprofit agencies, such as a municipality, college, or university responsible for operating a museum, may apply on behalf of museums. Under the IMS definition, a museum is a public or private nonprofit institution organized on a permanent basis for educational or aesthetic purposes, and which: owns or uses and cares for tangible objects, whether animate or inanimate; exhibits them to the general public on a regular basis. "Museums" includes aquariums and zoological parks, botanical gardens and arboreta, and nature centers; art, history (including historic buildings and sites), natural history, children's general, and specialized museums; science and technology centers; and planetariums. Federal museums are ineligible.

Range: $87,000 to $441,000. **Average:** $249,000.

Activity: new program listing in 2005 (CFDA on-line version); FY 05, 4 projects funded.

HQ: IMLS, 1800 M St. NW - 9th Floor, Washington, DC 20036-5802 Phone: (202) 653-4685.

Internet: www.imls.gov (Note: no field offices for this program.)

45.308 NATIVE AMERICAN/NATIVE HAWAIIAN MUSEUM SERVICES PROGRAM

Assistance: project grants (to 2 years).

Purposes: pursuant to MSLA as amended, for strengthening of museum programming, professional development, and museum services provided to Native Americans and Hawaii natives.

Eligible applicants/beneficiaries: Indian tribes, bands, nations, or other organized groups or communities including Alaska native villages, regional corporations, or village corporations—eligible for BIA programs; nonprofit organizations serving and representing Hawaii natives. Museums, libraries, schools, and IHEs are ineligible; however, they may participate in project partnerships.

Range: $6,700 to $20,000.

Activity: new program listing in 2005 (CFDA on-line version). FY 05, 45 grants awarded.

HQ: IMLS, Office of Library Services, State Library Program, 1800 M St. NW - 9th fl., Washington, DC 20036-5802 Phone: (202) 653-4678.

Internet: www.imls.gov (Note: no field offices for this program.)

45.309 MUSEUM GRANTS FOR AFRICAN AMERICAN HISTORY AND CULTURE

Assistance: project grants. (50 percent/to 2 years).

Purposes: pursuant to Museum and Library Services Act, to develop and/or strengthen knowledge, skills, and other expertise of current staff at African American museums; to attract new staff and retain skilled professionals. Grant funds may not be used for: construction, endowment fund contributions, social activities, ceremonies, entertainment, collection acquisition, or pre-grant costs.

Eligible applicants/beneficiaries: a unit of state or local government or a private not-for-profit organization with IRS tax-exempt status, located in 50 states, territories or possessions and a museum whose primary purpose is African American life, art, history and/or culture, or a historically black college or university. Museums located within a parent organization may also qualify if they meet certain criteria.

Range: $5,000 to $150,000.

Activity: new program in 2006.

HQ: IMLS, 1800 M St. NW - 9th fl., Washington, DC 20036-5802 Phone: (202) 653-4685, -4703.

Internet: www.imls.gov (Note: no field offices for this program.)

45.310 GRANTS TO STATES

Assistance: formula grants (66 percent).

Purposes: pursuant to MSLA, to support a broad range of library and information services, either directly or through subgrants, including: establishing or enhancing electronic linkages among or between libraries and with educational, school, or information services; promoting targeted services to diverse geographic, cultural, and socio-economic audiences in urban and rural communities; acquiring or sharing computer systems and telecommunications technologies. Recipients must have an approved five-year state plan.

Eligible applicants/beneficiaries: state library administrative agencies, including in territories and possessions.

Range: formula based on population. No range reported.

Activity: FY 06, 59 awards.

HQ: Office of Library Services, IMLS, 1800 M St. NW - 9th Floor, Washington, DC 20036-5802 Phone: (202) 653-4678.

Internet: www.imls.gov (Note: no field offices for this program.)

45.311 NATIVE AMERICAN AND NATIVE HAWAIIAN LIBRARY SERVICES

Assistance: project grants. (100 percent/to 2 years).

Purposes: pursuant to the Museum and Library Services Act of 2003, to provide library services to Native Americans, including: support of core library operations; technical assistance projects for training tribal library staff; establishing or enhancing electronic linkages among libraries and with educational, school, or information services; acquiring or sharing computer systems and telecommunications technologies; targeted services to those having difficulty using a library and to underserved communities.

Eligible applicants/beneficiaries: recognized tribes, Alaska native villages, organizations primarily serving Hawaii natives.

Range/Average: N.A.

Activity: FY 05, 251 grants.

HQ: Office of Library Services, IMLS, 1800 M St. NW - 9th Floor, Washington, DC 20036-5802 Phone: (202) 653-4665.

Internet: www.imls.gov (Note: no field offices for this program.)

45.312 NATIONAL LEADERSHIP GRANTS

Assistance: project grants (67 percent; above $250,000, 50 percent/to 3 years).

Purposes: pursuant to MSLA, to enhance the quality of library and museum services nationwide and to provide coordination between libraries and museums. Funded activities may include: research and demonstration projects; preservation or digitization of library materials and resources; model cooperative library-museum programs; Building Digital Resources projects.

Eligible applicants/beneficiaries: libraries including those that are nonfederal, public, school, academic, archives, and private nonprofit; also, special libraries, research libraries, library agencies; consortia, and IHEs—applying individually or in partnerships, including with other public, nonprofit organizations. "Museums" includes aquariums and zoological parks, botanical gardens and arboreta, and nature centers; art, history (including historic buildings and sites), natural history, children's general, and specialized museums; science and technology centers; and planetariums. Federal museums are ineligible.

Range: libraries, $50,000 to $1,000,000; museums, $25,000 to $1,000,000.

Activity: FY 05, 35 library, 14 museum grants.

HQ: IMLS, 1800 M St. NW - 9th Floor, Washington, DC 20036-5802 Phone: Library Building Digital Resources, Research, Demonstration, (202) 653-4667; Advanced Learning Communities, (202) 653-4768; Museums, (202) 653- 4644.

Internet: wwww.imls.gov (Note: no field offices for this program.)

45.313 LAURA BUSH 21st CENTURY LIBRARIAN PROGRAM

Assistance: project grants (to 4 years).

Purposes: pursuant to Museum and Library Services Act of 2003, to recruit and educate new librarians and faculty prepared to teach masters of library science students; to support pertinent research. Current priorities include master's level programs, doctoral programs, preprofessional programs, research, building institutional capacity, continuing education. Grants require a 50 percent match, minus funds for student support; the matching requirement is waived for projects involving research only.

Eligible applicants/beneficiaries: libraries including those that are nonfederal, public, school, academic, archives, and private nonprofit; also, special libraries, research libraries, library agencies; consortia, and IHEs—applying individually or in partnerships, including with other public, nonprofit organizations.

Range: $50,000 to $1,000,000.

Activity: new program in FY 03; FY 05, 38 projects funded.

HQ: IMLS, 1800 M St. NW - 9th Floor, Washington, DC 20036-5802 Phone: Doctoral, Research, Capacity Building Programs, (202) 653-4662; Master's, Preprofessional, Continuing Education Programs, (202) 653-4663.

Internet: www.imls.gov (Note: no field offices for this program.)

NATIONAL LABOR RELATIONS BOARD

46.001 LABOR-MANAGEMENT RELATIONS ("NLRB")

Assistance: specialized services; investigation of complaints.

Purposes: pursuant to the Labor-Management Relations Act of 1947 as amended, to avoid or minimize industrial strife affecting interstate commerce, by providing orderly procedures to protect the rights of employers, employees, labor organizations, and the general public; to prevent unlawful interference with those rights. Services are provided to employee organizations voting on whether to be represented by a labor organization, and to employers or unions regarding unfair labor practices—only after charges or petitions are filed.

Eligible applicants/beneficiaries: any covered employer, employee, labor organization, or person believing that a violation has occurred, or wishing to vote on whether to be represented by a labor organization. "Employees" exclude: agricultural laborers, domestic workers; individuals employed by spouse or parent; independent contractors; employees subject to the Railway Labor Act; certain others not covered by the Act. Federal, state, and local governments and most government corporations, except the U.S. Postal Service, are ineligible employers.

Range/Average: N.A.

Activity: FY 05, intake 29,879 cases.

HQ: Division of Information, National Labor Relations Board, 1099 14th St. NW, Washington, DC 20570 Phone: (202) 273-1991.

Internet: www.nlrb.gov.

NATIONAL SCIENCE FOUNDATION

47.041 ENGINEERING GRANTS ("ENG")

Assistance: project grants (6 months-3 years).

Purposes: pursuant to the National Science Foundation Act of 1950 (NSFA) as amended, for engineering research and education programs in virtually all phases of engineering science and technological innovation and practice. Funding may support such activities as: research in emerging areas; industry-university cooperative research centers; biomedical engineering research; research equipment and instrumentation grants; undergraduate student research; graduate fellowships; faculty enhancement; inter-disciplinary studies; small business innovation research; small business technology transfer programs. Cost sharing is required except for solicited proposals, conferences, publications, travel, and logistical support. Funds may not support inventions, product development, marketing, or research requiring security classifications.

Eligible applicants/beneficiaries: public and private IHEs; nonprofit institutions; profit organizations including small businesses; state, and local government agencies; unaffiliated individuals.

Range: $5,000 to $4,000,000. **Average:** $120,000.

Activity: FY 05, 8,692 grants.

HQ: Program Director, Grant Opportunities for Academic Liaison with Industry, Directorate for Engineering-NSF, 4201 Wilson Blvd., Arlington, VA 22230 Phone: (703) 292-7082.

Internet: www.eng.nsf.gov; e-mail, *general inquiries,* enginfo@nsf.gov (Note: no field offices for this program.)

47.049 MATHEMATICAL AND PHYSICAL SCIENCES ("MPS")

Assistance: project grants. (to 100 percent/3-5 years).

Purposes: pursuant to NSFA as amended, for mostly basic research in physics, chemistry, astronomical and mathematical sciences, and materials, including multidisciplinary research. Grants may support: start-of-the-art user facilities; science and technology centers; institutes; undergraduate student research; developing research opportunities for women, minority, and disabled scientists and engineers; instrumentation; laboratory improvement; research workshops, symposia, and conferences; faculty enhancement; curriculum development. Cost sharing is required, except for symposia, conferences, publications, travel, education, training, or facilities.

Eligible applicants/beneficiaries: public and private IHEs; nonprofit, nonacademic research institutions; private profit organizations; foreign institutions; state and local governments; other federal agencies; certain unaffiliated scientists.

Range: $10,000 to $45,000,000. **Average:** $130,000.

Activity: FY 05, 2,073 grants.

HQ: Assistant Director, MPS-NSF, 4201 Wilson Blvd., Arlington, VA 22230 Phone: (703) 292-8801.

Internet: www.nsf.gov (Note: no field offices for this program.)

47.050 GEOSCIENCES ("GEO")

Assistance: project grants (1-5 years).

Purposes: pursuant to NSFA as amended, for basic research and studies in the atmospheric (e.g., meteorology, climate, paleoclimate), earth, and ocean sciences and in related biological, chemical, and physical disciplines. Grants may support science and technology centers, undergraduate student research, facility enhancement, instrumentation, laboratory equipment, and research opportunities for women, minority, and disabled scientists and engineers. Cost sharing is required, except for symposia, conferences, publications, travel, education, training, facilities, ship operations, or equipment.

Eligible applicants/beneficiaries: public and private IHEs, nonprofit nonacademic research institutions, private profit organizations, certain unaffiliated scientists.

Range: $1,000 to $60,000,000. **Average:** $147,857.

Activity: FY 05, 1,321 awards.

HQ: NSF, 4201 Wilson Blvd., Arlington, VA 22230 Phone: *atmospheric sciences,* (703) 292-8520, FAX (703) 292-9022; *earth sciences,* (703) 292-8550, FAX (703) 292-9025; *ocean sciences,* (703) 292-8580, FAX (703) 292-9085.

Internet: URL, NSF, www.nsf.gov; *geosciences,* www.geo.nsf.gov (Note: no field offices for this program.)

47.070 COMPUTER AND INFORMATION SCIENCE AND ENGINEERING ("CISE")

Assistance: project grants. (cost sharing/6 months-3 years).

Purposes: pursuant to NSFA as amended, for research improving the fundamental understanding of computer and information science and engineering; to enhance the training and education of scientists and engineers; and, to provide access to very advanced computing and networking capabilities. Ineligible uses of funds include fellowships, scholarships, product development and marketing.

Eligible applicants/beneficiaries: public and private IHEs; nonprofit and profit organizations; small businesses; state and local government agencies, certain unaffiliated scientists.

Range: $2,000 to $19,000,000. **Average:** $136,000.

Activity: FY 05, 1,088 awards.

HQ: Assistant Director, CISE-NSF, 4201 Wilson Blvd., Arlington, VA 22230 Phone: (703) 292-8900.

Internet: www.cise.nsf.gov (Note: no field offices for this program.)

47.074 BIOLOGICAL SCIENCES ("BIO")

Assistance: project grants. (to 100 percent/to 5 years).

Purposes: pursuant to NSFA as amended, for mostly basic research in the biological sciences, including cellular and molecular biosciences, integrative organismal biology, environmental biology, biological infrastructure, and plant genomes. Grants may be used to purchase multi-user scientific equipment and for instrument development; research workshops, symposia, and conferences; doctoral, postdoctoral fellowships including for minority scientists. Cost sharing is required, except for symposia, conferences, publications, travel, education, or training.

Eligible applicants/beneficiaries: public and private IHEs, nonprofit nonacademic research institutions, private profit organizations, certain unaffiliated scientists.

Range: $2,000 to $12,389,000. **Average:** $184,040.

Activity: FY 05, 1,355 grants.

HQ: Assistant Director, BIO-NSF, 4201 Wilson Blvd., Arlington, VA 22230 Phone: (703) 292-8400.

Internet: www.nsf.gov/bio (Note: no field offices for this program.)

47.075 SOCIAL, BEHAVIORAL, AND ECONOMIC SCIENCES ("SBE")

Assistance: project grants. (to 100 percent/to 5 years).

Purposes: pursuant to NSFA as amended, for basic research in the social, behavioral and economic sciences in such disciplines as: anthropological and geographic sciences; cognitive, psychological, and language science; economic, decision, and management sciences; social and political science; infrastructure, methods, and science studies; educational attainment in science, mathematics, and engineering. Grants may support: science and technology centers, including climate change; science of learning centers, workshops, symposia, and conferences; doctoral and postdoctoral fellowships; junior faculty research; graduate traineeships; mid-career development; undergraduate student research; research opportunities for women, minorities, and disabled scientists and engineers.

Eligible applicants/beneficiaries: public and private IHEs, nonprofit nonacademic research institutions, private profit organizations, certain unaffiliated scientists.

Range: $1,100 to $4,980,000. **Average:** $85,000.

Activity: FY 05, 1,006 grants.

HQ: Directorate for Social, Behavioral and Economic Sciences-NSF, 4201 Wilson Blvd., Arlington, VA 22230 Phone: (703) 292-8700; Division of Science Resources Statistics, (703) 292-8780; Division of Social and Economic Sciences, (703) 292-8760; Division of Behavioral and Cognitive Sciences, (703) 292-8740.

Internet: www.nsf.gov; *science resources,* www.nsf.gov/sbe/srs; *social, economic sciences,* www.nsf.gov/sbe/ses; *behavioral, cognitive sciences,* www.nsf.gov/sbe/bcs (Note: no field offices for this program.)

47.076 EDUCATION AND HUMAN RESOURCES ("EHR")

Assistance: project grants (to 5 years).

Purposes: pursuant to NSFA as amended, for programs improving the effectiveness of science, mathematics, engineering, and technology education—through programs that support research and the development of models and strategies, including in: elementary, secondary, informal science education, and lifelong learning; undergraduate, graduate, and postdoctoral education; human resource development; research, evaluation, and dissemination; experimental programs. Grants may support fellowships for up to three years, scholarships, equipment purchases, salaries, and other expenses.

Eligible applicants: public and private two- and four-year IHEs; SEAs and LEAs; tribal entities; nonprofit and private organizations; professional societies; science academies and centers; science museums and zoological parks; research laboratories; other informal science education institutions.

Eligible beneficiaries: pre-school, elementary, secondary, and undergraduate science, mathematics, and engineering teachers and faculty; secondary, undergraduate, and graduate students.

Range: $3,000 to $15,000,000. **Average:** $255,472.

Activity: FY 05, 759 awards; 128 H1-B Nonimmigrant Petitioner institutional awards for 9,700 scholarships.

HQ: Assistant Director, EHR-NSF, 4201 Wilson Blvd. (Rm.805), Arlington, VA 22230 Phone: (703) 292-8600.

Internet: www.nsf.gov/dir/index.jsp?org=EHR (Note: no field offices for this program.)

47.078 POLAR PROGRAMS ("OPP")

Assistance: project grants. (to 100 percent/1-3 years).

Purposes: pursuant to NSFA as amended, for basic research in the Arctic and Antarctic regions, focused on the solid earth, glacial and sea ice, terrestrial ecosystems, the oceans, the atmosphere and beyond. Support is available for science and technology centers, undergraduate student research, postdoctoral fellowships, facility enhancement, instrumentation, laboratory equipment, and research opportunities for women, minority, and handicapped scientists and engineers. Cost sharing is required, except for symposia, conferences, publications, travel, education, training, facilities, ship operations, or equipment.

Eligible applicants/beneficiaries: public and private IHEs, nonprofit nonacademic research institutions, private profit organizations, certain unaffiliated scientists.

Range: $1,000 to $5,000,000. **Average:** $180,500.

Activity: FY 05, 284 awards.

HQ: National Science Foundation, 4201 Wilson Blvd., Arlington, VA 22230 Phone: Arctic Sciences, (703) 292-8029, FAX (703) 292-9082; Antarctic Sciences, (703) 292-8033, FAX (703) 292-9079; Polar Research, (703) 292-8032, FAX (703) 292-9080.

Internet: www.nsf.gov/od/opp (Note: no field offices for this program.)

47.079 INTERNATIONAL SCIENCE AND ENGINEERING (OISE) ("International")

Assistance: project grants. (to 100 percent/to 3 years).

Purposes: pursuant to NSFA as amended, for international partnerships fostering scientific basic research collaborations, discovery, and education abroad for U.S. students and junior faculty. Activities eligible for funding include graduate traineeships, postdoctoral fellowships, undergraduate research experiences, workshops, planning visits, and research opportunities for women, minorities, and scientists and engineers with disabilities—in all disciplinary fields supported by NSF.

Eligible applicants/beneficiaries: public and private IHEs, nonprofit nonacademic research institutions, profit organizations, certain unaffiliated scientists, multilateral science and technology organizations.

Range: $500 to $2,000,000. **Average:** $40,000.

Activity: new program listing in 2005; FY 05, 335 awards.

HQ: Office of International Science and Engineering-NSF, 4201 Wilson Blvd., Suite 935, Arlington, VA 22230 Phone: (703) 292-8710.

Internet: www.nsf.gov (Note: no field offices for this program.)

47.080 OFFICE OF CYBERINFRASTRUCTURE ("OCI")

Assistance: project grants (to 3 years).

Purposes: pursuant to NSFA as amended, to acquire, develop, and provide state-of-the-art cyberinfrastructure resources, tools, and services essential to 21st-century science and engineering research and education. Major program focus: the "OptiPuter" project's inventions and applications in such areas as next-generation access grids available to science, engineering, teaching and education, Doppler radar weather forecasting, and other enhancements of the possibilities of cyberinfrastructure.

Eligible applicants/beneficiaries: public and private IHEs; nonprofit and profit organizations including small businesses; federal, state, and local government agencies—with most funding allocated to academic institutions.

Range: $10,000 to $20,000,000. **Average:** $340,000.

Activity: new program listing in 2006 (CFDA on-line); FY 05, 75 awards.

HQ: Office of the Director, OCI-NSF, 4201 Wilson Blvd., Arlington, VA 22230 Phone: (703) 292-8970.

Internet: www.nsf.gov/oci/ (Note: no field offices for this program.)

47.081 OFFICE OF EXPERIMENTAL PROGRAM TO STIMULATE COMPETITIVE RESEARCH ("020 EPSCoR")

Assistance: project grants (6 months to 3 years).

Purposes: pursuant to the National Science Foundation Act of 1950 as amended, to assist those jurisdictions that have historically received lesser amounts of academic research and development funding and accelerate the movement of more researchers and institutions from EPSCoR jurisdictions into the mainstream of NSF support. Funds may be used for research, product development, resources, tools and services, salaries and wages, equipment and supplies, travel, publication costs, and other direct and indirect costs.

Eligible applicants/beneficiaries: public and private colleges and universities; non-profit, non-academic organizations; for-profit organizations; state and local governments; and unaffiliated scientists under special circumstances.

Range: $99,472 to $9,200,000. **Average:** $5,918,265.

Activity: FY 06, 14 proposals and 11 awards; FY 07, 18 proposals and 11 awards.

HQ: Office of the Director, National Science Foundation, 4201 Wilson Blvd., Arlington, VA 22230. Telephone: (703) 292-8970.

Internet: www.nsf.gov/oia. (Note: no field offices for this program.)

RAILROAD RETIREMENT BOARD

57.001 SOCIAL INSURANCE FOR RAILROAD WORKERS

Assistance: direct payments/unrestricted use.

Purposes: pursuant to the Social Security Act, Railroad Unemployment Insurance Act, Railroad Retirement Act of 1974, and amendments, to pay benefits to railroad workers and their beneficiaries, including retirement, death, disability, unemployment, or sickness insurance.

Eligible applicants/beneficiaries: Railroad Retirement Act benefits—for employee, spouse, and survivor benefits, the employee must have had 10 or more years of railroad service. Annuities—beginning January 2002 or later, 5 years of railroad service rendered after 1995. For survivors, the employees must have been insured at death. Railroad Unemployment Insurance Act—employees with certain minimum earnings in railroad wages; new employees must have worked for a railroad at least five months in a calendar (base) year.

Average: age annuities, monthly maximum $3,547, average $1,693; disability, monthly maximum $3,510, average $1,825; employee supplemental annuities, monthly maximum $70, average $42; spouse benefits, monthly maximum $1,693, average $645; widows/widowers, monthly maximum $3,547, average $1,064; widowed parents, monthly maximum $3,062, average $1,388; children, monthly maximum $2,017, average $789; unemployment sickness, weekly maximum/2006-07 benefit year $285, estimated average $285.

Activity: FY 05, 659,000 total beneficiaries; 36,404 retirement awards; 28,676 unemployment insurance beneficiaries.

HQ: Public Affairs, Railroad Retirement Board, 844 N. Rush St., Chicago, IL 60611-2092 Phone: (312) 751-4777.

Internet: www.rrb.gov.

SECURITIES AND EXCHANGE COMMISSION

58.001 SECURITIES—INVESTIGATION OF COMPLAINTS AND SEC INFORMATION ("Complaints and Inquiries")

Assistance: technical information; investigation of complaints.

Purposes: pursuant to the Securities Act of 1933, Securities and Exchange Act of 1934, Securities Investor Protection Act of 1970, amendments, and related acts, to provide assistance to or on behalf of securities investors, including educational materials and public educational activities; to represent individual investors in SEC rule-making proceedings. SEC's public files contain financial and other information about companies, broker-dealers, investment companies, investment advisers, transfer agents, and banks, which may be examined at SEC offices; or, copies may be obtained from SEC's Public Reference Branch. Investors believing they have been defrauded, or that another party has violated the federal securities laws, may present their complaint and/or information to the SEC. A public action taken by SEC does not necessarily result in monetary benefits to investors; however, aggrieved investors may find the information disclosed by the commission in its actions helpful in any private action brought to recover losses.

Eligible applicants/beneficiaries: anyone may seek information or file a complaint.

Range/Average: N.A.

Activity: FY 05, 76,221 complaints, inquiries, and other investor contacts.

HQ: Office of Investor Education and Assistance, SEC, 100 F St. NE, Washington, DC 20549-0213 Phone: (202) 551-6551, FAX (202) 942-9634; Public Reference Branch (MS 1-2), (202) 942-8090, FAX (202) 628-9001.

Internet: www.sec.gov; *questions, complaints,* www.sec.gov/complaint.shtml; e-mail, help@sec.gov; e-mail, Public Reference Branch, publicinfo@sec.gov.

SMALL BUSINESS ADMINISTRATION

NOTE: *In the following SBA program descriptions, "small business" means a business independently owned and operated, not dominant in its field, and meeting certain size standards in terms of numbers of employees and annual revenues. Unless otherwise indicated, SBA excludes from its financial assistance programs: nonprofit enterprises (except for disaster loans and sheltered workshops); lending or investment enterprises; gambling enterprises; and, real estate speculators.*

59.006 8(A) BUSINESS DEVELOPMENT PROGRAM ("Section 8(a) Program")

Assistance: specialized services (to 9 years).

Purposes: pursuant to the Small Business Act of 1953 as amended, for SBA to enter into procurement contracts with other federal agencies and for subcontracts, in turn, with socially and economically disadvantaged businesses. The program incorporates contract, technical, and managerial assistance to participants, and access to financial resources.

Eligible applicants/beneficiaries: small businesses at least 51 percent owned, controlled, and managed by U.S. citizens, determined by SBA to be socially and economically disadvantaged; disadvantaged tribes, Alaska native corporations, or native Hawaiian organizations.

Range/Average: N.A.

Activity: FY 01, 32,000 contract actions valued at $6.59 billion (latest data reported).

HQ: Associate Administrator/8(a) Business Development, SBA, 409 Third St. SW, Washington, DC 20416 Phone: (no number provided).

Internet: www.sba.gov.

59.007 7(J) TECHNICAL ASSISTANCE ("Section 7(j) Program")

Assistance: project grants (100 percent).

Purposes: pursuant to the Small Business Act of 1953 as amended, for projects conducted by qualified entities to provide business management, technical assistance, and services in obtaining financing—to businesses that are socially and economically disadvantaged, located in areas of high unemployment or low income, or participants in program **59.006**. Funds also may be used to establish and strengthen business service agencies including trade associations and cooperatives.

Eligible applicants/beneficiaries: state and local governments; educational institutions; public or private organizations and businesses; lending and financial institutions and sureties; tribes; qualified individuals.

Range/Average: N.A.

Activity: FY 01, 14 cooperative agreement, 3 contract awards (latest data reported).

HQ: Associate Administrator/Management and Technical Assistance, Office of Business Development, SBA, 409 Third St. SW, Washington, DC 20416 Phone: (202) 205-7343.

Internet: www.sba.gov.

59.008 DISASTER ASSISTANCE LOANS ("DL - Section 7(b) Loans")

Assistance: direct loans. (to 4-8 percent/3-30 years).

Purposes: pursuant to the Small Business Act of 1953 as amended and the Disaster Relief Act of 1970, for victims of declared physical disasters to restore or replace uninsured damaged or destroyed real or personal property. Loan terms depend on the applicant's access to credit. Provisions of the Flood Disaster Protection Act of 1973 and National Flood Insurance Reform Act of 1994 apply. Collateral is required on loans of more than $10,000.

Eligible applicants/beneficiaries: homeowners, renters, businesses, and charitable and nonprofit organizations. Agricultural enterprises are ineligible.

Range: homes, to $240,000, plus $200,000 in special cases to refinance existing liens, and $48,000 additional for protective measures; businesses, to $1,500,000 with higher amounts available for major source of employment. **Average:** homes, $25,000; businesses, $75,000.

Activity: FY 04, 25,000 loans.

HQ: Office of Disaster Assistance, SBA, 409 Third St. SW, Washington, DC 20416 Phone: (202) 205-6734.

Internet: www.sba.gov/DISASTER; e-mail, disaster.assistance@sba.gov.

59.009 PROCUREMENT ASSISTANCE TO SMALL BUSINESSES

Assistance: specialized services.

Purposes: pursuant to the Small Business Act of 1953 as amended and the Economic Opportunity Act of 1964, to assist small businesses in all phases of obtaining government procurement contracts and subcontracts, as well as of federal property sold. SBA: advocates small business participation in federal contracts and subcontracts, including application of small business "set-asides;" consults with other federal procuring agencies to optimize small business participation; manages the Central Contractor Registration's Dynamic Small Business Search, a nationwide Internet information database on small businesses interested in obtaining federal contracts or subcontracts.

Eligible applicants/beneficiaries: existing and potential small businesses.

Range/Average: N.A.

Activity: FY 04, $11.2 billion in set-asides.

HQ: Associate Administrator/Government Contracting, SBA, 409 Third St. SW, Washington, DC 20416 Phone: (202) 205-6460.

Internet: www.sba.gov.

59.011 SMALL BUSINESS INVESTMENT COMPANIES ("SBIC - SSBIC")

Assistance: direct loans; guaranteed/insured loans; advisory services/counseling (guaranteed/insured loans, to 10-15 years).

Purposes: pursuant to the Small Business Investment Act of 1958 as amended, for privately owned and managed SBA-licensed small business investment companies, including specialized SBICs (SSBICs) assisting socially or economically disadvantaged enterprises, to provide equity capital, in turn, to small businesses—through long-term loans or equity purchases. SBA guarantees debentures issued by the investment companies to maximize leveraging of private funds, by up to 300 percent within maximums established by SBA and for terms of 10 years; participating securities may be guaranteed for up to 15 years. The investment companies provide continuing management and other assistance to firms that obtain the loans.

Eligible applicants: chartered SBICs with private capital of at least $3,000,000 for those not receiving SBA leveraging, or $5,000,000 if receiving SBA leveraging.

Eligible beneficiaries: small businesses (single proprietorship, partnership, or corporation); SSBIC beneficiaries must also be socially or economically disadvantaged enterprises.

Range: $50,000 to $119,000,000. **Average:** $18,200,000.

Activity: as of FY 05, participation by 448 SBICs with capital resources of $25.7 billion.

HQ: Associate Administrator/Investment, Investment Division, SBA, 409 Third St. SW, Washington, DC 20416 Phone: (202) 205-6510.

Internet: www.sba.gov (Note: no field offices for this program.)

59.012 7(A) LOAN GUARANTEES ("Regular Business Loans - Section 7(a) Loans")

Assistance: guaranteed/insured loans.

Purposes: pursuant to the Small Business Act of 1953 as amended, for small businesses to construct, expand, or convert business facilities; to purchase equipment or materials; for working capital. Eligible loan uses also include design, manufacture, marketing, installation, or servicing of specific energy measures. Program components include SBA's: Low Documentation Loan Program (Low Doc); Cap Line Program; SBAExpress Program; International Trade.

Eligible applicants/beneficiaries: small businesses that meet eligibility standards.

Range: to $2,000,000. **Average:** $150,000.

Activity: FY 04, 81,000 loans guaranteed.

HQ: Director, Loan Programs Division, SBA, 409 Third St. SW, Washington, DC 20416 Phone: (202) 205-6570.

Internet: www.sba.gov/financing.

59.016 SURETY BOND GUARANTEES ("Surety Bond Guarantees")

Assistance: insurance (70-90 percent).

Purposes: pursuant to the Small Business Act of 1953 as amended and the Inspector General Act of 1978, to guarantee bonds issued by commercial surety companies for bid, payment, and performance or other bonds provided to small businesses on contracts up to $2,000,000.

Eligible applicants: surety companies holding certificates of authority from the Secretary of the Treasury.

Eligible beneficiaries: small contractors with gross annual receipts of no more than $6,000,000 as averaged for the last three fiscal years; certain manufacturers. (Applications are submitted directly to insurance agents or brokers.)

Range: $475 to $2,000,000. **Average:** contract, $268,000; guarantee, $213,000.

Activity: FY 04, 5,573 bid bonds approved, 2,230 final bond guarantees issued.

HQ: Associate Administrator, Office of Surety Guarantees, SBA, 409 Third St. SW, Washington, DC 20416 Phone: (202) 205-6540.

Internet: www.sba.gov.

59.026 SERVICE CORPS OF RETIRED EXECUTIVES ("SCORE")

Assistance: advisory services/counseling; training.

Purposes: pursuant to the Small Business Act of 1953 as amended, to operate the SCORE program through which retired or active business executives volunteer their services to counsel and train new and existing small business persons. Out-of-pocket expenses of volunteers may be reimbursed.

Eligible applicants/beneficiaries: existing and potential small businesses.

Range/Average: N.A.

Activity: 11,500 volunteers serve in the 50 states and in possessions.

HQ: Office of Business and Community Initiatives, SBA, 409 Third St. SW, Washington, DC 20024 Phone: (202) 205-6762, (800) 634- 0245; National SCORE Office, (same address), (202) 205-6762; (800) 634-0245.

Internet: www.sba.gov; SCORE, www.score.org.

59.037 SMALL BUSINESS DEVELOPMENT CENTERS ("SBDC")

Assistance: project grants; specialized services; advisory services/counseling; technical information (formula based, 50 percent).

Purposes: pursuant to the Small Business Act of 1953 as amended, for SBDCs to provide management counseling, training, and technical assistance to existing or potential small businesses.

Eligible applicants/beneficiaries: public or private IHEs including land grant, community, or junior colleges; certain existing SBDCs.

Range: $500,000 to $5,927,000. **Average:** $1,298,000.

Activity: FY 04, 280,000 individuals counseled, 27,000 training sessions.

HQ: SBDC Office, SBA, 409 Third St. SW - 6th floor, Washington, DC 20416 Phone: (202) 205-6766, FAX (202) 205-7727.

Internet: www.sba.gov/sbdc.

59.041 504 CERTIFIED DEVELOPMENT LOANS ("Section 504 Loans")

Assistance: guaranteed/insured loans (10-20 years).

Purposes: pursuant to the Small Business Investment Act of 1958 as amended, to assist small businesses in acquiring fixed assets, through the sale of debentures to private investors. Loans may cover acquisition of land, buildings, equipment, construction, expansion, renovation, or modernization. Ten percent of project costs must be provided by the small business concern, and 50 percent by a private lender.

Eligible applicants/beneficiaries: nonprofit certified development companies.

Range: to $1,000,000. **Average:** $480,000.

Activity: FY 04, 8,168 loans approved.

HQ: Office of Financial Assistance, SBA, 409 Third St. SW, Washington, DC 20416 Phone: (202) 205-6490.

Internet: www.sba.gov.

59.043 WOMEN'S BUSINESS OWNERSHIP ASSISTANCE

Assistance: project grants (50-67 percent/to 5 years).

Purposes: pursuant to the Small Business Act of 1953 as amended, Women's Business Ownership Act of 1988, and Women's Business Center Sustainability Act of 1999, to establish women's business centers to assist new or existing small businesses owned and controlled by women, through financial, management, procurement, marketing, training, and counseling services. Services are also provided through the Online Women's Business Center.

Eligible applicants/beneficiaries: experienced private nonprofit organizations.

Range: $75,000 to $150,000.

Activity: FY 05, 144,000 clients trained and counseled at 90 funded centers.

HQ: Office of Women's Business Ownership, SBA, 409 Third St. SW, Washington, DC 20416 Phone: (202) 205-6673.

Internet: www.sba.gov/womeninbusiness; www.onlinewbc.gov.

59.044 VETERANS BUSINESS DEVELOPMENT ("VBOP")

Assistance: project grants (matching/1-5 years).

Purposes: pursuant to the Small Business Act of 1953 as amended, to establish and operate Veterans Business Outreach Centers to provide long-term training, counseling, and mentoring to veterans starting or operating small businesses.

Eligible applicants/beneficiaries: educational institutions; private businesses; veterans nonprofit community-based organizations; federal, state, and local entities.

Range: $75 to $1,500 per client.

Activity: N.A.

HQ: Associate Administrator, Office of Veterans Business Development, SBA, 409 Third St. SW - 5th Floor, Washington, DC 20416 Phone: (202) 205-6773.

Internet: www.sba.gov.

59.046 MICROLOAN PROGRAM

Assistance: formula grants; direct loans (loans, to 10 years).

Purposes: to provide loan funds or loan guaranties to eligible intermediary lenders that, in turn, will make short-term, fixed- rate loans to newly established or growing small businesses for working capital or for the acquisition of supplies or equipment; to make grants to intermediaries to provide intensive marketing, management, and technical assistance to borrowers; to make grants to nonprofit entities to assist low-income individuals in obtaining private sector financing for their businesses.

Eligible applicants: intermediary lenders meeting SBA requirements.

Eligible beneficiaries: small businesses, minority entrepreneurs, nonprofit entities, women, low-income and other persons.

Average: $12,000.

Activity: not quantified specifically.

HQ: Microenterprise Development Branch (MC 7881), Office of Financial Assistance, SBA, 409 Third St. SW - 8th Floor, Washington, DC 20416 Phone: (202) 205-6490.

Internet: www.sba.gov.

59.049 SMALL DISADVANTAGED BUSINESSES ("OSBDC&E")

Assistance: direct loans (from 3 years).

Purposes: pursuant to the Small Business Act of 1953 as amended, to ensure compliance with "Adarand vs. Pena," relative to federal action programs that use racial or ethnic criteria as a basis for decision-making. The program assists the government in finding firms capable of providing services under procurement contracts.

Eligible applicants/beneficiaries: certified socially and economically disadvantaged small business concerns.

Range/Average: N.A.

Activity: FY 04, 1,000 new certifications issued.

HQ: OSBDC&E, SBA, 409 Third St. SW, Washington, DC 20416 Phone: (no number provided).

Internet: www.sba.gov/sdb (Note: no field offices for this program.)

59.050 PRIME TECHNICAL ASSISTANCE ("PRIME")

Assistance: project grants. (50 percent/1-5 years).

Purposes: pursuant to the Riegle Community Development and Regulatory Improvement Act of 1994 as amended and Gramm-Leach- Bliley Act, to increase the number of microenterprises and enhance their management capabilities, by: providing training and technical assistance in starting or expanding their businesses; providing training and capacity building services to enhance existing or new microenterprise development organizations (MDOs) that provide training programs and services; conducting research and development of "best practices" in the field.

Eligible applicants: established nonprofit MDOs or programs, including collaboratives, that are accountable to local communities and working in conjunction with a state or local government or tribe; certain tribes acting on their own.

Eligible beneficiaries: disadvantaged entrepreneurs and microenterprises.

Average: N.A.

Activity: N.A.

HQ: Office of Financial Assistance, SBA, 409 Third St. SW, Washington, DC 20416 Phone: (202) 205-6491.

Internet: www.sba.gov/inv; www.sba.gov/financing/sbaloan/microloans.html (Note: no field offices for this program.)

59.051 NEW MARKETS VENTURE CAPITAL PROGRAM

Assistance: project grants; guaranteed/insured loans. (grants, 50 percent/grants and loans, to 10 year).

Purposes: pursuant to the Small Business Investment Act of 1958 as amended, to promote economic development and the creation of wealth and job opportunities in low-income areas—through development venture capital investments in smaller enterprises located in such areas. Program loan recipients must match 30 percent of capital funds obtained from SBA (derived from SBA- guaranteed debentures); they may make equity capital investments in the enterprises at 1 percent interest above the cost of federal borrowing, requiring no repayment in years 1 to 5, interest-only payments in years 6 to 10, and a balloon payment at maturity, and with no prepayment penalty after year 1. Grant recipients provide related management and technical assistance to the enterprises.

Eligible applicants/beneficiaries: new for-profit companies; existing specialized small business investment companies (SSBICs).

Range: from $1,500,000.

Activity: N.A.

HQ: New Markets Venture Capital Program, Investment Division, SBA, 409 Third St. SW - Ste.6300, Washington, DC 20416 Phone: (202) 205-6510.

Internet: www.sba.gov/INV/NMVC (Note: no field offices for this program.)

59.052 NATIVE AMERICAN OUTREACH

Assistance: project grants.

Purposes: pursuant to the Small Business Act as amended, for entrepreneurial development programs and services provided to American Indians and Alaska and Hawaii natives, located in disadvantaged and under-served reservations and tribal areas, and seeking to establish, develop, and expand small businesses. Projects must include a strong outreach component stressing participation in under-served areas. Project examples: small business incubator activities; training; marketing outreach.

Eligible applicants/beneficiaries: organizations with experience in training, counseling, developing, and measuring small business development in Indian country.

Range/Average: N.A.

Activity: new program listing in 2005.

HQ: Office of Native American Affairs, SBA, 409 Third St. SW, Washington, DC 20416 Phone: (no number provided).

Internet: www.sba.gov/naa/ (Note: no field offices for this program.)

59.053 OMBUDSMAN AND REGULATORY FAIRNESS BOARDS

Assistance: project grants.

Purposes: pursuant to the Small Business Regulatory Fairness Act of 1996, to serve the small business community by receiving comments regarding unfair or excessive actions by federal agencies or agency employees conducting compliance or enforcement activities. Comments may be confidential or not, and be discussed with appropriate federal agency personnel to seek a timely response to an excessive or unfair federal regulatory issue. Hearings may be held throughout the country to receive testimony and commentary. Comments also may be submitted online, by FAX, mail, or personal delivery.

Eligible applicants/beneficiaries: small businesses, nonprofit organizations, or small government entities (representing fewer than 50,000 persons).

Range/Average: N.A.

Activity: new program listing in 2005.

HQ: Office of the National Ombudsman, SBA, 409 Third St. SW, Washington, DC 20416 Phone: (no number provided).

Internet: www.sba.gov/ombudsman (Note: no field offices for this program.)

59.054 7(A) EXPORT LOAN GUARANTEES ("Export Loans")

Assistance: guaranteed/insured loans.

Purposes: pursuant to the Small Business Act of 1953 as amended, for small businesses to increase their ability to compete in international markets by enhancing their ability to export, through: the Export Working Capital Program, providing 90 percent loan guarantees; the Export Express Loan Program, with 85 percent loan guarantees; the International Trade Loan Program, with 75 percent loan guarantees. Loans may be used: to construct, expand, or convert facilities; to purchase building equipment or materials; for export working capital.

Eligible applicants/beneficiaries: small businesses meeting SBA size standards, that are independently owned and operated, and not dominant in their field.

Range/Average: N.A.

Activity: new program listing in 2005; FY 04, 2,316 loans to exporters.

HQ: Associate Administrator, Office of International Trade, SBA, 409 Third St. SW, Washington, DC 20416 Phone: (202) 205-6720.

Internet: www.sba.gov.

59.055 HISTORICALLY UNDERUTILIZED BUSINESS ZONES (HUBZONE)

Assistance: project grants.

Purposes: pursuant to the HUBZone Act of1997, SBA Authorization and Manufacturing Assistance Act of 2004, and HUBZones in Native America Act of 2000, to provide federal contracting assistance for qualified SBCs located in historically underutilized business zones in an effort to increase employment opportunities, investment, and economic development in such areas.

Eligible applicants/beneficiaries: firms who are: SBA-defined small business; at least 51 percent owned/controlled by one or more U.S. citizens, a Community Development Corporation, agricultural cooperative, or Indian tribe; principle office located in a HUBZone; and at least 35 percent of employees are residents of a HUBZone.

Range/Average: N.A.

Activity: FY 04: 2,294 HUBZone small businesses certified and 505 program examinations completed.

HQ: Director, HUBZone Program, SBA, 409 Third St. SW, Washington, DC 20416 Phone: (no number provided).

Internet: www.sba.gov/hubzone.

59.070 DRUG-FREE WORKPLACE PROGRAM

Assistance: project grants; financial/technical assistance; dissemination of educational materials (2 years (cooperative agreements)).

Purposes: pursuant to the Small Business Act, to enable eligible intermediaries to assist small businesses financially and technically in establishing DFWP programs.

Eligible applicants: current small business owners.

Eligible beneficiaries: small businesses, including those owned by low-income and handicapped individuals located in high unemployment areas.

Range/Average: $100,000 to $250,000.

Activity: FY 07, 453 small businesses implemented full or partial drug-free workplace programs; 2,731 small businesses educated about the benefits of a drug free workplace program; 1,506 small businesses financially assisted; and 1,745 small businesses technically assisted.

HQ: Associate Administrator, Office of Small Business Development Centers, 409 3rd, SW, Washington, DC 20416. Phone: (202) 205-6766, FAX: (202) 205-7727.

Internet: www.sba.gov/sbdc.

DEPARTMENT OF VETERANS AFFAIRS

NOTE: *In DVA programs providing benefits directly to veterans, eligibility factors may include all or some of the following: discharge under other than dishonorable conditions; former prisoners of war; Medal of Honor award in peacetime and unable to pay the cost of necessary care; wartime service resulting in need of treatment for a full or partial service-connected or nonservice-connected disability; or for a disease; receiving a DVA pension or age 65 or older and with wartime or peacetime active service; discharged for a disability, or receiving compensation for and suffering from a permanent disability, with no adequate means of support; degree of disability; receiving compensation or allowances based on need of regular aid and attendance or housebound; income within certain limits, although eligibility based on financial income may be established by making a copyament for some services. For some programs, time and duration of service may affect eligibility.*

Details may be obtained from DVA medical centers or outpatient clings, from DVA Veterans Benefits Administration field offices (see 64.115 or other centers listed in Part IV).

VETERANS HEALTH ADMINISTRATION

64.005 GRANTS TO STATES FOR CONSTRUCTION OF STATE HOME FACILITIES ("State Home Construction")

Assistance: project grants. (to 65 percent/to 5 years).

Purposes: to acquire or construct state domiciliary or nursing home facilities for veterans; to expand, remodel, alter, or equip existing buildings to provide domiciliary, nursing home, or hospital care to veterans in state homes.

Eligible applicants/beneficiaries: states.

Range: $23,000 to $14,312,000. **Average:** $2,532,000.

Activity: FY 03 estimate, 42 grant approvals (latest data received).

HQ: Chief Consultant, Geriatrics and Extended Care Strategic Healthcare Group (114), DVA, Washington, DC 20420 Phone: (202) 273-8356.

Internet: www.va.gov (Note: no field offices for this program.)

64.007 BLIND REHABILITATION CENTERS ("Blind Center")

Assistance: specialized services.

Purposes: to provide personal and social adjustment programs and medical or health-related services to blind veterans at DVA medical centers with blind rehabilitation centers.

Eligible applicants/beneficiaries: blind veterans meeting certain general requirements (*see NOTE preceding* **64.005**). Active duty armed forces personnel may be transferred to a center.

Range/Average: N.A.

Activity: FY 05, 2,089 veterans benefited at the 10 centers.

HQ: Blind Rehabilitation Service (117B), Patient Care Services, DVA, Washington, DC 20420 Phone: (202) 273-8482, -8483.

Internet: www.va.gov/blindrehab.

64.008 VETERANS DOMICILIARY CARE ("DRRTP")

Assistance: specialized services.

Purposes: to provide inpatient medical care and physical, social, and psychological support services to ambulatory veterans disabled by age or illness, and not requiring acute care or skilled nursing services; for rehabilitation services preparing veterans for independent community living, or assisting them in reaching their optimal level of functioning in a protective environment.

Eligible applicants/beneficiaries: veterans meeting specific criteria (*see NOTE preceding* **64.005**).

Range/Average: N.A.

Activity: FY 05, 30,472 veterans served; average daily census, 9,015.

HQ: Chief Consultant, Office of Mental Health Services (116), DVA, Washington, DC 20420 Phone: (202) 273-8443, -8446.

Internet: www.va.gov.

64.009 VETERANS MEDICAL CARE BENEFITS ("Hospitalization and Medical Services")

Assistance: specialized services.

Purposes: to provide hospital outpatient medical, dental, medicine, medical supplies, home health, podiatric, optometric, surgical, and mental health services to enrolled veterans and their dependents, including reimbursement for some travel costs. Services are provided at DVA facilities or under fee-basis hometown care programs when properly authorized.

Eligible applicants/beneficiaries: veterans meeting specific criteria (*see NOTE preceding* **64.005**); veterans dependents and survivors that are ineligible for Medicare, CHAMPUS (Civilian Health and Medical Program of the Uniformed Service), or CHAMPVA (Civilian Health and Medical Program, Veterans Affairs).

Range/Average: N.A.

Activity: FY 05, 811,280 inpatients served in VA, state, and contract facilities; 58,236,000 total outpatient visits.

HQ: Director, Health Administration Services (10C3), DVA, Washington, DC 20420 Phone: (202) 273-8302, -8303.

Internet: www.va.gov.

64.010 VETERANS NURSING HOME CARE

Assistance: specialized services.

Purposes: to provide skilled nursing home care to veterans in DVA, state, or contracts facilities. Also provided are related medical services, supportive personal care, and individual adjustment services.

Eligible applicants/beneficiaries: veterans requiring skilled nursing care and related medical services, and meeting specific criteria (*see NOTE preceding* **64.005**).

Range/Average: N.A.

Activity: FY 05, 99,158 patients treated; average daily census, 34,375.

HQ: Nursing Home Care Program Chief, Geriatrics and Extended Strategic Health Group (114), DVA, Washington, DC 20420 Phone: (202) 273-8540.

Internet: www.va.gov.

64.011 VETERANS DENTAL CARE

Assistance: specialized services.

Purposes: to provide dental services for veterans.

Eligible applicants/beneficiaries: veterans meeting specific criteria (*see NOTE preceding* **64.005**).

Range/Average: N.A.

Activity: FY 05, 548,734 staff examinations, and 33,048 staff treatments by DVA staff, 26,007 fee cases.

HQ: Director, Health Administration Services (10C3), DVA, Washington, DC 20420 Phone: (202) 273-8302, -8303.

Internet: www.va.gov.

64.012 VETERANS PRESCRIPTION SERVICE ("Medicine For Veterans")

Assistance: sale, exchange, or donation of property and goods.

Purposes: to provide prescription drugs and expendable medical supplies from DVA pharmacies to veterans and certain dependents and survivors. Small co-payments may be required.

Eligible applicants/beneficiaries: veterans meeting specific criteria (*see NOTE preceding* **64.005**); wives and dependent children under CHAMP-VA (Civilian Health and Medical Program, Veterans Affairs).

Range/Average: N.A.

Activity: N.A.

HQ: Chief Consultant, Pharmacy Benefits Management, DVA, Washington, DC 20420 Phone: (202) 273-8429.

Internet: www.va.gov.

64.013 VETERANS PROSTHETIC APPLIANCES ("Prosthetics Services")

Assistance: sale, exchange, or donation of property and goods.

Purposes: to provide prosthetic and related appliances, equipment, and services to disabled veterans, including artificial limbs, artificial eyes, wheelchairs, aids for the blind, hearing aids, braces, orthopedic shoes, eyeglasses, crutches and canes, automobile adaptive equipment, and medical equipment, implants, and supplies—as well as training in the use of the foregoing.

Eligible applicants/beneficiaries: disabled veterans meeting specific criteria (*see NOTE preceding* **64.005**).

Range: $10 to $25,000. **Average:** $118.

Activity: FY 05, 5,700,000 prosthetic items and services provided (latest data reported).

HQ: Chief, Prosthetic and Clinical Logistics Officer (10f), DVA, Washington, DC 20420 Phone: (202) 254-0440, FAX (202) 254-0470.

Internet: www.vawwl.va.gov/prosthetics.

64.014 VETERANS STATE DOMICILIARY CARE

Assistance: formula grants (to 50 percent).

Purposes: pursuant to the Act of August 27, 1888 as amended, to provide domiciliary care services in state homes to veterans disabled by age or illness—to assist them in attaining physical, mental, and social well-being through rehabilitative programs.

Eligible applicants: states.

Eligible beneficiaries: veterans meeting specific criteria (*see NOTE preceding* **64.005**) including state admission requirements.

Range: $5,000 to $3,600,000. **Average:** $427,000.

Activity: FY 05, 5,333 patients treated; average daily census, 5,877.

HQ: Chief, State Home Per Diem Program, Assistant Chief Medical Director/Geriatrics and Extended Care (114B), DVA, Washington, DC 20420 Phone: (202) 273-8538.

Internet: www.va.gov.

64.015 VETERANS STATE NURSING HOME CARE

Assistance: formula grants (to 50 percent).

Purposes: to provide skilled nursing home care and related medical services to veterans in state veterans homes.

Eligible applicants: states.

Eligible beneficiaries: veterans eligible for care in a DVA facility, needing nursing home care, and meeting other specific criteria (*see NOTE preceding* **64.005**),including state admission requirements.

Range: $669,284 to $12,447,376. **Average:** $6,558,330.

Activity: FY 05, 36,533 patients treated; average daily census, 17,794.

HQ: Chief, State Home Per Diem Program, Assistant Chief Medical Director/Geriatrics and Extended Care (114), DVA, Washington, DC 20420 Phone: (202) 273-8538.

Internet: www.va.gov.

64.016 VETERANS STATE HOSPITAL CARE

Assistance: formula grants (to 50 percent).

Purposes: to provide inpatient hospital care to veterans in state veterans homes.

Eligible applicants: states.

Eligible beneficiaries: veterans meeting specific criteria (*see NOTE preceding* **64.005**), including state requirements.

Range: $2,022 to $3,217,481. **Average:** $1,609,752.

Activity: FY 05, 1,285 patients treated; average daily census, 174.

HQ: Chief, State Home Per Diem Program, Assistant Chief Medical Director/Geriatrics and Extended Care (114), DVA, Washington, DC 20420 Phone: (202) 273-8538.

Internet: www.va.gov.

64.018 SHARING SPECIALIZED MEDICAL RESOURCES ("Sharing Contracts - Exchange of Use or Mutual Use")

Assistance: specialized services.

Purposes: for exchanges between DVA and communities, or mutual use of, advanced medical techniques and specialized resources which otherwise might not be available to DVA or to the communities.

Eligible applicants/beneficiaries: medical schools; federal, state, local, public or private hospitals; clinics; research centers; blood and organ banks.

Range/Average: N.A.

Activity: FY 05, 4,816 contracts.

HQ: Director, Sharing and Purchasing Office (175), Veterans Health Administration, DVA, 810 Vermont Ave. NW, Washington, DC 20420 Phone: (202) 273-8406.

Internet: www.va.gov.

64.019 VETERANS REHABILITATION—ALCOHOL AND DRUG DEPENDENCE ("Substance Abuse Treatment Program, Mental Health and Behavioral Sciences Service")

Assistance: specialized services.

Purposes: to provide medical, social, vocational, and rehabilitation therapies to alcohol- and drug-dependent veterans, in DVA medical centers and clinics. Services include detoxification, substance abuse rehabilitation, individual and group and family therapy, psychotropic medications, psychiatric counseling, social services, vocational rehabilitation.

Eligible applicants/beneficiaries: veterans meeting specific criteria (*see NOTE preceding* **64.005**).

Range/Average: N.A.

Activity: FY 05, 100,000 veterans served.

HQ: Director, Mental Health and Behavioral Sciences Services (11C), DVA, Washington, DC 20420 Phone: (202) 273-8437.

Internet: www.va.gov.

64.022 VETERANS HOME BASED PRIMARY CARE

Assistance: specialized services.

Purposes: to provide primary health care services through DVA interdisciplinary teams to homebound veterans whose caregivers are capable and willing to assist in their care.

Eligible applicants/beneficiaries: veterans requiring intermittent skilled nursing care and related medical services, and meeting specific criteria (*see NOTE preceding* **64.005**).

Range/Average: N.A.

Activity: FY 05, 11,994 veterans received home care on the average day.

HQ: Home Based Primary Care Program Coordinator, Geriatrics and Extended Care Strategic Healthcare Group (114), DVA, Washington, DC 20420 Phone: (202) 273-6488, -8540.

Internet: www.va.gov (Note: no field offices for this program.)

64.024 VA HOMELESS PROVIDERS GRANT AND PER DIEM PROGRAM

Assistance: project grants (to 65 percent).

Purposes: pursuant to the Homeless Veterans Comprehensive Service Programs Act of 1992, to establish new programs and service centers to provide supportive housing and services for homeless veterans. Funds may be used to: acquire, renovate, or alter facilities; provide outreach and transportation services; pay operating costs. Per diem payments may be provided on behalf of VA-referred or -authorized veterans. Operating costs may be partially supported with grant funds.

Eligible applicants/beneficiaries: project grants—public or private nonprofit entities. For per diem payments, programs must have been established after 10 November 1992.

Range: $12,610 to $541,000.

Activity: cumulative estimate since program inception, 14 services centers, 2,500 new community-based beds, 20 vans purchased.

HQ: Program Manager, Homeless Providers Grant and Per Diem Program, Mental Health Strategic Healthcare Group (116E), DVA, 810 Vermont Ave. NW, Washington, DC 20420 Phone: (202) 273-8966, -8443; *toll-free*, (877) 322-0334.

Internet: www.va.gov (Note: no field offices for this program.)

64.026 VETERANS STATE ADULT DAY HEALTH CARE

Assistance: project grants (50 percent).

Purposes: for community-based, nonresidential programs providing skilled nursing and rehabilitative therapy services to veterans with medical or disabling conditions, including at least physical or occupational therapy, or speech-language pathology or audiology, and personal and psychological or counseling services as appropriate.

Eligible applicants/beneficiaries: veterans meeting state as well as DVA requirements (*see NOTE preceding* **64.005**).

Range: $35.17 per diem per veteran; state grants, $82,951 to $245,311. **Average:** $164,131.

Activity: new program listing in 2005 (CFDA on-line). FY 06 estimate, 96 participant slots at 2 recognized program locations.

HQ: Chief, State Home Per Diem Program, Assistant Chief Medical Director/Geriatrics and Extended Care (114), DVA, Washington, DC 20420 Phone: (202) 273-8538.

Internet: www.va.gov.

VETERANS BENEFITS ADMINISTRATION

64.100 AUTOMOBILES AND ADAPTIVE EQUIPMENT FOR CERTAIN DISABLED VETERANS AND MEMBERS OF THE ARMED FORCES

Assistance: direct payments/specified use.

Purposes: for disabled veterans and service-persons to purchase automobiles or other conveyances with adaptive equipment. Funds also may be used for repairs, replacements, or reinstallation. Adaptive equipment may be provided for no more than two conveyances during any four-year period, unless one of the vehicles becomes unavailable to the veteran.

Eligible applicants/beneficiaries: active duty personnel and veterans with honorable service and service-persons with a service-connected disability caused by loss of use or permanent loss of one or both feet, one or both hands, or a permanent impairment.

Range: no maximum for adaptive equipment; $11,000 maximum for automobile or other conveyance.

Activity: FY 06, 1,461 vehicles purchased.

HQ: DVA, Washington, DC 20420 Phone: (202) 273-7210.

Internet: www.va.gov.

64.101 BURIAL EXPENSES ALLOWANCE FOR VETERANS

Assistance: direct payments/specified use.

Purposes: for the plot or internment expenses of certain veterans not buried in a national cemetery; for funeral and burial expenses of veterans whose death results from a service-connected disability; for transportation of the remains of service- connected, disabled veterans to a national cemetery. Headstones or markers and an American flag to drape the casket may also be provided.

Eligible applicants/beneficiaries: burial and plot allowances—the person bearing the veteran's burial expense or the funeral director, if unpaid, on behalf of veterans: discharged under other than dishonorable conditions; discharged or released from active duty for a disability incurred or aggravated in line of duty; or, at time of death, entitled to compensation or pension or indigent or properly hospitalized at VA expense. Flags—next of kin, friend, or associate.

Range: to $300 for plot or interment expenses; to $300 for burial allowance if death is not service-connected; to $2,000 if death is service-connected.

Activity: FY 05, 81,254 burial allowances; 540,000 flags.

HQ: DVA, Washington, DC 20420 Phone: (202) 273-7210.

Internet: www.va.gov.

64.103 LIFE INSURANCE FOR VETERANS ("GI Insurance")

Assistance: direct loans; insurance.

Purposes: pursuant to the War Risk Insurance Act, World War Veterans Act, National Service Life Insurance Act, and Servicemen's Indemnity and Insurance Act, and amendments, to provide: life insurance protection for veterans of WW-I and -II, the Korean, Vietnam, and Gulf era conflicts, and for those with service-connected disabilities, separated from active duty on April 25, 1951 or later, and current members of the uniformed services and their spouses; mortgage protection life insurance for veterans receiving specially adapted housing; policy loans at varying interest rates. The programs are closed for new issues except Service-Disabled Veterans Insurance, Mortgage Protection Life Insurance, Service Members' Group Life Insurance, and Veterans Group Life Insurance.

Eligible applicants/beneficiaries: veterans meeting specific criteria (*see NOTE preceding* **64.005**). If the eligible applicant is mentally incompetent, a fiduciary recognized by DVA may apply on behalf of the veteran for Service-Disabled Veterans Insurance—benefits of which may also be granted under certain conditions for mentally incompetent veterans who were otherwise eligible for such insurance but, due to their incompetence, died without filing an application. Spouses and dependent children are automatically covered unless the member declines or reduces the coverage.

Range/Average: N.A.

Activity: as of FY 05, 6,000,000 policies in force.

HQ: Regional Office and Insurance Center, DVA, P.O. Box 42954, Philadelphia, PA 19101 Phone: (800) 669-8477.

Internet: www.insurance.va.gov (Note: no other field offices for this program.)

64.104 PENSION FOR NON-SERVICE-CONNECTED DISABILITY FOR VETERANS ("Pension")

Assistance: direct payments/unrestricted use.

Purposes: for wartime veterans with total and permanent nonservice-connected disabilities. Income and asset restrictions are prescribed.

Eligible applicants/beneficiaries: veterans with 90 days or more of honorable active wartime service in the Armed Forces or, if less than 90 days, released or discharged from service because of a service-connected disability, or permanently and totally disabled for reasons not due to service. Pension is not payable to those whose estates are so large that it is reasonable they use the estate for maintenance.

Range: $10,579 annually, reduced by countable income for veteran without dependents ($17,651 if in need of aid and attendance, and $12,929 if housebound); $13,855 for a veteran with one dependent ($20,924, if in need of aid and attendance, $16,205, if housebound); plus,$1,806 each additional dependent. Also, an additional $2,400 if a veteran of WW-I or Mexican Border Period.

Activity: FY 05, pensions to 337,787 veterans.

HQ: DVA, Washington, DC 20420 Phone: (202) 273-7210.

Internet: www.va.gov.

64.105 PENSION TO VETERANS SURVIVING SPOUSES, AND CHILDREN ("Death Pension")

Assistance: direct payments/unrestricted use.

Purposes: for needy dependents of deceased wartime veterans whose deaths were not due to service.

Eligible applicants/beneficiaries: unmarried surviving spouses and children of deceased veterans with at least 90 days of honorable active wartime service or, if less than 90 days, discharged for a service-connected disability. A child must be unmarried and under age 18, between age 18 and 23 if in school, or disabled before age 18 and continuously incapable of self-support. Pensions are not payable to those whose estates are so large that it is reasonable they use the estate for maintenance.

Range: $7,094 annually, reduced by countable income for a spouse without children ($11,340 if in need of aid and attendance, and $8,670 if housebound), $9,287 for spouse with one child ($13,529 if in need of aid and attendance, and $10,860 if housebound), plus $1,806 for each additional child.

Activity: FY 05, 211,240 cases.

HQ: DVA, Washington, DC 20420 Phone: (202) 273-7210.

Internet: www.va.gov.

64.106 SPECIALLY ADAPTED HOUSING FOR DISABLED VETERANS ("Paraplegic Housing")

Assistance: direct payments/specified use.

Purposes: to provide suitable adapted housing with special fixtures and facilities to severely disabled veterans, including construction, remodeling, or mortgage reduction payments.

Eligible applicants/beneficiaries: veterans with permanent, total, and compensable disabilities.

Range: 50 percent of cost to purchase, construct, or remodel a suitable housing unit, with $50,000 maximum; to $10,000 for special residential adaptations.

Activity: FY 05 estimate, 668 grants.

HQ: DVA, Washington, DC 20420 Phone: (202) 273-7355.

Internet: www.homeloans.va.gov/SAH.

64.109 VETERANS COMPENSATION FOR SERVICE-CONNECTED DISABILITY ("Compensation")

Assistance: direct payments/unrestricted use.

Purposes: for disabled veterans, in amounts reflecting the average impairment in the earning capacity the disability would cause in civilian occupations.

Eligible applicants/beneficiaries: persons suffering disabilities during service in the Armed Forces, incurred in or aggravated by service in the line of duty. Separation from service must have been under other than dishonorable conditions.

Range: monthly, from $112 for a 10 percent degree of disability, to $6,845 for very severe disabilities.

Activity: FY 05, 2,600,583 cases.

HQ: DVA, Washington, DC 20420 Phone: (202) 273-7210.

Internet: www.va.gov.

64.110 VETERANS DEPENDENCY AND INDEMNITY COMPENSATION FOR SERVICE-CONNECTED DEATH ("DIC")

Assistance: direct payments/unrestricted use.

Purposes: for survivors of deceased veterans whose death resulted from a service-connected disability or while on active duty.

Eligible applicants/beneficiaries: surviving spouses, children, and parent(s) of deceased veterans.

Range: DIC monthly, from $438 for one child when no spouse is entitled; $1,033 to $2,365 for a surviving spouse, with $257 additional if in need of aid and attendance, or $122 if housebound; surviving spouse is entitled to an additional $257 for each child under 18; parents, $5 to $507 depending on income and whether single or married, with $274 additional if in need of aid and attendance. Death Compensation, monthly from $87 for surviving spouse to $121 for widow/widower with one child; plus $29 each additional child; additional $79 if widow/widower or dependent parent in need of aid and attendance; assistance for parent, $75 for one, $80 for two.

Activity: FY 05, 326,272 cases.

HQ: DVA, Washington, DC 20420 Phone: (202) 273-7203.

Internet: www.va.gov.

64.114 VETERANS HOUSING—GUARANTEED AND INSURED LOANS ("VA Home Loans")

Assistance: guaranteed/insured loans.

Purposes: for housing for veterans, certain service personnel, or their surviving unremarried spouses—covering home construction or purchases, repairs, improvements, or refinancing. Eligible loans include those covering standard single-family units, condominiums, or manufactured homes and lots—for their own use; also, for solar heating or cooling or other energy conservation improvements. Applicants must have sufficient present and prospective income to meet loan repayment terms, and a satisfactory credit record.

Eligible applicants/beneficiaries: veterans meeting specific criteria (*see NOTE preceding* **64.005**). Also, unremarried surviving spouses of eligible veterans deceased in service or as a result of service-connected disabilities.

Average: to 50 percent for loans of $45,000 or less; $22,500 for loans between $45,000 and $56,250; $36,000 or 40 percent, whichever is less, for loans between $56,250 to $144,000; for loans greater than $144,000 or for VA loan refinancing, basically 25 percent of established loan limits.

Activity: FY 05, 149,399 insured loans.

HQ: DVA, Washington, DC 20420 Phone: (202) 273-7390.

Internet: www.va.gov.

64.115 VETERANS INFORMATION AND ASSISTANCE ("Veterans Services")

Assistance: advisory services/counseling.

Purposes: to provide information and assistance to all veterans—including of the PHS, NOAA, and certain WW-II Merchant Marines—relating to the full range of benefits to which they are entitled.

Eligible applicants/beneficiaries: generally, veterans, their dependents or beneficiaries, their representatives or other interested parties.

Range/Average: N.A.

Activity: annually, 21,000,000 contacts.

HQ: DVA, Washington, DC 20420 Phone: (202) 273-7210.

Internet: www.va.gov.

64.116 VOCATIONAL REHABILITATION FOR DISABLED VETERANS

Assistance: direct payments/unrestricted use; direct payments/specified use; direct loans; advisory services/counseling.

Purposes: pursuant to the Veterans' Rehabilitation and Education Amendments of 1980, to provide counseling, no-interest loans, and payments for tuition, fees, related costs, and subsistence for up to four years to disabled veterans and hospitalized service- members pending discharge—to obtain vocational training and suitable employment and to achieve maximum independence in daily living.

Eligible applicants/beneficiaries: veterans of WW-II and later service, with a compensable service-connected disability; certain hospitalized service-members pending discharge or release from service, in need of vocational rehabilitation because of an employment handicap.

Range: full cost of tuition, books, fees, supplies, and services; monthly full-time allowances range from $488.50 for a single veteran to $714.05 for a veteran with two dependents, plus $52.06 for each additional dependent in excess of two; no-interest loans of up to $977 and a work-study allowance not higher than 25 times the minimum hourly wage times the number of weeks of the veteran's period of enrollment.

Activity: FY 05, 92,703 participants, 4,445 loans.

HQ: Vocational Rehabilitation and Employment Service (28), Veterans Benefits Administration, DVA, Washington, DC 20420 Phone: (202) 273-7419.

Internet: www.va.gov; www.vetsuccess.gov.

64.117 SURVIVORS AND DEPENDENTS EDUCATIONAL ASSISTANCE

Assistance: direct payments/specified use.

Purposes: to provide educational opportunities for dependents of certain deceased or disabled veterans—covering pursuit of associate, bachelor, or graduate degree, licensing and certification tests, diplomas, apprenticeships and on-the-job training, preparatory courses, restorative or vocational training. Education must be completed within ten years of the date that the disability was incurred, or from the date of death of the veteran.

Eligible applicants/beneficiaries: spouses, surviving spouses, and children between age 18 and 26—of veterans deceased because of service-connected disabilities; of living veterans with service-connected disabilities considered permanently and totally disabling; of those deceased because of any cause while such disabilities were in existence; of service-members listed for more than 90 days as missing in action; or, of prisoners of war.

Range: monthly, institutional training—full time, $827; three-quarters time, $621; half-time, $413. Tutorial assistance, to $1,200. Work-study allowances also may be paid.

Activity: FY 05, 74,360 participants.

HQ: DVA, Washington, DC 20420 Phone: (202) 273-7132.

Internet: www.gibill.va.gov.

64.118 VETERANS HOUSING—DIRECT LOANS FOR CERTAIN DISABLED VETERANS

Assistance: direct loans (below-market interest).

Purposes: for disabled veterans to purchase, construct, or improve homes, including farm residences, with specially adapted features and facilities.

Loans are coordinated with grants obtained under **64.106** (Specially Adapted Housing for Disabled Veterans).

Eligible applicants/beneficiaries: disabled veterans serving on active duty on or after September 16, 1940, and eligible under **64.106** (Specially Adapted Housing for Disabled Veterans).

Range: to $33,000.

Activity: FY 05, no loans; FY 06-07 estimate, no loans.

HQ: DVA, Washington, DC 20420 Phone: (202) 273-7390.

Internet: www.va.gov.

64.119 VETERANS HOUSING—MANUFACTURED HOME LOANS

Assistance: guaranteed/insured loans. (to 95 percent/15-25 years).

Purposes: for manufactured homes (new or used), or homes and lots, or lots only—purchased or refinanced for their own use by veterans, servicemembers, and certain unremarried surviving spouses of veterans.

Eligible applicants/beneficiaries: veterans meeting specific criteria (*see NOTE preceding* **64.005**). Also, unremarried surviving spouses of eligible veterans deceased in service or as a result of service-connected disabilities.

Range: maximum guaranteed amount, $20,000 or 40 percent of the loan, whichever is less. **Average:** loan amount, $29,596.

Activity: FY 05, no loans; FY 06-07 estimate, no loans.

HQ: DVA, Washington, DC 20420 Phone: (202) 273-7390.

Internet: www.va.gov.

64.120 POST-VIETNAM ERA VETERANS' EDUCATIONAL ASSISTANCE ("Voluntary-Contributory Matching Program")

Assistance: direct payments/specified use.

Purposes: for educational, vocational, or professional training to persons entering the Armed Services after 31 December 1976 and before 1 July 1985, as well as those who served during certain other periods. Payments are provided on the basis of a $2 to $1 match of federal to participant contribution. Enrollments in avocational or recreational courses may not be covered. Participants must have satisfactorily contributed to the program, consisting of a monthly deduction of $25 to $100 from military pay, up to a maximum of $2,700, for deposit in a special training fund. Participants may make lump-sum contributions. Applicants must complete their education within ten years after release from service, with certain exceptions.

Eligible applicants/beneficiaries: basically, veterans serving honorably on active duty for more than 180 days beginning on or after 1 January 1977, or discharged after such date because of a service-connected disability; veterans serving for more than 180 days and continuing on active duty and completing their first period of obligated service (or six years of active duty, whichever comes first). No persons on active duty may initiate contributions to this program after March 31, 1987. Certain more recent veterans may elect Montgomery GI Bill benefits (see **64.124**), provided their basic pay was reduced by $1,200, based on dates of duty periods.

Range: $8,100 maximum; $1,200 maximum tutorial assistance. Work study allowances also may be provided.

Activity: FY 05, 723 participants.

HQ: DVA, Washington, DC 20420 Phone: (202) 273-7132.

Internet: www.va.gov.

64.124 ALL-VOLUNTEER FORCE EDUCATIONAL ASSISTANCE ("Montgomery GI Bill Active Duty - MGIB - Chapter 30")

Assistance: direct payments/specified use.

Purposes: for the educational expenses of veterans enrolling in approved educational, professional, or vocational programs, including flight training if already licensed. Participants must have agreed to reductions in their military pay while in service, as nonrefundable contributions toward their participation. $100 monthly is deducted from the basic pay for the first twelve months, unless the veteran specifically elects not to participate in the program; such deductions are nonrefundable except in the case of the death of the veteran within a certain time frame. DOD may provide supplementary contributions to participants' funds as inducements to reenlist, paid while they are enrolled in educational programs. Applicants must complete their education within ten years after release from service, with certain exceptions.

Eligible applicants/beneficiaries: basically, veterans with an honorable discharge and military personnel on active duty on or after 1 July 1985, and with a minimum of two years service. Participants without the required obligated service must have been discharged for a service-related disability, for hardship, for a pre-existing medical or physical or mental condition, for involuntary separation due to reduction in force. Certain others may also meet eligibility requirements as described in **64.120**; full criteria may be obtained from DVA.

Range: monthly, $816 to $1,900 for 36 months full-time; work- study allowances based on minimum wage rates; tutorial assistance, to $1,200.

Activity: FY 06 estimate, 370,248 trainees.

HQ: DVA, Washington, DC 20420 Phone: (202) 273-7132.

Internet: www.gibill.va.gov.

64.125 VOCATIONAL AND EDUCATIONAL COUNSELING FOR SERVICEMEMBERS AND VETERANS ("Chapter 36 Counseling")

Assistance: advisory services/counseling.

Purposes: pursuant to Veterans Education and Employment Programs Amendments, to provide vocational and educational counseling to service-members or veterans, in the identification of personal objectives including the development of employment plans.

Eligible applicants/beneficiaries: service-members applying within 180 days of projected discharge or release from active duty; veterans within one year of discharge or release.

Range/Average: N.A.

Activity: FY 05, 9,500 participants.

HQ: Vocational Rehabilitation and Employment Service (28), Veterans Benefits Administration, DVA, Washington, DC 20420 Phone: (202) 273-7419.

Internet: www.va.gov.

64.126 NATIVE AMERICAN VETERAN DIRECT LOAN PROGRAM ("VA Native American Veterans Housing Loan Program")

Assistance: direct loans.

Purposes: for certain native American veterans to purchase, construct, improve, or refinance homes that they will occupy, including manufactured homes, located on trust lands.

Eligible applicants/beneficiaries: qualifying native American veterans certified by a recognized tribal government, and certain surviving unremarried spouses of native American veterans.

Average: to $80,000 (more in high-cost areas).

Activity: FY 06-07 estimate, 30 loans.

HQ: DVA, Washington, DC 20420 Phone: (202) 273-7377.

Internet: www.va.gov.

64.127 MONTHLY ALLOWANCE FOR CHILDREN OF VIETNAM VETERANS BORN WITH SPINA BIFIDA

Assistance: direct payments/unrestricted use.

Purposes: to provide financial assistance to children of Vietnam veterans, born with spina bifida.

Eligible applicants/beneficiaries: natural children of Vietnam veterans, born with spina bifida, except spina bifida occulta, regardless of age or marital status, conceived after the date on which the veteran first served in Vietnam (between 9 January 1962 and 7 May 1975).

Range: $254 to $1,500 monthly, based on the degree of disability.

Activity: FY 07 estimate, 1,234 children assisted.

HQ: DVA, Washington, DC 20420 Phone: (202) 273-7210.

Internet: www.va.gov.

64.128 VOCATIONAL TRAINING AND REHABILITATION FOR VIETNAM VETERANS' CHILDREN WITH SPINA BIFIDA AND OTHER COVERED BIRTH DEFECTS

Assistance: direct payments/specified use.

Purposes: to provide vocational training and rehabilitation to certain children of Vietnam and Korea veterans, born with spina bifida or other covered birth defects.

Eligible applicants/beneficiaries: natural children of Vietnam veterans, born with spina bifida, except spina bifida occulta, regardless of age or marital status, conceived after the date on which the veteran first served in Vietnam (between 9 January 1962 and 7 May 1975); and some Korea veterans. DVA must determine that it is feasible for the child to achieve a vocational goal within 2 to 4 years.

Average: N.A.

Activity: FY 05, 20 new cases; FY 06-07 estimate, 40 new cases.

HQ: DVA, Washington, DC 20420 Phone: (202) 273-7419.

Internet: www.va.gov.

NATIONAL CEMETERY SYSTEM

64.201 NATIONAL CEMETERIES

Assistance: specialized services.

Purposes: pursuant to the National Cemeteries Act of 1973, to provide burial space, headstones and markers, and perpetual care for deceased veterans, members of the Armed Forces, Reservists, and National Guard members whose service was terminated other than dishonorably, and certain dependents—in national cemeteries.

Eligible applicants/beneficiaries: next of kin or, if there is no living kin, a friend of the decedent or public assistance officer on their behalf, of deceased: veterans, members of the Armed Forces (Army, Navy, Air Force, Marine Corps, Coast Guard) dying while on active duty; members of the Reserve or Army or National Guard dying while on active duty for training; 20-year reservists and National Guard and certain other of their dependents; enlisted personnel entering military duty after September 7, 1980, and/or becoming commissioned officers after October 16, 1981, and serving for a minimum of two years; spouses of eligible veterans or members of the Armed Forces lost or buried at sea or determined to be permanently missing or missing in action; minor children and certain unmarried adult children of eligible veterans; U.S. citizens serving in the Armed Forces of any government allied with the U.S. during any wars, and holding U.S. citizenship at time of death; certain commissioned officers of the PHS, NOAA, and others.

Range/Average: N.A.

Activity: FY 05, 93,245 interments in the 122 national cemeteries under DVA jurisdiction; FY 06 estimate, 101,800.

HQ: Director, Memorial Programs Service (41A), National Cemetery Administration-DVA, 810 Vermont Ave. NW, Washington, DC 20420 Phone: (202) 273-5226.

Internet: www.va.gov.

64.202 PROCUREMENT OF HEADSTONES AND MARKERS AND/OR PRESIDENTIAL MEMORIAL CERTIFICATES

Assistance: direct payments/specified use; specialized services.

Purposes: pursuant to the National Cemeteries Act of 1973 and Veterans' Disability Compensation and Survivors' Benefits Act of 1978, for headstones and markers for the graves or memorial plots in national, post, and state veterans cemeteries, or for the unmarked graves or memorial plots in private cemeteries—of deceased eligible veterans; also, costs of transportation and installation and maintenance, replacement of illegible markers. Presidential Memorial Certificates may also be provided.

Eligible applicants: private cemetery burials—next of kin or nonmembers of the deceased's family, after ascertaining that the grave is unmarked and that a government monument is preferred over a privately purchased one. Monuments must be of a type permitted on the grave of the deceased. If burial or memorial plot is in a national cemetery or state veterans cemetery, the director of the cemetery orders the headstone or marker, after completion of the interment in the cemetery, or upon need for replacement.

Eligible beneficiaries: deceased veterans of wartime or peacetime service, discharged under conditions other than dishonorable; members of the Reserve and the Army and Air National Guard dying while performing or as a result of performing active duty for training; commissioned officers of the PHS and the NOAA, Merchant Marine Seamen, and certain others participating in wartime activities. Spouses and certain dependents also may be eligible.

Range/Average: N.A.

Activity: FY 05, 363,627 applications; 368,901markers or headstones, and 487,809 Certificates.

HQ: Director, Memorial Programs Service (41A1), National Cemetery Administration-DVA, 5109 Russell Rd., Quantico, VA 22134-3903 Phone: (202) 501-3100; issues relating to headstone and marker, (202) 501-3027; application assistance, tracer information, problems with shipments arriving C.O.D., eligibility matters, inscription matters, (800) 697-6947; Presidential Memorial Certificates, (202) 565-4259.

Internet: www.va.gov.

64.203 STATE CEMETERY GRANTS

Assistance: project grants. (to 100 percent/to 3 years).

Purposes: pursuant to the Veterans Housing Benefits Act of 1978, to establish, expand, or improve state-owned veterans cemeteries for the interment of eligible veterans and their dependents.

Eligible applicants/beneficiaries: states.

Range: $4,305 to $10,966,000. **Average:** $1,653,582.

Activity: FY 06-07 estimate, 5 to 10 applications.

HQ: Director, State Cemetery Grants Service (41E), National Cemetery Administration-DVA, 810 Vermont Ave. NW, Washington, DC 20420 Phone: (202) 565-4084, -6801, FAX (202) 565-6141.

Internet: www.va.gov (Note: no field offices for this program.)

ENVIRONMENTAL PROTECTION AGENCY

66.001 AIR POLLUTION CONTROL PROGRAM SUPPORT

Assistance: formula grants (60 percent; tribes, 90-95 percent).

Purposes: pursuant to the Clean Air Act of 1990 (CAA) as amended, to plan, establish, improve, and maintain air pollution prevention and control programs. Funding priorities: attain and maintain national ambient standards for criteria pollutants (ozone, particulate matter, visibility, carbon monoxide, lead, sulfur dioxide, and nitrogen dioxide) that endanger human health and the environment; eliminate unacceptable risks of cancer and other health problems from air toxics emissions; reduce the destructive effects of acid rain deposition on land and water systems. Projects involve such strategies as: regulation of stationary sources, mobile source emissions testing and trip reduction measures, participation in interstate emissions trading program, and other innovative early reduction and voluntary measures taken locally. Funding supports cost of monitoring, personnel, training, and operations; construction costs are ineligible.

Eligible applicants/beneficiaries: municipal, intermunicipal, state, tribal, interstate, intertribal agencies, including possessions and territories.

Range: $5,500 to $7,200,000. **Average:** $1,440,000.

Activity: FY 06, 109 agencies funded.

HQ: National Air Grant Coordinator (MC 6102A), OAR-EPA, 1200 Pennsylvania Ave., NW, Washington, DC 20460 Phone: *state/local,* (202) 564-1234, FAX (202) 564-1352; *tribal,* (202) 564-7416, FAX (202) 564-1352.

Internet: www.epa.gov.

66.032 STATE INDOOR RADON GRANTS ("SIRG")

Assistance: project grants. (to 50 percent; tribes, 100 percent/to 5 years).

Purposes: pursuant to the Indoor Radon Abatement Act and Toxic Substances Control Act (TSCA), to develop and implement programs and projects to reduce radon risks in homes, schools, and other buildings. Eligible activities include radon surveys, public information and educational materials, radon control programs, purchase and maintenance of analytic equipment, training, administrative costs, data storage and management, mitigation demonstrations, toll-free hotlines, and promotion of environmental justice through outreach to low-income and culturally-diverse populations. Financial assistance may be provided to individuals only if such costs relate to demonstration projects or to the purchase and analysis of radon measurement devices.

Eligible applicants: states, territories and possessions, tribes.

Eligible beneficiaries: local, municipal, district, or areawide organizations; IHEs; nonprofit organizations; low-income persons, homeowners.

Range: $10,000 to $500,000. **Average:** states, $150,000; tribes, $30,000.

Activity: currently, 49 states, DC, Guam, and 35 tribal nations with radon programs.

HQ: Office of Radiation and Indoor Air (6604J), OAR-EPA, 1310 L St. NW, Washington, DC 20005 Phone: (202) 343-9117, FAX (202) 343- 2394.

Internet: www.epa.gov/iaq.

66.033 OZONE TRANSPORT COMMISSION

Assistance: project grants. (60-100 percent/to 2 years).

Purposes: pursuant to Section 106 (interstate pollution) and Section 111 (interstate ozone pollution) of CAA of 1990 as amended, to develop or recommend regional air quality control implementation plans for reducing ozone pollution. Funds may be used to support interstate pollution projects, including public education and outreach.

Eligible applicants/beneficiaries: state agencies or commissions designated by the governors of the New England and Mid-Atlantic states, and DC, representing affected states and political subdivisions.

Average: $635,000 (single grant).

Activity: single grant.

HQ: OAR-EPA (6102A), 1200 Pennsylvania Ave. NW, Washington, DC 20460 Phone: (202) 564-1082, FAX (202) 564-1352.

Internet: www.epa.gov/air.

66.034 SURVEYS, STUDIES, INVESTIGATIONS, DEMONSTRATIONS AND SPECIAL PURPOSE ACTIVITIES RELATING TO THE CLEAN AIR ACT

Assistance: project grants. (100 percent/to 5 years).

Purposes: pursuant to CAA of 1963 as amended, for surveys, studies, investigations, demonstrations, and special purpose assistance relating to the causes, effects (including upon health and welfare), extent, prevention, and control of air pollution—including air quality, acid deposition, climate change, global programs, indoor environments, mobile source technology, and community-driven approaches to transportation. Funding priorities include: indoor environments, especially those affecting children; air toxics, including the National Air Toxics Assessment program, National Toxics Inventory, and Air Toxics Monitoring Network; mobile source technologies; truck engine idle reduction technologies; National Clean Diesel Campaign; climate protections, including outreach and public education efforts; other issues.

Eligible applicants/beneficiaries: states, territories and possessions, tribes; international organizations; IHEs; other public and private nonprofit institutions.

Range: $5,000 to $750,000. **Average:** $150,000.

Activity: not quantified specifically.

HQ: *Program information,* OAR-EPA (6102A), 1200 Pennsylvania Ave. NW, Washington, DC 20460 Phone: (202) 564-1514, FAX (202) 564-1352 *Grants management information*: Grants Administration Division

(3903R), EPA, 1200 Pennsylvania Ave. NW, Washington, DC 20460 Phone: (no number provided).

Internet: www.epa.gov/air.

66.035 COMMUNITY ACTION FOR A RENEWED ENVIRONMENT (CARE) PROGRAM ("CARE")

Assistance: project grants. (cost sharing/to 5 years).

Purposes: pursuant to CAA, Clean Water Act (CWA), Solid Waste Disposal Act (SWDA), TSCA, Federal Insecticide Fungicide, and Rodenticide Act (FIFRA), Safe Drinking Water Act (SDWA), Marine Protection, Research, and Sanctuaries Act (MPRSA), and amendments, for analyses, studies, evaluations, surveys, investigations, conferences, demonstrations, and special projects that empower communities to reduce risks from exposure to toxic pollutants in the air, water, and land—through collaborative local action. "Level I" agreements support problem assessments and identification of potential solutions; "Level II" agreements support risk reduction projects.

Eligible applicants/beneficiaries: local public, private, and quasi-public nonprofit institutions and organizations; tribal governments, native American organizations; interstate, intrastate organizations, IHEs.

Range: to $300,000. **Average:** "Level I," $90,000; "Level II," $275,000.

Activity: new program in FY 05; FY 05, 12 grants; FY 06 estimate, 17 grants.

HQ: *Grants management information*: Grants Administration Division (3903R), EPA, 1200 Pennsylvania Ave. NW, Washington, DC 20460 Phone: (202) 564-9226, FAX (202) 564-7739.

Internet: www.epa.gov/care.

66.036 CLEAN SCHOOL BUS USA ("CSBUSA")

Assistance: project grants. (95 percent/2 years).

Purposes: to minimize children's exposure to diesel exhaust through necessary upgrades to diesel school bus fleets, through partnerships with educators, industry, transportation experts, public health officials, and community leaders. Projects involve: reducing school bus idling; retrofit of 1991-2004 model year buses with devices that reduce pollution; replacement of pre-1990 buses with new, clean-technology buses.

Eligible applicants/beneficiaries: local, state, and tribal governments; nonprofit organizations.

Range: to $1,500,000. **Average:** $250,000.

Activity: new program in FY 05; FY 05, grants awarded to 37 school districts.

HQ: OAR-EPA, 1200 Pennsylvania Ave. NW, Washington, DC 20460 Phone: (202) 343-9541, FAX (202) 343-2804.

Internet: www.epa.gov/cleanschoolbus.

66.037 INTERNSHIPS, TRAINING, WORKSHOPS AND FELLOWSHIPS FOR THE OFFICE OF AIR AND RADIATION

Assistance: project grants. (100 percent/to 3 years).

Purposes: pursuant to CAA as amended, for internships, training, workshops, fellowships, and technical monitoring supporting the Clean Air Act, including: developing career-oriented personnel; technical training of state, local, territorial, and tribal environmental control agencies; pertinent academic training; student support, traineeships, internships; personnel recruitment.

Eligible applicants/beneficiaries: states, territories and possessions, tribes, tribal governments; international organizations; IHEs; other public and private nonprofit institutions including hospitals, laboratories.

Range: $50,000 to $1,750,000. **Average:** $500,000.

Activity: new program listing in 2006 (CFDA on-line).

HQ: OAR-EPA, Washington, DC 20460 Phone: (202) 564-5373; FAX 564-1352.

Internet: www.epa.gov/air.

66.038 TRAINING, INVESTIGATIONS, AND SPECIAL PURPOSE ACTIVITIES OF FEDERALLY-RECOGNIZED INDIAN TRIBES CONSISTENT WITH THE CLEAN AIR ACT (CAA), TRIBAL SOVEREIGNTY AND THE PROTECTION AND MANAGEMENT OF AIR QUALITY

Assistance: project grants (to 5 years).

Purposes: Clean Air Act of 1963, Section 103, as amended to support federally-recognized Indian Tribes' efforts to understand, assess and characterize air quality, and design methods and plans to protect and improve air quality on tribal lands through surveys, studies, research, training, investigations, and special purpose activities. Funding is available to support recipient's allowable direct costs for approved Tribal air resource activities that will protect public health and the environment or that are in accordance with established EPA policies and regulations. Assistance agreement awards under this program may involve or relate to geospatial information (see, http://geodata.epa.gov).

Eligible applicants/beneficiaries: federally-recognized Indian Tribes and Intertribal Consortia.

Range: $25,000 to $500,000. **Average:** $75,000.

Activity: N.A.

HQ: Grants and Interagency Agreement Management Division, EPA, Room 3903R, Washington, DC 20460. Phone: (202) 564-7416, FAX: (202) 501-1153.

Internet: www.epa.gov/air/tribal.

66.039 NATIONAL CLEAN DIESEL FUNDING ASSISTANCE PROGRAM ("DERA National Program")

Assistance: project grants (to 5 years).

Purposes: pursuant to the Interior, Environment and Related Agencies Appropriations Act of 2008 and the Energy Policy Act of 2005, to award grants and low-cost revolving loans to eligible entities in order to fund the costs of a retrofit technology that significantly reduces emissions through development and implementation of a certified engine configuration, verified technology, or emerging technology for buses (including school buses), medium-duty or heavy-duty trucks, marine engines, locomotives, or nonroad engines or vehicles used in construction, handling of cargo (including at port or airport), agriculture, mining, or energy production. Funds may also be used for programs or projects to reduce long-duration idling using verified technology involving a vehicle or equipment described above, or the creation of low-cost revolving loan programs to finance diesel emissions reduction projects. (Note: funding priorities the same as **66.040**.)

Eligible applicants: qualified regional, state, local, tribal agency, port authority, city, county, municipal agency, school district, or metropolitan planning organization (MPO) with jurisdiction over transportation or air quality; nonprofit organizations or institutions that represent or provide pollution reduction or educational services to persons or organizations that own or operate diesel fleets or have as its principal purpose, the promotion of transportation or air quality.

Eligible beneficiaries: state, local, public nonprofit institution/organization, general public.

Range: smaller grants, $100,000 to $300,000; larger grants, $500,000 to $2 million. **Average:** smaller grants, $125,000; larger grants, $650,000.

Activity: N.A. New program in FY 08.

HQ: Environmental Protection Agency, 1200 Pennsylvania Ave. NW - MS 6405J, Washington, DC 20460. Phone: (202) 343-9541, FAX: (202) 343-2803.

Internet: www.epa.gov/cleandiesel.

66.040 STATE CLEAN DIESEL GRANT PROGRAM ("DERA State Program")

Assistance: project grants (to 7 years).

Purposes: pursuant to the Interior, Environment and Related Agencies Appropriations Act of 2008 and the Energy Policy Act of 2005, to award assistance agreements to States to develop and implement such grant and low-cost revolving loan programs in the state as are appropriate to meet state needs and goals relating to the reduction of diesel emissions. Priority shall be given to projects which: maximize public health benefits; are most cost-effective; serve areas with the highest population density, that are poor air quality areas; serve areas that receive a disproportionate quantity of air pollution from diesel fleets or that use a community-based multi-stakeholder collaborative process to reduce toxic emissions; include a certified engine configuration, verified technology, or emerging technology that has a long expected useful life; will maximize the useful life of any certified engine configuration, verified technology, or emerging technology used or funded by the eligible entity; conserve diesel fuel; and utilize ultra low sulfur diesel fuel.

Eligible applicants: 50 states.

Eligible beneficiaries: state, local, public nonprofit institution/organization, general public.

Range: $300,000 to $3,000,000. **Average:** $300,000.

Activity: N.A. New program in FY 08.

HQ: Environmental Protection Agency, 1200 Pennsylvania Avenue, NW - MS 6405J, Washington, DC 20460. Phone: (202) 343-9541, FAX: (202) 343-2803.

Internet: http://www.epa.gov/cleandiesel.

66.110 HEALTHY COMMUNITIES GRANT PROGRAM

Assistance: project grants. (95 percent/1-2 years).

Purposes: pursuant to CAA, CWA, Resource Conservation and Recovery Act (RCRA), TSCA, SDWA, FIFRA, National Environmental Education Act, Pollution Prevention Act (PPA), MPRSA, CERCLA, Indian Environmental General Assistance Program Act, and amendments, for projects only in the New England states that: are located in and directly benefit one or more EPA-designated "Target Investment Areas," "Environmental Justice Areas of Potential Concern," "Places with High Risks from Toxic Air Pollution," "Sensitive Populations," or "Urban Areas;" and, that will achieve measurable environmental and public health results as defined by EPA. Current program priorities include projects involving asthma, capacity building, healthy indoor/outdoor environments, healthy schools, preserving and restoring urban natural resources and open/green space, smart growth, and water quality monitoring or analyses. Projects may provide or support educational opportunities for students, interns, or citizens to learn more about science, biology, and water quality monitoring.

Eligible applicants/beneficiaries: for activities only within the New England states—local public, private, quasi-public nonprofit institutions and organizations; tribal governments; K- 12 schools or school districts; grassroots and community-based organizations; IHEs with substantial community involvement.

Range: $9,900 to $30,000. **Average:** $27,335.

Activity: new program in 2005; FY 05, 23 grants; FY 06-07 estimate, 20-25 grants, per year.

HQ: Region 1-EPA, 1 Congress St. - Ste.1100, Boston, MA 02114. Phone: (617) 918-1797; Toll Free: (888) 372-7341; TTY: (617) 918-2028, FAX: (617) 918-0797.

Internet: www.epa.gov/region01/index.html (Note: the field office serves as headquarters.)

66.111 REGIONAL ENVIRONMENTAL PRIORITY PROJECTS

Assistance: project grants (to 5 years).

Purposes: pursuant to CWA, FIFRA, CAA, SWDA, SDWA, and TSCA, for investigations, experiments, training, demonstrations, surveys, studies, and special purpose assistance to protect public health and prevent, reduce, and eliminate pollution—only in Iowa, Kansas, Missouri, and Nebraska. Projects may be single or multi- media, addressing places, sectors, or innovations, and focused on critical ecosystems, sensitive populations, or agriculture.

Eligible applicants/beneficiaries: only within EPA Region 7—states, territories, possessions, tribes; IHEs, hospitals, laboratories; other public or private nonprofit organizations; profit groups; individuals.

Range/Average: N.A.

Activity: new program listing in 2005 (CFDA on-line version).

HQ: Region 7-EPA, 901 N, Fifth St., Kansas City, Kansas 66101 Phone: (913) 551-7782, -7193; FAX (913) 551-9782, -9183.

Internet: www.epa.gov/region07/economics/index.htm (Note: the field office serves as headquarters.)

66.112 SURVEYS, STUDIES, INVESTIGATIONS, TRAINING, DEMONSTRATIONS, AND SPECIAL PURPOSE GRANTS FOR REGIONAL GEOGRAPHIC INITIATIVES ("Region 8 Regional Priorities Grant Program")

Assistance: project grants (to 5 years).

Purposes: pursuant to Clean Water Act, FIFRA, Safe Drinking Water Act, National Environmental Policy Act, and other acts, to support projects in Region 8 states, including: surveys, studies, training, demonstrations, and/or investigations, and special purpose assistance associated with air quality, acid deposition, drinking water, water quality, hazardous waste, toxic substances, and pesticides; projects to prevent, reduce, and eliminate pollution; evaluation of economic and social consequences of alternative strategies and mechanisms; educational outreach to targeted audiences associated with specific public health and environmental risks.

Eligible applicants/beneficiaries: state agencies, local and tribal governments, U.S. territories and possessions, public and private universities, colleges, hospitals, laboratories and other public or private nonprofit institutions. Applicants need not be located within the boundaries of EPA Region 8, but must propose a project that affects Region 8.

Range/Average: N.A.

Activity: new program in 2006; FY 06-07 estimate, 10 awards.

HQ: Region 8-EPA, 999 18th St - Suite 300, Denver, CO 80202 Phone: (303) 312-6569, FAX (303) 312-6339.

Internet: www.epa.gov/regional/rgi.htm (Note: field office serves as headquarters for this program.)

66.113 REGION 3 ENVIRONMENTAL PRIORITY PROJECTS ("Regional Geographic Initiatives")

Assistance: project grants. (100 percent/to 2 years).

Purposes: pursuant to CWA, FIFRA, CAA, SWDA, SDWA, and TSCA, for investigations, experiments, training, demonstrations, surveys, studies, and special purpose assistance associated with air quality, acid deposition, drinking water, water quality, hazardous waste, toxic substances, or pesticides—only in Delaware, DC, Maryland, Pennsylvania, Virginia, and West Virginia.

Eligible applicants/beneficiaries: only within EPA Region 3—states, local governments; IHEs, hospitals, laboratories; other public or private nonprofit organizations.

Range: $25,000 to $150,000. **Average:** $100,000.

Activity: new program listing in 2006 (CFDA on-line).

HQ: Region 3- EPA, 1650 Arch St., Philadelphia, PA 19103 Phone: (215) 814-5384, FAX (215) 814-5261.

Internet: www.epa.gov/region03/grants/index.htm (Note: the field office serves as headquarters for this program.)

66.115 SURVEYS, STUDIES, INVESTIGATIONS, TRAINING, DEMONSTRATIONS, AND SPECIAL PURPOSE GRANTS FOR EPA REGION 10 REGIONAL GEOGRAPHIC INITIATIVE

Assistance: project grants (to 5 years).

Purposes: pursuant to CWA, FIFRA, CAA, SWDA, SDWA, and TSCA, and other acts, to support projects only in EPA Region 10 states (Alaska, Idaho, Oregon and Washington) related to regional environmental priorities and including: surveys, studies, training, demonstrations and/or investigations, and special purpose assistance.

Eligible applicants/beneficiaries: state agencies, local and tribal governments, U.S. territories and possessions, public and private universities, colleges, hospitals, laboratories and other public or private nonprofit institutions.

Range: $10,000 to $50,000. **Average:** $42,000.

Activity: FY 06, 9 awards.

HQ: Region 10-EPA, 1200 6th Ave, Seattle, WA 98101 Phone: (206) 553-6911, FAX (206) 553-6984.

Internet: www.epa.gov/r10earth; http://yosemite.epa.gov/R10/HOMEPAGE.NSF/webpage/Grants (Note: field office serves as headquarters for this program.)

66.116 REGIONAL GEOGRAPHIC INITIATIVE/ENVIRONMENTAL PRIORITY PROJECTS

Assistance: project grants (2 years).

Purposes: pursuant to CWA, FIFRA, CAA, SWDA, SDWA, and TSCA, for investigations, experiments, training, demonstrations, surveys, studies, and special purpose assistance associated with air quality, acid deposition, drinking water, water quality, hazardous waste, toxic substances, or pesticides within the Region VI area of Arkansas, Louisiana, New Mexico, Oklahoma, and Texas.

Eligible applicants/beneficiaries: state and local governments, U.S. territories and possessions, Indian tribes, universities and colleges, hospitals, laboratories, and other public and private nonprofit institutions.

Average: $250,000.

Activity: new program listing in 2006 (CFDA on-line).

HQ: Region 6-EPA, 1445 Ross Ave-Suite 1200, Dallas, TX 75202-2733 Phone: (214) 665-8461, FAX (214) 665-7284.

Internet: www.epa.gov/docx/earth1r6///gandf (Note: field office serves as headquarters for this program.)

66.117 REGION 9 MULTI-MEDIA AND GEOGRAPHIC PRIORITY PROJECTS ("R9 RGI and EPP grants")

Assistance: project grants.

Purposes: pursuant to Clean Air Act, Section 103; Clean Water Act, Section 104; Safe Drinking Water Act, Sections 1442; Solid Waste Disposal Act, Section 8001; National Environmental Education Act, Section 6, and others: to fund projects, including surveys, studies, investigations, demonstrations, training, and outreach, that address more than one medium or vector of human health or ecological risk; to prevent, reduce, and eliminate pollution; identify, develop, and demonstrate pollution control techniques and technology; to evaluate the economic, social, and environmental effects of alternative mechanisms and strategies; and to promote coordination and collaboration between and among federal, state, and local governmental and non-governmental organizations. Projects funded under this program must be carried out within the area of U.S. EPA's Region 9, comprised of the states and tribal lands of Arizona, California, Hawaii, or Nevada, and of the Pacific islands associated with the United States. Multi-media priorities for FY2007 include agriculture in the Central Valley, Pacific Island infrastructure, and information management support.

Eligible applicants/beneficiaries: funding is available only for projects conducted within the geographic boundaries of EPA's Region 9, which includes states and tribal lands of Arizona, California, Hawaii, Nevada, Navajo Nations land in New Mexico, and the Pacific islands associated with the United States. Interstate, state, tribal, intrastate, and local government agencies, districts, and councils; and public and private universities and colleges, hospitals, laboratories, and research facilities; and public or private non-governmental, non-profit institutions are eligible to apply, unless restricted by the authorizing statutes. Non-profit organizations must have documentation of non-profit status from the U.S. Internal Revenue Service or their state of incorporation, except that non-profits organizations as defined in Section 501(c)(4) of the Internal Revenue Code that engage in lobbying as defined in Section 3 of the Lobbying Disclosure Act 1995 or superseding legislation are ineligible. For certain competitive funding opportunities under this CFDA description, the Agency may limit eligibility to compete to a number or subset of eligible applicants consistent with the Agency's Assistance Agreement Competition Policy.

Range: $5,000 to $160,000. **Average:** $51,000.

Activity: not quantified specifically.

HQ: Special Assistant, Office of the Regional Administrator, Region 9, EPA, 75 Hawthorne Street (ORA-1), San Francisco, CA 94105. Phone: (415) 972-3501; FAX: (415) 947-3588.

Internet: http://www.epa.gov/region09/funding.

66.202 CONGRESSIONALLY MANDATED PROJECTS ("Congressional Earmarks")

Assistance: project grants.

Purposes: for investigations, experiments, training, demonstrations, and surveys directed by Congress in the EPA annual appropriation or in the annual Appropriations Conference Report—pertaining to activities within EPA's broad purview.

Eligible applicants/beneficiaries: as designated by Congress.

Range: $100,000 to $5,000,000.

Activity: new program listing in 2006 (CFDA on-line).

HQ: EPA, Washington, DC 20460 Phone: OAR, (202) 564-1514; OW, (202) 564-4613; Office of Wastewater Management; (202) 564-0672; Office of Ground Water and Drinking Water, (202) 564-3843; OPPPTS, (202) 564-0547, -0548; OSWER, (202) 566-1893; OECA, (202) 564-2271; Office of Research and Development, (202) 564-4763; Office of Environmental Information, (202) 564-6064; Office of International Affairs, (202) 564-6619; Office of Administrator, (202) 564-0418; Office of the Inspector General, (202) 564-2648.

Internet: www.epa.gov/epahome/finance.htm; www.epa.gov/ocfo/budget/index.htm.

66.305 COMPLIANCE ASSISTANCE SUPPORT FOR SERVICES TO THE REGULATED COMMUNITY AND OTHER ASSISTANCE PROVIDERS ("Compliance Assistance Centers")

Assistance: project grants. (to 100 percent/to 5 years).

Purposes: pursuant to SWDA as amended and RCRA, to develop projects to improve environmental compliance within identified commercial or industrial sectors. Funds may be used to create compliance assistance tools utilizing industry and commercial communication channels to deliver the assistance tools, including internet communications, toll-free telephone assistance lines, satellite training, other interactive technologies.

Eligible applicants/beneficiaries: nonprofit organizations, IHEs, and state, local, and tribal governments.

Range: $65,000 to $150,000 per year. **Average:** $90,000.

Activity: FY 05, 15 centers supported through 10 cooperative agreements.

HQ: OECA-EPA, 1200 Pennsylvania Ave. NW, Washington, DC 20460 Phone: Compliance Centers Team, Platform Development, U.S.-Mexico Border Environmental Issues Leads, (202) 564-7076, FAX (202) 564-0037; Industry Leads, (202) 564-1459, FAX (202) 564-0009; Chemical

Manufacturing Center Lead, (202) 564-7071, FAX,(202) 564-0037; Local Government Center Lead, (202) 564-7049, FAX (202) 564-0037.

Internet: www.epa.gov/compliance/assistance/centers/index.html; www.assistancecenters.net (Note: no field offices for this program.)

66.306 ENVIRONMENTAL JUSTICE COLLABORATIVE PROBLEM- SOLVING COOPERATIVE AGREEMENT PROGRAM ("EJCPS")

Assistance: project grants (100 percent/3 years).

Purposes: pursuant to the CWA, SDWA, SWDA, CAA, TSCA, FIFRA, and MPRSA, for projects by affected groups demonstrating the utility of the Federal Interagency Working Group Model on Collaborative Problem-Solving, toward the solution of community environmental and public health issues. Funds may support such activities as: capacity-building; partnerships and collaborative involvement with industry and federal, state, and local governments, academia, and environmental organizations; establishing health clinics or medical screening programs or replacing diesel buses with buses using clean fuels; outreach and community education.

Eligible applicants/beneficiaries: organizations designated nonprofit by IRS or by state, territory, commonwealth, or tribe in which it is located.

Average: $100,000.

Activity: new program listing in 2004; FY 05, no awards.

HQ: Director, Office of Environmental Justice (2201A), EPA, 1200 Pennsylvania Ave. NW, Washington, DC 20460 Phone: (202) 564-5396, FAX,(202) 501-0740; Environmental Justice Hotline (800) 962-6215.

Internet: www.epa.gov/compliance/environmentaljustice (Note: no field offices for this program.)

66.309 SURVEYS, STUDIES, INVESTIGATIONS AND SPECIAL PURPOSE ACTIVITIES RELATING TO ENVIRONMENTAL JUSTICE ("EJSS")

Assistance: project grants (100 percent/1-5 years).

Purposes: pursuant to the CWA, SDWA, SWDA, CAA, TSCA, FIFRA, MPRSA, and CERCLA, for surveys, studies, investigations, and special activities addressing broad environmental and public health issues, emphasizing environmental justice.

Eligible applicants/beneficiaries: states, territories, possessions, tribes and public and private IHEs, hospitals, libraries, and other institutions.

Range/Average: N.A.

Activity: new program in FY 06 (CFDA on-line version); 10 awards anticipated.

HQ: Grants Administration Division (3903R), EPA, 1200 Pennsylvania Ave. NW, Washington, DC 20460 Phone: (202) 564-2602, FAX (202) 501-0740.

Internet: www.epa.gov/compliance/environmentaljustice/index.html (Note: no field offices for this program.)

66.310 CAPACITY BUILDING GRANTS AND COOPERATIVE AGREEMENTS FOR COMPLIANCE ASSURANCE AND ACTIVITIES IN INDIAN COUNTRY AND OTHER TRIBAL AREAS ("Office of Enforcement and Compliance Assurance Tribal Resources")

Assistance: project grants. (100 percent/multi-year).

Purposes: pursuant to CWA, FIFRA, CAA, SWDA, SDWA, TSCA, MPRSA, National Environmental Policy Act, and Indian Environmental General Assistance Program Act, to build and improve the capacity to foster environmental enforcement and compliance assurance activities in Indian country and other tribal areas including in Alaska. Eligible project activities include: inspections; assessment; surveys; performance measurement; data quality improvement; enforcement; training including through fellowships, scholarships, traineeships, conferences, and technical assistance; experiments and demonstrations; construction; dissemination and information exchange. Funds should support activities directly related to the National Tribal Compliance Assurance Priority and other specified priorities in Indian country.

Eligible applicants/beneficiaries: responsible tribal, federal, and state organizations; consortia.

Range: $5,000 to $100,000 per year. **Average:** $29,000.

Activity: new program listing in 2005 (CFDA on-line version). Not quantified specifically.

HQ: Office of Compliance, OECA-EPA, 1200 Pennsylvania Ave. NW, Washington, DC 20460 Phone: (202) 564-2516, FAX (202) 564-7083.

Internet: www.epa.gov/compliance/state/grants/index.htm.

66.418 CONSTRUCTION GRANTS FOR WASTEWATER TREATMENT WORKS

Assistance: project grants (55-85 percent; insular areas, 100 percent).

Purposes: pursuant to CWA as amended, for construction of municipal wastewater treatment works, including privately owned individual systems, required to meet state or federal water quality standards. Projects may include industrial wastes, provided pretreatment or entry prevention into funded projects is included. Users must be charged.

Eligible applicants/beneficiaries: any municipal, intermunicipal, state, or interstate agency; Indian tribal governments. Also available to each U.S. territory and possession. (Currently, only DC, VI, and Outer Pacific Islands being newly funded; others apply to state revolving funds—see **66.458**.

Range: $100,000 to $15,000,000 per fiscal year. **Average:** $7,550,000.

Activity: FY 05 estimate, 2 grants; FY 06 estimate, 3 grants.

HQ: Municipal Assistance Branch (4204M), Municipal Support Division, Office of Wastewater Management, OW-EPA, 1200 Pennsylvania Ave. NW, Washington, DC 20460 Phone: (202) 564-0648, FAX (202) 501-2396.

Internet: www.epa.gov/owm.cwfinance/index.htm.

66.419 WATER POLLUTION CONTROL STATE, INTERSTATE, AND TRIBAL PROGRAM SUPPORT ("106 Grants")

Assistance: formula (matching).

Purposes: pursuant to CWA as amended, for activities to prevent and abate surface- and groundwater pollution from point and nonpoint sources, including: planning, monitoring, assessments, permitting, studies, surveillance and enforcement, training, technical assistance, and public information; restoration of impaired watersheds. Funds may not be used for waste treatment plant construction, operation, or maintenance.

Eligible applicants/beneficiaries: state, interstate, tribal, and territorial agencies.

Range: $60,000 to $11,200,000 per fiscal year. **Average:** $5,630,000.

Activity: FY 05, 180 grants; FY 06 estimate, 180-200 grants.

HQ: State, Interstate and Tribal Coordinator, Office of Wastewater Management (4201), OW-EPA, 1200 Pennsylvania Ave. NW, Washington, DC 20460 Phone: (202) 564-8831, FAX (202) 501-2399.

Internet: www.epa.gov/owm.cwfinance/ipollutioncontrol.htm.

66.424 SURVEYS, STUDIES, DEMONSTRATIONS AND SPECIAL PURPOSE GRANTS—SECTION 1442 OF THE SAFE DRINKING WATER ACT

Assistance: project grants.

Purposes: pursuant to SDWA Section 1442 as amended, to support research, studies, and demonstrations associated with source water and drinking water; to develop and expand capabilities of pertinent programs. Priorities include: contaminants in drinking water; source water protection and treatment methods; measures to protect water quality in the distribution system and at the tap; tribal source water program support; tribal operator certification program; tribal capacity development; tribal administration of the Drinking Water Infrastructure Grants to identify health effects associated with drinking water contaminants.

Eligible applicants/beneficiaries: states, territories and possessions, tribes, IHEs, hospitals, laboratories, other public and private nonprofit institutions, and individuals.

Range: $50,000 to $800,000 per fiscal year. **Average:** $425,000.

Activity: FY 05, 3 grants.

HQ: *Program information,* Office of Groundwater and Drinking Water (4604M), OW-EPA, 1200 Pennsylvania Ave. NW, Washington, DC 20460 Phone: (202) 564- 3817, FAX (202) 564-3754; Immediate Office, (202) 564-4633, FAX (202) 564-0348 *Grants management information*: Grants Administration Division (3903R), EPA, 1200 Pennsylvania Ave. NW, Washington, DC 20460 Phone: (202) 564-2602, FAX (202) 501-0740.

Internet: www.epa.gov/safewater.

66.432 STATE PUBLIC WATER SYSTEM SUPERVISION

Assistance: formula grants (75 percent).

Purposes: pursuant to the Public Health Service Act (PHSA), SDWA, and amendments, to develop and implement programs implementing public water system supervision adequate to enforce SDWA provisions, including program plan development, adoption of applicable regulations, data management, system inventories, public participation, technical assistance, laboratory certification, and enforcement.

Eligible applicants/beneficiaries: state agencies, territories and possessions, tribes treated as states.

Range: $124,000 to $6,142,800. **Average:** $1,685,550.

Activity: FY 05, 55 grants.

HQ: Office of Ground Water and Drinking Water (4604M), OW-EPA, Washington, DC 20460 Phone: (202) 564-3829, FAX (202) 564-3755.

Internet: www.epa.gov/safewater/pws/pwsgrant.html.

66.433 STATE UNDERGROUND WATER SOURCE PROTECTION

Assistance: formula grants (75 percent; tribes, 90 percent).

Purposes: pursuant to SDWA and amendments, to develop and implement underground injection control programs. Funds may be used for such purposes as state regulation review, plan development, data management, inventory of injection facilities, identification of aquifers, technical assistance, public participation, enforcement activities.

Eligible applicants/beneficiaries: states, tribes.

Range: $33,000 to $988,000 per fiscal year. **Average:** $178,000.

Activity: FY 05-06, funding to 43 states and tribes with primary responsibility for 36 full and 7 partial programs.

HQ: Prevention Branch, Drinking Water Protection Division (4606M), Office of Ground Water and Drinking Water, OW-EPA, 1200 Pennsylvania Ave. NW, Washington, DC 20460 Phone: (202) 564-4688, FAX (202) 564-3756.

Internet: www.epa.gov/OGWDW/Safewater/UIC.html.

66.436 SURVEYS, STUDIES, INVESTIGATIONS, DEMONSTRATIONS, AND TRAINING GRANTS AND COOPERATIVE AGREEMENTS - SECTION 104(B)(3) OF THE CLEAN WATER ACT

Assistance: project grants.

Purposes: pursuant to CWA Section 104(b)(3) as amended, for coordination and acceleration of research, investigations, experiments, training, demonstrations, surveys, and studies relating to the causes, effects including health and welfare effects, extent, prevention, reduction, and elimination of water pollution. Priorities include: water quality improvement, watersheds management, aquatic ecosystem restoration, pollutant trading, fish contamination and consumption, nonpoint source management, wetlands protection, coastal and estuarine management, treatment technologies, and environmental management systems. Project examples: watershed education program for broadcast meteorologists; atmospheric mercury deposition study; watershed protection and restoration guides.

Eligible applicants/beneficiaries: states, territories and possessions, tribes, IHEs, hospitals, laboratories, other public and private nonprofit institutions, and individuals.

Range: $15,000 to $4,970,000 per fiscal year. **Average:** $2,493,000.

Activity: not quantified specifically.

HQ: Office of Groundwater and Drinking Water (4604M), OW-EPA,1200 Pennsylvania Ave. NW, Washington, DC 20460 Phone: (202) 564-3817, FAX (202) 564-3754; *and* phone: Office of Wetlands, Oceans and Watersheds, (202) 566-1254; Office of Wastewater Management, (202) 564-0672; Office of Science and Technology, (202) 566-1453; Immediate Office, (202) 566-4633.

Internet: www.epa.gov/ow.

66.437 LONG ISLAND SOUND PROGRAM ("Long Island Sound Study - LISS")

Assistance: project grants (50-95 percent).

Purposes: pursuant to CWA as amended by the Long Island Sound Restoration Act of 2000, to implement elements of the Long Island Sound Study (LISS) Comprehensive Conservation and Management Plan (CCMP), with special emphasis on implementation projects, research and planning, enforcement, and citizen involvement and education projects.

Eligible applicants/beneficiaries: state, interstate, and regional water control agencies and organizations.

Range: $20,000 to $500,000. **Average:** $467,000.

Activity: new program listing in 2004; FY 05, no awards; FY 06 estimate, 3 awards.

HQ: Ocean and Coastal Protection Division, Office of Wetlands, Oceans and Watersheds, OW-EPA, 1301 Pennsylvania Ave. NW, Washington, DC 20004. Phone: (202) 566-1256, FAX (202) 566-1334.

Internet: www.epa.gov/region01/eco/lis.

66.439 TARGETED WATERSHEDS GRANTS

Assistance: project grants (75 percent; tribes, to 100 percent).

Purposes: pursuant to CWA as amended, for watershed partnerships to develop innovative, community-based approaches aimed at preventing, reducing, or eliminating water pollution—involving local, state, tribal, and interstate agencies and other public or nonprofit organizations. Funds may be used for research, investigations, experiments, training, demonstrations, surveys, and studies.

Eligible applicants/beneficiaries: state, local, interstate, public agencies; private nonprofit institutions and organizations; tribal governments; territories, possessions; IHEs, individuals.

Range: $300,000 to $1,300,000. **Average:** $800,000.

Activity: FY 05, 12 awards.

HQ: Office of Wetlands, Oceans, and Watersheds, OW-EPA, 1200 Pennsylvania Ave. NW - Rm.7136E, Washington, DC 20460 Phone: (202) 566-1304, FAX (202) 566-1326.

Internet: www.epa.gov/twg.

66.454 WATER QUALITY MANAGEMENT PLANNING ("Section 205(j)(2)")

Assistance: formula grants (100 percent).

Purposes: pursuant to CWA as amended and Water Quality Act of 1987, for water quality management planning, with priority encouraged for watershed restoration. States must allocate 40 percent of funds to regional and interstate agencies. Program examples: performing waste load allocations; point and nonpoint source planning.

Eligible applicants/beneficiaries: state water quality management agencies.

Range: $100,000 to $1,500,000. **Average:** $800,000.

Activity: FY 04, 57 state and territorial grants awarded.

HQ: Assessment and Watershed Protection Division (4503T), OW-EPA, 1200 Pennsylvania Ave. NW, Washington, DC 20004 Phone: (301) 694-7329, FAX: (202) 566-1545.

Internet: www.epa.gov/ow/owow.htm.

66.456 NATIONAL ESTUARY PROGRAM ("NEP")

Assistance: project grants (50-75 percent/to 3 years).

Purposes: pursuant to CWA as amended, to develop and implement comprehensive conservation and management plans to protect and restore the coastal resources of 28 estuaries holding priority for funding. Funds must be used to develop master environmental plans based on relationships between pollutant loading and ecological impacts.

Eligible applicants/beneficiaries: within the priority geographic areas—regional, interstate, state water pollution control agencies; state coastal zone management agencies; public or private nonprofit organizations; individuals.

Average: base grant of $492,600 for each NEP.

Activity: 28 NEP estuaries received funding.

HQ: Chief, Coastal Management Branch, Oceans and Coastal Protection Division, Office of Wetlands, Oceans, and Watersheds (4504T), OW-EPA, Washington, DC 20460. Phone: (202) 566-1200, FAX (202) 566-1336.

Internet: www.epa.gov/owow/estuaries.

66.458 CAPITALIZATION GRANTS FOR CLEAN WATER STATE REVOLVING FUNDS ("CW State Revolving Fund")

Assistance: formula grants (80 percent).

Purposes: pursuant to CWA as amended and Water Quality Act of 1987, to establish state revolving loan funds to finance wastewater treatment facilities and other water quality management activities. Capitalization grants deposited in the revolving funds may be used to provide loans to finance construction of publicly owned wastewater treatment works, to execute a nonpoint source management program, and to develop and execute estuary conservation and management plans.

Eligible applicants: states, PR; (DC, possessions, tribes and territorial agencies use **66.418**.)

Eligible beneficiaries: loans from revolving funds—community, intermunicipal, interstate, and tribal agencies.

Range: $6,500,000 to $147,000,000. **Average:** $26,000,000.

Activity: annually, 51 grants.

HQ: State Revolving Fund Branch, Municipal Support Division (4204M), Office of Wastewater Management, OW-EPA, Washington, DC 20460 Phone: (202) 564-0686, FAX (202) 501-2403.

Internet: www.epa.gov/owm.cwfinance/index.htm.

66.460 NONPOINT SOURCE IMPLEMENTATION GRANTS ("319 Program")

Assistance: formula grants (60-90 percent).

Purposes: pursuant to Clean Water Act, Title III, to assist in implementing EPA-approved Section 319 nonpoint source management programs that promote the development and implementation of watershed-based plans, focusing on watersheds with water quality impairments caused by nonpoint sources, which result in improved water quality in impaired waters.

Eligible applicants/beneficiaries: states (including DC, VI, PR, American Samoa, Northern Marianas, Pacific Trust Territories), tribes and intertribal consortia.

Range: FY 06: states & territories, $538,700 to $10,650,400; tribes, $30,000 to $50,000; competitive, to $150,000. **Average:** states & territories, $3,560,257.

Activity: FY 05-06, 56 awards.

HQ: Assessment and Watershed Protection Division, Nonpoint Source Control Branch, Office of Wetlands, Oceans and Watersheds (4503T), EPA, Ariel Rios Bldg, 1200 Pennsylvania Ave. NW, Washington, DC 20460 Phone: (202) 566-1203, FAX (202) 566-1545.

Internet: www.epa.gov/owow/nps.

66.461 REGIONAL WETLAND PROGRAM DEVELOPMENT GRANTS

Assistance: project grants (75 percent).

Purposes: pursuant to CWA as amended, to develop new or enhance existing regional wetlands protection management and restoration programs, with priority to: strengthening comprehensiveness of programs; monitoring and assessment; compensatory mitigation; protection of vulnerable wetlands and aquatic resources. Funds may support research, investigations, experiments, training, demonstrations, surveys, and studies—relating to the causes, effects, extent, prevention, reduction and elimination of water pollution.

Eligible applicants/beneficiaries: appropriate state, interstate, and local agencies—including those involved with wetlands or water quality regulation, planning offices, wild and scenic rivers, fish and wildlife, agriculture and transportation departments, coastal zone management, similar functions; inter-tribal consortia; IHEs that are agencies of the state.

Range: $11,000 to $496,000. **Average:** $254,000.

Activity: FY 05, 65 cooperative agreements were awarded.

HQ: Wetlands Division, Office of Wetlands, Oceans and Watersheds (4502T), OW-EPA, 1200 Pennsylvania Ave. NW, Washington, DC 20460 Phone: (202) 566-1225, FAX (202) 566-1349.

Internet: www.epa.gov/owow/wetlands/initiative/#financial.

66.462 NATIONAL WETLAND PROGRAM DEVELOPMENT GRANTS

Assistance: project grants (75 percent).

Purposes: pursuant to CWA as amended, for comprehensive national wetlands program development by promoting the coordination and acceleration of research, investigations, experiments, training, and studies—relating to the causes, effects, extent, prevention, reduction and elimination of water pollution. Projects also may involve such activities as training and information dissemination.

Eligible applicants/beneficiaries: nonprofit, nongovernmental capable of advancing programs on a national basis; interstate and intertribal agencies.

Range: $10,000 to $140,000. **Average:** $75,000.

Activity: new program in FY 05; FY 05, 5 awards; FY 06 estimate, 5 awards.

HQ: Wetlands Division, Office of Wetlands, Oceans and Watersheds (4502T), OW-EPA, 1200 Pennsylvania Ave. NW, Washington, DC 20460 Phone: (202) 566-1225, FAX (202) 566-1349.

Internet: www.epa.gov/owow/wetlands/initiative/#financial.

66.463 WATER QUALITY COOPERATIVE AGREEMENTS

Assistance: project grants.

Purposes: pursuant to CWA as amended, to develop, implement, and demonstrate innovative approaches relating to the causes, effects, extent, prevention, reduction, and elimination of water pollution, including watershed approaches for combined sewer overflow, sanitary sewer overflows, and storm water discharge problems, pretreatment and sludge program activities, alternative ways to measure the effectiveness of point source programs, trading, water efficiency, asset management, and sustainable infrastructure. Projects should promote the coordination and acceleration of research, investigations, experiments, training, and studies—relating to the causes, effects, extent, prevention, reduction and elimination of water pollution. In most EPA regions, funds also may be used for internships to high school students working at wastewater treatment plants, under the Youth and the Environment Program.

Eligible applicants/beneficiaries: state, interstate agencies; tribes; IHEs; individuals; other public or nonprofit organizations.

Range: $10,000 to $300,000. **Average:** EPA HQ awards, $100,000; regional awards, $120,000.

Activity: FY 05, 75 grants.

HQ: Office of Wastewater Management (4204M), OW-EPA, 1200 Pennsylvania Ave NW - Rm.7324J, Washington, DC 20460 Phone: (202) 564-0672, FAX (202) 501-2397.

Internet: www.epa.gov/owm.cwfinance/index.htm.

66.466 CHESAPEAKE BAY PROGRAM

Assistance: project grants (50-95 percent).

Purposes: pursuant to CWA, for research, experiments, investigations, training, demonstrations, surveys, or studies related to reducing pollution and improving the quality of living resources in the Chesapeake Bay; for the implementation of Chesapeake Bay interstate management programs; for small watershed grants to local organizations to build citizen-based stewardship. Project examples: nonpoint source implementation programs; biological nutrient removal; living resources restoration studies and surveys; mainstem monitoring.

Eligible applicants/beneficiaries: within the Chesapeake Bay basin—state and local governments, interstate agencies, IHEs, other nonprofit organizations, individuals.

Range: $8,200 to $2,800,000. **Average:** $1,404,000.

Activity: FY 05, 18 awards.

HQ: Office of Water (4101M), EPA, 1200 Pennsylvania Ave. NW, Washington, DC 20460 Phone: (202) 546-4633, FAX: (202) 564-0348.

Internet: www.epa.gov/region03/chesapeake.

66.467 WASTEWATER OPERATOR TRAINING GRANT PROGRAM (TECHNICAL ASSISTANCE)

Assistance: project grants. (75 percent/to 3 years).

Purposes: pursuant to the Federal Water Pollution Control Act as amended, to provide on-site technical assistance to operations and maintenance (O&M) personnel at publicly owned wastewater treatment works, as well as classroom training.

Eligible applicants/beneficiaries: state agencies; possessions, territories, and tribes; state-designated nonprofit agencies.

Range: $14,000 to $71,000. **Average:** $40,000.

Activity: FY 05, 754 small facilities assisted; FY 06 estimate, 650 small facilities to receive assistance.

HQ: Office of Wastewater Management (4204M), OW-EPA, 1200 Pennsylvania Ave NW, Washington, DC 20460 Phone: (202) 564-0648, FAX (202) 501-2396.

Internet: www.epa.gov/owm/mab/smcomm/104g/index.htm.

66.468 CAPITALIZATION GRANTS FOR DRINKING WATER STATE REVOLVING FUND
("Drinking Water State Revolving Fund - DWSRF")

Assistance: formula grants (80 percent).

Purposes: pursuant to SDWA Amendments of 1966, to capitalize DWSRFs to finance infrastructure needed to achieve and maintain compliance with SDWA requirements, through loans or other assistance; to establish new programs to prevent contamination through source water protection and enhanced water systems management.

Eligible applicants: capitalization grants—states, PR. Direct grants—DC, territories, tribes.

Eligible beneficiaries: loans—public, private, or nonprofit community drinking water systems.

Range: $14,000 (for tribes) to $84,848,000 (for states). **Average:** states, $46,567,000; tribes, $330,000; territories, $685,000.

Activity: DWSRFs established in all states and PR. FY 05, states made 544 loans; 4 awards to territories, 38 awards to tribes.

HQ: Infrastructure Branch (4606M), Drinking Water Protection Division, Office of Groundwater and Drinking Water, OW-EPA, 1200 Pennsylvania Ave. NW, Washington, DC 20460 Phone: (202) 564-3848, FAX (202) 564-1836.

Internet: www.epa.gov/safewater/dwsrf.html.

66.469 GREAT LAKES PROGRAM

Assistance: project grants; use of property, facilities, and equipment; technical information. (grants, 65-100 percent/grants, 1-2 years).

Purposes: pursuant to CWA, to restore and maintain the chemical, physical, and biological integrity of the Great Lakes Basin Ecosystem. Funds may be used for such activities as surveys, research, experiments, training, studies, and demonstrations relating to: contaminated sediment remediation; pollution prevention, reduction, or elimination; habitat protection and restoration; invasive aquatic and terrestrial species, emphasizing prevention; and, similar efforts. Great Lakes Legacy Act projects, requiring a 35 percent match, entail cooperative agreements for contaminant remediation.

Eligible applicants/beneficiaries: state water pollution control agencies; interstate and other public and private nonprofit agencies; institutions; organizations; tribes; individuals.

Range: $4,000 to $700,000. **Average:** $352,000.

Activity: FY 05, 70 awards.

HQ: Great Lakes National Program Office (G-17J), OW-EPA, 77 W. Jackson Blvd., Chicago, IL 60604-3590 Phone: (312) 886-4013, FAX: (312) 353-2018.

Internet: www.epa.gov/glnpo/fund (Note: no other field offices for this program.)

66.471 STATE GRANTS TO REIMBURSE OPERATORS OF SMALL WATER SYSTEMS FOR TRAINING AND CERTIFICATION COSTS ("Operator Certification Expense Reimbursement Grants")

Assistance: formula grants. (80-100 percent/2 years).

Purposes: pursuant to SDWA Amendments, to reimburse operators of community and nontransient noncommunity water systems serving 3,300 or fewer persons—for costs of training and certification needed to meet EPA guidelines.

Eligible applicants: states, PR, and territories.

Eligible beneficiaries: small systems operators, tribes, Alaska native villages.

Range: $14,000 to $9,643,000. **Average:** $4,829,000.

Activity: to date, all states, PR, Northern Marianas, Guam funded; FY 05,1 award to states; 3 awards to territories.

HQ: Protection Branch (4606M), Drinking Water Protection Division, Office of Groundwater and Drinking Water, OW-EPA, 1200 Pennsylvania Ave. NW, Washington, DC 20460 Phone: (202) 564- 3836, FAX (202) 564-3755.

Internet: www.epa.gov/safewater/opcert/opcert.htm.

66.472 BEACH MONITORING AND NOTIFICATION PROGRAM IMPLEMENTATION GRANTS

Assistance: project grants.

Purposes: pursuant to CWA as amended and Beaches Environmental Assessment and Coastal Health Act of 2000, to develop and implement water quality monitoring and public notification programs for coastal recreation waters adjacent to beaches or similar points of public access—including developing protocols, public outreach and education to users.

Eligible applicants/beneficiaries: coastal and Great Lakes states, territories, tribes. Local governments may receive grants after the first year of program operation.

Range: $150,000 to $530,000. **Average:** $340,000.

Activity: FY 06 estimate, awards to all 35 coastal and Great Lake states, territories, and tribes.

HQ: OW-EPA (4305T), 1200 Pennsylvania Ave. NW, Washington, DC 20460 Phone: (202) 566-0399, FAX (202) 566-0409.

Internet: www.epa.gov/waterscience/beaches.

66.473 DIRECT IMPLEMENTATION TRIBAL COOPERATIVE AGREEMENTS ("DITCA")

Assistance: project grants. (100 percent/1-3 years).

Purposes: to build tribal capacity to carry out EPA-approved environmental programs for tribes, including such activities as developing protocols for interfacing inspections, permit and enforcement actions, training tribal employees to receive federal credentials.

Eligible applicants/beneficiaries: tribes and inter-tribal consortia.

Range: $10,000 to $100,000. **Average:** $55,000.

Activity: FY 05, 7 awards; FY 06 estimate, 13 awards.

HQ: *program information:* American Indian Environmental Office (4104M), OW-EPA, 1200 Pennsylvania Ave. NW, Washington, DC 20460 Phone: (202) 564-0289, FAX (202) 564-0298 *Grants management information,* Grants Administration Division (3903R), EPA, 1200 Pennsylvania Ave. NW, Washington, DC 20460 Phone: (202) 564- 5084, FAX (202) 565-2047.

Internet: www.epa.gov/indian/index.htm.

66.474 WATER PROTECTION GRANTS TO THE STATES

Assistance: formula grants (from 1 year).

Purposes: pursuant to SDWA and Department of Defense and Emergency Supplemental Appropriations for Recovery from and Response to Terrorist Acts on the Unites States Act of 2002, for coordination of protection activities pertaining to critical water infrastructure, including work with water utilities and local, state, and federal agencies. Funded activities may include vulnerability assessments and related security enhancements, communications improvement, duty officer programs, toll-free numbers, emergency response and recovery planning, technical assistance, training, and education.

Eligible applicants/beneficiaries: states, tribes, territories, possessions.

Range: $17,000 to $302,000. **Average:** $159,000.

Activity: FY05, awards made to 50 states, DC and 5 territories.

HQ: Water Security Division (Mail Code 140), U.S. EPA, 26 W. Martin Luther King Dr., Cincinnati, OH 45268 Phone: (513) 569-7864, FAX (513) 569-7191.

Internet: http://cfpub.epa.gov/safewater/watersecurity/financeassist.cfm (Note: field office serves as headquarters for this program.)

66.475 GULF OF MEXICO PROGRAM ("Gulf of Mexico Allliance Regional partnership Projects")

Assistance: project grants.

Purposes: pursuant to CWA, to expand and strengthen cooperative efforts to restore and protect the health and productivity of the Gulf of Mexico and its region—including activities in the Mississippi River Basin designed to reduce Gulf hypoxia. Funded activities may include surveys, studies, investigations, research, and demonstrations that are approved by the Gulf of Mexico Program Office. Project examples include: implementation of restoration actions for impaired coastal segments; shellfish habitat restoration; water quality monitoring; characterization of mercury data.

Eligible applicants/beneficiaries: state and local governments, interstate agencies, tribes, IHEs, individuals, and other public or nonprofit organizations.

Range: $11,300 to $225,000. **Average:** $92,500.

Activity: FY 05, 26 agreements funded.

HQ: EPA/Gulf of Mexico Program Office, Mail Code EPA/GMPO, Stennis Space Cntr., MS 39529 Phone: (228) 688-1281, FAX (228) 688-2709.

Internet: www.epa.gov/gmpo (Note: field office serves as headquarters for this program.)

66.478 WATER SECURITY TRAINING AND TECHNICAL ASSISTANCE AND WATER SECURITY INITIATIVE CONTAMINATION WARNING SYSTEM PILOTS

Assistance: project grants.

Purposes: pursuant to SDWA as amended, Public Health Security and Bioterrorism Preparedness and Response Act of 2002, and Department of Defense and Emergency Supplemental Appropriations for Recovery from and Response to Terrorist Attacks on the United States Act of 2002, to improve drinking water system security through training and technical assistance for water utilities, provided by eligible nonprofit organizations. Program focus is helping states, tribes, and local authorities in completing vulnerability assessments, emergency response plans, security enhancements.

Eligible applicants/beneficiaries: capable public and private nonprofit organizations.

Range/Average: N.A.

Activity: FY 03, 5 grants for systems serving populations under 50,000; 2 grants estimated for systems serving populations between 50,000 and 100,000. FY 04, continuation grants issued. FY 05-06, no new awards.

HQ: Water Security Division (Mail Code 140), U.S. EPA, 26 W. Martin Luther King Dr., Cincinnati, OH 45268 Phone: (513) 569-7864, FAX (513) 569-7191.

Internet: http://cfpub.epa.gov/safewater/watersecurity/financeassist.cfm (Note: field office serves as headquarters.)

66.479 WETLAND PROGRAM GRANTS—STATE/TRIBAL ENVIRONMENTAL OUTCOME WETLAND DEMONSTRATION PROGRAM

Assistance: project grants (75 percent).

Purposes: pursuant to CWA as amended, for projects proposing to demonstrate the extent to which the implementation of both regulatory and non-regulatory wetland programs result in positive environmental outcomes—in particular, no net loss, net gain, and protection of vulnerable wetlands. Projects may involve the coordination and acceleration of research, investigations, experiments, training, surveys, and studies relating to the causes, effects, extent, prevention, reduction, and elimination of water pollution.

Eligible applicants/beneficiaries: state and tribal wetland agencies.

Range: $200,000 to $300,000. **Average:** $250,000.

Activity: new program in FY 05; 25 awards made in FY 05.

HQ: Wetlands Division, Office of Wetlands, Oceans and Watersheds (4502T), OW-EPA, 1200 Pennsylvania Ave. NW, Washington, DC 20460 Phone: (202) 566-1382, FAX (202) 566-1349.

Internet: www.epa.gov/owow/wetlands/grantpilot.

66.480 ASSESSMENT AND WATERSHED PROTECTION PROGRAM GRANTS

Assistance: project grants (to 5 years).

Purposes: pursuant to CWA, to coordinate and accelerate watershed research, investigations, experiments, training, demonstrations surveys, and studies relating to the causes, effects, extent, prevention, reduction, and elimination of water pollution. Current program priorities include: Total Maximum Daily Load (TMDL) technical conference; advancing the TMDL program nationally; TMDL technical support.

Eligible applicants/beneficiaries: state, local governments; tribes; territories and possessions; interstate or intertribal consortia; public or private nonprofit, nongovernmental organizations; individuals.

Range: $10,000 to $300,000. **Average:** $80,000.

Activity: new program listing in 2005; FY 05, 14 proposals funded.

HQ: *program information,* OWOW-EPA, Office of Wetlands, Oceans and Watersheds (4502T), OW-EPA, 1200 Pennsylvania Ave. NW, Washington, DC 20460 Phone: (202) 566-1254; Assessment and Watershed Protection Division, (202) 566-1206 *Grants management information*: OW-EPA, 1200 Pennsylvania Ave. NW, Washington, DC 20460.

Internet: www.epa.gov/owow/funding.html.

66.481 LAKE CHAMPLAIN BASIN PROGRAM

Assistance: project grants (75 percent).

Purposes: pursuant to CWA as amended, to assist the states of New York and Vermont in protecting and preserving the Lake Champlain ecosystem, through implementation of elements of the "Lake Champlain Basin Management Plan, Opportunities for Action." Funds may be used to assist research, surveys, studies, modeling, technical, field, restoration, and other supporting work.

Eligible applicants/beneficiaries: state, interstate, and regional water pollution control agencies; public or nonprofit agencies and organizations. (Awards are made in consultation with the Lake Champlain Program Steering Committee.)

Range: $75,000 to $1,199,000. **Average:** $637,000.

Activity: new program listing in 2005. (Program began in 1991; awards are not quantified specifically.)

HQ: New England Regional Office, EPA, 1 Congress St. - Ste.1100- CWN, Boston, MA 02114-2023 Phone: (617) 918-1606, FAX (617) 918-0606 *Or,* Region 2 Office, EPA, 290 Broadway - 24th floor, New York, NY 10007-1866 Phone: (212) 637-3779, FAX (212) 637-3889.

Internet: www.epa.gov/NE/eco/lakechamplain/index.html (Note: the field offices serve as headquarters for this program.)

66.508 SENIOR ENVIRONMENTAL EMPLOYMENT PROGRAM ("SEE")

Assistance: project grants (100 percent/1-3 years).

Purposes: pursuant to the Environmental Programs Assistance Act of 1984, to employ older Americans in temporary full- or part- time jobs to provide technical assistance in pollution prevention, abatement, and control projects. Funded project examples: nonagricultural pesticide surveys; monitoring asbestos compliance in schools; research, general administrative, and clerical tasks; review and monitoring of the import car program.

Eligible applicants: nonprofit organizations designated by DOL under the Older Americans Act of 1965.

Eligible beneficiaries: federal, state, and local environmental agencies; individuals age 55 or older.

Range: $1,248 to $987,250. **Average:** $98,700.

Activity: FY 05, 15 new awards, 345 cooperative agreements; as of June, 2006, 24 new awards.

HQ: Director, SEE Program (3661A), Office of Administration and Resources Management, EPA, 1200 Pennsylvania Ave. NW, Washington, DC 20460 Director, SEE Program, (202) 564-0410, (202) 564-0735.

Internet: www.epa.gov/epahrist/see/brochure (Note: no field offices for this program.)

66.509 SCIENCE TO ACHIEVE RESULTS (STAR) RESEARCH PROGRAM ("STAR Program")

Assistance: project grants (2-5 years).

Purposes: pursuant to CAA, CWA, SWDA, SDWA, FIFRA, and TSCA, for research: to determine the environmental and human health effects of air and water quality, hazardous waste, toxic substances, and pesticides; to identify, develop, and demonstrate effective pollution control techniques; to explore and develop strategies and mechanisms for use by those in economic, social, governmental, and environmental systems in decision-making. Support may be provided for environmental research centers. Awards are made only in response to requests for competitive proposals; unsolicited proposals are not accepted.

Eligible applicants/beneficiaries: U.S. IHEs, hospitals, and nonprofit organizations; state, local, tribal governments, territories, and possessions.

Range: new grants, $150,000 to $15,000,000 total per grant. **Average:** $475,000.

Activity: FY 05, 40 grants.

HQ: Grants Administration Division (3903R), EPA, 1200 Pennsylvania Ave. NW, Washington, DC 20460 Phone: *eligibility questions,* (202) 343-9862, FAX (202) 233-0680.

Internet: www.epa.gov.ncer.

66.510 SURVEYS, STUDIES, INVESTIGATIONS AND SPECIAL PURPOSE GRANTS WITHIN THE OFFICE OF RESEARCH AND DEVELOPMENT

Assistance: project grants. (100 percent/to 5 years).

Purposes: pursuant to CAA, CWA, SWDA, RCRA, SDWA, FIFRA, TSCA, amendments, and MPRSA, to determine the environmental effects of air quality, drinking water, water quality, hazardous waste, toxic substances, and pesticides; to identify, develop, and demonstrate effective pollution control techniques. Generally, awards are made only in response to requests for competitive proposals, and unsolicited proposals are not funded.

Eligible applicants/beneficiaries: state, local, tribal governments and agencies; territories, possessions; IHEs, hospitals, laboratories, nonprofit organizations; individuals.

Range: $5,000 to $500,000. **Average:** $100,000.

Activity: annually, 50 awards.

HQ: Office of Research and Development-EPA, 1200 Pennsylvania Ave. NW, Washington, DC 20460 Phone: *applications, procedures information,* (202) 564-4763, FAX (202) 565-2903.

Internet: www.epa.gov/ord/htm/grantopportunity.htm.

66.511 OFFICE OF RESEARCH AND DEVELOPMENT CONSOLIDATED RESEARCH/TRAINING

Assistance: project grants. (100 percent/to 5 years).

Purposes: pursuant to CAA, CWA, SWDA, RCRA, SDWA, FIFRA, TSCA, CERCLA, amendments, and MPRSA, for research and engineering to determine the environmental effects of air quality, drinking water, water quality, hazardous waste, toxic substances, and pesticides; to identify, develop, and demonstrate effective pollution control techniques; to perform risk assessments to characterize the potential adverse health effects of human exposures to environmental hazards—in broad areas such as environmental chemistry and physics, environmental engineering, health and ecological effects of pollution, environmental economics and decision sciences. Generally, unsolicited proposals are not funded.

Eligible applicants/beneficiaries: state, local, tribal governments and agencies; territories, possessions; IHEs, hospitals, laboratories, nonprofit organizations; individuals.

Range: $75,000 to $950,000. **Average:** $250,000.

Activity: annually, 125 awards.

HQ: Office of Research and Development-EPA, 1200 Pennsylvania Ave. NW, Washington, DC 20460 Phone: *applications, procedures information,* (202) 564-4763, FAX (202) 565-2903.

Internet: www.epa.gov/ord/htm/grantopportunity.htm.

66.512 REGIONAL ENVIRONMENTAL MONITORING AND ASSESSMENT PROGRAM (REMAP) RESEARCH PROJECTS ("REMAP Research Projects")

Assistance: project grants.

Purposes: pursuant to the Clean Water Act, Section 104, as amended, for statistical monitoring of the conditions of national ecological resources, toward the testing of the applicability of EMAP's probalistic approach to answer questions about ecological conditions at regional and local levels—resulting in improved monitoring tools and probability-based data for resolving issues.

Eligible applicants/beneficiaries: states, territories, possessions, local and tribal governments; IHEs, hospitals, other nonprofit organizations; consortia.

Range: incremental funding for new projects, $92,000 to $192,000; incremental funding for previously awarded projects, $89,000 to $192,000. **Average:** new projects, $172,000.

Activity: new program listing in 2005; FY 05, 6 awards anticipated.

HQ: Mid-Continent Ecology Division, Office of Research and Development-EPA, 6201 Congdon Blvd., Duluth, MN 55804 Phone: *applications, procedures information,* (218) 529-5198; *administrative questions,* (218) 529-5016.

Internet: www.epa.gov/emap/remap.

66.513 GREATER RESEARCH OPPORTUNITIES (GRO) FELLOWSHIPS FOR UNDERGRADUATE/GRADUATE ENVIRONMENTAL STUDY

Assistance: project grants (100 percent).

Purposes: pursuant to CAA, CWA, SWDA, SDWA, TSCA, and FIFRA, to provide graduate and undergraduate fellowships in fields of study related to the environment, including environmental engineering, atmospheric sciences, geology, economics, geography, urban/regional planning, biochemistry, biological sciences, genetics, public health, ecological sciences, and related fields—to strengthen the research capacity especially of IHEs that receive limited funding in the field, including particularly institutions with substantial minority enrollment. Two years of study in specific disciplines may be supported for undergraduates and master's students; doctoral candidates, for three years. Awards are competitive.

Eligible applicants/beneficiaries: U.S. citizens and lawfully admitted permanent residents demonstrating high scientific ability.

Range: per fellowship: undergraduates, $30,000 to $41,500; graduates, $55,000 to $110,000. **Average:** undergraduates, $35,000; graduates, $33,386.

Activity: new program listing in 2004; FY 06, 15 new undergraduate awards, 21 new graduate awards.

HQ: *Grants management information*: Grants Administration Division (3903R), EPA, 1200 Pennsylvania Ave. NW, Washington, DC 20460 Phone: *graduate fellowships information,* (202) 343-9737, FAX (202)

343-0680; *undergraduate fellowships information,* (202) 343-9741, FAX (202) 343-0680.

Internet: www.epa.gov/ncer (Note: no field offices for this program.)

66.514 SCIENCE TO ACHIEVE RESULTS (STAR) FELLOWSHIP PROGRAM ("STAR Program")

Assistance: project grants (100 percent).

Purposes: pursuant to CAA, CWA, SWDA, SDWA, TSCA, and FIFRA, to provide graduate fellowships in the fields of study cited under **66.514**. Two years of study may be supported for master's students; doctoral candidates, for three years. Awards are competitive.

Eligible applicants/beneficiaries: U.S. citizens and lawfully admitted permanent residents demonstrating high scientific ability.

Range: $55,000 to $111,000 total per fellowship. **Average:** $80,000.

Activity: new program listing in 2004; FY 05, 135 awards.

HQ: *Grants management information*: Grants Administration Division (3903R), EPA, 1200 Pennsylvania Ave. NW, Washington, DC 20460 Phone: *graduate fellowships information,* (202) 343-9737, FAX (202) 343-0680; *undergraduate fellowships information,* (202) 343-9741, FAX (202) 343-0680.

Internet: www.epa.gov/ncer (Note: no field offices for this program.)

66.515 GREATER OPPORTUNITIES: RESEARCH PROGRAM

Assistance: project grants (2-5 years).

Purposes: pursuant to CAA, CWA, SWDA, RCRA, SDWA, TSCA, and FIFRA, to stimulate and nurture environmental and educational opportunities at IHEs that receive limited funding in environmental fields, particularly institutions with substantial minority enrollment. Projects are invited for research concerning the applications of nanotechnology in environmentally benign manufacturing and processing, monitoring devices and sensors, and treatment and remediation technology. Generally, awards are made only in response to requests for competitive proposals; unsolicited proposals are not funded. Eligible beneficiaries/beneficiaries: four-year IHEs as described under "Purposes".

Eligible applicants/beneficiaries: U.S. public and private nonprofit institutions/organizations including four-year IHEs as described under "Purposes".

Range: $275,000 to $350,000 total per grant. **Average:** $325,000.

Activity: new program listing in 2004; FY 05, 6 awards.

HQ: Grants Administration Division (3903R), EPA, 1200 Pennsylvania Ave. NW, Washington, DC 20460 Phone: (202) 343-9858, FAX (202) 233-0680.

Internet: www.epa.gov/ncer.

66.516 P3 AWARD: NATIONAL STUDENT DESIGN COMPETITION FOR SUSTAINABILITY

Assistance: project grants.

Purposes: pursuant to CAA, CWA, SWDA, SDWA, TSCA, and FIFRA, for design projects in wide-ranging categories, conducted by interdisciplinary student teams to: define a technical challenge to environmental sustainability; discuss the relationship of the challenge to people, prosperity, and the planet; and, develop a design approach to address the challenge. Categories may include such topics as water quality and quantity, protection of ecosystem health, green chemistry and engineering, biotechnology, energy production and distribution, conservation of materials and energy, product design, mobility, information technology, and delivery of resources.

Eligible applicants/beneficiaries: teams of graduate and undergraduate students attending U.S. IHEs (*For additional details, see request for applications at web site*: http://www.epa.gov.ncer).

Range: Phase I: $7,000 to $10,000; Phase II: $35,000 to $75,000. **Average:** Phase I: $9,800; Phase II: $69,000.

Activity: new program in FY 04. FY 05, Phase I, 41 awards; Phase II, 6 awards.

HQ: Grants Administration Division (3903R), EPA, 1200 Pennsylvania Ave. NW, Washington, DC 20460 Phone: (202) 343-9689, FAX (202) 233-0680.

Internet: www.epa.gov/ncer.

66.517 REGIONAL APPLIED RESEARCH EFFORTS (RARE)

Assistance: project grants (to 5 years).

Purposes: pursuant to National Environmental Policy Act of 1969, Clean Air Act, Clean Water Act, Solid Waste Disposal Act, Resource Conservation and Recovery Act of 1976, Safe Drinking Water Act, and others, as amended, to determine the environmental effects of air quality, drinking water, water quality, hazardous waste, toxic substances, and pesticides and identify, develop, and demonstrate effective pollution control techniques. Some funding priorities for Fiscal Year 2007 include: conducting high priority air pollutants research, ecological risk assessment, water quality, watersheds and drinking water research, research to improve human health (including children's) risk assessment, pollution prevention and new technologies. Assistance agreement awards under this program may involve or relate to geospatial information (refer to http://geodata.epa.gov).

Eligible applicants/beneficiaries: states, territories and possessions, and U.S. Tribal nations, including DC, public and private state universities and colleges, hospitals, laboratories, state and local government departments, other public or private nonprofit institutions, and in some cases, individuals who have demonstrated unusually high scientific ability.

Range: $20,000 to $100,000. **Average:** $60,000.

Activity: 5 grants per year.

HQ: EPA, 1200 Pennsylvania Ave. Washington, D.C. 20460. Phone: (202) 564-4763; FAX: (202) 565-2903.

Internet: http://www.epa.gov/ord/htm/grantopportunity.htm.

66.518 STATE SENIOR ENVIRONMENTAL EMPLOYMENT PROGRAM ("SSEE")

Assistance: project grants (100 percent/1-3 years).

Purposes: pursuant to the Environmental Programs Assistance Act of 1984, for states to employ Americans, age 55 or older, in temporary full- or part-time positions to provide technical assistance to federal, state, and local environmental agencies for projects involving pollution prevention, abatement, and control—ranging from inspections of large capacity cesspools to clerical work for environmental staff offices.

Eligible applicants: private, nonprofit organizations designated by the DOL secretary under OAA.

Eligible beneficiaries: state environmental agencies; individuals age 55 or older.

Average: $48,800.

Activity: new program listing in 2005. FY 04, 1 cooperative agreement (with the state of Hawaii); 1 additional amendment made in FY 05.

HQ: Director, SEE Program (3661A), Office of Administration and Resources Management, EPA, 1200 Pennsylvania Ave. NW, Washington, DC 20460 Director, SEE Program, (202) 564-0410, (202) 564-0735(Note: no field offices for this program.)

Internet: http://epa.gov/epahrist/see/brochure (Note: no field offices for this program.)

66.600 ENVIRONMENTAL PROTECTION CONSOLIDATED GRANTS—PROGRAM SUPPORT ("Consolidated Program Support Grants")

Assistance: project grants.

Purposes: pursuant to CAA, CWA, SWDA, RCRA, SDWA, FIFRA, SWDA, MPRSA, CERCLA, amendments, and other acts, to provide an alternative funding mechanism to territories and possessions within the purview of EPA Regions 2 and 9 to develop an integrated approach to pollution control programs, by consolidating activities funded under such programs as **66.001**, **66.418**, **66.419**, **66.432**, **66.433**, **66.454**, **66.468**, **66.473**, **66.700**, **66.801**. Applicants eligible for two or more of the programs may consolidate applications into one, and receive a single total award. Funding for this program is the aggregate total of the programs that may be consolidated; it is not appropriated separately.

Eligible applicants/beneficiaries: agencies in territories and possessions within the purview of EPA Regions 2 and 9.

Range: $2,000,000 to $4,000,000 per territory/per fiscal year. **Average:** $8,500,000 total per fiscal year.

Activity: N.A.

HQ: *for information on programs of interest, contact appropriate HQ or field offices for individual programs..*

Internet: Region 2, www.epa.gov.region2; Region 9, www.epa.gov/region9.

66.604 ENVIRONMENTAL JUSTICE SMALL GRANT PROGRAM ("EJCGP")

Assistance: project grants. (100 percent/2 years).

Purposes: pursuant to pursuant to CWA, SDWA, SWDA, CAA, TSCA, FIFRA, MPRSA, AND CERCLA, to design, demonstrate, or disseminate practices, methods, or techniques related to environmental justice, including multi-media projects. Funding is available for activities that examine issues related to a community's exposure to multiple environmental harms and risks, extending to socio- economic, institutional, and public policy issues and the natural sciences. Research training may be supported. Ineligible uses of funds include: research related only to contamination from petroleum products unless other issues also are involved; organizational support; capacity building; program development; any construction activities; lobbying; underwriting legal actions.

Eligible applicants/beneficiaries: only affected nonprofit, incorporated community-based organizations unaffiliated with larger national, state, or regional organizations.

Average: $50,000.

Activity: FY 05, 25 awards.

HQ: Office of Environmental Justice (2201A), EPA, 1200 Pennsylvania Ave. NW, Washington, DC 20460 Phone: (202) 564-2602, FAX (202) 501-1162; Environmental Justice Hotline, (800) 962-6215.

Internet: www.epa.gov/compliance/environmentaljustice/grants.

66.605 PERFORMANCE PARTNERSHIP GRANTS ("PPGs")

Assistance: formula grants; project grants.

Purposes: to provide an alternative assistance delivery mechanism giving grant recipients greater flexibility in addressing environmental priorities; to improve environmental performance; to achieve savings in administrative costs; and, to strengthen partnerships between EPA and grant recipients. For application and administrative purposes, recipients may combine two or more grant programs specifically identified by EPA. Funding for this program is included in the grant programs that may be involved; it is not appropriated separately.

Eligible applicants/beneficiaries: states, interstate agencies; territories; tribes—eligible to combine two or more of 20 specific EPA categorical grant programs.

Average: N.A.

Activity: FY 05, 125 grants, including 38 to state environmental agencies, 29 to state agricultural agencies, and 58 to tribal agencies.

HQ: Office of Congressional and Intergovernmental Relations (1306A), Office of the Administrator-EPA, 1200 Pennsylvania Ave. NW, Washington DC 20460 Phone: Program Manager, (202) 564-3792, FAX (202) 501-1545; *tribes,* Office of Water, American Indian Environmental Office Phone: (202) 564-0303, FAX (202) 564-0298.

Internet: www.epa.gov/ocir.

66.608 ENVIRONMENTAL INFORMATION EXCHANGE NETWORK GRANT PROGRAM AND RELATED ASSISTANCE

Assistance: project grants. (100 percent/2 years).

Purposes: to develop a nationwide Environmental Information Exchange Network, an internet- and standards-based information network—facilitating electronic reporting, exchange, and integration of environmental data from many sources, concerning the natural environment and related human health issues. Funds support development of: related information technology infrastructure and management capabilities; exchanging data with EPA and other users, through the development of data standards and formats; collaborative innovative projects address the business needs of government agencies at all levels.

Eligible applicants/beneficiaries: states, territories and possessions, tribes and tribal consortia; authorized regional air pollution control agencies.

Range: Environmental Program & Management (EPM): $100,00 to $258,000 for two years; State & Tribal Air Grants (STAG): $75,000 to $1,000,000 for two years. **Average:** STAG: $300,000; EPM: $179,000.

Activity: FY 05 estimate, 60 awards to all states, DC, 3 territories and 40 tribes.

HQ: Program Manager, Office of Information Collection, Office of Environmental Information (2823T), EPA, 1200 Pennsylvania Ave. NW, Washington, DC 20460 Phone: (202) 566-0196, -2142, FAX (202) 566-1684, -1624.

Internet: www.epa.gov/oei (Note: no field offices for this program.)

66.609 PROTECTION OF CHILDREN AND OLDER ADULTS (ELDERLY) FROM ENVIRONMENTAL HEALTH RISKS ("Children's Environmental Health and the Aging Initiative")

Assistance: project grants (cost sharing/to 5 years).

Purposes: pursuant to CAA, CWA, SDWA, TSCA, SWDA, FIFRA, MPRSA, CERCLA, and National Environmental Policy Act, to reduce environmental health threats to children or the elderly, through such activities as: supporting efforts to create health school environments; building capacity to address childhood asthma and other children's environmental health issues, as well as to reduce environmental health hazards affecting older persons; implementing a National Agenda for the Environment and the Aging to help protect the health of older persons; civic engagement in pertinent activities and projects; related international efforts; public outreach and communications.

Eligible applicants/beneficiaries: states and state agencies, territories and possessions, tribes, IHEs, hospitals, laboratories, public and private nonprofit organizations.

Range: $5,000 to $150,000. **Average:** aging initiatives, $23,000; children, $49,000; health professionals for children, $145,000.

Activity: FY 05, 19 awards to aging initiatives, 7 awards for child-related projects.

HQ: Office of Children's Health Protection (1107A), Office of the Administrator-EPA, 1200 Pennsylvania Ave. NW, Washington, DC 20460 Phone: FAX (202) 564-2763; Children's Health, (202) 564- 2192; Aging Initiative, (202) 564-3651.

Internet: www.epa.gov/children (Note: no field offices for this program.)

66.610 SURVEYS, STUDIES, INVESTIGATIONS AND SPECIAL PURPOSE GRANTS WITHIN THE OFFICE OF THE ADMINISTRATOR

Assistance: project grants. (cost sharing/to 5 years).

Purposes: pursuant to CAA, CWA, SDWA, TSCA, SWDA, FIFRA, MPRSA, CERCLA, and National Environmental Policy Act, for surveys, studies, investigations, and special purpose assistance associated with air quality, acid deposition, drinking water quality, hazardous waste, toxic substances, and pesticides; to identify, develop and demonstrate necessary pollution control techniques; to evaluate the economic and social consequences of alternative strategies and mechanisms. Current funding priorities include: providing environmental health information and analysis to state legislatures; building state capacity to reduce environmental hazards affecting health and the environment; supporting environmental education training.

Eligible applicants/beneficiaries: states and state agencies, territories and possessions, tribes, IHEs, hospitals, laboratories, public and private nonprofit organizations.

Range: $500 to $500,000. **Average:** $150,000.

Activity: not quantified specifically.

HQ: *grants management information*: Grants Administration Division (3903R), EPA, 1200 Pennsylvania Ave. NW, Washington, DC 20460 Phone: (202) 343-9689, FAX (202) 233-0680 *Program information,* Office of the Administrator-EPA Phone: (202) 564-1347, FAX (202) 564-2733.

Internet: www.epa.gov/adminweb (Note: no field offices for this program.)

66.611 ENVIRONMENTAL POLICY AND INNOVATION GRANTS

Assistance: project grants (cost sharing/to 5 years). (cost sharing/to 5 years).

Purposes: pursuant to CAA, CWA, SDWA, TSCA, SWDA, FIFRA, and CERCLA, for analyses, studies, evaluations, and conferences leading to reduced pollutants generated and to conservation of natural resources; to improve economic information and analytic methods to support studies, surveys, analyses, evaluations, conferences, workshops, and demonstration projects relating to the benefits, costs, and impacts of environmental programs, as well as of incentive-based and voluntary environmental management strategies and mechanisms. Current funding priorities include innovative projects relating to smart growth, performance result demonstrations, economic analysis, economic analytical and statistical methods development.

Eligible applicants/beneficiaries: states, tribes, territories, possessions; IHEs, hospitals, laboratories, other public or private nonprofit institutions; individuals.

Range: $15,000 to $200,000. **Average:** $45,000.

Activity: not quantified specifically.

HQ: *grants information,* Grants Administration Division (3903R), EPA, 1200 Pennsylvania Ave. NW, Washington, DC 20460 Phone: (202) 343-9689, FAX (202) 233-0680 *Program information,* Office of Policy, Economics and Innovation, Office of the Administrator-EPA, (202) 566-0949, FAX (202) 566- 3001.

Internet: www.epa.gov/opei.

66.612 SURVEYS, STUDIES, INVESTIGATIONS, TRAINING DEMONSTRATIONS AND EDUCATIONAL OUTREACH RELATED TO ENVIRONMENTAL INFORMATION AND THE RELEASE OF TOXIC CHEMICALS

Assistance: project grants.

Purposes: pursuant to the Clean Water Act, Federal Insecticide, Fungicide, and Rodenticide Act, Clean Air Act, Solid Waste Disposal Act, Safe Drinking Water Act, Toxic Substances Control Act, to provide funding in support of surveys, studies, investigations, training/demonstrations, educational outreach and special purpose assistance as they relate to environmental information and the release of toxic chemicals.

Eligible applicants: states, District of Columbia, U.S. territories, federally recognized Indian tribes and intertribal consortia, public and private colleges and universities, and other public or private nonprofit organizations. Nonprofit organizations exempt from taxation under Section 501(c)(4) of the Internal Revenue Code that lobby are not eligible for financial assistance.

Eligible beneficiaries: general public; state, territory, city, town, county, regional governments, federally recognized Indian tribes and intertribal consortia, and public institutions and industries subject to EPA regulatory reporting requirements.

Range: $15,000 to $350,000. **Average:** $200,000.

Activity: N.A.

HQ: Grants and Interagency Agreements Management Division, EPA, 3903R, Washington, DC 20460. Phone: (202) 566-1230.

Internet: www.epa.gov/oei.

66.700 CONSOLIDATED PESTICIDE ENFORCEMENT COOPERATIVE AGREEMENTS

Assistance: project grants (100 percent).

Purposes: pursuant to FIFRA as amended, to develop and maintain comprehensive pesticide programs addressing all aspects of enforcement, and special initiatives; to sponsor cooperative surveillance, monitoring, and analytical procedures; to encourage state regulatory activities. Funding priorities include: worker protection; pesticides used to protect public health; inspection of production facilities, retailing, and application practices; civil and criminal prosecution of violations. Grant funds may be used to pay for inspection and laboratory equipment and supplies, personnel salaries, other administrative costs.

Eligible applicants/beneficiaries: state agencies, territories and possessions, tribes.

Range: $32,000 to $747,000. **Average:** $250,000.

Activity: annually, 85 awards.

HQ: Office of Compliance, OECA-EPA, (MC 2225A), 1200 Pennsylvania Ave. NW, Washington, DC 20460 Phone: (202) 564-5033, FAX (202) 564-0085.

Internet: www.epa.gov/compliance.

66.701 TOXIC SUBSTANCES COMPLIANCE MONITORING COOPERATIVE AGREEMENTS

Assistance: project grants (75-100 percent).

Purposes: pursuant to TSCA as amended, to: establish and operate compliance toxic substance monitoring and enforcement programs, including PCBs, asbestos in schools, lead-based paint, and sector-based activities; encourage state regulatory activities; establish worker training and accreditation standards. Grant funds may cover costs of inspection supplies and equipment, personnel, and administration.

Eligible applicants/beneficiaries: state agencies, territories and possessions, tribes.

Range: $18,000 to $208,000. **Average:** $102,000.

Activity: annually, 74 awards.

HQ: OECA-EPA, 1200 Pennsylvania Ave. NW, Washington, DC 20460 Phone: *PCB, asbestos programs,* Chief, National Compliance Monitoring Policy Branch (2223A), Compliance Assessment and Media Programs Division, (202) 564-4131, FAX (202) 564-0050; *lead-based paint program information,* (202) 564-7037, FAX (202) 564-0009.

Internet: www.epa.gov/compliance.

66.707 TSCA TITLE IV STATE LEAD GRANTS CERTIFICATION OF LEAD-BASED PAINT PROFESSIONALS ("State Lead Certification Grants")

Assistance: project grants.

Purposes: pursuant to TSCA as amended, to develop and conduct accredited training and certification programs for persons and contractors engaged in lead-based paint activities, and accredit training programs; for pre-renovation education programs, requiring distribution of lead-hazard information prior to building renovations.

Eligible applicants/beneficiaries: state agencies, territories and possessions, tribes.

Range: $16,000 to $350,000. **Average:** $200,000.

Activity: as of May, 2006, 39 states, PR, DC and 3 tribes with approved training and certification programs, 2 states with pre-renovation education programs.

HQ: Director, National Program Chemicals Division (7404T), Office of Pollution Prevention and Toxics, OPPTS-EPA, 1200 Pennsylvania Ave. NW, Washington, DC 20460 Phone: (202) 566-0500, FAX (202) 566-0470.

Internet: www.epa.gov/lead.

66.708 POLLUTION PREVENTION GRANTS PROGRAM ("PPIS Grant Program")

Assistance: project grants. (50 percent/to 3 years).

Purposes: pursuant to the Pollution Prevention Act of 1990, to support two programs. Pollution Prevention Grants ("P2cover innovative activities promoting preventative approaches to environmental performance and addressing various sectors of concern, including industrial toxics, agriculture, energy, transportation; projects focus on institutionalizing multimedia pollution prevention, establishing prevention goals, providing direct technical assistance and outreach to businesses, and collecting and analyzing data. Pollution Prevention Information Network ("PPIN Grants seek to coordinate work among technical assistance providers, to minimize duplication of effort in information collection, synthesis, dissemination, and training.

Eligible applicants/beneficiaries: state agencies and universities, territories and possessions, tribes. Participation is encouraged through partnerships with business and other environmental assistance providers.

Range: $20,000 to $140,000. **Average:** $80,000.

Activity: annually, 60 P2, 10 PPIN grants awarded.

HQ: Pollution Prevention Division, Office of Pollution Prevention, Pesticides and Toxics (7409-M), OPPTS-EPA, 1200 Pennsylvania Ave. NW, Washington, DC 20460 Phone: (202) 564-8857, FAX (202) 564-8899.

Internet: P2 Grants, *www.epa.gov/oppt/p2home/grants/ppis/ppis.htm; PPIN Grants, www.epa.gov/oppt/p2home/grants/ppin/ppin.htm.*

66.709 MULTI-MEDIA CAPACITY BUILDING GRANTS FOR STATES AND TRIBES

Assistance: project grants (100 percent/2-3 years).

Purposes: pursuant to CWA, FIFRA, CAA, SWDA, SDWA, TSCA, MPRSA, National Environmental Policy Act, and Indian Environmental General Assistance Program Act, to build and improve capacity to foster environmental enforcement and compliance assurance activities—including through economic, social science, statistical research, development, studies, demonstrations, investigations, public education, training, and fellowships. Program emphasis: inspector training, program planning and performance measurement, outcome measurement, public access to information, data management, permit compliance system modernization.

Eligible applicants/beneficiaries: state agencies, territories, multijurisdictional state organizations, tribes; certain state or tribal IHEs.

Range: $35,000 to $278,000. **Average:** $130,000.

Activity: FY 04, 12 projects funded.

HQ: Office of Compliance, OECA-EPA, 1200 Pennsylvania Ave. NW, Washington, DC 20460 Phone: (202) 564-8318, FAX (202) 564-0034.

Internet: www.epa.gov/compliance/state/grants/stag/index.html.

66.714 PESTICIDE ENVIRONMENTAL STEWARDSHIP REGIONAL GRANTS ("PESP Regional Grants")

Assistance: project grants. (100 percent/to 2 years).

Purposes: pursuant to FIFRA as amended, to reduce risk from the use of pesticides in agricultural and nonagricultural settings, through research, monitoring, demonstration, and related activities.

Eligible applicants/beneficiaries: states, state universities, territories, possessions, tribes.

Range: $20,000 to $50,000. **Average:** $50,000.

Activity: FY 05, 10 grants.

HQ: Pesticide Environmental Stewardship Program, Biopesticides and Pollution Prevention Division (7511-C), OPPTS-EPA, 1200 Pennsylvania Ave. NW, Washington, DC 20460 Phone: (703) 308-8107, (800) 972-7717, FAX (703) 308-7026.

Internet: www.epa.gov/oppbppd1/PESP/regional_grants.html.

66.715 TRIBAL EDUCATIONAL OUTREACH ON LEAD POISONING AND BASELINE ASSESSMENT OF TRIBAL CHILDREN'S EXISTING AND POTENTIAL EXPOSURE AND RISKS ASSOCIATED WITH LEAD ("Tribal Lead Grants")

Assistance: project grants. (100 percent/2 years).

Purposes: pursuant to TSCA as amended, for activities relating to blood-lead screening of tribal children; for outreach to educate Indian families about lead-based paint hazards.

Eligible applicants/beneficiaries: tribes, tribal consortia.

Range: assessment projects, to $75,000; outreach/education, to $75,900. **Average:** assessment, $54,771; outreach/education, $47,634.

Activity: FY 05, 17 grants; FY 06 estimate, 15-25 awards.

HQ: Director, National Program Chemicals Division (7404T), Office of Pollution Prevention and Toxics, OPPTS-EPA, 1200 Pennsylvania Ave. NW, Washington, DC 20460 Phone: (202) 566-0516, FAX (202) 566- 0469.

Internet: www.epa.gov/lead.

66.716 SURVEYS, STUDIES, INVESTIGATIONS, TRAINING DEMONSTRATIONS AND EDUCATIONAL OUTREACH

Assistance: project grants.

Purposes: pursuant to FIFRA and TSCA, to protect the public health, the environment, ecosystems, and most threatened species from potential risk from future toxic chemicals; to explore such emerging issues as risks to the environment and ecosystems from biotechnology, endocrine disrupters, and lead poisoning.

Eligible applicants/beneficiaries: states, territories, possessions, tribal governments, native American organizations; public and private IHEs, hospitals, laboratories, and other nonprofit institutions; individuals.

Range: $1,000 to $1,500,000. **Average:** $500,000.

Activity: FY 05, Office of Pesticide Programs (OPP): 13 awards.

HQ: *grants management information*: Grants Administration Division (3903R), EPA, 1200 Pennsylvania Ave. NW, Washington, DC 20460 Phone: *Program information,* Immediate Office, OPPTS, (202) 564-0547, FAX (202) 564-0550; Office of Pollution Prevention and Toxics, (202) 564-0911, FAX (202) 564-8251; Office of Pesticide Programs, (703) 3057711, FAX (702) 305-5060; Office of Science Coordination Policy, (202) 564-8430, FAX (202) 564-8452.

Internet: www.epa.gov/oppts.html.

66.717 SOURCE REDUCTION ASSISTANCE

Assistance: project grants. (95 percent/to 2 years).

Purposes: pursuant to CAA, CWA, FIFRA, SDWA, SWDA, TSCA, amendments, and Executive Orders, for source reduction, pollution prevention, and resource conservation activities that: promote integration of pollution prevention into environmental media regulatory programs; disseminate pollution prevention news, innovative technologies, and technical assistance; encourage and promote activities to assist in the purchasing of environmentally preferable products and services; support the pollution prevention information network through work in measurement of "P2" information activities and services (re: **66.708**).

Eligible applicants/beneficiaries: state, local, tribal, and special districts governments, territories and possessions, independent school districts, state IHEs, nonprofits including community-based grassroots organizations.

Range: $5,000 to $100,000. **Average:** $70,000.

Activity: FY 05, 30 awards.

HQ: Pollution Prevention Division, Office of Pollution Prevention, Pesticides and Toxics (7409-M), OPPTS-EPA, 1200 Pennsylvania Ave. NW, Washington, DC 20460 Phone: (202) 564-8857, FAX (202) 564-8899.

Internet: www.epa.gov/oppt/p2home/grants/index.htm.

66.718 NATIONAL COMMUNITY-BASED LEAD OUTREACH AND TRAINING GRANT PROGRAM

Assistance: project grants (100 percent).

Purposes: pursuant to Toxic Substances Control Act (TSCA), to reduce childhood lead poisoning by providing outreach to low income communities. For fiscal year 2008, funding preference will be given to outreach activities identifying children's risks to lead hazards.

Eligible applicants: local governments; national, community-based, nonprofit, and faith-based organizations; community action agencies, institutions of higher learning, school groups, trainers, and environmental consultants.

Eligible beneficiaries: local, public nonprofit institutions or organizations, health and education professionals, builders, contractors, developers, homeowners, property owners, preschools, low income residents and communities.

Range: $76,925 to $250,000. **Average:** $207,802.

Activity: FY 07, 80 proposals received, 15 awards granted; FY 08 and FY 09, anticipated: 50 to 80 proposals yielding 6 to 8 grants totally $2 million.

HQ: National Program Chemical Division (7404T), OPPTS-EPA, 1200 Pennsylvania Ave. NW, Washington, DC 20460-0001. Phone: (202) 566-0516, FAX: (202) 566-0469.

Internet: www.epa.gov/lead.

66.801 HAZARDOUS WASTE MANAGEMENT STATE PROGRAM SUPPORT

Assistance: formula grants (75 percent).

Purposes: pursuant to SWDA and RCRA as amended, to develop and implement authorized hazardous waste management programs to control the generation, transportation, treatment, storage, and disposal of hazardous wastes, including: permitting; oversight of corrective actions; facilities inspection; inspection of wastes generators; waste minimization.

Eligible applicants/beneficiaries: state agencies, territories, possessions.

Range: $200,000 to $8,400,000. **Average:** $2,080,000.

Activity: not quantified specifically.

HQ: Office of Solid Waste (5303W), OSWER-EPA, Washington, DC 20460 Phone: (703) 308-8630, FAX (703) 308-8609; *Grants management information*: Grants Administration Division (3903R), EPA, 1200 Pennsylvania Ave. NW, Washington, DC 20460.

Internet: www.epa.gov/epaoswer/osw.

66.802 SUPERFUND STATE, POLITICAL SUBDIVISION, AND INDIAN TRIBE SITE-SPECIFIC COOPERATIVE AGREEMENTS ("Superfund")

Assistance: project grants (50-100 percent; tribes, 100 percent).

Purposes: pursuant to CERCLA as amended, to conduct site characterization activities at potential or confirmed hazardous waste sites; to undertake remedial planning and implementation at sites on the National Priorities List (NPL) of the National Oil and Hazardous Substances Contingency Plan. Project funds may be used to: conduct nontime-critical removal actions; inspect, assess, investigate, study, and prepare remedial designs; conduct remedial actions at uncontrolled sites listed on the NPL;

identify responsible parties, conduct settlement negotiations, and take enforcement actions. Matching fund requirements: none if site was privately owned and operated at time of waste disposal prior to development of the NPL, and 10 percent for subsequent activities; 50 percent for sites state or locally operated; 10 percent for infrastructure development.

Eligible applicants/beneficiaries: states, political subdivisions, tribal governments, territories and possessions.

Range: $30,000 to $1,000,000. **Average:** $500,000.

Activity: not quantified specifically.

HQ: State, Tribe and Site Identification Branch, Assessment and Remediation Division, Office of Superfund Remediation and Technology Innovation (5204G), OSWER-EPA, Washington, DC 20460 Phone: (703) 299-3438, FAX (703) 299-3438.

Internet: www.epa.gov/superfund.

66.804 STATE AND TRIBAL UNDERGROUND STORAGE TANKS PROGRAM ("UST Program")

Assistance: formula grants (75 percent; tribes, 100 percent).

Purposes: pursuant to SWDA, RCRA, Demonstration Cities and Metropolitan Development Act, and amendments, to develop and implement underground hazardous substances storage tank programs to operate in lieu of the federal program. Funds may be used to: promote effective compliance; ensure routine and correct monitoring by owners and operators; establish state statutory and regulatory authority.

Eligible applicants/beneficiaries: state and territorial agencies, tribes, intertribal consortia.

Range: states/territories, $80,000 to $187,000; tribes/intertribal consortia, $20,000 to $150,000. **Average:** states/territories, $187,000; tribes/intertribal consortia, $62,000.

Activity: FY 05, 66 awards.

HQ: Immediate Office, Office of Underground Storage Tanks (5401G), OSWER-EPA, 1200 Pennsylvania Ave. NW, Washington, DC 20460 Phone: (703) 603-7148, FAX (703) 603-0175.

Internet: www.epa.gov/oust.

66.805 LEAKING UNDERGROUND STORAGE TANK TRUST FUND PROGRAM ("LUST")

Assistance: formula grants (90 percent; tribes, 100 percent).

Purposes: pursuant to SWDA, RCRA, Demonstration Cities and Metropolitan Development Act, and amendments, to correct releases of petroleum from underground storage tanks; to conduct related enforcement and cost recovery activities; to oversee clean-ups by responsible parties. Trust funds may be used for responses where tank owners and operators are unknown, unwilling, or unable to undertake corrective actions; owners and operators are liable to states for costs incurred when the trust fund is used, and are subject to cost recovery actions.

Eligible applicants/beneficiaries: state and territorial agencies, tribes, intertribal consortia.

Range: states/territories, $43,000 to $3,400,000; tribes, $22,000 to $140,000. **Average:** states, $910,000; territories, $45,000; tribes, $48,000.

Activity: FY 05, 50 states, 6 territories, 10 tribes funded; 14,000 clean-ups completed.

HQ: Immediate Office, Office of Underground Storage Tanks (5401G), OSWER-EPA, 1200 Pennsylvania Ave. NW, Washington, DC 20460 Phone: (703) 603-7148, FAX (703) 603-0175.

Internet: www.epa.gov/oust.

66.806 SUPERFUND TECHNICAL ASSISTANCE GRANTS (TAG) FOR COMMUNITY GROUPS AT NATIONAL PRIORITY LIST (NPL) SITES ("TAG")

Assistance: project grants. (from 80 percent/3 years).

Purposes: pursuant to CERCLA and SARA as amended, for community groups to hire technical advisors to assist in: interpreting technical information concerning the assessment of potential hazards at waste sites; selecting and designing appropriate remedies at sites eligible for clean-up under the Superfund program; providing community information. Grant funds may not pay the costs of developing new information, underwriting legal actions or political activity, or travel by recipients.

Eligible applicants/beneficiaries: qualified, incorporated groups affected by an actual or threatened release at any Superfund facility.

Average: initial award, $50,000.

Activity: cumulatively since 1988 program inception, 286 awards.

HQ: Community Involvement and Outreach Center, Office of Superfund Remediation and Technology Innovation (5204G), OSWER- EPA, 1200 Pennsylvania Ave. NW, Washington, DC 20460 Phone: (703) 603-8889, FAX (703) 603-9102.

Internet: www.epa.gov/superfund.

66.808 SOLID WASTE MANAGEMENT ASSISTANCE GRANTS

Assistance: project grants (95-100 percent/3 years).

Purposes: pursuant to SWDA and RCRA as amended, to promote use of integrated solid waste management systems to solve municipal generation and management problems at the local, regional, and national levels. Funds may be used for training, surveys, public education materials and programs, studies, and demonstrations. Funding priorities include developing partnerships and education and outreach activities.

Eligible applicants/beneficiaries: federal, state, interstate, intrastate, and local public authorities; private nonprofit organizations and agencies, institutions (including non-profit hospitals and educational institutions); tribes.

Range: $5,000 to $1,367,000. **Average:** $100,000.

Activity: FY 05, 75 project awards.

HQ: *grants management information*, Grants Administration Division (3903F), EPA, Washington, DC 20460 Phone: (202) 260- 9266 *Program information*, OSWER-EPA (5305W), Washington, DC 20460 Phone: (703) 308-8460, FAX(703) 308-7904.

Internet: www.epa.gov/epaoswer/osw.

66.809 SUPERFUND STATE AND INDIAN TRIBE CORE PROGRAM COOPERATIVE AGREEMENTS

Assistance: project grants (90 percent).

Purposes: pursuant to CERCLA as amended, for CERCLA response actions that are not site-specific. Funding supports personnel hiring and training, emergency response procedural planning, enforcement, legislative development.

Eligible applicants/beneficiaries: states, territories and possessions, tribal governments, tribal consortia.

Range: $50,000 to $500,000. **Average:** $200,000.

Activity: not quantified specifically.

HQ: State, Tribe and Site Identification Branch, Assessment and Remediation Division, Office of Superfund Remediation and Technology Innovation (5204G), OSWER-EPA, Washington, DC 20460 Phone: (703) 299-3438, FAX (703) 299-3438.

Internet: www.epa.gov/superfund.

66.810 CHEMICAL EMERGENCY PREPAREDNESS AND PREVENTION (CEPP) TECHNICAL ASSISTANCE GRANTS PROGRAM ("CAA Section 112 and SARA Title III State Grants Program")

Assistance: project grants. (75 percent/1-2 years).

Purposes: pursuant to CAA and TSCA, for chemical accident emergency preparedness and prevention planning (CEPP) activities relating to the Risk Management Program under CAA; for community right-to-know programs established to prevent or eliminate unreasonable risk to community health and environment. Funding priorities are: capacity building to implement and enforce CAA chemical accident prevention provisions, and to integrate chemical accident prevention activities, planning efforts, and community right-to-know programs; community issues; and, partnerships among states and tribes and local emergency planning committees, industry, emergency responders, and the general public. Project funds may be used to develop technical assistance and materials to be used directly or by others. Project examples: educational videos; Hazardous Vulnerability Analysis Plans.

Eligible applicants: states, local agencies, tribes, DC, PR, VI, Northern Marianas.

Eligible beneficiaries: local emergency planning committees, local emergency responders.

Range: $20,000 to $30,000. **Average:** $25,000 per one year award.

Activity: FY 05, 3 awards; FY 06-07 estimate, 3 awards.

HQ: Grant Program Manager, Office of Emergency Management (5104A), OSWER-EPA, 1200 Pennsylvania Ave. NW, Washington, DC 20460 Phone: (202) 564-6174, FAX (202) 564-8211.

Internet: www.epa.gov/emergencies.

66.812 HAZARDOUS WASTE MANAGEMENT GRANT PROGRAM FOR TRIBES

Assistance: project grants (100 percent).

Purposes: to develop and implement hazardous waste management programs, including: building capacity to improve and maintain regulatory compliance; developing solutions to address waste mismanagement affecting tribal lands.

Eligible applicants/beneficiaries: tribal governments, including those involving Alaska natives; consortia.

Range: $18,000 to $100,000. **Average:** $56,000.

Activity: FY 05, 6 awards.

HQ: Office of Solid Waste (5303W), OSWER-EPA, Washington, DC 20460 Phone: (703) 308-8458, FAX (703) 308- 8638.

Internet: www.epa.gov/tribalmsw; *grants information,* www.epa.gov/ogd.

66.813 ALTERNATIVE OR INNOVATIVE TREATMENT TECHNOLOGY RESEARCH, DEMONSTRATION, TRAINING, AND HAZARDOUS SUBSTANCE RESEARCH GRANTS

Assistance: project grants. (cost sharing/to 5 years).

Purposes: pursuant to CERCLA as amended, for programs involving: research, evaluation, testing, development, and demonstration of alternative or innovative treatment technologies that may be used in response actions to achieve more permanent protection of human health and welfare and the environment; technology transfer including the development, collection, evaluation, coordination, and dissemination of information for response action; training and evaluation of training needs in handling and removal of hazardous substances; research on the detection, assessment, and evaluation of human health and environmental risks of hazardous substances.

Eligible applicants/beneficiaries: states, territories, possessions, tribes; public and private IHEs, hospitals, laboratories, and other nonprofits; individuals; certain projects by profit organizations.

Range: $30,000 to $50,000. **Average:** $40,000.

Activity: FY 05, 16 grants.

HQ: *grants information,* Grants Administration Division (3903R), EPA, 1200 Pennsylvania Ave. NW—3903R, Washington, DC 20460 Phone: (no number provided) *Program information,* Contracts Management Branch, Resources Management Division 1200 Pennsylvania Ave. NW-5202G, Washington, DC 20460 Phone: (703) 603-9042, FAX (703) 603-9133.

Internet: www.epa.gov/superfund/index.htm.

66.814 BROWNFIELDS TRAINING, RESEARCH, AND TECHNICAL ASSISTANCE GRANTS AND COOPERATIVE AGREEMENTS

Assistance: project grants (to 100 percent/1-5 years).

Purposes: pursuant to CERCLA as amended, for training, research, and technical assistance to individuals and organizations to facilitate the inventory of brownfield properties, assessments, clean-up, community involvement, or site preparation. Grant matching requirements have not been established.

Eligible applicants/beneficiaries: general purpose local government units; land clearance authorities or other quasi- governmental entities operating under the supervision of, or as agent of a local government; regional councils or groups of local governments; redevelopment agencies established by state legislatures; tribes, Alaska native corporations, and the Metlakatla Indian Community; nonprofit organizations including IHEs.

Range: to $762,000. **Average:** $137,000.

Activity: FY 05, 6 new awards; incremental funding also provided for ongoing projects.

HQ: Office of Brownfields Cleanup and Redevelopment, OSWER-EPA, Washington, DC 20460 Phone: (202) 566-2777, FAX (202) 566-2757.

Internet: www.epa.gov/brownfields.

66.815 BROWNFIELD JOB TRAINING COOPERATIVE AGREEMENTS

Assistance: project grants. (to 100 percent/2 years).

Purposes: pursuant to CERCLA as amended, for training, research, and technical assistance to individuals and organizations to facilitate the inventory of brownfield properties, assessments, clean-up, community involvement, or site preparation. Proposed projects showing evidence of leveraged funding receive priority consideration for approval.

Eligible applicants/beneficiaries: general purpose local government units; land clearance authorities or other quasi- governmental entities operating under the supervision of, or as agent of a local government; regional councils or groups of local governments; redevelopment agencies established by state legislatures; tribes, Alaska native corporations, and the Metlakatla Indian Community; nonprofit organizations including IHEs.

Range: to $200,000. **Average:** $197,831.

Activity: FY 06, 12 grants.

HQ: Office of Brownfields Cleanup and Redevelopment, OSWER-EPA, Washington, DC 20460 Phone: (202) 566-2777, FAX (202) 566-2757.

Internet: www.epa.gov/brownfields.

66.816 HEADQUARTERS AND REGIONAL UNDERGROUND STORAGE TANKS PROGRAM

Assistance: project grants (100 percent/to 5 years).

Purposes: pursuant to SWDA, Hazardous and Solid Waste Amendments of 1984, SARA, RCRA, Demonstration Cities and Metropolitan Development Act, and amendments, for activities promoting the prevention, identification, corrective action, enforcement, and management of releases from underground storage tank systems, including: training on a regional and national scale; an "electronic newsletter" to provide technical information to state and tribal regulators, the general public, and the regulated community; state-federal partnerships providing technical assistance and forums for information exchange.

Eligible applicants/beneficiaries: public authorities including state, inter- and intrastate, tribal, intertribal, and local consortia; public and private nonprofit agencies and institutions.

Range: $138,000 to $220,300. **Average:** $180,000.

Activity: FY 05, 2 awards; FY 06, 1 award.

HQ: Immediate Office, Office of Underground Storage Tanks (5401G), OSWER-EPA, 1200 Pennsylvania Ave. NW, Washington, DC 20460 Phone: (703) 603-7148, FAX (703) 603-0175.

Internet: www.epa.gov/oust.

66.817 STATE AND TRIBAL RESPONSE PROGRAM GRANTS

Assistance: formula grants (80-100 percent).

Purposes: pursuant to CERCLA as amended and Small Business Liability Relief and Brownfields Revitalization Act, to establish or enhance state and tribal capacity for brownfields response programs; to capitalize revolving loan funds for clean-up activities; and, to support insurance mechanisms. Programs must ensure maintenance of a public record of completed projects and of planned sites. Applicants must provide a 20 percent share of the cost projects that capitalize a revolving loan fund; otherwise, the federal share is 100 percent.

Eligible applicants/beneficiaries: states and tribes.

Range: $50,000 to $1,500,000. **Average:** $500,000.

Activity: FY 05, 97 grants; FY 06 estimate, 90 grants.

HQ: Office of Brownfields Cleanup and Redevelopment, OSWER-EPA, Washington, DC 20460 Phone: (202) 566-2777, FAX (202) 566-2757.

Internet: www.epa.gov/brownsfields.

66.818 BROWNFIELDS ASSESSMENT AND CLEANUP COOPERATIVE AGREEMENTS

Assistance: project grants. (80-100 percent/3-5 years).

Purposes: pursuant to CERCLA as amended by the Small Business Liability Relief and Brownfields Revitalization Act, to conduct inventories, characterizations, assessments, planning, and community involvement activities related to brownfield sites; to capitalize revolving loan funds and provide subgrants (maximum, 40 percent of grants funds) for clean-up activities; to carry out clean-up activities at brownfield sites owned by the grant recipient. Assessment grants do not require matching funds; grants to establish revolving loan funds or provide subgrants require a 20 percent match, which may be waived by EPA in cases of financial hardship.

Eligible applicants/beneficiaries: general purpose local government units; land clearance authorities or other quasi- governmental entities operating under the supervision of, or as agent of a local government; regional councils or groups of local governments; redevelopment agencies established by state legislatures; tribes, Alaska native corporations, and the Metlakatla Indian Community; nonprofit organizations including IHEs.

Range: assessment grants, to $200,000 per site for sites contaminated by hazardous substances or pollutants; to $350,000 for sites contaminated by petroleum; revolving loan funds, to $1,000,000. **Average:** assessments, clean-ups, $200,000; revolving funds, $1,000,000.

Activity: FY 06, 292 grants awarded.

HQ: Office of Brownfields Cleanup and Redevelopment, OSWER-EPA, Washington, DC 20460 Phone: (202) 566-2777, FAX (202) 566-2757 Additional phone: (202) 566-2744; Superfund Call Center, (800) 553-7672.

Internet: wwww.epa.gov/brownfields.

66.926 INDIAN ENVIRONMENTAL GENERAL ASSISTANCE PROGRAM (GAP) ("GAP for Tribes")

Assistance: project grants. (100 percent/to 4 years).

Purposes: pursuant to the Indian Environmental General Assistance Program Act of 1992 as amended, to administer environmental regulatory programs on Indian lands; to provide EPA technical assistance in the development of multimedia programs to address environmental issues. Funds may be used: to plan, develop, and establish capability to implement environmental protection programs including development and implementation of solid and hazardous waste programs; to conduct assessments and monitoring; to foster compliance with federal environmental statutes. Project examples: water quality assessment program; environmental assessment inventory; establishment of environmental codes; radon and underground storage tank projects.

Eligible applicants/beneficiaries: tribal governments, including those involving Alaska natives; consortia.

Range: $75,000 to $400,000. **Average:** $110,000.

Activity: FY 05, 490 tribes benefited.

HQ: American Indian Environmental Office (4104M), EPA, 1200 Pennsylvania Ave. NW, Washington, DC 20460 Phone: (202) 564-0303, FAX (202) 564-0298.

Internet: www.epa.gov/indian/grant.htm.

66.931 INTERNATIONAL FINANCIAL ASSISTANCE PROJECTS SPONSORED BY THE OFFICE OF INTERNATIONAL AFFAIRS

Assistance: project grants. (to 100 percent/to 5 years).

Purposes: pursuant to CWA, SWDA, RCRA, CAA, TSCA, FIFRA, SDWA, amendments, National Environmental Policy Act, and MPRSA, for multilateral international efforts to reduce significant risks to human health and ecosystems, caused by pollution that crosses national boundaries—including: issues concerning air quality, water, and toxins relating to the borders between the U.S. and Mexico, Canada (particularly the Great Lakes region), and the Arctic region; reviews and analytical studies of environmental aspects of international trade issues; and, providing technical assistance, capacity building, and on-the-ground projects in priority countries—including those conducted in cooperation with such organizations as the World Health Organization and the United Nations Environment Program, concerning such issues as global climate and clean fuels.

Eligible applicants/beneficiaries: states, territories, possessions, tribes; public and private IHEs, hospitals, laboratories, and other nonprofit organizations.

Range: $15,000 to $325,000. **Average:** $90,000.

Activity: FY 05, 6 new grants; FY 06 estimate, 5 new grants.

HQ: *grants information,* Grants Administration Division (3903R), EPA, 1200 Pennsylvania Ave. NW, Washington, DC 20460 Phone: (no number provided) *Program information,* Office of International Affairs-EPA, 1200 Pennsylvania Ave. NW, Washington, DC. Phone: (202) 564-6614, FAX (202) 565-2408.

Internet: www.oia.epa.gov (Note: no field offices for this program.)

66.940 ENVIRONMENTAL POLICY AND STATE INNOVATION GRANTS

Assistance: project grants. (100 percent/to 4 years).

Purposes: pursuant to CAA, CWA, SWDA, SDWA, TSCA, FIFRA, CERCLA, and amendments, for projects involving: analyses, studies, evaluations, and conferences leading to reduced generation of pollutants and conservation of natural resources; promotion of comprehensive cross-media approaches; encouragement and promotion of stewardship programs reflecting "beyond compliance" performance and offering incentives for superior environmental performance; systems-oriented change enabling better results from programs, processes, or sector-wide innovation; building in measurement and evaluation essential to transferability of the innovation.

Eligible applicants/beneficiaries: state environmental regulatory agencies including in territories and possessions. (EPA may make a separate competition available to federally certified Tribes.)

Range: $50,000 to $300,000. **Average:** $180,000.

Activity: new program in FY 05. FY 06 estimate, 7 awards.

HQ: Grants Administration Division (3903R), EPA, 1200 Pennsylvania Ave. NW, Washington, DC 20460 Phone: (202) 566-0949, FAX(202) 566-3001.

Internet: www.epa.gov/innovation/stategrants.

66.950 ENVIRONMENTAL EDUCATION AND TRAINING PROGRAM ("EETP")

Assistance: project grants (75 percent/5 years).

Purposes: pursuant to the National Environmental Education Act, to train professionals in the development and delivery of environmental education programs. Funds may be used to develop programs involving such activities as: classroom training; demonstration projects; program and curriculum development; international exchanges involving the U.S., Mexico, and Canada; library acquisitions; conferences; networking.

Eligible applicants/beneficiaries: IHEs, nonprofit organizations or consortia of institutions to deliver environmental training and support for education professionals.

Average: single grant awarded, $8.5 million every 5 years.

Activity: 1 grant only, to the University of Wisconsin/Stevens Point (funded through 30 September 2005).

HQ: Environmental Education Specialist, Office of Environmental Education (1704A), EPA, 1200 Pennsylvania Ave. NW, Washington, DC 20460 Phone: (202) 564-0454, FAX (202) 564-2754.

Internet: www.epa.gov/enviroed.

66.951 ENVIRONMENTAL EDUCATION GRANTS ("EEG")

Assistance: project grants. (75 percent/1-2 years).

Purposes: pursuant to the National Environmental Education Act, to design, demonstrate, or disseminate practices, methods, or techniques related to environmental education and training, including: development of curricula and educational tools and materials; teacher and faculty training programs; international exchanges involving the U.S., Mexico, and Canada; projects to understand and assess specific environmental and ecological issues or problems. Funding priorities include: capacity building across a state or multiple states; education reform; community issues focus; health and threats to health from environmental pollution, especially as children are affected; teaching skills; career development; environmental justice.

Eligible applicants/beneficiaries: IHEs, local and state education agencies, environmental agencies, nonprofit organizations or consortia, licensed noncommercial educational broadcasting entities.

Range: $2,000 to $150,000. **Average:** HQ, $80,000; regional, $10,000 to $15,000.

Activity: FY 05, 10 grants from HQ, 135 from regional offices.

HQ: Environmental Education Grant Program (1704A), Office of Environmental Education, EPA, 1200 Pennsylvania Ave. NW, Washington, DC 20460. Phone: (202) 564-0451, FAX (202) 564-2754.

Internet: www.epa.gov/enviroed.

66.952 NATIONAL NETWORK FOR ENVIRONMENTAL MANAGEMENT STUDIES FELLOWSHIP PROGRAM ("NNEMS Fellowship Program")

Assistance: project grants. (100 percent/to 3 years).

Purposes: pursuant to CAA, CWA, SDWA, SWDA, FIFRA, CERCLA, and amendments, to enable students to participate in research projects directly related to their fields of study. Current priorities include: environmental policy, regulation, and law; environmental management and administration; environmental science; public relations and communications; computer programming and development. Stipends are awarded for three months full-time to three years part-time, throughout the fellowship period—for work performed at EPA headquarters, regional offices, or laboratories.

Eligible applicants/beneficiaries: U.S. citizens and permanent residents enrolled at accredited IHEs as graduate or undergraduate students, with satisfactory educational performance and appropriate related course completion.

Range: 3-months/full-time, $7,100 to $11,300. **Average:** $10,000.

Activity: new program listing in 2005 (CFDA on-line version). Annually, 35 NEMS research projects eligible for participation by fellowship awardees. Since 1986, 1,370 fellowships awarded. FY 06 estimate, 25 awards.

HQ: Environmental Education Grant Program (1704A), Office of Environmental Education, EPA, 1200 Pennsylvania Ave. NW, Washington, DC 20460 Phone: (202) 564-0443, FAX (202) 564-2754 *Or,* NNEMS Fellowship Program, Tetra Tech EM, Inc., 1881 Campus Commons Dr. - Ste.200, Reston, VA 20191 Phone: (800) 358-8769.

Internet: www.epa.gov/enviroed (Note: no field offices for this program.)

NATIONAL GALLERY OF ART

68.001 NATIONAL GALLERY OF ART EXTENSION SERVICE

Assistance: use of property, facilities, and equipment.

Purposes: to provide educational materials from the National Gallery of Art for use in art and humanities programs. Available audiovisual materials relate to collections of paintings, sculptures, and special exhibitions in the gallery; included are video cassettes, CD-ROMS, DVDs, slide programs, teaching packets. The service is free of charge, except for return mailing costs.

Eligible applicants/beneficiaries: schools, colleges, libraries, museums, clubs, community organizations, noncommercial educational television stations, and individuals.

Range/Average: N.A.

Activity: FY 05, 140,403 showings with a total audience of some 21,243,902 persons.

HQ: Department of Education Resources, National Gallery of Art, Washington, DC 20565 Phone: (202) 842-6273, (202) 737-4215.

Internet: www.nga.gov/education/classsroom/loanfinder; e-mail, ExtProg@nga.gov (Note: no field offices for this program.)

OVERSEAS PRIVATE INVESTMENT CORPORATION

70.002 FOREIGN INVESTMENT FINANCING

Assistance: guaranteed/insured loans (5-15 years).

Purposes: pursuant to the Foreign Assistance Act of 1969, to finance investments in developing countries and emerging economies. Projects must contribute to the economic and social development of host countries and have a positive impact on the U.S. economy. Borrowers must provide a significant equity investment. Direct loans may be approved only for private sector projects with significant involvement by U.S. small businesses. Examples of funded projects include power generation, cellular telephone networks, retail petroleum.

Eligible applicants/beneficiaries: U.S. citizens, corporations, partnerships, other associations beneficially owning more than 50 percent of the entity, or foreign corporations at least 95 percent owned be such entity, or any other 100 percent U.S.-owned foreign entity.

Range: $10,000,000 to $320,000,000; small businesses, $100,000 to $46,300,000; non-small businesses, $1,350,000 to $250,000,000. **Average:** small businesses, $7,143,245; non-small businesses, $45,641,379.

Activity: since 1971, over $164 billion in investments supported in more than 150 countries.

HQ: Information Officer, OPIC, 1100 New York Ave. NW, Washington, DC 20527. Phone: (202) 336-8799.

Internet: www.opic.gov; email, info@opic.gov (Note: no field offices for this program.)

70.003 FOREIGN INVESTMENT INSURANCE ("Political Risk Insurance")

Assistance: insurance. (90 percent/to 20 years).

Purposes: pursuant to the Foreign Assistance Act of 1969, to insure U.S. investments in developing countries and emerging markets against the political risks of inconvertibility, expropriation, and political violence. The investments must contribute to the economic and social development of host countries, and not adversely affect U.S. employment or the economy. Special programs insure: contractors and exporters against arbitrary drawings of letters of credit posted as bid, performance, or advance payment guarantees; petroleum exploration, development, and production; leasing operations; debt financing including securities.

Eligible applicants/beneficiaries: U.S. citizens, corporations, partnerships, other associations beneficially owning more than 50 percent of the entity, or foreign corporations at least 95 percent owned be such entity, or any other 100 percent U.S.-owned foreign entity.

Range: to $250,000,000. **Average:** $12,244,695.

Activity: since 1971, over $164 billion in investments supported in more than 150 countries.

HQ: Information Officer, OPIC, 1100 New York Ave. NW, Washington, DC 20527. Phone: (202) 336-8799.

Internet: www.opic.gov; email, info@opic.gov (Note: no field offices for this program.)

NUCLEAR REGULATORY COMMISSION

77.006 U.S. NUCLEAR REGULATORY COMMISSION NUCLEAR EDUCATION GRANT PROGRAM

Assistance: project grants.

Purposes: pursuant to Energy Policy Act of 2005, to provide assistance to IHEs in support or improvement of courses, studies, training, curricula, and disciplines relevant to fields that the NRC determines critical to its mission, including: nuclear safety, security, and environmental protection. Funds may be used for salaries, materials and supplies, equipment, travel, and publication, research, and training costs.

Eligible applicants/beneficiaries: U.S. public and private IHEs.

Range: $200,000 to $4,700,000.

Activity: new program listing in 2006 (CFDA on-line version).

HQ: U.S. Nuclear Regulatory Commission, Two White Flint North, 11545 Rockville Pike, Rockville, MD 20852; Mail Stop T-7-1-2 Washington, DC 20555-0001 Phone: (301) 415-7856.

Internet: www.nrc.gov (Note: no field offices for this program.)

77.007 U.S. NUCLEAR REGULATORY COMMISSION MINORITY SERVING INSTITUTIONS PROGRAM (MSIP)

Assistance: project grants; direct payments/specified use.

Purposes: pursuant to Energy Policy Act of 2005, to provide assistance to minority serving programs, activities, symposiums, and training for the exchange and transfer of knowledge and skills regarding fields that the NRC determines critical to its mission, including: nuclear safety, security, and environmental protection. Funds may be used for instruction, training, developmental learning, research and development, program evaluation, technical assistance, facilities and equipment acquisition, internships, fellowships, scholarships, tuition and housing assistance.

Eligible applicants/beneficiaries: U.S. public and private Minority Serving Institutions, their students and faculty and organizations that provide services to Minority Serving Institutions.

Range/Average: N.A.

Activity: new program listing in 2006 (CFDA on-line version).

HQ: U.S. Nuclear Regulatory Commission, Two White Flint North, 11545 Rockville Pike, Rockville, MD 20852; Mail Stop T-7-1-2 Washington, DC 20555-0001 Phone: (301) 415-7380.

Internet: www.nrc.gov (Note: no field offices for this program.)

77.008 U.S. NUCLEAR REGULATORY COMMISSION SCHOLARSHIP AND FELLOWSHIP PROGRAM

Assistance: grants.

Purposes: pursuant to Energy Policy Act of 2005 (Section 243), to provide scholarships and fellowships to qualified students interested in pursuing an education in science, engineering, or another field of study in a critical skill area related to the Commission's regulatory mission. Recipients must be enrolled in a professional degree or graduate program offered by a four year institution of higher education in the United States and must commit to employment by the Commission.

Eligible applicants: four year U.S. public and private institutions of higher education.

Eligible beneficiaries: undergraduate and graduate students.

Range/Average: $50,000.

Activity: new program, FY 07; 8-10 awards, resulting in approximately 40-50 fellowships/scholarships.

HQ: NRC, Washington, D.C. 20555-0001. Phone:(301) 415-7000.

Internet: www.nrc.gov (Note: no field offices for this program.)

COMMODITY FUTURES TRADING COMMISSION

78.004 COMMODITY FUTURES REPARATIONS CLAIMS

Assistance: investigation of complaints.

Purposes: pursuant to the Commodity Exchange Act as amended, Futures Trading Acts, Commodity Futures Modernization Act of 2000, related acts, and amendments, to respond to customer complaints and inquiries concerning commodity futures trading; to conduct hearings and rulings on reparations complaints regarding monetary damages resulting from violations of the acts or regulations, by persons or firms registered under the Act.

Eligible applicants/beneficiaries: market users and the general public.

Range/Average: N.A.

Activity: FY 04 estimate, 100 reparations complaints accepted.

HQ: Office of the Executive Director, Office of Proceedings, Commodity Futures Trading Commission, 1155 21st St. NW, Washington, DC 20581. Phone: (202) 418-5250.

Internet: www.cftc.gov.

DEPARTMENT OF ENERGY

81.003 GRANTING OF PATENT LICENSES ("DOE Patents Available for Licensing")

Assistance: technical information.

Purposes: pursuant to the Atomic Energy Act of 1954 and Department of Energy Organization Act of 1977 (DOEOA) as amended, to license some 1,200 DOE-owned U.S. and 200 foreign patents, encouraging widespread use of the licensed inventions. Licenses usually are nonexclusive and revocable, but may be exclusive or partially so under some circumstances such as for commercialization. Copies of patents may be obtained for a modest fee from the U.S. Patent and Trademark Office (see **11.900**).

Eligible applicants/beneficiaries: individuals, firms, or corporations with satisfactory commercialization plans.

Range/Average: N.A.

Activity: FY 06 estimate, 6 licenses to be granted; FY 07 estimate, 6 licenses to be granted.

HQ: Office of Assistant General Counsel/Technology Transfer and Intellectual Property, DOE, Washington, DC 20585. Phone: (202) 586-2802.

Internet: www.doe.gov (Note: no field offices for this program.)

81.022 USED ENERGY-RELATED LABORATORY EQUIPMENT GRANTS ("Used Equipment Grants")

Assistance: sale, exchange, or donation of property and goods.

Purposes: pursuant to the Atomic Energy Act of 1954, DOEOA, and Energy Reorganization Act of 1974 as amended, to grant used energy-related laboratory equipment for use in energy-oriented research or instructional programs in the life, physical, and environmental sciences and engineering.

Eligible applicants/beneficiaries: U.S. nonprofit IHEs, hospitals, technical institutes, museums.

Range/Average: N.A.

Activity: not quantified specifically.

HQ: Office of Science, DOE, 1000 Independence Ave. SW, Washington, DC 20585. Phone: (202) 586-7231.

Internet: erle.osti.gov/erle.

81.036 INVENTIONS AND INNOVATIONS ("I&I")

Assistance: project grants; technical information; advisory services/counseling. (grants, to 100 percent/grants, 1-2 years).

Purposes: pursuant to the Federal Nonnuclear Energy Research and Development Act of 1974 and DOEOA as amended, to support development and commercialization of energy-saving inventions, by providing limited financial assistance and technical assistance in evaluating and launching promising concepts. Funding may not include equity capital.

Eligible applicants/beneficiaries: U.S. citizens and small businesses.

Range: up to $250,000, depending on stage of idea. **Average:** $150,000.

Activity: since 1977 program inception, 500 inventions supported.

HQ: Weatherization and Intergovernmental Program (EE-2K), OEERE-DOE, 1000 Independence Ave. SW, Washington, DC 20585. Phone: (202) 586-2212.

Internet: www.eere.energy.gov/inventions.

81.041 STATE ENERGY PROGRAM

Assistance: formula grants (100 percent).

Purposes: pursuant to the Energy Policy and Conservation Act, DOEOA as amended, and related acts, to develop, implement, or modify state energy conservation plans. Funds may cover costs of plan development or modification, but not research, demonstrations, subsidies, or tax credits.

Eligible applicants/beneficiaries: states, territories, possessions.

Range: $200,000 to $2,000,000.

Activity: 56 states and territories participate.

HQ: Weatherization and Intergovernmental Program (EE-2K), OEERE-DOE, 1000 Independence Ave. SW, Washington, DC 20585. Phone: (no number provided).

Internet: www.eere.energy.gov/state_energy_program.

81.042 WEATHERIZATION ASSISTANCE FOR LOW-INCOME PERSONS

Assistance: formula grants (100 percent).

Purposes: pursuant to the Energy Conservation and Production Act, DOEOA, Energy Security Act of 1980, State Energy Efficiency Programs Improvement Act of 1990, amendments, and other acts, for weatherization measures in the homes of low-income households, especially the elderly and the handicapped. Funds may cover such costs as attic insulation, storm windows, furnace and cooling system modifications, replacement furnaces and boilers.

Eligible applicants/beneficiaries: states and certain tribal organizations. If a state does not apply, general purpose local government units, community action agencies, or other nonprofit agencies may apply.

Average: $2,744 per household.

Activity: to date, 5,300,000 homes weatherized.

HQ: Office of Weatherization and Intergovernmental Program (EE-2K), Office of Energy Efficiency and Renewable Energy-DOE, Forrestal Bldg., Washington, DC, 20585. Phone: (202) 586-4074.

Internet: www.eere.energy.gov/weatherization.

81.049 OFFICE OF SCIENCE FINANCIAL ASSISTANCE PROGRAM ("Basic Energy Sciences; High Energy Physics; Fusion Energy Sciences; Biological and Environmental Research; Advanced Scientific Computing Research")

Assistance: project grants. (to 100 percent/to 5 years).

Purposes: pursuant to the Atomic Energy Act of 1954, Federal Nonnuclear Energy Research and Development Act of 1974, DOEOA, Energy Reorganization Act of 1974, and amendments, for fundamental energy research, training, and related activities in the basic sciences and in advanced technology concepts and assessments in related fields. Funds may be obtained for work in such fields as basic energy sciences, high energy and nuclear physics, fusion energy, biological and environmental research, advanced scientific computing. Graduate student support may be provided.

Eligible applicants/beneficiaries: IHEs, profit and nonprofit organizations, state and local governments, unaffiliated individuals.

Range: $10,000 to $2,000,000. **Average:** $200,000.

Activity: not quantified specifically.

HQ: Grants and Contracts Division, Office of Science-DOE, 19901 Germantown Rd., Germantown, MD 20874-1290. Phone: (301) 903- 5212.

Internet: www.science.doe.gov/production/grants/grants.html.

81.057 UNIVERSITY COAL RESEARCH

Assistance: project grants. (75-100 percent/to 3 years).

Purposes: pursuant to the Atomic Energy Act of 1954 as amended, Federal Nonnuclear Energy Research and Development Act of 1974, DOEOA, and Energy Reorganization Act of 1974, for research on the physics and chemistry involved in the conversion and utilization of coal. Projects must involve teaching faculty and funded student participation.

Eligible applicants/beneficiaries: U.S. IHEs.

Range: $50,000 to $400,000. **Average:** $154,000.

Activity: FY 05, 22 grants.

HQ: Office of Advanced Research, Assistant Secretary/Fossil Energy-DOE, Washington, DC 20585. Phone: (301) 903-2786.

Internet: www.netl.doe.gov/coal/Advanced%20Research.

81.064 OFFICE OF SCIENTIFIC AND TECHNICAL INFORMATION ("OSTI")

Assistance: technical information.

Purposes: for OSTI to conduct its centralized technical information management program for the collection, organization, preservation, and distribution of domestic and international nuclear and other energy research findings in electronic and printed form; to provide pertinent technical services and information to DOE and its contractors.

Eligible applicants/beneficiaries: state and local governments, universities that are DOE contractors, and other organizations. Public access is available through NTIS and GPO.

Range/Average: N.A.

Activity: FY 05, 38,000,000 user transactions for OSTI web products.

HQ: Office of Program Integration, OSTI-DOE, 1 Science.gov Way, Oak Ridge, TN 37831. Phone: (865) 576-1194.

Internet: www.osti.gov (Note: no field offices for this program.)

81.065 NUCLEAR WASTE DISPOSAL SITING ("Consultation and Cooperation Financial Assistance")

Assistance: direct payments/specified use; project grants (grants, to 100 percent).

Purposes: pursuant to the Nuclear Waste Policy Act and amendments, to develop repositories for the disposal of high- level radioactive waste and spent nuclear fuel; for related research, development, and demonstration projects. Funds may be used to: review potential economic, social, health and safety, and environmental impacts; develop requests for impact and mitigation assistance; monitor, test, or evaluate activities; provide public information.

Eligible applicants/beneficiaries: Nevada and affected local governments and tribes where DOE is considering nuclear waste disposal activities.

Range: $40,000 to $5,000,000.

Activity: approximately 10 grants.

HQ: Office of Repository Development-DOE, Las Vegas, NV 89134. Phone: (702) 794-1368.

Internet: www.ocrwm.doe.gov (Note: the field office serves as headquarters for this program.)

81.079 REGIONAL BIOMASS ENERGY PROGRAMS

Assistance: project grants. (to 100 percent/2 months-1 year).

Purposes: pursuant to DOEOA as amended, to develop and transfer biomass energy technologies to the scientific and industrial communities; for outreach, public education, and behavior modification activities. Regional programs are tailored to specific regions for feedstock production, conversion technologies, and feasibility studies.

Eligible applicants/beneficiaries: profit and nonprofit organizations; intrastate, interstate, state, local government agencies; universities.

Range/Average: N.A.

Activity: not quantified specifically.

HQ: Office of Biomass Program-DOE, Washington, DC 20585. Phone: (no number provided).

Internet: www.eere.energy.gov.

81.086 CONSERVATION RESEARCH AND DEVELOPMENT ("Conservation")

Assistance: project grants. (to 100 percent/2 months to 2 years).

Purposes: pursuant to DOEOA as amended and Federal Nonnuclear Energy Research and Development Act of 1974, for long-term research in energy conservation technology in buildings, industry, FreedomCAR and vehicle technologies and hydrogen, fuel cells, and infrastructure. Project examples include research on high-performance heat pumps, thermally efficient commercial buildings, vehicle engines, high temperature materials, industrial separation processes.

Eligible applicants/beneficiaries: profit and nonprofit organizations, state and local governments.

Range: $50,000 to $500,000.

Activity: not quantified specifically.

HQ: OEERE-DOE OEERE- DOE, 1000 Independence Ave. SW, Washington, DC 20585 Phone: (no number provided).

Internet: www.eere.energy.gov (Note: no field offices for this program.)

81.087 RENEWABLE ENERGY RESEARCH AND DEVELOPMENT ("Renewable Energy")

Assistance: project grants. (to 100 percent/2 months-1 year).

Purposes: pursuant to DOEOA, for research and development projects in energy technologies, including solar, distributed energy and electric reliability, biomass, wind and hydropower, hydrogen, and geothermal.

Eligible applicants/beneficiaries: profit and nonprofit organizations; intrastate, interstate, and local agencies; universities.

Range: $50,000 to $1,000,000.

Activity: not quantified specifically.

HQ: OEERE- DOE, 1000 Independence Ave. SW, Washington, DC 20585 Phone: (no number provided).

Internet: www.eere.doe.gov (Note: no field offices for this program.)

81.089 FOSSIL ENERGY RESEARCH AND DEVELOPMENT

Assistance: project grants.

Purposes: pursuant to the Federal Nonnuclear Energy Research and Development Act of 1974, Energy Policy and Conservation Act, DOEOA, and other acts, for fundamental research and technology development to promote the use of environmentally and economically superior technologies for supply, conversion, delivery, and utilization of fossil fuels.

Eligible applicants/beneficiaries: states, local governments, universities, governmental entities, consortia, nonprofit institutions, commercial corporations, joint federal-industry corporations, territories, individuals.

Range: $20,000 to $65,000,000.

Activity: FY 05, 533 awards.

HQ: Fossil Energy Program (FE-3), DOE, 19901 Germantown Rd., Germantown, MD 20874. Phone: (301) 903-3514.

Internet: www.netl.doe.gov.

81.104 OFFICE OF ENVIRONMENTAL CLEANUP AND ACCELERATION

Assistance: project grants. (to 100 percent/to 5 years).

Purposes: pursuant to the Atomic Energy Act, DOEOA, Hazardous Materials Transportation Uniform Safety Act of 1990, amendments, and other acts, to develop new or improved technology systems to: eliminate or reduce known or recognized potential risks to the public and to the environment; reduce overall clean-up costs; develop new clean-up methods. Major remediation and waste management areas include: transuranic waste; high-level waste; groundwater and soils; deactivation and decommissioning; nuclear materials.

Eligible applicants/beneficiaries: public and quasi-public agencies, private industry, individuals, groups, educational institutions, nonprofit organizations, state and local governments, tribal governments, territories and possessions.

Range: $200,000 to $7,000,000.

Activity: not quantified specifically.

HQ: Office of Environmental Cleanup and Acceleration, Office of Environmental Management, DOE, Washington, DC 20585. Phone: (no number provided).

Internet: www.em.doe.gov (Note: no field offices for this program.)

81.105 NATIONAL INDUSTRIAL COMPETITIVENESS THROUGH ENERGY, ENVIRONMENT, AND ECONOMICS ("NICE3")

Assistance: project grants. (50 percent/to 3 years).

Purposes: pursuant to DOEOA and Energy Policy Act of 1992 as amended, to develop new processes and/or equipment to reduce the generation of high-volume wastes and greenhouse gases in industry, including agriculture and mining, and to conserve energy and energy-intensive feed stocks. Emphasis is on states with industries with the highest energy consumption and the greatest levels of generation of pollutants. State funding must include industrial partner monies.

Eligible applicants/beneficiaries: commercial firms with proposals endorsed by state agencies; state agencies, territories, possessions, tribes.

Range: $455,000 to $525,000. **Average:** $475,000.

Activity: cumulative energy savings of 34.5 trillion Btu; this program is in close-out; no appropriations for grant funding.

HQ: Weatherization and Intergovernmental Program (EE-2K), OEERE-DOE, 1000 Independence Ave. SW, Washington, DC 20585. Phone: (202) 586-2212.

Internet: www.eere.energy.gov/wip/program/nice3.html.

81.106 TRANSPORT OF TRANSURANIC WASTES TO THE WASTE ISOLATION PILOT PLANT: STATES AND TRIBAL CONCERNS, PROPOSED SOLUTIONS

Assistance: project grants (100 percent).

Purposes: pursuant to the National Security and Military Application of Nuclear Energy Authorization Act and Waste Isolation Pilot Land Withdrawal Act as amended, to support cooperative efforts among the tribes, states, and DOE on the Waste Isolation Pilot Plant shipping corridors in developing plans and procedures for the safe transportation of transuranic waste from temporary storage facilities to the plant. Project elements include accident prevention, emergency preparedness training, and public information activities.

Eligible applicants/beneficiaries: Western Governors' Association, Southern Governors' Association, State of New Mexico, and affected tribal governments.

Range: $50,000 to $24,223,000.

Activity: not quantified specifically.

HQ: Federal Disposition Options, Office of Environmental Management-DOE, Washington, DC 20585. Phone: (301) 903-7416.

Internet: www.em.doe.gov.

81.108 EPIDEMIOLOGY AND OTHER HEALTH STUDIES FINANCIAL ASSISTANCE PROGRAM

Assistance: project grants (100 percent).

Purposes: pursuant to the Atomic Energy Act of 1954, Federal Nonnuclear Energy Research and Development Act of 1977, Energy Reorganization Act of 1974, and amendments, for research, education, conferences, communication, and other activities relating to the health of DOE workers and others potentially exposed to health hazards associated with energy production, transmission, and use. Grant funds may support costs relating to project administration, training, publications, and epidemiological studies and research.

Eligible applicants/beneficiaries: IHEs, businesses, nonprofit institutions.

Range: $50,000 to $7,000,000. **Average:** $1,000,000.

Activity: not quantified specifically.

HQ: Office of Health Programs-DOE (EH-7/270CC), Germantown, MD 20874-1290. Phone: (301) 903-1244.

Internet: tis.eh.doe.gov/health (Note: no field offices for this program.)

81.112 STEWARDSHIP SCIENCE GRANT PROGRAM ("Defense Science")

Assistance: project grants (100 percent).

Purposes: pursuant to the Atomic Energy Act of 1954, Federal Nonnuclear Energy Research and Development Act of 1974, DOEOA, amendments, and other laws, for basic and applied research in science and technology relevant to stockpile stewardship; to promote inter-action among researchers and scientists at DOE laboratories; to train scientists in specific areas related to long-term research; to complement the DOE Advanced Simulation and Computing Academic Strategic Alliances Program by emphasizing primarily experimental research in forefront areas.

Eligible applicants/beneficiaries: U.S. public and private IHEs.

Range: $100,000 to $2,000,000. **Average:** $380,000.

Activity: not quantified specifically.

HQ: Office of Defense Science-DOE (NA-113/Forrestal), 1000 Independence Ave, Washington, DC 20585. Phone: (202) 586-5782, FAX (202) 586-8005.

Internet: www.nnsa.doe.gov/ssaa (Note: no field offices for this program.)

81.113 DEFENSE NUCLEAR NONPROLIFERATION RESEARCH

Assistance: project grants. (100 percent/to 3 years).

Purposes: pursuant to the Atomic Energy Act of 1954, Federal Nonnuclear Energy Research and Development Act of 1974, DOEOA, National Defense Authorization Act of 2000, amendments, and other acts, for basic and applied research and development on verification technologies that enhance U.S. national security and reduce global danger from the proliferation of special nuclear materials and weapons of mass destruction.

Eligible applicants/beneficiaries: public and private nonprofit IHEs and nongovernmental organizations; federal agencies.

Range: $100,000 to $250,000/year.

Activity: less than 20 grants expected per year.

HQ: Office of Nonproliferation Research and Engineering (NA-22), Office of Defense Nuclear Nonproliferation, National Nuclear Security Administration-DOE, Washington, DC 20585. Phone: (202) 586-5751.

Internet: www.nnsa.doe.gov/na-20 (Note: no field offices for this program.)

81.114 UNIVERSITY REACTOR INFRASTRUCTURE AND EDUCATION SUPPORT

Assistance: project grants (to 100 percent).

Purposes: pursuant to the Atomic Energy Act of 1954, DOEOA, amendments, and Energy Reorganization Act of 1974, for research design, equipment upgrades, graduate and undergraduate student support, analysis, and assessments in science and technology in fields related to nuclear energy.

Eligible applicants/beneficiaries: individuals, partnerships, corporations, associations, joint ventures, IHEs, nonprofit organizations.

Range: $50,000 to $300,000.

Activity: not quantified specifically.

HQ: Office of Nuclear Energy (NE-40), DOE, 19901 Germantown Rd., Germantown, MD 20874. Phone: (301) 903- 1536.

Internet: www.ne.doe.gov/university/university1.html.

81.117 ENERGY EFFICIENCY AND RENEWABLE ENERGY INFORMATION DISSEMINATION, OUTREACH, TRAINING AND TECHNICAL ANALYSIS/ASSISTANCE

Assistance: project grants. (to 100 percent/6 months-5 years).

Purposes: pursuant to DOEOA, Energy Policy Act of 1992, Energy Reorganization Act of 1974, and amendments, to stimulate increased energy efficiency and use of renewable and alternative energy in transportation, buildings, industry, and the federal sector through information dissemination, outreach, training, and related technical assistance.

Eligible applicants/beneficiaries: public and private profit and nonprofit organizations, state and local governments, tribal organizations, Alaska native American organizations, universities.

Range/Average: N.A.

Activity: FY 05, 137 awards.

HQ: Program Execution Support, Office of Business Administration (EE-3A), OEERE-DOE, 1000 Independence Ave, SW, Washington, DC 20585. Phone: (no number provided).

Internet: www.eere.energy.gov (Note: no field offices for this program.)

81.119 STATE ENERGY PROGRAM SPECIAL PROJECTS

Assistance: project grants (to 100 percent).

Purposes: pursuant to DOEOA and National Energy Conservation Policy Act of 1978, amendments, and other acts, to assist states in implementing specific DOE deployment activities and initiatives in such programmatic areas as building codes and standards, alternative fuels, industrial efficiency, and solar and renewable energy technologies.

Eligible applicants/beneficiaries: states, territories, and possessions.

Range: $20,000 to $1,000,000. **Average:** $99,518.

Activity: not quantified specifically.

HQ: Weatherization and Intergovernmental Program (EE-2K), OEERE-DOE, 1000 Independence Ave. SW, Washington, DC 20585. Phone: (no number provided).

Internet: www.eere.energy.gov/state_energy_program.

81.121 NUCLEAR ENERGY RESEARCH, DEVELOPMENT AND DEMONSTRATION ("NE RD&D")

Assistance: project grants (to 100 percent).

Purposes: pursuant to the Atomic Energy Act of 1954, DOEOA, amendments, and Energy Reorganization Act of 1974, for research, development, demonstrations, and deployment in science and technology fields related to nuclear energy to address key issues affecting the future worldwide use of nuclear energy including such areas as advanced reactors, proliferation-resistant fuel and reactor concepts, modeling and analysis, reactor physics. Projects may include development, demonstrations, studies, economic analyses, new regulatory or licensing requirements, and similar activities.

Eligible applicants/beneficiaries: federal, state, and local governments; public or private nonprofit or profit organizations, IHEs; consortia; individuals.

Range: $100,000 to $500,000. **Average:** $350,000.

Activity: not quantified specifically.

HQ: Office of Nuclear Energy, Office of Advanced Nuclear Research (NE-20), Germantown Bldg., 1000 Independence Ave. SW, Washington, DC 20585-1290. Phone: (301) 903-1652.

Internet: www.nuclear.gov.

81.122 ELECTRICITY DELIVERY AND ENERGY RELIABILITY, RESEARCH, DEVELOPMENT AND ANALYSIS

Assistance: project grants. (100 percent/to 3 years).

Purposes: pursuant to DOEOA as amended, Energy Tax Act of 1978, Energy Security Act of 1980, Superconductivity and Competitiveness Act of 1988, and Energy Policy Act of 1992, for research, development, demonstration, technology transfer, and education and outreach activities intended to: modernize and expand the national electricity delivery system; assure the security of the energy infrastructure and reduce its vulnerability; develop an effective emergency response system to protect and restore its capabilities in case of disruption or attack.

Eligible applicants/beneficiaries: private profit and nonprofit organizations, state and local governments.

Range: FY 05, $82,000 to $640,500. **Average:** $340,000.

Activity: new program in FY 05.

HQ: Office of Electricity Delivery and Energy Reliability, DOE, Washington, DC. Phone: (202) 586-1411.

Internet: www.oe.energy.gov (Note: no field offices for this program.)

81.123 NATIONAL NUCLEAR SECURITY ADMINISTRATION (NNSA) MINORITY SERVING INSTITUTIONS (MSI) PROGRAM ("NNSA")

Assistance: project grants. (100 percent/to 3 years).

Purposes: pursuant to the Atomic Energy Act of 1954, DOEOA, Energy Reorganization Act of 1974, National Nuclear Security Administration Act, and amendments, to establish a research partnership with HBCUs, HSIs, and TCUs to increase their participation in national security-related research, and to train HBCU graduates for NNSA employment.

Eligible applicants/beneficiaries: HBCUs, HSIs, and TCUs.

Range: $100,000 to $4,000,000.

Activity: FY 05, 24 awards.

HQ: Office of Diversity and Outreach (NA-61), NNSA-DOE, 1000 Independence Ave. SW, Washington, DC 20585. Phone: (202) 586-8023, FAX (202) 586-2531.

Internet: www.nnsa.doe.gov; email, diversity.outreach@nnsa.doe.gov (Note: no field offices for this program.)

81.124 PREDICTIVE SCIENCE ACADEMIC ALLIANCE PROGRAM (PSAAP) ("Office of Advanced Simulation and Computing (ASC)")

Assistance: project grants.

Purposes: pursuant to Atomic Energy Act of 1954, Energy Reorganization Act of 1974, Federal Nonnuclear Energy Research and Development Act of 1974, and others, as amended, to foster the science of building integrated, multi-scale, and multi-physics codes with the primary focus on code validation and verification to help advance the newly emergent predictive science in academia; to promote and sustain scientific interactions between the academic community and scientists at the NNSA laboratories; and to train scientists in specific areas of long-term research relevant to DOE stockpile stewardship. Funds are used to explore research ideas that do not unnecessarily duplicate work already in progress or contemplated by DOE.

Eligible applicants/beneficiaries: U.S. public/private education institutions with Ph.D. granting programs.

Range: $1,600,000-$3.400,000 per institution, per FY.

Activity: new program in FY 07 (online).

HQ: Office of Advanced Simulation and Computing, NA-114/Forrestal, 1000 Independence Avenue, Washington, DC 20585. Phone: (202) 586-7050; FAX: (202 586-0405.

Internet: www.sandia.gov/NNSA/ASC/univ/psaap.html (Note: no field offices for this program.)

81.126 FEDERAL LOAN GUARANTEES FOR INNOVATIVE ENERGY TECHNOLOGIES

Assistance: guaranteed/insured loans (to 30 years).

Purposes: pursuant to Energy Policy Act of 2005 and Title XVII, to encourage early commercial use in the U.S. of new or significantly improved technologies in energy projects that avoid, reduce, or sequester air pollutants or anthropogenic emissions of greenhouse gases through the use of Federal loan guarantees. This is a "self-pay" program and applicants will pay the subsidy costs as determined by the credit subsidy calculation.

Eligible applicants/beneficiaries: corporations, companies, partnerships, associations, societies, trusts, joint ventures or stock companies, or governmental nonfederal entities that have the authority to enter into a loan guarantee for a loan or other debt obligation of an Eligible Project. Examples of funded projects include: renewable energy systems, such as wind photovoltaics, biomass and hydropower projects, advanced fossil energy technology including gasification, efficient end use technologies and hydrogen fuel cell technology.

Range/Average: N.A.

Activity: new program in 2006.

HQ: Loan Guarantee Program Office, DOE, 1000 Independence Ave. SW, Washington, DC 20585 Phone: (202) 586-8336.

Internet: www.lgprogram.energy.gov; e-mail, lgprogram@hq.doe.gov (Note: no field offices for this program.)

DEPARTMENT OF EDUCATION

84.002 ADULT EDUCATION—STATE GRANT PROGRAM

Assistance: formula grants. (75 percent; territories, 88 percent/to 27 months).

Purposes: pursuant to the Adult Education and Family Literacy Act, Chapter 2, and WIA, for education and workplace, family, and English literacy services, and civics education programs for adults and out-of-school youth at least age 16 lacking mastery of basic educational skills or without a high school diploma or English language proficiency. Portions of grant amounts may be spent for: state leadership activities; professional development; teacher training; correctional education and services to other institutionalized individuals.

Eligible applicants: designated State agencies, LEAs, other public or private nonprofit organizations, including libraries, public housing authorities, IHEs, literacy organizations.

Eligible beneficiaries: out-of-school adults age 16 and older lacking basic educational skills, a high school diploma, or proficiency of English.

Range: $855,000 to $64,223,000.

Activity: FY 05, 2,800,000 participants.

HQ: Division of Adult Education and Literacy, OVAE-DOED, 400 Maryland Ave. SW, Washington, DC 20202-7100. Phone: (202) 205- 5698.

Internet: www.ed.gov/fund/grant//find//AdultEd/f- ogrant.html (Note: no field offices for this program.)

84.004 CIVIL RIGHTS TRAINING AND ADVISORY SERVICES

Assistance: project grants. (100 percent/3 years).

Purposes: pursuant to the Civil Rights Act of 1964 as amended, Title IV, for educational equity assistance centers to provide technical assistance and training services to school districts, relating to compliance with civil rights laws pertaining to race, gender, and national origin. Project funds may be used for information dissemination, staff and community training, and developing curriculum materials specifically for the instruction of students with limited English proficiency relevant to program purposes.

Eligible applicants: private nonprofit organizations, public agencies.

Eligible beneficiaries: educational personnel and elementary and secondary students.

Average: $711,000.

Activity: 10 centers grants awarded.

HQ: School Support and Technology Programs, OESE-DOED, 400 Maryland Ave. SW, Washington, DC 20202. Phone: (202) 260-2638.

Internet: www.ed.gov/programs/equitycenters/index.html; www.ed.gov/about/contacts/gen/othersites/equity.html (Note: no field offices for this program.)

84.007 FEDERAL SUPPLEMENTAL EDUCATIONAL OPPORTUNITY GRANTS ("FSEOG")

Assistance: direct payments/specified use (75 percent).

Purposes: pursuant to the Higher Education Act of 1965 (HEA) as amended, Title IV, for undergraduate postsecondary study by students in financial need. Institutions may receive an administrative cost allowance.

Eligible applicants: public, private nonprofit, postsecondary vocational, and proprietary IHEs.

Eligible beneficiaries: needy undergraduate students meeting citizenship or residency requirements, enrolled or enrolling as regular students, maintaining satisfactory academic progress, in compliance with Selective Service requirements, and neither owing a refund on a Title IV grant or in default on a Title IV loan.

Average: $766.

Activity: FY 05, 1,286,843 student awards.

HQ: OFSA-DOED, 400 Maryland Ave. SW, Washington, DC 20202-5446. Phone: Student Financial Aid Information Center, (800) 433-3243.

Internet: ifap.ed.gov.

84.010 TITLE I GRANTS TO LOCAL EDUCATIONAL AGENCIES ("Title I Basic, Concentration, Targeted and Education Finance Incentive Grants")

Assistance: formula grants (100 percent).

Purposes: pursuant to the Elementary and Secondary Education Act of 1965 (ESEA), Title I, Part A, to supplement state and local funding for extra instructional activities for children failing to meet academic standards or at-risk. Programs in schools with at least a 40 percent poverty rate may be operated on a schoolwide basis; other schools must operate targeted assistance programs for children failing or at-risk of failing to meet challenging state academic standards.

Eligible applicants: SEAs including in outlying areas; BIA. LEAs and tribal schools are subgrantees.

Eligible beneficiaries: children at risk of failing to meet State academic standards.

Range: $29,138,015 to $1,776,542,957.

Activity: 15,800,000 public and nonpublic school children in 51,000 schools served.

HQ: OESE-DOED, 400 Maryland Ave. SW, Washington, DC 20202-6132. Phone: (202) 260-0826.

Internet: www.ed.gov/programs/titleiparta/index.html (Note: no field offices for this program.)

84.011 MIGRANT EDUCATION—STATE GRANT PROGRAM

Assistance: formula grants (100 percent).

Purposes: pursuant to ESEA as amended, Title I, Part C, for comprehensive educational programs for migratory children, including: academic, remedial, bilingual, compensatory, multicultural, and vocational instruction; preschool services; health services; career education services.

Eligible applicants: SEAs; consortia.

Eligible beneficiaries: children age 0-21, of migratory agricultural workers or fishers that have moved across school districts during the last 36 months.

Range: $69,000 to $126,875,000. **Average:** $7,316,000.

Activity: 2005 school year, 737,700 students served.

HQ: Office of Migrant Education, OESE-DOED, 400 Maryland Ave. SW, Washington, DC 20202-6135. Phone: (202) 260-1334.

Internet: www.ed.gov/programs/mep/index.html (Note: no field offices for this program.)

84.013 TITLE I PROGRAM FOR NEGLECTED AND DELINQUENT CHILDREN

Assistance: formula grants (100 percent).

Purposes: pursuant to ESEA as amended, Title I, Part D, for education programs and related services for institutionalized neglected or delinquent children, including children under age 21 in state institutions, adult correctional institutions, or state- operated community day schools. Funds may cover supplemental instruction in core academic subjects, tutoring, counseling, services facilitating transition to schools. Juvenile institutions must provide at least 20 hours of instruction per week; adult institutions, at least 15 hours from nonfederal funds.

Eligible applicants: SEAs. Related state agencies may receive subgrants.

Eligible beneficiaries: children under age 21 in an adult correctional institution, a community day school, or a State institution for neglected or delinquent children.

Range: FY 05, $63,035 to $3,405,378.

Activity: FY 05, 211,000 children served in 400 institutions.

HQ: Student Achievement and School Accountability Programs, OESE-DOED (FB-6 - Rm.3W214), 400 Maryland Ave. SW, Washington, DC 20202-6132. Phone: (202) 260-4412.

Internet: www.ed.gov/programs/titleipartd/index.html (Note: no field offices for this program.)

84.015 NATIONAL RESOURCE CENTERS AND FELLOWSHIPS PROGRAM FOR LANGUAGE AND AREA OR LANGUAGE AND INTERNATIONAL STUDIES

Assistance: project grants. (100 percent/to 3 years).

Purposes: pursuant to HEA as amended, Title VI, for instruction in modern foreign languages and in area and international studies. Center grants may be awarded for undergraduate training only, or they may be comprehensive involving undergraduate, graduate, and professional training—supporting costs of instruction programs, administration, library resources and staff, lectures and conferences. Fellowships may be awarded for graduate language study combined with area studies and world affairs, covering tuition, fees, and basic subsistence.

Eligible applicants: accredited US IHEs with resources and commitment to language and international studies.

Eligible beneficiaries: graduate students that are U.S. citizens, nationals, or permanent residents.

Average: FY 05, center awards $239,000; fellowships awards $227,000.

Activity: FY 05, 120 centers funded; 124 fellowships grants.

HQ: OPE-DOED, 400 Maryland Ave. SW, Washington, DC 20202-5331. Phone: (202) 502-7630.

Internet: www.ed.gov/programs/iegpsnrc; www.ed.gov/programs/iegpsflasf (Note: no field offices for this program.)

84.016 UNDERGRADUATE INTERNATIONAL STUDIES AND FOREIGN LANGUAGE PROGRAMS

Assistance: project grants. (50 percent/1-3 years).

Purposes: pursuant to HEA as amended, Title VI, for undergraduate international studies and foreign language program strengthening and improvement. Funds may cover costs of administration, curriculum and faculty development, lectures and conferences, library enhancement, travel.

Eligible applicants/beneficiaries: accredited IHEs, public and private nonprofit agencies and organizations.

Average: FY 05, new awards $79,000; continuations $79,000.

Activity: FY 05, 57 grants.

HQ: International Studies Branch, International Education and Graduate Programs Service, Office of International Education and Foreign Language Studies, OPE-DOED, 400 Maryland Ave. SW, Washington, DC 20202-5332. Phone: (202) 502-7629.

Internet: www.ed.gov/programs/iegpsugisf (Note: no field offices for this program.)

84.017 INTERNATIONAL RESEARCH AND STUDIES

Assistance: project grants. (100 percent/1-3 years).

Purposes: pursuant to HEA as amended, Title VI, to improve education and training in modern foreign languages, area, and other international studies through studies, surveys, research, experimentation, and development of specialized instructional materials and publications. Funds may not support student or teacher training.

Eligible applicants/beneficiaries: public and private agencies, organizations, institutions; individuals.

Average: FY 05, new awards $119,000; continuations $141,000.

Activity: FY 05, 46 grants; 1 SBIR project.

HQ: International Education and Graduate Program Service, OPE-DOED, 400 Maryland Ave. SW, Washington, DC 20202-5331. Phone: (202) 502-7636.

Internet: www.ed.gov/programs/iegpsirs (Note: no field offices for this program.)

84.018 OVERSEAS PROGRAMS—SPECIAL BILATERAL PROJECTS

Assistance: project grants. (100 percent/4-6 weeks).

Purposes: pursuant to MECEA as amended, to pay the travel and tuition costs of educators participating in short-term training seminars abroad, on topics in the social sciences and humanities.

Eligible applicants/beneficiaries: U.S. citizens or permanent residents with appropriate language proficiency and a bachelor's degree, that are: undergraduate faculty members or full-time elementary or junior high school teachers, administrators, supervisors, curriculum development specialists, or administrators.

Average: $211,000.

Activity: FY 05, 144 participants in 10 projects.

HQ: International Studies Branch, International Education and Graduate Programs Service, Office of International Education and Foreign Language Studies, OPE-DOED, 400 Maryland Ave. SW, Washington, DC 20202-5332. Phone: (202) 502-7691.

Internet: www.ed.gov/programs/iegpssap (Note: no field offices for this program.)

84.019 OVERSEAS PROGRAMS—FACULTY RESEARCH ABROAD

Assistance: project grants. (100 percent/3-12 months).

Purposes: pursuant to MECEA as amended, for fellowships for research abroad by college faculty members, relevant to foreign languages and cultures. Generally, grants are unavailable for projects focusing primarily on Western Europe, nor in countries where the U.S. has no formal diplomatic relations. Awards provide stipends in lieu of salary and cover travel costs, fees to foreign institutions, expenses for expendable materials and supplies, services.

Eligible applicants: IHEs.

Eligible beneficiaries: U.S. citizens, nationals, or permanent residents that: are IHE employees; have been engaged in teaching relevant to the foreign language or area specialization for the previous two years; are not engaged in dissertation research for a Ph.D.

Average: FY 05, new awards $63,000; new fellowships $53,000.

Activity: FY 05, 26 fellowships.

HQ: Advanced Training and Research Team, International Education and Graduate Program Service, OPE-DOED, 400 Maryland Ave. SW, Washington, DC 20202-5331. Phone: (202) 502-7633.

Internet: www.ed.gov/programs/iegpsfra (Note: no field offices for this program.)

84.021 OVERSEAS PROGRAMS—GROUP PROJECTS ABROAD

Assistance: project grants. (100 percent/5 weeks to 36 months).

Purposes: pursuant to MECEA, for groups of teachers, faculty, and graduate or upper-classmen to conduct studies abroad in modern foreign languages and area studies. Funds may cover costs incurred abroad including round-trip travel, rent for instructional facilities, maintenance stipends, books, teaching materials, clerical, and related costs.

Eligible applicants: IHEs; state departments of education; private nonprofit educational organizations; consortia.

Eligible beneficiaries: U.S. citizens, nationals, or permanent residents that are faculty members or teachers at all levels, or graduate students or upper-classmen planning teaching careers in foreign language or area studies.

Average: $74,000.

Activity: FY 05, 60 projects with 995 participants.

HQ: International Studies Team, International Education and Grants Programs Service, OPE-DOED, 400 Maryland Ave. SW, Washington, DC 20202-5332. Phone: (202) 502-7624.

Internet: www.ed.gov/programs/iegpsgpa (Note: no field offices for this program.)

84.022 OVERSEAS PROGRAMS—DOCTORAL DISSERTATION RESEARCH ABROAD

Assistance: project grants. (100 percent/6-12 months).

Purposes: pursuant to MECEA as amended, for fellowships to graduate students to complete dissertation research abroad in modern foreign languages and area studies, to develop research knowledge and capability in areas not widely included in American curricula. Generally, no grants are available for projects focusing primarily on Western Europe, nor in countries where the U.S. has no formal diplomatic relations. Grants may cover stipends, travel costs, tuition to host institutions, dependents allowances, insurance, project expenses.

Eligible applicants: IHEs.

Eligible beneficiaries: U.S. citizens, nationals, or permanent residents that are graduate students already admitted to a doctoral degree candidacy program, plan teaching careers in the U.S. upon graduation, and have appropriate language skills. (DOED recommends applicants to the Fulbright scholarship board for approval.)

Average: $29,000.

Activity: FY 05, 153 fellowships.

HQ: International Education Programs Service, OPE-DOED, 400 Maryland Ave. SW, Washington, DC 20202-5331. Phone: (202) 502-7632.

Internet: www.ed.gov/programs/iegpsddrap (Note: no field offices for this program.)

84.027 SPECIAL EDUCATION—GRANTS TO STATES

Assistance: formula grants (100 percent).

Purposes: pursuant to the Individuals with Disabilities Act (IDEA) as amended, to provide special education and related services to children and youth, age 3-21, with disabilities, including those in private schools.

Eligible applicants: SEAs; territories and possessions; BIA. LEAs apply to SEAs for funds.

Eligible beneficiaries: children with disabilities.

Range: $14,975,978 to $1,132,572,659.

Activity: FY 05, 6,800,000 children served.

HQ: Office of the Assistant Secretary for Special Education Programs-DOED, 400 Maryland Ave. SW, Washington, DC 20202. Phone: (202) 245-7629.

Internet: www.ed.gov/about/offices/list/osers/osep/index.html (Note: no field offices for this program.)

84.031 HIGHER EDUCATION—INSTITUTIONAL AID

Assistance: project grants. (50-100 percent/to 5 years).

Purposes: pursuant to HEA as amended, Title III, to help colleges and universities address their fiscal and management problems. The Strengthening Institutions Program includes tribally controlled and Alaska native- and Hawaii native-serving institutions; funds may be used to plan, develop, and implement programs for faculty development, and for administrative expenses, improvement of academic programs, library and equipment purchases, and student services. The Historically Black Colleges and Universities (HBCU) Program provides funds for undergraduate and graduate programs, which may be used: to acquire scientific equipment; to construct, maintain, and improve classroom, library, and other instructional facilities; for faculty exchanges and fellowships; to purchase library materials; to provide tutoring, counseling, and other student services; for administrative management and equipment. Graduate HBCU program funds may be used to establish or maintain endowments. HBCU projects over $1,000,000 require a 50 percent match.

Eligible applicants/beneficiaries: IHEs with a low average educational and general expenditure, substantial percentage of students receiving Pell Grants or other federal need-based financial aid; HBCUs established prior to 1964.

Range: HBCU, from $500,000.

Activity: FY 05, 500 grants.

HQ: Office of Higher Education Programs, OPE-DOED, 1990 K St. NW, Washington, DC 20006-8500. Phone: (202) 502-7777.

Internet: www.ed.gov/programs/iduestitle3a (Note: no field offices for this program.)

84.032 FEDERAL FAMILY EDUCATION LOANS

Assistance: guaranteed/insured loans. (100 percent/5-30 years).

Purposes: pursuant to HEA as amended, Title IV, to provide federal reinsurance on loans insured by state or private nonprofit guaranty agencies for vocational, graduate, or undergraduate student educational expenses. Loans are obtained from banks, credit unions, savings and loan associations, pension funds, insurance companies, and schools. Repayment of Stafford loans begins six months after termination of at least half-time enrollment; for PLUS loans, repayment begins 60 days after disbursement of the last installment, and generally extends five to ten years, except that Consolidation Loans may extend up to 30 years. Deferments and forbearance of payment may be granted for certain periods.

Eligible applicants/beneficiaries: Stafford loans-generally, any U.S. citizen, national, or permanent resident enrolled or accepted for enrollment for at least half-time as an undergraduate, graduate, professional, or vocational student at a participating postsecondary school.

Range/Average: varies according to type of loan.

Activity: FY 05, 12,300,000 loans.

HQ: Office of Postsecondary Education, OFSA-DOED, 400 Maryland Ave. SW, Washington, DC 20202-5446. Phone: Student Financial Aid Information Center, (800) 433-3243.

Internet: www.ifap.ed.gov.

84.033 FEDERAL WORK-STUDY PROGRAM

Assistance: direct payments/specified use (50-75 percent).

Purposes: pursuant to HEA as amended, Title IV, to provide part- time employment to postsecondary students. The program contributes up to 75 percent of student earnings in jobs in public or nonprofit organizations, or 50 percent when a profit organization hires the student-plus administrative cost allowances to the educational institution. At least 5 percent of allocated funds must support students employed in community service.

Eligible applicants: public, private nonprofit, postsecondary vocational, and proprietary IHEs.

Eligible beneficiaries: undergraduate, graduate, or professional students meeting citizenship and residency requirements, demonstrating financial need, maintaining satisfactory academic progress, in compliance with Selective Service requirements, and neither owing a refund or in default on a Title IV loan.

Average: $1,447.

Activity: FY 05, $1,184,204 awarded to 818,386 students.

HQ: OFSA-DOED, 400 Maryland Ave. SW, Washington, DC 20202-5446. Phone: Student Financial Aid Information Center, (800) 433-3243.

Internet: ifap.ed.gov.

84.037 PERKINS LOAN CANCELLATIONS

Assistance: direct payments/specified use; direct payments/unrestricted use.

Purposes: pursuant to HEA as amended, Title IV, to reimburse institutions for their share of loans canceled for Perkins loan recipients that: become teachers; perform full-time active military service; and, certain other recipients.

Eligible applicants: public, private nonprofit, postsecondary vocational, and proprietary IHEs.

Eligible beneficiaries: Federal Perkins and National Direct and Defense Loan borrowers for loans made 23 July 1992 or after, with an outstanding balance as of 7 October 1998-loan cancellation is available for full-time service as: teachers in designated elementary or secondary school having a high enrollment of children from low-income families; full-time staff members in Head Start programs; members of the Armed Forces (in an area of hostilities); volunteers in the Peace Corps or ACTION programs as full-time law enforcement or corrections officers; full-time special education teachers; full-time teachers of math, science, foreign languages, bilingual education or other areas having a shortage of teachers; full-time nurses or medical technicians; full-time employees of public or private nonprofit child or family service agencies. Cancellation provisions differ for loans made before 23 July 1992.

Range/Average: N.A.

Activity: not quantified specifically.

HQ: OFSA-DOED, 400 Maryland Ave. SW, Washington, DC 20202-5347. Phone: Student Financial Aid Information Center, (800) 433-3243.

Internet: ifap.ed.gov.

84.038 FEDERAL PERKINS LOAN PROGRAM—FEDERAL CAPITAL CONTRIBUTIONS

Assistance: direct payments/specified use (75 percent).

Purposes: pursuant to HEA as amended, Title IV, for educational institutions to make low-interest loans to needy undergraduate, graduate, and professional students for their educational expenses. The institutions receive an administrative cost allowance.

Eligible applicants: public, private nonprofit, postsecondary vocational, and proprietary IHEs.

Eligible beneficiaries: undergraduate, graduate, or professional students meeting citizenship and residency requirements, demonstrating financial need, maintaining satisfactory academic progress, in compliance with Selective Service requirements, and neither owing a refund or in default on a Title IV loan.

Range: graduate, professional students, to $6,000 annually and $40,000 cumulative maximum including undergraduate loans; undergraduates, to $4,000 annually and $20,000 cumulative maximum. (Maximums may be 20 percent more for study abroad.) **Average:** $2,003.

Activity: FY 04, 630,495 loans.

HQ: OFSA-DOED, 400 Maryland Ave. SW, Washington, DC 20202-5446. Phone: Student Financial Aid Information Center, (800) 433-3243.

Internet: ifap.ed.gov.

84.040 IMPACT AID—FACILITIES MAINTENANCE

Assistance: project grants (100 percent).

Purposes: pursuant to ESEA as amended, Title VIII, to construct, enlarge, maintain, restore, or improve school facilities owned by DOED and operated by LEAs, and to transfer such facilities to LEAs.

Eligible applicants: LEAs.

Eligible beneficiaries: public elementary and secondary school children.

Range/Average: N.A.

Activity: not quantified specifically.

HQ: Impact Aid Programs, OESE-DOED, 400 Maryland Ave. SW - Rm.3E105 (FB-6), Washington, DC 20202-6244. Phone: (202) 260-3858.

Internet: www.ed.gov/about/offices/list/oese/impactaid/index.html; email, impact.aid@ed.gov (Note: no field offices for this program.)

84.041 IMPACT AID

Assistance: formula grants (100 percent).

Purposes: pursuant to ESEA as amended, Title VIII, for operating costs of LEAs where enrollments or the tax base are adversely affected by federal activities including: federal acquisition of real property; employment of parents on federal property or in the uniformed services; significant numbers of children residing on federal land including Indian lands; sudden increases in school enrollment. Special additional funds are provided based on related enrollments of handicapped children, which must be used for special programs. Payments for construction may be used for construction and renovation, debt service, or other capital fund activities.

Eligible applicants: LEAs.

Eligible beneficiaries: public elementary and secondary school children.

Range/Average: N.A.

Activity: FY 05, 1,280 LEAs received grants serving 1,037,000 children.

HQ: Impact Aid Programs, OESE-DOED, 400 Maryland Ave. SW - Rm.3E105 (FB-6), Washington, DC 20202-6244. Phone: (202) 260-3858.

Internet: www.ed.gov/about/offices/list/oese/impactaid/index.html; email, impact.aid@ed.gov (Note: no field offices for this program.)

84.042 TRIO—STUDENT SUPPORT SERVICES

Assistance: project grants. (100 percent/4-5 years).

Purposes: pursuant to HEA as amended, Title IV, to provide supportive services to disadvantaged college students to enhance their potential to complete their programs, to facilitate their transition from two-year to four-year programs of study, or to graduate or professional programs. Projects may include personal and academic counseling, career guidance, instruction, mentoring, tutoring, and special services to students with limited language proficiency. Grants may be awarded to students under certain conditions. At least two-thirds of project participants must be physically handicapped or low-income, first-generation college students.

Eligible applicants: IHEs and consortia.

Eligible beneficiaries: low-income, first generation college students or disabled students.

Average: FY 05, new awards $280,000; continuation awards $306,000.

Activity: FY 05, 959 awards serving 203,212 students.

HQ: Federal TRIO Programs, OPE-DOED, 400 Maryland Ave. SW, Washington, DC 20202-5249. Phone: (202) 502-7694, -7097.

Internet: www.ed.gov/programs/triostudsupp; email, trio@ed.gov (Note: no field offices for this program.)

84.044 TRIO—TALENT SEARCH

Assistance: project grants. (100 percent/to 5 years).

Purposes: pursuant to HEA as amended, Title IV, to identify disadvantaged youth with potential for postsecondary education; to encourage them to return to or continue in and graduate from secondary schools and enroll in postsecondary education; to publicize the availability of financial aid; to provide special tutoring. Two-thirds of project participants must be low-income, potential first-generation college students.

Eligible applicants: IHEs; public and private agencies and organizations; combinations of IHEs and others; some secondary schools.

Eligible beneficiaries: individuals residing in target areas or attending a target school. Participants must be age 11-27 (exceptions allowed).

Average: FY 05, continuations $309,000.

Activity: FY 05, 468 grants; 384,588 individuals served.

HQ: Federal TRIO Programs, OPE-DOED, 400 Maryland Ave. SW, Washington, DC 20202-5249. Phone: (202) 502-7539.

Internet: www.ed.gov/programs/triotalent; email, trio@ed.gov (Note: no field offices for this program.)

84.047 TRIO—UPWARD BOUND

Assistance: project grants. (100 percent/to 5 years).

Purposes: pursuant to HEA as amended, Title IV, for programs providing academic instruction, personal and academic counseling, tutoring, career guidance, and special instruction to prepare participants for postsecondary education and for careers in which persons from disadvantaged backgrounds are under-represented. Stipends may be paid to students ($40 monthly during the academic year, $60 monthly during special summer residential programs). Two-thirds of the participants must be low-income, potential first-generation college students.

Eligible applicants: IHEs; public and private agencies and organizations; combinations of IHEs and others; some secondary schools.

Eligible beneficiaries: low-income individuals and potential first-generation college students. Except for veterans, eligible regardless of age, participants must be age 13-19 and have completed the eighth grade but not have entered the twelfth grade (exceptions allowed).

Average: new awards, $343,000; new math/science awards, $293,000.

Activity: FY 05, 800 awards; 61,359 students served; 127 awards for math/science centers projects.

HQ: Federal TRIO Programs, OPE-DOED, 400 Maryland Ave. SW, Washington, DC 20202-5249. Phone: (202) 502-7545.

Internet: www.ed.gov/programs/trioupbound; email, trio@ed.gov.

84.048 CAREER AND TECHNICAL EDUCATION—BASIC GRANTS TO STATES

Assistance: formula grants. (states, 50 percent; outlying areas, 100 percent/states, 27 months).

Purposes: pursuant to the Carl D. Perkins Vocational and Technical Education Act of 1998 (CDPVTEA), Title I, to expand and improve vocational education programs, including special programs for single parents, single pregnant women, displaced homemakers, criminal offenders in correctional institutions, and for individuals participating in programs to eliminate sex bias and stereotyping.

Eligible applicants: states, outlying areas. Subgrants may be awarded to LEAs and postsecondary institutions.

Eligible beneficiaries: wide range of individuals pursuing vocational education and training.

Range: FY 05, $640,000 to $128,963,000.

Activity: not quantified specifically.

HQ: Division of High School, Postsecondary and Career Education, OVAE-DOED, 400 Maryland Ave. SW, Washington, DC 20202-7241. Phone: (202) 245-7735.

Internet: www.ed.gov/students/prep/job/cte/index.html (Note: no field offices for this program.)

84.051 CAREER AND TECHNICAL EDUCATION—NATIONAL PROGRAMS

Assistance: project grants. (100 percent/to 5 years).

Purposes: pursuant to CDPVTEA as amended, for research, development, demonstration, dissemination, evaluation, and assessment activities to improve vocational and technical education.

Eligible applicants/beneficiaries: universities; university consortia and a public or private nonprofit organization.

Range/Average: N.A.

Activity: not quantified specifically.

HQ: Policy, Research and Evaluation Staff, OVAE-DOED, 400 Maryland Ave. SW, Washington, DC 20202-7242. Phone: (202) 245- 7818.

Internet: www.ed.gov/about/offices/list/ovae/index.html (Note: no field offices for this program.)

84.060 INDIAN EDUCATION—GRANTS TO LOCAL EDUCATIONAL AGENCIES

Assistance: formula grants; project grants. (100 percent/to 5 years).

Purposes: pursuant to ESEA as amended, Title VII, for education programs serving Indian students to assure that they are based on state content and student performance standards. Among the types of activities that may be funded are culturally related programs including native languages, early childhood and family programs emphasizing school readiness, enrichment programs, school-to-work transition, drop-out prevention.

Eligible applicants: LEAs that enroll at least 10 Indian children or in which Indians constitute at least 25 percent of the total enrollment, except those serving Indian children in Alaska, California, and Oklahoma or located on or near an Indian reservation.

Eligible beneficiaries: Indian children, BIA funded schools.

Range: $4,000 to $2,112,000. **Average:** $198 per student.

Activity: FY 05, awards to 1,144 LEAs, 65 BIA grant/contract, 50 BIA-operated schools, serving 481,627 Indian students.

HQ: Office of Indian Education, OESE-DOED, 400 Maryland Ave. SW, Washington, DC 20202. Phone: (202) 260-1683.

Internet: www.ed.gov/about/offices/list/oese/oie/programs.html (Note: no field offices for this program.)

84.063 FEDERAL PELL GRANT PROGRAM ("Pell Grants")

Assistance: direct payments/specified use.

Purposes: pursuant to HEA as amended, Title IV, for grants to undergraduate postsecondary students demonstrating financial need, to attend public or private nonprofit colleges, vocational-technical schools, universities, hospital schools of nursing, or for-profit proprietary institutions. Award amount reflects family income and assets.

Eligible applicants/beneficiaries: U.S. citizens or eligible noncitizens with a high school diploma, enrolled as undergraduate students and making satisfactory academic progress. Eligible males, age 18 or over and born after December 31, 1959, must have registered with the Selective Service.

Range: $400 to $4,050 annually. **Average:** $2,456.

Activity: FY 05, 5,129,000 grants awarded.

HQ: OFSA-DOED, 400 Maryland Ave. SW, Washington, DC 20202-5446. Phone: Student Financial Aid Information Center, (800) 433-3243.

Internet: www.ifap.ed.gov.

84.066 TRIO—EDUCATIONAL OPPORTUNITY CENTERS

Assistance: project grants. (100 percent/to 5 years).

Purposes: pursuant to HEA as amended, Title IV, to establish and operate educational opportunity centers to provide academic and financial information to qualified adults interested in pursuing postsecondary education, and to assist them in applying for admission. Tutoring and counseling may be provided for participants not enrolled in an Upward Bound or a Student Support Services project. Two-thirds of the participants must be low-income potential first-generation college students.

Eligible applicants: IHEs; public and private agencies and organizations; combinations of IHEs and others; some secondary schools.

Eligible beneficiaries: residents of target areas, at least age 19 (exceptions allowed).

Average: FY 05, continuation awards $352,000.

Activity: FY 05, 139 awards assisting 217,565 participants.

HQ: Federal TRIO Programs, OPE-DOED, 400 Maryland Ave. SW, Washington, DC 20202-5249. Phone: (202) 502-7547.

Internet: www.ed.gov/programs/trioeoc, email, ope.trio@ed.gov (Note: no field offices for this program.)

84.069 LEVERAGING EDUCATIONAL ASSISTANCE PARTNERSHIP ("LEAP")

Assistance: formula grants (50 percent).

Purposes: pursuant to HEA as amended, Title IV, to provide scholarships of up to $5,000 to postsecondary students with substantial financial need, enrolled at postsecondary institutions. Grant amounts are reduced for students enrolled less than full time.

Eligible applicants: state and territorial agencies.

Eligible beneficiaries: postsecondary education students with substantial financial need.

Range: student awards, to $5,000. **Average:** $1,000.

Activity: FY 05, awards to 166,928 students.

HQ: OFSA-DOED, 400 Maryland Ave. SW, Washington, DC 20202-5447. Phone: Student Financial Aid Information Center, (800) 433-3243.

Internet: www.ifap.ed.gov.

84.083 WOMEN'S EDUCATIONAL EQUITY ACT PROGRAM

Assistance: project grants. (100 percent/to 4 years).

Purposes: pursuant to ESEA as amended, Title V, to promote gender equity for women and girls at all levels of education, including their increased participation in such areas as math, science, and computer science courses. Grants may be awarded for implementation projects or for research to develop model programs.

Eligible applicants/beneficiaries: public and private nonprofit agencies, institutions, and organizations; student and community groups; individuals.

Average: implementation grants $175,000.

Activity: FY 05, 17 implementation grants.

HQ: Office of Innovation and Improvement, OESE-DOED, 400 Maryland Ave. SW, Washington, DC 20202. Phone: (202) 260-0964.

Internet: www.ed.gov/programs/equity/index.html.

84.101 CAREER AND TECHNICAL EDUCATION—INDIAN SET-ASIDE

Assistance: project grants. (100 percent/to 2 years).

Purposes: pursuant to CDPVTEA, Title I, to plan, conduct, and administer Indian vocational and technical education programs or portions of programs.

Eligible applicants/beneficiaries: tribes, tribal organizations, Alaska native entities.

Range/Average: N.A.

Activity: 35 projects funded.

HQ: Division of High School, Postsecondary and Career Education, OVAE-DOED, 400 Maryland Ave. SW, Washington, DC 20202-7242. Phone: (202) 205-9353.

Internet: www.ed.gov/programs/cteivep/index.html (Note: no field offices for this program.)

84.103 TRIO STAFF TRAINING PROGRAM

Assistance: project grants. (100 percent/1-2 years).

Purposes: pursuant to HEA as amended, Title IV, to train present or new staff and leadership personnel for federal TRIO programs (special programs for students from disadvantaged backgrounds - **84.042**, **84.044**, **84.047**, **84.066**, **84.217**). Grants support seminars, workshops, internships, and publications.

Eligible applicants: IHEs, public and nonprofit private agencies and organizations.

Eligible beneficiaries: leadership personnel, staff of projects under the federal TRIO programs, individuals preparing for TRIO leadership.

Average: $408,000.

Activity: FY 05, 13 grants involving 3,688 TRIO projects staff.

HQ: Federal TRIO Programs, OPE-DOED, 400 Maryland Ave. SW, Washington, DC 20202-5249. Phone: (202) 502-7733, -7735.

Internet: www.ed.gov/programs/triotrain; email, trio@ed.gov (Note: no field offices for this program.)

84.116 FUND FOR THE IMPROVEMENT OF POSTSECONDARY EDUCATION ("FIPSE")

Assistance: project grants. (to 100 percent/1-3 years).

Purposes: pursuant to HEA as amended, Title VII, to develop innovative programs to improve access to and quality of postsecondary education. Examples of funded projects include cooperation between colleges and business, uses of technology, improved access for Blacks, Hispanics, and other minorities.

Eligible applicants/beneficiaries: two- and four-year IHEs, community organizations, libraries, museums, consortia, student groups, local government agencies.

Average: FY 05, continuation grants $145,000.

Activity: FY 05, 80 grants.

HQ: FIPSE, OPE-DOED, Washington, DC 20202-5175. Phone: (202) 502-7506.

Internet: www.ed.gov/programs/fipsecomp (Note: no field offices for this program.)

84.120 MINORITY SCIENCE AND ENGINEERING IMPROVEMENT ("MSEIP")

Assistance: project grants. (to 100 percent/1-3 years).

Purposes: pursuant to HEA as amended, Title III, to improve undergraduate science and engineering education programs at predominantly minority institutions to better prepare their students, particularly women, for graduate work or careers in which they are under-represented. Eligible uses of funds include salaries, purchase of equipment and instructional materials, faculty development, and inservice training.

Eligible applicants/beneficiaries: private and public nonprofit two- and four-year IHEs whose enrollments are predominantly American Indian, Alaska native, Black, Hispanic, Pacific Islander, or any combination of these or other underrepresented minority; nonprofit science organizations; professional scientific societies; private organizations with science and engineering facilities; quasi-governmental entities with a significant scientific or engineering mission.

Average: FY 05, new awards $99,000; continuation awards $83,000.

Activity: FY 05, 98 awards.

HQ: Institutional Development and Undergraduate Education Service, OPE-DOED, Washington, DC 20202. Phone: (202) 219-7038.

Internet: www.ed.gov/programs/iduesmsi (Note: no field offices for this program.)

84.126 REHABILITATION SERVICES—VOCATIONAL REHABILITATION GRANTS TO STATES

Assistance: formula grants (79 percent).

Purposes: pursuant to the Rehabilitation Act of 1973 as amended, for vocational rehabilitation services to persons with mental and/or physical disabilities resulting in employment handicaps that may reasonably be expected to increase their employability. Services include: assessment; counseling; vocational and other training; reader services for the blind, interpreter services for the deaf; job placement; medical and related services, prosthetic and orthotic devices; rehabilitation technology; transportation to obtain services; construction and establishment of community rehabilitation facilities; services to families of handicapped persons.

Eligible applicants: state agencies, territories, possessions.

Eligible beneficiaries: individuals with physical and/or mental impairments which constitute or result in a substantial impediment to employment.

Range: FY 05, $7,566,973 to $248,655,290.

Activity: FY 05, 984,337 persons served.

HQ: Rehabilitation Services Administration, OSERS-DOED, 400 Maryland Ave. SW, Washington, DC 20202-2500. Phone: (202) 245-7598.

Internet: www.ed.gov/programs/rsabvrs/index.html (Note: no field offices for this program.)

84.128 REHABILITATION SERVICES—SERVICE PROJECTS

Assistance: project grants. (50-100 percent/3-5 years).

Purposes: pursuant to the Rehabilitation Act of 1973 as amended, for vocational rehabilitation demonstrations and special projects for disabled persons, holding promise of expanding and otherwise improving services over and above those provided by **84.126**. Special programs include recreation projects, migrant and seasonal worker projects.

Eligible applicants: Recreational projects - states, public agencies, nonprofit organizations. Migrant and seasonal farm worker projects - designated state agencies including territories and possessions; nonprofit and local agencies in collaboration with state agencies.

Eligible beneficiaries: individuals with disabilities; individuals with significant disabilities.

Range/Average: N.A.

Activity: FY 05, 24 recreational, 13 migrant and seasonal farm worker projects.

HQ: Rehabilitation Services Administration, OSERS-DOED, 400 Maryland Ave. SW, Washington, DC 20202-2647. Phone: migrant, seasonal workers, (202) 245-7557; recreational, (202) 245-7377.

Internet: www.ed.gov/programs/rsamigrant/index.html; www.ed.gov/programs/rsarecreation/index.html (Note: no field offices for this program.)

84.129 REHABILITATION LONG-TERM TRAINING

Assistance: project grants. (90 percent/to 5 years).

Purposes: pursuant to the Rehabilitation Act of 1973 as amended, for academic training programs for personnel involved in vocational rehabilitation for the disabled. Training grants cover such specialties as rehabilitation counseling, independent living, rehabilitation medicine, physical and occupational therapy, prosthetics-orthotics, speech-language, pathology and audiology, rehabilitation of the deaf and the blind, rehabilitation technology. At least 75 percent of grant funds must be used for scholarships.

Eligible applicants: IHEs, state vocational rehabilitation agencies including territories and possessions; other public or nonprofit agencies and organizations.

Eligible beneficiaries: individuals preparing for employment in the field of rehabilitation for the disabled.

Range: $70,000 to $100,000. **Average:** $100,000.

Activity: annually, 1,500 students supported.

HQ: Rehabilitation Services Administration, OSERS-DOED, 400 Maryland Ave. SW, Washington, DC 20202-2649. Phone: (202) 245-7458.

Internet: www.ed.gov/offices/OSERS/RSA (Note: no field offices for this program.)

84.132 CENTERS FOR INDEPENDENT LIVING

Assistance: project grants. (to 100 percent/to 5 years).

Purposes: pursuant to the Rehabilitation Act of 1973 as amended, to establish and operate centers for independent living for significantly disabled persons - providing a broad range of services to residents such as information and referrals, training in independent living skills, peer counseling, and individual and systems advocacy. Individuals with disabilities must be employed by and substantially involved in policy direction and management of the centers. Personnel training may be provided with grants funds.

Eligible applicants: principally, previously funded private nonprofit agencies. If funds are available, other centers for independent living and state agencies, including territories and possessions, become eligible.

Eligible beneficiaries: persons with such significant physical, mental cognitive, or sensor impairments that independent living services are needed to attain independence in the home or community.

Range: $793,000 to $7,431,000. **Average:** $1,395,000.

Activity: 340 centers supported.

HQ: Rehabilitation Services Administration, OSERS-DOED, 400 Maryland Ave. SW, Washington, DC 20202. Phone: (202) 245-7378.

Internet: www.ed.gov/programs/cil/index.html (Note: no field offices for this program.)

84.133 NATIONAL INSTITUTE ON DISABILITY AND REHABILITATION RESEARCH

Assistance: project grants. (cost sharing/to 5 years).

Purposes: pursuant to the Rehabilitation Act of 1973 as amended, for research, demonstrations, dissemination and utilization projects, rehabilitation personnel career training, and research fellowships - involving broad ranges of programs and services for persons of all ages with physical and mental disabilities, especially the severely disabled.

Eligible applicants/beneficiaries: states; public, private, or nonprofit agencies and organizations; IHEs; tribes and tribal organizations. Individuals may obtain fellowships.

Range/Average: N.A.

Activity: FY 05, 270 projects funded.

HQ: National Institute on Disability and Rehabilitation Research, OSERS-DOED, 400 Maryland Ave. SW, Washington, DC 20202-2500. Phone: (202) 245-7462.

Internet: www.ed.gov/about/offices/list/osers/nidrr/index.html (Note: no field offices for this program.)

84.141 MIGRANT EDUCATION—HIGH SCHOOL EQUIVALENCY PROGRAM ("HEP")

Assistance: project grants. (100 percent/to 5 years).

Purposes: pursuant to HEA, Title IV, to assist migrant students obtain the equivalent of a secondary school diploma and subsequently to gain employment or to attend college or obtain other postsecondary education or training. Program funds may be used to recruit students and to provide academic and support services and stipends.

Eligible applicants: IHEs or private nonprofit agencies in cooperation with IHEs.

Eligible beneficiaries: students age 16 or older, lacking a high school diploma, in migrant or seasonally employed families, or that participated or were eligible to participate in the Title I Migrant Education Program or JTPA 402.

Average: $2,642 per student.

Activity: 2005, 7,092 students served in 50 projects.

HQ: Office of Migrant Education, OESE-DOED, 400 Maryland Ave. SW - Rm. 3E227, Washington, DC 20202. Phone: (202) 260-8103.

Internet: www.ed.gov/programs/hep/index.html (Note: no field offices for this program.)

84.144 MIGRANT EDUCATION—COORDINATION PROGRAM

Assistance: project grants. (100 percent/to 5 years).

Purposes: pursuant to ESEA, Title I, to improve interstate and intrastate coordination of migrant education among SEAs and LEAs. Incentive grants may be provided to SEAs that participate in an approved consortium.

Eligible applicants: SEAs, LEAs, IHEs, other public or nonprofit private entities.

Eligible beneficiaries: migratory children of migratory agricultural workers or fishers.

Range/Average: N.A.

Activity: FY 05, 35 consortium incentive grants.

HQ: Office of Migrant Education, OESE-DOED, 400 Maryland Ave. SW (Rm. 3E331), Washington, DC 20202-6135. Phone: (202) 260-1391.

Internet: www.ed.gov/about/offices/list/oese/ome/index.html (Note: no field offices for this program.)

84.145 FEDERAL REAL PROPERTY ASSISTANCE PROGRAM

Assistance: sale, exchange, or donation of property and goods (to 30 years).

Purposes: pursuant to the Federal Property and Administrative Services Act of 1949 as amended and Department of Education Organization Act of 1979, to convey surplus federal real property for educational purposes, including all educational levels, vocational education or rehabilitation, libraries, central administration facilities, educational radio and television, rehabilitation and training, research, correctional education centers. Examples include: improved or unimproved land; former Nike sites; total military bases.

Eligible applicants/beneficiaries: states and their political subdivisions and instrumentalities; tax-supported or tax-exempt organizations or private nonprofit institutions.

Range/Average: N.A.

Activity: annually, 10 transfers.

HQ: Federal Real Property Assistance Program, Office of the Administrator/Management Services, DOED, 400 Maryland Ave. SW, Washington, DC 20202 Phone: (202) 401-0500.

Internet: www.ed.gov.

84.149 MIGRANT EDUCATION—COLLEGE ASSISTANCE MIGRANT PROGRAM ("CAMP")

Assistance: project grants (100 percent/to 5 years).

Purposes: pursuant to HEA, Title IV, to provide supportive and instructional services and other assistance to migrants enrolling full-time in college for the first academic year. Funds may be used to provide tutoring, counseling, assistance in obtaining financial aid, follow-up services, and inservice training for project staff.

Eligible applicants: IHEs or private nonprofit agencies in cooperation with IHEs.

Eligible beneficiaries: first-year college students engaged, or whose families are engaged, in migrant or other seasonal farm work, or that participated or were eligible to participate in the Title I Migrant Education Program or JTPA 402.

Average: $6,500 per student.

Activity: 2,400 students currently being served at 45 institutions.

HQ: Office of Migrant Education, OESE-DOED, 400 Maryland Ave. SW, Washington, DC 20202 Phone: (202) 260-8103; Toll-Free: (800) 872-5327.

Internet: www.ed.gov/programs/camp/index.html (Note: no field offices for this program.)

84.153 BUSINESS AND INTERNATIONAL EDUCATION PROJECTS

Assistance: project grants. (50 percent/1-2 years).

Purposes: pursuant to HEA as amended, Title VI, for innovations and improvements in international business education curricula. Participating institutions must enter into agreements with businesses, trade organizations, or associations engaged in international economic activity.

Eligible applicants/beneficiaries: IHEs.

Average: FY 05: continuations, $79,000; new awards, $85,000.

Activity: FY 05, 55 awards.

HQ: International Education and Graduate Programs Service, OPE- DOED, 400 Maryland Ave. SW, Washington, DC 20202-5332 Phone: (202) 502-7626.

Internet: www.ed.gov/programs/iegpsbie (Note: no field offices for this program.)

84.160 TRAINING INTERPRETERS FOR INDIVIDUALS WHO ARE DEAF AND INDIVIDUALS WHO ARE DEAF-BLIND

Assistance: project grants (cost sharing/to 5 years).

Purposes: pursuant to the Rehabilitation Act of 1973 as amended, to train prospective or improve the skills of present manual, oral, and cued speech interpreters providing services to deaf or deaf-blind persons—through classroom instruction, workshops, seminars, and field placement. Curriculum may include such specialty areas as interpreting in medical, legal, or rehabilitation settings.

Eligible applicants/beneficiaries: public or private nonprofit agencies and organizations; IHEs.

Range: $120,000 to $160,000.

Activity: N.A.

HQ: Rehabilitation Services Administration, OSERS-DOED, 400 Maryland Ave. SW, Washington, DC 20202-2736. Phone: (202) 245- 7489.

Internet: www.ed.gov/students/college/aid/rehab/catinter.html (Note: no field offices for this program.)

84.161 REHABILITATION SERVICES—CLIENT ASSISTANCE PROGRAM ("CAP")

Assistance: formula grants (100 percent).

Purposes: pursuant to the Rehabilitation Act of 1973 as amended, to help persons with disabilities obtain information about and benefits of Rehabilitation Act and ADA projects, programs, facilities, and services, whether as clients or applicants for services—and to help them overcome problems with service delivery systems including assistance and advocacy in pursuing legal, administrative, and other appropriate remedies. Grants may not support class action suits.

Eligible applicants/beneficiaries: states and territories, through public or private agencies designated by the governor.

Range: $120,762 to $1,224,186.

Activity: FY 05, 57,600 clients served.

HQ: Rehabilitation Services Administration, OSERS-DOED, 400 Maryland Ave. SW, Washington, DC 20202-2500. Phone: (202) 245-7258.

Internet: www.ed.gov/programs/rsacap/index.html.

84.165 MAGNET SCHOOLS ASSISTANCE

Assistance: project grants. (100 percent/to 3 years).

Purposes: pursuant to ESEA as amended, Title V, for magnet school projects that are part of approved desegregation plans designed to bring together students from different social, economic, racial, and ethnic backgrounds. Funds may be used for planning and promotional activities to develop, expand, continue, or enhance academic instruction; to pay or subsidize teacher and staff salaries; to purchase books, materials, equipment. Funds may not be used for transportation or activities that do not augment academic improvement. Project examples: science and math magnet projects; performing arts magnet programs; Montessori programs.

Eligible applicants/beneficiaries: LEAs.

Range: $200,000 to $3,400,000.

Activity: FY 05, 52 awards.

HQ: Magnet Schools Assistance Program, School Improvement Programs, Office of Innovation and Improvement, OESE-DOED, 400 Maryland Ave. SW, Washington, DC 20202-6140. Phone: (202) 260- 2476.

Internet: www.ed.gov/programs/magnet/index.html (Note: no field offices for this program.)

84.169 INDEPENDENT LIVING—STATE GRANTS

Assistance: formula grants (50 percent).

Purposes: pursuant to the Rehabilitation Act of 1973 as amended, for states to maximize the leadership, empowerment, independence, and productivity of individuals with disabilities and their integration into the mainstream American society—through independent living services. Funds may be used to: support statewide independent living councils; support center operations; demonstrate ways to expand and improve services; increase the capacities of public or nonprofit organizations and agencies to develop comprehensive approaches and systems; conduct studies and analyses; train the disabled and service personnel; provide outreach to unserved or underserved populations.

Eligible applicants/beneficiaries: designated state agencies, territories, possessions.

Average: $432,000.

Activity: 78 state units funded.

HQ: Rehabilitation Services Administration, OSERS-DOED, 400 Maryland Ave. SW, Washington, DC 20202 Phone: (202) 245-7404.

Internet: www.ed.gov/programs/rsailstate/index.html (Note: no field offices for this program.)

84.170 JAVITS FELLOWSHIPS

Assistance: project grants. (100 percent/to 4 years).

Purposes: pursuant to HEA as amended, Title VII, for fellowships to graduate degree candidates demonstrating exceptional promise, financial need, and intending to pursue doctoral degrees in the arts, humanities, or social sciences—or terminal master's degrees.

Eligible applicants/beneficiaries: U.S. citizens, nationals, or permanent residents.

Average: $30,000; institutional allowance, $12,000.

Activity: FY 04, 234 awards.

HQ: International Education and Graduate Programs, OPE-DOED, 400 Maryland Ave, SW, Washington, DC 20202 Phone: (202) 502-7569.

Internet: www.ed.gov/programs/iegpsjavits; e-mail, ope- javits-programs@ed.gov. (Note: no field offices for this program.)

84.173 SPECIAL EDUCATION—PRESCHOOL GRANTS

Assistance: formula grants. (100 percent/15 months).

Purposes: pursuant to IDEA as amended, for free appropriate public educational programs for preschool children with disabilities, requiring special education and related services. States may also use funds to develop and implement elements of comprehensive statewide service delivery systems.

Eligible applicants: SEAs, DC, PR.

Eligible beneficiaries: children age 3-5 (optionally, age 2 and to reach age 3 during the school year), determined to be mentally retarded, hearing impaired, speech or language impaired, visually handicapped, seriously emotionally disturbed, autistic, orthopedically impaired, or other health-impaired.

Range: $247,636 to $38,677,085.

Activity: all eligible agencies funded; 701,949 children served.

HQ: Office of Special Education Programs, OSERS-DOED, 400 Maryland Ave. SW, Washington, DC 20202 Phone: (202) 245-7553.

Internet: www.ed.gov/about/offices/list/osers/osep/programs.htm (Note: no field offices for this program.)

84.177 REHABILITATION SERVICES—INDEPENDENT LIVING SERVICES FOR OLDER INDIVIDUALS WHO ARE BLIND

Assistance: project grants. (90 percent/to 5 years).

Purposes: pursuant to the Rehabilitation Act of 1973 as amended, to provide independent living services for blind persons age 55 or older, whose vision impairments make competitive employment extremely difficult, but for whom independent living in their own homes or communities is feasible. Program funds may be used to pay such costs as: vision correction or modification; eyeglasses or other visual aids; services and equipment to enhance mobility and self-care; training in braille; teaching services in household management; public education activities.

Eligible applicants/beneficiaries: state agencies, territories, possessions.

Average: $630,000.

Activity: 56 projects funded.

HQ: Rehabilitation Services Administration, OSERS-DOED, 400 Maryland Ave. SW- (Rm.5057 PCP), Washington, DC 20202 Phone: (202) 245-7404.

Internet: www.ed.gov/programs/rsailob/index.html (Note: no field offices for this program.)

84.181 SPECIAL EDUCATION—GRANTS FOR INFANTS AND FAMILIES

Assistance: formula grants. (100 percent/to 27 months).

Purposes: pursuant to IDEA as amended, to develop and implement statewide, comprehensive, coordinated, multidisciplinary, inter- agency systems to provide early intervention services for handicapped infants and toddlers and their families. Grants may support expanded or improved services.

Eligible applicants/beneficiaries: states, territories, possessions.

Range: $2,160,000 to $53,695,000. **Average:** $8,309,000.

Activity: FY 05, 286,080 participants served.

HQ: Office of Special Education Programs, OSERS-DOED, 400 Maryland Ave. SW, Washington, DC 20202 Phone: (202) 245-7629.

Internet: www.ed.gov/about/offices/list/osers/osep/programs.html (Note: no field offices for this program.)

84.184 SAFE AND DRUG-FREE SCHOOLS AND COMMUNITIES—NATIONAL PROGRAMS

Assistance: project grants. (to 100 percent/1-4 years).

Purposes: pursuant to ESEA as amended, Title IV, for prevention and education activities concerning the illegal use of drugs and violence at all educational levels.

Eligible applicants/beneficiaries: public and private and nonprofit organizations, individuals.

Range/Average: N.A.

Activity: FY 05, 86 safe schools/healthy students initiative, 254 mentoring awards; 150 other grants.

HQ: Office of Safe and Drug-Free Schools, DOED, 400 Maryland Ave. SW, Washington, DC 20202-6123 Phone: (202) 260-3954.

Internet: www.ed.gov/about/offices/list/osdfs/programs.html#state (Note: no field offices for this program.)

84.185 BYRD HONORS SCHOLARSHIPS

Assistance: formula grants. (100 percent/to 4 years).

Purposes: pursuant to HEA as amended, Title IV, for $1,500 annual merit scholarships to recognize and promote student excellence and achievement. Each participating state is allotted at least 10 scholarships, based on population.

Eligible applicants: SEAs including territories and possessions.

Eligible beneficiaries: U.S. citizens or residents that are public or private high school graduates, accepted for enrollment at IHEs, demonstrating promise of continued outstanding academic achievement.

Range/Average: scholarships, to $1,500.

Activity: FY 04, 27,114 scholarships.

HQ: Higher Education Programs, OPE-DOED, 400 Maryland Ave. SW, Washington, DC 20024-5251 Phone: (202) 502-7657.

Internet: www.ed.gov/programs/iduesbyrd (Note: no field offices for this program.)

84.186 SAFE AND DRUG-FREE SCHOOLS AND COMMUNITIES—STATE GRANTS

Assistance: formula grants (100 percent).

Purposes: pursuant to ESEA as amended, Title IV, to establish alcohol, drug, tobacco, and violence prevention and education programs in local school systems, coordinated with related federal, state, and community efforts and resources including parent involvement. At least 20 percent of awarded funds must be distributed to community-based organizations.

Eligible applicants: state departments of education, governors, insular areas, native Hawaiian organizations.

Eligible beneficiaries: SEAs, LEAs, tribal governments, public and private nonprofit organizations including community action agencies, parent groups, and other community-based organizations.

Range: $2,135,000 to $53,743,000. **Average:** $8,212,000.

Activity: awards to all states, insular areas, and BIA.

HQ: Office of Safe and Drug-Free Schools, DOED, 400 Maryland Ave. SW-Room 3E314, Washington, DC 20202-6123 Phone: (202) 205-8134.

Internet: www.ed.gov/about/offices/list/osdfs/programs.html#state (Note: no field offices for this program.)

84.187 SUPPORTED EMPLOYMENT SERVICES FOR INDIVIDUALS WITH SIGNIFICANT DISABILITIES ("Supported Employment State Grants")

Assistance: formula grants (100 percent).

Purposes: pursuant to the Rehabilitation Act of 1973 as amended, for time-limited services leading to supported employment for severely handicapped persons whose potential to engage in a training program has been properly evaluated. Funds may be used for most program operating costs including systematic client training, skilled job trainers to accompany workers for intensive on-the-job training, job development, follow-up services.

Eligible applicants/beneficiaries: state vocational rehabilitation agencies, territories and possessions.

Range: states, $300,000 to $4,120,381.

Activity: N.A.

HQ: Rehabilitation Services Administration, OSERS-DOED, 400 Maryland Ave. SW, Washington, DC 20202-2500 Phone: (202) 245-7598.

Internet: www.ed.gov/programs/rsasupemp/index.html (Note: no field offices for this program.)

84.191 ADULT EDUCATION—NATIONAL LEADERSHIP ACTIVITIES

Assistance: project grants. (100 percent/12-18 months).

Purposes: pursuant to the Adult Education and Family Literacy Act as amended, for the improvement and expansion nationally of adult basic education through applied research, development, demonstration, dissemination, evaluation, and related activities. Project examples: evaluations of "what works" for adult basic education and ESL, the funding set-aside for corrections education, and distance learning initiative.

Eligible applicants/beneficiaries: public or private agencies, institutions, organizations; business concerns; individuals.

Range/Average: N.A.

Activity: not quantified specifically.

HQ: Division of Adult Education and Literacy, OVAE-DOED, 400 Maryland Ave. SW, Washington, DC 20202-7240 Phone: (202) 245-7814.

Internet: www.ed.gov/about/offices/list/ovae/pi/AdultEd/index.htm (Note: no field offices for this program.)

84.196 EDUCATION FOR HOMELESS CHILDREN AND YOUTH

Assistance: formula grants (100 percent).

Purposes: pursuant to MVHAA, to develop and implement plans to coordinate and improve education programs for homeless children and youth; to identify homeless children and ensure that they enroll in, attend, and achieve success in school. States may provide subgrants to LEAs for direct services to homeless children and youth including tutoring, summer enrichment programs, purchases of supplies, school personnel training.

Eligible applicants/beneficiaries: state departments of education and outlying areas; schools funded by DOI, serving Indian students.

Average: states, $1,179,000.

Activity: awards to 50 states, DC, PR, VI, Guam, Samoa, Palau, Northern Marianas, and BIA.

HQ: OESE-DOED, 400 Maryland Ave. SW, Washington, DC 20202-6132 Phone: (202) 260-4412.

Internet: www.ed.gov/programs/homeless/index.html (Note: no field offices for this program.)

84.200 GRADUATE ASSISTANCE IN AREAS OF NATIONAL NEED ("GAANN")

Assistance: project grants. (75 percent/3-5 years).

Purposes: pursuant to HEA as amended, Title VII, for graduate fellowships for up to five years that will help sustain and enhance the capacity for teaching and research in academic areas of national need, designated by the Secretary of Education.

Eligible applicants: IHEs.

Eligible beneficiaries: needy graduate students with excellent academic records and planning teaching or research careers. They must be U.S. citizens, nationals, permanent residents, or permanent residents of the Trust Territory of the Pacific Islands or citizens of Freely Associated States.

Average: continuation grants, $209,000; continuation fellowships, $41,000.

Activity: FY 05, 145 grants awarded providing 736 fellowships.

HQ: International Education and Graduate Programs Service, OPE- DOED, 400 Maryland Ave. SW, Washington, DC 20202-5247. Phone: (202) 502-7767.

Internet: www.ed.gov/programs/iegpsgaann/; e-mail, ope.gaann.program@ed.gov. (Note: no field offices for this program.)

84.203 STAR SCHOOLS

Assistance: project grants. (50-75 percent/to 5 years).

Purposes: pursuant to ESEA as amended, Title V, for telecommunications partnerships to encourage improved instruction in mathematics, science, foreign languages, vocational education, literacy skills, and other subjects. Funds may be used: to develop telecommunications facilities and to acquire equipment, instructional programming; for technical assistance; for teacher training. Priority is given to projects that will meet the needs of traditionally underserved populations.

Eligible applicants/beneficiaries: partnerships organized on a statewide or multistate basis (1) by public agencies or corporations or, (2) that include at least one SEA or LEA, and three or more of the following: LEAs with a significant number of schools eligible for Title I funds (or operated by DOI for Indian children); SEAs; adult and family education programs; teaching training centers; public or private agencies with relevant experience, or public broadcasting entities; or a public or private elementary or secondary school.

Range/Average: N.A.

Activity: FY 05, 10 grants.

HQ: Technology in Education Programs, OII-DOED, 400 Maryland Ave. SW- Rm. 4W219, FB-6, Washington, DC 20208-5900. Phone: (202) 205-5633.

Internet: www.ed.gov/programs/starschools/index.html. (Note: no field offices for this program.)

84.206 JAVITS GIFTED AND TALENTED STUDENTS EDUCATION GRANT PROGRAM

Assistance: project grants. (100 percent/to 3 years).

Purposes: pursuant to ESEA as amended, Title V, for programs designed to meet the special educational needs of gifted and talented elementary and secondary students, including: personnel professional development; exemplary programs; innovative learning strategies; SEA leadership and assistance to local entities in planning, operating, and improving programs; research, technical assistance, and information dissemination.

Eligible applicants/beneficiaries: SEAs, LEAs, IHEs, public and private agencies and organizations, including tribes and Hawaii native organizations.

Average: $468,000.

Activity: FY 05, 11 awards; National Center for Research and Development in the Education of Gifted and Talented Children and Youth also funded.

HQ: Jacob J. Javits Gifted and Talented Students Education, OESE- DOED, 400 Maryland Ave. SW, Washington, DC 20202. Phone: (202) 260-7813.

Internet: www.ed.gov/programs/javits/index.htm/. (Note: no field offices for this program.)

84.213 EVEN START—STATE EDUCATIONAL AGENCIES

Assistance: formula grants; project grants. (subgrants, 50-90 percent/subgrants, to 4 years).

Purposes: pursuant to ESEA as amended, Title I, for education projects involving low-income parents in the early education of their children, and to provide literacy training and adult and parenting education. Subgrants may support participant recruitment and screening, program design and coordination, instruction of children and parents, staff training.

Eligible applicants/beneficiaries: SEAs. Subgrants—partnerships of LEAs and community-based organizations, public agencies, IHEs, or other nonprofit organizations, with priority to projects in Empowerment Zones or Enterprise Communities.

Range: $1,014,000 to $27,702,000. **Average:** $3,901,000.

Activity: 1,000 projects funded in all states.

HQ: Student Achievement and School Accountability Programs, OESE-DOED, 400 Maryland Ave. SW, Washington, DC 20202-6132. Phone: (202) 205-8736.

Internet: www.ed.gov/programs/evenstartformula/index.html. (Note: no field offices for this program.)

84.214 EVEN START—MIGRANT EDUCATION

Assistance: project grants (60-90 percent/to 4 years).

Purposes: pursuant to ESEA as amended, Title I, for education projects involving parents of migratory children in the early education of their children from birth-age 7, including adult literacy and adult basic and parenting education. Funds may support participant recruitment and screening, program design and coordination, instruction of children and parents, staff training.

Eligible applicants/beneficiaries: SEAs, LEAs, other entities including nonprofit community-based organizations.

Range/Average: N.A.

Activity: 28 projects operating.

HQ: Office of Migrant Education, OESE-DOED, FOB 6 - Rm.3E313, 400 Maryland Ave. SW, Washington, DC 20202-6134. Phone: (202) 260-9533.

Internet: www.ed.gov/programs/mep/index.html (Note: no field offices for this program.)

84.215 FUND FOR THE IMPROVEMENT OF EDUCATION ("FIE")

Assistance: project grants (100 percent).

Purposes: pursuant to ESEA as amended, Title V, for projects of national significance to improve the quality of education, to assist all students to meet challenging state content standards, and contribute to the achievement of elementary and secondary students. Projects may support a wide range of activities.

Eligible applicants/beneficiaries: SEAs, LEAs, IHEs, public and private organizations.

Range/Average: N.A.

Activity: N.A.

HQ: OERI-DOED, 555 New Jersey Ave. NW, Washington, DC 20208-5645. Phone: (202) 401-2492.

Internet: www.ed.gov/programs/fie/index.html. (Note: no field offices for this program.)

84.217 TRIO—MCNAIR POST-BACCALAUREATE ACHIEVEMENT

Assistance: project grants. (100 percent/4-5 years).

Purposes: pursuant to HEA as amended, Title IV, to prepare low- income, first-generation college students and students from under-represented groups for graduate study. Services may include: opportunities for research and other scholarly activities; summer internships; seminars; tutoring; academic counseling; securing graduate admission and financial assistance; mentoring; exposure to cultural events.

Eligible applicants/beneficiaries: IHEs or combinations of IHEs.

Average: new awards, $247,000; continuations, $235,000.

Activity: FY 05, 178 grants, serving 4,236 students.

HQ: Federal TRIO Programs, OPE-DOED, 400 Maryland Ave. SW, Washington, DC 20202-5249. Phone: (202) 502-7730, -7694.

Internet: www.ed.gov/programs/triomcnair/; e-mail, trio@ed.gov. (Note: no field offices for this program.)

84.220 CENTERS FOR INTERNATIONAL BUSINESS EDUCATION

Assistance: project grants. (50-90 percent/3 years).

Purposes: pursuant to HEA as amended, Title VI, for inter- disciplinary faculty research to promote international competitiveness of U.S. business. Activities must include: center advisory councils to plan and design activities and programs; collaboration in the center's establishment and operation among the business, management, foreign language, international studies, and other professional schools or departments; assurance that the center's programs are open to students concentrating in these areas.

Eligible applicants/beneficiaries: public and nonprofit private IHEs, or combinations thereof.

Average: $357,000.

Activity: FY 05, 30 grants.

HQ: International Studies Branch, Center for International Education, 400 Maryland Ave., SW, Washington, DC 20202-5332. Phone: (202) 502-7700.

Internet: www.ed.gov/programs/iegpscibe/. (Note: no field offices for this program.)

84.224 ASSISTIVE TECHNOLOGY

Assistance: project grants; technical information.

Purposes: pursuant to the Assistive Technology Act of 1998, to develop and implement comprehensive consumer-responsive statewide programs of technology-related assistance and services for persons of all ages with disabilities, and to their family members, guardians, advocates, and authorized representatives. States may provide assistance directly to individuals or to statewide community-based organizations.

Eligible applicants/beneficiaries: states, DC, PR, outlying areas; Governor-designated applicants.

Range/Average: N.A.

Activity: FY 05, awards to 33 states.

HQ: National Institute on Disability and Rehabilitation Research, OSERS-DOED, 400 Maryland Ave. SW, Washington, DC 20202-2500. Phone: (202) 245-7319. (Note: no field offices for this program.)

Internet: www.ed.gov/about/offices/list/nidrr/index.html. (Note: no field offices for this program.)

84.229 LANGUAGE RESOURCE CENTERS

Assistance: project grants. (100 percent/to 3 years).

Purposes: pursuant to HEA as amended, Title VI, to establish, strengthen, and operate foreign language resource centers to improve teaching and learning at IHEs, through: research on the use of advanced educational technology; development of new teaching materials based on the research; development and application of performance testing; teacher training; publication of instructional materials in the less commonly taught languages; dissemination of project results.

Eligible applicants/beneficiaries: IHEs or combinations of IHEs.

Average: $346,000.

Activity: FY 05, 14 awards.

HQ: International Education and Graduate Programs Service, OPE- DOED, 400 Maryland Ave. SW, Washington, DC 20202-5331. Phone: (202) 502-7636.

Internet: www.ed.gov/programs/iegpslrc/. (Note: no field offices for this program.)

84.234 PROJECTS WITH INDUSTRY ("PWI")

Assistance: project grants (80 percent/to 5 years).

Purposes: pursuant to the Rehabilitation Act of 1973 as amended, for programs preparing persons with disabilities for employment in the competitive labor market, by partnering with private industry to provide job training, placement, and career advancement services.

Eligible applicants/beneficiaries: employers, profit and nonprofit organizations, labor unions, state vocational rehabilitation agencies. New awards are available only in unserved or under-served areas.

Average: $235,000.

Activity: FY 04, 86 awards.

HQ: OSERS-DOED, 400 Maryland Ave. SW, Washington, DC 20202-2740. Phone: (202) 245-7281.

Internet: www.ed.gov/programs/rsapwi/index.html.

84.235 REHABILITATION SERVICES DEMONSTRATION AND TRAINING PROGRAMS

Assistance: project grants (100 percent/to 5 years).

Purposes: pursuant to the Rehabilitation Act of 1973 as amended, to expand and improve vocational rehabilitation and related services for the disabled and severely disabled. Projects may include demonstrations involving such activities as: increasing client choice; service delivery; technical assistance; systems change; special studies and evaluations; transition services; supportive employment; services to unserved, underserved, or populations, and to low-incidence disabilities; transportation; parent information and training; Braille training.

Eligible applicants/beneficiaries: states, public or nonprofit organizations.

Range/Average: N.A.

Activity: FY 05, 62 projects funded.

HQ: Rehabilitation Services Administration, OSERS-DOED, 400 Maryland Ave. SW, Washington, DC 20202-2500 Phone: (202) 245-7458.

Internet: www.ed.gov/offices/OSERS/RSA/Programs/Discretionary/demotrain.html (Note: no field offices for this program.)

84.240 PROGRAM OF PROTECTION AND ADVOCACY OF INDIVIDUAL RIGHTS ("PAIR")

Assistance: project grants (100 percent).

Purposes: pursuant to the Rehabilitation Act of 1973 as amended, for systems for protection and advocacy of the rights of persons with disabilities—including services upholding their individual legal and human rights beyond the scope of the Client Assistance Program, and for persons ineligible for programs under the Developmental Disabilities Assistance

(DDA) and Bill of Rights Act and the Protection and Advocacy for Individuals with Mental Illness Act (PAIMI).

Eligible applicants/beneficiaries: state-designated protection and advocacy agencies, including territories.

Range: $168,000 to $1,692,000.

Activity: FY 05, 87,300 persons served.

HQ: Rehabilitation Services Administration, OSERS-DOED, 400 Maryland Ave. SW, Washington, DC 20202-2500 Phone: (202) 245-7273.

Internet: www.ed.gov/programs/rsapair/index.html (Note: no field offices for this program.)

84.243 TECH-PREP EDUCATION

Assistance: formula grants, project grants. (100 percent/27 months).

Purposes: pursuant to CDPVTEA, for planning and demonstrations by educational consortia to develop and operate four-year programs to provide "tech-prep" education programs leading to two- year associate degrees or certificates, establishing proficiency in mathematics, science, communications, and technologies. The four years must include the two years preceding and following graduation from secondary school, including apprenticeships. Funds may support curriculum development, inservice teacher and counselor training.

Eligible applicants/beneficiaries: state vocational education boards. Subgrants—consortia of LEAs, intermediate education agencies or area vocational education schools serving secondary students, BIA-funded secondary schools, nonprofit and proprietary IHEs, offering two-year associate degrees, and two-year apprenticeship programs that follow secondary instruction.

Range: $58,000 to $11,563,000.

Activity: Tech-Prep consortia in 50 states, DC, PR, and VI.

HQ: OVAE Division of High School, Postsecondary and Career Education, OVAE-DOED, 400 Maryland Ave. SW, Washington, DC 20202-7241. Phone: (202) 245-7735.

Internet: www.ed.gov/about/offices/ovae/pi/cte/tphome.html. (Note: no field offices for this program.)

84.245 TRIBALLY CONTROLLED POSTSECONDARY CAREER AND TECHNICAL INSTITUTIONS

Assistance: project grants. (100 percent/to 5 years).

Purposes: pursuant to CDPVTEA, for the maintenance and operation of tribally controlled postsecondary vocational and technical institutions.

Eligible applicants/beneficiaries: chartered and accredited tribally controlled postsecondary vocational institutions that: have operated for at least three years; enroll at least 100 full- time students (a majority of which are Indians); and, meet other requirements.

Range: $3,000,000 to $4,375,000.

Activity: FY 05, 2 awards.

HQ: OVAE Division of High School, Postsecondary and Career Education, OVAE-DOED, 400 Maryland Ave. SW, Washington, DC 20202-7242. Phone: (202) 245-7737.

Internet: www.ed.gov/programs/tcpvi/index.html. (Note: no field offices for this program.)

84.246 REHABILITATION SHORT-TERM TRAINING

Assistance: project grants. (cost sharing/1-3 years).

Purposes: pursuant to the Rehabilitation Act of 1973 as amended, for special training seminars, institutes, workshops, and other short-term courses in technical matters relating to the delivery of vocational, medical, social, and psychological services—in fields directly related to the vocational and independent living rehabilitation of persons with disabilities.

Eligible applicants/beneficiaries: IHEs, state vocational rehabilitation agencies including territories and possessions; other public or nonprofit agencies and organizations.

Range: $100,000 to $250,000.

Activity: not quantified specifically.

HQ: Rehabilitation Services Administration, OSERS-DOED, 400 Maryland Ave. SW, Washington, DC 20202-2649. Phone: (202) 245-7458.

Internet: www.ed.gov/offices/OSERS/RSA.

84.250 REHABILITATION SERVICES—AMERICAN INDIANS WITH DISABILITIES

Assistance: project grants. (90 percent/to 5 years).

Purposes: pursuant to the Rehabilitation Act of 1973 as amended, to establish and operate tribal vocational rehabilitation service projects serving American Indians with disabilities, residing on reservations.

Eligible applicants/beneficiaries: tribal governments or consortia on federal or state reservations.

Range: $250,000 to $400,000.

Activity: FY 05, 72 projects funded.

HQ: Rehabilitation Services Administration, OSERS-DOED, 400 Maryland Ave. SW, Washington, DC 20202-2500. Phone: (202) 245-7485.

Internet: www.ed.gov/about/offices/list/osers/osep/programs.html. (Note: no field offices for this program.)

84.256 FREELY ASSOCIATED STATES—EDUCATION GRANT PROGRAM

Assistance: project grants. (100 percent/3 years).

Purposes: pursuant to ESEA as amended, Title I, for educational activities including teacher training, curriculum development, instructional materials, general school improvement, and schoolwide reform.

Eligible applicants/beneficiaries: LEAs in Micronesia, Marshall Islands, Palau.

Range: $250,000 to $500,000.

Activity: annually, 7-10 awards.

HQ: School Support and Technology Programs, OESE-DOED, FOB 6 - Rm.3E245, 400 Maryland Ave. SW, Washington, DC 20202-6140. Phone: (202) 260-2543.

Internet: www.ed.gov/programs/tfasegp/index.html.

84.257 NATIONAL INSTITUTE FOR LITERACY ("NIL")

Assistance: project grants (100 percent).

Purposes: pursuant to the Adult Education and Family Literacy Act, to coordinate literacy services and services; to serve as a national resource for adult education and literacy programs through dissemination. Program is governed by an interagency group made up of DOED, DOL, and HHS. Project examples: inter- agency systems; internet-based literacy information system.

Eligible applicants/beneficiaries: public and private nonprofit institutions.

Range/Average: N.A.

Activity: not quantified specifically.

HQ: National Institute for Literacy, DOED, 1775 I St. NW, Washington, DC 20006. Phone: (202) 233-2025.

Internet: www.nifl.gov. (Note: no field offices for this program.)

84.258 EVEN START—INDIAN TRIBES AND TRIBAL ORGANIZATIONS

Assistance: project grants (50-90 percent/to 4 years).

Purposes: pursuant to ESEA as amended, Title I, to operate family-centered education projects involving low-income parents in the early education of their children from birth-age 7, and to provide literacy training, and adult and parenting education. Funds may support participant recruitment and screening, program design and coordination, instruction of children and parents, staff training.

Eligible applicants/beneficiaries: tribes and tribal organizations.

Range: $100,000 to $200,000.

Activity: FY 05 estimate, 29 grants.

HQ: OESE-DOED, 400 Maryland Ave. SW, Washington, DC 20202-6132. Phone: (202) 260-0999.

Internet: www.ed.gov/programs/evenstartindian/index.html. (Note: no field offices for this program.)

84.259 NATIVE HAWAIIAN CAREER AND TECHNICAL EDUCATION

Assistance: project grants (100 percent/to 5 years).

Purposes: pursuant to CDPVTEA, for vocational education projects conducted by organizations primarily serving and representing Hawaii natives.

Eligible applicants/beneficiaries: organizations recognized by the governor, primarily serving and representing Hawaii natives.

Range/Average: N.A.

Activity: not quantified specifically.

HQ: Division of High School, Postsecondary and Career Education, OVAE-DOED, 400 Maryland Ave. SW, Washington, DC 20202-7242 Phone: (202) 245-7737, -7792.

Internet: www.ed.gov/programs/ctenhvep/index.html (Note: no field offices for this program.)

84.263 REHABILITATION TRAINING—EXPERIMENTAL AND INNOVATIVE TRAINING

Assistance: project grants. (cost sharing/to 5 years).

Purposes: pursuant to the Rehabilitation Act of 1973 as amended, to develop new and improved methods of training rehabilitation personnel, relating to vocational and independent living services provided to persons with disabilities.

Eligible applicants/beneficiaries: IHEs, state vocational rehabilitation agencies including territories and possessions; other public or nonprofit agencies and organizations.

Range/Average: N.A.

Activity: not quantified specifically.

HQ: Rehabilitation Services Administration, OSERS-DOED, 400 Maryland Ave. SW, Washington, DC 20202-2649 Phone: (202) 245-7458.

Internet: www.ed.gov/offices/OSERS/RSA (Note: no field offices for this program.)

84.264 REHABILITATION TRAINING—CONTINUING EDUCATION

Assistance: project grants (cost sharing/to 5 years).

Purposes: pursuant to the Rehabilitation Act of 1973 as amended, for regional or area training centers providing continuing education for rehabilitation counselors, administrators, independent living specialists, audiologists, rehabilitation teachers for the blind, and rehabilitation technology specialists—providing vocational, independent living, and client assistance services to the disabled.

Eligible applicants/beneficiaries: IHEs, state vocational rehabilitation agencies including territories and possessions; other public or nonprofit agencies and organizations.

Range/Average: N.A.

Activity: not quantified specifically.

HQ: Rehabilitation Services Administration, OSERS-DOED, 400 Maryland Ave. SW, Washington, DC 20202-2649 Phone: (202) 245-7458.

Internet: www.ed.gov/offices/OSERS/RSA (Note: no field offices for this program.)

84.265 REHABILITATION TRAINING—STATE VOCATIONAL REHABILITATION UNIT IN-SERVICE TRAINING

Assistance: project grants. (90 percent/to 3 years).

Purposes: pursuant to the Rehabilitation Act of 1973 as amended, for special projects to train state vocational rehabilitation unit personnel. Projects must address: recruitment and retention of professionals; planning needs; issues of leadership development and capacity building; training on provisions of the Act and amendments.

Eligible applicants/beneficiaries: state vocational rehabilitation agencies including territories and possessions.

Range: $7,400 to $240,000. **Average:** $70,000.

Activity: 13,000 rehabilitation personnel participating.

HQ: Rehabilitation Services Administration, OSERS-DOED, 400 Maryland Ave. SW, Washington, DC 20202-2649. Phone: (202) 245-7458.

Internet: www.ed.gov/offices/OSERS/RSA (Note: no field offices for this program.)

84.268 FEDERAL DIRECT STUDENT LOANS

Assistance: direct loans (10-30 years).

Purposes: pursuant to HEA as amended, Title IV, to provide education loans for any school year to vocational, undergraduate, professional, and graduate postsecondary students and their parents—directly from DOED rather than through private lenders. Subsidized loans are based on financial need; unsubsidized loans are not. Standard, extended, consolidated, and graduated repayment plans are available. Generally, repayment begins six months after termination of at least half-time enrollment.

Eligible applicants/beneficiaries: U.S. citizens, nationals, or permanent residents enrolled or accepted for at least half-time enrollment at a participating postsecondary school. Parents may borrow for dependent students under the Direct PLUS program. School enrollment is not required for Direct Consolidation Loans which are available to students, married couples, or parents if they are unable to obtain consolidated loans under **84.032** (Federal Family Education Loans). Students must maintain satisfactory academic progress, be in compliance with Selective Service requirements, and neither owe a refund nor be in default on a Title IV grant or loan.

Range/Average: N.A.

Activity: FY 05, 3,600,000 loans.

HQ: Federal Direct Loans, OFSA-DOED, Washington, DC 20202. Phone: Student Financial Aid Information Center, (800) 443-3243.

Internet: www.ed.gov/programs/iegpsiipp.

84.269 INSTITUTE FOR INTERNATIONAL PUBLIC POLICY

Assistance: project grants. (50 percent/to 5 years).

Purposes: pursuant to HEA as amended, Title VI, to establish an institute of international public policy to conduct a program to increase the numbers of African-Americans and other under- represented minorities in the international service, including with private international voluntary organizations and the U.S. Foreign Service. Funds may support a junior year abroad, graduate fellowships, internships, intensive academic programs such as summer institutes, or intensive language training.

Eligible applicants/beneficiaries: a consortium of institutions eligible for assistance under HEA Title III, Part B, and an IHE serving substantial numbers of African-Americans or other under- represented minority students.

Average: one award only, $1,616,000 in FY 05.

Activity: FY 05, 1 award.

HQ: International Education and Graduate Programs Service, OPE- DOED, 400 Maryland Ave. SW, Washington, DC 20202-5332. Phone: (202) 502-7626.

Internet: www.ed.gov/programs/iegpsiipp/. (Note: no field offices for this program.)

84.274 AMERICAN OVERSEAS RESEARCH CENTERS

Assistance: project grants. (100 percent/3 years).

Purposes: pursuant to HEA as amended, Title VI, to establish or operate overseas research centers that are consortia of IHEs to promote postgraduate research, exchanges, and area studies. Funds may cover the costs of: faculty and staff stipends, salaries, travel, and research; student travel; maintenance and operations; teaching and research materials; conferences; publications.

Eligible applicants/beneficiaries: tax-exempt permanent overseas centers receiving over 50 percent of their funding from public or private U.S. sources.

Average: $83,000.

Activity: FY 05, 12 awards.

HQ: International Education and Graduate Programs Service, OPE- DOED, 400 Maryland Ave. SW, Washington, DC 20202-5331. Phone: (202) 502-7634.

Internet: www.ed.gov/programs/iegpsaorc/. (Note: no field offices for this program.)

84.275 REHABILITATION TRAINING—GENERAL TRAINING

Assistance: project grants. (100 percent/1-5 years).

Purposes: pursuant to the Rehabilitation Act of 1973 as amended, for education programs for rehabilitation personnel providing services to persons with disabilities through such programs as: vocational, medical, social, and psychological rehabilitation; supported employment; independent living client assistance. Specialties include rehabilitation counselors, administrators, audiologists, teachers of the blind, rehabilitation teachers, and rehabilitation technology specialists.

Eligible applicants: IHEs, state vocational rehabilitation agencies including territories and possessions; other public or nonprofit agencies and organizations.

Eligible beneficiaries: individuals working in the field of rehabilitation of individuals with disabilities.

Range/Average: N.A.

Activity: clearinghouse for rehabilitation training materials.

HQ: Rehabilitation Services Administration, OSERS-DOED, 400 Maryland Ave. SW, Washington, DC 20202-2649. Phone: (202) 245-7458.

Internet: www.ed.gov.offices/OSERS/RSA (Note: no field offices for this program.)

84.282 CHARTER SCHOOLS

Assistance: project grants. (100 percent/to 3 years).

Purposes: pursuant to ESEA as amended, Title V, for the planning, development, and initial implementation of charter schools which provide enhanced parental choice while exempt from many statutory and regulatory requirements, in return for which the schools establish plans to improve student academic achievement and stimulate the creativity and commitment of teachers, parents, and the public.

Eligible applicants/beneficiaries: SEAs. If SEAs do not participate, authorized public chartering agencies or other public entities may apply.

Average: SEAs, $3,000,000.

Activity: 1,200 schools supported.

HQ: Parental Options and Information, OII-DOED, 400 Maryland Ave. SW, Washington, DC 20202. Phone: (202) 260-1882.

Internet: www.ed.gov/programs/charter/index.html (Note: no field offices for this program.)

84.283 COMPREHENSIVE CENTERS

Assistance: project grants; technical information. (grants, 100 percent/grants, to 5 years).

Purposes: pursuant to the Education Sciences Reform Act of 2002, to support not less than 20 comprehensive centers provide training, technical assistance, and professional development in reading, mathematics, and technology—particularly to school districts and schools that fail to meet their state's definition of adequate yearly progress. Sixteen centers focus on such areas as: implementation and administration of programs authorized under ESEA; using scientifically valid teaching methods and assessment tools in mathematics, science, reading and language arts, English language acquisition, education technology; facilitating communication between education experts, school officials, teachers, parents, and librarians; related information dissemination. Five content centers focus on accountability, instruction, teacher quality, innovation and improvement, and high schools.

Eligible applicants/beneficiaries: public or private nonprofit entities or consortia.

Average: $2,081,000.

Activity: FY 05, 21 center awards.

HQ: School Support and Technology Programs, OESE-DOED, 400 Maryland Ave. SW, Washington, DC 20202-6140. Phone: (202) 401-0039.

Internet: www.ed.gov/about/contacts/gen/othersites/compcenters.html; www.ed.gov/pubs/ExcellAcctTeach/part-5.html (Note: no field offices for this program.)

84.286 READY TO TEACH

Assistance: project grants. (50 percent/to 3 years).

Purposes: pursuant to ESEA as amended, Title V, for a national telecommunications-based program to improve teaching in core curriculum areas. Projects must: use the public broadcasting infrastructure, the internet, and school digital networks to deliver video and data in an integrated service to train teachers in the use of materials and learning technologies; be conducted in cooperation with appropriate SEAs, LEAs, state, and local profit public telecommunications entities; ensure that a significant portion of project benefits will be available to schools with a high percentage of children counted for the purpose of ESEA Title I, Part A. The program also provides digital educational programming grants, enabling development, production, and distribution of innovative educational video programming.

Eligible applicants: public telecommunications entities or partnership of such entities.

Eligible beneficiaries: elementary and secondary school teachers.

Range/Average: N.A.

Activity: FY 05, 2 national telecommunications awards; 2 digital educational programming awards.

HQ: Technology in Education Programs, OII-DOED, 400 Maryland Ave. SW, Washington, DC 20202. Phone: (202) 205-5880.

Internet: www.ed.gov/programs/readyteach/index.html (Note: no field offices for this program.)

84.287 TWENTY-FIRST CENTURY COMMUNITY LEARNING CENTERS

Assistance: formula grants (100 percent).

Purposes: pursuant to ESEA as amended, Title IV, for community learning centers to provide academic enrichment opportunities in core subjects for children and literacy programs for families, in rural and inner-city areas.

Eligible applicants: state departments of education.

Eligible beneficiaries: residents within communities served by learning centers.

Range: $4,856,000 to $137,175,000.

Activity: FY 05, 1,320,000 students served.

HQ: 21st Century Community Learning Centers, OESE-DOED, 400 Maryland Ave. SW, Washington, DC 20202-6100. Phone: (202) 260-2514.

Internet: www.ed.gov/programs/21stcclc/index.html (Note: no field offices for this program.)

84.293 FOREIGN LANGUAGE ASSISTANCE

Assistance: project grants. (50 percent/3 years).

Purposes: pursuant to ESEA as amended, Title V, for innovative model programs of foreign language study in public elementary and secondary schools.

Eligible applicants: SEAs, LEAs.

Eligible beneficiaries: elementary and secondary school children.

Range: $33,000 to $175,000.

Activity: FY 05, 127 awards.

HQ: Office of English Language Acquisition, OESE-DOED, 400 Maryland Ave. SW, Washington, DC 20202. Phone: (202) 245-7133.

Internet: www.ed.gov/programs/flap/index.html (Note: no field offices for this program.)

84.295 READY-TO-LEARN TELEVISION

Assistance: project grants. (100 percent/to 5 years).

Purposes: pursuant to ESEA as amended, Title II, to develop: educational programming for preschool and early elementary school children and their families; educational television, programming, and ancillary materials to increase school readiness for young children with limited English proficiency; family literacy programs; support materials and services promoting effective use of educational programming.

Eligible applicants: qualified public telecommunications entities.

Eligible beneficiaries: young children, their parents, child care workers, Head Start providers.

Range/Average: N.A.

Activity: not quantified specifically.

HQ: Technology in Education Programs, OII-DOED, 500 Maryland Ave. SW, Washington, DC 20202. Phone: (202) 205-449.

Internet: www.ed.gov/programs/rtltv/index.html(Note: no field offices for this program.)

84.298 STATE GRANTS FOR INNOVATIVE PROGRAMS

Assistance: formula grants (100 percent).

Purposes: pursuant to ESEA as amended, Title V, for reforms in elementary and secondary education by LEAs and SEAs. Funds may be used for such related purposes as: implementing programs that rely on scientifically-based research; providing library services and instructional and media materials; improving services to disadvantaged students; class-size reduction programs.

Eligible applicants: states, DC, PR, and insular areas.

Eligible beneficiaries: public and private elementary and secondary students.

Range: $985,000 to $24,694,000. **Average:** $3,789,000.

Activity: not quantified specifically.

HQ: School Support and Technology Programs, OESE-DOED, FOB 6 - Rm.3E245, 400 Maryland Ave. SW, Washington, DC 20202-6140. Phone: (202) 260-2540.

Internet: www.ed.gov/programs/innovative/index.html; www.ed.gov/policy/elsec/leg/esea02/pg57.html (Note: no field offices for this program.)

84.304 CIVIC EDUCATION—COOPERATIVE EDUCATION EXCHANGE PROGRAM

Assistance: project grants (100 percent).

Purposes: pursuant to ESEA as amended, Title II, for international K-12 education exchange activities between the U.S. and eligible countries, in civics, government, and economics education—in Eastern and Central European countries, Lithuania, Latvia, Estonia, the independent states of the former Soviet Union, Republic of Ireland, Northern Ireland, and approved developing countries.

Eligible applicants/beneficiaries: Center for Civic Education and the National Council Economic Education (each receiving 37.5 of available funds); independent nonprofit education organizations experienced in program areas.

Range/Average: N.A.

Activity: FY 05, 4 awards.

HQ: Office of Safe and Drug-Free Schools, DOED, 400 Maryland Ave. SW, Washington, DC 20202. Phone: (202) 205-8061.

Internet: www.ed.gov/programs/coopedexchange/index.html (Note: no field offices for this program.)

84.305 EDUCATION RESEARCH, DEVELOPMENT AND DISSEMINATION

Assistance: project grants. (100 percent/1-5 years).

Purposes: pursuant to the Education Sciences Reform Act of 2002, to develop and distribute research-based information supporting learning and improved academic achievement. Grants may fund basic and applied research, development, dissemination, evaluations, and demonstrations.

Eligible applicants/beneficiaries: SEAs, LEAs, IHEs, public and private agencies and organizations, institutions, individuals, or consortia.

Range/Average: N.A.

Activity: not quantified specifically.

HQ: Institute of Education Sciences, DOED, 555 New Jersey Ave. NW, Washington, DC 20202. Phone: (202) 219-2079.

Internet: www.ed.gov/about/offices/list/ies/index.html (Note: no field offices for this program.)

84.310 PARENTAL INFORMATION AND RESOURCE CENTERS

Assistance: project grants. (first year, 100 percent/1-4 years).

Purposes: pursuant to ESEA as amended, Title V, to establish parental information and resource centers to: (1) assist parents in helping their children to meet state and local standards; (2) obtain information about the range of programs, services, and resources available nationally and locally to parents and school personnel; (3) help parents use the technology applied in their children's education; (4) plan, implement, and fund activities for parents that coordinate child education with other appropriate programs; (5) coordinate and integrate early childhood and school-age education programs. At least 50 percent of grant funds must be used to serve areas with high concentrations of low-income families, to serve parents that are severely educationally or economically disadvantaged. After the first year of grant-funded activities, cost sharing is required.

Eligible applicants: nonprofit organizations; nonprofit organizations in consortia with LEAs.

Eligible beneficiaries: preschool and school-aged children and their parents.

Average: $615,000.

Activity: FY 05, 72 awards.

HQ: Parental Options and Information, OII-DOED, FB-6 - Rm.3E209, 400 Maryland Ave. SW, Washington, DC 20202. Phone: (202) 260-2476.

Internet: www.ed.gov/programs/pirc/index.html (Note: no field offices for this program.)

84.315 CAPACITY BUILDING FOR TRADITIONALLY UNDERSERVED POPULATIONS

Assistance: project grants. (100 percent/1-5 years).

Purposes: pursuant to the Rehabilitation Act of 1973 as amended, to enhance the capacity and increase the participation of HBCUs, Hispanic serving IHEs, other IHEs where minority enrollment is at least 50 percent, and tribes in competitions for Rehabilitation Act funds. Projects should focus on recruiting minorities into vocational rehabilitation and related service careers.

Eligible applicants/beneficiaries: states; public and nonprofit agencies; profit organizations.

Range: $225,000 to $250,000.

Activity: not quantified specifically.

HQ: Rehabilitation Services Administration, OSERS-DOED, 400 Maryland Ave. SW, Washington, DC 20202-2649. Phone: (202) 245-7300.

Internet: www.ed.gov/about/offices/list/osers/rsa/index.html.

84.318 EDUCATION TECHNOLOGY STATE GRANTS ("Enhancing Education through Technology Program")

Assistance: formula grants.

Purposes: pursuant to ESEA as amended, Title II, to improve student academic achievement through the use of technology in schools; to assist students to become technologically literate by the end of the eighth grade; to integrate technology with teacher training and curriculum development to establish successful research-based instructional methods. At least 95 percent of grant funds to SEAs must be subgranted to LEAs.

Eligible applicants: states, territories and possessions, BIA.

Eligible beneficiaries: elementary and secondary schools, students, and teachers.

Range: $2,400,000 to $65,557,000.

Activity: not quantified specifically.

HQ: School Support and Technology Programs, OESE-DOED, FOB 6 - Rm.3E241, 400 Maryland Ave. SW, Washington, DC 20202-6140. Phone: (202) 260-3778.

Internet: www.ed.gov/programs/edtech/index.html (Note: no field offices for this program.)

84.323 SPECIAL EDUCATION—STATE PERSONNEL DEVELOPMENT

Assistance: project grants. (100 percent/1-5 years).

Purposes: pursuant to IDEA as amended, to reform and improve systems for providing educational, early intervention, and transitional services to infants, toddlers, and children with disabilities and their families—including professional development, technical assistance, and information dissemination about best practices.

Eligible applicants: SEAs.

Eligible beneficiaries: infants, toddlers, and children with disabilities and their families.

Range/Average: N.A.

Activity: FY 05, 49 grants.

HQ: Office of Special Education Programs, OSERS-DOED, 400 Maryland Ave. SW (Rm. 4019 PCP), Washington, DC 20202-2600. Phone: (202) 245-7571.

Internet: www.ed.gov/about/offices/list/osers/osep/index.html (Note: no field offices for this program.)

84.324 RESEARCH IN SPECIAL EDUCATION

Assistance: project grants. (to 100 percent/1-5 years).

Purposes: pursuant to the Education Sciences Reform Act of 2002, for applied research to improve services provided and results achieved under IDEA, for infants, toddlers, and children with disabilities—including educational and early intervention services and professional practices.

Eligible applicants: SEAs, LEAs, IHEs, public agencies, private nonprofit organizations, tribes and tribal organizations, profit organizations, outlying areas.

Eligible beneficiaries: infants, toddlers, children, and others with disabilities and their families.

Range: $150,000 to $1,000,000 per year.

Activity: annually, 75-100 awards.

HQ: Office of Special Education Programs, OSERS-DOED, 400 Maryland Ave. SW (Rm. 4019 PCP), Washington, DC 20202-2600. Phone: (202) 219-1309, -0377.

Internet: www.ed.gov/offices/OSERS/OSEP (Note: no field offices for this program.)

84.325 SPECIAL EDUCATION—PERSONNEL DEVELOPMENT TO IMPROVE SERVICES AND RESULTS FOR CHILDREN WITH DISABILITIES

Assistance: project grants. (to 100 percent/1-5 years).

Purposes: pursuant to IDEA as amended, to prepare personnel to serve infants, toddlers, and children with disabilities—in special and regular education, related services, and early intervention. Projects must emphasize use of skills and knowledge derived from research and experience.

Eligible applicants: SEAs, LEAs, IHEs, public agencies, private nonprofit organizations, tribes and tribal organizations, profit organizations, outlying areas.

Eligible beneficiaries: infants, toddler, and children with disabilities and their families.

Range: $196,000 to $1,350,000.

Activity: FY 05, 380 awards.

HQ: Office of Special Education Programs, OSERS-DOED, 400 Maryland Ave. SW (Rm. 4019 PCP), Washington, DC 20202-2600. Phone: (202) 245-7620.

Internet: www.ed.gov/about/offices/list/osers/osep/index.html (Note: no field offices for this program.)

84.326 SPECIAL EDUCATION—TECHNICAL ASSISTANCE AND DISSEMINATION TO IMPROVE SERVICES AND RESULTS FOR CHILDREN WITH DISABILITIES

Assistance: project grants. (to 100 percent/1-5 years).

Purposes: pursuant to IDEA as amended, to provide technical assistance and disseminate information to improve early intervention, education, and transitional services and results for children with disabilities and their families—through institutes, regional resource centers, clearinghouses, and similar methods.

Eligible applicants: SEAs, LEAs, IHEs, public agencies, private nonprofit organizations, tribes and tribal organizations, profit organizations, outlying areas.

Eligible beneficiaries: infants, toddler, and children with disabilities and their families.

Range: $25,000 to $3,000,000. **Average:** $760,000.

Activity: FY 05, 100 awards.

HQ: Office of Special Education Programs, OSERS-DOED, 400 Maryland Ave. SW (Rm. 4019 PCP), Washington, DC 20202-2600. Phone: (202) 245-7291.

Internet: www.ed.gov/about/offices/list/osers/osep/index.html (Note: no field offices for this program.)

84.327 SPECIAL EDUCATION—TECHNOLOGY AND MEDIA SERVICES FOR INDIVIDUALS WITH DISABILITIES

Assistance: project grants. (to 100 percent/1-5 years).

Purposes: pursuant to IDEA as amended, for the development, demonstration, and utilization of technology; for educational media activities designed to be of educational value; and, for captioning, video description, and cultural activities—for children with disabilities and their families.

Eligible applicants: SEAs, LEAs, IHEs, public agencies, private nonprofit organizations, tribes and tribal organizations, profit organizations, outlying areas.

Eligible beneficiaries: infants, toddler, and children with disabilities and their families.

Range: $200,000 to $1,500,000. **Average:** $425,000.

Activity: FY 05, 80 new and continuation awards.

HQ: Office of Special Education Programs, OSERS-DOED, 400 Maryland Ave. SW (Rm. 4098 PCP), Washington, DC 20202-2600. Phone: (202) 245-7291.

Internet: www.ed.gov/about/offices/list/osers/osep/index.html (Note: no field offices for this program.)

84.328 SPECIAL EDUCATION—PARENT INFORMATION CENTERS

Assistance: project grants. (to 100 percent/1-5 years).

Purposes: pursuant to IDEA as amended, to ensure that children with disabilities and their parents: receive training and information on their rights under the Act; can participate effectively in planning and decision-making related to early intervention, special education, and transitional services, including the development of Individual Education Programs (IEPs).

Eligible applicants: parent organizations as defined in IDEA, SEAs, LEAs, public charter schools that are LEAs under state law, IHEs, public agencies, private nonprofit organizations, outlying areas, freely associated states, Indian tribes or tribal organizations, for-profit organizations.

Eligible beneficiaries: infants, toddlers, and other individuals with disabilities and their families.

Range: $100,000 to $648,554. **Average:** $218,000.

Activity: FY 05, 100 awards.

HQ: Office of Special Education Programs, OSERS-DOED, 400 Maryland Ave. SW (Rm. 4065 PCP), Washington, DC 20202-2600. Phone: (202) 245-7329.

Internet: www.ed.gov/about/offices/list/osers/osep/index.html (Note: no field offices for this program.)

84.329 SPECIAL EDUCATION—STUDIES AND EVALUATIONS

Assistance: project grants. (to 100 percent/1-5 years).

Purposes: pursuant to IDEA as amended, to evaluate progress in implementing IDEA. Projects cover state and local efforts to provide a free appropriate public education to children with disabilities and early intervention services to infants and toddlers that would be at risk of having substantial development delays without such services.

Eligible applicants: SEAs, LEAs, IHEs, public agencies, private nonprofit organizations, tribes and tribal organizations, profit organizations, outlying areas.

Eligible beneficiaries: infants, toddlers, children, and others with disabilities and their families.

Range/Average: N.A.

Activity: not quantified specifically.

HQ: Office of Special Education Programs, OSERS-DOED, 400 Maryland Ave. SW, Washington, DC 20202-2500. Phone: (202) 219-1011.

Internet: www.ed.gov/about/offices/list/osers/osep/index.html (Note: no field offices for this program.)

84.330 ADVANCED PLACEMENT PROGRAM

Assistance: project grants.

Purposes: pursuant to ESEA as amended, Title I, to cover part or all of the cost of Advanced Placement Test Fees for low-income persons enrolled in an advanced placement class and planning to take a test.

Eligible applicants: SEAs, LEAs, nonprofit organizations.

Eligible beneficiaries: low-income individuals who are enrolled in an advanced placement class and plan to take an advanced placement test.

Range/Average: N.A.

Activity: FY 05, 46 incentive grants with 50 states participating.

HQ: Improvement Programs, OII-DOED, 400 Maryland Ave. SW, Washington, DC 20202-6140. Phone: (202) 260-2502.

Internet: www.ed.gov/programs/apfee/index.html (Note: no field offices for this program.)

84.331 GRANTS TO STATES FOR INCARCERATED YOUTH OFFENDERS

Assistance: formula grants. (100 percent/2 years).

Purposes: pursuant to HEA as amended, Title VIII, to assist and encourage incarcerated youth offenders to acquire postsecondary education and vocational training, and to provide them with employment counseling and related services during their incarceration and pre-release periods, and subsequently.

Eligible applicants: designated state correctional education agencies, territories and possessions.

Eligible beneficiaries: persons age 25 or younger, incarcerated in state prisons including pre-release facilities or alternative programs such as boot camps, eligible for release or parole within five years, and possessing a secondary school diploma or equivalent.

Range: $27,000 to $2,408,000.

Activity: FY 05, 50 grants.

HQ: Office of Safe and Drug-Free Schools, DOED, 400 Maryland Ave. SW, Washington, DC 20202-7242. Phone: (202) 219-1743.

Internet: www.ed.gov/programs/transitiontraining/index.html (Note: no field offices for this program.)

84.332 COMPREHENSIVE SCHOOL REFORM DEMONSTRATION ("CSR")

Assistance: formula grants. (100 percent/subgrants, to 3 years).

Purposes: pursuant to ESEA as amended, Title I, to substantially improve student achievement, particularly in Title I schools, through implementation of comprehensive school reform programs that are based on reliable research and effective practices and that emphasize basic academics and parental involvement. Funded projects must also include: comprehensive schools designs with aligned components; professional development; measurable goals and benchmarks; support within the school; parental and community involvement; external technical support and assistance; evaluation strategies; coordination of resources.

Eligible applicants/beneficiaries: SEAs. Subgrants—LEAs applying as collaboratives.

Average: $3,734,000.

Activity: not quantified specifically.

HQ: CSRD, OESE-DOED, 400 Maryland Ave. SW, Washington, DC 20202. Phone: (202) 260-1335.

Internet: www.ed.gov/programs/compreform/index.html (Note: no field offices for this program.)

84.333 DEMONSTRATION PROJECTS TO ENSURE STUDENTS WITH DISABILITIES RECEIVE A HIGHER EDUCATION

Assistance: project grants. (to 100 percent/3 years).

Purposes: pursuant to HEA as amended, Title VII, for model demonstration projects providing technical assistance or professional development for higher education faculty, to provide students with disabilities a quality postsecondary education.

Eligible applicants: IHEs of which at least two provide professional development for students with learning disabilities.

Eligible beneficiaries: faculty and administration in postsecondary education and students with disabilities.

Average: $287,000.

Activity: 24 grants awarded.

HQ: OPE-DOED, 400 Maryland Ave. SW, Washington, DC 20202-5131. Phone: (202) 502-7808.

Internet: www.ed.gov/programs/disabilities (Note: no field offices for this program.)

84.334 GAINING EARLY AWARENESS AND READINESS FOR UNDERGRADUATE PROGRAMS ("GEAR-UP")

Assistance: project grants. (50 percent/to 5 years).

Purposes: pursuant to HEA, Title IV, to assist low-income students with a secondary diploma, or equivalent, in obtaining the financial assistance necessary to attend an IHE; to provide supportive services to elementary, middle, and secondary students at risk of becoming school drop-outs, including counseling, mentoring, academic support; to provide outreach and relevant information to students and their parents. Services are provided under the Early Intervention Component. Federal grants may be provided under the Scholarship Component, to students participating in the Early Intervention component or in a TRIO program.

Eligible applicants: states; partnerships of LEAs, IHEs, and at least two community organizations including businesses, professional associations, philanthropic organizations, state agencies, parent groups.

Eligible beneficiaries: low-income students and students in high-poverty schools.

Average: new state grants, $2,907,000; continuations state grants, $1,744,000; new partnership grants, $1,213,000; continuation partnership grants, $753,000.

Activity: FY 05, 39 state, 213 partnership grants.

HQ: GEAR-UP, OPE-DOED, 400 Maryland Ave. SW, Washington, DC 20202-5131. Phone: (202) 502-7676.

Internet: www.ed.gov/programs/gearup; email, gearup@ed.gov (Note: no field offices for this program.)

84.335 CHILD CARE ACCESS MEANS PARENTS IN SCHOOL

Assistance: project grants (4 years).

Purposes: pursuant to HEA as amended, Title IV, to support participation of low-income parents in postsecondary education by providing campus-based child care services. Grants may be used to support or establish child care programs, including before or after-school services—but not for construction other than minor renovations. Grant amounts may not exceed one percent of the total amount of Pell grants awarded by the IHE for the preceding year.

Eligible applicants: IHEs that awarded $350,000 or more in Pell grants for the preceding year.

Eligible beneficiaries: low-income students enrolled in postsecondary programs.

Average: new awards, $88,000; continuation awards, $47,000.

Activity: FY 05, 237 awards.

HQ: Higher Education Programs, OPE-DOED, 400 Maryland Ave. SW, Washington, DC 20202-5131. Phone: (202) 502-7634.

Internet: www.ed.gov/programs/campisp (Note: no field offices for this program.)

84.336 TEACHER QUALITY ENHANCEMENT GRANTS

Assistance: project grants. (50-75 percent/3-5 years).

Purposes: pursuant to HEA, Title II, for projects to reform teacher preparation programs and certification and licensure requirements, providing alternatives to traditional preparation for teaching, and to develop and implement effective mechanisms for teacher recruitment, pay, removal, and social promotion.

Eligible applicants/beneficiaries: states and partnerships with LEAs with high percentages of households below the poverty line and of secondary teachers not teaching within their specialty, and high rate of teacher turnover. IHEs must demonstrate specific teacher training performance standards.

Average: new state grant awards, $2,642,000; continuation state grant awards, $1,875,000; new teacher recruitment grants, $840,000; continuation partnership grants, $1,227,000.

Activity: FY 05, 7 state, 30 partnership, 20 teacher recruitment grants.

HQ: Teacher Quality Programs, OPE-DOED, 400 Maryland Ave. SW, Washington, DC 20202. Phone: (202) 502-7878.

Internet: www.ed.gov/programs/heatqp (Note: no field offices for this program.)

84.337 INTERNATIONAL EDUCATION—TECHNOLOGICAL INNOVATION AND COOPERATION FOR FOREIGN INFORMATION ACCESS

Assistance: project grants (67 percent).

Purposes: pursuant to HEA as amended, Title VI, to develop innovative techniques or programs using new electronic technologies to collect, organize, preserve, and disseminate information on world regions and countries other than the U.S.—addressing U.S. teaching and research needs in international education and foreign languages.

Eligible applicants/beneficiaries: IHEs, public or nonprofit private libraries, or consortia.

Average: $170,000.

Activity: 10 awards.

HQ: International Education and Graduate Programs Service, OPE- DOED, 400 Maryland Ave. SW, Washington, DC 20202-5332. Phone: (202) 502-7628.

Internet: www.ed.gov/programs/iegpsticfia (Note: no field offices for this program.)

84.343 ASSISTIVE TECHNOLOGY—STATE GRANTS FOR PROTECTION AND ADVOCACY

Assistance: project grants. (100 percent/to 6 years).

Purposes: pursuant to the Assistive Technology Act of 1998, for protection and advocacy services related to acquiring, using, or maintaining assistive technology services and devices for persons with disabilities, as provided in the Developmental Disabilities Assistance and Bill of Rights Act.

Eligible applicants: designated protection and advocacy agencies in states and outlying areas.

Eligible beneficiaries: people with disabilities who may benefit from assistive technology services and devices.

Range: $50,000 to $421,079.

Activity: FY 05, 56 grants.

HQ: National Institute on Disability and Rehabilitation Research, OSERS-DOED, 400 Maryland Ave. SW, Washington, DC 20202-2500. Phone: (202) 245-7385.

Internet: www.ed.gov/programs/rsapair/awards.html (Note: no field offices for this program.)

84.345 UNDERGROUND RAILROAD EDUCATIONAL AND CULTURAL PROGRAM

Assistance: project grants (20 percent).

Purposes: pursuant to HEA as amended, Title VIII, to support research, display, interpretation, and collection of artifacts relating to the history of the underground railroad.

Eligible applicants/beneficiaries: nonprofit educational organizations meeting program purposes.

Average: $1,102,000.

Activity: FY 05, 2 awards.

HQ: OPE-DOED, 400 Maryland Ave. SW, Washington, DC 20202. Phone: (202) 502-7507.

Internet: www.ed.gov/programs/ugroundrr/index.html (Note: no field offices for this program.)

84.349 EARLY CHILDHOOD EDUCATOR PROFESSIONAL DEVELOPMENT

Assistance: project grants. (100 percent/to 4 years).

Purposes: pursuant to ESEA as amended, Title II, for professional development of early childhood educators working in urban or rural high-poverty communities and serving primarily low-income families. Training must be research-based and designed to improve pedagogy that will improve children's language ability and literacy skills.

Eligible applicants/beneficiaries: IHEs, state higher education agencies, LEAs, SEAs; other public and private agencies and organizations including child care consortia and Head Start programs.

Average: $2,910,000.

Activity: FY 05, 5 awards.

HQ: Early Childhood Educator Professional Development, OESE-DOED, 400 Maryland Ave. SW, Washington, DC 20202-6132. Phone: (202) 260-0792.

Internet: www.ed.gov/programs/eceducator/index.html, email, ece-profdev@ed.gov (Note: no field offices for this program.)

84.350 TRANSITION TO TEACHING

Assistance: project grants. (100 percent/3 years).

Purposes: pursuant to ESEA, Title II, to recruit, train, and place talented individuals from other fields, as well as recent college graduates, into licensed teaching positions in K-12 classrooms in high-need areas, and to support them during their first years in the classroom.

Eligible applicants/beneficiaries: LEA, SEAs, educational service centers, nonprofit agencies and other organizations; partnerships of the foregoing.

Average: $361,000.

Activity: FY 05, 124 continuation awards.

HQ: Teacher Quality Programs, OII-DOED, 400 Maryland Ave. SW, Washington, DC 20202-6100. Phone: (202) 260-0223.

Internet: www.ed.gov/programs/transitionteach/index.html (Note: no field offices for this program.)

84.351 ARTS IN EDUCATION

Assistance: project grants. (100 percent/3-5 years).

Purposes: pursuant to ESEA as amended, Title V, to improve systemic education reform by strengthening arts education as an integral part of elementary and secondary school curricula; to assist students in learning to challenge state content standards in the arts; to enable students to demonstrate competence in the arts in accordance with the National Education Goals; to improve the educational performance and future potential of at-risk students; to provide comprehensive and coordinated educational and cultural services. Project selection is coordinated with NEA, NEH, and other arts organizations.

Eligible applicants/beneficiaries: SEAs, LEAs, IHEs; museums and other cultural institutions; other public and private agencies; private profit organizations for certain activities.

Range/Average: N.A.

Activity: FY 05, 90 awards.

HQ: OESE-DOED, 400 Maryland Ave. SW, Washington, DC 20202. Phone: (202) 401-3813.

Internet: www.ed.gov/programs/artsed/index.html (Note: no field offices for this program.)

84.354 CREDIT ENHANCEMENT FOR CHARTER SCHOOL FACILITIES

Assistance: project grants. (100 percent/to 5 years).

Purposes: pursuant to ESEA as amended, Title V, for charter schools to leverage funds to finance the cost of acquiring, constructing, and renovating facilities. Grant funds must be deposited in approved reserve accounts, to be used to access private sector capital through bond or other financing instruments.

Eligible applicants/beneficiaries: public governmental or private nonprofit entities, or consortia.

Range: \$2,000,000 to \$10,000,000.

Activity: FY 05, 5 awards.

HQ: Parental Options and Information, OII-DOED, 400 Maryland Ave. SW (Rm. 3C140, FB-6), Washington, DC 20202-6140. Phone: (202) 401-0307.

Internet: www.ed.gov/programs/charterfacilities/index.html (Note: no field offices for this program.)

84.356 ALASKA NATIVE EDUCATIONAL PROGRAMS

Assistance: project grants (100 percent).

Purposes: pursuant to ESEA as amended, Title VII, for projects that recognize and address the unique education needs of Alaska native students, parents, and teachers. Activities eligible for funding include: curriculum and education development programs; student enrichment programs in science and mathematics; professional development; Even Start and Headstart activities; family literacy services; dropout prevention programs.

Eligible applicants/beneficiaries: Alaska native educational organizations or entities with experience in developing programs, or partnerships including Alaska native organizations.

Range/Average: N.A.

Activity: FY 05, 55 awards.

HQ: School Improvement Programs, OESE-DOED, 400 Maryland Ave. SW, Washington, DC 20202-6140. Phone: (202) 401-0281.

Internet: www.ed.gov/programs/alaskanative/index.html (Note: no field offices for this program.)

84.357 READING FIRST STATE GRANTS

Assistance: project grants. (100 percent/to 6 years).

Purposes: pursuant to ESEA as amended, Title I, to ensure that every student can read at grade level or above by the end of the third grade, by establishing reading programs for students in kindergarten through third grade that are based on scientific reading research. Projects also focus on teacher development, including special education teachers, preparing them to identify specific reading barriers facing their students.

Eligible applicants/beneficiaries: SEAs, BIA, territories, and possessions.

Range: \$2,491,000 to \$146,982,000. **Average:** \$19,161,000.

Activity: all eligible agencies funded.

HQ: Reading First Program, OESE-DOED, FOB 6 - Rm.3W311, 400 Maryland Ave. SW, Washington, DC 20202-6100. Phone: (202) 401-4877.

Internet: www.ed.gov/programs/readingfirst/index.html; email, reading.first@ed.gov (Note: no field offices for this program.)

84.358 RURAL EDUCATION

Assistance: formula grants.

Purposes: pursuant to ESEA as amended, Title VI, to help improve the quality of teaching and learning in rural school districts. Components include:

"Small, Rural School Achievement Program," for activities including Improving Teacher Quality, Educational Technology, Language Instruction for Limited English Proficient and Immigrant Students, Safe and Drug-Free Schools and Communities, 21st Century Community Learning Centers, and Innovative Programs; "Rural and Low-Income School Program," for teacher recruitment and retention, professional development, educational technology, and parental involvement.

Eligible applicants/beneficiaries: Small, Rural Achievement—essentially, LEAs where average daily attendance at all schools is less than 600, or in counties with population density less than 10 persons per square mile. Rural and Low- Income Schools—SEAs, for redistribution to LEAs ineligible for Small, Rural Achievement funds and meeting other criteria. If an SEA does not apply, funds may be awarded to eligible LEAs.

Average: Small, Rural Achievement, $18,000; Rural and Low- Income Schools, $71,000.

Activity: FY 05, 4,630 Small, Rural achievement grants; Rural, Low-Income, 1,195 grants.

HQ: School Support and Technology Programs, OESE-DOED, 400 Maryland Ave. SW, Washington, DC 20202. Phone: (202) 401-0039.

Internet: www.ed.gov/programs/reapsrsa/index.html; e-mail, reap@ed.gov (Note: no field offices for this program.)

84.359 EARLY READING FIRST

Assistance: project grants. (100 percent/to 6 years).

Purposes: pursuant to ESEA as amended, Title I, to enhance the early language, literacy, and prereading development of preschool age children, particularly those from low-income families, through instructional strategies and professional development based on scientific reading research—with monitoring and assessment components. Funds must be used in existing public or private preschool programs serving low-income families.

Eligible applicants/beneficiaries: LEAs eligible for a subgrant under **84.357**; public or private organizations of agencies serving Head Start, child care, Even Start Family Literacy, school labs, or similar agencies; collaboratives.

Average: $3,089,000.

Activity: FY 05, 8,550 children, 700 teachers served.

HQ: Early Reading First Program, OESE-DOED, 400 Maryland Ave. SW, Washington, DC 20202. Phone: (202) 260-0968, -2533.

Internet: www.ed.gov/programs/earlyreading/index.html (Note: no field offices for this program.)

84.360 DROPOUT PREVENTION PROGRAM

Assistance: project grants. (100 percent/to 3 years).

Purposes: pursuant to ESEA as amended, Title I, to help schools implement effective dropout prevention and re-entry programs, including: identifying at-risk students including in middle schools; providing special services to at-risk students; identifying drop-outs and encouraging them to re-enter school; implementing other comprehensive approaches such as breaking large schools into smaller learning communities. Authorized activities include: professional development; reduction in pupil- teacher ratios; counseling and mentoring for at-risk students; implementing comprehensive school reform models.

Eligible applicants/beneficiaries: SEAs and LEAs serving communities with dropout rates above the state average.

Average: $2,310,000.

Activity: FY 05, 2 grants.

HQ: OVAE-DOED, 400 Maryland Ave. SW, Washington, DC 20202-6100. Phone: (202) 205-3804.

Internet: www.ed.gov/programs/dropout/index.html (Note: no field offices for this program.)

84.361 VOLUNTARY PUBLIC SCHOOL CHOICE

Assistance: project grants. (100 percent/to 5 years).

Purposes: pursuant to ESEA as amended, Title V, to establish or expand programs of public school choice, with funding for: planning or designing programs; making tuition transfer payments to public elementary or secondary schools to which students transfer; capacity-enhancing activities that enable high-demand public elementary or secondary schools to accommodate transfers; public education campaigns to inform students and parents about the program; similar costs.

Eligible applicants/beneficiaries: SEAs; LEAs; partnerships of SEAs, LEAs, or other public, nonprofit, or profit entities.

Average: $1,900,000.

Activity: FY 05, 13 awards.

HQ: Parental Options and Information, OII-DOED, 400 Maryland Ave. SW, Washington, DC 20202-6140. Phone: (202) 260-1999.

Internet: www.ed.gov/programs/choice/index.html (Note: no field offices for this program.)

84.362 NATIVE HAWAIIAN EDUCATION

Assistance: project grants. (100 percent/to 5 years).

Purposes: pursuant to ESEA as amended, Title VII, to develop innovative educational programs to assist native Hawaiians and to supplement and expand education programs and authorities. Funds may support: early education and care programs; operation of family-based education centers; beginning reading and literacy activities; programs addressing the needs of gifted and talented students; professional development; assistance enabling students to enter and complete postsecondary education.

Eligible applicants/beneficiaries: native Hawaiian educational organizations or community-based organizations; experienced public and private nonprofit organizations, agencies, and institutions; consortia.

Range/Average: N.A.

Activity: FY 05, 60 awards.

HQ: Academic Improvement and Teacher Quality Programs, OESE-DOED, 400 Maryland Ave. SW (Rm. 3C126, FB-6), Washington, DC 20202-6140. Phone: (202) 260-1091.

Internet: www.ed.gov/programs/nathawaiian/index.html (Note: no field offices for this program.)

84.363 SCHOOL LEADERSHIP

Assistance: project grants.

Purposes: pursuant to ESEA as amended, Title II, to develop innovative programs that recruit, train, and mentor principals and assistant principals. Funds may be used for: financial incentives to aspiring new principals; stipends to principals to mentor new principals; professional development programs in instructional leadership and management; incentives for teachers or individuals from other fields wanting to become principals and that are effective in training new principals.

Eligible applicants/beneficiaries: high-need LEAs applying singly or in consortia or partnerships that include nonprofit organizations and IHEs.

Average: new awards, $503,000; continuation awards, $408,000.

Activity: FY 05, 30 awards.

HQ: Teacher Quality Programs, OII-DOED, 400 Maryland Ave. SW, Washington, DC 20202-6140. Phone: (202) 205-5009.

Internet: www.ed.gov/programs/leadership/index.html (Note: no field offices for this program.)

84.364 LITERACY THROUGH SCHOOL LIBRARIES

Assistance: project grants.

Purposes: pursuant to ESEA as amended, Title I, to improve student literacy skills and achievement by increasing access to up-to-date school library materials, technologically advanced school library media centers, and well-trained professionally certified school library media specialists. Funds may be used for pertinent library acquisitions, internet links and other resource-sharing networks, professional development and collaborative activities, and student library access during non- school hours.

Eligible applicants/beneficiaries: LEAs with a child poverty rate of at least 20 percent.

Average: $100,000.

Activity: FY 05, 85 awards.

HQ: Academic Improvement and Teacher Quality Programs, OESE-DOED, 400 Maryland Ave. SW, Washington, DC 20202-6100. Phone: (202) 401-3751.

Internet: www.ed.gov/program/lsl/index.html (Note: no field offices for this program.)

84.365 ENGLISH LANGUAGE ACQUISITION GRANTS

Assistance: formula grants; project grants.

Purposes: pursuant to ESEA as amended, Title III, to ensure that limited English proficient (LEP) children and youth, including immigrants, attain proficiency and meet the same state academic content and achievement standards as all children. Outlying areas and native American applicants may use project funds for appropriate special activities for up to five years, including: hiring tutors and for special professional development and training; developing students' native language skills. Training must be based upon scientifically based research and improve teacher instruction and enhance their ability to understand and use curricula, assessment measures, and instruction strategies for LEP students.

Eligible applicants/beneficiaries: formula funds (95 percent of which must be allocated as subgrants to SEAs)—states and outlying areas with approved state plans. Project grants—tribal educational authorities, BIA-operated or -funded elementary or secondary schools, nonprofit native Hawaiian or native American Pacific Islander language organizations.

Range: formula grants, $500,000 to $149,565,827.

Activity: FY 05, 148 grants.

HQ: Office of English Language Acquisition, OESE-DOED, 400 Maryland Ave. SW, Washington, DC 20202-6510. Phone: (202) 245-7149.

Internet: www.ed.gov/programs/sfgp/nrgcomp.html (Note: no field offices for this program.)

84.366 MATHEMATICS AND SCIENCE PARTNERSHIPS

Assistance: project grants. (100 percent/to 3 years).

Purposes: pursuant to ESEA as amended, Title II, to improve student academic achievement in mathematics and science through projects supporting partnerships of organizations representing preschool through higher education. Funds may be used for such activities as: developing more rigorous curricula aligned with state and local content standards; distance learning projects for teachers; teacher recruitment among mathematics, science, and engineering majors through the use of signing and performance incentives, stipends, and scholarships.

Eligible applicants/beneficiaries: partnerships of SEAs with IHE mathematics, science, or engineering departments, and a high-need LEA. Other organizations may participate.

Range: $888,000 to $24,513,000. **Average:** $3,173,000.

Activity: FY 05, all states supported.

HQ: Academic Improvement and Teacher Quality Programs, OESE-DOED, 400 Maryland Ave. SW, Washington, DC 20202-6254. Phone: (202) 260-3710.

Internet: www.ed.gov/programs/mathsci/index.html (Note: no field offices for this program.)

84.367 IMPROVING TEACHER QUALITY STATE GRANTS

Assistance: formula grants (to 2 years).

Purposes: pursuant to ESEA as amended, Title II, to increase student achievement by improving teacher and principal quality and increasing their numbers, through such efforts as: recruiting and retaining highly qualified teachers, principals, and assistant principals; professional development addressing subject matter knowledge and related activities.

Eligible applicants/beneficiaries: states with approved consolidated state plans.

Average: $55,250,000.

Activity: all SEAs funded.

HQ: OESE-DOED, 400 Maryland Ave. SW, Washington, DC 20202. Phone: (202) 260-9737.

Internet: www.ed.gov/programs/teacherqual/index.html (Note: no field offices for this program.)

84.369 GRANTS FOR STATE ASSESSMENTS AND RELATED ACTIVITIES

Assistance: formula grants (to 27 months).

Purposes: pursuant to ESEA as amended, Title VI, for the development of the additional state assessments and standards required currently by ESEA—or, if a state has developed those assessments, to support their administration or to carry out other activities related to ensuring that the state's schools and LEAs are held accountable for results.

Eligible applicants/beneficiaries: states.

Range: $3,331,278 to $33,952,540. **Average:** $7,615,000.

Activity: not quantified specifically.

HQ: Compensatory Education Programs, OESE-DOED, 400 Maryland Ave. SW, Washington, DC 20202-6132. Phone: (202) 260-1824.

Internet: (none provided). (Note: no field offices for this program.)

84.370 DC SCHOOL CHOICE INCENTIVE PROGRAM

Assistance: project grants. (100 percent/to 5 years).

Purposes: pursuant to the DC School Choice Incentive Act of 2003, to establish scholarship programs to provide students with expanded elementary and secondary school choice options. Scholarship funds may be used to pay tuition and fees and transportation expenses to participating DC nonpublic schools of their choice.

Eligible applicants: an educational entity of the District of Columbia government; a nonprofit organizations or a consortium of same.

Eligible beneficiaries: elementary and secondary students residing in DC, from households with income not exceeding 185 percent of the poverty line.

Range/Average: N.A.

Activity: not quantified specifically.

HQ: OII-DOED, 400 Maryland Ave. SW, Washington, DC 20202-5961. Phone: (202) 205-1729.

Internet: www.ed.gov/programs/dcchoice/index.html (Note: no field offices for this program.)

84.371 STRIVING READERS

Assistance: project grants. (100 percent/to 5 years).

Purposes: pursuant to ESEA as amended, Title I, to raise student achievement by improving the reading skills of middle and high school students reading below grade level, in Title I-eligible schools that are at risk of not meeting or not meeting ESEA annual progress requirements—including implementation and evaluation of research-based reading interventions. Project grants support costs such as: supplemental literacy intervention strategies; cross-disciplinary strategies including professional development for subject matter teachers; additional staff time for extra periods of instruction; age-appropriate reading materials; assessment instruments.

Eligible applicants: one or more LEAs receiving Title I funds with one or more high schools or middle schools with significant numbers of students reading below grade level; or, intermediate service agencies on behalf of eligible LEAs; or, partnerships that may include public or private institutions of higher education, eligible nonprofit or for-profit organizations, and LEAs that have one or more high schools or middle schools with significant numbers of students reading below grade level.

Eligible beneficiaries: students in grades 6-12.

Average: $3,000,000.

Activity: new program listing in 2006 (CFDA on-line). FY 05, 8 awards.

HQ: OESE-DOED, 400 Maryland Ave. SW, Washington, DC 20202. Phone: (202) 401-2563.

Internet: www.ed.gov/programs/strivingreaders; e-mail, strivingreaders@ed.gov (Note: no field offices for this program.)

84.372 STATEWIDE DATA SYSTEMS

Assistance: project grants. (100 percent/1-3 years).

Purposes: pursuant to Educational Technical Assistance Act of 2002, for SEAs to design, develop, and implement statewide, longitudinal data systems to manage, analyze, disaggregate, and use individual student data—consistent with ESEA.

Eligible applicants/beneficiaries: SEAs.

Range/Average: N.A.

Activity: approximately 15 states received support in 2005.

HQ: Institute of Education Sciences, National Center for Education Statistics, DOED, 400 Maryland Ave., SW, Washington, DC 20202 Phone: (202) 502-7411.

Internet: www.ed.gov/programs/lds/index.html (Note: no field offices for this program.)

84.373 SPECIAL EDUCATION—TECHNICAL ASSISTANCE ON STATE DATA COLLECTION

Assistance: project grants. (100 percent/1-5 years).

Purposes: pursuant to IDEA, to provide technical assistance to improve state capacity to meet IDEA data collection requirements.

Eligible applicants: SEAs, LEAs, public charter schools that are LEAs under state law, IHEs, other public agencies, private nonprofit and profit organizations, tribes and tribal organizations, outlying areas, freely associated states.

Eligible beneficiaries: infants, toddler, and children with disabilities, and other individuals with disabilities, and their families.

Range: $150,000 to $1,250,000.

Activity: new program listing in 2006 (CFDA on-line).

HQ: Division of Research to Practice, OSERS-DOED, 400 Maryland Ave. SW, Washington, DC 20202-2600. Phone: (202) 245-7291.

Internet: www.ed.gov/about/offices/list/osers/osep/index.html (Note: no field offices for this program.)

84.374 TEACHER INCENTIVE FUND ("TIF")

Assistance: project grants. (100 percent/to 5 years).

Purposes: pursuant to ESEA as amended, Title V, for programs that develop and implement performance-based teacher and principal compensation systems in high-need schools, including incentives to assume individual responsibilities and leadership roles. Programs must include gains in student achievement as well as classroom evaluations conducted multiple times during each school year.

Eligible applicants/beneficiaries: LEAs, public charter schools that are LEAs under state law, SEAs; or, partnerships of an LEA, an SEA, or both, and at least one profit organization.

Range: $300,000 to $5,000,000.

Activity: new program listing in 2006 (CFDA on-line). 25-30 awards anticipated.

HQ: OESE-DOED, 400 Maryland Ave. SW, Washington, DC 20202. Phone: (202) 260-5619.

Internet: www.ed.gov/programs/teacherincentive (Note: no field offices for this program.)

84.375 ACADEMIC COMPETITIVENESS GRANTS

Assistance: direct payments/specified use. (100 percent/1 year).

Purposes: pursuant to HEA as amended, Title IV, to provide first- or second-year full-time undergraduate students that have completed a rigorous course of study in high school with need- based grant assistance to help meet educational expenses.

Eligible applicants/beneficiaries: first- or second-year full- time undergraduate students that are: U.S. citizens; eligible for a Pell grant; first-time undergraduates—and meet other requirements.

Range: first-year students, $750; second-year, $1,300. **Average:** $911.

Activity: new program listing in 2006 (CFDA on-line). FY 06 estimate, 439,000 students to be awarded funds.

HQ: Office of Postsecondary Education-DOED, 400 Maryland Ave. SW, Washington, DC 20202. Phone: Student Financial Aid Information Center, (800) 433-3243.

Internet: www.ifap.ed.gov.

84.376 NATIONAL SCIENCE AND MATHEMATICS ACCESS TO RETAIN TALENT (SMART) GRANTS ("SMART Grants")

Assistance: direct payments/specified use.

Purposes: pursuant to HEA as amended, Title IV, to provide third- and fourth-year full-time undergraduates, majoring in designated technical fields or foreign languages, with need-based grant assistance to meet educational expenses.

Eligible applicants/beneficiaries: third- and fourth-year undergraduate students that are: U.S. citizens; eligible for a Pell grant; enrolled at a public or private nonprofit or profit proprietary IHE; pursuing a major in physical, life, or computer sciences, mathematics, technology, engineering or a critical foreign language; obtaining a cumulative GPA of at least 3.0; cannot be owed a refund on a Title IV grant or be in default on a Title IV loan; registered with the Selective Service.

Range: to $4,000. **Average:** $3,980.

Activity: new program listing in 2006 (CFDA on-line). FY 06 estimate, 98,000 students to receive awards.

HQ: Office of Postsecondary Education-DOED, 400 Maryland Ave. SW, Washington, DC 20202. Phone: Student Financial Aid Information Center, (800) 433-3243.

Internet: www.ifap.ed.gov.

84.377 SCHOOL IMPROVEMENT GRANTS

Assistance: project grants (100 percent/to 27 months).

Purposes: pursuant to the Elementary and Secondary Education Act (ESEA), as amended to strengthen the capacity of states to carry out their program improvement responsibilities required under Sections 1116 and 1117 of Title I of the ESEA by implementing effective school improvement strategies and providing resources to LEAs to carry out those strategies. An SEA must allocate at least 95 percent of the amount of the funds it receives directly to LEAs for schools that have been identified for improvement, corrective action, or restructuring to carry out activities under Section 1116(b), while retaining up to 5 percent of the grant amount received for administration, evaluation, and technical assistance expenses. At the LEA level, these funds may be used for any reasonable costs associated with carrying out school improvement, corrective action, or restructuring activities described in Section 1116(b).

Eligible applicants: SEAs with approved state plan amendments.

Eligible beneficiaries: LEAs must have one or more schools identified for school improvement, corrective action, or restructuring under Section 1116(b) of Title I.

Range/Average: N.A.

Activity: N.A. New program in FY 08.

HQ: Office of Elementary and Postsecondary Education-DOED, 400 Maryland Ave. SW, Washington, DC 20202. Phone: (202) 260-4412.

Internet: www.ed.gov/oese. (Note: no field offices for this program.)

84.378 COLLEGE ACCESS CHALLENGE GRANT PROGRAM ("CACGP")

Assistance: formula grants (to 66 percent/to 2 years).

Purposes: pursuant to the Higher Education Act of 1965, as amended to foster partnerships among federal, state and local government entities and philanthropic organizations through matching challenge grants aimed at increasing the number of underrepresented students who enter and remain in postsecondary education. No more than 6 percent of the total amount of the sum of the federal share provided and nonfederal share required may be used for administrative purposes. The minimum allotment for each State for a fiscal year cannot be an amount that is less than 0.5 percent of the total amount appropriated for the program.

Eligible applicants: state agencies with jurisdiction over higher education, or other agencies designated by the Governor of each state. In cases where the State fails to meet program requirements, the Secretary may award funds to philanthropic organizations.

Eligible beneficiaries: underrepresented students and families.

Range/Average: N.A.

Activity: N.A. New program in FY 08.

HQ: College Access Challenge Grant Program, Office of Postsecondary Education-DOED, 400 Maryland Ave. SW, Washington, DC 20202. Phone: (202) 502-7807.

Internet: www.ed.gov/programs/cacg. (Note: no field offices for this program.)

84.379 TEACHER EDUCATION ASSISTANCE FOR COLLEGE AND HIGHER EDUCATION GRANTS (TEACH GRANTS) ("TEACH Grants")

Assistance: direct payments/specified use (100 percent).

Purposes: pursuant to the College Cost Reduction and Access Act of 2007 and Higher Education Act of 1965, as amended to provide annual grants of up to $4,000 to eligible undergraduate and graduate students who agree to teach specified high-need subjects at schools serving primarily disadvantaged populations for four years within eight years of graduation.

Eligible applicants/beneficiaries: undergraduate and graduate students with a 3.25 GPA completing coursework or requirements necessary to begin a career in teaching. Graduate students must be teachers or retirees from another occupation with expertise in a field in which there is a shortage of teachers or pursuing high-quality alternative certification. Students must attend an IHE that provides high-quality teacher preparation and professional development services; is financially sound; and provides, or assists in the provision, of pedagogical coursework, supervision and support services to teachers.

Range: to $4,000 per student, per year; grant reduced for part-time students. **Average:** FY 08, $2,774.

Activity: New program in 2008. FY 08, awards to 31,000 students.

HQ: Office of Postsecondary Education-DOED, 400 Maryland Ave. SW, Washington, DC 20202. Phone: (800) 433-2343.

Internet: www.ifap.ed.gov.

84.380 SPECIAL EDUCATION—OLYMPIC EDUCATION PROGRAMS

Assistance: project grants (to 5 years).

Purposes: pursuant to the Special Olympic Sports and Empowerment Act, to promote the expansion of Special Olympics and the design and implementation of Special Olympics education programs.

Eligible applicants: Special Olympics.

Eligible beneficiaries: individuals with intellectual disabilities.

Range/Average: N.A.

Activity: N.A. New program in FY 08.

HQ: Office of Special Education Programs, OSERS-DEOD, 400 Maryland Ave. SW, Room 4103-PCP, Washington, DC 20202-2600. Phone: (202) 245-7277.

Internet: www.ed.gov/about/overview/budget/budget08/08action.pdf. (Note: no field offices for this program.)

84.381 BACCALAUREATE DEGREES IN SCIENCE, TECHNOLOGY, ENGINEERING, MATHEMATICS, AND CRITICAL FOREIGN LANGUAGES AND MASTER'S DEGREES IN SCIENCE, TECHNOLOGY, ENGINEERING, MATHEMATICS, AND CRITICAL FOREIGN LANGUAGES ("BD-STEM-CFL MD-STEM-CFL")

Assistance: project grants (50 percent).

Purposes: pursuant to America Creating Opportunities to Meaningfully Promote Excellence in Technology, Education, and Science Act of 2007, to develop and implement programs that provide courses of study in science, technology, engineering, mathematics or critical foreign languages integrated with teacher education and lead to a baccalaureate or master's degree with concurrent teacher certification.

Eligible applicants/beneficiaries: institutions of higher education that receive a grant on behalf of science, technology, engineering, mathematics, or a critical foreign language departments or on behalf of a department or school with a competency-based degree program in those areas and include teacher certification.

Range/Average: FY 08, $225,000 per year.

Activity: N.A. New program in FY 08.

HQ: Teacher and Student Development Services Program, Office of Postsecondary Education-DOED, 1900 K Street NW, Washington, DC 20006. Phone: (202) 502-7774.

Internet: www.ed.gov/programs/tct. (Note: no field offices for this program.)

84.382 STRENGTHENING MINORITY-SERVING INSTITUTIONS

Assistance: project grants (100 percent/to 2 years).

Purposes: pursuant to the Higher Education Act of 1965 as amended by section 802 of the College Cost Reduction and Access Act (CCRAA) of 2007, to strengthen Predominantly Black Institutions (PBI); Asian American and Native American Pacific Islander-Serving Institutions (AANAPISI); and Native American-Serving Non-tribal Institutions (NASNTI) that propose to carry out activities to improve and expand the capacity to serve minority students.

Eligible applicants: PBIs: undergraduate enrollment of at least 40 percent Black American students; AANAPISI and NASNTI: undergraduate enrollment not less than 10 percent Asian American and Native American Pacific Islander and Native American students, respectively.

Eligible beneficiaries: undergraduates who are low-income, first-generation, and/or minority students.

Range/Average: PBI, $600,000 per year; AANAPISI, $1,000,000 to $1,500,000 per year; NASNTI, $1,000,000 to $1,500,000 per year.

Activity: N.A. New program in FY 08.

HQ: Teacher and Student Development Services Program, Office of Postsecondary Education-DOED, 1900 K Street NW, 6th FL, Washington, DC 20006. Phone: (202) 502-7777.

Internet: PBI: www.ed.gov/programs/pbi; AANAPISI: www.ed.gov/programs/aanapiccraa; NASNTI: www.ed.gov/programs/nasnticcraa.

84.938 HURRICANE EDUCATION RECOVERY

Assistance: formula grants.

Purposes: pursuant to Hurricane Education Recovery Act and Emergency Supplemental Appropriations Act to Address Hurricanes in the Gulf of Mexico and Pandemic Influenza, 2006, to assist in meeting the educational needs of individuals and educational institutions affected by Hurricanes Katrina and Rita in the Gulf of Mexico during 2005. Funds may be used to defray expenses related to the restart, reopening, and re-enrollment of students in affected elementary and secondary schools.

Eligible applicants/beneficiaries: SEAs in affected areas. LEAs, nonpublic schools, and postsecondary educations are subgrantees.

Range/Average: N.A.

Activity: new program listing in 2006 (CFDA on-line).

HQ: Impact Aid Programs, OESE-DOED, 400 Maryland Ave. SW - Rm.3E105 (FB-6), Washington, DC 20202-6244. Phone: (202) 260-3858.

Internet: www.ed.gov; hurricanehelpforschools.gov/proginfo/index.html; email, impact.aid@ed.gov (Note: no field offices for this program.)

SCHOLARSHIP AND FELLOWSHIP FOUNDATIONS

HARRY S TRUMAN SCHOLARSHIP FOUNDATION

85.001 HARRY S TRUMAN SCHOLARSHIP PROGRAM

Assistance: direct payments/specified use.

Purposes: pursuant to the Harry S Truman Memorial Scholarship Act, for scholarships for full-time students pursuing careers in public service, financed by a permanent trust fund endowment.

Eligible applicants/beneficiaries: U.S. citizens or nationals in their college junior year, nominated by their IHEs. Applicants must rank in the upper quarter of their class, and their studies should permit admission to a graduate or professional program for a career in public service.

Range: $2,000 to $15,000/year. **Average:** $12,000/year.

Activity: since 1977 program inception, 2,405 scholarships.

HQ: Executive Secretary, Harry S Truman Scholarship Foundation, 712 Jackson Pl. NW, Washington, DC 20006. Phone: (202) 395-4831.

Internet: www.truman.gov (Note: no field offices for this program.)

CHRISTOPHER COLUMBUS FELLOWSHIP FOUNDATION

85.100 CHRISTOPHER COLUMBUS FELLOWSHIP PROGRAM

Assistance: project grants; specialized services.

Purposes: pursuant to the Christopher Columbus Quincentenary Coins and Fellowship Foundation Act, for research, study, and labor designed to produce new discoveries in all fields, for the benefit of mankind.

Eligible applicants/beneficiaries: U.S. citizens.

Range: $10,000 to $25,000.

Activity: awards honor and sponsor individual inventors, as well as group efforts.

HQ: Executive Director, Christopher Columbus Scholarship Foundation, 110 Genesee St. - Ste. 390, Auburn, NY 13021. Phone: (315) 258-0090, FAX (315) 258-0093.

Internet: www.columbusfdn.org (Note: no field offices for this program.)

BARRY GOLDWATER SCHOLARSHIP AND EXCELLENCE IN EDUCATION

85.200 BARRY M. GOLDWATER SCHOLARSHIP PROGRAM

Assistance: direct payments/specified use.

Purposes: for scholarships to outstanding students to pursue careers in mathematics, the natural sciences, and engineering—financed by a permanent trust fund endowment.

Eligible applicants/beneficiaries: U.S. citizens, nationals, or lawful resident aliens that are full-time college sophomores and juniors at two- and four-year IHEs, ranking in the upper fourth of their class.

Range: to $7,500/year. **Average:** $6,650.

Activity: since 1988 program inception, 3,962 scholars selected.

HQ: President, Barry M. Goldwater Scholarship Foundation, 6225 Brandon Ave. - Ste. 315, Springfield, VA 22150-2519. Phone: (703) 756-6012, FAX (703) 756-6015.

Internet: www.act.org/goldwater; e-mail, goldh2o@erols.com (Note: no field offices for this program.)

WOODROW WILSON INTERNATIONAL CENTER FOR SCHOLARS

85.300 WOODROW WILSON CENTER FELLOWSHIPS IN THE HUMANITIES AND SOCIAL SCIENCES

Assistance: project grants (4-9 months).

Purposes: pursuant to the Woodrow Wilson Memorial Act of 1968, to foster scholarship and promote exchange of views between scholars and decision makers. The Center sponsors research, meetings, and publications in such areas as history, economics, politics, international relations, the environment, the humanities, and other areas. Fellows are in residence at the Center's main offices in Washington, D.C., where they receive office space, use of special libraries and personal computers, part-time research assistance, and publications services.

Eligible applicants/beneficiaries: citizens of any country, with backgrounds in government, business, the professions, or academia—with English language proficiency. For academic participants, eligibility is limited to the postdoctoral level.

Range: $7,000 to $85,000 including travel, support for dependents, 75 percent of health insurance.

Activity: 2004-2005, 23 fellows supported.

HQ: Woodrow Wilson International Center for Scholars, 1300 Pennsylvania Ave. NW, Washington, DC 20004. Phone: (202) 691-4000.

Internet: www.wilsoncenter.org; e-mail, fellowships@wwics.si.edu (Note: no field offices for this program.)

MORRIS K. UDALL SCHOLARSHIP AND EXCELLENCE IN NATIONAL ENVIRONMENTAL POLICY FOUNDATION

85.400 MORRIS K. UDALL SCHOLARSHIP PROGRAM

Assistance: direct payments/specified use.

Purposes: pursuant to the Morris K. Udall Scholarship and Excellence in National Environmental and Native American Public Policy Act of 1992, for internships, scholarships, and fellowships to develop increased opportunities for young Americans to prepare for careers related to the environment; for native Americans and Alaska natives intending to pursue careers in health care and tribal public policy. The program is financed by a permanent trust fund endowment.

Eligible applicants/beneficiaries: U.S. citizens, nationals, or permanent resident aliens that are college sophomores or juniors, nominated by accredited IHEs.

Average: $5,000.

Activity: as of FY 06, 836 scholarships awarded.

HQ: Executive Director, Morris K. Udall Foundation, 130 S. Scott Ave., Tucson, AZ 85701. Phone: (520) 670-5529, -5542, FAX (520) 670-5530.

Internet: www.udall.gov (Note: no field offices for this program.)

85.401 MORRIS K. UDALL FELLOWSHIP PROGRAM

Assistance: direct payments/specified use.

Purposes: pursuant to the Morris K. Udall Scholarship and Excellence in National Environmental and Native American Public Policy Act of 1992, for internships, scholarships, and fellowships to develop increased opportunities for young Americans to prepare for careers related to the environment; for native Americans and Alaska natives intending to pursue careers in health care and tribal public policy. The program is financed by a permanent trust fund endowment.

Eligible applicants/beneficiaries: U.S. citizens and permanent residents that are full-time doctoral degree candidates in their final year of writing their dissertation in environmental public policy and conflict resolution.

Average: $24,000.

Activity: as of FY 06, 22 fellowships.

HQ: Executive Director, Morris K. Udall Foundation, 130 S. Scott Ave., Tucson, AZ 85701. Phone: (520) 670-5529, -5609, FAX (520) 670-5530.

Internet: www.udall.gov (Note: no field offices for this program.)

85.402 MORRIS K. UDALL NATIVE AMERICAN CONGRESSIONAL INTERNSHIP PROGRAM

Assistance: direct payments/specified use.

Purposes: pursuant to the Morris K. Udall Scholarship and Excellence in National Environmental and Native American Public Policy Act of 1992, for internships, scholarships, and fellowships to develop increased opportunities for young Americans to prepare for careers related to the environment; for native Americans and Alaska natives intending to pursue careers in health care and tribal public policy. The program is financed by a permanent trust fund endowment. Interns receive round- trip air fare to Washington, D.C., lodging, a per diem for meals and incidentals, and a $1,200 stipend at the conclusion of the internship.

Eligible applicants/beneficiaries: members of recognized tribes or Alaska natives that are matriculated college seniors or graduate or law students with a minimum 3.2 GPA, and interested in tribal government and policy.

Average: $3,160 to $3,685 per intern per 10-week program.

Activity: as of FY 06, 114 internships in various Congressional offices and the White House.

HQ: Executive Director, Morris K. Udall Foundation, 130 S. Scott Ave., Tucson, AZ 85701. Phone: (520) 670-5187, FAX (520) 670-5530.

Internet: www.udall.gov (Note: no field offices for this program.)

JAMES MADISON MEMORIAL FELLOWSHIP FOUNDATION

85.500 JAMES MADISON MEMORIAL FELLOWSHIP PROGRAM

Assistance: direct payments/specified use.

Purposes: pursuant to the James Madison Memorial Fellowship Act, for fellowships to future and current secondary school (grades 7- 12) American history, government, or social studies teachers—toward a deeper understanding of American government, as well the spirit of civic participation that inspired the nation's founders. Recipients are obligated to perform one year of teaching for each year of study supported by a fellowship. Payments cover actual costs of tuition, room and board, fees, and books.

Eligible applicants/beneficiaries: Junior Fellows (2-year maximum)—college seniors or college graduates. Senior Fellows (5-year maximum)—experienced, full-time teachers of grades 7- 12, pursuing a Master's level degree. All candidates must be U.S. citizens or nationals.

Range: to $12,000 for one year; $24,000 maximum total award.

Activity: since 1992 program inception, 800 fellowship awards. Currently, 83 active junior, 268 active senior fellowships.

HQ: Director of Administration and Finance, James Madison Memorial Fellowship Foundation, 2000 K St. NW - Ste.303, Washington, DC 20006. Phone: (202) 653-8700, FAX (202) 653-6045.

Internet: www.jamesmadison.com (Note: no field offices for this program.)

SMITHSONIAN INSTITUTE FELLOWSHIP FOUNDATION

85.601 SMITHSONIAN INSTITUTION FELLOWSHIP PROGRAM

Assistance: project grants (10 weeks to 1 year).

Purposes: for graduate and predoctoral students and postdoctoral and senior investigators to conduct research in association with Smithsonian professional staff. Fellowships and internships presently cover: animal behavior; ecology; environmental science emphasizing the tropics; anthropology and archaeology; astrophysics and astronomy; earth sciences and paleobiology; evolutionary and systemic biology; history of science and technology, history of art, especially American, contemporary African, and Asian art, American crafts, decorative arts; social and cultural history of the U.S.; folklife.

Eligible applicants/beneficiaries: postdoctoral fellowships—scholars holding the degree or equivalent for less than 7 years. Senior fellowships—scholars holding the degree or equivalent for 7 years of more. Predoctoral fellowships—candidates who have completed preliminary coursework and exams. Graduate Student fellowships—candidates enrolled in a graduate program of study with at least one semester completed.

Range: $4,500 to $40,000.

Activity: new program in FY 05.

HQ: Office of Fellowships, Smithsonian Institution, Victor Bldg. - Ste. 9300, Washington, DC 20013-7012. Phone: (202) 275-0655.

Internet: www.si.edu/research+study; email, siofg@si.edu (Note: no field offices for this program.)

PENSION BENEFIT GUARANTY CORPORATION

86.001 PENSION PLAN TERMINATION INSURANCE ("ERISA")

Assistance: insurance.

Purposes: pursuant to the Employee Retirement Income Security Act of 1974 as amended (ERISA), Pension Protection Act of 1987, Retirement Protection Act of 1994, Job Creation and Worker Assistance Act of 2002, Pension Funding Act Equity Act of 2004, and other acts, to insure voluntary private pension plans; to provide for uninterrupted payment of pension benefits to participants and beneficiaries in PBGC-covered plans; to maintain premiums charged by PBGC at the lowest level consistent with fulfilling its obligations. Insurance coverage is mandatory for any pension plan established or maintained by an employer or an employee organization engaged in or affecting commerce, except such plans as those covering: individual accounts; federal, state, local employees; church employees; nonresident aliens; select groups of management or highly compensated employees; professional service employers with fewer than 25 participants; other specific groups. Single-employer plans may terminate in a standard termination only if sufficient assets exist to provide all benefits—and in a voluntary distress termination only if the sponsoring employer can satisfy specified distress criteria. Benefits are paid within limits specified by law.

Eligible applicants/beneficiaries: private businesses and organizations that maintain defined benefit plans; participants in such plans.

Range: $10 to $3,971.59 in monthly benefits per retiree.

Activity: 30,300 plans insured with 44,100,000 participants; FY 05, 682,820 participants received benefits.

HQ: Pension Benefit Guaranty Corporation, 1200 K St. NW, Washington, DC 20005-4026. Phone: (202) 326-4000.

Internet: www.pbgc.gov.

ARCHITECTURAL AND TRANSPORTATION BARRIERS COMPLIANCE BOARD

88.001 ARCHITECTURAL AND TRANSPORTATION BARRIERS COMPLIANCE BOARD ("Access Board")

Assistance: technical information.

Purposes: pursuant to the ADA, Rehabilitation Act of 1973, and Architectural Barriers Act of 1968 as amended, and other laws, to enforce federal laws requiring accessibility for physically handicapped persons in federally funded buildings and facilities; to establish related guidelines and requirements; to provide technical assistance and training on design guidelines and standards; to conduct pertinent research.

Eligible applicants/beneficiaries: general public; federal, state, and local agencies.

Range/Average: N.A.

Activity: not quantified specifically.

HQ: Director, Office of Technical and Information Services, ATBCB, 1331 F St. NW - Ste.1000, Washington, DC 20004-1111. Phone: (202) 272-0080, TTY (202) 272-0082, FAX (202) 272-0081; *technical assistance,* (800) 872-2253, TTY (800) 993-2822.

Internet: www.access-board.gov; e-mail, info@access-board.gov (Note: no field offices for this program.)

NATIONAL ARCHIVES AND RECORDS ADMINISTRATION

89.001 NATIONAL ARCHIVES REFERENCE SERVICES—HISTORICAL RESEARCH

Assistance: use of property, facilities, and equipment; advisory services/counseling; technical information.

Purposes: pursuant to the National Archives and Records Administration Act of 1984 and other acts, to provide reference services to the public and researchers in obtaining access to records and historical materials of the federal government in the National Archives, Presidential Libraries, and Regional Records Services. Conferences, workshops, and other outreach activities may be conducted. Restrictions apply to records subject to the Freedom of Information Act, such as national security.

Eligible applicants/beneficiaries: general public.

Range/Average: N.A.

Activity: FY 05 (aggregate of all sources), 14,230,880 reference services.

HQ: Office of Records Services, National Archives and Records Administration, College Park, MD 20740-6001. Phone: (301) 837- 3110; Office of Regional Records Services, (301) 837-1982; Office of Presidential Libraries, (301) 837-3250.

Internet: www.archives.gov.

89.003 NATIONAL HISTORICAL PUBLICATIONS AND RECORDS GRANTS

Assistance: project grants.

Purposes: pursuant to the National Archives and Records Administration Act of 1984 and other acts, for preservation, publication, and use of documentary sources relating to U.S. history. Projects may involve: collaborative efforts with the states, including training; publication in book, microform, or electronic editions of papers and documents of national historical significance.

Eligible applicants/beneficiaries: state and local governments, territorial agencies, tribes; educational and other nonprofit institutions including IHEs, libraries, historical societies, museums, university presses, archives; individuals.

Range: $5,000 to $750,000. **Average:** $85,000.

Activity: FY 06, 100 awards; FY 07 estimated 0 awards.

HQ: National Historical Publications and Records Commission, National Archives and Records Administration, National Archives Bldg., Washington, DC 20408. Phone: (202) 357-5010, FAX (202) 357-5914.

Internet: www.archives.gov/grants; e-mail, nhprc@nara.gov (Note: no field offices for this program.)

89.005 COOPERATIVE AGREEMENTS TO SUPPORT THE PROGRAMS OF THE NATIONAL ARCHIVES AND RECORDS ADMINISTRATION (NARA)

Assistance: direct payments/specified use.

Purposes: to undertake a wide-range of activities for the public purpose of carrying out programs of the National Archives and Records Administration.

Eligible applicants/beneficiaries: state and local governments, other public entities, educational institutions or private nonprofit organizations (including foundations or institutes organized to support the National Archives and Records Administration or the Presidential archival depositories).

Range: to $25,000 per cooperative agreement. **Average:** $19,950.

Activity: new program in 2006; FY 05, 2 awards.

HQ: Policy and Planning Staff, National Archives and Records Administration, 8601 Adelphi Rd-Room 4100, College Park, MD 20740 Phone: (301) 837- 1850.

Internet: www.archives.gov.

INDEPENDENT BOARDS AND COMMISSIONS

DENALI COMMISSION

90.100 DENALI COMMISSION PROGRAM

Assistance: project grants.

Purposes: pursuant to the Denali Commission Act of 1998, to support the Denali Commission as a federal-state partnership to provide critical utilities and infrastructure throughout Alaska, particularly in distressed communities. Project examples: bulk fuel tank storage at isolated site; remote hydroelectric generation; health care infrastructure planning and construction.

Eligible applicants/beneficiaries: Alaska state and local government agencies, public and private profit and nonprofit organizations, individuals.

Range: $200,000 to $10,000,000. **Average:** $5,000,000.

Activity: not quantified specifically.

HQ: Denali Commission, 510 L St. - Ste. 410, Anchorage, AK 99501. Phone: (907) 271-1414.

Internet: www.denali.gov (Note: no field offices for this program.)

DELTA REGIONAL AUTHORITY

90.200 DELTA REGIONAL DEVELOPMENT ("Delta Program")

Assistance: project grants.

Purposes: pursuant to FSRIA, for 240 specific counties in the eight states in the Delta Region (Mississippi River), in partnership with the federal government, to remedy severe and chronic economic distress by stimulating economic development in distressed communities—by leveraging other federal and state programs focused on: basic infrastructure development transportation improvements; business development; and job training services. States each prepare annual development plans related to a strategic program for which funding is requested in that year; the plans are submitted for approval to the Delta Regional Authority (DRA) which is led by a federal co-chairman and the eight state governors; once approved, individual projects are administered by the federal agency involved, a local development district, or the DRA. Funding is reflected in programs **90.201** and **90.202**.

Eligible applicants/beneficiaries: eight states, public and nonprofit entities in the Delta region. Inquiries and proposals should be submitted to appropriate Local Development Districts (listed on the DRA web site, below).

Range/Average: N.A.

Activity: new program listing in 2005 (CFDA on-line).

HQ: Executive Director, Delta Regional Authority, 236 Sharkey Ave. - Ste. 400, Clarksdale, MS 38614. Phone: (662) 624-8600.

Internet: www.dra.gov (Note: no field offices for this program.)

90.201 DELTA AREA ECONOMIC DEVELOPMENT ("Supplemental and Direct Grants")

Assistance: project grants. (50-90 percent/to 18 months).

Purposes: pursuant to FSRIA, to provide supplemental funds under federal grant-in-aid programs for high-priority projects in state development plans as described in **90.200**. Projects must involve: basic public infrastructure in distressed counties and isolated areas of distress; transportation infrastructure to facilitate economic development; business development emphasizing entrepreneurship; job training or employment-related education, using existing public educational institutions in the region. Recent project examples: water and sewer systems for industrial parks, with tenants committed; IHE workforce training with committed company participation; business incubators.

Eligible applicants/beneficiaries: eight states, public and nonprofit entities in the Delta region. Inquiries and proposals should be submitted to appropriate Local Development Districts (listed on the DRA web site, below).

Range: $25,000 to $200,000.

Activity: new program listing in 2005 (CFDA on-line). FY 05, 48 projects approved.

HQ: Executive Director, Delta Regional Authority, 236 Sharkey Ave. - Ste. 400, Clarksdale, MS 38614. Phone: (662) 624-8600.

Internet: www.dra.gov (Note: no field offices for this program.)

90.202 DELTA LOCAL DEVELOPMENT DISTRICT ASSISTANCE ("LDD")

Assistance: project grants. (50 percent/1 year).

Purposes: pursuant to FSRIA, for the administrative and technical services costs of certified development districts in multicounty districts, including pertinent professional and technical development—in furtherance of projects and programs outlined in **90.200**.

Eligible applicants/beneficiaries: certified multicounty organizations in the Delta Region.

Range: $5,090 to $19,800. **Average:** $9,209.

Activity: new program listing in 2005 (CFDA on-line). FY 05, 43 planning districts aided.

HQ: Executive Director, Delta Regional Authority, 236 Sharkey Ave. - Ste. 400, Clarksdale, MS 38614. Phone: (662) 624-8600.

Internet: www.dra.gov (Note: no field offices for this program.)

JAPAN US FRIENDSHIP COMMISSION

90.300 JAPAN-U.S. FRIENDSHIP COMMISSION GRANTS

Assistance: project grants. (cost sharing/6-18 months).

Purposes: to promote educational, artistic, and cultural exchange and research between Japan and the U.S.

Eligible applicants/beneficiaries: public, state, and private IHEs; "501(c)(3)" organizations other than IHEs.

Range/Average: N.A.

Activity: N.A.; new program listing in 2004.

HQ: Japan-U.S. Friendship Commission, 1201 15th St. NW - Ste. 330, Washington, DC 20005. Phone: (no number provided).

Internet: www.jusfc.gov (Note: no field offices for this program.)

ELECTIONS ASSISTANCE COMMISSION

90.400 HELP AMERICA VOTE COLLEGE PROGRAM

Assistance: project grants.

Purposes: pursuant to the Help America Vote Act of 2002, to recruit and train college students to assist state and local governments in the administration of elections by serving as nonpartisan poll workers or assistants.

Eligible applicants/beneficiaries: state and private IHEs; "501(c)(3)" organizations other than IHEs; other nonprofit organizations.

Range: to $20,000.

Activity: FY 04, 15 colleges, universities and nonprofit groups assisted.

HQ: Director, Help America Vote College Program, U.S. Elections Assistance Commission, 1225 New York Ave. NW - Ste. 1100, Washington, DC 20005. Phone: (202) 566-3100.

Internet: www.eac.gov (Note: no field offices for this program.)

90.401 HELP AMERICA VOTE ACT REQUIREMENTS PAYMENTS

Assistance: direct payments/specified use (95 percent).

Purposes: pursuant to the Help America Vote Act of 2002, to reimburse states for costs incurred in obtaining voting equipment and in meeting standards required by the Act.

Eligible applicants/beneficiaries: states, DC, and outlying areas.

Range/Average: N.A.

Activity: new program listing in 2005 (CFDA on-line).

HQ: Director, Help America Vote College Program, U.S. Elections Assistance Commission, 1225 New York Ave. NW - Ste. 1100, Washington, DC 20005. Phone: (202) 566-3100.

Internet: www.eac.gov (Note: no field offices for this program.)

90.402 HELP AMERICA VOTE MOCK ELECTION PROGRAM

Assistance: project grants (100 percent).

Purposes: pursuant to the Omnibus Appropriations Act for Fiscal Year 2008, to promote voter participation and education in American elections through a program of simulated Federal elections (held at least 5 days before the actual general Federal election) that permits participation by students enrolled in a secondary education program. Nonallowable activities and expenditures include: construction, indirect costs, voter registration and Get-Out-The-Vote (GOTV) efforts.

Eligible applicants: state election offices and non-profit organizations, including faith-based, community-based, and tribal organizations who can demonstrate prior experience operating a program of simulated elections aimed at students enrolled in a secondary education program.

Eligible beneficiaries: students in secondary education programs.

Range: FY 08 estimate, not less than $10,000. **Average:** FY 08 estimate, $20,000.

Activity: New program; FY 08 estimate, 1-35 awards.

HQ: Help America Vote Mock Election Program, Election Assistance Commission, 1225 New York Ave. NW, Suite 1100, Washington, DC 20005. Phone: (202) 566-3100.

Internet: www.eac.gov. (Note: no field offices for this program.)

UNITED STATES INSTITUTE OF PEACE

91.001 UNSOLICITED GRANT PROGRAM

Assistance: project grants.

Purposes: pursuant to the United States Institute of Peace Act and the Department of Defense Authorization Act of 1985, for education, training, research, and public information projects in international peace and conflict resolution. Unsolicited grant awards may support: research by scholars; curricula and materials development for secondary through postgraduate programs; media programming, including materials for television and radio; development of data bases, bibliographies, collections.

Eligible applicants/beneficiaries: domestic or foreign nonprofit organizations; official public institutions; individuals including U.S. citizens and foreign nationals.

Average: $38,000.

Activity: since FY 89, 1,150 awards.

HQ: Unsolicited Grant Program, U.S. Institute of Peace, 1200 17th St. NW - Ste. 200, Washington, DC 20036-3006. Phone: (202) 429- 3842.

Internet: www.usip.org; e-mail, grants@usip.org (Note: no field offices for this program.)

91.002 SOLICITED GRANT PROGRAM

Assistance: project grants (100 percent).

Purposes: pursuant to the United States Institute of Peace Act and the Department of Defense Authorization Act of 1985, for competitive grants to support research, education, library and information technology—on international peace and conflict resolution and on themes and topics identified by the Institute.

Eligible applicants/beneficiaries: domestic or foreign nonprofit organizations; official public institutions; individuals including U.S. citizens and foreign nationals.

Average: $40,000.

Activity: since 1989, over 424 awards.

HQ: Solicited Grant Program, U.S. Institute of Peace, 1200 17th St. NW - Ste. 200, Washington, DC 20036-3006. Phone: (202) 429- 3842.

Internet: www.usip.org; e-mail, grants@usip.org (Note: no field offices for this program.)

DEPARTMENT OF HEALTH AND HUMAN SERVICES

NOTES: *In HHS programs:*

"NRSA" *refers to National Research Service Awards available to institutions, individuals, or both. Only domestic nonprofit organizations may apply for institutional awards. Individual applicants must: be U.S. citizens, noncitizen nationals, or lawful permanent residents; have a professional or scientific degree (M.D., Ph.D., D.D.S., D.V.M., Sc.D., D.Eng., or equivalent domestic or foreign degree); arrange sponsorships by a public or private nonprofit institution with appropriate staff and facilities; comply with applicable service or payback requirements. Predoctoral awards may be available to recipients with a baccalaureate degree and some work completed toward a graduate degree.*

"SBIR" *refers to the Small Business Innovation Research program. SBIR grants fund the development of technological innovations that may lead to commercialization of products and processes. Phase I contracts, usually up to $100,000 covering six months of research activity, are to establish technical merit and feasibility. Phase II funding, ranging to $750,000 for up to two years, is for continuation of Phase I activities. Primary employment of the principal investigator named in the firm's proposal must be with the small business.*

"STTR" *refers to the Small Business Technology Transfer program. STTR Phase I grants, up to $100,000 for one year of activity, fund cooperative research and development by small businesses and research institutions to determine scientific, technical, and commercial merit and feasibility. Phase II funding, up to $500,000 for two years, reflects results of Phase I research. At least 40 percent of project activities must be performed by the small business concern, and at least 30 percent by the research institution.*

SBIR *and* **STTR** *program contracts must involve domestic small businesses—i.e., for-profit, independently owned, not dominant in the field, and with no more than 500 employees—conducting research in the U.S. or its possessions. Participation by minority, women-owned, and socially and economically disadvantaged businesses is fostered and encouraged.*

Internet: *NIH SBIR and STTR program basic grant solicitation and contract information: e-mail, ASKHIH@odrockml.od.hih.gov".*

93.001 CIVIL RIGHTS AND PRIVACY RULE COMPLIANCE ACTIVITIES

Assistance: investigation of complaints.

Purposes: pursuant to the Civil Rights Act, Age Discrimination Act of 1975, ADA, Small Business Job Protection Act of 1996 (SBJPA), Health Insurance Portability and Accountability Act of 1996 (HIPAA), related acts, and amendments, to ensure equal opportunities for, and nondiscrimination on any basis against, applicants for or beneficiaries of HHS assistance through any HHS-assisted program or facility—and that the privacy of their health information will be protected under the HIPAA Privacy Rule; to encourage compliance with nondiscrimination regulations by providing technical assistance to recipients of HHS assistance, through workshops, designing model compliance plans, and training responsible state and local officials. Under SBJPA, the Office of Civil Rights investigates complaints and takes steps to assure that individuals are not discriminated against in adoption or foster care placement decisions.

Eligible applicants/beneficiaries: anyone believing that they have been discriminated against in any HHS program, or wanting information or technical assistance to assure compliance with applicable laws.

Range/Average: N.A.

Activity: FY 05 (sampling), 9,802 discrimination complaints filed, 8,423 complaint actions completed; 3,969 grant compliance reviews.

HQ: Deputy Director, Management Operations Division, Office for Civil Rights, OS-HHS, HHH Bldg. - Rm.509-F6, 200 Independence Ave. SW, Washington, DC 20201. Phone: (202) 619-1333; Director, Office for Civil Rights, (same address), (202) 619-0403.

Internet: www.hhs.gov/ocr.

93.003 PUBLIC HEALTH AND SOCIAL SERVICES EMERGENCY FUND

Assistance: project grants (100 percent).

Purposes: pursuant to the Public Health Service Act (PHSA), to provide supplemental funding for public health and social service emergencies resulting from disasters. Funds are allocated to HHS agencies for award. (Note: see planned additional uses under "Activity," below.)

Eligible applicants/beneficiaries: federal agencies, state and local governments, service providers in disaster areas.

Range/Average: N.A.

Activity: FY 05-06, funds to be used to prepare the public health system and hospitals for future emergencies, for a reserve of medical supplies for use in possible mass casualty events, for research into new treatments and diagnostic tools to cope with possible bioterrorism incident.

HQ: Director, Division of Financial Management, SAMHSA-HHS, Parklawn Bldg., 1 Choke Cherry Rd., Rockville, MD 20857. Phone: (240) 276-1660. Deputy Director, Financial Management Office, CDCP-HHS, 1600 Clifton Rd., Atlanta, GA 30333. Phone: (404) 639- 7400.

Internet: www.hhs.gov (Note: no field offices for this program.)

93.004 COOPERATIVE AGREEMENTS TO IMPROVE THE HEALTH STATUS OF MINORITY POPULATIONS

Assistance: project grants. (100 percent/to 5 years).

Purposes: pursuant to PHSA as amended, for activities to improve the health status and quality of life of racial and ethnic minorities, consistent with the mission of the HHS Office of Minority Health. Funds may not be used to provide health care, for construction, or to supplant ongoing project activities. Project example: provider education and sensitivity training on cultural practices and their influence on patient compliance with medication and therapeutic treatment interventions.

Eligible applicants/beneficiaries: public and private nonprofit entities; faith based organizations.

Range: $25,000 to $614,000. **Average:** $186,000.

Activity: FY 06 estimate, 9 continuation awards.

HQ: Director, Division of Program Operations, Office of Minority Health, Office of Public Health and Science, OS-HHS, 1101 Wooten Pkwy. - Ste.600, Rockville, MD 20852. Phone: (240) 453-8444.

Internet: www.omhrc.gov (Note: no field offices for this program.)

93.006 STATE AND TERRITORIAL AND TECHNICAL ASSISTANCE CAPACITY DEVELOPMENT MINORITY HIV/AIDS DEMONSTRATION PROGRAM

Assistance: project grants. (100 percent/to 3 years).

Purposes: pursuant to PHSA as amended, for demonstrations involving state offices of minority health and community-based organizations in HIV/AIDS health education and prevention strategies—to coordinate statewide responses to the crisis in minority communities; to increase access to services and treatment for minorities; to provide technical assistance and capacity development to minority community-based organizations. Funds may not be used to provide health care, for construction, or to supplant ongoing project activities.

Eligible applicants/beneficiaries: state and territorial offices of minority health, or agencies functioning in that capacity; minority-serving community-based organizations.

Range: $144,127 to $1,200,000. **Average:** $430,649.

Activity: FY 06 and FY 07 estimate, 17 continuation awards.

HQ: Director, Division of Program Operations, Office of Minority Health, Office of Public Health and Science, OS-HHS, 1101 Wooten Pkwy. - Ste. 700, Rockville, MD 20852. Phone: (240) 453-8444.

Internet: www.omhrc.gov (Note: no field offices for this program.)

93.007 PUBLIC AWARENESS CAMPAIGNS ON EMBRYO ADOPTION

Assistance: project grants. (100 percent/to 1 year).

Purposes: for public awareness campaigns on embryo adoption.

Eligible applicants/beneficiaries: "particular" experienced public agencies, nonprofit, and profit organizations; collaboratives. Subgrants may be awarded.

Range: $200,000 to $250,000.

Activity: FY 06, 3-4 new, 4 continuation awards.

HQ: Office of Population Affairs, Office of Public Health and Science, OS-HHS, 1101 Wooten Pkwy. - Ste. 700, Rockville, MD 20852. Phone: (240) 453-2828. *Grants management information*: Office of Grants Management, Office of Public Health and Science, OS-HHS, 1101 Wooten Pkwy. - Ste. 550, Rockville, MD 20852. Phone: (240) 453-2888.

Internet: www.osophs.dhhs.gov/ophs (Note: no field offices for this program.)

93.008 MEDICAL RESERVE CORPS SMALL GRANT PROGRAM

Assistance: project grants. (100 percent/to 3 years).

Purposes: pursuant to PHSA as amended, for development of community Medical Reserve Corps (MRCs) units to increase capacity at the community level to respond to emergencies that have medical consequences, and to improve public health through volunteerism on an ongoing basis. Funds may be used: to establish community-based, citizen-volunteer MRCs; for organizing, volunteer recruitment, assessment of risks and vulnerability, strategy development, planning, training, drills and practices, supplies, and equipment.

Eligible applicants/beneficiaries: local government entities; local nonprofit, nongovernmental community-based organizations, including nonprofit Citizen Corps Councils of the USA Freedom Corps.

Range: $10,000 to $50,000. **Average:** $50,000.

Activity: FY 06 estimate, 40-75 new awards.

HQ: Office of the Surgeon General, USPHS, OS-HHS, 5600 Fishers Lane - Rm.18-66, Rockville, MD 20817. Phone: (301) 443-2528. *Grants management information*: Office of Grants Management, Office of Public Health and Science, OS-HHS, 1101 Wooten Pkwy. - Ste. 550, Rockville, MD 20852. Phone: (240) 453-8822.

Internet: www.medicalreservecorps.gov (Note: no field offices for this program.)

93.009 COMPASSION CAPITAL FUND ("CCF")

Assistance: project grants. (80-100 percent/to 3 years).

Purposes: pursuant to SSA as amended, for charitable organizations to emulate model social service programs; for research on the "best practices" of social service organizations. Funds are provided to intermediary organizations, experienced in capacity building, to provide long-term technical assistance to smaller so-called faith-based and community organizations in such areas as strategic planning, financial management, board development, fund development, and outcome measurement. The intermediary organizations provide one-time $50,000 (unmatched) sub-awards to the smaller organizations, with priority to those that: have not received federal funds; will serve the homeless, elders in need, families in transition from welfare to work, at-risk youth, those in need of intensive rehabilitation such as addicts or prisoners, provide marriage education and preparation services. The sub-awards may not fund direct services; rather, they must improve efficiency and capacity.

Eligible applicants/beneficiaries: intermediaries—county, municipal, special district, and tribal governments; IHEs; profit and nonprofit "501(c)(3)" organizations; faith-based organizations. Sub-awards—nonprofit organizations with and without "501(c)(3)" status, other than IHEs; tribal governments; faith-based organizations.

Range: $50,000 to $500,000.

Activity: FY 05, 24 continuation awards, 33 new awards to intermediary organizations, 200 mini-grants.

HQ: Program Manager, Office of Community Services, ACF-HHS, 370 L'Enfant Promenade - 5th Floor West, Washington, DC 20447. Phone: (202) 260-2583, FAX (202) 401-4839.

Internet: www.acf.dhhs.gov (Note: no field offices for this program.)

93.010 COMMUNITY-BASED ABSTINENCE EDUCATION ("CBAE")

Assistance: project grants. (100 percent/to 3 years).

Purposes: pursuant to SSA, Section 510(a-h), for community-based abstinence education projects to reduce out-of-wedlock childbearing and sexually-transmitted disease among adolescents age 9-18. (Note: program provisions approximate **93.235**.)

Eligible applicants/beneficiaries: public and private nonprofit organizations, state and local government agencies, tribal or ethnic and faith-based organizations, hospitals, clinics, school districts.

Range: $200,000 to $600,000. **Average:** $425,000.

Activity: FY 06, 152 grants; FY 07 estimate, 202 grants.

HQ: Family and Youth Services Bureau, ACF-HHS, 1250 Maryland Ave. SW, Washington, DC 20024. Phone: (no number provided). *Grants management information*: Office of Grants Management, Division of Discretionary Grants, 370 L'Enfant Promenade SW, Washington, DC 20447. Phone: (no number provided).

Internet: www.acf.hhs.gov/programs/fysb (Note: no field offices for this program.)

93.012 IMPROVING, ENHANCING, AND EVALUATING OUTCOMES OF COMPREHENSIVE HEART HEALTH CARE PROGRAMS FOR HIGH-RISK WOMEN

Assistance: project grants.

Purposes: pursuant to PHSA, to improve and enhance existing heart health care programs and to enable tracking and evaluation of outcome data through demonstration projects. Projects must provide a continuum of services through the integration of five inter-related components: Education and Awareness; Screening and Risk Assessment; Diagnostic Testing and Treatment; Lifestyle Modification and Rehabilitation; Tracking and Evaluation. Grantees must target high-risk women in at least of the following groups: age 60 or older; racial and ethnic minorities; women living in rural communities. Funds may cover such costs as personnel and consultants; supplies and software; domestic travel; educational, promotional, and evaluation materials. Funds may not support direct health care services or equipment for patients nor building costs.

Eligible applicants/beneficiaries: existing public or private hospitals, clinics, or health centers; academic health centers and state, county, and local health departments—providing heart health care services to women and with three of the five components previously mentioned in place. Special encouragement to apply is given to enterprise communities and empowerment zones, tribal organizations, religious organizations and those serving rural or frontier communities.

Range: $50,000 to $150,000.

Activity: FY 05, 6 new grants; FY 06, 6 continuation grants.

HQ: Senior Science Advisor, Office on Women's Health, Office of Public Health and Science, OS-HHS, 200 Independence Ave. SW - Rm. 719E, Washington, DC 20201. Phone: (no number provided). *Grants management information*: Office of Grants Management, 1101 Wootton Pkwy, Ste. 550, Rockville, MD 20852. Phone: (240) 453-8822.

Internet: www.4woman.gov/owh (Note: no field offices for this program.)

93.013 AMBASSADORS FOR CHANGE PROGRAM

Assistance: project grants. (100 percent/to 3 years).

Purposes: for the enhancement of programs conducted by the National Centers of Excellence in Women's Health ("COEs and the National Community Centers of Excellence in Women's Health ("CCOEs" - see **93.290**), through the integration of components including: leadership development for women; training for lay, allied health, and professional health care providers; public education and outreach, especially to minority women; comprehensive health service delivery, including gender and age- appropriate preventive services, and allied health professionals as members of comprehensive care teams; basic science, clinical, and community-based research. Community centers must replicate their national model in another community. Funding is through cooperative agreements, to be used mainly for staff and coordination activities, including travel.

Eligible applicants/beneficiaries: previously funded COE and CCOE programs whose funding has ended and are without remaining option years.

Range: $25,000 to $50,000.

Activity: new program listing in 2006 (CFDA on-line); 6 grantees anticipated.

HQ: Office on Women's Health, Office of Public Health and Science, OS-HHS, 200 Independence Ave. SW - Rm. 712E, Washington, DC 20201. Phone: (no number provided). *Grants management information*: Division of Program Management, Office on Women's Health-HHS, Parklawn Bldg. - Rm. 16A-55, 5600 Fishers Lane, Rockville, MD 20857. Phone: (no number provided).

Internet: www.4woman.gov/owh (Note: no field offices for this program.)

93.014 STEPS TO HEALTHIER GIRLS PROGRAM

Assistance: project grants (100 percent).

Purposes: to increase number of girls who regularly engage in 60 minutes per day of physical activity and girls' knowledge of healthy weight, nutrition, the ill effects of tobacco and the importance of a healthy environment. Funds may be used for personnel, consultants, grant-related office supplies, software, educational, promotional and evaluation materials.

Eligible applicants/beneficiaries: Girl Scouts of USA.

Range: $60,000.

Activity: new program in 2006.

HQ: Office on Women's Health, OS-HHS, 200 Independence Ave. SW - Rm. 712E, Washington, DC 20201 Phone: (no number provided).

Internet: www.4woman.gov/owh.

93.015 HIV PREVENTION PROGRAMS FOR WOMEN

Assistance: project grants. (100 percent/to 2 years).

Purposes: to increase awareness of HIV prevention information, of access to related services, and of testing of women in specific categories of women: Living in the Rural South; Attending Minority Institutions; Living in the Rural and Frontier Indian Country; Incarcerated and Newly Released; Living in the U.S. Virgin Islands and Puerto Rico. Funding is through cooperative agreements, and may not be used for direct health care services or equipment.

Eligible applicants/beneficiaries: public IHEs; HBCUs; Hispanic- Serving Institutions; tribal IHEs; private nonprofit community- based organizations; tribal organizations; religious organizations.

Range/Average: N.A.

Activity: new program listing in 2006 (CFDA on-line).

HQ: Office on Women's Health, Office of Public Health and Science, OS-HHS, 200 Independence Ave. SW - Rm. 712E, Washington, DC 20201. Phone: (no number provided). *Grants management information*: Office of Grants Management, 1101 Wootton Pkwy, Ste. 550, Rockville, MD 20852. Phone: (240) 453-8822.

Internet: www.4woman.gov/owh (Note: no field offices for this program.)

93.017 STRENGTHENING THE MANAGEMENT AND SERVICES OF THE WOMEN'S AND CHILDREN'S HOSPITALS IN KABUL

Assistance: project grants. (100 percent/to 3 years).

Purposes: pursuant to PHSA, to develop leadership and to improve management and operations at health institutions in Kabul, Afghanistan. Funding is through cooperative agreements, intended for activities covering facilities operation, professionals training, and related activities—but not to provide direct health care services or equipment for patients, nor real property improvements.

Eligible applicants/beneficiaries: nonprofit entities with offices in the U.S. or partner country or incorporated in or with U.S. headquarters; organizations or consortia including religious and community-based organizations with pertinent experience.

Range: $200,000 to $1,500,000.

Activity: new program listing in 2006 (CFDA on-line).

HQ: Office of Global Affairs-HHS, 200 Independence Ave. SW - Rm. 639-H, Washington, DC 20201. Phone: (202) 690-6174; FAX (202) 690-7127. *Program, technical assistance*: Office of Global Affairs-OS-HHS, 5600 Fishers Lane - Ste. 18-101, Rockville, MD 20857. Phone: (240) 453-8822.

Internet: www.globalhealth.gov/oirh.shtml (Note: no field offices for this program.)

93.018 STRENGTHENING PUBLIC HEALTH SERVICES AT THE OUTREACH OFFICES OF THE U.S.-MEXICO BORDER HEALTH COMMISSION

Assistance: project grants (100 percent).

Purposes: pursuant to PHSA, to improve the health of residents along the U.S.-Mexico border, through: targeted outreach and health promotion activities; evaluation and assessments; health data analysis; Health Border/Healthy Gente activities. Funding is through cooperative agreements covering costs of personnel, consultants, educational materials, software, and related travel—but not direct patient care services or equipment, nor real estate-related improvements.

Eligible applicants/beneficiaries: border state departments of health, working with the U.S.-Mexico Border Health Commission.

Range: $250,000 to $500,000.

Activity: new program listing in 2006 (CFDA on-line).

HQ: Office of Global Affairs-HHS, 200 Independence Ave. SW - Rm. 639-H, Washington, DC 20201. Phone: (202) 690-6174; FAX (202) 690-7127. *Program, technical assistance*: Office of Global Affairs-OS-HHS, 5600 Fishers Lane - Ste. 18-101, Rockville, MD 20857. Phone: (240) 453-8822.

Internet: www.globalhealth.gov/oirh.shtml (Note: no field offices for this program.)

93.041 SPECIAL PROGRAMS FOR THE AGING—TITLE VII, CHAPTER 3—PROGRAMS FOR PREVENTION OF ELDER ABUSE, NEGLECT, AND EXPLOITATION

Assistance: formula grants. (100 percent/1-4 years).

Purposes: pursuant to the Older Americans Act of 1965 (OAA) as amended, to develop, strengthen, and carry out comprehensive and coordinated programs for the prevention and treatment of abuse, neglect, and exploitation of older persons. Eligible project activities include public education and outreach, counseling, development and analysis of information and data systems, technical assistance and training for professionals and paraprofessionals. States must submit plans covering 2-4 years.

Eligible applicants/beneficiaries: states and territories with state agencies on aging, designated by the governors.

Range: $3,197 to $511,900. **Average:** $92,274.

Activity: annually, 56 grants.

HQ: Director, Office of Deputy Assistant Secretary/Policy and Programs, AOA-HHS, Washington, DC 20001. Phone: (202) 401-4634.

Internet: www.aoa.gov.

93.042 SPECIAL PROGRAMS FOR THE AGING—TITLE VII, CHAPTER 2—LONG-TERM CARE OMBUDSMAN SERVICES FOR OLDER INDIVIDUALS ("State Grants for Long-Term Care Ombudsman Services")

Assistance: formula grants.

Purposes: pursuant to OAA as amended, to develop or strengthen ombudsman services programs for older persons living or seeking to live in nursing homes or long-term care facilities, to: provide for the investigation and resolution of complaints by or on behalf of residents; promote policies and practices to improve the quality of life and care; consumer and provider education activities. States must submit plans covering 2-4 years.

Eligible applicants/beneficiaries: states and territories with state agencies on aging, designated by the governors.

Range: $8,763 to $1,416,144. **Average:** $250,360.

Activity: annually, 56 grants.

HQ: Director, Long-Term Care Ombudsman Programs, AOA-HHS, Washington, DC 20001. Phone: (202) 357-3516.

Internet: www.aoa.gov.

93.043 SPECIAL PROGRAMS FOR THE AGING—TITLE III, PART D—DISEASE PREVENTION AND HEALTH PROMOTION SERVICES

Assistance: formula grants. (85 percent/1-4 years).

Purposes: pursuant to OAA as amended, to develop or strengthen programs for preventive health services ineligible for reimbursement under Medicare and for health promotion, at senior centers or alternative sites. Eligible project activities include health risk assessments, routine health and nutrition screening, home injury control and safety screening, physical fitness programs, coordination of community mental health services, gerontological counseling, referrals and follow-ups. States must submit plans covering 2-4 years.

Eligible applicants/beneficiaries: states and territories with state agencies on aging, designated by the governors.

Range: $13,465 to $2,176,053. **Average:** $384,704.

Activity: annually, 56 grants; no grants anticipated for FY 08.

HQ: Office for Community-Based Services, AOA-HHS, Washington, DC 20001. Phone: (202) 357-3546.

Internet: www.aoa.gov.

93.044 SPECIAL PROGRAMS FOR THE AGING—TITLE III, PART B—GRANTS FOR SUPPORTIVE SERVICES AND SENIOR CENTERS

Assistance: formula grants. (85 percent/1-4 years).

Purposes: pursuant to OAA as amended, to provide comprehensive and coordinated supportive services and to operate multipurpose facilities for older persons, including senior centers, developed according to approved 2-4 year state plans; to maximize support provided to older Americans to enable them to remain in their homes and communities. In addition to supportive nutrition services, funds may cover transportation service, in-home services, and caregiver support, as well as acquisition, construction, or renovation costs.

Eligible applicants/beneficiaries: states and territories with state agencies on aging, designated by the governors.

Range: $220,595 to $35,130,320. **Average:** $6,302,726.

Activity: annually, 56 grants.

HQ: Office for Community-Based Services, AOA-HHS, Washington, DC 20001. Phone: (202) 357-3546.

Internet: www.aoa.gov.

93.045 SPECIAL PROGRAMS FOR THE AGING—TITLE III, PART C—NUTRITION SERVICES

Assistance: formula grants. (85 percent/1-4 years).

Purposes: pursuant to OAA as amended, to provide meals, nutrition education, and related services for the elderly—including at least one hot or other appropriate meal per day, five or more days per week (except in rural areas). Meals may be served in a congregate setting or delivered to the home.

Eligible applicants: states and territories with state agencies on aging, designated by the governors.

Eligible beneficiaries: persons age 60 and over and their spouses; certain disabled or handicapped persons under age 60.

Range: congregate services, $241,237 to $35,184,631; home services, $113,885 to $18,402,694. **Average:** congregate, $6,892,495; home, $3,253,851.

Activity: annually, 56 grants.

HQ: Office for Community-Based Services, AOA-HHS, Washington, DC 20001. Phone: (202) 357-3546.

Internet: www.aoa.gov.

93.047 SPECIAL PROGRAMS FOR THE AGING—TITLE VI, PART A, GRANTS TO INDIAN TRIBES—PART B, GRANTS TO NATIVE HAWAIIANS

Assistance: project grants (100 percent (formula-based)).

Purposes: pursuant to OAA as amended, for supportive services to older Indians and Alaska and Hawaii natives, including nutrition services, multipurpose center improvements and staffing, transportation, information and referral assistance, and multifaceted caregiver services.

Eligible applicants: tribal organizations and public or private nonprofit organizations that serve native Hawaiian elders, serving at least 50 clients.

Eligible beneficiaries: Indians age 60 or older and, for nutrition services, their spouses; certain others under age 60.

Range: tribes, $73,620 to $180,467; Hawaii natives, $47,430 to $852,005. **Average:** tribes, $99,963; Hawaii, $449,718.

Activity: FY 05, 2 native Hawaii, 237 tribal organizations funded.

HQ: Director, Office of American Indian, Alaskan Native, and Native Hawaiian Programs, AOA-HHS, Washington, DC 20201. Phone: (202) 357-3500.

Internet: www.aoa.gov.

93.048 SPECIAL PROGRAMS FOR THE AGING—TITLE IV— AND TITLE II — DISCRETIONARY PROJECTS

Assistance: project grants. (75 percent/1-3 years).

Purposes: pursuant to OAA as amended, for development and testing of innovative programs in the field of aging—to develop knowledge of the problems and needs of the elderly. Funds may be used to: demonstrate new methods and practices; evaluate existing programs and services; conduct applied research and analysis; train professionals.

Eligible applicants/beneficiaries: public or private nonprofit agencies, organizations, and institutions.

Range: $11,750 to $2,937,312. **Average:** $250,000.

Activity: FY 05, 367 awards; FY 06 estimated 250 awards.

HQ: Center for Planning and Policy Department, AOA-HHS, Washington, DC 20201. Phone: (202) 357-3443.

Internet: www.aoa.gov.

93.051 ALZHEIMER'S DISEASE DEMONSTRATION GRANTS TO STATES ("Alzheimer's Demonstration Program")

Assistance: project grants. (55-75 percent/3 years).

Purposes: pursuant to PHSA as amended, Home Health Care and Alzheimer's Disease Amendments Act of 1990, and HPEPA, to plan, establish, and operate model programs for persons with Alzheimer's disease and related disorders, their families, and care-givers, including home health and personal care, companion services, short-term care in health facilities, other respite care services.

Eligible applicants: state agencies.

Eligible beneficiaries: individuals with Alzheimer's disease, families of those individuals, and care providers of those individuals.

Range: $150,000 to $311,150. **Average:** $277,487.

Activity: cumulatively, first 10 years of program, 15,000 client families served.

HQ: Center for Wellness and Community-Based Services, AOA-HHS, Washington, DC 20201. Phone: (202) 357-3452, 401-4634.

Internet: www.aoa.gov/alz.

93.052 NATIONAL FAMILY CAREGIVER SUPPORT, TITLE III, PART E

Assistance: formula grants; project grants. (formula, 75 percent; project grants, 100 percent/formula grants, 1-4 years).

Purposes: pursuant to OAA as amended, to provide multi-faceted systems of support services for family caregivers and grandparents or older individuals who are relative-caregivers, including: information about, and assistance in gaining access to, available services; individual counseling, organizational support groups, caregiver training in making decisions and solving problems relating to their roles; temporary respite care relief for the caregivers; supplemental complementary services.

Eligible applicants: formula grants—state and territorial governments, with subgrants to area agencies on aging. Project grants—tribal organizations, native Hawaiian organizations.

Eligible beneficiaries: family caregivers.

Range: $14,720 to $15,532,999. **Average:** $633,253.

Activity: annually, 56 awards.

HQ: *formula grants,* Center for Wellness of Community-Based Services, AOA-HHS, Washington, DC 20201. Phone: (202) 357-3586. *Project grants,* Office for American Indian, Alaskan Natives and Native Hawaiian Programs, AOA-HHS, Washington, DC 20201. Phone: (202) 357-3501.

Internet: www.aoa.gov.

93.053 NUTRITION SERVICES INCENTIVE PROGRAM

Assistance: formula grants.

Purposes: pursuant to OAA as amended, to reward effective performance by states and tribes in the efficient delivery or meals to older adults, through the use of cash or USDA commodities in congregate or home-delivered meals. The funding incentives are based on the number of meals served in the prior fiscal year in proportion to all other states and tribes.

Eligible applicants/beneficiaries: state agencies and tribal organizations receiving funds through OAA Titles III and VI.

Range: $324 to $14,224,141. **Average:** $507,774.

Activity: FY 04, about 248,000,000 meals served.

HQ: Office for Community-Based Services, AOA-HHS, Washington, DC 20201. Phone: (202) 357-3546.

Internet: www.aoa.gov.

93.054 NATIONAL FAMILY CAREGIVER SUPPORT, TITLE VI, PART C, GRANTS TO INDIAN TRIBES AND NATIVE HAWAIIANS

Assistance: project grants (100 percent).

Purposes: pursuant to the Older Americans Act as amended, to assist Indian Tribal Organizations in providing multifaceted systems of support services for family caregivers, grandparents or older individuals who are relative caregivers. Services may include: information about and assistance and access to services for caregivers, individual counseling and caregiver training, respite care, and supplemental services, on a limited basis, to complement caregiver services.

Eligible applicants: approved Indian Tribal and Native Hawaiian organizations.

Eligible beneficiaries: family caregivers, grandparents, and older individuals who are relative caregivers.

Range: $14,510 to $59,310. **Average:** $31,048.

Activity: FY 07 and 08,109 grants estimated.

HQ: Office for American Indian, Alaskan Natives and Native Hawaiian Programs, AOA-HHS, Washington, DC 20201. Phone: (202) 357-3501.

Internet: www.aoa.gov.

93.061 INNOVATIONS IN APPLIED PUBLIC HEALTH RESEARCH

Assistance: project grants. (100 percent/to 3 years).

Purposes: pursuant to PHSA as amended, for applied public health research to translate biomedical science results into effective programs that directly affect the quality and length of life. Preference in project selection is given to proposals with participatory research involving affected communities.

Eligible applicants/beneficiaries: public and private profit and nonprofit organizations; governments and their agencies including territories and possessions; IHEs, hospitals, community-based organizations, women- and minority-owned businesses, Indian tribes and tribal organizations, research institutions, faith-based organizations.

Range/Average: N.A.

Activity: new program in FY 04.

HQ: Office of Public Health Research (D-72), CDCP-HHS, 1600 Clifton Rd., Atlanta, GA 30333. Phone: (404) 693-4639. *Grants management information*: Grants Management Specialist, Procurement and Grants Office, CDCP-HHS, 2920 Brandywine Rd., Atlanta, GA 30341. Phone: (770) 488-2696.

Internet: www.cdc.gov (Note: no field offices for this program.)

93.063 CENTERS FOR GENOMICS AND PUBLIC HEALTH

Assistance: project grants. (100 percent/1-4 years).

Purposes: pursuant to PHSA as amended, to provide information, technical assistance, and training to community, state, and regional organizations in genomics and population health for the health workforce. Funds may not support direct patient care, capital outlays, or research involving human subjects.

Eligible applicants/beneficiaries: IHEs, research institutions.

Range: $450,000 to $900,000.

Activity: new program in FY 04; 3 public health schools funded.

HQ: Office of Genomics and Disease Prevention, CDCP-HHS, 1600 Clifton Rd. N.E. (Mail Stop K-89), Atlanta, GA 30333. Phone: (no number provided). *Grants management information*: Procurement and Grants Office, CDC-HHS, 2920 Brandywine Rd. (Mail Stop K-75), Atlanta, GA 30341. Phone: (770) 488-2722.

Internet: www.cdc.gov (Note: no field offices for this program.)

93.064 LABORATORY TRAINING, EVALUATION, AND QUALITY ASSURANCE PROGRAMS ("Quality Assurance in Pathology and Laboratory Medicine")

Assistance: project grants. (100 percent/to 3 years).

Purposes: pursuant to PHSA as amended, to improve laboratory genetic testing practices relevant to clinical and public health settings; to determine standardized approaches to quality assurance in pathology and laboratory medicine, applicable in diverse settings including community hospitals, academic medical centers, and independent laboratories.

Eligible applicants/beneficiaries: public and private nonprofit organizations, IHEs, research institutions, hospitals, community organizations; state and local governments and their agents, including in territories and possessions.

Range: $100,000 to $225,000.

Activity: new program in FY 04.

HQ: PHPPO-DLS, CDCP-HHS, 4770 Buford Hwy, Atlanta, GA 30333. Phone: (770) 488-8070, FAX (770) 488-8278. *Grants management information*: Grants Management Specialist, Procurement and Grants Office, CDCP-HHS, 2920 Brandywine Rd., Atlanta, GA 30341. Phone: (770) 488-2748.

Internet: www.cdc.gov.

93.065 LABORATORY LEADERSHIP, WORKFORCE TRAINING AND MANAGEMENT DEVELOPMENT, IMPROVING PUBLIC HEALTH LABORATORY INFRASTRUCTURE

Assistance: project grants. (100 percent/to 5 years).

Purposes: pursuant to PHSA as amended, to improve public health laboratory infrastructure; for state-of-the-art training to prepare laboratorians to deal with public health threats with emerging infectious diseases or other biologic and chemical threats; to improve laboratory leadership capabilities; to enhance inter-laboratory communications.

Eligible applicants/beneficiaries: state governments, specifically state public health laboratories; organizations representing state public health laboratories with an established training network.

Range: $4,200,000 to $4,800,000. **Average:** $4,700,000.

Activity: new program listing in 2005.

HQ: Project Officer, CDCP-HHS, Atlanta, GA. Phone: (404) 498-2230. *Grants management information*: Grants Management Specialist, Procurement and Grants Office, CDCP-HHS, 2920 Brandywine Rd., Atlanta, GA 30341. Phone: (770) 488-2748.

Internet: www.cdc.gov; www.phppo.cdc.gov/dls (Note: no field offices for this program.)

93.066 STATE VITAL STATISTICS IMPROVEMENT PROGRAM

Assistance: project grants. (100 percent/1-3 years).

Purposes: pursuant to PHSA as amended, to assist states in improving the timeliness, quality, and sustainability of the decentralized vital statistics system by adopting national consensus standards and guidelines, in all 57 registration areas. These will be systems that can: provide quality and timely data for public health surveillance and medical research; meet citizen needs for legal copies of their birth and death records, as well as meet federal needs for related record verification and authentication; produce comparable vital registration and statistics systems in each state; use national standards and guidelines, including certificates of birth, death, and fetal death; support national security and privacy requirements; integrate with other public health systems; use internet technology.

Eligible applicants/beneficiaries: appropriate public and private nonprofit organizations.

Average: $171,500.

Activity: new program listing in 2004.

HQ: Project Officer, Division of Vital Statistics, National Center for Health Statistics, CDCP-HHS, 3311 Toledo Rd. - Rm. 7315, Hyattsville, MD 20782. Phone: (301) 458-4467. *Grants management information*: Grants Management Specialist, Acquisition and Assistance Field Branch, CDC Procurement and Grants Office, P.O. Box 18070, Cochran Mill Rd., Pittsburg, PA 15236. Phone: (412) 386-6826.

Internet: www.cdc.gov.

93.067 GLOBAL AIDS

Assistance: project grants. (100 percent/1-5 years).

Purposes: pursuant to PHSA as amended, for activities conducted with other countries, international organizations, U.S. Department of State, USAID, and other partners to achieve the United Nations General Assembly Special Session on HIV/AIDS goal of reducing prevalence among persons age 15-24. Research may not be funded under this program.

Eligible applicants/beneficiaries: limited competition, or single eligibility by authorizing legislation.

Range: $75,000 to $775,000.

Activity: new program in FY 05.

HQ: Lead Contract Specialist, International Branch, CDCP-HHS, 2920 Brandywine Rd., Atlanta, GA 30341. Phone: (770) 488-2632.

Internet: www.cdc.gov (Note: no field offices for this program.)

93.068 CHRONIC DISEASES: RESEARCH, CONTROL, AND PREVENTION

Assistance: project grants. (100 percent/1-5 years).

Purposes: pursuant to PHSA as amended, to prevent and control chronic diseases and disorders through research, development, capacity building, and intervention; to use research data to improve detection, diagnosis, treatment, and care of chronic diseases and their complications; to develop new related knowledge that will improve health and quality of life and eliminate health disparities among segments of the population. CDCP will have substantial involvement in project activities.

Eligible applicants/beneficiaries: state and local governments or their bona fide agents, including in territories and possessions; public, private, profit, and nonprofit organizations including small, minority and women-owned businesses, IHEs, research institutions, faith-based organizations, Indian tribes and tribal organizations; some foreign institutions may be eligible for certain programs.

Range: $100,000 to $1,500,000. **Average:** $500,000.

Activity: new program listing in 2005 (CFDA on-line).

HQ: Office of Extramural Research, National Center for Chronic Disease Prevention and Health Promotion, CDCP-HHS, 4770 Buford Hwy. NE (Mail Stop K-92), Atlanta, GA. Phone: (770) 488-8390. *Grants management information*: Grants Management Officer, Grants Management Branch, Procurement and Grants Office, CDC, 2920 Brandywine Rd. (Rm. 3000), Atlanta, GA 30341. Phone: (770) 488-2722.

Internet: www.cdc.gov (Note: no field offices for this program.)

93.069 PUBLIC HEALTH EMERGENCY PREPAREDNESS

Assistance: project grants (100 percent/5 years).

Purposes: pursuant to Public Health Service Act, to develop emergency-ready public health departments intended to support the National Response Plan (NRP) and the National Incident Management System (NIMS) by working with state, local, and tribal governments, the private sector, and non-governmental agencies to upgrade, evaluate and integrate state and local public health jurisdictions and prepare for and respond to terrorism, pandemic influenza, and other public health emergencies.

Eligible applicants/beneficiaries: state health departments of all 50 states, DC, the nation's three largest municipalities (New York, Chicago, Los Angeles county), PR, VI, American Samoa, Guam, Micronesia, Palau, Marshall Islands and Northern Marianas.

Range: $423,673 to $54,211,969.

Activity: as of 2002, 62 grantees, including 50 states, 8 territories, and 4 large municipalities; 150 Laboratory Response Networks (LRNs) with at least one in every state.

HQ: Branch Chief, Program Services Branch, Division of State and Local Readiness, Coordinating Office of Terrorism Preparedness and Emergency Response, CDCP-HHS, 1600 Clifton Rd. NE (Mail Stop D29), Atlanta, GA 30333 Phone: (404) 639-5998 *Grants management information*: Grants Management Officer, Grants Management Branch, Procurement and Grants Office, CDC-HHS, 2920 Brandywine Rd., Atlanta, GA 30341 Phone: (770) 488-2771.

Internet: www.cdc.gov (Note: no field offices for this program.)

93.086 HEALTHY MARRIAGE PROMOTION AND RESPONSIBLE FATHERHOOD GRANTS

Assistance: project grants; technical information (project grants, to 5 years).

Purposes: pursuant to SSA (as included in the Deficit Reduction Act of 2005), for: (1) healthy marriage promotion activities helping couples that chose marriage for themselves have access to marriage education services; (2) responsible fatherhood promotion activities designed to reverse the rise in father absence; (3) demonstration projects to test the effectiveness of tribal governments and consortia in coordinating services to tribal families at risk of child abuse, or neglect of child welfare services; (4) federal technical assistance to grant recipients. Projects must assure voluntary participation by services recipients; they must also incorporate strong domestic violence prevention components.

Eligible applicants/beneficiaries: "Healthy Marriage Grants"—public and private entities including state, local, and special district government entities, public and private IHEs, tribes and tribal organizations, nonprofit and profit organizations, faith-based and community organizations.

Range: Healthy Marriage, $250,000 to $5,000,000; Responsible Fatherhood, $200,000 to $2,000,000; Tribal TANF TA, $25,000 to $100,000. **Average:** Healthy Marriage, $1,000,000; Responsible Fatherhood, $700,000; Tribal TANF TA, $80,000.

Activity: new program listing in 2006 (CFDA on-line).

HQ: Office of Family Assistance, ACF-HHS, 370 L'Enfant Promenade - 5th Floor East, Washington, DC 20447. Phone: (202) 401-9317; FAX (202) 205-5887.

Internet: www.acf.hhs.gov/healthymarriage/index.html (Note: no field offices for this program.)

93.087 ENHANCE THE SAFETY OF CHILDREN AFFECTED BY PARENTAL METHAMPHETAMINE OR OTHER SUBSTANCE ABUSE

Assistance: project grants (75-85 percent/3-5 years).

Purposes: pursuant to Child and Family Service Improvement Act of 2006, to provide through interagency collaboration and integration of program activities that are designed to increase the well-being of, improve permanency outcomes for, and enhance the safety of children who are in an out-of-home placement or are at risk of being placed in an out-of-home placement as a result of parent's or caretaker's methamphetamine or other substance abuse. Funding may include: family-based comprehensive long-term substance abuse treatment; early intervention and preventative services; children/family counseling; mental health services; and parenting skills training.

Eligible applicants/beneficiaries: public and private entities including state, local, and special district government entities, public and private IHEs, tribes and tribal organizations, nonprofit and profit organizations/institutions.

Range: $500,000 to $1,000,000.

Activity: new program listing in 2006 (CFDA on-line).

HQ: Director, Office on Child Abuse and Neglect, Children's Bureau, ACF-HHS, 1250 Maryland Ave. SW, Washington, DC 20024 Phone: (202) 260-5140.

Internet: www.acf.hhs.gov/program/cb (Note: no field offices for this program.)

93.100 HEALTH DISPARITIES IN MINORITY HEALTH

Assistance: project grants. (100 percent/to 2 years).

Purposes: pursuant to PHSA as amended and Disadvantaged Minority Health Improvement Act of 1990, to support elimination of health disparities among racial and ethnic populations through small- scaled projects addressing a demonstrated health problem or issue. Funds may not support health care, construction, or ongoing project costs.

Eligible applicants: private nonprofit community-based minority organizations.

Eligible beneficiaries: Pacific islanders, Blacks, African- Americans, Hispanics, Latinos, native Americans, Alaska natives, native Hawaiians, or their subgroups.

Range: $30,028 to $50,000. **Average:** $49,146.

Activity: FY 05, final program year; noncompeting applications only.

HQ: Director, Division of Program Operations, Office of Minority Health, Office of Public Health and Science, OS-HHS, 1101 Wooten Pkwy. - Ste. 700, Rockville, MD 20852. Phone: (301) 594-0769. *Grants management information*: Director, Office of Grants Management, Office of Public Health and Science, 1101 Wootton Pkwy. - Ste. 550, Rockville, MD 20852. Phone: (301) 594-0758.

Internet: www.omhrc.gov (Note: no field offices for this program.)

93.103 FOOD AND DRUG ADMINISTRATION—RESEARCH

Assistance: project grants. (100 percent/1-5 years).

Purposes: pursuant to PHSA and Small Business Innovation Research Program Reauthorization Act of 1992 (SBIRPRA) as amended and Radiation Control for Health Safety Act of 1968, for research, demonstration, education, and dissemination activities in a broad range of areas, AIDS, biologics, blood and blood products, therapeutics, vaccine and allergenic projects, drug hazards, human and veterinary drugs, medical devices and diagnostics products, orphan product development, and radiation-emitting devices and materials, food safety and additives. SBIR awards are made (*see Notes preceding **93.001***).

Eligible applicants/beneficiaries: public or private nonprofit IHEs, institutions, state and local governments, hospitals, laboratories, commercial and nonprofit organizations.

Range: $5,000 to $3,000,000. **Average:** $225,970.

Activity: FY 07 estimate, 23 new, 65 continuation grants; SBIR, 33 Phase I, 2 Phase II awards.

HQ: Chief Grants Management Officer, Division of Contracts and Procurement Management, Office of Acquisition and Grant Services, FDA-HHS (HFA-500), 5600 Fishers Lane - Rm. 2107, Rockville, MD 20857. Phone: (301) 827-7182; *SBIR information,* (301) 827-7179; FAX: (301) 827-7101.

Internet: www.fda.gov (Note: no field offices for administration of this program; however, district offices are listed in Part IV for information purposes.)

93.104 COMPREHENSIVE COMMUNITY MENTAL HEALTH SERVICES FOR CHILDREN WITH SERIOUS EMOTIONAL DISTURBANCES (SED) ("CMHS Child Mental Health Service Initiative")

Assistance: project grants. (33-75 percent/to 6 years).

Purposes: pursuant to PHSA as amended, for community-based care systems for children and adolescents with serious emotional disturbances, and their families—ensuring that: services are provided collaboratively across child-serving systems; each child or adolescent served receives an individualized service plan developed with the participation of the family and, where appropriate, of the child; each plan designates a case manager; funding is provided for the required mental health services. Project funds may be used to pay: administrative costs including staff salaries, travel, supplies, communications, and space and equipment rental; for pertinent training including in providing therapeutic foster or group home care, intensive home-based or intensive day treatment services. Ineligible expenses include real estate-related costs, residential care or services in centers serving more than 10 children, unrelated training, non- mental health services including medical and educational services, and protection and advocacy.

Eligible applicants: states and their political subdivisions, tribal governments.

Eligible beneficiaries: children under age 22 with diagnosed SED or serious behavioral or mental disorders.

Range: $46,507,927 to $58,022,823. **Average:** $56,538,504.

Activity: FY 06 estimate, 44 continuation awards.

HQ: Chief, Child Adolescent and Family Branch, Division of Knowledge Development and Systems Change, CMHS-SAMHSA-HHS, 1 Choke Cherry Rd., Rockville, MD 20857. Phone: (240) 276-1980. *Grants management information*: Grants Management Officer, SAMHSA-HHS, 1 Choke Cherry Rd., Rockville, MD 20857. Phone: (240) 276-1421.

Internet: www.hhs.gov (Note: no field offices for this program.)

93.105 BILINGUAL/BICULTURAL SERVICE DEMONSTRATION GRANTS

Assistance: project grants. (100 percent/3 years).

Purposes: pursuant to PHSA as amended, to improve and expand the capacity for bilingual/bicultural competence of health care professionals in providing services to minority communities with limited English proficiency (LEP), including professional and paraprofessional staff training and providing interpreters and translators—but not providing health care services or augmentation of ongoing project activities.

Eligible applicants/beneficiaries: public or private nonprofit minority community-based organizations or health care facilities serving targeted LEP communities.

Range: $100,000 to $200,000. **Average:** $150,000.

Activity: FY 05 estimate, 20 new awards; FY 06-07, continuation awards only.

HQ: Director, Division of Program Operations, Office of Minority Health, Office of Public Health and Science, Office of the Secretary, 1101 Wootton Pkwy. - Ste. 600, Rockville, MD 20852. Phone: (240) 453-8444. *Grants management information*: Office of Public Health and Science, Office of Grants Management, 1101 Wootton Pkwy. - Ste. 550, Rockville, MD 20852. Phone: (240) 453-8822.

Internet: www.omhrc.gov (Note: no field offices for this program.)

93.107 MODEL STATE-SUPPORTED AREA HEALTH EDUCATION CENTERS ("MODEL AHEC")

Assistance: formula grants. (50 percent/to 3 years).

Purposes: pursuant to PHSA as amended and HPEPA, to encourage regionalization of health professions schools by establishing model Area Health Education Centers (see **93.824**), involving collaborative partnerships of university health centers with local planning, educational, and clinical resources; for health careers programs for students in grades 9-12. Emphasis is on recruitment and community-based training of primary care students, residents, and providers.

Eligible applicants/beneficiaries: schools of allopathic medicine or osteopathy and consortia operating AHECs and no longer receiving assistance under **93.824**.

Range: $165,174 to $908,457. **Average:** $364,526.

Activity: FY 05, 38 grants.

HQ: Chief, AHEC Branch, Division of State, Community and Public Health, Bureau of Health Professions, HRSA-HHS, Parklawn Bldg. - Rm.9-05, 5600 Fishers Lane, Rockville, MD 20857. Phone: (301) 443- 6950. *Grants management information*: Director, Division of Grants Management, Health Resources and Services Administration-HHS, 5600 Fishers Lane - Rm. 11A-16, Rockville, MD 20857. Phone: Health Services, (301) 443-2385; Research and Training, (301) 443-3099; Government and Special Focus, (301) 443-3288.

Internet: www.hrsa.gov.

93.110 MATERNAL AND CHILD HEALTH FEDERAL CONSOLIDATED PROGRAMS ("Special Projects of Regional and National Significance (SPRNS)")

Assistance: project grants.

Purposes: pursuant to the Social Security Act of 1935 (SSA) as amended, for special projects of regional or national significance involving training, services, research, and demonstrations in maternal and child health services, including: genetic disease testing, counseling, and information dissemination; operation of comprehensive hemophilia diagnosis and treatment centers. A portion of grant funds, if appropriated, may be used to provide other services including home visitations, increased participation of obstetricians and pediatricians, maternal and child health centers for women and infants, rural health services, community-based services for children with special health care needs.

Eligible applicants/beneficiaries: training grants—public or private nonprofit IHEs. Research grants—public or private nonprofit IHEs, agencies, and organizations. Hemophilia and genetics grants and other special project grants—any public or private entity.

Range: $4,500 to $1,000,000. **Average:** $183,358.

Activity: FY 06 estimate, 500-600 projects; FY 07 estimate, 450-500 projects.

HQ: Associate Administrator, Maternal and Child Health Bureau, HRSA-HHS, 5600 Fishers Lane - Rm. 18-05, Rockville, MD 20857. Phone: (301) 443-2170. *Grants management information*: Director, Division of Grants Management, Health Resources and Services Administration-HHS, 5600 Fishers Lane - Rm. 11A-16, Rockville, MD 20857. Phone: Health Services, (301) 443-2385; Research and Training, (301) 443-3099; Special Focus, (301) 443-3288.

Internet: www.hrsa.gov.

93.111 ADOLESCENT FAMILY LIFE RESEARCH GRANTS

Assistance: project grants. (100 percent/to 3 years).

Purposes: pursuant to PHSA as amended, for research and information dissemination activities concerning societal causes and consequences of adolescent sexual activity, contraceptive use, pregnancy and child rearing.

Eligible applicants/beneficiaries: state and local government agencies; private nonprofit and profit organizations; IHEs.

Range: $108,000 to $151,000. **Average:** $145,000.

Activity: FY 06 estimate, 5 continuation, 3 new project awards.

HQ: Office of Adolescent Pregnancy Programs, Office of Population Affairs, OS-HHS, 1101 Wootton Pkwy. - Ste. 700, Rockville, MD 20852. Phone: (240) 453-2828. *Grants management information*: Director, Office of Grants Management, Office of Public Health and Science-HHS, 1101 Wootton Pkwy. - Ste. 550 Rockville, MD 20853. Phone: (240) 453-8822.

Internet: www.opa.osophs.dhhs.gov (Note: no field offices for this program.)

93.113 BIOLOGICAL RESPONSE TO ENVIRONMENTAL HEALTH HAZARDS

Assistance: project grants. (100 percent/to 5 years).

Purposes: pursuant to PHSA as amended and Small Business Research and Development Enhancement Act of 1992 (SBRDEA), for research and research training on the chemical and physical causes of pathological changes in molecules, cells, tissues, and organs, toward the prevention of neurological, behavioral, and developmental abnormalities, and respiratory diseases, cancer, and other disorders. Grants also support studies of toxicity in metals, natural and synthetic chemicals, pesticides, asbestos and silica, and natural toxins—and their effects on human organ systems, metabolism, endocrine and immune systems, and other biological functions. The Environmental Health Sciences Education Program may fund projects to improve student understanding of environmental health issues and to expand career awareness in health sciences research and services occupations, by developing educational materials for grades K-12. Independent Scientist Awards, Mentored Research Scientist Development Awards, Mentored Clinical Scientist Development Awards, Academic Career Awards, and other programs may also be funded including centers on children's health and disease. SBIR and STTR awards are made (*see Notes preceding* **93.001**).

Eligible applicants/beneficiaries: research grants and cooperative agreements, science education grants, independent scientist awards, mentored clinical and research scientist awards, academic career awards—IHEs, hospitals, state or local governments, nonprofit research institutions, or profit organizations for research by a named principal investigator. Candidates for academic career development awards must have a clinical or research doctorate and peer-reviewed independent research support, and they must devote at least 75 percent effort. Candidates for mentored clinical scientist awards must have clinical training; those holding a Ph.D. degree are ineligible, as are researchers that have served as principal investigators on PHS-supported research projects.

Range: research grants, $71,500 to $2,039,442; SBIR grants, up to $100,000 (Phase I), up to $750,000 (Phase II); STTR grants, up to $100,000 (Phase I), up to $500,000 (Phase II). **Average:** research grants, $346,893.

Activity: FY 06 estimate, 495 awards.

HQ: Division of Extramural Research and Training, NIEHS, NIH-HHS, P.O. Box 12233, Research Triangle Park, NC 27709. Phone: Research Grants, (919) 541-0797, -3289; Environmental Justice, Science Education Grants, (919) 541-4980; Independent Scientist Awards, Mentored Research Scientist Development Award, Mentored Clinical Research Scientist Development Award, Academic Career Award, (919) 541-1445; AREA, SBIR and STTR Grant Programs, (919) 541-0781.

Internet: www.niehs.nih.gov (Note: no field offices for this program.)

93.116 PROJECT GRANTS AND COOPERATIVE AGREEMENTS FOR TUBERCULOSIS CONTROL PROGRAMS

Assistance: projects grants. (100 percent/to 5 years).

Purposes: pursuant to PHSA as amended, TB Prevention Amendments Act of 1990 as amended, and other acts, for tuberculosis control and prevention activities. Funds may cover such costs as patient outreach, directly observed therapy to assure its completion, morbidity surveillance, personnel, equipment, supplies, program assessment, and services. Costs of construction and inpatient care are ineligible uses.

Eligible applicants/beneficiaries: official public health agencies of state and local governments, territories and possessions.

Range: $78,860 to $15,272,295. **Average:** $1,554,360.

Activity: annually, 68 continuation awards.

HQ: National Center for HIV, STD, and TB Prevention, CDCP-HHS, 1600 Clifton Rd. NE (Mail Stop E10), Atlanta, GA 30333. Phone: (404) 639-5337. *Grants management information*: Grants Management Officer, Grants Management Branch, Procurement and Grants Office, CDC-HHS, 1600 Clifton Rd. (Mail Stop E15), Atlanta, GA 30333. Phone:(404) 639-0941.

Internet: www.cdc.gov (Note: no field offices for this program.)

93.117 GRANTS FOR PREVENTIVE MEDICINE ("Preventive Medicine")

Assistance: project grants. (100 percent/3 years).

Purposes: pursuant to PHSA as amended and HPEPA, to plan, develop, maintain, or improve postgraduate training programs in preventive medicine. Financial assistance may be provided to residency trainees. Grants may not used for construction or direct patient services.

Eligible applicants: public or private schools of medicine, osteopathy, or public health.

Eligible beneficiaries: U.S. citizens, nationals, and lawful permanent residents.

Range: $100,338 to $423,605. **Average:** $166,654.

Activity: FY 05, 31 enrollees and 36 graduates/completers.

HQ: Division of State, Community, and Public Health, Center for Public Health, Bureau of Health Professions, HRSA-HHS, Parklawn Bldg. - Rm. 8A-19, 5600 Fishers Lane, Rockville, MD 20857. Phone: (301) 443-5244. *Grants management information*: Director, Division of Grants Management, Health Resources and Services Administration, Department of Health and Human Services, 5600 Fishers Lane - Rm. 11A-16, Rockville, MD 20857. Phone: Health Services, (301) 443-2385; Research and Training, (301) 443-3099; Special Focus, (301) 443-3288.

Internet: www.hrsa.gov (Note: no field offices for this program.)

93.118 ACQUIRED IMMUNODEFICIENCY SYNDROME (AIDS) ACTIVITY

Assistance: project grants. (100 percent/to 5 years).

Purposes: pursuant to PHSA as amended, to develop and implement HIV prevention programs of public education and information.

Eligible applicants/beneficiaries: public and private nonprofit and profit organizations including IHEs and research institutions; state and local governments, territories and possessions; small and minority- and women-owned businesses.

Range: $130,560 to $1,000,000. **Average:** $153,650.

Activity: FY 05, 5 awards; FY 06 and FY 07, estimated 23 awards.

HQ: Division of HIV/AIDS Prevention (A43), CDCP-HHS, 1600 Clifton Rd., Atlanta, GA 30333. Phone: (404) 639-6285. *Grants management information*: Grants Management Officer, Procurement and Grants Office, CDC, 2920 Brandywine Rd. - Rm. 3000, Atlanta, GA 30341. Phone: (770) 498-1911.

Internet: www.cdc.gov (Note: no field offices for this program.)

93.121 ORAL DISEASES AND DISORDERS RESEARCH

Assistance: project grants. (100 percent/to 5 years).

Purposes: pursuant to PHSA as amended and SBRDEA, for research and research training in the oral health sciences, in such areas as craniofacial, oral, and dental health promotion and disease prevention, diagnostics, and therapeutics. Grant programs support basic, clinical, and transitional research, from molecular biology to patient-oriented and community-based clinical investigations—including etiology, pathogenesis, epidemiology, prevention, diagnosis, and treatment—within overlapping programs: Inherited Diseases and Disorders (e.g., cleft lip and palate, other craniofacial birth defects, developmentally related disorders), as well as occlusion defects acquired through trauma; Infectious Diseases such as dental caries, periodontitis, oral manifestations of HIV/AIDS, herpes, hepatitis, and other diseases; Neoplastic Diseases; Chronic Disabling Diseases; Biomaterials, Biomimetics and Tissue Engineering; Behavior, Health Promotion and Environment. Also supported are: Comprehensive Oral Research Centers of Discovery; Research Training and Careers; Diversity in Research; Clinical Trials and Clinical Core Centers; and Technology Transfer. NRSA, SBIR, and STTR awards are available (*see Notes preceding* **93.001**).

Eligible applicants/beneficiaries: research grants—scientists at universities, medical and dental schools, hospitals, laboratories, other public, private, nonprofit, or profit institutions. Career development award candidates must comply with requirements similar to those applying to the NRSA program.

Range: projects, $1,000 to $5,613,000; NRSA, $8,000 to $677,000; SBIR Phase II, up to $750,000. **Average:** projects, $318,000; NRSA, $154,000 SBIR Phase I, $100,000.

Activity: FY 07 estimate, 451 noncompeting, 169 competing research grants; 8 research centers; 90 career development, 337 NRSA positions; 27 other research grants; 34 SBIR/STTR awards.

HQ: Division of Extramural Research, National Institute of Dental and Craniofacial Research, NIH-HHS, Bethesda, MD 20892. Phone: Division of Basic and Translational Sciences, (301) 594-2419; Division of Extramural Activities, (301) 594-2904; Division of Population Health Promotion Sciences, (301) 496-9469; Division of Intramural Research, (301) 496-2687.

Internet: www.hhs.gov (Note: no field offices for this program.)

93.123 HEALTH PROFESSIONS PREGRADUATE SCHOLARSHIP PROGRAM FOR INDIANS

Assistance: project grants (100 percent).

Purposes: pursuant to the Indian Health Care Improvement Act as amended, for four-year scholarships for American Indians and Alaska natives to complete pregraduate education leading to a baccalaureate degree in premedicine or pre-dentistry. Part-time attendance may be supported for a maximum of eight years.

Eligible applicants/beneficiaries: American Indians or Alaska natives accepted or enrolled in a pregraduate program.

Range: $18,913 to $27,217. **Average:** $20,049.

Activity: FY 06-07 estimate, 61 awards.

HQ: IHS Scholarship Program, IHS-HHS, 801 Thompson Ave. - Ste. 120, Rockville, MD 20852. Phone: (301) 443-6197. *Grants management information*: Grants Management Officer, Division of Acquisition and Grants Operations, IHS-HHS, same address. Phone: (301) 443-0243.

Internet: www.ihs.gov (Note: no field offices for this program.)

93.124 NURSE ANESTHETIST TRAINEESHIPS

Assistance: project grants. (100 percent/1 year).

Purposes: pursuant to PHSA as amended and HPEPA, for nurse anesthetist traineeships for up to 18 months of full-time study by registered nurses in nurse anesthetist master's education programs.

Eligible applicants: accredited schools of nursing, academic health centers, and other public and private nonprofit institutions.

Eligible beneficiaries: U.S. citizens, noncitizen nationals, or permanent residents with 12 months of completed nurse anesthetist master's training.

Range: $431 to $38,057. **Average:** $16,667.

Activity: FY 05, 75 awards.

HQ: Division of Nursing, Bureau of Health Professions, HRSA-HHS, Parklawn Bldg. - Rm.9-36, 5600 Fishers Lane, Rockville, MD 20857. Phone: (301) 443-5787. *Grants management information*: Director, Division of Grants Management, Health Resources and Services Administration, HHS, 5600 Fishers Lane - Rm. 11A-16, Rockville, MD 20857. Phone: Health Services, (301) 443-2385; Research and Training, (301) 443-3099; Government and Special Focus, (301) 443-3288.

Internet: www.hrsa.gov (Note: no field offices for this program.)

93.127 EMERGENCY MEDICAL SERVICES FOR CHILDREN ("EMS for Children")

Assistance: project grants. (100 percent/to 3 years).

Purposes: pursuant to PHSA as amended, for demonstration projects to expand and improve emergency medical services for children needing critical care or treatment for trauma.

Eligible applicants/beneficiaries: states, schools of medicine.

Range: $109,492 to $1,200,000. **Average:** $192,130.

Activity: FY 06 estimate, 78 projects funded; FY 07 estimate, no funding available.

HQ: EMSC Program Director, Maternal and Child Health Bureau, HRSA-HHS, 5600 Fishers Lane - Rm.18A-38, Rockville, MD 20857. Phone: (no number provided). *Grants management information*: Director, Division of Grants Management, Health Resources and Services Administration, HHS, 5600 Fishers Lane - Rm. 11A-16, Rockville, MD 20857. Phone:

Health Services, (301) 443-2385; Research and Training, (301) 443-3099; Government and Special Focus, (301) 443-3288.

Internet: www.hrsa.gov (Note: no field offices for this program.)

93.129 TECHNICAL AND NON-FINANCIAL ASSISTANCE TO HEALTH CENTERS ("State and Regional Primary Care Associations")

Assistance: project grants. (100 percent/to 5 years).

Purposes: pursuant to PHSA as amended, to provide technical and nonfinancial assistance to health centers and NHSC delivery sites, relative to: collaborative activities on state or market area levels; involvement of state agencies in providing primary care to medically underserved populations; developing shared services and joint purchasing arrangements; providing training, assessment of community health needs, expertise in dealing with the homeless, public housing residents, farm workers, and rural and other special populations, as well as in managing and maximizing nonfederal resources; expanding the health center network.

Eligible applicants/beneficiaries: state primary care associations currently working with BHPC-supported providers; other community-based providers.

Range: $188,000 to $1,175,000.

Activity: FY 06 estimate, 51 associations funded.

HQ: Director, Division of State and Community Assistance, Bureau of Primary Health Care, HRSA-HHS, 5600 Fishers Lane - Rm.15C-26, Rockville, MD 20857. Phone: (301) 594-4488. *Grants management information*: Director, Division of Grants Management, Health Resources and Services Administration, HHS, 5600 Fishers Lane - Rm. 11A-16, Rockville, MD 20857. Phone: Health Services, (301) 443-2385; Research and Training, (301) 443-3099; Government and Special Focus, (301) 443-3288.

Internet: www.hrsa.gov (Note: no field offices for this program.)

93.130 COOPERATIVE AGREEMENTS TO STATES/TERRITORIES FOR THE COORDINATION AND DEVELOPMENT OF PRIMARY CARE OFFICES ("State Primary Care Offices")

Assistance: project grants.

Purposes: pursuant to PHSA, to coordinate local, state, and federal resources contributing to primary care service delivery and workforce issues to meet the needs of medically under-served populations, through health centers and other community-based providers. Emphasis is on: coordination of Medicaid, Children's Health Insurance program, state offices of rural health, and other health care financing services, maternal and child health; health systems development; National Health Service Corps monitoring; and recruitment and retention of primary care practitioners.

Eligible applicants/beneficiaries: states, state agencies, statewide public or nonprofit entities operating in one state only.

Average: $192,000.

Activity: annually, 53 awards.

HQ: Shortage Designation Branch, Office of Workforce, Evaluation and Quality Assurance, Bureau of Health Professions, HRSA-HHS, 5600 Fishers Lane - Rm.8C-26, Rockville, MD 20857. Phone: (301) 594-0816. *Grants management information*: Director, Division of Grants Management, Health Resources and Services Administration, HHS, 5600 Fishers Lane - Rm. 11A-16, Rockville, MD 20857. Phone: Health Services, (301) 443-2385; Research and Training, (301) 443-3099; Government and Special Focus, (301) 443-3288.

Internet: www.hrsa.gov (Note: no field offices for this program.)

93.134 GRANTS TO INCREASE ORGAN DONATIONS

Assistance: project grants. (100 percent/3 years).

Purposes: pursuant to PHSA as amended, for activities to increase the number of organ donors. Funds may not be used for activities reimbursable under Medicare.

Eligible applicants/beneficiaries: public and private nonprofit organ procurement, donation, and transplantation organizations.

Range: clinical interventions, $184,807 to $638,101; social, behavioral interventions, $165,000 to $510,000; minority organ donation, $312 to $687,620. **Average:** clinical, $371,066; social, behavioral, $377,000; minority organ donation, $526,982; hospitals and organ procurement, $75,000.

Activity: FY 06 estimate, 11 noncompeting clinical intervention awards; 12 noncompeting, 4-5 competing social, behavioral intervention awards.

HQ: Division of Transplantation, Healthcare Systems Bureau, HRSA- HHS, 5600 Fishers Lane - Rm.12C-06, Rockville, MD 20857. Phone: (301) 443-3124. *Grants management information*: Director, Division of Grants Management, Health Resources and Services Administration, HHS, 5600 Fishers Lane - Rm. 11A-16, Rockville, MD 20857. Phone: Health Services, (301) 443-2385; Research and Training, (301) 443-3099; Government and Special Focus, (301) 443-3288.

Internet: www.hrsa.gov (Note: no field offices for this program.)

93.135 CENTERS FOR RESEARCH AND DEMONSTRATION FOR HEALTH PROMOTION AND DISEASE PREVENTION ("Prevention Research Centers")

Assistance: project grants. (100 percent/1-5 years).

Purposes: pursuant to PHSA as amended, to establish, maintain, and operate academic-based centers for research and demonstration programs in health promotion and disease prevention; to establish linkages between ongoing related basic and applied research; for field testing and evaluation of new methods and strategies; to streamline the development and delivery of new techniques; to involve communities in prevention research.

Eligible applicants/beneficiaries: schools of medicine, osteopathy, and public health.

Range: $740,000 to $770,000. **Average:** $755,000.

Activity: FY 05 estimate, 28 continuation, 5 new grants.

HQ: Director, Prevention Research Center Program, Division of Adult and Community Health (K-45), National Center for Chronic Disease Prevention and Health Promotion, CDCP-HHS, 4770 Buford Hwy. NE, Atlanta, GA 30341-3724. Phone: (770) 488-5919. *Grants management information*: Grants Management Officer/Contracting Officer, Branch B, Procurement and Grants Office, CDC-HHS, 2920 Brandywine Rd. (Mailstop E-18), Atlanta, GA 30341. Phone: (770) 488-2754.

Internet: www.cdc.gov/prc (Note: no field offices for this program.)

93.136 INJURY PREVENTION AND CONTROL RESEARCH AND STATE AND COMMUNITY BASED PROGRAMS

Assistance: project grants. (100 percent/1-5 years).

Purposes: pursuant to PHSA as amended and other acts, for injury prevention and control research and demonstrations; to integrate aspects of engineering, public health, behavioral sciences, medicine, and other disciplines; to apply and evaluate current and new interventions, methods, and strategies; for injury control research centers in academic institutions to develop improved approaches to research and training; for public health programs for injury control; to develop and evaluate existing and new methods and techniques of injury surveillance, and to develop, expand, or improve injury control programs to reduce morbidity, mortality, severity, disability, and cost from injuries.

Eligible applicants/beneficiaries: research and centers grants—nonprofit and profit organizations. State and community program grants—official state public health agencies; territories and possessions; jurisdictions of more than 1,000,000 population. Community-based programs—public and private nonprofit and profit organizations.

Range: injury control research projects, $200,000 to $300,000; state, community-based, $40,000 to $300,000; youth violence prevention, $150,000 to $425,000; violence against women, $85,000 to $800,000; applied research for traumatic brain injury, $100,000 to $150,000; surveillance and traumatic brain injury, $16,000 to $500,000; other unintentional injuries, $50,000 to $1,050,000. **Average:** injury control research centers, $905,500; injury control research, $250,000; state, community-based, $170,000; youth violence prevention, $275,000; violence against women, $600,000; applied research for traumatic brain injury, $125,000; surveillance and traumatic brain injury, $258,000; other unintentional injuries, $550,000.

Activity: FY 05 (sampling), 11 centers, 38 individual grants; most existing grants continued.

HQ: National Center for Injury Prevention and Control, CDCP-HHS, 4770 Buford Hwy. NE, Atlanta, GA 30341-3724. Phone: *individual research grants,* (770) 488-1508, FAX (770) 488- 1670; *research centers,* (770) 488-4823, FAX (770) 488-1670; *community-based grant programs,* (770) 488-4710, FAX (770) 488-1662.

Internet: www.cdc.gov (Note: no field offices for this program.)

93.137 COMMUNITY PROGRAMS TO IMPROVE MINORITY HEALTH GRANT PROGRAM

Assistance: project grants. (100 percent/3 years).

Purposes: pursuant to PHSA as amended, for demonstration projects conducted by minority community health coalitions to modify behavioral or environmental conditions implicated in the health problems of minority groups—including HIV/AIDS, cancer, cardiovascular disease and stroke, chemical dependency, diabetes, homicide, suicide, unintentional injuries, infant mortality. Projects involve: coordination of integrated community-based screening and outreach services to minority groups and low-income communities; linkages for access and treatment to those at high risk; overcoming socio-cultural and linguistic barriers; working with nontraditional partners in projects to increase educational understanding of health issues. No health care services are provided under this program.

Eligible applicants/beneficiaries: private nonprofit community- based organizations serving Asians, Pacific islanders, African Americans, Latinos, Hispanics, native Americans, Alaska natives, native Hawaiians, or subgroups.

Range: $181,266 to $270,000. **Average:** $200,000.

Activity: FY 06 estimate, 24 continuation awards; 15 new awards.

HQ: Director, Division of Program Operations, Office of Minority Health, Office of Public Health and Science, OS-HHS, 1101 Wooten Pkwy. - Ste. 700, Rockville, MD 20852. Phone: (240) 453-8444. *Grants management information*: Office of Grants Management, Office of Public Health and Science, 1101 Wootton Pkwy. - Ste. 550, Rockville, MD 20852. Phone: (240) 453-8822.

Internet: www.omhrc.gov (Note: no field offices for this program.)

93.138 PROTECTION AND ADVOCACY FOR INDIVIDUALS WITH MENTAL ILLNESS ("PAIMI")

Assistance: formula grants. (100 percent/2 years).

Purposes: pursuant to PHSA, Protection and Advocacy for Individuals with Mental Illness Act of 1986, and Developmental Disabilities Assistance and Bill of Rights Act, as amended, to plan, develop, administer, and expand programs to protect and advocate the rights of the mentally ill, and to investigate incidents of their abuse and neglect including in public and private care and treatment facilities and nonmedical community- based facilities for children and youth. Limited funds may be used for training and technical assistance provided to staff.

Eligible applicants: state and local government agencies, public or private organizations designated by governors; territories, possessions.

Eligible beneficiaries: mentally ill persons with severe emotional impairments while inpatients or residents in care or treatment facilities, in their own homes, or living in the community; persons in process of being admitted or transported to such facilities, or involuntarily confined in detention facilities, jails, or prisons.

Range: $190,400 to $2,657,883. **Average:** $384,248.

Activity: annually, 57 grants (to all states and territories).

HQ: Program Officer, Protection and Advocacy Program, Division of State and Community Systems Development, CMHS-SAMHSA-HHS, 1 Choke Cherry Rd., Rockville, MD 20857. Phone: (240) 276-1741. *Grants management information*: Grants Management Officer, Division of Grants Management, Substance Abuse and Mental Health Services Administration, HHS, Rm. 7-1091, 1 Choke Cherry Rd., Rockville, MD 20857. Phone: (240) 276-1404.

Internet: www.samhsa.gov (Note: no field offices for this program.)

93.140 INTRAMURAL RESEARCH TRAINING AWARD ("IRTA")

Assistance: project grants.

Purposes: pursuant to HPEPA, to provide developmental training and practical research experience at the NIH for pre- or post- doctoral participants, in disciplines related to biomedical research, medical library research, and related fields. IRTA components include: postdoctoral (1-5 years), for physicians and other doctoral researchers; predoctoral (1 month-3 years), for students enrolled in doctoral degree programs in biomedical sciences, or accepted into graduate, doctoral, or medical degree programs; postbaccalaureate (1-2 years), for recent college graduates, particularly minorities, women, and persons with disabilities; technical (2-3 years), for training of professionals; student (1 month-1 year), for promising high school, undergraduate, and graduate students.

Eligible applicants/beneficiaries: postdoctoral awards—candidates with a Ph.D., M.D., D.D.S., D.M.D., D.V.M., or equivalent degree and not more than five years of postdoctoral research experience; predoctoral awards—students applying for, enrolled in, or accepted into graduate, doctoral, or medical degree programs; postbaccalaureate—candidates that graduated no more than one year prior to activation of the traineeship and intending to apply to graduate or medical school in biomedical research within one year; technical—candidates that graduated from a U.S. college or university with a bachelor's or master's degree in any discipline; student—candidates at least age 16 and enrolled at least half-time in high school, or accepted for or enrolled in an accredited U.S. college or university. Recipients must be U.S. citizens or permanent resident aliens.

Range: postdoctoral stipends, $33,800 to $67,000; predoctoral, $20,900 to $29,600; postbaccalaureate, $20,200 to $24,800; technical, $22,000 to $30,900; student, $1,200 to $2,900.

Activity: FY 06 estimate, 4,048 awards.

HQ: Executive Director/Intramural Research, NIH-HHS, Shannon Bldg. - Rm. 140, Bethesda, MD 20892. Phone: (301) 496-4920.

Internet: www.nih.gov (Note: no field offices for this program.)

93.142 NIEHS HAZARDOUS WASTE WORKER HEALTH AND SAFETY TRAINING ("Superfund Worker Training Program")

Assistance: project grants. (100 percent/to 5 years).

Purposes: pursuant to PHSA and SARA as amended, to develop and administer model education and training programs in worker health and safety practices for persons involved in hazardous waste generation, treatment, storage, removal, disposal, containment, transportation, or emergency response. Direct costs of classroom and practical training may be supported. Some SBIR and STTR awards may be made (*see Notes preceding* **93.001**).

Eligible applicants/beneficiaries: public or private nonprofit entities. Small business may apply for SBIR and STTR awards.

Range: $549,588 to $3,824,655. **Average:** $1,470,444.

Activity: FY 06 estimate, 18 noncompeting renewal grants.

HQ: Program Director, Worker Training and Education Program, NIEHS, NIH-HHS, P.O. Box 12233, Research Triangle Park, NC 27709. Phone: (919) 541-0217. *Grants management information*: Grants Management Officer, Grants Management Branch, Division of Extramural Research and Training, NIH-HHS, P.O. Box 12233, Research Triangle Park, NC 27709. Phone: (919) 541-1373.

Internet: www.niehs.nih.gov/wetp/home.htm (Note: no field offices for this program.)

93.143 NIEHS SUPERFUND HAZARDOUS SUBSTANCES—BASIC RESEARCH AND EDUCATION ("NIEHS Superfund Research Program")

Assistance: project grants. (100 percent/to 5 years).

Purposes: pursuant to PHSA, CERCLA, and SARA, as amended, to establish linkages between biomedical research and related engineering, geoscience, and ecological research. Funds may support basic research and advanced or graduate training activities on an inter-disciplinary, multiproject basis, covering: methods and technologies to detect hazardous substances in the environment; advanced techniques for the detection, assessment, and evaluation of the effects of hazardous substances on humans; environmental and occupational health and safety and the engineering aspects of hazardous waste control; related graduate training in the geosciences. SBIR awards are available (*see Notes preceding* **93.001**).

Eligible applicants/beneficiaries: IHEs. Subcontracts are permitted with state and local governments, public or private organizations, or persons or organizations involved with the generation, assessment, treatment of hazardous substances, or operation or ownership or facilities containing hazardous substances.

Range: $1,125,130 to $3,824,655. **Average:** $1,936,637.

Activity: FY 06 estimate, 9 noncompeting grants; 6-7 competing awards.

HQ: Director, Superfund Hazardous Substance Basic Research and Training Program, Division of Extramural Research and Training, NIEHS-NIH-

HHS, P.O. Box 12233, Research Triangle Park, NC 27709. Phone: (919) 541-0797. *Grants management information*: Grants Management Officer, Grants Management Branch, Division of Extramural Research and Training, NIH-HHS, P.O. Box 12233, Research Triangle Park, NC 27709. Phone: (919) 541-2749.

Internet: www.niehs.nih.gov (Note: no field offices for this program.)

93.145 AIDS EDUCATION AND TRAINING CENTERS

Assistance: project grants. (100 percent/3-5 years).

Purposes: pursuant to PHSA as amended and Ryan White CARE Act Amendments of 2000, for the education and training of primary care providers and others, on the diagnosis, treatment and prevention of HIV disease; for faculty training in related disciplines; to develop and disseminate pertinent curricula and resource materials; to develop protocols for the medical care of women with HIV disease, including prenatal and other gynecological care.

Eligible applicants/beneficiaries: public and private nonprofit entities, schools, academic health science centers.

Range: $445,081 to $4,815,031. **Average:** $2,233,333.

Activity: FY 07 estimate, 15 competitive and noncompetitive awards.

HQ: Division of Training and Technical Assistance/AIDS ETCs, HIV/AIDS Bureau, HRSA-HHS, 5600 Fishers Lane - Rm. 7-2946, Rockville, MD 20857. Phone: (301) 443-6364, FAX (301) 443-9887. *Grants management information*: Director, Division of Grants Management, Health Resources and Services Administration, NIH-HHS, 5600 Fishers Lane - Rm. 11A-16, Rockville, MD 20857. Phone: Health Services, (301) 443-2385; Research and Training, (301) 443-3099; Government and Special Focus, (301) 443-3288.

Internet: www.hrsa.gov (Note: no field offices for this program.)

93.150 PROJECTS FOR ASSISTANCE IN TRANSITION FROM HOMELESSNESS ("PATH")

Assistance: formula grants (75 percent; territories, 100 percent).

Purposes: pursuant to PHSA as amended and SBMHAA, to support services for homeless persons with serious mental illness, with serious mental illness and substance abuse, or at imminent risk of so becoming. Funds may support such services as: outreach; community mental health; screening and diagnosis; habilitation and rehabilitation; substance abuse treatment services; referrals to housing, primary health, job training; staff training; case management; supportive and supervisory services in residential settings. Funds may not be used for emergency shelters or construction, inpatient psychiatric of substance abuse treatment, cash payments to recipients of mental health or substance abuse services.

Eligible applicants/beneficiaries: states, territories, possessions. Subgrants must be provided to political subdivisions and private nonprofit entities including veterans and other community-based organizations.

Range: $50,000 to $1,680,000. **Average:** $347,000.

Activity: annually, 56 grants.

HQ: PATH Program, Homeless Programs Branch, Division of Knowledge Development and Systems Change, CMHS-SAMHSA-HHS, 1 Choke Cherry Rd., Rockville, MD 20857. Phone: (240) 276-1894. *Grants management information*: Grants Management Officer, SAMHSA, 1 Choke Cherry Rd., Rockville, MD 20857. Phone: (240) 276-1404.

Internet: www.samhsa.gov (Note: no field offices for this program.)

93.153 COORDINATED SERVICES AND ACCESS TO RESEARCH FOR WOMEN, INFANTS, CHILDREN, AND YOUTH ("Ryan White CARE Act Title IV Program")

Assistance: project grants. (100 percent/to 5 years).

Purposes: pursuant to PHSA as amended and Ryan White CARE Amendments Act of 2000, to improve access to primary medical care, research, and support services within for women, infants, children, and youth with HIV/AIDS or at risk, and to provide support services for their families; to link care systems with proven clinical research; to provide related client education.

Eligible applicants/beneficiaries: public and private nonprofit entities providing primary care.

Range: $285,000 to $2,320,869. **Average:** $766,222.

Activity: annually, 91 projects.

HQ: Division of Community Based Programs, HIV-AIDS Bureau, HRSA-HHS, 5600 Fishers Lane - Rm. 7A-30, Rockville, MD 20857. Phone: (301) 443-9051. *Grants management information*: Director, Division of Grants Management, Health Resources and Services Administration, NIH-HHS, 5600 Fishers Lane - Rm. 11A-16, Rockville, MD 20857. Phone: Health Services, (301) 443-2385; Research and Training, (301) 443-3099; Government and Special Focus, (301) 443-3288.

Internet: www.hrsa.gov (Note: no field offices for this program.)

93.155 RURAL HEALTH RESEARCH CENTERS

Assistance: project grants. (100 percent/to 4 years).

Purposes: to operate rural health research centers and to provide one-year research grants to new investigators to establish an information base and policy analysis capability on the full range of rural health issues, including financing, recruitment and retention of health professionals, access to care, and rural delivery systems.

Eligible applicants/beneficiaries: public and private nonprofit and profit entities including IHEs, research organizations, foundations, and community entities.

Range: centers, $400,000 to $600,000; research grants, $100,000 to $200,000. **Average:** centers, $500,000; research grants, $150,000.

Activity: FY 06 estimate, 8 center, 4 research awards.

HQ: Director, Rural Research Centers, Office of Rural Health Policy, HRSA-HHS, Parklawn Bldg. - Rm. 9A-55, 5600 Fishers Lane, Rockville, MD 20857. Phone: (301) 443-0835. *Grants management information*: Director, Division of Grants Management, Health Resources and Services Administration, NIH-HHS, 5600 Fishers Lane - Rm. 11A-16, Rockville, MD 20857. Phone: Health Services, (301) 443-2385; Research and Training, (301) 443-3099; Government and Special Focus, (301) 443-3288.

Internet: www.hrsa.gov (Note: no field offices for this program.)

93.156 GERIATRIC TRAINING FOR PHYSICIANS, DENTISTS AND BEHAVIORAL/MENTAL HEALTH PROFESSIONALS ("Geriatric Fellowships")

Assistance: project grants. (100 percent/5 years).

Purposes: pursuant to PHSA as amended and HPEPA, for training programs for current and future faculty in geriatric medicine, dentistry, and behavioral and mental health professionals. Funds may support: one-year retraining programs for physician faculty members in departments of internal or family medicine, gynecology, geriatrics, behavioral or mental health, and dentist faculty members at schools of dentistry or hospital departments of dentistry; two-year fellowships for physicians and dentists with relevant advanced training or experience in medical or dental education.

Eligible applicants/beneficiaries: public or private nonprofit schools of medicine or osteopathy, teaching hospitals, graduate medical education programs.

Range: $326,846 to $650,544. **Average:** $492,162.

Activity: FY 05, 6 new, 7 continuation awards.

HQ: Division of State, Community, and Public Health, Bureau of Health Professions, HRSA-HHS, Parklawn Bldg. - Rm. 8-05, 5600 Fishers Lane, Rockville, MD 20857. Phone: (301) 443-5794. *Grants management information*: Director, Division of Grants Management, Health Resources and Services Administration, NIH-HHS, 5600 Fishers Lane - Rm. 11A-16, Rockville, MD 20857. Phone: Health Services, (301) 443-2385; Research and Training, (301) 443-3099; Government and Special Focus, (301) 443-3288.

Internet: www.hrsa.gov (Note: no field offices for this program.)

93.157 CENTERS OF EXCELLENCE ("COEs")

Assistance: project grants. (100 percent/3 years).

Purposes: pursuant to PHSA as amended and HPEPA, to establish, strengthen, or expand programs to enhance the academic performance of underrepresented minority students in the health professions, though linkages with IHEs, local school districts, and other community-based entities. Funds may be used for such costs as: faculty recruitment, training, and retention, including through the payment of stipends and fellowships; library resource development and enhancement; student recruitment and academic performance enhancement programs; curriculum development;

facilitating faculty and student research on issues particularly affecting minority groups; student stipends.

Eligible applicants/beneficiaries: schools of medicine, osteopathy, dentistry, pharmacy; private nonprofit schools with graduate training programs in behavioral and mental health; certain HBCUs.

Range: $310,000 to $5,280,000. **Average:** $659,995.

Activity: FY 06 estimate, 0 continuation, 4 competitive grants.

HQ: Chief, Diversity Branch, Division of Health Careers Diversity and Development, Bureau of Health Professions, HRSA-HHS, Parklawn Bldg. - Rm. 8-55, 5600 Fishers Lane, Rockville, MD 20857. Phone: (301) 443-2100. *Grants management information*: Director, Division of Grants Management, Health Resources and Services Administration, NIH-HHS, 5600 Fishers Lane - Rm. 11A-16, Rockville, MD 20857. Phone: Health Services, (301) 443-2385; Research and Training, (301) 443-3099; Government and Special Focus, (301) 443-3288.

Internet: www.hrsa.gov (Note: no field offices for this program.)

93.161 HEALTH PROGRAM FOR TOXIC SUBSTANCES AND DISEASE REGISTRY

Assistance: project grants. (100 percent/1-5 years).

Purposes: pursuant to CERCLA and RCRA as amended, to reduce or eliminate illness, disability, and death resulting from public or worker exposure to toxic substances at spill and waste disposal sites. Services may include: health assessments; health effects studies; exposure and disease registries; technical assistance; consultation; information dissemination; specialized services and assistance including responses to public health emergencies; training; research of chemical toxicity.

Eligible applicants/beneficiaries: states and their political subdivisions, territories, possessions, IHEs, tribal governments.

Range: $130,000 to $300,000. **Average:** $200,000.

Activity: FY 06 estimate, 14 continuation grants.

HQ: Office of Financial and Administrative Services, Agency for Toxic Substances and Disease (E-28), CDCP-HHS, 1600 Clifton Rd. NE, Atlanta, GA 30333. Phone: (404) 498-0272, FAX (404) 498-0059. *Grants management information*: Grants Management Officer, Procurement and Grants Office, CDC-HHS, 2920 Brandywine Rd., Atlanta, GA 30341. Phone: (770) 488-2745, FAX: (770) 488-2777.

Internet: www.atsdr.cdc.gov (Note: no field offices for this program.)

93.162 NATIONAL HEALTH SERVICE CORPS LOAN REPAYMENT PROGRAM ("NHSC Loan Repayment Program")

Assistance: project grants.

Purposes: pursuant to PHSA as amended and National Health Service Corps Amendments Act of 1987, for the repayment of NHSC participants' qualifying government and commercial health professions undergraduate and graduate education loans. Up to $25,000 per year may be awarded during the first two years of practice at selected NHSC service sites, and up to $35,000 in the third and subsequent years—plus a 39 percent tax assistance payment. Priority currently is given to primary care physicians, dentists, certified nurse-midwives and nurse practitioners, physician assistants, clinical psychologists, clinical social workers, psychiatric nurse specialists, marriage and family therapists, licensed professional counselors, dental hygienists.

Eligible applicants/beneficiaries: U.S. citizens with a degree in health professions or in professional practice, licensed in a state, and eligible for appointment in the federal civil service or holding a commission in the PHS. Applicants may not: be in default on any federal debt; have a court judgment against them; have an existing service obligation.

Range: $3,896 to $50,000. **Average:** $45,408.

Activity: FY 06 estimate, 1,478 awards; FY 07 estimate, 1,624 awards.

HQ: Chief, Applications and Award Branch, NHSC Division, Bureau of Health Professions, HRSA-HHS, 5600 Fishers Lane - Rm. 8A-55, Rockville, MD 20857. Phone: (301) 594-4400; *public information*, (800) 221-9393. *Grants management information*: Director, Division of Grants Management, Health Resources and Services Administration, NIH-HHS, 5600 Fishers Lane - Rm. 11A-16, Rockville, MD 20857. Phone: Health Services, (301) 443-2385; Research and Training, (301) 443-3099; Government and Special Focus, (301) 443-3288.

Internet: www.hrsa.gov (Note: no field offices for this program.)

93.164 INDIAN HEALTH SERVICE EDUCATIONAL LOAN REPAYMENT ("IHS Loan Repayment Program")

Assistance: project grants (100 percent).

Purposes: pursuant to the Indian Health Care Amendments of 1988, for payments of up to $20,000 annually toward participants' health professions education loans during each year of service at IHS priority sites or certain other sites—plus 20 percent for tax liability on the grant award. A minimum of two years of service is required.

Eligible applicants/beneficiaries: students enrolled in their final year in a program leading to a degree, or graduate students enrolled in approved programs; or, degreed and licensed professionals, eligible for or holding a PHS or civil service appointment in the HIS; or employees of an Indian health program.

Range: $3,000 to $48,000 for a two-year service obligation. **Average:** $43,315.

Activity: FY 06 estimate, 245 new, 240 continuation awards; FY 07 estimate, 230 new, 220 continuation awards.

HQ: Chief, Loan Repayment Program, IHS-HHS, 801 Thompson Ave. - Ste. 120, Rockville, MD 20852. Phone: (301) 443-3396.

Internet: www.ihs.gov.

93.165 GRANTS TO STATES FOR LOAN REPAYMENT PROGRAM ("State Loan Repayment Program")

Assistance: project grants. (50 percent/to 5 years).

Purposes: pursuant to PHSA, for state educational loan repayment programs for health professionals agreeing to serve full-time for a minimum of two years in a health manpower shortage area. State programs must be similar to **93.162**.

Eligible applicants/beneficiaries: states.

Range: $5,000 to $620,822. **Average:** $108,625.

Activity: FY 06, 34 awards.

HQ: Division of State, Community and Public Health, Bureau of Health Professions, HRSA-HHS, Parklawn Bldg. - Rm. 9-05, 5600 Fishers Lane, Rockville, MD 20857. Phone: (301) 443-1648. *Grants management information*: Director, Division of Grants Management, Health Resources and Services Administration, NIH-HHS, 5600 Fishers Lane - Rm. 11A-16, Rockville, MD 20857. Phone: Health Services, (301) 443-2385; Research and Training, (301) 443-3099; Government and Special Focus, (301) 443-3288.

Internet: www.hrsa.gov (Note: no field offices for this program.)

93.172 HUMAN GENOME RESEARCH

Assistance: project grants. (100 percent/1-5 years).

Purposes: pursuant to PHSA as amended and SBRDEA, to obtain genetic and physical maps and to determine the deoxyribonucleic acid (DNA) sequences of the genomes of humans and model organisms to be used as resources in biomedical research, medicine, and biotechnology—including consideration of the ethical, legal, and social implications. NRSA, SBIR, and STTR awards are available (*see Notes preceding* **93.001**).

Eligible applicants/beneficiaries: public or private, profit or nonprofit IHEs, hospitals, laboratories, other institutions; state and local governments; small businesses.

Range: $7,148 to $9,587,489. **Average:** $610,048.

Activity: FY 05 estimate, 76 competing research project grants; 31 research center, 28 research career, 18 other research- related, and 157 full-time research trainee positions.

HQ: National Human Genome Research Institute, NIH-HHS, Bethesda, MD 20892. Phone: program, research centers, SBIR, (301) 496-7531; ethical, legal, and social implications, (301) 402-4997. *Grants management information*: Grants Management Officer, National Human Genome Research Institute, NIH-HHS, Bethesda, MD 20892. Phone: (301) 402-0733.

Internet: www.nih.gov (Note: no field offices for this program.)

93.173 RESEARCH RELATED TO DEAFNESS AND COMMUNICATION DISORDERS

Assistance: project grants. (100 percent/to 5 years).

Purposes: pursuant to PHSA as amended and SBRDEA, to investigate solutions to problems of patients with deafness or disorders of human communication such as hearing, balance, voice, speech, language, and the senses of taste, touch, and smell. Focus may be on etiology, pathology, detection, treatment, and prevention of all forms of hearing disorders and other communication processes, primarily through basic and applied research in anatomy, audiology, biochemistry, bioengineering, epidemiology, genetics, immunology, microbiology, molecular biology, the neurosciences, otolaryngology, psychology, pharmacology, physiology, speech and language pathology, and other scientific disciplines. Funds may support research centers, as well as mentored and unmentored career awards. NRSA, SBIR, and STTR awards are available (*see Notes preceding* **93.001**).

Eligible applicants/beneficiaries: public, private, nonprofit, or profit institutions; SBIR firms; individuals.

Range: $75,000 to $1,500,000. **Average:** $309,000.

Activity: FY 06 estimate, 1,160 awards; FY 07 estimate, 1135 awards.

HQ: National Institute on Deafness and Other Communication Disorders, NIH-HHS, Executive Plaza South - Rm. 400-C, Bethesda, MD 20892-7180. Phone: (301) 496-5061. *Grants management information*: National Institute on Deafness and Other Communications Disorders, NIH, Executive Plaza South, - Rm.400-B, Bethesda, MD 20892. Phone: (301) 402-0909.

Internet: www.nidcd.nih.gov (Note: no field offices for this program.)

93.178 NURSING WORKFORCE DIVERSITY ("Disadvantaged Assistance")

Assistance: project grants. (100 percent/3 years).

Purposes: pursuant to PHSA as amended and HPEPA, to increase nursing education opportunities for individuals from disadvantaged backgrounds, by providing student $250 monthly stipends, with a $7,000 annual maximum scholarship, and pre-entry preparation and retention activities. Funds also may be used for project personnel salaries, consultant fees, supplies and equipment, travel, and related costs.

Eligible applicants/beneficiaries: schools of nursing, nursing centers, academic health centers, state and local governments, and other public and nonprofit private entities—with above average rates of admission, retention, and graduation of individuals from disadvantaged backgrounds and ethnic and racial minorities, or with plans for improving such rates.

Range: $42,954 to $419,606. **Average:** $266,590.

Activity: FY 06 estimate, 25 new, 35 continuation grants.

HQ: Division of Nursing, Bureau of Health Professions, HRSA-HHS, Parklawn Bldg. - Rm.9-36, 5600 Fishers Lane, Rockville, MD 20857. Phone: (301) 443-6193. *Grants management information*: Director, Division of Grants Management, Health Resources and Services Administration, HHS, 5600 Fishers Lane - Rm. 11A-16, Rockville, MD 20857. Phone: Health Services, (301) 443-2385; Research and Training, (301) 443-3099; Government and Special Focus, (301) 443-3288.

Internet: www.hrsa.gov (Note: no field offices for this program.)

93.181 PODIATRIC RESIDENCY TRAINING IN PRIMARY CARE

Assistance: project grants. (100 percent/to 3 years).

Purposes: pursuant to PHSA as amended and HPEPA, for preventive and primary care residency training programs for podiatrists, including financial assistance to residents.

Eligible applicants/beneficiaries: collaboratives of health professions schools, academic health centers, state or local governments, public and private nonprofit entities, community- based organizations.

Range: $205,291 to $286,362. **Average:** $245,826.

Activity: FY 05, 2 continuation awards; FY 06, program zeroed out.

HQ: Dentistry, Psychology and Special Projects Branch, Division of Medicine and Dentistry, Bureau of Health Professions, HRSA- HHS, 5600 Fishers Lane - Rm. 9A-27, Rockville, MD 20857. Phone: (301) 443-4880. *Grants management information*: Director, Division of Grants Management, Health Resources and Services Administration, HHS, 5600 Fishers Lane - Rm. 11A-16, Rockville, MD 20857. Phone: Health Services, (301) 443-2385; Research and Training, (301) 443-3099; Government and Special Focus, (301) 443-3288.

Internet: www.hrsa.gov (Note: no field offices for this program.)

93.184 DISABILITIES PREVENTION ("Disability and Health")

Assistance: project grants. (to 100 percent/3-5 years).

Purposes: pursuant to PHSA as amended, to provide a national focus for the prevention of secondary conditions in persons with selected disability domains, including mobility, personal care, communication, and learning—through cooperative agreements and research projects designed to: build state capacity to coordinate prevention and education activities and to conduct surveillance; provide related technical assistance to communities; employ epidemiological methods to set priorities and target interventions; conduct research on the disabled and their physical, medical, cognitive, emotional, or psychosocial conditions; support a national limb loss information center to serve as an information clearinghouse and to conduct peer education and training sessions with hospitals and limb loss support groups; support the National Center on Physical Activity and Disability to provide information and promote physical activity for the disabled; conduct related activities.

Eligible applicants/beneficiaries: cooperative agreements—state health departments or other state agencies, including in territories or possessions with existing agreements. Research grants—public and private nonprofit entities, universities, nonprofit medical centers, rehabilitation hospitals, disability service organizations, tribal governments.

Range: state capacity projects, $125,000 to $350,000.

Activity: FY 06, 16 states funded.

HQ: Project Officer, Division of Human Development and Disability, National Center on Birth Defects and Developmental Disabilities (E88),

CDCP-HHS, 1600 Clifton Rd. NE., Atlanta, GA 30333. Phone: (404) 498-3957. *Grants management information*: Grants Management Officer, Procurement and Grants Office, CDC-HHS, 2920 Brandywine Rd., Atlanta, GA 30341. Phone: (770) 488-2728.

Internet: www.cdc.gov (Note: no field offices for this program.)

93.185 IMMUNIZATION RESEARCH, DEMONSTRATION, PUBLIC INFORMATION AND EDUCATION—TRAINING AND CLINICAL SKILLS IMPROVEMENT PROJECTS

Assistance: project grants. (100 percent/1-5 years).

Purposes: pursuant to PHSA as amended, for research, demonstration, and information dissemination projects on vaccine- preventable diseases and conditions. Funds may be used to conduct project activities including, in certain circumstances, purchasing vaccine.

Eligible applicants/beneficiaries: states and their political subdivisions, other public and private nonprofit entities.

Range: $5,000 to $500,000. **Average:** $185,000.

Activity: not quantified specifically.

HQ: Associate Director/Management and Operations, National Immunization Program (E-05), CDCP-HHS, 1600 Clifton Rd. NE, Atlanta, GA 30333. Phone: (404) 639-8900, FAX (404) 639-8626. *Grants management information*: Procurement and Grants Office, CDCP-HHS, 2920 Brandywine Rd. - Rm. 3618, Atlanta, GA 30341. Phone: (770) 488-2716.

Internet: www.cdc.gov (Note: no field offices for this program.)

93.186 NATIONAL RESEARCH SERVICE AWARD IN PRIMARY CARE MEDICINE

Assistance: project grants. (100 percent/3-5 years).

Purposes: pursuant to PHSA as amended and the National Institutes of Health Revitalization Act of 1993, for postdoctoral research training programs in primary medical care. Individuals receiving awards incur one month of service obligation for each of the first 12 months of the NRSA support, after which no further service obligation is incurred; the continued training serves to discharge the payback obligation (*see Notes preceding* **93.001**).

Eligible applicants/beneficiaries: domestic public or private nonprofit organizations; state or local governments and territories. Individuals must be U.S. citizens, noncitizen nationals, or lawful permanent residents.

Range: $188,550 to $825,861. **Average:** $400,423.

Activity: FY 06 estimate, 19 continuation awards.

HQ: Dentistry, Psychology and Special Projects Branch, Division of Medicine and Dentistry, Bureau of Health Professions, HRSA- HHS, 5600 Fishers Lane - Rm. 9A-27, Rockville, MD 20857. Phone: (301) 443-6785. *Grants management information*: Director, Division of Grants Management, Health Resources and Services Administration, HHS, 5600 Fishers Lane - Rm. 11A-16, Rockville, MD 20857. Phone: Health Services, (301)

443-2385; Research and Training, (301) 443-3099; Government and Special Focus, (301) 443-3288.

Internet: www.hrsa.gov (Note: no field offices for this program.)

93.187 UNDERGRADUATE SCHOLARSHIP PROGRAM FOR INDIVIDUALS FROM DISADVANTAGED BACKGROUNDS ("NIH Undergraduate Scholarship Program; UGSP")

Assistance: project grants. (100 percent/to 4 years).

Purposes: pursuant to PHSA as amended, for scholarships to persons from disadvantaged backgrounds, pursuing undergraduate education preparing them for professions in the biomedical or bio-behavioral sciences at NIH. Recipients must agree: to serve full-time for at least ten consecutive weeks as an NIH employee during each year of the scholarship period; within 60 days of obtaining a degree, to serve one year as a full-time NIH employee for each year of scholarship assistance received, unless deferred.

Eligible applicants/beneficiaries: U.S. citizens, nationals, or permanent residents from disadvantaged backgrounds, enrolled or accepted at IHEs for full-time study, and maintaining good academic standing.

Range: $1,714 to $20,000 per academic year. **Average:** $12,000 per scholar.

Activity: FY 06 estimate, 20 awards; FY 07 estimate, 20 awards.

HQ: Office of Intramural Research, NIH-HHS, 2 Center Dr. - Rm. 2E24, Bethesda, MD 20892-0230. Phone: (888) 352-3001, FAX (301) 480-3123.

Internet: ugsp.info.nih.gov; e- mail, ugsp@nih.gov (Note: no field offices for this program.)

93.189 HEALTH EDUCATION AND TRAINING CENTERS ("HETC")

Assistance: project grants. (100 percent/to 3 years).

Purposes: pursuant to PHSA as amended and HPEPA, establish, maintain, and operate multi-disciplinary HETCs to improve the supply, distribution, quality, and efficiency of personnel providing health services—in rural and inner-city communities, in Florida, and in U.S.-Mexico border areas. Funds must be expended mainly in the service area of the recipient's program.

Eligible applicants/beneficiaries: schools of allopathic or osteopathic medicine or nursing; consortia.

Range: border-HETC, $100,000 to $556,010; non-border, $239,508 to $326,615. **Average:** border, $355,462; non-border, $296,069.

Activity: FY 05, 5 border grants, 6 non-border grants.

HQ: Chief, AHEC Branch, Division of State, Community and Public Health, Bureau of Health Professions, HRSA-HHS, Parklawn Bldg. - Rm. 9-05, 5600 Fishers Lane, Rockville, MD 20857. Phone: (301) 443- 6950. *Grants management information*: Director, Division of Grants Management, Health Resources and Services Administration-HHS, 5600 Fishers Lane - Rm. 11A-16, Rockville, MD 20857. Phone: Health Services, (301)

443-2385; Research and Training, (301) 443-3099; Government and Special Focus, (301) 443-3288.

Internet: www.hrsa.gov (Note: no field offices for this program.)

93.191 ALLIED HEALTH SPECIAL PROJECTS

Assistance: project grants. (100 percent/3 years).

Purposes: pursuant to PHSA as amended and HPEPA, to establish and expand training programs in the allied health professions that will: expand enrollments in disciplines in short supply or most needed by the elderly; provide rapid transition training programs for participants with baccalaureate degrees in health-related sciences; provide career advancement training for practicing allied health professionals; establish or expand clinical training sites in medically underserved or rural communities; develop curriculum in prevention and health promotion, geriatrics, long-term care, home health and hospice care, and ethics; expand or establish interdisciplinary and training programs; link academic centers to clinical centers; support graduate programs in behavioral and mental health practice. Funds may be used for the costs of personnel, equipment, consultants, guest lecturers, space rental, or renovation—but not for construction, land acquisition, financial support to students.

Eligible applicants/beneficiaries: health professions schools, academic health centers, state or local governments, public or private nonprofit entities.

Range: $92,799 to $214,390. **Average:** $155,238.

Activity: FY 05, 9 new, 18 continuation awards.

HQ: Division of State, Community and Public Health, Bureau of Health Professions, HRSA-HHS, Parklawn Bldg. - Rm. 8-05, 5600 Fishers Lane, Rockville, MD 20857. Phone: (301) 443-5794. *Grants management information*: Director, Division of Grants Management, Health Resources and Services Administration-HHS, 5600 Fishers Lane - Rm. 11A-16, Rockville, MD 20857. Phone: Health Services, (301) 443-2385; Research and Training, (301) 443-3099; Government and Special Focus, (301) 443-3288.

Internet: www.hrsa.gov (Note: no field offices for this program.)

93.192 QUENTIN N. BURDICK PROGRAM FOR RURAL INTERDISCIPLINARY TRAINING
("Interdisciplinary Training for Health Care for Rural Areas")

Assistance: project grants. (100 percent/to 3 years).

Purposes: pursuant to PHSA as amended and HPEPA, for interdisciplinary training projects for health care professionals in rural areas, in delivering health services; for relevant demonstration and research projects; to recruit and retain health care practitioners. Grants may be used for student stipends, postdoctoral fellowships, faculty training, and purchase or rental of transportation and telecommunications equipment.

Eligible applicants/beneficiaries: health professions schools; academic health centers; state or local governments; public and private nonprofit entities. Applications must be submitted jointly by at least two eligible applicants, designating rural health care agencies for clinical treatment or training hospitals, community or migrant health centers, long-term care facilities, or facilities operated by the IHS, tribal, or native Hawaiian health care providers.

Range: $133,709 to $344,077. **Average:** $250,107.

Activity: FY 05, 5 new, 18 continuation awards.

HQ: Division of State, Community, and Public Health, Bureau of Health Professions, HRSA-HHS, Parklawn Bldg. - Rm. 8A-09, 5600 Fishers Lane, Rockville, MD 20857. Phone: (301) 443-6867. *Grants management information*: Director, Division of Grants Management, Health Resources and Services Administration, NIH-HHS, 5600 Fishers Lane - Rm. 11A-16, Rockville, MD 20857. Phone: Health Services, (301) 443-2385; Research and Training, (301) 443-3099; Government and Special Focus, (301) 443-3288.

Internet: www.hrsa.gov (Note: no field offices for this program.)

93.193 URBAN INDIAN HEALTH SERVICES ("Urban Indian Alcohol and Substance Abuse Program; Urban Mental Health; Urban Immunization and Health Promotion/Disease Prevention")

Assistance: project grants. (100 percent/to 5 years).

Purposes: pursuant to the Indian Health Care Improvement Act as amended, for health-related services to Indians residing in urban areas, including: alcohol and substance abuse prevention, treatment, rehabilitation, and education; mental health needs assessment and services; health promotion and disease prevention; immunization.

Eligible applicants/beneficiaries: urban Indian organizations.

Range: $114,578 to $573,126. **Average:** $209,846.

Activity: FY 06 estimate, 34 continuation grants; FY 07, 34 continuation grants.

HQ: Urban Programs, IHS-HHS, 801 Thompson Ave. - Ste. 200, Rockville, MD 20852. Phone: (301) 443-4680. *Grants management information*: Grants Management Officer, Division of Grants Operations, IHS-HHS, 801 Thompson Ave. - Ste. 100, Rockville, MD 20852. Phone: (301) 443-5204.

Internet: www.ihs.gov (Note: no field offices for this program.)

93.197 CHILDHOOD LEAD POISONING PREVENTION PROJECTS—STATE AND LOCAL CHILDHOOD LEAD POISONING PREVENTION AND SURVEILLANCE OF BLOOD LEAD LEVELS IN CHILDREN ("CLPPP")

Assistance: project grants. (100 percent/to 3 years).

Purposes: pursuant to PHSA as amended, Preventive Health Amendments of 1992, and Children's Health Act of 2000, for childhood lead poisoning prevention projects in communities with demonstrated high-risk populations. Funds are to be used: for screening and testing; to identify sources of lead exposure; to monitor medical and environmental management of cases, including follow-up; for public and technical education activities, including staff training; to enhance primary prevention activities in collaboration with other government and community- based organizations; to establish state-based surveillance systems. Ineligible uses of funds include medical care or treatment, remediation of lead sources; however, an acceptable plan must be submitted with assurances that such activities will be carried out.

Eligible applicants/beneficiaries: state health or other departments or agencies; territories and possessions; tribal governments; consortia of the foregoing; five specified local governments.

Range: $75,000 to $1,700,000.

Activity: annually, 42 state, local grants.

HQ: Program Services Team Leader, Lead Poisoning Prevention Branch, National Center for Environmental Health, CDCP-HHS (F-30), 4770 Buford Hwy., Atlanta, GA 30341. Phone: (770) 488-7493, FAX (770) 498-3635. *Grants management information*: Grants Management Branch, CDC, 2920 Brandywine Rd. - Rm. 3000, Atlanta, GA 30341. Phone: (770) 488-2745, FAX (770) 488-2777.

Internet: www.cdc.gov (Note: no field offices for this program.)

93.202 CAPACITY BUILDING AMONG AMERICAN INDIAN TRIBES

Assistance: project grants. (100 percent/1-5 years).

Purposes: pursuant to CERCLA as amended, to enhance tribal ability to collaborate with the Agency for Toxic Substances and Disease Registry in conducting public health activities related to potential human exposures from the Hanford Nuclear Reservation, including outreach materials to community members.

Eligible applicants/beneficiaries: affected tribal governments.

Range: $40,000 to $60,000. **Average:** $50,000.

Activity: FY 03 estimate, 9 continuation awards; no new awards anticipated.

HQ: Division of Health Assessment and Consultation, Agency for Toxic Substances and Disease (E-32), CDCP-HHS, 1600 Clifton Rd. NE, Atlanta, GA 30333. Phone: (404) 498-0457. *Grants management information*: Grants Management Officer, Procurement and Grants Office, CDC-HHS, 2920 Brandywine Rd. - Rm. 3000, Atlanta, GA 30341. Phone: (770) 488-2743, FAX: (770) 488-2777.

Internet: www.atsdr.cdc.gov (Note: no field offices for this program.)

93.204 SURVEILLANCE OF HAZARDOUS SUBSTANCE EMERGENCY EVENTS

Assistance: project grants. (100 percent/1-5 years).

Purposes: pursuant to CERCLA as amended and SARA, to develop state-based surveillance systems for monitoring hazardous substance emergency events, to enable states to: assess the burden of adverse health effects created by unexpected, sudden releases; describe the situations and persons most likely impacted; define the risk factors; and, work with appropriate agencies to implement prevention activities. Funds may cover the costs of personnel, travel, supplies, and services.

Eligible applicants/beneficiaries: state public health departments, tribal governments, possessions and territories.

Range: $60,000 to $80,000. **Average:** $79,000.

Activity: FY 03 estimate (most recent data), 16 continuation awards.

HQ: Division of Health Studies, Agency for Toxic Substances and Disease Registry, CDCP-HHS (E-31), 1600 Clifton Rd. NE, Atlanta, GA 30333. Phone: (404) 498-0268, FAX (404) 498-0058. *Grants management information*: Grants Management Officer, Procurement and Grants Office, CDC-HHS, 2920 Brandywine Rd. - Rm. 3000, Mail Stop E-75, Atlanta, GA 30341. Phone: (770) 488-2745, FAX: (770) 488-2777.

Internet: www.atsdr.cdc.gov (Note: no field offices for this program.)

93.206 HUMAN HEALTH STUDIES—APPLIED RESEARCH AND DEVELOPMENT

Assistance: project grants. (100 percent/1-5 years).

Purposes: pursuant to CERCLA as amended and SARA, for studies on human health effects of hazardous substances identified at hazardous waste sites, as identified by the Agency for Toxic Substances and Disease Registry, including: birth defects and reproductive disorders; cancers; immune function disorders; kidney and liver dysfunction; lung and respiratory diseases; neurotoxin disorders.

Eligible applicants/beneficiaries: state public health departments, tribal governments, possessions and territories, and state research institutions and IHEs.

Range: $50,000 to $500,000. **Average:** $100,000.

Activity: FY 05, 20 continuation awards.

HQ: Office of Financial and Administrative Services, Agency for Toxic Substances and Disease (E-28), CDCP-HHS, 1600 Clifton Rd. NE, Atlanta, GA 30333. Phone: (404) 498-0270, FAX (404) 498-0059. *Grants management information*: Grants Management Officer, Procurement and Grants Office, CDC-HHS, 2920 Brandywine Rd. - Rm. 3000, Atlanta, GA 30341. Phone: (770) 488-2743, FAX: (770) 488-2745.

Internet: www.atsdr.cdc.gov (Note: no field offices for this program.)

93.208 GREAT LAKES HUMAN HEALTH EFFECTS RESEARCH

Assistance: project grants. (100 percent/1-3 years).

Purposes: pursuant to CERCLA as amended, SARA, and Great Lakes Critical Programs Act of 1990, for research on the impact on human health of fish consumption in the Great Lakes basin, focusing on populations identified as having a higher risk of long-term adverse health effects from exposure to contaminants—especially native Americans and other minority groups, sport anglers, the urban poor, the elderly. The research is intended to study the effects of contaminants on human reproductive and developmental, behavioral, immunologic, neurologic, and endocrinologic health. Findings are coordinated with other Public Health Service research programs and activities, to ameliorate adverse impacts of persistent toxic substances.

Eligible applicants/beneficiaries: in the Great Lakes states—state and local health agencies, state IHEs and research institutions, and tribal governments.

Range: $72,000 to $175,000. **Average:** $119,000.

Activity: annually, 10 continuation grants.

HQ: Division of Toxicology, Agency for Toxic Substances and Disease Registry, HHS (E-29), 1600 Clifton Rd. NE, Atlanta, GA 30333. Phone: (404) 498-0717, FAX (404) 498-0094. *Grants management information*: Grants Management Officer, Procurement and Grants Office, CDC-HHS, 2920 Brandywine Rd. - Rm. 3000, Atlanta, GA 30341. Phone: (770) 488-2745, FAX: (770) 488-2777.

Internet: www.atsdr.cdc.gov (Note: no field offices for this program.)

93.209 CONTRACEPTION AND INFERTILITY RESEARCH LOAN REPAYMENT PROGRAM ("CIR LRP")

Assistance: direct payments/specified use.

Purposes: pursuant to PHSA as amended, to provide incentives to health professionals to work in reproductive research related to contraceptive development or infertility diagnosis and treatment, by providing assistance in repaying their education loans. The program pays up to $35,000 of loan principal and interest for each year of service commitment, not to exceed one-half of remaining loan balance—plus up to 39 percent to offset tax liability. Participants must agree to commit to a period of obligated service of at least two years.

Eligible applicants/beneficiaries: U.S. citizens, nationals, or permanent residents that are health and allied health professionals, including physicians, Ph.D.-level scientists, nurses, physician assistants, or graduate students and postgraduate research fellows.

Range: $2,975 to $70,000. **Average:** $47,286.

Activity: FY 07 estimate, 21 contracts.

HQ: Director, Office of Extramural Research, National Institute of Child Health and Human Development, NIH-HHS, Bldg.61E - Rm. 2C01, Bethesda, MD 20892-7510. Phone: (301) 435-6856.

Internet: www.nichd.nih.gov (Note: no field offices for this program.)

93.210 TRIBAL SELF-GOVERNANCE PROGRAM: IHS COMPACTS/FUNDING AGREEMENTS

Assistance: project grants.

Purposes: pursuant to ISDEAA as amended, to establish and operate programs to provide planning and negotiation resources to tribes interested in participating in the Tribal Self-Governance Program—enabling them to enter into compacts to assume programs, services, and functions of the IHS and HHS that are otherwise available to Indians or tribes.

Eligible applicants/beneficiaries: recognized tribes.

Range/Average: N.A.

Activity: FY 05, 71 compact, 91 funding agreements awards covering 11 hospitals, 71 health centers, 1 school health center, 189 health stations.

HQ: Director, Office of Tribal Self-Governance, IHS-HHS, 801 Thompson Ave. - Ste. 240, Rockville, MD 20852. Phone: (301) 443-7821. *Grants management information*: Grants Management Officer, Division of Grants Operations, HIS, 801 Thompson Ave., TMP, Ste. 360, Rockville, MD 20852. Phone: (301) 443-5204.

Internet: www.ihs.gov (Note: no field offices for this program.)

93.211 TELEHEALTH NETWORK GRANTS

Assistance: project grants. (100 percent/to 3 years).

Purposes: pursuant to PHSA as amended by the Health Care Safety Net Amendments of 2002, to demonstrate the use of telehealth technologies to support and promote long-distance clinical health care, patient and professional health-related education; to collect information for a systematic evaluation of such projects. Projects are meant for rural areas, frontier communities, and medically-underserved populations. Up to 40 percent of grant funds may be used for equipment (non-transmission).

Eligible applicants/beneficiaries: public nonprofit health care providers or consortia, that are members of an existing or proposed telemedicine network including for-profit entities.

Range: $200,000 to $250,000.

Activity: FY 05, 15 grants.

HQ: Office for the Advancement of Telehealth, HRSA-HHS, 5600 Fishers Lane - Rm. 7C-22, Rockville, MD 20857. Phone: (301) 443-0076. *Grants management information*: Director, Division of Grants Management, Health Resources and Services Administration, NIH-HHS, 5600 Fishers Lane - Rm. 11A-16, Rockville, MD 20857. Phone: Health Services, (301) 443-2385; Research and Training, (301) 443-3099; Government and Special Focus, (301) 443-3288.

Internet: www.hrsa.gov (Note: no field offices for this program.)

93.212 CHIROPRACTIC DEMONSTRATION PROJECT GRANTS

Assistance: project grants. (100 percent/3 years).

Purposes: pursuant to PHSA as amended and HPEPA, for demonstration projects in which chiropractors and medical doctors collaborate to identify and treat spinal and lower-back conditions. Project funds may be used for related research activities, personnel, equipment, supplies, domestic travel, consultants and guest lecturers, rent, renovations, and other direct project costs—but not for land acquisition, facilities construction, foreign travel, or student support.

Eligible applicants/beneficiaries: health professions schools, academic health centers, state or local governments, public or private nonprofit entities, and nonprofit colleges and schools of chiropractic.

Range: $369,572 to $473,373. **Average:** $435,942.

Activity: FY 06 estimate, 4 new awards.

HQ: Division of State, Community, and Public Health, Bureau of Health Professions, HRSA-HHS, Parklawn Bldg. - Rm. 8-05, 5600 Fishers Lane, Rockville, MD 20857. Phone: (301) 443-5794. *Grants management information*: Director, Division of Grants Management, Health Resources and Services Administration, NIH-HHS, 5600 Fishers Lane - Rm. 11A-16, Rockville, MD 20857. Phone: Health Services, (301) 443-2385; Research and Training, (301) 443-3099; Government and Special Focus, (301) 443-3288.

Internet: www.hrsa.gov (Note: no field offices for this program.)

93.213 RESEARCH AND TRAINING IN COMPLEMENTARY AND ALTERNATIVE MEDICINE
("National Center for Complementary and Alternative Medicine")

Assistance: project grants. (100 percent/to 5 years).

Purposes: pursuant to PHSA as amended, to foster collaboration between biomedical researchers and practitioners of alternative, complementary, or unconventional medical treatments, by: supporting and coordinating evaluations of alternative medical practices; identifying areas of clinical and preclinical research needing further development; developing clinical databases in conjunction with the National Library of Medicine; developing further international contacts; establishing an intra- and extramural clinical research fellowship program in alternative medicine. Grants may support costs of personnel, consultants, equipment, supplies, patient costs, animals, travel, and related items.

Eligible applicants/beneficiaries: IHEs, hospitals, public agencies, nonprofit research institutions, profit organizations, individuals.

Range: training, $22,000 to $412,000; projects, $125,000 to $3,000,000. **Average:** projects, $317,000.

Activity: FY 06 estimate, 293 grants; FY 07 estimate, 290 grants.

HQ: Division of Extramural Research, National Center for Complementary and Alternative Medicine, NIH-HHS, 6707 Democracy Blvd. - Ste. 401, Bethesda, MD 20892-5475. Phone: (301) 496-4792, FAX (301) 402-4741.

Internet: nccam.nih.gov (Note: no field offices for this program.)

93.217 FAMILY PLANNING—SERVICES

Assistance: project grants. (from 90 percent/3-5 years).

Purposes: pursuant to PHSA as amended and Family Planning Services and Population Research Acts, for educational, counseling, and comprehensive medical and social services involving family planning, with priority to the low-income. Grants may be used for contraceptive, infertility, and special services to adolescents. Funds may not be used in programs where abortion is a method of family planning, nor for personnel salaries paid from other federal funds, nor for building construction.

Eligible applicants/beneficiaries: city, county, local, regional, or state governmental or private nonprofit entities in states, territories, and possessions; "faith-based" organizations.

Range: $47,791 to $16,962,215. **Average:** $2,519,960.

Activity: annually, 91 grantees funded.

HQ: Director, Office of Family Planning, Office of Population Affairs, 1101 Wootton Pkwy. - Ste. 700, Rockville, MD 20852. Phone: (240) 453-2888. *Grants management information*: Director, Office of Grants Management, Office of Public Health and Science, HHS, 1101 Wootton Pkwy. - Ste. 550, Rockville, MD 20853. Phone: (240) 453-8822.

Internet: www.opa.osophs.dhhs.gov.

93.220 CLINICAL RESEARCH LOAN REPAYMENT PROGRAM FOR INDIVIDUALS FROM DISADVANTAGED BACKGROUNDS ("NIH Clinical Research Loan Repayment Program; CR LRP")

Assistance: project grants. (100 percent/2 years minimum).

Purposes: pursuant to PHSA as amended, for repayment of extant educational loans incurred by persons from disadvantaged backgrounds, engaged in clinical research as employees of the NIH. Payments may be made up to $35,000 per year, plus $13,650 annually for tax reimbursements.

Eligible applicants/beneficiaries: U.S. citizens, nationals, or permanent residents from disadvantaged backgrounds, with: an M.D., Ph.D., D.O., D.D.S., D.M.D., D.P.M., B.S.N., A.D.N., or equivalent degree; qualified undergraduate or graduate educational loan debt exceeding 20 percent of their NIH salary; a contract commitment of at least two years of service to NIH; no existing service obligation to federal, state, or other entities.

Range: $4,000 to $70,000; tax reimbursements, $1,977 to $34,598. **Average:** $68,454.

Activity: FY 06 estimate, 12 awards; FY 07 estimate, 12 awards.

HQ: Office of Loan Repayment and Scholarship, NIH-HHS, 6011 Executive Blvd. - Rm. 206, Bethesda, MD 20892-7650. Phone: *helpline,* (866) 849-4047, FAX (866) 849-4046.

Internet: www.lrp.nih.gov; e-mail, lrp@nih.gov (Note: no field offices for this program.)

93.223 DEVELOPMENT AND COORDINATION OF RURAL HEALTH SERVICES

Assistance: project grants. (100 percent/3 years).

Purposes: pursuant to PHSA, to develop and disseminate information to assist rural communities and rural health care organizations in developing and coordinating rural health care services—including information from federal and state agencies, workshops, conferences, research reports, recruitment efforts, and reports from national health care associations.

Eligible applicants/beneficiaries: nonprofit private organizations representing national, state, and local rural health constituencies.

Average: one award only.

Activity: FY 06, 1 continuation award.

HQ: Director, Rural Research Centers, Office of Rural Health Policy, HRSA-HHS, Parklawn Bldg. - Rm. 9A-55, 5600 Fishers Lane, Rockville,

MD 20857. Phone: (301) 443-0835. *Grants management information*: Director, Division of Grants Management, Health Resources and Services Administration, NIH-HHS, 5600 Fishers Lane - Rm. 11A-16, Rockville, MD 20857. Phone: Health Services, (301) 443-2385; Research and Training, (301) 443-3099; Government and Special Focus, (301) 443-3288.

Internet: www.hrsa.gov (Note: no field offices for this program.)

93.224 CONSOLIDATED HEALTH CENTERS (COMMUNITY HEALTH CENTERS, MIGRANT HEALTH CENTERS, HEALTH CARE FOR THE HOMELESS, PUBLIC HOUSING PRIMARY CARE, AND SCHOOL BASED HEALTH CENTERS)

Assistance: project grants (to 5 years).

Purposes: pursuant to PHSA and Health Centers Consolidation Act of 1996, to increase access to comprehensive primary and preventive health care and improve the health status of underserved and vulnerable populations, including at centers providing care through or to community, migrant, homeless, public housing, and school-based populations. Projects should improve the availability, accessibility, and organization of health care. Project funds may not be used for inpatient services or to make cash payments to service recipients.

Eligible applicants/beneficiaries: public or private nonprofit entities.

Range: $200,000 to $11,000,000.

Activity: FY 05, 13,900,000 patients served.

HQ: Director, Division of Health Center Management, Bureau of Primary Health Care, HRSA-HHS, 5600 Fishers Lane - Rm. 16C-26, Rockville, MD 20857. Phone: (301) 594-4420. *Grants management information*: Director, Division of Grants Management, Health Resources and Services Administration, NIH-HHS, 5600 Fishers Lane - Rm. 11A-16, Rockville, MD 20857. Phone: Health Services, (301) 443-2385; Research and Training, (301) 443-3099; Government and Special Focus, (301) 443-3288.

Internet: www.hrsa.gov (Note: no field offices for this program.)

93.225 NATIONAL RESEARCH SERVICE AWARDS—HEALTH SERVICES RESEARCH TRAINING

Assistance: project grants. (100 percent/3-5 years).

Purposes: pursuant to PHSA, for fellowships for full-time postdoctoral training in health services research for up to three years, and to predoctoral candidates from under-represented minority groups for up to five years—with grants to institutions providing the training (*see Notes preceding* **93.001**). Training is in health services research and research methods, epidemiology, biostatistics, geriatrics, health administration and public health, medical information sciences, health policy and management, organizational behavior, clinical outcomes and effectiveness, primary care, health care quality, health economics and financing, child health, and vulnerable populations. Postdoctoral fellowship recipients must meet service payback requirements.

Eligible applicants/beneficiaries: domestic public or private nonprofit organizations including state and local governments and territories—with existing training programs. Fellowship recipients must be U.S. citizens, noncitizen nationals, or lawful permanent residents.

Range: individuals, $32,000 to $60,000; institutions, $120,000 to $500,000. **Average:** individuals, $45,000; institutions, $250,000.

Activity: FY 06 estimate, 10 fellowships, 27 institutional grants; FY 07 estimate, 10 fellowships, 27 institutional grants.

HQ: Division of Research Education, Agency for Healthcare Research and Quality, HHS, 540 Gaither Rd., Rockville, MD 20850. Phone: (301) 427-1527, -1528; Grants Management Specialist, (301) 427-1453, -1454.

Internet: www.ahrq.gov (Note: no field offices for this program.)

93.226 RESEARCH ON HEALTHCARE COSTS, QUALITY AND OUTCOMES

Assistance: project grants. (100 percent/to 5 years).

Purposes: pursuant to PHSA as amended, for research and evaluations, demonstration projects, research networks, multidisciplinary centers, and information dissemination on health care and systems for delivery of care. Major issue categories include: quality measurement and improvement; outcomes and cost-effectiveness; clinical practice including primary and practice-oriented research; health care technologies, facilities, and equipment; costs, productivity, organization, and market forces; health promotion and disease prevention, including clinical preventive services; health statistics, surveys, data base development, epidemiology; medical liability.

Eligible applicants/beneficiaries: federal, state, local government agencies; tribal governments; territories and possessions; sponsored organizations; public or private nonprofit organizations; minority and specialized groups; IHEs; individuals; and, profit organizations for cooperative agreements.

Range: $5,000 to $2,800,000. **Average:** $310,000.

Activity: FY 06 estimate, 325 grants; FY 07 estimate, 304 grants.

HQ: Division of Research Education, Agency for Healthcare Research and Quality, HHS, 540 Gaither Rd., Rockville, MD 20850. Phone: Center for Outcomes and Evidence, (301) 427-1600; Center for Quality Improvement and Patient Safety, (301) 427-1349; Center for Primary Care, Prevention and Partnerships, (301) 427-1500; Center for Financing, Access, and Cost Trends, (301) 427-1406; Center for Delivery, Organization, and Markets, (301) 427-1410; Grants Management, (301) 427-1447.

Internet: www.ahrq.gov (Note: no field offices for this program.)

93.228 INDIAN HEALTH SERVICE—HEALTH MANAGEMENT DEVELOPMENT PROGRAM

Assistance: project grants.

Purposes: pursuant to ISDEAA, to increase the capability of American Indians and Alaska natives to operate existing IHS health care programs involving curative, preventive, and rehabilitative health services. Funds may be used for feasibility studies, planning, tribal health management structure development, evaluation.

Eligible applicants/beneficiaries: tribes and tribal organizations.

Range: management, $50,000 to $100,000; services projects, $85,000 to $185,000. **Average:** management, $79,690; services, $182,140.

Activity: FY 06 estimate, 20 new, 7 continuing tribal management project awards, 20 continuing health services awards; FY 07 estimate, 23 new, 7 continuing tribal management project awards, 20 continuing health services awards.

HQ: *management programs,* Program Analyst, Office of Tribal Programs, IHS-HHS, 801 Thompson Ave. - Ste. 120, Rockville, MD 20852. Phone: (301) 443-1104. *Health services projects, grants management information*: Grants Management Officer, Division of Grants Operations, IHS-HHS, 801 Thompson Ave. - Ste. 360, Rockville, MD 20852. Phone: (301) 443-5204.

Internet: www.ihs.gov/nonmedicalprograms/tmg/index.asp.

93.229 DEMONSTRATION COOPERATIVE AGREEMENTS FOR DEVELOPMENT AND IMPLEMENTATION OF CRIMINAL JUSTICE TREATMENT NETWORKS

Assistance: project grants. (100 percent/to 5 years).

Purposes: pursuant to PHSA as amended, for integrated criminal justice treatment networks of a consortium of criminal justice, substance abuse treatment, primary health and mental health care, and allied social services and job placement agencies involved with adult male or female offenders and juvenile justice populations. Each network must develop strategies to link existing partnerships into a comprehensive continuum of services in metropolitan areas with populations of 200,000 to 1,000,000, with the pivotal points of referral and supervision either in the courts or community probations and parole agencies.

Eligible applicants/beneficiaries: state alcohol and drug abuse agencies applying on behalf of consortia state and local officials and public and nonprofit private entities. If the state does not apply, consortia may submit applications through nonprofit entities, in coordination with state agencies.

Average: one award only.

Activity: annually, 1 award.

HQ: Division of Practice and Systems Development, CSAT-SAMHSA-HHS, 1 Choke Cherry Rd., Rockville, MD 20857. Phone: (240) 276-1576. *Grants management information*: Grants Management Officer, Office of Program Support, SAMHSA-HHS, 1 Choke Cherry Rd., Rockville, MD 20857. Phone: (240) 276-1421.

Internet: www.samhsa.gov (Note: no field offices for this program.)

93.230 CONSOLIDATED KNOWLEDGE DEVELOPMENT AND APPLICATION (KD&A) PROGRAM

Assistance: project grants. (100 percent/3 years).

Purposes: pursuant to PHSA as amended, to provide immediately usable, practical knowledge to services providers on the efficacy of substance abuse and mental health services in crucial selected areas—based on questions arising from consumers and their families, providers, and public and private agencies and organizations including at state and federal policymaking and legislative levels. Activities are undertaken in service settings. Dissemination occurs through multiple channels including technology. Specific study topics are announced annually.

Eligible applicants/beneficiaries: state and local governments; private nonprofit and profit entities such as community-based organizations, IHEs, and hospitals.

Range: $162,500 to $1,200,000. **Average:** $351,500.

Activity: N.A.

HQ: SAMHSA-HHS, 1 Choke Cherry Rd. - Rm. 7-1091, Rockville, MD 20857. Phone: CSAP, (240) 276-2447; CSAT, (240) 276-1681.

Internet: www.samhsa.gov (Note: no field offices for this program.)

93.231 EPIDEMIOLOGY COOPERATIVE AGREEMENTS

Assistance: project grants. (100 percent/to 3 years).

Purposes: pursuant to the Indian Health Care Improvement Act as amended, to develop tribal epidemiology centers and public health infrastructure to coordinate and participate in disease surveillance and prevention projects, as well as investigations and studies of national scope. Project activities include convening of meetings, technical assistance and consultation, training, site visits, coordination on a national basis.

Eligible applicants/beneficiaries: tribes; tribal, urban tribal organizations; consortia.

Range: $399,500 to $540,000. **Average:** $469,750.

Activity: FY 06 estimate, 12 projects; FY 07 estimate, 12 projects.

HQ: Division of Epidemiology, IHS Headquarters West, HHS, 5300 Homestead Rd. NE, Albuquerque, NM 87110. Phone: (505) 248-4132. *Grants management information*: Grants Management Officer, Division of Grants Operations, IHS-HHS, 801 Thompson Ave. - Ste. 360, Rockville, MD 20852. Phone: (301) 443-5204.

Internet: www.ihs.gov (Note: no field offices for this program.)

93.232 LOAN REPAYMENT PROGRAM FOR GENERAL RESEARCH ("NIH General Loan Repayment Program; GR- LRP")

Assistance: project grants. (100 percent/3 years).

Purposes: pursuant to PHSA as amended, for repayment of extant educational loans incurred by scientific professionals engaged in laboratory or clinical research as employees of the NIH for a minimum of three years.

Eligible applicants/beneficiaries: U.S. citizens, nationals, or permanent residents from disadvantaged backgrounds, with: an M.D., Ph.D., D.O., D.D.S., D.M.D., D.P.M., B.S.N., A.D.N., or equivalent degree; qualified undergraduate or graduate educational loan debt exceeding 20 percent of their NIH salary; a contract commitment of at least two years of service to NIH; no existing service obligation to federal, state, or other entities.

Range: loan repayment awards (for initial 3-year contracts), $6,000 to $105,000; tax reimbursements, $2,966 to $51,896. **Average:** $85,316, including loan and tax reimbursement.

Activity: FY 06 estimate, 91 awards; FY 07 estimate, 91 awards.

HQ: Division of Loan Repayment and Scholarship, NIH-HHS, 6011 Executive Blvd. - Rm. 206, Bethesda, MD 20892-7650. Phone: *helpline,* (866) 849-4047, FAX (866) 849-4046.

Internet: www.lrp.nih.gov; e-mail, lrp@nih.gov (Note: no field offices for this program.)

93.233 NATIONAL CENTER ON SLEEP DISORDERS RESEARCH

Assistance: project grants. (100 percent/1-5 years).

Purposes: pursuant to PHSA, for research, training, information dissemination, and other activities relating to sleep and sleep disorders, including biological and circadian rhythm research, basic understanding of sleep, chronobiological and other sleep related research; to coordinate center activities with other federal agencies and with public and nonprofit organizations. NRSA, SBIR, and STIR funding is available (*see Notes preceding* **93.001**).

Eligible applicants/beneficiaries: nonprofit and profit organizations; individuals.

Range: $85,573 to $964,467. **Average:** $350,233.

Activity: FY 06 estimate, 173 research grants, 10 NRSAs.

HQ: Director, National Center on Sleep Disorders Research, National Heart, Lung, and Blood Institute, NIH-HHS, Bethesda, MD 20892. Phone: (301) 435-0199; Administrative Office, (301) 435-6373. *Grants management information*: Grants Management Officer, Grants Operation Branch, Office of Program Policy and Procedures, National Heart, Lung and Blood Institute, NIH-HHS, Bethesda, MD 20892. Phone: (301) 435-0144.

Internet: www.nhlbi.nih.gov/sleep (Note: no field offices for this program.)

93.234 TRAUMATIC BRAIN INJURY STATE DEMONSTRATION GRANT PROGRAM ("TBI")

Assistance: project grants. (67 percent/1-3 years).

Purposes: pursuant to PHSA as amended, to improve access to health and other TBI-related service for persons of all ages and their families. Planning grants support development of four state-level core capacity components to provide TBI services. Implementation grants are for states with the four core capacity components in place. Post-demonstration grants fund activities begun during the state implementation phase.

Eligible applicants/beneficiaries: state governments.

Range: $73,465 to $200,000. **Average:** $136,318.

Activity: FY 06 estimate, 45 projects supported.

HQ: Division of Services for Children with Special Health Care Needs, Maternal and Child Health Bureau, 5600 Fishers Lane - Rm. 18A-18,

Rockville, MD 20857. Phone: (301) 443-2370. *Grants management information*: Director, Division of Grants Management, Health Resources and Services Administration-HHS, 5600 Fishers Lane - Rm. 11A-16, Rockville, MD 20857. Phone: Health Services, (301) 443-2385; Research and Training, (301) 443-3099; Government and Special Focus, (301) 443-3288.

Internet: www.hrsa.gov (Note: no field offices for this program.)

93.235 ABSTINENCE EDUCATION PROGRAM

Assistance: formula grants (57 percent).

Purposes: pursuant to SSA, Section 510, to provide abstinence education and, at state option, mentoring, counseling, and adult supervision to promote abstinence from sexual activity outside of marriage—focusing on groups most likely to bear children out of wedlock. (Note: program provisions approximate **93.010**.)

Eligible applicants/beneficiaries: governor-designated agencies.

Range: $13,501 to $7,055,240. **Average:** $847,458.

Activity: estimate, 59 grants annually.

HQ: Family and Youth Services Bureau, ACF-HHS, 1250 Maryland Ave. SW, Washington, DC 20024. Phone: (no number provided). *Grants management information*: Office of Grants Management, Division of Discretionary Grants, 370 L'Enfant Promenade SW, Washington, DC 20447. Phone: (no number provided).

Internet: www.acf.hhs.gov/programs/fysb (Note: no field offices for this program.)

93.236 GRANTS FOR DENTAL PUBLIC HEALTH RESIDENCY TRAINING

Assistance: project grants. (100 percent/3 years).

Purposes: pursuant to PHSA and HPEPA, to plan and develop new or to maintain and improve existing dental public health residency training programs; to provide financial assistance to trainees. Grants may not be used for construction or for direct patient services.

Eligible applicants/beneficiaries: public or private schools of public health or dentistry; experienced, qualified nonprofit and community-based organizations.

Range: $59,665 to $159,714. **Average:** $107,674.

Activity: FY 06 estimate, 5 new awards.

HQ: Division of Medicine and Dentistry, Bureau of Health Professions, HRSA-HHS, Parklawn Bldg. - Rm. 9A-27, 5600 Fishers Lane, Rockville, MD 20857. Phone: (301) 443-1707. *Grants management information*: Director, Division of Grants Management, Health Resources and Services Administration-HHS, 5600 Fishers Lane - Rm. 11A-16, Rockville, MD 20857. Phone: Health Services, (301) 443-2385; Research and Training, (301) 443-3099; Government and Special Focus, (301) 443-3288.

Internet: www.hrsa.gov (Note: no field offices for this program.)

93.237 SPECIAL DIABETES PROGRAM FOR INDIANS—DIABETES PREVENTION AND TREATMENT PROJECTS ("Indian Health")

Assistance: project grants. (100 percent/to 5 years).

Purposes: for primary, secondary, and tertiary diabetes prevention and treatment services and related data collection among American Indians and Alaskan natives.

Eligible applicants/beneficiaries: tribes, tribal and urban Indian organizations operating IHS health programs.

Range: non-competitive, $46,000 to $5,000,000; competitive receive one of two amounts, $324,300 or $397,100. **Average:** non-competitive, $350,350.

Activity: estimate, 330 non-competitive and 66 competitive grants annually.

HQ: Director, Diabetes Program, IHS-HHS, 5300 Homestead Rd. NE, Albuquerque, NM 87110. Phone: (505) 248-4182, FAX (505) 248-4188. *Grants management information*: Grants Management Officer, Division of Grants Operations, IHS-HHS, 801 Thompson Ave. - Ste. 360, Rockville, MD 20852. Phone: (301) 443-5204, FAX (301) 443-9602.

Internet: www.ihs.gov/medicalprograms/diabetes; www.ihs.gov/nonmedicalprograms/gogp (Note: no field offices for this program.)

93.238 COOPERATIVE AGREEMENTS FOR STATE TREATMENT OUTCOMES AND PERFORMANCE PILOT STUDIES ENHANCEMENT

Assistance: project grants. (100 percent/3 years).

Purposes: pursuant to PHSA as amended, to collect information on treatment services funded with Substance Abuse Pilot Treatment Block Grant; to monitor common substance abuse treatment effectiveness data across various state management information systems; for evaluation programs to design or enhance state management information systems or outcome management systems that examine treatment effectiveness and costs through standardized performance and outcome measures while incorporating common data measures on an interstate basis.

Eligible applicants/beneficiaries: projects—single state authorities. Technical assistance centers—domestic nonprofit and profit entities including community-based organizations, IHEs, and hospitals.

Range: $300,000 to $500,000. **Average:** $459,839.

Activity: FY 05, 1 award.

HQ: Division for State and Community Assistance, CSAT-SAMHSA-HHS, 1 Choke Cherry Rd., Rockville, MD 20857. Phone: (240) 276-2406. *Grants management information*: Grants Management Officer, Office of Program Support, SAMHSA-HHS, 1 Choke Cherry Rd. - Rm. 7-1091, Rockville, MD 20857. Phone: (240) 276-1421.

Internet: www.samhsa.gov (Note: no field offices for this program.)

93.239 POLICY RESEARCH AND EVALUATION GRANTS

Assistance: project grants (to 100 percent).

Purposes: pursuant to the Social Security Act, for research relevant to policy development and evaluation of current and proposed programs, covering: issues of long-term care, disability, and personal assistance services including informal care giving; health care delivery issues including financing; welfare reform outcomes and policies affecting children and youth; community development; science policy development; reduction of poverty.

Eligible applicants/beneficiaries: nonprofit organizations, state and local government agencies, IHEs, individuals, some profit organizations.

Range: $300,000 to $1,200,000. **Average:** $575,000.

Activity: FY 05, 4 states funded for closeout of innovation grants, funding provided for continuation of national poverty and three area poverty centers.

HQ: Grants Officer, Assistant Secretary/Planning and Evaluation, OS-HHS, HHH Bldg. - Rm. 405F, 200 Independence Ave. SW, Washington, DC 20201. Phone: (202) 690-8794.

Internet: www.aspe.hhs.gov (Note: no field offices for this program.)

93.240 STATE CAPACITY BUILDING ("Site Specific Activities Cooperative Agreement Program")

Assistance: project grants. (100 percent/3-5 years).

Purposes: pursuant to CERCLA, SARA, and RCRA as amended, for public health agency capacity building in coordination with the Agency for Toxic Substances and Disease Registry, to conduct: health consultations; public health assessments; exposure investigations; community involvement; health education; public health studies.

Eligible applicants/beneficiaries: state public health agencies including possessions and territories, tribal governments.

Range: $150,627 to $700,000. **Average:** $350,000.

Activity: FY 05 estimate, 33 continuation awards.

HQ: Funding Resource Specialist, Office of Financial and Administrative Services, Agency for Toxic Substances and Disease Registry, (E-28), CDCP-HHS, 1600 Clifton Rd. NE, Atlanta, GA 30333. Phone: (404) 498-0624, FAX (404) 498-0059. *Grants management information*: Grants Management Officer, Procurement and Grants Office, CDC-HHS, 2920 Brandywine Rd. - Rm. 3000, Atlanta, GA 30341. Phone: (770) 488-2745, FAX: (770) 488-2777.

Internet: www.atsdr.cdc.gov (Note: no field offices for this program.)

93.241 STATE RURAL HOSPITAL FLEXIBILITY PROGRAM

Assistance: project grants.

Purposes: for states to work with rural communities and hospitals to develop and implement rural health plans and integrated care networks, to improve emergency medical services, and to designate critical access hospitals.

Eligible applicants/beneficiaries: states with rural health plans already submitted to the Centers for Medicare and Medicaid Services (CMS). Other states submit applications to CMS regional offices.

Range: $200,000 to $650,000. **Average:** $484,977.

Activity: annually, 45 continuation awards.

HQ: Health Systems Advisor, Office of Rural Health Policy, 5600 Fishers Lane - Rm. 9A-55, Rockville, MD 20857. Phone: (301) 443-0835. *Grants management information*: Director, Division of Grants Management, Health Resources and Services Administration-HHS, 5600 Fishers Lane - Rm. 11A-16, Rockville, MD 20857. Phone: Health Services, (301) 443-2385; Research and Training, (301) 443-3099; Government and Special Focus, (301) 443-3288.

Internet: www.hrsa.gov (Note: no field offices for this program.)

93.242 MENTAL HEALTH RESEARCH GRANTS

Assistance: project grants. (100 percent/to 5 years).

Purposes: pursuant to PHSA as amended and SBRDEA, for research on basic brain and behavioral processes underlying mental and behavioral disorders and mental health—employing theoretical, laboratory, clinical, methodological, and field studies involving clinical, subclinical, and normal subjects and populations of all age ranges, as well as animal, computational, and mathematical models. Areas eligible for support include HIV/AIDS behavior, neurosciences including molecular genetics, behavioral sciences, epidemiology, clinical assessment, etiology, treatment, prevention, and services. Grants support clearly defined projects or small groups of related research activities, and research conferences. Program Project and Center grants support large- scale, broad-based interdisciplinary research programs. Small grants (to $50,000 for two years) support small-scale exploratory and pilot studies or exploration of an unusual research opportunity. SBIR and STTR awards are made (*see Notes preceding* **93.001**).

Eligible applicants/beneficiaries: public, private, profit, or nonprofit agencies including state and local governments, federal agencies, IHEs, hospitals, academic or research institutions.

Range: $25,234 to $2,930,750. **Average:** $385,976.

Activity: FY 06 estimate, 2,491 grants; FY 07 estimate, 2500 grants.

HQ: NIMH, NIH-HHS, 6001 Executive Blvd., Bethesda, MD 20892. Phone: (301) 443-9700; *Grants management information*: Grants Management Officer, NIMH, NIH-HHS, 6001 Executive Blvd. - Rm.6115, Bethesda, MD 20892-9605. Phone: (301) 443-2811.

Internet: www.nih.gov (Note: no field offices for this program.)

93.243 SUBSTANCE ABUSE AND MENTAL HEALTH SERVICES—PROJECTS OF REGIONAL AND NATIONAL SIGNIFICANCE ("PRNS")

Assistance: project grants. (100 percent/1-5 years).

Purposes: pursuant to PHSA as amended and Children's Health Act of 2000, to address priority substance abuse treatment, prevention, and mental health needs of regional and national significance, through grants and cooperative agreements for: knowledge, development, and application projects for treatment and rehabilitation, and their evaluation; training and technical assistance; targeted capacity response programs; systems change, including projects involving statewide family networks and client-oriented and consumer-run self-help activities; programs to foster child health and development.

Eligible applicants/beneficiaries: state and local governments; private non-profit and profit entities such as community-based organizations, IHEs, and hospitals.

Average: $1,083,333.

Activity: FY 05-06 estimate, 600 grants.

HQ: SAMHSA-HHS, 1 Choke Cherry Rd. - Rm. 7-1091, Rockville, MD 20857. Phone: CSAP, (240) 276-2447; CSAT, (240) 276-1681; CMHS, (240) 276-1824. *Grants management information*: Division of Grants Management, SAMHSA, 1 Choke Cherry Rd., Rockville, MD 20857. Phone: (240) 276-1400.

Internet: www.samhsa.gov (Note: no field offices for this program.)

93.244 MENTAL HEALTH CLINICAL AND AIDS SERVICE-RELATED TRAINING GRANTS

Assistance: project grants. (100 percent/to 5 years).

Purposes: pursuant to PHSA as amended, for training programs in the mental health professions, including administrative costs, trainee stipends, and other allowances to trainees—with payback agreements required in some instances. Specific program objectives are to increase the number of qualified minority personnel in the field, and the number of mental health personnel trained to deal with the special problems of children, adolescents, the elderly, the seriously mentally ill, and rural populations. Eligible disciplines include: psychiatry, psychology, social work, psychiatric nursing, and marriage and family therapy. Awards may be made to faculty scholars and for state human resource development.

Eligible applicants: public or private nonprofit institutions and organizations, state and local government agencies.

Eligible beneficiaries: U.S. citizens, nationals, lawful permanent residents.

Range: $225,000 to $300,000. **Average:** $250,000.

Activity: FY 05, 6 awards.

HQ: Human Resource Planning and Development Branch, CMHS-SAMHSA- HHS, 1 Choke Cherry Rd., Rockville, MD 20857. Phone: General,(240) 276-1387; HIV/AIDS Program, (240) 276-1962. *Grants management information*: Grants Management Officer, SAMHSA-HHS, 1 Choke Cherry Rd., Rockville, MD 20857. Phone: (240) 276-1421.

Internet: www.samhsa.gov (Note: no field offices for this program.)

93.247 ADVANCED EDUCATION NURSING GRANT PROGRAM

Assistance: project grants. (100 percent/3 years).

Purposes: pursuant to PHSA as amended and HPEPA, to enhance advanced nursing education and practice including: master's and doctoral programs; combined RN and master's degree programs; post-nursing master's certificate programs; or, for nurse midwives, in certificate programs existing on 12 November 1998, to serve as nurse practitioners, clinical nurse specialist, nurse midwives, nurse administrators, public health nurses, or other specialties.

Eligible applicants/beneficiaries: schools of nursing, academic health centers; other public or private nonprofit or profit entities including community-based organizations.

Range: $90,000 to $450,516. **Average:** $250,000.

Activity: FY 05, 43 new, 114 continuation awards.

HQ: Division of Nursing, Bureau of Health Professions, HRSA-HHS, Parklawn Bldg. - Rm. 9-36, 5600 Fishers Lane, Rockville, MD 20857. Phone: (301) 443-6333. *Grants management information*: Director, Division of Grants Management, Health Resources and Services Administration-HHS, 5600 Fishers Lane - Rm. 11A-16, Rockville, MD 20857. Phone: Health Services, (301) 443-2385; Research and Training, (301) 443-3099; Government and Special Focus, (301) 443-3288.

Internet: www.hrsa.gov (Note: no field offices for this program.)

93.249 PUBLIC HEALTH TRAINING CENTERS GRANT PROGRAM

Assistance: project grants. (100 percent/5 years).

Purposes: pursuant to PHSA as amended and HPEPA, for graduate- level and specialized public health educational programs to strengthen the technical, scientific, managerial, and leadership competencies of the current and future public health work force—particularly with respect to providing health care services to medically underserved populations including such groups as the elderly, immigrants, refugees, and the disadvantaged. Centers must: designate specific geographic service areas in a location removed from the main teaching facilities; assess personnel needs of such areas and design programs to meet those needs; establish or strengthen field placements for students; involve faculty members and students in collaborative projects to enhance services. Project funds may not be used for student stipends, construction, or patient services.

Eligible applicants/beneficiaries: accredited schools of public health and other public or private nonprofit institutions.

Range: $200,000 to $400,000. **Average:** $303,000.

Activity: FY 05, 14 public health training centers funded.

HQ: Public Health Advisor, Division of Community, State and Public Health, Bureau of Health Professionals, Heath Resources and Services Administration, 5600 Fishers Lane - Rm. 8A-17, Rockville, MD 20857. Phone: (301) 443-6864. *Grants management information*: Director, Division of Grants Management, Health Resources and Services Administration-HHS, 5600 Fishers Lane - Rm. 11A-16, Rockville, MD 20857. Phone: Health Services, (301) 443-2385; Research and Training, (301) 443-3099; Government and Special Focus, (301) 443-3288.

Internet: www.hrsa.gov (Note: no field offices for this program.)

93.250 GERIATRIC ACADEMIC CAREER AWARDS

Assistance: direct payments/specified use. (100 percent/5 years).

Purposes: pursuant to PHSA as amended and HPEPA, to provide financial incentives for junior faculty at schools of allopathic and osteopathic medicine to pursue academic careers in geriatrics.

Eligible applicants/beneficiaries: junior faculty members of accredited schools of allopathic and osteopathic medicine who: are board-certified or -eligible in internal medicine, family practice, or psychiatry; have completed geriatrics fellowship programs; are U.S. citizens, nationals, or lawful permanent residents.

Average: $59,658.

Activity: FY 05, 12 new, 92 continuation awards.

HQ: Division of State, Community, and Public Health, Bureau of Health Professions, HRSA-HHS, Parklawn Bldg. - Rm. 8-05, 5600 Fishers Lane, Rockville, MD 20857. Phone: (301) 443-5794. *Grants management information*: Director, Division of Grants Management, Health Resources and Services Administration, NIH-HHS, 5600 Fishers Lane - Rm. 11A-16, Rockville, MD 20857. Phone: Health Services, (301) 443-2385; Research and Training, (301) 443-3099; Government and Special Focus, (301) 443-3288.

Internet: www.hrsa.gov (Note: no field offices for this program.)

93.251 UNIVERSAL NEWBORN HEARING SCREENING

Assistance: project grants. (100 percent/3-5 years).

Purposes: pursuant to PHSA, to implement universal newborn child hearing screening prior to hospital discharge with linkage to a medical home, and diagnostic evaluation and enrollment in a program of early intervention.

Eligible applicants/beneficiaries: states; one technical assistance organization.

Range: $101,615 to $150,000. **Average:** $125,000.

Activity: FY 06 estimate, 1 new, 51 continuation state projects; 1 continuation technical assistance grant.

HQ: Integrated Services Branch, Division of Services for Children with Special Needs, Maternal and Child Health Bureau, HRSA-HHS, 5600 Fishers Lane - Rm. 18A-18, Rockville, MD 20857. Phone: (301) 443-9023. *Grants management information*: Director, Division of Grants Management, Health Resources and Services Administration, NIH-HHS, 5600 Fishers Lane - Rm. 11A-16, Rockville, MD 20857. Phone: Health Services, (301) 443-2385; Research and Training, (301) 443-3099; Government and Special Focus, (301) 443-3288.

Internet: www.hrsa.gov (Note: no field offices for this program.)

93.252 HEALTHY COMMUNITIES ACCESS PROGRAM

Assistance: project grants. (100 percent/to 3 years).

Purposes: pursuant to PHSA, for communities and consortia of health care providers to develop or strengthen integrated health care systems that coordinate health services for the uninsured or under-insured, including those with chronic conditions. Grants may support activities directly providing or ensuring the provision of primary, secondary, and tertiary services, as well as substance abuse treatment and mental health services. A maximum of 15 percent of granted funds may be used to provide direct patient care and services, including reimbursable services, supplies, capital equipment. Grants funds may not be used for construction or reserve requirements for state licensure.

Eligible applicants/beneficiaries: consortia or networks of community-wide health care providers, including local and tribal governments, hospitals, medical and dental societies, foundations, and community-based nonprofit organizations.

Range: $355,000 to $1,200,000.

Activity: FY 05, 104 grants; no grants will be funded in FY 06 or FY 07.

HQ: Health Center Infrastructure Branch, Division of Health Center Development, Bureau of Primary Health Care, HRSA-HHS, 5600 Fishers Lane, Rockville, MD 20857. Phone: (301) 594-4300. *Grants management information*: Director, Division of Grants Management, Health Resources and Services Administration, NIH-HHS, 5600 Fishers Lane - Rm. 11A-16, Rockville, MD 20857. Phone: Health Services, (301) 443-2385; Research and Training, (301) 443-3099; Government and Special Focus, (301) 443-3288.

Internet: www.hrsa.gov (Note: no field offices for this program.)

93.253 POISON CONTROL STABILIZATION AND ENHANCEMENT GRANTS ("Poison Control Centers; PCC")

Assistance: project grants.

Purposes: pursuant to the Poison Control Center Enhancement and Awareness Act, Amendments of 2003, to strengthen poisoning prevention and treatment programs and services; to enable non- certified or new centers to obtain certification; to create collaborative approaches among PCCs and with other health entities; to expand access to services. Previous projects also have established a toll-free phone number and nationwide media campaign, developed uniform patient management guidelines.

Eligible applicants/beneficiaries: state-designated poison control centers.

Range: $30,000 to $2,100,000. **Average:** $300,000.

Activity: FY 05-06 estimate, 69 grants.

HQ: Poison Control Program, Healthcare Systems Bureau, HRSA-HHS, 5600 Fishers Lane - Rm. 13-103, Rockville MD 20857. Phone: (301) 443-6192. *Grants management information*: Director, Division of Grants Management, Health Resources and Services Administration, NIH-HHS, 5600 Fishers Lane - Rm. 11A-16, Rockville, MD 20857. Phone: Health Services, (301) 443-2385; Research and Training, (301) 443-3099; Government and Special Focus, (301) 443-3288.

Internet: www.hrsa.gov (Note: no field offices for this program.)

93.254 INFANT ADOPTION AWARENESS TRAINING ("IAATP")

Assistance: project grants. (100 percent/1-3 years).

Purposes: pursuant to PHSA and Children's Health Act of 2000, to develop and implement programs to train designated health center staff in providing adoption information and referrals to pregnant women on an equal basis, with all other courses of action included in nondirective counseling.

Eligible applicants/beneficiaries: private nonprofit national, regional, or local organizations whose primary purposes are adoption.

Range: $400,000 to $6,000,000. **Average:** $600,000.

Activity: FY 05, 6 awards.

HQ: Administration on Children, Youth, and Families, Children's Bureau, 1250 Maryland Ave. SW - Rm. 8354, Washington, DC 20024. Phone: (202) 205-8060, FAX (202) 401-5917.

Internet: www.acf.hhs.gov/programs/cb (Note: no field offices for this program.)

93.255 CHILDREN'S HOSPITALS GRADUATE MEDICAL EDUCATION PAYMENT ("CHGME Payment Program")

Assistance: direct payments/specified use.

Purposes: pursuant to SSA, PHSA as amended, Children's Health Act of 2000, and Healthcare Research and Quality Act of 1999, to operate graduate medical residency programs in pediatrics and other specialties at children's teaching hospitals—to help offset the disparity in funding levels versus other types of federally supported teaching hospitals.

Eligible applicants/beneficiaries: public or private nonprofit and profit children's teaching hospitals with accredited residency training programs, with a Medicare provider agreement in effect and excluded from the Medicare Inpatient Prospective Payment system.

Range: $6,335 to $21,115,646.44. **Average:** $4,806,820,90.

Activity: FY 06, 61 hospitals funded.

HQ: Division of Medicine and Dentistry, Bureau of Health Professions, HRSA-HHS, 5600 Fishers Lane - Rm. 9A-27, Rockville, MD 20857. Phone: (301) 443-6190. *Grants management information*: Director, Division of Grants Management, Health Resources and Services Administration, NIH-HHS, 5600 Fishers Lane - Rm. 11A-16, Rockville, MD 20857. Phone: Health Services, (301) 443-2385; Research and Training, (301) 443-3099; Government and Special Focus, (301) 443-3288.

Internet: www.hrsa.gov (Note: no field offices for this program.)

93.256 STATE PLANNING GRANTS HEALTH CARE ACCESS FOR THE UNINSURED

Assistance: project grants.

Purposes: for states to develop plans to provide access to health insurance coverage for all citizens. Plans must set forth proposed programs that are similar in scope to the Federal Employees Health Benefit Plan, Medicaid, state employee plans, or similar plans.

Eligible applicants/beneficiaries: governor-designated agencies or individuals, including in territories, that have not previously a state planning grant.

Range/Average: N.A.

Activity: FY 05, SPG grants awarded to 52 states, territories and DC; FY 06, no funding anticipated.

HQ: Director, State Planning Grants Program, Healthcare Systems Bureau, HRSA-HHS, 5600 Fishers Lane - Rm. 11C-26, Rockville, MD 20857. Phone: (301) 443-0938, FAX (301) 443-8196. *Grants management information*: Director, Division of Grants Management, Health Resources and Services Administration, NIH-HHS, 5600 Fishers Lane - Rm. 11A-16, Rockville, MD 20857. Phone: Health Services, (301) 443-2385; Research and Training, (301) 443-3099; Government and Special Focus, (301) 443-3288.

Internet: www.hrsa.gov (Note: no field offices for this program.)

93.257 GRANTS FOR EDUCATION, PREVENTION, AND EARLY DETECTION OF RADIOGENIC CANCERS AND DISEASES ("Radiation Exposure Screening and Education Program")

Assistance: project grants.

Purposes: pursuant to PHSA, for new or expanded programs to: screen individuals, as described in the Radiation Exposure Compensation Act, for cancer as a preventative health measure; provide referrals for medical treatment and provide follow-up services; develop and disseminate public information and education for the detection, prevention, and treatment of radiogenic cancers and diseases; facilitate putative applicants in the documentation of claims under the Radiation Exposure Compensation Act. Project funds may not support inpatient services or cash payments to patients.

Eligible applicants/beneficiaries: within states with uranium mines or mills or involved in uranium transport (Arizona, Colorado, Idaho, New Mexico, North Dakota, Oregon, South Dakota, Texas, Utah, Washington, and Wyoming)—cancer centers designated by the National Cancer Institute, DVA health facilities, federally qualified health centers, state or local agencies currently providing health care services, IHS health care facilities, nonprofit organizations.

Average: $300,000.

Activity: FY 06 estimate, 7 grants; FY 07 estimate, 7 grants.

HQ: Director, Division of Health Center Management, Bureau of Primary Health Care, HRSA-HHS, 5600 Fishers Lane - Rm. 16C-26, Rockville, MD 20857. Phone: (301) 594-4420. *Grants management information*: Director, Division of Grants Management, Health Resources and Services Administration, NIH-HHS, 5600 Fishers Lane - Rm. 11A-16, Rockville,

MD 20857. Phone: Health Services, (301) 443-2385; Research and Training, (301) 443-3099; Government and Special Focus, (301) 443-3288.

Internet: www.hrsa.gov (Note: no field offices for this program.)

93.259 RURAL ACCESS TO EMERGENCY DEVICES GRANT ("RAED")

Assistance: project grants.

Purposes: pursuant to the Cardiac Arrest Survival Act of 2000, for state community partnerships to purchase Access to Emergency Devices (AEDs) and to obtain training on their use. Funds may also support: medical dispatcher training addressing the use of AEDs for the lay person until arrival of EMS personnel; maintenance costs; data reporting costs.

Eligible applicants/beneficiaries: rural community partnerships including first response entities (e.g., fire, EMS, police), profit and nonprofit entities, statewide or regional offices.

Range: $50,000 to $300,000.

Activity: FY 06 estimate, 49 continuation awards.

HQ: Office of Rural Health Policy, HRSA-HHS, Parklawn Bldg. - Rm. 9A-55, 5600 Fishers Lane, Rockville, MD 20857. Phone: (301) 443-0246. *Grants management information*: Director, Division of Grants Management, Health Resources and Services Administration, NIH-HHS, 5600 Fishers Lane - Rm. 11A-16, Rockville, MD 20857. Phone: Health Services, (301) 443-2385; Research and Training, (301) 443-3099; Government and Special Focus, (301) 443-3288.

Internet: www.hrsa.gov (Note: no field offices for this program.)

93.260 FAMILY PLANNING—PERSONNEL TRAINING

Assistance: project grants. (100 percent/to 3-5 years).

Purposes: pursuant to PHSA and the Family Planning Services and Population Research Act of 1970 as amended, to train paramedical and paraprofessional personnel in family planning services, particularly in rural areas. Programs where abortion as a method of family planning are ineligible for assistance.

Eligible applicants/beneficiaries: city, county, local, regional, or state governments and private nonprofit entities in states, territories, and possessions.

Range: $238,000 to $472,000. **Average:** $355,000.

Activity: FY 07 estimate, 11 grants.

HQ: Director, Office of Family Planning, Office of Population Affairs, HHS, 1101 Wootton Pkwy. - Ste. 700, Rockville, MD 20852. Phone: (240) 453-2888. *Grants management information*: Director, Office of Grants Management, Office of Public Health and Science, HHS, 1101 Wootton Pkwy. - Ste. 550, Rockville, MD 20853. Phone: (240) 453-8822.

Internet: www.opa.osophs.dhhs.gov (Note: no field offices for this program.)

93.262 OCCUPATIONAL SAFETY AND HEALTH PROGRAM

Assistance: project grants. (100 percent/1-5 years).

Purposes: pursuant to PHSA as amended and Occupational Safety and Health Act of 1970, for research in occupational disease and injury prevention, including projects involving new or improved procedures, methods, techniques, or systems; to train specialized professional and paraprofessional personnel in occupational medicine, nursing, safety, and in industrial hygiene and occupational safety. Grants may be used for: educational resource centers to provide primarily graduate multidisciplinary training; long-term training programs for undergraduate, graduate, technical, or professional trainees. SBIR awards are made (*see Notes preceding* **93.001**).

Eligible applicants/beneficiaries: domestic and foreign public or private profit and nonprofit organizations; federal, state, local, tribal governments agencies; IHEs; research institutions; hospitals; individuals, with special encouragement to apply to women, minorities, and persons with disabilities.

Range: research, $50,000 to $5,000,000; training, $28,000 to $1,500,000.

Activity: FY 06 estimate, 250 grants.

HQ: Office of Extramural Programs, NIOSH (E74), CDCP-HHS, 1600 Clifton Rd. NE, Atlanta, GA 30333. Phone: (404) 498-2530. *Grants management information*: Grants Management Specialist, Acquisition and Assistance Field Branch, CDC Procurement and Grants Office, 626 Cochrans Mill Rd., P.O. Box 18070, Pittsburg, PA 15236. Phone: (412) 386-6826.

Internet: www.cdc.gov/niosh/oep (Note: no field offices for this program.)

93.264 NURSE FACULTY LOAN PROGRAM ("NFLP")

Assistance: direct loans. (90 percent/1 year).

Purposes: pursuant to PHSA as amended and Nurse Reinvestment Act of 2002, for schools of nursing to capitalize student loan funds to increase the number of nursing faculty. The program provides up to 90 percent funding for such funds; in turn, schools may award loans of to $30,000 per academic year to students, or the amount of the student's financial need. Loan cancellation ensues for students completing a four-year employment service requirement as nursing faculty, up to 85 percent of the total principal and interest.

Eligible applicants: public and private nonprofit and profit schools of nursing offering full-time advanced degree programs.

Eligible beneficiaries: full-time, graduate nursing students that are U.S. citizens, nationals, or lawful permanent residents.

Range: $13,834 to $392,952. **Average:** $70,029.

Activity: FY 04-05 (academic period), 349 loans, 92 agreements with nursing schools.

HQ: Division of Nursing, Bureau of Health Professions, HRSA-HHS, Parklawn Bldg. - Rm. 9-36, 5600 Fishers Lane, Rockville, MD 20857. Phone:

(301) 443-1399, FAX (301) 443-0791. *Grants management information*: Director, Division of Grants Management, Health Resources and Services Administration-HHS, 5600 Fishers Lane - Rm. 11A-16, Rockville, MD 20857. Phone: Health Services, (301) 443-2385; Research and Training, (301) 443-3099; Government and Special Focus, (301) 443-3288.

Internet: www.hrsa.gov (Note: no field offices for this program.)

93.265 COMPREHENSIVE GERIATRIC EDUCATION PROGRAM ("CGEP")

Assistance: project grants. (100 percent/3 years).

Purposes: pursuant to PHSA as amended and Nurse Reinvestment Act of 2002, for programs to train and educate nursing personnel in providing geriatric care. Funds may support student and faculty training programs, curriculum development, continuing education, salaries, travel costs, supplies, and equipment.

Eligible applicants/beneficiaries: schools of nursing, academic health centers, health care facilities, programs leading to certified nurse assistant, partnerships, and other public or private nonprofit and profit entities.

Range: $58,000 to $216,000. **Average:** $157,000.

Activity: FY 05, 17 continuation awards, 11 new awards.

HQ: Division of Nursing, Bureau of Health Professions, HRSA-HHS, Parklawn Bldg. - Rm. 9-36, 5600 Fishers Lane, Rockville, MD 20857. Phone: (301) 443-6333. *Grants management information*: Director, Division of Grants Management, Health Resources and Services Administration-HHS, 5600 Fishers Lane - Rm. 11A-16, Rockville, MD 20857. Phone: Health Services, (301) 443-2385; Research and Training, (301) 443-3099; Government and Special Focus, (301) 443-3288.

Internet: www.hrsa.gov (Note: no field offices for this program.)

93.266 RAPID EXPANSION OF ANTIRETROVIRAL THERAPY PROGRAMS FOR HIV-INFECTED PERSONS IN SELECTED COUNTRIES IN AFRICA AND THE CARIBBEAN UNDER THE PRESIDENT'S EMERGENCY PLAN FOR AIDS RELIEF ("Global AIDS")

Assistance: project grants. (100 percent/1-5 years).

Purposes: pursuant to PHSA as amended and United States Leadership Against HIV/AIDS, Tuberculosis and Malaria Act of 2003, to rapidly expand antiretroviral therapy ("ART") to low-income HIV-infected persons in the 15 countries targeted under the President's Emergency Plan for AIDS Relief (PEDFAR); to develop sustainable indigenous capacity to continue such programs after projects end.

Eligible applicants/beneficiaries: organizations with three years experience in providing ART in three or more of the targeted countries.

Range: $20,000,000 to $50,100,000. **Average:** $25,000,000.

Activity: new program in FY 04; 2 awards.

HQ: Global Program, HIV/AIDS Bureau, HRSA-HHS, 5600 Fishers Lane - Ste. 7-05, Rockville, MD 20857. Phone: (301) 443-1993. *Grants management information*: Director, Division of Grants Management, Health Resources and Services Administration-HHS, 5600 Fishers Lane - Rm. 11A-16, Rockville, MD 20857. Phone: Health Services, (301) 443-2385; Research and Training, (301) 443-3099; Government and Special Focus, (301) 443-3288.

Internet: www.hrsa.gov (Note: no field offices for this program.)

93.267 STATE GRANTS FOR PROTECTION AND ADVOCACY SERVICES

Assistance: formula grants. (100 percent/2 years).

Purposes: pursuant to PHSA as amended, for state protection and advocacy systems to provide outreach and services to individuals with traumatic brain injury, including: information, referrals, and advice; individual and family advocacy; legal representation; specific assistance in self-advocacy.

Eligible applicants/beneficiaries: state protection and advocacy systems including in territories.

Range: $20,000 to $124,221. **Average:** $52,632.

Activity: annually, 57 awards.

HQ: Program Officer, Protection and Advocacy for Traumatic Brain Injury Program, Division of Services for Children with Special Healthcare Needs, 5600 Fishers Lane - Rm. 18A-18, Rockville, MD 20857. Phone: (301) 443-2370. *Grants management information*: Director, Division of Grants Management, Health Resources and Services Administration-HHS, 5600 Fishers Lane - Rm. 11A-16, Rockville, MD 20857. Phone: Health Services, (301) 443-2385; Research and Training, (301) 443-3099; Government and Special Focus, (301) 443-3288.

Internet: www.hrsa.gov (Note: no field offices for this program.)

93.268 IMMUNIZATION GRANTS ("Section 301 and 317, Public Health Service Act; Immunization Program Section 1928 of the Social Security Act; Vaccines for Children Program")

Assistance: project grants (to 100 percent).

Purposes: pursuant to PHSA as amended, Health Services and Centers Amendments of 1978, Preventive Health Amendments of 1984, and SSA, to plan, organize, and conduct immunization programs for the control of vaccine-preventable diseases; to purchase, store, supply, and deliver vaccine; for assessment, surveillance, outbreak control, information and education, and volunteer activities; compliance with compulsory school immunization laws. Vaccine purchased with grant funds may be given to private practitioners but may not be sold to patients.

Eligible applicants/beneficiaries: states and, in consultation with state health authorities, political subdivisions and other public entities.

Range: Section 317 grants, $167,222 to $41,918,911; VFC grants, $248,440 to $153,808,159. **Average:** Section 317 grants, $6,362,486; VFC grants, $16,299,866.

Activity: annually, 64 Section 317 grants, 61 VFC grants.

HQ: Director, Immunization Services Division, CDCP-HHS, 1600 Clifton Rd. NE, Atlanta, GA 30333. Phone: (404) 639-8208, FAX (404) 639-8627. *Grants management information*: Grants Management Specialist, Procurement and Grants Office, CDCP-HHS, 2920 Brandywine Rd. - Rm. 3623, Atlanta, GA 30341. Phone: (770) 488-2738.

Internet: www.cdc.gov (Note: no field offices for this program.)

93.269 COMPLEX HUMANITARIAN EMERGENCY AND WAR-RELATED INJURY PUBLIC HEALTH ACTIVITIES

Assistance: project grants (100 percent/to 5 years).

Purposes: pursuant to the Public Health Service Act, to bring public health and epidemiologic principles to the aid of populations affected by complex humanitarian emergencies and war-related injuries. Grants and cooperative agreements may be used for personnel, salaries, consultant costs, survey costs, training, equipment, supplies, travel, patient costs, miscellaneous items, and indirect costs.

Eligible applicants: only Landmine Survivors Network may apply for non-research activities supported by the CDC.

Eligible beneficiaries: general public.

Range: FY 09 estimated, $50,000 to $250,000.

Activity: FY 04 through FY 08, CDC provided: a technical advisor to UNICEF to oversee and complete measles vaccination of more than 2 million children in Southern Sudan; technical assistance to UNICEF and other global partners for the annual emergency food security and nutrition assessment in Darfur of over 4.1 million affected persons; surveillance data on injury collected in post-conflict areas of 11 countries.

HQ: International Emergency and Refugee Health Branch, CDCP-HHS, 1600 Clifton Rd. NE, Atlanta, GA 30341-3717. Phone: (770) 488-0683, Grants management information: Grants Management Specialist, Procurement and Grants Office, CDCP-HHS, 2920 Brandywine Rd., MS K75, Atlanta, GA 30341. Phone: (770) 488-8382.

Internet: www.cdc.gov. (Note: no field offices for this program.)

93.270 ADULT VIRAL HEPATITIS PREVENTION AND CONTROL

Assistance: project grants (to 5 years).

Purposes: pursuant to the Public Health Service Act, to assist State and local health agencies, health related organizations and other governmental and nongovernmental organizations in their efforts to decrease the incidence of new infections of hepatitis A, hepatitis B and hepatitis C viruses and to decrease risks for chronic liver disease including cirrhosis and liver cancer in persons with chronic hepatitis B and hepatitis C infections.

Eligible applicants: local health agencies and other governmental and non-governmental health-related organizations in the states, DC, and territories.

Eligible beneficiaries: general public.

Range/Average: $50,000 to $100,000.

Activity: FY 08, 62 awards for hepatitis prevention; 7 awards for surveillance activities.

HQ: National Center for HIV, Viral Hepatitis, STD, TB Prevention, CDC-HHS,1600 Clifton Road, NE, Mailstop G-37, Atlanta, GA 30333. Phone: (404) 718-8540. Grants Management Officer, Grants Management Branch, Procurement and Grants Office, CDC, 8 Corporate Square, Room 1044-MS E15, Atlanta, GA 30329. Phone: (404) 639-8864.

Internet: www.cdc.gov. (Note: no field offices for this program.)

93.271 ALCOHOL RESEARCH CAREER DEVELOPMENT AWARDS FOR SCIENTISTS AND CLINICIANS ("Research Career ("K") Awards")

Assistance: project grants. (100 percent/5 years).

Purposes: pursuant to PHSA as amended, for research training related to alcohol abuse and alcoholism prevention, treatment, and rehabilitation. Funds may support five-year fellowships and some research costs, including work by senior investigators. Programs include Mentored Research Scientist Development, Mentored Clinical Scientist Development, Independent Scientist, Mentored Patient-Oriented Career Development, Mid-career Investigator in Patient Oriented Research, Mentored Quantitative Research Career Development, Senior Scientist, and Academic Career Awards.

Eligible applicants/beneficiaries: research centers, medical schools, departments of psychiatry, nonmedical academic departments, psychiatric hospitals or hospitals with psychiatric services, community mental health centers, biomedical research institutes, and departments of behavioral science. Researchers must have scholastic degree and previous training, and they must be U.S. citizens, nationals, or lawful permanent residents.

Range: $92,000 to $259,000. **Average:** $133,000.

Activity: FY 06 estimate, 94 awards.

HQ: NIAAA, NIH-HHS, 5635 Fishers Lane, Bethesda, MD 20892-9304. Phone: Division of Metabolism and Health Effects, (301) 443-0799; Division of Treatment and Recovery, (301) 443-1208; Division of Epidemiology and Prevention Research, (301) 443-1274; Division of Neuroscience and Behavior, (301) 443-7722. *Grants management information*: Grants Management Officer, NIAAA, NIH-HHS, 5635 Fishers Lane - Rm. 3023, Bethesda, MD 20892-9304. Phone: (301) 443-4704.

Internet: www.nih.gov (Note: no field offices for this program.)

93.272 ALCOHOL NATIONAL RESEARCH SERVICE AWARDS FOR RESEARCH TRAINING ("NRSA Program")

Assistance: project grants. (100 percent/to 6 years).

Purposes: pursuant to PHSA as amended, for NRSA programs providing training in clinical research, treatment assessment research, problems of health promotion and alcoholism prevention, and basic biological and behavioral processes (*see Notes preceding* **93.001**). Individual grants may cover up to five years for predoctoral or up to three years of postdoctoral full- time research training; M.D. and Ph.D. fellowships are for up to 6 years; senior fellowships are for up to two years. Special predoctoral fellowships are available for students with disabilities and for minority students. Postdoctoral recipients must meet payback requirements through a period of research and/or teaching after training is completed.

Eligible applicants/beneficiaries: domestic public or private nonprofit organizations. Predoctoral applicants must be enrolled in a doctoral degree program. Postdoctoral applicants must have a doctoral degree. Awardees must be U.S. citizens, nationals, or lawful permanent residents.

Range: $16,000 to $542,000. **Average:** $113,000.

Activity: FY 06 estimate, 55 fellowship, 30 institutional grants.

HQ: NIAAA, NIH-HHS, 5635 Fishers Lane, Bethesda, MD 20892-9304. Phone: Division of Metabolism and Health Effects, (301) 443-0799; Division of Treatment and Recovery, (301) 402-4344; Division of Epidemiology and Prevention Research, (301) 443-1274; Division of Neuroscience and Behavior, (301) 443-7722. *Grants management information*: Grants Management Officer, NIAAA, NIH-HHS, 5635 Fishers Lane - Rm. 3023, Bethesda, MD 20892-9304. Phone: (301) 443-4704.

Internet: www.nih.gov (Note: no field offices for this program.)

93.273 ALCOHOL RESEARCH PROGRAMS

Assistance: project grants. (100 percent/to 5 years).

Purposes: pursuant to PHSA as amended and SBRDEA, for research on alcoholism and alcohol-related problems in such disciplines and subject areas as biomedical and genetic factors, psychological and environmental factors, medical disorders, health services, and prevention and treatment. Research Project Grants support clearly defined projects or small groups of related research activities, and research conferences. Program Project grants support large-scale, broad-based interdisciplinary research programs. Small Grants, limited to $50,000 for up to two years, are for small-scale exploratory and pilot studies or exploration of an unusual research opportunity. Exploratory/Developmental Grants are for a maximum of $275,000 total for up to two years. SBIR and STTR awards are available (*see Notes preceding* **93.001**).

Eligible applicants/beneficiaries: public, private profit and nonprofit agencies including state, local, or regional government agencies, IHEs, hospitals, academic or research institutions.

Range: $40,000 to $1,515,000. **Average:** $359,000.

Activity: FY 06 estimate, 801 grants.

HQ: NIAAA, NIH-HHS, 5635 Fishers Lane, Bethesda, MD 20892-9304. Phone: Division of Metabolism and Health Effects, (301) 443-0799; Division of Treatment and Recovery, (301) 443-1208; Division of Epidemiology and Prevention Research, (301) 443-1274; Division of Neuroscience and Behavior, (301) 443-7722. *Grants management information*: Grants

Management Officer, NIAAA, NIH-HHS, 5635 Fishers Lane - Rm. 3023, Bethesda, MD 20892-9304. Phone: (301) 443-4704.

Internet: www.nih.gov (Note: no field offices for this program.)

93.275 SUBSTANCE ABUSE AND MENTAL HEALTH SERVICES - ACCESS TO RECOVERY

Assistance: project grants. (100 percent/1-3 years).

Purposes: pursuant to PHSA as amended, to implement voucher programs for substance abuse clinical treatment and recovery support services, enabling clients to obtain free services from providers of their choice.

Eligible applicants/beneficiaries: chief executives of states, territories, and tribal organizations.

Range: to $15,000,000.

Activity: FY 06 estimate, 5 grants; FY 07 estimate, zero grants.

HQ: CSAT-SAMHSA-HHS, 1 Choke Cherry Rd., Rockville, MD 20857. Phone: (240) 276-1575. *Grants management information*: Grants Management Officer, Office of Program Support, SAMHSA-HHS, 1 Choke Cherry Rd., Rockville, MD 20857. Phone: (240) 276-1407, FAX (240) 276-1430.

Internet: www.samhsa.gov (Note: no field offices for this program.)

93.276 DRUG-FREE COMMUNITIES SUPPORT PROGRAM GRANTS ("Drug-Free Community Grants")

Assistance: project grants. (to 50 percent/1 year).

Purposes: pursuant to the Drug-Free Communities Act of 1997, to increase the capacity of community coalitions to reduce substance abuse among adults through collaborative activities; to disseminate state-of-the-art information on practices and initiatives proven to be effective in reducing substance abuse among youth.

Eligible applicants/beneficiaries: nonprofit, charitable, educational community coalitions collaborating with community entities, including government agencies, in a substantial voluntary effort—established for at least six months and with a five-year strategic plan. Note: proposals are submitted to the Office of Justice Programs, and approved by OJJDP and the Office of National Drug Control Policy.

Range: to $100,000.

Activity: FY 06 estimate, 120 grants.

HQ: Substance Abuse and Mental Health Services Administration, Center for Substance Abuse Prevention, 1 Choke Cherry Rd. - Rm. 4-1089, Rockville, MD 20857. Phone: (240) 276-1270. *Grants management information*: Grants Management Officer, Substance Abuse and Mental Health Services Administration, Division of Grants Management, 1 Choke Cherry Rd. - Rm. 7-1097, Rockville, MD 20857. Phone: (240) 276-1421.

Internet: www.usdoj.gov (Note: no field offices for this program.)

93.279 DRUG ABUSE AND ADDICTION RESEARCH PROGRAMS

Assistance: project grants. (100 percent/to 5 years).

Purposes: pursuant to PHSA as amended and SBRDEA, for epidemiologic, basic, clinical, and applied research on the etiology, treatment, prevention, and consequences of drug addiction, including HIV/AIDS. Research project grants support clearly defined projects or small groups of related research activities, and research conferences. Program project and center grants support large-scale, broad-based interdisciplinary research programs. Small grants (up to $50,000 per year for up to two years) support less experienced investigators, testing of new methods and techniques, small-scale exploratory and pilot studies or exploration of an unusual research opportunity. SBIR and STTR awards are available (*see Notes preceding* **93.001**).

Eligible applicants/beneficiaries: public, private, profit and nonprofit organizations; foreign or domestic agencies, including state, local or regional government agencies; IHEs; hospitals; academic or research institutions.

Range: $23,000 to $907,000. **Average:** $141,000.

Activity: FY 07 estimate, 2,376 grants.

HQ: National Institute on Drug Abuse, NIH-HHS, Neurosciences Bldg., 6001 Executive Bldg., Bethesda, MD 20892. Phone: Division of Basic Neurosciences and Behavioral Research, (301) 443-1887; Division of Pharmacotherapies and Medical Consequences of Drug Abuse (301) 443-6173; Division of Epidemiology, Services and Prevention Research, (301) 443-6504; Division of Clinical Neuroscience and Behavioral Research, (301) 443-4877; Director of the Center for the Clinical Trials Network, (301) 443-6697; NIDA Deputy Coordinator of Research Training, (301) 443-6071; SBIR, (301) 443-6071. *Grants management information*: Grants Management Officer, NIDA, NIH-HHS, Neuroscience Bldg., 6001 Executive Blvd., Bethesda, MD 20892. Phone:(301) 443-6710.

Internet: www.nih.gov; www.nida.nih.gov; www.drugabuse.gov (Note: no field offices for this program.)

93.280 NATIONAL INSTITUTES OF HEALTH LOAN REPAYMENT PROGRAM FOR CLINICAL RESEARCHERS ("NIH LRP-CR")

Assistance: project grants. (100 percent/from 2 years).

Purposes: pursuant to PHSA, to attract and retain health professionals to clinical research careers by offering extant educational loan repayment for participants agreeing to engage in clinical research at least half-time in a qualifying institution for at least two years. Research must be patient-oriented and conducted with human subjects in an out- or inpatient setting to clarify a problem in human physiology, pathophysiology or disease, or epidemiologic or behavioral studies, outcomes or health services research, or developing new technologies, therapeutic interventions, or clinical trials. Maximum annual benefit is $35,000 in loan repayment and $13,650 in federal tax reimbursement.

Eligible applicants/beneficiaries: U.S. citizens, nationals, or permanent residents with: a Ph.D., M.D., D.D.S., D.M.D., D.O., D.P.M., Pharm.D.,

D.C., N.D., or equivalent doctoral degree from an accredited institution; qualifying educational debt in excess of 20 percent of annual salary (half of which must be paid by program participant); a contract to conduct research supported by a nonprofit foundation, professional association, or other institution, or a U.S. or other state or local government agency. Full-time federal employees are ineligible.

Range: loan repayments per initial two-year contract period, $2,298 to $70,000; tax reimbursements, $1,040 to $31,679. **Average:** $48,718 including tax reimbursements.

Activity: annually, 935 awards.

HQ: Division of Loan Repayment, NIH, 6011 Executive Blvd. - Rm. 206, MSC 7650, Bethesda, MD 20892-7650. Phone: (866) 849-4047, FAX (866) 849-4046.

Internet: www.lrp.nih.gov (Note: no field offices for this program.)

93.281 MENTAL HEALTH RESEARCH CAREER/SCIENTIST DEVELOPMENT AWARDS
("Research Career/Scientist Development ("K" Series) Awards")

Assistance: project grants. (100 percent/to 5 years).

Purposes: pursuant to PHSA as amended, for research training in the problems of mental illness, behavioral disorders, and HIV/AIDS—through Mentored Research Scientist, Mentored Clinical Scientist, Mentored Scientist Development for New Minority Faculty, Mentored Patient-Oriented Career Development, Mid-career Investigator in Patient Oriented Research, Independent Scientist, and Senior Scientist Awards. Some research costs may be supported.

Eligible applicants/beneficiaries: research centers, medical schools, departments of psychiatry, nonmedical academic departments, psychiatric hospitals or hospitals with psychiatric services, community mental health centers, biomedical research institutes, and departments of behavioral science. Researchers must have scholastic degree and previous training, and they must be U.S. citizens, nationals, or lawful permanent residents.

Range: $59,400 to $428,924. **Average:** $147,000.

Activity: FY 06 estimate, 498 awards; FY 07 estimate, 506 awards.

HQ: NIMH, NIH-HHS, 6001 Executive Blvd., Bethesda, MD 20892. Phone: (301) 443-9700. *Grants management information*: Grants Management Officer, NIMH, NIH-HHS, 6001 Executive Blvd. - Rm.6112, Bethesda, MD 20892-9605. Phone: (301) 443-2811.

Internet: www.nih.gov (Note: no field offices for this program.)

93.282 MENTAL HEALTH NATIONAL RESEARCH SERVICE AWARDS FOR RESEARCH TRAINING
("NRSA Program")

Assistance: project grants. (100 percent/to 6 years).

Purposes: pursuant to PHSA as amended, for NRSA programs providing research training in mental health problems (*see Notes preceding* **93.001**).

Included are: basic biomedical, clinical neuroscience, and behavioral research; epidemiology of mental disorders; etiology, description, diagnosis, and pathogenesis of mental disorders; treatment development, assessment, and evaluation; public health intervention and prevention approaches. Grants for up to six years are directed toward young scientists at the predoctoral or postdoctoral level for full-time work. Career Opportunities in Research (COR) Honors Undergraduate grants are available to minority trainees competing successfully for entry into Ph.D. degree programs. Postdoctoral students receiving support for less than 12 months must meet payback requirements through an equivalent period of research and/or teaching after training is completed.

Eligible applicants/beneficiaries: training grants—domestic public or private nonprofit organizations. Applicants for predoctoral support must have completed at least two years of graduate work and be enrolled in a doctoral degree program. Postdoctoral applicants must have a PhD., Psy.D., M.D., D.D.S., Sc.D., D.N.S., D.O., D.S.W., or equivalent degree. Applicants for individual awards must be U.S. citizens, nationals, or lawful permanent residents. COR Honors Undergraduate program awards—four-year IHEs or health professional schools whose enrollment is drawn substantially from ethnic groups.

Range: postdoctoral, $35,568 to $51,036. **Average:** predoctoral stipends, $22,772; COR honors undergraduate, $10,956.

Activity: FY 06 estimate, 300 individual, 182 institutional grants; FY 07 estimate, 299 individual, 181 institutional grants.

HQ: NIMH, NIH-HHS, 6001 Executive Blvd., Bethesda, MD 20892. Phone: (301) 443-9700; *Grants management information*: Grants Management Officer, NIMH, NIH-HHS, 6001 Executive Blvd. - Rm.6122, Bethesda, MD 20892-9605. Phone: (301) 443-2811.

Internet: www.nih.gov (Note: no field offices for this program.)

93.283 CENTERS FOR DISEASE CONTROL AND PREVENTION—INVESTIGATIONS AND TECHNICAL ASSISTANCE

Assistance: project grants. (50-100 percent/1-3 years).

Purposes: pursuant to PHSA, Federal Mine Safety and Health Amendments Act of 1977 as amended, and Occupational Safety and Health Act of 1970, to strengthen state and local disease prevention and control programs, including communicable and chronic diseases such as tuberculosis, childhood immunization, tobacco use, diabetes, oral health, and sexually transmitted diseases. Services include investigations, epidemic aid, occupational safety and health programs, epidemiology, consultation, personnel training, responses to public health emergencies.

Eligible applicants/beneficiaries: states and their political subdivisions, local health authorities, and organizations with specialized health interests; IHES and research institutions; certain private, public nonprofit organizations.

Range: diabetes, $625,000 to $855,000 (only data provided).

Activity: not quantified specifically.

HQ: Extramural Program Teal Leader, National Center for Chronic Disease Prevention and Health Promotion, CDCP-HHS. Phone: (770) 488-5549. *Grants management information*: Grants Management Branch, Procurement and Grants Office, CDCP-HHS, 2920 Brandywine Rd. - Rm. 3000, Atlanta, GA 30341. Phone: (770) 488-2700.

Internet: www.cdc.gov (Note: no field offices for this program.)

93.284 INJURY PREVENTION PROGRAM FOR AMERICAN INDIANS AND ALASKAN NATIVES—COOPERATIVE AGREEMENTS ("Injury Prevention")

Assistance: project grants.

Purposes: pursuant to PHSA as amended, to provide injury prevention health services to American Indians and Alaska natives, through capacity building, implementation of interventions, and training.

Eligible applicants/beneficiaries: tribes, tribal organizations, urban Indian organizations, nonprofit organizations.

Range: capacity building, to $75,000; interventions, to $10,000.

Activity: annually, 33 grants.

HQ: Injury Prevention Program Manager, IHS-HHS, 801 Thompson Ave. - Ste. 120, Rockville, MD 20852. Phone: (301) 443-1054. *Grants management information*: Grants Management Officer, Division of Grants Operations, HIS, 801 Thompson Ave. - Ste. 360, Rockville, MD 20852. Phone: (301) 443-5204.

Internet: www.ihs.gov (Note: no field offices for this program.)

93.285 NATIONAL INSTITUTES OF HEALTH PEDIATRIC RESEARCH LOAN REPAYMENT PROGRAM ("PR-LRP")

Assistance: project grants. (100 percent/from 2 years).

Purposes: pursuant to PHSA as amended, to attract and retain health professionals to pediatric research careers by offering repayment of extant education loans for participants agreeing to engage in pediatric research for two years minimum in a qualifying nonprofit institution. Payments may be made up to $35,000 per year, plus $13,650 annually for tax reimbursements.

Eligible applicants/beneficiaries: U.S. citizens, nationals, or permanent residents from disadvantaged backgrounds, with: an M.D., Ph.D., D.O., D.D.S., D.M.D., D.P.M., B.S.N., A.D.N., or equivalent degree; qualified undergraduate or graduate educational loan debt exceeding 20 percent of their salary; a contract commitment of at least two years of service; no existing service obligation to federal, state, or other entities.

Range: two-year contract repayment amounts, $2,394 to $70,000; tax reimbursements, $934 to $31,679. **Average:** $50,843 including tax reimbursements.

Activity: annually, 391 awards.

HQ: Division of Loan Repayment, NIH, 6011 Executive Blvd. - Rm. 206, MSC 7650, Bethesda, MD 20892-7650. Phone: (866) 849-4047, FAX (866) 849-4046.

Internet: www.lrp.nih.gov; email, lrp@nih.gov (Note: no field offices for this program.)

93.286 DISCOVERY AND APPLIED RESEARCH FOR TECHNOLOGICAL INNOVATIONS TO IMPROVE HUMAN HEALTH

Assistance: project grants. (100 percent/to 5 years).

Purposes: pursuant to PHSA, for hypothesis-, design-, technology-, or device-driven research relating to the discovery, design, development, validation, and applications of technologies in biomedical imaging and bioengineering. The program includes biomaterials, biosensors and biotransducers, nanotechnology, imaging device development, biomedical imaging technology development, image exploitation, contrast agents, informatics, and computer sciences—related to imaging, molecular and cellular imaging, bio-electrics/biomagnetics, organ and whole body imaging, screening for diseases and disorders, imaging technology assessment, and related disciplines. NRSAs, SBIR, and STTR awards are available (*see Notes preceding* **93.001**).

Eligible applicants/beneficiaries: corporations, public or private institutions, nonprofit or profit entities, individuals.

Range: $2,000 to $1,914,284. **Average:** $337,038.

Activity: FY 06 estimate, 799 awards; FY 07 estimate, 829 awards.

HQ: National Institute of Biomedical Imaging and Bioengineering, NIH-HHS, 6707 Democracy Blvd., Bethesda, MD 20892. Phone: (301) 496-9388, FAX (301) 480-4973. *Business contact*: National Institute of Biomedical Imaging and Bioengineering, NIH-HHS, same address. Phone: (301) 451-6773, FAX (301) 480-4530.

Internet: www.nibib.nih.gov (Note: no field offices for this program.)

93.288 NATIONAL HEALTH SERVICE CORPS SCHOLARSHIP PROGRAM ("NHSC Scholarship Program")

Assistance: project grants. (100 percent/1-4 years).

Purposes: pursuant to PHSA, for scholarships to full-time students in the health professions. Disciplines include: allopathic and osteopathic medicine, and dentistry; family nurse practitioners; nurse midwifery; primary care physician assistants; and, other disciplines needed by the NHSC. Scholarship recipients must perform one year of service in a federally-designated health manpower shortage area for each year of support received, or a minimum of two years; however, service deferments may be granted to complete residencies in family practice, internal medicine, pediatrics, and OB/GYN. Service sites also may be located in the territories or possessions.

Eligible applicants/beneficiaries: U.S. citizens or nationals, enrolled or accepted in an accredited U.S. school.

Range: $1,157 monthly stipend plus tuition and other fees.

Activity: FY 06 estimate, 100 new, 86 continuation awards; FY 07 estimate, 100 new, 86 continuation awards.

HQ: Chief, Applications and Award Branch, NHSC Division, Bureau of Health Professions, HRSA-HHS, 5600 Fishers Lane - Rm. 8A-55, Rockville, MD 20857. Phone: (301) 594-4400; *public information*, (800) 221-9393. *Grants management information*: Director, Division of Grants Management, Health Resources and Services Administration, NIH-HHS, 5600 Fishers Lane - Rm. 11A-16, Rockville, MD 20857. Phone: Health Services, (301) 443-2385; Research and Training, (301) 443-3099; Government and Special Focus, (301) 443-3288.

Internet: www.hrsa.gov (Note: no field offices for this program.)

93.289 PRESIDENT'S COUNCIL ON PHYSICAL FITNESS AND SPORTS ("PCPFS")

Assistance: advisory services/counseling.

Purposes: to provide professional assistance in the design, development, improvement, and implementation of physical fitness programs, as well as expanded exercise and sports participation opportunities for all age groups. This is accomplished through publications, media campaigns, and a web site, in coordination with school systems, government agencies, employee and industrial organizations, recreation and park departments, communications media, etc.—not with organizations with a commercial interest in physical fitness. No funding is provided.

Eligible applicants/beneficiaries: general public.

Range/Average: N.A.

Activity: not quantified specifically.

HQ: Public Affairs Specialist, President's Council on Physical Fitness and Sports, Office of Public Health and Science, OS-HHS, 200 Pennsylvania Ave. SW - Ste. 738H, Washington, DC 20201-0004. Phone: (202) 690-9000, FAX (202) 690-5211.

Internet: www.fitness.gov (Note: no field offices for this program.)

93.290 NATIONAL COMMUNITY CENTERS OF EXCELLENCE IN WOMEN'S HEALTH ("CCOE")

Assistance: project grants. (100 percent/to 5 years).

Purposes: for community-based programs integrating, coordinating, and strengthening linkages in women's health in the following components: comprehensive health service delivery; training for lay and professional health providers; community-based research; public education and outreach; leadership development for women as health care consumers and providers; technical assistance. Funds may be used for staffing, supplies, consultants, equipment, and travel.

Eligible applicants/beneficiaries: public or private nonprofit community-based hospitals or organizations, or community health centers serving underserved women. Note: existing programs and organizations in certain states and PR are ineligible.

Average: all awards are for $150,000.

Activity: FY 04, 14 awards.

HQ: Office on Women's Health, 0S-HHS, Parklawn Bldg. - Rm. 16A-55, 5600 Fishers Lane, Rockville, MD 20857. Phone: (no number provided). *Grants management information*: Office of Public Health and Science, Office of Grants Management, 1101 Wootton Pkwy. - Ste. 550, Rockville, MD 20852. Phone: (240) 453-8822.

Internet: www.4woman.gov/owh/CCOE/index.htm (Note: no field offices for this program.)

93.291 SURPLUS PROPERTY UTILIZATION ("Federal Property Assistance Program")

Assistance: sale, exchange, or donation of property and goods.

Purposes: pursuant to the Federal Property and Administrative Services Act of 1949 and SBMHAA as amended, to convey or lease surplus federal real properties needed and usable in health programs including research—e.g., land and buildings for use as hospitals, clinics, public health administration, water and sewer systems, rehabilitation programs, and facilities for the homeless. Discounts of up to 100 percent of value may be granted. Deed restrictions apply for 30 years for land, and lesser periods for improvements.

Eligible applicants/beneficiaries: states, political subdivisions and instrumentalities; tax-supported public and nonprofit health institutions.

Range/Average: N.A.

Activity: FY 05, transferred 66.47 acres of land and 86 buildings.

HQ: Director, Division of Property Management, Program Support Center, HHS, Parklawn Bldg. - Rm. 5B-17, 5600 Fishers Lane, Rockville, MD 20857. Phone: (301) 443-2265, FAX (202) 443-0084.

Internet: www.psc.gov; e-mail, rpb@psc.gov (Note: no field offices for this program.)

93.294 MENTORING PARTNERSHIP PROGRAM—PROTEGE ("Protege")

Assistance: project grants (100 percent/to 2 years).

Purposes: to strengthen organizational infrastructure and program services of small nonprofit organizations so that they may deliver improved HIV/AIDS prevention and support services to women most at risk for acquiring HIV/AIDS and women with positive HIV serostatus. The majority of awarded funds must be used to support staff and program implementation. Funds may not be used for construction, building alterations, equipment, medical treatment, or renovations.

Eligible applicants/beneficiaries: nonprofit community-based, faith-based, national or tribal organizations; colleges and universities; hospitals and clinics; research institution; state, local or tribal government agencies.

Range: to $50,000 per award.

Activity: new program in 2006; 4 awards anticipated.

HQ: Office on Women's Health, Office of Public Health and Science, OS-HHS, 200 Independence Ave. SW - Rm. 712E, Washington, DC 20201. Phone: (no number provided). *Grants management information*: Division of Program Management, Office on Women's Health-HHS, Parklawn Bldg. - Rm. 16A-55, 5600 Fishers Lane, Rockville, MD 20857. Phone: (no number provided).

Internet: www.4woman.gov/owh.

93.295 INTERGENERATIONAL APPROACHES TO HIV/AIDS PREVENTION EDUCATION WITH WOMEN ACROSS THE LIFESPAN PILOT PROGRAM ("Intergenerational")

Assistance: project grants (100 percent/to 2 years).

Purposes: to educate African American, Native American/American Indian, Hispanic/Latino, and Asian/Pacific Islander females 12+ years old about and/or increase their knowledge of HIV/AIDS prevention; to know their serostatus; to gain competencies in cross-generational communications about sexual health; and to connect with a primary healthcare physician and/or navigate other systems of care.

Eligible applicants/beneficiaries: nonprofit community-based, faith-based, national or tribal organizations; colleges and universities; hospitals and clinics; research institution; state, local or tribal government agencies.

Range: to $250,000 per award.

Activity: new program in 2006; 4 awards anticipated.

HQ: Office on Women's Health, OS-HHS, 200 Independence Ave. SW - Rm. 712E, Washington, DC 20201 Phone: (no number provided). *Grants program information/technical assistance* Phone: (202) 260-8420; Budget/Business aspects of application, Phone: (240) 453-8822.

Internet: www.4woman.gov/owh.

93.296 STATE PARTNERSHIP GRANT PROGRAM TO IMPROVE MINORITY HEALTH

Assistance: project grants. (100 percent/to 5 years).

Purposes: pursuant to PHSA, for the development of partnerships with state and territorial offices of minority health—to develop and implement strategies to improve minority health and to eliminate health disparities including in adult and child immunization, asthma, cancer, diabetes, heart disease and stroke, HIV, infant mortality, and mental health. Project activity examples: development of plans of action; strengthened capacity to collect, analyze, and report data and to conduct evaluations; implementation of culturally and linguistically appropriate services; partnering with health professions schools to track progress of minority students to increase the number of minority graduates. Funds may not be used to provide health care treatment, for construction, or to supplant ongoing project activities.

Eligible applicants/beneficiaries: official state and territorial offices of minority health.

Range: $115,000 to $175,000. **Average:** $149,000.

Activity: new program listing in 2006 (CFDA on-line). FY 05, 32 new awards; FY 06 estimate, 32 continuation awards.

HQ: *program information* Director, Division of Program Operations, Office of Minority Health, Office of Public Health and Science, OS-HHS, 1101 Wooten Pkwy. - Ste.600, Rockville, MD 20852 Phone: (240) 453-8444 Grants management, Phone: (240) 453-8822.

Internet: www.omhrc.gov (Note: no field offices for this program.)

93.300 NATIONAL CENTER FOR HEALTH WORKFORCE ANALYSIS ("NCHWA")

Assistance: project grants. (to 100 percent/to 5 years).

Purposes: pursuant to PHSA as amended and HPEPA, to develop information describing the health professions workforce and to analyze related issues, enabling decision-making on future directions in the field and in nursing programs in response to societal and professional needs. Funds may be used for targeted information collection and analysis, to develop a nonfederal analytic and research infrastructure, and for program evaluation and assessment.

Eligible applicants/beneficiaries: state and local governments, health professions schools, schools of nursing, academic health centers, community-based health facilities, and other public or private nonprofit entities.

Range: $50,000 to $400,000. **Average:** $250,000.

Activity: FY 05, 6 continuation awards; FY 06 and FY 07, no new or continuation awards.

HQ: NCHWA, Bureau of Health Professions, HRSA-HHS, 5600 Fishers Lane - Rm. 9-105, Rockville, MD 20857. Phone: (301) 443-5452. *Grants management information*: Director, Division of Grants Management, Health Resources and Services Administration-HHS, 5600 Fishers Lane - Rm. 11A-16, Rockville, MD 20857. Phone: Health Services, (301) 443-2385; Research and Training, (301) 443-3099; Government and Special Focus, (301) 443-3288.

Internet: www.hrsa.gov (Note: no field offices for this program.)

93.301 SMALL RURAL HOSPITAL IMPROVEMENT GRANT PROGRAM

Assistance: project grants.

Purposes: pursuant to SSA, to implement "PPS"; to comply with legislative health improvement requirements; to reduce medical errors and support quality improvement.

Eligible applicants/beneficiaries: small rural hospitals, including in territories.

Range: $38,720 to $909,920. **Average:** $319,840.

Activity: FY 05, 1,600 awards through 46 state rural health offices.

HQ: Office of Rural Health Policy, 5600 Fishers Lane - Rm. 9A-55, Rockville, MD 20857. Phone: (301) 443-0835, FAX (301) 443-2669. *Grants management information*: Director, Division of Grants Management, Health Resources and Services Administration-HHS, 5600 Fishers Lane - Rm. 11A-16, Rockville, MD 20857. Phone: Health Services, (301) 443-2385; Research and Training, (301) 443-3099; Government and Special Focus, (301) 443-3288.

Internet: www.hrsa.gov (Note: no field offices for this program.)

93.303 NURSING SCHOLARSHIP PROGRAM

Assistance: direct payments/specified use (100 percent/1-4 years).

Purposes: pursuant to the Nurse Reinvestment Act of 2002 and the Public Health Service Act as amended, to increase the supply of registered nurses (RN) in approved health care facilities with a critical shortage of nurses by providing service-obligated scholarships to full and part-time nursing students. Scholarships pay tuition and required fees to the school, a monthly stipend to students and a single annual payment to the student to assist with other reasonable educational expenses, including: books, supplies, equipment, uniforms, travel, for the provision of clinical service, etc. The program requires one year of service with a minimum 2-year service commitment post graduation.

Eligible applicants: U.S. citizen or national, enrolled or accepted for enrollment in a fully accredited US academic institution with a graduate, baccalaureate, or associate degree or diploma nursing program. The applicant must be free of any Federal judgment liens or service obligation, have not defaulted on a federal debt and have no conflicting service obligations. Financial need is also reviewed as part of the eligibility determination.

Eligible beneficiaries: U.S. citizens or nationals enrolled or accepted for enrollment in a fully accredited graduate, baccalaureate, associate degree or diploma nursing program.

Range: $20,000 to $220,000 per award. **Average:** $55,000 per award.

Activity: FY 06, 218; FY 07 estimate, 196; FY 08 estimate, 257.

HQ: Director, Division of Grants Management, HRSA-HHS, 5600 Fishers Lane - Rm.11A-16, Rockville, MD 20857. Phone: (301) 443-2728. Chief, Health Services Branch, Phone: (301) 443-3262; Chief, Research and Training Branch, Phone: (301) 443-3099; Chief, Government and Special Focus Branch, Phone: (301) 443-3288.

Internet: www.hrsa.gov.

93.307 MINORITY HEALTH AND HEALTH DISPARITIES RESEARCH

Assistance: project grants. (100 percent/1-5 years).

Purposes: pursuant to PHSA and SBRDEA, to support basic, clinical, social, and behavioral research; to promote research infrastructure and training; to foster emerging programs; to disseminate information—reaching out to minority and other health disparity communities. The Excellence in Partnerships for Community Outreach, Research on Health Disparities and Training Program ("Project EXPORT provides funds to centers conducting inter-disciplinary minority health and other health disparities research intervention activities. The Research Endowment Program grants provide income for: teaching programs in the biomedical and behavioral sciences and related areas; facilities; student and faculty recruitment and retention; instructional delivery systems and information technology; scholarships, tutoring and counseling programs, and student service programs. The Health Disparities Research-Loan Repayment Program (HDR-LRP) provides for repayment of existing educational loan debt incurred by health professionals engaged in research on minority health or other health disparity issues; recipients must contract for two-year periods minimum, with extensions available. The Research Infrastructure in Minority Institutions (RIMI) Program assists nondoctoral degree institutions in developing their research infrastructure through collaborations with research-intensive universities. SBIR and STIR funding also is available (*see Notes preceding* **93.001**).

Eligible applicants/beneficiaries: grants—individuals, public and private nonprofit and profit institutions. Endowment grants—"Section 736" health professions schools with net endowment assets less than 50 percent of the national average for similar institutions. HDR-LRP—U.S. citizens, nationals, or permanent residents, with qualifying outstanding educational loan debt equal to or less than 20 percent of the applicant's annual salary, with no service obligations to federal, state, or other entities, nor judgment liens arising from federal debt.

Range: EXPORT, $227,251 to $1,621,536; endowment grants, $937,500 to $5,000,000; HDR-LRP, $3,906 to $106,057; RIMI, $417,287 to $970,833. **Average:** EXPORT, $870,333; endowment, $3,267,090; HDR- LRP, $43,502; RIMI, $826,381.

Activity: FY 06 estimates, 0 new EXPORT, 13 endowment, 209 HDR- LRP, 20 SBIR and STTR awards.

HQ: Director, Division of Research and Training Activities, National Center on Minority Health and Health Disparities (NCMHD), NIH-HHS, 6707 Democracy Blvd. - Ste. 800, Bethesda, MD 20892-5465. Phone: (301) 402-1366. *Grants management information*: same address and telephone.

Internet: www.ncmhd.nih.gov; www.nih.gov (Note: no field offices for this program.)

93.308 EXTRAMURAL LOAN REPAYMENT FOR INDIVIDUALS FROM DISADVANTAGED BACKGROUNDS CONDUCTING CLINICAL RESEARCH

Assistance: project grants. (100 percent/2 to 4 years).

Purposes: pursuant to PHSA as amended, for repayment of existing educational loan debt incurred by health professionals from disadvantaged backgrounds, engaged in patient-oriented clinical research with human subjects, or research on the causes and consequences of disease in inpatient or outpatient settings. Recipients must contact for two-year periods minimum, with one- year extensions available.

Eligible applicants/beneficiaries: U.S. citizens, nationals, or permanent residents with: a Ph.D., M.D., D.D.S., D.M.D., D.O., D.P.M., Pharm.D., D.C., N.D., or equivalent doctoral degree from an accredited institution; qualifying educational debt in excess of 20 percent of annual salary (half of which must be paid by program participant); a contract to conduct research supported by a nonprofit foundation, professional association, or other institution, or a U.S. or other state or local government agency. Full-time federal employees are ineligible.

Range: for two-year period, $4,252 to $106,057 in loan repayments, plus $3,000 to $28,000 in tax reimbursements. **Average:** loan repayments, $45,000; tax payments, $18,000.

Activity: annually, 35 awards.

HQ: NCMHD, Loan Repayment Program, 6707 Democracy Blvd. - Ste. 800, Bethesda, MD 20892-5465. Phone: (301) 402-1366, FAX (301) 480-4049.

Internet: www.ncmhd.nih.gov (Note: no field offices for this program.)

93.310 TRANS-NIH RESEARCH SUPPORT

Assistance: project grants; training. (project grants, 100 percent/project grants, to 5 years).

Purposes: pursuant to PHSA, for new initiatives addressing major opportunities and gaps in biomedical research that no NIH Institute could address alone, but the which the agency as a whole can pursue to stimulate biomedical research progress and to catalyze changes that will serve to transform new scientific knowledge into tangible public health benefits.

Eligible applicants/beneficiaries: domestic public or private profit and nonprofit organizations, IHEs, hospitals, laboratories, or other institutions, state and local government units, individuals; foreign organizations for certain initiatives.

Range: $2,300 to $3,800,000. **Average:** $620,000.

Activity: not quantified specifically.

HQ: Assistant Director/Roadmap Coordination, Office of the Director, NIH-HHS, Bethesda, MD 20892. Phone: (301) 402-4217. *Scientific/research contact,* Program Director, Office of Extramural Programs-NIH-HHS, Bethesda, MD 20892. Phone: (301) 435- 2690.

Internet: www.nihroadmap.nih.gov (Note: no field offices for this program.)

93.342 HEALTH PROFESSIONS STUDENT LOANS, INCLUDING PRIMARY CARE LOANS/LOANS FOR DISADVANTAGED STUDENTS ("HPSL/PCL/LDS")

Assistance: direct loans (90 percent).

Purposes: pursuant to PHSA and HPEPA, to capitalize and administer student loan funds to provide long-term, low-interest loans to full-time students in financial need or from disadvantaged backgrounds, preparing for the health professions. Students may borrow amounts annually to cover reasonable living expenses, tuition, and educational expenses. Third- and fourth- year medical and osteopathic medicine students may borrow additional funds to repay earlier educational loans; they must agree to enter and complete a primary health care residency training program not later than four years after graduating, and to practice primary health care until the loan is paid in full. Payback service provisions apply. The loan interest rate is 5 percent.

Eligible applicants: accredited public or nonprofit private schools located in states, territories, or possessions, providing a course of study leading to a degree of doctor of medicine, dentistry, osteopathy, pharmacy, optometry, podiatry, or veterinary medicine, or B.S. in pharmacy—or an equivalent degree. For LDS, applicant schools must have student recruitment and retention programs, minority health issues curricula, clinic services for minority groups, and mentor programs.

Eligible beneficiaries: full-time students in need of a loan, enrolled or accepted in an eligible course of study—that are U.S. citizens, nationals, or permanent residents of a state or territories or possessions.

Range: $25,000 to $150,000. **Average:** $11,000.

Activity: FY 05 estimate, 16,437 students supported.

HQ: Division of Health Careers Diversity and Development, Bureau of Health Professions, HRSA-HHS, 5600 Fishers Lane - Rm. 8-34, Rockville, MD 20857. Phone: (301) 443-4776.

Internet: www.bhpr.hrsa.gov/dsa (Note: no field offices for this program.)

93.358 ADVANCED EDUCATION NURSING TRAINEESHIPS

Assistance: project grants.

Purposes: pursuant to PHSA as amended and HPEPA, to provide financial support through traineeships for 36 months to nurses at the master's or doctoral level, preparing full-time for careers as nurse educators, clinical specialists, practitioners, administrators, midwives, public health nurses, and other approved specialties—and for nurse anesthetists for one year only.

Eligible applicants: schools of nursing, academic health centers, public or private nonprofit entities.

Eligible beneficiaries: U.S. citizens, nationals, or permanent residents licensed as registered nurses, enrolled full-time in graduate courses toward a master's degree or doctoral program.

Range: $682 to $249,573. **Average:** $46,110.

Activity: FY 05, 347 grants.

HQ: Division of Nursing, Bureau of Health Professions, HRSA-HHS, Parklawn Bldg. - Rm. 9-36, 5600 Fishers Lane, Rockville, MD 20857. Phone: (301) 443-6333. *Grants management information*: Director, Division of Grants Management, Health Resources and Services Administration-HHS, 5600 Fishers Lane - Rm. 11A-16, Rockville, MD 20857. Phone: Health Services, (301) 443-2385; Research and Training, (301) 443-3099; Government and Special Focus, (301) 443-3288.

Internet: www.hrsa.gov (Note: no field offices for this program.)

93.359 NURSE EDUCATION, PRACTICE AND RETENTION GRANTS ("NEPR")

Assistance: project grants. (100 percent/to 5 years).

Purposes: pursuant to PHSA as amended and Nurse Reinvestment Act of 2002, to expand enrollment in baccalaureate nursing programs; to develop and implement internship and residency programs to encourage mentoring and the development of specialties; to provide education in new technologies including distance learning methodologies. Practice methodologies include: establishing or expanding nursing practice arrangements in non-institutional settings to demonstrate methods to improve access to primary health care in medically underserved areas; providing care for underserved populations and other high-risk groups such as the elderly, persons with HIV-AIDS, substance abusers, the homeless, and victims of domestic violence; providing managed care, quality improvement, and other skills needed to practice in existing and emerging organized health care systems; developing cultural competencies; promoting career mobility, cross training, or specialty training.

Eligible applicants/beneficiaries: collegiate schools of nursing, health care facilities, or partnerships involving academic health centers, state and local governments, and other public or private nonprofit or profit entities and community-based organizations.

Range: $25,000 to $400,000. **Average:** $242,000.

Activity: FY 06 estimate, 56 new, 98 continuation grants.

HQ: Division of Nursing, Bureau of Health Professions, HRSA-HHS, Parklawn Bldg. - Rm. 9-36, 5600 Fishers Lane, Rockville, MD 20857. Phone: (301) 443-6193. *Grants management information*: Director, Division of Grants Management, Health Resources and Services Administration, HHS, 5600 Fishers Lane - Rm. 11A-16, Rockville, MD 20857. Phone: Health Services, (301) 443-2385; Research and Training, (301) 443-3099; Government and Special Focus, (301) 443-3288.

Internet: www.hrsa.gov (Note: no field offices for this program.)

93.361 NURSING RESEARCH

Assistance: project grants. (100 percent/to 5 years).

Purposes: pursuant to PHSA as amended and SBRDEA, for clinical and basic research to establish a scientific basis for the care of individuals across the life span—from management of patients during illness and recovery to the reduction of risks for disease and disability and the promotion of healthy lifestyles, and extending to: patients, families, and care givers; special needs of at-risk and underserved populations; improving clinical care settings; translating scientific advances into cost-effective health care; bioethical issues. The Centers Program: promotes interdisciplinary research; supports research training and career development activities; concentrates research resources on selected research areas through Core Centers for Nursing Research. NRSA, SBIR, and STTR awards are available (*see Notes preceding* **93.001**).

Eligible applicants/beneficiaries: research—any corporation, public or private institution or agency, SBIR firm, or other legal entity whether profit or nonprofit; individuals. NRSA applicants must be registered professional nurses with a baccalaureate or master's degree in nursing or a related field.

Range: research grants, $3,000 to $747,870; NRSAs, $2,266 to $52,304 (individual), $46,352 to $482,930 (institutional). **Average:** research grants, $319,375; NRSAs, $30,587 (individual), $283,316 (institutional).

Activity: FY 05, 357 research grants, 80 NRSA individual awards, 155 NRSA institutional awards.

HQ: National Institute of Nursing Research, NIH-HHS, 6707 Democracy Blvd. - Rm. 710, Bethesda, MD 20817. Phone: (301) 594-6906. *Grants management information*: Grants Management Officer, National Institute of Nursing Research, NIH-HHS, same address. Phone: (301) 594-6869.

Internet: www.nih.gov/ninr (Note: no field offices for this program.)

93.364 NURSING STUDENT LOANS ("NSL")

Assistance: direct loans (90 percent).

Purposes: pursuant to PHSA as amended and HPEPA, for nursing schools to make 5 percent interest, long-term loans to full- or half-time students with financial needs. The maximum loan in any one year is $2,500, except $4,000 for each of the final two years of study; the total borrowed may not exceed $13,000.

Eligible applicants/beneficiaries: accredited public and private nonprofit schools of nursing. Students must be U.S. citizens, nationals, or permanent residents.

Range: $1,500 to $101,555. **Average:** $23,051.

Activity: FY 04, 143 nursing school awards; FY 05 no awards.

HQ: Division of Health Careers Diversity and Development, Bureau of Health Professions, HRSA-HHS, 5600 Fishers Lane - Rm. 8-42, Rockville, MD 20857. Phone: (301) 443-4776. *Grants management information*: Director, Division of Grants Management, Health Resources and Services Administration, HHS, 5600 Fishers Lane - Rm. 11A-16, Rockville, MD 20857. Phone: Health Services, (301) 443-2385; Research and Training, (301) 443-3099; Government and Special Focus, (301) 443-3288.

Internet: www.hrsa.gov (Note: no field offices for this program.)

93.365 SICKLE CELL TREATMENT DEMONSTRATION PROGRAM ("SCTDP")

Assistance: project grants (100 percent).

Purposes: pursuant to American Jobs Creation Act of 2004, to develop and establish partnerships to enhance the prevention and treatment of sickle cell disease through coordination of service delivery, genetic counseling and testing, bundling of technical services, training of health professionals, and patient and provider education.

Eligible applicants/beneficiaries: federally-qualified health centers, nonprofit hospitals or clinics, university health centers providing primary care.

Average: $320,000 per award.

Activity: new program listing in 2006 (CFDA on-line).

HQ: Genetic Services Branch, Division of Services for Children with Special Health Needs, Maternal and Child Health Bureau, HRSA-HHS, 5600 Fishers Lane - Rm. 18A-19, Rickville MD 20857. Phone: (301) 443-1080. *Grants management information*: Director, Division of Grants Management, Health Resources and Services Administration, HHS, 5600 Fishers Lane - Rm. 11A-16, Rockville, MD 20857. Phone: Health Services, (301) 443-2385; Research and Training, (301) 443-3099; Government and Special Focus, (301) 443-3288.

Internet: www.hrsa.gov (Note: no field offices for this program.)

93.389 NATIONAL CENTER FOR RESEARCH RESOURCES ("DBT, DCRR, DCM, DRI")

Assistance: project grants. (50-100 percent/1-5 years).

Purposes: pursuant to PHSA as amended and SBRDEA, for primary research to discover and develop critical resources, models, and technologies; to provide biomedical researchers with access to diverse instrumentation, technologies, basic and clinical research facilities, animal models, genetic stocks, biomaterials, and similar resources—enabling advances in biomedicine leading to lifesaving drugs, devices, and therapies. Awards are provided through program mechanisms including: Biomedical Technology Resource (BTR) grants; research project grants; Shared Instrumentation Grants (SIG); High End Instrumentation (HEI); Exploratory Grants. The Division of Clinical Research Resources helps translate scientific knowledge into effective patient care through General Clinical Research Centers (GCRC); such programs as Research Career Development, Mentored Clinical Research Scholar, National Gene Vector Laboratories (NGVL), Science Educational Partnership Award (SEPA); NRSA, SBIR, and STTR awards are available (*see Notes preceding* **93.001**). The Division of Comparative Medicine (DCM) supports National Primate Research Centers (NPRC), Biological Models and Materials Research (BMMR), and Laboratory Animal Science (LAS) programs. The Division of Research Infrastructure (DRI) supports enhancement of the research environment at minority institutions through grants supporting programs including: Research Centers in Minority Institutions (RCMI); Clinical Research Infrastructure Initiative (RCRII); Institutional Development Awards (IDA); Animal Facilities Improvement; and, Research Facilities Improvement Program (RFIP).

Eligible applicants/beneficiaries: BTR grants—U.S. nonprofit health professional schools, other academic institutions, hospitals, state and local health agencies, research organizations. SIG and HEI awards—institutions only. GCRCs—schools, research hospitals, and other institutions.

Research career development—public or private domestic, nonfederal organizations, and IHEs on behalf of candidates. SEPA—IHEs, professional organizations, school systems, scientific societies, science museums, and similar applicants. DCM—IHEs, hospitals, nonprofit and profit organizations. DRI programs—predominantly minority institutions, organizations with historically low success rate in obtaining NIH funding, and nonprofit and some profit organizations, depending on program.

Range: research projects, $42,000 to $1,107,000; research centers, $17,000 to $12,208,000; other research, $3,000 to $2,506,000; research training, $29,000 to $405,000; R&D, $4,000 to $4,103,000; construction, $250,000 to $4,000,000.

Activity: FY 06 estimate (representative), 119 research projects, 105 clinical research centers, 51 BTRs, 51 CMCs, 73 R&D awards.

HQ: National Center for Research Resources, NIH-HHS, Bethesda, MD 20892. Phone: BTR, (301) 435-0755; Division of Clinical Research Resources, (301) 435-0790; DCM, (301) 435-0744; DRI, (301) 435-0788. *Grants management information*: Grants Management Officer, Office of Grants Management, National Center for Research Resources, NIH-HHS, Bethesda, MD 20892. Phone: (301) 435-0844.

Internet: www.ncrr.nih.gov (Note: no field offices for this program.)

93.392 CANCER CONSTRUCTION

Assistance: project grants (50 percent).

Purposes: pursuant to PHSA as amended, to renovate existing or build new cancer research facilities to meet basic research or clinical space requirements, or laboratory safety, biohazard containment, and animal care standards. Proposed facilities must be part of an existing or developing cancer research program, and used for grant purposes for at least 20 years.

Eligible applicants/beneficiaries: public or private nonprofit agencies, institutions, corporations, organizations, or associations—in the states, possessions, or territories.

Range/Average: N.A.

Activity: FY 05-06, no awards. (Note: CFDA indicates that most funding for activities covered by this program have been obtained through National Center for Research Resources, **93.389**.).

HQ: Associate Director/Space and Facilities Planning, Office of Management, National Cancer Institute, NIH-HHS, 6116 Executive Blvd., - Ste. 600, Bethesda, MD 20892-8343. Phone: (301) 496-8534. *Grants management information*: Grants Management Officer, National Cancer Institute, EPS-234, Bethesda, MD 20892. Phone: (301) 496-7753.

Internet: www.nih.gov (Note: no field offices for this program.)

93.393 CANCER CAUSE AND PREVENTION RESEARCH

Assistance: project grants. (100 percent/to 5 years).

Purposes: pursuant to PHSA as amended and SBRDEA, for research into the causes of cancer and to develop prevention mechanisms. Programs include: epidemiology; chemical, physical, and biological carcinogenesis; nutrition; immunology; field studies and statistics; organ site. Grant funds may be used for personnel and consultants, equipment, patient costs, laboratory animals, alterations, and renovations. SBIR and STTR awards are made (*see Notes preceding* **93.001**).

Eligible applicants/beneficiaries: IHEs, hospitals, public agencies, nonprofit research institutions, or profit organizations.

Range: $32,200 to $5,358,941. **Average:** $411,347.

Activity: FY 06 estimate, 1,691 awards; FY 07 estimate, 1,696 awards.

HQ: National Cancer Institute, NIH-HHS, 6130 Executive Blvd., Bethesda, MD 20892. Phone: Division of Cancer Control and Population Science, (301) 496-9600; Division of Cancer Prevention, (301) 496-6616.

Internet: www.nih.gov; www.cancer.gov; www.cancercontrol.cancer.gov (Note: no field offices for this program.)

93.394 CANCER DETECTION AND DIAGNOSIS RESEARCH

Assistance: project grants. (100 percent/to 5 years).

Purposes: pursuant to PHSA as amended and SBRDEA, for research to improve cancer screening, early detection, and diagnostic techniques and methods. Grant funds may be used for patient costs, laboratory animals, equipment, renovations, alterations, personnel and consultant costs. SBIR and STTR awards are made (*see Notes preceding* **93.001**).

Eligible applicants/beneficiaries: IHEs, hospitals, public agencies, nonprofit research institutions, or profit organizations.

Range: $60,000 to $5,287,695. **Average:** $415,783.

Activity: FY 06 estimate, 729 awards; FY 07 estimate, 709 awards.

HQ: Associate Director, Cancer Diagnosis Program, Division of Cancer Treatment and Diagnosis, National Cancer Institute (EPN- 6035A), NIH-HHS, 6130 Executive Blvd., Bethesda, MD 20892. Phone: (301) 496-8639. *Grants management information*: Grants Management Officer, National Cancer Institute, NIH-HHS, EPS-234, Bethesda, MD 20892. Phone: (301) 496-7753.

Internet: www.nih.gov (Note: no field offices for this program.)

93.395 CANCER TREATMENT RESEARCH

Assistance: project grants. (100 percent/to 5 years).

Purposes: pursuant to PHSA as amended and SBRDEA, for fundamental, applied, and clinical cancer treatment research in all modes of therapy including surgery, radiotherapy, chemotherapy, and biological therapy. Supportive approaches include nutrition, stem cell and bone marrow transplantation, blood component replacement, toxicology, pharmacology. Grant funds may be used for patient costs, laboratory animals, alterations, renovations, personnel and consultant costs. SBIR and STTR awards are made (*see Notes preceding* **93.001**).

Eligible applicants/beneficiaries: IHEs, hospitals, public agencies, nonprofit research institutions, or profit organizations.

Range: $56,928 to $6,893,995. **Average:** $422,250.

Activity: FY 06 estimate, 1,365 grants; FY 07 estimate, 1350 grants.

HQ: Division of Cancer Treatment and Diagnosis, National Cancer Institute, NIH-HHS, Bldg. 31/3A44, 9000 Rockville Pike, Bethesda, MD 20892. Phone: (301) 496-4291. *Grants management information*: Grants Management Officer, National Cancer Institute, NIH-HHS, EPS-234, Bethesda, MD 20892. Phone: (301) 496-7753.

Internet: www.nci.nih.gov (Note: no field offices for this program.)

93.396 CANCER BIOLOGY RESEARCH

Assistance: project grants. (100 percent/to 5 years).

Purposes: pursuant to PHSA as amended and SBRDEA, for cancer biology research, including in the areas of nutrition, tumor biology, genetics, and immunology—toward the prevention, detection, diagnosis, and treatment of neoplastic diseases. Grant funds may be used for patient costs, laboratory animals, renovations, alterations, personnel and consultant costs. SBIR and STTR awards are made (*see Notes preceding* **93.001**).

Eligible applicants/beneficiaries: IHEs, hospitals, public agencies, nonprofit research institutions, or profit organizations.

Range: $58,055 to $2,880,629. **Average:** $347,764.

Activity: FY 06 estimate, 1,668 grants; FY 07 estimate, 1605 grants.

HQ: Deputy Director, Division of Cancer Biology, National Cancer Institute (EPN-5050), NIH-HHS, 6130 Executive Blvd., Bethesda, MD 20892. Phone: (301) 594-8782. *Grants management information*: Grants Management Officer, National Cancer Institute, NIH-HHS, EPS-234, Bethesda, MD 20892. Phone: (301) 496-7753.

Internet: www.nih.gov (Note: no field offices for this program.)

93.397 CANCER CENTERS SUPPORT GRANTS ("CCSG")

Assistance: project grants. (100 percent/to 5 years).

Purposes: pursuant to PHSA as amended, to provide core funding for comprehensive and specialized cancer centers, supporting the coordination of interdisciplinary programs ranging from basic research to clinical investigation to population science. Funds may be used for professional staff, centralized shared resources and services, and recruitment. Generally, research projects are not supported as such; rather, grants enhance ongoing research.

Eligible applicants/beneficiaries: U.S. nonprofit institutions with a peer-reviewed cancer research base of $4,000,000.

Range: $10,219 to $10,029,153. **Average:** $2,988,500.

Activity: FY 06 estimate, 152 center awards; FY 07 estimate, 152 center awards.

HQ: Chief, Cancer Centers Branch, Office of Centers, Training and Resources, NIH-HHS, 6116 Executive Blvd. - Ste. 700, Bethesda, MD 20892. Phone: (301) 496-8531. *Grants management information*: Grants

Management Officer, National Cancer Institute, NIH-HHS, EPS-234, Bethesda, MD 20892. Phone: (301) 496-7753.

Internet: www.nci.nih.gov/cancercenters (Note: no field offices for this program.)

93.398 CANCER RESEARCH MANPOWER

Assistance: project grants. (100 percent/to 5 years).

Purposes: pursuant to PHSA as amended, for biomedical training programs in basic, clinical, and cancer prevention research, and for fellowships to trainees under the NRSA program (*see Notes preceding* **93.001**). Cancer Education Grants are also available to promote cancer education programs. Various career awards provide short-term support for students.

Eligible applicants/beneficiaries: IHEs, hospitals, public agencies, or non-profit research institutions; U.S. citizens or permanent residents. Cancer Education Grants, career awards—profit organizations.

Range: $25,375 to $1,309,042. **Average:** $178,175.

Activity: FY 06 estimate, 986 awards; FY 07, 996 awards.

HQ: Chief, Cancer Training Branch, National Cancer Institute, NIH-HHS, 6116 Executive Blvd. - Rm. 7019, Bethesda, MD 20892. Phone: (301) 496-8580. *Grants management information*: Grants Management Officer, National Cancer Institute, NIH-HHS, EPS-234, Bethesda, MD 20892. Phone: (301) 496-7753.

Internet: www.cancer.gov (Note: no field offices for this program.)

93.399 CANCER CONTROL

Assistance: project grants. (100 percent/to 5 years).

Purposes: pursuant to PHSA as amended, for basic and applied research in cancer prevention and interventions. Programs include chemo-prevention; cancer communications; diet, nutrition, and physical activity; screening and early detection; biobehavioral mechanisms; tobacco control; special populations research; cancer survivorship; health services and outcomes research; surveillance research. Grant funds may be used for patient costs, renovations, alterations, personnel and consultant costs, and laboratory animals. SBIR and STTR awards are made (*see Notes preceding* **93.001**).

Eligible applicants/beneficiaries: IHEs, hospitals, public agencies, non-profit research institutions, or profit organizations.

Range: $16,733 to $17,418,204. **Average:** $1,044,185.

Activity: FY 06 estimate, 199 awards; FY 07 estimate, 199 awards.

HQ: Director, Division of Cancer Prevention, National Cancer Institute, NIH-HHS, 6130 Executive Blvd, Rockville, MD 20852. Phone: (301) 496-6616. Director, Division of Cancer Control and Population Science, National Cancer Institute, same address. Phone: (301) 594-6776. *Grants management information*: Grants Management Officer, National Cancer Institute, NIH-HHS, EPS-234, Bethesda, MD 20892. Phone: (301) 496-7753.

Internet: www.nih.gov; www.cancer.gov; www.cancercontrol.cancer.gov; www.cancer.gov/prevention (Note: no field offices for this program.)

93.441 INDIAN SELF-DETERMINATION ("Indian Self-Determination 638 Contracts")

Assistance: direct payments/specified use.

Purposes: pursuant to Contract Disputes Act of 1978 and ISDEAA, as amended, to enable Indian tribes to assume the management and operation of programs, functions, services, and activities for delivery of health care to Indian people through self-determination contracts.

Eligible applicants/beneficiaries: federally-recognized tribes or tribal organizations.

Range: $31,963 to $25,950,652. **Average:** $1,722,872.

Activity: as of FY 04, contracts support tribally-operated facilities: 3 hospitals, 97 health centers, 1 school health center, 65 health stations.

HQ: Health Promotion/Disease Prevention Coordinator IHS-HHS, 801 Thompson Ave. - Ste. 220, Rockville, MD 20852 Phone: (301) 443-1104.

Internet: www.ihs.gov.

93.442 SPECIAL DIABETES PROGRAM FOR INDIANS (SDPI) COMPETITIVE GRANT PROGRAM ("SDPI")

Assistance: project grants. (100 percent/5 years).

Purposes: for demonstration projects to implement and evaluate primary prevention of diabetes or prevention of cardiovascular disease in Indians with diabetes.

Eligible applicants/beneficiaries: IHS hospitals or clinics; tribes; Urban Indian Health Programs; consortia.

Range: $200,000 to $300,000 per year.

Activity: new program listing in 2004; 60 awards anticipated.

HQ: IHS National Diabetes Program, IHS-HHS, 5300 Homestead Rd. NE, Albuquerque, NM 87110. Phone: (505) 248-4182, FAX (505) 248-4188. *Grants management information*: Division of Grants Operations, HIS, 801 Thompson Ave. - Ste. 360, Rockville, MD 20852. Phone: (301) 443-5204, FAX (301) 443-9602.

Internet: www.ihs.gov/medicalprograms/diabetes; email, diabetesprogram@mail.ihs.gov (Note: no field offices for this program.)

93.443 HEALTH PROMOTION/DISEASE PREVENTION PROGRAM FOR AMERICAN INDIANS AND ALASKA NATIVES

Assistance: project grants. (100 percent/to 3 years).

Purposes: to create healthier American Indian/Alaskan Native communities by developing, implementing, and coordinating innovative and effective community and clinic-based intervention programs designed to promote health and prevent chronic disease and disability.

Eligible applicants: Federally-recognized tribes, tribal, urban Indian and primarily Indian and Native Alaskan nonprofit organizations.

Eligible beneficiaries: individuals who are members of an eligible applicant tribe, band, group or village within the scope of the Indian Health and medical service program.

Range: to $100,000 per grant.

Activity: new program added in 2005; FY 06 estimate, 13 new grants; FY 07 estimate, 13 continuing grants.

HQ: Health Promotion/Disease Prevention Coordinator IHS-HHS, 801 Thompson Ave. - Ste. 300, Rockville, MD 20852 Phone: (301) 443-5204; Grants Management information, Phone: (301) 443-5204.

Internet: www.ihs.gov.

93.447 STATE HEALTH FRAUD TASK FORCE GRANTS

Assistance: project grants (100 percent).

Purposes: pursuant to PHSA, to assist and educate health professionals and persons with serious illnesses of the dangers and magnitude of health fraud; to assist law enforcement agencies in identifying and prosecuting health fraud perpetrators; to obtain and disseminate information on the use of fraudulent drugs and therapies, as well as on approved drugs and therapies; to provide health fraud information to all state health agencies and community-based organizations. Funds may be used: to hold conferences and workshops; to develop and disseminate publications; for travel.

Eligible applicants/beneficiaries: one existing state health fraud task force per state, with consideration to states in the process of organizing a task force.

Range: $13,600 to $15,000. **Average:** $14,900.

Activity: FY 05, 11 awards.

HQ: Division of Federal-State Relations, Office of Regional Operations, Office of Regulatory Affairs, FDA-HHS (HFC-150), 5600 Fishers Lane - Rm. 12-07, Rockville, MD 20857. Phone: (301) 827-2906. *Grants management information*: Grants Management Specialist, Division of Contracts and Grants Management, Office of Acquisition and Grant Services, FDA, 5630 Fishers Lane, Rockville, MD 20857. Phone: (301) 827-7177, FAX (301) 827-7101.

Internet: www.fda.gov (Note: no field offices for this program.)

93.448 FOOD SAFETY AND SECURITY MONITORING PROJECT

Assistance: project grants. (100 percent/1-3 years).

Purposes: pursuant to the Public Health Security and Bioterrorism Preparedness and Response Act of 2002, to expand participation in networks to enhance federal, state, tribal, and local food safety and security testing programs; to promote a continuing, reliable capability and capacity for laboratory sample analyses of foods and food products for the rapid detection and identification of toxic chemicals or toxins. Funding supports provision of supplies, personnel, facility upgrades, training, and participation in proficiency testing to establish additional reliable laboratory sample analysis capacity and analysis of surveillance samples.

Eligible applicants/beneficiaries: state, local, and tribal government food emergency response laboratories.

Range: to $350,000 annually.

Activity: new program in FY 05.

HQ: Division of Field Science, Office of Regulatory Affairs (HFC- 140), FDA-HHS, 5600 Fishers Lane - Rm. 1207, Rockville, MD 20857. Phone: (301) 827-2899. *Grants management information*: Division of Contracts and Grants Management, FDA-HHS (HFA-500), 5600 Fishers Lane - Rm. 2107, Rockville, MD 20857. Phone: (301) 827-7182.

Internet: www.fda.gov/ora/fed_state/default.htm; www.grants.gov (Note: contacts are with program headquarters; however, district offices are listed in Part IV for information purposes.)

93.449 RUMINANT FEED BAN SUPPORT PROJECT

Assistance: project grants. (100 percent/to 3 years).

Purposes: pursuant to the Public Health Security and Bioterrorism Preparedness and Response Act of 2002, to increase surveillance throughout commercial feed channels to prevent the introduction or amplification of "BSE" in the U.S.A. Funds must supplement annual state program appropriations, and may be used for inspections or salvagers of food and feed and transporters of animal feed and ingredients, supplies, training, laboratory equipment for feed sample testing.

Eligible applicants/beneficiaries: state and tribal feed/BSE regulatory programs.

Average: $250,000.

Activity: new program in FY 05.

HQ: Division of Federal-State Relations, Office of Regulatory Affairs, HFC-140, 5600 Fishers Lane - Rm. 1207, Rockville, MD 20857. Phone: (301) 827-2899.

Internet: www.fda.gov/ora/fed_state/default.htm; www.grants.gov (Note: contacts are with program headquarters; however, district offices are listed in Part IV for information purposes.)

93.550 TRANSITIONAL LIVING FOR HOMELESS YOUTH

Assistance: project grants. (90 percent/5 years).

Purposes: pursuant to the Runaway, Homeless, and Missing Children Protection Act of 2003, to establish and operate transitional living projects for homeless youth age 16-21, including pregnant and parenting youth—providing shelter, skills training, and support services to help them make a successful transition toward productive adulthood and self-sufficiency. Living accommodations may be provided as host family homes, agency-supervised apartments, or scattered-site units rented directly by young persons with agency support.

Eligible applicants/beneficiaries: states, localities, private nonprofit entities, and networks unless they are part of the justice system; tribal governments applying as private nonprofit agencies; community-based organizations.

Range: $100,000 to $200,000. **Average:** $195,000.

Activity: FY 06 estimate, 207 grants; FY 07 estimate, 193 grants.

HQ: Associate Commissioner, Family and Youth Services Bureau, ACF-HHS, 1250 Maryland Ave., SW, Washington, DC 20024. Phone: (202) 205-8102.

Internet: www.acf.hhs.gov/programs/fysb.

93.551 ABANDONED INFANTS

Assistance: project grants. (90 percent/to 4 years).

Purposes: pursuant to the Abandoned Infants Assistance Act of 1988 as amended, for demonstration projects to prevent the abandonment of infants and young children, especially those exposed to HIV/AIDS or drug-affected, and to provide them and their families with appropriate services; to find homes for them, whether with their natural families or in foster care; to conduct residential programs; to provide respite care for families and care givers; to recruit and train service providers including foster parents, case management, and hospital staff; to provide technical assistance in planning, developing and operating projects.

Eligible applicants/beneficiaries: state, local, tribal governments; territories, possessions; nonprofit organizations; universities.

Range: $100,000 to $475,000. **Average:** $450,000.

Activity: FY 06 estimate, 31 grants; FY 07 estimate, 31 grants.

HQ: Children's Bureau, ACF-HHS, 1250 Maryland Ave., SW, Washington, DC 20024. Phone: (202) 205-8060.

Internet: www.acf.hhs.gov/programs/cb (Note: no field offices for this program.)

93.556 PROMOTING SAFE AND STABLE FAMILIES

Assistance: formula grants (75 percent).

Purposes: pursuant to SSA as amended, Adoption and Safe Families Act of 1997, and Promoting Safe and Stable Families Amendments of 2001, for community-based family support services promoting the safety and well-being of children and families by enhancing family functioning and child development; for family preservation services for those at risk or in crisis, including reunification, adoption promotion and support, preplacement and prevention, follow-up after foster or respite care, and improving parenting skills; for infant safe haven programs.

Eligible applicants/beneficiaries: states, territories, and certain tribes.

Range: state grants, $437,470 to $43,424,375; tribe grants, $10,198 to $910,697; discretionary grants, $100,000 to $700,000. **Average:** $250,000.

Activity: FY 06 estimate, 81 grants; FY 07 estimate, 81 grants.

HQ: Deputy Associate Commissioner, Children's Bureau, ACF-HHS, 1250 Maryland Ave., SW, Washington, DC 20024. Phone: (202) 205-8618.

Internet: www.acf.hhs.gov/programs/cb.

93.557 EDUCATION AND PREVENTION GRANTS TO REDUCE SEXUAL ABUSE OF RUNAWAY, HOMELESS AND STREET YOUTH ("Street Outreach Program" - "SOP")

Assistance: project grants. (90 percent/3 years).

Purposes: pursuant to VCCLEA and Runaway, Homeless, and Missing Children Protection Act of 2003, to provide street-based services to runaway, homeless, and "street youth" that have been subjected to or are at risk of sexual abuse, prostitution, or sexual exploitation—including education and outreach, emergency shelter, survival aid, case management, treatment and counseling, information and referral, crisis intervention, and follow-up support.

Eligible applicants/beneficiaries: private nonprofit agencies including nonfederally recognized tribes and urban Indian organizations.

Range: $100,000 to $200,000 for three years. **Average:** $100,000.

Activity: FY 06 estimate, 140 grants; FY 07 estimate, 140 grants.

HQ: Associate Commissioner, Family and Youth Services Bureau, ACF-HHS, 1250 Maryland Ave., SW, Washington, DC 20024. Phone: (202) 205-8102.

Internet: www.acf.hhs.gov/programs/fysb.

93.558 TEMPORARY ASSISTANCE FOR NEEDY FAMILIES ("TANF")

Assistance: formula grants.

Purposes: pursuant to SSA as amended and PRWORA, to provide cash grants, work opportunities, and other services to needy families so that their children can be cared for in their own homes; to reduce dependency by promoting job preparation, work, and marriage; to reduce and prevent out-of-wedlock pregnancies; and, to encourage the formation and maintenance of two-parent families. Permitted uses of funds are flexible, based on state plans developed in consultation with local governments and private organizations, including: assistance to low-income households in meeting home heating and cooling costs; uses permitted under the predecessor Aid to Families with Dependent Children (AFDC), Job Opportunities and Basic Skills Training (JOBS), and Emergency Assistance (EA) programs; transferring limited amounts to the Child Care and Development Block Grant (CCDBG) and Social Services Block Grant (SSBG) programs; to meet contingencies. "High Performance Bonus" and "Decrease in Illegitimacy Bonus" funds may be awarded to states meeting specific maintenance-of-effort requirements relating to superseded programs. Most families may receive assistance for no more than five years.

Eligible applicants/beneficiaries: states, tribes, specified Alaskan entities, territories.

Range: states, $21,781,446 to $3,733,817,784; tribes, $77,195 to $31,174,026.

Activity: FY 06 estimate, all states, DC, 3 territories, 65 tribal programs funded.

HQ: Director, Office of Family Assistance, ACF-HHS, Aerospace Bldg. - 5th floor, 370 L'Enfant Promenade SW, Washington, DC 20447. Phone: (no number provided).

Internet: www.acf.dhhs.gov/program/ofa; www.acf.dhhs.gov/programs/dts.

93.560 FAMILY SUPPORT PAYMENTS TO STATES—ASSISTANCE PAYMENTS ("Adult Programs in the Territories")

Assistance: formula grants (75 percent).

Purposes: to provide the federal share of assistance payments to aged, blind or disabled persons in Guam, PR, and VI—enabling recipients to pay for food, shelter, clothing, and other daily living needs.

Eligible applicants: Guam, PR, and VI.

Eligible beneficiaries: needy aged, blind or disabled persons in Guam, PR, and VI.

Range: $700,000 to $21,000,000. **Average:** $7,700,000.

Activity: 3 awards annually.

HQ: Director, Office of Family Assistance, ACF-HHS, Aerospace Bldg. - 5th floor, 370 L'Enfant Promenade SW, Washington, DC 20447. Phone: (202) 401-9275.

Internet: www.acf.dhhs.gov/programs/ofa.

93.563 CHILD SUPPORT ENFORCEMENT

Assistance: formula grants (66-90 percent).

Purposes: pursuant to SSA, Title IV-D, as amended, to enforce the collection of child support obligations of absent parents, and to locate absent parents, establish paternity, and obtain child, spousal, and medical support.

Eligible applicants: state agencies, DC, PR, VI, and Guam; tribes.

Eligible beneficiaries: all TANF, foster care maintenance, and Medicaid payments applicants or recipients assigning support rights to the states; all ceasing to receive TANF payments; individuals authorizing the continuation of support enforcement services; other individuals authorizing the continuation of support enforcement services; other individuals applying for services.

Average: $75,391,889.

Activity: annually, 54 grants. FY 07 estimated collections, $25 billion.

HQ: Director, Planning, Research and Evaluation Division, Office of Child Support Enforcement, ACF-HHS, 370 L'Enfant Promenade SW - 4th floor, Washington, DC 20447. Phone: (202) 401-5374.

Internet: www.acf.dhhs.gov/programs/cse.

93.564 CHILD SUPPORT ENFORCEMENT RESEARCH

Assistance: project grants. (to 95 percent/from 17 months).

Purposes: pursuant to SSA as amended, for innovative research and demonstration projects of regional and national significance to improve the administrative and services delivery aspects of child support payment enforcement programs.

Eligible applicants/beneficiaries: state agencies.

Range: $83,000 to $120,000.

Activity: FY 06 estimate, 8 new, 10 continuation grants.

HQ: Director, Planning, Research and Evaluation Division, Office of Child Support Enforcement, ACF-HHS, 370 L'Enfant Promenade SW - 4th floor, Washington, DC 20447. Phone: (202) 690-6275.

Internet: www.acf.dhhs.gov/programs/cse.

93.566 REFUGEE AND ENTRANT ASSISTANCE—STATE ADMINISTERED PROGRAMS

Assistance: formula grants.

Purposes: pursuant to the Refugee Act of 1980 and Refugee Education Assistance Act of 1980 as amended, for resettlement assistance to eligible refugees from foreign countries including Cuban and Haitian entrants, asylees, victims of a severe form of trafficking, and certain Amerasians from Vietnam—including maintenance payments for up to eight months, medical and social services, English language training, case management, employment services. States may contract with other providers to offer such services.

Eligible applicants/beneficiaries: designated state agencies.

Range: FY 05 total cash, medical and administration, $132,277,000,000.

Activity: FY 06, ceiling of 70,000 refugees; arrivals of 20,000 Cuban/Haitian entrants, 24,000 asylees, 1,000 victims of trafficking.

HQ: Office of Refugee Resettlement, ACF-HHS, 370 L'Enfant Promenade SW - 8th floor, Washington, DC 20447. Phone: (202) 401-4579.

Internet: www.acf.hhs.gov/programs/orr (Note: no field offices for this program.)

93.567 REFUGEE AND ENTRANT ASSISTANCE—VOLUNTARY AGENCY PROGRAMS

Assistance: project grants. (67 percent/3 years).

Purposes: pursuant to the Refugee Act of 1980 as amended, to assist refugees in becoming self-supporting. Funds may be used for cash allowances, job training and development, English language training, case management, social services, and medical support. The federal share is up to $2,000 per refugee.

Eligible applicants/beneficiaries: private nonprofit agencies with a Reception and Placement Grant from the Department of State or DHS.

Average: voluntary agencies, $6,000,000; local affiliates, $200,000.

Activity: FY 06, 9 agencies funded.

HQ: Office of Refugee Resettlement, ACF-HHS, 370 L'Enfant Promenade SW - 8th Floor West, Washington, DC 20447. Phone: (202) 401-4559.

Internet: www.acf.hhs.gov/programs/orr (Note: no field offices for this program.)

93.568 LOW-INCOME HOME ENERGY ASSISTANCE

Assistance: formula grants (100 percent).

Purposes: pursuant to the Community Opportunities, Accountability, Training, and Educational Services Act of 1998 (COATES), for Energy Assistance Block Grants to states, enabling them to make payments to or on behalf of eligible low-income households for their home energy costs, either heating or cooling. Recipients may also receive energy crisis and weatherization assistance. Funds may support training and technical assistance to state and other jurisdictions administering the program. Supplemental funds may be allocated to grantees that leverage nonfederal resources with their LIHEAP funds, under the Residential Energy Assistance Challenge Program (REACH).

Eligible applicants/beneficiaries: block grants—states, DC, tribal governments, specified territories. Training and technical assistance grants—states, tribes, tribal organizations, territories, public agencies, private nonprofit organizations, businesses applying jointly with private nonprofit organizations.

Range: $1,123,000,000 to $236,007,613. **Average:** $30,352,000.

Activity: FY 06 estimate, 5,000,000 households assisted.

HQ: Director, Division of Energy Assistance, Office of Community Services, ACF-HHS, 370 L'Enfant Promenade SW, Washington, DC 20447. Phone: (202) 401-9351, FAX (202) 401-5661.

Internet: www.acf.hhs.gov/programs/liheap (Note: no field offices for this program.)

93.569 COMMUNITY SERVICES BLOCK GRANT

Assistance: formula grants.

Purposes: pursuant to COATES, for anti-poverty programs and projects, conducted by local community action agencies and organizations, to eliminate the causes of poverty—including employment services, elderly services, housing, educational services, health care, emergency health and food assistance, services to migrant and seasonal farm workers, coordination of various governmental and private services.

Eligible applicants: states, territories, tribes, tribal organizations.

Eligible beneficiaries: locally-based nonprofit community anti- poverty agencies and other eligible entities providing services to low-income individuals and families.

Range/Average: N.A.

Activity: FY 05, 231 grants; FY 06 estimate, 227 grants.

HQ: Division of State Assistance, Office of Community Services, ACF-HHS, 370 L'Enfant Promenade SW, Washington, DC 20447. Phone: (202) 401-9343.

Internet: www.acf.hhs.gov/programs/ocs (Note: no field offices for this program.)

93.570 COMMUNITY SERVICES BLOCK GRANT—DISCRETIONARY AWARDS ("Community Economic Development")

Assistance: project grants. (100 percent/1-5 years).

Purposes: pursuant to COATES, for program activities to alleviate the causes of poverty in distressed communities. Eligible activities include those that: promote full-time permanent jobs for the poor; provide income or ownership opportunities for community members; address needs for rural water and waste-water treatment; provide character-building activities for youth, including sports and physical fitness; assist migrant and seasonal farm workers; promote electronic communication and access to program information. Special consideration is given to projects designated for Empowerment Zones or Enterprise Communities.

Eligible applicants/beneficiaries: economic development projects—private, locally initiated and governed nonprofit community development corporations.

Range: to $700,000.

Activity: FY 05, 56 awards; FY 06 estimate, 53 awards.

HQ: Team Leader, Division of Community Discretionary Programs, Office of Community Services, ACF-HHS, 370 L'Enfant Promenade SW, Washington, DC 20447. Phone: (202) 401-3446.

Internet: www.acf.hhs.gov/programs/ocs (Note: no field offices for this program.)

93.571 COMMUNITY SERVICES BLOCK GRANT FORMULA AND DISCRETIONARY AWARDS COMMUNITY FOOD AND NUTRITION PROGRAMS

Assistance: formula grants; direct payments/specified use. (grants and payments, 100 percent/direct payments, to 17 months).

Purposes: pursuant to COATES, for community-based, local, statewide, and national food and nutrition initiatives to coordinate existing private and public resources for low-income populations. Funds must be subgranted to eligible agencies. Competitive grants may be awarded for innovative approaches, including outreach and public education activities to inform unserved or underserved target groups, including displaced workers, of available nutrition services.

Eligible applicants/beneficiaries: formula grants—states, territories, possessions. Direct grants—state and local public and private nonprofit agencies.

Range: formula grants, $715 to $363,440; direct grants, $50,000. **Average:** formula grants, $182,078.

Activity: FY 06, 104 grants.

HQ: Division of State Assistance, Office of Community Services, ACF-HHS, 370 L'Enfant Promenade SW, Washington, DC 20447. Phone: (202) 401-9343.

Internet: www.acf.hhs.gov/programs/ocs (Note: no field offices for this program.)

93.575 CHILD CARE AND DEVELOPMENT BLOCK GRANT ("CCDF")

Assistance: formula grants.

Purposes: pursuant to the Child Care and Development Block Grant Act of 1990 and PRWORA, to develop and provide child care policies and fee-based services, mainly for working low-income families. Activities must include: comprehensive consumer education to parents and the public; increasing parental choice; resource and referral services; infant and toddler, and school- age services; implementation of state health, safety, licensing, and registration standards; staff training; research, demonstration, and evaluation projects; to improve resettlement services for refugees. Funds may not support any real estate or major construction costs.

Eligible applicants: states, territories, possessions; tribal governments and organizations, Alaska native and native Hawaiian organizations.

Eligible beneficiaries: children under age 13 (19 if disabled), residing with a family with income not above 85 percent of the state median, in which at least one parent has a job or attends a job training or educational program, or needing or receiving protective services.

Range: (including funding under **93.596**) states, DC, PR, $8,196,763 to $535,672,762; tribes, $22,837 to $9,813,443; territories, $1,700,190 to $4,063,930. **Average:** $93,000,000; tribes, $381,000; territories, $2,600,000.

Activity: FY 06, 313 grants.

HQ: Child Care Bureau, ACF-HHS, 1250 Maryland Ave. SW - 8th Floor, Washington, DC 20024. Phone: (202) 690-6782.

Internet: www.acf.dhhs.gov/programs/ccb.

93.576 REFUGEE AND ENTRANT ASSISTANCE—DISCRETIONARY GRANTS

Assistance: project grants. (to 100 percent/1-5 years).

Purposes: pursuant to the Refugee Act of 1980 and Refugee Education Assistance Act of 1980 as amended, for projects promoting refugee self-sufficiency or addressing their special needs. Project examples: relocation from high welfare dependency areas to communities with favorable employment prospects; vocational training and employment services; micro-loans for start-up businesses.

Eligible applicants/beneficiaries: state and local governments, private non-profit organizations.

Range: $5,000 to $19,000,000.

Activity: FY 06 estimate, 260 discretionary, 49 targeted assistance grants.

HQ: Office of Refugee Resettlement, ACF-HHS, 370 L'Enfant Promenade SW - 8th Floor West, Washington, DC 20447. Phone: *targeted assistance,* (202) 401-4556; *discretionary,* (202) 401-5363.

Internet: www.acf.hhs.gov/programs/orr (Note: no field offices for this program.)

93.579 U.S. REPATRIATION

Assistance: project grants. (100 percent/5 years).

Purposes: pursuant to SSA, to provide temporary assistance, care, and treatment to citizens returning to the U.S. from foreign travel—required because of physical or mental illness, destitution, or because of war, threat of war, or a similar crisis. Assistance may include money, food, shelter, clothing, and transportation. Costs must be repaid to the federal government.

Eligible applicants/beneficiaries: international social service organizations.

Average: FY 04, one award, $833,662.

Activity: annual estimate, 175-200 citizens assisted.

HQ: Office of Refugee Resettlement, ACF-HHS, 370 L'Enfant Promenade SW - 8th floor, Washington, DC 20447. Phone: (202) 401-4845.

Internet: www.acf.hhs.gov/programs/orr (Note: no field offices for this program.)

93.581 IMPROVING THE CAPABILITY OF INDIAN TRIBAL GOVERNMENTS TO REGULATE ENVIRONMENTAL QUALITY

Assistance: project grants. (80-100 percent/1-3 years).

Purposes: pursuant to the Native American Programs Act of 1974 as amended and Indian Environmental Regulatory Enhancement Act, to plan, develop, and implement tribal environmental regulatory programs pertaining to Indian lands, including: environmental protection regulations, ordinances, and laws; technical and operating capacity relating to both tribal and federal requirements; employee training and education; monitoring and enforcement; tribal court enforcement systems.

Eligible applicants/beneficiaries: tribes, incorporated nonfederally-recognized tribes, Alaska native villages, tribal governments, and consortia.

Range: $50,000 to $250,000.

Activity: FY 06 estimate, 16 grants.

HQ: Administration for Native Americans, ACF-HHS, 370 L'Enfant Promenade SW, Washington, DC 20447. Phone: (202) 401-5590.

Internet: www.acf.dhhs.gov/programs/ana (Note: no field offices for this program.)

93.582 MITIGATION OF ENVIRONMENTAL IMPACTS TO INDIAN LANDS DUE TO DEPARTMENT OF DEFENSE ACTIVITIES

Assistance: project grants. (95-100 percent/1-3 years).

Purposes: pursuant to the Department of Defense Appropriations Act, to identify DOD environmental impacts to tribal lands and Alaska native villages, and to plan, develop, and implement mitigation programs.

Eligible applicants/beneficiaries: tribes; incorporated nonfederally-recognized and state-recognized tribes; Alaska native villages, tribes, or tribal governing bodies; nonprofit Alaska native regional associations or corporations or native organizations or consortia.

Range/Average: N.A.

Activity: FY 05, 2 awards; FY 06 estimate, 8-10 grants; FY 07 estimate, 0 awards.

HQ: Administration for Native Americans, ACF-HHS, 370 L'Enfant Promenade SW, Washington, DC 20447. Phone: (877) 922-9262.

Internet: www.acf.dhhs.gov/programs/ana (Note: no field offices for this program.)

93.583 REFUGEE AND ENTRANT ASSISTANCE—WILSON/FISH PROGRAM ("Wilson/Fish Program"- "Fish/Wilson Program")

Assistance: project grants. (100 percent/to 4 years).

Purposes: pursuant to the Refugee Act of 1980 and Refugee Education Assistance Act of 1980 as amended, for demonstration projects promoting early employment and self-sufficiency of refugees, including certain Amerasian immigrants, asylees, Cuban and Haitian entrants, and certified victims of a severe form of trafficking—developed as innovative approaches to the state- administered program (**93.566**), including the provision of integrated services, cash and medical assistance, social services, case management, and coordination among voluntary resettlement agencies and services providers.

Eligible applicants/beneficiaries: states, voluntary and other nonprofit resettlement organizations.

Range/Average: N.A.

Activity: FY 06, 11 continuation projects funded.

HQ: Office of Refugee Resettlement, ACF-HHS, 370 L'Enfant Promenade SW - 8th Floor West, Washington, DC 20447. Phone: (202) 205-5933.

Internet: www.acf.hhs.gov/programs/orr (Note: no field offices for this program.)

93.584 REFUGEE AND ENTRANT ASSISTANCE—TARGETED ASSISTANCE GRANTS ("TAP; TAG")

Assistance: formula grants. (100 percent/3 years).

Purposes: pursuant to the Immigration and Nationality Act, Refugee Assistance Extension Act of 1986, VTVPA, amendments, and related acts, for employment-related and other social services for refugees, asylees, Amerasians, victims of a severe form of trafficking, and entrants in areas of high concentrations and high welfare rates, including: job development and placement; on- the-job training; business and employer incentives; job-related and vocational English language training.

Eligible applicants: state agencies providing assistance to counties and similar areas.

Eligible beneficiaries: refugees admitted within last five years, Cuban and Haitian entrants, certain Amerasians from Vietnam and their accompanying family members, certified victims of a severe form of trafficking.

Range: $125,199 to $11,126,128.

Activity: FY 05, 48 counties in 27 states funded.

HQ: Office of Refugee Resettlement, ACF-HHS, Division of Budget, Policy, and Data Analysis, 370 L'Enfant Promenade SW - 8th Floor, Washington, DC 20447. Phone: (202) 401-4579.

Internet: www.acf.hhs.gov/programs/orr (Note: no field offices for this program.)

93.586 STATE COURT IMPROVEMENT PROGRAM

Assistance: formula grants (75 percent).

Purposes: to improve the performance of state courts in their role in the continuum of care provided for families and children at risk. Funds may be used to assess areas in need of correction or added attention and to implement reforms.

Eligible applicants/beneficiaries: the highest state court in each state, DC, and PR.

Range: $98,224 to $1,226,900. **Average:** $259,869.

Activity: annually, 52 grants.

HQ: Children's Bureau, ACF-HHS, 1250 Maryland Ave. SW, Washington, DC 20024. Phone: (202) 205-8709.

Internet: www.acf.hhs.gov/programs/cb.

93.587 PROMOTE THE SURVIVAL AND CONTINUING VITALITY OF NATIVE AMERICAN LANGUAGES

Assistance: project grants. (80-100 percent/1-3 years).

Purposes: pursuant to the Native Americans Programs Act of 1974 as amended and Native Americans Languages Act of 1992, to plan and implement programs to assure the survival and continuing vitality of native American languages. Project examples: development of specialized school curricula; language training programs including language immersion camps and master/apprentice programs; compilation and transcription of oral narratives.

Eligible applicants/beneficiaries: tribes; incorporated nonfederally-recognized and state-recognized tribes; Alaska native villages, tribes, or tribal governing bodies; nonprofit Alaska native regional associations or corporations or native organizations or consortia; incorporated nonprofit multipurpose community-based Indian organizations; urban Indian centers; public and private nonprofit agencies, tribally controlled community colleges, postsecondary vocation.

Range: Category I, $50,000 to $100,000; Category II, $50,000 to $175,000.

Activity: FY 06 estimate, 25 grants; FY 07 estimate, 25 grants.

HQ: Administration for Native Americans, ACF-HHS, 370 L'Enfant Promenade SW, Washington, DC 20447. Phone: (202) 690-5787.

Internet: www.acf.dhhs.gov/programs/ana (Note: no field offices for this program.)

93.590 COMMUNITY-BASED CHILD ABUSE PREVENTION GRANTS

Assistance: formula grants.

Purposes: pursuant to the Child Abuse Prevention and Treatment Act as amended, to establish, operate, or expand statewide networks of community-based family resource programs to prevent child abuse and neglect.

Eligible applicants: states, some territories and possessions.

Eligible beneficiaries: children, families; organizations dealing with family resource programs.

Range: $200,000 to $4,000,000. **Average:** $717,263.

Activity: annually, 60 grants.

HQ: Office on Child Abuse and Neglect, ACF-HHS, 1250 Maryland Ave. SW - 8th Floor, Washington, DC 20024. Phone: (202) 205-2629.

Internet: www.friendsnrc.org (Note: no field offices for this program.)

93.591 FAMILY VIOLENCE PREVENTION AND SERVICES/GRANTS FOR BATTERED WOMEN'S SHELTERS—GRANTS TO STATE DOMESTIC VIOLENCE COALITIONS

Assistance: formula grants (100 percent).

Purposes: pursuant to the Family Violence Prevention and Services Act, Child Abuse Prevention, Adoption and Family Services Act, VCCLEA, VTVPA, Child Abuse Prevention and Treatment Act, Keeping Children and Families Safe Act of 2003, amendments, and other acts, for prevention and intervention activities conducted by state domestic violence coalitions, including: program coordination with and technical assistance to local programs and services providers; encouraging appropriate responses to domestic violence cases; working with judicial and law enforcement officials to develop appropriate responses to child custody and visitation issues involving domestic violence; public education campaigns; training; related activities.

Eligible applicants/beneficiaries: statewide nonprofit coalitions in states, some territories and possessions.

Average: states, $237,037.

Activity: annually, 53 grants.

HQ: Family and Youth Services Bureau, ACF-HHS, 1250 Maryland Ave. SW, Washington, DC 20024. Phone: (202) 401-5529.

Internet: www.acf.hhs.gov/programs/fysb (Note: no field offices for this program.)

93.592 FAMILY VIOLENCE PREVENTION AND SERVICES/GRANTS FOR BATTERED WOMEN'S SHELTERS—DISCRETIONARY GRANTS

Assistance: project grants. (varying match/1-5 years).

Purposes: pursuant to the Family Violence Prevention and Services Act, Child Abuse Prevention, Adoption and Family Services Act, Child Abuse Prevention and Treatment Act, VCCLEA, VTVPA, Keeping Children and Families Safe Act of 2003, amendments, and other acts, to prevent family violence through projects and activities intended to improve the design, delivery, and coordination of services addressing the problem. Project activities may involve information gathering, research, demonstrations, evaluation, establishing specialized national resource centers, a national hotline, and public education.

Eligible applicants/beneficiaries: public and private nonprofit agencies, tribes, Alaska native villages or regional corporations.

Range: $30,000 to $1,494,779. **Average:** $260,142.

Activity: annually, 44 grants.

HQ: Family and Youth Services Bureau, ACF-HHS, 1250 Maryland Ave. SW, Washington, DC 20024. Phone: (202) 401-5529.

Internet: www.acf.hhs.gov/programs/fysb (Note: no field offices for this program.)

93.593 JOB OPPORTUNITIES FOR LOW-INCOME INDIVIDUALS ("JOLI Program")

Assistance: project grants. (to 100 percent/to 3 years).

Purposes: pursuant to the Family Support Act as amended and PRWORA, to create new permanent employment and business opportunities for TANF recipients and others through: participant training, supportive, and follow-up activities; expansion of existing businesses through technical and financial assistance; self-employment and micro-enterprises; new business ventures; nontraditional employment initiatives leading to self-sufficiency. Projects must: involve cooperative relationships with local TANF agencies, involving supportive services and client referrals, with encouragement to establish partnerships with child support enforcement agencies; include a strong evaluation component.

Eligible applicants: nonprofit IRS Section 501(c) organizations including community development corporations and charitable and tribal organizations.

Eligible beneficiaries: TANF recipients and other low-income individuals.

Range: to $500,000.

Activity: FY 06 estimate, 10 grants.

HQ: Team Leader, Division of Community Discretionary Programs, Office of Community Services, ACF-HHS, 370 L'Enfant Promenade SW, Washington, DC 20447. Phone: (202) 401-5483.

Internet: www.acf.hhs.gov/programs/ocs/index.html (Note: no field offices for this program.)

93.594 TRIBAL WORK GRANTS ("Native Employment Works; NEW")

Assistance: formula grants.

Purposes: pursuant to SSA as amended, to allow tribes to operate programs to make work available to their members.

Eligible applicants/beneficiaries: tribes or Alaska native organizations that conducted JOBS programs in FY 95.

Range: $5,187 to $1,752,666. **Average:** $97,862.

Activity: annually, 78 grants.

HQ: Division of Tribal TANF Management, Office of Family Assistance, Administration for Children and Families, HHS, Aerospace Bldg., 370 L'Enfant Promenade, SW - 5th Floor, Washington, DC 20447. Phone: (202) 401-5308.

Internet: www.acf.hhs.gov/programs.

93.595 WELFARE REFORM RESEARCH, EVALUATIONS AND NATIONAL STUDIES

Assistance: project grants. (75 percent/1-5 years).

Purposes: pursuant to PRWORA, for research on the benefits, effects, and costs of various welfare reform interventions; for studies on the effects of different programs on welfare dependency, illegitimacy, teen pregnancy, employment rates, child well-being, and related areas; for demonstrations; for analyses and evaluations.

Eligible applicants/beneficiaries: governmental entities, IHEs, nonprofit and profit organizations.

Range: $90,260 to $6,000,000. **Average:** $712,000.

Activity: annually, 18 grants.

HQ: Office of Planning, Research and Evaluation, Administration for Children and Families, HHS, 370 L'Enfant Promenade SW - 7th Floor, Washington, DC 20447. Phone: (202) 401-4535, FAX (202) 205-3598.

Internet: www.acf.hhs.gov/programs/opre.

93.596 CHILD CARE MANDATORY AND MATCHING FUNDS OF THE CHILD CARE AND DEVELOPMENT FUND ("Child Care and Development Fund (CCDF)")

Assistance: formula grants (matching/2 years).

Purposes: pursuant to SSA, PRWORA, Child Care and Development Block Grant Act of 1990, and amendments, to assist low-income families with child care by: developing flexible child care programs and policies; promoting choices by working parents in selecting suitable child care; providing consumer education information to help parents make informed child care choices; implementing state health, safety, licensing, and registration standards. At least 70 percent of grant funds must be used to provide child care assistance to families: receiving assistance under a state TANF program; attempting to work to "transition" off temporary assistance programs through work activities, or at risk of becoming dependent on temporary assistance programs. The matching rate is the same as under the Medicaid program.

Eligible applicants: states, DC, tribal governments and organizations, Alaska native corporations.

Eligible beneficiaries: children under age 13 (19 if disabled), residing with a family with income not above 85 percent of the state median, in which at least one parent has a job or attends a job training or educational program, or needing or receiving protective services.

Range: states, $8,196,763 to $535,672,762; tribes, $22,837 to $9,813,443; territories, $1,700,190 to $4,063,930. **Average:** states, $93,000,000; tribes, $381,000; territories, $2,600,000.

Activity: FY 06, 292 grants; FY 07 estimate, 292 grants.

HQ: Child Care Bureau, ACF-HHS, 1250 Maryland Ave. SW - 8th Floor, Washington, DC 20024. Phone: (202) 690-6782, FAX (202) 690-5600.

Internet: www.acf.dhhs.gov/programs/ccb.

93.597 GRANTS TO STATES FOR ACCESS AND VISITATION PROGRAMS

Assistance: project grants (90 percent).

Purposes: pursuant to SSA, for programs that support and facilitate access and visitation by noncustodial parents with their children. Eligible project activities include mediation, counseling, education, development of parenting plans, visitation enforcement, and development of guidelines for visitation and alternative custody arrangements.

Eligible applicants/beneficiaries: states, DC, PR, VI, Guam.

Range/Average: N.A.

Activity: FY 06 estimate, 54 grants; FY 07 estimate, 62 grants.

HQ: Director, Consumer Services, Office of Child Support Enforcement, Aerospace Bldg., 370 L'Enfant Promenade SW - 4th Floor, Washington, DC 20447. Phone: (202) 401- 9373.

Internet: www.acf.dhhs.gov/programs/cse.

93.598 SERVICES TO VICTIMS OF A SEVERE FORM OF TRAFFICKING

Assistance: project grants.

Purposes: pursuant to VTVPA, to provide victims of a severe form of trafficking access to benefits and services to the same extent as refugees, including case management, referrals and funded cash, medical assistance, special mental health and other services, and community and local outreach.

Eligible applicants: state and local governments; private nonprofit organizations.

Eligible beneficiaries: adults and children certified by HHS as victims of a severe form of trafficking, in consultation with the Attorney General.

Range/Average: N.A.

Activity: FY 05, 230 victims certified as eligible for assistance.

HQ: Office of Refugee Resettlement, ACF-HHS, 370 L'Enfant Promenade SW - 8th floor, Washington, DC 20447. Phone: (866) 401-5510, (202) 401-4825, -9207.

Internet: www.acf.dhhs.gov/programs/orr (Note: no field offices for this program.)

93.599 CHAFEE EDUCATION AND TRAINING VOUCHERS PROGRAM ("ETV")

Assistance: formula grants (80 percent).

Purposes: pursuant to SSA, Chafee Foster Care Independence Act of 1999, and Promoting Safe and Stable Families Amendments of 2001, to make vouchers available for education and training, including postsecondary, to youths that have aged out of foster care or that have been adopted from the foster care system after age 16 until they reach age 23—as long as they are participating in the Chafee Foster Care Independence Program (program **93.674**) at age 21. Vouchers in amounts up to $5,000 per year may be used for the cost of attending an IHE.

Eligible applicants: state governments, DC, PR.

Eligible beneficiaries: youth otherwise eligible for services under program **93.674**, including those who have left foster care because they attained age 18 and not yet attained age 21; youth likely to remain in foster care until age 18.

Range: $92,716 to $8,547,517. **Average:** $879,469.

Activity: annually, 52 grants.

HQ: Children's Bureau, ACF HHS, 1250 Maryland Ave. SW - 8th Floor, Washington DC 20024. Phone: (202) 205-8086.

Internet: www.acf.hhs.gov/programs/cb.

93.600 HEAD START

Assistance: project grants (80 to 100 percent).

Purposes: pursuant to COATES, to promote school readiness through Head Start Programs offering comprehensive health, education, nutrition, social, and other services to economically disadvantaged preschool children, including children of migratory workers and on Indian reservations; to involve parents in the program. Training and technical assistance grants may be awarded to Head Start agencies and to agencies providing services. At least 90 percent of project enrollment must be from families with incomes below OMB poverty guidelines or receiving public assistance; at least 10 percent must be available for children with disabilities.

Eligible applicants: local governments, tribes, public or private nonprofit and profit agencies. Subcontracts with other agencies are permitted.

Eligible beneficiaries: children from birth until their entry into school systems.

Range: $133,000 to $199,043,000. **Average:** $4,120,000.

Activity: annually, 1,604 grants.

HQ: Head Start Bureau, ACF-HHS, 330 C St. SW, Washington, DC 20447. Phone: (202) 205-8572.

Internet: www2.acf.dhhs.gov/programs/hsb.

93.601 CHILD SUPPORT ENFORCEMENT DEMONSTRATIONS AND SPECIAL PROJECTS

Assistance: project grants. (100 percent/17 weeks).

Purposes: pursuant to SSA and PRWORA, for regional and national projects and demonstrations to improve the effectiveness of child support enforcement efforts on the regional and national levels, advancing the requirements of PRWORA.

Eligible applicants/beneficiaries: state human services umbrella and other state and local public agencies; nonprofit organizations; tribes and tribal organizations; consortia.

Range: $100,000 to $200,000. **Average:** $150,000.

Activity: FY 06 estimate, 6 grants; FY 07 estimate, 6 grants.

HQ: Deputy Director, Division of State, Tribal, and Local Assistance, Office of Child Support Enforcement, ACF-HHS, 370 L'Enfant Promenade SW - 4th Floor, Washington, DC 20447. Phone: (202) 401-4849.

Internet: www.acf.dhhs.gov/programs/cse.

93.602 ASSETS FOR INDEPENDENCE DEMONSTRATION PROGRAM

Assistance: project grants. (50 percent/5 years).

Purposes: pursuant to the Assets for Independence Act and COATES as amended, for demonstration projects to establish and evaluate the social, civic, psychological, and economic effects of providing incentives to individuals and families with limited incomes to save a portion of their earned income to: obtain a postsecondary education; purchase first homes; capitalize small businesses; transfer assets to IDAs of family members. 85 percent of federal and matching funds must be used to match deposits in Individual Development Accounts (IDAs) by participants. The maximum federal contribution is $2,000 per individual and $4,000 per household.

Eligible applicants: national, state, regional, and community- based organizations; tax-exempt nonprofit organizations; state or local agencies; tribal governments applying jointly with nonprofit organizations; low-income credit unions; community development financial institutions collaborating with community-based organizations.

Eligible beneficiaries: individuals and members of households eligible for TANF or with adjusted incomes not exceeding the earned income amount specified in Section 32 of the Internal Revenue Code. Maximum net worth provisions apply.

Range: to $1,000,000. **Average:** $350,000.

Activity: FY 06 estimate, 62 grants; FY 07 estimate, 62 grants.

HQ: Office of Community Services, ACF-HHS, 370 L'Enfant Promenade SW, Washington, DC 20447. Phone: (202) 401-4626.

Internet: www.acf.hhs.gov/assetbuilding; e-mail, AFIProgram@acf.hhs.gov (Note: no field offices for this program.)

93.603 ADOPTION INCENTIVE PAYMENTS

Assistance: formula grants.

Purposes: pursuant to SSA and Adoption Promotion Act of 2003, to provide incentives to states to increase the annual number of foster child, special needs, and older child adoptions. Funds may also be used for post-adoption services to children.

Eligible applicants/beneficiaries: states, DC, PR.

Range: $16,000 to $3,486,000. **Average:** $559,000.

Activity: FY 05, 26 grants.

HQ: Division of Program Implementation, Children's Bureau, ACF- HHS, 1250 Maryland Ave. SW, Washington, DC 20024. Phone: (202) 205-6733.

Internet: www.acf.hhs.gov/programs/cb.

93.604 ASSISTANCE FOR TORTURE VICTIMS

Assistance: project grants.

Purposes: pursuant to the Torture Victims Relief Act of 1998 and amendments, to provide services and rehabilitation for victims of torture, with special emphasis on applicants for asylum. Eligible uses of funds include treatment, social and legal services, providing research and training for care providers.

Eligible applicants/beneficiaries: public or private organizations and institutions.

Range: $150,705 to $440,000.

Activity: FY 06, 27 grants, 1 contract, 1 interagency program.

HQ: Office of Refugee Resettlement, Administration for Children and Families, HHS, 370 L'Enfant Promenade SW - 8th Floor West, Washington, DC 20447. Phone: (202) 205-5933, FAX (202) 401-5772.

Internet: www.acf.hhs.gov/programs/orr (Note: no field offices for this program.)

93.612 NATIVE AMERICAN PROGRAMS

Assistance: project grants. (80-100 percent/1-3 years).

Purposes: pursuant to the Native American Programs Act of 1974, OAA, and amendments, to improve the social and economic conditions of native Americans within their communities. Funds may be used for such activities as: governance projects; economic and social development projects; financial assistance; training and technical assistance; research, demonstration, and evaluation.

Eligible applicants/beneficiaries: public and private nonprofit agencies including governing bodies of tribes on federal and state reservations, Alaska native villages and regional corporations, agencies serving Hawaii natives, organizations in urban or rural non-reservation areas, native American Pacific Islanders.

Range: tribal, urban grants, $50,000 to $500,000; NAHMI grants, $50,000 to $200,000. **Average:** tribal, $125,000.

Activity: FY 06 estimate, 85 grants; FY 07 estimate, 85 grants.

HQ: Administration for Native Americans, ACF-HHS, 370 L'Enfant Promenade SW - 8th Floor West, Washington, DC 20447. Phone: (202) 690-5787.

Internet: www.acf.hhs.gov/programs/ana (Note: no field offices for this program.)

93.613 PRESIDENT'S COMMITTEE FOR PEOPLE WITH INTELLECTUAL DISABILITIES ("PCPID")

Assistance: advisory services/counseling.

Purposes: to advise and assist the President on matters pertaining to persons with intellectual disabilities, including mental retardation, through studies and coordination of federal, state, and local efforts; to provide public information; to mobilize support for related activities.

Eligible applicants/beneficiaries: general public.

Range/Average: N.A.

Activity: not quantified specifically.

HQ: Executive Director, President's Committee for People with Intellectual Disabilities, ACF-HHS, Washington, DC 20447. Phone: (202) 619-0634.

Internet: www.acf.hhs.gov/programs/pcpid (Note: no field offices for this program.)

93.616 MENTORING CHILDREN OF PRISONERS ("MCP")

Assistance: project grants. (75 percent/3 years).

Purposes: pursuant to the Safe and Stable Families Act of 2001, to establish or expand and operate programs using a network of public and private entities to provide mentoring services for children of prisoners.

Eligible applicants/beneficiaries: state or local government units, tribes and tribal organizations, private nonprofit community groups—in areas with substantial numbers of children or prisoners.

Range: $100,000 to $1,000,000.

Activity: FY 05, 218 grants; FY 06 estimate, 218 grants; FY 07 estimate, 185 grants.

HQ: Associate Commissioner, Family and Youth Services Bureau, ACF-HHS, 1250 Maryland Ave., SW, Washington, DC 20024. Phone: (202) 205-8102.

Internet: www.acf.hhs.gov/programs/fysb (Note: no field offices for this program.)

93.617 VOTING ACCESS FOR INDIVIDUALS WITH DISABILITIES—GRANTS TO STATES ("Election Assistance for Individuals with Disabilities; (EAID)")

Assistance: formula grants.

Purposes: pursuant to the Help America Vote Act, to provide greater accessibility to polling places for persons with disabilities. Funds may be used to: make polling places accessible, including the path of travel, entrances, exits, and voting areas of each polling place; provide opportunity for voting access and participation, including privacy and independence; train election officials, poll workers, and election volunteers in elections for federal office; provide appropriate information dissemination.

Eligible applicants/beneficiaries: states, territories and possessions.

Range: from $100,000.

Activity: annually, 55 grants.

HQ: Administration on Developmental Disabilities, ACF-HHS, 200 Independence Ave. SW, Washington, DC 20201. Phone: (202) 690-5962.

Internet: www.acf.hhs.gov/programs.add (Note: no field offices for this program.)

93.618 VOTING ACCESS FOR INDIVIDUALS WITH DISABILITIES—GRANTS FOR PROTECTION AND ADVOCACY SYSTEMS

Assistance: formula grants; project grants.

Purposes: pursuant to the Help America Vote Act, to ensure full participation by persons with disabilities in the electoral process. Funds may be used to improve access and participation, and to provide training and technical assistance to protection and advocacy systems.

Eligible applicants/beneficiaries: states, territories and possessions with an approved Protection and Advocacy System in place.

Range: P&As, $70,000 or $30,000.

Activity: not quantified specifically.

HQ: Administration on Developmental Disabilities, ACF-HHS, 200 Independence Ave. SW, Washington, DC 20201. Phone: (202) 690-5962.

Internet: www.acf.hhs.gov/programs.add (Note: no field offices for this program.)

93.623 BASIC CENTER GRANT ("BCP")

Assistance: project grants. (to 90 percent/to 3 years).

Purposes: pursuant to the Runaway, Homeless, and Missing Children Protection Act of 2003, to establish or strengthen the operation of locally controlled, community-based centers for runaway and homeless youth and their families. Grants fund services must be delivered outside the law enforcement, child welfare, mental health, and juvenile justice systems. Centers provide services in residential settings normally accommodating no more than 20 youth, including activities such as individual and family counseling, temporary shelter for youth under age 18 for up to 15 days, food, clothing, transitional and after-care assistance. The program funds a national toll-free communication system, personnel training, research, demonstration, and service projects.

Eligible applicants/beneficiaries: states, localities, private entities, and coordinated networks of such agencies operating outside the law enforcement structure or juvenile justice system; Indian organizations.

Range: $100,000 to $200,000. **Average:** $128,000.

Activity: FY 05, 342 grants; FY 06 estimate, 328 grants; FY 07 estimate, 328 grants.

HQ: Associate Commissioner, Family and Youth Services Bureau, ACF-HHS, 1250 Maryland Ave., SW, Washington, DC 20024. Phone: (202) 205-8102.

Internet: www.acf.hhs.gov/programs/fysb.

93.630 DEVELOPMENTAL DISABILITIES BASIC SUPPORT AND ADVOCACY GRANTS ("State Councils on Developmental Disabilities and Protection and Advocacy Systems")

Assistance: formula grants (75-100 percent).

Purposes: pursuant to the Mental Retardation Facilities and Construction Act of 1963, Developmental Disabilities Assistance and Bill of Rights Act, and amendments, to plan and provide comprehensive and coordinated services to developmentally disabled persons, enabling them to reach their maximum potential in the community and to assure the protection of their legal and human rights. Funds may support state and local costs of planning and administration of services.

Eligible applicants: designated state agencies, territories and possessions.

Eligible beneficiaries: persons with developmental disabilities attributable to a mental and/or physical impairment manifested before age 22, resulting in functional limitations and reflecting lifelong need for services in at least three of seven functional areas—including self-care, receptive and expressive language, learning, mobility, self-direction, capacity for independent living, economic self-sufficiency, infants and children to age 9 showing high probability of a developmental disability.

Average: basic support, $450,000; protection and advocacy, $200,000.

Activity: annually, 112 grants.

HQ: Administration on Developmental Disabilities, ACF-HHS, 370 L'Enfant Promenade SW, Washington, DC, 20447. Phone: (202) 690-5976, -5905.

Internet: www.acf.dhhs.gov/programs/add.

93.631 DEVELOPMENTAL DISABILITIES PROJECTS OF NATIONAL SIGNIFICANCE

Assistance: project grants (varying match).

Purposes: pursuant to the Mental Retardation Facilities and Construction Act of 1963, Developmental Disabilities Assistance and Bill of Rights Act, and amendments, to increase and support the independence, productivity, and integration into communities of developmentally disabled persons. Grants support such activities as family support activities, education of policy makers, data collection and analysis, federal inter-agency initiatives, technical assistance including for developing information and referral systems, improved supportive services, services to minorities with disabilities, transitional services for youth, nationally significant projects.

Eligible applicants/beneficiaries: state, local, public, or private nonprofit agencies and organizations.

Range: $50,000 to $300,000.

Activity: FY 05, 53 grants; FY 06 estimate, 43 grants; FY 07 estimate, 43 grants.

HQ: Administration on Developmental Disabilities, ACF-HHS, 370 L'Enfant Promenade SW, Washington, DC, 20447. Phone: (202) 690-5985.

Internet: www.acf.dhhs.gov/programs/add.

93.632 UNIVERSITY CENTERS FOR EXCELLENCE IN DEVELOPMENTAL DISABILITIES EDUCATION, RESEARCH, AND SERVICE ("UCEDD")

Assistance: project grants. (75-90 percent/5 years).

Purposes: pursuant to the Mental Retardation Facilities and Construction Act of 1963, Developmental Disabilities Assistance and Bill of Rights Act, and amendments, to administer and operate university- or college-related programs for the developmentally disabled, including: interdisciplinary training for personnel; basic and applied research; information dissemination; community demonstration projects including direct services to developmentally disabled persons—e.g., family and individual support, educational, vocational, clinical, health and prevention services.

Eligible applicants/beneficiaries: public or nonprofit entities associated with or integral parts of IHEs.

Average: $500,000.

Activity: FY 05, 65 grants; FY 06 estimate, 68 grants; FY 07 estimate, 67 grants.

HQ: Administration on Developmental Disabilities, ACF-HHS, 370 L'Enfant Promenade SW, Washington, DC, 20447. Phone: (202) 690-5982.

Internet: www.acf.dhhs.gov/programs.add (Note: no field offices for this program.)

93.643 CHILDREN'S JUSTICE GRANTS TO STATES

Assistance: formula grants. (100 percent/2 years).

Purposes: pursuant to the Child Abuse Prevention and Treatment Act, VOCA, and amendments, for improved response to, and investigation and prosecution of, child abuse and neglect cases, particularly cases of sexual abuse and exploitation—including experimental, model, and demonstration programs, and legal and procedural reforms. Projects must be designed to achieve reforms in such areas as: investigative, administrative, and judicial handling of cases; inter-jurisdictional matters, with emphasis on reducing trauma to victims and their families; performance of court-appointed attorneys and guardians.

Eligible applicants/beneficiaries: states, territories, possessions.

Range: $50,000 to $1,900,000. **Average:** $346,938.

Activity: FY 05, grants to 48 states (including DC), 4 territorial governments; FY 06 estimate, grants to 49 states (including DC), 4 territorial governments.

HQ: Office on Child Abuse and Neglect, ACF-HHS, 1250 Maryland Ave. SW - 8th Floor, Washington, DC 20024. Phone: (202) 205-8714.

Internet: www.acf.dhhs.gov/programs/cb (Note: no field offices for this program.)

93.645 CHILD WELFARE SERVICES—STATE GRANTS

Assistance: formula grants (75 percent).

Purposes: pursuant to SSA as amended, for state, local, and tribal child welfare services to enable children in need of welfare services to remain in their own homes or to provide alternative permanent homes. Grants may cover costs of: personnel providing protective services; licensing and standard-setting for private child care organizations; return of runaway children; prevention and reunification services.

Eligible applicants/beneficiaries: state agencies, tribes, territories and possessions.

Range: states, $322,663 to $33,061,365; tribes, $1,652 to $1,013,367. **Average:** states, $5,081,580.

Activity: annually, 194 grants awarded.

HQ: Children's Bureau, ACF-HHS, 1250 Maryland Ave. SW, Washington, DC 20024. Phone: (202) 205-7243.

Internet: www.acf.hhs.gov/programs/cb.

93.647 SOCIAL SERVICES RESEARCH AND DEMONSTRATION

Assistance: project grants. (75 percent/1-3 years).

Purposes: pursuant to SSA as amended, for innovative research projects to test, demonstrate, and evaluate new concepts in social services for children and families.

Eligible applicants/beneficiaries: governmental entities, IHEs, nonprofit or profit organizations.

Range: $90,260 to $6,000,000. **Average:** $712,000.

Activity: FY 06 estimate, 19 awards.

HQ: Office of Planning, Research and Evaluation, Administration for Children and Families, HHS, 370 L'Enfant Promenade SW - 7th Floor, Washington, DC 20447. Phone: (202) 401-4535, FAX (202) 205-3598.

Internet: www.acf.hhs.gov/programs/opre.

93.648 CHILD WELFARE SERVICES TRAINING GRANTS

Assistance: project grants (to 100 percent).

Purposes: pursuant to SSA as amended, for programs to train current and prospective child welfare program personnel, including traineeship stipends. Previous projects examples include professional education for child welfare practices and cross-program training.

Eligible applicants/beneficiaries: IHEs.

Range: $75,000 to $350,000. **Average:** $155,333.

Activity: FY 05, 47 grants; FY 06 estimate, 48 grants; FY 07 estimate, 48 grants.

HQ: Children's Bureau, ACF-HHS, 1250 Maryland Ave., SW, Washington, DC 20024. Phone: (202) 205-8405.

Internet: www.acf.hhs.gov/programs/cb.

93.652 ADOPTION OPPORTUNITIES

Assistance: project grants. (to 100 percent/1-5 years).

Purposes: pursuant to the Child Abuse Prevention and Treatment and Adoption Reform Act of 1978 as amended, for projects to improve adoption practices including: adoption education and training; recruitment on the national level; child placement in kinship care arrangements, pre-adoptive, or adoptive homes; operation of national center for special needs adoption; minority recruitment, post-legal adoption services; improving the placement rate in foster care; barrier elimination across jurisdictional boundaries.

Eligible applicants/beneficiaries: state and local government entities, public and private nonprofit licensed agencies, community-based organizations, adoptive family groups, minority groups, sectarian institutions.

Range: $200,000 to $1,000,000. **Average:** $300,000.

Activity: FY 05, 44 grants; FY 06 estimate, 48 grants; FY 07 estimate, 53 grants.

HQ: Children's Bureau, ACF-HHS, 1250 Maryland Ave., SW, Washington, DC 20024. Phone: (202) 205-8354.

Internet: www.acf.hhs.gov/programs/cb (Note: no field offices for this program.)

93.658 FOSTER CARE—TITLE IV-E

Assistance: formula grants (50-83 percent).

Purposes: pursuant to SSA as amended, Title IV-E, for the operation of state and local foster child programs, including payments on behalf of the children, and training and administrative costs.

Eligible applicants/beneficiaries: states, DC, PR.

Range: $1,188,294 to $1,081,924,410. **Average:** $88,767,615.

Activity: annually, 53 grants, over 230,000 children receiving monthly benefits.

HQ: Children's Bureau, ACF- HHS, 1250 Maryland Ave. SW, Washington, DC 20024. Phone: (202) 654-2527.

Internet: www.acf.hhs.gov/programs/cb.

93.659 ADOPTION ASSISTANCE

Assistance: formula grants.

Purposes: pursuant to SSA as amended, Title IV-E, for adoption subsidy payments for adopted children with special needs. The subsidies are available from the time of adoption placement to age 18 (or older for certain handicaps).

Eligible applicants: states, DC, PR.

Eligible beneficiaries: children that are recipients of or eligible for AFDC, AFDC-FC, or SSI, and have special needs, e.g., a special factor or condition requiring adoption assistance for placement.

Range: $477,145 to $291,220,931. **Average:** $32,925,478.

Activity: annually, 52 grants, over 360,000 children assisted monthly.

HQ: Children's Bureau, ACF- HHS, 1250 Maryland Ave. SW, Washington, DC 20024. Phone: (202) 205-6733.

Internet: www.acf.hhs.gov/programs/cb.

93.667 SOCIAL SERVICES BLOCK GRANT

Assistance: formula grants (100 percent).

Purposes: pursuant to SSA, Jobs Training Bill, Medicaid and Medicare Patient and Program Act of 1987, Family Support Act of 1988, and amendments, to provide social services to: prevent, reduce, or eliminate dependency; achieve or maintain self- sufficiency; prevent neglect, abuse, or exploitation of persons; prevent or reduce inappropriate institutional care; enable individuals to secure admission or referral for institutional care when other forms of care are inappropriate; supplement comprehensive community revitalization in designated Empowerment Zones and Enterprise Communities (EZ/EC). Funds may be used for activities relating to preventive health, mental health, substance abuse, and maternal and child health, as well as low- income home energy assistance. Ineligible uses include cash payments for subsistence or for room and board, medical care, health or prison facility social services, educational services, and most real estate costs—unless specifically approved by HHS.

Eligible applicants/beneficiaries: states, territories and possessions.

Range: $56,000 to $207,311,000. **Average:** $30,263,000.

Activity: FY 05, 57 grants; FY 06 estimate, 108 grants.

HQ: Division of State Assistance, Office of Community Services, ACF-HHS, 370 L'Enfant Promenade SW, Washington, DC 20447. Phone: (202) 401-9343.

Internet: www.acf.hhs.gov/programs/ocs/ssbg.

93.669 CHILD ABUSE AND NEGLECT STATE GRANTS

Assistance: formula grants. (100 percent/to 5 years).

Purposes: pursuant to the Child Abuse Prevention, Adoption and Family Services Act of 1988, JJDPA, Child Abuse Prevention and Treatment Act, Keeping Children and Families Safe Act of 2003, amendments, and other acts, to operate, improve, and augment state child protective systems, including such activities as: reporting, investigation, management, legal representation, and prosecution of cases of child abuse and neglect; research; treatment of and services to abused children and their families; personnel training; public education and information; community- based programs.

Eligible applicants/beneficiaries: states, territories and possessions.

Range: $54,227 to $3,367,810. **Average:** $505,185.

Activity: FY 05, 54 grants; FY 06 estimate, 56 grants; FY 07 estimate, 56 grants.

HQ: Children's Bureau, ACF-HHS, 1250 Maryland Ave. SW - 8th Floor, Washington, DC 20024. Phone: (202) 205-8709.

Internet: www.acf.dhhs.gov/programs/cb.

93.670 CHILD ABUSE AND NEGLECT DISCRETIONARY ACTIVITIES

Assistance: project grants. (varying match/to 5 years).

Purposes: pursuant to the Child Abuse Prevention and Treatment Act and Child Abuse Prevention, Adoption and Family Services Act of 1988 as amended, and Keeping Children and Families Safe Act of 2003, for research, demonstration service improvement, information dissemination, and technical assistance projects—toward the prevention, identification, assessment, and treatment of child abuse and neglect.

Eligible applicants/beneficiaries: states, local governments, public and private nonprofit agencies and organizations, tribes.

Range: $80,000 to $1,988,200. **Average:** $300,000.

Activity: FY 05, 70 grants; FY 06 estimate, 41 grants; FY 07 estimate, 56 grants.

HQ: Research and Innovation Division, Children's Bureau, 1250 Maryland Ave. SW - 8th Floor, Washington, DC 20024. Phone: (202) 205-8172.

Internet: www.acf.hhs.gov/programs/cb (Note: no field offices for this program.)

93.671 FAMILY VIOLENCE PREVENTION AND SERVICES/GRANTS FOR BATTERED WOMEN'S SHELTERS—GRANTS TO STATES AND INDIAN TRIBES

Assistance: formula grants (65-80 percent).

Purposes: pursuant to the Family Violence Prevention and Services Act, Child Abuse Prevention, Adoption and Family Services Act of 1988, VCCLEA, VTVPA, Keeping Children and Families Safe Act of 2003, amendments, and other laws, for the prevention of family violence; to provide immediate shelter and other assistance to victims and their dependents. The program emphasizes community- based projects that provide shelter, counseling, advocacy, and self-help services to victims and their children—without income eligibility standards. Funds may not be used to make payments to victims.

Eligible applicants/beneficiaries: states, tribes, territories and possessions.

Range: states, $718,710 to $7,204,366; tribes, $20,332 to $2,013,157.

Activity: annually, 225 grants.

HQ: Family and Youth Services Bureau, Administration on Children, Youth, and Families, 1250 Maryland Ave. SW, Washington, DC 20024. Phone: (202) 401-5529.

Internet: www.acf.hhs.gov/programs/fysb (Note: no field offices for this program.)

93.674 CHAFEE FOSTER CARE INDEPENDENCE PROGRAM ("CFCIP")

Assistance: formula grants (80 percent).

Purposes: pursuant to SSA as amended and Foster Care Independence Act of 1999, and Promoting Safe and Stable Families Amendments of 2001, for state and local programs designed to assist youth receiving foster care maintenance payments to make the transition to independent living. Funds may be used for skill development, mentoring activities, postsecondary education, supportive services, or training related to program purposes, including voucher payments.

Eligible applicants: states, DC, PR.

Eligible beneficiaries: youth age 18 and over, currently or formerly receiving foster care payments, until they reach age 21.

Range: $500,000 to $25,012,729. **Average:** $2,692,228.

Activity: annually, 52 grants.

HQ: Children's Bureau, Administration for Children and Families, 1250 Maryland Ave. SW - 8th Floor, Washington, DC 20024. Phone: (202) 205-8086.

Internet: www.acf.dhhs.gov/programs/cb.

93.676 UNACCOMPANIED ALIEN CHILDREN PROGRAM

Assistance: project grants.

Purposes: pursuant to the Homeland Security Act of 2002, to develop plans and policies to coordinate and implement care and placement services for unaccompanied alien children in federal custody by reason of their immigration status.

Eligible applicants/beneficiaries: state and local governments, private nonprofit and profit organizations.

Range/Average: N.A.

Activity: FY 05, 19 continuation grants, 16 contracts, 5 interagency agreements; FY 06 estimate, 23 new grants, 5 continuation grants, 16 contracts, 5 interagency agreements.

HQ: Director, Division of Unaccompanied Children Services, HHS, 370 L'Enfant Promenade SW - 8th Floor West, Washington, DC 20447. Phone: (202) 401-5523.

Internet: www.acf.hhs.gov/programs/orr (Note: no field offices for this program.)

93.760 RURAL PACE (PROGRAM OF ALL-INCLUSIVE CARE FOR THE ELDERLY) PROVIDER GRANT PROGRAM

Assistance: project grants.

Purposes: pursuant to the Deficit Reduction Act of 2005, to provide services in a geographic area that is rural, in whole or part, and has received a site development grant under Section 5302 of Public Law 109-171. A rural area is a county that is not part of a Metropolitan Statistical Area (MSA) as defined by the Office of Management and Budget.

Eligible applicants/beneficiaries: any public or private non-profit entity organized for charitable purposes defined as a PACE provider by section 1894(a)(3) or 1934(a)(3) of the Social Security Act. In addition, each potential applicant must meet the full statutory definition of a rural area.

Range: pilot sites, to $750,000; outlier, to $500,000.

Activity: new program listing in 2006 (CFDA on-line).

HQ: Office of Operations Management, Acquisitions and Grants Group, CMS-HHS, 7500 Security Blvd. (Mail Stop C2-21-15), Baltimore, MD 21244-1850. Phone: (410) 786-5158.

Internet: www.cms.hhs.gov (Note: no field offices for this program.)

93.767 STATE CHILDREN'S INSURANCE PROGRAM ("CHIP; SCHIP")

Assistance: formula grants (to 85 percent).

Purposes: pursuant to the Medicare, Medicaid and State Children's Health Insurance Program Balanced Budget Refinement Act of 1999, Medicare, Medicaid, and State Children's Health Insurance Program Improvement Act of 2000, for states to initiate and expand child health assistance to uninsured low-income children, including under state Medicaid programs. Coverage may not discriminate on the basis of diagnosis nor pre-existing condition, and must be coordinated with other public and private programs. The cost of abortions may be covered only to save the life of the mother or if the pregnancy resulted from rape or incest.

Eligible applicants: states, possessions and territories with HHS-approved state plans.

Eligible beneficiaries: targeted low-income children whose family income exceeds Medicaid limits by no more than 50 percent, ineligible for Medicaid and not covered by other health insurance—not including families eligible for a state health benefits plan through employment with a state public agency.

Range: $467,775 (territories) to $646,682,123.

Activity: FY 04, 6,100,000 unduplicated ever-enrolled enrollees.

HQ: Center for Medicaid and State Operations, CMS-HHS, 7500 Security Blvd., Baltimore, MD 21244. Phone: (410) 786-3870.

Internet: www.cms.hhs.gov.

93.768 MEDICAID INFRASTRUCTURE GRANTS TO SUPPORT THE COMPETITIVE EMPLOYMENT OF PEOPLE WITH DISABILITIES ("Ticket To Work Infrastructure Grants")

Assistance: project grants.

Purposes: pursuant to the Ticket-to-Work and Work Incentives Improvement Act of 1999, for states to enhance employment options for persons with disabilities, by creating health systems change through the Medicaid program and removing barriers to employment. Projects are expected to be designed to provide personal assistance services and Medicaid buy-ins to sustain adequate health coverage, even if relocation to another state is needed. Funds may not be used to provide direct services to clients except on a one-time, last resort, emergency basis to sustain competitive employment.

Eligible applicants: single state Medicaid agencies or partner agencies.

Eligible beneficiaries: employed persons with disabilities, age 16-65, and: meeting established income, asset, and resource standards; or, ceasing eligibility for Medicaid because of medical improvements but still with severe medically determined impairments.

Range: $500,000 to $2,750,000. **Average:** $500,000.

Activity: through FY 05, 49 states and DC approved for funding.

HQ: Center for Medicaid and State Operations, CMS-HHS, 7500 Security Blvd., Baltimore, MD 21244-1850. Phone: (410) 786-3870.

Internet: www.cms.hhs.gov/contracts.

93.769 DEMONSTRATION TO MAINTAIN INDEPENDENCE AND EMPLOYMENT

Assistance: project grants.

Purposes: pursuant to the Ticket-to-Work and Work Incentives Improvement Act of 1999, for states to assist workers by providing the necessary medical assistance benefits and services they require to manage the progression of their conditions and remain employed. Projects are to provide benefits equivalent to those provided by Medicaid to the categorically needy and to workers with physical or mental impairments and, without medical assistance, will result in disabilities.

Eligible applicants: states.

Eligible beneficiaries: employed persons with disabilities, age 16-65, and: meeting established income, asset, and resource standards; or, ceasing eligibility for Medicaid because of medical improvements but still with severe medically determined impairments.

Range: $284,253 to $3,980,308. **Average:** $2,132,280.

Activity: as of FY 04, 6 states and DC funded.

HQ: Center for Medicaid and State Operations, CMS-HHS, 7500 Security Blvd., Baltimore, MD 21244-1850. Phone: (410) 786-3870.

Internet: www.cms.hhs.gov/contracts.

93.770 MEDICARE—PRESCRIPTION DRUG COVERAGE ("Medicare Part D")

Assistance: direct payments/specified use.

Purposes: pursuant to SSA and Medicare Prescription Drug, Improvement and Modernization Act of 2003 (Medicare Modernization Act - "MMA"), to provide prescription drugs to Medicare beneficiaries through their voluntary participation in prescription drug plans, with a subsidy provided to low-income beneficiaries.

Eligible applicants: nongovernmental entities organized and licensed under state laws as risk-bearing entities to offer health insurance in state in which they offer plans.

Eligible beneficiaries: individuals entitled to Medicare benefits under Part A or enrolled in Part B, residing in an approved plan's service area, and not enrolled in a Medicare Advantage plan other than a Medicare savings account plan or private fee- for-service plan that does not provide qualified prescription drug coverage.

Range/Average: N.A.

Activity: new program listing in 2005. (Note: program began in 2006.)

HQ: CMS-HHS, 7500 Security Blvd., Baltimore, MD 21244-1850. Phone: eligibility and enrollment, (410) 786-9064; benefits, beneficiary protections, (214) 767-6435; plan bidding process, (410) 786-3198.

Internet: www.cms.hhs.gov (Note: no field offices for this program.)

93.773 MEDICARE—HOSPITAL INSURANCE ("Medicare A")

Assistance: direct payments/specified use.

Purposes: pursuant to SSA, Medicare, Medicaid, and State Children's Health Insurance Program Improvement Act of 2000, MMA, amendments, and other acts, to provide insurance coverage for treatment in hospitals and other care facilities for covered services to persons age 65 or over, to certain disabled persons, and to those with chronic renal disease. Benefits may be paid to participating and emergency hospitals, skilled nursing facilities, home health agencies, and hospice agencies—for inpatient hospital services and post-hospital extended care services incurred during a benefit period. For 2005, the beneficiary is responsible for a $912 inpatient hospital deductible, and varying coinsurance amounts according to the type and length of care received. Home health services are paid in full.

Eligible applicants/beneficiaries: persons age 65 or over and certain disabled persons. Nearly everyone that reached 65 before 1968 is eligible, including those ineligible for cash Social Security benefits. Those reaching age 65 in 1968 or after and ineligible need some work credit to qualify for hospital insurance benefits, the amount of which depends on their age. Hospital insurance is also available to persons age 65 or over and otherwise ineligible, through payment of a monthly premium. Certain federal, state, and local government employees are also eligible.

Range/Average: N.A.

Activity: FY 05, 41,874,000 persons insured; FY 06 estimate, 42,489,000 persons insured; FY 07 estimate, 43,201,000 persons insured.

HQ: Center for Medicare & Medicaid Services, 7500 Security Blvd. - Rm. C5-19-16, Baltimore, MD 212444. Phone: (410) 786-3418.

Internet: www.medicare.gov; www.cms.hhs.gov.

93.774 MEDICARE—SUPPLEMENTARY MEDICAL INSURANCE ("Medicare Part B")

Assistance: direct payments/specified use (50-100 percent).

Purposes: pursuant to SSA as amended, Medicare, Medicaid, and State Children's Health Insurance Program Improvement Act of 2000, MMA, amendments, and other acts, to provide medical insurance protection for covered services furnished by physicians and other suppliers of medical services to elderly or disabled persons and to those with chronic renal disease, including services provided by hospitals, skilled nursing facilities, and home health agencies. The beneficiary is responsible for an annual $110 deductible before benefits may begin, effective in FY 05; thereafter, Medicare pays a percentage of charges for covered services, varying from

50 to 100 percent. The enrollee pays a monthly premium ($78.20 in 2005). Some states and other third- parties pay the premium on behalf of qualifying individuals.

Eligible applicants/beneficiaries: all persons age 65 and over, and those under age 65 eligible for hospital insurance benefits (see **93.773**)—voluntarily enrolled for supplementary medical insurance. Eligibility is available to U.S. citizen-residents or lawful permanent residents residing in the U.S. continuously for the previous five years.

Range/Average: N.A.

Activity: FY 04, 38,706,000 enrollees; FY 05 estimate, 39,237,000 enrollees; FY 06 estimate, 39,751,000 enrollees.

HQ: Center for Beneficiary Choices, CMS-HHS, 7500 Security Blvd. Rm. C5-19-16, Baltimore, MD 21244. Phone: (410) 786-3418.

Internet: www.cms.hhs.gov.

93.775 STATE MEDICAID FRAUD CONTROL UNITS ("SMFCUs")

Assistance: formula grants (75-90 percent).

Purposes: pursuant to SSA as amended, to investigate and prosecute fraud and patient abuse in state Medicaid programs.

Eligible applicants/beneficiaries: specified state government entities.

Range: $299,000 to $34,638,000. **Average:** $3,248,468.

Activity: currently, 48 states, DC certified.

HQ: Director, Medicaid Fraud Unit Oversight Division, Office of Evaluation and Inspections, Office of Inspector General, OS-HHS, Cohen Bldg. - Rm. 5656, 330 Independence Ave. SW, Washington, DC 20201. Phone: (202) 260-3711.

Internet: www.dhhs.gov (Note: no field offices for this program.)

93.776 HURRICANE KATRINA RELIEF

Assistance: project grants.

Purposes: pursuant to Deficit Reduction Act of 2005, to reimburse states affected by Hurricane Katrina for the nonfederal share of specified hurricane-related medical care expenditures and associated administrative costs, and for the total uncompensated care costs for affected states; to provide the nonfederal share of medical care expenditures furnished to Title XIX and XXI individuals under existing states plan, to affected counties or parishes. With HHS approval, funds may also be used by states to restore access to health care in communities impacted by Hurricane Katrina.

Eligible applicants/beneficiaries: CMS Title XIX and XXI participants.

Range: to $2,000,000,000 for 2006 and beyond.

Activity: new program listing in 2006 (CFDA on-line).

HQ: Centers for Medicare and State Operations, CMS-HHS (MS S2-01-16), 7500 Security Blvd., Baltimore, MD 21244. Phone: (410) 786-8693; financial questions, (410) 786-2013.

Internet: www.cms.hhs.gov.

93.777 STATE SURVEY AND CERTIFICATION OF HEALTH CARE PROVIDERS AND SUPPLIERS

Assistance: formula grants.

Purposes: pursuant to SSA as amended, to monitor health care providers and suppliers to assure their compliance with federal regulatory health and safety standards and conditions of participation in Medicare and Medicaid programs.

Eligible applicants/beneficiaries: designated state agencies.

Range: $15,000 to $28,063,819. **Average:** $4,668,142.

Activity: FY 06 estimate, 53 state and territorial agencies funded to provide monitoring of 55,000 certified providers and suppliers.

HQ: Director, Survey and Certification Group, CMS-HHS, 7500 Security Blvd., Baltimore, MD 21244. Phone: (410) 786-9493.

Internet: www.cms.hhs.gov/contracts.

93.778 MEDICAL ASSISTANCE PROGRAM ("Medicaid; Title XIX")

Assistance: formula grants (50-83 percent).

Purposes: pursuant to SSA as amended, for medical assistance payments on behalf of recipients of cash assistance, children, pregnant women, certain elderly, and other eligible groups. States must provide: hospital in- and outpatient care; rural health clinic services; federally qualified health center services; other laboratory and X-ray services; nursing facility services; home health services for persons over age 21; family planning services; early and periodic screening, diagnosis, and treatment for persons under age 21; pediatric or family nurse practitioner services; nurse-midwife services. States may use funds to pay for Medicare premiums, copayments, and deductible payments of eligible beneficiaries.

Eligible applicants: state and local welfare agencies.

Eligible beneficiaries: low-income persons over age 65 or blind or disabled, members of families with dependent children, low- income children and pregnant women; certain Medicare beneficiaries; in some states, medically-needy persons may apply to a state or local welfare agency for medical assistance.

Range: $2,663,000 to $26,401,883,000. **Average:** $3,582,162,000.

Activity: FY 05, 49,100,000 Medicaid enrollees; FY 06 estimate, 51,600,000 Medicaid enrollees; FY 07 estimate, 52,900,000 Medicaid enrollees.

HQ: Center for Medicaid and State Operations, CMS-HHS, 7500 Security Blvd. - Rm. C4-25-02, Baltimore, MD 21244. Phone: (410) 786-3870.

Internet: www.cms.hhs.gov/contracts.

93.779 CENTERS FOR MEDICARE AND MEDICAID SERVICES (CMS) RESEARCH, DEMONSTRATIONS AND EVALUATIONS ("CMS Research")

Assistance: project grants. (to 95 percent/to 2 years).

Purposes: pursuant to the SSA and Small Business Innovation Development Act of 1982 as amended, for analyses, experiments, demonstrations, and pilot projects to resolve major health care financing issues or to improve the administration of the Medicare and Medicaid programs. Funds may be provided as SBIR grants (*see Notes preceding **93.001***), Hispanic health services grants, HBCU grants, IHE grants.

Eligible applicants/beneficiaries: private nonprofit or profit organizations; public agencies including state Medicaid agencies.

Range: $25,000 to $1,000,000. **Average:** $235,000.

Activity: FY 06 estimate, 24 new cooperative agreements, 20 new contract awards; FY 07, 20 new cooperative agreements, 17 new contract awards.

HQ: Director, Office of Research, Development, and Information, CMS-HHS, Central Bldg. - Rm. C3-20-11, 7500 Security Blvd., Baltimore, MD 21244-1850. Phone: (410) 786-0948.

Internet: www.cms.hhs.gov/contracts.

93.780 GRANTS TO STATES FOR OPERATION OF QUALIFIED HIGH-RISK POOLS

Assistance: formula grants.

Purposes: pursuant to the Trade Act of 2002, for the operation of qualified state high-risk health insurance pools by providing federal funding for up to 50 percent of losses incurred by the pool for a given state fiscal year.

Eligible applicants/beneficiaries: states that: (1) operate a qualified high-risk pool as defined in section 2744(c)(2) of PHSA; restrict premiums charged under the pool to no more than 150 percent of applicable standard risk rates for the state; offer a choice of two or more coverage options through the pool; have in effect a mechanism reasonably designed to ensure continues funding of losses after then end of FY 04; incurred losses in the state's FY 02, 03, or 04.

Range/Average: N.A.

Activity: not quantified specifically.

HQ: Centers for Medicare and State Operations, CMS-HHS (MS S2-01-16), 7500 Security Blvd., Baltimore, MD 21244. Phone: (410) 786-5957.

Internet: www.cms.hhs.gov/riskpool.

93.781 SEED GRANTS TO STATES FOR QUALIFIED HIGH-RISK POOLS

Assistance: project grants.

Purposes: pursuant to the Trade Act of 2002, to establish and for initial operation of qualified state high-risk health insurance pools for individuals who cannot purchase individual coverage because of pre-existing medical conditions.

Eligible applicants/beneficiaries: states that did not have qualified high-risk pools as of 6 August 2002.

Range: to $1,000,000.

Activity: not quantified specifically.

HQ: Centers for Medicare and State Operations, CMS-HHS (MS S2-01-16), 7500 Security Blvd., Baltimore, MD 21244. Phone: (410) 786-5957.

Internet: www.cms.hhs.gov/riskpool.

93.783 MEDICARE TRANSITIONAL DRUG ASSISTANCE PROGRAM FOR STATES

Assistance: direct payments/specified use.

Purposes: pursuant to MMA, for transitional assistance to certain low-income Medicare beneficiaries enabling them to purchase prescription drugs. Credits are provided to beneficiaries through private discount card sponsors.

Eligible applicants: nongovernmental, single legal entities doing business in the U.S., with three years of private sector experience in pharmacy benefit management, and serving at least 1,000,000 covered persons.

Eligible beneficiaries: Medicare beneficiaries with incomes not more than 135 percent of the poverty line, and not receiving outpatient coverage from other sources including Medicaid, TRICARE, group health insurance or federal employee health benefit plans unless the drug is covered through Part C Medicare+Choice plan or Medigap plan.

Range: to $600 per beneficiary.

Activity: not quantified specifically.

HQ: Health Plan Benefits Group, Center for Beneficiary Choices, CMS-HHS, 7500 Security Blvd., Baltimore, MD 21244. Phone: (410) 786-1164.

Internet: www.cms.hhs.gov (Note: no field offices for this program.)

93.784 FEDERAL REIMBURSEMENT OF EMERGENCY HEALTH SERVICES FURNISHED TO UNDOCUMENTED ALIENS

Assistance: direct payments/specified use.

Purposes: pursuant to MMA, to reimburse providers for their otherwise unreimbursed costs associated with furnishing emergency health services required under the Emergency Medical Treatment and Active Labor Act (EMTALA), to undocumented and certain other aliens.

Eligible applicants: states.

Eligible beneficiaries: hospitals, certain physicians, ambulance services that provide emergency health care under EMTALA.

Range/Average: N.A.

Activity: new program in FY 05.

HQ: Hospital and Ambulatory Group, Center for Medicare Management, CMS-HHS, 7500 Security Blvd., Baltimore, MD 21244. Phone: (410) 786-9317.

Internet: (none). (Note: no field offices for this program.)

93.785 PILOT PROGRAM FOR NATIONAL AND STATE BACKGROUND CHECKS—DIRECT PATIENT ACCESS FOR LONG-TERM CARE

Assistance: project grants (100 percent).

Purposes: pursuant to MMA, for pilot programs to develop procedures to conduct background checks on prospective direct patient access employees.

Eligible applicants/beneficiaries: state agencies.

Range: $500,000 to $5,000,000.

Activity: new program in FY 04; FY 05, 7 grants.

HQ: Survey & Certification Group, CMS-HHS, 7500 Security Blvd., Baltimore, MD 21244. Phone: (410) 786-6773.

Internet: www.cms.hhs.gov/medicaid/survey-cert/bcp.asp (Note: no field offices for this program.)

93.786 STATE PHARMACEUTICAL ASSISTANCE PROGRAMS ("SPAPs")

Assistance: formula grants.

Purposes: pursuant to MMA, for states with SPAPs to educate SPAP participants about Medicare Part D coverage, including technical assistance, phone support, and counseling in selecting and enrolling in Part D plans.

Eligible applicants/beneficiaries: states with CMS-approved transitional assistance grant applications (program **93.783**).

Range/Average: N.A.

Activity: new program in FY 05 (CFDA on-line).

HQ: Division of Financial Management, Center for Medicaid and State Operations, CMS-HHS, 7500 Security Blvd., Baltimore, MD 21244. Phone: (410) 786-9291.

Internet: www.cms.hhs.gov (Note: no field offices for this program.)

93.789 ALTERNATIVES TO PSYCHIATRIC RESIDENTIAL TREATMENT FACILITIES FOR CHILDREN ("Demonstration Projects Regarding Home and Community-Based Alternatives to Psychiatric Residential Treatment Facilities for Children")

Assistance: project grants (to 5 years).

Purposes: pursuant to Deficit Reduction Act of 2005, to provide funding to 10 states for development of demonstration programs that provide home and community-based services to youth as alternatives to Psychiatric Residential Treatment Facilities (PRTFs).

Eligible applicants: any single State Medicaid Agency, State Mental Health Agency or instrumentality of the state (meaning states, DC, or U.S. territories or possessions). Only one application per state.

Eligible beneficiaries: individuals under the age of 21 who require the need for a PRTF.

Range: $2,100,000 to $50,000,000.

Activity: new program in 2006; 10 awards, estimated.

HQ: Center for Medicaid and State Operations, CMS-HHS, 7500 Security Blvd, MS S2-14-26, Baltimore, MD 21244 Phone: (410) 786-2267.

Internet: www.cms.hhs.gov (Note: no field offices for this program.)

93.791 MONEY FOLLOWS THE PERSON REBALANCING DEMONSTRATION

Assistance: project grants (to 5 years).

Purposes: pursuant to Deficit Reduction Act of 2005, to give states the option to rebalance their long-term support programs to allow Medicaid programs to be more sustainable, while helping individuals to achieve independence by proposing a system of home and community-based care, subject to approval by the CMS. States will be reimbursed for home and community-based services under this program.

Eligible applicants: any single State Medicaid Agency, State Mental Health Agency or instrumentality of the state (meaning states, DC, or U.S. territories or possessions). Only one application per state.

Eligible beneficiaries: individuals who have resided in state for at least 6 months (possibly up to 2 years as specified in some states) previous to start of Money Follows the Person (MFP) Rebalancing Demonstration; who are in an inpatient facility; who receive Medicaid benefits for services furnished by the facility and who would continue to require those services.

Range/Average: N.A.

Activity: new program in 2006.

HQ: CMS-HHS (MS S2-14-26), 7500 Security Blvd., Baltimore, MD 21244 Phone: (410) 786-8287.

Internet: www.cms.hhs.gov/NewFreedomInitiative/02_WhatsNew.asp (Note: no field offices for this program.)

93.793 MEDICAID TRANSFORMATION GRANTS

Assistance: project grants. (100 percent/to 2 years).

Purposes: pursuant to Deficit Reduction Act of 2005, to provide Federal payments to states for the adoption of innovative methods to improve effectiveness and efficiency in providing Medical Assistance. Funds may not be used for the state's share of Medicaid program costs or as supplemental Disproportionate Share Hospital (DHS) payments.

Eligible applicants/beneficiaries: 51 State Medicaid Agencies and Medicaid Agencies in the Federal Territories only.

Range/Average: N.A.

Activity: new program in 2006.

HQ: Health Insurance Specialist, CMS-HHS, 7500 Security Blvd, MS S2-01-16, Baltimore, MD 21244 Phone: (410) 786-5957, -6177.

Internet: www.cms.hhs.gov/MedicaidTransGrant (Note: no field offices for this program.)

93.794 REIMBURSEMENT OF STATE COSTS FOR PROVISION OF PART D DRUGS

Assistance: direct payments/specified use.

Purposes: pursuant to SSA as amended, Section 402, to reimburse states for costs of providing Part D drugs "dual eligible" Part D recipients (i.e., beneficiaries under both Medicare and Medicaid) and other low-income beneficiaries, including certain administrative and educational services costs—provided between 1 January and 15 February 2006.

Eligible applicants/beneficiaries: states.

Range/Average: N.A.

Activity: new program listing in 2006 (CFDA on-line).

HQ: CMS (MS C1-26-12), 7500 Security Blvd., Baltimore, MD 21244. Phone: (410) 786-4578.

Internet: www.cms.hhs.gov.

93.822 HEALTH CAREERS OPPORTUNITY PROGRAM ("HCOP")

Assistance: project grants. (100 percent/3 years).

Purposes: pursuant to PHSA as amended and HPEPA, to assist students from disadvantaged backgrounds to undertake education preparing them to enter a health or allied health professions schools, including graduate programs. Projects provide preparatory services, including recruitment, counseling, mentoring, preliminary education and health research training, information on financial aid, primary care exposure activities, and stipends.

Eligible applicants/beneficiaries: accredited schools of medicine, osteopathy, public health, dentistry, veterinary medicine, optometry, pharmacy, allied health, chiropractic, podiatry; public and private nonprofit schools with programs to train physician assistants or offering graduate programs in behavioral and mental health.

Range: $150,000 to $1,400,000. **Average:** $443,113.

Activity: FY 05, 50 continuation, 34 new awards. FY 06 estimate, 4 continuation, 0 new awards; FY 07 estimate, 0 awards.

HQ: Chief, Diversity Branch, Division of Health Careers Diversity and Development, Bureau of Health Professions, HRSA-HHS, Parklawn Bldg. - Rm. 8-55, 5600 Fishers Lane, Rockville, MD 20857. Phone: (301) 443-2100. *Grants management information*: Director, Division of Grants Management, Health Resources and Services Administration, NIH-HHS, 5600 Fishers Lane - Rm. 11A-16, Rockville, MD 20857. Phone: Health Services, (301) 443-2385; Research and Training, (301) 443-3099; Government and Special Focus, (301) 443-3288.

Internet: www.hrsa.gov (Note: no field offices for this program.)

93.824 BASIC/CORE AREA HEALTH EDUCATION CENTERS ("AHEC")

Assistance: project grants. (from 50-75 percent/3 years).

Purposes: pursuant to PHSA as amended and HPEPA, to improve the distribution, diversity, supply, and quality of health service delivery system personnel, by encouraging regionalization of health professions schools and involving students in grades 9-12 in health careers programs. Program funds may be used to plan, develop, and operate AHECs, linked with academic resources of university health sciences centers, to initiate education system incentives to attract and retain health care personnel in scarcity areas, emphasizing community-based training of primary care oriented students, residents, and providers—but not for construction, patient services, or stipends.

Eligible applicants/beneficiaries: public or nonprofit schools of medicine or osteopathy, consortia; accredited schools of nursing in states without AHECs.

Range: $252,991 to $2,582,605. **Average:** $1,059,770.

Activity: FY 05, 13 awards.

HQ: Chief, AHEC Branch, Division of State Community and Public Health, Bureau of Health Professions, HRSA-HHS, 5600 Fishers Lane - Rm. 9-05, Rockville, MD 20857. Phone: (301) 443-6950. *Grants management information*: Director, Division of Grants Management, Health Resources and Services Administration, NIH-HHS, 5600 Fishers Lane - Rm. 11A-16, Rockville, MD 20857. Phone: Health Services, (301) 443-2385; Research and Training, (301) 443-3099; Government and Special Focus, (301) 443-3288.

Internet: www.hrsa.gov (Note: no field offices for this program.)

93.837 HEART AND VASCULAR DISEASES RESEARCH

Assistance: project grants. (100 percent/1-5 years).

Purposes: pursuant to PHSA as amended and SBRDEA, for research and research training in prevention, education, and control activities related to heart and vascular diseases. Project funds may support salaries, equipment, and patient hospitalization costs required to perform the research effort. NRSA, SBIR, and STTR awards are available (*see Notes preceding* **93.001**).

Eligible applicants/beneficiaries: nonprofit and profit organizations engaged in biomedical research.

Range: $16,000 to $4,444,879. **Average:** $441,745.

Activity: FY 06 estimate, 2,829 research grants, 300 NRSAs; FY 07 estimate, 2,843 research grants, 301 NRSAs.

HQ: Director, Division of Heart and Vascular Diseases, National Heart, Lung, and Blood Institute, NIH-HHS, Bethesda, MD 20892. Phone: (301) 435-0466; SBIR, (301) 435-0266. *Grants management information*: Grants Management Officer, Grants Operations Branch, National Heart, Lung, and Blood Institute, NIH-HHS, Bethesda, MD 20892. Phone: (301) 435-0166.

Internet: www.nih.gov (Note: no field offices for this program.)

93.838 LUNG DISEASES RESEARCH

Assistance: project grants. (100 percent/to 5 years).

Purposes: pursuant to PHSA as amended and SBRDEA, for research and research training concerning lung diseases, and to improve their prevention and treatment. Project funds may support salaries, equipment, and patient hospitalization costs required to perform the research effort. NRSA, SBIR, and STTR awards are available (*see Notes preceding* **93.001**).

Eligible applicants/beneficiaries: nonprofit and profit organizations engaged in biomedical research.

Range: $97,509 to $903,938. **Average:** $284,034.

Activity: FY 06 estimate, 1,241 research grants, 90 NRSAs; FY 07 estimate, 1,247 research grants, 90 NRSAs.

HQ: Director, Division of Lung Diseases, National Heart, Lung, and Blood Institute, NIH-HHS, Bethesda, MD 20892. Phone: (301) 435-0233. *Grants management information*: Grants Management Officer, Grants Operation Branch, Office of Program Policy and Procedures, National Heart, Lung and Blood Institute, NIH-HHS, Bethesda, MD 20892. Phone: (301) 435-0144.

Internet: www.nhlbi.nih.gov (Note: no field offices for this program.)

93.839 BLOOD DISEASES AND RESOURCES RESEARCH

Assistance: project grants. (100 percent/to 5 years).

Purposes: pursuant to PHSA as amended and SBRDEA, for research and research training toward the improved diagnosis, treatment, and prevention of nonmalignant blood diseases; for research on stem cell biology and transplantation; to improve the availability, safety, and use of blood and blood products. Project funds may support salaries, equipment, and patient hospitalization costs required to perform the research effort. NRSA, SBIR, and STTR awards are available (*see Notes preceding* **93.001**).

Eligible applicants/beneficiaries: nonprofit and profit organizations engaged in biomedical research.

Range: $126,799 to $2,526,971. **Average:** $511,012.

Activity: FY 06 estimate, 794 research grants, 79 NRSAs; FY 07 estimate, 798 research grants, 80 NRSAs.

HQ: Director, Division of Blood Diseases and Resources, National Heart, Lung, and Blood Institute, NIH-HHS, Bethesda, MD 20892. Phone: (301) 435-0080. *Grants management information*: Grants Management Officer, Grants Operation Branch, Office of Program Policy and Procedures, National Heart, Lung and Blood Institute, NIH-HHS, Bethesda, MD 20892. Phone: (301) 435-0144.

Internet: www.nhlbi.nih.gov (Note: no field offices for this program.)

93.846 ARTHRITIS, MUSCULOSKELETAL AND SKIN DISEASES RESEARCH

Assistance: project grants. (100 percent/to 5 years).

Purposes: pursuant to PHSA as amended and SBRDEA, for basic research, research training, and clinical investigations concerning all aspects and forms of arthritis and musculoskeletal and skin diseases, including a centers program for large-scale research. NRSA, SBIR, and STTR awards are available (*see Notes preceding* **93.001**).

Eligible applicants/beneficiaries: individuals, public and private nonprofit or profit institutions proposing to establish, expand, and improve research activities in health sciences and related fields.

Range: research grants, $5,000 to $3,100,000; NRSAs, $25,000 to $370,000. **Average:** research grants, $318,000; NRSAs, $107,000.

Activity: FY 06 estimate, 1,237 research grants including 52 SBIR and STTR awards, 306 NRSAs; FY 07 estimate, 1,212 research grants including 51 SBIR and STTR awards, 305 NRSAs.

HQ: Director, Extramural Program, National Institute of Arthritis and Musculoskeletal and Skin Diseases, NIH-HHS, 6701 Democracy Blvd. - Ste. 800, Bethesda, MD 20892. Phone: (301) 594-2463. *SBIR and grants management information*: Grants Management Officer, Extramural Program, National Institute of Arthritis and Musculoskeletal and Skin Diseases, NIH-HHS, 6701 Democracy Blvd. - Ste. 800, Bethesda, MD 20892. Phone: (301) 594-3278.

Internet: www.hhs.gov (Note: no field offices for this program.)

93.847 DIABETES, ENDOCRINOLOGY AND METABOLISM RESEARCH

Assistance: project grants. (100 percent/to 5 years).

Purposes: pursuant to PHSA as amended and SBRDEA, for basic and clinical biomedical research and research training in: diabetes and related complications, including its etiology, pathogenesis, prevention, diagnosis, and treatment; endocrinology, including the normal and abnormal functions of the pituitary, thyroid, parathyroid, adrenal, pineal, and thymus glands, as well as the action of hormones, hormone biosynthesis, secretion, metabolism, binding to protein carriers and subsequent release, and the kinetics of binding; metabolic processes of diseases such as membrane structure, function, and transport phenomena, as well as inherited disorders including cystic fibrosis, including their causes, prevention, and treatment. NRSA, SBIR, and STTR awards are available (*see Notes preceding* **93.001**).

Eligible applicants/beneficiaries: individuals, public and private nonprofit or profit institutions proposing to establish, expand, and improve research activities in health sciences and related fields.

Range: research grants, $16,600 to $2,098,000; NRSAs, $3,000 to $263,700. **Average:** research grants, $180,100; NRSAs, $61,600.

Activity: FY 05, 1,495 research grants, 135 NRSAs, 51 SBIRs; FY 06 estimate, 1,439 research grants, 134 NRSAs, 49 SBIRs.

HQ: Director, Division of Diabetes, Endocrinology, and Metabolic Diseases, National Institute of Diabetes and Digestive and Kidney Diseases, NIH-HHS, 6707 Democracy Blvd. - Rm. 689, Bethesda, MD 20892-2560. Phone: (301) 496-7349. *Grants management information*: Chief Grants Management Officer, Grants Management Branch, Division of Extramural Activities, NIDDKD-NIH, 2 Democracy Plaza - Rm. 731, 6707 Democracy Blvd., Bethesda, MD 20892. Phone: (301) 594-8854.

Internet: www.niddk.nih.gov (Note: no field offices for this program.)

93.848 DIGESTIVE DISEASES AND NUTRITION RESEARCH

Assistance: project grants. (100 percent/to 5 years).

Purposes: pursuant to PHSA as amended and SBRDEA, for basic and clinical biomedical research and research training in digestive and liver diseases, nutrition, and obesity. Support is provided through investigator-initiated awards, cooperative agreements, contracts, centers. NRSA, SBIR, and STTR awards are available (*see Notes preceding* **93.001**).

Eligible applicants/beneficiaries: individuals, public and private nonprofit or profit institutions proposing to establish, expand, and improve research activities in health sciences and related fields.

Range: research grants, $26,547 to $1,438,500; NRSAs, $19,000 to $214,500. **Average:** research grants, $164,900; NRSAs, $71,775.

Activity: FY 06 estimate, 1,207 research grants, 124 NRSAs, 44 SBIRs.

HQ: Director, Division of Digestive Diseases and Nutrition, National Institute of Diabetes and Digestive and Kidney Diseases, 2 Democracy Plaza - Rm. 675, 6707 Democracy Blvd., Bethesda, MD 20892. Phone: (301) 594-7680. *Grants management information*: Chief Grants Management Officer, Grants Management Branch, Division of Extramural Activities, NIDDKD-NIH, 2 Democracy Plaza - Rm. 731, 6707 Democracy Blvd., Bethesda, MD 20892. Phone: (301) 594-8854.

Internet: www.niddk.nih.gov (Note: no field offices for this program.)

93.849 KIDNEY DISEASES, UROLOGY AND HEMATOLOGY RESEARCH

Assistance: project grants. (100 percent/to 5 years).

Purposes: pursuant to PHSA as amended and SBRDEA, for basic and clinical biomedical research and research training concerning kidney diseases, urology, and hematology, and for the development of improved diagnostic tools and therapies. NRSA, SBIR, STTR awards are available (*see Notes preceding* **93.001**).

Eligible applicants/beneficiaries: individuals, public and private nonprofit or profit institutions proposing to establish, expand, and improve research activities in health sciences and related fields.

Range: research grants, $15,000 to $1,647,000; NRSAs, $9,168 to $220,160. **Average:** research grants, $171,000; NRSAs, $73,720.

Activity: FY 06 estimate, 1,078 research awards, 103 NRSAs, 41 SBIR grants.

HQ: Director, Division of Kidney, Urologic and Hematologic Diseases, National Institute of Diabetes and Digestive and Kidney Diseases, NIH-HHS, 6707 Democracy Blvd. - Rm. 645, Bethesda, MD 20892-2560. Phone: (301) 496-6325. *Grants management information*: Chief Grants Management Officer, Grants Management Branch, Division of Extramural Activities, NIDDKD-NIH, 2 Democracy Plaza - Rm. 731, 6707 Democracy Blvd., Bethesda, MD 20892. Phone: (301) 594-8854.

Internet: www.niddk.nih.gov (Note: no field offices for this program.)

93.853 EXTRAMURAL RESEARCH PROGRAMS IN THE NEUROSCIENCES AND NEUROLOGICAL DISORDERS

Assistance: project grants. (100 percent/to 5 years).

Purposes: pursuant to PHSA as amended and SBRDEA, for clinical and basic research and research training concerning neurological disorders and stroke, and their diagnosis, prevention, epidemiology, and treatment through development of drugs and neural prostheses. Programs supported include research on stroke, traumatic brain and spinal cord injuries, Parkinson's and Alzheimer's diseases, brain tumors; cellular, molecular, and systems neuroscience, developmental neurobiology and disorders, and neurogenetics, epilepsy, multiple sclerosis, AIDS, immune disorders, and sleep and pain disorders. Special programs include a number of career development awards (such as those cited within "Ranges", below), including Re-Entry into the Neurological Sciences awards for scientists that have been away from research for a least three years to re-establish their skills. NRSA, SBIR, and STTR awards are available (*see Notes preceding* **93.001**).

Eligible applicants/beneficiaries: research grants—any public or private nonprofit or profit institution. Career program awards—U.S. citizens or permanent residents nominated and sponsored by a public or private nonprofit institution.

Range: research grants, $50,000 to $5,944,257; Mentored Research Career Development Awards, $38,415 to $295,768; Independent Scientist Research Career Awards, $70,766 to $174,258; NRSAs, $41,342 to $76,129. **Average:** research grants, $385,129; Mentored Career, $159,945; Independent Scientist, $157,083; NRSAs, $43,356.

Activity: FY 05 estimate, 519 competing research grants, 140 NRSAs.

HQ: National Institute of Neurological Disorders and Stroke, NIH- HHS, 6001 Executive Blvd., Bethesda, MD 20892. Phone: Director, Division of Extramural Research (Ste. 3309), (301) 496-9248; Repair and Plasticity (Ste. 2204), (301) 496-1447; Neural Environment (Ste. 2115), (301) 496-1431; Neurodegeneration (Ste. 2223), (301) 496-5680; Systems & Cognitive Neuroscience (Ste. 2113), (301) 496-9964; Channels, Synapses & Circuits (Ste. 2142), (301) 496-1917; Neurogenetics (Ste. 2133), (301) 496-5745; International Activities (Ste. 2110), (301) 496-0012; Clinical Trials (Ste. 2216), (301) 496-9135; Technology Development (Ste. 2137), (301) 496-1779; Grants Management (Ste. 3258), (301) 496-9231; Contracts Management (Ste. 3280), (301) 496-1813; Minority Health and Research (Ste. 2151), (301) 496-3102; Training and Career Development (Ste. 2138), (301) 496-4188.

Internet: www.ninds.nih.gov (Note: no field offices for this program.)

93.855 ALLERGY, IMMUNOLOGY AND TRANSPLANTATION RESEARCH

Assistance: project grants. (100 percent/to 7 years).

Purposes: pursuant to PHSA as amended and SBRDEA, to establish, expand, and improve basic and clinical biomedical research and research training in allergic and immunologic diseases and related areas, including asthma, AIDS, transplantation biology, and related areas including genetics. Research Career Development Awards are available to institutions for up to five years, to train young scientists for independent research careers.

NRSA, SBIR, and STTR awards are available (*see Notes preceding* **93.001**).

Eligible applicants/beneficiaries: IHEs, hospitals, laboratories, and other public or private, profit or nonprofit, institutions, state and local governments, small businesses, individuals.

Range: grants, $5,000 to $6,618,348; NRSAs, $11,510 to $1,591,964. **Average:** grants, $594,678; NRSAs, $178,949.

Activity: FY 06 estimate, 1,765 awards.

HQ: Director, Division of Extramural Activities, National Institute of Allergy and Infectious Diseases, NIH-HHS, Bethesda, MD 20892. Phone: (301) 496-7291. *Grants management information*: Grants Management Officer, Grants Management Branch, National Institute of Allergy and Infectious Diseases, NIH-HHS, Bethesda, MD 20892. Phone: (301) 496-7075.

Internet: www.niaid.nih.gov (Note: no field offices for this program.)

93.856 MICROBIOLOGY AND INFECTIOUS DISEASES RESEARCH

Assistance: project grants. (100 percent/to 7 years).

Purposes: pursuant to PHSA as amended and SBRDEA, for basic, applied, and clinical biomedical research and research training related to microbiology and infectious diseases. Program aims include the control of disease caused by infectious or parasitic agents, including AIDS, retroviruses, Reye's Syndrome. Studies are supported on the mechanisms of antibiotics, as well as epidemiological observations in hospitalized patients or community populations. Research Career Development Awards are available to institutions for up to five years, to train young scientists for careers in independent research. NRSA, SBIR, and STTR awards are available (*see Notes preceding* **93.001**).

Eligible applicants/beneficiaries: IHEs, hospitals, laboratories, and other public or private, profit or nonprofit, institutions, state and local governments, small businesses, individuals.

Range: research grants, $5,000 to $12,477,542; NRSAs, $9,094 to $812,799. **Average:** research grants, $546,671; NRSAs, $140,784.

Activity: FY 05, 3,688 grants; FY 06 estimate, 4,327 grants; FY 07 estimate, 4,383 grants.

HQ: Director, Division of Extramural Activities, National Institute of Allergy and Infectious Diseases, NIH-HHS, Bethesda, MD 20892. Phone: (301) 496-7291. *Grants management information*: Grants Management Officer, Grants Management Branch, National Institute of Allergy and Infectious Diseases, NIH-HHS, Bethesda, MD 20892. Phone: (301) 496-7075.

Internet: www.niaid.nih.gov (Note: no field offices for this program.)

93.859 BIOMEDICAL RESEARCH AND RESEARCH TRAINING

Assistance: project grants. (100 percent/to 5 years).

Purposes: pursuant to PHSA as amended, for research and research training in basic biomedical sciences not targeted to specific diseases or disorders. Biomedical science fields supported include: cell biology and biophysics;

genetics and development biology; pharmacology, physiology, and biological chemistry; bio- informatics and computational biology. Special training programs include: Minority Access to Research Careers which supports research training at the undergraduate, graduate, and faculty levels; Minority Biomedical Research Support.

Eligible applicants/beneficiaries: U.S. citizens, non-citizen nationals, permanent residents.

Range: $20,000 to $7,500,000.

Activity: annually, approximately 4,400 grants.

HQ: National Institute of General Medical Sciences, 45 Center Drive, Bethesda, MD 20892-6200. Phone: Division of Cell Biology and Biophysics, (301) 594-0828; Division of Genetics and Developmental Biology, (301) 594-0943; Division of Pharmacology, Physiology, and Biological Chemistry, (301) 594-3827; Division of Minority Opportunities in Research, (301) 594-3900; Division of Extramural Activities, (301) 594-3910; Bioinformatics and Computational Biology, (301) 451-6446.

Internet: www.nigms.nih.gov (Note: no field offices for this program.)

93.865 CHILD HEALTH AND HUMAN DEVELOPMENT EXTRAMURAL RESEARCH

Assistance: project grants. (100 percent/to 5 years).

Purposes: pursuant to PHSA as amended and SBRDEA, for fundamental and clinical, biomedical, and behavioral research and research training associated with growth and development biologic and reproductive functions, and population dynamics; also, to conduct research on the impact of disabilities, diseases, and defects, toward the restoration, increase, and maximization of the capabilities of persons so afflicted. NRSA, SBIR, and STTR awards are available (*see Notes preceding* **93.001**).

Eligible applicants/beneficiaries: IHEs; medical, dental, nursing, and public health schools; state and local health departments; hospitals; laboratories; other public or private profit or nonprofit organizations; individuals.

Range: research grants, $50,000 to $5,000,000; NRSA basic stipend first year beyond the doctoral degree, $36,996. **Average:** research grants, $379,400.

Activity: FY 06 estimate, 1,830 research grants, 808 NRSAs.

HQ: Director, Center for Research for Mothers and Children, National Institute of Child Health and Human Development, NIH- HHS, Bldg. 61E - Rm. 4B05, Bethesda, MD 20892-7510. Phone: (301) 496-5097, FAX (301) 480-7773. *Grants management information*: Chief, Grants Management Branch, NIH-HHS, Bldg. 61E - Rm. 8A01, Bethesda, MD 20892-7510. Phone: (301) 435-6975, FAX (301) 402-0915.

Internet: www.nichd.nih.gov (Note: no field offices for this program.)

93.866 AGING RESEARCH

Assistance: project grants. (100 percent/to 5 years).

Purposes: pursuant to PHSA as amended and SBRDEA, for biomedical, social, and behavioral research and research training associated with the aging process and the diseases, special problems, and needs people as they age—including geriatric research and research into genetic diseases and Alzheimer's, and social aspects of care and aging. NRSA, SBIR, and STTR awards are available (*see Notes preceding* **93.001**).

Eligible applicants/beneficiaries: IHEs; medical, dental, nursing, and public health schools; state and local health departments; hospitals; laboratories; other public or private profit or nonprofit organizations; individuals.

Range: research grants, $5,000 to $4,000,000; institutional NRSAs, $31,878 to $724,776; individual NRSA, basic stipend first year beyond doctoral degree, $35,568. **Average:** research grants, $361,940; institutional NRSAs, $279,882.

Activity: FY 06 estimate, 390 competing research project grants, 103 competing NRSAs.

HQ: National Institute on Aging, NIH-HHS, Bethesda, MD 20892. Phone: biology of aging, (301) 496-4996; geriatrics and clinical research, (301) 496-6761; behavioral and social research, (301) 496-3136; neuroscience and neuropsychology of aging research, (301) 496-9350; small business innovation research, (301) 496-9322; grants management, (301) 496-1472.

Internet: www.nia.nih.gov (Note: no field offices for this program.)

93.867 VISION RESEARCH

Assistance: project grants. (100 percent/to 5 years).

Purposes: pursuant to PHSA as amended, SBRDEA, and other acts, for basic, clinical, and applied research and research training projects addressing the leading causes of blindness and impaired vision, including retinal and corneal diseases, diabetic retinopathy, macular degeneration, cataract, glaucoma, strabismus, and amblyopia; for related projects including enhancement of the rehabilitation, training, and quality of life of persons who are partially-sighted or blind. Conference grants, core grants, mentored clinical scientist development awards, clinical vision research development awards, clinical study planning grants, and small grants for data analysis may be offered. NRSA, SBIR, and STTR awards are available (*see Notes preceding* **93.001**).

Eligible applicants/beneficiaries: research grants, cooperative agreements, career development awards—IHEs, hospitals, laboratories, federal institutions; other public or private nonprofit and profit organizations including small businesses; state and local governments. Foreign institutions may apply for research grants only.

Range: research grants and cooperative agreements, $2,889 to $7,011,704; institutional NRSAs, $18,842 to $521,402; individual NRSAs, $24,624 to $56,308. **Average:** research grants and cooperative agreements, $333,101; institutional NRSAs, $189,957; individual NRSAs, $47,095.

Activity: FY 03 estimate, 1,460 grants including 267 NRSAs, 54 SBIR and STTR awards (latest data reported).

HQ: Research Resources Officer, National Eye Institute, NIH-HHS (EPS 350), 6120 Executive Blvd., Bethesda, MD 20892-7164. Phone: (301) 451-2020. *Grants management information*: Chief, Grants Management Branch, National Eye Institute, NIH-HHS, EPS 350, 6120 Executive Blvd., Bethesda, MD 20892-7164. Phone: (301) 451-2020.

Internet: www.nei.nih/gov (Note: no field offices for this program.)

93.879 MEDICAL LIBRARY ASSISTANCE

Assistance: project grants. (100 percent/to 5 years).

Purposes: pursuant to PHSA as amended and SBRDEA, for training programs for professional medical library personnel; for fellowships; to expand or improve existing medical libraries; for biomedical publications; for research in medical informatics and related computer sciences; for similar uses, including computer and telecommunications technology. SBIR and STTR awards are made (*see Notes preceding* **93.001**).

Eligible applicants/beneficiaries: training grants—nonfederal public and nonprofit private institutions. Fellowships—pre- or postdoctoral candidates that are U.S. citizens, nationals, or lawful permanent residents. Other grants—depending on category, domestic public, private, nonprofit, profit health sciences institutions and organizations.

Range: $25,000 to $2,000,000. **Average:** research grants, $353,000; knowledge management grants, $138,000; scholarly works grants, $66,600.

Activity: FY 06 estimate, 208 grants; FY 07 estimate, 210 grants.

HQ: Extramural Programs, National Library of Medicine, NIH-HHS, Bethesda, MD 20894. Phone: (301) 496-4621, (301) 594-4882. *Grants management information*: Grants Management Officer, same address. Phone: (301) 496-4221; *grant review contact,* (301) 496-4253.

Internet: www.nlm.nih.gov/ep (Note: no field offices for this program.)

93.884 GRANTS FOR TRAINING IN PRIMARY CARE MEDICINE AND DENTISTRY ("Primary Care Training")

Assistance: project grants. (100 percent/3 years).

Purposes: pursuant to PHSA as amended and HPEPA, for graduate education and residency programs leading to the practice of family medicine including geriatrics, general internal medicine, general pediatrics, general dentistry, or pediatric dentistry, as well as training of physician assistants in primary care. Grant funds may be used: to plan, develop, and operate or participate in approved programs; provide financial assistance to participants; for faculty development and improving academic administrative units to strengthen clinical instruction. Grants may not be used for construction or patient services.

Eligible applicants/beneficiaries: accredited public or private nonprofit schools of medicine or osteopathy, hospitals, or other entities.

Range: $256,700 to $600,235. **Average:** $211,624.

Activity: FY 06 estimate, 149 family medicine continuation awards; 47 general internal medicine/pediatrics continuation awards; 30 general/pediatric dentistry continuation awards.

HQ: Primary Care Medical Education Branch, Division of Medicine and Dentistry, Bureau of Health Professions, HRSA-HHS, Parklawn Bldg. - Rm. 9A-20, 5600 Fishers Lane, Rockville, MD 20857. Phone: (301) 443-1467. *Grants management information*: Director, Division of Grants Management, Health Resources and Services Administration, HHS, 5600 Fishers Lane - Rm. 11A-16, Rockville, MD 20857. Phone: Health Services, (301) 443-2385; Research and Training, (301) 443-3099; Government and Special Focus, (301) 443-3288.

Internet: www.hrsa.gov (Note: no field offices for this program.)

93.887 HEALTH CARE AND OTHER FACILITIES ("Renovation or Construction Projects")

Assistance: project grants. (100 percent/3-5 years).

Purposes: to construct, renovate, expand, repair, equip, or modernize health care facilities and other related facilities.

Eligible applicants/beneficiaries: state and local governments including their IHEs, quasi-governmental agencies, private IHEs, private profit and nonprofit entities. Entities are eligible if specifically earmarked in Congressional appropriation.

Range: $10,000 to $19,641,298. **Average:** $551,504.

Activity: FY 05, 766 projects; FY 06 and 07 estimate, no awards.

HQ: Facilities Monitoring Branch, Division of Facilities Compliance and Recovery, Healthcare Systems Bureau, HRSA-HHS, Parklawn Bldg.- Rm. 10-105, 5600 Fishers Lane, Rockville, MD 20857. Phone: (301) 443-5656. *Grants management information*: Director, Division of Grants Management, Health Resources and Services Administration, HHS, 5600 Fishers Lane - Rm. 11A-16, Rockville, MD 20857. Phone: Health Services, (301) 443-2385; Research and Training, (301) 443-3099; Government and Special Focus, (301) 443-3288.

Internet: www.hrsa.gov (Note: no field offices for this program.)

93.888 SPECIALLY SELECTED HEALTH PROJECTS

Assistance: project grants. (100 percent/3-5 years).

Purposes: for programs selected by the U.S. Congress as needed for improved health care.

Eligible applicants/beneficiaries: state and local governments including their IHEs, quasi-governmental agencies, private IHEs, private profit and nonprofit entities. Entities are eligible if specifically earmarked in Congressional appropriation.

Range: $45,250 to $24,945,000. **Average:** $1,164,135.

Activity: new program in FY 04.

HQ: Division of Grants Policy, Office of Federal Assistance Management, HRSA-HHS, 5600 Fishers Lane - Rm. 11A-55, Rockville, MD 20857. Phone: (no number provided).

Internet: www.hrsa.gov (Note: no field offices for this program.)

93.889 NATIONAL BIOTERRORISM HOSPITAL PREPAREDNESS PROGRAM

Assistance: project grants.

Purposes: pursuant to the Public Health Security and Bioterrorism Preparedness and Response Act of 2002, for health care entities to upgrade their ability to deliver coordinated and effective care to victims of terrorism and other public health emergencies requiring mass immunization, treatment, isolation, and quarantine in the aftermath of bioterrorism or other outbreaks of infectious disease; for needs assessment updates; for continuation, refinement, and implementation of approved work plans.

Eligible applicants/beneficiaries: state health departments including territories and possessions; and, New York City, Chicago, and Los Angeles.

Range: $330,787 to $39,203,268.

Activity: new program listing in 2004 (CFDA on-line).

HQ: National Bioterrorism Hospital Preparedness Branch, Healthcare Systems Bureau, Division of Health Care Preparedness, HRSA-HHS, Parklawn Bldg. - Rm. 13-103, 5600 Fishers Lane, Rockville, MD 20857. Phone: (301) 443-0924. *Grants management information*: Director, Division of Grants Management, Health Resources and Services Administration, HHS, 5600 Fishers Lane - Rm. 11A-16, Rockville, MD 20857. Phone: Health Services, (301) 443-2385; Research and Training, (301) 443-3099; Government and Special Focus, (301) 443-3288.

Internet: www.hrsa.gov (Note: no field offices for this program.)

93.890 HEALTHY COMMUNITIES ACCESS PROGRAM (HCAP) DEMONSTRATION AUTHORITY ("HCAP")

Assistance: project grants.

Purposes: pursuant to PHSA as amended, for Historically Black Health Professions Schools (HBHPSs) to: develop patient-based research infrastructure with HCAP providers; to establish joint and collaborative programs of medical research and data collection between HBHPSs and HCAPs whose goal is to improve the health status of medically underserved populations; support the related cost of patient care, data collection, and academic training resulting from affiliations with HCAP providers.

Eligible applicants/beneficiaries: HBHPSs affiliated with HCAPs.

Range: $706,762 to $933,118.

Activity: new program in FY 05 (CFDA on-line); FY 05, 4 grants.

HQ: Division of State and Community Assistance, Bureau of Primary Health Care, HRSA-HHS, 5600 Fishers Lane - Rm. 15C-04, Rockville, MD 20857. Phone: (301) 594-4488. *Grants management information*: Director, Division of Grants Management, Health Resources and Services Administration, HHS, 5600 Fishers Lane - Rm. 11A-16, Rockville, MD 20857. Phone: Health Services, (301) 443-2385; Research and Training, (301) 443-3099; Government and Special Focus, (301) 443-3288.

Internet: www.hrsa.gov (Note: no field offices for this program.)

93.891 ALCOHOL RESEARCH CENTER GRANTS

Assistance: project grants. (100 percent/5 years).

Purposes: pursuant to PHSA as amended, for long-term, core support of alcohol research centers, focusing multi-disciplinary attention on the problems of alcohol use and alcoholism. The activities of investigators from biomedical, behavioral, and social sciences are coordinated at such centers.

Eligible applicants/beneficiaries: state and local governments; domestic public or private nonprofit institutions—for centers affiliated with an institution such as a university, medical center, or research center with resources to sustain long-term coordinated research programs, as well as research and clinical training.

Range: $645,000 to $2,093,000. **Average:** $1,693,000.

Activity: FY 06 estimate, 20 grants.

HQ: NIAAA, NIH-HHS, 5635 Fishers Lane, Bethesda, MD 20892-9304. Phone: Division of Metabolism and Health Effects, (301) 443-0799; Division of Treatment and Recovery, (301) 402-4344; Division of Epidemiology and Prevention Research, (301) 443-1274; Division of Neuroscience and Behavior, (301) 443-7722. *Grants management information*: Grants Management Officer, NIAAA, NIH-HHS, 5635 Fishers Lane - Rm. 3023, Bethesda, MD 20892-9304. Phone: (301) 443-4704.

Internet: www.niaaa.nih.gov (Note: no field offices for this program.)

93.908 NURSING EDUCATION LOAN REPAYMENT PROGRAM

Assistance: project grants (100 percent).

Purposes: pursuant to PHSA as amended and Nurse Reinvestment Act of 2002, to repay education loans on behalf of nurses entering full-time employment at IHS or native Hawaiian health centers, public hospitals, migrant or rural health clinics, or certain other health facilities with critical shortages of nurses. Repayment agreements are made for not less than two consecutive years of service; amounts range from 30 percent of the unpaid initial principal and interest of qualified loans in return for the first year of service, to 85 percent for three years.

Eligible applicants/beneficiaries: licensed or license-eligible registered nurses that: will have received a diploma or academic degree; will begin full-time employment (32 hours or more per week) for two or three years at an eligible health facility; have unpaid educational loans obtained for their nursing education; are U.S. citizens, nationals, or permanent legal residents.

Range: 2-year contracts, $11,157 to $112,745; 1-year contracts, $3,329 to $39,175. **Average:** 2-year contracts, $28,079; 1-year contracts, $10,853.

Activity: FY 05, 860 contracts; FY 06 estimate, 744 contracts; FY 07 estimate, 744 contracts.

HQ: Chief, Nursing Education Loan Repayment Branch, Division of Nursing, Bureau of Health Professions, HRSA-HHS, Parklawn Bldg. - Rm. 9-36, 5600 Fishers Lane, Rockville, MD 20857. Phone: (301) 443-6633. *Grants management information*: Director, Division of Grants Management, Health Resources and Services Administration, HHS, 5600 Fishers

Lane - Rm. 11A-16, Rockville, MD 20857. Phone: Health Services, (301) 443-2385; Research and Training, (301) 443-3099; Government and Special Focus, (301) 443-3288.

Internet: www.hrsa.gov (Note: no field offices for this program.)

93.910 FAMILY AND COMMUNITY VIOLENCE PREVENTION PROGRAM ("Family Life Centers")

Assistance: project grants. (100 percent/4 years).

Purposes: pursuant to PHSA as amended, to establish family life centers on the campuses of 24 minority IHEs, to prevent minority- related violence and to improve health and human services to minorities, through: assessments of, and coordination with, related local community resources; design and implementation of educational interventions addressing interpersonal family violence; outreach services to students from dysfunctional families. Funds may not be used to provide health care, nor for construction or demonstration projects.

Eligible applicants/beneficiaries: an IHE representing four-year, primarily minority undergraduate institutions and a two-year tribal college.

Average: one cooperative agreement award, $7,400,000.

Activity: FY 06 estimate, 1 continuation award representing 26 participating institutions.

HQ: Director, Division of Program Operations, Office of Minority Health, Office of Public Health and Science, OS-HHS, 1101 Wooten Pkwy. - Ste. 600, Rockville, MD 20852. Phone: (240) 453-8444. *Grants management information*: Office of Grants Management, Office of Public Health and Science, 1101 Wootton Pkwy. - Ste. 550, Rockville, MD 20852. Phone: (240) 453-8822.

Internet: www.fcvp.gov (Note: no field offices for this program.)

93.912 RURAL HEALTH CARE SERVICES OUTREACH AND RURAL HEALTH NETWORK DEVELOPMENT PROGRAM

Assistance: project grants (100 percent).

Purposes: pursuant to the Health Care Safety Net Amendment, to expand access to, coordinate, restrain the cost of, and improve essential rural health care services by developing integrated systems or networks in rural areas and regions—including mental health services, emergency services, prenatal care, free clinical services, prevention services, professionals training, and transportation services.

Eligible applicants/beneficiaries: rural public or private nonprofit entities that include three or more health care providers; organizations exclusively providing services to migrant and seasonal farm workers; tribal, quasi-tribal entities delivering services on reservations or tribal areas.

Range: outreach, $130,000 to $150,000; network development, $170,000 to $180,000.

Activity: FY 06 estimate, 65 new and 43 continuation outreach grants, 23 new and 15 continuation network development grants.

HQ: Outreach Program Coordinator or Network Development Program Coordinator, Office of Rural Health Policy, Director, Rural Research Centers, Office of Rural Health Policy, HRSA-HHS, Parklawn Bldg. - Rm. 9A-55, 5600 Fishers Lane, Rockville, MD 20857. Phone: (301) 443-0835. *Grants management information*: Director, Division of Grants Management, Health Resources and Services Administration, NIH-HHS, 5600 Fishers Lane - Rm. 11A-16, Rockville, MD 20857. Phone: Health Services, (301) 443-2385; Research and Training, (301) 443-3099; Government and Special Focus, (301) 443-3288.

Internet: www.hrsa.gov (Note: no field offices for this program.)

93.913 GRANTS TO STATES FOR OPERATION OF OFFICES OF RURAL HEALTH

Assistance: project grants. (to 75 percent/to 5 years).

Purposes: pursuant to PHSA as amended, to improve health care in rural areas by establishing state offices of rural health. Funds must support information clearinghouses, coordination of state and federal programs, technical assistance, health professionals recruitment activities.

Eligible applicants/beneficiaries: states.

Range: $100,000 to $150,000.

Activity: annually 50 continuation grants.

HQ: State Office of Rural Health Grant Program, Office of Rural Health Policy, HRSA-HHS, Parklawn Bldg. - Rm. 9A-55, 5600 Fishers Lane, Rockville, MD 20857. Phone: (301) 443-2669. *Grants management information*: Director, Division of Grants Management, Health Resources and Services Administration, NIH-HHS, 5600 Fishers Lane - Rm. 11A-16, Rockville, MD 20857. Phone: Health Services, (301) 443-2385; Research and Training, (301) 443-3099; Government and Special Focus, (301) 443-3288.

Internet: www.hrsa.gov (Note: no field offices for this program.)

93.914 HIV EMERGENCY RELIEF PROJECT GRANTS

Assistance: project grants.

Purposes: pursuant to PHSA as amended and Ryan White Comprehensive AIDS Resources Emergency (CARE) Act Amendments of 2000, to assist areas most severely affected by the HIV epidemic, in developing, organizing, and operating programs providing a continuum of health and support services—including: HIV- related outpatient and ambulatory services; case management and comprehensive treatment services for patients and their families; substance abuse and mental health treatment; inpatient services to prevent unnecessary hospitalization or to expedite discharge; services to infants, women, and children with or exposed to HIV disease.

Eligible applicants/beneficiaries: metropolitan areas with populations of 500,000 or more, reporting more than 2,000 cases of AIDS during the most recent five years, per CDCP data.

Range: $850,000 to $120,000,000. **Average:** $11,518,147.

Activity: FY 06 estimate, 51 competing continuation grants.

HQ: Division of Service Systems, HIV/AIDS Bureau, HRSA-HHS, Parklawn Bldg. - Rm. 7A-55, 5600 Fishers Lane, Rockville, MD 20857. Phone: (301) 443- 6745. *Grants management information*: Director, Division of Grants Management, Health Resources and Services Administration, NIH-HHS, 5600 Fishers Lane - Rm. 11A-16, Rockville, MD 20857. Phone: Health Services, (301) 443-2385; Research and Training, (301) 443-3099; Government and Special Focus, (301) 443-3288.

Internet: www.hrsa.gov (Note: no field offices for this program.)

93.917 HIV CARE FORMULA GRANTS

Assistance: formula grants (to 100 percent).

Purposes: pursuant to PHSA as amended and Ryan White Comprehensive AIDS Resources Emergency (CARE) Act Amendments of 2000, to improve the quality, availability, and organization of health care and support services for persons with HIV disease and their families. Funds may be used: to provide outpatient and ambulatory health and support services, including case management and comprehensive treatment services, substance abuse treatment, and mental health treatment; for inpatient case management services to prevent unnecessary hospitalization or to expedite discharge; to establish and operate consortia; to provide home and community-based care services; to assure the continuity of health insurance coverage; to provide therapeutics to treat individuals with HIV disease.

Eligible applicants/beneficiaries: states, territories and possessions.

Range: $50,000 to $171,786,592. **Average:** $17,963,976.

Activity: annually, 59 awards.

HQ: Division of Service Systems, HIV/AIDS Bureau, HRSA-HHS, Parklawn Bldg. - Rm. 7A-55, 5600 Fishers Lane, Rockville, MD 20857. Phone: (301) 443- 6745. *Grants management information*: Director, Division of Grants Management, Health Resources and Services Administration, NIH-HHS, 5600 Fishers Lane - Rm. 11A-16, Rockville, MD 20857. Phone: Health Services, (301) 443-2385; Research and Training, (301) 443-3099; Government and Special Focus, (301) 443-3288.

Internet: www.hrsa.gov (Note: no field offices for this program.)

93.918 GRANTS TO PROVIDE OUTPATIENT EARLY INTERVENTION SERVICES WITH RESPECT TO HIV DISEASE

Assistance: project grants. (100 percent/to 5 years).

Purposes: pursuant to PHSA as amended and the Ryan White Comprehensive AIDS Resources Emergency (CARE) Act Amendments of 2000, to improve the availability, accessibility, and organization of ambulatory services to persons infected with HIV or at high risk, and to offer early intervention services, including: counseling and testing; partner involvement in risk reduction; transmission prevention; primary care diagnosis and treatment; case management. Capacity building funding may be provided to develop new or expanded programs particularly in rural, underserved, and minority areas. Funds may not be used to acquire real property or to provide inpatient or residential care.

Eligible applicants/beneficiaries: public or private nonprofit: community health centers; family planning grantees under PHS Section 1001, other than states; comprehensive programs of primary health care; comprehensive hemophilia diagnostic and treatment centers.

Range: $100,000 to $650,000—planning, to $50,000; capacity development, to $150,000. **Average:** $350,000.

Activity: FY 05, 359 early intervention awards, 14 capacity development grants.

HQ: Division of Community Based Programs, HIV-AIDS Bureau, HRSA-HHS, 5600 Fishers Lane - Rm. 7A-30, Rockville, MD 20857. Phone: (301) 443-7602, -1377. *Grants management information*: Director, Division of Grants Management, Health Resources and Services Administration, NIH-HHS, 5600 Fishers Lane - Rm. 11A-16, Rockville, MD 20857. Phone: Health Services, (301) 443-2385; Research and Training, (301) 443-3099; Government and Special Focus, (301) 443-3288.

Internet: www.hrsa.gov (Note: no field offices for this program.)

93.919 COOPERATIVE AGREEMENTS FOR STATE-BASED COMPREHENSIVE BREAST AND CERVICAL CANCER EARLY DETECTION PROGRAMS

Assistance: project grants. (75 percent/1-5 years).

Purposes: pursuant to the Breast and Cervical Cancer Mortality Prevention Act of 1990, to develop comprehensive breast and cervical cancer early detection programs; to increase screening and follow-up among all groups of women, especially those that are low-income, uninsured, under-insured, minority, or native Americans. Funds may be used for public education and outreach, referrals services, staff training, project monitoring and evaluation—but not for treatment services.

Eligible applicants/beneficiaries: state health agencies, territories and possessions, tribes and tribal organizations.

Range: $145,000 to $8,400,000. **Average:** $2,100,000.

Activity: annually, 50 states, DC, 13 American Indian and Alaska native tribes, 4 territories funded.

HQ: Program Services Branch, Division of Cancer Prevention and Control, National Center for Chronic Disease Prevention and Health Promotion (K57), CDCP-HHS, 4770 Buford Hwy. NE, Atlanta, GA 30341. Phone: (404) 488-4880. *Grants management information*: Grants Management Officer, Grants Management Branch, Procurement and Grants Office, CDC, 2920 Brandywine Rd. - Rm. 3000, Atlanta, GA 30341. Phone: (770) 488-2722.

Internet: www.cdc.gov/cancer (Note: no field offices for this program.)

93.923 DISADVANTAGED HEALTH PROFESSIONS FACULTY LOAN REPAYMENT (FLRP) AND MINORITY FACULTY FELLOWSHIP PROGRAM (MFFP)

Assistance: project grants; direct payments/specified use. (project grants, 50-100 percent/project grants, to 3 years).

Purposes: pursuant to PHSA as amended and HPEPA, to repay educational loans owed by health professionals from disadvantaged backgrounds, or to provide fellowships to minority faculty, serving for at least two years on the full-time or part-time faculty of a school of medicine, nursing, osteopathy, dentistry, pharmacy, podiatry, optometry, veterinary medicine, public health, allied health, or graduate programs in clinical psychology. Unless waived, schools are required to pay 50 percent of the repayment or fellowship amount due for each year of service.

Eligible applicants/beneficiaries: FLRP—health professionals from disadvantaged backgrounds with degrees or enrolled in approved graduate training programs, or enrolled as full-time students in their final course of study. MFFP—health professions schools with programs in the fields designated.

Range: loan repayments, $2,740 to $55,600 (including funds to cover tax liability); minority fellowships, $4,100 to $59,156 (including funds to cover tax liability). **Average:** loan repayments, $16,300; fellowships, $25,548.

Activity: FY 05, 48 awards total.

HQ: *faculty program,* Division of Health Careers Diversity and Development, Bureau of Health Professions, HRSA-HHS, 5600 Fishers Lane - Rm. 8-42, Rockville, MD 20857. Phone: (301) 443-4776. *Minority faculty fellowship program,* Division of Health Careers, Chief, Diversity Branch, Division of Health Careers Diversity and Development, Bureau of Health Professions, HRSA-HHS, Parklawn Bldg. - Rm. 8-55, 5600 Fishers Lane, Rockville, MD 20857. Phone: (301) 443-2100. *Grants management information*: Director, Division of Grants Management, Health Resources and Services Administration, NIH-HHS, 5600 Fishers Lane - Rm. 11A-16, Rockville, MD 20857. Phone: Health Services, (301) 443-2385; Research and Training, (301) 443-3099; Government and Special Focus, (301) 443-3288.

Internet: www.hrsa.gov (Note: no field offices for this program.)

93.924 RYAN WHITE HIV/AIDS DENTAL REIMBURSEMENTS/COMMUNITY-BASED DENTAL PARTNERSHIP

Assistance: direct payments/specified use; project grants (project grants, to 5 years).

Purposes: pursuant to PHSA as amended and Ryan White CARE Act Amendments of 2000, to reimburse the uncompensated costs incurred for oral health services to patients with HIV/AIDS, by dental schools, and postdoctoral dental education and dental hygiene education programs; to increase access to oral health care services for HIV-positive individuals, while providing education and clinical training for dental and hygiene provided located in community-based settings through "dental partnerships.".

Eligible applicants/beneficiaries: public or private nonprofit schools of dentistry and dental hygiene, and accredited postgraduate dental education programs in the states, territories, and possessions.

Range: reimbursements, $831 to $1,079,951; partnership projects, $184,748 to $403,042. **Average:** reimbursements, $141,418; projects, $276,692.

Activity: FY 05, 12 partnership programs funded; 66 reimbursement awards.

HQ: Division of Community Based Programs, HIV-AIDS Bureau, HRSA-HHS, 5600 Fishers Lane - Rm. 7A-30, Rockville, MD 20857. Phone: (301) 443-1434. *Grants management information*: Director, Division of Grants Management, Health Resources and Services Administration, NIH-HHS, 5600 Fishers Lane - Rm. 11A-16, Rockville, MD 20857. Phone: Health Services, (301) 443-2385; Research and Training, (301) 443-3099; Government and Special Focus, (301) 443-3288.

Internet: www.hrsa.gov (Note: no field offices for this program.)

93.925 SCHOLARSHIPS FOR HEALTH PROFESSIONS STUDENTS FROM DISADVANTAGED BACKGROUNDS ("SDS")

Assistance: project grants.

Purposes: pursuant to PHSA as amended and HPEPA, for annual scholarships to full-time students from disadvantaged backgrounds, awarded by health professions schools that maintain special programs for enrollees, including recruiting and retaining students from disadvantaged backgrounds. At least 16 percent of funds must be allocated to schools providing scholarships only to nurses, and giving preference to former EFN and SDS recipients.

Eligible applicants: public or private nonprofit schools of medicine, nursing, osteopathy, dentistry, pharmacy, podiatry, optometry, veterinary medicine, chiropractic, allied health, or offering graduate programs in public health, behavioral and mental health, or physician assistants.

Eligible beneficiaries: U.S. citizens, nationals, or lawful permanent residents of states, territories, or possessions.

Range: $1,000 to $650,000. **Average:** $94,848.

Activity: FY 05, grants to 471 schools.

HQ: Division of Health Careers Diversity and Development, Bureau of Health Professions, HRSA-HHS, 5600 Fishers Lane - Rm. 8-42, Rockville, MD 20857. Phone: (301) 443-4776. *Grants management information*: Director, Division of Grants Management, Health Resources and Services Administration, NIH-HHS, 5600 Fishers Lane - Rm. 11A-16, Rockville, MD 20857. Phone: Health Services, (301) 443-2385; Research and Training, (301) 443-3099; Government and Special Focus, (301) 443-3288.

Internet: www.hrsa.gov (Note: no field offices for this program.)

93.926 HEALTHY START INITIATIVE

Assistance: project grants. (100 percent/to 4 years).

Purposes: pursuant to PHSA, to eliminate disparities in perinatal and maternal health by enhancing community service systems and infrastructure, and state infrastructures, directing resources and interventions to improve access to, utilization, and full participation of comprehensive service projects for high-risk women and infants. Funds may be used to implement community- driven, multifaceted approaches integrating various health education, social and support services—including outreach, case management, screening and referral, peer mentoring by trained community members, and home visiting programs to promote access and use of preconceptional, perinatal, and inter- conceptional services. Projects must have a community-base consortium of individuals and organizations, including persons served, to collaborate with their state agency and to implement a local health system action plan.

Eligible applicants/beneficiaries: in urban and rural communities with significant disparities in perinatal health—public or private entities including community-based organizations, tribes, and tribal organizations; states needing to build their infrastructure and capacity to address and support eligible communities.

Range: $270,000 to $2,350,000. **Average:** $939,031.

Activity: FY 05, 102 projects; FY 06 estimate, 103 projects; FY 07 estimate, 99 projects.

HQ: Division of Healthy Start and Perinatal Services, Maternal and Child Health Bureau, HRSA-HHS, Parklawn Bldg. - Rm. 18-12, 5600 Fishers Lane, Rockville, MD 20857. Phone: (301) 443-0543. *Grants management information*: Director, Division of Grants Management, Health Resources and Services Administration, NIH-HHS, 5600 Fishers Lane - Rm. 11A-16, Rockville, MD 20857. Phone: Health Services, (301) 443-2385; Research and Training, (301) 443-3099; Government and Special Focus, (301) 443-3288.

Internet: www.hrsa.gov (Note: no field offices for this program.)

93.928 SPECIAL PROJECTS OF NATIONAL SIGNIFICANCE ("SPNS")

Assistance: project grants. (100 percent/to 5 years).

Purposes: pursuant to PHSA as amended and Ryan White CARE Act Amendments of 2000, to advance knowledge and skills in the delivery of health and support services to persons with HIV disease. Funds support innovative projects: for which implementation, costs, utilization, and outcomes can be evaluated rigorously; providing models unlikely to exist without SPNS support; that extend the care model to previously underserved or unserved populations.

Eligible applicants/beneficiaries: public and private nonprofit entities including state or local health departments, hospitals, IHEs, community-based service organizations, IHEs; national service provider organizations.

Range: $75,000 to $599,98. **Average:** $283,190.

Activity: FY 06 estimate, 49 continuation, 15 new awards; FY 07 estimate, 35 continuation, 17 new awards.

HQ: Chief, Demonstration Project Development and Evaluation Branch, Division of Science and Policy, HIV/AIDS Bureau, HRSA- HHS, 5600 Fishers Lane - Rm. 7C-07, Rockville, MD 20857. Phone: (301) 443-3327.

Grants management information: Director, Division of Grants Management, Health Resources and Services Administration, NIH-HHS, 5600 Fishers Lane - Rm. 11A-16, Rockville, MD 20857. Phone: Health Services, (301) 443-2385; Research and Training, (301) 443-3099; Government and Special Focus, (301) 443-3288.

Internet: www.hrsa.gov (Note: no field offices for this program.)

93.932 NATIVE HAWAIIAN HEALTH SYSTEMS

Assistance: project grants. (to 83.3 percent/to 3 years).

Purposes: pursuant to the Native Hawaiian Health Care Improvement Act, for programs raising the health status of native Hawaiians living in Hawaii, by providing comprehensive health promotion and disease prevention and primary health care services. Outreach, case management, and referral components should integrate traditional health concepts with western medicine, employing existing health resources as much as possible.

Eligible applicants/beneficiaries: Papa Ola Lokahi (a consortium of Hawaiian and native Hawaiian organizations); Native American Health Care Systems as specifically defined in Hawaii state laws.

Range: $1,300,000 to $2,400,000.

Activity: annually, 6 grants.

HQ: Director, Division of Health Center Management, Bureau of Primary Health Care, HRSA-HHS, 5600 Fishers Lane - Rm. 16C-26, Rockville, MD 20857. Phone: (301) 594-4485. *Grants management information*: Director, Division of Grants Management, Health Resources and Services Administration, NIH-HHS, 5600 Fishers Lane - Rm. 11A-16, Rockville, MD 20857. Phone: Health Services, (301) 443-2385; Research and Training, (301) 443-3099; Government and Special Focus, (301) 443-3288.

Internet: www.hrsa.gov (Note: no field offices for this program.)

93.933 DEMONSTRATION PROJECTS FOR INDIAN HEALTH

Assistance: project grants. (100 percent/to 5 years).

Purposes: pursuant to PHSA as amended, to promote improved health care among American Indians and Alaska natives, through research, studies, and demonstration projects addressing such issues as elder care, women's health care, and children and youth initiative.

Eligible applicants/beneficiaries: tribes, tribal organizations, nonprofit intertribal or urban Indian organizations contracting with IHS, public or private nonprofit health and education entities, state and local health agencies.

Range: $27,000 to $300,000. **Average:** $115,000.

Activity: FY 05, 44 projects.

HQ: Elders Health, Nashville Area Health Consultant, IHS-HHS, 45 Vernon St., Northampton, MA 01060. Phone: (413) 584-0790. Indian Women's Health Demonstration, Division of Nursing Services, IHS-HHS, 801 Thompson Ave. - Ste. 300, Rockville, MD 20852. Phone: (301) 443-1840. Children & Youth Initiative, Maternal and Child Health Coordinator, Office of Public Health, 801 Thompson Ave. - Ste. 300, Rockville, MD 20852.

Phone: (301) 443-5070. Grants Management, Indian Health Service, 801 Thompson Ave. - Ste. 360, Rockville, MD 20852. Phone: (301) 443-5204.

Internet: www.ihs.gov (Note: no field offices for this program.)

93.936 NATIONAL INSTITUTES OF HEALTH ACQUIRED IMMUNODEFICIENCY SYNDROME RESEARCH LOAN REPAYMENT PROGRAM ("AIDS LRP")

Assistance: project grants. (100 percent/from 2 years).

Purposes: pursuant to PHSA as amended, for partial repayment of educational loans owed by physicians, registered nurses, and scientists employed by NIH in AIDS research. Recipients must have qualified educational debt exceeding 20 percent of their annual salary, and they must engage in research for a minimum of two years. Continuation contracts are available.

Eligible applicants/beneficiaries: NIH AIDS researchers with an M.D., Ph.D., D.D.S., D.O., D.M.D., D.V.M., D.P.M., A.D.N., B.S.N., or equivalent degree, that: are U.S. citizens, nationals, or permanent residents; have no existing service obligation to federal, state, or other entities.

Range: $4,000 to $70,000 (2 years); tax reimbursement, $1,977 to $34,598. **Average:** loan, $53,162 including tax reimbursement.

Activity: FY 05, 11 awards; FY 06 estimate, 12 awards; FY 07 estimate, 12 awards.

HQ: Division of Loan Repayment, NIH-HHS, 6011 Executive Blvd. - Rm. 206, Bethesda, MD 20892-7650. Phone: *helpline,* (866) 849-4047, FAX (866) 849-4046.

Internet: www.lrp.nih.gov (Note: no field offices for this program.)

93.938 COOPERATIVE AGREEMENTS TO SUPPORT COMPREHENSIVE SCHOOL HEALTH PROGRAMS TO PREVENT THE SPREAD OF HIV AND OTHER IMPORTANT HEALTH PROBLEMS ("SHEPSA")

Assistance: project grants. (100 percent/to 5 years).

Purposes: pursuant to PHSA as amended, to develop and implement health education programs for HIV and other health problems for school-age populations (elementary through college), parents, and school, health, and education personnel. Funds may support personnel salaries, training, data collection, monitoring, preparation and dissemination of information including audiovisuals, technical assistance; special outreach to minority, special needs, and high-risk youth. Funds may not be used for research, surveys, computer or office equipment purchases, office space costs, construction or renovation—unless specifically approved.

Eligible applicants/beneficiaries: states, territories and possessions; large urban school districts with high HIV-AIDS rates; national nongovernmental organizations.

Range: $87,000 to $650,000. **Average:** $299,000.

Activity: FY 04, 73 grants.

HQ: Program Development and Services Branch, Division of Adolescent and School Health, National Center for Chronic Disease Prevention and Health Promotion (K31), CDCP-HHS, 4770 Buford Hwy., Atlanta, GA 30341. Phone: (770) 488-6130, FAX (770) 488-6163. *Grants management information*: Grants Management Officer, Grants Management Branch, Procurement and Grants Office, CDCP, 2920 Brandywine Rd. - Rm. 2306, Atlanta, GA 30341. Phone: (770) 488-2754.

Internet: www.cdc.gov/healthyyouth (Note: no field offices for this program.)

93.939 HIV PREVENTION ACTIVITIES—NON-GOVERNMENTAL ORGANIZATION BASED

Assistance: project grants. (to 100 percent/to 5 years).

Purposes: pursuant to PHSA as amended, to promote coordination for primary and secondary HIV prevention efforts among community- based organizations, HIV education and prevention service agencies, and national and regional nonprofit organizations. Project examples include street outreach, risk reduction, and community intervention programs.

Eligible applicants/beneficiaries: nongovernmental public and private nonprofit entities.

Range: $95,000 to $2,250,000. **Average:** $367,200.

Activity: FY 05, 209 awards; FY 06 estimate, 218 awards; FY 07 estimate, 218 awards.

HQ: Division of HIV/AIDS Prevention (A43), CDCP-HHS, 1600 Clifton Rd., Atlanta, GA 30333. Phone: (404) 639-6285. *Grants management information*: Grants Management Officer, Procurement and Grants Office, CDC, 2920 Brandywine Rd. - Rm. 3000, Atlanta, GA 30341. Phone: (770) 498-1911.

Internet: www.cdc.gov (Note: no field offices for this program.)

93.940 HIV PREVENTION ACTIVITIES—HEALTH DEPARTMENT BASED

Assistance: project grants. (to 100 percent/1-5 years).

Purposes: pursuant to PHSA as amended, for state and local health departments to develop, implement, and evaluate primary and secondary HIV prevention programs. Project activities may include: health education and risk reduction for drug users; public information; minority initiatives; counseling, testing, referral, and partner notification.

Eligible applicants/beneficiaries: states and, in consultation with state health authorities, political subdivisions, territories and possessions.

Range: $126,000 to $27,528,000. **Average:** $4,634,000.

Activity: FY 05, 65 awards; FY 06 estimate, 68 awards; FY 07 estimate, 68 awards.

HQ: Division of HIV/AIDS Prevention (A43), CDCP-HHS, 1600 Clifton Rd., Atlanta, GA 30333. Phone: (404) 639-0928. *Grants management information*: Grants Management Officer, Procurement and Grants Office,

CDC, 2920 Brandywine Rd. - Rm. 3000, Atlanta, GA 30341. Phone: (770) 498-1911.

Internet: www.cdc.gov (Note: no field offices for this program.)

93.941 HIV DEMONSTRATION, RESEARCH, PUBLIC AND PROFESSIONAL EDUCATION PROJECTS

Assistance: project grants. (to 100 percent/1-5 years).

Purposes: pursuant to PHSA as amended, to develop, test, and disseminate improved HIV prevention strategies at the community level. Applicants are encouraged to involve research groups in the program.

Eligible applicants/beneficiaries: states and political subdivisions, other public and private nonprofit entities.

Range: $69,400 to $1,356,000. **Average:** $214,325.

Activity: FY 05, 17 awards; FY 06 estimate, 60 awards; FY 07 estimate, 60 awards.

HQ: Division of HIV/AIDS Prevention (A43), CDCP-HHS, 1600 Clifton Rd., Atlanta, GA 30333. Phone: (404) 639-1955. *Grants management information*: Grants Management Officer, Procurement and Grants Office, CDC, 2920 Brandywine Rd. - Rm. 3000, Atlanta, GA 30341. Phone: (770) 498-1911.

Internet: www.cdc.gov (Note: no field offices for this program.)

93.942 RESEARCH, TREATMENT AND EDUCATION PROGRAMS ON LYME DISEASE IN THE UNITED STATES ("Lyme Disease")

Assistance: project grants. (100 percent/to 3 years).

Purposes: pursuant to PHSA as amended, to develop and implement improved measures for the primary and secondary prevention of Lyme disease, including: surveillance activities; ecological and epidemiological studies; diagnostic tests; public education; use of primate models.

Eligible applicants/beneficiaries: public and private nonprofit organizations able to provide services in areas where Lyme disease is found, including IHEs, research institutions, state and local health departments.

Range: $100,000 to $700,000. **Average:** $350,000.

Activity: annually, 10 continuation grants.

HQ: Office of Extramural Research (C-19), National Center for Infectious Diseases, CDCP-HHS, 1600 Clifton Rd. NE, Atlanta, GA 30333. Phone: (404) 639-0043; FAX (404) 639-2469. *Grants management information*: Grants Management Branch, Procurement and Grants Office, CDC, 2920 Brandywine Rd., Atlanta, GA 30341. Phone: (770) 488-2628, FAX (770) 488-2777.

Internet: www.cdc.gov.

93.943 EPIDEMIOLOGIC RESEARCH STUDIES OF ACQUIRED IMMUNODEFICIENCY SYNDROME (AIDS) AND HUMAN IMMUNODEFICIENCY VIRUS (HIV) INFECTION IN SELECTED POPULATION GROUPS

Assistance: project grants. (100 percent/1-3 years).

Purposes: pursuant to PHSA as amended, for research of HIV- related epidemiologic issues concerning risks of transmission, the natural history and transmission of the disease in certain populations, and development and evaluation of behavioral recommendations to reduce AIDS and HIV infection—particularly as they affect minority populations.

Eligible applicants/beneficiaries: states and their political subdivisions, agents, or instrumentalities; public or private nonprofit or profit organizations.

Range: $49,585 to $757,500. **Average:** $237,840.

Activity: FY 05, 53 awards; FY 06 estimate, 13 awards; FY 07 13 awards.

HQ: National Center for HIV, STD, and TB Prevention (A-43), CDC-HHS, 1600 Clifton Rd. NE, Atlanta, GA 30333. Phone: (404) 639-1955. *Grants management information*: Grants Management Branch, Procurement and Grants Office, CDC, 2920 Brandywine Rd. - Rm. 3000, Atlanta, GA 30341. Phone: (770) 498-1911.

Internet: www.cdc.gov (Note: no field offices for this program.)

93.944 HUMAN IMMUNODEFICIENCY VIRUS (HIV)/ACQUIRED IMMUNODEFICIENCY SYNDROME (AIDS) SURVEILLANCE

Assistance: project grants. (100 percent/1-5 years).

Purposes: pursuant to PHSA as amended, to continue and strengthen HIV/AIDS surveillance programs; to effect, maintain, measure, and evaluate the extent of incidence and prevalence throughout the U.S. and its territories; to provide information for targeting and implementing prevention activities. Funds may support staffing costs, purchase of computer hardware and software, laboratory costs.

Eligible applicants/beneficiaries: state and local governments including territories and possessions currently receiving HIV/AIDS surveillance cooperative agreements.

Range: $4,000 to $4,705,000. **Average:** $579,650.

Activity: FY 05, 104 awards; FY 06 estimate, 120 awards; FY 07 estimate, 120 awards.

HQ: Division of HIV/AIDS Prevention (A43), CDCP-HHS, 1600 Clifton Rd., Atlanta, GA 30333. Phone: (404) 639-1955. *Grants management information*: Grants Management Officer, Procurement and Grants Office, CDC, 2920 Brandywine Rd. - Rm. 3000, Atlanta, GA 30341. Phone: (770) 498-1911.

Internet: www.cdc.gov (Note: no field offices for this program.)

93.945 ASSISTANCE PROGRAMS FOR CHRONIC DISEASE PREVENTION AND CONTROL

("State Cardiovascular Health Programs (CVH); Arthritis State-Based Program; National Arthritis Action Plan; Epilepsy Program; Lupus Program, and Racial and Ethnic Approaches to Community Health (REACH)")

Assistance: project grants (80-100 percent/3-5 years).

Purposes: pursuant to PHSA as amended, to prevent and control chronic diseases, including cardiovascular diseases and arthritis; to establish new chronic disease prevention programs such as Racial and Ethnic Approaches to Community Health (REACH) programs. Funds may support costs associated with planning, implementing, and evaluating programs—but not direct curative or rehabilitative services.

Eligible applicants/beneficiaries: *all programs,* health agencies of the states and U.S. territories and possessions. REACH—public and private community-based organizations.

Range: CVH core capacity building, $250,000 to $350,000; basic implementation, $900,000 to $1,350,000; arthritis, to $250,000. **Average:** CVH core, $300,000; basic implementation, $1,250,000; REACH: Interventions, $800,000; AI/AN core capacity, $300,000; elderly, $250,000.

Activity: FY 06-07—CVH, 33 state programs funded; arthritis, 36 state establishment grants; REACH, 31 awards.

HQ: Deputy Director, Division of Adult and Community Health (K47), National Center for Chronic Disease Prevention and Health Promotion, CDCP-PHS-HHS, 4770 Buford Hwy., Atlanta, GA 30333. Phone: (770) 488-8004. *Grants management information*: Grants Management Officer, Procurement and Grants Office, CDC, 2920 Brandywine Rd. - Rm. 3000, Atlanta, GA 30341. Phone: (770) 488-2754.

Internet: www.cdc.gov/nccdphp.

93.946 COOPERATIVE AGREEMENTS TO SUPPORT STATE-BASED SAFE MOTHERHOOD AND INFANT HEALTH INITIATIVE PROGRAMS ("Infant Health and Pre-term Delivery Initiative; PRAMS; MCHEP; ART; VAW; Maternal Health Research")

Assistance: project grants. (100 percent/to 5 years).

Purposes: pursuant to PHSA as amended, for: (1) Pregnancy Risk Assessment and Monitoring Systems (PRAMS), to establish and maintain state-specific, population-based surveillance of selected maternal behaviors that occur during pregnancy and early infancy, and to generate state-specific data for planning and assessing perinatal health programs; (2) Maternal and Child Health Epidemiology Programs (MCHEP) to develop state multidisciplinary teams to assist states in using epidemiological and surveillance data to address the health problems of women, infants, and children, related to pregnancy, in vitro fertilization, violence around pregnancy, pre-term delivery, and reproductive health complications. Funds also may support related other types of surveillance, research, and demonstration projects.

Eligible applicants/beneficiaries: state and territorial public health agencies designated as vital U.S. registration areas; New York City public health agency; tribal governments. Prevention research—public and private nonprofit agencies including universities.

Range: PRAMS, $100,000 to $150,000. **Average:** $125,000.

Activity: 29 ongoing PRAMS agreements.

HQ: Division of Reproductive Health, National Center for Chronic Disease Prevention and Health Promotion, CDCP-HHS, Atlanta, GA 30341. Phone: (770) 488-5200. *Grants management information*: Grants Management Branch, Procurement and Grants Office, CDC, 2920 Brandywine Rd. - Rm. 3000, Atlanta, GA 30341. Phone: (770) 488-2754.

Internet: www.cdc.gov (Note: no field offices for this program.)

93.947 TUBERCULOSIS DEMONSTRATION, RESEARCH, PUBLIC AND PROFESSIONAL EDUCATION

Assistance: project grants. (to 100 percent/3-5 years).

Purposes: pursuant to PHSA as amended, for research into the prevention and control of tuberculosis nationally and internationally; for demonstration projects; for public information and education programs; for education, training, and clinical skills improvement for health professionals including allied health personnel. Funds may not be used for inpatient care.

Eligible applicants/beneficiaries: states, political subdivisions; public and private nonprofit entities.

Range: $135,000 to $915,000. **Average:** $350,000.

Activity: annually, 4 awards.

HQ: National Center for HIV, STD, and TB Prevention, CDCP-HHS, 1600 Clifton Rd. NE (Mail Stop E10), Atlanta, GA 30333. Phone: (404) 639-5336. *Grants management information*: Grants Management Officer, Grants Management Branch, Procurement and Grants Office, CDC-HHS, 1600 Clifton Rd. (Mail Stop E15), Atlanta, GA 30333. Phone:(404) 639-0941.

Internet: www.cdc.gov (Note: no field offices for this program.)

93.952 TRAUMA CARE SYSTEMS PLANNING AND DEVELOPMENT ("Rural EMS/Trauma Care")

Assistance: project grants. (to 100 percent/to 3 years).

Purposes: pursuant to PHSA as amended, for research and demonstration projects designed to improve the availability and quality of emergency medical services in rural areas. Funds may be used to develop: innovative uses of communications technologies, or new technology; model curricula for training EMS personnel including first responders, emergency medical technicians, nurses, physicians, and paramedics—with respect to patient care as well as to management of EMS systems; making EMS training more accessible in rural areas through telecommunications, home studies, and other methods; innovative protocols and agreements to increase patient access to pre- hospital care and transportation equipment; evaluations of protocols.

Eligible applicants/beneficiaries: public or private nonprofit entities.

Range: $15,000 (territories) to $40,000 (states).

Activity: annually, 50 states, territories participating.

HQ: Trauma-EMS Branch, Healthcare Systems Bureau, Healthcare Systems Bureau, Division of Healthcare Emergency Preparedness, HRSA-HHS, Parklawn Bldg. - Rm. 13-103, 5600 Fishers Lane, Rockville, MD 20857.

Phone: (no number provided). *Grants management information*: Director, Division of Grants Management, Health Resources and Services Administration, HHS, 5600 Fishers Lane - Rm. 11A-16, Rockville, MD 20857. Phone: Health Services, (301) 443-2385; Research and Training, (301) 443-3099; Government and Special Focus, (301) 443-3288.

Internet: www.hrsa.gov (Note: no field offices for this program.)

93.954 TRIBAL RECRUITMENT AND RETENTION OF HEALTH PROFESSIONALS INTO INDIAN HEALTH PROGRAMS

Assistance: project grants.

Purposes: pursuant to the Indian Health Care Improvement Act as amended, to establish and operate programs designed to recruit for and retain health professionals in Indian health programs and facilities, including those operated by HIS.

Eligible applicants/beneficiaries: tribes or Indian health organizations, with preference to proposed participants in the IHS Loan Repayment Program (**93.164**).

Range: $60,000 to $100,000. **Average:** $82,900.

Activity: annually, 6 continuation grants.

HQ: Leader, Health Professions Manager, IHS-HHS, 801 Thompson Ave. - Ste. 120, Rockville, MD 20852. Phone: (301) 443-5710. *Grants management information*: Grants Management Officer, Division of Grants Operations, IHS-HHS, 801 Thompson Ave. - Ste. 360, Rockville, MD 20852. Phone: (301) 443-5204.

Internet: www.ihs.gov (Note: no field offices for this program.)

93.958 BLOCK GRANTS FOR COMMUNITY MENTAL HEALTH SERVICES ("CMHS Block Grant")

Assistance: formula grants.

Purposes: pursuant to PHSA as amended, to provide comprehensive community mental health services to adults with a serious mental illness and to children with serious emotional disturbance; for program monitoring; for technical assistance in related planning and implementation. Services must be provided through qualified community programs including community mental health centers or child mental health, psycho-social rehabilitation, mental health peer-support, or mental health primary consumer-directed programs. Funds may not be used for inpatient services, cash payments to patients, most real estate or major equipment costs.

Eligible applicants/beneficiaries: state and territorial governments; tribal organizations.

Range: $50,000 to $54,955,073. **Average:** $27,502,536.

Activity: annually, 59 awards.

HQ: State Planning and System Development Branch, CMHS-SAMHSA-HHS, 1 Choke Cherry Rd. - Rm. 2-1093, Rockville, MD 20857. Phone: (240) 276-1736. Division of Practice and Systems Development, CSAT-SAMHSA- HHS, 1 Choke Cherry Rd., Rockville, MD 20857. Phone:

(240) 276- 1576. *Grants management information*: Grants Management Officer, Office of Program Support, SAMHSA-HHS, 1 Choke Cherry Rd. - Rm. 7-1091, Rockville, MD 20857. Phone: (240) 276-1404.

Internet: www.samhsa.gov (Note: no field offices for this program.)

93.959 BLOCK GRANTS FOR PREVENTION AND TREATMENT OF SUBSTANCE ABUSE ("Substance Abuse Prevention and Treatment (SAPT) Block Grant")

Assistance: formula grants.

Purposes: pursuant to PHSA as amended, to develop and implement prevention, treatment, and rehabilitation activities directed to the diseases of alcohol and drug abuse. At least 20 percent of funds allocated must support education and counseling programs concerning alcohol and substance abuse and tobacco use, for persons not requiring treatment; at least 5 percent of funds must increase treatment services for pregnant women and women with dependent children. States must require treatment programs for intravenous drug abusers, stipulating prompt admittance of such individuals into treatment. States must provide tuberculosis services such as counseling, testing, treatment, and early intervention for substance abusers at risk for HIV disease—either directly or through public or nonprofit entities.

Eligible applicants/beneficiaries: state and territory governments; the Red Lake Band of Chippewa Indians.

Range: $110,614 to $252,450,447. **Average:** $126,285,530.

Activity: annually, 60 awards.

HQ: Division for State and Community Assistance, CSAT-SAMHSA-HHS, 1 Choke Cherry Rd. - Rm. 5-1057, Rockville, MD 20857. Phone: (240) 276-2891. *Grants management information*: Grants Management Officer, Office of Program Support, SAMHSA-HHS, 1 Choke Cherry Rd. - Rm. 7-1091, Rockville, MD 20857. Phone: (240) 276-1404.

Internet: www.samhsa.gov (Note: no field offices for this program.)

93.962 HEALTH ADMINISTRATION TRAINEESHIPS PROGRAM

Assistance: project grants. (100 percent/3 years).

Purposes: pursuant to PHSA as amended and HPEPA, for traineeships for graduate students enrolled in health program or hospital administration, or health policy analysis and planning; for programs to prepare students for employment with public or private nonprofit entities, such as practice-education linkages.

Eligible applicants: public or private nonprofit educational entities.

Eligible beneficiaries: enrolled U.S. citizens or permanent residents, with priority to students demonstrating a commitment to public or nonprofit employers.

Range: $11,387 to $110,457. **Average:** $60,922.

Activity: FY 05, 30 continuation awards.

HQ: Center for Public Health of the Bureau of Health Professions, HRSA-HHS, Parklawn Bldg. - Rm. 8A-19, 5600 Fishers Lane, Rockville, MD

20857. Phone: (301) 443-3231. *Grants management information*: Director, Division of Grants Management, Health Resources and Services Administration, Department of Health and Human Services, 5600 Fishers Lane - Rm. 11A-16, Rockville, MD 20857. Phone: Health Services, (301) 443-2385; Research and Training, (301) 443-3099; Special Focus, (301) 443-3288.

Internet: www.hrsa.gov (Note: no field offices for this program.)

93.964 PUBLIC HEALTH TRAINEESHIPS

Assistance: formula grants. (100 percent/to 3 years).

Purposes: pursuant to PHSA as amended and HPEPA, for traineeships for graduate students of public health. Training must be in: biostatistics; epidemiology; environmental health; toxicology; public health nutrition; maternal and child health.

Eligible applicants/beneficiaries: schools, programs of public health; other accredited public and private nonprofit institutions.

Range: $8,109 to $148,850. **Average:** $50,150.

Activity: FY 05, 34 awards.

HQ: Division of State, Community, and Public Health, Center for Public Health, Bureau of Health Professions, HRSA-HHS, Parklawn Bldg. - Rm. 8A-19, 5600 Fishers Lane, Rockville, MD 20857. Phone: (301) 443-1973. *Grants management information*: Director, Division of Grants Management, Health Resources and Services Administration, Department of Health and Human Services, 5600 Fishers Lane - Rm. 11A-16, Rockville, MD 20857. Phone: Health Services, (301) 443-2385; Research and Training, (301) 443-3099; Special Focus, (301) 443-3288.

Internet: www.hrsa.gov (Note: no field offices for this program.)

93.965 COAL MINERS RESPIRATORY IMPAIRMENT TREATMENT CLINICS AND SERVICES ("Black Lung Clinics")

Assistance: project grants.

Purposes: pursuant to the Federal Mine Safety and Health Act and Black Lung Benefits Act, for broad support of coal miners respiratory impairments treatment clinics and services, including patient and family member education to maximize the patient's ability for self-care.

Eligible applicants/beneficiaries: state, public or private entities.

Range: $125,000 to $1,246,000.

Activity: annually, 15 grants.

HQ: Director, Division of Health Center Management, Bureau of Primary Health Care, HRSA-HHS, 5600 Fishers Lane - Rm. 16C-05, Rockville, MD 20857. Phone: (301) 594-4420. *Grants management information*: Director, Division of Grants Management, Health Resources and Services Administration, NIH-HHS, 5600 Fishers Lane - Rm. 11A-16, Rockville, MD 20857. Phone: Health Services, (301) 443-2385; Research and Training, (301) 443-3099; Government and Special Focus, (301) 443-3288.

Internet: www.hrsa.gov (Note: no field offices for this program.)

93.969 GERIATRIC EDUCATION CENTERS ("GECs")

Assistance: project grants. (100 percent/5 years).

Purposes: pursuant to PHSA as amended and HPEPA, to develop collaborative arrangements among health professions schools and health care facilities, focusing on multi-disciplinary training of health professionals in geriatric health care, including faculty training and retraining; to provide students with clinical training in nursing homes, chronic and acute care hospitals, ambulatory care centers, and senior centers; to develop and disseminate pertinent curricula; provide continuing education for health professionals. Funds may not be used for trainee costs or for land acquisition or construction activities.

Eligible applicants/beneficiaries: accredited health professions schools; schools of allied health; physician assistant training programs.

Range: $148,310 to $432,540. **Average:** $342,848.

Activity: FY 05, 18 new, 32 continuation awards.

HQ: Division of State, Community, and Public Health, Bureau of Health Professions, HRSA-HHS, Parklawn Bldg. - Rm. 8-05, 5600 Fishers Lane, Rockville, MD 20857. Phone: (301) 443-5794. *Grants management information*: Director, Division of Grants Management, Health Resources and Services Administration, NIH-HHS, 5600 Fishers Lane - Rm. 11A-16, Rockville, MD 20857. Phone: Health Services, (301) 443-2385; Research and Training, (301) 443-3099; Government and Special Focus, (301) 443-3288.

Internet: www.hrsa.gov (Note: no field offices for this program.)

93.970 HEALTH PROFESSIONS RECRUITMENT PROGRAM FOR INDIANS

Assistance: project grants (100 percent).

Purposes: pursuant to the Indian Health Care Improvement Act as amended, to establish and operate programs to recruit American Indians and Alaska natives into education or training programs at health or allied health professions schools; to increase the number of nurses, nurse midwives, nurse practitioners, and nurse anesthetists delivering health care services to Americans Indians and Alaska natives; to place health professional residents for short-term assignments at IHS facilities.

Eligible applicants/beneficiaries: public or private nonprofit health or educational entities, with preference to tribes and tribal or urban Indian health organizations.

Range: $300,000 to $500,000. **Average:** $224,600.

Activity: annually, 11 continuation projects.

HQ: *health professions, health residents recruitment,* Leader, Health Professions Manager, IHS-HHS, 801 Thompson Ave. - Ste. 120, Rockville, MD 20852. Phone: (301) 443-5710. *Nursing recruitment,* Nurse Consultant, Nursing Program, IHS-HHS, same address (Ste. 300). Phone: (301) 443-1026. *Grants management information*: Grants Management Officer,

Division of Grants Management, IHS, 801 Thompson Ave. - Ste. 360, Rockville, MD 20852. Phone: (301) 443-5204.

Internet: www.ihs.gov (Note: no field offices for this program.)

93.971 HEALTH PROFESSIONS PREPARATORY SCHOLARSHIP PROGRAM FOR INDIANS

Assistance: project grants.

Purposes: pursuant to the Indian Health Care Improvement Act as amended, for compensatory pre-professional health education scholarships to American Indians and Alaska natives, covering up to two years of full-time study. Eligible disciplines are pre- nursing, -pharmacy, -medical technology, -physical therapy, -engineering, and pre-sanitation.

Eligible applicants/beneficiaries: persons of American Indian or Alaska native descent, with high school completed and accepted into an eligible program.

Range: $17,500 to $26, 019. **Average:** $17,366.

Activity: FY 05, 54 new, 44 continuation awards; FY 06 estimate, 98 continuation awards; FY 07 estimate, 98 continuation awards.

HQ: Scholarship Branch, Division of Health Professions Support, 801 Thompson Ave. - Ste. 450A, Rockville, MD 20852. Phone: (301) 443-6197. *Grants management information*: Grants Management Officer, Division of Grants Operations, HIS, same address (Ste. 360), Phone: (301) 443-0243.

Internet: www.ihs.gov.

93.972 HEALTH PROFESSIONS SCHOLARSHIP PROGRAM

Assistance: project grants. (100 percent/to 4 years).

Purposes: pursuant to the Indian Health Care Amendments of 1988, for scholarships to American Indians and Alaska natives enrolling full- or part-time in health professions schools, to prepare them for careers serving Indians in: allopathic or osteopathic medicine; dentistry; baccalaureate or graduate nursing; graduate public health nutrition; graduate medical social work; graduate speech pathology/audiology; optometry; pharmacy; health care administration. Grantees must serve one year in the IHS or an Indian health organization for each year of support received through the program, with a minimum of two years—with deferments for certain types of advanced training.

Eligible applicants/beneficiaries: native American Indians or Alaskans enrolled as members of a tribe, accepted for study at a U.S. educational institution in a medical/health career education program deemed necessary by the IHS, and eligible for or holding an appointment to the PHS or for civil service in IHS.

Range: $24,128 to $38,222. **Average:** $24,694.

Activity: annually, 78 new, 196 continuing awards.

HQ: Scholarship Branch, Division of Health Professions Support, 801 Thompson Ave. - Ste. 120, Rockville, MD 20852. Phone: (301) 443-6197.

Grants management information: Grants Management Officer, Division of Grants Operations, HIS, same address (Ste. 360), Phone: (301) 443-0243.

Internet: www.ihs.gov.

93.974 FAMILY PLANNING—SERVICE DELIVERY IMPROVEMENT RESEARCH GRANTS ("SDI")

Assistance: project grants (100 percent).

Purposes: pursuant to PHSA as amended and Family Planning Services and Population Research Acts, for research studies to improve family planning services delivery. Funds may not be used in programs where abortion is a method of family planning.

Eligible applicants/beneficiaries: public or private nonprofit entities, including in territories and possessions.

Range: $150,000 to $550,000.

Activity: annually, 15 continuation grants.

HQ: Office of Population Affairs, HHS, 1101 Wootton Pkwy. - Ste. 700, Rockville, MD 20852. Phone: (240) 453-2888. *Grants management information*: Office of Grants Management, Office of Public Health and Science, HHS, same address (Ste. 550). Phone: (240) 453-8822.

Internet: www.opa.osophs.dhhs.gov (Note: no field offices for this program.)

93.977 PREVENTIVE HEALTH SERVICES—SEXUALLY TRANSMITTED DISEASES CONTROL GRANTS

Assistance: project grants. (to 100 percent/1-5 years).

Purposes: pursuant to PHSA and amendments, for surveillance activities to prevent sexually transmitted disease, including reporting, screening, case follow-up including notification of sex partners; interstate epidemiological referral; personnel education and training; studies and demonstrations; development of control strategies and activities.

Eligible applicants/beneficiaries: any state, and in consultation with state authorities, political subdivisions.

Range: $19,000 to $5,100,000. **Average:** $850,000.

Activity: annually, 65 grants.

HQ: Division of STD Prevention (E-02), National Center for HIV, STD, and TB Prevention, CDCP-HHS, 1600 Clifton Rd. NE, Atlanta, GA 30333. Phone: (404) 639-8259, FAX (404) 639-8608. *Grants management information*: Grants Management Officer, Grants Management Branch, Procurement and Grants Office, CDC-HHS, 2920 Brandywine Rd., Atlanta, GA 30341. Phone: (404) 639-0941.

Internet: www.cdc.gov (Note: no field offices for this program.)

93.978 PREVENTIVE HEALTH SERVICES—SEXUALLY TRANSMITTED DISEASES RESEARCH, DEMONSTRATIONS, AND PUBLIC INFORMATION AND EDUCATION GRANTS

Assistance: project grants. (100 percent/1-5 years).

Purposes: pursuant to PHSA and amendments, for applied research, demonstrations, personnel training activities, and public education activities concerning the prevention and control of sexually transmitted diseases. Participants in the applied research may receive reimbursements from grant funds.

Eligible applicants/beneficiaries: states, political subdivisions, public or private nonprofit institutions.

Range: $125,000 to $450,000. **Average:** $313,809.

Activity: annually, 10 prevention training center grants.

HQ: Division of STD Prevention (E-02), National Center for HIV, STD, and TB Prevention, CDCP-HHS, 1600 Clifton Rd. NE, Atlanta, GA 30333. Phone: (404) 639-8259. *Grants management information*: Grants Management Officer, Grants Management Branch, Procurement and Grants Office, CDC-HHS, 2920 Brandywine Rd., Atlanta, GA 30341. Phone: (404) 639-0941.

Internet: www.cdc.gov (Note: no field offices for this program.)

93.982 MENTAL HEALTH DISASTER ASSISTANCE AND EMERGENCY MENTAL HEALTH

Assistance: project grants. (100 percent/9-12 months).

Purposes: pursuant to the Robert T. Stafford Disaster Relief and Emergency Assistance Act, for supplemental emergency mental health counseling services to victims of major disasters; to train workers to provide such counseling.

Eligible applicants/beneficiaries: state or local nonprofit agencies recommended by the state governor.

Range: $47,000 to $3,705,061. **Average:** $1,000,000.

Activity: FY 04, 10 grants; FY 05-06, no awards.

HQ: Emergency Services and Disaster Relief Branch, CMHS-SAMHSA-HHS, Rockville, MD 20857. Phone: (no number provided). *Grants management information*: Grants Management Officer, SAMHSA, HHS, 1 Choke Cherry Rd., Rockville, MD 20857. Phone: (240) 276-1421.

Internet: www.samhsa.gov.

93.988 COOPERATIVE AGREEMENTS FOR STATE-BASED DIABETES CONTROL PROGRAMS AND EVALUATION OF SURVEILLANCE SYSTEMS ("DCPs")

Assistance: project grants. (80-84 percent/5 years).

Purposes: pursuant to PHSA as amended and Health Services and Centers Amendments Act of 1978, to plan, implement, and evaluate state-based diabetes control programs including: determining the size and nature diabetes-related problems; developing new strategies to prevention; establishing partnerships to prevent diabetes problems; increasing awareness of prevention and control opportunities among the public, health care and business communities, and diabetes patients; improving access to quality care. Direct curative or rehabilitative services to patients may not be provided with grant funds.

Eligible applicants/beneficiaries: official state and territorial health agencies.

Range: core capacity program, $75,000 to $350,000; implementation programs, $300,000 to $800,000. **Average:** core capacity, $250,000; implementation, $500,000.

Activity: estimate, 33capacity-building, 26 implementation awards.

HQ: Program Development Branch, Division of Diabetes Translation, National Center for Chronic Disease Prevention and Health Promotion, CDCP-HHS, 1600 Clifton Rd. NE, Atlanta, GA 30333. Phone: (770) 488-5033. *Grants management information*: Grants Management Officer, Grants Management Branch, Procurement and Grants Office, CDC, 2929 Brandywine Rd., Atlanta, GA 30341. Phone: (770) 488-2722.

Internet: www.cdc.gov (Note: no field offices for this program.)

93.989 INTERNATIONAL RESEARCH AND RESEARCH TRAINING

Assistance: project grants. (100 percent/to 5 years).

Purposes: pursuant to PHSA as amended, for research and research training to reduce disparities in global health and toward the international exchange of ideas and information. Research is supported in the basic biological, behavioral, and social sciences, including economics, demography, and ethics. Grants may support stipends, foreign living allowances, travel, and minimal other costs required to perform research in a foreign country.

Eligible applicants/beneficiaries: IHEs, hospitals, laboratories, federal institutions, state and local governments, and other public or private nonprofit of profit institutions.

Range: regular research, education project, training grants, $100,000 to $1,300,000; career awards, $50,000 to $150,000; cooperative agreements, $300,000 to $700,000; small grants, $30,000 to $45,000.

Activity: FY 05 (representative), 120 Fogarty international research collaboration, 11 clinical-operational-mental health services, 17 environmental and occupational, 30 global infectious diseases training grants, 25 AIDS training and research continuation awards.

HQ: Fogarty International Center, NIH-HHS, Bldg. 31 - Rm. B2C39, MSC 2220, Bethesda, MD 20892-2220. Phone: (301) 496-1653.

Internet: www.fic.nih.gov; www.fic.nih.gov/programs/grants.html (Note: no field offices for this program.)

93.990 NATIONAL HEALTH PROMOTION

Assistance: project grants. (100 percent/to 3 years).

Purposes: pursuant to PHSA as amended, for national membership organizations from various sectors to participate in the National Health Promotion Program to educate the public about good health habits and programs designed to prevent disease and disability. Funds may be used to develop promotion programs and materials to be used by schools, medical treatment sites, work sites, and community health promotion programs; to identify the needs of special population groups; to fill gaps identified in the "Healthy People 2010: National Health Promotion and Disease Prevention Objectives.".

Eligible applicants/beneficiaries: public or private nonprofit organizations.

Range: $75,000 to $275,000.

Activity: FY 04, 22 new awards for a 3-year project period.

HQ: Office of Disease Prevention and Health Promotion, OS-HHS, 1100 Wootton Pkwy. - Ste. 550, Rockville, MD 20853. Phone: (240) 453-8280. *Grants management information*: Office of Grants Management, Office of Public Health and Science, HHS, (same address). Phone: (240) 453-8822.

Internet: www.health.gov/healthypeople (Note: no field offices for this program.)

93.991 PREVENTIVE HEALTH AND HEALTH SERVICES BLOCK GRANT ("PHHS Block Grants")

Assistance: formula grants. (100 percent/2 years).

Purposes: pursuant to PHSA, Health Omnibus Programs Extension Act of 1988, and amendments, for state preventive health service programs, including emergency medical services program improvement (but not program operations costs), health incentive activities, hypertension programs, rodent control, fluoridation programs, health education, risk reduction programs, home health services, services for victims of sex offenses including prevention of sex offenses, and other services related to the accomplishment of "Year 2000/2010" objectives.

Eligible applicants/beneficiaries: state and Pacific territorial governments, certain tribes.

Range: $29,046 to $9,429,807. **Average:** $2,117,686.

Activity: annually, all states and territories, two tribes funded.

HQ: Project Officer, National Center for Chronic Disease Prevention and Health Promotion (K30), CDCP-HHS, 4770 Buford Hwy. NE, Atlanta, GA 30341-3724. Phone: (770) 488-5282. *Grants management information*: Grants Management Officer/Contracting Officer, Branch B, Procurement and Grants Office, CDC, 2920 Brandywine Rd. - Rm. 2306, Atlanta, GA 30341. Phone: (770) 488-2754.

Internet: www.cdc.gov (Note: no field offices for this program.)

93.993 PUBLIC HEALTH RESEARCH ACCREDITATION PROJECT

Assistance: project grants. (100 percent/to 3 years).

Purposes: pursuant to PHSA as amended, to develop pilot measures to assess the ability of the public health infrastructure to assess and monitor research involving human subjects. Projects will assess the role of accreditation of human research protection programs to enhance protections afforded to persons involved in public health research, including epidemiologic, health services, social and behavioral intervention, as well as traditional biomedical research and clinical trials.

Eligible applicants/beneficiaries: public or private, nonprofit or profit organizations actively engaged in accreditation of human research protection programs.

Range/Average: N.A.

Activity: new program listing in 2004.

HQ: Procurement and Grants Office, CDCP-HHS, 2920 Brandywine Rd., Atlanta, GA 30341-4146. Phone: general questions, technical information management, (770) 488-2700; management, budget matters, Contracts Specialist, (770) 488-2696; technical assistance, (404) 639-7262.

Internet: www.cdc.gov (Note: no field offices for this program.)

93.994 MATERNAL AND CHILD HEALTH SERVICES BLOCK GRANT TO THE STATES ("MCH Block Grants")

Assistance: formula grants (57 percent).

Purposes: pursuant to SSA as amended, for a broad range of health and related services including preventive and primary care services to pregnant women, mothers, infants, and children including children with special health needs. Funds may support such costs as program planning, administration, education, and evaluation. Ineligible uses of funds are most inpatient services, cash payments for health services, major equipment purchases, construction costs, or research or training other than by public or nonprofit entities.

Eligible applicants/beneficiaries: states and insular areas.

Range: $159,139 to $48,441,501. **Average:** $9,980,508.

Activity: annually, 59 block grants.

HQ: Division of State and Community Health, Maternal and Child Health Bureau, HRSA-HHS, 5600 Fishers Lane - Rm. 18-31, Rockville, MD 20857. Phone: (301) 443-2204. *Grants management information*: Director, Division of Grants Management, Health Resources and Services Administration-HHS, 5600 Fishers Lane - Rm. 11A-16, Rockville, MD 20857. Phone: Health Services, (301) 443-2385; Research and Training, (301) 443-3099; Government and Special Focus, (301) 443-3288.

Internet: www.hrsa.gov (Note: no field offices for this program.)

93.995 ADOLESCENT FAMILY LIFE—DEMONSTRATION PROJECTS ("AFL")

Assistance: project grants. (to 70 percent/to 5 years).

Purposes: pursuant to PHSA as amended, to establish innovative, comprehensive, and integrated approaches to the delivery of care services to pregnant and parenting adolescents, especially those under age 17; to promote abstinence from sexual relations through age-appropriate education on sexuality and decision making skills as the most effective method of preventing adolescent pregnancy and avoiding sexually transmitted diseases including HIV/AIDS. Funds may support costs of: care and prevention services; coordination of services among local providers; appropriate supplemental services.

Eligible applicants/beneficiaries: public organizations including city, county, regional, and state governments; private nonprofit organizations.

Range: $250,000 to $375,000.

Activity: FY 06 estimate, 100 continuation, 50 new grants.

HQ: Office of Adolescent Pregnancy Programs, Office of Population Affairs, OS-HHS, 1101 Wootton Pkwy. - Ste. 700, Rockville, MD 20852. Phone: (240) 453-2828. *Grants management information*: Director, Office of Grants Management, Office of Public Health and Science-HHS, 1101 Wootton Pkwy. - Ste. 550 Rockville, MD 20853. Phone: (240) 453-8822.

Internet: www.opa.osophs.dhhs.gov (Note: no field offices for this program.)

93.996 BIOTERRORISM TRAINING AND CURRICULUM DEVELOPMENT PROGRAM ("BTCDP")

Assistance: project grants. (100 percent/to 2 years).

Purposes: pursuant to the Public Health Security and Bioterrorism Preparedness and Response Act of 2002, to prepare a workforce of health care professionals to address the medical consequences of bioterrorism and other public health emergency preparedness and response issues. Funding may support multidisciplinary and collaborative: provision of continuing education for practicing providers; undergraduate and graduate curriculum development in health professions schools; drills, exercises, and simulations. Linkages and relationships must be demonstrated with such entities as awardees of the CDC Public Health Preparedness and Response for Bioterrorism Program and HRSA Bioterrorism Hospital Preparedness Programs, academic health centers, other service providers, and consumers.

Eligible applicants/beneficiaries: academic health centers, public and private nonprofit accredited or licensed health professions schools, multistate or multi-institutional consortia, professional organizations and societies, and community-based organizations.

Range: continuing education projects, $684,510 to $1,500,000; curriculum development, $77,130 to $200,000. **Average:** continuing education projects, $1,271,460; curriculum development, $152,526.

Activity: FY 05, 19 continuing education, 13 curriculum development awards.

HQ: Emergency Training Branch, Division of Healthcare Preparedness, Healthcare Systems Bureau, HRSA, 5600 Fishers Lane - Rm. 13-103, Rockville, MD 20857. Phone: (301) 443-4912, FAX (301) 443-4922. *Grants management information*: Director, Division of Grants Management, Health Resources and Services Administration, NIH-HHS, 5600 Fishers Lane - Rm. 11A-16, Rockville, MD 20857. Phone: Health Services, (301) 443-2385; Research and Training, (301) 443-3099; Government and Special Focus, (301) 443-3288.

Internet: www.hrsa.gov (Note: no field offices for this program.)

CORPORATION FOR NATIONAL AND COMMUNITY SERVICE

94.002 RETIRED AND SENIOR VOLUNTEER PROGRAM ("RSVP")

Assistance: project grants. (70-90 percent/3 years).

Purposes: pursuant to the Domestic Volunteer Service Act of 1973 as amended and National and Community Service Trust Act of 1993 (NCSA), for programs engaging retired persons as volunteers in community service projects—e.g., intergenerational activities, in-home care, consumer education, public safety, and health and human service activities. Grant funds cover program costs including staff salaries and reimbursements to volunteers for their out-of-pocket expenses, primarily for transportation. Technical assistance and materials toward establishing and operating programs are available.

Eligible applicants: public agencies including state and local government agencies, private nonprofit organizations.

Eligible beneficiaries: volunteers at least age 55.

Range: to $847,000. **Average:** $68,800.

Activity: over 485,000 volunteers serving in over 65,000 local organizations, contributing 77,000,000 hours of volunteer service.

HQ: National Senior Service Corps, RSVP, CNCS, 1201 New York Ave. NW, Washington, DC 20525. Phone: (202) 606-6715.

Internet: www.nationalservice.org.

94.003 STATE COMMISSIONS

Assistance: project grants (cost sharing).

Purposes: pursuant to NCSA as amended, to operate independent, bipartisan state commissions to oversee funded AmeriCorps programs. Commissions generally include 15 to 25 members appointed by governors.

Eligible applicants/beneficiaries: state governments, DC, PR.

Range: $125,000 to $750,000.

Activity: not quantified specifically.

HQ: CNCS, 1201 New York Ave. NW, Washington, DC 20525. Phone: (202) 606-6715.

Internet: www.nationalservice.org.

94.004 LEARN AND SERVE AMERICA—SCHOOL AND COMMUNITY BASED PROGRAMS

Assistance: project grants. (50-90 percent/to 5 years).

Purposes: pursuant to NCSA as amended, to encourage elementary and secondary schools and community-based agencies to establish, develop, and offer service-learning opportunities for school-age youth—in such areas as health, education, public safety, and environment; to educate teachers about service-learning and incorporate its concepts into classrooms; to coordinate adult volunteers serving in schools; to introduce young people to career opportunities. Funds may be used for: planning and capacity building; program operating costs including grants to local partnerships for service-learning projects; programs involving adult volunteers in educating students; teacher and staff training and technical assistance.

Eligible applicants/beneficiaries: SEAs, State Commissions on National Service, territories, tribes, public or private nonprofit entities.

Range: $20,000 to $2,376,360. **Average:** $298,610.

Activity: FY 02, 1,500,000 youth involved (latest data reported).

HQ: CNCS, 1201 New York Ave. NW, Washington, DC 20525. Phone: (202) 606-6715.

Internet: www.nationalservice.org.

94.005 LEARN AND SERVE AMERICA—HIGHER EDUCATION

Assistance: project grants. (to 50 percent/to 3 years).

Purposes: pursuant to NCSA as amended and HEA of 1965, for service-learning projects engaging graduate and undergraduate college students and faculty members in meeting community needs, while enhancing student academic and civic learning; to build capacity and strengthen the service infrastructure of IHEs. Eligible project activities include tutoring, mentoring, health outreach and education, primary and preventive health care, conflict resolution, neighborhood clean-up and revitalization, and prevention of gang violence and substance abuse activities.

Eligible applicants/beneficiaries: IHEs, consortia of IHEs, and nonprofit organizations or public agencies including states in partnerships with IHEs.

Range: $40,000 to $320,000. **Average:** $188,600.

Activity: FY 03 estimate, 62 continuation grants supporting some 30,000 students participating at 300 IHEs (latest data reported).

HQ: CNCS, 1201 New York Ave. NW, Washington, DC 20525. Phone: (202) 606-6715.

Internet: www.nationalservice.org.

94.006 AMERICORPS

Assistance: project grants.

Purposes: pursuant to NCSA as amended, to plan or operate national and community service programs addressing community education, public safety, human, and environmental needs—by encouraging volunteers to serve part- or full-time. AmeriCorps members serve for one year, and receive education awards for postsecondary education or to pay off student loans. Examples include volunteers serving as mentors, tutors, teaching assistants, role models—in after-school, immunization, low- income housing renovation, "crime watch", environmental projects.

Eligible applicants/beneficiaries: states, tribes, territories, national non-profit organizations, professional corps, and multi- state organizations.

Range: $200,000 (state programs) to $3,000,000 (national programs).

Activity: FY 06-07, 67,350 AmeriCorps members.

HQ: CNCS, 1201 New York Ave. NW, Washington, DC 20525. Phone: (202) 606-6715.

Internet: www.nationalservice.org.

94.007 PLANNING AND PROGRAM DEVELOPMENT GRANTS

Assistance: project grants.

Purposes: pursuant to NCSA as amended, for innovative demonstration projects that build the ethic of service among Americans of all ages and backgrounds—including through the AmeriCorps Education Award Program, AmeriCorps Promise Fellows Program, and Martin Luther King Day of Service Program, and Disability Outreach grants for programs ensuring participation of the disabled in national and community service.

Eligible applicants/beneficiaries: demonstration grants—state and local government agencies, nonprofit organizations. Disability grants—operating AmeriCorps programs, state commissions, national nonprofit organizations.

Range: demonstration grants, $25,000 to $500,000; Martin Luther King Day of Service grants, to $5,000.

Activity: not quantified specifically.

HQ: CNCS, 1201 New York Ave. NW, Washington, DC 20525. Phone: (202) 606-6715.

Internet: www.nationalservice.org.

94.009 TRAINING AND TECHNICAL ASSISTANCE

Assistance: project grants.

Purposes: pursuant to the NCSA as amended, for training and technical assistance services to CNCS grantees in such areas as program and financial management, fund raising, sustainability, membership development and training, and program evaluation. Services are provided through national, regional, and state workshops, publications, on-site consultations.

Eligible applicants/beneficiaries: federal, state, and local agencies and other government units; tribes; IHEs; nonprofit and community-based organizations; some for-profit companies.

Range: $100,000 to $1,500,000.

Activity: not quantified specifically.

HQ: CNCS, 1201 New York Ave. NW, Washington, DC 20525. Phone: (202) 606-6915, FAX (202) 208-4151.

Internet: www.nationalservice.org.

94.011 FOSTER GRANDPARENT PROGRAM ("FGP")

Assistance: project grants (from 90 percent).

Purposes: pursuant to the Domestic Volunteer Service Act of 1973 as amended and National and Community Service Trust Act of 1993, to engage older volunteers with limited incomes in providing supportive services to infants, children, or youth with special or exceptional needs. Programs may be conducted in the children's homes or in residential or nonresidential facilities including preschools. Grant funds may be used: to pay stipends to low- income foster grandparents serving as volunteers, and to provide their transportation, physical exams, and meals; for staff salaries and travel, equipment, and space costs. Technical assistance and materials toward establishing and operating programs are available.

Eligible applicants: state and local government agencies, private nonprofit organizations.

Eligible beneficiaries: persons at least age 60, low-income, and physically, mentally, and emotionally capable of serving clients on a person-to-person basis; non-low-income individuals may serve as volunteers without stipends.

Range: to $1,949,000. **Average:** $318,333.

Activity: FY 05, 342 local projects nationwide funded, over 31,000 volunteers contributed 27.9 million hours of service for 263,000 children.

HQ: Foster Grandparent Program, National Senior Service Corps, CNCS, 1201 New York Ave. NW, Washington, DC 20525. Phone: (202) 606-6715.

Internet: www.nationalservice.org.

94.013 VOLUNTEERS IN SERVICE TO AMERICA ("AmeriCorps-VISTA")

Assistance: specialized services.

Purposes: pursuant to the Domestic Volunteer Service Act of 1973 as amended, to provide volunteers from all walks of life and age groups, working in projects addressing the problems of poverty such as health, illiteracy, substance abuse prevention and education, hunger, homelessness, housing, unemployment. Volunteers may be recruited locally or referred by CNCS; they serve full-time for one year, living at subsistence levels of support among the people they serve.

Eligible applicants/beneficiaries: federal, state, or local government agencies or private nonprofit organizations.

Range/Average: N.A.

Activity: FY 05, 6,707 volunteers, 1,200 projects in 50 states, DC, PR.

HQ: Director, VISTA, CNCS, 1201 New York Ave. NW, Washington, DC 20525. Phone: (202) 606-5000, (800) 424-8867.

Internet: www.nationalservice.org.

94.016 SENIOR COMPANION PROGRAM ("SCP")

Assistance: project grants. (from 90 percent/3 years).

Purposes: pursuant to the Domestic Volunteer Service Act of 1973 as amended and National and Community Service Trust Act of 1993, for the operating costs of the Senior Companion Program, including stipends, transportation, physical exams, insurance, and meals for low-income older volunteers. SCP participants serve as companions to other adults, primarily older persons with special needs. Services to the adults may be provided in their homes or in residential or nonresidential facilities, including such activities as helping hospital patients during their recuperation, arranging for community social services, working with the terminally ill. Respite care services, including to Alzheimer's patients and their families, are also provided.

Eligible applicants: state and local government agencies, private nonprofit organizations.

Eligible beneficiaries: persons at least age 60, low-income, and physically, mentally, and emotionally capable of serving clients on a person-to-person basis; non-low-income individuals may serve as volunteers without stipends.

Range: to $689,000. **Average:** $237,500.

Activity: FY 05, over 16,000 volunteers contributed 13.9 million hours of service to 58,000 people through 224 organizations.

HQ: Senior Companion Program, CNCS, 1201 New York Ave. NW, Washington, DC 20525. Phone: (202) 606-5000, ext. 189; (800) 424-8867.

Internet: www.nationalservice.org.

SOCIAL SECURITY ADMINISTRATION

96.001 SOCIAL SECURITY—DISABILITY INSURANCE

Assistance: direct payments/unrestricted or specified use.

Purposes: pursuant to SSA as amended, to replace part of the earnings lost because of a physical or mental impairment preventing a person from working. Disability is defined as a medically determined physical or mental impairment that has lasted or is expected to last at least 12 months, or to result in death. There is a five-month waiting period. Costs of vocational rehabilitation for certain beneficiaries are eligible.

Eligible applicants/beneficiaries: disabled workers under full retirement age (66 for workers age 62 in 2005) if they have worked for a sufficient period of time under Social Security. Certain family members of disabled workers also are eligible for benefits, including: unmarried children under age 18, or 19 for full-time elementary and secondary students; disabled unmarried children under age 22; spouse caring for child under age 16 or disabled, receiving benefits on worker's Social Security record; spouses age 62 or over; divorced spouses age 62 or over, married to the worker for at least 10 years. Benefits are subject to an earnings test, and may be reduced by amounts received under other programs. Certain restrictions apply for impairments: based on drug addiction or alcoholism; based on felony- and confinement-related impairments. Coverage credits under the social security systems of certain foreign governments may be taken into account. Effective after 2003, lawfully admitted aliens may be eligible if they have a work-authorized Social Security Number. Applicants should contact local Social Security offices for additional details.

Range: to $2,099 monthly for a disabled worker; to $3,148.60 for a family. **Average:** individual, $880; family, $1,496.

Activity: FY 05 estimate, 8,005,000 benefit recipients monthly (average).

HQ: Office of Public Inquiries, SSA, Annex - Rm. 4100, Baltimore, MD 21235. Phone: (410) 965-2736.

Internet: www.socialsecurity.gov.

96.002 SOCIAL SECURITY—RETIREMENT INSURANCE

Assistance: direct payments/unrestricted use.

Purposes: pursuant to SSA as amended, to pay monthly cash benefits to retired workers and their eligible auxiliaries.

Eligible applicants/beneficiaries: retired workers age 62 and over that have worked the required number of years under Social Security. Certain family members also are eligible for benefits, including: unmarried children under age 18, or 19 for full-time elementary and secondary students; disabled unmarried children under age 22; spouse caring for child under age 16 or disabled, receiving benefits on worker's Social Security record; spouses age 62 or over; divorced spouses age 62 or over, married to the worker for at least 10 years. Benefit payments to eligible workers applying before full-benefit retirement age (66 for workers age 62 in 2005) are reduced permanently. Benefit amounts may be reduced for a spouse receiving a government pension based on his or her work in non-covered employment. Coverage credits under the social security systems of certain foreign governments may be taken into account to meet eligibility requirements. Effective after 2003, lawfully admitted aliens may be eligible if they have a work-authorized Social Security Number. All applicants should contact local Social Security offices for additional details and restrictions.

Range: to $1,939 monthly for an individual retiring at full-retirement age; to $3,394.10 for a family receiving benefits. **Average:** individual, $942 monthly; retired worker and eligible spouse, $1,574 monthly.

Activity: FY 04, 32,709,000 monthly benefit recipients (average); FY 05 estimate, 33,066,000 monthly benefit recipients (average); FY 06 estimate, 33,535,000 monthly benefit recipients (average).

HQ: Office of Public Inquiries, SSA, Annex - Rm. 4100, Baltimore, MD 21235. Phone: (410) 965-2736.

Internet: www.socialsecurity.gov.

96.004 SOCIAL SECURITY—SURVIVORS INSURANCE

Assistance: direct payments/specified or unrestricted uses.

Purposes: pursuant to SSA as amended, to pay monthly cash benefits to a deceased worker's dependents if the deceased was insured for survivors' insurance protection.

Eligible applicants/beneficiaries: widows or widowers age 60 or over; surviving divorced spouses age 60 or over, married to the deceased worker for at least 10 years; survivors with a child in their care under age 16 or disabled; disabled widows, widowers, or divorced spouses age 50-59; unmarried children under age 18, or under 19 if in elementary or secondary school, or age 18 or older if disabled before age 22; dependent parents age 62 or over. Earnings tests and benefit limits apply, except for beneficiaries age 70 or over. Under certain conditions, a lump-sum death payment of $255 is payable to survivors. Benefits are subject to an earnings test, and may be reduced by amounts received under other programs. Benefit amounts are reduced for a spouse receiving a government pension based on his or her work in non-covered employment. Coverage credits under the social security systems of certain foreign governments may be taken into account to meet eligibility requirements. Effective after 2003, lawfully admitted aliens may be eligible if they have a work-authorized Social Security Number. Applicants should contact local Social Security offices for additional details.

Range: to $1,939 monthly. **Average:** for an aged widow or widower alone, $920 monthly; with two or more eligible children, $1,905 monthly.

Activity: FY 04, monthly benefits to 6,779,000 survivors (average); FY 05 estimate, monthly benefits to 6,747,000 survivors (average); FY 06 estimate, monthly benefits to 6,728,000 survivors (average).

HQ: Office of Public Inquiries, SSA, Annex - Rm. 4100, Baltimore, MD 21235. Phone: (410) 965-2736.

Internet: www.socialsecurity.gov.

96.006 SUPPLEMENTAL SECURITY INCOME

Assistance: direct payments/unrestricted or specified uses.

Purposes: pursuant SSA as amended, to provide supplemental income to persons aged 65 and over and to blind or disabled persons with incomes and financial resources below specified levels.

Eligible applicants/beneficiaries: persons age 65 or over or blind or disabled, meeting U.S. citizenship or residence requirements, and with income and assets below certain levels.

Range: to $579 monthly for individuals; to $869 for an individual with an eligible spouse. **Average:** $404 monthly.

Activity: FY 04, monthly benefits to 6,666,000 persons (average); FY 05 estimate, monthly benefits to 6,821,000 persons (average); FY 06 estimate, monthly benefits to 7,020,000 persons (average).

HQ: Office of Public Inquiries, SSA, Annex - Rm. 4100, Baltimore, MD 21235. Phone: (410) 965-2736.

Internet: www.socialsecurity.gov.

96.007 SOCIAL SECURITY—RESEARCH AND DEMONSTRATION ("SSA Research and Demonstration")

Assistance: project grants. (75-95 percent/3 months-5 years).

Purposes: pursuant to SSA as amended, for social, economic, and demographic research and demonstration projects and experiments to improve the management, administration, and effectiveness of facets of SSA programs.

Eligible applicants/beneficiaries: state and local governments, educational institutions, hospitals, public and private nonprofit and profit organizations.

Range: $100,000 to $1,750,000.

Activity: FY 05, 52 continuation awards FY 06 estimate, 62 continuation awards, 1 new award.

HQ: Grants Management Officer, Office of Operations Contracts and Grants, Office of Acquisition and Grants, DCFAM, SSA, 7111 Security Blvd., Baltimore, MD 21244. Phone: (410) 965-9518.

Internet: www.socialsecurity.gov (Note: no field offices for this program.)

96.008 SOCIAL SECURITY—WORK INCENTIVES PLANNING AND ASSISTANCE PROGRAM

Assistance: project grants. (75-95 percent/3 months-5 years).

Purposes: pursuant to SSA, Ticket-to-Work Incentives Improvement Act of 1999, Workforce Improvement Act of 1998, and other acts, for: statewide benefits planning and assistance programs, including information on the availability of protection and advocacy services, to all Social Security Disability Insurance and SSI beneficiaries; ongoing outreach to beneficiaries with disabilities and families eligible to participate in state or federal work incentives programs; to disseminate information to SSA beneficiaries with disabilities, including transition-to-work youth, about work incentives and related issues.

Eligible applicants/beneficiaries: state or local governments; public, private, profit or nonprofit organizations—including such organizations as centers for independent living, protection and advocacy organizations, tribal entities, client assistance programs, state vocational rehabilitation agencies, developmental disabilities councils, Workforce Investment Boards.

Range: $50,000 to $300,000.

Activity: annually, 56 cooperative agreements with all states and territories.

HQ: Project Officer, Office of Employment Support Programs, ODISP-SSA, 107 Altmeyer Bldg., 6401 Security Blvd., Baltimore, MD 21235. Phone: (410) 965-1729.

Internet: www.socialsecurity.gov/work (Note: no field offices for this program.)

96.009 SOCIAL SECURITY STATE GRANTS FOR WORK INCENTIVES ASSISTANCE TO DISABLED BENEFICIARIES

Assistance: project grants. (formula based/3 months-5 years).

Purposes: pursuant to SSA, Ticket-to-Work Incentives Improvement Act of 1999, Workforce Improvement Act of 1998, and other acts, to provide information, advice, and advocacy to disabled SSA beneficiaries, about obtaining vocational rehabilitation and other services to help them obtain or regain gainful employment. Some program cost-sharing will be required.

Eligible applicants/beneficiaries: state protection and advocacy systems.

Range: $50,000 to $438,275. **Average:** $117,982.

Activity: not quantified specifically.

HQ: Project Officer, Office of Employment Support Programs, ODISP-SSA, 107 Altmeyer Bldg., 6401 Security Blvd., Baltimore, MD 21235. Phone: (410) 965-8658.

Internet: www.socialsecurity.gov/work/ServiceProviders/pafactsheet.html (Note: no field offices for this program.)

96.020 SPECIAL BENEFITS FOR CERTAIN WORLD WAR II VETERANS ("Special Veterans Benefits; SVB")

Assistance: direct payments/unrestricted use.

Purposes: pursuant to SSA and Foster Care Independence Act of 1999, to pay special benefits to certain World War II veterans that are eligible for SSI benefits and reside outside the U.S.

Eligible applicants/beneficiaries: World War II veterans age 65 or older as of December 14, 1999, residing outside the U.S. (including specific Filipino veterans), meeting length and dates of service requirements, and with other benefit income that is less than 75 percent of the SSI benefit rate.

Range: SVB, to $452.25 monthly; federal, $342.68 monthly.

Activity: currently, 2,550 beneficiaries residing in the Philippines.

HQ: SSA, Office of Public Inquiries, Windsor Park Bldg., 6401 Security Blvd., Baltimore, MD 21235. Phone: (401) 965-2736.

Internet: www.socialsecurity.gov.

DEPARTMENT OF HOMELAND SECURITY

97.001 PILOT DEMONSTRATION OR EARMARKED PROJECTS ("Earmarked Projects or One-Time Funded Programs")

Assistance: project grants.

Purposes: pursuant to the Homeland Security Act and U.S.A. Patriot Act of 2001 (USAPA), for special programs or projects by entities specified in Congressional appropriations.

Eligible applicants/beneficiaries: nonfederal entities—e.g., state, local, tribal governments; private, public, profit, or nonprofit organizations, or individuals specified in Congressional appropriations.

Range/Average: N.A.

Activity: new program in FY 03.

HQ: Office of Grant Policy and Oversight-DHS, 245 Murray Lane - Rm. 214, Washington, DC 20523. Phone: (202) 205-9193.

Internet: www.dhs.gov/dhspublic/display?theme=37&content=3608 (Note: no field offices for this program.)

97.002 RESEARCH PROJECTS ("Earmarked Research Projects or One-Time Funded Research Programs")

Assistance: project grants.

Purposes: pursuant to the Homeland Security Act and USAPA, for research programs or projects by entities specified in Congressional appropriations.

Eligible applicants/beneficiaries: nonfederal entities—e.g., state, local, tribal governments; private, public, profit, or nonprofit organizations, or individuals specified in Congressional appropriations.

Range/Average: N.A.

Activity: new program in FY 03.

HQ: Office of Grant Policy and Oversight-DHS, 245 Murray Lane - Rm. 214, Washington, DC 20523. Phone: (202) 205-9193.

Internet: www.dhs.gov/dhspublic/display?theme=37&content=3608 (Note: no field offices for this program.)

97.004 STATE DOMESTIC PREPAREDNESS EQUIPMENT SUPPORT PROGRAM

Assistance: formula grants. (100 percent/to 3 years).

Purposes: pursuant to USAPA, to enhance the capacity of state and local first responders to respond to Weapons of Mass Destruction (WMD) terrorist incidents involving nuclear, biological, chemical, incendiary, and explosive devices. Funds may be used to: conduct comprehensive threat and needs assessments; develop and implement Statewide Domestic Preparedness Strategies; purchase equipment; plan and conduct of exercises. Program initially listed as a DOJ program, and transferred to DHS in CFDA 2003; CFDA indicates program has been renamed "State Homeland Security Grant Program, (**97.073**), and merged into "Homeland Security Grant Program (**97.067**); however, this program has not been deleted in CFDA. (Note: re web site given under "HQ", below, CFDA cites web site as active.)

Eligible applicants/beneficiaries: states, territories, possessions.

Range/Average: N.A.

Activity: not quantified specifically.

HQ: Office of State and Local Government Coordination and Preparedness, Office for Domestic Preparedness-DHS, 245 Murray Lane - Bldg. 410, Washington, DC 20523. Phone: (800) 368-6498.

Internet: www.ojp.usdoj.gov (Note: no field offices for this program.)

97.005 STATE AND LOCAL HOMELAND SECURITY TRAINING PROGRAM

Assistance: project grants. (100 percent/to 3 years).

Purposes: pursuant to USAPA, to develop and conduct training programs for state and local first responders to incidents involving WMD domestic terrorist incidents involving nuclear, biological, chemical, incendiary, and explosive devices—for personnel involved in fire-fighting, law enforcement, emergency medical services, emergency management, public works, and public health.

Eligible applicants: the National Domestic Preparedness Consortium. Others that may become eligible will be so notified.

Eligible beneficiaries: state and local government units.

Range/Average: N.A.

Activity: over 390,000 first responders trained.

HQ: Office of State and Local Government Coordination and Preparedness, Office for Domestic Preparedness-DHS, 245 Murray Lane - Bldg. 410, Washington, DC 20523. Phone: (800) 368-6498.

Internet: www.ojp.usdoj.gov/odp (Note: no field offices for this program.)

97.006 STATE AND LOCAL HOMELAND SECURITY EXERCISE SUPPORT

Assistance: project grant. (100 percent/to 3 years).

Purposes: pursuant to the USAPA, to plan and conduct exercises for national, state, and local first responders to incidents of terrorism involving WMD including nuclear, biological, chemical, incendiary and explosive devices. (Note: program initially listed as a DOJ program, and transferred to DHS in CFDA 2003.)

Eligible applicants: public or private organizations with expertise and experience in providing program assistance.

Eligible beneficiaries: state and local units of government.

Range/Average: N.A.

Activity: not quantified specifically.

HQ: Office of State and Local Government Coordination and Preparedness, Office for Domestic Preparedness-DHS, 245 Murray Lane, Washington, DC 20523. Phone: (202) 282-8000.

Internet: www.ojp.usdoj.gov/odp (Note: no field offices for this program.)

97.007 HOMELAND SECURITY PREPAREDNESS TECHNICAL ASSISTANCE PROGRAM

Assistance: project grants. (100 percent/to 3 years).

Purposes: pursuant to USAPA, to enhance the capacity of state and local first responders to respond to WMD terrorist incidents involving nuclear, biological, chemical, incendiary, and explosive devices. Funds may be used to develop, plan, and implement programs and to sustain and maintain specialized equipment.

Eligible applicants: public or private organizations with expertise and experience in providing program assistance.

Eligible beneficiaries: state and local units of government.

Range/Average: N.A.

Activity: not quantified specifically.

HQ: Office of State and Local Government Coordination and Preparedness, Office for Domestic Preparedness-DHS, 245 Murray Lane, Bldg. 410, Washington, DC 20523. Phone: (800) 368-6498.

Internet: www.ojp.usdoj.gov/odp (Note: no field offices for this program.)

97.008 URBAN AREAS SECURITY INITIATIVE ("UASI")

Assistance: project grants. (100 percent/2.5 years).

Purposes: pursuant to USAPA, to address the unique needs of large urban areas and mass transit authorities to be prepared for and respond to threats of incidents of terrorism. Funds may be used for equipment, training, exercises, and planning.

Eligible applicants/beneficiaries: states containing selected cities.

Range/Average: N.A.

Activity: not quantified specifically.

HQ: Office of State and Local Government Coordination and Preparedness, Office for Domestic Preparedness-DHS, 245 Murray Lane, Bldg. 410, Washington, DC 20523. Phone: (800) 368-6498.

Internet: www.dhs.gov (Note: no field offices for this program.)

97.009 CUBAN/HAITIAN ENTRANT PROGRAM

Assistance: project grants. (100 percent/1-4 years).

Purposes: pursuant to the Refugee Education Assistance Act of 1980 as amended, for primary resettlement services to eligible Cubans and Haitians paroled into communities by DHS for humanitarian reasons; for Cuban and Haitian entrants living in south Florida and requiring secondary resettlement assistance. (Program initially listed as a DOJ program, and transferred to DHS in CFDA 2003.)

Eligible applicants/beneficiaries: public or private nonprofit organizations or agencies; certain profit organizations.

Range: to $4,500,000.

Activity: FY 04 estimate, 19,000 entrants served.

HQ: Parole and Humanitarian Assistance Branch, Immigration and Customs Enforcement, Office of International Affairs-DHS, 425 I St. NW, (ATTN: 800 N. Capitol St. - 3rd Fl.), Washington, DC 20536. Phone: (no number provided).

Internet: www.dhs.gov.

97.010 CITIZENSHIP EDUCATION AND TRAINING

Assistance: technical information.

Purposes: pursuant to the Immigration and Nationality Act of 1952 as amended, to provide instruction and training materials in citizenship responsibilities for immigrants interested becoming U.S. citizens and in learning English and U.S. history and government. Free federal textbooks on citizenship at various reading levels are provided. (Program initially listed as a DOJ program, and transferred to DHS in CFDA 2003.)

Eligible applicants/beneficiaries: public schools or other educational groups conducting classes under supervision of public schools.

Range/Average: N.A.

Activity: annually, 4,200 textbooks distributed.

HQ: DHS, 245 Murray Dr. SW, Washington, DC 20528. Phone: (202) 282-8000.

Internet: www.dhs.gov.

97.011 BOATING SAFETY

Assistance: specialized services; technical information; training.

Purposes: for the Coast Guard Auxiliary to provide: boating safety education and training; Vessel Safety Checks; assistance in patrolling regattas and parades, and to boaters in distress; publications. (Program initially listed as a USCG-DOT program, and transferred to DHS in CFDA 2003.)

Eligible applicants/beneficiaries: U.S. citizens at least age 17 may apply for membership in the Auxiliary.

Range/Average: N.A.

Activity: 112,000 vessel safety examinations; 220,000 public school students enrolled in courses; 2,256 regatta and 23,000 safety patrols, 3,733 public assists, 311 lives saved.

HQ: Commandant (G-OCX), U.S. Coast Guard-DHS, 2100 Second St. SW - Rm. 3501, Washington, DC 20593-0001. Phone: (202) 267-1001.

Internet: www.cgaux.org.

97.012 BOATING SAFETY FINANCIAL ASSISTANCE

Assistance: formula grants. (50-100 percent/1 year).

Purposes: for states to develop and operate recreational boating safety programs. Funds may support: education, maintenance, and enforcement activities; costs of facilities acquisition and construction or repair of access sites; personnel training; administration. (Program initially listed as a USCG-DOT program, and transferred to DHS in CFDA 2003.)

Eligible applicants/beneficiaries: states, territories, and possessions with approved boating safety programs; national nonprofit service organizations.

Range: states, $342,000 to $4,603,000; organizations (100 percent funding), $6,000 to $495,000. **Average:** states, $1,000,000; organizations, $95,000.

Activity: 50 states, several territories and possessions, 15 national organizations funded.

HQ: Office of Boating Safety (G-PCB), U.S. Coast Guard-DHS, 2100 Second St. SW, Washington, DC 20593. Phone: states, (202) 267-0857; nonprofits, (202) 267-0974.

Internet: www.uscgboating.org; www.dhs.gov (Note: no field offices for this program.)

97.013 STATE ACCESS TO THE OIL SPILL LIABILITY TRUST FUND

Assistance: project grants (100 percent).

Purposes: pursuant to the Oil Pollution Act of 1990, to reimburse states for costs incurred in responding to actual or threatened discharges of oil occurring after 18 August 1990. Eligible expenses include engaged state officials' salaries, personnel and materials transportation, equipment, and similar costs. (Program initially listed as a USCG-DOT program, and transferred to DHS in CFDA 2003.)

Eligible applicants/beneficiaries: governors of states, territories, and possessions.

Range: $250,000 maximum per incident.

Activity: not quantified specifically.

HQ: DHS, 245 Murray Dr. SW, Washington, DC 20528. Phone: (202) 494-9118.

Internet: www.dhs.gov (Note: no field offices for this program.)

97.014 BRIDGE ALTERATION ("Truman-Hobbs Act")

Assistance: direct payments/specified use.

Purposes: pursuant to the Rivers and Harbors Appropriations Act of 1899, Bridge Act of 1906 as amended, and Truman-Hobbs Act, for the alteration of obstructive bridges to render navigation reasonably free, easy, and unobstructed. Project funds may not be used for such activities as those providing special benefits to bridge owners, nor solely to achieve savings in repair or maintenance costs or to increase carrying capacity. (Program initially listed as a USCG-DOT program, and transferred to DHS in CFDA 2003.)

Eligible applicants/beneficiaries: any state, county, municipality, or other political subdivision, or any corporation, association, partnership, or individual—owning or jointly owning a lawful bridge over U.S. navigable waters used and operated to carry railroad or highway traffic.

Range: $14,740,000 to $42,800,000.

Activity: 27 projects completed; 9 projects under design and construction.

HQ: DHS, 245 Murray Dr. SW, Washington, DC 20528. Phone: (202) 282-8000.

Internet: www.dhs.gov.

97.015 SECRET SERVICE—TRAINING ACTIVITIES

Assistance: training.

Purposes: to acquaint local law enforcement officials with the functions of the Secret Service and the techniques used to detect counterfeit money and documents and to protect dignitaries. Bank tellers, department store cashiers, and other money handlers may be briefed in the detection of counterfeit currency and documents by Secret Service regional offices. (Program initially listed as a Department of the Treasury program, and transferred to DHS in CFDA 2003.)

Eligible applicants/beneficiaries: sworn members of police agencies.

Range/Average: N.A.

Activity: annually, 3,200 participants.

HQ: DHS, U.S. Secret Service, 245 Murray Dr. SW, Washington, DC 20528. Phone: (202) 282-8000.

Internet: www.dhs.gov.

97.016 REIMBURSEMENT FOR FIREFIGHTING ON FEDERAL PROPERTY

Assistance: direct payments/specified use.

Purposes: pursuant to the Federal Fire Prevention and Control Act of 1974 as amended, to reimburse fire service organizations for their direct expenses and losses from firefighting operations on federal property. (Program initially listed as a FEMA program, and transferred to DHS in CFDA 2003.)

Eligible applicants/beneficiaries: volunteer and paid fire departments of states, territories, possessions, and federal Indian lands.

Range: to $500,000, with no stated limit.

Activity: FY 03, no claims approved (most recent data).

HQ: FEMA-DHS, 245 Murray Lane - Bldg. 410, Washington, DC 20523. Phone: (no number provided).

Internet: www.dhs.gov (Note: no field offices for this program.)

97.018 NATIONAL FIRE ACADEMY TRAINING ASSISTANCE ("Student Stipend Reimbursement Program")

Assistance: direct payments/specified use.

Purposes: pursuant to the Federal Fire Prevention and Control Act of 1974 as amended, for limited stipends, travel expenses, and lodging costs of attending resident or regional programs the National Fire Academy. (Program initially listed as a FEMA program, and transferred to DHS in CFDA 2003.)

Eligible applicants/beneficiaries: members of fire departments and others with significant responsibility for fire prevention and control. Federal and private industry employees and foreign students may attend courses, but are ineligible for payments.

Average: resident courses, $330; regional, $112.

Activity: annually, over 4,200 stipends paid.

HQ: Emergency Preparedness and Response, FEMA-DHS, 245 Murray Lane, Bldg. 410, Washington, DC 20523. Phone: (no number provided).

Internet: www.dhs.gov (Note: no field offices for this program.)

97.019 NATIONAL FIRE ACADEMY EDUCATIONAL PROGRAM

Assistance: training.

Purposes: pursuant to the Federal Fire Prevention and Control Act of 1974 as amended, to increase the professional level of the fire service and others responsible for fire prevention and control through training at the National Fire Academy or at off- campus locations. Training is provided on specific subjects to specific audiences. (Program initially listed as a FEMA program, and transferred to DHS in CFDA 2003.)

Eligible applicants/beneficiaries: members of fire departments; others with significant responsibility for fire prevention and control.

Range/Average: N.A.

Activity: 5,239 national facility, 787 regional, 2,872 "State Weekend," 60,000 train-the-trainer program participants.

HQ: Emergency Preparedness and Response, FEMA-DHS, 245 Murray Lane, Bldg. 410, Washington, DC 20523. Phone: (no number provided).

Internet: www.dhs.gov (Note: no field offices for this program.)

97.020 HAZARDOUS MATERIALS TRAINING PROGRAM ("SARA Title III Training Program")

Assistance: project grants. (80 percent/1 year).

Purposes: pursuant to CERCLA as amended and SARA, for education and training programs for tribal government personnel to improve emergency planning, preparedness, mitigation, response, and recovery capabilities—with emphasis on hazardous chemicals and related emergencies. (Program initially listed as a FEMA program, and transferred to DHS in CFDA 2003.)

Eligible applicants/beneficiaries: tribal governments.

Range: $2,000 to $251,000. **Average:** $84,000.

Activity: not quantified specifically.

HQ: FEMA-DHS, 245 Murray Lane, Bldg. 410, Washington, DC 20523. Phone: (800) 621-FEMA(3363).

Internet: www.dhs.gov.

97.021 HAZARDOUS MATERIALS ASSISTANCE PROGRAM ("CERCLA Implementation")

Assistance: project grants.

Purposes: pursuant to CERCLA as amended and SARA, for planning, exercising, and educational projects enhancing emergency management capabilities for dealing with oil and hazardous materials releases. Limited funding is available for costs of certain training and equipment purchases. (Program initially listed as a FEMA program, and transferred to DHS in CFDA 2003.)

Eligible applicants/beneficiaries: states, locals, tribes, territories, State Emergency Response Committees, Local Emergency Planning Commissions.

Range: to $20,000.

Activity: not quantified specifically.

HQ: FEMA-DHS, 245 Murray Lane, Bldg. 410, Washington, DC 20523. Phone: (800) 621-FEMA(3363).

Internet: www.dhs.gov.

97.022 FLOOD INSURANCE ("National Flood Insurance Program" - "NFIP")

Assistance: insurance.

Purposes: pursuant to the National Flood Insurance Act of 1968, to insure property owners against losses from floods, mudflow, and flood-caused erosion—at or below normal actuarial rates; to promote flood plain management practices. Flood insurance must be purchased as a condition of obtaining any form of federal financial assistance, including disaster assistance and mortgage loan insurance from VA, FmHA, and FHA, when projects are located within flood hazard areas where flood insurance is available. Special program provisions apply for properties within the Coastal Barrier Resource System. Maximum amounts of coverage and other requirements apply, according to type and location of structure; details are available from FEMA regional offices or responsible state offices. (Program initially listed as a FEMA program, and transferred to DHS in CFDA 2003.)

Eligible applicants: states and their political subdivisions that submit completed applications to FEMA consistent with program regulations.

Eligible beneficiaries: residential, business, and municipal property owners in states or political subdivisions that have enacted NFIP flood plain management measures.

Range: claims paid: $1 to $1,900,000. **Average:** $29,000.

Activity: as of FY 02, 19,706 communities participating; 4,365,000 policies in force, representing $597 billion in insurance (latest available data).

HQ: FEMA-DHS, 245 Murray Lane - Bldg. 410, Washington, DC 20523 Phone: (800) 621-FEMA(3363).

Internet: www.dhs.gov.

97.023 COMMUNITY ASSISTANCE PROGRAM—STATE SUPPORT SERVICES ELEMENT ("CAP-SSSE")

Assistance: project grants (75 percent).

Purposes: pursuant to the National Flood Insurance Act of 1968 and Flood Disaster Protection Act of 1973 as amended, to identify, prevent, and resolve flood plain management issues in communities participating in the NFIP, through the adoption of flood loss reduction measures. Project examples: community assistance visits, ordinance assistance, coordination meetings with FEMA regional offices, community rating system application assistance and review workshops. (Program initially listed as a FEMA program, and transferred to DHS in CFDA 2003.)

Eligible applicants/beneficiaries: states and through the states, NFIP communities and local governments.

Range: $50,000 to $350,000.

Activity: FY 04, 50 awards.

HQ: FEMA-DHS, 245 Murray Lane - Bldg. 410, Washington, DC 20523 Phone: (800) 621-FEMA(3363).

Internet: www.dhs.gov.

97.024 EMERGENCY FOOD AND SHELTER NATIONAL BOARD PROGRAM

Assistance: formula grants.

Purposes: pursuant to SBMHAA as amended, to supplement and expand ongoing programs providing shelter, food, and supportive services for needy families and individuals; for projects to create more effective and innovative local programs; for minimum rehabilitation of existing mass shelter or feeding facilities, bringing them into compliance with local building codes. Eligible expenses include: costs of food and its transport, food preparation and serving equipment; mass shelter and other shelter, such as hotels and motels; rent or mortgage payments assistance for one month only; limited facility repairs; utility payments. Ineligible costs include such expenses as rental security or other deposits, cash payments to the homeless, major property improvements. (Program initially listed as a FEMA program, and transferred to DHS in CFDA 2003.)

Eligible applicants/beneficiaries: jurisdictions approved by the Emergency Food and Shelter Program National Board chaired by FEMA or State Set-Aside Committees, may award grants to: public or private nonprofit organizations, community action agencies, food banks, food pantries; specialized community groups such as domestic violence centers; native American organizations; organizations providing food and shelter to AIDS patients, handicapped persons, the elderly, teenage runaways, and others with emergency needs.

Range: $2,000 to $5,864,000.

Activity: assistance to 11,000 social service agencies in 2,500 jurisdictions, 10 training sessions with 700 participants.

HQ: FEMA-DHS, 245 Murray Lane - Bldg. 410, Washington, DC 20523 Phone: (800) 621-FEMA(3363).

Internet: www.dhs.gov.

97.025 NATIONAL URBAN SEARCH AND RESCUE (US&R) RESPONSE SYSTEM ("US&R")

Assistance: project grants (100 percent).

Purposes: pursuant to the Earthquake Hazards Reduction Act of 1977 and Stafford Act as amended, to develop national immediately deployable urban search and rescue task forces to locate, extricate, and provide medical treatment to victims of structural collapse during a disaster. Funds may be used for training, exercises, and to acquire and maintain specialized equipment. (Program initially listed as a FEMA program, and transferred to DHS in CFDA 2003.)

Eligible applicants/beneficiaries: 28 jurisdictions designated by FEMA as members of the National Urban Search and Rescue Response System.

Average: $592,915 per grantee.

Activity: FY 06, 28 grants.

HQ: FEMA-DHS, 245 Murray Lane - Bldg. 410, Washington, DC 20523 Phone: (800) 621-FEMA(3363).

Internet: www.dhs.gov (Note: no field offices for this program.)

97.026 EMERGENCY MANAGEMENT INSTITUTE—TRAINING ASSISTANCE ("Student Stipend Reimbursement Program - SEP")

Assistance: direct payments/specified use.

Purposes: pursuant to the Stafford Act, National Security Act of 1947, Defense Production Act of 1950, Earthquake Hazards Reduction Act of 1977, and amendments, for emergency management personnel to obtain training at the Emergency Management Institute and selected other locations. Programs embody the Comprehensive Emergency Management System by unifying the elements of planning, preparedness, mitigation, response, and recovery. Travel and per diem costs are reimbursed for state and local participants. (Program initially listed as a FEMA program, and transferred to DHS in CFDA 2003.)

Eligible applicants/beneficiaries: state, local, and tribal emergency management personnel.

Average: FY 03, $380 stipend. (Students pay for their own meals.)

Activity: FY 03, 8,947 participants; 3,625 stipends paid (latest available data).

HQ: Preparedness Directorate, FEMA-DHS, 245 Murray Lane - Bldg. 410, Washington, DC 20523 Phone: (301) 447-1000.

Internet: http://training.fema.gov/EMIWeb/contactus.asp; www.dhs.gov.

97.027 EMERGENCY MANAGEMENT INSTITUTE (EMI)—INDEPENDENT STUDY PROGRAM

Assistance: training.

Purposes: pursuant to the Stafford Act, National Security Act of 1947, Defense Production Act of 1950, Earthquake Hazards Reduction Act of 1977, and amendments, to offer home study courses in emergency management practices, of which 32 are available. Examples include: Emergency Program Manager; Radiological Emergency Management; A Citizen's Guide to Disaster Assistance; Building for the Earthquakes of Tomorrow: Engineering Principles and Practices for Retrofitting Flood Prone Residential Buildings; Animals in Disaster; and, refresher and other specialized courses. (Program initially listed as a FEMA program, and transferred to DHS in CFDA 2003.)

Eligible applicants/beneficiaries: general public, emergency management personnel, public officials. Some courses are restricted to certain audiences.

Range/Average: N.A.

Activity: FY 04 estimate, 207,000 enrollments.

HQ: Preparedness Directorate, FEMA-DHS, 245 Murray Lane - Bldg. 410, Washington, DC 20523 Phone: (301) 447-1000.

Internet: http://training.fema.gov/EMIWeb/contactus.asp; www.dhs.gov.

97.028 EMERGENCY MANAGEMENT INSTITUTE (EMI)—RESIDENT EDUCATIONAL PROGRAM

Assistance: training.

Purposes: pursuant to the Stafford Act, National Security Act of 1947, Defense Production Act of 1950, Earthquake Hazards Reduction Act of 1977, and amendments, to provide training of federal, state, local, and tribal emergency management personnel involved in emergency and disaster response. Training emphasizes planning, mitigation, response, and recovery—embodied in the Comprehensive Emergency Management System. (Program initially listed as a FEMA program, and transferred to DHS in CFDA 2003.)

Eligible applicants/beneficiaries: official emergency management personnel.

Range/Average: N.A.

Activity: FY 05 estimate, 8,947 participants.

HQ: Preparedness Directorate, FEMA-DHS, 245 Murray Lane - Bldg. 410, Washington, DC 20523 Phone: (301) 447-1000.

Internet: http://training.fema.gov/EMIWeb/contactus.asp; www.dhs.gov.

97.029 FLOOD MITIGATION ASSISTANCE ("FMA")

Assistance: project grants. (base amount plus 75 percent/2 years).

Purposes: pursuant to the National Flood Insurance Reform Act of 1994, to implement measures that reduce or eliminate long-term risks of flood damage to buildings, manufactured homes, and other insurable structures under the NFIP. Funds may support planning, engineering and planning services, and such implementation activities as elevation or dry flood-proofing of structures, minor structural projects, beach nourishment. (Program initially listed as a FEMA program, and transferred to DHS in CFDA 2003.)

Eligible applicants/beneficiaries: planning and project grants—states and communities participating in the NFIP. Technical assistance grants—state agencies.

Range/Average: N.A.

Activity: not quantified specifically.

HQ: FEMA-DHS, 245 Murray Lane - Bldg. 410, Washington, DC 20523 Phone: (800) 621-FEMA(3363).

Internet: www.dhs.gov.

97.030 COMMUNITY DISASTER LOANS

Assistance: direct loans (generally, 5 years).

Purposes: pursuant to the Stafford Act, for local governments in declared disaster areas, suffering substantial loss of tax and other revenue and demonstrating a need for financial assistance. Funds may be used only to maintain existing municipal operating functions. (Program initially listed as a FEMA program, and transferred to DHS in CFDA 2003.)

Eligible applicants/beneficiaries: local governments in designated disaster areas.

Range: to 25 percent of the applicant's FY operating budget.

Activity: none.

HQ: FEMA-DHS, 245 Murray Lane - Bldg. 410, Washington, DC 20523 Phone: (800) 621-FEMA(3363).

Internet: www.dhs.gov.

97.031 CORA BROWN FUND

Assistance: direct payments/specified use.

Purposes: pursuant to the Stafford Act as amended, to help victims of natural disasters that will not obtain assistance through other government or private programs. The fund was established by the late Cora C. Brown of Kansas City, Missouri, who left a portion of her estate to the U.S. government to help victims of natural disasters not caused by or attributed to war. (Program initially listed as a FEMA program, and transferred to DHS per CFDA 2003.)

Eligible applicants/beneficiaries: individuals, families, and groups in need of disaster-related home repair and rebuilding and other services.

Range/Average: N.A.

Activity: none.

HQ: Emergency Preparedness and Response, FEMA-DHS, 245 Murray Lane - Bldg. 410, Washington, DC 20523 Phone: (202) 646-4528.

Internet: www.dhs.gov.

97.032 CRISIS COUNSELING

Assistance: project grants. (100 percent/60 days).

Purposes: pursuant to the Stafford Act as amended and the Crisis Counseling Assistance and Training Act, to provide immediate crisis counseling services to victims of major natural disasters to relieve mental health problems, at no cost to the victims. Funding may support: such services as screening, diagnostic and counseling techniques, outreach, and public education; training of providers. (Program initially listed as a FEMA program, and transferred to DHS in CFDA 2003.)

Eligible applicants/beneficiaries: states or public or private agencies designated by the governor.

Range/Average: N.A.

Activity: FY 01, responses to 54 major disasters in 31 states or territories (latest available data).

HQ: FEMA-DHS, 245 Murray Lane - Bldg. 410, Washington, DC 20523 Phone: (800) 621-FEMA(3363).

Internet: www.dhs.gov.

97.033 DISASTER LEGAL SERVICES

Assistance: direct payments/specified use.

Purposes: pursuant to the Stafford Act as amended, to provide free legal services to persons affected by natural disasters, including legal advice, counseling, and representation in nonfee- generating cases. (Program initially listed as a FEMA program, and transferred to DHS per CFDA 2003.)

Eligible applicants/beneficiaries: low-income individuals, families, groups.

Range/Average: N.A.

Activity: N.A.

HQ: FEMA-DHS, 245 Murray Lane - Bldg. 410, Washington, DC 20523 Phone: (800) 621-FEMA(3363).

Internet: www.dhs.gov.

97.034 DISASTER UNEMPLOYMENT ASSISTANCE ("DUA")

Assistance: direct payments/specified use; specialized services (to 26 weeks).

Purposes: pursuant to the Stafford Act as amended, to provide weekly unemployment benefits to persons left jobless by natural disasters and ineligible for regular unemployment insurance benefits. (Program initially listed as a FEMA program, and transferred to DHS in CFDA 2003.)

Eligible applicants/beneficiaries: disaster victims.

Range/Average: N.A.

Activity: N.A.

HQ: FEMA-DHS, 245 Murray Lane - Bldg. 410, Washington, DC 20523 Phone: (800) 621-FEMA(3363).

Internet: www.dhs.gov.

97.036 DISASTER GRANTS - PUBLIC ASSISTANCE (PRESIDENTIALLY DECLARED DISASTERS)

Assistance: project grants (75 percent).

Purposes: pursuant to the Stafford Act, to provide supplemental assistance in alleviating suffering and hardship resulting from declared major disasters or emergencies. Eligible program costs include the removal of wreckage and debris on public and private lands, emergency protective measures, emergency transportation or communications, restoration of eligible facilities. (Program initially listed as a FEMA program, and transferred to DHS in CFDA 2003.)

Eligible applicants/beneficiaries: state and local governments, other state political subdivisions, territories and possessions, tribal governments, Alaska native villages or organizations, certain private nonprofit organizations.

Range: small projects, to $57,500.

Activity: FY 01, 47 disasters and 13 emergencies declared (latest available data).

HQ: FEMA-DHS, 245 Murray Lane - Bldg. 410, Washington, DC 20523 Phone: (800) 621-FEMA(3363).

Internet: www.dhs.gov.

97.039 HAZARD MITIGATION GRANT ("HMGP")

Assistance: project grants. (75 percent/2 years).

Purposes: pursuant to the Stafford Act, for measures to permanently reduce or eliminate future damages and losses from natural hazards through safer building practices, improving existing structures, and supporting infrastructure. Funds may be used: to acquire, relocate, modify, or demolish structures; for seismic rehabilitation or retrofitting of structures; for initial implementation of vegetation management programs; to provide pertinent training to architects, engineers, building officials, and others; to bring structures into compliance with floodplain management requirements.

Eligible applicants/beneficiaries: state and local governments, other public entities, authorized tribal organizations, Alaska native villages or organizations, private nonprofit organizations.

Range/Average: N.A.

Activity: not quantified specifically. (Program initially listed as a FEMA program, and transferred to DHS per CFDA 2003.)

HQ: FEMA-DHS, 245 Murray Lane - Bldg. 410, Washington, DC 20523 Phone: (800) 621-FEMA(3363).

Internet: www.dhs.gov.

97.040 CHEMICAL STOCKPILE EMERGENCY PREPAREDNESS PROGRAM ("CSEPP")

Assistance: projects grants.

Purposes: pursuant to the Department of Defense Authorization Act of 1986, to enhance emergency preparedness capabilities at the eight chemical agent stockpile facilities maintained by DOD. Funding has paid for operational siren systems, demographic surveys, dedicated radio and telephone systems, public training courses and exercises. (Program initially listed as a FEMA program, and transferred to DHS in CFDA 2003.)

Eligible applicants/beneficiaries: the states of Alabama, Arkansas, Colorado, Illinois, Indiana, Kentucky, Maryland, Oregon, Utah, and Washington and the Confederated Tribes Umatilla Indian Reservation. Local governments and tribes may receive subgrants.

Range: $60,000 to $13,000,000. **Average:** $8,100,000.

Activity: not quantified specifically.

HQ: FEMA-DHS, 245 Murray Lane - Bldg. 410, Washington, DC 20523 Phone: (202) 282-8000.

Internet: www.dhs.gov.

97.041 NATIONAL DAM SAFETY PROGRAM ("Dam Safety State Assistance Program")

Assistance: project grants (100 percent).

Purposes: pursuant to the Water Resources Development Act of 1996, to establish, improve, and maintain safety programs covering nonfederal dams. States meeting specific criteria may use funds for such activities as permitting and approval of project plans, legislative modifications and regulations development, enforcement activities, emergency response, program staffing, public education, and training. (Program initially listed as a FEMA program, and transferred to DHS in CFDA 2003.)

Eligible applicants/beneficiaries: states, PR.

Range: $26,000 to $281,000.

Activity: N.A.

HQ: FEMA-DHS, 245 Murray Lane - Bldg. 410, Washington, DC 20523 Phone: (800) 621-FEMA(3363).

Internet: www.dhs.gov.

97.042 EMERGENCY MANAGEMENT PERFORMANCE GRANTS ("EMPG")

Assistance: formula grants. (to 50 percent/2 years).

Purposes: pursuant to the Stafford Act as amended, to develop, maintain, and improve comprehensive emergency management capabilities, by combining several funding streams into a consolidated grant. The key functional areas are: Laws and Authorities; Hazard Identification and Risk Assessment; Hazard Management; Resource Management; Planning; Direction, Control, and Coordination; Communications and Warning; Operations and Procedures; Logistics and Facilities; Training; Exercises; Public Education and Information; Finance and Administration. (Program initially listed as a FEMA program, and transferred to DHS in CFDA 2003.)

Eligible applicants/beneficiaries: states, DC, territories, possessions.

Range: $50,000 to $14,300,000.

Activity: FY 02, all states and territories funded (latest available data).

HQ: Preparedness Directorate, FEMA-DHS, 245 Murray Lane - Bldg. 410, Washington, DC 20523 Phone: (800) 368-6498.

Internet: www.ojp.usdoj.gov/odp.

97.043 STATE FIRE TRAINING SYSTEMS GRANTS ("National Fire Academy Training Grants")

Assistance: project grants.

Purposes: for state fire training systems to deliver National Fire Academy courses and programs. (Program initially listed as a FEMA program, and transferred to DHS in CFDA 2003.)

Eligible applicants/beneficiaries: 50 state fire training systems.

Range: $23,000 to $30,000 per state.

Activity: 50 grants annually.

HQ: FEMA-DHS, 245 Murray Lane - Bldg. 410, Washington, DC 20523 Phone: (no phone number).

Internet: www.dhs.gov.

97.044 ASSISTANCE TO FIREFIGHTERS GRANT ("Fire Grants")

Assistance: project grants (70-90 percent).

Purposes: pursuant to the Federal Fire Prevention and Control Act of 1974 as amended by the Defense Authorization Bill of 2001, for direct assistance to fire departments for costs of firefighting operations and firefighter safety. Applicants must compete for grants which may be used for a broad range of eligible expenses including equipment and vehicles, training, public education, personnel, arson prevention, emergency medical services—with funding limits on certain categories. (Program initially listed as a FEMA program, and transferred to DHS in CFDA 2003.)

Eligible applicants/beneficiaries: fire departments in states, territories and possessions, local authorities, tribal nations—including their emergency medical services units.

Range: $900 to $700,000. **Average:** $51,000.

Activity: FY 03 estimate, 8,722 awards.

HQ: Preparedness Directorate, FEMA-DHS, 245 Murray Lane - Bldg. 410, Washington, DC 20523 Phone: (800) 368-6498.

Internet: www.dhs.gov.

97.045 COOPERATING TECHNICAL PARTNERS ("CTP")

Assistance: project grants (100 percent/1-2 years).

Purposes: pursuant to the National Flood Insurance Act of 1968 (Housing and Urban Development Acts of 1968 and 1969), Flood Disaster Protection Act of 1973, amendments, and National Flood Insurance Reform Act of 1994, to increase local involvement in and ownership of the development and maintenance of flood hazard maps produced for the NFIP. Project examples: Refinement of Zone A Boundaries; Digital Flood Insurance Rate Map Preparation. (Program initially listed as a FEMA program, and transferred to DHS in CFDA 2003.)

Eligible applicants/beneficiaries: states, territories, possessions, regional agencies, and communities participating in the NFIP.

Range: $35,000 to $6,000,000.

Activity: 173 agreements as of 13 April 2004.

HQ: FEMA-DHS, 245 Murray Lane - Bldg. 410, Washington, DC 20523 Phone: (800) 621-FEMA(3363).

Internet: www.dhs.gov.

97.046 FIRE MANAGEMENT ASSISTANCE GRANT

Assistance: project grants; specialized services (grants, 75 percent).

Purposes: pursuant to the Stafford Act, for the mitigation, management, and control of any fire on public (nonfederal) or privately owned forest or grassland that threatens to become a major disaster. (Program initially listed as a FEMA program, and transferred to DHS in CFDA 2003.)

Eligible applicants/beneficiaries: state and tribal governments.

Range/Average: N.A.

Activity: FY 01, 15 grants authorized (latest available data).

HQ: FEMA-DHS, 245 Murray Lane - Bldg. 410, Washington, DC 20523 Phone: (800) 621-FEMA(3363).

Internet: www.dhs.gov.

97.047 PRE-DISASTER MITIGATION ("PDM")

Assistance: project grants. (75-90 percent/to 2 years).

Purposes: pursuant to the Stafford Act as amended by the Disaster Mitigation Act of 2000, for cost-affective hazard mitigation activities that are part of a comprehensive mitigation program and reduce injuries, fatalities, and property destruction. (Program initially listed as a FEMA program, and transferred to DHS in CFDA 2003.)

Eligible applicants/beneficiaries: states, territories, possessions, tribal governments. Subgrants may be awarded to local and tribal governments participating in the NFIP.

Range: from $500,000 per state.

Activity: N.A.

HQ: FEMA-DHS, 245 Murray Lane - Bldg. 410, Washington, DC 20523 Phone: (800) 621-FEMA(3363).

Internet: www.dhs.gov.

97.048 DISASTER HOUSING ASSISTANCE TO INDIVIDUALS AND HOUSEHOLDS IN PRESIDENTIAL DECLARED DISASTER AREAS

Assistance: direct payments/specified use. (75 percent/to 18 months).

Purposes: pursuant to the Stafford Act as amended, for individuals and households affected by disasters to enable them to: obtain temporary housing; make repairs to their primary residences; build replacement new permanent housing; meet such other needs as medical, dental, funeral, personal property, transportation costs. (Program initially listed as a FEMA program, and transferred to DHS in CFDA 2003.)

Eligible applicants/beneficiaries: U.S. citizens, noncitizen nationals, or qualified aliens whose primary residences: have been damaged or destroyed by declared major disasters; are not covered by insurance; are located in an insular area outside continental U.S. or in other remote locations where alternative housing resources are unavailable. (Note: states apply for funds under **97.050**.)

Range/Average: N.A.

Activity: N.A.

HQ: Emergency Preparedness and Response, FEMA-DHS, 245 Murray Lane - Bldg. 410, Washington, DC 20523 Phone: (202) 646-3943.

Internet: www.dhs.gov.

97.049 PRESIDENTIAL DECLARED DISASTER ASSISTANCE—DISASTER HOUSING OPERATIONS FOR INDIVIDUALS AND HOUSEHOLDS

Assistance: direct payments/specified use (to 18 months).

Purposes: pursuant to the Stafford Act as amended, for individuals and households affected by disasters, who lack available housing resources and would be unable to rent alternative housing. (Program initially listed as a FEMA program, and transferred to DHS in CFDA 2003.)

Eligible applicants/beneficiaries: U.S. citizens, noncitizen nationals, or qualified aliens whose primary residences have been damaged or destroyed by declared major disasters and are not covered by insurance.

Range/Average: N.A.

Activity: N.A.

HQ: Emergency Preparedness and Response, FEMA-DHS, 245 Murray Lane - Bldg. 410, Washington, DC 20523 Phone: (202) 646-3943.

Internet: www.dhs.gov.

97.050 PRESIDENTIAL DECLARED DISASTER ASSISTANCE TO INDIVIDUALS AND HOUSEHOLDS—OTHER NEEDS ("Individual and Household Other Needs")

Assistance: project grants. (75 percent/to 18 months).

Purposes: pursuant to the Stafford Act as amended, for individuals and households affected by disasters to pay necessary expenses and address serious needs that cannot be met through other forms of assistance or through insurance. Assistance may be used to meet medical, dental, funeral, personal property, transportation needs. (Program initially listed as a FEMA program, and transferred to DHS in CFDA 2003.)

Eligible applicants/beneficiaries: states. (NOTE: if states do not apply, assistance to individuals is provided under **97.048**.)

Range/Average: N.A.

Activity: N.A.

HQ: Emergency Preparedness and Response, FEMA-DHS, 245 Murray Lane - Bldg. 410, Washington, DC 20523 Phone: (202) 646-3943.

Internet: www.dhs.gov.

97.052 EMERGENCY OPERATIONS CENTERS

Assistance: project grants (phase I: 100 percent; phase II: 50 percent).

Purposes: pursuant to the Robert T. Stafford Disaster Relief and Emergency Assistance Act (Stafford Act) and the Departments of Veterans Affairs, Housing and Urban Development, and Independent Agencies Appropriations Act of 2000, to supplement and assist state and local capabilities to respond to emergencies or disasters including terrorist attacks. Grants to states are to encourage the development of Emergency Operations Centers (EOCs) that provide flexibility, sustainability, security, survivability, and interoperability. A Phase I grant of $50,000 will be awarded to each state to complete a vulnerability assessment of its existing state EOC. If a state has already completed a vulnerability assessment, it may apply to use the funds to conduct initial assessments of local EOCs. Phase II grants will be used to address the most immediate EOC deficiencies nationwide.

Eligible applicants/beneficiaries: states (including territories) and local governments.

Range/Average: $50,000 minimum to each state.

Activity: N.A.

HQ: Office of National Preparedness, FEMA-HHS, 500 C Street, SW, Washington, DC 20472. Phone: (202) 646-4090; FAX: (202) 646-4053. Phone (24-hour operator): (202) 566-1600.

Internet: www.fema.gov.

97.053 CITIZEN CORPS

Assistance: project grants. (100 percent/2.5 years).

Purposes: pursuant to the Stafford Act, for Citizen Corps Council organization activities involving volunteer groups that enhance homeland security through outreach to individuals, communities, and families to increase their preparedness and strengthen homeland security. Funds may support: training, equipping, and maintaining Community Emergency Response Teams (CERTs); liability coverage for participants; public outreach and education activities. 75 percent of funds made available to states must be allocated to local governments.

Eligible applicants/beneficiaries: states, territories, possessions, local governments and tribes.

Range: $55,000 to $1,662,000. **Average:** $375,000.

Activity: new program listing in 2003.

HQ: Preparedness Directorate, FEMA-DHS, 245 Murray Lane - Bldg. 410, Washington, DC 20523 Phone: (202) 646-3640 or (800) 368-6498.

Internet: www.citizenscorps.gov.

97.055 INTEROPERABLE COMMUNICATIONS EQUIPMENT

Assistance: project grants (75 percent).

Purposes: pursuant to the Homeland Security Act of 2002, Federal Fire Prevention and Control Act of 1974, and other acts, for demonstration projects on multidisciplinary and/or inter- jurisdictional uses of equipment and technologies to increase communications inter-operability among fire services, law enforcement, and emergency medical services. Funds may support purchases of equipment or services to participate in public safety, commercial, or other shared networks and portable gateway solutions.

Eligible applicants/beneficiaries: local governments nominated by state or territorial governments.

Range: $50,000 to $6,000,000.

Activity: new program in FY 03; 14 grants anticipated.

HQ: Office of National Preparedness, FEMA, 500 C Street, SW, Washington, DC 20472 Phone: (202) 646-3850, FAX (202) 646-3061.

Internet: www.fema.gov.

97.056 PORT SECURITY GRANT PROGRAM

Assistance: project grants (75 percent).

Purposes: for regulated seaports and terminals to enhance port security through: security assessments and mitigation strategies; enhanced facility and operational security—e.g., terminal and commuter or ferry vessels access control, and physical, cargo, and passenger security. Funds may support such costs as for planning, training, exercises, equipment, and administration.

Eligible applicants/beneficiaries: federally regulated public and private ports or terminals designated as "critical"; consortia of local stakeholder groups such as river groups, ports, and terminal associations.

Range/Average: N.A.

Activity: new program listing in 2003. 120 grants awarded for 154 projects.

HQ: Transportation Infrastructure Security Division, Preparedness Directorate, FEMA-DHS, 245 Murray Lane - Bldg. 410, Washington, DC 20523 Phone: (800) 368-6498.

Internet: www.portsecuritygrants.dottsa.net (Note: no field offices for this program.)

97.057 INTERCITY BUS SECURITY GRANTS

Assistance: project grants.

Purposes: to protect inter-city bus systems and the traveling public from terrorism, especially explosives and nonconventional threats. Funds may support such costs as for planning, training, exercises, equipment, and administration.

Eligible applicants/beneficiaries: not provided in CFDA 2005. (Previous edition listed "private or public operators of over-the-road buses including operators of regular route, charter, tour, and other services; bus associations; other associations related to intercity bus industry—i.e., transportation industry organizations involved directly in training and providing technical assistance with an emphasis on security.").

Average: $3,000.

Activity: FY 05, 25 projects funded.

HQ: Transportation Infrastructure Security Division, Preparedness Directorate, FEMA-DHS, 245 Murray Lane - Bldg. 410, Washington, DC 20523 Phone: (800) 368-6498.

Internet: www.ojp.usdoj.gov/odp.htm (Note: no field offices for this program.)

97.058 OPERATION SAFE COMMERCE (OSC) COOPERATIVE AGREEMENT PROGRAM ("OSC")

Assistance: project grants. (100 percent/18 months).

Purposes: to explore commercially viable options to enhance cargo security, including business processes and technology prototypes supporting containerized cargo supply chain security management while facilitating the flow of trade. Funds may support such costs as for personnel, equipment, supplies, services or consultants, facilities, and administration.

Eligible applicants/beneficiaries: load centers (defined as the Ports of Los Angeles/Long Beach, Seattle/Tacoma, and the Port Authority of New York/New Jersey).

Range/Average: no funding available under this program.

Activity: new program listing in 2003. 18 projects approved, during last funding period.

HQ: Transportation Infrastructure Security Division, Preparedness Directorate, FEMA-DHS, 245 Murray Lane - Bldg. 410, Washington, DC 20523 Phone: (800) 368-6498.

Internet: www.tsa.gov/public/index.jsp; www.ojp.usdoj.gov/odp (Note: no field offices for this program.)

97.059 TRUCK SECURITY PROGRAM

Assistance: project grants (100 percent/2.5 years).

Purposes: to promote security awareness among all segments of the commercial motor carriers and transportation community, by training drivers to observe and report any suspicious activities or items that may threaten the critical elements of the nation's highway transportation system. Funds may support such costs as for equipment, supplies, services or consultants, facilities, and administration.

Eligible applicants/beneficiaries: as directed by Congress.

Average: N.A.

Activity: new program in FY 03. One award anticipated.

HQ: Transportation Infrastructure Security Division, Preparedness Directorate, FEMA-DHS, 245 Murray Lane - Bldg. 410, Washington, DC 20523 Phone: (800) 368-6498.

Internet: www.ojp.usdoj.gov/odp (Note: no field offices for this program.)

97.060 PORT SECURITY RESEARCH & DEVELOPMENT GRANT

Assistance: project grants (75 percent/to 18 months).

Purposes: pursuant to the Maritime Transportation Security Act of 2002 and Homeland Security Act of 2002, to identify technology solutions for port security through research and development to provide end products meeting or exceeding specific priorities: Cargo Information Action Center; Passengers and Vehicles Screening on Ferries; Transparency of Vessel Ownership; Operation Restore.

Eligible applicants/beneficiaries: national laboratories, private nonprofit organizations, IHEs, and others.

Range/Average: N.A.

Activity: new program listing in 2004.

HQ: Office of Acquisition (TSA-25), TSA-DHS, 701 S. 12th St., Arlington, VA 22202 Phone: (571) 227-1587.

Internet: http://tsa.gov (Note: no field offices for this program.)

97.061 CENTERS FOR HOMELAND SECURITY ("University- Based HS Centers")

Assistance: project grants. (100 percent/to 3 years).

Purposes: pursuant to the Homeland Security Act of 2002 as amended and Emergency Wartime Supplemental Appropriation Act of 2003, to establish a coordinated, university-based system to enhance homeland security, complementing other DHS and other federal agency activities—to develop and deploy specific homeland security technologies and capabilities. Funds may be used for: targeted research area that leverage the multidisciplinary capabilities of universities; involve U.S. graduate and undergraduate students.

Eligible applicants/beneficiaries: IHEs.

Range: $1,000,000 to $6,000,000.

Activity: new program in FY 04. FY 05 estimate, 6 new awards anticipated.

HQ: University Programs, DHS, 245 Murray Lane - Bldg. 410, Washington, DC 20523 Phone: (no number provided).

Internet: www.dhs.gov; e-mail, universityprograms@dhs.gov (Note: no field offices for this program.)

97.062 SCHOLARS AND FELLOWS, AND EDUCATIONAL PROGRAMS ("DHS Scholars and Fellows")

Assistance: direct payments/specified use.

Purposes: pursuant to the Homeland Security Act of 2002 as amended, to develop and increase the number of undergraduate and graduate students attaining advanced degrees and working in areas of importance to homeland security. Tuition and fee payments are paid to universities; students receive monthly stipends.

Eligible applicants/beneficiaries: U.S. citizens enrolled full- time as juniors, graduate students, or postdoctoral fellows in computer science, engineering, life or physical sciences, math, psychology, social sciences, DVM/PhD, and certain humanities.

Range: school year 2004-05: graduates, $2,300 monthly stipend; undergraduates, $1,000 monthly stipend. **Average:** school year 2004-05: graduates, $44,000 annually; undergraduates, $27,000 annually.

Activity: new program listing in 2004. 105 scholars and fellows.

HQ: University Programs, DHS, 245 Murray Lane - Bldg. 410, Washington, DC 20523 Phone: (no number provided).

Internet: www.dhs.gov; e-mail, universityprograms@dhs.gov (Note: no field offices for this program.)

97.064 DEBRIS REMOVAL INSURANCE

Assistance: project grants (insurance). (100 percent/to 25 years).

Purposes: to incorporate a captive insurance company by the City of New York, N.Y. to insure the city and its contractors for claims arising from debris removal at the World Trade Center following the terrorist attacks of September 11, 2001.

Eligible applicants/beneficiaries: the State of New York to insure the City of New York and its debris removal contractors.

Range/Average: N.A.

Activity: new program in FY 04.

HQ: Recovery Division, Emergency Preparedness and Response, FEMA-DHS, 245 Murray Lane - Bldg. 410, Washington, DC 20523 Phone: (202) 646- 3587.

Internet: www.fema.gov/rrr/pa.

97.065 HOMELAND SECURITY ADVANCED RESEARCH PROJECTS AGENCY ("HSARPA")

Assistance: project grants.

Purposes: pursuant to the Homeland Security Act of 2002 as amended, for basic and applied research and technology development projects in areas of science and technology supporting homeland security, including: development, testing, evaluation, and deployment of critical homeland security technologies; prototyping and deployment technologies addressing security vulnerabilities. SBIR contracts may be awarded.

Eligible applicants/beneficiaries: public, private, nonprofit, profit entities and organizations; federally funded R&D centers; universities, individuals, specialized groups.

Range/Average: N.A.

Activity: new program in FY 04.

HQ: HSARPA, S&T Directorate, DHS, 245 Murray Lane - Bldg. 410, Washington, DC 20528 Phone: (no number provided).

Internet: www.dhs.gov; www.hsarpabaa.com (Note: no field offices for this program.)

97.066 HOMELAND SECURITY INFORMATION TECHNOLOGY AND EVALUATION PROGRAM ("ITEP")

Assistance: project grants (to 100 percent).

Purposes: to foster and identify novel uses of existing "state-of-the-market" information technology that will remove barriers and improve information sharing and integration of state and local public safety interoperability communications.

Eligible applicants/beneficiaries: chief executive officers of states and territories.

Range/Average: N.A.

Activity: new program in FY 04.

HQ: (no address provided). Phone: *ODP help line*, (800) 368- 6498.

Internet: www.dhs.gov (Note: no field offices for this program.)

97.067 HOMELAND SECURITY GRANT PROGRAM ("HSGP")

Assistance: formula grants (2 years).

Purposes: pursuant to the U.S.A. Patriot Act of 2001, to enhance the capacity of state and local emergency responders to prevent, respond to, and recover from a terrorism incident involving chemical, biological, radiological, nuclear, and explosive (CBRNE) devices and cyber attacks. The program encompasses: (1) State Homeland Security Program (SHSP); (2) Urban Areas Security Initiative (UASI); (3) Law Enforcement Terrorism Prevention Program (LETPP); (4) Citizen Corps Program (CCP); (5) Emergency Management Performance Grants; (6) Metropolitan Medical Response System. (See note in program description for **97.004**.)

Eligible applicants/beneficiaries: states, territories, possessions. Local government units may receive subgrants.

Range/Average: N.A.

Activity: new program in FY 04.

HQ: Office of State and Local Government Coordination and Preparedness, Office for Domestic Preparedness-DHS, 810 7th St. NW, Washington, DC 20531 Phone: (800) 368-6498.

Internet: www.dhs.gov; www.ojp.usdoj.gov/odp (Note: no field offices for this program.)

97.068 COMPETITIVE TRAINING GRANTS

Assistance: project grants. (100 percent/3 years).

Purposes: for training initiatives that prepare the nation to prevent, deter, respond to, and recover from terrorism incidents, covering a broad range of issues including: continuity of operations planning; increasing threat awareness among public officials, public health personnel and the medical community, and public safety and public works personnel; technicians and operating personnel training.

Eligible applicants/beneficiaries: state, local, tribal, and territorial governments; national public safety associations, IHEs, private corporations working with the nonprofit sector, nonprofit organizations, including faith-based organizations.

Range/Average: N.A.

Activity: new program in FY 04; to date, 910,000 first responders trained.

HQ: Preparedness Directorate, Office of Grants & Training, FEMA-DHS, 245 Murray Lane - Bldg. 410, Washington, DC 20523 Phone: (800) 368-6498.

Internet: www.dhs.gov (Note: no field offices for this program.)

97.069 AVIATION RESEARCH GRANTS

Assistance: project grants; use of property, facilities, and equipment.

Purposes: pursuant to the Federal Aviation Administration Research, Engineering and Development Authorization Act of 1990, Aviation Security Improvement Act of 1990, and Aviation Security Act of 2001, for innovative, advanced, and applied research and development in areas of potential benefit to the long-term growth of civil aviation security—specifically, in system security technology.

Eligible applicants/beneficiaries: public and private nonprofit organizations; IHEs; profit organizations.

Range: $25,000 to $5,000,000.

Activity: new program listing in 2004.

HQ: Aviation Research Grants Program (ACT-50), Hughes Technical Center, TSA-HHS, Atlantic City International Airport, NJ 08405 Phone: (609) 485-4424, FAX (609) 485-6509.

Internet: www.tsa.gov; www.its.tc.faa.gov/logistics/grants (Note: the field office serves as headquarters for this program.)

97.070 MAP MODERNIZATION MANAGEMENT SUPPORT ("MMMS")

Assistance: project grants (100 percent/1-2 years).

Purposes: pursuant to the Housing and Urban Development Act of 1968 ("National Flood Insurance Act of 1968as amended, Housing and Urban Development Act of 1969, Flood Disaster Protection Act of 1973 as amended, and National Flood Insurance Reform Act of 1994, to increase local involvement in and ownership of management of the development and maintenance of flood hazard maps produced for the National Flood Insurance Program ("NFIP").

Eligible applicants/beneficiaries: states, communities, territories, possessions participating in NFIP.

Range: from $25,000. **Average:** FY 03, $35,000.

Activity: new program listing in 2004.

HQ: FEMA-DHS, 245 Murray Lane - Bldg. 410, Washington, DC 20523 Phone: (800) 621-FEMA(3363).

Internet: www.dhs.gov.

97.071 METROPOLITAN MEDICAL RESPONSE SYSTEM ("MMRS")

Assistance: project grants. (100 percent/2 years).

Purposes: pursuant to the National Defense Authorization Act of 1997 as amended by the Nunn-Lugar-Domenici Amendment, for the 124 highly populated jurisdictions (as of end-FY 03) to develop plans, conduct training and exercises, and acquire pharmaceuticals and personal protective equipment—to achieve the enhanced capability needed to respond to a mass casualty event caused by WMD with their locally controlled and operated resources until significant external resources arrive (e.g., from HRSA, CDC, and OSLGC programs). Key MMRS components require: activation and notification procedures; concept of operations plans; forward movement of patients, coordinated with the National Defense Medical System; hospital and health care system surge capacity management; provision of specially trained responders and equipment through exercises, drills, public information dissemination; coordinated response protocols; a bioterrorism plan including customized pharmaceuticals and plans for the prophylaxis of an affected population for up to 1,000 chemical and 10,000 biological victims.

Eligible applicants/beneficiaries: 124 highly populated jurisdictions.

Range: $250,000 to $700,000.

Activity: new program listing in 2004.

HQ: Preparedness Directorate, Office of Grants & Training, FEMA-DHS, 245 Murray Lane - Bldg. 410, Washington, DC 20523 Phone: (800) 368-6498.

Internet: www.ojp.usdoj.gov/odp (Note: no field offices for this program.)

97.072 NATIONAL EXPLOSIVES DETECTION CANINE TEAM PROGRAM

Assistance: project grants (100 percent/5 years).

Purposes: pursuant to the Federal Aviation Reauthorization Act of 1996, Homeland Security Act of 2002, and Aviation and Transportation Security Act, for cooperative agreements to employ canine teams to deter and detect the introduction of explosives devices into the transportation system, including rail stations, airports, passenger terminals, seaports, surface carriers, and support facilities. The canine teams consist of a highly trained dog and trainer, with a three-team minimum.

Eligible applicants/beneficiaries: designated state and local law enforcement agencies.

Range: $150,500 to $1,000,000.

Activity: new program listing in 2004. Currently, 79 award recipients.

HQ: Director, National Explosives Detection Canine Team Program, TSA-DHS, 601 South 12th St. - Rm.8E18S, Arlington, VA 22202 Phone: (no number provided).

Internet: www.tsa.gov (links: Security and Law Enforcement, Canine and Explosives Program); (Note: no field offices for this program.)

97.073 STATE HOMELAND SECURITY PROGRAM ("SHSP")

Assistance: formula grants (24 months).

Purposes: pursuant to the U.S.A. Patriot Act, to enhance the capacity of state and local governments to prevent, respond to, and recover from a terrorism incident involving chemical, biological, radiological, nuclear, and explosive (CBRNE) devices and cyber attacks. The program supports costs of homeland security and emergency operations: planning; equipment purchases; CBRNE-related and cyber security training and exercises, and attendance at ODP-approved courses; management and administration; evaluations. (See note in program description for **97.004**.)

Eligible applicants/beneficiaries: state administrative agencies (SAAs), territories, and possessions. SAAs are obligated to allocated funds to local government units including authorities, commissions, tribes, special districts, and similar entities.

Range/Average: N.A.

Activity: new program listing in 2004 (CFDA on-line).

HQ: Preparedness Directorate, Office of Grants & Training, FEMA-DHS, 245 Murray Lane - Bldg. 410, Washington, DC 20523 Phone: (800) 368-6498.

Internet: www.ojp.usdoj.gov/odp (Note: no field offices for this program.)

97.074 LAW ENFORCEMENT TERRORISM PREVENTION PROGRAM ("LETPP")

Assistance: formula grants. (100 percent/30 months).

Purposes: pursuant to the U.S.A. Patriot Act, for prevention activities by state and local law enforcement communities, including: information sharing to preempt terrorist attacks; target hardening to reduce vulnerability of selected high-value targets; recognition and mapping of potential or developing threats; interoperable communications; interdiction of terrorists or terrorist intervention activities. Grant funds may be used for planning, organization, training, exercises, and equipment.

Eligible applicants/beneficiaries: state administrative agencies (SAAs), territories, and possessions. SAAs are obligated to allocated funds to local government units including authorities, commissions, tribes, special districts, and similar entities.

Range/Average: N.A.

Activity: new program in FY 04 (CFDA on-line).

HQ: Preparedness Directorate, Office of Grants & Training, FEMA-DHS, 245 Murray Lane - Bldg. 410, Washington, DC 20523 Phone: (800) 368-6498.

Internet: www.ojp.usdoj.gov/odp (Note: no field offices for this program.)

97.075 RAIL AND TRANSIT SECURITY GRANT PROGRAM

Assistance: project grants. (100 percent/30 months).

Purposes: pursuant to the U.S.A. Patriot Act, for rail and transit systems to develop a sustainable program to enhance their security and overall preparedness to prevent, respond to, and recover from acts of terrorism. Eligible uses of project funds include planning, organization, training, exercises, equipment, and limited management expenses.

Eligible applicants: state administrative agencies.

Eligible beneficiaries: rail and transit operators and industry associations.

Average: N.A.

Activity: new program in FY 05 (CFDA on-line).

HQ: Transportation Infrastructure Security Division, Office of Grants and Training, Preparedness Directorate, FEMA-DHS, 245 Murray Lane - Bldg. 410, Washington, DC 20523 Phone: (800) 368-6498.

Internet: www.ojp.usdoj.gov/odp (Note: no field offices for this program.)

97.076 NATIONAL CENTER FOR MISSING AND EXPLOITED CHILDREN ("NCMEC")

Assistance: project grants.

Purposes: to prevent the abduction, abuse, and sexual exploitation of children through activities supporting investigative and forensics; to promote awareness of the child pornography tip line and Project Alert; to operate a national resource center and clearinghouse.

Eligible applicants/beneficiaries: a designated nonprofit organization.

Range/Average: N.A.

Activity: new program listing in 2005; over 150,000 calls on toll-free hotline; cyber tip hotline, over 165,000 reports.

HQ: NCMEC, U.S. Secret Service-DHS, 245 Murray Lane - Bldg.410, Washington, DC 20523 Phone: Secret Service, (202) 406-9277; Project Alert, ICE, (703) 293-8006.

Internet: www.dhs.gov (Note: no field offices for this program.)

97.077 HOMELAND SECURITY RESEARCH TESTING, EVALUATION, AND DEMONSTRATION OF TECHNOLOGIES RELATED TO NUCLEAR DETECTION

Assistance: project grants; use of property, facilities, and equipment; sale, exchange, donation of property and goods; technical information.

Purposes: pursuant to the Homeland Security Act of 2002, to provide funding and/or property to conduct testing, evaluation, and demonstration of homeland security technologies intended to identify, counter, or respond to terrorist threats.

Eligible applicants/beneficiaries: state, local, and tribal governments; private, public profit or nonprofit organizations; individuals.

Range/Average: N.A.

Activity: new program in FY 05.

HQ: Logistics and Property Manager, Science and Technology Directorate (no additional address provided in CFDA) Phone: (202) 254-5667.

Internet: www.dhs.gov (Note: no field offices for this program.)

97.078 BUFFER ZONE PROTECTION PROGRAM (BZPP) ("BZPP")

Assistance: project grants.

Purposes: to plan, equip, and manage protective actions toward the protection, securing, and reducing of vulnerabilities of identified critical infrastructure and key resource sites. State Administrative Agencies allocate funds to jurisdictions in which sites are located.

Eligible applicants: State Administrative Agencies, including in territories and possessions.

Eligible beneficiaries: responsible state and local governmental jurisdictions.

Range/Average: N.A.

Activity: new program in FY 05.

HQ: Preparedness Directorate, Office of Grants & Training, FEMA-DHS, 245 Murray Lane - Bldg. 410, Washington, DC 20523 Phone: (800) 368-6498.

Internet: www.ojp.usdoj.gov/odp; www.dhs.gov; e-mail, askcsid@dhs.gov (Note: no field offices for this program.)

97.079 PUBLIC ALERT RADIOS FOR SCHOOLS

Assistance: project grants.

Purposes: to disseminate public alerts and warnings by providing Public Alert Radios to K-12 schools designated by DHS.

Eligible applicants/beneficiaries: K-12 schools in locations identified by DHS.

Range/Average: N.A.

Activity: new program in FY 05.

HQ: Information Analysis and Infrastructure Protection Directorate-DHS, 245 Murray Lane - Bldg.410, Washington, DC 20528 Phone: (202) 282-8396; alternate/NOAA, (301) 713-1824.

Internet: www.dhs.gov/dhspublic/display?theme=52 (Note: no field offices for this program.)

97.080 INFORMATION ANALYSIS INFRASTRUCTURE PROTECTION (IAIP) PILOT PROJECTS ("IAIP")

Assistance: project grants.

Purposes: pursuant to the Department of Homeland Security Act, for pilot or demonstration projects to explore the feasibility and viability of commercially available protective measure technology to nonfederal entities.

Eligible applicants/beneficiaries: state, local, and tribal governments; private, public profit or nonprofit organizations; individuals.

Range/Average: N.A.

Activity: new program in FY 05.

HQ: Information Analysis and Infrastructure Protection Directorate-DHS, 245 Murray Lane - Bldg.410, Washington, DC 20528 Phone: (202) 282-8753.

Internet: www.dhs.gov (Note: no field offices for this program.)

97.081 LAW ENFORCEMENT TRAINING AND TECHNICAL ASSISTANCE

Assistance: specialized services; training.

Purposes: pursuant to OCCSSA as amended, to provide advanced and specialized training to state, local, tribal, and campus law enforcement agency personnel, either at the Federal Law Enforcement Training Center or at selected sites; to provide technical assistance to agencies on request. Participant expenses may be partially or wholly subsidized.

Eligible applicants/beneficiaries: state, local, tribal, and campus law enforcement, fire, and emergency management specialists; prosecutors and city attorneys; domestic violence advocates; certain applicants from private organizations sponsored by law enforcement or public safety agencies.

Range: 50 to 100 percent of tuition costs (FY 05).

Activity: new program listing in 2005; 3,000 state, local, tribal, and campus law enforcement officers trained annually.

HQ: Federal Law Enforcement Training Center, National Center for State and Local Law Enforcement Training, 1131 Chapel Crossing Rd. - Townhouse 393, Glynco, GA 31524 Phone: (800) 74FLETC, FAX (912) 267-2894.

Internet: www.fletc.gov.osl; e-mail, stateandlocaltraining@dhs.gov (Note: no field offices for this program.)

97.082 EARTHQUAKE CONSORTIUM

Assistance: project grants (100 percent).

Purposes: pursuant to the Earthquake Hazards Reduction Act of 1977 as amended, to develop earthquake preparedness and response plans, prepare inventories, and conduct seismic safety inspection of critical structures and lifelines—including the development of multistate groups for such purposes. Project examples include education and training for community and state officials.

Eligible applicants/beneficiaries: restricted to Central U.S. Earthquake Consortium, Western States Seismic Policy Council, Northeast States Emergency Consortium, and Cascadia Region Earthquake Workgroup.

Range: $75,000 to $450,000.

Activity: new program listing in 2005.

HQ: Mitigation Division, FEMA-DHS, 500 C Street, SW, Washington, DC 20472 Phone: (202) 646- 2727.

Internet: www.fema.gov (Note: no field offices for this program.)

97.083 STAFFING FOR ADEQUATE FIRE AND EMERGENCY RESPONSE ("SAFER")

Assistance: project grants. (to 90 percent/5 years).

Purposes: to recruit, hire, and retain firefighters in local communities, and help the communities meet industry minimum standards. Grant recipients may not use funds to supplant pre-existing local funding, and they must retain personnel under the program for at least one year beyond the grant period. Matching requirements increase from year to year.

Eligible applicants/beneficiaries: specific jurisdictions in states, possessions, and territories.

Range: $10,000 to $2,000,000 ($100,000 maximum per position). **Average:** $500,000.

Activity: new program in FY 05.

HQ: Fire Grants Program Office, Office for State and Local Government Coordination and Preparedness-DHS, 245 Murray Lane - Bldg. 410. Washington, DC 20523 Phone: (866) 274-0960.

Internet: www.firegrantsupport.com/safer/sguidance.aspx; e-mail, fire-grants@dhs.gov (Note: no field offices for this program.)

97.084 HURRICANE KATRINA CASE MANAGEMENT INITIATIVE PROGRAM

Assistance: project grants. (100 percent/2 years).

Purposes: pursuant to Homeland Security Act of 2002 and Stafford Act, to provide case management services for displaced persons from areas affected by Hurricane Katrina.

Eligible applicants/beneficiaries: National Case Management Consortium, consisting of 6-12 FEMA-designated private nonprofit organizations.

Average: $66,000,000.

Activity: new program in FY 06 (CFDA on-line).

HQ: Federal Coordinating Officer, FEMA-DHS, 245 Murray Lane - Bldg. 410. Washington, DC 20523 Phone: (202) 646-4395, FAX (202) 646-2730.

Internet: www.fema.gov (Note: no field offices for this program.)

97.085 9/11 HEROES STAMP PROGRAM

Assistance: direct payments/unrestricted use.

Purposes: pursuant to the 9/11 Heroes Stamp Act of 2001, to use the proceeds of the Hero postal stamp sales to provide assistance to personal representatives of emergency relief personnel killed or permanently physically disabled while serving in the line of duty in connection with the September 11, 2001 terrorist attacks. FEMA will distribute funds equally among eligible claimants until program funds have been liquidated.

Eligible applicants/beneficiaries: personal representatives of emergency relief personnel killed or permanently physically disabled while serving in the line of duty in connection with the September 11, 2001 terrorist attacks, at the World Trade Center, Pentagon, or Shanksville, Pennsylvania site.

Average: approximately $10,000 per claimant.

Activity: new program in FY 06 (CFDA on-line).

HQ: Hero Stamp Program, U.S. Fire Administration, National Emergency Training Center, FEMA-DHS, 16825 S. Seton Ave., Emmitsburg, MD 21727 Phone: (866) 887-9107.

Internet: www.usfa.fema.gov; e-mail, FEMA- HeroesStamp@dhs.gov (Note: no field offices for this program.)

97.086 HOMELAND SECURITY OUTREACH, EDUCATION, AND TECHNICAL ASSISTANCE

Assistance: project grants; technical information.

Purposes: pursuant to the Homeland Security Act of 2002, for outreach, education, and technical assistance projects to increase public awareness of homeland security issues; to help communities forge partnerships across agencies and disciplines to address preparedness and response.

Eligible applicants/beneficiaries: state, local, tribal governments; private, public, profit, and nonprofit organizations; individuals.

Range/Average: N.A.

Activity: new program in FY 06 (CFDA on-line).

HQ: Director, Grants and Financial Assistance Division, Office of Procurement Operations, DHS, Washington, DC Phone: (202) 772- 9826.

Internet: www.dhs.gov (Note: no field offices for this program.)

97.087 ALTERNATIVE HOUSING PILOT PROGRAM

Assistance: project grants (100 percent).

Purposes: pursuant to Emergency Supplemental Appropriations Act for Defense, the Global War on Terror, and Hurricane Recovery of 2006, to fund pilot housing projects in the Gulf Coast Region which will be alternatives to FEMA Disaster Housing and evaluate the efficacy of non-traditional short and intermediate-term housing for potential future use in a catastrophic disaster environment.

Eligible applicants: eligible Gulf Coast states affected by Hurricane Katrina (Alabama, Florida, Louisiana, Mississippi, and Texas). State governors will designate appropriate state agencies to apply and administer funds.

Eligible beneficiaries: individuals/families.

Range/Average: N.A.

Activity: new program listing in 2006.

HQ: FEMA-DHS, 245 Murray Dr, SW, Washington, DC 20528 Phone: (800) 336-0327.

Internet: www.fema.gov.

97.088 DISASTER ASSISTANCE PROJECTS

Assistance: project grants.

Purposes: pursuant to the Homeland Security Act, Stafford Act, and Public Health Bioterrorism and Public Health Emergencies Act of 2002, for specified projects identified by Congress or a DHS program office.

Eligible applicants/beneficiaries: nonfederal entities invited to apply by DHS or specified in appropriation statute.

Range/Average: N.A.

Activity: new program listing in 2006 (CFDA on-line).

HQ: FEMA-DHS, 245 Murray Lane - Bldg. 410, Washington, DC 20523 Phone: (202) 646-4397.

Internet: www.fema.gov (Note: no field offices for this program.)

97.089 REAL ID PROGRAM

Assistance: project grants.

Purposes: pursuant to the Homeland Security Act and Real ID Act, for projects integrating hardware, software, and information management systems to implement the Real ID Act, establishing national standards for issuing drivers licenses.

Eligible applicants/beneficiaries: state, territorial agencies responsible for issuing drivers licenses.

Range/Average: N.A.

Activity: new program listing in 2006 (CFDA on-line).

HQ: Office of Grants and Training, Preparedness Directorate, DHS, 245 Murray Lane - Bldg. 410, Washington, DC 20523 Phone: (800) 368-6498.

Internet: www.ojp.usdoj.gov/odp (Note: no field offices for this program.)

97.090 LAW ENFORCEMENT OFFICER REIMBURSEMENT AGREEMENT PROGRAM

Assistance: direct payments/specified use (100 percent).

Purposes: to support deployment of local law enforcement officers at airport screening checkpoints.

Eligible applicants/beneficiaries: state, local, or other public institutions/organizations responsible for commercial airport operations within their jurisdiction, as specified in U.S. statute or TSA program guidance document and regulations.

Range/Average: N.A.

Activity: new program listing in 2006.

HQ: Program Manager, TSA-DHS, TSA-18 E-8 205S, 601 South 12th St, Arlington, VA 22203 Phone: (571) 227-1528.

Internet: www.tsa.gov (Note: no field offices for this program.)

97.091 HOMELAND SECURITY BIOWATCH PROGRAM

Assistance: project grants; use of property, facilities, equipment; sale, exchange, or donation of property and goods; technical information.

Purposes: pursuant to the Homeland Security Act of 2002, to provide funding for testing, evaluation, and demonstration of homeland security technologies intended to identify, counter, or respond to terrorist threats. Financial and non-financial assistance may be used for: salaries, materials and supplies, equipment, travel, publication costs, subcontractor and supporting costs required for technical and other activities.

Eligible applicants/beneficiaries: state and local governments or as specified by U.S. Appropriation Statute.

Range/Average: N.A.

Activity: new program listing in 2006.

HQ: Director, Grants and Financial Assistance Division, Office of Procurement Operations, DHS, 245 Murray Lane - Bldg. 410, Washington, DC 20523 Phone: (202) 772-9826.

Internet: www.dhs.gov (Note: no field offices for this program.)

97.092 REPETITIVE FLOOD CLAIMS ("RFC")

Assistance: project grants (1-2 years).

Purposes: pursuant to National Flood Insurance of 1968 and Bunning-Bereuter-Blumenauer Flood Insurance Reform Act of 2004, as amended, to assist states, tribal governments, and communities with the reduction or elimination of long-term risk of flood damage to structures insured under the NFIP that have had one or more claims for flood damages through mitigation activities that are in the best interest of the National Flood Insurance Fund (NFIF).

Eligible applicants/beneficiaries: state emergency management agencies of states, DC, and federally-recognized tribal governments.

Range/Average: N.A.

Activity: new program listing in 2006; 28 awards estimated.

HQ: FEMA-DHS, 245 Murray Lane - Bldg. 410, Washington, DC 20523 Phone: (202) 646-3321.

Internet: www.dhs.gov.

97.093 FIRE SERVICE HAZARDOUS MATERIALS PREPAREDNESS AND RESPONSE

Assistance: direct payments/specified use.

Purposes: provide information to the fire and emergency services community, emergency managers, and other local government officials concerning issues related to the planning, mitigation, prevention, and response to hazardous materials incidents, which include acts of terrorism.

Eligible applicants/beneficiaries: one private nonprofit institution/organization designated by Congressional Statute or DHS. Unsolicited applications are not accepted.

Range: one award of $50,000 per year.

Activity: new program listing in 2006.

HQ: U.S. Fire Administration, DHS, 245 Murray Lane - Bldg. 410, Washington, DC 20523 Phone: (800) 238-3358.

Internet: www.dhs.gov (Note: no field offices for this program.)

97.094 PREVENTION ADVOCACY RESOURCES AND DATA EXCHANGE PROGRAM ("PARADE")

Assistance: project grants.

Purposes: pursuant to Homeland Security Act of 2002, U.S.A. Patriot Act of 2001, Federal Fire Prevention and Control Act of 1974 and others, as amended, to assist state and local fire marshals with implementation of programs and to conduct networking activities with their counterparts, including exchange of fire prevention/protection related materials, risk analysis, hazard reduction, best practices, and trend analysis.

Eligible applicants/beneficiaries: state or metropolitan fire department marshal or appointed International Fire Marshal's Association (IFMA) representative in each of the ten regions served by the program.

Range: $3,000 per region.

Activity: new program listing in 2006; 10 awards anticipated.

HQ: U.S. Fire Administration, DHS, 245 Murray Lane - Bldg. 410, Washington, DC 20523 Phone: (800) 238-3358.

Internet: www.dhs.gov (Note: no field offices for this program.)

97.095 SAFE KIDS WORLDWIDE

Assistance: project grants.

Purposes: to reduce fire deaths and injuries among children under the age of 14, by providing support to local coalitions and their high-risk communities. Funds may be used to develop fire and burn education, for prevention materials, to teach fire safety awareness and techniques, and provide fire safety equipment.

Eligible applicants/beneficiaries: qualified nonprofit organization designated by DHS, statutes, and regulations. Unsolicited applications are not accepted.

Range: one grant of $200,000.

Activity: new program listing in 2006; one grant.

HQ: U.S. Fire Administration, DHS, 245 Murray Lane - Bldg. 410, Washington, DC 20523 Phone: (800) 238-3358.

Internet: www.dhs.gov (Note: no field offices for this program.)

97.096 COMMERCIAL EQUIPMENT DIRECT ASSISTANCE PROGRAM (CEDAP) ("CEDAP")

Assistance: sale, exchange, or donation of property and goods.

Purposes: pursuant to DHS Appropriations Act of 2006, to develop technology transfer programs to assist smaller communities in acquiring and using commercially available technologies to prevent, deter, and respond to terrorist attacks as identified in State homeland security strategies.

Eligible applicants/beneficiaries: first responders in state, local, tribal and U.S. territories and possessions in rural communities and jurisdictions smaller than 50,000 population.

Range: equipment value: $3,000 to $75,000.

Activity: new program listing in 2006.

HQ: Preparedness Directorate, Office of Grants & Training, DHS, 810 Seventh St, NW, Washington, DC 20531 Phone: (800) 368-6498.

Internet: www.rkb.mipt.org (Note: no field offices for this program.)

97.097 TRAINING RESOURCE AND DATA EXCHANGE (TRADE)

Assistance: project grants.

Purposes: to support the national exchange of fire/emergency service training related materials and information.

Eligible applicants/beneficiaries: specialized group: TRADE network participants are directors of fire service training systems from 50 states and senior executive training officers from the nation's largest fire departments.

Range: $5,340 to $17,255 per region.

Activity: new program listing in 2006; one grant per each TRADE region.

HQ: U.S. Fire Administration, DHS, 245 Murray Dr, SW - Bldg. 410, Washington, DC 20523 Phone: (301) 447-1483.

Internet: www.usfa.fema.gov/training/nfa/trade (Note: no field offices for this program.)

97.098 DISASTER DONATIONS MANAGEMENT PROGRAM

Assistance: project grants (100 percent).

Purposes: pursuant to Homeland Security Act of 2002, Federal Grant and Cooperative Act and others, as amended, to distribute technology solutions to U.S. state and local government and voluntary agencies via the Aidmatrix Foundation/FEMA partnership, increasing their capacity to respond quickly and effectively to a disaster.

Eligible applicants/beneficiaries: restricted to named government, voluntary/non-profit agencies.

Range/Average: N.A.

Activity: new program listing in 2006.

HQ: FEMA-DHS, 245 Murray Dr. SW, Washington, DC 20528 Phone: (312) 408-5337.

Internet: www.fema.gov (Note: no field offices for this program.)

97.099 RESIDENTIAL FIRE SAFETY & FIRE SPRINKLER INITIATIVES

Assistance: project grants.

Purposes: pursuant to Homeland Security Act of 2002, Patriot Act of 2001, Federal Fire Prevention and Control Act or 1974, as amended, to support residential fire safety initiatives, including: promoting public awareness of fire protection systems (e.g. smoke alarms and automatic sprinkler systems) through provision of educational materials, public service announcement kits, and newsletter/media releases.

Eligible applicants/beneficiaries: nonfederal entities invited to apply by DHS. Unsolicited applications will not be accepted.

Range/Average: N.A.

Activity: new program listing for 2007 (CFDA on-line).

HQ: U.S. Fire Administration, DHS, 245 Murray Dr, SW-Bldg. 410, Washington, DC 20523 Phone: (800) 238-3358.

Internet: www.dhs.gov (Note: no field offices for this program.)

97.100 AIRPORT CHECKED BAGGAGE SCREENING PROGRAM

Assistance: direct payments/specified use.

Purposes: to support U.S. commercial airports in implementing and maintaining security compliance requirements of baggage handling systems. Funds may be used for improvements involving replacement or reconfiguration of baggage conveyor systems or terminal areas, installation of explosive detection systems in order to screen passengers/luggage. This program requires an airline passenger boarding-based cost sharing or match agreement.

Eligible applicants/beneficiaries: state, local, or other public entities/agencies responsible for commercial airport operations within their jurisdiction.

Range/Average: N.A.

Activity: new program listing for 2007 (CFDA on-line).

HQ: Transportation Security Administration, Security Technology Division, DHS, 245 Murray Dr, SW-Bldg. 410, Washington, DC 20523 Phone: (571) 227-1035.

Internet: (no web site address provided) (Note: no field offices for this program.)

97.103 DEGREES AT A DISTANCE PROGRAM

Assistance: project grants.

Purposes: pursuant to Homeland Security Act of 2002, U.S.A. Patriot Act of 2001, Federal Fire Prevention and Control Act of 1974, and others, to support curriculum development, regional meeting support, program marketing, course material printing, publications and initiation of institutional agreements with local two-year college degree programs and colleges/universities designated by the National Fire Academy, to participate in the Degrees at a Distance Program (DDP).

Eligible applicants: only colleges/universities designated by U.S. Fire Administration are eligible. Unsolicited applications will not be accepted.

Eligible beneficiaries: general public.

Range/Average: N.A.

Activity: new program, June 2007 (online).

HQ: U. S. Fire Administration, DHS, 16825 South Seton Avenue, Emmitsburg, Maryland 21727. Phone: (800) 238-3358.

Internet: www.usfa.dhs.gov (Note: no field offices for this program.)

97.104 HOMELAND SECURITY-RELATED SCIENCE, TECHNOLOGY, ENGINEERING AND MATHEMATICS (HS STEM) CAREER DEVELOPMENT PROGRAM ("HS-STEM Career Development Program")

Assistance: project grants (100 percent).

Purposes: to provide funding for the establishment of a scientific career development program at colleges and universities, who, in turn, provide scholarships and fellowships to students.

Eligible applicants: specific information on applicant eligibility is identified in funding opportunity announcement and program guidance.

Eligible beneficiaries: public and private institutions/organizations (colleges and universities).

Range/Average: N.A.

Activity: new program, June 2007 (online).

HQ: Chief Procurement Officer, Grants and Financial Assistance Division, Office of Procurement Operations, DHS, 245 Murray Lane, S.W., Building 410, Washington, DC 20523. Phone: (202) 447-5608.

Internet: www.dhs.gov (Note: no field offices for this program.)

97.105 FIREFIGHTER/EMERGENCY MEDICAL SERVICES (EMS) OUTREACH, TECHNOLOGY TRANSFER, INFORMATION DISSEMINATION, AND TECHNICAL ASSISTANCE

Assistance: project grants (100 percent).

Purposes: pursuant to Homeland Security Act of 2002, U.S.A. Patriot Act of 2001, Federal Fire Prevention and Control Act of 1974, as amended to support firefighter/emergency medical service (EMS) health and safety issues, technology transfer, technical assistance, and information dissemination/outreach efforts concerning emergency/first responder issues including communications operability and interoperability, and to enhance operational safety.

Eligible applicants: specialized group; applicant eligibility identified in the funding opportunity announcement and application/program guidance. No unsolicited applications will be accepted.

Eligible beneficiaries: specialized group, general public.

Range/Average: N.A.

Activity: N.A.

HQ: Department of Homeland Security, 245 Murray Drive SW, Building 410, Washington, DC 20528. Phone: (800) 621-FEMA.

Internet: www.fema.gov. (Note: no field offices for this program.)

97.106 SECURING THE CITIES

Assistance: project grants; use of property, facilities, and equipment; sale, exchange, or donation of property and goods; dissemination of technical information.

Purposes: pursuant to the Homeland Security Act of 2002, as amended to prevent a Radiological/Nuclear (RN) attack on high risk urban areas by enhancing regional capabilities to detect, identify, and interdict illicit radioactive materials in and around urban areas. Financial and non-financial assistance may be provided for the following: salaries, materials and supplies, equipment, travel, publication costs, subcontractor and supporting costs required for technical and other activities necessary to achieve the objective.

Eligible applicants: specific applicant eligibility identified in the funding opportunity announcement and application/program guidance, or as specified by U.S. Appropriation Statute.

Eligible beneficiaries: federal, state, local and Indian tribal governments, interstate or intrastate governmental organizations, private, public or non-profit organizations.

Range/Average: N.A.

Activity: FY 07, one award for a pilot implementation of a regional preventive radiological and nuclear detection architecture in NYC metropolitan area; FY 08, one award anticipated.

HQ: Assessments, Domestic Nuclear Detection Office, DHS, MS 7100, 245 Murray Drive SW, Building 410, Washington, DC 20528. Phone: (202) 254-7412.

Internet: www.dhs.gov. (Note: no field offices for this program.)

97.107 NATIONAL INCIDENT MANAGEMENT SYSTEM ("NIMS")

Assistance: project grants (100 percent).

Purposes: pursuant to the Homeland Security Act of 2002 and the Department of Homeland Security Appropriations Act of 2007, to support the development, integration, and deployment of incident management systems. This includes establishing operational, technical and programmatic standards in support of nationwide implementation of the NIMS model, a unified approach to incident management and standard command and management structures.

Eligible applicants: specific applicant eligibility identified in the funding opportunity announcement and application/program guidance.

Eligible beneficiaries: state, local, and Indian Tribal governments, U.S. territories and possessions, public, private and nonprofit institutions and organizations.

Range/Average: N.A.

Activity: not quantified specifically.

HQ: FEMA-DHS, 245 Murray Drive SW, Building 410, Washington, DC 20528. Phone: (800) -621-FEMA.

Internet: www.fema.gov/emergency/nims/index.shtm. (Note: no field offices for this program.)

97.108 HOMELAND SECURITY, RESEARCH, TESTING, EVALUATION, AND DEMONSTRATION OF TECHNOLOGIES

Assistance: project grants; use of property, facilities, and equipment; sale, exchange, or donation of property and goods; dissemination of technical information.

Purposes: pursuant to the Homeland Security Act of 2002, to provide funding and/or property for the purpose of conducting research, testing, evaluation, and demonstration of homeland security technologies intended to identify, counter, or respond to terrorist threats. Financial and nonfinancial assistance may be provided for the following: salaries, materials and supplies, equipment, travel, publication costs, subcontractor and supporting costs required for technical and other activities necessary to achieve the objective.

Eligible applicants: state, local, and Indian Tribal governments, private, public, profit or nonprofit organizations, or individuals specified by U.S. Appropriation Statute, including U. S. and international institutions of higher education and educational laboratories.

Eligible beneficiaries: federal, state, local, and Indian Tribal governments, private, public, profit or nonprofit organizations, and individuals.

Range/Average: N.A.

Activity: N.A.

HQ: Grants and Financial Assistance Division, Office of Procurement Operations, DHS, 245 Murray Lane, S.W., Building 410, Washington, DC 20523. Phone: (202) 447-5589.

Internet: www.dhs.gov. (Note: no field offices for this program.)

97.109 DISASTER HOUSING ASSISTANCE GRANT

Assistance: project grants (100 percent).

Purposes: pursuant to the Homeland Security Act and the Robert T. Stafford Disaster Relief and Emergency Assistance Act (Stafford Act), to provide temporary housing assistance and case management for families who were displaced by Hurricanes Katrina and Rita. DHAP would be implemented in the form of a rental assistance program that would continue providing housing subsidies for families for the next 18 months after termination of Federal Emergency Management Agency's (FEMA) initial temporary housing program. Public Housing Agencies (PHAs) will administer the DHAP to families that have been determined eligible by FEMA through HUD's web-based Disaster Information System.

Eligible applicants/beneficiaries: individuals and families determined eligible for FEMA housing assistance.

Range/Average: N.A.

Activity: N.A.

HQ: Department of Homeland Security, 245 Murray Drive SW, Building 410, Washington, DC 20528. Phone: (800) 621-FEMA.

Internet: www.fema.gov. (Note: no field offices for this program.)

97.110 SEVERE LOSS REPETITIVE PROGRAM ("SLR")

Assistance: project grants (75-90 percent).

Purposes: pursuant to the National Flood Insurance Act of 1968, as amended by the Bunning-Bereuter-Blumenauer Flood Insurance Reform Act of 2004, to assist states and local governments to reduce or eliminate the long-term risk of flood damage to residential properties insured under the National Flood Insurance Program (NFIP) that meet the definition of severe repetitive loss property, and to reduce losses to the National Flood Insurance Fund (NFIF) by funding projects that result in the greatest savings to the NFIF in the shortest time period. Eligible activities under the SLR program include: acquisition and relocation of at-risk structures and the conversion of property to open space; elevation of existing structures to the Base Flood Elevation (BFE) or an ABFE Advisory Base Flood Elevation (ABFE) or higher (for the SRL program Mitigation Reconstruction is only permitted when traditional elevation cannot be implemented); minor physical localized flood control projects; and dry-flood proofing (historic properties only).

Eligible applicants: state emergency management agencies or a similar state office, DC, U.S. territories, and federally-recognized Indian tribal governments. Specific information on sub-applicant eligibility and application procedures for Indian tribal governments provided in SRL program guidance.

Eligible beneficiaries: states, territories, local, and federally-recognized Indian tribal governments and homeowners.

Range/Average: N.A.

Activity: N.A.

HQ: Chief, Program Implementation Section, Risk Reduction Branch, Mitigation Division, FEMA, 500 C Street SW, Washington, DC 20472. Phone: (202) 646-3428.

Internet: www.fema.gov/government/mitigation.shtm.

97.111 REGIONAL CATASTROPHIC PREPAREDNESS GRANT PROGRAM ("RCPGP")

Assistance: project grants (75 percent).

Purposes: pursuant to the U.S. Troop Readiness, Veterans' Care, Katrina Recovery, and Iraq Accountability Appropriations Act of 2007, and Consolidated Appropriations Act of 2008, to support an integrated planning system that provides for regional all-hazard planning for catastrophic events and the development of necessary plans, protocols, and procedures to manage a catastrophic event. Objectives include: creating regional planning processes and planning communities through the establishment of a Catastrophic Planning Working Group; identifying and assessing priority areas of concern using both capabilities-based and scenario-based planning models; developing enhanced regional plans and addressing shortcomings in jurisdiction plans to support both the management of a catastrophic incident and to enable enduring government; and linking planning efforts to resource allocations.

Eligible applicants: specific applicant eligibility identified in the funding opportunity announcement and application/program guidance.

Eligible beneficiaries: state and local governments.

Range/Average: N.A.

Activity: FY 08 estimated, 9 applications and 9 awards.

HQ: Department of Homeland Security, 245 Murray Lane SW, Bldg. 410, Washington, DC 20528. Grants and Training, Phone: (800) 368-6498.

Internet: www.ojp.usdoj.gov/odp. (Note: no field offices for this program.)

97.112 BORDER INFRASTRUCTURE IMPROVEMENT PROJECTS

Assistance: project grants.

Purposes: pursuant to the Homeland Security Act of 2002, as amended, to provide funding, technical assistance and other resources in order to implement border security infrastructure improvement projects and initiatives.

Eligible applicants: specific applicant eligibility identified in the funding opportunity announcement and application/program guidance.

Eligible beneficiaries: states, local governments, territories, nonprofit and private organizations.

Range/Average: N.A.

Activity: N.A.

HQ: DHS, 245 Murray Drive SW, Building 410, Washington, DC 20528. Phone: (800) -621-FEMA.

Internet: www.dhs.gov. (Note: no field offices for this program.)

UNITED STATES AGENCY FOR INTERNATIONAL DEVELOPMENT

98.001 USAID FOREIGN ASSISTANCE FOR PROGRAMS OVERSEAS

Assistance: project grants (to 5 years).

Purposes: pursuant to the Foreign Assistance Act of 1961 as amended, to advance U.S. foreign policy objectives by supporting economic growth, agriculture and trade, global health, democracy, conflict prevention, and humanitarian assistance projects. Funds usually are awarded competitively to U.S. nongovernmental and educational institutions, for projects conducted in developing countries virtually throughout the world.

Eligible applicants: any type of applicant.

Eligible beneficiaries: foreign governments, public or private institutions or organizations, or individuals.

Range: $4,200,000 to $4,700,000. **Average:** $4,300,000.

Activity: new program listing in 2004. Active projects under way in more than 100 countries.

HQ: USAID, 1300 Pennsylvania Ave. NW, Washington, DC 20523 Phone: (202) 712-4810.

Internet: www.usaid.gov; e-mail, pinquiries@usaid.gov (Note: no field offices for this program.)

98.002 COOPERATIVE DEVELOPMENT PROGRAM ("CDP")

Assistance: project grants (3-5 years).

Purposes: pursuant to the Foreign Assistance Act of 1961 as amended, to support cooperative development organizations in the establishment and management of cooperatives worldwide. Funds may support feasibility studies and technical assistance or advisory services to cooperatives, private voluntary and other nongovernmental organizations, governments, and groups of individuals interested in developing new or existing cooperatives. Program emphasis is on developing, testing, and implementing solutions to major issues facing international cooperative development, including governance, modern management, cooperatives legislation and regulation, and achieving scale and salience.

Eligible applicants/beneficiaries: U.S. cooperatives and recognized cooperative development organizations.

Range: $1,000,000 to $5,000,000 over five years.

Activity: new program listing in 2004. FY 02, 8 continuation grants through FY 04.

HQ: Cooperative Coordinator, Office of Private and Voluntary Cooperation, Bureau for Democracy, Conflict and Humanitarian Assistance, USAID, Washington, DC 20523 Phone: (202) 712-5226.

Internet: www.usaid.gov/hum_response/pvc/coop.html (Note: no field offices for this program.)

98.003 OCEAN FREIGHT REIMBURSEMENT PROGRAM ("OFR")

Assistance: project grants. (100 percent/2 years).

Purposes: pursuant to the Foreign Assistance Act of 1961, to pay transportation charges for overseas shipments of commodities used in privately funded development and humanitarian assistance programs for the relief and rehabilitation of friendly people. Shipments must consist only of approved commodities—e.g., medical and educational supplies, agricultural and building equipment—only to approved countries that receive shipments duty-free.

Eligible applicants/beneficiaries: U.S. private voluntary organizations registered with USAID, receiving at least 20 percent of their funding for international programs from nongovernmental sources.

Range: $2,500 to $150,000 per year.

Activity: new program listing in 2004. FY 04, 59 grants awarded.

HQ: Ocean Freight Program Officer, Cooperative Coordinator, Office of Private and Voluntary Cooperation, Bureau for Democracy, Conflict and Humanitarian Assistance, USAID, Washington, DC 20523 Phone: (202) 712-4795.

Internet: www.usaid.gov; keyword: ofr. (Note: no field offices for this program.)

98.004 NON-GOVERNMENTAL ORGANIZATION STRENGTHENING ("NGO")

Assistance: project grants (70 percent/to 5 years).

Purposes: pursuant to the Foreign Assistance Act of 1961 as amended, to improve the capacities of local indigenous nongovernmental organizations, networks, and intermediate service organizations in developing countries.

Eligible applicants: U.S. private voluntary organizations registered with USAID, receiving at least 20 percent of their funding for international programs from nongovernment sources, and current matching grant recipients.

Eligible beneficiaries: foreign private institutions or organizations.

Range: $1,300,000 to $3,250,000. **Average:** $2,400,000.

Activity: new program listing in 2004. FY 03, 13 cooperative agreements awarded through FY 08.

HQ: (no address/phone provided).

Internet: www.usaid.gov/our_work/crosscutting_programs/private_voluntary_cooperation/ngo.html (Note: no field offices for this program.)

98.005 INSTITUTIONAL CAPACITY BUILDING (ICB) ("ICB")

Assistance: project grants. (75-90 percent/to 5 years).

Purposes: pursuant to the Foreign Assistance Act of 1961 as amended, to strengthen the capacity of new and experienced "Food for Peace Title II Partners" to plan and implement food security programs, including in emergency situations. Funds may support establishing systems, training, food security assessments and aid logistics, and strengthening mechanisms.

Eligible applicants/beneficiaries: U.S. private voluntary organizations or cooperatives registered with USAID.

Range: to $3,500,000 per organization for 5 years.

Activity: new program listing in 2004.

HQ: Grants Manager, Program Operations Division, Office of Food for Peace, USAID, 1300 Pennsylvania Ave. NW, Washington, DC 20523 Phone: (no number provided).

Internet: www.usaid.gov (Note: no field offices for this program.)

98.006 FOREIGN ASSISTANCE TO AMERICAN SCHOOLS AND HOSPITALS ABROAD ("ASHA")

Assistance: project grants. (cost sharing/2-5 years).

Purposes: pursuant to the Foreign Assistance Act of 1961 as amended, to strengthen foreign schools and hospitals best demonstrating American ideas and practices. Project examples: upgrading of a training facility; construction and equipping of private health care ward; construction of telecommunication laboratory.

Eligible applicants/beneficiaries: U.S. nonprofit organizations demonstrating a continuing supportive relationship with overseas institutions.

Range: $15,000,000 to $20,000,000 per year. **Average:** $17,000,000.

Activity: new program listing in 2004.

HQ: Office of American School and Hospitals Abroad, Bureau for Democracy, Conflict and Humanitarian Assistance, USAID, Washington, DC 20523 Phone: (no number provided).

Internet: www.usaid.gov (Note: no field offices for this program.)

98.007 FOOD FOR PEACE DEVELOPMENT ASSISTANCE PROGRAM ("DAP")

Assistance: project grants; sale, exchange, or donation of property and goods. (cost sharing/to 5 years).

Purposes: pursuant to the Agriculture, Trade and Development Assistance Act of 1954 as amended, to improve access, availability, and utilization of food in food-insecure environments abroad. Program focus: improving household nutrition and health status, especially in children and mothers; increasing agricultural productivity including field production, post- harvest handling, transformation, and marketing. Applicants may request commodities and cash for program implementation.

Eligible applicants/beneficiaries: U.S. private voluntary organizations or cooperatives registered with USAID; registration with the Office of Food Peace also is required.

Range: $1,000,000 to $25,000,000 over 5-7 years.

Activity: new program listing in 2004.

HQ: Development Programs Division, Office of Food for Peace, USAID, 1300 Pennsylvania Ave. NW, Washington, DC 20523 Phone: (no number provided).

Internet: www.usaid.gov (Note: no field offices for this program.)

98.008 FOOD FOR PEACE EMERGENCY PROGRAM ("EP")

Assistance: project grants; sale, exchange, or donation of property and goods.

Purposes: pursuant to the Agriculture, Trade and Development Assistance Act of 1954 as amended, to improve access, availability, and utilization of food in food-insecure environments abroad—especially in emergency situations in which hunger and malnutrition need to be prevented. Applicants may request commodities and cash for program implementation.

Eligible applicants/beneficiaries: U.S. private voluntary organizations or cooperatives registered with USAID; registration with the Office of Food Peace also is required.

Range/Average: N.A.

Activity: new program listing in 2004.

HQ: Emergency Programs Division, Office of Food for Peace, USAID, 1300 Pennsylvania Ave. NW, Washington, DC 20523 Phone: (no number provided).

Internet: www.usaid.gov (Note: no field offices for this program.)

98.009 JOHN OGONOWSKI FARMER-TO-FARMER PROGRAM ("Development Assistance Program")

Assistance: project grants (5-10 years).

Purposes: pursuant to the Farm Security and Rural Investment Act of 2002 and Agriculture, Trade and Development Assistance Act of 1954, to improve global food production and marketing by transferring technical skills of the U.S. agricultural community to farmers in developing and middle-income countries, emerging markets, sub-Saharan African countries, and Caribbean Basin countries.

Eligible applicants/beneficiaries: agricultural producers, agriculturalists, IHEs and their foundations, private agribusinesses willing to waive profits and fees, private organizations—which must be registered with USAID.

Range: $1,500,000 to $16,000,000 covering 5-9 years. **Average:** $10,600,000 per year.

Activity: new program listing in 2004. Currently, 8 participating private voluntary organizations.

HQ: Farmer-to-Farmer Program, USAID, Washington, DC 20523 Phone: (202) 712-4086, FAX (202) 216-3579; Technical Advisor, (202) 712-5837, FAX (202) 216-3579; Program Analyst, (202) 219-0476, FAX (202) 219-0508.

Internet: www.usaid.gov/our_work/agriculture/farmer_to_farmer.html (Note: no field offices for this program.)

98.010 DENTON PROGRAM

Assistance: specialized services.

Purposes: to use empty space on U.S. military carriers to transport eligible donated goods for humanitarian relief, at little or no cost to nongovernmental organizations. The program is jointly administered by USAID, Department of State, and DOD.

Eligible applicants/beneficiaries: U.S. private voluntary organizations, nongovernmental organizations, or small organizations.

Average: $50,000 per year for inspections.

Activity: new program listing in 2004. FY 03, 25 shipments serving 13 countries (latest available data).

HQ: Denton Program Officer, Office of Private and Voluntary Cooperation, Bureau for Democracy, Conflict and Humanitarian Assistance, USAID, Washington, DC 20523 Phone: (202) 712-4795.

Internet: www.usaid.gov/hum_response/pvc; www.dentonfunded.ida.org (Note: no field offices for this program.)

98.011 GLOBAL DEVELOPMENT ALLIANCE ("GDA")

Assistance: project grants (50 percent/to 5 years).

Purposes: pursuant to the Foreign Assistance Act of 1961 as amended, for activities by public-private alliances promoting such international objectives as: advancing the growth of democracy and good governance; strengthening world economic growth, development, and stability, while expanding opportunities for U.S. business; improving health, education, environmental conditions for the global population; minimizing the human costs of displacement, conflicts, and natural disasters.

Eligible applicants/beneficiaries: U.S. and non-U.S. nongovernmental organizations, private businesses, foundations, business and trade associations, international organizations, IHEs; U.S. cities and states, other federal agencies, host country parastals, individual and group philanthropies, other similar organizations.

Range: projects, $300,000 to $1,000,000.

Activity: new program listing in 2004. Currently, activities ongoing in more than 100 countries.

HQ: GDA Secretariat, USAID, Washington, DC 20523 Phone: (202) 712-4272.

Internet: www.usaid.gov/our_work/global_partnerships/gda (Note: no field offices for this program.)

98.012 USAID DEVELOPMENT PARTNERSHIPS FOR UNIVERSITY COOPERATION AND DEVELOPMENT

Assistance: project grants.

Purposes: for U.S. IHEs to collaborate with counterpart institutions in developing countries to conduct projects that address critical development needs in those countries.

Eligible applicants/beneficiaries: U.S. IHEs, including community colleges.

Range: $14,300,000 to $31,000,000. **Average:** $22,600,000.

Activity: new program listing in 2005. To date, 226 partnerships financed in 59 countries; 313 IHEs involved overseas.

HQ: Higher Education Community Liaison, USAID, 1300 Pennsylvania Ave. NW, Washington, DC 20523 Phone: (202) 712-1531, FAX (202) 216-3229.

Internet: www.usaid.gov; www.HEDProgram.org (Note: no field offices for this program.)

PART III

Program Funding Levels

Summary Tables

Four tables are presented:

- *Table 1. Estimated Outlays/Credits for Domestic Assistance Programs, by Federal Administrative Entity* (FY 05, 06, 07, 08), beginning on page 843.
- *Table 2. Summary of Estimated Outlays/Credits, by Federal Department or Agency* (FY 05, 06, 07, 08), beginning on page 881.
- *Table 3. The Fifty Largest Domestic Assistance Programs in FY 2007, by Funds Outlayed and/or Credited* (page 885).
- *Table 4. The Fifty Smallest Domestic Assistance Programs in FY 2007, by Funds Outlayed and/or Credited* (page 886).

The tables are based on information in the *Catalog of Federal Domestic Assistance 2007* and prior editions. The tables offer a general perspective of government funding for specific programs and agencies, in relation to one another and to other federal activities. Such a perspective can be useful in several ways to persons or organizations interested in certain programs and in government assistance, including:

- Having identified programs meeting given needs, prospective applicants can use the tables to compare relative funding levels.
- Tables 1 and 2 show funding levels for four federal fiscal years. To our knowledge tables compiled specifically for the domestic assistance programs exist nowhere else—i.e., apart from the costs of other administering agency functions. Perhaps such a compilation adds a new dimension to perspectives of federal domestic assistance.
- Tables 3 and 4 answer some questions frequently posed to the editor.

Important Notes on the Tables, Footnotes

Certain inconsistencies in the source material cannot be corrected. Therefore, the tables should be used only as a general guide to the availability of funding.

In Table 2, the first two digits in the five-digit number preceding the name of the administering agency correspond to the program number series identifying programs in Part II—e.g., 11.000 preceding DEPARTMENT OF COMMERCE encompasses all department programs including administrative sub-units.

The following footnotes are employed:

* amount shown is a "credit" rather than an actual cash outlay. In the tables, amounts loaned or insured by the government are classified as credits.

(a) funding for the program cannot be separately identified from other agency expenses.

e amount was estimated in the source material, the significance of which is discussed on page 19, following the heading **Range**.

\i includes funding for this and for one or more other programs; program descriptions in Part II explain such cases.

(n) program did not exist during the reported fiscal year.

(o) funding is included in an amount reported for another program, as noted in the Part II program descriptions.

\p includes value of property or goods awarded; such amounts are not necessarily appropriated funds.

\r program supports or is supported by a revolving fund.

\t program includes support from or is supported by a federal trust fund.

\u user charges, fees, or other nonfederal funds help support the program, including loan repayments; amounts shown are not necessarily or entirely appropriated funds.

Table 1. Estimated Outlays/Credits for All Domestic Assistance Programs, by Administrative Entity

Program number	ADMINISTRATIVE ENTITY/SUB-UNIT Program Title (abridged)	FY 2005 in $thousands	FY 2006 in $thousands	FY 2007 in $thousands	FY 2008 in $thousands
	DEPARTMENT OF AGRICULTURE				
10.001	Agricultural Research	17,997	16,497	20,295 e	20,295 e
10.025	Plant, Animal Disease, Pest Control \ t	138,229	115,563 e	164,399 e	0 e
10.028	Wildlife Services	363	365	365 e	0 e
10.029	Avian Influenza Indemnity Program	0	0	0 e	0 e
10.051	Commodity Loans, Deficiency Payments \ u	9,691,206*	9,493,384*	9,493,384*e	0*e
10.053	Dairy Indemnity	10,000	0	0 e	0 e
10.054	Emergency Conservation	0	199,800	0 e	0 e
10.055	Direct, Counter-Cyclical Payments \ u	12,455,246	8,123,433	8,123,433	0 e
10.056	Farm Storage Facility Loans \ u	15,289*	1,238*	1,238*e	0*e
10.066	Livestock Assistance Program \ u	475,100	326,775	326,775 e	0 e
10.069	Conservation Reserve Program	1,788,334	1,859,176	1,969,880 e	0 e
10.070	Colorado River Salinity Control	0	394	10 e	0 e
10.072	Wetlands Reserve	250,922	191,049	239,345 e	500,500 e
10.073	Crop Disaster Program	2,395,405	374,233	0 e	0 e
10.077	Livestock Compensation Program	0	0	0 e	0 e
10.078	Bioenergy Program	100,000	100,000	60,000 e	0 e
10.079	Emerson Humanitarian Trust \ t	73,052	0	0 e	0 e
10.080	Milk Income Loss Contract	9,112	415,000	330,000 e	0 e
10.081	Lamb Meat Adjustment Assistance	14,230	0	0 e	0 e
10.082	Tree Assistance Program	2,952	29,015	0 e	0 e
10.084	Dairy Market Loss Assistance \ u	0	10,000	0 e	0 e
10.085	Tobacco Transition Payments \ u	938,844	960,261	952,000 e	0 e
10.153	Market News	30,595	30,759	32,182	32,745 e
10.155	Marketing Agreements and Orders	15,800	15,141	15,493	16,798 e
10.156	Federal-State Marketing Improvement	3,816	3,809	1,334	3,209 e
10.162	Inspection Grading, Standardization \ t	190,082	196,825	192,129	198,132 e
10.163	Market Protection and Promotion	31,651	29,409	28,053	29,456 e
10.164	Wholesale Farmers, Alternative Markets	2,736	3,679	3,721	3,781 e
10.165	Perishable Agricultural Commodities	9,397	9,999	10,557	10,052 e
10.167	Transportation Services	2,716	2,649	2,719	2,783 e
10.168	Farmers' Market Promotion	0	1,000	1,000	1,000 e
10.169	Specialty Crop Block Grant	0	6,930	6,930	8,440
10.200	Agricultural Research, Special	126,457	132,145	13,682	16,955 e
10.202	Cooperative Forestry Research	20,979	20,794	28,356	19,376 e
10.203	Agricultural Experiment Stations	168,462	166,770	304,477	154,804 e
10.205	1890 Land-Grant Colleges	34,622	35,094	38,366	36,252 e
10.206	Agricultural Research—Competitive	165,013	166,789	175,143	240,084 e
10.207	Animal Health and Disease Research	4,702	4,654	4,651	0 e
10.210	Food, Sciences—Fellowships	2,857	3,504	3,507	4,277 e
10.212	Small Business Innovation Research	15,302	15,765	15,599 e	12,814 e
10.215	Sustainable Agriculture Research	11,606	11,490	11,490	8,553 e
10.216	1890 Institution Capacity Building	11,645	11,305	11,616	11,583 e
10.217	Higher Education Challenge Grants	5,238	5,173	5,174	5,227 e
10.219	Biotechnology Risk Assessment	0	2,012	1,685	1,685 e
10.220	Multicultural Scholars Program	952	938	932 e	948 e
10.221	Tribal Colleges Education Equity	2,232	2,228	3,342	2,227 e
10.222	Tribal Colleges Endowment	2,093	2,474	3,120	3,264 e
10.223	Hispanic Serving Institutions	5,376	5,679	5,687	5,364 e
10.224	FRA—Research, Education, Extension	0	0	0 e	0 e
10.225	Community Food Projects	4,800	4,800	4,800	4,800 e
10.226	Secondary Agriculture Education	952	932	931	950 e
10.227	1994 Institutions Research Program	1,009	959	1,445	999 e
10.228	Alaska, Hawaii Native Education	3,333	3,089	3,089	2,848 e
10.250	Agricultural, Rural Research	75,796	76,850	84,222 e	0 e
10.253	Food Assistance, Nutrition Research \ u	0	76,850 e	84,222 e	0 e
10.254	Invasive Species Management \ u	0	76,850 e	84,222 e	0 e
10.255	Economic Development Grants \ u	0	76,850 e	84,222 e	0 e
10.256	Consumer Data Initiative \ u	0	76,850 e	84,222 e	0 e
10.290	Agricultural Market Research	0	2,921	2,874	2,874 e

Please see "Important Notes on the Tables, Footnotes," page 842

Table 1. *(continued)*

Program number	ADMINISTRATIVE ENTITY/SUB-UNIT Program Title (abridged)	FY 2005 in $thousands	FY 2006 in $thousands	FY 2007 in $thousands	FY 2008 in $thousands
10.303	Integrated Programs	41,913	41,363	41,335	1,312 e
10.304	Homeland Security-Agricultural	8,571	9,504	9,504	13,706 e
10.305	International Science, Education	952	918	950	1,910 e
10.306	Biodiesel	960	960	960	960 e
10.307	Organic Agriculture Research	2,880	2,836	2,837	2,880 e
10.308	Instruction/Insular Area Activities	476	471	469	475 e
10.309	Specialty Crop Research	(n)	(n)	(n)	28,440
10.350	Assistance/Cooperatives	(o)	(o)	(o)	(o)
10.352	Value-Added Producer Grants	14,600	21,204	21,638	19,000 e
10.404	Emergency Loans \ u	23,570*	100,000*	69,788*e	0*e
10.405	Farm Labor Housing \ r, u	30,358	13,860	13,860 e	0 e
		41,999*	38,117*	41,580*e	0*e
10.406	Farm Operating Loans \ u	1,440,531*	1,842,364*	1,669,110*e	0*e
10.407	Farm Ownership Loans \ u	1,298,945*	1,615,876*	1,422,750*e	0*e
10.410	Very Low/Moderate Income Housing \ u	1,143,756*	4,091,000*	1,027,374*e	0*e
10.411	Rural Site/Self-Help Loans \ u	2,745*	9,980*	5,000*e	0*e
10.415	Rural Rental Housing Loans \ u	99,200*	34,652*	36,382*e	0*e
10.417	Housing Repair Loans, Grants \ u	31,596	30,120	29,700 e	0 e
		34,720*	34,650*	36,800*e	0*e
10.420	Rural Self-Help Housing	37,214	34,016	37,062 e	0 e
10.421	Tribal Corporation Loans \ u	0*	2,000*	3,960*e	0*e
10.427	Rural Rental Assistance Payments	587,264	646,571	487,000 e	0 e
10.433	Rural Housing Preservation Grants	8,584	10,000	9,900 e	0 e
10.435	State Mediation Grants	3,968	4,208	4,208 e	0 e
10.437	Interest Assistance Program \ u	283,423*	271,886*	272,250*e	0*e
10.438	Section 538 Rural Rental Housing	99,200*	99,000*	197,997*e	0*e
10.441	Technical, Supervisory Assistance	2,038	1,000	1,000 e	0 e
10.442	Housing Application Packaging	27	35	35 e	0 e
10.443	Outreach/Farmers, Ranchers	5,593	5,651	5,667 e	6,653 e
10.444	Housing—Disaster Loans, Grants \ u	5,800	38	0 e	0 e
		2,000*	3,100*	0*e	0*e
10.445	Housing—Disaster Loans \ u	0*	1,800,000*	0*e	0*e
10.446	Rural Community Development \ u	6,600	6,000 e	6,200	6,000 e
10.447	Housing Preservation Restructuring	(n)	(n)	(n)	20,000 e
10.449	Boll Weevil Eradication Loans	83,070*	100,000*	59,400*e	0*e
10.450	Crop Insurance \ u	2,344,708	2,298,140	2,803,070 e	3,663,065 e
		2,343,581*	3,590,032*	5,266,271*e	6,569,971*e
10.451	Noninsured Assistance \ u	109,619	380,067	327,744 e	0 e
10.452	Disaster Reserve Assistance	456	24,775	0 e	0 e
10.454	Dairy Options Pilot Program \ u	0	0	0 e	0 e
10.455	Community Outreach, Assistance \ u	6,889	5,000 e	5,000 e	0 e
10.456	Non-Insurance Risk Management \ u	8,200	4,000	4,000 e	0 e
10.457	Commodity Partnerships \ u	5,238	5,500 e	5,500 e	0 e
10.458	Crop Insurance Education \ u	4,401	4,500 e	4,500 e	0 e
10.459	Commodity Partnerships, Small \ u	316	312	500 e	500 e
10.475	Intrastate Meat, Poultry Inspection	43,477	42,940	46,500 e	47,446 e
10.477	Meat, Poultry and Egg Inspection \ t	787,781	791,462	847,549 e	884,786 e
10.479	Food Safety	2,528	1,000	1,000	0 e
10.500	Cooperative Extension Service	427,485	431,569	431,248	410,099 e
10.551	Food Stamps	28,535,000	33,050,942	30,319,569	33,616,777 e
10.553	School Breakfast Program	1,937,416	2,082,855 e	2,228,842	2,367,186 e
10.555	School Lunch Program \ p	7,023,830	8,545,341 e	8,955,074 e	9,341,948 e
10.556	Special Milk Program	16,637	14,998 e	14,225	15,006 e
10.557	Nutrition/Women, Infants, Children	3,615,164	3,765,230 e	5,547,777	6,250,280 e
10.558	Child, Adult Care Food Program \ p	2,134,418	2,156,445 e	2,284,301	2,286,629 e
10.559	Summer Food Service \ p	273,202	290,201 e	297,933	312,637 e
10.560	State Expenses/Child Nutrition \ p	145,710	156,061 e	162,844	171,178 e
10.561	State Grants/Food Stamp Program	2,388,219	2,510,000	2,508,553	2,620,000 e
10.565	Commodity Supplemental Food \ p	(a)	0	107,828	139,830 e
10.566	Nutrition Assistance/Puerto Rico	1,495,346	1,517,776	1,551,167	1,622,521 e
10.567	Food Distribution/Indian \ p	78,429	79,000 e	77,534	88,477 e
10.568	Emergency Food—Administrative	50,085	55,500	50,310	49,650 e
10.569	Emergency Food—Commodities \ p	140,000	140,000 e	140,000	140,000 e
10.572	WIC Farmers' Market Nutrition	19,840	19,800	22,109	23,860 e

Please see "Important Notes on the Tables, Footnotes," page 842

Table 1. *(continued)*

Program number	ADMINISTRATIVE ENTITY/SUB-UNIT Program Title (abridged)	FY 2005 in $thousands	FY 2006 in $thousands	FY 2007 in $thousands	FY 2008 in $thousands
10.574	Team Nutrition Grants	10,038	10,038 e	9,382	13,269 e
10.576	Senior Farmers Market Nutrition	15,000	15,000	16,203	16,200 e
10.578	WIC Grants to States	17,300	18,000	14,000 e	0 e
10.579	Child Nutrition Discretionary \ p	0	0 e	2,998 e	0 e
10.580	Food Stamp Program Outreach	0	0	989	0 e
10.582	Fresh Fruit, Vegetable Program	2,281	15,000 e	9,036	12,410 e
10.600	Foreign Market Development \ u	34,500	34,500	34,500 e	0 e
10.601	Market Access Program \ u	140,000	100,000	0 e	0 e
10.603	Emerging Markets Program \ u	10,000	10,000	10,000 e	0 e
10.604	Assistance/Specialty Crops \ u	2,000	2,000	2,000 e	0 e
10.605	Quality Samples Program \ u	2,500	2,500	2,500 e	0 e
10.606	Food for Progress \ u	122,000	158,000	169,000 e	225,000 e
10.607	Section 416(B) \ u	8,000	12,000	0 e	0 e
10.608	Food for Education \ u	50,338	87,000	98,000 e	98,000 e
10.609	Trade Adjustment Assistance \ r	90,000	90,000 e	90,000 e	0 e
10.652	Forestry Research	13,762	14,000	14,000 e	0 e
10.664	Cooperative Forestry Assistance	38,270	38,107 e	40,069 e	0 e
10.665	Schools and Roads—States	359,277	366,463	0 e	0 e
10.666	Schools and Roads—Counties	5,655	6,038	6,287 e	0 e
10.670	Forest-Dependent Communities	3,642	9,000	0 e	0 e
10.671	Southeast Alaska Economic Disaster	10,000	12,000	0	0 e
10.672	Rural Development, Forestry	3,974	3,951	0 e	0 e
10.673	Wood in Transportation	478	416	0 e	0 e
10.674	Forest Products Lab: Technology Unit	0	4,431	0 e	0 e
10.675	Urban and Community Forestry	35,999	28,413 e	30,130	17,436 e
10.676	Forest Legacy	64,134	57,939	57,107	0 e
10.677	Forest Land Enhancement	20,000	0	0	0
10.678	Forest Stewardship	32,012	31,884	40,069 e	0 e
10.679	Collaborative Forest Restoration	4,101	4,101	4,101 e	0 e
10.680	Forest Health Protection	38,107	40,000	40,000 e	0 e
10.681	Wood Education	0	1,700	1,700	1,000 e
10.684	International Forestry Programs	(n)	(n)	362	0 e
10.700	National Agricultural Library	24,085	24,586	22,801 e	21,561 e
10.760	Water, Waste Disposal Systems \ i, u	525,206	357,754	349,385 e	349,385 e
		924,290*	1,010,640*	1,065,000*e	1,155,236*e
10.761	Technical Assistance, Training	18,114	17,726	18,359	16,215 e
10.762	Solid Waste Management	0	3,465	3,465 e	3,465 e
10.763	Community Water Assistance	10,677	6,749	6,959	7,000 e
10.766	Community Facilities Loans, Grants \ u	19,920	17,000	17,000 e	0 e
		621,193*	510,000*	510,000*e	0*e
10.767	Intermediary Relending Program \ u	33,939*	33,870*	33,870*	33,772*e
10.768	Business and Industry Loans \ u	678,110*	766,314*	830,435*	990,000*e
10.769	Rural Business Enterprise Grants	41,277	41,807	41,926	44,223 e
10.770	Water, Waste Disposal	42,909	40,098	41,085 e	40,750 e
10.771	Rural Cooperative Development	5,000	4,357	3,587	4,900 e
10.772	Empowerment Zones Program	12,170	12,000 e	11,698	10,724 e
10.773	Rural Business Opportunity Grants	3,075	3,140	6,940	5,779 e
10.774	Sheep Industry Improvement \ r	(o)	(o)	(o)	(o)
10.775	Renewable Energy Systems	22,237	21,209	20,553	15,888 e
		10,100*	24,159*	55,846*	204,954*e
10.778	Economic Impact of Cooperatives	(n)	495	500 e	492 e
10.850	Rural Electrification Loans \ u	4,319,115*	5,400,000*	6,142,001*e	0*e
10.851	Rural Telephone Loans \ u	568,000*	689,760*	672,753*	690,000*e
10.854	Rural Economic Development \ r, u	8,120	10,000	9,963	10,000 e
		24,302*	25,110*	26,167*	33,121*e
10.855	Distance Learning, Telemedicine	2,050	26,503	15,000	24,750 e
		2,682*	4,124*	127,914*	0*e
10.856	1890 Land Grant Outreach	1,199	1,500	1,500 e	0 e
10.857	State Bulk Fuel Revolving Fund \ r	0	0	500	0
10.858	RUS Denali Commission	15,000	15,000	15,000	15,000 e
10.859	High Energy Cost Communities	5,118	23,504	3,929 e	21,900 e
10.860	Rural Business Investment	0	1,000	0 e	0 e
		0*	24,294*	0*e	0*e
10.861	Public Television Digital Transition	0	4,970	4,950	0

Please see "Important Notes on the Tables, Footnotes," page 842

Table 1. *(continued)*

Program number	ADMINISTRATIVE ENTITY/SUB-UNIT Program Title (abridged)		FY 2005 in $thousands	FY 2006 in $thousands	FY 2007 in $thousands	FY 2008 in $thousands
10.862	Household Water Well System		992	300	990	990
10.863	Community Connect Grant Program		17,876	9,000	0 e	0 e
10.864	Fund/Financing Water, Wastewater \ r		497	495	495	0 e
10.886	Rural Broadband Access Loans		602,947*	329,209*	923,186*	300,000*e
10.901	Resource Conservation, Development		52,002	50,787 e	25,933 e	0 e
10.902	Soil and Water Conservation		753,083	722,871	634,320 e	0 e
10.903	Soil Survey		88,241	89,212	90,426 e	91,354 e
10.904	Watershed Protection		80,664	104,939	35,233 e	0 e
10.905	Plant Materials for Conservation		13,073	10,953	12,243 e	10,858 e
10.906	Watershed Surveys and Planning		6,845	6,010	6,056 e	0 e
10.907	Snow Survey, Water Forecasting		10,231	10,509	10,849 e	10,760 e
10.910	Rural Abandoned Mine Program		0	0	0 e	0 e
10.912	Environmental Quality Incentives		995,497	992,376	995,560 e	1,000,000 e
10.913	Farm, Ranch Lands Protection		111,788	10,500	50,000 e	0 e
10.914	Wildlife Habitat Incentive		45,818	42,661	43,236 e	0 e
10.916	Watershed Rehabilitation		27,819	31,245	15,300 e	0 e
10.917	Agricultural Management Assistance		13,780	4,940	5,000 e	0 e
10.918	Water Conservation-Environmental		64,541	69,785	70,093 e	0 e
10.919	Klamath Basin-Environmental Quality		10,111	11,258	8,360 e	0 e
10.920	Grassland Reserve Program		71,266	37,916	15,907 e	0 e
10.921	Conservation Security Program		201,568	257,220	259,270 e	316,212 e
10.922	Healthy Forests Program		0	2,475	2,476 e	2,476 e
10.923	Watershed Protection Program		0	246,954	213,143 e	150,792 e
10.950	Agricultural Statistics Reports		151,329	159,172	160,300 e	0 e
10.960	Technical Agricultural Assistance		5,081	7,000	7,000 e	0 e
10.961	Scientific Cooperation and Research		916	830	830 e	0 e
10.962	International Training		5,090	1,002	1,500 e	1,200 e
10.994	Peanut Quota Buyout Program		5,581	12,300	0 e	0 e
10.995	Hard White Wheat Incentive \ u		3,169	7,100	0 e	0 e
10.999	Storage, Transportation Lease Agreements		(n)	(n)	1,774,995 e	6,607 e
	DEPARTMENT TOTAL:	OUTLAYS	76,630,176	77,912,849	76,910,751	68,076,275
		CREDITS*	24,387,913*	31,944,759*	29,990,456*	9,977,054*
	DEPARTMENT OF COMMERCE					
	BUREAU OF THE CENSUS					
11.001	Census Bureau Data Products		328	352	275 e	0 e
11.002	Census Customer Services		94	96 e	67 e	0 e
11.003	Census Geography		38,598	37,302 e	40,210 e	0 e
11.004	Intergovernmental Services		5,354	4,998 e	12,639 e	0 e
11.005	Census Special Tabulations		9,383	4,419 e	1,433 e	0 e
11.006	Personal Census Search		180	180	180	0 e
	Subtotal:	Outlays	53,937	47,347	54,804	0
		Credits*	0*	0*	0*	0*
	ECONOMICS AND STATISTICS ADMINISTRATION					
11.025	Measures and Analyses		73,567	75,721	76,507 e	0 e
11.026	National Trade Data Bank \ r, u		0	0	0	0 e
	Subtotal:	Outlays	73,567	75,721	76,507	0
		Credits*	0*	0*	0*	0*
	INTERNATIONAL TRADE ADMINISTRATION					
11.106	Antidumping Duty		61,741	64,134	0 e	0 e
11.108	Commercial Service		223,255	222,839 e	237,291 e	0 e
11.110	Manufacturing and Services		48,376	32,266	47,328	0 e
11.111	Foreign-Trade Zones/U.S.		1,130	1,021	0 e	0 e
11.112	Export Market Development		1,794	2,000	2,000	0 e
11.113	ITA Special Projects		494	500	500	0 e
	Subtotal:	Outlays	336,790	322,760	287,119	0
		Credits*	0*	0*	0*	0*

Please see "Important Notes on the Tables, Footnotes," page 842

Table 1. *(continued)*

Program number	ADMINISTRATIVE ENTITY/SUB-UNIT Program Title (abridged)		FY 2005 in $thousands	FY 2006 in $thousands	FY 2007 in $thousands	FY 2008 in $thousands
	BUREAU OF EXPORT ADMINISTRATION					
11.150	Licensing Services, Information		1,582	1,714	1,753 e	0 e
	Subtotal:	Outlays	1,582	1,714	1,753	0
		Credits*	0*	0*	0*	0*
	ECONOMIC DEVELOPMENT ADMINISTRATION					
11.300	Public Works, Economic Development		179,451	158,089	158,089 e	248,900 e
11.302	Support for Planning Organizations		27,282	27,000	27,000	27,000 e
11.303	Technical Assistance		9,207	8,203 e	0	0 e
11.307	Economic Adjustment Assistance		53,158	44,154	44,155	42,300 e
11.312	Research and Evaluation		445	481	481	470
11.313	Trade Adjustment Assistance		10,577	12,814 e	12,814 e	12,900 e
	Subtotal:	Outlays	280,120	250,741	242,539	331,570
		Credits*	0*	0*	0*	0*
	NATIONAL OCEANIC AND ATMOSPHERIC ADMINISTRATION					
11.400	Geodetic Surveys and Services		15,279	15,927 e	17,218 e	0 e
11.405	Anadromous Fish Conservation		1,873	1,900 e	1,900 e	0 e
11.407	Interjurisdictional Fisheries		3,090	3,500 e	3,700 e	0 e
11.408	Fishermen's Contingency Fund		166	175 e	175 e	0 e
11.413	Fishery Products Inspection		17,069	17,923 e	18,000 e	0 e
11.415	Fisheries Finance Program \ u		64,000*	157,816*e	64,000*e	0*e
11.417	Sea Grant Support		59	51,150 e	51,250 e	0 e
11.419	Coastal Zone Management		126,242	123,147 e	73,546 e	0 e
11.420	Estuarine Research Reserves		24,444	25,661 e	23,178 e	0 e
11.426	Coastal Ocean Science		6,600	6,000	1,000 e	0 e
11.427	Fisheries Development		0	0 e	0 e	0 e
11.429	Marine Sanctuary Program		19,103	18,710 e	12,072 e	0 e
11.430	Undersea Research		15,000	8,400 e	8,000 e	0 e
11.431	Climate, Atmospheric Research		47,000	36,000 e	45,000 e	0 e
11.432	Oceanic, Atmospheric Research		112,681	120,000 e	0 e	0 e
11.433	Marine Fisheries Initiative		1,979	950 e	2,500 e	0 e
11.434	Cooperative Fishery Statistics		5,937	5,000 e	5,000 e	0 e
11.435	Southeast Area Monitoring		1,155	1,140 e	1,140 e	0
11.436	Columbia River Fisheries		12,744	13,200 e	13,200 e	0 e
11.437	Pacific Fisheries		20,421	20,000 e	20,000 e	0 e
11.438	Pacific Coast Salmon Recovery		94,998	95,000 e	95,000 e	0 e
11.439	Marine Mammal Data Program		24,185	25,000 e	25,000 e	0 e
11.440	Environmental Sciences		20,000	21,000 e	22,000 e	0 e
11.441	Fishery Management Councils		21,531	22,000 e	22,000 e	0 e
11.443	Short Term Climate Fluctuations		0	0 e	0 e	0 e
11.444	Hawaii Fisheries/Aquaculture		515	525 e	525 e	0 e
11.445	Hawaii Stock Management		468	500 e	500 e	0 e
11.449	Independent Education and Science		0	10 e	10 e	0 e
11.450	Automated Flood Warning Systems		445	384	425	0 e
11.452	Unallied Industry Projects		13,842	14,000 e	14,000 e	0 e
11.454	Unallied Management Projects		11,959	12,000 e	12,000 e	0 e
11.455	Cooperative Science, Education		6,138	6,200 e	6,200 e	0 e
11.457	Chesapeake Bay Studies		13,354	13,500 e	13,500 e	0 e
11.459	Weather and Air Quality Research		0	0	0 e	0 e
11.460	Oceanic and Atmospheric Projects		24,200	28,500 e	0 e	0 e
11.462	Hydrologic Research		0	0 e	0 e	0 e
11.463	Habitat Conservation		35,703	32,500 e	32,500 e	0 e
11.467	Meteorologic, Hydrologic Projects		4,763	4,983 e	4,983 e	0 e
11.468	Applied Meteorological Research		5,512	1,544 e	1,544 e	0 e
11.469	Congressionally Identified Projects		18,040	20,180 e	0 e	0 e
11.472	Unallied Science Program		33,005	34,000 e	34,000 e	0 e
11.473	Coastal Services Center		35,281	32,500 e	27,000 e	0 e
11.474	Atlantic Coastal Fisheries		7,250	9,250 e	9,250 e	0 e
11.477	Fisheries Disaster Relief		11,700,000	0 e	0 e	0 e

Please see "Important Notes on the Tables, Footnotes," page 842

Table 1. *(continued)*

Program number	ADMINISTRATIVE ENTITY/SUB-UNIT Program Title (abridged)		FY 2005 in $thousands	FY 2006 in $thousands	FY 2007 in $thousands	FY 2008 in $thousands
11.478	Coastal Ocean Program		28,400	11,000 e	16,000 e	0 e
11.480	Ocean Service Intern Program		0	0 e	0 e	0 e
11.481	Educational Partnership Program		14,439	14,400 e	14,400 e	0 e
	Subtotal:	Outlays	12,544,870	867,759	647,716	0
		Credits*	64,000*	157,816*	64,000*	0*
	NATIONAL TELECOMMUNICATIONS AND INFORMATION ADMINISTRATION					
11.550	Public Telecommunications Facilities		21,565	0	22,450	19,457 e
11.554	Digital-to-Analog Conversion		(n)	(n)	10,000 e	10,000 e
11.555	Interoperable Communications Grant		(n)	(n)	968,385	0 e
11.556	TV Converter Box Coupon		(n)	(n)	429,424 e	471,870 e
	Subtotal:	Outlays	21,565	0	1,430,259	501,327
		Credits*	0*	0*	0*	0*
	NATIONAL INSTITUTE FOR STANDARDS AND TECHNOLOGY					
11.601	Calibration Program \ r		7,850	7,864 e	7,877 e	0 e
11.603	Standard Reference Data System \ r		4,070	4,211 e	4,281 e	0 e
11.604	Standard Reference Materials \ r		9,994	11,932 e	12,025 e	0 e
11.606	Weights and Measures Service \ r		4,532	4,532	4,532 e	0 e
11.609	Measurement, Engineering Research \ r		25,760	27,406 e	34,362 e	0 e
11.610	Standards and Certification \ r		700	700 e	700 e	0 e
11.611	Manufacturing Extension Partnership		86,400	96,500 e	35,000 e	0 e
11.612	Advanced Technology Program		96,921	47,227 e	0 e	0 e
11.617	Congressionally-Identified Projects		51,700	137,266 e	0 e	0 e
	Subtotal:	Outlays	287,927	337,638	98,777	0
		Credits*	0*	0*	0*	0*
	NATIONAL TECHNICAL INFORMATION SERVICE					
11.650	National Technical Information \ r, u		15,858	48,718 e	41,000 e	0 e
	Subtotal:	Outlays	15,858	48,718	41,000	0
		Credits*	0*	0*	0*	0*
	OFFICE OF THE SECRETARY					
11.702	Postsecondary Internships		1,262	1,270	1,270 e	0 e
	Subtotal:	Outlays	1,262	1,270	1,270	0
		Credits*	0*	0*	0*	0*
	MINORITY BUSINESS DEVELOPMENT AGENCY					
11.800	Minority Business Development		8,700	8,400 e	8,400 e	0 e
11.801	Native American Business Development		1,592	1,592 e	1,592 e	0 e
11.803	Minority Business Committee		1,633	1,655 e	1,655 e	0 e
	Subtotal:	Outlays	11,925	11,647	11,647	0
		Credits*	0*	0*	0*	0*
	PATENT AND TRADEMARK OFFICE					
11.900	Patent and Trademark Information		1,508,392	1,683,086 e	1,842,966 e	0 e
	Subtotal:	Outlays	1,508,392	1,683,086	1,842,966	0
		Credits*	0*	0*	0*	0*
	DEPARTMENT TOTAL:	OUTLAYS	15,137,795	3,648,401	4,736,357	832,897
		CREDITS*	1,572,392*	1,840,902*	1,906,966*	0*

DEPARTMENT OF DEFENSE

Program number	ADMINISTRATIVE ENTITY/SUB-UNIT Program Title (abridged)		FY 2005 in $thousands	FY 2006 in $thousands	FY 2007 in $thousands	FY 2008 in $thousands
	DEFENSE LOGISTICS AGENCY					
12.002	Procurement Technical Assistance		12,000	12,000	0 e	0 e
	Subtotal:	Outlays	12,000	12,000	0	0
		Credits*	0*	0*	0*	0*

Please see "Important Notes on the Tables, Footnotes," page 842

Table 1. *(continued)*

Program number	ADMINISTRATIVE ENTITY/SUB-UNIT Program Title (abridged)		FY 2005 in $thousands	FY 2006 in $thousands	FY 2007 in $thousands	FY 2008 in $thousands
	DEPARTMENT OF THE ARMY, OFFICE OF THE CHIEF OF ENGINEERS					
12.100	Aquatic Plant Control		0	0 e	0 e	0 e
12.101	Beach Erosion Control Projects		2,800	2,500	0 e	0 e
12.102	Emergency Flood Control Works		0	0 e	0 e	0 e
12.103	Emergency Flood Response		5,000	0 e	0 e	0 e
12.104	Flood Plain Management		8,500	9,000 e	0 e	0 e
12.105	Essential Highways, Public Works		13,000	9,000 e	0 e	0 e
12.106	Flood Control Projects		30,600	25,000 e	0 e	0 e
12.107	Navigation Projects		5,900	7,000 e	0 e	0 e
12.108	Snagging and Clearing		1,600	200 e	0 e	0 e
12.109	Protection, Clearing Channels		50	0 e	0 e	0 e
12.110	Planning Assistance to States		5,800	6,500 e	0 e	0 e
12.111	Flood Prevention		500	1,000 e	0 e	0 e
12.112	Payments to States/Taxes		5,000	0 e	0	0 e
12.113	Reimbursements/Technical Services		27,546	41,453 e	43,545 e	0 e
12.114	Collaborative Research, Development		4,660	5,306 e	6,000 e	0 e
12.116	DOD Appropriation Act of 2003		0	10,000	0 e	0 e
	Subtotal:	Outlays	110,956	116,959	49,545	0
		Credits*	0*	0*	0*	0*
	DEPARTMENT OF THE NAVY, OFFICE OF THE CHIEF OF NAVAL RESEARCH					
12.300	Basic, Applied Scientific Research		470,000	480,000 e	480,000 e	0 e
12.350	DOD HIV/AIDS Prevention		0	10,000 e	10,000 e	0 e
12.351	Combating WMD—Basic Research		(n)	20	13,298	38,000
12.352	Combating WMD—Advanced Research		(n)	(n)	500 e	1,000 e
12.360	Chemical, Biological Defense		(n)	(n)	3,753 e	10,000 e
	Subtotal:	Outlays	470,000	490,020	507,551	49,000
		Credits*	0*	0*	0*	0*
	NATIONAL GUARD BUREAU					
12.400	Military Construction		59,130	66,363 e	0 e	0 e
12.401	National Guard Operations		244,000	150,000 e	100,000 e	0 e
12.404	Civilian Youth Opportunities		62,300	62,500 e	62,500 e	0 e
	Subtotal:	Outlays	365,430	278,863	162,500	0
		Credits*	0*	0*	0*	0*
	U.S. ARMY MEDICAL COMMAND					
12.420	Military Medical Research		137,380	56,530 e	140,000 e	0 e
	Subtotal:	Outlays	137,380	56,530	140,000	0
		Credits*	0*	0*	0*	0*
	U.S. ARMY MATERIEL COMMAND					
12.431	Basic Scientific Research		150,000	150,000	0 e	0 e
	Subtotal:	Outlays	150,000	150,000	0	0
		Credits*	0*	0*	0*	0*
	ASSISTANT SECRETARY (STRATEGY AND REQUIREMENTS)					
12.550	International Education \ t		1,171	6,500	12,000 e	12,000 e
12.551	National Security—Scholarships \ t		2,000	2,000	2,000 e	0 e
12.552	National Security—Fellowships		(n)	2,000	2,000 e	0 e
12.553	National Flagship Language Fellowships		(n)	6,500	12,000 e	12,000 e
12.554	Heritage Language Speakers Grants		(n)	2,000	2,000 e	0 e
12.555	Heritage Language Speakers Scholarships		(n)	2,000	2,000 e	0 e
	Subtotal:	Outlays	3,171	21,000	32,000	24,000
		Credits*	0*	0*	0*	0*
	OFFICE OF ECONOMIC ADJUSTMENT					
12.607	Community Economic Planning \ t		1,171	15,000	60,000	45,000 e
12.610	Joint Land Use Studies \ t		610	1,240	1,200 e	0 e
12.611	Community Planning Assistance		0	1,900	2,000 e	2,000 e
12.614	Advance Planning \ t		519	3,500	1,500 e	1,500 e
	Subtotal:	Outlays	2,300	21,640	64,700	48,500
		Credits*	0*	0*	0*	0*

Please see "Important Notes on the Tables, Footnotes," page 842

Table 1. *(continued)*

Program number	ADMINISTRATIVE ENTITY/SUB-UNIT Program Title (abridged)		FY 2005 in $thousands	FY 2006 in $thousands	FY 2007 in $thousands	FY 2008 in $thousands
	OFFICE OF THE SECRETARY OF DEFENSE					
12.630	Research/Science, Engineering		224,196	220,000 e	215,000 e	0 e
	Subtotal:	Outlays	224,196	220,000	215,000	0
		Credits*	0*	0*	0*	0*
	SECRETARIES OF MILITARY DEPARTMENTS					
12.700	Obsolete DOD Property \ p		2,500	2,750 e	0 e	0 e
	Subtotal:	Outlays	2,500	2,750	0	0
		Credits*	0*	0*	0*	0*
	DEPARTMENT OF THE AIR FORCE, MATERIEL COMMAND					
12.800	Defense Research Sciences		263,000	260,000 e	275,000 e	0 e
	Subtotal:	Outlays	263,000	260,000	275,000	0
		Credits*	0*	0*	0*	0*
	NATIONAL SECURITY AGENCY					
12.900	Language Grant Program		50	50 e	0 e	0 e
12.901	Mathematical Sciences Grants		2,900	2,600 e	3,000 e	0 e
12.902	Information Security		1,400	1,000 e	2,000 e	0 e
	Subtotal:	Outlays	4,350	3,650	5,000	0
		Credits*	0*	0*	0*	0*
	ADVANCED RESEARCH PROJECTS AGENCY					
12.910	Research and Technology		50,000	50,000	0 e	0 e
	Subtotal:	Outlays	50,000	50,000	0	0
		Credits*	0*	0*	0*	0*
	DEPARTMENT TOTAL:	OUTLAYS	1,795,283	1,683,412	1,451,296	121,500
		CREDITS*	0*	0*	0*	0*

DEPARTMENT OF HOUSING AND URBAN DEVELOPMENT

Program number	Program Title (abridged)	FY 2005 in $thousands	FY 2006 in $thousands	FY 2007 in $thousands	FY 2008 in $thousands
14.103	Interest Reduction—Housing \ u	(a)	(a)	(a)	(a)
14.108	Rehabilitation Mortgage Insurance \ u	431,175*	406,456*	420,631*e	583,421 e
14.110	Manufactured Home Loan Insurance \ i, u	66,936*	57,228*	58,638*e	58,638*e
14.112	Construction, Rehab/Condominiums \ u	(o)*	(o)*	(o)*	(o)*
14.117	Mortgage Insurance—Homes \ i, u	58,017,003*	51,782,950*	44,418,000*e	66,118,045*e
14.119	Homes for Disaster Victims \ u	(o)*	(o)*	(o)*	(o)*
14.122	Mortgage Insurance—Renewal Areas \ u	(o)*	(o)*	(o)*	(o)*
14.123	Mortgage Insurance—Declining Areas \ u	(o)*	(o)*	(o)*	(o)*
14.126	Mortgage Insurance—Cooperatives \ u	(o)*	(o)*	(o)*	(o)*
14.127	Manufactured Home Parks \ u	(o)*	(o)*	(o)*	(o)*
14.128	Mortgage Insurance—Hospitals \ u	431,175*	365,766*e	675,000*e	900,000*e
14.129	Mortgage Insurance—Nursing Homes \ u	1,220,728*	1,690,527*	1,869,000*e	3,179,000*e
14.132	Sales/Cooperative Housing \ u	(o)*	(o)*	(o)*	(o)*
14.133	Mortgage Insurance—Condominiums \ i, u	12,878,737*	21,155,602*	12,163,144*e	0*e
14.134	Mortgage Insurance—Rental Housing \ u	(o)*	(o)*	(o)*	(o)*
14.135	Mortgage Insurance—Market Rate \ i, u	2,244,821*	1,520,810*	1,362,000*e	3,624,750*e
14.138	Mortgage Insurance—Elderly \ u	(o)*	(o)*	(o)*	(o)*
14.139	Rental Housing/Renewal Areas \ u	(o)*	(o)*	(o)*	(o)*
14.142	Property Improvement Loans \ u	50,901*	43,649*	43,496*e	43,496*e
14.149	Rent Supplements, Housing	(a)*	(a)*	(a)*	(a)*
14.151	Supplemental Loan Insurance \ u	0*	4,300*	3,225*e	5,950*e
14.155	Existing Multifamily Projects \ u	1,870,334*	2,425,579*	1,830,750*	3,932,500*e
14.157	Supportive Housing/Elderly \ i, u	1,009,328	890,599	890,000 e	889,000 e
14.159	Graduated Payment Mortgage \ u	(o)*	(o)*	(o)*	(o)*
14.162	Manufactured Home Lot Loans \ u	(o)*	(o)*	(o)*	(o)*
14.163	Single Family Cooperative Housing \ u	(o)*	(o)*	(o)*	(o)*
14.164	Operating Assistance/Multifamily \ u	0	0	0 e	0 e
14.165	Homes—Military Impacted Areas \ u	(o)*	(o)*	(o)*	(o)*
14.167	Operating Loss Loans \ u	2,859*	1,467*	1,650*e	3,025*e

Please see "Important Notes on the Tables, Footnotes," page 842

Table 1. *(continued)*

Program number	ADMINISTRATIVE ENTITY/SUB-UNIT Program Title (abridged)	FY 2005 in $thousands	FY 2006 in $thousands	FY 2007 in $thousands	FY 2008 in $thousands
14.168	Land Sales	577	694	650 e	650 e
14.169	Housing Counseling Assistance	44,659	39,080	41,080 e	50,000 e
14.171	Manufactured Home Standards \ t	9,016	9,411	13,401 e	16,000 e
14.172	Growing Equity Mortgages \ u	(o)*	(o)*	(o)*	(o)*
14.175	Adjustable Rate Mortgages \ u	(o)*	(o)*	(o)*	(o)*
14.181	Supportive Housing/Disabilities \ u	296,333	268,966	255,000 e	250,000 e
14.183	Home Equity Conversion Mortgages \ u	(o)*	(o)*	(o)*	(o)*
14.184	Mortgages/Single Room Occupancy \ u	(o)*	(o)*	(o)*	(o)*
14.188	HFA Risk Sharing Program \ u	197,324*	158,758*	111,750*e	154,250*e
14.189	QPE Risk Sharing \ u	17,965*	10,167*	6,750*e	10,500*e
14.191	Multifamily Housing Coordinators	(o)	(o)	(o)	(o)
14.195	Section 8—Special Allocations	6,318,000	8,096,509	8,665,000 e	8,633,000 e
14.197	Multifamily Housing Reform \ u	199,000	175,000	206,000 e	67,000 e
14.198	Officer Next Door Sales Program \ u	(o)	(o)	(o)	(o)
14.199	Multifamily Property Disposition \ p	1,000	0	0 e	100 e
14.218	CDBG/Entitlement	2,876,923	2,592,790	2,592,790 e	1,937,306 e
14.219	CDBG/Small Cities	5,858	5,296 e	4,245 e	0 e
14.225	CDBG/Insular Area	6,944	6,930 e	6,930 e	7,000 e
14.227	CDBG/Technical Assistance	1,389	0	0 e	3,000 e
14.228	CDBG/State	1,227,109	12,605,900 e	886,029	0 e
14.231	Emergency Shelter Grants	158,720	160,779	160,000 e	160,000 e
14.235	Supportive Housing Program	770,071	668,662 e	829,426 e	964,063 e
14.238	Shelter Plus Care	255,006	248,985 e	303,897 e	353,227 e
14.239	HOME Investment Partnerships	1,858,016	1,757,250	1,757,250 e	1,966,640 e
14.241	Housing/Persons with AIDS	281,728	286,110	286,110 e	300,100 e
14.244	Empowerment Zones Program	9,920	0	0 e	0 e
14.246	CDBG/Economic Development	18,808	9,900	9,900 e	0 e
14.247	Self-Help Homeownership	24,800	0	39,600 e	39,700 e
14.248	CDBG—Section 108 Loans	275,000*	137,500*	137,500*e	0*e
14.249	Section 8—SRO	31,529	20,690	20,730 e	21,081 e
14.250	Rural Development	23,808	16,830	16,830 e	0 e
14.251	Neighborhood Initiative	(n)	356,400	0 e	0 e
14.252	Section 4 Capacity Building	(n)	33,000	29,590 e	30,000 e
14.310	Teacher Next Door Initiative \ p, u	(o)	(o)	(o)	(o)
14.311	Single Family Property Disposition \ i, p	4,216,688	3,737,514	5,571,351 e	4,225,355 e
14.313	Dollar Home Sales \ p	(o)	(o)	(o)	(o)
14.314	Assisted Living Conversion	(o)	(o)	(o)	(o)
14.315	Emergency Capital Repair	(o)	(o)	(o)	(o)
14.316	Housing Counseling Training	(n)	3,875 e	4,500 e	0 e
14.400	Equal Opportunity in Housing	(a)	(a)	(a)	(a)
14.401	FHAP—State, Local	23,696	29,680	26,394 e	25,841 e
14.402	Non-Discrimination/Age	(a)	(a)	(a)	(a)
14.404	Non-Discrimination/Disability	(a)	(a)	(a)	(a)
14.405	Non-Discrimination/Race, Color	(a)	(a)	(a)	(a)
14.406	Non-Discrimination/CDBG	(a)	(a)	(a)	(a)
14.407	Architectural Barriers	(a)	(a)	(a)	(a)
14.408	Fair Housing Initiatives	21,590	20,000	20,400 e	20,180 e
14.412	Employment/Lower Income	(a)	(a)	(a)	(a)
14.414	Non-Discrimination/Public Entities	(a)	(a)	(a)	(a)
14.415	Non-Discrimination/Sex	(a)	(a)	(a)	(a)
14.506	General Research and Technology	45,816	32,226	36,261 e	39,400 e
14.511	Community Outreach Partnership	6,646	0	0 e	5,940 e
14.514	Hispanic-Serving Institutions	6,646	5,940	5,940 e	5,650 e
14.515	Alaska/Hawaii Institutions	3,968	2,970	2,970 e	2,825 e
14.516	Doctoral Dissertation Research	393	396	300 e	300 e
14.517	Early Doctoral Student Research	119	143	105 e	100 e
14.519	Tribal Colleges and Universities	2,976	2,574	2,574 e	2,449 e
14.520	Historically Black Colleges	9,920	8,910	8,910 e	8,476 e
14.850	Public and Indian Housing	2,439,790	3,564,010 e	3,864,000 e	4,000,000 e
14.856	Section 8 Moderate Rehabilitation	190,812	236,444	203,127 e	166,712 e
14.862	Indian CDBG	70,769	70,231	59,400 e	57,420 e
14.865	Indian Housing Loans	145,345*	190,461*	251,000*e	367,000*e
14.866	Distressed Public Housing	164,894	99,000	99,000 e	0 e
14.867	Indian Housing Block Grants	659,264	613,308	623,700 e	626,965 e

Please see "Important Notes on the Tables, Footnotes," page 842

Table 1. *(continued)*

Program number	ADMINISTRATIVE ENTITY/SUB-UNIT Program Title (abridged)	FY 2005 in $thousands	FY 2006 in $thousands	FY 2007 in $thousands	FY 2008 in $thousands
14.869	Tribal Housing Activities	17,926*	13,338*	17,000*e	17,000*e
14.870	Residents—Supportive Services	25,521	37,620	37,620 e	23,800 e
14.871	Section 8 Housing Choice Vouchers	13,857,745	14,550,206	15,804,828 e	16,000,000 e
14.872	Public Housing Capital Fund	2,555,422	2,439,000	2,439,000 e	2,024,000 e
14.873	Hawaii Housing Block Grants	9,444	0	8,727 e	5,940 e
14.874	Native Hawaiian Housing	37,403*	0*	43,000*e	41,504*e
14.875	Public Housing Neighborhood Networks	4,564	7,425	7,425 e	0 e
14.876	ROSS—Elderly, Disabled	7,715	37,620	37,620 e	23,800 e
14.877	Public Housing, Family Self-Sufficiency	8,973	9,310	21,993 e	0 e
14.878	Main Street Rejuvenation	(n)	500	2,500 e	0 e
14.879	Mainstream Vouchers	(n)	9,920,000	0 e	0 e
14.900	Lead-Based Paint Hazards	93,600	84,911	76,400 e	86,000 e
14.901	Healthy Homes Demonstrations	5,000	4,370	5,000 e	5,000 e
14.902	Lead Technical Studies Grants \ i	3,000	3,000	3,000 e	3,000 e
14.903	Operation Lead Elimination Action	8,000	14,610	17,300 e	17,300 e
14.904	Lead Outreach Grants	2,000	2,000 e	2,000 e	2,000
14.905	Lead Hazard Reduction Demonstration	49,400	59,615	54,700 e	0
14.906	Healthy Homes Technical Studies	2,000	1,200	2,000 e	2,000 e
	DEPARTMENT TOTAL: OUTLAYS	39,924,913	63,848,389	46,063,503	43,068,320
	CREDITS*	77,905,632*	79,964,558*	63,412,534*	79,039,079*
	DEPARTMENT OF THE INTERIOR				
15.020	Aid to Tribal Governments	35,492	38,101	36,270 e	33,887 e
15.021	Consolidated Tribal Government	64,629	61,352	63,185 e	69,240 e
15.022	Tribal Self-Governance	295,588	138,079	141,849 e	139,036 e
15.024	Indian Self-Determination	85,406	133,599	143,628 e	149,628 e
15.025	Children, Elderly, Families	20,855	20,865	21,032 e	21,690 e
15.026	Indian Adult Education	2,105	2,395	2,355 e	2,324 e
15.027	Tribally Controlled Colleges	51,985	55,545 e	54,721 e	54,721 e
15.028	Community College Endowments	947	1,292	4,586 e	1,292 e
15.029	Tribal Courts	8,417	8,358	8,169 e	11,604 e
15.030	Indian Law Enforcement	106,641	110,037	116,560 e	132,159 e
15.031	Indian Community Fire Protection	965	904	904 e	948 e
15.032	Indian Economic Development	2,000	1,807	1,941 e	1,477 e
15.033	Road Maintenance	7,281	7,394	7,443 e	7,015 e
15.034	Agriculture on Indian Lands	3,325	3,731	3,485 e	3,659 e
15.035	Forestry on Indian Lands	13,978	13,905	14,011 e	14,324 e
15.036	Indian Rights Protection	386	392	393 e	416 e
15.037	Water Resources on Indian Lands	8,166	8,204	7,880 e	6,702 e
15.038	Minerals, Mining/Indian Lands	979	981	1,225 e	1,401 e
15.039	Fish, Wildlife, Parks/Indian Lands	31,494	2,274	2,340 e	2,390 e
15.040	Real Estate Programs-Indian Lands	3,669	3,389	3,606 e	3,988 e
15.041	Environmental Management	6,326	6,354	6,319 e	5,952 e
15.042	Indian School Equalization	189,312	191,795	194,049 e	198,329 e
15.043	Indian Child and Family Education	9,674	9,627	7,602 e	9,615 e
15.044	Indian Schools—Transportation	25,244	27,352	27,413 e	31,105 e
15.045	Indian Children/Severe Disabilities	3,732	3,704	3,713 e	3,774 e
15.046	Administrative Costs/Indian Schools	45,704	44,553	44,060 e	44,060 e
15.047	Indian Education Facilities	40,303	40,185	40,354 e	41,327 e
15.048	BIA Facilities	1,202	1,408	1,384 e	1,441 e
15.049	Irrigation Operations, Maintenance	6,195	8,869	8,210 e	8,202 e
15.050	Indian Hunting, Fishing Rights	43	46	43 e	0 e
15.051	Endangered Species/Indian Lands	1,510	834	153 e	873 e
15.052	Litigation Support/Indian Rights	1,453	2,325	2,324 e	1,764 e
15.053	Attorney Fees-Indian Rights	978	1,826	1,826 e	1,386 e
15.055	Alaskan Indian Allotments	136	235	136 e	0 e
15.057	Navajo-Hopi Settlement	225	228	230 e	239 e
15.058	Indian Post Secondary Schools	(a)	(a)	(a)	(a)
15.059	Graduate Student Scholarships	1,731	2,198	2,198 e	2,198 e
15.060	United Tribes Technical College	3,451	0	0 e	0 e
15.061	United Sioux Tribes	444	0	0 e	0 e

Please see "Important Notes on the Tables, Footnotes," page 842

Table 1. *(continued)*

Program number	ADMINISTRATIVE ENTITY/SUB-UNIT Program Title (abridged)	FY 2005 in $thousands	FY 2006 in $thousands	FY 2007 in $thousands	FY 2008 in $thousands
15.062	Replacement, Repair—Schools	179,208	131,138	122,700 e	69,129 e
15.063	Improvement—Detention Facilities	3,600	7,292	7,293 e	10,000 e
15.064	Fire Protection-BIA Facilities	541	533	533 e	533 e
15.065	Safety of Dams/Indian Lands	17,990	16,381	16,656 e	16,497 e
15.108	Indian Employment Assistance	7,367	7,221	7,262 e	6,924 e
15.113	Indian Social Services—Welfare	63,950	63,041	59,332 e	59,332 e
15.114	Indian—Higher Education	24,316	27,537	27,077 e	26,726 e
15.124	Indian Loans—Economic \ u	6,332*	76,703*	82,170*e	105,000*e
15.130	Indian Education—Schools	14,694	16,371	12,000 e	16,500 e
15.141	Indian Housing Assistance	16,017	15,817	15,812 e	15,817 e
15.144	Indian Child Welfare Act	10,300	10,909	10,063 e	10,974 e
15.146	Ironworker Training Program	515	0	0 e	0 e
15.147	Tribal Courts-Trust Reform	5,384	5,330	0 e	0 e
15.214	Disposals of Mineral Material \ p	(a)	(a)	(a)	(a)
15.222	Inspection Agreements	1,133	1,000 e	1,000	0 e
15.224	Cultural Resource Management	(a)	(a)	(a)	(a)
15.225	Recreation Resource Management	3,628	3,500 e	3,500 e	0 e
15.226	Payments in Lieu of Taxes	226,410	232,134	198,000 e	0 e
15.227	Receipts/State, Local Governments	356,306	269,095 e	256,733 e	0 e
15.228	Wildland Urban Fire Assistance	15,982	8,100 e	8,500 e	0 e
15.229	Wild Horse, Burro Resource Management	1,458	1,490 e	1,490 e	0 e
15.231	Fish, Wildlife, Plant Conservation	4,200	4,000 e	4,000 e	0 e
15.242	National Fire Plan—Rural Assistance	8,449	9,000 e	10,000 e	0 e
15.250	Surface Coal Mining	56,837	56,365	56,365	60,559 e
15.252	Abandoned Mine Land Reclamation	147,523	145,353	145,353	285,400 e
15.253	Not-for-Profit AMD Reclamation	2,000	1,500	1,500	1,500 e
15.254	Summer Watershed Intern	50	60	65	70 e
15.255	Coal Mining, Applied Science Agreements	(n)	1,200 e	1,200 e	1,400 e
15.421	Alaska Coastal Marine Institute	1,000	1,000	500	750 e
15.422	LSU Coastal Marine Institute	2,000	2,000	1,400	1,000 e
15.423	Minerals Management Service Studies	3,000	1,000 e	2,400	1,500 e
15.424	Marine Minerals Activities	0	750	1,280 e	0 e
15.425	Offshore Research, TEES	400	400	400 e	400 e
15.426	Coastal Impact Assistance	(n)	0	250,000 e	250,000 e
15.427	Oil and Gas Royalty Management \ t	9,100	8,960	9,490 e	10,200 e
15.504	Water Reclamation and Reuse	25,896	23,902	10,100	9,780 e
15.506	Desalination Research, Development	3,800	0	0	2,275 e
15.507	Water 2025	11,000	1,312	9,200	11,000 e
15.508	Desert Terminal Lakes	1,500	106,600	7,000	75,000 e
15.509	Colorado River Basin Salinity Control	(n)	15,838	16,409 e	7,850 e
15.510	Water Rights Settlement, Ute	(n)	55,440	57,420 e	35,000 e
15.511	Cultural Resources Management	(n)	(a)	(a)	(a)
15.512	Central Valley Project Improvement	(n)	15,000	5,500 e	0 e
15.513	Federal Property Disposition	(n)	359	368 e	376 e
15.514	Emergency Drought Relief	(n)	479 e	475 e	436 e
15.515	Federal Resource Protection	(n)	(a)	(a)	(a)
15.516	Fort Peck Water Supply	(n)	16,000 e	5,000 e	0 e
15.517	Fish and Wildlife Coordination Act	(n)	(a)	(a)	(a)
15.518	Garrison Diversion Unit	(n)	27,597 e	24,221 e	17,642 e
15.519	Indian Tribal Water Resources	(n)	(a)	(a)	(a)
15.520	Lewis and Clark Rural Water System	(n)	17,500	21,000 e	26,000 e
15.521	Lower Rio Grande Irrigation Projects	(n)	1,671 e	1,200 e	0 e
15.522	Mni Wiconi Water Supply Project	(n)	27,597	24,221	26,309
15.523	Perkins County Rural Water System	(n)	975	125 e	0 e
15.524	Recreation Resources Management	(n)	(a)	(a)	(a)
15.525	Rocky Boy's Regional Water	(n)	5,750	7,000	0 e
15.526	San Gabriel Basin Restoration	(n)	10,519	753	400 e
15.527	San Luis, Central Valley Project	(n)	2,323	3,500 e	(a)
15.528	St. Mary Storage Rehabilitation	(n)	349	0 e	0 e
15.529	Endangered Fish Recovery	(n)	9,082	11,480 e	1,600 e
15.530	Water Conservation	(n)	(a)	(a)	(a)
15.531	Yakima River Basin Water	(n)	3,305	9,866	6,500 e
15.532	Central Valley Project	(n)	724	1,705	1,000 e
15.533	California Water Security	(n)	2,800	1,000 e	1,000 e

Please see "Important Notes on the Tables, Footnotes," page 842

Table 1. *(continued)*

Program number	ADMINISTRATIVE ENTITY/SUB-UNIT Program Title (abridged)	FY 2005 in $thousands	FY 2006 in $thousands	FY 2007 in $thousands	FY 2008 in $thousands
15.602	Conservation Law Training	505	520 e	0 e	0 e
15.605	Sport Fish Restoration \ t	294,691	0	349,089	364,965 e
15.608	Fish and Wildlife Management	2,173	2,169 e	250 e	0 e
15.611	Wildlife Restoration	227,456	231,108 e	243,768 e	0 e
15.614	Coastal Wetlands \ t	13,400	15,200	18,973	20,490 e
15.615	Endangered Species Fund	70,618	80,001	81,001	81,001 e
15.616	Clean Vessel Act \ t	10,249	10,000 e	12,500 e	13,000 e
15.619	Rhinoceros, Tiger Conservation	1,472	1,713	1,400 e	1,400 e
15.620	African Elephant Conservation \ t	1,397	1,384	1,300 e	1,300 e
15.621	Asian Elephant Conservation	1,436	1,269	1,300 e	1,300 e
15.622	Sportfishing, Boating Safety \ t	8,466	8,000 e	12,500 e	13,100 e
15.623	Wetlands Conservation	62,157	71,602 e	70,216 e	0 e
15.625	Wildlife Conservation	(n)	(n)	(n)	0 e
15.626	Hunter Education and Safety	8,000	1,269	1,300 e	1,300 e
15.628	Multi-State Conservation Grants \ t	6,000	6,000	6,000 e	6,000 e
15.629	Great Apes Conservation	1,379	1,419	1,300 e	1,300 e
15.630	Coastal Program	11,700	12,954	12,984	12,900 e
15.631	Partners for Fish, Wildlife	47,000	50,151	42,660	42,600 e
15.632	Private Stewardship/Imperiled Species	6,558	6,913 e	8,930 e	0 e
15.633	Landowner Incentive	19,119	18,915 e	21,302 e	0 e
15.634	State Wildlife Grants	62,089	59,556	60,755	69,492 e
15.635	Neotropical Migratory Bird	3,923	3,952 e	3,841 e	0 e
15.636	Alaska Subsistence Management	5,913	5,915 e	5,915 e	0 e
15.637	Migratory Bird Joint Ventures	1,210	3,500	4,019	5,000 e
15.638	Tribal Landowner Incentive	2,874	2,104	1,776 e	0 e
15.639	Tribal Wildlife Grants	5,926	5,917	6,343 e	5,282 e
15.640	Wildlife—Latin America	519	580	492 e	492 e
15.641	Wildlife—Mexico	668	657	635	330 e
15.642	Challenge Cost Share	6,831	9,754 e	12,000 e	0 e
15.643	Alaska Migratory Bird Co-Management	200	223 e	221 e	0 e
15.644	Junior Duck Stamp Conservation \ p	215	119 e	164 e	0 e
15.645	Marine Turtle Conservation	99	622	641	620 e
15.647	Migratory Bird Conservation	132	84	251	200 e
15.648	Anadromous Fish Restoration	9,203	8,338 e	8,755 e	0 e
15.649	National Resource Conservation Training	(n)	0	0 e	0 e
15.650	Research Grants	(n)	0	0 e	0 e
15.651	Wildlife Without Borders—Africa	(n)	(n)	250 e	250 e
15.653	Outreach, Communication Program \ t	(n)	11,300	11,800 e	12,000 e
15.654	Visitor Facility Enhancements	(n)	345	0 e	0 e
15.655	Migratory Bird Conservation	(n)	2,279	2,205 e	1,909 e
15.805	State Water Resources Research	6,123	6,080	5,171	0 e
15.807	Earthquake Hazards Reduction	10,096	12,744	12,800 e	12,800 e
15.808	Geological Survey—Research, Data	33,233	46,000	41,000 e	41,000 e
15.809	National Spatial Data	1,084	1,185	1,319	1,275 e
15.810	National Geologic Mapping Program	6,655	6,514	6,683 e	6,680 e
15.811	GAP Analysis Program	1,712	1,800	1,800	1,800 e
15.812	Cooperative Research Units Program	12,794	13,564	15,406	16,000 e
15.813	Minority Natural Resource Training	(n)	(n)	150 e	150 e
15.814	Geological, Geophysical Data	(n)	(n)	180	400
15.850	Indian Arts, Crafts Development	1,054	1,052 e	1,057 e	0 e
15.875	Economic, Social, Political Development	214,110	199,902	187,822	186,737 e
15.904	Historic Preservation	68,552	39,658	42,663 e	39,658 e
15.910	National Natural Landmarks	993	985 e	985 e	0 e
15.912	National Historic Landmarks	785	758	787 e	790 e
15.914	National Register/Historic Places	1,745	1,706	1,700 e	1,700 e
15.915	Technical Preservation Services	1,600	1,600	1,600 e	1,600 e
15.916	Outdoor Recreation	89,736	27,995	27,995 e	0 e
15.918	Federal Surplus Real Property	648	145	145	155 e
15.921	Rivers, Trails Conservation	8,185	8,015	7,697 e	7,600 e
15.922	Native American Graves Protection	2,451	2,400	2,400 e	2,350 e
15.923	Preservation Technology, Training	336	300	300 e	250 e
15.925	National Maritime Heritage	0	0	0 e	0 e
15.926	American Battlefield Protection	365	350	492	490 e
15.927	Hydropower Recreation Assistance	801	801	818	852 e

Please see "Important Notes on the Tables, Footnotes," page 842

Table 1. *(continued)*

Program number	ADMINISTRATIVE ENTITY/SUB-UNIT Program Title (abridged)	FY 2005 in $thousands	FY 2006 in $thousands	FY 2007 in $thousands	FY 2008 in $thousands
15.928	Civil War Battlefield Acquisition	6,000	0	0 e	0 e
15.929	Save America's Treasures	29,805	29,559	13,000	20,000 e
15.930	Chesapeake Bay Gateways	(n)	905 e	480 e	550 e
15.931	Youth Service Conservation Activities	(n)	10,400	12,000 e	11,000
15.978	Upper Mississippi Monitoring	2,044	2,942	2,950	2,421 e
	DEPARTMENT TOTAL: OUTLAYS	3,702,010	3,400,934	3,821,280	3,088,034
	CREDITS*	6,332*	76,703*	82,170*	105,000*
	DEPARTMENT OF JUSTICE				
16.001	Narcotics, Drugs—Laboratory	4,161	4,360	4,280	4,287 e
16.003	Narcotics, Drugs/Publications	2	3	1	3 e
16.004	Narcotics, Drugs Training	0	3,062	3,100	3,116 e
16.005	Public Education on Drug Abuse	760	778	0	0 e
16.012	ATF-Training Assistance	1,800	2,500	2,500 e	3,200 e
16.013	Court Training Grants	(n)	(n)	(n)	0 e
16.014	Domestic, Dating, Sexual Violence Prevention	(n)	(n)	(n)	0 e
16.016	Culturally Specific Services	(n)	(n)	(n)	0 e
16.017	Sexual Assault Services	(n)	(n)	(n)	0 e
16.100	Desegregation of Public Education	5,547	5,629 e	5,890 e	6,084 e
16.101	Equal Employment Opportunity	9,385	9,522 e	9,963 e	10,292 e
16.103	Fair Housing and Equal Credit	13,352	13,541 e	14,168 e	14,636 e
16.104	Protection of Voting Rights	11,589	16,626 e	17,400 e	17,973 e
16.105	Institutionalized Persons	11,922	12,096 e	12,656 e	13,074 e
16.108	Disabilities Act Assistance	16,394	16,626 e	17,400 e	17,973 e
16.109	Civil Rights Prosecution	12,395	12,567 e	13,140 e	15,287 e
16.110	Education, Enforcement—Immigration	5,059	4,464 e	4,672 e	4,826 e
16.200	Community Relations Service	9,465	9,536 e	10,229 e	0 e
16.202	Offender Reentry Program	1,592	14,902	39,719 e	0 e
16.203	Sex Offender Management	4,273	3,270	4,665 e	0 e
16.300	FBI Advanced Police Training	15,072	15,464 e	15,866 e	0 e
16.301	FBI Crime Laboratory	165,496	167,444 e	186,164 e	0 e
16.302	FBI Field Police Training	10,456	10,770 e	10,985 e	0 e
16.303	FBI Fingerprint Identification	146,038	150,419 e	154,932 e	0 e
16.304	National Crime Information Center	23,494	24,199 e	24,925 e	0 e
16.305	Uniform Crime Reports	24,614	23,352 e	26,113 e	0 e
16.307	DNA Index System	7,165	7,947 e	7,947 e	0 e
16.308	Indian Country Investigations	1,115	1,166 e	1,198 e	0 e
16.309	Law Enforcement Assistance—NICS	23,452	24,156 e	24,881 e	0 e
16.320	Services for Trafficking Victims	13,730	16,660	9,774	0 e
16.321	Antiterrorism Emergency Reserve	878	33,510	51,773	50,000
16.523	Juvenile Accountability Incentives	69,433	46,744	46,617 e	0 e
16.524	Legal Assistance for Victims	28,370	39,212	32,915	32,789 e
16.525	Crimes Against Women/Campuses	9,052	8,909	8,563	8,123 e
16.526	Technical Assistance, Training	10,723	9,944	9,270	9,270 e
16.527	Supervised Visitation/Children	13,890	11,353	12,957	11,138 e
16.528	Elder Abuse, Neglect, Exploitation	4,539	4,593	4,032	4,388 e
16.529	Violence/Women with Disabilities	7,153	11,230	6,448 e	6,448 e
16.540	Juvenile Justice—States	69,500	78,788 e	74,588 e	0 e
16.541	Developing, Testing—New Programs	442	0	0	0 e
16.543	Missing Children's Assistance	47,160	47,840	47,387 e	0 e
16.547	Victims of Child Abuse	27,980	13,200	27,331 e	0 e
16.548	Delinquency Prevention Program	23,686	9,333	4,662 e	0 e
16.550	State Justice Statistics Program	2,160	2,100	2,500 e	0 e
16.554	Criminal History Improvement	27,833	9,418	9,385 e	0 e
16.556	State Violence Coalition Grants	8,952	9,598	8,969	8,969 e
16.557	Tribal Violence Coalition Grants	3,418	6,226	3,038	3,038 e
16.560	NIJ Research, Evaluation, Development	57,628	55,052	54,298 e	0 e
16.562	Graduate Research Fellowships	40	0	0 e	0 e
16.566	Dubois Fellowship Program	75	0	0 e	0 e
16.571	Public Safety Officers' Benefits	50,880	56,782	68,583 e	0 e
16.575	Crime Victim Assistance	372,807	395,918	370,600	268,064

Please see "Important Notes on the Tables, Footnotes," page 842

Table 1. *(continued)*

Program number	ADMINISTRATIVE ENTITY/SUB-UNIT Program Title (abridged)	FY 2005 in $thousands	FY 2006 in $thousands	FY 2007 in $thousands	FY 2008 in $thousands
16.576	Crime Victim Compensation	169,653	143,418	165,716	268,064
16.578	Federal Surplus Property Transfer	0	0	0	0 e
16.579	Byrne Formula Grant Program	64	0	0 e	0 e
16.580	Byrne Law Enforcement Assistance	189,838	212,196	189,256 e	0 e
16.582	Victim Assistance/Discretionary	28,626	28,327	29,527 e	28,283 e
16.583	Children's Justice/Indian	2,996	2,899	3,000 e	3,000 e
16.585	Drug Court Program	43,382	7,899	9,360 e	0 e
16.586	Violent Offender Incarceration	1,269	0	1,269 e	0 e
16.587	Violence Against Women/Indian	9,220	38,666	38,799 e	0
16.588	Violence Against Women	184,587	126,030	109,794	120,083 e
16.589	Rural Domestic Violence	28,316	38,666	38,799 e	0 e
16.590	Arrest Policies/Enforcement	51,804	60,354	56,022	50,842 e
16.593	Substance Abuse Treatment/Prisoners	33,147	9,753	9,360 e	0 e
16.595	Community Capacity Development Office	60,415	48,248	46,922	0 e
16.596	Correctional Grant/Tribes	22	13,858	7,488 e	0 e
16.597	Motor Vehicle Theft Protection Act	65	0	0 e	0 e
16.601	Corrections—Training	7,289	6,835	6,500 e	6,500 e
16.602	Corrections—Research	3,297	1,758	1,750 e	1,750 e
16.603	Corrections—Technical Assistance	4,815	4,952	5,250 e	5,250 e
16.606	Criminal Alien Assistance	2,933	295,468	379,097 e	0 e
16.607	Bulletproof Vest Partnership	13,911	38,032	28,153 e	0 e
16.608	Tribal Court Assistance	7,520	7,476	8,424 e	0 e
16.609	Community Prosecution	12,074	16,560	19,594 e	0 e
16.610	Regional Information Sharing	39,489	39,722	39,719	0 e
16.611	Closed-Circuit TV/Child Abuse	357	41	928 e	0 e
16.612	National White Collar Crime Center	8,916	8,885	8,885 e	0 e
16.613	Scams Targeting the Elderly	2,883	0	0 e	0 e
16.614	Anti-Terrorism Training	0	0	0 e	0 e
16.615	Public Safety Educational Assistance	852	882	3,814 e	0 e
16.616	Indian Alcohol and Drug Prevention	6,183	4,125	4,680 e	0 e
16.710	Public Safety, Community Policing	595,282	498,928	555,446	4,000 e
16.726	Juvenile Mentoring Program	9,853	70	9,323 e	0 e
16.727	Enforcing Underage Drinking Laws	25,679	23,896	23,309 e	0 e
16.730	Safe Start	11,133	10,134	9,409 e	0 e
16.731	Tribal Youth Program	9,831	9,405	9,323	0 e
16.734	Special Data Collections	(a)	(a)	(a)	(a)
16.735	Protecting Inmates, Communities	22,941	0	0	0 e
16.736	Transitional Housing/Victims	12,333	15,734	12,522	12,522 e
16.737	Gang Resistance Education, Training	15,151	32,061	23,309 e	0 e
16.738	Byrne Memorial Justice Assistance	493,498	290,710	473,154 e	0 e
16.739	National Prison Rape Statistics	20,354	13,510	13,868 e	0 e
16.740	Victim Information Notification	0	13,045	8,885 e	0 e
16.741	Forensic DNA Capacity Enhancement	0	39,535	44,250 e	0 e
16.742	Coverdell Forensic Sciences	9,598	18,264	17,361	0 e
16.743	Forensic DNA Backlog Reduction	0	18,728	18,728 e	0 e
16.744	Anti-Gang Initiative	0	35,339	42,776 e	0 e
16.745	Criminal and Mental Health Collaboration	0	4,653	4,680 e	0 e
16.746	Capital Case Litigation	0	931	936 e	0 e
16.747	Crime Victims' Rights Act	(n)	1,974 e	1,974 e	0 e
16.748	DNA Backlog Reduction	(n)	14,447	14,447 e	0 e
16.749	Radiation Exposure Compensation	(n)	51,000 e	38,000 e	31,000 e
16.750	Adam Walsh Act Grant	(n)	(n)	6,040	18,960
16.751	Byrne Competitive Grant	(n)	(n)	(n)	16,000 e
16.752	High-Tech Crime Prevention	(n)	(n)	(n)	5,000
16.753	Congressionally Recommended Awards	(n)	(n)	(n)	187,500
	DEPARTMENT TOTAL: OUTLAYS	3,514,503	3,668,223	4,006,330	1,271,732
	CREDITS*	0*	0*	0*	0*

Please see "Important Notes on the Tables, Footnotes," page 842

Table 1. *(continued)*

Program number	ADMINISTRATIVE ENTITY/SUB-UNIT Program Title (abridged)		FY 2005 in $thousands	FY 2006 in $thousands	FY 2007 in $thousands	FY 2008 in $thousands
	DEPARTMENT OF LABOR					
	BUREAU OF LABOR STATISTICS					
17.002	Labor Force Statistics		326,854	327,715	328,336	342,076 e
17.003	Prices and Cost of Living Data		169,204	172,927	177,797	192,149 e
17.004	Productivity and Technology Data		10,466	10,695	10,995,429	11,332 e
17.005	Compensation, Working Conditions		84,753	86,308	87,408	91,248 e
	Subtotal:	Outlays	591,277	597,645	11,588,970	636,805
		Credits*	0*	0*	0*	0*
	EMPLOYEE BENEFITS SECURITY ADMINISTRATION					
17.150	Employee Benefits Security		131	134	135	143 e
	Subtotal:	Outlays	131	134	135	143
		Credits*	0*	0*	0*	0*
	EMPLOYMENT AND TRAINING ADMINISTRATION					
17.201	Registered Apprenticeship, Training		21,000	22,000	22,000 e	23,000 e
17.207	Employment Service \ t		892,000	828,000	792,000 e	747,000 e
17.225	Unemployment Insurance \ t		35,791,000	34,657,000	35,050,000 e	37,392,000 e
17.235	Senior Community Service		437,000	432,000	432,000 e	350,000 e
17.245	Trade Adjustment Assistance		269,000	259,000	260,000 e	260,000 e
17.258	WIA Adult Program		891,000	857,000	861,000 e	712,000 e
17.259	WIA Youth Activities		971,494	928,000	932,000 e	828,000 e
17.260	WIA Dislocated Workers		1,454,000	1,274,000	1,224,000 e	1,056,000 e
17.261	Pilots, Demonstration, Research		132,000	136,000	82,000 e	91,000 e
17.264	Migrant, Seasonal Farmworkers		76,000	80,000	80,000 e	0 e
17.265	Native American Employment		70,000	68,000	68,000 e	58,000 e
17.266	Work Incentives Grant		18,000	28,000	23,000 e	0 e
17.267	WIA Incentive Grants—Section 503		17,000	17,000	16,000 e	10,000 e
17.268	H-1B Job Training Grants		47,000	95,000	111,000 e	94,000 e
17.269	Job Training Grants		0	124,000	249,000 e	150,000 e
17.270	Prisoner Reentry		0	20,000	20,000 e	0 e
17.271	Work Opportunity Tax Credit		18,000	18,000	18,000 e	18,000 e
17.272	Permanent Labor Certification, Foreign		9,000	42,000	50,000 e	63,000 e
17.273	Temporary Labor Certification, Foreign		49,000	22,000	22,000 e	24,000 e
17.274	Youth Build Program		(n)	0	50,000 e	50,000 e
	Subtotal:	Outlays	41,162,494	39,907,000	40,362,000	41,926,000
		Credits*	0*	0*	0*	0*
	EMPLOYMENT STANDARDS ADMINISTRATION					
17.301	Federal, Construction Contractors		80	81	83 e	84 e
17.302	Longshore and Harbor Workers		148	147	144 e	150 e
17.303	Wage, Hour Standards \ i		164	167	170	182 e
17.306	Consumer Credit Protection		(o)	(o)	(o)	(o)
17.307	Coal Mine Workers' Compensation \ t		359	626	577 e	536 e
17.308	Farm Labor Contractors		(o)	(o)	(o)	(o)
17.309	Labor Organization Reports		42	45	45 e	57 e
17.310	Occupational Illness Compensation		618	886,000	964 e	1,197 e
	Subtotal:	Outlays	1,411	887,066	1,983	2,206
		Credits*	0*	0*	0*	0*
	OCCUPATIONAL SAFETY AND HEALTH ADMINISTRATION					
17.502	Susan Harwood Training		10,217	10,175	10,116 e	0 e
17.503	State Program		91,013	91,093	91,093 e	91,093 e
17.504	Consultation Agreements		53,362	53,357 e	53,357 e	0 e
17.505	OSHA Data Initiative		1,533	1,528	1,351 e	1,351 e
	Subtotal:	Outlays	156,125	156,153	155,917	92,444
		Credits*	0*	0*	0*	0*

Please see "Important Notes on the Tables, Footnotes," page 842

Table 1. *(continued)*

Program number	ADMINISTRATIVE ENTITY/SUB-UNIT Program Title (abridged)		FY 2005 in $thousands	FY 2006 in $thousands	FY 2007 in $thousands	FY 2008 in $thousands
	MINE SAFETY AND HEALTH ADMINISTRATION					
17.600	Mine Health and Safety Grants		7,973	7,973	8,204 e	8,941 e
17.601	Mine Health, Safety Counseling		25,111	26,079	29,237 e	28,200 e
17.602	Mine Health, Safety Education		11,300	10,800	12,400 e	11,900 e
17.603	Brookwood-Sago Grant		(n)	(n)	500	500 e
	Subtotal:	Outlays	44,384	44,852	50,341	49,541
		Credits*	0*	0*	0*	0*
	OFFICE OF THE SECRETARY, WOMEN'S BUREAU					
17.700	Women's Bureau		9,478	9,666	9,666	9,832 e
	Subtotal:	Outlays	9,478	9,666	9,666	9,832
		Credits*	0*	0*	0*	0*
	OFFICE OF DISABILITY EMPLOYMENT POLICY					
17.720	Disability Employment Policy		47,164	27,655	27,712	18,602 e
	Subtotal:	Outlays	47,164	27,655	27,712	18,602
		Credits*	0*	0*	0*	0*
	OFFICE OF THE ASSISTANT SECRETARY FOR VETERANS' EM					
17.801	Disabled Veterans Outreach		81,187	77,319	77,494	79,805 e
17.802	Veterans Employment Program		7,505	7,425	7,435 e	7,351 e
17.803	Uniformed Services/Rights		(a)	(a)	(a)	(a)
17.804	Local Veterans Employment		75,567	77,726	76,372	76,466 e
17.805	Homeless Veterans Reintegration		18,888	21,077	20,285 e	23,630 e
17.806	Preference/Federal Employment		(a)	(a)	(a)	(a)
17.807	Transition Assistance Program		55,914	2,828 e	3,128 e	0 e
	Subtotal:	Outlays	239,061	186,375	184,714	187,252
		Credits*	0*	0*	0*	0*
	DEPARTMENT TOTAL:	OUTLAYS	42,251,525	41,816,546	52,381,438	42,922,825
		CREDITS*	0*	0*	0*	0*

DEPARTMENT OF STATE

Program number	ADMINISTRATIVE ENTITY/SUB-UNIT Program Title (abridged)		FY 2005 in $thousands	FY 2006 in $thousands	FY 2007 in $thousands	FY 2008 in $thousands
	BUREAU OF OCEANS AND INTERNATIONAL ENVIRONMENTAL A					
19.204	Fishermen's Guaranty Fund		0	0	500 e	0 e
	Subtotal:	Outlays	0	0	500	0
		Credits*	0*	0*	0*	0*
	BUREAU OF INTELLIGENCE AND RESEARCH					
19.300	Study/Eastern Europe		4,600	4,200 e	4,200 e	0 e
	Subtotal:	Outlays	4,600	4,200	4,200	0
		Credits*	0*	0*	0*	0*
	BUREAU OF EDUCATIONAL AND CULTURAL AFFAIRS					
19.400	Educational Exchange—Graduate		54,700	57,700 e	60,700 e	0 e
19.401	Lecturers and Research Scholars		41,550	42,550 e	43,550 e	0 e
19.402	International Visitors Program		10,612	11,012 e	11,360 e	0 e
19.403	Young Political Leaders		890	890	890 e	0 e
19.408	Exchange—Secondary, Postsecondary		10,250	10,890 e	12,390 e	0 e
19.409	Art Exchanges on International Issues		1,000	1,200 e	1,000 e	0 e
19.410	Exchange—Bundestag Youth		3,176	3,256	3,256 e	0 e
19.415	Professional Exchanges		5,545	5,800 e	7,050 e	0 e
19.418	American Studies Institutes		3,000	3,118	3,200 e	0 e
19.421	English Language Fellow Program		4,973	6,800	6,800 e	0 e
19.423	English Language Specialist		729	600 e	600 e	0 e
19.425	Gilman International Scholarship		2,600	3,712	5,000 e	0 e
19.430	International Education, Research		725	1,625 e	1,625 e	0 e
19.431	Scholar-In-Residence		1,000	1,300	1,300 e	0 e

Please see "Important Notes on the Tables, Footnotes," page 842

Table 1. *(continued)*

Program number	ADMINISTRATIVE ENTITY/SUB-UNIT Program Title (abridged)		FY 2005 in $thousands	FY 2006 in $thousands	FY 2007 in $thousands	FY 2008 in $thousands
19.432	Overseas Educational Advising		1,720	1,775 e	1,775 e	0 e
	Subtotal:	Outlays	142,470	152,228	160,496	0
		Credits*	0*4	0*	0*	0*
	BUREAU OF NEAR EASTERN AFFAIRS					
19.500	Middle East Partnership Initiative		74,400	99,000	120	0 e
	Subtotal:	Outlays	74,400	99,000	120	0
		Credits*	0*	0*	0*	0*
	BUREAU OF POPULATION, REFUGEES, AND MIGRATION					
19.510	U.S. Refugee Admissions		55,440	55,363	74,600 e	0 e
19.511	Refugee Assistance/East Asia		22,758	22,621	0 e	0 e
19.517	Refugee Assistance/Africa		229,342	245,590	0 e	0 e
19.518	Refugee Assistance/Western Hemisphere		25,373	19,476 e	0 e	0 e
19.519	Refugee/Near East, South Asia		157,940	14,619 e	0	0 e
19.520	Refugee Assistance/Europe		50,000	44,371 e	40,000 e	0 e
19.522	Refugee/Strategic Global Priorities		58,704	67,900	63,000	0 e
	Subtotal:	Outlays	599,557	469,940	177,600	0
		Credits*	0*	0*	0*	0*
	DEPARTMENT TOTAL:	OUTLAYS	821,027	725,368	342,916	0
		CREDITS*	0*	0*	0*	0*
	DEPARTMENT OF TRANSPORTATION					
	FEDERAL AVIATION ADMINISTRATION					
20.100	Aviation Education		0	0	0 e	0 e
20.106	Airport Improvement Program \ t		3,590,507	3,423,404 e	2,647,000 e	0 e
20.108	Aviation Research \ t		30,000	30,000 e	0 e	0 e
20.109	Air Transportation Centers \ t		7,800	7,800 e	0 e	0 e
	Subtotal:	Outlays	3,628,307	3,461,204	2,647,000	0
		Credits*	0*	0*	0*	0*
	FEDERAL HIGHWAY ADMINISTRATION					
20.200	Highway Research, Development		(o)	(o)	(o)	(o)
20.205	Highway Planning, Construction \ i, t		26,451,172	24,244,734	26,000,000 e	0 e
20.215	Highway Training, Education \ t		(o)	(o)	(o)	(o)
20.218	National Motor Carrier Safety \ t		184,375	184,375	197,000	202,000 e
20.219	Recreational Trails \ t		(o)	(o)	(o)	(o)
20.223	Transportation Infrastructure Finance \ u		(n)*	42,000*	1,228,000*e	0*e
20.231	Registration Information Management \ t		4,960	5,015	5,967	0 e
20.232	Commercial Driver License State \ t		0	25,000	25,000	25,000 e
20.233	Border Enforcement Grants \ t		(n)	32,000	32,000 e	32,000 e
20.234	Safety Data Improvement Program \ t		0	1,000	2,000 e	0 e
20.235	Commercial Operator Training \ t		1,000	1,000	1,000 e	0 e
20.236	Thermal Imaging Inspection \ t		0	1,412	0	0 e
20.237	Commercial Vehicle Information		0	25,000	25,000 e	0 e
20.238	Commercial Drivers License Information \ t		(n)	5,000	7,000 e	8,000 e
20.240	Fuel Tax Evasion Enforcement \ t		0	1,000	1,000 e	0 e
	Subtotal:	Outlays	26,641,507	24,525,536	26,295,967	267,000
		Credits*	0*	42,000*	1,228,000*	0*
	FEDERAL RAILROAD ADMINISTRATION					
20.301	Railroad Safety		51,501,000	531,500 e	0 e	0 e
20.303	Grants/Railroad Safety		1,025	41,367	1,400 e	0 e
20.312	High Speed Ground Transportation \ t		21,500	21,500	20,000 e	0 e
20.313	Railroad Research and Development		980	984	980 e	0 e
20.314	Railroad Development		0	0	3,500	66,100 e
20.315	Railroad Passenger Corporation Grants		(n)	1,293,633	1,293,633	1,325,000
20.316	Railroad Rehabilitation \ u		(n)*	189,784*	234,039*e	638,000*e

Please see "Important Notes on the Tables, Footnotes," page 842

Table 1. *(continued)*

Program number	ADMINISTRATIVE ENTITY/SUB-UNIT Program Title (abridged)		FY 2005 in $thousands	FY 2006 in $thousands	FY 2007 in $thousands	FY 2008 in $thousands
20.317	Intercity Rail Assistance		(n)	0	0 e	0 e
	Subtotal:	Outlays	51,524,505	1,888,984	1,319,513	1,391,100
		Credits*	0*	189,784*	234,039*	638,000*
	FEDERAL TRANSIT ADMINISTRATION					
20.500	Capital Investment Grants \ t		3,421,571	1,565,699 e	0 e	0 e
20.505	Metropolitan Planning Grants \ t		59,902	123,211 e	0 e	0 e
20.507	Urbanized Area Formula Grants \ t		4,000,000	1,565,699	5,540,822	4,230,751
20.509	Nonurbanized Areas		490,702	294,480 e	0	0 e
20.513	Elderly, Persons with Disabilities \ t		152,330	95,093 e	0	0 e
20.514	Transit Planning, Research \ t		27,435	37,200	34,415 e	0 e
20.515	State Planning and Research \ t		12,513	25,730 e	0 e	0 e
20.516	Job Access—Reverse Commute \ t		126,760	123,211 e	0 e	0 e
20.518	Over-the-Road Bus Accessibility \ t		6,950	6,950 e	0 e	0 e
20.519	Clean Fuels		0	17,607	43,000 e	0 e
20.521	New Freedom Program		0	78,000	81,000	0 e
20.522	Alternatives Analysis		(n)	24,750	25,000	0 e
	Subtotal:	Outlays	8,298,163	3,957,630	5,724,237	4,230,751
		Credits*	0*	0*	0*	0*
	NATIONAL HIGHWAY TRAFFIC SAFETY ADMINISTRATION					
20.600	State, Community Highway Safety \ t		160,000	160,000	167,000 e	0 e
20.601	Drunk Driving Prevention \ t		120,000	125,000	131,000	139,000 e
20.602	Occupant Protection \ t		19,840	25,000	25,000	0 e
20.605	Drunk Driving Safety Incentives \ t		(n)	85,000	85,000 e	0 e
20.607	Alcohol Open Container \ t		112,000	112,000	112,000 e	0 e
20.608	Penalties/Repeat Offenders \ t		173,000	173,000	173,000 e	0 e
20.609	Safety Belt Performance Grants \ t		124,500	124,500	124,500 e	124,500 e
20.610	Traffic Safety Information System		0	34,500	34,500 e	34,500 e
20.611	Prohibit Racial Profiling Incentive \ t		0	15,000	7,500	0 e
20.612	Motorcyclist Safety Incentive \ t		0	6,000	7,000 e	7,000
20.613	Child Safety/Booster Seats Incentive \ t		0	6,000	6,000	0 e
20.614	Highway Safety Grants		0	35,000	40,000	0 e
	Subtotal:	Outlays	709,340	901,000	912,500	305,000
		Credits*	0*	0*	0*	0*
	RESEARCH AND SPECIAL PROGRAMS ADMINISTRATION					
20.700	Pipeline Safety		19,209	19,331	19,518	20,000 e
20.701	University Transportation Centers		(n)	76,700	76,700	0 e
20.703	Hazardous Materials Training		0	12,800	12,800	27 e
20.704	RITA Hydrogen		4,000	3,000	3,000	0 e
20.720	State Damage Prevention Grants		(n)	(n)	(n)	1,500 e
20.721	Pipeline Safety		(n)	1,010	1,021	1,043
20.760	University Transportation		76,700	76,700	76,700	0 e
20.761	Biobased Transportation		(n)	12,500	12,500	0 e
20.762	Research Grants		0	706	1,000	1,000 e
20.763	Hydrogen Alternative Fuel		(n)	1,000	1,000	1,000
20.764	Hydrogen Storage Research		(n)	0	41,200 e	400 e
	Subtotal:	Outlays	99,909	203,747	245,439	24,970
		Credits*	0*	0*	0*	0*
	MARITIME ADMINISTRATION					
20.801	Ports, Intermodal Transportation		143	145	145 e	0 e
20.802	Federal Ship Financing \ u		38,482*	0*e	0*e	0*e
20.803	Maritime War Risk Insurance \ u		0	0	0	0 e
20.806	State Marine Schools		10,490	10,611	0 e	0 e
20.807	U.S. Merchant Marine Academy		55,914	63,854	0 e	0 e
20.808	Capital Construction Fund		141	143	0 e	0 e
20.810	Supplementary Training		85	0	0 e	0 e
20.812	Construction Reserve Fund		11	11	0 e	0 e
20.813	Maritime Security Fleet Program		99,577	154,400	0	0 e
20.814	Small Shipyard Assistance		(n)	(n)	(n)	10,000 e
	Subtotal:	Outlays	166,361	229,164	145	10,000
		Credits*	38,482*	0*	0*	0*

Please see "Important Notes on the Tables, Footnotes," page 842

Table 1. *(continued)*

Program number	ADMINISTRATIVE ENTITY/SUB-UNIT Program Title (abridged)		FY 2005 in $thousands	FY 2006 in $thousands	FY 2007 in $thousands	FY 2008 in $thousands
	OFFICE OF THE SECRETARY					
20.900	Transportation—Consumer Affairs		1,825	1,871	1,645	2,046 e
20.901	Essential Air Services \ t		102,000	109,000	50,000 e	0 e
20.904	Bonding Assistance		(n)	0	0	0
20.905	Disadvantaged—Short-Term Lending		7,642*	0*	0*	0*
20.910	Small Business Assistance		(n)	0	1,350 e	0 e
20.930	Small Community Air Service \ t		18,953	10,000 e	10,000 e	0 e
20.931	Transportation Planning		6,351	4,689	3,000 e	0 e
	Subtotal:	Outlays	129,129	125,560	65,995	2,046
		Credits*	7,642*	0*	0*	0*
	DEPARTMENT TOTAL:	OUTLAYS	91,197,221	35,292,825	37,210,796	6,230,867
		CREDITS*	46,124*	231,784*	1,462,039*	638,000*
	DEPARTMENT OF THE TREASURY					
	INTERNAL REVENUE SERVICE					
21.003	Taxpayer Service		1,120,967	1,128,045 e	1,096,746 e	1,074,688 e
21.004	Federal Tax Information/States		0	0	0 e	0 e
21.006	Tax Counseling/Elderly		3,950	3,950	3,950 e	4,000 e
21.008	Low-Income Taxpayer Clinics		8,000	8,000	8,000	9,000 e
	Subtotal:	Outlays	1,132,917	1,139,995	1,108,696	1,087,688
		Credits*	0*	0*	0*	0*
	UNDER SECRETARY FOR DOMESTIC FINANCE					
21.020	Community Development Program		50,519	27,219	27,387	55,000 e
21.021	Bank Enterprise Award		17,008	11,993 e	11,168 e	20,000 e
	Subtotal:	Outlays	67,527	39,212	38,555	75,000
		Credits*	0*	0*	0*	0*
	DEPARTMENT TOTAL:	OUTLAYS	1,200,444	1,179,207	1,147,251	1,162,688
		CREDITS*	0*	0*	0*	0*
	APPALACHIAN REGIONAL COMMISSION					
23.001	Appalachian Regional Development		(o)	(o)	(o)	(o)
23.002	Appalachian Area Development		62,682	61,784 e	58,917	73,000 e
23.003	Highway System		325,065	395,296 e	423,820	470,000 e
23.009	Development District Assistance		6,239	6,233 e	6,135	7,000 e
23.011	Research, Technical Assistance		1,200	900 e	764	1,000 e
	DEPARTMENT TOTAL:	OUTLAYS	395,186	464,213	489,636	551,000
		CREDITS*	0*	0*	0*	0*
	OFFICE OF PERSONNEL MANAGEMENT					
27.001	Federal Civil Service		(a)	(a)	(a)	(a)
27.002	Employment Assistance/Veterans		(a)	(a)	(a)	(a)
27.003	Federal Student Employment		(a)	(a)	(a)	(a)
27.005	Federal Employment/Disabled		(a)	(a)	(a)	(a)
27.006	Federal Summer Employment		(a)	(a)	(a)	(a)
27.011	Intergovernmental Mobility		(a)	(a)	(a)	(a)
27.013	Presidential Management Intern \ r		(a)	(a)	(a)	(a)
	DEPARTMENT TOTAL:	OUTLAYS	0	0	0	0
		CREDITS*	0*	0*	0*	0*
	COMMISSION ON CIVIL RIGHTS					
29.001	Clearinghouse Services		8,740	8,740 e	8,740 e	0 e
	DEPARTMENT TOTAL:	OUTLAYS	8,740	8,740	8,740	0
		CREDITS*	0*	0*	0*	0*

Please see "Important Notes on the Tables, Footnotes," page 842

Table 1. *(continued)*

Program number	ADMINISTRATIVE ENTITY/SUB-UNIT Program Title (abridged)		FY 2005 in $thousands	FY 2006 in $thousands	FY 2007 in $thousands	FY 2008 in $thousands
	EQUAL EMPLOYMENT OPPORTUNITY COMMISSION					
30.001	Title VII/Civil Rights \ i		326,848	326,804 e	331,228 e	0 e
30.002	Fair Employment Agencies \ i		32,539	32,579 e	28,000 e	0 e
30.005	Private Bar Program		(a)	(a)	(a)	(a)
30.008	Age Discrimination		(o)	(o)	(o)	(o)
30.009	Indian Tribes		(o)	(o)	(o)	(o)
30.010	Discrimination Equal Pay Act		(o)	(o)	(o)	(o)
30.011	Title I ADA, Investigations		(o)	(o)	(o)	(o)
	DEPARTMENT TOTAL:	OUTLAYS	359,387	359,383	359,228	0
		CREDITS*	0*	0*	0*	0*
	FEDERAL COMMUNICATIONS COMMISSION					
32.001	Information, Investigation		(a)	(a)	(a)	(a)
	DEPARTMENT TOTAL:	OUTLAYS	0	0	0	0
		CREDITS*	0*	0*	0*	0*
	FEDERAL MARITIME COMMISSION					
33.001	Shipping—Complaints		733	997 e	1,047 e	0 e
	DEPARTMENT TOTAL:	OUTLAYS	733	997	1,047	0
		CREDITS*	0*	0*	0*	0*
	FEDERAL MEDIATION AND CONCILIATION SERVICE					
34.001	Labor Mediation, Conciliation		44,439	42,601	42,849 e	43,800 e
34.002	Labor Management Cooperation		1,488	396 e	396 e	0 e
	DEPARTMENT TOTAL:	OUTLAYS	45,927	42,997	43,245	43,800
		CREDITS*	0*	0*	0*	0*
	FEDERAL TRADE COMMISSION					
36.001	Fair Competition Counseling		200,477	210,080	223,635 e	240,239 e
	DEPARTMENT TOTAL:	OUTLAYS	200,477	210,080	223,635	240,239
		CREDITS*	0*	0*	0*	0*
	GENERAL SERVICES ADMINISTRATION					
39.002	Real Property Disposal \ p		25,377	22,559	51,547 e	41,973 e
39.003	Personal Property Donation \ p		11,236	11,485	11,507 e	12,645 e
39.007	Personal Property Sale \ p, r		15,331	15,063	16,128	23,999 e
39.009	Federal Citizen Information Center \ r, u		20,016	24,112	29,686 e	24,863 e
	DEPARTMENT TOTAL:	OUTLAYS	71,960	73,219	108,868	103,480
		CREDITS*	0*	0*	0*	0*
	GOVERNMENT PRINTING OFFICE					
40.001	Depository Libraries		31,697	33,004 e	43,000 e	0 e
40.002	Government Publications Sales \ p, r		29,000	24,800 e	0 e	0 e
	DEPARTMENT TOTAL:	OUTLAYS	60,697	57,804	43,000	0
		CREDITS*	0*	0*	0*	0*

Please see "Important Notes on the Tables, Footnotes," page 842

Table 1. *(continued)*

Program number	ADMINISTRATIVE ENTITY/SUB-UNIT Program Title (abridged)		FY 2005 in $thousands	FY 2006 in $thousands	FY 2007 in $thousands	FY 2008 in $thousands
	LIBRARY OF CONGRESS					
42.001	Books for the Blind, Handicapped		53,403	54,518	38,040	75,623 e
42.002	Copyright Service \ i, u		46,097	51,676	48,651	51,562 e
42.008	Semiconductor Chip Protection \ u		(o)	(o)	(o)	(o)
42.009	Vessel Hull Design Protection \ u		(o)	(o)	(o)	(o)
	DEPARTMENT TOTAL:	OUTLAYS	99,500	106,194	86,691	127,185
		CREDITS*	0*	0*	0*	0*
	NATIONAL AERONAUTICS AND SPACE ADMINISTRATION					
43.001	Aerospace Education Services		10,300	10,336	6,340 e	0 e
43.002	Technology Transfer		28,600	42,853	24,200 e	31,000 e
	DEPARTMENT TOTAL:	OUTLAYS	38,900	53,189	30,540	31,000
		CREDITS*	0*	0*	0*	0*
	NATIONAL CREDIT UNION ADMINISTRATION					
44.001	Credit Union Charter \ u		233,000*	238,000*	268,000*e	274,000*e
44.002	Revolving Loan Program \ u		4,574*	2,879*	7,300*e	2,500*e
	DEPARTMENT TOTAL:	OUTLAYS	0	0	0	0
		CREDITS*	237,574*	240,879*	275,300*	276,500*
	NATIONAL FOUNDATION ON THE ARTS AND THE HUMANITIES					
	NATIONAL ENDOWMENT FOR THE ARTS					
45.024	Organizations and Individuals		61,113	61,001	60,191 e	61,765 e
45.025	Partnership Agreements		39,083	41,434	40,128 e	41,177 e
	Subtotal:	Outlays	100,196	100,196	100,196	100,196
		Credits*	0*	0*	0*	0*
	NATIONAL ENDOWMENT FOR THE HUMANITIES					
45.129	Federal-State Partnership		36,886	38,721	38,818	31,215 e
45.130	Challenge Grants		12,703	10,456	10,274	9,479 e
45.149	Preservation and Access		22,422	24,520	23,905	17,671 e
45.160	Fellowships and Stipends		8,891	7,158	6,796	5,450 e
45.161	Research		7,131	8,748	8,970	6,759 e
45.162	Teaching, Learning, Curriculum		3,536	3,426	2,224	2,401 e
45.163	Professional Development		11,177	11,020	14,359	9,400 e
45.164	Public Programs		14,424	15,511	13,847	11,910 e
45.168	We the People		11,217	115,239	15,239	15,239 e
45.169	Digital Humanities Initiative		(a)	(a)	(a)	(a)
	Subtotal:	Outlays	128,387	234,799	134,432	109,524
		Credits*	0*	0*	0*	0*
	FEDERAL COUNCIL ON THE ARTS AND THE HUMANITIES					
45.201	Arts and Artifacts Indemnity		0*	0*e	0*e	0*e
	Subtotal:	Outlays	0	0	0	0
		Credits*	0*	0*	0*	0*
	INSTITUTE OF MUSEUM AND LIBRARY SERVICES					
45.301	Museum for America Grants		16,864	17,152	17,152	22,165 e
45.302	Museum Assessment Program		446	442	442	471 e
45.303	Conservation Project Support		2,788	2,772	2,772	3,801 e
45.304	Conservation Assessment Program		815	807	807	814 e
45.307	21st Century Museum Professionals		992	1,671	1,500 e	2,141 e
45.308	Native American/Hawaiian Museum		843	911	911	945 e
45.309	African American History Grants		0	842	842	1,350 e
45.310	State Library Program		160,704	163,746	163,746	171,500 e

Please see "Important Notes on the Tables, Footnotes," page 842

Table 1. *(continued)*

Program number	ADMINISTRATIVE ENTITY/SUB-UNIT Program Title (abridged)		FY 2005 in $thousands	FY 2006 in $thousands	FY 2007 in $thousands	FY 2008 in $thousands
45.311	Native American, Hawaiian Library		3,472	3,638	3,638	3,717 e
45.312	National Leadership Grants		19,840	20,295	20,295	20,925 e
45.313	Librarians for the 21st Century		22,816	23,760	23,760	26,500 e
	Subtotal:	Outlays	229,580	236,036	235,865	254,329
		Credits*	0*	0*	0*	0*
	DEPARTMENT TOTAL:	OUTLAYS	458,163	571,031	470,493	464,049
		CREDITS*	0*	0*	0*	0*
	NATIONAL LABOR RELATIONS BOARD					
46.001	Labor-Management Relations \ u		249,973	249,940	249,888 e	0 e
	DEPARTMENT TOTAL:	OUTLAYS	249,973	249,940	249,888	0
		CREDITS*	0*	0*	0*	0*
	NATIONAL SCIENCE FOUNDATION					
47.041	Engineering Grants		557,090	585,460	629,990	636,870 e
47.049	Mathematical, Physical Sciences		1,069,360	1,086,610	1,150,730	1,167,310 e
47.050	Geosciences		697,170	703,950	745,850	752,660 e
47.070	Computer, Information Science		490,200	496,350	526,680	534,530 e
47.074	Biological Sciences		576,780	580,900	608,540	612,020 e
47.075	Social, Behavioral, Economic		196,800	201,230	214,540	215,130 e
47.076	Education and Human Resources		843,540	700,260	695,650	725,600 e
47.078	Polar Programs		122,540	122,420	145,920	151,200 e
47.079	International Science, Engineering		33,960	34,880	40,360	41,340 e
47.080	Office of Cyberinfrastructure		126,115	127,140	182,420	185,330 e
47.081	Competitive Research		(n)	98,220	102,110	111,100 e
	DEPARTMENT TOTAL:	OUTLAYS	4,713,555	4,737,420	5,042,790	5,133,090
		CREDITS*	0*	0*	0*	0*
	RAILROAD RETIREMENT BOARD					
57.001	Social Insurance/Railroad Workers \ t		9,265,000	9,534,000	9,907,000 e	10,178,000 e
	DEPARTMENT TOTAL:	OUTLAYS	9,265,000	9,534,000	9,907,000	10,178,000
		CREDITS*	0*	0*	0*	0*
	SECURITIES AND EXCHANGE COMMISSION					
58.001	Investigation of Complaints		888,227	888,117 e	904,846 e	0 e
	DEPARTMENT TOTAL:	OUTLAYS	888,227	888,117	904,846	0
		CREDITS*	0*	0*	0*	0*
	SMALL BUSINESS ADMINISTRATION					
59.006	8(a) Business Development		35,066	29,582	41,191	35,952 e
59.007	(7j) Technical Assistance		3,116	2,289	3,340	2,472 e
59.008	Physical Disaster Loans		0*	0*e	0*e	0*e
59.009	Procurement Assistance		24,118	28,091	26,667	35,614 e
59.011	Small Business Investment Companies		15,874	3,648	4,382	4,960
			355,290*	477,300*	707,470*e	3,000,000*e
59.012	Small Business Loans		14,336,672*	13,799,941*	17,541,823*	17,546,173*e
59.016	Bond Guarantees \ u		493,258*	517,830*	544,750*e	811,124*e
59.026	Service Corps of Retired Executives		18,507	16,932	9,799	19,430 e
59.037	Small Business Development Center		103,541	103,007	101,241	104,726 e
59.041	Certified Development Company Loans		14,190	16,046	16,028	18,369
			5,000,000*	5,700,500*	6,282,000*	7,500,000*e
59.043	Women's Business Ownership		23,555	22,033	20,432	23,193 e

Please see "Important Notes on the Tables, Footnotes," page 842

Table 1. *(continued)*

Program number	ADMINISTRATIVE ENTITY/SUB-UNIT Program Title (abridged)		FY 2005 in $thousands	FY 2006 in $thousands	FY 2007 in $thousands	FY 2008 in $thousands
59.044	Veterans Entrepreneurial Training		3,253	3,590	4,180 e	4,727 e
59.046	Microloan Program		15,668	1,702	1,775	1,955
			21,553*	32,825*	33,861*	25,000*e
59.049	Disadvantaged Business Certification		1,614	1,772	1,235	2,130 e
59.050	Microenterprise Development Grants		14,129	1,926	1,863	0 e
59.051	Operational Assistance Grants		349	317	361	0 e
59.052	Native American Economic Development		3,530	3,740	1,415	3,505 e
59.053	Ombudsman, Fairness Boards		1,469	1,270	1,407	0 e
59.054	7(a) Export Loans		682,175	4,304	5,258	5,231 e
59.055	Historically Underutilized Business Zones		6,789	7,496	6,767	8,790 e
59.070	Drug-Free Workplace		(n)	(n)	859	1,086
	DEPARTMENT TOTAL:	OUTLAYS	966,943	247,745	248,200	272,140
		CREDITS*	20,206,773*	20,528,396*	25,109,904*	28,882,297*
	DEPARTMENT OF VETERANS AFFAIRS					
	VETERANS HEALTH ADMINISTRATION					
64.005	Construction/State Homes		123,109	87,933	73,515 e	165,000 e
64.007	Blind Rehabilitation Centers		69,238	72,403	80,654 e	87,775 e
64.008	Veterans Domiciliary Care		379,089	351,958	386,728 e	396,199 e
64.009	Veterans Medical Care Benefits		29,708,964	31,697,755	32,326,744 e	36,789,140 e
64.010	Veterans Nursing Home Care		3,174,233	3,050,891	3,316,900	3,505,986 e
64.011	Veterans Dental Care		389,957	400,468	490,700 e	524,021 e
64.012	Veterans Prescription Service \ p		4,226,712	4,284,888	4,510,000 e	5,001,950 e
64.013	Veterans Prosthetic Appliances \ p		1,038,558	1,118,980	1,231,512 e	1,339,131 e
64.014	Veterans State Domiciliary Care		43,528	41,452	45,332 e	49,245 e
64.015	Veterans State Nursing Homes		381,674	413,343	451,305 e	508,794 e
64.016	Veterans State Hospital Care		8,285	3,444	4,226 e	4,470 e
64.018	Sharing Specialized Medical Resources		687,000	728,000	798,000 e	868,000 e
64.019	Alcohol and Drug Dependence		342,415	358,292	355,854 e	357,993 e
64.022	Home Based Primary Care		134,253	168,550	158,927	207,546 e
64.024	Homeless Providers Grants		62,180	63,621	92,180 e	107,180 e
64.026	State Adult Day Health Care		245	237	228 e	291 e
	Subtotal:	Outlays	40,769,440	42,842,215	44,322,805	49,912,721
		Credits*	0*	0*	0*	0*
	VETERANS BENEFITS ADMINISTRATION					
64.100	Automobiles, Adaptive Equipment		53,514	50,737	51,800 e	53,000 e
64.101	Burial Expenses Allowance		153,340	141,349	201,197 e	227,533 e
64.103	Life Insurance \ t, u		2,536,907	3,303,928	3,371,152 e	2,714,683 e
			0*	0*	0*	0*
64.104	Pension/Non-Service Connected		2,651,724	2,747,281	2,814,409 e	2,883,173 e
64.105	Pension/Survivors		730,786	777,752	830,506 e	889,162 e
64.106	Specially Adapted Housing		28,229	25,780	26,520 e	26,520 e
64.109	Service-Connected Disability		24,445,389	26,469,578	29,603,277 e	32,681,865 e
64.110	Dependency, Indemnity Compensation		4,197,473	4,363,348	4,505,306 e	4,660,982 e
64.114	Veterans Housing—Loans \ u		22,543,614*	24,464,918*	24,490,503*e	29,104,463*e
64.115	Veterans Information, Assistance		(a)	(a)	(a)	(a)
64.116	Vocational Rehabilitation \ u		573,290	574,270	626,948 e	672,005 e
			3,096*	2,808*	2,403*e	3,287*e
64.117	Dependents Educational Assistance		388,719	413,136	450,234 e	479,277 e
64.118	Housing—Disabled Veterans \ u		0*	0*	0*e	0*e
64.119	Manufactured Home Loans \ u		0*	0*	0*e	0*e
64.120	Post-Vietnam Era Educational \ t		2,842	2,366	1,922 e	1,626 e
64.124	All-Volunteer Force Educational		1,887,239	1,937,037	2,014,608 e	2,066,195 e
64.125	Vocational, Educational Counseling		5,875	5,121	6,000 e	6,000 e
64.126	Native American Direct Loan \ u		6,157*	2,786*	7,378*e	3,668*e
64.127	Allowance/Spina Bifida		17,015	17,573	18,247 e	18,676 e
64.128	Training/Spina Bifida		1	2	2 e	0 e
	Subtotal:	Outlays	37,672,343	40,829,258	44,522,128	47,380,697
		Credits*	22,552,867*	24,470,512*	24,500,284*	29,111,418*

Table 1. *(continued)*

Program number	ADMINISTRATIVE ENTITY/SUB-UNIT Program Title (abridged)		FY 2005 in $thousands	FY 2006 in $thousands	FY 2007 in $thousands	FY 2008 in $thousands
	NATIONAL CEMETERY SYSTEM					
64.201	National Cemeteries		141,559	146,372	159,078 e	163,690 e
64.202	Headstones, Markers, Certificates		43,104	42,060	45,019 e	45,825 e
64.203	State Cemetery Grants		36,107	17,776	46,226 e	37,000 e
	Subtotal:	Outlays	220,770	206,208	250,323	246,515
		Credits*	0*	0*	0*	0*
	DEPARTMENT TOTAL:	OUTLAYS	78,662,553	83,877,681	89,095,256	97,539,933
		CREDITS*	22,552,867*	24,470,512*	24,500,284*	29,111,418*
	ENVIRONMENTAL PROTECTION AGENCY					
66.001	Air Pollution Control Support		172,759	175,494	154,747	173,200
66.032	State Indoor Radon Grants		6,915	7,439	7,439	8,074 e
66.033	Ozone Transport		635	635	639	635 e
66.034	Surveys, Studies/Clean Air Act		68,726	66,407	0 e	0 e
66.035	Community Action/Renewed Environment		1,760	2,700	3,400	3,500 e
66.036	Clean School Bus USA		7,440	6,900	6,900	6,900 e
66.037	Air and Radiation Training		(n)	(n)	(n)	1,250 e
66.038	Air Quality—Native American		(n)	(n)	(n)	7,750 e
66.039	Clean Diesel—National		(n)	(n)	(n)	35,000 e
66.040	Clean Diesel—State		(n)	(n)	(n)	15,000
66.110	Healthy Communities Grant Program		(a)	(a)	(a)	(a)
66.111	Environmental Priority Projects		(n)	362	392	350 e
66.112	Region 8 Geographic Initiatives		0	198	377	377
66.113	Region 3 Geographic Initiatives		0	141	412	500 e
66.114	Environmental Protection Grants		0	0	0	0
66.115	Region 10 Geographic Initiatives		1,500	333	350 e	0 e
66.116	Region 6 Geographic Initiatives		(n)	580	557	300
66.117	Region 9 Geographic Initiatives		(n)	641	389 e	344 e
66.202	Congressionally Mandated Projects		537,080	554,486	0	202,245 e
66.305	Compliance Assistance-Support		1,300	1,195	1,165	1,160
66.306	Environmental Justice Collaborative		0	1,000	1,000	0
66.309	Surveys, Studies, Investigations \ t		0	150	500	0 e
66.310	Compliance Assurance/Indian Country		1,450	1,390	1,390	1,390
66.418	Wastewater Treatment Works		1,669	6,541	7,994	8,000 e
66.419	Water Pollution Control		209,945	220,772	221,661	221,664 e
66.424	Surveys/Safe Drinking Water Act		1,290	975	1,067	9,330 e
66.432	Public Water System Supervision		100,462	98,279	98,279	99,100 e
66.433	Underground Water Source Protection		9,691	9,486	9,118	10,891 e
66.436	Surveys, Studies/Clean Water Act		22,000	14,361	25,730	15,000 e
66.437	Long Island Sound Program		2,794	767	1,363	467 e
66.439	Targeted Watershed Grants		17,062	10,400	14,200	0 e
66.454	Water Quality Management Planning		11,851	10,143	11,080	8,607 e
66.456	National Estuary Program		13,419	13,804	11,704	6,832 e
66.458	Clean Water State Revolving Funds \ r		1,053,899	872,898	1,017,074	687,554 e
66.460	Nonpoint Source Implementation		207,329	203,807	199,300	194,040 e
66.461	Regional Wetland Program Development		7,722	8,400	9,300	15,800 e
66.462	National Wetland Program Development		490	715	285	500 e
66.463	Water Quality Agreements		12,373	11,137	1,258	0 e
66.466	Chesapeake Bay Program		16,771	21,995	20,027	28,790 e
66.467	Wastewater Operator Training		1,448	1,182	1,182	0 e
66.468	Drinking Water/Revolving Fund \ r		798,188	837,495	837,495	842,167 e
66.469	Great Lakes Program		14,759	35,389	37,231	42,000 e
66.471	Small Water Systems		2,077	620	0	0 e
66.472	Beach Monitoring and Notification		9,920	9,707	10,573	9,900 e
66.473	Direct Implementation/Tribal		485	815	1,317	900 e
66.474	Water Protection Grants to States		4,889	4,927	4,926	4,950 e
66.475	Gulf of Mexico Program		1,817	2,615	955	2,000 e
66.478	Water Security Training, Assistance		0	0	20,200	18,000 e
66.479	Wetland Program Grants - State/Tribal		6,158	6,158	6,158	0 e
66.480	Assessment, Watershed Protection		1,078	1,078	1,100	550 e
66.481	Lake Champlain Basin Project		2,480	3,952	1,497	934 e

Please see "Important Notes on the Tables, Footnotes," page 842

Table 1. *(continued)*

Program number	ADMINISTRATIVE ENTITY/SUB-UNIT Program Title (abridged)	FY 2005 in $thousands	FY 2006 in $thousands	FY 2007 in $thousands	FY 2008 in $thousands
66.508	Senior Environmental Employment	59,340	60,431	53,058	53,000 e
66.509	Science to Achieve Results	64,300	65,924	61,510	65,421 e
66.510	Surveys, Studies/Office of Research	8,900	9,100	4,300	6,700 e
66.511	Consolidated Research, Training	35,900	24,500	34,000	32,000 e
66.512	REMAP Research Projects	596	2,045	2,210	0 e
66.513	Greater Opportunities Fellowship	1,577	1,485	1,529	1,528 e
66.514	STAR Fellowship Program	11,000	9,281	7,503	5,875 e
66.515	Greater Opportunities Research	1,145	1,121	1,153	0 e
66.516	Design Competition/Sustainability	600	1,250	1,245	1,272 e
66.517	Regional Applied Research Efforts	(n)	295	823 e	500 e
66.518	State Senior Environmental Employment	50	583	270	350 e
66.600	Consolidated Grants—Program Support	10,372	7,850	8,460	8,500 e
66.604	Environmental Justice Small Grant \ t	625	0	1,000	0
66.605	Performance Partnership Grants	326,186	365,577	372,689	392,000
66.608	Information Exchange Network	20,240	20,015	14,708	13,000 e
66.609	Health Protection/Children, Elderly	1,369	861	800 e	300 e
66.610	Surveys/Office of Administrator	908	510	473	500 e
66.611	Environmental Policy, Innovation	2,784	615	2,176,408	1,670 e
66.612	Toxic Chemical Information	(n)	0	0	250 e
66.700	Pesticide Enforcement	19,344	18,622	18,622	18,711
66.701	Toxic Substances Compliance	5,516	5,150	5,074	5,099 e
66.707	TSCA State Lead Grants	11,937	15,115	22,936	13,564 e
66.708	Pollution Prevention Grants	5,162	4,926	4,774 e	5,000 e
66.709	Multi-Media Capacity Building Grants	2,200	1,435	1,476	3,800 e
66.714	Pesticide Environmental Stewardship	332	503	503	502 e
66.715	Blood-Lead Screening/Tribal	915	915	971	500 e
66.716	Surveys, Studies, Training	3,861	4,142	4,222	4,117 e
66.717	Source Reduction Assistance	952	1,475	1,249 e	1,600 e
66.718	Lead Outreach Training	(n)	0	3,100 e	3,100 e
66.801	Hazardous Waste Management	103,168	101,944	101,944	103,346 e
66.802	Superfund—Site Specific \ t	58,000	70,000	50,000	50,000 e
66.804	Underground Storage Tanks	11,904	11,774	30,717	2,500 e
66.805	Leaking Storage Tank Trust Fund\ t	56,720	72,647	57,661	62,207 e
66.806	TAG/Community Groups/NPL Sites	541	332	610	500 e
66.808	Solid Waste Management Assistance	4,000	4,000	4,000	4,000 e
66.809	Superfund/Core Program	10,000	13,000	8,800	8,000 e
66.810	CEPP Technical Assistance	74	90	100	75 e
66.812	Hazardous Waste Management/Tribes	298	288	288	288 e
66.813	Treatment Technology Research	350	1,649	1,711	1,800 e
66.814	Brownfields Agreements	3,226	3,390	2,669	3,000 e
66.815	Brownfield Job Training	2,176	2,000	2,343	2,500 e
66.816	Underground Storage Tanks \ t	336	858	868	900 e
66.817	State and Tribal Response	49,600	49,300	49,300	49,300 e
66.818	Brownfields Assessment, Cleanup	74,267	74,000	70,700 e	70,700 e
66.926	Indian Environmental GAP	61,504	56,654	56,654	56,925 e
66.931	International Financial Assistance	5,935	5,600	4,300	3,700 e
66.940	Environmental Policy, State Innovation	0	1,430	1,611	1,000 e
66.950	Environmental Education, Training	1,699	1,699	837	1,699 e
66.951	Environmental Education Grants	2,885	2,885	1,343	2,885 e
66.952	Environmental Management Fellowship	404	273	221	300 e
	DEPARTMENT TOTAL: OUTLAYS	4,374,829	4,326,008	6,003,474	3,750,435
	CREDITS*	0*	0*	0*	0*
	NATIONAL GALLERY OF ART				
68.001	Art Extension Service	410	416	430 e	450 e
	DEPARTMENT TOTAL: OUTLAYS	410	416	430	450
	CREDITS*	0*	0*	0*	0*
	OVERSEAS PRIVATE INVESTMENT CORPORATION				
70.002	Foreign Investment Financing \ u	2,029,000*	2,000,000*e	1,950,000*e	0*e

Please see "Important Notes on the Tables, Footnotes," page 842

Table 1. *(continued)*

Program number	ADMINISTRATIVE ENTITY/SUB-UNIT Program Title (abridged)		FY 2005 in $thousands	FY 2006 in $thousands	FY 2007 in $thousands	FY 2008 in $thousands
70.003	Foreign Investment Insurance \ u		1,128,000*	1,000,000*e	1,200,000*e	0*e
	DEPARTMENT TOTAL:	OUTLAYS	0	0	0	0
		CREDITS*	3,157,000*	3,000,000*	3,150,000*	0*
	NUCLEAR REGULATORY COMMISSION					
77.006	Nuclear Education Grants		(n)	0 e	4,700 e	0 e
77.007	Minority Serving Institutions		(n)	0 e	900 e	0 e
77.008	Scholarship and Fellowship, Science		(n)	0	400	400
	DEPARTMENT TOTAL:	OUTLAYS	0	0	6,000	400
		CREDITS*	0*	0*	0*	0*
	COMMODITY FUTURES TRADING COMMISSION					
78.004	Commodity Futures Reparations		67,850	70,400 e	70,400 e	0 e
	DEPARTMENT TOTAL:	OUTLAYS	67,850	70,400	70,400	0
		CREDITS*	0*	0*	0*	0*
	DEPARTMENT OF ENERGY					
81.003	Granting of Patent Licenses		(a)	(a)	(a)	(a)
81.022	Energy-Related Equipment \ p		(a)	(a)	(a)	(a)
81.036	Inventions and Innovations		16,341	11,954	2,753	0 e
81.041	State Energy Program		43,644	34,606	45,382	50,000 e
81.042	Weatherization Assistance		226,329	234,057	204,357	166,667 e
81.049	Office of Science		830,000	830,000	830,000	830,000 e
81.057	University Coal Research		116,000	3,000	2,755	2,400 e
81.064	Scientific, Technical Information		8,800	8,700	8,700	8,700 e
81.065	Nuclear Waste Disposal Siting		14,449	20,200	16,585 e	22,345 e
81.079	Regional Biomass Programs		35,000	1,320	395	58,050 e
81.086	Conservation Research, Development		85,676	85,232	71,883 e	90,000 e
81.087	Renewable Energy Research		217,048	216,943	225,949	300,000 e
81.089	Fossil Energy Research, Development		235,000	287,727 e	468,184 e	434,000 e
81.104	Office of Environmental Cleanup		26,358	18,000 e	13,000 e	30,000 e
81.105	National Industrial Competitiveness		0	0	1,634	0 e
81.106	Transport/Transuranic Waste		35,115	6,382	5,632	6,346 e
81.108	Epidemiology, Health Studies		12,000	18,000	18,000	18,000 e
81.112	Stewardship Science		14,751	16,000	17,700	16,600 e
81.113	Nuclear Nonproliferation Research		15,510	11,625	7,000	11,500 e
81.114	University Reactor Infrastructure		23,810	26,730	12,132	0 e
81.117	Energy Efficiency—Renewable		24,611	20,055	29,436	35,000 e
81.119	State Energy Special Projects		16,637	4,649	5,340	5,447 e
81.121	Nuclear Energy Research, Development		74,817	91,191	143,029 e	150,000 e
81.122	Electricity Delivery, Reliability		1,408	11,616	14,579	11,000 e
81.123	HBCU Program		22,320	15,150	9,214	8,500 e
81.124	Predictive Science		(n)	(n)	(n)	8,000 e
81.126	Innovative Energy Loans \ u		(n)	(n)	(n)	9,000,000 e
	DEPARTMENT TOTAL:	OUTLAYS	2,095,624	1,973,137	2,153,639	11,262,555
		CREDITS*	0*	0*	0*	0*
	DEPARTMENT OF EDUCATION					
84.002	Adult Education—State Grant		569,672	563,975	563,975 e	544,122 e
84.004	Civil Rights Training		7,185	7,113	7,113 e	6,989 e
84.007	Educational Opportunity Grants		778,720	775,462	770,933 e	757,465 e
84.010	Title I Grants		12,739,571	12,713,125	12,838,123 e	13,898,875 e
84.011	Migrant Education		380,428	376,524	376,524 e	369,771 e
84.013	Neglected and Delinquent Children		49,600	49,797	49,797 e	48,927 e
84.015	Language, Area Studies		56,919	57,750	57,979 e	59,552 e

Table 1. *(continued)*

Program number	ADMINISTRATIVE ENTITY/SUB-UNIT Program Title (abridged)	FY 2005 in $thousands	FY 2006 in $thousands	FY 2007 in $thousands	FY 2008 in $thousands
84.016	Undergraduate International Studies	4,490	4,400	4,300 e	4,380 e
84.017	International Research and Studies	6,052	5,830	5,823 e	5,930 e
84.018	Overseas—Bilateral Projects	1,895	2,039	2,420 e	2,018 e
84.019	Overseas—Faculty Research Abroad	1,391	1,395	1,395 e	1,395 e
84.021	Overseas—Group Projects Abroad	4,468	4,273	3,888 e	4,722 e
84.022	Overseas—Doctoral Dissertation	4,452	4,400	4,445 e	4,721 e
84.027	Special Education—State Grants	10,589,746	10,582,961	10,782,961 e	10,947,511 e
84.031	Higher Education—Institutional Aid	421,476	419,630	419,630 e	546,458 e
84.032	Family Education Loans	97,240,000*	118,717,000*	98,261,000*e	90,182,000*e
84.033	Work-Study Program	990,257	999,523	980,354 e	980,492 e
84.037	Perkins Loan Cancellations	66,132	65,471	65,471 e	64,327 e
84.038	Perkins Loans	0*	4,731*	0*e	0*e
84.040	Impact Aid—Facilities Maintenance	7,901	4,950	4,950 e	4,864 e
84.041	Impact Aid	1,075,018	1,223,503	1,223,503 e	1,235,853 e
84.042	TRIO—Student Support Services	277,773	272,762	271,567 e	281,032 e
84.044	TRIO—Talent Search	144,649	145,330	143,077 e	142,884 e
84.047	TRIO—Upward Bound	309,939	311,050	300,817 e	290,826 e
84.048	Vocational Education—States	1,167,578	1,155,902	1,162,294 e	1,142 e
84.051	Vocational Education—National	11,757	9,164	10,000 e	7,860 e
84.060	Indian Education—LEAs	96,166	95,331	95,331 e	96,613 e
84.063	Pell Grant Program	12,364,997	17,345,230	13,660,771 e	16,256,000 e
84.066	TRIO—Educational Opportunity	48,972	49,598	47,007 e	47,057 e
84.069	Leveraging Educational Assistance	65,643	64,987	64,987 e	63,852 e
84.083	Women's Educational Equity	2,956	2,926	1,879 e	1,846 e
84.101	Vocational Education—Indians	14,929	14,780	14,769 e	14,511 e
84.103	TRIO Staff Training Program	5,299	4,000	3,331 e	4,000 e
84.116	Fund/Postsecondary Education	162,108	21,989	21,989 e	120,333 e
84.120	Minority Science, Engineering	8,818	8,730	8,730 e	8,577 e
84.126	Rehabilitation Services—State	2,603,845	2,602,845	2,685,771 e	2,802,755 e
84.128	Rehabilitation Services—Projects	4,845	4,797	4,797 e	4,713 e
84.129	Rehabilitation Training	18,446	19,267	19,267 e	19,524 e
84.132	Centers for Independent Living	75,392	74,638	74,638 e	73,334 e
84.133	Disability, Rehabilitation Research	107,783	106,705	106,705 e	105,741 e
84.141	Migrant Education—High School	18,737	18,550	18,550 e	18,226 e
84.144	Migrant Education—Coordination	10,000	10,000	10,000 e	12,500 e
84.145	Federal Real Property Assistance \ p	(a)	(a)	(a)	(a)
84.149	Migrant Education—College	15,532	15,377	15,377 e	15,108 e
84.153	Business, International Education	4,491	4,400	4,340 e	4,420 e
84.160	Training Interpreters for Deaf	2,100	2,093	2,093 e	2,084 e
84.161	Rehabilitation—Client Assistance	11,901	11,782	11,782 e	11,576 e
84.165	Magnet Schools	107,771	106,693	106,693 e	104,829 e
84.169	Independent Living	22,816	22,588	22,588 e	22,193 e
84.170	Javits Fellowships	9,797	9,699	9,699 e	9,530 e
84.173	Special Education—Preschool	384,597	380,751	380,751 e	374,099 e
84.177	Rehabilitation Services—Blind	33,227	32,895	32,895 e	32,320 e
84.181	Infants, Families/Disabilities	440,808	436,400	436,400 e	435,654 e
84.184	Drug-Free Schools—National	234,580	222,335	230,929 e	218,632 e
84.185	Byrd Honors Scholarships	40,672	40,590	40,590 e	40,284 e
84.186	Safe/Drug-Free Schools—State	437,381	346,500	346,500 e	294,759 e
84.187	Supported Employment	37,379	29,700	29,700 e	29,181 e
84.191	Adult Education—National Leadership	9,096	9,005	9,005 e	7,860 e
84.196	Homeless Children, Youth	62,496	61,871	61,871 e	64,067 e
84.200	Graduate Assistance/National Need	30,371	30,067	30,067 e	29,542 e
84.203	Star Schools	20,832	14,850	11,513 e	0 e
84.206	Javits Gifted/Talented Students	11,022	9,596	7,596 e	7,463 e
84.213	Even Start—State	202,836	89,080	75,700 e	0 e
84.214	Even Start—Migrant	7,878	2,800	2,000 e	0
84.215	Improvement of Education	257,114	11,668	16,051 e	121,934 e
84.217	TRIO/Post-Baccalaureate	41,935	41,935	45,355 e	43,636 e
84.220	International Business Education	10,700	10,650	10,650 e	10,840 e
84.224	Assistive Technology	20,289	30,452	30,452 e	29,920 e
84.229	Language Resource Centers	4,850	4,800	4,844 e	5,030 e
84.234	Projects with Industry	21,799	19,538	17,293 e	19,197 e
84.235	Rehabilitation Services/Training	25,607	6,511	8,756 e	10,151 e
84.240	Protection and Advocacy	16,656	16,489	16,489 e	16,201 e

Please see "Important Notes on the Tables, Footnotes," page 842

Table 1. *(continued)*

Program number	ADMINISTRATIVE ENTITY/SUB-UNIT Program Title (abridged)	FY 2005 in $thousands	FY 2006 in $thousands	FY 2007 in $thousands	FY 2008 in $thousands
84.243	Tech-Prep Education	105,812	104,754	104,753 e	102,923 e
84.245	Tribal Vocational/Technical	7,440	7,366	7,366 e	7,546 e
84.246	Rehabilitation Short-Term Training	450	750	750 e	750 e
84.250	Rehabilitation—Indians/Disabilities	31,964	33,024	34,025 e	34,892 e
84.256	Freely Associated States—Education	4,980	3,818 e	3,818 e	3,818 e
84.257	Institute for Literacy	4,010	3,570	3,989 e	3,906 e
84.258	Even Start—Indian	4,502	1,485	1,000 e	0 e
84.259	Hawaiian Vocational Education	(n)	2,956	2,954 e	2,902 e
84.263	Rehabilitation Training—Innovative	299	0	0 e	500 e
84.264	Rehabilitation Training—Continuing	10,052	10,071	10,071 e	8,090 e
84.265	Rehabilitation Training—State Unit	5,290	5,766	5,766 e	5,766 e
84.268	Federal Direct Student Loans	28,615,000*	12,176,000*	13,022,000*e	14,103,000*e
84.269	International Public Policy	1,616	1,600	1,600 e	1,600 e
84.274	Overseas Research Centers	1,056	1,000	1,000 e	1,000 e
84.275	Rehabilitation Training—General	300	300	300 e	300 e
84.282	Charter Schools	216,952	214,782	214,782 e	0 e
84.283	Comprehensive Centers	56,825	56,257	56,257 e	56,257 e
84.286	Ready to Teach	14,291	10,890	10,890 e	10,700 e
84.287	Community Learning Centers	991,077	981,166	981,166 e	1,081,166 e
84.293	Foreign Language Assistance	17,856	21,780	23,780 e	25,655 e
84.295	Ready-To-Learn TV	23,312	24,255	24,255 e	23,831 e
84.298	State Grants/Innovative Programs	198,400	99,000	99,000 e	0 e
84.304	Civic Education—Exchange	12,194	12,072	12,072	11,861 e
84.305	Education Research, Development	164,194	162,552	162,552 e	159,696 e
84.310	Parental Assistance Centers	41,886	39,600	39,600 e	38,908 e
84.315	Capacity Building	2,597	2,291	2,291 e	2,900 e
84.318	Education Technology State Grants	496,000	272,250 e	272,250 e	267,494 e
84.323	State Personnel Development	50,653	50,146	0 e	22,598 e
84.324	Research in Special Education	83,104	71,840	71,840 e	70,585 e
84.325	Personnel/Children with Disabilities	90,626	89,720	89,720 e	88,153 e
84.326	Technical/Children with Disabilities	52,396	48,903	48,903 e	48,049 e
84.327	Technology/Individuals/Disabilities	38,816	38,428	38,428 e	39,301 e
84.328	Parent Information Centers	26,964	25,704	25,704 e	26,528 e
84.329	Studies, Evaluations	0	9,900	9,900 e	9,460 e
84.330	Advanced Placement Program	29,760	32,175	37,026 e	43,540 e
84.331	Incarcerated Youth Offenders	21,824	22,770	22,770 e	22,372 e
84.332	Comprehensive School Reform	205,344	7,920	2,352 e	1,605 e
84.333	Disabilities—Higher Education	6,944	6,875	6,875 e	6,775 e
84.334	Awareness, Readiness—Undergraduate	306,488	303,423	303,423 e	303,423 e
84.335	Child Care/Parents in School	15,970	15,810	15,810 e	15,534 e
84.336	Teacher Quality Enhancement Grants	68,337	59,895	59,895 e	33,662 e
84.337	Education—Technology/Foreign Access	1,700	1,700	1,700 e	1,700 e
84.341	Community Technology Centers	4,690	0 e	0 e	0 e
84.343	Assistive Technology/Protection	4,385	4,341	4,341 e	4,265 e
84.344	TRIO—Dissemination Partnership	4,387	0	0 e	0 e
84.345	Underground Railroad Education	2,204	1,980	1,980 e	1,945 e
84.349	Early Childhood Educator	14,696	14,549	14,550 e	0 e
84.350	Transition to Teaching	44,933	44,484	44,484 e	43,707 e
84.351	Arts in Education	35,633	35,277	35,277 e	37,533 e
84.353	Tech-Prep Demonstration Grants	4,900	0 e	0 e	0 e
84.354	Credit Enhancement/Charter School	36,981	36,611	36,611 e	36,611 e
84.356	Alaska Native Educational Programs	34,224	33,908	33,907 e	33,315 e
84.357	Reading First State Grants	1,041,600	1,029,234	1,029,234 e	393,012 e
84.358	Rural Education	170,624	168,918	168,918 e	171,854 e
84.359	Early Reading First	104,160	103,118	117,666 e	125,549 e
84.360	Dropout Prevention Programs	4,930	4,851	0 e	0 e
84.361	Voluntary Public School Choice	26,543	26,278	26,278 e	25,819 e
84.362	Native Hawaiian Education	34,224	33,908	33,907 e	33,315 e
84.363	School Leadership	14,880	14,731	14,731 e	14,474 e
84.364	Literacy through School Libraries	19,683	19,486	19,485 e	19,145 e
84.365	English Language Acquisition	631,468	620,522	620,522 e	649,869 e
84.366	Mathematics, Science Partnerships	178,560	182,160	182,160 e	178,978 e
84.367	Improving Teacher Quality	2,916,605	2,887,439	2,887,439 e	2,935,248 e
84.369	State Assessments, Activities	411,860	407,563	407,563 e	408,732 e

Please see "Important Notes on the Tables, Footnotes," page 842

Table 1. *(continued)*

Program number	ADMINISTRATIVE ENTITY/SUB-UNIT Program Title (abridged)		FY 2005 in $thousands	FY 2006 in $thousands	FY 2007 in $thousands	FY 2008 in $thousands
84.370	DC School Choice Incentive Program		13,800	13,860 e	13,860 e	14,800 e
84.371	Striving Readers		24,800	29,700	31,870	35,371
84.372	Statewide Data Systems		0	24,552	24,552	48,293
84.373	Special Education Data Collection		0	15,000	14,927 e	14,930 e
84.374	Teacher Incentive Funds		0	99,000	99,000 e	97,270 e
84.375	Academic Competitiveness Grants		0	340,000	350,000 e	440,000 e
84.376	Science and Mathematics Grants		0	310,000 e	230,000 e	260,000 e
84.377	School Improvement Grants		(n)	(n)	125,000	500,000 e
84.378	College Access Challenge Grant		(n)	(n)	(n)	66,000 e
84.379	Teacher Education Grants		(n)	(n)	(n)	86,000 e
84.380	Special Education—Olympic		(n)	(n)	(n)	11,790 e
84.381	Degrees in STEM-CFL		(n)	(n)	(n)	1,965 e
84.382	Minority-Serving Institutions		(n)	(n)	(n)	25,000
84.938	Hurricane Education Recovery		0	1,600,000	30,000 e	0 e
	DEPARTMENT TOTAL:	OUTLAYS	56,995,589	63,181,851	58,316,735	61,122,744
		CREDITS*	125,855,000*	130,897,731*	111,283,000*	104,285,000*

SCHOLARSHIP AND FELLOWSHIP FOUNDATIONS

Program number	Program Title		FY 2005	FY 2006	FY 2007	FY 2008
	HARRY S TRUMAN SCHOLARSHIP FOUNDATION					
85.001	Truman Scholarship Program \ t		2,000	2,000 e	2,000 e	0 e
	Subtotal:	Outlays	2,000	2,000	2,000	0
		Credits*	0*	0*	0*	0*
	CHRISTOPHER COLUMBUS FELLOWSHIP FOUNDATION					
85.100	Columbus Fellowship Program \ t		620	552 e	535 e	290 e
	Subtotal:	Outlays	620	552	535	290
		Credits*	0*	0*	0*	0*
	BARRY GOLDWATER SCHOLARSHIP AND EXCELLENCE IN EDUCATION					
85.200	Goldwater Scholarship Program \ t		2,800	3,000 e	300,000 e	0 e
	Subtotal:	Outlays	2,800	3,000	300,000	0
		Credits*	0*	0*	0*	0*
	WOODROW WILSON INTERNATIONAL CENTER FOR SCHOLARS					
85.300	Wilson Fellowships		1,208	1,391 e	1,405 e	0 e
	Subtotal:	Outlays	1,208	1,391	1,405	0
		Credits*	0*	0*	0*	0*
	MORRIS K. UDALL SCHOLARSHIP AND EXCELLENCE IN NATIONAL ENVIRONMENTAL POLICY FOUNDATION					
85.400	Udall Scholarship Program		400	400	400	400 e
85.401	Udall Fellowship Program		48	48	48	48 e
85.402	Udall Congressional Internships		140	140	170	170 e
	Subtotal:	Outlays	588	588	618	618
		Credits*	0*	0*	0*	0*
	JAMES MADISON MEMORIAL FELLOWSHIP FOUNDATION					
85.500	Madison Fellowship Program \ t		1,085	1,150	1,091	1,125 e
	Subtotal:	Outlays	1,085	1,150	1,091	1,125
		Credits*	0*	0*	0*	0*
	SMITHSONIAN INSTITUTE FELLOWSHIP FOUNDATION					
85.601	Smithsonian Institution Fellowship		0	850 e	1,000 e	0 e
	Subtotal:	Outlays	0	850	1,000	0
		Credits*	0*	0*	0*	0*
	DEPARTMENT TOTAL:	OUTLAYS	8,301	9,531	306,649	2,033
		CREDITS*	0*	0*	0*	0*

Please see "Important Notes on the Tables, Footnotes," page 842

Table 1. *(continued)*

Program number	ADMINISTRATIVE ENTITY/SUB-UNIT Program Title (abridged)		FY 2005 in $thousands	FY 2006 in $thousands	FY 2007 in $thousands	FY 2008 in $thousands
	PENSION BENEFIT GUARANTY CORPORATION					
86.001	Pension Plan Termination Insurance \ u		3,314,800	4,639,000	4,890,000 e	4,606,000 e
	DEPARTMENT TOTAL:	OUTLAYS	3,314,800	4,639,000	4,890,000	4,606,000
		CREDITS*	0*	0*	0*	0*
	ARCHITECTURAL AND TRANSPORTATION BARRIERS COMPLIANCE BOARD					
88.001	Compliance Board		5,160	4,354,000 e	5,427,000 e	0 e
	DEPARTMENT TOTAL:	OUTLAYS	5,160	4,354,000	5,427,000	0
		CREDITS*	0*	0*	0*	0*
	NATIONAL ARCHIVES AND RECORDS ADMINISTRATION					
89.001	Historical Research		82,899	51,161	52,780 e	55,346 e
89.003	National Historical Publications		6,399	5,006	5,000 e	0 e
89.005	National Archives Support		35	62	35	0 e
	DEPARTMENT TOTAL:	OUTLAYS	89,333	56,229	57,815	55,346
		CREDITS*	0*	0*	0*	0*
	INDEPENDENT BOARDS AND COMMISSIONS					
	DENALI COMMISSION					
90.100	Denali Commission Program \ t		110,000	139,000	111,000	106,000 e
	Subtotal:	Outlays	110,000	139,000	111,000	106,000
		Credits*	0*	0*	0*	0*
	DELTA REGIONAL AUTHORITY					
90.200	Delta Regional Development		(a)	(a)	(a)	(a)
90.201	Delta Area Economic Development		4,389	7,800 e	8,000 e	0 e
90.202	Delta Local Development District		396	396 e	396 e	0 e
	Subtotal:	Outlays	4,785	8,196	8,396	0
		Credits*	0*	0*	0*	0*
	JAPAN US FRIENDSHIP COMMISSION					
90.300	Japan-US Friendship Grants		2,655	2,655	2,655 e	2,655 e
	Subtotal:	Outlays	2,655	2,655	2,655	2,655
		Credits*	0*	0*	0*	0*
	ELECTIONS ASSISTANCE COMMISSION					
90.400	Help America Vote—Pollworker		0	250	0 e	750 e
90.401	Help America Vote Act Requirements		0	0 e	0 e	0 e
90.402	Help America Vote—Mock Elections		(n)	(n)	(n)	(n)
	Subtotal:	Outlays	0	250	0	750
		Credits*	0*	0*	0*	0*
	UNITED STATES INSTITUTE OF PEACE					
91.001	Unsolicited Grant Program		2,187	1,850 e	2,000 e	0 e
91.002	Solicited Grant Program		1,827	1,200 e	2,500 e	0 e
	Subtotal:	Outlays	4,014	3,050	4,500	0
		Credits*	0*	0*	0*	0*
	DEPARTMENT TOTAL:	OUTLAYS	121,454	153,151	126,551	109,405
		CREDITS*	0*	0*	0*	0*

Please see "Important Notes on the Tables, Footnotes," page 842

Table 1. *(continued)*

Program number	ADMINISTRATIVE ENTITY/SUB-UNIT Program Title (abridged)	FY 2005 in $thousands	FY 2006 in $thousands	FY 2007 in $thousands	FY 2008 in $thousands
	DEPARTMENT OF HEALTH AND HUMAN SERVICES				
93.001	Civil Rights, Privacy Rule	34,952	34,646	34,909	37,062 e
93.003	Health, Social Services Emergency	0	409	0 e	0 e
93.004	Health Status/Minority Populations	5,991	7,293 e	7,842 e	0 e
93.006	Minority HIV/AIDS Demonstration	8,678	6,700 e	6,700 e	0 e
93.007	Public Awareness/Embryo Adoption	950	1,500	1,500	0 e
93.008	Medical Reserve Corps	8,350	8,350	8,350 e	0 e
93.009	Compassion Capital Fund	54,549	64,306 e	64,350 e	75,000 e
93.010	Community-Based Abstinence Education	88,421	95,807	96,418	124,148 e
93.012	Heart Health Care/High-Risk Women	750	900	0 e	0 e
93.013	Ambassadors for Change	(n)	(n)	(n)	0
93.014	Steps to Healthier Girls	(n)	(n)	(n)	0 e
93.015	HIV Prevention, Women	(n)	(n)	(n)	0 e
93.017	Kabul Women's and Children's Health	2,175	2,175	0 e	0 e
93.018	US/Mexico Border Health	0	1,286	0 e	0 e
93.041	Aging—Prevention of Abuse, Neglect	5,167	5,142	5,146 e	5,146 e
93.042	Aging—Long-Term Care Ombudsman	14,162	14,860	14,936	15,421 e
93.043	Aging—Disease Prevention	21,616	21,385	21,400 e	0 e
93.044	Aging—Senior Centers	354,136	350,354	350,595 e	350,595 e
93.045	Aging—Nutrition Services	570,100	566,834	587,224 e	564,399 e
93.047	Aging—Indian, Native Hawaiian	26,398	26,116	26,134 e	26,134 e
93.048	Aging—Discretionary Projects	56,552	37,702	37,191 e	48,618 e
93.051	Alzheimer's Disease Demonstration	11,786	11,660	11,668 e	0 e
93.052	National Family Caregiver Support	162,048	162,408 e	160,428 e	0 e
93.053	Nutrition Services Incentive	148,596	147,774	147,846 e	147,110 e
93.054	Family Caregiver Support	(n)	6,237	6,241 e	6,241 e
93.061	Applied Public Health Research	25,000	27,777	27,000 e	27,000 e
93.063	Centers/Genomics, Public Health	600	900	900	900 e
93.064	Laboratory Training, Evaluation	425	425	1,405	2,400 e
93.065	Improving Public Health Laboratory	11,772	12,360	11,395	12,000 e
93.066	Vital Statistics Re-Engineering	172	172 e	172 e	0 e
93.067	Global Aids	392,527	499,758	800,000 e	900,000 e
93.068	Research, Control, Prevention	2,000	1,018	300 e	2,000 e
93.069	Public Health Emergency Preparedness	(n)	1,081,532	920,075 e	698,267 e
93.086	Healthy Marriage and Fatherhood	0	150,000 e	150,000 e	0 e
93.087	Children's Safety, Parental Drug Use	(n)	0	40,000 e	35,000 e
93.100	Health Disparities/Minority	1,000	1,000 e	0 e	0 e
93.103	FDA—Research	21,277	22,000	24,500 e	25,200 e
93.104	CMHS/Serious Emotional Disturbances	46,508	0	82,278	62,059 e
93.105	Bilingual/Bicultural Service	2,500	2,500	2,500 e	0 e
93.107	Model Area Health Education Centers	13,852	14,000	14,000 e	14,800 e
93.110	Maternal, Child Health Programs	114,145	112,300 e	115,231 e	104,021 e
93.111	Adolescent Family Life Research	1,139	1,040	1,040 e	0 e
93.113	Biological Response/Health Hazards	167,896	293,694	303,847 e	291,954 e
93.116	Tuberculosis Control Programs	108,190	103,023	101,348 e	101,348 e
93.117	Preventive Medicine	1,200	1,250	1,250 e	1,250 e
93.118	AIDS Activity	1,684	3,049	2,951 e	3,138 e
93.121	Oral Diseases/Disorders Research	296,956	293,341 e	288,744 e	0 e
93.123	Pregraduate Scholarship/Indians	1,365	1,365 e	1,365 e	0 e
93.124	Nurse Anesthetist Traineeships	1,250	1,250	1,250 e	1,250 e
93.127	Emergency Medical Services/Children	14,349	15,370	15,679 e	0 e
93.129	Assistance to Health Centers	28,949	29,000	34,000 e	34,000 e
93.130	State Primary Care Offices	10,200	9,800 e	9,800 e	0 e
93.134	Organ Donations	7,518	9,274	8,309 e	11,067 e
93.135	Centers/Health Promotion	25,300	24,400	24,500 e	0 e
93.136	Injury Prevention, Control Research	107,463	104,356 e	105,000 e	105,000 e
93.137	Community Minority Health	6,500	6,500 e	6,500 e	0 e
93.138	Advocacy/Mental Illness	33,656	0	33,320	33,320 e
93.140	Intramural Research Training	44,935	49,428 e	49,428 e	0 e
93.142	Hazardous Waste Worker Training	28,741	26,876	26,906 e	28,765 e
93.143	Hazardous Substances Research	51,095	47,515	46,568 e	47,046 e
93.145	AIDS Education, Training Centers	33,538	33,164	33,159 e	28,000 e

Please see "Important Notes on the Tables, Footnotes," page 842

Table 1. *(continued)*

Program number	ADMINISTRATIVE ENTITY/SUB-UNIT Program Title (abridged)	FY 2005 in $thousands	FY 2006 in $thousands	FY 2007 in $thousands	FY 2008 in $thousands
93.150	Transition from Homelessness	52,399	51,873	51,873 e	51,873 e
93.153	Research/Women, Infants, Youth	67,043	66,191 e	66,191 e	66,191 e
93.155	Rural Health Research Centers	10,000	4,449	4,750 e	4,750
93.156	Geriatric Fellowships	6,287	0	7,000 e	7,000 e
93.157	Centers of Excellence	31,800	11,378	11,393 e	0 e
93.161	Toxic Substances, Disease Registry	9,705	3,728	4,168 e	7,482 e
93.162	NHSC Loan Repayment	55,216	58,440	59,000 e	60,000 e
93.164	IHS Loan Repayment	17,525	16,411 e	16,924 e	0 e
93.165	State Loan Repayment	3,700	7,000	7,000 e	7,000 e
93.172	Human Genome Research	348,135	0	0 e	0 e
93.173	Deafness, Communication Disorders	394,171	389,623	393,668 e	393,682 e
93.178	Nursing Workforce Diversity	16,270	15,105	15,243 e	16,107 e
93.181	Podiatric Residency Training	418	0	0 e	0 e
93.184	Disabilities Prevention	17,770	16,689	16,729	17,340 e
93.185	Immunization Research, Demonstration	11,004	11,004	9,000 e	9,000 e
93.186	NRSA/Primary Care	7,615	7,608	7,716 e	7,716 e
93.187	Undergraduate Scholarships	844	768 e	768 e	0 e
93.189	Health Education, Training Centers	3,554	0	0	0 e
93.191	Allied Health Special Projects	4,100	1,980	1,980 e	1,980 e
93.192	Rural Interdisciplinary Training	5,752	3,870	4,600	0 e
93.193	Urban Indian Health Services	7,797	7,817 e	7,817 e	0 e
93.197	Childhood Lead Poisoning Prevention	31,000	33,690	33,700	28,093 e
93.202	Capacity Building/Indian Tribes	100	100 e	0	0 e
93.204	Hazardous Substance Emergency	2,000	800	1,394	3,492 e
93.206	Health Studies/Research	1,930	200	156	36 e
93.208	Great Lakes Health Effects	1,260	1,000	1,020	1,083 e
93.209	Contraception, Infertility LRP	993	1,004	1,000 e	1,000 e
93.210	Tribal Self-Governance	974,120	1,028,890 e	1,082,840 e	0 e
93.211	Telehealth Network Grants	3,774	6,236	6,432	6,432 e
93.212	Chiropractic Demonstration Projects	1,308	1,841	1,802 e	1,817 e
93.213	Complementary/Alternative Medicine	86,496	86,067	85,484 e	85,538 e
93.217	Family Planning—Services	253,643	253,643	253,643	0 e
93.220	Loan Repayment/Disadvantaged	563	483 e	483 e	0 e
93.223	Rural Health Services	756	300	300 e	300 e
93.224	Consolidated Health Centers	1,570,481	1,740,557	1,943,484 e	1,943,484 e
93.225	Health Services Research Training	7,615	7,615	7,716 e	7,700 e
93.226	Research/Healthcare Cost, Quality	101,061	109,785	149,344 e	149,344 e
93.228	IHS—Health Management	6,019	5,343 e	5,430 e	0 e
93.229	Criminal Justice Treatment	1,000	1,000 e	1,000 e	0 e
93.230	Knowledge Development, Application	49,003	32,457	23,314	500 e
93.231	Epidemiology Agreements	4,436	6,000 e	6,000 e	6,000 e
93.232	Loan Repayment/General Research	4,921	5,286 e	5,286 e	0 e
93.233	Sleep Disorders Research	50,558	52,938	52,938 e	52,938 e
93.234	Traumatic Brain Injury	2,225	4,585	5,403 e	0 e
93.235	Abstinence Education	40,914	41,807	50,000 e	50,000 e
93.236	Dental Public Health Training	646	466	455 e	455 e
93.237	Special Diabetes Program/Indians	135,600	135,600	135,600 e	0 e
93.238	Treatment Outcomes Studies	800	0 e	0 e	0 e
93.239	Policy Research	2,382	2,300 e	0 e	0 e
93.240	State Capacity Building	8,783	9,705	10,894	12,682 e
93.241	State Rural Hospital Flexibility	22,200	22,230	21,800 e	21,800 e
93.242	Mental Health Research	980,502	963,717	963,079 e	946,006 e
93.243	Substance Abuse, Mental Health	241,246	0	480,211	351,706 e
93.244	Mental Health Clinical, AIDS	3,022	5,586 e	0 e	0 e
93.247	Advanced Education Nursing	37,888	36,623	33,419	33,419 e
93.249	Public Health Training Centers	4,912	4,483	4,500 e	4,500
93.250	Geriatric Academic Career Awards	6,055	0	0 e	0 e
93.251	Universal Newborn Hearing Screening	8,584	8,453 e	8,376 e	0 e
93.252	Healthy Communities Access Program	72,302	0	0 e	0 e
93.253	Poison Control Centers	19,018	19,753 e	12,174	8,500 e
93.254	Infant Adoption Awareness Training	12,802	12,674	12,674	12,674 e
93.255	Children's Hospitals Education	300,000	297,000	297,000 e	301,650 e
93.256	Health Care Access/Uninsured	9,500	0	0 e	0 e
93.257	Radiogenic Cancers, Diseases	1,623	1,917	1,575 e	1,586 e

Please see "Important Notes on the Tables, Footnotes," page 842

Table 1. *(continued)*

Program number	ADMINISTRATIVE ENTITY/SUB-UNIT Program Title (abridged)	FY 2005 in $thousands	FY 2006 in $thousands	FY 2007 in $thousands	FY 2008 in $thousands
93.259	Rural Access/Emergency Devices	7,313	1,500	1,500	1,500 e
93.260	Family Planning—Personnel	7,213	7,213	7,213 e	0 e
93.262	Occupational Safety, Health Program	101,218	104,900	105,000 e	104,000 e
93.264	Nurse Faculty Loan Program	4,622*	4,580*	4,600*e	4,600*e
93.265	Comprehensive Geriatric Education	3,250	3,171	3,095	2,803 e
93.266	Global AIDS Relief	50,100	109,785	149,344 e	149,344
93.267	Protection, Advocacy Services	2,976	2,970 e	2,970 e	0 e
93.268	Immunization Grants	1,508,387	2,168,892	2,936,725 e	2,875,912 e
93.269	Humanitarian Public Health	(n)	(n)	(n)	(n)
93.270	Viral Hepatitis Prevention	(n)	(n)	8,135	9,500 e
93.271	Alcohol Research Career Awards	11,870	11,441	11,781 e	12,051 e
93.272	Alcohol Research Training	9,731	10,889	11,284 e	11,284 e
93.273	Alcohol Research Programs	264,533	259,034	260,567 e	260,630 e
93.275	Mental Health—Access to Recovery	30,042	0	103,957	95,963 e
93.276	Drug-Free Communities Support	20,221	75,118	57,717 e	36,500 e
93.279	Drug Abuse, Addiction Research	34,789	35,389	37,808 e	37,848 e
93.280	NIH Loan Repayment/Researchers	42,512	42,244 e	42,202 e	0 e
93.281	Mental Health/Development Awards	74,188	71,740	72,281 e	72,382 e
93.282	Mental Health Research Training	57,894	55,144	54,868 e	54,868 e
93.283	Disease Control—Investigations	121,365	129,787	171,848 e	72,864 e
93.284	Injury Prevention—Indians/Alaskans	1,475	1,475 e	1,475 e	0 e
93.285	NIH Pediatric Research LRP	17,377	17,344 e	17,328 e	0 e
93.286	Discovery and Applied Research	298,209	298,088	298,314 e	300,463 e
93.288	NHSC Scholarship	24,656	24,656	15 e	15,000 e
93.289	Physical Fitness and Sports	1,989	1,211	1,288	1,270 e
93.290	Centers/Women's Health	1,670	1,050	0 e	0 e
93.291	Surplus Property Utilization	400	641 e	792 e	686 e
93.294	Mentoring Partnership Program	0	200	0 e	0 e
93.295	HIV/AIDS Prevention, Intergenerational	0	1,000	0 e	0 e
93.296	Minority Health Improvement Grants	4,783	4,979 e	4,979 e	4,979 e
93.300	Health Workforce Analysis	1,500	1,500 e	0 e	0 e
93.301	Small Rural Hospital Improvement	14,700	14,491 e	14,700 e	14,800 e
93.303	Nursing Scholarship Program	(n)	9,724	10,000 e	14,000 e
93.307	Minority Health, Disparities Research	149,623	128,249	149,523 e	149,973 e
93.308	Loan Repayment/Clinical Research	1,562	1,562 e	1,562 e	0 e
93.310	Trans-NIH Research	188,000	256,000 e	353,000 e	0 e
93.342	Health Professions Student Loans	16,493*	13,069*	22,051*	12,250*e
93.358	Advanced Nursing Traineeships	16,000	16,000 e	16,000 e	16,000 e
93.359	Nurse Education, Practice, Retention	36,468	589	1,200	1,800 e
93.361	Nursing Research	114,017	121,176	120,937 e	119,461 e
93.364	Nursing Student Loans \ r	0*	571*e	2,200*e	2,200*e
93.365	Sickle Cell Treatment	0	1,279 e	1,280 e	1,280 e
93.389	National Center/Research Resources	1,082,371	1,061,105	1,115,884 e	1,069,627 e
93.392	Cancer Construction	0	0	0	0
93.393	Cancer Cause, Prevention	719,744	638,419	675,494 e	665,744 e
93.394	Cancer Detection, Diagnosis	285,928	304,447	299,830 e	296,547 e
93.395	Cancer Treatment Research	563,811	575,006	552,681 e	546,177 e
93.396	Cancer Biology Research	560,681	580,272	563,618 e	542,875 e
93.397	Cancer Centers Support	454,252	463,860	487,505 e	495,505 e
93.398	Cancer Research Manpower	178,531	180,621	182,702 e	184,902 e
93.399	Cancer Control	231,809	213,482	217,879 e	221,379 e
93.441	Indian Self-Determination	(n)	509,600 e	0 e	0 e
93.442	Special Diabetes Program/Indians	23,300	23,300 e	23,300 e	0 e
93.443	Native American Health Promotion	1,292	1,300 e	1,300 e	0 e
93.447	State Health Fraud Task Force	164	168 e	49 e	50 e
93.448	Food Safety, Security Monitoring	2,493	3,080 e	3,083 e	3,154 e
93.449	Ruminant Feed Ban Support Project	1,831	1,831	2,000 e	2,000 e
93.550	Transitional Living/Homeless Youth	37,634	39,392	39,409	39,399 e
93.551	Abandoned Infants	11,955	11,835	11,835	11,835 e
93.556	Promoting Safe and Stable Families	390,333	421,160	381,160	386,160 e
93.557	Street Outreach Program	15,078	14,898	14,897	14,887 e
93.558	Temporary Assistance/Families	17,266,850	17,040,628 e	17,120,658 e	0 e
93.560	Family Support Payments	33,000	38,000	38,000	38,000 e
93.563	Child Support Enforcement	4,083,491	4,196,528	4,414,678 e	3,962,713 e

Please see "Important Notes on the Tables, Footnotes," page 842

Table 1. *(continued)*

Program number	ADMINISTRATIVE ENTITY/SUB-UNIT Program Title (abridged)	FY 2005 in $thousands	FY 2006 in $thousands	FY 2007 in $thousands	FY 2008 in $thousands
93.564	Child Support Enforcement Research	1,800	1,800	1,800 e	1,800 e
93.566	Refugee and Entrant Assistance	211,414	243,627	243,986	289,557 e
93.567	Refugees, Entrants—Agencies	50,000	50,000	60,000	60,000 e
93.568	Low-Income Home Energy Assistance	2,161,752	0 e	0 e	0 e
93.569	Community Services Block Grant	636,789	629,978 e	630,425 e	0 e
93.570	CSBG—Discretionary	34,536	34,291	34,315	0 e
93.571	CSBG—Community Food, Nutrition	7,080	0 e	0	0 e
93.575	Child Care, Development Block Grant	2,082,921	2,062,081	2,062,081	2,062,081 e
93.576	Refugee, Entrant—Discretionary	71,500	71,239	75,536	67,705 e
93.577	Early Learning Fund	35,712	0	0	0 e
93.579	U.S. Repatriation Program	1,000	1,000	1,000 e	1,300 e
93.581	Indian/Environmental Quality	1,416	1,762	1,500	1,500 e
93.582	Environmental Impacts/Indian Lands	207	75	1,200	0
93.583	Refugee, Entrant Assistance-Wilson	19,000	16,913	17,272	23,000 e
93.584	Refugee, Entrant Assistance—Targeted	44,173	43,731 e	43,731 e	43,731 e
93.586	State Court Improvement	13,253	32,940	32,940	32,940 e
93.587	Native American Languages	3,553	1,554	2,500	2,500 e
93.590	Community-Based Child Abuse Prevention	42,857	42,430	42,430	42,430 e
93.591	Domestic Violence Coalitions	12,563	12,473	12,473	12,473 e
93.592	Family Violence—Discretionary	15,787	125,050	126,510 e	126,510 e
93.593	Job Opportunities/Low-Income	5,436	5,378 e	5,382 e	0 e
93.594	Tribal Work Grants	7,558	7,558	7,558	7,558 e
93.595	Welfare Reform Research \ i	107,527	97,147	97,218	101,880 e
93.596	Child Care, Development	2,717,000	2,917,000	2,917,000	2,917,000 e
93.597	Access and Visitation Programs	10,000	10,000	10,000 e	12,000 e
93.598	Victims of Trafficking	5,690	2,407	2,202	6,085 e
93.599	Chafee Vouchers	46,612	46,157	46,157	46,157 e
93.600	Head Start	6,779,725	6,691,742	6,740,071	6,740,071 e
93.601	Child Support Enforcement	1,551	1,572	1,700 e	1,500 e
93.602	Assets/Independence Demonstration	24,702	24,435	24,452	24,452 e
93.603	Adoption Incentive Payments	14,488	17,808	5,000	13,500 e
93.604	Assistance for Torture Victims	9,618	9,513	9,476	9,372 e
93.612	Native American Programs	23,583	37,804	37,753	37,853
93.613	President's Committee/Disabilities	552	565	588	612 e
93.616	Mentoring Children of Prisoners	49,044	49,037	54,006 e	59,451 e
93.617	Voting/Individuals with Disabilities	9,919	10,879	10,890 e	10,890 e
93.618	Voting/P & A Systems	4,796	4,830	4,830	4,830 e
93.623	Basic Center Grant	48,644	47,979	48,074	48,064 e
93.630	Developmental Disabilities/Basic	110,605	110,462	110,489	110,489 e
93.631	Developmental Disabilities/Projects	11,542	11,355	11,414	11,414 e
93.632	Developmental Disabilities/University	31,549	33,190	33,213	33,213 e
93.643	Children's Justice Grants	17,000	17,000	17,000	17,000 e
93.645	Child Welfare Services	289,650	286,754 e	286,754 e	286,754 e
93.647	Social Services Research	107,527	97,147	97,218 e	101,880
93.648	Child Welfare Services Training	7,409	7,335	7,335	7,335 e
93.652	Adoption Opportunities	27,116	27,848	26,848	26,848 e
93.658	Foster Care	4,371,198	4,325,363	4,475,000	4,593,000 e
93.659	Adoption Assistance	1,712,125	1,791,460	2,027,000	2,159,000 e
93.667	Social Services Block Grant	1,700,000	1,700,000 e	1,700,000 e	1,200,000 e
93.669	Child Abuse, Neglect State Grants	27,280	27,007	27,007	27,007 e
93.670	Child Abuse, Neglect Discretionary	31,640	25,446	25,780	36,138 e
93.671	Family Violence/States, Indians	100,504	99,784	99,784	99,784 e
93.674	Chafee Foster Care Independence	139,996	140,000	140,000	140,000 e
93.676	Unaccompanied Alien Children	43,405	61,276	61,862	114,763 e
93.760	Rural Elderly Care	0	7,500	5,000	2,500 e
93.767	State Children's Insurance Program	4,725,018	4,538,772	5,940,730	6,640,000 e
93.768	Medicaid Infrastructure/Disabled	25,639	30,777	37,075	40,200 e
93.769	Independence, Employment	15,000	72,666	36,080	2,000 e
93.770	Medicare Prescription Drugs \ t	531,618	31,717,610	49,103,284	45,087,000 e
93.773	Medicare—Hospital Insurance \ t	184,309,000	183,570,891	204,535,775	226,122,000 e
93.774	Medicare—Supplementary \ t	149,778,249	159,657,881	180,941,362	187,935,000 e
93.775	Medicaid Fraud Control	149,400	161,600	174,800 e	183,540 e
93.776	Hurricane Katrina Relief	0	1,863,913	370,784	19,064 e
93.777	State Survey/Providers, Suppliers	416,413	425,124	427,185	467,009

Please see "Important Notes on the Tables, Footnotes," page 842

Table 1. *(continued)*

Program number	ADMINISTRATIVE ENTITY/SUB-UNIT Program Title (abridged)	FY 2005 in $thousands	FY 2006 in $thousands	FY 2007 in $thousands	FY 2008 in $thousands
93.778	Medicaid	193,197,944	195,012,679	203,499,801	204,052,706 e
93.779	Medicare, Medicaid Research	77,331	62,394	57,317	33,701 e
93.780	Grants to States/High-Risk Pools	40,000	75,046 e	0	0
93.781	Seed Grants/High-Risk Pools	0	2,450	1,450	0 e
93.783	Medicare Drug Assistance/States \ t	1,124,809	228,594	9,815	0 e
93.784	Reimbursement/Undocumented Aliens	250	170,000	219,919	225,000 e
93.785	Background Checks—Long-Term Care	11,504	9,997	16	1,184 e
93.786	State Pharmaceutical Assistance	62,500	62,500	20,274	0 e
93.789	Children's Treatment Alternatives	21,000	0	21,326	37,168 e
93.791	Money Follows the Person	0	0	45,935	350,470 e
93.793	Medicaid Transformation Grants	0	0	75,000	75,000 e
93.794	Part D State Cost Reimbursement \ t	0	292,436	233,000	0 e
93.822	Health Careers Opportunity Program	32,790	3,878	3,957	9,825 e
93.824	Area Health Education Centers	13,777	13,900	13,900 e	13,200 e
93.837	Heart, Vascular Diseases Research	1,327,584	1,570,605	1,570,605 e	1,570,605 e
93.838	Lung Diseases Research	557,295	531,460	531,460 e	531,460 e
93.839	Blood Diseases, Resources Research	398,565	411,308	411,308 e	411,308 e
93.846	Arthritis/Skin Diseases Research	412,182	407,077	411,858 e	404,776 e
93.847	Diabetes, Endocrinology, Metabolism	580,702	567,990	576,281 e	567,411 e
93.848	Digestive Diseases, Nutrition	421,978	414,649	420,622 e	414,239 e
93.849	Kidney Diseases, Urology, Hematology	374,980	384,060	389,635 e	383,689 e
93.853	Neuroscience, Neurological Disorders	1,349,102	1,325,701	1,322,030 e	1,323,610 e
93.855	Allergy, Immunology, Transplantation	604,062	649,575	654,705 e	656,722 e
93.856	Microbiology, Infectious Diseases	2,108,678	1,993,108	2,008,375 e	2,014,425 e
93.859	Biomedical Research, Training	1,849,215	1,845,062	1,859,512 e	1,839,855 e
93.865	Child Health, Development Research	929,389	873,263	882,894	877,944 e
93.866	Aging Research	890,322	879,755	885,172 e	870,787 e
93.867	Vision Research	523,968	538,750	533,329 e	533,749 e
93.879	Medical Library Assistance	66,619	69,247	67,568 e	67,568 e
93.884	Primary Care Medicine, Dentistry	81,898	37,907	45,532	47,346
93.887	Renovation/Health Care Facilities	422,452	0 e	0 e	0 e
93.888	Specially Selected Health Projects	18	0 e	0 e	0 e
93.889	Bioterrorism Hospital Preparedness	466,000	460,217	415,032	398,059 e
93.890	Healthy Communities Access Program	3,200	0	0 e	0 e
93.891	Alcohol Research Center Grants	30,201	29,687	27,276 e	27,276 e
93.908	Nursing Education Loan Repayment	18,715	19,245	19,000 e	27,000 e
93.910	Family Life Centers	7,400	7,400	0 e	0 e
93.912	Rural Health Outreach, Development	33,212	24,527 e	24,097 e	24,097 e
93.913	Offices of Rural Health	7,400	7,209 e	7,400 e	7,400 e
93.914	HIV Emergency Relief Project Grants	587,426	587,426 e	537,645 e	537,645 e
93.917	HIV Care Formula Grants	1,059,875	1,059,875	1,195,500 e	1,195,500 e
93.918	Outpatient Early Intervention/HIV	187,148	182,240	181,850 e	181,850 e
93.919	Breast, Cervical Cancer Detection	161,285	155,586	158,086 e	158,086 e
93.923	Disadvantaged Health Faculty Loan	1,108	1,088	1,071	0 e
93.924	HIV/AIDS Dental Reimbursements	9,334	12,654 e	12,654 e	12,654 e
93.925	Health Professions Scholarships	44,673	44,059	44,000 e	7,733 e
93.926	Healthy Start Initiative	95,781	97,069	96,669 e	95,669 e
93.928	Projects of National Significance	25,000	24,902	24,755	25,000 e
93.932	Hawaiian Health Systems	12,288	12,735	12,545	125,450 e
93.933	Demonstration Projects/Indian Health	11,959	11,959	11,959 e	0 e
93.936	AIDS Research Loan Repayment	452	610 e	610 e	0 e
93.938	School Health Programs/HIV	34,059	35,594 e	35,594	35,594 e
93.939	HIV Prevention—Non-Governmental	80,138	78,565	81,101 e	81,060 e
93.940	HIV Prevention—Health Department	301,206	292,719	331,086 e	333,799 e
93.941	HIV Demonstration, Research	5,427	12,733	19,062 e	11,483 e
93.942	Research, Treatment/Lyme Disease	3,493	3,144	2,986	2,450 e
93.943	Epidemiologic Research/AIDS, HIV	12,606	6,605	5,085	5,138 e
93.944	HIV/AIDS Surveillance	71,234	67,014	68,070 e	71,171 e
93.945	Chronic Disease Prevention, Control	71,909	62,096 e	60,262 e	0 e
93.946	Motherhood, Infant Health Initiative	4,600	5,500 e	5,500 e	0 e
93.947	Tuberculosis Demonstration	1,385	1,209	1,697 e	1,697 e
93.952	Trauma Care	1,611	0	0 e	0 e
93.954	Tribal Recruitment/Health	580	580 e	580 e	0 e
93.958	Block Grants/Mental Health	410,953	406,843	406,843 e	406,843 e

Please see "Important Notes on the Tables, Footnotes," page 842

Table 1. *(continued)*

Program number	ADMINISTRATIVE ENTITY/SUB-UNIT Program Title (abridged)	FY 2005 in $thousands	FY 2006 in $thousands	FY 2007 in $thousands	FY 2008 in $thousands
93.959	Block Grants/Substance Abuse	1,686,777	1,670,661	1,670,661 e	1,670,661 e
93.962	Health Administration Traineeships	1,035	0	0 e	0 e
93.964	Public Health Traineeships	1,483	1,290	1,257 e	1,258 e
93.965	Coal Miners Respiratory Impairment	5,890	5,800 e	5,800 e	5,800 e
93.969	Geriatric Education Centers	17,142	0	17,000 e	17,000 e
93.970	Health Professions/Indians	3,520	3,520 e	3,520 e	0 e
93.971	Health Preparatory/Indians	2,519	2,519 e	2,519 e	0 e
93.972	Health Professions Scholarship	9,604	9,604 e	9,604 e	0 e
93.974	Family Planning—Service Research	5,456	5,456	5,456 e	0 e
93.977	STD Control	5,400	105,454	104,844 e	104,283 e
93.978	STD Research	111,000	5,580	5,034 e	5,034 e
93.982	Mental Health Disaster Assistance	5,811	0	64,312	0 e
93.988	Diabetes Control Programs	28,864	28,547	29,859 e	29,859 e
93.989	International Research, Training	51,920	50,962	50,033	50,100 e
93.990	National Health Promotion	4,000	4,000	4,000 e	0 e
93.991	Health Services Block Grant	106,100	92,937 e	93,327 e	0 e
93.993	Public Health Research Accreditation	100	100	0	0
93.994	Maternal, Child Health Block Grant	585,970	561,618	561,618 e	573,958 e
93.995	Adolescent Family Life	25,000	25,000	25,000 e	0 e
93.996	Bioterrorism Training, Curriculum	26,600	21,000	21,000	0 e
	DEPARTMENT TOTAL: OUTLAYS	616,398,208	659,378,157	729,802,284	733,386,725
	CREDITS*	21,115*	18,220*	28,851*	19,050*
	CORPORATION FOR NATIONAL AND COMMUNITY SERVICE				
94.002	Retired, Senior Volunteer Program	58,528	59,685 e	59,685 e	0 e
94.003	State Commissions	11,904	12,516 e	12,516 e	0 e
94.004	Learn and Serve/School, Community	31,992	27,844 e	25,616 e	0 e
94.005	Learn and Serve/Higher Education	10,644	9,281 e	8,539 e	0 e
94.006	AmeriCorps	287,680	264,830 e	258,960 e	0 e
94.007	Planning, Program Development	13,227	16,281 e	9,029 e	0 e
94.009	Training, Technical Assistance	13,227	16,281 e	9,029 e	0 e
94.011	Foster Grandparent Program	111,424	110,937 e	110,943	0 e
94.013	Volunteers in Service to America	94,240	95,460 e	95,470 e	0 e
94.016	Senior Companion Program	45,905	46,964 e	46,964 e	0 e
	DEPARTMENT TOTAL: OUTLAYS	678,771	660,079	636,751	0
	CREDITS*	0*	0*	0*	0*
	SOCIAL SECURITY ADMINISTRATION				
96.001	Social Security—Disability \ t	83,765,000	90,644,000 e	96,988,000	102,854,000 e
96.002	Social Security—Retirement \ t	343,652,000	383,413,000	406,880,000 e	428,032,000 e
96.004	Survivors Insurance \ t	65,581,000	67,801,000	69,830,000	71,704,000 e
96.006	Supplemental Security Income	33,661,000	37,510,765	36,481,898	41,225,000 e
96.007	Research and Demonstration \ t	17,079	23,756 e	22,855 e	0 e
96.008	Benefits Planning, Outreach \ t	23,000	23,000	23,000 e	23,000 e
96.009	Incentives/Disabled Beneficiaries \ t	7,000	7,000	7,000 e	7,000 e
96.020	Benefits/World War II Veterans	9,544	10,000 e	11,000 e	0 e
	DEPARTMENT TOTAL: OUTLAYS	526,715,623	579,432,521	610,243,753	643,845,000
	CREDITS*	0*	0*	0*	0*
	DEPARTMENT OF HOMELAND SECURITY				
97.001	Earmarked Projects	(a)	(a)	(a)	(a)
97.002	Research Projects	(a)	(a)	(a)	(a)
97.004	State Domestic Preparedness	(a)	(a)	(a)	(a)
97.005	State, Local Training Program	165,000	125,461	84,077	0 e
97.006	State, Local Exercise Support	50,000	0	0 e	0 e
97.007	Preparedness Technical Assistance	30,000	1,565	1,550	0 e
97.008	Urban Areas Security Initiative	854,657	(o)	(o)	(o)

Please see "Important Notes on the Tables, Footnotes," page 842

Table 1. *(continued)*

Program number	ADMINISTRATIVE ENTITY/SUB-UNIT Program Title (abridged)	FY 2005 in $thousands	FY 2006 in $thousands	FY 2007 in $thousands	FY 2008 in $thousands
97.009	Cuban/Haitian Entrant Program	9,000	10,292	8,688	10,000 e
97.010	Citizenship Education, Training	30	30 e	30 e	0 e
97.011	Boating Safety	16,400	3,455	6,429	7,504 e
97.012	Boating Safety Financial \ t	57,000	109,488 e	111,916 e	110,284 e
97.013	Oil Spill Trust Fund \ t	0	0	0 e	0 e
97.014	Bridge Alteration	0	18,015	16,029	16,400 e
97.015	Secret Service—Training Activities	0	0	0 e	0 e
97.016	Firefighting/Federal Property	0	1	0 e	0 e
97.018	National Fire Academy Training	1,265	1,464	1,500 e	1,500 e
97.019	Fire Academy Educational Program	3,387	5,136 e	5,200 e	5,200 e
97.020	Hazardous Materials Training	205	0	0 e	0 e
97.021	Hazardous Materials Assistance	106	0	0	0 e
97.022	Flood Insurance \ r	112,593*	118,763*e	128,588*e	138,786*e
97.023	Community Assistance Program \ r	8,901	7,500 e	7,500 e	7,500 e
97.024	Emergency Food, Shelter	153,000	151,470 e	151,470 e	153,000 e
97.025	National Urban Search, Rescue	25,070	17,101 e	17,101 e	0 e
97.026	EMI—Training Assistance	1,300	1,407 e	1,242 e	1,242 e
97.027	EMI—Independent Study	422	874 e	870 e	881 e
97.028	EMI—Resident Education	0	3,500 e	3,500 e	3,500 e
97.029	Flood Mitigation Assistance	20,000	28,000 e	31,000 e	0 e
97.030	Community Disaster Loans	567*	1,270,501*	0*	0*e
97.031	Cora Brown Fund \ t	0	0	0 e	0 e
97.032	Crisis Counseling	42,896	96,149	38,863 e	0 e
97.033	Disaster Legal Services	30	361	51 e	0 e
97.034	Disaster Unemployment Assistance	88,752	392,016 e	62,000 e	0 e
97.036	Disaster Grants—Public Assistance	4,313,443	7,181,452	4,154,462	5,314,729 e
97.039	Hazard Mitigation Grant	184,503	382,706 e	0	0 e
97.040	Chemical Stockpile Emergency	54,871	62,117 e	54,887 e	88,156 e
97.041	Dam Safety	3,376	3,212 e	3,212 e	0 e
97.042	Emergency Management Performance	178,828	177,656 e	194,000	0 e
97.043	State Fire Training Systems Grants	1,400	1,344 e	1,200 e	1,200 e
97.044	Assistance to Firefighters Grant	633,500	539,500	547,000 e	0 e
97.045	Cooperating Technical Partners	40,000	56,000	54,000	0 e
97.046	Fire Management Assistance	140,198	68,144	62,180	106,474 e
97.047	Pre-Disaster Mitigation	150,000	100,000 e	0 e	0 e
97.048	Individual, Household Housing	0	3,580,522	189,367	0 e
97.049	Disaster Housing Operations	2,376	4,747,802 e	80,576 e	0 e
97.050	Individuals, Households/Other	66,189	86,033 e	5,426 e	0 e
97.052	Emergency Operations Centers	(n)	(n)	(n)	(n)
97.053	Citizen Corps	13,486	1,295	550	0 e
97.055	Interoperable Communications	0	0	0 e	0 e
97.056	Port Security Grant Program	146,357	168,053	312,270	210,000 e
97.057	Intercity Bus Security	9,657	9,503	11,640	0 e
97.058	Operation Safe Commerce	0	0	0 e	0 e
97.059	Truck Security	5,000	4,802	11,640	9,000 e
97.060	Port Security Research, Development	0	0	0 e	0 e
97.061	Centers for Homeland Security	40,285	0	24,714	29,750 e
97.062	Scholars and Fellows	29,715	0	3,500	7,300 e
97.064	Debris Removal Insurance	0	0	0 e	0 e
97.065	Advanced Research Projects Agency	5,351	0	0 e	0 e
97.066	Information Technology, Evaluation	630	0	0 e	0 e
97.067	Homeland Security Grant Program \ i	2,610,000	1,670,922	1,666,460	0 e
97.068	Competitive Training Grants	30,000	28,809	29,100	0 e
97.069	Aviation Research Grants	15,535	23,721	0	0 e
97.070	Map Modernization Management Support	5,600	5,200	5,200	0 e
97.071	Metropolitan Medical Response System	22,281,408	(a)	(a)	(a)
97.072	Explosives Detection Canine Team	28,000	28,900	21,300	31,000 e
97.073	State Homeland Security Program	1,062,285	(a)	(a)	(a)
97.074	Law Enforcement Terrorism Prevention	386,286	(a)	(a)	(a)
97.075	Rail and Transit Security	150,000	143,241	271,780	0 e
97.076	Center/Missing, Exploited Children	5,200	5,445 e	6,000	6,000 e
97.077	Testing, Evaluation, Demonstration \ p	0	1,000 e	0 e	0 e
97.078	Buffer Zone Protection Plan	92,000	50,000	50,000	0 e
97.079	Public Alert Radios for Schools	500	2,270 e	2,930 e	1,500 e

Please see "Important Notes on the Tables, Footnotes," page 842

Table 1. *(continued)*

Program number	ADMINISTRATIVE ENTITY/SUB-UNIT Program Title (abridged)		FY 2005 in $thousands	FY 2006 in $thousands	FY 2007 in $thousands	FY 2008 in $thousands
97.080	IAIP Pilot Projects		0	0	17,352	0 e
97.081	Law Enforcement Training, Technical		1,116	1,137	1,155	1,155 e
97.082	Earthquake Consortium		885	925 e	925 e	0 e
97.083	Staffing/Fire, Emergency		65,000	110,000 e	115,000 e	0 e
97.084	Hurricane Katrina Case Management \ t		(n)	0	0	0
97.085	9/11 Heroes Stamp Program \ t		(n)	10,565 e	0 e	0 e
97.086	Outreach, Education, Technical		(n)	4,813	2,346	0 e
97.087	Alternative Housing Pilot Program		(n)	(n)	388,000 e	0 e
97.088	Disaster Assistance Projects		0	0	0 e	0 e
97.089	Real ID Program		0	6,000 e	6,000 e	0 e
97.090	Law Enforcement Reimbursement		63,612	67,365	66,295	65,050 e
97.091	Homeland Security Biowatch \ p		14,764	25,500 e	25,500 e	0 e
97.092	Repetitive Flood Claims		0	9,800 e	10,000 e	10,000 e
97.093	Hazardous Materials Preparedness		50	50 e	50 e	50 e
97.094	Resources and Data Exchange		0	30 e	30 e	30 e
97.095	Safe Kids Worldwide		225	200 e	200 e	200 e
97.096	Commercial Equipment Assistance \ p		40,000	34,629 e	38,651 e	40,000 e
97.097	Training Resource and Data Exchange		93	93 e	93 e	0 e
97.098	Disaster Donations		(n)	1,400 e	0 e	0 e
97.099	Fire Safety Initiatives, Residential		(n)	130	130 e	0 e
97.100	Airport Checked Baggage Screening		(n)	240,447	187,822 e	0 e
97.103	Degrees at a Distance		(n)	0	95 e	70 e
97.104	STEM Career Development		(n)	0	6,000 e	0 e
97.105	Firefighter/EMS Assistance		(n)	0	75	0 e
97.106	Securing Cities \ p		(n)	0	3,250	30,000 e
97.107	Incident Management System		(n)	6,815	6,815	5,700 e
97.108	Homeland Security Technologies \ p		(n)	0	593	0 e
97.109	Disaster Housing Grants		(n)	0	204,000 e	365,000 e
97.110	Flood Loss Program		(n)	40,000	40,000	80,000 e
97.111	Catastrophic Preparedness Grant		(n)	35,000 e	35,000 e	0 e
	DEPARTMENT TOTAL:	OUTLAYS	34,399,145	20,697,833	9,467,787	6,719,375
		CREDITS*	113,160*	1,389,264*	128,588*	138,786*

UNITED STATES AGENCY FOR INTERNATIONAL DEVELOPMENT

Program number	Program Title (abridged)		FY 2005 in $thousands	FY 2006 in $thousands	FY 2007 in $thousands	FY 2008 in $thousands
97.112	Border Improvement		(n)	(n)	(n)	88,000
98.001	Foreign Assistance Programs		4,061	4,510	4,698 e	0 e
98.002	Cooperative Development Program		5,500	5,500	5,500	0 e
98.003	Ocean Freight Reimbursement		2,700	2,000	2,700 e	0 e
98.004	NGO Strengthening		6,159	6,159	6,159 e	0 e
98.005	Institutional Capacity Building		5,000	5,000	0 e	0 e
98.006	American Schools, Hospitals Abroad		19,840	19,800	16,000 e	0 e
98.007	Food for Peace DAP \ p		328,829	350,000 e	350,000 e	0 e
98.008	Food for Peace Emergency Program \ p		1,193,826	609,225	0 e	0 e
98.009	John Ogonowski Farmer-to-Farmer		10,580	10,381	10,600 e	0 e
98.010	Denton Program		50	50 e	50 e	0 e
98.011	Global Development Alliance		359,000	377,000 e	395,000 e	0 e
98.012	USAID/University Partnerships		12,000	18,000 e	25,000 e	0 e
	DEPARTMENT TOTAL:	OUTLAYS	1,947,545	1,407,625	815,707	88,000
		CREDITS*	0*	0*	0*	0*
	GRAND TOTAL:	**OUTLAYS**	**1,619,873,460**	**1,674,998,842**	**1,763,709,996**	**1,746,407,522**
		CREDITS*	**276,061,882***	**294,603,708***	**261,330,092***	**252,472,184***
	GRAND TOTAL: OUTLAYS + CREDITS		**1,895,935,342**	**1,969,602,550**	**2,025,040,088**	**1,998,879,706**

Please see "Important Notes on the Tables, Footnotes," page 842

Table 2. Summary of Estimated Outlays/Credits, by Federal Department or Agency (FY 05, 06, 07, 08)

Program number	DEPARTMENT OR AGENCY	FY 2005 in $thousands	FY 2006 in $thousands	FY 2007 in $thousands	FY 2008 in $thousands
10.000	**DEPARTMENT OF AGRICULTURE**				
	Total Outlays	76,630,176	77,912,849	76,910,751	68,076,275
	Total Credits	24,387,913	31,944,759	29,990,456	9,977,054
	TOTAL OUTLAYS + CREDITS	101,018,089	109,857,608	106,901,207	78,053,329
11.000	**DEPARTMENT OF COMMERCE**				
	Total Outlays	15,137,795	3,648,401	4,736,357	832,897
	Total Credits	1,572,392	1,840,902	1,906,966	0
	TOTAL OUTLAYS + CREDITS	16,710,187	5,489,303	6,643,323	832,897
12.000	**DEPARTMENT OF DEFENSE**				
	Total Outlays	1,795,283	1,683,412	1,451,296	121,500
	Total Credits	0	0	0	0
	TOTAL OUTLAYS + CREDITS	1,795,283	1,683,412	1,451,296	121,500
14.000	**DEPARTMENT OF HOUSING AND URBAN DEVELOPMENT**				
	Total Outlays	39,924,913	63,848,389	46,063,503	43,068,320
	Total Credits	77,905,632	79,964,558	63,412,534	79,039,079
	TOTAL OUTLAYS + CREDITS	117,830,545	143,812,947	109,476,037	122,107,399
15.000	**DEPARTMENT OF THE INTERIOR**				
	Total Outlays	3,702,010	3,400,934	3,821,280	3,088,034
	Total Credits	6,332	76,703	82,170	105,000
	TOTAL OUTLAYS + CREDITS	3,708,342	3,477,637	3,903,450	3,193,034
16.000	**DEPARTMENT OF JUSTICE**				
	Total Outlays	3,514,503	3,668,223	4,006,330	1,271,732
	Total Credits	0	0	0	0
	TOTAL OUTLAYS + CREDITS	3,514,503	3,668,223	4,006,330	1,271,732
17.000	**DEPARTMENT OF LABOR**				
	Total Outlays	42,251,525	41,816,546	52,381,438	42,922,825
	Total Credits	0	0	0	0
	TOTAL OUTLAYS + CREDITS	42,251,525	41,816,546	52,381,438	42,922,825
19.000	**DEPARTMENT OF STATE**				
	Total Outlays	821,027	725,368	342,916	0
	Total Credits	0	0	0	0
	TOTAL OUTLAYS + CREDITS	821,027	725,368	342,916	0
20.000	**DEPARTMENT OF TRANSPORTATION**				
	Total Outlays	91,197,221	35,292,825	37,210,796	6,230,867
	Total Credits	46,124	231,784	1,462,039	638,000
	TOTAL OUTLAYS + CREDITS	91,243,345	35,524,609	38,672,835	6,868,867
21.000	**DEPARTMENT OF THE TREASURY**				
	Total Outlays	1,200,444	1,179,207	1,147,251	1,162,688
	Total Credits	0	0	0	0
	TOTAL OUTLAYS + CREDITS	1,200,444	1,179,207	1,147,251	1,162,688
23.000	**APPALACHIAN REGIONAL COMMISSION**				
	Total Outlays	395,186	464,213	489,636	551,000
	Total Credits	0	0	0	0
	TOTAL OUTLAYS + CREDITS	395,186	464,213	489,636	551,000
27.000	**OFFICE OF PERSONNEL MANAGEMENT**				
	Total Outlays	0	0	0	0
	Total Credits	0	0	0	0
	TOTAL OUTLAYS + CREDITS	0	0	0	0

Please see "Important Notes on the Tables, Footnotes," page 842

Table 2. *(continued)*

Program number	Department or Agency	FY 2005 in $thousands	FY 2006 in $thousands	FY 2007 in $thousands	FY 2008 in $thousands
29.000	**COMMISSION ON CIVIL RIGHTS**				
	Total Outlays	8,740	8,740	8,740	0
	Total Credits	0	0	0	0
	TOTAL OUTLAYS + CREDITS	8,740	8,740	8,740	0
30.000	**EQUAL EMPLOYMENT OPPORTUNITY COMMISSION**				
	Total Outlays	359,387	359,383	359,228	0
	Total Credits	0	0	0	0
	TOTAL OUTLAYS + CREDITS	359,387	359,383	359,228	0
32.000	**FEDERAL COMMUNICATIONS COMMISSION**				
	Total Outlays	0	0	0	0
	Total Credits	0	0	0	0
	TOTAL OUTLAYS + CREDITS	0	0	0	0
33.000	**FEDERAL MARITIME COMMISSION**				
	Total Outlays	733	997	1,047	0
	Total Credits	0	0	0	0
	TOTAL OUTLAYS + CREDITS	733	997	1,047	0
34.000	**FEDERAL MEDIATION AND CONCILIATION SERVICE**				
	Total Outlays	45,927	42,997	43,245	43,800
	Total Credits	0	0	0	0
	TOTAL OUTLAYS + CREDITS	45,927	42,997	43,245	43,800
36.000	**FEDERAL TRADE COMMISSION**				
	Total Outlays	200,477	210,080	223,635	240,239
	Total Credits	0	0	0	0
	TOTAL OUTLAYS + CREDITS	200,477	210,080	223,635	240,239
39.000	**GENERAL SERVICES ADMINISTRATION**				
	Total Outlays	71,960	73,219	108,868	103,480
	Total Credits	0	0	0	0
	TOTAL OUTLAYS + CREDITS	71,960	73,219	108,868	103,480
40.000	**GOVERNMENT PRINTING OFFICE**				
	Total Outlays	60,697	57,804	43,000	0
	Total Credits	0	0	0	0
	TOTAL OUTLAYS + CREDITS	60,697	57,804	43,000	0
42.000	**LIBRARY OF CONGRESS**				
	Total Outlays	99,500	106,194	86,691	127,185
	Total Credits	0	0	0	0
	TOTAL OUTLAYS + CREDITS	99,500	106,194	86,691	127,185
43.000	**NATIONAL AERONAUTICS AND SPACE ADMINISTRATION**				
	Total Outlays	38,900	53,189	30,540	31,000
	Total Credits	0	0	0	0
	TOTAL OUTLAYS + CREDITS	38,900	53,189	30,540	31,000
44.000	**NATIONAL CREDIT UNION ADMINISTRATION**				
	Total Outlays	0	0	0	0
	Total Credits	237,574	240,879	275,300	276,500
	TOTAL OUTLAYS + CREDITS	237,574	240,879	275,300	276,500
45.000	**NATIONAL FOUNDATION ON THE ARTS AND THE HUMANITIES**				
	Total Outlays	458,163	571,031	470,493	464,049
	Total Credits	0	0	0	0
	TOTAL OUTLAYS + CREDITS	458,163	571,031	470,493	464,049
46.000	**NATIONAL LABOR RELATIONS BOARD**				
	Total Outlays	249,973	249,940	249,888	0
	Total Credits	0	0	0	0
	TOTAL OUTLAYS + CREDITS	249,973	249,940	249,888	0

Please see "Important Notes on the Tables, Footnotes," page 842

Table 2. *(continued)*

Program number	Department or Agency	FY 2005 in $thousands	FY 2006 in $thousands	FY 2007 in $thousands	FY 2008 in $thousands
47.000	**NATIONAL SCIENCE FOUNDATION**				
	Total Outlays	4,713,555	4,737,420	5,042,790	5,133,090
	Total Credits	0	0	0	0
	TOTAL OUTLAYS + CREDITS	4,713,555	4,737,420	5,042,790	5,133,090
57.000	**RAILROAD RETIREMENT BOARD**				
	Total Outlays	9,265,000	9,534,000	9,907,000	10,178,000
	Total Credits	0	0	0	0
	TOTAL OUTLAYS + CREDITS	9,265,000	9,534,000	9,907,000	10,178,000
58.000	**SECURITIES AND EXCHANGE COMMISSION**				
	Total Outlays	888,227	888,117	904,846	0
	Total Credits	0	0	0	0
	TOTAL OUTLAYS + CREDITS	888,227	888,117	904,846	0
59.000	**SMALL BUSINESS ADMINISTRATION**				
	Total Outlays	966,943	247,745	248,200	272,140
	Total Credits	20,206,773	20,528,396	25,109,904	28,882,297
	TOTAL OUTLAYS + CREDITS	21,173,716	20,776,141	25,358,104	29,154,437
64.000	**DEPARTMENT OF VETERANS AFFAIRS**				
	Total Outlays	78,662,553	83,877,681	89,095,256	97,539,933
	Total Credits	22,552,867	24,470,512	24,500,284	29,111,418
	TOTAL OUTLAYS + CREDITS	101,215,420	108,348,193	113,595,540	126,651,351
66.000	**ENVIRONMENTAL PROTECTION AGENCY**				
	Total Outlays	4,374,829	4,326,008	6,003,474	3,750,435
	Total Credits	0	0	0	0
	TOTAL OUTLAYS + CREDITS	4,374,829	4,326,008	6,003,474	3,750,435
68.000	**NATIONAL GALLERY OF ART**				
	Total Outlays	410	416	430	450
	Total Credits	0	0	0	0
	TOTAL OUTLAYS + CREDITS	410	416	430	450
70.000	**OVERSEAS PRIVATE INVESTMENT CORPORATION**				
	Total Outlays	0	0	0	0
	Total Credits	3,157,000	3,000,000	3,150,000	0
	TOTAL OUTLAYS + CREDITS	3,157,000	3,000,000	3,150,000	0
77.000	**NUCLEAR REGULATORY COMMISSION**				
	Total Outlays	0	0	6,000	400
	Total Credits	0	0	0	0
	TOTAL OUTLAYS + CREDITS	0	0	6,000	400
78.000	**COMMODITY FUTURES TRADING COMMISSION**				
	Total Outlays	67,850	70,400	70,400	0
	Total Credits	0	0	0	0
	TOTAL OUTLAYS + CREDITS	67,850	70,400	70,400	0
81.000	**DEPARTMENT OF ENERGY**				
	Total Outlays	2,095,624	1,973,137	2,153,639	11,262,555
	Total Credits	0	0	0	0
	TOTAL OUTLAYS + CREDITS	2,095,624	1,973,137	2,153,639	11,262,555
84.000	**DEPARTMENT OF EDUCATION**				
	Total Outlays	56,995,589	63,181,851	58,316,735	61,122,744
	Total Credits	125,855,000	130,897,731	111,283,000	104,285,000
	TOTAL OUTLAYS + CREDITS	182,850,589	194,079,582	169,599,735	165,407,744
85.000	**SCHOLARSHIP AND FELLOWSHIP FOUNDATIONS**				
	Total Outlays	8,301	9,531	306,649	2,033
	Total Credits	0	0	0	0
	TOTAL OUTLAYS + CREDITS	8,301	9,531	306,649	2,033

Please see "Important Notes on the Tables, Footnotes," page 842

Table 2. *(continued)*

Program number	Department or Agency	FY 2005 in $thousands	FY 2006 in $thousands	FY 2007 in $thousands	FY 2008 in $thousands
86.000	**PENSION BENEFIT GUARANTY CORPORATION**				
	Total Outlays	3,314,800	4,639,000	4,890,000	4,606,000
	Total Credits	0	0	0	0
	TOTAL OUTLAYS + CREDITS	3,314,800	4,639,000	4,890,000	4,606,000
88.000	**ARCHITECTURAL AND TRANSPORTATION BARRIERS COMPLIANCE BOARD**				
	Total Outlays	5,160	4,354,000	5,427,000	0
	Total Credits	0	0	0	0
	TOTAL OUTLAYS + CREDITS	5,160	4,354,000	5,427,000	0
89.000	**NATIONAL ARCHIVES AND RECORDS ADMINISTRATION**				
	Total Outlays	89,333	56,229	57,815	55,346
	Total Credits	0	0	0	0
	TOTAL OUTLAYS + CREDITS	89,333	56,229	57,815	55,346
90.000	**INDEPENDENT BOARDS AND COMMISSIONS**				
	Total Outlays	121,454	153,151	126,551	109,405
	Total Credits	0	0	0	0
	TOTAL OUTLAYS + CREDITS	121,454	153,151	126,551	109,405
93.000	**DEPARTMENT OF HEALTH AND HUMAN SERVICES**				
	Total Outlays	616,398,208	659,378,157	729,802,284	733,386,725
	Total Credits	21,115	18,220	28,851	19,050
	TOTAL OUTLAYS + CREDITS	616,419,323	659,396,377	729,831,135	733,405,775
94.000	**CORPORATION FOR NATIONAL AND COMMUNITY SERVICE**				
	Total Outlays	678,771	660,079	636,751	0
	Total Credits	0	0	0	0
	TOTAL OUTLAYS + CREDITS	678,771	660,079	636,751	0
96.000	**SOCIAL SECURITY ADMINISTRATION**				
	Total Outlays	526,715,623	579,432,521	610,243,753	643,845,000
	Total Credits	0	0	0	0
	TOTAL OUTLAYS + CREDITS	526,715,623	579,432,521	610,243,753	643,845,000
97.000	**DEPARTMENT OF HOMELAND SECURITY**				
	Total Outlays	34,399,145	20,697,833	9,467,787	6,719,375
	Total Credits	113,160	1,389,264	128,588	138,786
	TOTAL OUTLAYS + CREDITS	34,512,305	22,087,097	9,596,375	6,858,161
98.000	**UNITED STATES AGENCY FOR INTERNATIONAL DEVELOPMENT**				
	Total Outlays	1,947,545	1,407,625	815,707	88,000
	Total Credits	0	0	0	0
	TOTAL OUTLAYS + CREDITS	1,947,545	1,407,625	815,707	88,000
	GRAND TOTAL: OUTLAYS	**1,619,873,460**	**1,674,998,842**	**1,763,709,996**	**1,746,407,522**
	CREDITS	**276,061,882**	**294,603,708**	**261,330,092**	**252,472,184**
	GRAND TOTAL: OUTLAYS + CREDITS	**1,895,935,342**	**1,969,602,550**	**2,025,040,088**	**1,998,879,706**

Please see "Important Notes on the Tables, Footnotes," page 842

Table 3. The Fifty Largest Domestic Assistance Programs in FY 2007, by Funds Outlayed or Credited

Program number	PROGRAM TITLE (abridged)	Outlays in $thousands	Credits in $thousands	Totals in $thousands	Rank
96.002	Social Security—Retirement \ t	406,880,000	0	406,880,000	1
93.773	Medicare—Hospital Insurance \ t	204,535,775	0	204,535,775	2
93.778	Medicaid	203,499,801	0	203,499,801	3
93.774	Medicare—Supplementary \ t	180,941,362	0	180,941,362	4
84.032	Family Education Loans	0	98,261,000	98,261,000	5
96.001	Social Security—Disability \ t	96,988,000	0	96,988,000	6
96.004	Survivors Insurance \ t	69,830,000	0	69,830,000	7
93.770	Medicare Prescription Drugs \ t	49,103,284	0	49,103,284	8
14.117	Mortgage Insurance—Homes \ i, u	0	44,418,000	44,418,000	9
96.006	Supplemental Security Income	36,481,898	0	36,481,898	10
17.225	Unemployment Insurance \ t	35,050,000	0	35,050,000	11
64.009	Veterans Medical Care Benefits	32,326,744	0	32,326,744	12
10.551	Food Stamps	30,319,569	0	30,319,569	13
64.109	Service-Connected Disability	29,603,277	0	29,603,277	14
20.205	Highway Planning, Construction \ i, t	26,000,000	0	26,000,000	15
64.114	Veterans Housing—Loans \ u	0	24,490,503	24,490,503	16
59.012	Small Business Loans	0	17,541,823	17,541,823	17
93.558	Temporary Assistance/Families	17,120,658	0	17,120,658	18
14.871	Section 8 Housing Choice Vouchers	15,804,828	0	15,804,828	19
84.063	Pell Grant Program	13,660,771	0	13,660,771	20
84.268	Federal Direct Student Loans	0	13,022,000	13,022,000	21
84.010	Title I Grants	12,838,123	0	12,838,123	22
14.133	Mortgage Insurance—Condominiums \ i, u	0	12,163,144	12,163,144	23
17.004	Productivity and Technology Data	10,995,429	0	10,995,429	24
84.027	Special Education—State Grants	10,782,961	0	10,782,961	25
57.001	Social Insurance/Railroad Workers \ t	9,907,000	0	9,907,000	26
10.051	Commodity Loans, Deficiency Payments \ u	0	9,493,384	9,493,384	27
10.555	School Lunch Program \ p	8,955,074	0	8,955,074	28
14.195	Section 8—Special Allocations	8,665,000	0	8,665,000	29
10.055	Direct, Counter-Cyclical Payments \ u	8,123,433	0	8,123,433	30
10.450	Crop Insurance \ u	2,803,070	5,266,271	8,069,341	31
93.600	Head Start	6,740,071	0	6,740,071	32
59.041	Certified Development Company Loans	16,028	6,282,000	6,298,028	33
10.850	Rural Electrification Loans \ u	0	6,142,001	6,142,001	34
93.767	State Children's Insurance Program	5,940,730	0	5,940,730	35
14.311	Single Family Property Disposition \ i, p	5,571,351	0	5,571,351	36
10.557	Nutrition/Women, Infants, Children	5,547,777	0	5,547,777	37
20.507	Urbanized Area Formula Grants \ t	5,540,822	0	5,540,822	38
88.001	Compliance Board	5,427,000	0	5,427,000	39
86.001	Pension Plan Termination Insurance \ u	4,890,000	0	4,890,000	40
64.012	Veterans Prescription Service \ p	4,510,000	0	4,510,000	41
64.110	Dependency, Indemnity Compensation	4,505,306	0	4,505,306	42
93.658	Foster Care	4,475,000	0	4,475,000	43
93.563	Child Support Enforcement	4,414,678	0	4,414,678	44
97.036	Disaster Grants—Public Assistance	4,154,462	0	4,154,462	45
14.850	Public and Indian Housing	3,864,000	0	3,864,000	46
64.103	Life Insurance \ t, u	3,371,152	0	3,371,152	47
64.010	Veterans Nursing Home Care	3,316,900	0	3,316,900	48
93.268	Immunization Grants	2,936,725	0	2,936,725	49
93.596	Child Care, Development	2,917,000	0	2,917,000	50

Please see "Important Notes on the Tables, Footnotes," page 842

Table 4. The Fifty Smallest Domestic Assistance Programs in FY 2007, by Funds Outlayed or Credited*

Program number	PROGRAM TITLE (abridged)	Outlays in $actual	Credits in $actual	Totals in $actual	Rank
16.003	Narcotics, Drugs/Publications	1,000	0	1,000	1
64.128	Training/Spina Bifida	2,000	0	2,000	2
11.449	Independent Education and Science	10,000	0	10,000	3
10.070	Colorado River Salinity Control	10,000	0	10,000	4
93.288	NHSC Scholarship	15,000	0	15,000	5
93.785	Background Checks—Long-Term Care	16,000	0	16,000	6
97.094	Resources and Data Exchange	30,000	0	30,000	7
97.010	Citizenship Education, Training	30,000	0	30,000	8
10.442	Housing Application Packaging	35,000	0	35,000	9
89.005	National Archives Support	35,000	0	35,000	10
15.050	Indian Hunting, Fishing Rights	43,000	0	43,000	11
17.309	Labor Organization Reports	45,000	0	45,000	12
85.401	Udall Fellowship Program	48,000	0	48,000	13
93.447	State Health Fraud Task Force	49,000	0	49,000	14
97.093	Hazardous Materials Preparedness	50,000	0	50,000	15
98.010	Denton Program	50,000	0	50,000	16
97.033	Disaster Legal Services	51,000	0	51,000	17
15.254	Summer Watershed Intern	65,000	0	65,000	18
11.002	Census Customer Services	67,000	0	67,000	19
97.105	Firefighter/EMS Assistance	75,000	0	75,000	20
17.301	Federal, Construction Contractors	83,000	0	83,000	21
97.097	Training Resource and Data Exchange	93,000	0	93,000	22
97.103	Degrees at a Distance	95,000	0	95,000	23
66.810	CEPP Technical Assistance	100,000	0	100,000	24
14.517	Early Doctoral Student Research	105,000	0	105,000	25
19.500	Middle East Partnership Initiative	120,000	0	120,000	26
15.523	Perkins County Rural Water System	125,000	0	125,000	27
97.099	Fire Safety Initiatives, Residential	130,000	0	130,000	28
17.150	Employee Benefits Security	135,000	0	135,000	29
15.055	Alaskan Indian Allotments	136,000	0	136,000	30
17.302	Longshore and Harbor Workers	144,000	0	144,000	31
20.801	Ports, Intermodal Transportation	145,000	0	145,000	32
15.918	Federal Surplus Real Property	145,000	0	145,000	33
15.813	Minority Natural Resource Training	150,000	0	150,000	34
15.051	Endangered Species/Indian Lands	153,000	0	153,000	35
93.206	Health Studies/Research	156,000	0	156,000	36
15.644	Junior Duck Stamp Conservation \ p	164,000	0	164,000	37
85.402	Udall Congressional Internships	170,000	0	170,000	38
17.303	Wage, Hour Standards \ i	170,000	0	170,000	39
93.066	Vital Statistics Re-Engineering	172,000	0	172,000	40
11.408	Fishermen's Contingency Fund	175,000	0	175,000	41
15.814	Geological, Geophysical Data	180,000	0	180,000	42
11.006	Personal Census Search	180,000	0	180,000	43
97.095	Safe Kids Worldwide	200,000	0	200,000	44
15.643	Alaska Migratory Bird Co-Manage	221,000	0	221,000	45
66.952	Environmental Management Fellowship	221,000	0	221,000	46
64.026	State Adult Day Health Care	228,000	0	228,000	47
15.057	Navajo-Hopi Settlement	230,000	0	230,000	48
15.651	Wildlife Without Borders—Africa	250,000	0	250,000	49
15.608	Fish and Wildlife Management	250,000	0	250,000	50

*Excluding programs without allocations when data were compiled

Please see "Important Notes on the Tables, Footnotes," page 842

PART IV

Field Office Contacts

NOTE: Field offices manage specific programs, or they may provide information about programs. However, if the program description in Part II states "Note: no field offices for this program," contacts should be with the headquarters office. "PART I - Obtaining Federal Assistance" offers observations concerning field office contacts, especially in the discussion of the entry heading "⑩ *Program headquarters address, phone number, and web sites*" on pages 21-22.

DEPARTMENT OF AGRICULTURE

AGRICULTURAL RESEARCH SERVICE

10.001 **REGIONAL OFFICES**

BELTSVILLE—Bldg. 003 - Rm.203, BARC-West, Beltsville, MD 20705. Phone: FTS (301)504-7019.

MIDSOUTH—Delta States Research Center, P.O. Box 225, Stoneville, MS 38776. Phone: FTS (601)686-5345.

MIDWEST—Northern Regional Research Center, 1815 N. University St., Peoria, IL 61604. Phone: FTS (700)360-4618.

NORTH ATLANTIC—Eastern Regional Research Center, 600 E. Mermaid Lane, Philadelphia, PA 19118. Phone: FTS (215)233-6551.

NORTHERN PLAINS—National Resources Research Center, Bldg.D - Ste. 310, 2150 Centre Ave., Ft. Collins, CO 80525-5526. Phone: FTS (303)229-5513.

PACIFIC WEST—Western Regional Research Center, 800 Buchanan St., Albany, CA 94710. Phone: FTS (510)559-6016.

SOUTH ATLANTIC—Russell Research Center, College Station Rd., Athens, GA 30604-5677. Phone: FTS (706)546-3532.

SOUTHERN PLAINS—7607 Eastmark Dr. - Ste. 230, College Station, TX 77840. Phone: FTS (979)960-9444.

ANIMAL AND PLANT HEALTH INSPECTION SERVICE

10.025 and 10.028 **REGIONAL OFFICES**

Plant Protection and Quarantine

CENTRAL *(Arkansas, Iowa, Kansas, Louisiana, Missouri, Nebraska, North Dakota, Oklahoma, South Dakota, Texas)*—3505 Boca Chica Blvd. - Ste. 360, Brownsville, TX 78521-4065. Phone: (956)504-4150.

10.025 and 10.028 *(cont.)* **EASTERN** *(Connecticut, Delaware, District of Columbia, Illinois, Indiana, Maine, Maryland, Massachusetts, Michigan, Minnesota, New Hampshire, New Jersey, New York, Ohio, Pennsylvania, Rhode Island, Vermont, Virginia, West Virginia, Wisconsin)*—Blason II - 2nd fl., 505 S. Lenola Rd., Moorestown, NJ 08057-1549. Phone: (609)968-4970.

SOUTHEAST *(Alabama, Florida, Georgia, Kentucky, Mississippi, North Carolina, Puerto Rico, South Carolina, Tennessee, Virgin Islands)*—Bldg. 1, 3505 25th Ave., Gulfport, MS 39501. Phone: (601)863-1813.

WESTERN *(Alaska, Arizona, California, Colorado, Guam, Hawaii, Idaho, Montana, Nevada, New Mexico, Oregon, Utah, Washington, Wyoming)*—9580 Micron Ave. - Ste. I, Sacramento, CA 95827. Phone: (916)857-6065.

Veterinary Services

CENTRAL *(Arkansas, Iowa, Kansas, Louisiana, Missouri, Nebraska, North Dakota, Oklahoma, South Dakota, Texas)*—100 W. Pioneer Pkwy. - Ste. 100, Arlington, TX 76010. Phone: (817)276-2201.

NORTHERN *(Illinois, Indiana, Maryland, Massachusetts, Michigan, Minnesota, New Jersey, New York, Ohio, Pennsylvania, Virginia, West Virginia, Wisconsin)*—1 Winner's Circle - Ste. 100, Albany, NY 12205. Phone (518)453-0103.

SOUTHEAST *(Alabama, Florida, Georgia, Kentucky, Mississippi, North Carolina, Puerto Rico, South Carolina, Tennessee*—500 E. Zack St. - Ste. 410, Tampa, FL 33602-3945. Phone: (813)228-2952.

WESTERN *(Alaska, Arizona, California, Colorado, Hawaii, Idaho, Montana, Nevada, New Mexico, Oregon, Utah, Washington, Wyoming)*—384 Inverness Dr. S. - Ste. 150, Englewood, CO 80112. Phone (303)784-6202.

Wildlife Service

EASTERN *(Alabama, Arkansas, Connecticut, Delaware, District of Columbia, Florida, Georgia, Illinois, Indiana, Iowa, Louisiana, Kentucky, Maine, Maryland, Massachusetts, Michigan, Minnesota, Mississippi, Missouri, New Hampshire, New Jersey, New York, North Carolina, Ohio, Pennsylvania, Puerto Rico, Rhode Island, South Carolina, Tennessee, Vermont, Virginia, Virgin Islands, West Virginia, Wisconsin)*—3322 West End Ave. - Ste. 301, Nashville, TN 37203. Phone: (615)736-2007.

WESTERN *(Alaska, Arizona, California, Colorado, Guam, Hawaii, Idaho, Kansas, Montana, Nebraska, Nevada, New Mexico, North Dakota, Oklahoma, Oregon, South Dakota, Texas, Utah, Washington, Wyoming)*—12345 W. Alameda Pkwy. - Ste. 204, Lakewood, CO 80228. Phone: (303)969-6560.

- National Wildlife Research Center, 1201 Oakridge Dr., Ft. Collins, CO 80525. Phone: (970)223-1588.

10.029 Applicants may obtain information about assistance from county offices by contacting those listed under **10.051**.

FARM SERVICE AGENCY

10.051 thru 10.056

STATE OFFICES

Alabama—4121 Carmichael Rd. - Ste. 600, Montgomery, AL 36106-5013. Phone: (334)279-3500. *For mail:* P.O. Box 235013.

Alaska—800 W. Evergreen - Ste. 216, Palmer, AK 99645-6389. Phone: (907)745-7982.

Arizona—77 E. Thomas Rd. - Ste. 240, Phoenix, AZ 85012-3318. Phone: (602)640-5200.

Arkansas—Federal Bldg. - Rm.5416, 700 W. Capitol Ave., Little Rock, AR 72201-3225. Phone: (501)301-3000.

California—430 G St. - Ste. 4161, Davis, CA 95616-4161. Phone: (530)792-5538.

Caribbean Area—Fernandez Junzos Station, Cobian's Plaza - Ste. 309,P.O. Box 11188, 1607 Ponce DeLeon Ave., Santurce, PR 00909-0001. Phone: (809)729-6872.

Colorado—655 Parfet St. - Ste. E-305, Lakewood, CO 80215-5517. Phone: (303)236-2866.

Connecticut—88 Day Hill Rd., Windsor, CT 06095. Phone: (860)285-8483.

Delaware—1201 College Park Dr. - Ste. 101, Dover, DE 19904-8713. Phone: (302)678-2547.

Florida—440 NW 25th Place - Ste. 1, Gainesville, FL 32606. Phone: (352)379-4500.

Georgia—Federal Bldg. - Rm.102, 355 E. Hancock Ave., Athens, GA 30603-1907. Phone: (706)546-2266.

Hawaii—300 Ala Moana Blvd. - Rm.5106, P.O. Box 50008, Honolulu, HI 96850. Phone: (808)541-2644.

Idaho—9173 W. Barners - Ste. B, Boise, ID 83705-1511. Phone: (208)378-5650.

Illinois—3500 W Avenue, P.O. Box 19273, Springfield, IL 62794-9273. Phone: (217)241-6600.

Indiana—5981 Lakeside Blvd., Indianapolis, IN 46278. Phone: (317)290-3030, ext.317.

Iowa—10500 Buena Vista Ct., Des Moines, IA 50322. Phone: (515)254-1540, ext.600.

Kansas—3600 Anderson Ave., Manhattan, KS 66502-2511. Phone: (785)539-3531.

Kentucky—771 Corporate Dr. - Ste. 100, Lexington, KY 40503-5478. Phone: (606)224-7601.

Louisiana—3737 Government St., Alexandria, LA 71302-3395. Phone: (318)473-7721.

Maine—444 Stillwater Ave. - Ste. 1, Bangor, ME 04402-0406. Phone: (207)990-9140.

Maryland—River Center - Ste. E, 8335 Guilford Rd., Columbia, MD 21046. Phone: (410)381-4550.

Massachusetts—445 West St., Amherst, MA 01002-2957. Phone: (413)256-0232.

Michigan—3001 Coolidge Rd. - Ste. 100, East Lansing, MI 48823-6321. Phone: (517)337-6659, ext.1201.

Minnesota—400 Farm Credit Service Bldg., 375 Jackson St., St. Paul, MN 55101-1852. Phone: (612)602-7700.

Mississippi—6310 I-55 North, P.O. Box 14995, Jackson, MS 39211. Phone: (601)965-4300.

Missouri—Parkade Plaza, 601 Business Loop 70 West - Ste. 225, Columbia, MO 65203. Phone: (573)876-0925.

Montana—10 E. Babcock - Rm.557, P.O. Box 670, Bozeman, MT 59715. Phone: (406)587-6872.

Nebraska—7131 A St., P.O. Box 57975, Lincoln, NE 68510-7975. Phone: (402)437-5581.

Nevada—1755 E. Plumb Lane - Ste. 202, Reno, NV 89502-3207. Phone: (702)784-5411.

New Hampshire—22 Bridge St. - 4th fl., P.O. Box 1388, Concord, NH 03302-1338. Phone: (603)224-7941.

New Jersey—Mastoris Professional Plaza, Bldg. 2 - Ste. E, 163 Rt. 130, Bordentown, NJ 08505-2249. Phone: (609)298-3446.

New Mexico—6200 Jefferson St. NE, Albuquerque, NM 87109. Phone: (505)761-4900.

New York—441 S. Salina St. - (5th fl.) Ste. 356, Syracuse, NY 13202-2455. Phone: (315)477-6303.

North Carolina—4407 Bland Rd. - Ste. 175, Raleigh, NC 27609-6296. Phone: (919)875-4800.

North Dakota—1025 28th St. SW, P.O. Box 3046, Fargo, ND 58108. Phone: (701)239-5205.

10.051 thru 10.056 *(cont.)*

Ohio—Federal Bldg. - Rm.540, 200 N. High St., Columbus, OH 43215. Phone: (614)469-6735.

Oklahoma—100 USDA - Ste. 102, Farm Rd. and McFarland St., Stillwater, OK 74074-2653. Phone: (405)742-1130.

Oregon—7620 SW Mohawk, P.O. Box 1300, Tualatin, OR 97062-8121. Phone: (503)692-6830.

Pennsylvania—One Credit Union Pl. - Ste. 320, Harrisburg, PA 17110-2994. Phone: (717)237-2113.

Rhode Island—West Bay Office Complex - Rm.40, 60 Quaker Lane, Warwick, RI 02886-0111. Phone: (401)828-8232.

South Carolina—1927 Thurmond Mall - Ste. 100, Columbia, SC 29201-2375. Phone: (803)806-3830.

South Dakota—Federal Bldg. - Rm.308, 200 4th St. SW, Huron, SD 57350-2478. Phone: (605)352-1160.

Tennessee—U.S. Courthouse - Rm.579, 801 Broadway, Nashville, TN 37203-3816. Phone: (615)736-5555.

Texas—Commerce National Bank Bldg. - 2nd fl., 2405 Texas Ave. S., College Station, TX 77840. Phone: (409)260-9207. *For mail:* P.O. Box 2900, College Station, TX 77841-0001.

Utah—125 S. State St. - Rm.4239, P.O. Box 11350, Salt Lake City, UT 84147-0350. Phone: (801)524-5013.

Vermont—Executive Square Office Bldg., 346 Shelburne St., Burlington, VT 05401-4995. Phone: (802)658-2803.

Virginia—Culpeper Bldg. - Ste. 138, 1606 Santa Rosa Rd., Richmond, VA 23229. Phone: (804)287-1500.

Washington—Rock Pointe Tower - Ste. 568, 316 W. Boone Ave., Spokane, WA 99201-2350. Phone: (509)323-3000.

West Virginia—New Federal Bldg. - Rm.239, 75 High St., P.O. Box 1049, Morgantown, WV 26507-1049. Phone: (304)291-4351.

Wisconsin—6515 Watts Rd. - Rm.100, Madison, WI 53719-2797. Phone: (608)276-8732, ext.100.

Wyoming—951 Werner Ct. - Ste. 130, Casper, WY 82601-1307. Phone: (307)261-5231.

10.062 and 10.064 10.062 and 10.064

10.066 and 10.069 10.066 and 10.069

10.070 and 10.072 10.070 and 10.072

10.073 thru 10.077 10.073 thru 10.077

10.080 thru 10.085 10.080 thru 10.085

AGRICULTURAL MARKETING SERVICE

COTTON DIVISION

Grading, Marketing Services (including Market News)

3275 Appling Rd., Memphis, TN 38133. Phone: (901)384-3000.

Standardization and Quality Assurance Branch

3275 Appling Rd., Memphis, TN 38133. Phone: (901)384-3015.

DAIRY DIVISION

Dairy Inspection, Grading Branch and Laboratory

Bldg. A - Ste. 370, 800 Roosevelt Rd., Glen Ellyn, IL 60137. Phone: (708)790-6920.

Market News Service

2811 Agricultural Dr., Madison, WI 53704-6777. Phone: (608)224-5080.

FRUIT AND VEGETABLE DIVISION

Fresh and Processed Products

Alabama—1557 Reeves St., P.O. Box 1368, Dothan, AL 36302. Phone: (334)792-5185.

Arizona—1688 W. Adams - Rm.415, Phoenix, AZ 85007. Phone: (602)542-0880.

California—1320 E. Olympic Ave. - Rm.212, Los Angeles, CA 90021. Phones: (213)894-2489, -6553.

- 1220 N St. - Rm.A-270, P.O. Box 942871, Sacramento, CA 94271-0001. Phones: (916)654-0810, -0813, -0815.

Colorado—2331 W. 31st Ave., Denver, CO 80211. Phones: (303)844-4570, 477-0093.

Connecticut—Connecticut Regional Market, 101 Reserve Rd. - Rm.5, Hartford, CT 06114. Phone: (860)240-3446.

Delaware—2320 S. DuPont Hwy., Dover, DE 19901. Phone: (302)736-4811.

District of Columbia/Maryland—Baltimore-Washington Terminal Market Office, 8610 Baltimore-Washington Blvd. - Ste. 212, Jessup, MD 20794. Phones: (301)317-4387, -4587.

Florida—Techniport Bldg. - Rm.556, 5600 NW 36th St., Miami, FL 33122. Phone: (305)870-9542.

Georgia—Administration Bldg. - Rm.205, 16 Forest Pkwy., Forest Park, GA 30050. Phone: (404)366-7522.

Hawaii—1428 S. King St., P.O. Box 22159, Honolulu, HI 96823-2159. Phone: (808)973-9566.

Idaho—2270 Old Penitentiary Rd., Boise, ID 83712. Phone: (208)332-8670.

Indiana—Greenfield, IN 46140-0427. Phone: (317)462-5897.

Kentucky—No. 1 Produce Terminal, Louisville, KY 40218. Phones: (502)595-4266, -4278.

Louisiana—U.S. Postal Service Bldg. - Rm.11036, 701 Loyola Ave., New Orleans, LA 70113. Phones: (504)589-6741, -6742.

Maine—744 Main St. - Ste. 4, P.O. Box 1058, Presque Isle, ME 04769. Phone: (207)764-2100.

Massachusetts—Boston Market Terminal Bldg. - Rm.1, 34 Market St., Everett, MA 02149. Phones: (617)389-2480, -2481.

10.153 thru 10.163 *(cont.)*

Michigan—90 Detroit Union Produce Union Terminal, 7201 W. Fort St., Detroit, MI 48209. Phones:(313)226-6059, -6225.

Minnesota—90 W. Plato Blvd., St. Paul, MN 55107. Phones: (612)296-8557, -0593.

Missouri—Gumble Bldg. - Rm.502, 801 Walnut St., Kansas City, MO 64106. Phone: (816)374-6273.

- Unit 1 Produce Row - (1st fl.) Rm.100, St. Louis, MO 63102. Phone: (314)425-4514, -4515.

New Jersey—Federal Bldg. - Rm.1430, 970 Broad St., Newark, NJ 07102. Phone: (201)645-2636.

New York—Division of Food Safety and Inspection Service, Capital Plaza - Bldg. 2 (2nd fl.), 1 Winners Circle, Albany, NY 12235. Phones: (518)457-1211, -2090, -1982.

- 465B Hunts Point Market, Bronx, NY 10474. Phones: (718)991-7665, -7669.

Ohio—3716 Croton Ave., Cleveland, OH 44115. Phone: (216)522-2135.

- Division of Food, Dairy and Drugs, Bldg. 2, 8995 E. Main St., Reynoldsburg, OH 43068. Phone: (614)728-6350.

Oklahoma—2800 N. Lincoln Blvd., Oklahoma City, OK 73105. Phone: (405)521-3864.

Oregon—635 Capitol St. NE, Salem, OR 97310-0110. Phone: (503)986-4629.

Pennsylvania—2301 N. Cameron St. - Rm.112, Harrisburg, PA 17110. Phones: (717)787-5107, -5108.

- 210 Produce Bldg., 3301 S. Galloway St., Philadelphia, PA 19148. Phones: (215)336-0845, -0846.
- Pittsburgh Produce Terminal Bldg. - Rm.206, 2100 Smallman St., Pittsburgh, PA 15222. Phones: (412)261-6435.

Puerto Rico—Federal-State Inspection, GSA Service Center, 651 Federal Dr. - Ste. 103-05, Guaynabo, PR 00965. Phones: (787)783-2230, -4116.

Tennessee—3211 Alcoa Hwy., Knoxville, TN 37920. Phone: (423)577-2633.

- Melrose Station, P.O. Box 40627, Nashville, TN 37204. Phone: (615)360-0169.

Texas—1406 Parker St. - Ste. 203, Dallas, TX 75215. Phones: (214)767-5337, -5338.

- 8001 E N. Mesa - Ste. 303, El Paso, TX 79932. Phone: (505)589-3753.
- 3100 Produce Row - Rm.1A, Houston, TX 77023. Phones: (713)923-2557, -2558.
- Administration Bldg. - Rm.244, 1500 S. Zarzamora St., San Antonio, TX 78207. Phone: (210)222-2751.
- 1301 W. Expressway, P.O. Box 107, San Juan,TX 78589. Phones: (210)787-4091, -6881.

Utah—350 N. Redwood Rd. - Rm.217, Salt Lake City, UT 84116. Phone: (801)538-7187.

Washington—National Resources Bldg. - 2nd fl., 1111 Washington St., Olympia, WA 98504-2560. Phone: (360)902-1831.

Market News Branch

Arizona—522 N. Central Ave. - Rm.106, Phoenix, AZ 85004. Phone: (602)379-3066.

California—2202 Monterey St. - Ste. 104-A, Fresno, CA 93721. Phone: (209)487-5178.

- 1320 E. Olympic Blvd. - Ste. 212, Los Angeles, CA 90021-1907. Phone: (213)894-3077.
- 630 Sansome St. - Rm.727, San Francisco, CA 94111. Phone: (415)705-1300.

Colorado—Greeley Producers Bldg., 711 "O" St., Greeley, CO 80631. Phones: (970)351-7097, -8256.

Florida—Brickell Plaza Bldg. - Ste. 424, 909 SE 1st Ave., Miami, FL 33131. Phone: (305)373-2955.

- (*Seasonal*)775 Warner Ln., Orlando, FL 32803. Phone: (407)897-5950.

Georgia—203 Administration Bldg., 16 Forest Pkwy., Forest Park, GA 30050. Phones: (404)763-7297, 361-1376.

- Georgia State Farmers Market - Stall 39, 502 Smith Ave., U.S. Hwy. 84, P.O. Box 1447, Thomasville, GA 31799. Phone: (912)228-1208.

Idaho—1820 E. 17th St. - Ste. 130, Idaho Falls, ID 83404. Phone: (208)526-0166.

Illinois—Kluczynski Bldg. - Rm.512, 230 S. Dearborn St., Chicago, IL 60604. Phone: (312)353-0111.

Maryland—Maryland Wholesale Produce Market, Bldg. B - Rm.101, 7460 Conowingo Ave., Jessup, MD 20794. Phones: (410)799-4840, -4841; Washington DC only: (301)621-1261.

Massachusetts—Boston Market Terminal - Rm.10, 34 Market St., Everett, MA 02149. Phones: (617)387-4498, -4615, -4681.

Michigan—Federal Bldg. - Rm.201, 175 Territorial Rd., P.O. Box 1204, Benton Harbor, MI 49023. Phones: (616)925-3270, -3271.

- Union Produce Terminal - Rm.53, 7201 W. Fort St., Detroit, MI 48209. Phone: (313)841-1111.

Missouri—Unit 1, Produce Row - Rm.101, St. Louis, MO 63102-1418. Phone: (314)425-4520.

New York—5A NYC Terminal Market, Halleck St. at Edgewater Rd., Bronx, NY 10474-7355. Phone: (718)542-2225.

Pennsylvania—3301 S. Galloway St. - Rm.261, Philadelphia, PA 19148. Phone: (215)597-4536.

- 2100 Smallman St. - Rm.207, Pittsburgh, PA 15222. Phone: (412)644-5847.

Texas—1406 Parker - Rm.201, Dallas, TX 75215. Phones: (214)767-5375, -5376, -5377.

Washington—Interwest Savings Bank - Ste. 302, 15111 8th Ave. SW, Seattle, WA 98148-0099. Phones: (206)764-3753, -3804.

- Agricultural Service Center - Rm.4, 2015 S. 1st St., Yakima, WA 98903. Phones: (509)575-2492, -2493.

Marketing Field Service

California—2202 Monterey St. - Ste. 102-B, Fresno, CA 93721. Phone: (209)487-5901.

Florida—301 3rd St. NW - Ste. 206, P.O. Box 2276, Winterhaven, FL 33881. Phones: (941)299-4770, -4886.

Oregon—1220 SW 3rd Ave. - Rm.369, Portland, OR 97204. Phones: (503)326-2724, -2725.

Texas—1313 E. Hackberry, McAllen, TX 78501. Phone: (956)682-2833.

Processed Products Branch

EASTERN—Regional Director, Bldg. A - Ste. 380, 800 Roosevelt Rd., Glen Ellyn, IL 60137-5875. Phone: (630)790-6957.

Florida—6966 NW 36th Ave., Miami, FL 33147-6506. Phone: (305)835-7626.

- 98 3rd St. SW, Winter Haven, FL 33880-2909. Phone: (941)294-7416.

Georgia—1555 St. Joseph Ave., East Point, GA 30344-2591. Phone: (404)763-7495.

Indiana—4318 Technology Dr., South Bend, IN 46628-9752. Phone: (219)287-5407.

10.153 thru 10.163 (cont.)

Louisiana (*Inspection Point of East Point, GA*)—Commerce Bldg. - Ste. 3, 1942 Williams Blvd., Kenner, LA 70062-6285. Phone: (504)466-0343.

Maine—165 Lancaster St., Portland, ME 04101-2499. Phone: (207)772-1588.

Maryland (*Inspection Point of Hunt Valley, MD*)—102 Maryland Ave., Easton, MD 21601-3409. Phone: (410)822-3383.

- Hunt Valley Professional Bldg., 9 Schilling Rd., Hunt Valley, MD 21031-1106. Phone: (410)962-4946.

Michigan (*Inspection Point of South Bend, IN*)—c/o Vroom Cold Storage, Russell Rd., Hart, MI 49420-0113. Phone: (616)873-5654.

Minnesota (*Inspection Point of Ripon, WI*)—2126 Hoffman Rd., Mankato, MN 56001-5863. Phone: (507)387-6101.

New Jersey—Park Plaza, Professional Bldg. - Ste. 304, 622 Georges Rd., North Brunswick, NJ 08902-3313. Phone: (908)545-0939.

New York (*Inspection Point of North Brunswick, NJ*)—Genesee Valley Regional Market, 900 Jefferson Rd. - Rm.110, Rochester, NY 14623-3289. Phones: (716)424-2092, -2096.

Oklahoma (*Inspection Point of Weslaco, TX*)—716 S. 2nd St. - Ste. 106, Stillwater, OK 74960-4806. Phone: (918)696-6333.

Puerto Rico—Federal State Inspection Service, GSA Center - Ste. 103-05, 651 Federal Dr., Guaynabo, PR 00965-1030. Phones: (809)783-2230, -4116.

Texas—Federal Bldg. - Rm.1011, 2320 La Branch St., Houston, TX 77004-1036. Phone: (713)659-3836.

- (*Inspection Point of Weslaco, TX*)—319 Market St., Laredo, TX 78040-8529. Phone: (210)726-2258.
- 117 S. Westgate, Weslaco, TX 78596-2701. Phones: (210)968-2772, -2126.

Virginia—No.1 N. 14th St. - Rm.332, Richmond, VA 23219-3691. Phone: (804)786-0930.

Wisconsin—742 E. Fond du Lac St., Ripon, WI 54971-9555. Phone: (414)748-2287.

WESTERN—Regional Director, 2202 Monterey St. - Ste. 102-C, Fresno, CA 93721-3175. Phone: (209)487-5891.

California—2202 Monterey St. - Ste. 102-A, Fresno, CA 93721-3129. Phone: (209)487-5210.

- (*Inspection Point of Fresno*)—45-116 Commerce St. - Ste. 15, Indio, CA 92201-3440. Phone: (619)347-1057.
- 1320 E. Olympic Rd. - Rm.212, Los Angeles, CA 90021-1948. Phone: (213)894-3173.

Hawaii—State of Hawaii Department of Agriculture, 1428 S. King St., P.O. Box 22159, Honolulu, HI 96823-2159. Phone: (808)973-9566.

Oregon (*Inspection Point of Yakima, WA*)—111 S. Main St., Milton-Freewater, OR 97862-1342. Phone: (541)938-3251.

- 340 High St. NE, Salem, OR 97301-3631. Phone: (503)399-5761.

Washington—32 N. 3rd St. - Rm.212, Yakima, WA 98901-2791. Phone: (509)575-5869.

LIVESTOCK DIVISION

Livestock and Grain Market News Branch

Alabama—1445 Federal Dr. - Rm.107, P.O. Box 3336, Montgomery, AL 36109-0336. Phone: (334)223-7488.

Arizona—Stockyards Bldg. - Rm.102, 5001 E. Washington St., Phoenix, AZ 85034-2010. Phone: (602)379-4376.

Arkansas—2301 S. University - Rm.110-B, Little Rock, AR 72203-3910. Phone: (501)671-2203.

Colorado—711 "O" St., Greeley, CO 80631-9540. Phone: (970)353-9750.

Florida—775 Warner Lane, Orlando, FL 32803. Phone: (407)897-2708.

Georgia—Georgia State Farmers Market, 502 Smith Ave. - Stall 38, Thomasville, GA 31792-0086. Phone: (912)226-2198.

Illinois—Illinois Department of Agriculture, Division of Marketing, State Fairgrounds, P.O. Box 19281, Springfield, IL 62794-9281. Phone: (217)782-4925.

Iowa—210 Walnut St. - Rm.767, Des Moines, IA 50309-2106. Phone: (515)284-4460.

- 800 Cunningham Dr. - Rm.225, Sioux City, IA 51107-2437. Phone: (712)252-3286.

Kansas—100 Military Ave. - Ste. 217, Dodge City, KS 67801-4945. Phone: (316)227-8881.

Kentucky—1321 Story Ave., Louisville, KY 40206-1884. Phone: (502)582-5287.

Louisiana—Capitol Station, 5825 Florida Blvd., Baton Rouge, LA 70821-3334. Phone: (504)922-1328.

Minnesota—New Livestock Exchange Bldg. - Ste. 208, S. St. Paul, MN 55075-5598. Phone: (612)451-1565.

Missouri—601 Illinois Ave. - Rm.210, St. Joseph, MO 64504-1396. Phone: (816)238-0678.

Montana—Public Auction Yards Bldg. - Rm.206, 112 S. 18th and Minnesota Ave., Billings, MT 59103-1191. Phone: (406)657-6285.

Nebraska—213 Livestock Exchange Bldg., 29th and O St., Omaha, NE 68107-2603. Phone: (402)731-4520.

New Mexico—2507 N. Telshor Blvd. - Ste. 4, Las Cruces, NM 88001. Phone: (505)521-4928.

Oklahoma—Livestock Exchange Bldg. - Rm.140, 2501 Exchange Ave., Oklahoma City, OK 73108-2477. Phone: (405)232-5425.

Oregon—1220 SW 3rd Ave. - Rm.1772, Portland, OR 97204-2899. Phone: (503)326-2237.

Pennsylvania—c/o New Holland Sales Stables, 101 W. Fulton St., P.O. Box 155, New Holland, PA 17557. Phone: (717)354-2391.

South Carolina—Youngblood Bldg., 1001 Bluff Rd., Columbia, SC 29201-3405. Phone: (803)737-4491.

South Dakota—803 E. Rice St. - Rm.103, Sioux Falls, SD 57103-0193. Phone: (605)338-4061.

Tennessee—Melrose Station, Ellington Agriculture Center, Hogan Rd., Nashville, TN 37204-0627. Phone: (615)781-5406.

Texas—Livestock Exchange Bldg. - 1st fl., 101 S. Manhattan St., P.O. Box 30217, Amarillo, TX 79104-0217. Phone: (806)372-6361.

- Producers Livestock Auction Bldg., San Angelo, TX 76903-0160. Phone: (915)653-1778.

Washington—988 Juniper St., Moses Lake, WA 98837-2250. Phone: (509)765-3611.

Wyoming—1834 E. A St., Torrington, WY 82240-1813. Phone: (307)532-4146.

Meat Grading and Certification

Colorado—400 Livestock Exchange Bldg., Denver, CO 80216-2139. Phone: (303)294-7676.

10.153 thru 10.163 *(cont.)*

Illinois—Bldg. A - Ste. 330, 800 Roosevelt Rd., Glen Ellyn, IL 60137-5832. Phone: (708)790-6905.

Iowa—210 Walnut St. - Rm.575-A, Des Moines, IA 50309-2106. Phone: (515)284-7166.

Nebraska—204 Livestock Exchange Bldg., 29th and O St., Omaha, NE 68107-2603. Phone: (402)733-4833.

Texas—Livestock Exchange Bldg., 101 S. Manhattan St., P.O. Box 30217, Amarillo, TX 79104. Phone: (806)373-7111.

POULTRY DIVISION

Poultry Grading Branch

EAST MIDWEST *(Alabama, Arkansas, Louisiana, Mississippi, Oklahoma, Tennessee, Texas)*—1 Natural Resources Dr. - Rm.110, Little Rock, AR 72215-8521. Phone: (501)324-5955.

EASTERN *(Connecticut, Delaware, District of Columbia, Florida, Georgia, Maine, Maryland, Massachusetts, New Hampshire, New Jersey, New York, North Carolina, Pennsylvania, Puerto Rico, Rhode Island, South Carolina, Vermont, Virgin Islands, Virginia, West Virginia)*—635 Cox Rd. - Ste. G, Gastonia, NC 28054-3441. Phone: (704)867-3871.

WEST MIDWEST *(Illinois, Indiana, Iowa, Kansas, Kentucky, Michigan, Minnesota, Missouri, Nebraska, North Dakota, Ohio, South Dakota, Wisconsin)*—Federal Bldg. - Rm.777, 210 Walnut St., Des Moines, IA 50309-2100. Phone: (515)284-4581.

WESTERN *(Alaska, Arizona, California, Colorado, Hawaii, Idaho, Montana, New Mexico, Nevada, Oregon, Utah, Washington, Wyoming)*—2909 Coffee Rd. - Ste. 4, Modesto, CA 95355-3188. Phone: (209)522-5251.

Poultry Market News Branch

California—Bldg. 6 - Section E, 5600 Rickenbacker Rd., Bell, CA 90201-6418. Phones: (213)269-4154; *Recorded messages 24 hrs./day*: (213)260-4676.

Connecticut—Connecticut Department of Agriculture, Marketing Division, State Office Bldg. - Rm.263, 165 Capital Ave., Hartford, CT 06106-1688. Phone: (860)566-3671.

District of Columbia—AMS, PY Division, USDA National Poultry Supervisor/National Egg Supervisor, South Bldg. - Rm.3960, Washington, DC 20090-6456. Phone: (202)720-6911.

Georgia—60 Forsyth St. SW - Rm.6M80, Atlanta, GA 30303. Phones: FTS (404)562-5830, -5856.

Iowa—210 Walnut St. - Rm.951, Des Moines, IA 50309-2103. Phone: (515)284-4545 (*recorded messages 24 hrs./day*).

Louisiana—Louisiana Department of Agriculture, Wilson Bldg., Baton Rouge, LA 70821-3334. Phone: (504)922-1328.

Mississippi—352 E. Woodrow Wilson, Jackson, MS 39296-4629. Phone: (601)965-4662.

North Carolina—North Carolina Department of Agriculture, State Agriculture Bldg. - Rm.402, 2 W. Edenton St., P.O. Box 27647, Raleigh, NC 27611-7647. Phone: (919)733-7252.

Texas—Texas Department of Agriculture, Capitol Station, 1700 N. Congress Ave., Austin, TX 78711-2847. Phones: (512)463-7628; (toll-free within state, 1-800-252-3407).

Virginia—Virginia Department of Agriculture and Consumer Services, 116 Reservoir St., Harrisonburg, VA 22801-4232. Phone: (540)434-0779.

SCIENCE DIVISION

Alabama—Supervisory Chemist, Aflatoxin Laboratories, 3119 Wesley Way, Dothan, AL 36301-2020. Phone: (334)794-5070.

- Laboratory Supervisor, 1557 Reeves St., P.O. Box 1368, Dothan, AL 36302. Phone: (334)792-5185.

Florida—Supervisory Chemist, Eastern Laboratories, 98 3rd St. SW - Ste. 211, Winter Haven, FL 33880-2909. Phone: (941)299-7958.

Georgia—Laboratory Supervisor, 1211 Schley Ave., Albany, GA 31707. Phone: (912)430-8490.

- Laboratory Supervisor, P.O. Box 488, Ashburn, GA 31714. Phone: (912)567-3703.
- Laboratory Supervisor, 610 N. Main St., Blakely, GA 31723. Phone: (912)723-4570.
- Laboratory Supervisor, P.O. Box 272, Dawson, GA 31742. Phone: (912)995-7257.

Illinois—Laboratory Director, Midwestern Laboratory, 3570 N. Avondale Ave., Chicago, IL 60618-5391. Phone: (312)353-6525.

North Carolina—Laboratory Supervisor, 301 W. Pearl St., P.O. Box 279, Aulander, NC 27805. Phone: (919)345-1661, ext.156.

- Laboratory Director, Eastern Laboratory, 2311-B Aberdeen Blvd., Gastonia, NC 28054-0614. Phone: (704)867-3873.
- Laboratory Address, 645 Cox Rd., Gastonia, NC 28054-0614. Phone: (704)867-1882.

Oklahoma—Laboratory Supervisor, 107 S. 4th St., Madill, OK. 73446. Phone: (405)795-5615.

Virginia—Pesticide Records Branch, 8700 Centreville Rd. - Ste. 200, Manassas, VA 22110-0031, Phones: (703)330-7826; Residue Branch, (703)330-2300.

- Laboratory Supervisor, 308 Culloden St., P.O. Box 1130, Suffolk, VA 23434. Phone: (757)925-2286.

TOBACCO DIVISION

Tobacco Inspection and Market News

LEXINGTON REGION *(Indiana, Kentucky, Maryland, Missouri, North Carolina, Ohio, Tennessee, Virginia, West Virginia (burley), and Connecticut, Massachusetts, Pennsylvania, Wisconsin cigar areas)*—771 Corporate Dr. - Ste. 500, Lexington, KY 40503. Phone: (606)224-1088.

RALEIGH REGION *(Alabama, Florida, Georgia, North Carolina, South Carolina, Virginia(Flue-cured, Tobacco and Naval Stores Inspection))*—1306 Annapolis Dr. - Rm.205, Raleigh, NC 27608-0001. Phone: (919)856-4584.

10.165 REGULATORY BRANCH REGIONAL OFFICES (Perishable Agricultural Commodities Act)

Arizona—Federal Bldg. - Rm.7, 300 W. Congress St., P.O. Box FB30, Tucson, AZ 85701-1319. Phone: (520)670-4793.

Illinois—Bldg. A - Ste. 360, 800 Roosevelt Rd., Glen Ellyn, IL 60137-5832. Phone: (630)790-6929.

New Jersey—622 Georges Rd. - Ste. 303, North Brunswick, NJ 08902-3303. Phone: (908)846-8222.

Texas—1200 E. Copeland Rd. - Ste. 404, Arlington, TX 76011-4938. Phone: (817)885-7805.

Virginia—8700 Centerville Rd. - Ste. 206, Manassas, VA 22110. Phone: (703)330-4455.

10.352 Listed under **10.405**.

10.404 Listed under **10.051**.

RURAL DEVELOPMENT (Rural Housing Service - Rural Business-Cooperative Service)

10.405 STATE OFFICES

Alabama—Sterling Center - Ste. 601, 4121 Carmichael Rd., Montgomery, AL 36106-3683. Phone: (334)279-3400.

Alaska—800 W. Evergreen - Ste. 201, Palmer, AK 99645-6539. Phone: (907)745-2176.

Arizona—3003 N. Central Ave. - Ste. 900, Phoenix, AZ 85012-2906. Phone: (602)280-8700.

Arkansas—700 W. Capitol Ave. - Rm.3416, P.O. Box 2778, Little Rock, AR 72201-3325. Phone: (501)301-3200.

California—430 G St. - Agency 4169, Davis, CA 95616-4169. Phone: (530)792-5800.

Colorado—655 Parfet St. - Rm.E-100, Lakewood, CO 80215. Phone: (303)236-2801.

Connecticut—*See* **Massachusetts**.

Delaware *(Delaware, Maryland)*—5201 S. Dupont Hwy., P.O. Box 400, Camden, DE 19934-9998. Phone: (302)697-4300.

Florida *(Florida, Virgin Islands)*—Federal Bldg., 4440 NW 25th Place, Gainesville, FL 32614-7010. Phone: (352)338-3400.

Georgia—Stephens Federal Bldg., 355 E. Hancock Ave., Athens, GA 30601-2768. Phone: (706)546-2162.

Hawaii—Federal Bldg. - Rm.311, 154 Waianuenue Ave., Hilo, HI 96720. Phone: (808)933-3000.

Idaho—9173 W. Barnes Dr. - Ste. A1, Boise, ID 83709. Phone: (208)378-5600.

Illinois—Illini Plaza - Ste. 103, 1817 S. Neil St., Champaign, IL 61820. Phone: (217)398-5235.

Indiana—5975 Lakeside Blvd., Indianapolis, IN 46278. Phone: (317)290-3100.

Iowa—Federal Bldg. - Rm.873, 210 Walnut St., Des Moines, IA 50309. Phone: (515)284-4663.

Kansas—1200 SW Executive Dr., P.O. Box 4653, Topeka, KS 66605. Phone: (785)271-2700.

Kentucky—771 Corporate Plaza - Ste. 200, Lexington, KY 40503. Phone: (606)224-7300.

Louisiana—3727 Government St., Alexandria, LA 71302. Phone: (318)473-7920.

Maine—444 Stillwater Ave. - Ste. 2, Bangor, ME 04402-0405. Phone: (207)990-9106.

Maryland— *See* **Delaware**.

Massachusetts *(Connecticut, Massachusetts, Rhode Island)*—451 West St., Amherst, MA 01002. Phone: (413)253-4300.

Michigan—3001 Coolidge Rd. - Ste. 200, East Lansing, MI 48823. Phone: (517)337-6635.

Minnesota—410 Agribank Bldg., 375 Jackson St., St. Paul, MN 55101-1853. Phone: (651)602-7800.

Mississippi—Federal Bldg. - Ste. 831, 100 W. Capitol St., Jackson, MS 39269. Phone: (601)965-4316.

Missouri—Parkade Center - Ste. 235, 601 Business Loop - 70 West, Columbia, MO 65203. Phone: (573)876-0976.

Montana—900 Technology Blvd. - (Unit 1) Ste. B, P.O. Box 850, Bozeman, MT 59715. Phone: (406)585-2580.

Nebraska—Federal Bldg. - Rm.152, 100 Centennial Mall North, Lincoln, NE 68508. Phone: (402)437-5551.

Nevada—1390 S. Curry St., Carson City, NV 89703-9910. Phone: (702)887-1222.

New Hampshire— *See* **Vermont**.

New Jersey—Tarnsfield Plaza - Ste. 22, 790 Woodland Rd., Mt. Holly, NJ 08060. Phone: (609)265-3600.

New Mexico—6200 Jefferson St. NE - Rm.255, Albuquerque, NM 87109. Phone: (505)761-4950.

New York—The Galleries of Syracuse, 441 S. Salina St. - Ste. 357, Syracuse, NY 13202-2541. Phone: (315)477-6400.

North Carolina—4405 Bland Rd. - Ste. 260, Raleigh, NC 27609. Phone: (919)873-2000.

North Dakota—Federal Bldg. - Rm.208, 220 E. Rosser, Bismarck, ND 58502-1737. Phone: (701)250-4781.

Ohio—Federal Bldg. - Rm.507, 200 N. High St., Columbus, OH 43215-2477. Phone: (614)469-5606.

Oklahoma—100 USDA - Ste. 108, Stillwater, OK 74074-2654. Phone: (405)742-1000.

Oregon—101 SW Main St. - Ste. 1410, Portland, OR 97204-3222. Phone: (503)414-3300.

Pennsylvania—One Credit Union Pl. - Ste. 330, Harrisburg, PA 17110-2996. Phone: (717)237-2299.

Puerto Rico—New San Juan Office Bldg. - Rm.501, 159 Carlos E. Chardon St., Hato Rey, PR 00918-5481. Phone: (787)766-5095.

Rhode Island— *See* **Massachusetts**.

South Carolina—Thurmond Federal Bldg. - Rm.1007, 1835 Assembly St., Columbia, SC 29201. Phone: (803)765-5163.

South Dakota—Huron Federal Bldg. - Rm.210, 200 4th St. SW, Huron, SD 57350. Phone: (605)352-1100.

Tennessee—3322 West End Ave. - Ste. 300, Nashville, TN 37203-1084. Phone: (615)783-1300.

Texas—Federal Bldg. - Ste. 102, 101 S. Main, Temple, TX 76501. Phone: (254)742-9700.

Utah—Federal Bldg. - Rm.4311, 125 S. State St., P.O. Box 11350, Salt Lake City, UT 84147-0350. Phone: (801)524-4063.

Vermont *(New Hampshire, Vermont)*—City Center - 3rd fl., 89 Main St., Montpelier, VT 05602. Phone: (802)828-6010.

Virgin Islands— *See* **Florida**.

Virginia—Culpeper Bldg. - Ste. 238, 1606 Santa Rosa Rd., Richmond, VA 23229. Phone: (804)287-1550.

Washington—1835 Black Lake Blvd. SW - Ste. B, Olympia, WA 98512-5715. Phone: (360)704-7740.

West Virginia—Federal Bldg. - Rm.320, 75 High St., Morgantown, WV 26505-7500. Phone: (304)291-4791.

Wisconsin—4949 Kirschling Court, Stevens Point, WI 54481. Phone: (715)345-7600.

Wyoming—Federal Bldg. - Rm.1005, 100 E. B St., P.O. Box 820, Casper, WY 82602. Phone: (307)261-6300.

10.406 and 10.407 Listed under **10.051**.

10.410 thru 10.420 Listed under **10.405**.

10.421 Listed under **10.051**.

10.427 and 10.433 Listed under **10.405**.

10.437 Listed under **10.051**.

10.438 thru 10.442 Listed under **10.405**.

10.443 Contact appropriate office listed under **10.051**, **10.405**, or **10.900**.

10.444 thru 10.446 Listed under **10.405**.

RISK MANAGEMENT AGENCY

10.450 REGIONAL SERVICE OFFICES

REGION 1 *(Connecticut, Delaware, Maine, Maryland, Massachusetts, New Hampshire, New Jersey, New York, North Carolina, Pennsylvania, Rhode Island, Vermont, Virginia, West Virginia)*—4407 Bland Rd. - Ste. 160, Raleigh, NC 27609. Phone: (919)875-4880.

REGION 2 *(Alabama, Florida, Georgia, Puerto Rico, South Carolina, Virgin Islands)*—106 S. Patterson St. - Ste. 250, Valdosta, GA 31601-5609. Phone: (912)242-3044.

REGION 3 *(Arkansas, Kentucky, Louisiana, Mississippi, Tennessee)*—8 River Bend Place, Jackson, MS 39208. Phone: (601)965-4771.

REGION 4 *(Illinois, Indiana, Michigan, Ohio)*—3500 W. Wabash - Ste. B, Springfield, IL 62707. Phone: (217)241-6601.

REGION 5 *(Iowa, Minnesota, Wisconsin)*—Minnesota World Trade Center, 30 E. 7th St. - Ste. 910, St. Paul, MN 55101-4901. Phone: (651)290-3304.

REGION 6 *(Montana, North Dakota, South Dakota, Wyoming)*—3490 Gabel Rd. - Ste. 100, Billings, MT 59102-6440. Phone: (406)657-6447.

REGION 7 *(Colorado, Kansas, Missouri, Nebraska)*—3401 SW Van Buren St., Topeka, KS 66611-2227. Phone: (785)266-0248.

REGION 8 *(New Mexico, Oklahoma, Texas)*—205 NW 63rd St. - Ste. 170, Oklahoma City, OK 73116-8209. Phone: (405)879-2700.

REGION 9 *(Arizona, California, Hawaii, Nevada, Utah)*—430 G St. - Ste. 4168, Davis, CA 95616-4168. Phone: (530)792-5870.

REGION 10 *(Alaska, Idaho, Oregon, Washington)*—112 N. University Rd. - Ste. 205, Spokane, WA 99206-5295. Phone: (509)353-2147.

COMPLIANCE FIELD OFFICES

CENTRAL *(Colorado, Kansas, Missouri, Nebraska)*—6501 Beacon Dr., Kansas City, MO 64131. Phone: (816)926-7963.

EASTERN *(Alabama, Connecticut, Delaware, Florida, Georgia, Maine, Maryland, Massachusetts, New Hampshire, New Jersey, New York, North Carolina, Pennsylvania, Puerto Rico, Rhode Island, South Carolina, Vermont, Virginia, West Virginia)*—4407 Bland Rd. - Ste. 280, Raleigh, NC 27609. Phone: (919)875-4930.

MIDWEST *(Illinois, Indiana, Ohio, Michigan)*—6045 Lakeside Blvd., Indianapolis, IN 46278. Phone: (317)290-3050.

NORTHERN *(Iowa, Minnesota, Montana, North Dakota, South Dakota, Wisconsin, Wyoming)*—3440 Federal Dr. - Ste. 200, Eagan, MN 55122-1301. Phone: (612)725-3730.

SOUTHERN *(Kentucky, Louisiana, Mississippi, New Mexico, Oklahoma, Tennessee, Texas)*—1111 W. Mockingbird Lane - Ste. 280, Dallas, TX 75247-5016. Phone: (214)767-7700.

WESTERN *(Alaska, Arizona, California, Hawaii, Idaho, Nevada, Oregon, Utah, Washington)*—430 G St. - Ste. 4167, Davis, CA 95616-4167. Phone: (530)792-5850.

10.451 and 10.452 Listed under **10.051**.

10.455 Listed under **10.450**.

10.456 Risk Management Agency, Research and Evaluation Division, 6501 Beacon Dr., Stop 0813, Kansas City, MO 64133-4676. Phones: (816)926-6343; FAX (816)926-7343. **Internet:** e-mail,"www.RMARED.Applications@rma.usda.gov".

10.457 thru 10.459 Listed under **10.450**.

FOOD SAFETY AND INSPECTION SERVICE

Meat, Poultry, and Egg Products Inspection

10.475 and 10.477 DISTRICT OFFICES

Arkansas *(DISTRICT 35: Arkansas, Louisiana, Oklahoma)*—Country Club Center - Ste. 201, 4700 S. Thompson Bldg. B, Springdale, AR 72764. Phone: (501)751-8412.

California *(DISTRICT 5: California)*—Bldg. 2C, 620 Central Ave., Alameda, CA 94501. Phone: (510)337-5000.

Colorado *(DISTRICT 15: Arizona, Colorado, New Mexico, Nevada, Utah)*—665 S. Broadway - Ste. B, Boulder, CO 80303. Phone: (303)497-5411.

Georgia *(DISTRICT 85: Florida, Georgia, Puerto Rico, Virgin Islands)*—Bldg. 1924 - Ste. 3R90, 100 Alabama St. SW, Atlanta, GA 30303. Phone: (404)562-5900.

Illinois *(DISTRICT 50: Illinois, Indiana, Ohio)*—1919 S. Highland Ave. - Ste. 115C, Lombard, IL 60148. Phone: (630)620-7474.

Iowa *(DISTRICT 25: Iowa, Nebraska)*—Federal Bldg. - Rm.985, 210 Walnut St., Des Moines, IA 50309. Phone: (515)727-8960.

Kansas *(DISTRICT 30: Kansas, Missouri)*—4920 Bob Billings Pkwy, Lawrence, KS 66049. Phone: (785)841-5600.

Maryland *(DISTRICT 75: Delaware, Maryland, Virginia, Washington D.C., West Virginia)*—5601 Sunnyside Ave. - Ste. 1-2288B, Beltsville, MD 20705-5200. Phone: (301)504-2136.

Minnesota *(DISTRICT 20: Minnesota, Montana, North Dakota, South Dakota, Wyoming)*—Butler Square West - Ste. 989C, 100 N. 6th St., Minneapolis, MN 55403. Phone: (612)370-2400.

Mississippi *(DISTRICT 90: Alabama, Mississippi, Tennessee)*—715 S. Pear Orchard Rd. - Ste. 101, Ridgeland, MS 39157. Phone: (601)965-4312.

New York *(DISTRICT 65: Connecticut, Maine, Massachusetts, New Hampshire, New York, Rhode Island, Vermont)*—230 Washington Ave., Albany, NY 12203-6870. Phone: (518)452-6870.

North Carolina *(DISTRICT 80: Kentucky, North Carolina, South Carolina)*—6020 Six Forks Rd., Raleigh, NC 27609. Phone: (919)844-8400.

Oregon *(DISTRICT 10: Alaska, American Samoa, Guam, Hawaii, Idaho, Northern Mariana Islands, Oregon, Washington)*—530 Center St. NW, Salem, OR 97301. Phone: (503)399-5831.

Pennsylvania *(DISTRICT 60: New Jersey, Pennsylvania)*—Mellon Independence Center - Ste. 4100-A, 701 Market St., Philadelphia, PA 19106-1576. Phone: (215)597-4219, ext.106.

10.475 and 10.477 (cont.) **Texas** *(DISTRICT 40: Texas)*—1100 Commerce - Rm.516, Dallas, TX 75242-0598. Phone: (214)767-9116.

Wisconsin *(DISTRICT 45: Michigan, Wisconsin)*—2810 Crossroads Dr. - Ste. 3500, Madison, WI 53718-7969. Phone: (608)240-4080.

FOOD AND NUTRITION SERVICE

10.550 thru 10.580 REGIONAL OFFICES

MID-ATLANTIC *(Delaware, District of Columbia, Maryland, New Jersey, Pennsylvania, Puerto Rico, Virgin Islands, Virginia, West Virginia)*—Mercer Corporate Park, 300 Corporate Blvd., Robinsville, NJ 08691. Phone: (609)259-5025.

MIDWEST *(Illinois, Indiana, Michigan, Minnesota, Ohio, Wisconsin)*—77 W. Jackson Blvd - 20th fl., Chicago, IL 60604-3507. Phone: (312)353-6664.

MOUNTAIN PLAINS *(Colorado, Iowa, Kansas, Missouri, Montana, Nebraska, North Dakota, South Dakota, Utah, Wyoming)*—1244 Speer Blvd. - Ste. 903, Denver, CO 80204. Phone: (303)844-0300.

NORTHEAST *(Connecticut, Maine, Massachusetts, New Hampshire, New York, Rhode Island, Vermont)*—10 Causeway St. - Rm.501, Boston MA 02222-1068. Phone: (617)565-6370.

SOUTHEAST *(Alabama, Florida, Georgia, Kentucky, Mississippi, North Carolina, South Carolina, Tennessee)*—Martin Luther King, Jr. Federal Annex - (1st fl.) Rm.8T36, 61 Forsythe St. SW, Atlanta, GA 30303. Phone: (404)562-1801, -1802

SOUTHWEST *(Arkansas, Louisiana, New Mexico, Oklahoma, Texas)*—1100 Commerce St. - Rm.555, Dallas, TX 75242. Phone: (214)290-9800.

WESTERN *(Alaska, American Samoa, Arizona, California, Guam, Hawaii, Idaho, Nevada, Northern Marianas, Oregon, Washington, Freely Associated States of the Pacific)*—550 Kearny St. - Rm.400, San Francisco, CA 94108. Phone: (415)705-1310.

10.609 Consult local phone directory for nearest county FSA office or state offices listed under **10.051** or via: **Internet:** "www.fsa.usda.gov/edso/statedefault.htm".

FOREST SERVICE

10.652 RESEARCH HEADQUARTERS - Forest and Range Experiment Stations

INTERMOUNTAIN *(Idaho, Montana, Nevada, Utah, Wyoming-western one-third)*—324 25th St., Ogden, UT 84401. Phone: (801)625-5421.

NORTH CENTRAL *(Illinois, Indiana, Iowa, Michigan, Minnesota, Missouri, Wisconsin)*—1992 Folwell Ave., St. Paul, MN 55108. Phone: (612)649-5252.

NORTHEASTERN *(Connecticut, Kentucky, Maine, Massachusetts, New Hampshire, New Jersey, New York, Ohio, Pennsylvania, Vermont, West Virginia)*—5 Radnor Corporate Center - Ste. 200, Radnor, PA 19087-4585. Phone: (610)975-4207.

PACIFIC NORTHWEST *(Alaska, Oregon, Washington)*—Portland, OR 97208-3890. Phone: (503)326-5644.

PACIFIC SOUTHWEST *(California, Hawaii)*—Berkeley, CA 94701-0245. Phone: (510)559-6317.

ROCKY MOUNTAIN *(Arizona, Colorado, Kansas, Nebraska, New Mexico, North Dakota, Panhandle, South Dakota, Texas-western, Wyoming-eastern two-thirds)*—240 W. Prospect Rd., Ft. Collins, CO 80526-2098. Phone: (970)498-1139.

SOUTHERN *((Alabama, Arkansas, Florida, Georgia, Louisiana, Mississippi, North Carolina, Oklahoma-except Panhandle, Puerto Rico, South Carolina, Tennessee, Texas-eastern, Virginia)*—200 Weaver Blvd., P.O. Box 2680, Asheville, NC 28802. Phone: (704)257-4301.

Forest Products Laboratory: One Gifford Pinchot Dr., Madison, WI 53705-2398. Phone: (608)231-9315.

10.664 thru 10.674

REGIONAL OFFICES

Note: to contact local Forest Supervisor or Ranger District Offices, consult phone directory under USDA, or the appropriate regional office, following.

REGION 1 *(Idaho-northern, Montana, North Dakota, South Dakota-northwestern corner)*—Federal Bldg., P.O. Box 7669, Missoula, MT 59807. Phone: (406)329-3280.

REGION 2 *(Colorado, Kansas, Nebraska, South Dakota-except northwestern corner, Wyoming-eastern two-thirds)*—740 Simms St., P.O. Box 25127, Lakewood, CO 80255. Phone: (303)275-5741.

REGION 3 *(Arizona, New Mexico)*—P.O. Box 1689, Santa Fe, NM 87504. Phone: (505)842-3344.

REGION 4 *(Idaho-southern, Nevada, Utah, Wyoming-western one-third)*—Federal Office Bldg., 324 25th St., Ogden, UT 84401. Phone: (801)625-5239.

REGION 5 *(California, Hawaii)*—1323 Club Dr., Vallejo, CA 94592. Phone: (707)562-8910.

REGION 6 *(Oregon, Washington)*—333 SW 1st St., Portland, OR 97208-3623. Phone: (503)808-2355, -2348.

REGION 8 *(Alabama, Arkansas, Florida, Georgia, Kentucky, Louisiana, Mississippi, North Carolina, Oklahoma, Puerto Rico, South Carolina, Tennessee, Texas, Virginia, Virgin Islands)*—1720 Peachtree Rd. NW, Atlanta, GA 30367. Phone: (404)347-7486.

REGION 9 *(Connecticut, Delaware, Illinois, Indiana, Iowa, Maine, Maryland, Massachusetts, Michigan, Minnesota, Missouri, New Hampshire, New Jersey, New York, Ohio, Pennsylvania, Rhode Island, Vermont, West Virginia, Wisconsin)*—5 Radnor Corporate Center - Ste. 200, P.O. Box 6775, Radnor, PA 19087-4555. Phone: (610)975-4103.

REGION 10 *(Alaska)*—3301 C St. - Ste. 522, Anchorage, AK 99503-3956. Phone: (907)271-2519.

State and Private Forestry Areas

NORTHEASTERN AREA *(Covers states listed under Region 9, foregoing)*—5 Radnor Corporate Center, P.O. Box 6775, Radnor, PA 19087-8775. Phone: (610)975-4103.

10.675 Contact the State and Private Forestry office addresses and phone numbers via: **Internet:** "www.fs.fed.us/ucf/Regional_Offices.htm".

10.676 Contacts for the Regional and Area State and Private Forestry offices and for addresses and phone numbers of Regional Foresters and Area Director of the Forest Service can be found via: **Internet:** "www.fs.fed.us/spf/coop/library/flp_region_coord.shtml".

10.677 Same as **10.676** via **Internet:** "http://www.fs.fed.us/contactus/regions.shtml".

10.678

FOREST STEWARDSHIP

ALASKA *(Alaska)*—3301 C St. - Ste. 522, Anchorage, AK 99503. Phones: (907)271-2550; FAX (907)271-2897.

INTERMOUNTAIN *(Idaho, Montana, North Dakota, Nevada, Utah)*—Federal Bldg., 324 25th St., Ogden, UT 84401. Phones: (801)625-5189; FAX (801)625-5127.

NORTHEASTERN *(Connecticut, Delaware, Illinois, Indiana, Iowa, Massachusetts, Maryland, Maine, Michigan, Minnesota, Missouri, New Jersey, New Hampshire,*

10.678 (cont.) *New York, Ohio, Pennsylvania, Rhode Island, Vermont, Wisconsin, West Virginia)*—11 Campus Blvd. - Ste. 200, Newtown Square, PA 19073. Phones: (610)557-4029; FAX (610)557-4136.

PACIFIC NORTHWEST *(Oregon, Washington)*—333 SW 1st Ave., P.O. Box 3623, Portland, OR 97208. Phones: (503)808-2355; FAX (503)808-2339.

PACIFIC SOUTHWEST *(California, Hawaii)*—1323 Club Drive, Vallejo, CA 94592. Phones: (707)562-8918; FAX (707)562-9054.

ROCKY MOUNTAIN *(Colorado, Kansas, Nebraska, South Dakota, Wyoming)*—P.O. Box 25127, Lakewood, CO 80225. Phones: (303)275-5239; FAX (303)275-5754.

SOUTHERN *(Alabama, Arkansas, Florida, Georgia, Kentucky, Louisiana, Mississippi, North Carolina, Oklahoma, South Carolina, Tennessee, Texas, Virginia)*—1720 Peachtree Rd. NW - Ste. 8508, Atlanta, GA 30367. Phones: (404)347-1649; FAX (404)347-2776.

SOUTHWESTERN *(Arizona, New Mexico)*—517 Gold Ave. SW, Albuquerque, NM 87102. Phones: (505)842-3229; FAX (505)842-3800.

10.679 and 10.680 Listed under **10.664**.

10.760 thru 10.773 Listed under **10.405**.

10.775 *Obtain information contacts for each state from headquarters office.*

10.854 Listed under **10.405**.

10.856 Listed under **10.405** or via **Internet:** e-mail,"CSGrants@usda.gov".

10.860 and 10.862 Listed under **10.405**

10.864 Listed under **10.405**.

NATURAL RESOURCES CONSERVATION SERVICE

10.900 thru 10.950

REGIONAL OFFICES

EAST—1400 Wilson Blvd. - Ste. 1100, Arlington, VA 22209. Phone: (703)312-7282.

MIDWEST—One Gifford Pinchot Dr. - Rm.204, Madison, WI 53705-3210. Phone: (608)264-5281.

NORTHERN PLAINS—100 Centennial Mall North - Rm.152, Lincoln, NE 68508. Phone: (402)437-5315.

SOUTH CENTRAL—Bldg. 23, 501 W. Felix St., P.O. Box 6459, Ft. Worth, TX 76115. Phone: (817)334-5224, ext.3700.

SOUTHEAST—1720 Peachtree Rd. NW - Ste. 716-N, Atlanta, GA 30367. Phone: (404)347-6105.

WEST—650 Capitol Mall - Rm.6072, Sacramento, CA 95814. Phone: (916)498-5284.

STATE OFFICES

Alabama—3381 Skyway Dr., Auburn, AL 36830. Phone: (334)887-4500.

Alaska—949 E. 36 Ave. - Ste. 400, Anchorage, AK 99508-4302. Phone: (907)271-2424.

Arizona—3003 N. Central Ave. - Ste. 800, Phoenix, AZ 85012-2945. Phone: (602)280-8808.

Arkansas—Federal Bldg. - Rm.5404, 700 W. Capitol Ave., P.O. Box 2323, Little Rock, AR 72201-3228. Phone: (501)324-5445.

California—2121-C 2nd St. - Ste. 102, Davis, CA 95616-5475. Phone: (916)757-8215.

Colorado—655 Parfet St. - Rm.E200C, Lakewood, CO 80215-5517. Phone: (303)236-2886, ext.202.

Connecticut—16 Professional Park Rd., Storrs, CT 06268-1299. Phone: (203)487-4014.

Delaware—1203 College Park Dr. - Ste. 101, Dover, DE 19904-8713. Phone: (302)678-4160.

Florida—2614 NW 43rd St., Box 141510, Gainesville, FL 32606-6611. Phone: (904)338-9500.

Georgia—Federal Bldg., 355 E. Hancock Ave., P.O. Box 13, Athens, GA 30601-2769. Phone: (706)546-2272.

Hawaii—300 Ala Moana Blvd. - Rm.4316, P.O. Box 50004, Honolulu, HI 96850-0002. Phone: (808)541-2601.

Idaho—3244 Elder St. - Rm.124, Boise, ID 83705-4711. Phone: (208)378-5700.

Illinois—1902 Fox Dr., Champaign, IL 61820-7335. Phone: (217)398-5267.

Indiana—6013 Lakeside Blvd., Indianapolis, IN 46278-2933. Phone: (317)290-3200.

Iowa—Federal Bldg. - Ste. 693, 210 Walnut St., Des Moines, IA 50309-2180. Phone: (515)284-6655.

Kansas—760 S. Broadway, Salina, KS 67401. Phone: (913)823-4565.

Kentucky—771 Corporate Dr. - Ste. 110, Lexington, KY 40503-5479. Phone: (606)224-7350.

Louisiana—3737 Government St., Alexandria, LA 71302-3727. Phone: (318)473-7751.

Maine—5 Godfrey Dr., Orono, ME 04473. Phone: (207)866-7241.

Maryland—John Hansen Business Center - Ste. 301, 339 Busch's Frontage Rd., Annapolis, MD 21401-5534. Phone: (410)757-0861.

Massachusetts—451 West St., Amherst, MA 01002-2995. Phone: (413)253-4351.

Michigan—1405 S. Harrison Rd. - Rm.101, East Lansing, MI 48823-5243. Phone: (517)337-6701, ext.1201.

Minnesota—600 Farm Credit Bldg., 375 Jackson St., St. Paul, MN 55101-1854. Phone: (612)290-3675.

Mississippi—Federal Bldg. - Ste. 1321, 100 W. Capital St., Jackson, MS 39269-1399. Phone: (601)965-5205.

Missouri—Parkade Center - Ste. 250, 601 Business Loop - 70 West, Columbia, MO 65203-2546. Phone: (573)876-0901.

Montana—Federal Bldg. - Rm.443, 10 E. Babcock St., Bozeman, MT 59715-4704. Phone: (406)587-6813.

Nebraska—Federal Bldg. - Rm.152, 100 Centennial Mall N., Lincoln, NE 68508-3866. Phone: (402)437-5327.

Nevada—Bldg. F - Ste. 201, 5301 Longley Lane, Reno, NV 89511-1805. Phone: (702)784-5863.

New Hampshire—Federal Bldg., 2 Madbury Rd., Durham, NH 03824-1499. Phone: (603)433-0505.

New Jersey—1370 Hamilton St., Somerset, NJ 08873-3157. Phone: (908)246-1205.

New Mexico—6200 Jefferson NE - Rm.305, Albuquerque, NM 87109-3734. Phone: (505)761-4400.

New York—441 S. Salina St. - (Ste. 354) Rm.520, Syracuse, NY 13202-2450. Phone: (315)477-6504.

10.900 thru 10.950 *(cont.)* **North Carolina**—4405 Bland Rd. - Ste. 205, Raleigh, NC 27609-6293. Phone: (919)873-2102.

North Dakota—Federal Bldg. - Rm.270, 220 E. Rosser Ave. and 3rd St., Bismarck, ND 58502-1458. Phone: (701)250-4421.

Ohio—Federal Bldg. - Rm.522, 200 N. High St., Columbus, OH 43215-2478. Phone: (614)469-6962.

Oklahoma—100 USDA - Ste. 203, Stillwater, OK 74074-2624. Phone: (405)742-1204.

Oregon—Federal Bldg. - (16th fl.) Ste. 1300, 101 SW Main St., Portland, OR 97204-3221. Phone: (503)414-3201.

Pacific Basin Area—FHB Bldg. - Ste. 301, 400 Route 9, Guam 96927. Phone: (9-011-671)472-7490.

Pennsylvania—One Credit Union Place - Ste. 340, Harrisburg, PA 17110-2993. Phone: (717)782-2202.

Puerto Rico—IBM Bldg. - Ste. 604, 654 Munoz Rivera Ave., Hato Rey, PR 00918-4123. Phone: (no number provided).

Rhode Island—60 Quaker Lane - Ste. 46, Warwick, RI 02886-0111. Phone: (401)828-1300.

South Carolina—Thurmond Federal Bldg. - Rm.950, 1835 Assembly St., Columbia, SC 29201-2489. Phone: (803)765-5681.

South Dakota—Federal Bldg., 200 4th St. SW, Huron, SD 57350-2475. Phone: (605)352-1200.

Tennessee—675 U.S. Courthouse, 801 Broadway, Nashville, TN 37203-3878. Phone: (615)736-5471.

Texas—Poage Federal Bldg., 101 S. Main St., Temple, TX 76501-7682. Phone: (817)774-1214.

Utah—Bennett Federal Bldg. - Rm.4402, 125 S. State St., Salt Lake City, UT 84147. Phone: (801)524-5050.

Vermont—69 Union St., Winooski, VT 05404-1999. Phone: (802)951-6795.

Virginia—Culpeper Bldg. - Ste. 209, 1606 Santa Rosa Rd., Richmond, VA 23229-5014. Phone: (804)287-1691.

Washington—W. 316 Boone Ave. - Ste. 450, Spokane, WA 99201-2348. Phone: (509)323-2900.

West Virginia—75 High St. - Rm.301, Morgantown, WV 26505. Phone: (304)291-4153.

Wisconsin—6515 Watts Rd. - Ste. 200, Madison, WI 53719-2726. Phone: (608)264-5577.

Wyoming—Federal Office Bldg. - Rm.3124, 100 E. B St., Casper, WY 82601. Phones: (307)261-5201, -1911.

10.994 and 10.995 Listed under **10.051**.

DEPARTMENT OF COMMERCE

BUREAU OF THE CENSUS

11.001 thru 11.005

REGIONAL OFFICES

California—15350 Sherman Way - Ste. 300, Van Nuys, CA 91406-4224. Phones: (818)904-6393, -6427.

Colorado—6900 W. Jefferson Ave. - Ste. 100, Denver, CO 80235-2032. Phones: (303)969-6750, -6777.

Georgia—101 Marietta St. NW - Ste. 3200, Atlanta, GA 30303-2700. Phones: (404)730-3832, -3835.

Illinois—2255 Enterprise Dr. - Ste. 5501, Westchester, IL 60154-5800. Phones: (708)562-1377, -1788.

Kansas—1211 N. 8th St., Kansas City, KS 66101-2129. Phones: (913)551-6728, -6789.

Massachusetts—4 Copley Place - Ste. 301, Boston, MA 02117-9108. Phones: (617)424-4501, -0547.

Michigan—1395 Brewery Park Blvd. - Ste. 100, Detroit, MI 48207-2635. Phones: (313)259-1158, -5045.

New York—395 Hudson St. - Ste. 800, New York, NY 10014. Phones: (212)584-3400, 478-4800.

North Carolina—901 Center Park Dr. - Ste. 106, Charlotte, NC 28217-2935. Phones: (704)424-6400, 344-6444.

Pennsylvania—833 Chestnut St.- Ste. 504, Philadelphia, PA 19103-2395. Phones: (215)717-1800, -0755.

Texas—8585 N. Stemmons Fwy. - Ste. 800S, Dallas, TX 75247-3841. Phones: (214)253-4401, 655-5362.

Washington—Key Tower - Ste. 5100, 700 5th Ave., Seattle, WA 98104-5018. Phones: (206)553-5837, -5857.

11.006 **Personal Census Records Service**—Technical Services Supervisor, Personal Census Search Unit, U.S Census Bureau, P.O. Box 1545, Jeffersonville, IN 47131. Phone: (812)218-3046.

INTERNATIONAL TRADE ADMINISTRATION (including Export Assistance Centers)

11.108 thru 11.112 **Alabama**—Medical Forum Bldg. - Rm.707, 950 22nd St. N., Birmingham, AL 35203. Phones: (205)731-1331; FAX (205)731-0076.

Alaska—431 W. 7th Ave. - Ste. 108, Anchorage, AK 99501. Phones: (907)271-6237; FAX (907)271-6242.

Arizona—2901 N. Central Ave. - Ste. 970, Phoenix, AZ 85012. Phones: (602)640-2513; FAX (602)640-2518.

- 255 W. Alameda - 3rd fl., Tucson, AZ 85701. Phones: (520)670-5540; FAX (520)791-5413.

Arkansas—425 W. Capitol Ave. - Ste. 700, Little Rock, AR 72201. Phones: (501)324-5794; FAX (501)324-7380.

California—390-B Fir Ave., Clovis, CA 93611. Phones: (559)325-1619; FAX (559)325-1647.

- 550 Shaw Ave., Fresno, CA 93710. Phones: (559)325-1619; FAX (559)325-1647.
- One World Trade Center - Ste. 1670, Long Beach, CA 90831. Phones: (562)980-4550; FAX (562)980-4561.
- 11150 Olympic Blvd. - Ste. 975, Los Angeles, CA 90064. Phones: (310)235-7104; FAX (310)235-7220.
- c/o Monterey Institute of International Studies, 411 Pacific St. - Ste. 316A, Monterey, CA 93940. Phones: (831)641-9850; FAX (831)641-9849.

11.108 thru 11.112 *(cont.)*

- Orange County Export Assistance Center, 3300 Irvine Ave. - Ste. 305, Newport Beach, CA 92660. Phones: (949)660-1688; FAX (949)660-8039.
- 530 Water St. - Ste. 740, Oakland, CA 94607. Phones: (510)273-7350; FAX (510)251-7352.
- Inland Empire Export Assistance Center, 2940 Inland Empire Blvd. - Ste. 121, Ontario, CA 91764. Phones: (909)466-4134; FAX (909)466-4140.
- 917 7th St. - 2nd fl., Sacramento, CA 95814. Phones: (916)498-5155; FAX (916)498-5923.
- 6363 Greenwich Dr. - Ste. 230, San Diego, CA 92122. Phones: (619)557-5395; FAX (619)557-6176.
- 250 Montgomery St. - 14th fl., San Francisco, CA 94104. Phones: (415)705-2300; FAX (415)705-2297.
- 101 Park Center Plaza - Ste. 1001, San Jose, CA 95113. Phones: (408)271-7300; FAX (408)271-7307.
- 4040 Civic Center Dr. - Ste. 200, San Rafael, CA 94903. Phones: (415)883-1966; FAX (415)883-2711.
- 5201 Great American Pkwy. - Ste. 456, Santa Clara, CA 95054. Phones: (408)970-4610; FAX (408)970-4618.

Colorado—1625 Broadway - Ste. 680, Denver, CO 80202. Phones: (303)844-6623; FAX (303)844-5651.

Connecticut—213 Court St. - Rm.903, Middletown, CT 06457-3346. Phones: (860)638-6950; FAX (860)638-6970.

Delaware—*See* **Pennsylvania**, Philadelphia office.

Florida—14010 Roosevelt Blvd. - Ste. 704, Clearwater, FL 33762. Phones: (727)893-3738; FAX (727)449-2889.

- 200 E. Las Olas Blvd. - Ste. 1600, Ft. Lauderdale, FL 33301. Phones: (954)356-6640; FAX (954)356-6644.
- 777 NW 72nd Ave - Mailbox 3L2, Miami, FL 33126-3009. Phones: (305)526-7425; FAX (305)526-7434.
- Eola Park Centre - Ste. 1270, 200 E. Robinson St., Orlando, FL 32801. Phones: (407)648-6235; FAX (407)648-6756.
- 325 John Knox Rd. - Ste. 201 Tallahassee, FL 32303. Phones: (850)942-9635; FAX (850)922-9595.

Georgia—Centergy One Bldg. - Ste. 1055, 75 5th St., NW, Atlanta, GA 30308. Phones: (912)652-4204; FAX (912)652-4241.

- 111 E. Liberty St. - Ste. 202, Savannah, GA 31401. Phones: (404)657-1900; FAX (404)657-1970.

Hawaii—521 Ala Moana Blvd. - Rm.214, Honolulu, HI 96813. Phones: (808)522-8040; FAX (808)522-8045.

Idaho *(Portland, OR district)*—700 W. State St. - 2nd fl., Boise, ID 83720. Phones: (208)334-3857; FAX (208)334-2783.

Illinois—200 W. Adams St. - Ste. 2450, Chicago, IL 60603. Phones: (312)353-8045; FAX (312)353-8120.

- 610 Central Ave. - Ste. 150, Highland Park, IL 60035. Phones: (847)681-8010; FAX (847)681-8012.
- 515 N. Court St., P.O. Box 1747, Rockford, IL 61103. Phones: (815)987-8123; FAX (815)963-7943.

Indiana—Indianapolis Export Assistance Center, Pennwood One - Ste. 106, 11405 N. Pennsylvania St., Carmel, IN 46032. Phones: (317)582-2300; FAX (317)582-2301.

Iowa—700 Locust St. - Ste. 100, Des Moines, IA 50309-3739. Phones: (515)288-8614; FAX (515)288-1437.

Kansas *(Kansas City, MO district)*—209 E. William - Ste. 300, Wichita, KS 67202-4012. Phones: (316)263-4067; FAX (316)263-8306.

Kentucky—601 W. Broadway - Rm.634B, Louisville, KY 40202. Phones: (502)582-5066; FAX (502)582-6573.

- 140 E. Main St., Lexington, KY 40507. Phones: (606)677-6160; FAX (606)677-6161.

Louisiana—Delta Export Assistance Center, 2 Canal St. - Ste. 2710, New Orleans, LA 70130. Phones: (504)589-6546; FAX (504)589-2337.

- Business Education Bldg.- 119H, One University Place, Shreveport, LA 71129. Phones: (318)676-3064; FAX (318)676-3063.

Maine *(Boston, MA District)*—511 Congress St., Portland, ME 04101. Phones: (207)541-7400; FAX (207)541-7420.

Maryland—World Trade Center - Ste. 2432, 401 E. Pratt St., Baltimore, MD 21202. Phones: (410)962-4539; FAX (410)962-4529.

Massachusetts—World Trade Center - Ste. 307, 164 Northern Ave., Boston, MA 02210-2071. Phones: (617)424-5990; FAX (617)424-5992.

Michigan—425 S. Main St. - Ste. 103, Ann Arbor, MI 48104. Phones: (734)741-2430; FAX (734)741-2432.

- 211 W. Fort St. - Ste. 2220, Detroit, MI 48226. Phones: (313)226-3650; FAX (313)226-3657.
- 301 W. Fulton St. - Ste. 718-S, Grand Rapids, MI 49504. Phones: (616)458-3564; FAX (616)458-3872.
- Oakland Pointe Office Bldg. - Ste. 1300 West, 250 Elizabeth Lake Rd., Pontiac, MI 48341. Phones: (248)975-9600; FAX (248)975-9606.

Minnesota—45 S. 7th St. - Ste. 2240, Minneapolis, MN 55402. Phones: (612)348-1638; FAX (612)348-1650.

Mississippi—704 E. Main St., Raymond, MS 39154. Phones: (601)857-0128; FAX (601)857-0026.

Missouri—2345 Grand - Ste. 650, Kansas City, MO 64108. Phones: (816)410-9201; FAX (816)410-9208.

- 8182 Maryland Ave. - Ste. 303, St. Louis, MO 63105. Phones: (314)425-3302; FAX (314)425-3381.

Montana—c/o Montana World Trade Center - Ste. 257, Gallagher Business Bldg., Missoula, MT 59812. Phones: (406)243-2098; FAX (406)243-5259.

Nebraska—11135 "O" St., Omaha, NE 68137. Phones: (402)221-3664; FAX (402)221-3668.

Nevada—1755 E. Plumb Lane - Ste. 152, Reno, NV 89502. Phones: (702)784-5203; FAX (702)784-5343.

New Hampshire *(Boston, MA district)*—17 New Hampshire Ave., Portsmouth, NH 03801-2838. Phones: (603)334-6074; FAX (603)334-6110.

New Jersey—One Gateway Center - 9th fl., Newark, NJ 07102. Phones: (973)645-4682; FAX (973)645-4783.

- Bldg.4 - Ste. 105, 3131 Princeton Pike, Trenton, NJ 08648. Phones: (609)989-2100; FAX (609)989-2395.

New Mexico *(Dallas, TX District)*—c/o New Mexico Department of Economic Development, 1100 St. Francis Dr., Santa Fe, NM 87503. Phones: (505)827-0350; FAX (505)827-0263.

New York—111 W. Huron St. - Rm.1304, Buffalo, NY 14202. Phones: (716)551-4191; FAX (716)551-5290.

11.108 thru 11.112 *(cont.)*

- Long Island Export Assistance Center, 1550 Franklin Ave. - Rm.207, Mineola, NY 11501. Phones: (516)739-1765; FAX (516)739-3310.
- Harlem Export Assistance Center, 163 W. 125th St. - Ste. 904, New York, NY 10027. Phones: (212)860-6200; FAX (212)860-6203.
- 6 World Trade Center - Rm.635, New York, NY 10048. Phones: (212)466-5222; FAX (212)264-1356.
- Westchester Export Assistance Center, 707 W. Chester Ave. - Ste. 209, White Plains, NY 10604. Phones: (914)682-6712; FAX (914)682-6698.

North Carolina—521 E. Morehead St. - Ste. 435, Charlotte, NC 28202. Phones: (704)333-4886; FAX (704)332-2681.

- 400 W. Market St. - Ste. 102, Greensboro, NC 27401. Phones: (336)333-5345; FAX (336)333-5158.

North Dakota—*See* **Minneapolis, MN** Export Assistance Center.

Ohio—36 E. 7th St. - Ste. 2650, Cincinnati, OH 45202. Phones: (513)684-2944; FAX (513)684-3227.

- Bank One Center - Ste. 700, 600 Superior Ave. E., Cleveland, OH 44114. Phones: (216)522-4750; FAX (216)522-2235.
- Two Nationwide Plaza - Ste. 1400, Columbus, OH 43215. Phones: (614)365-9510; FAX (614)365-9598.
- 300 Madison Ave., Toledo, OH 43604. Phones: (419)241-0683; FAX (419)241-0684.

Oklahoma—301 NW 63rd St. - Ste. 330, Oklahoma City, OK 73116. Phones: (405)608-5302; FAX (405)608-4211.

- 700 N. Greenwood Ave. - Ste. 1400, Tulsa, OK 74106. Phones: (918)581-7650; FAX (918)581-6263.

Oregon—1401 Willamette St., Eugene, OR 97401-4003. Phones: (541)465-6575; FAX (541)465-6704.

- One World Trade Center - Ste. 242, 121 SW Salmon St., Portland, OR 97204. Phones: (503)326-3001; FAX (503)326-6351.

Pennsylvania—One Commerce Square, 228 Walnut St. - Ste. 850, P.O. Box 11698, Harrisburg, PA 17108-1698. Phones: (717)221-4510; FAX (717)221-4505.

- The Curtis Center - Ste. 580W, Independence Square West, Philadelphia, PA 19106. Phones: (215)597-6101; FAX (215)597-6123.
- Federal Bldg. - Rm.2002, 1000 Liberty Ave., Pittsburgh, PA 15222. Phones: (412)395-5050; FAX (412)395-4875.

Puerto Rico *(Hato Rey)*—525 F.D. Roosevelt Ave. - Ste. 905, San Juan, PR 00918. Phones: (787)766-5555; FAX (787)766-5692.

Rhode Island *(Hartford, CT district)*—One West Exchange St., Providence, RI 02903. Phones: (401)528-5104; FAX (401)528-5067.

South Carolina—5300 International Blvd. - Ste. 201-C, North Charleston, SC 29418. Phones: (843)760-3794; FAX (843)760-3798.

- Thurmond Federal Bldg. - Ste. 172, 1835 Assembly St., Columbia, SC 29201. Phones: (803)765-5345; FAX (803)253-3614.
- Upstate Export Assistance Center, Park Central Office Park - Bldg. 1 (Ste. 109), 555 N. Pleasantburg Dr., Greenville, SC 29607. Phones: (864)271-1976; FAX (864)271-4171.

South Dakota—Siouxland Export Assistance Center, Augustana College - Rm.122, 2001 S. Summit Ave. Sioux Falls, SD 57197. Phones: (605)330-4264; FAX (605)330-4266.

Tennessee—c/o Centre for Enterprise, Buckman Hall - 3rd fl.(Ste. 348), 650 E. Parkway S., Memphis, TN 38104. Phones: (901)323-1543; FAX (901)320-9128.

- Old Historic City Hall - Ste. 300, 600 W. Summit Hill Dr., Knoxville, TN 37902-2011. Phones: (865)545-4637; FAX (865)545-4435.
- 211 Commerce St. - Ste. 100(3rd fl.), Nashville, TN 37201. Phones: (615)736-5161; FAX (615)736-2454.

Texas—1700 Congress - 2nd fl., Austin, TX 78701. Phones: (512)916-5939; FAX (512)916-5940. *For mail*: P.O. Box 12728, Austin, TX 78711.

- 2050 N. Stemmons Fwy. - Ste. 170, Dallas, TX 75207. Phones: (214)767-0542; FAX (214)767-8240. *For mail*: Dallas, TX 75342-0069.
- 711 Houston St., Ft. Worth, TX 76102. Phones: (817)212-2673; FAX (817)978-0178.
- 500 Dallas - Ste. 1160, Houston, TX 77002. Phones: (713)718-3062; FAX (713)718-3060.
- 203 S. St. Mary St. - Ste. 360, San Antonio, TX 78205. Phones: (210)228-9878; FAX (210)228-9874.

Utah—324 S. State St. - Ste. 221, Salt Lake City, UT 84111. Phones: (801)524-5116; FAX (801)524-5886.

Vermont—National Life Bldg. - 6th fl., Drawer 20, Montpelier, VT 05620-0501. Phones: (802)828-4508; FAX (802)828-3258.

Virginia—1911 N. Ft. Myer Dr. - Ste. 601, Arlington, VA 22209. Phones: (703)524-2885; FAX (703)524-2649.

- 400 N. 8th St. - Ste. 540, P.O. Box 10026, Richmond, VA 23240. Phones: (804)771-2246; FAX (804)771-2390.

Washington—2001 6th Ave. - Ste. 650, Seattle, WA 98121. Phones: (206)553-5615; FAX (206)553-7253.

- 801 W. Riverside Ave. - Ste. 400, Spokane, WA 99201. Phones: (509)353-2625; FAX (509)353-2449.
- 950 Pacific Ave. - Ste. 410, Tacoma, WA 98402. Phones: (253)593-6736; FAX (253)383-4676.

West Virginia—405 Capitol St. - Ste. 807, Charleston, WV 25301. Phones: (304)347-5123; FAX (304)347-5408.

- Wheeling Jesuit University/NTTC, 316 Washington Ave., Wheeling, WV 26003. Phones: (304)243-5493; FAX (304)243-5494.

Wisconsin—517 E. Wisconsin Ave. - Rm.596, Milwaukee, WI 53202. Phones: (414)297-3473; FAX (414)297-3470.

Wyoming—*See* **Denver, Colorado** Export Assistance Center.

11.150 Bureau of Export Administration

Western—3300 Irvine Ave. - Ste. 345, Newport Beach, CA 92660-3198. Phone: (714)660-0144.

- 101 Park Center Plaza - Ste. 1001, San Jose, CA 95113. Phone: (408)998-7402.

ECONOMIC DEVELOPMENT ADMINISTRATION

11.300 thru 11.313 REGIONAL OFFICES

Atlanta *(Alabama, Florida, Georgia, Kentucky, Mississippi, North Carolina, South Carolina, Tennessee)*—401 W. Peachtree St. NW - Ste. 1820, Atlanta, GA 30308-3510. Phone: (404)730-3002.

Austin *(Arkansas, Louisiana, New Mexico, Oklahoma, Texas)*—327 Congress Ave. - Ste. 200, Austin, TX 78701-5595. Phone: (512)381-8144.

11.300 thru 11.313 *(cont.)* **Chicago** *(Illinois, Indiana, Michigan, Minnesota, Ohio, Wisconsin)*—111 N. Canal St. - Ste. 855, Chicago, IL 60606-7204. Phone: (312)353-8143.

Denver *(Colorado, Iowa, Kansas, Missouri, Montana, Nebraska, North Dakota, South Dakota, Utah, Wyoming)*—1244 Speer Blvd. - Rm.670, Denver, CO 80204. Phone: (303)844-4715.

Philadelphia *(Connecticut, Delaware, District of Columbia, Maine, Maryland, Massachusetts, New Hampshire, New Jersey, New York, Pennsylvania, Puerto Rico, Rhode Island, Vermont, Virgin Islands, Virginia, West Virginia)*—Curtis Center, Independence Square West - Ste. 140 South, Philadelphia, PA 19106. Phone: (215)597-4603.

Seattle *(Alaska, American Samoa, Arizona, California, Guam, Hawaii, Idaho, Marshall Islands, Micronesia, Nevada, Northern Mariana Islands, Oregon, Washington)*—Jackson Federal Bldg. - Ste. 1856, 915 2nd Ave., Seattle, WA 98174. Phone: (206)220-7660.

NATIONAL OCEANIC AND ATMOSPHERIC ADMINISTRATION

11.405 thru 11.427

REGIONAL OFFICES

ALASKA—Juneau, AK 99802-1668. Phone: (907)586-7221.

NORTHEAST—One Blackburn Dr., Gloucester, MA 01930. Phone: (978)281-9250.

NORTHWEST—7600 Sand Point Way NE, Seattle, WA 98115. Phone: (206)526-6150.

SOUTHEAST—9721 Executive Center Dr. N. - Ste. 201, St. Petersburg, FL 33702. Phone: (727)570-5301.

SOUTHWEST—501 W. Ocean Blvd. - Ste. 4200, Long Beach, CA 90802-4213. Phone: (562)980-4001.

- Southwest Fisheries Science Center, La Jolla, CA 92038-0271. Phone: (619)546-7081.

FIELD AREAS

Virginia—Atlantic Marine Center, 439 W. York St., Norfolk, VA 23510-1114. Phone: (757)441-6776.

Washington—Pacific Marine Center, 1801 Fairview Ave. E., Seattle, WA 98102. Phone: (206)553-7656.

11.433 **NORTHEAST**—NMFS, One Blackburn Dr., Gloucester, MA 01930. Phone: (978)281-9267. **Internet:** e-mail, "Grants.Information@noaa.gov".

SOUTHEAST—State/Federal Liaison Office, NMFS, 263 13th Ave. S., St. Petersburg, FL 33701. Phone: (727)824-5324.

11.434 **SOUTHEAST**—Federal Program Officer, State/Federal Liaison Office, 263 13th Ave. S., St. Petersburg, FL 33701. Phones: (727)824-5324; FAX (727)824-5364.

11.435 **SOUTHEAST**—Federal Program Officer, State/Federal Liaison Branch, 263 13th Ave. S., St. Petersburg, FL 33701. Phones: (727)824-5324; FAX (727)824-5364.

11.436 **NORTHWEST**—Columbia River Fisheries Development Program, NMFS-NOAA, Salmon Recovery Division, Hatcheries and Inland Fisheries Branch, 1201 NE Lloyd Blvd., Portland, OR 97232-1274. Phones: (503)231-2009; FAX (503)872-2737.

Northwest Fisheries Science Center, NOAA-NMFS, 2725 Montlake Blvd. E., Seattle, WA 98112-2097. Phones: (206)860-3234; FAX (206)860-3467.

11.437 **ALASKA**—NMFS, Federal Program Officer, Juneau, AK 99802-1668. Phones: (907)586-7255; FAX (907)586-7255.

11.438 **ALASKA**—Pacific Coast Salmon Recovery Program, NMFS, Juneau, AK 99802-1668. Phone: (907)586-7280.

NORTHWEST—Pacific Salmon Treaty, NOAA-NMFS, 7600 Sand Point Way NE, Seattle, WA 98115. Phones: (206)526-4140; FAX (206)526-6534.

- NOAA-NMFS, 7600 Sand Point Way NE, Seattle, WA 98115. Phones: (206)526-6150; FAX (206)526-6426.

11.439 *Discretionary: Stranding Network Contacts*

ALASKA—NMFS, Federal Bldg. - 14th fl., 709 W. 9th St., Juneau, AK 99802-1668. Phone: (907)586-7824.

NORTHEAST—NMFS, One Blackburn Dr., Gloucester, MA 01930-2298. Phone: (978)281-9328.

NORTHWEST—NMFS, Bldg. 1, 7600 Sand Point Way, NE, Seattle, WA 98115. Phone: (206)526-6733.

SOUTHEAST—NMFS, 263 13th Ave. S., St. Petersburg, FL 33701. Phone: (727)824-5312.

SOUTHWEST—NMFS, 501 W. Ocean Blvd. - Ste. 4200, Long Beach, CA 90802-4213. Phone: (562)980-4017.

Nondiscretionary:

ALASKA—NOAA/NMFS, Juneau, AK 99802-1668. Phone: (907)586-7273.

NORTHWEST—NOAA/NMFS, 7600 Sand Point Way NE, Seattle, WA 98115. Phones: (206)526-6150; FAX (206)526-6426.

PACIFIC ISLANDS—NMFS, 1601 Kapiolani Blvd. - Ste. 1110, Honolulu, HI 96814-4700. Phone: (808)973-2935.

11.441 Listed under **11.405**.

11.444 and 11.445 **PACIFIC ISLANDS**—Pacific Islands Fisheries Science Center, NMFS, 2570 Dole St., Honolulu, HI 96822. Phones: (808)983-5374; FAX (808)983-2902.

11.449 NOAA/OAR, Bldg. 22, 325 Broadway, Boulder, CO 80303. Phone: (303)497-6731.

11.450 AFWS Operations Manager, Hydrologic Services Division, National Weather Service Eastern Region (W/ER2), Airport Corporate Center, 630 Johnson Ave., Bohemia, NY 11716. Phone: (631)244-0112.

11.452 **ALASKA**—NMFS, P.O. Box 12668, Juneau, AK 99802. Phone: (907)586-7280.

NORTHEAST—Director, State, Federal and Constituent Programs Office, NMFS, One Blackburn Dr., Gloucester, MA 01930-2298. Phones: (978)281-9243; FAX (978)281-9117. **Internet:** e-mail, "Grants.Information@noaa.gov".

NORTHWEST—NMFS, 7600 Sand Point Way NE, Seattle, WA 98115. Phones: (206)526-6115; FAX (206)526-4461.

SOUTHEAST—State/Federal Liaison Branch, 263 13th Ave. S., St. Petersburg, FL 33701. Phones: (727)824-5364; FAX (727)824-5364.

SOUTHWEST—Federal Programs Officer, 501 W. Ocean Blvd. - Ste. 4200, Long Beach, CA 90802. Phones: (562)980-4033; FAX (562)980-4047.

PACIFIC ISLANDS AREA OFFICE—Program Analyst, 1601 Kapiolani Blvd. - Ste. 1110, Honolulu, HI 96814. Phones: (808)973-2935, ext.213; FAX (808)973-2941.

11.454 **ALASKA**—NMFS, Juneau, AK 99802-1668. Phone: (907)586-7845.

NORTHEAST—State, Federal and Constituent Programs Office, NMFS, One Blackburn Dr., Gloucester, MA 01930-2298. Phones: (978)281-9243; FAX (978)281-9117. **Internet:** e-mail, "Grants.Information@noaa.gov".

NORTHWEST—NMFS, 7600 Sand Point Way NE, Seattle, WA 98115. Phones: (206)526-6150; FAX (206)526-6426.

11.454 *(cont.)* **SOUTHEAST**—Federal Program Officer, State/Federal Liaison Branch, 263 13th Ave. S., St. Petersburg, FL 33701. Phones: (727)824-5324; FAX (727)824-5364.

SOUTHWEST—Federal Program Officer, 501 W. Ocean Blvd. - Ste. 4200, Long Beach, CA 90802-4213. Phones: (562)980-4033; FAX (562)980-4047.

11.455 **ALASKA**—Director, Alaska Fisheries Science Center - Bldg. 4, 7600 Sand Point Way NE, Seattle, WA 98115-6349. Phones: (206)526-4000; FAX (206)526-4004.

NORTHEAST—Chief/Office of Marine Ecosystem Studies, Northeast Fisheries Science Center, 28 Tarzwell Dr., Narragansett, RI 02882. Phones: (401)782-3211; FAX (401)782-3201.

NORTHWEST—Deputy Director, Northwest Fisheries Science Center, 2725 Montlake Blvd. E., Seattle, WA 98112-2097. Phones: (206)860-3200; FAX (206)860-3217.

SOUTHEAST—Federal Program Officer, State/Federal Liaison Branch, 263 13th Ave. S., St. Petersburg, FL 33701. Phones: (727)824-5324; FAX (727)824-5364.

SOUTHWEST—Deputy Science Director, Southwest Fisheries Science Center, 8604 La Jolla Shores Drive, La Jolla, CA 92038-1508. Phones: (858)546-7066; (858)546-7003.

11.457 Chesapeake Bay Office, NMFS-NOAA, 410 Severn Ave. - Ste. 107A, Annapolis, MD 21403. Phones: (410)267-5660; FAX (410)267-5666.

11.463 Listed under **11.405**

11.472 **ALASKA**—NMFS, Juneau, AK 99802-1668. Phones: (907)586-7845; FAX (907)586-7255.

NORTHEAST—Director, State, Federal and Constituent Programs Office, NMFS, One Blackburn Drive, Gloucester, MA 01930-2298. Phones: (978)281-9243; (978)281-9117. **Internet:** e-mail, "Grants.Information@noaa.gov".

NORTHWEST—NMFS, 7600 Sand Point Way NE, Seattle, WA 98115. Phones: (206)526-6115; FAX (206)526-4461.

SOUTHEAST—State/Federal Liaison Staff, 9721 Executive Center Drive N., St. Petersburg, FL 33702-2432. Phones: (727)570-5324; FAX (727)570-5364.

11.473 **SOUTHWEST**—Federal Program Officer, 501 W. Ocean Blvd. - Ste. 4200, Long Beach, CA 90802-4213. Phones: (562)980-4033; (562)980-4047. Director, NOAA Coastal Services Center, 2234 S. Hobson Ave., Charleston, SC 29405-2413. Phone: (843)740-1200.

11.474 **NORTHEAST**—State, Federal and Constituent Programs Division, NMFS, One Blackburn Dr., Gloucester, MA 01930. Phones: (978)281-9243; FAX (978)281-9117. **Internet:** e-mail, "Grants.Information@noaa.gov".

SOUTHEAST—Federal Program Officer, State/Federal Liaison Branch, 263 13th Ave. S., St. Petersburg, FL 33701. Phones: (727)824-5324; FAX (727)824-5364.

11.477 **ALASKA**—NMFS, Juneau, AK 99802-1668. Phones: (907)586-7845; FAX (907)586-7255.

NORTHEAST—Director, State,Federal and Constituent Programs Office, NMFS, One Blackburn Dr., Gloucester, MA 01930-2298. Phones: (978)281-9243; FAX (978)281-9117. **Internet:** e-mail, "Grants.Information@noaa.gov".

NORTHWEST—NMFS, Sustainable Fisheries Division, 7600 Sand Point Way NE, Seattle, WA 98115. Phones: (206)526-6113; FAX (206)526-4461.

SOUTHEAST—State/Federal Liaison Staff, 263 13th Ave. S., St. Petersburg, FL 33702-2432. Phones: (727)570-5324; FAX (727)570-5364.

SOUTHWEST—Federal Program Officer, 501 W. Ocean Blvd., Long Beach, CA 90802-4213. Phones: (562)980-4239; FAX (562)980-4047.

NATIONAL INSTITUTE OF STANDARDS AND TECHNOLOGY

11.603 and 11.604 Listed under **11.108**.

MINORITY BUSINESS DEVELOPMENT AGENCY

11.800 thru 11.803 **REGIONAL AND DISTRICT OFFICES**

REGIONS I, II, AND III *(Connecticut, Delaware, District of Columbia, Maine, Maryland, Massachusetts, New Hampshire, New Jersey, New York, Pennsylvania, Puerto Rico, Rhode Island, Vermont, Virgin Islands, West Virginia)*—26 Federal Plaza - Rm.3720, New York, NY 10278. Phone: (212)264-3262.

Massachusetts—10 Causeway St. - Rm.418., Boston, MA 02222-1041. Phone: (617)565-6850.

Pennsylvania—Federal Office Bldg. - Rm.10128, 600 Arch St., Philadelphia, PA 19106. Phone: (215)597-9236.

REGION IV *(Alabama, Florida, Georgia, Kentucky, Mississippi, North Carolina, South Carolina, Tennessee)*—401 W. Peachtree St. NW - Rm.1715, Atlanta, GA 30308-3516. Phone: (404)730-3300.

Florida—Federal Bldg. - Rm.1314, 51 SW 1st Ave., P.O. Box 25, Miami, FL 33130. Phone: (305)536-5054.

REGIONS V AND VII *(Illinois, Indiana, Iowa, Kansas, Michigan, Minnesota, Missouri, Nebraska, Ohio, Wisconsin)*—55 E. Monroe St. - Ste. 1406, Chicago, IL 60603. Phone: (312)353-0182.

REGIONS VI AND VIII *(Arkansas, Colorado, Louisiana, Montana, New Mexico, North Dakota, Oklahoma, South Dakota, Texas, Utah, Wyoming)*—1100 Commerce St. - Rm.7B23, Dallas, TX 75242. Phone: (214)767-8001.

REGIONS IX AND X *(Alaska, American Samoa, Arizona, California, Guam, Hawaii, Idaho, Nevada, Oregon, Washington)*—221 Main St. - Rm.1280, San Francisco, CA 94105. Phone: (415)744-3001.

California—9660 Flair Dr. - Ste. 455, El Monte, CA 91731. Phone: (818)453-8636.

PATENT AND TRADEMARK OFFICE

11.900 Listed under **11.108**.

DEPARTMENT OF DEFENSE

DEPARTMENT OF THE ARMY, CORPS OF ENGINEERS

12.100 thru 12.111 **Alabama** *(Mobile District)*—P.O. Box 2288, Mobile, AL 36628. Phone: (205)690-2511.

Alaska *(Alaska District)*—P.O. Box 898, Anchorage, AK 99506. Phone: (907)752-5233.

Arkansas *(Little Rock District)*—P.O. Box 867, Little Rock, AR 72203. Phone: (501)378-5531.

12.100 thru 12.111 *(cont.)*

California *(Los Angeles District)*—P.O. Box 2711, Los Angeles, CA 90053. Phone: (213)688-5300.

- *(Sacramento District)*—650 Capitol Mall, Sacramento, CA 95814. Phone: (916)448-2232.
- *(San Francisco District)*—211 Main St., San Francisco, CA 94105. Phone: (415)974-0358.
- *(South Pacific Division)*—630 Sansome St. - Rm.720, San Francisco, CA 94111. Phone: (415)556-0914.

District of Columbia—CDR, USACA/CEMP-RI, 20 Massachusetts Ave. NW, Washington, DC 20314. Phone: (202)504-4950.

Florida *(Jacksonville District)*—P.O. Box 4970, Jacksonville, FL 32232. Phone: (904)791-2241.

Georgia *(Savannah District)*—P.O. Box 889, Savannah, GA 31402. Phone: (912)944-5224, ext.224.

- *(South Atlantic Division)*—510 Title Bldg., 30 Pryor St. SW, Atlanta, GA 30335. Phone: (404)221-6711.

Hawaii *(Pacific Ocean Division)*—Ft. Shafter, HI 96858. Phone: (808)438-1500.

Illinois *(Chicago District)*—219 S. Dearborn St., Chicago, IL 60604. Phone: (312)353-6400.

- *(North Central Division)*—536 S. Clark St., Chicago, IL 60605. Phone: (312)353-6310.
- *(Rock Island District)*—Clock Tower Bldg., P.O. Box 2004, Rock Island, IL 61204. Phone: (309)788-6361.
- Constitution Engineering Research Laboratory, Champaign, IL 61820-1305. Phone: (217)373-6789.

Kentucky *(Louisville District)*—P.O. Box 59, Louisville, KY 40201. Phone: (502)582-5601.

Louisiana *(New Orleans District)*—P.O. Box 60267, New Orleans, LA 70160. Phone: (504)838-1121.

Maryland *(Baltimore District)*—P.O. Box 1715, Baltimore, MD 21203. Phone: (301)962-4545.

Massachusetts *(New England Division)*—424 Trapelo Rd., Waltham, MA 02254. Phone: (617)647-8220.

Michigan *(Detroit District)*—P.O. Box 1027, Detroit, MI 48231. Phone: (313)226-6762.

Minnesota *(St. Paul District)*—1135 USPO and Custom House, St. Paul, MN 55101. Phone: (612)725-7501.

Mississippi *(Lower Mississippi Valley Division)*—P.O. Box 80, Vicksburg, MS 39180. Phone: (601)634-5750.

- *(Vicksburg District)*—P.O. Box 60, Vicksburg, MS 39180. Phone: (601)634-5010.
- Waterways Experiment Station, Vicksburg, MS 39180-0631. Phone: (601)634-2424.

Missouri *(Kansas City District)*—700 Federal Bldg., Kansas City, MO 64106. Phone: (816)374-3201.

- *(St. Louis District)*—210 N. Tucker Blvd., St. Louis, MO 63101. Phone: (314)263-5660.

Nebraska *(Missouri River Division)*—Downtown Station, P.O. Box 103, Omaha, NE 68101. Phone: (402)221-7201.

- *(Omaha District)*—USPO and Courthouse - Rm.6014, Omaha, NE 68102. Phone: (402)221-3900.

New Hampshire—Cold Regions Research and Engineering Laboratory, Hanover, NH 03755-1290. Phone: (603)646-4390.

New Mexico *(Albuquerque District)*—P.O. Box 1580, Albuquerque, NM 87103. Phone: (505)766-2732.

New York *(Buffalo District)*—1776 Niagara St., Buffalo, NY 14207. Phone: (716)876-5454, ext.2200.

- *(New York District)*—26 Federal Plaza, New York, NY 10278. Phone: (212)264-0100.
- *(North Atlantic Division)*—90 Church St., New York, NY 10007. Phone: (212)264-7101.

North Carolina *(Wilmington District)*—P.O. Box 1890, Wilmington, NC 28402. Phone: (919)343-4501.

Ohio *(Ohio River Division)*—P.O. Box 1159, Cincinnati, OH 45201. Phone: (513)221-6000.

Oklahoma *(Tulsa District)*—P.O. Box 61, Tulsa, OK 74121. Phone: (918)581-7311.

Oregon *(North Pacific Division)*—P.O. Box 2870, Portland, OR 97208. Phone: (503)221-3700.

- *(Portland District)*—P.O. Box 2946, Portland, OR 97208. Phone: (503)221-6000.

Pennsylvania *(Philadelphia District)*—U.S. Custom House, 2nd and Chestnut St., Philadelphia, PA 19106. Phone: (215)597-4848.

- *(Pittsburgh District)*—Federal Bldg., 1000 Liberty Ave., Pittsburgh, PA 15222. Phone: (412)644-6800.

South Carolina *(Charleston District)*—P.O. Box 919, Charleston, SC 29402. Phone: (803)724-4229.

Tennessee *(Memphis District)*—B-202 Clifford Davis Federal Bldg., Memphis, TN 38103. Phone: (901)521-3221.

- *(Nashville District)*—P.O. Box 1070, Nashville, TN 37202. Phone: (615)251-5626.

Texas *(Ft. Worth District)*—P.O. Box 17300, Ft. Worth, TX 76102. Phone: (817)334-2300.

- *(Galveston District)*—P.O. Box 1229, Galveston, TX 77553. Phone: (409)766-3006.
- *(Southwestern Division)*—1114 Commerce St., Dallas, TX 75242. Phone: (214)767-2500.

Virginia *(Norfolk District)*—803 Front St., Norfolk, VA 23510. Phone: (804)441-3601.

- Humphreys Engineer Center Support Activity, Ft. Belvoir, VA 22060-5580. Phone: (202)355-2153.
- Topographic Engineering Center, Ft. Belvoir, VA 22060-5546. Phone: (202)355-2659.

Washington *(Seattle District)*—P.O. Box C-3755, Seattle, WA 98124. Phone: (206)764-3690.

- *(Walla Walla District)*—City-County Airport - Bldg. 602, Walla Walla, WA 99362. Phone: (509)522-6506.

West Virginia *(Huntington District)*—502 8th St., Huntington, WV 25721. Phone: (304)529-5395.

12.114 and 12.116 Research and Development Laboratories

USAE Hydrologic Engineering Center, 609 2nd St., Davis, CA 95616-4887. Phone: (916)756-1104.

USA Construction Engineering Research Laboratory, 2902 Newmark Dr., Champaign, IL 61821-1075. Phones: (800)872-2375, (800)252-7122.

12.114 and 12.116 *(cont.)* USAE Waterways Experiment Station, 3909 Falls Ferry Rd., Vicksburg, MS 39180-6199. Phones: (601)634-2512, (800)522-6937.

USA Cold Regions Research and Engineering Laboratory, 72 Lynn Rd., Hanover, NH 03755-1290. Phone: (603)646-4445.

USA Topographic Engineering Center, Cude Bldg. No. 2592, Ft. Belvoir, VA 22060-5546. Phone: (703)355-3133.

USAE Institute for Water Resources, Casey Bldg. No. 2594, Ft. Belvoir, VA 22060-5586. Phone: (703)355-3084.

DEPARTMENT OF THE ARMY, U.S. ARMY MEDICAL COMMAND

12.420 Commander, Army Medical Research Acquisition Activity, Attn: SGRD-RMA-RC, Ft. Detrick, Frederick, MD 21702-5014. Phone: (301)619-2036.

OFFICE OF THE SECRETARY (ECONOMIC SECURITY)

12.600 thru 12.614 **WESTERN REGION**—Office of Economic Adjustment, OASD(FM&P), 1325 J St. - Ste. 1500, Sacramento, CA 95814. Phone: (916)567-7365.

SECRETARIES OF MILITARY DEPARTMENTS

12.700 *Contact nearest military installation. Consult local phone directory.*

DEPARTMENT OF THE AIR FORCE, MATERIAL COMMAND

12.800 Air Force Office of Scientific Research, Bolling AFB - Ste. B115, 110 Duncan Ave., Washington, DC 20332-4990. Phone: (no number provided).

Armstrong Laboratory, 8005 9th St., Brooks AFB, TX 78235-5353. Phone: (no number provided).

Phillips Laboratory, 3651 Lowry Ave. SE, Kirkland AFB, NM 87117-5777. Phone: (505)846-4979.

Rome Laboratory, 26 Electronics Pkwy., Griffins AFB, NY 13441-4514. Phone: (315)330-7746.

Wright Laboratory, Bldg. 7, 2530 C St., Wright-Patterson AFB, OH 45433-7607. Phone: (513)255-4813.

DEPARTMENT OF HOUSING AND URBAN DEVELOPMENT

HOUSING - FEDERAL HOUSING COMMISSIONER

14.103 thru 14.195

FIELD OFFICES

Alabama—950 22nd St. N. - Ste. 900, Birmingham, AL 35203-5302. Phones: (205)731-2617; FAX (205)731-2593.

Alaska—3000 C St. - Ste. 401, Anchorage, AK 99503. Phones: (907)677-9800; FAX (907)677-9803.

Arizona—1 N. Central Ave. - Ste. 600, Phoenix, AZ 85004. Phones: (602)379-7100; FAX (602)379-3985.

- 160 N. Stone Ave., Tucson, AZ 85701-1467. Phones: (602)670-6000; FAX (602)670-6207.

Arkansas—TCBY Tower, 425 W. Capitol Ave. - Ste. 900, Little Rock, AR 72201-3488. Phones: (501)324-5931; FAX (501)324-6142.

California—2135 Fresno St. - Ste. 100, Fresno, CA 93721-1718. Phones: (559)487-5033, ext.232; FAX (559)487-5191.

- AT&T Center - Ste. 800, 611 W. 6th St., Los Angeles, CA 90017-3127. Phones: (213)894-8007; FAX (213)894-8110.
- 925 L St., Sacramento, CA 95814-2601. Phones: (916)498-5220, ext.322; FAX (916)498-5262.
- Symphony Towers - Ste. 1600, 750 B St., San Diego, CA 92101-8131. Phones: (619)557-5310; FAX (619)557-5312.
- 600 Harrison St. - 3rd fl., San Francisco, CA 94107-1300. Phones: (415)489-6400; FAX (415)489-6419.
- World Trade Tower, 1600 N. Broadway - Ste. 101, Santa Ana, CA 92706-3927. Phones: (714)796-5577; FAX (714)796-1285.

Colorado—1670 Broadway 23rd fl.,, Denver, CO 80202. Phones: (303)672-5440; FAX (303)672-5004.

Connecticut—One Corporate Center - 19th fl., 20 Church St., Hartford, CT 06103-3220. Phones: (860)240-4800; FAX (860)240-4850.

Delaware—One Rodney Square - Ste. 404, 920 King St., Wilmington, DE 19801. Phones: (302)573-6300; FAX (302)573-6259.

District of Columbia—820 1st St. NE - Ste. 300, Washington, DC 20002-4205. Phones: (202)275-9200; FAX (202)523-9212.

Florida—Southern Bell Tower - Ste. 2200, 301 W. Bay St., Jacksonville, FL 32202-5121. Phones: (904)232-2627; FAX (904)232-3759.

- Brickell Plaza Bldg., 909 SE 1st Ave., Miami, FL 33131-3028. Phones: (305)536-4456; FAX (305)536-5765.
- Langley Bldg. - Ste. 270, 3751 Maguire Blvd., Orlando, FL 32803-3032. Phones: (407)648-6441; FAX (407)648-6310.
- Timberlake Federal Bldg. Annex - Ste. 402, 501 E. Zack St., Tampa, FL 33602-3945. Phones: (813)228-2026; FAX (813)228-2431.

Georgia—Five Points Plaza, 40 Marietta St., Atlanta, GA 30303-2806. Phones: (404)331-4111; FAX (404)730-2392.

14.103 thru 14.195 *(cont.)*

Hawaii—3 Waterfront Plaza - Ste. 3A, 500 Ala Moana Blvd., Honolulu, HI 96813-4918. Phones: (808)522-8175, ext.256 or 259; FAX (808)522-8194.

Idaho—Plaza IV - Ste. 220, 800 Park Blvd., Boise, ID 83712-7743. Phones: (208)334-1990, ext.3007; FAX (208)334-9648.

Illinois—Metcalfe Federal Bldg., 77 W. Jackson Blvd., Chicago, IL 60604-3507. Phones: (312)353-5680; FAX (312)886-2729.

- 500 W. Monroe St. - Ste. 1SW, Springfield, IL 62704. Phones: (217)492-4120; FAX (217)492-4154.

Indiana—151 N. Delaware St. - Ste. 1200, Indianapolis, IN 46204-2526. Phones: (317)226-6303; FAX (317)226-6317.

Iowa—Federal Bldg.- Rm.239, 210 Walnut St., Des Moines, IA 50309-2155. Phones: (515)284-4512; FAX (515)284-4743.

Kansas—Gateway Tower II, 400 State Ave. - Rm.200, Kansas City, KS 66101-2406. Phones: (913)551-5462, ext.4; FAX (913)551-5469.

Kentucky—601 W. Broadway, Louisville, KY 40202. Phones: (502)582-5251; FAX (502)582-6074.

Louisiana—Boggs Federal Bldg. - 9th fl., 501 Magazine St., New Orleans, LA 70130-3099. Phones: (504)589-7201; FAX (504)589-6619.

- 401 Edwards St. - Ste. 1510, Shreveport, LA 71101-5513. Phones: (318)676-3440; FAX (318)676-3407.

Maine—Smith Federal Bldg. - Rm.101, 202 Harlow St., Bangor, ME 04401-4919. Phones: (207)945-0467; FAX (207)945-0533.

Maryland—City Crescent Bldg. - 5th fl., 10 S. Howard St., Baltimore, MD 21201-2505. Phones: (410)962-2520, ext.3474; FAX (410)962-1849.

Massachusetts—O'Neill Jr. Federal Office Bldg. - Rm.301, 10 Causeway St., Boston, MA 02222-1092. Phones: (617)994-8200; FAX (617)565-5257.

Michigan—McNamara Federal Bldg., 477 Michigan Ave., Detroit, MI 48226-2592. Phones: (313)226-7900; FAX (313)226-5611.

- Phoenix Bldg., 801 S. Saginaw St., Flint, MI 48502. Phones: (810)766-5112; FAX (810)766-5122.
- Trade Center Bldg., 50 Louis St. NW, Grand Rapids, MI 49503-2633. Phones: (616)456-2100; FAX (616)456-2114.

Minnesota—Kinnard Financial Center, 920 Second St. S., Minneapolis, MN 55402. Phones: (612)370-3000, ext.2045; FAX (612)370-3220.

Mississippi—McCoy Federal Bldg. - Rm.910, 100 W. Capitol St., Jackson, MS 39269-1096. Phones: (601)965-4757; FAX (601)965-4773.

Missouri—Young Federal Bldg. - Ste. 3207, 1222 Spruce St., St. Louis, MO 63103-2836. Phones: (314)539-6583; FAX (314)539-6384.

Montana—Power Block Bldg., 7 W. 6th Ave., Helena, MT 59601. Phones: (406)449-5050; FAX (406)449-4052.

Nebraska—Executive Tower Centre - Ste. 100, 10909 Mill Valley Rd., Omaha, NE 68154-3955. Phones: (402)492-3101; FAX (402)492-3150.

Nevada—300 S. Las Vegas Blvd. - Ste. 2900, Las Vegas, NV 89101-5833. Phones: (702)366-2100; FAX (702)388-6244.

- 3702 S. Virginia Ave., Reno, NV 89502-6581. Phones: (775)784-5383; FAX (775)784-5005.

New Hampshire—1000 Elm St. - 8th fl., Manchester, NH 03101-1730. Phones: (603)666-7510; FAX (603)666-7667.

New Jersey—Hudson Bldg. - 2nd fl., 800 Hudson Square, Camden, NJ 08102-1156. Phones: (856)757-5081; FAX (856)757-5373.

- One Newark Center - 13th fl., Newark, NJ 07102-5260. Phones: (973)622-7900; FAX (973)645-2323.

New Mexico—625 Silver Ave. SW - Ste. 100, Albuquerque, NM 87102-3185. Phones: (505)346-6463, ext.7332; FAX (505)346-6704.

New York—52 Corporate Circle, Albany, NY 12203-5121. Phones: (518)464-4200, ext.4204; FAX (518)464-4300.

- Lafayette Court - 5th fl., 465 Main St., Buffalo, NY 14203-1780. Phones: (716)551-5755, ext.5000; FAX (716)551-5752.
- 26 Federal Plaza - Ste. 3541, New York, NY 10278-0068. Phones: (212)264-8000; FAX (212)264-3068.
- 128 Jefferson St., Syracuse, NY 13202. Phones: (315)477-0616; FAX (315)477-0196.

North Carolina—Asheville Bldg. - Ste. 401, 1500 Pinecroft Rd., Greensboro, NC 27407-3838. Phones: (336)547-4001; FAX (336)547-4138.

North Dakota—Federal Bldg. - Rm.366, 657 2nd Ave., Fargo, ND 58108-2483. Phones: (701)239-5136; FAX (701)239-5249.

Ohio—15 E. 7th St., Cincinnati, OH 45202-2401. Phones: (513)684-3451; FAX (513)684-6224.

- Renaissance Bldg. - Ste. 500, 1350 Euclid Ave., Cleveland, OH 44115-1815. Phones: (216)522-4058, ext.7102; FAX (216)522-4067.
- 200 N. High St., Columbus, OH 43215-2463. Phones: (614)469-2540; FAX (614)469-2432.

Oklahoma—301 NW 6th St. - Ste. 200, Oklahoma City, OK 73102. Phones: (405)609-8509; FAX (405)609-8588.

- 1516 S. Boston St. - Ste. 100, Tulsa, OK 74119-4030. Phones: (918)581-7434; FAX (918)581-7440.

Oregon—400 SW 6th Ave. - Ste. 700, Portland, OR 97204-1632. Phones: (503)326-2561; FAX (503)326-2568.

Pennsylvania—The Wanamaker Bldg., 100 Penn Square East, Philadelphia, PA 19107-3380. Phones: (215)656-0600; FAX (215)656-3445.

- 339 6th Ave. - 6th fl., Pittsburgh, PA 15222-2515. Phones: (412)644-6428; FAX (412)644-4240.

Puerto Rico—New San Juan Office Bldg., 171 Carlos E. Chardon Ave., San Juan, PR 00918-0903. Phones: (787)766-5201; FAX (787)766-5995.

Rhode Island—10 Weybosset St. - 6th fl., Providence, RI 02903-2818. Phones: (401)528-5230; FAX (401)528-5312.

South Carolina—Thurmond Federal Bldg. - 13th fl., 1835 Assembly St., Columbia, SC 29201-2480. Phones: (803)765-5592; FAX (803)253-3043.

South Dakota—2400 W. 49th St. - Ste. I-201, Sioux Falls, SD 57105-6558. Phones: (605)330-4223; FAX (605)330-4428.

Tennessee—Duncan Federal Bldg. - 3rd fl., 710 Locust St., Knoxville, TN 37902-2526. Phones: (865)545-4384; FAX (865)545-4569.

- One Memphis Place - Ste. 1200, 200 Jefferson Ave., Memphis, TN 38103-2389. Phones: (901)544-3367; FAX (901)544-3697.
- 235 Cumberland Bend Dr. - Ste. 200, Nashville, TN 37228-1803. Phones: (615)736-5213, ext.7120; FAX (615)736-7848.

Texas—525 Griffin St. - Rm.860, Dallas, TX 75202-5007. Phones: (214)767-8300; FAX (214)767-8973.

- 801 Cherry St., Ft. Worth, TX 76113-2905. Phones: (817)978-5965; FAX (817)978-5567.
- 1301 Fannin - Ste. 2200, Houston, TX 77002. Phones: (713)718-3199; FAX (713)313-2319.
- Mahon Federal Bldg. and U.S. Courthouse - Rm.511, 1205 Texas Ave., Lubbock, TX 79401-4093. Phones: (806)472-7265, ext.3030; FAX (806)472-7275.

14.103 thru 14.195 *(cont.)*

- One Alamo Center, 106 S. St. Mary's St, Antonio, TX 78205. Phones: (210)475-6806; FAX (210)472-6804.

Utah—125 S. State St. - Ste. 3001, Salt Lake City, UT 84138. Phones: (801)524-6070; FAX (801)524-3439.

Vermont—159 Bank St. - 2nd fl., Burlington, VT 05401-4410. Phones: (802)951-6290; FAX (802)951-6298.

Virginia—The 3600 Centre, 600 E. Broad St. - 3rd fl., Richmond, VA 23219-4920. Phones: (804)771-2100; FAX (804)771-2090.

Washington—Seattle Federal Office Bldg. - Ste. 200, 909 1st Ave., Seattle, WA 98104-1000. Phones: (206)220-5101; FAX (206)220-5108.

- US Courthouse Bldg. - Rm.588, 920 W. Riverside, Spokane, WA 99201-1010. Phones: (509)353-0674; FAX (509)353-0682.

West Virginia—Kanawha Valley Bldg. - Ste. 708, 405 Capitol St., Charleston, WV 25301-1795. Phones: (304)347-7000, ext.101; FAX (304)347-7050.

Wisconsin—Reuss Federal Plaza - Ste. 1380, 310 W. Wisconsin Ave., Milwaukee, WI 53203-2289. Phones: (414)297-3214, ext.8001; FAX (414)297-3947.

Wyoming—Federal Bldg. - Rm.1010, 100 E. B St., Casper, WY 82601-1969. Phones: (307)261-6250; FAX (307)261-6245.

OFFICE OF NATIVE AMERICAN PROGRAMS

Alaska—3000 C St. - Ste. 401, Anchorage, AK 99503. Phones: (907)677-9800; FAX (907)667-9807.

Eastern/Woodlands (*Iowa, all states east of Mississippi River*)—77 W. Jackson Blvd. - Rm.2404, Chicago, IL 60604-3507. Phones: (800)735-3239; FAX (312)353-8936.

Northern Plains (*Colorado, Montana, Nebraska, North Dakota, South Dakota, Utah, Wyoming*)—UMB Plaza - 22nd fl., 1670 Broadway, Denver, CO 80202-4801. Phones: (303)672-5465; FAX (303)672-5003.

Northwest (*Idaho, Oregon, Washington*)—Seattle Federal Office Bldg. - Ste. 300, 909 1st Ave., Seattle, WA 98104-1000. Phones: (206)220-5270; FAX (206)220-5234.

Southern Plains (*Arkansas, Kansas, Louisiana, Missouri, Oklahoma,Texas*)—301 NW 6th St. - Ste. 200., Oklahoma City, OK 73102. Phones: (405)609-8532; FAX (405)609-8403.

Southwest (*Arizona, California, Nevada, New Mexico*)—1 N. Central Ave. - Ste. 600, Phoenix, AZ 85004-2361. Phones: (602)379-7200; FAX (602)379-3101.

14.197 Office of Multifamily Housing Assistance Restructuring:

- **Chicago**—Metcalfe Federal Bldg. - Rm.2301, 77 W. Jackson Blvd., Chicago, IL 60604. Phone: (312)886-4133, ext.2371.
- **District of Columbia**—The Portals Bldg. - Ste. 380, 1280 Maryland Ave. SW, Washington, DC 20024. Phone: (202)260-2746, ext.3768.

14.198 Listed under **14.103**.

14.199 Contact Multifamily Property Disposition Centers in the Atlanta and Fort Worth HUD offices listed under **14.103**.

COMMUNITY PLANNING AND DEVELOPMENT

14.218 thru 14.250 Office of Community Planning and Development. Addresses are listed under **14.103**.

14.310 thru 14.314 Listed under **14.103**.

FAIR HOUSING AND EQUAL OPPORTUNITY

14.400 thru 14.415 Director, Office of Fair Housing and Equal Opportunity, HUD Regional Office. Addresses are listed under **14.103**.

POLICY DEVELOPMENT AND RESEARCH

14.520 Listed under **14.103**.

PUBLIC AND INDIAN HOUSING

14.850 thru 14.867 Office of Public Housing *or* Office of Native American Programs. Addresses are listed under **14.103**.

14.870 thru 14.872 Listed under **14.103**.

DEPARTMENT OF THE INTERIOR

BUREAU OF INDIAN AFFAIRS

15.020 thru 15.025

AREA OFFICES

Alaska—Alaska Regional Office, Juneau, AK 99802-5520. Phone: (907)586-7177.

Arizona—Western Regional Office, (MS 100), Two Arizona Center - 12th fl., Phoenix, AZ 85001-0010. Phone: (602)379-6600.

California—Pacific Regional Office, Federal Office Bldg., 2800 Cottage Way, Sacramento, CA 95825-1846. Phone: (916)979-2600. *See also* **Arizona**.

District of Columbia—Deputy Commissioner of Indian Affairs, (MS 4140 MIB), 1849 C St. NW, Washington, DC 20240. Phone: (202)208-5116.

Minnesota—Midwest Regional Office, One Federal Dr. - Rm.550, St. Snelling, MN 55111. Phone: (612)713-4400, ext.1020.

Montana—Rocky Mountain Regional Office, 316 N. 26th St., Billings, MT 59101-1397. Phone: (406)247-7943.

New Mexico—Southwest Regional Office, 615 1st St. NW, P.O. Box 26567, Albuquerque, NM 87125-6567. Phone: (505)346-7590. *See also* **Arizona**.

- Navajo Regional Office, P.O. Box 1060, Gallup, NM 87305. Phone: (505)863-8314.

New York—*See* **Virginia**—Eastern Regional Office.

North Carolina—*See* **Virginia**—Eastern Regional Office.

North Dakota—*See* **South Dakota**.

Oklahoma—Southern Plains Office, Anadarko, OK 73005-0368. Phone: (405)247-6673, ext.257.

15.020 thru 15.025 *(cont.)*

- Eastern Oklahoma Regional Office, 101 N. 5th St., Muskogee, OK 74401-6206. Phone: (918)687-2295.

Oregon—Northwest Regional Office, 911 NE 11th Ave., Portland, OR 97232-4169. Phone: (503)231-6702. *See also* **Arizona**.

South Dakota—Great Plains Regional Office, 115 4th Ave. SE, Aberdeen, SD 57401-4382. Phone: (605)226-7343.

Utah—*See* **Arizona, New Mexico(Navajo), and Oregon.**

Virginia—Eastern Regional Office, 3701 N. Fairfax Dr. - Ste. 260, Arlington, VA 22203. Phone: (703)235-3006.

Washington—***See*** Oregon.

Wisconsin—***See*** Minnesota.

Wyoming—***See*** Montana.

FIELD AGENCIES

Alaska—Anchorage Field Office, 1675 C St. - Ste. 211, Anchorage, AK 99501-5198. Phone: (907)271-4088.

- Bethel Field Office, 1675 C St. - Ste. 279, Anchorage, AK 99501-5198. Phone: (907)271-4086.
- Fairbanks Agency, 101 12th Ave. - Rm.16, Fairbanks, AK 99701-6270. Phone: (907)456-0222.
- Metlakatla Field Office, P.O. Box 450, Metlakatla, AK 99926. Phone: (907)886-3791.

Arizona—Chinle Agency, P.O. Box 7-H, Chinle, AZ 86503. Phone: (520)674-5100.

- Colorado River Agency, Rt.1 - Box 9-C, Parker, AZ 85344. Phone: (520)669-7111.
- Ft. Apache Agency, P.O. Box 560, Whiteriver, AZ 85941. Phone: (520)338-5353.
- Ft. Defiance Agency, P.O. Box 619, Ft. Defiance, AZ 86504. Phone: (520)729-7217, -7218.
- Ft. Yuma Field Office, P.O. Box 11000, Yuma, AZ 85366-1000. Phone: (760)572-0248.
- Hopi Agency, P.O. Box 158, Keams Canyon, AZ 86034. Phone: (520)738-2228.
- Papago Agency, P.O. Box 578, Sells, AZ 85634. Phone: (520)383-3286.
- Pima Agency, P.O. Box 8, Sacaton, AZ 85247. Phone: (520)562-3326.
- Salt River Field Office, 10000 E. McDowell Rd., Scottsdale, AZ 85256. Phone: (602)640-2168.
- San Carlos Agency, P.O. Box 209, San Carlos, AZ 85550. Phone: (520)475-2321.
- Truxton Canon Field Office, P.O. Box 37, Valentine, AZ 86437. Phone: (520)769-2286.
- Western Navajo Agency, P.O. Box 127, Tuba City, AZ 86045. Phone: (520)283-2254, -2252.

California—Central California Agency, 1824 Tribute Rd. - Ste. J, Sacramento, CA 95815. Phone: (916)566-7121.

- Northern California Field Office, 1900 Churn Creek Rd. - Ste. 300, Redding, CA 96002. Phone: (530)246-5141.
- Palm Springs Field Office, 650 E. Tahquitz Canyon Way - Ste. A, P.O. Box 2245, Palm Springs, CA 92262. Phone: (760)416-2133.
- Southern California Agency, 2038 Iowa Ave. - Ste. 101, Riverside, CA 92507-0001. Phone: (909)276-6624.

Colorado—Southern Ute Agency, P.O. Box 315, Ignacio, CO 81137. Phone: (970)563-4511.

- Ute Mountain Ute Field Office, P.O. Box KK, Towaoc, CO 81334. Phone: (970)565-8473.

Florida—Seminole Agency, 6075 Sterling Rd., Hollywood, FL 33024. Phone: (954)356-7288.

Idaho—Ft. Hall Agency, P.O. Box 220, Ft. Hall, ID 83203. Phone: (208)238-2301.

- Northern Idaho Agency, P.O. Drawer 277, Lapwai, ID 83540. Phone: (208)843-2300.
- Plummer Subagency, 850 A St., P.O. Box 408, Plummer, ID 83851. Phone: (208)686-1887.

Kansas—Haskell Indian Nations University, 155 Indian Ave., Lawrence, KS 66046. Phone: (785)749-8404.

- Horton Field Office, P.O. Box 31, Horton, KS 66439. Phone: (785)486-2161.

Michigan—Michigan Field Office, 2901.5 I-75 Business Spur, Sault Ste. Marie, MI 49783. Phone: (906)632-6809.

Minnesota—Minnesota Agency, Federal Bldg. - Rm.418, 522 Minnesota Ave. NW, Bemidgi, MN 56601-3062. Phone: (218)751-2011.

- Red Lake Field Office, Red Lake, MN 56671. Phone: (218)679-3361.

Mississippi—Choctaw Field Office, 421 Powell St., Philadelphia, MS 39350. Phone: (601)656-1522.

Montana—Blackfeet Agency, P.O. Box 880, Browning, MT 59417. Phone: (406)338-7544.

- Crow Agency, P.O. Box 69, Crow Agency, MT 59022. Phone: (406)638-2672.
- Flathead Field Office, P.O. Box 40, Pablo, MT 59855-5555. Phone: (406)675-0242.
- Ft. Belknap Agency, R.R. 1 - P.O. Box 980, Harlem, MT 59526. Phone: (406)353-2901, ext.23.
- Ft. Peck Agency, P.O. Box 637, Poplar, MT 59255. Phone: (406)768-5312.
- Northern Cheyenne Agency, P.O. Box 40, Lame Deer, MT 59043. Phone: (406)477-8242.
- Rocky Boy's Field Office, R.R. 1 - P.O. Box 542, Box Elder, MT 59521. Phone: (406)395-4476.

Nebraska—Winnebago Agency, P.O. Box 18, Winnebago, NE 68071. Phone: (402)878-2502.

Nevada—Eastern Nevada Field Office, 1555 Shoshone Circle, Elko, NV 89801. Phone: (775)738-0569.

- Western Nevada Agency, 1677 Hot Springs Rd., Carson City, NV 89706. Phone: (775)887-3500.

New Mexico—Eastern Navajo Agency, P.O. Box 328, Crownpoint, NM 87313. Phone: (505)786-6100.

- Jicarilla Agency, P.O. Box 167, Dulce, NM 87528. Phone: (505)759-3951.
- Laguna Agency, P.O. Box 1448, Laguna, NM 87026. Phone: (505)552-6001.
- Mescalero Agency, P.O. Box 189, Mescalero, NM 88340. Phone: (505)671-4423.
- Northern Pueblos Agency, Fairview Station, P.O. Box 4269, Espanola, NM 87533. Phone: (505)753-1400.
- Ramah-Navajo Agency, Rt.2 - Box 14, Ramah, NM 87321. Phone: (505)775-3235.
- Shiprock Agency, P.O. Box 966, Shiprock, NM 87420. Phone: (505)368-3300.
- Southern Pueblos Agency, P.O. Box 1667, Albuquerque, NM 87103. Phone: (505)346-2424.
- Zuni Agency, P.O. Box 369, Zuni, NM 87327. Phone: (505)782-5591.

New York—New York Field Office, Syracuse, NY 13261-7366. Phone: (315)448-0620.

15.020 thru 15.025 *(cont.)*

North Carolina—Cherokee Agency, Cherokee, NC 28719. Phone: (704)497-9131.

North Dakota—Ft. Berthold Agency, P.O. Box 370, New Town, ND 58763. Phone: (701)627-4707.

- Ft. Totten Agency, P.O. Box 270, Ft. Totten, ND 58335. Phone: (701)766-4545.
- Standing Rock Agency, P.O. Box E, Ft. Yates, ND 58538. Phone: (701)854-3433.
- Turtle Mountain Agency, P.O. Box 60, Belcourt, ND 58316. Phone: (701)477-3191.

Oklahoma—Anadarko Agency, P.O. Box 309, Anadarko, OK 73005. Phone: (405)247-6677.

- Chickasaw Agency, 1500 N. Country Club Rd., P.O. Box 2240, Ada, OK 74821. Phone: (580)436-0784.
- Concho Field Office, El Reno, OK 73036-0068. Phone: (405)262-7481.
- Okmulgee Field Office, P.O. Box 370, Okmulgee, OK 74447. Phone: (918)756-3950.
- Osage Agency, P.O. Box 1539, Pawhuska, OK 74056. Phone: (918)287-1032.
- Miami Field Office, P.O. Box 391, Miami, OK 74355. Phone: (918)542-3396.
- Pawnee Agency, Pawnee, OK 74058-0440. Phone: (918)762-2585.
- Shawnee Field Office, 624 W. Independence - Ste. 114, Shawnee, OK 74801. Phone: (405)273-0317.
- Talihina Office, Drawer H, Talihina, OK 74571. Phone: (918)567-2207.
- Wewoka Agency, P.O. Box 1060, Wewoka, OK 74884. Phone: (405)257-6259.

Oregon—Siletz Field Office, P.O. Box 569, Siletz, OR 97380. Phone: (541)444-2679.

- Umatilla Agency, P.O. Box 520, Pendleton, OR 97801. Phone: (541)278-3786.
- Warm Springs Agency, P.O. Box 1239, Warm Springs, OR 97761. Phone: (541)553-2411.

South Dakota—Cheyenne River Agency, P.O. Box 325, Eagle Butte, SD 57625. Phone: (605)964-6611.

- Crow Creek Agency, P.O. Box 139, Ft. Thompson, SD 57339. Phone: (605)245-2311.
- Lower Brule Agency, P.O. Box 190, Lower Brule, SD 57548. Phone: (605)473-5512.
- Pine Ridge Agency, P.O. Box 1203, Pine Ridge, SD 57770. Phone: (605)867-5125.
- Rosebud Agency, P.O.Box 550, Rosebud, SD 57570. Phone: (605)747-2224.
- Sisseton Agency, P.O. Box 688, Agency Village, SD 57262. Phone: (605)698-3001.
- Yankton Agency, P.O. Box 577, Wagner, SD 57380. Phone: (605)384-3651.

Utah—Uintah and Ouray Agency, P.O. Box 130, Ft. Duchesne, UT 84026. Phone: (435)722-4300.

- Southern Paiute Field Office, P.O. Box 720, St. George, UT 84771. Phone: (435)674-9720.

Washington—Colville Agency, Nespelem, WA 99155-0111. Phone: (509)634-2316.

- Makah Field Office, P.O. Box 115, Neah Bay, WA 98357. Phone: (360)645-3232.
- Olympic Peninsula Agency, P.O. Box 48, Aberdeen, WA 98520. Phone: (360)533-9100.
- Puget Sound Field Office, 2707 Colby Ave. - Ste. 1101, Everett, WA 98201. Phone: (425)258-2651.
- Spokane Agency, P.O. Box 389, Wellpinit, WA 99040. Phone: (509)258-4561.
- Yakima Agency, P.O. Box 632(BIA) - P.O. Box 151(Tribal), Toppenish, WA 98948. Phone: (509)865-5121.

Wisconsin—Great Lakes Agency, 615 Main St. W., Ashland, WI 54806-0273. Phone: (715)682-4527.

Wyoming—Wind River Agency, P.O. Box 158, Ft. Washakie, WY 82514. Phone: (307)332-7810.

15.026 thru 15.028 EDUCATION LINE OFFICES

Alaska—Anchorage Education Field Office, 1675 C St., Anchorage, AK 99501. Phone: (907)271-4115.

Arizona—Chinle Agency-Education, Navajo Rt. 7, P.O. Box 6003, Chinle, AZ 86503. Phone: (520)674-5130, ext.201.

- Ft. Apache Agency-Education, Hwy. 73 and Elm St., P.O. Box 920, White River, AZ 85941. Phone: (520)338-5441.
- Ft. Defiance Agency-Education, Bldg. 38, Blue Canyon Hwy., Ft. Defiance, AZ 86504-0110. Phone: (520)729-7251.
- Hopi Agency-Education, Hwy. 264, P.O. Box 568, Keams Canyon, AZ 86034. Phone: (520)738-2262.
- Papago Agency-Education, South Bldg. 49, P.O. Box 38, Sells, AZ 85634. Phone: (520)383-3292.
- Pima Agency-Education, 400 N. 5th St., P.O. Box 10, Phoenix, AZ 85001. Phone: (602)379-3944.
- Western Navajo Agency-Education, Bldg. 407, Hwy. 160 and Warrior Dr., P.O. Box 746, Tuba City, AZ 86045. Phone: (520)283-2218.

California—Sacramento Area Education Office, 2800 Cottage Way, Sacramento, CA 95825. Phone: (916)979-2560, ext.234.

Kansas—Haskell Indian Nations University, 155 Indian Ave. - #1305, Lawrence, KS 66046-4800. Phone: (785)749-8404.

Minnesota—Minneapolis Area Education Office, 331 S. 2nd Ave., Minneapolis, MN 55401-2241. Phone: (612)373-1000, ext.1090.

Montana—Billings Area Education Office, 316 N. 26th St., Billings, MT 59101-1397. Phone: (406)247-7953.

New Mexico—Eastern Navajo Agency Education, Bldg. 222, 1 Main St., P.O. Box 328, Crownpoint, NM 87313. Phone: (505)786-6150.

- Northern Pueblos Agency-Education, Fairview Station, 1 Mile N. of Espanola - Hwy. 68, P.O. Box 4269, Espanola, NM 87533. Phone: (505)753-1465.
- Shiprock Agency-Education, Hwy. 666N, Shiprock, NM 87420-3239. Phone: (505)368-4427, ext.360.
- Southern Pueblos Agency-Education, 1000 Indian School Rd. NW, P.O. Box 1667, Albuquerque, NM 87103. Phone: (505)346-2431.
- Southwestern Indian Polytechnic Institute, 9169 Coors Rd. NW, P.O. Box 10146-9196, Albuquerque, NM 87184. Phone: (505)346-2343.

North Dakota—Standing Rock Agency-Education, Main St. off Hwy. 106, Agency Ave., P.O. Box E, Ft. Yates, ND 58538. Phone: (701)854-3497.

- Turtle Mountain Agency-Education, School St., P.O. Box 30, Belcourt, ND 58316. Phone: (701)477-6471, ext.211.

Oklahoma—Oklahoma Education Office, 4149 Highline Blvd. - Ste. 380, Oklahoma City, OK 73108. Phone: (605)945-6051, ext.301, (405)605-6057.

Oregon—Portland Area Education Office, 911 NE 11th Ave., Portland, OR 97232-4169. Phone: (503)872-2743.

South Dakota—Cheyenne River Agency-Education, 100 N. Main, P.O. Box 2020, Eagle Butte, SD 51625. Phone: (605)964-8722.

- Crow Creek/Lower Brule Agency-Education, 140 Education Ave., P.O. Box 139, Ft. Thompson, SD 57339. Phone: (605)245-2398.
- Pine Ridge Agency-Education, 101 Main St., P.O. Box 333, Pine Ridge, SD 57770. Phone: (605)867-1306.

15.026 thru 15.028 *(cont.)*

- Rosebud Agency-Education, 1001 Ave. D, P.O. Box 669, Mission, SD 57555. Phone: (605)856-4478, ext.261.

Virginia—South and Eastern States Agency-Education, 3701 N. Fairfax Dr. - Ste. 260, Arlington, VA 22203. Phone: (703)235-3233.

15.029 Listed under **15.020**.

15.030 LAW ENFORCEMENT DISTRICTS

(No phone numbers provided).

DISTRICT I *(All Indian reservations in Michigan, Minnesota, Nebraska, North Dakota, South Dakota, Wisconsin)*—Office of Law Enforcement, Bureau of Indian Affairs, 115 4th Ave. SE, (MC 302), Aberdeen, SD 57401.

DISTRICT II *(All Indian reservations in Kansas and western Oklahoma, all Indian tribes in eastern Oklahoma)*—Office of Law Enforcement, Bureau of Indian Affairs, 101 N. 5th St., Muskogee, OK 74401.

DISTRICT III *(All Indian reservations in Arizona, northern California, Nevada, Utah (excluding Navajo))*—Office of Law Enforcement, Bureau of Indian Affairs, Bldg. 2 - N. 5th St., Phoenix, AZ 85004. *For mail:* P.O. Box 10, Phoenix, AZ 85001.

DISTRICT IV *(All Indian reservations in southern Colorado, New Mexico, and all Navajo Indian reservations in Arizona, New Mexico, Utah)*—Office of Law Enforcement, Bureau of Indian Affairs, P.O. Box 26567, Albuquerque, NM 87125-6567.

DISTRICT V *(All Indian reservations in Alaska, Idaho, Montana, Oregon, Washington, Wyoming)*—Office of Law Enforcement, Bureau of Indian Affairs, 316 N. 26th St., Billings, MT 59101.

DISTRICT VI *(All Indian reservations in Alabama, Connecticut, Florida, Louisiana, Maine, Mississippi, New York, North Carolina, Rhode Island)*—Office of Law Enforcement, Bureau of Indian Affairs, 1849 C St. NW, (MS 4550 MIB), Washington, DC 20240-0001.

15.031 thru 15.041 Listed under **15.020**.

15.042 thru 15.046 Listed under **15.026**.

15.047 thru 15.058 Listed under **15.020**.

15.060 Contact BIA agency office listed under **15.020**, *or* United Tribes Technical College, 3315 University Dr., Bismarck, ND 58504. Phone: (701)255-3285, ext.334.

15.061 United Sioux Tribes Development Corporation, 1830 Lombardy Dr., Rapid City, SD 57701. Phone: (605)226-7426.

15.062 thru 15.113 Listed under **15.020**.

15.114 Listed under **15.026**.

15.124 Listed under **15.020**.

15.130 Listed under **15.026**.

15.141 and 15.144 Listed under **15.020**.

15.146 Contact BIA agency office listed under **15.020**, *or* Director, National Ironworkers Training Program for American Indians, 1819 Beach St., Broadview, IL 60153. Phone: (708)345-2344.

15.147 Listed under **15.020**.

BUREAU OF LAND MANAGEMENT

15.214 thru 15.242 STATE OFFICES

Alaska—6881 Abbott Loop Rd., Anchorage, AK 99507. Phone: (907)267-1323.

Arizona—222 N. Central Ave., P.O. Box 16563, Phoenix, AZ 95004-2203. Phone: (602)417-9266.

California—2800 Cottage Way - Ste. W-1834, Sacramento, CA 95825-1886. Phone: (916)978-4527.

Colorado—2850 Youngfield St., Lakewood, CO 80215-7076. Phone: (303)239-3677.

District of Columbia - Branch of Procurement Management *(For bureauwide inquiries)*—1849 C St. NW, (MS 1075-LS), Washington, DC 20240. Phone: (202)452-5170.

Idaho—1387 S. Vinnell Way, Boise, ID 83709-1657. Phone: (208)373-3909.

Montana—5001 Southgate Dr., P.O. Box 36800, Billings, MT 59107-6800. Phone: (406)896-5205.

Nevada—1340 Financial Blvd, P.O. Box 12000, Reno, NV 89520-0006. Phone: (702)861-6417.

New Mexico—435 Montano NE, Albuquerque, NM 87107. Phone: (505)761-8994.

Oregon—1515 SW 5th Ave., P.O. Box 2965, Portland, OR 97208. Phone: (503)952-6220.

Utah—324 S. State St. - Ste. 301, Salt Lake City, UT 84111-2303. Phone: (801)539-4172.

Virginia-Eastern States Office—7450 Boston Blvd., Springfield, VA 22153. Phone: (703)440-1596.

Wyoming—5353 Yellowstone Rd., P.O. Box 1828, Cheyenne, WY 82005. Phone: (307)775-6058.

OFFICE OF SURFACE MINING RECLAMATION AND ENFORCEMENT

15.250 thru 15.254 FIELD OFFICES

Alabama—135 Gemini Circle - Ste. 215, Homewood, AL 35209. Phone: (205)290-7282.

District of Columbia—1951 Constitution Ave. NW, Washington, DC 20240. Phone: (202)208-4006.

Indiana—575 N. Pennsylvania St. - Rm.301, Indianapolis, IN 46204. Phone: (317)226-6700.

Kentucky—2675 Regency Rd., Lexington, KY 40503-2922. Phone: (859)233-2494.

New Mexico—505 Marquette Ave. NW - Ste. 1200, Albuquerque, NM 87102. Phone: (505)248-5070.

15.250 thru 15.254 *(cont.)*

Oklahoma—5100 E. Skelly Dr. - Ste. 470, Tulsa, OK 74135. Phone: (918)581-6431.

Pennsylvania—Harrisburg Transportation Center - Ste. 3C, 415 Market St., Harrisburg, PA 17101. Phone: (717)782-4036.

Tennessee—530 Gay St. SW - Ste. 500, Knoxville, TN 37902. Phone: (423)545-4103.

Virginia—Powell Valley Square Shopping Center, 1941 Neeley Rd. - Ste. 201 (Compartment 116), Big Stone Gap, VA 24219. Phone: (540)523-4303.

West Virginia—1027 Virginia St. E., Charleston, WV 25301. Phone: (304)347-7162.

Wyoming—Federal Bldg. - Rm.2128, 100 E. "B" St., Casper, WY 82601-1918. Phone: (307)261-6555.

REGIONAL COORDINATING CENTERS

APPALACHIAN REGION—Three Parkway Center, Pittsburgh, PA 15220. Phone: (412)937-2828.

MID-CONTINENT REGION—Alton Federal Bldg., 501 Belle St. - Rm.216, Alton, IL 62002. Phone: (618)463-6460.

WESTERN REGION—1999 Broadway - Ste. 3320, Denver, CO 80202-5733. Phone: (303)844-1401.

BUREAU OF RECLAMATION

15.504 REGIONAL OFFICES

COMMISSIONER'S OFFICE—Denver Federal Center, P.O. Box 25007, Denver, CO 80225-0007. Phone: (303)445-2692.

GREAT PLAINS—P.O. Box 36900, Billings, MT 59107-6900. Phone: (406)247-7600.

LOWER COLORADO—Boulder City, NV 89006-1470. Phone: (702)293-8411.

MID-PACIFIC—Federal Office Bldg., 2800 Cottage Way, Sacramento, CA 95825-1898. Phone: (916)978-5000.

PACIFIC NORTHWEST—1150 N. Curtis Rd. - Ste. 100, Boise, ID 83706-1234. Phone: (208)378-5012.

UPPER COLORADO—125 S. State St. - Rm.6107, Salt Lake City, UT 84138-1102. Phone: (801)524-3600.

15.508 *Technical/Program Information:*

Bureau of Reclamation, Lahontan Basin Area Office, 705 N. Plaza St. - Rm.320, Carson City, NV 89701-4015. Phones: (775)882-3436; FAX (775)882-7592.

Acquistion Office:

Bureau of Reclamation, Mid-Pacific Regional Office, Acquisition Services, 2800 Cottage Way - Rm.E-1815, Sacramento, CA 95825-1898. Phones: (916)978-5130; FAX (916)978-5175, -5182. **Internet:** e-mail, "2WG4@mp.usbr.gov".

U.S. FISH AND WILDLIFE SERVICE

15.602 Federal Law Enforcement Training Center, Bldg. 69 - Rm.100, Glynco, GA 31524. Phone: (912)267-2370.

15.605 thru 15.634 REGIONAL OFFICES

REGION I *(California, Hawaii, Idaho, Nevada, Oregon, Washington)*—911 NE 11th Ave., Portland, OR 97232-4181. Phones: (503)872-2716; FAX (503)231-6118.

REGION II *(Arizona, New Mexico, Oklahoma, Texas)*—500 Gold Ave. SW - Rm.3018, P.O. Box 1306, Albuquerque, NM 87103. Phones: (505)248-6910; FAX (505)248-6282.

REGION III *(Illinois, Indiana, Iowa, Michigan, Minnesota, Missouri, Ohio, Wisconsin)*—Federal Bldg., 1 Federal Dr., Ft. Snelling, MN 55111. Phones: (612)713-5284; FAX (612)713-5301.

REGION IV *(Alabama, Arkansas, Florida, Georgia, Kentucky, Louisiana, Mississippi, North Carolina, Puerto Rico, South Carolina, Tennessee, Virgin Islands)*—1875 Century Blvd., Atlanta, GA 30345. Phones: (404)679-4006; FAX (404)679-4000.

REGION V *(Connecticut, Delaware, District of Columbia, Maine, Maryland, Massachusetts, New Hampshire, New Jersey, New York, Pennsylvania, Rhode Island, Vermont, Virginia, West Virginia)*—300 Westgate Center Dr., Hadley, MA 01035. Phones: (413)253-8308; FAX (413)253-8300.

REGION VI *(Colorado, Kansas, Montana, Nebraska, North Dakota, South Dakota, Utah, Wyoming)*—Denver Federal Center, P.O. Box 25486, Denver, CO 80025. Phones: (303)236-7920; FAX (303)236-8295.

REGION VII *(Alaska)*—1011 E. Tudor Rd., Anchorage, AK 99503. Phones: (907)786-3306; FAX (907)786-3542.

15.637 thru 15.643 Listed under **15.605**

15.644 REGIONAL OFFICES (Junior Duck Stamp Conservation and Design)

Alabama—Wheeler NWR, 2700 Refuge Hdqtrs. Rd., Decatur, AL 35603. Phone: (256)350-6639.

Alaska—Yukon Flats NWR, 101 12th Ave., Rte.264 - Box 14, Fairbanks, AK 99701. Phone: (907)456-0440. **Internet:** e-mail, “Education_Specialist@fws.gov”.

American Samoa—USFWS, 911 NE 11th Ave., Portland, OR 97232. Phone: (503)231-6164.

Arizona—Cabeza Prieta NWR, 1611 N. 2nd Ave., Ajo, AZ 85321. Phone: (520)387-6483.

Arkansas—One 4H Way, Little Rock, AR 72223. Phone: (501)821-6884.

California—Sacramento NWR Complex, 752 County Rd. 99W, Willows, CA 95988. Phone: (530)934-2801.

Colorado—Alamosa/Monte Vista NWR, 9383 El Rancho Lane, Alamosa, CO 81101. Phone: (719)589-4021.

Connecticut—CN Waterfowl Association, 29 Bowers Hill Rd., Oxford, CT 06478. Phone: (no number provided).

Delaware—DE Division/Fish and Wildlife, 4876 Hay Point Landing Rd., Smyrna, DE 19977. Phone: (302)653-2882, ext.104.

District of Columbia—DC Fish and Wildlife Division, 51 N. St. NE - Rm.5002, Washington, DC 20002. Phone: (202)535-2266.

Florida—J.N. Ding Darling NWR, 1 Wildlife Drive, Sanibel, FL 33957. Phone: (239)472-1100.

Georgia—GA Ecological Services, 247 S. Milledge, Athens, GA 30605. Phone: (706)613-9493.

Hawaii—USFWS, Pacific Islands Office, Rm.5-311 - Box 50187, 300 Ala Moana Blvd., Honolulu, HI 96850. Phone: (808)792-9530.

Idaho—Deer Flat NWR, 13751 Upper Embankment Rd., Nampa, ID 83686. Phone: (208)467-9378, -9379.

Illinois—IL DNR, Division of Education, 1 Natural Resources Way, Springfield, IL 62702. Phone: (217)524-4126.

Indiana—Muscatatuck NWR, 12985 E. US Hwy. 50, Seymour, IN 47274. Phone: (812)522-4352.

15.644 *(cont.)* **Iowa**—Neal Smith NWR, 9981 Pacific St., P.O. Box 399, Prairie City, IA 50228. Phone: (515)994-3400.

Kansas—Great Plains Nature Center, 6232 E. 29th N., Wichita, KS 67220. Phone: (316)683-5499, ext.108.

Kentucky—KY Department of Fish and Wildlife, #1 Game Farm Rd., Frankfort, KY 40601. Phone: (502)564-3400.

Louisiana—Natchitoches NFH, 615 South Dr., Natchitoches, LA 71457. Phone: (318)352-5324.

Maine—Rachel Carson NWR, 321 Port Rd., Wells, ME 04090. Phone: (207)646-9226.

Maryland—Patuxent Research Refuge, 10901 Scarlet Tanager Loop, Laurel, MD 20708-4027. Phone: (301)497-5761.

Massachusetts—MA Wildlife Federation, One Rabbit Hill Rd., Westboro, MA 01581. Phone: (508)792-7270, ext.110.

Michigan—MI Duck Hunter Tournament, 3517 Anna, Trenton, MI 48183. Phone: (734)676-1995.

Minnesota—MN Valley NWR, 3815 American Blvd. E., Bloomington, MN 55425. Phone: (952)858-0710.

Mississippi—MS Museum of Natural Science, 2148 Riverside Dr., Jackson, MS 39202. Phone: (601)354-7303.

Missouri—Big Muddy NWR, 4200 New Haven Dr., Columbia, MO 65102. Phone: (573)441-2799.

Montana—Lee Metcalf NWR, Outdoor Recreation Planner, P.O. Box 247, Stevensville, MT 59870. Phone: (406)777-5552.

Nebraska—Crescent Lake NWR Complex, 115 Railway, Scottsbluff, NE 69361. Phone: (308)635-7851.

Nevada—Stillwater NWR, 1000 Auction Rd., Fallon, NV 89406. Phone: (775)423-5128.

New Hampshire—NH Fish and Game Department, 11 Hazen Dr., Concord, NH 03301. Phone: (603)271-3211.

New Jersey—The Wetlands Institute, 1075 Stone Harbor Blvd., Stone Harbor, NJ 08247. Phone: (609)368-1211.

New Mexico—Bitter Lake NWR, 4065 Bitter Lakes Rd., Roswell, NM 88201. Phone: (505)622-6755, ext.29.

New York—Wertheim NWR, P.O. Box 21, 360 Smith Rd., Shirley, NY 11967. Phone: (631)874-4814.

North Carolina—USFWS Ecological Survey, 551 E. Pylon Dr., Raleigh, NC 27606. Phone: (919)856-4520, ext.25.

North Dakota—Tewaukon NWR, 9754 143 1/2 Ave. SE, Cayuga, ND 58013. Phone: (701)724-3598.

Ohio—Ottawa NWR, 14000 W. State Rte.2, Oak Harbor, OH 43449. Phone: (419)898-0014.

Oklahoma—Wichita Mountains Wildlife Refuge, Rte.1 - Box 448, Indiahoma, OK 73552. Phone: (580)429-3221.

Oregon—OR Coast NWR Complex, 2127 SE Marine Science Dr., Newport, OR 97365. Phone: (541)867-4550.

Pennsylvania—Erie NWR, 11296 Wood Duck Lane, Guys Mills, PA 16327. Phone: (814)789-3585.

Rhode Island—USFWS Division of Migratory Birds-R5, 300 Westgate Center Dr., Hadley, MA 01035. Phone: (413)253-8643.

South Carolina—SC Dept. of Natural Resources, 1000 Assembly St. #209, Columbia, SC 29202. Phone: (803)734-3885.

South Dakota—USFWS, Federal Bldg. - Rm.309, 200 4th St. SW, Huron, SD 57350. Phone: (605)352-5894.

Tennessee—Tennessee NWR, 3006 Dinkins Lane, Paris, TN 38242. Phone: (731)642-2091.

Texas—Santa Ana NWR, RR-2 - Box 202A, Alamo, TX 78516. Phone: (956)787-7630.

Utah—Bear River Bird Refuge, 58 S. 950 West, Brigham City, UT 84302. Phone: (435)723-5887, ext.16.

Vermont—Missisquoi NWR, 371 N. River St., Swanton, VT 05488. Phone: (802)868-4781.

Virginia—USFWS Division of Migratory Birds-R5, 300 Westgate Center Dr., Hadley, MA 01035. Phone: (413)253-8643.

Virgin Islands—VI Division of Fish and Wildlife, 45 Mars Hill, Frederiksted, VI 00840. Phone: (340)713-2422.

Washington—Nisqually NWR, 100 Brown Farm Rd., Olympia, WA 98516. Phone: (360)753-9467.

West Virginia—Ohio River Islands NWR, P.O. Box 1811, 3004 7th St., Parkersburg, WV 26102. Phone: (304)422-0752.

Wisconsin—Necedah NWR, W7996 20th St. W., Necedah, WI 54646. Phone: (608)565-2551.

Wyoming—National Museum of Wildlife Art, P.O. Box 6825, 2820 Rungius Rd., Jackson, WY 83002. Phone: (307)733-5771.

15.645

USFWS, University of West Georgia, Department of Biology, Carrollton, GA 30118-6300. Phones: (770)214-9293; FAX (678)839-6548.

15.647

Division of Migratory Birds, USFWS, 1 Federal Dr., Fort Snelling, MN 55111-4056. Phones: (612)713-5473, 5470; FAX (612)713-5393.

U.S. GEOLOGICAL SURVEY

15.808 REGIONAL OFFICES

Biological Resources Division

CENTRAL *(Arkansas, Colorado, Iowa, Kansas, Louisiana, Minnesota, Missouri, Montana, Nebraska, New Mexico, North Dakota, Oklahoma, South Dakota, Texas, Wyoming)*—Regional Chief Biologist, Denver Federal Center Bldg, 020 - Rm.A1419, (MS 300), Denver, CO 80225. Phone: (303)236-2739, ext.238.

EASTERN *(Alabama, Connecticut, District of Columbia, Florida, Georgia, Illinois, Indiana, Kentucky, Maine, Maryland, Massachusetts, Michigan, Mississippi, New Hampshire, New Jersey, New York, North Carolina, Ohio, Pennsylvania, Puerto Rico, Rhode Island, South Carolina, Tennessee, Vermont, Virginia, West Virginia, Wisconsin)*—Acting Regional Chief Biologist, National Center - Rm.4A100, (MS 300), 12201 Sunrise Valley Dr., Reston, VA 20192. Phone: (703)648-4060.

WESTERN *(Alaska, Arizona, California, Hawaii, Idaho, Nevada, Oregon, Utah, Washington)*—Regional Chief Biologist, 909 1st Ave. - Ste. 800, Seattle, WA 98104. Phone: (206)220-4600.

Geologic Division

CENTRAL—Federal Center, (MS 911), Denver, CO 80225. Phone: (303)236-5435.

15.808 (cont.) **EASTERN**—953 National Center, Reston, VA 20192. Phone: (703)648-6662.

WESTERN—345 Middlefield Rd., (MS 919), Menlo Park, CA 94025. Phone: (415)650-5102.

National Mapping Division

Mapping Application Center—National Center, (MS 567), Reston, VA 20192. Phone: (703)648-6002.

Midcontinent Mapping Center—1400 Independence Rd., (MS 300), Rolla, MO 65401. Phone: (573)308-3800.

Rocky Mountain Mapping Center—Denver Federal Center, (MS 508), Bldg. 810, Box 25046, Denver, CO 80225-0046. Phone: (303)202-4040.

South Dakota - Earth Resources Observation Systems Data Center—Mundt Federal Bldg., Sioux Falls, SD 57198. Phone: (605)594-6123.

Western Mapping Center—345 Middlefield Rd., (MS 531), Menlo Park, CA 94025-3591. Phone: (415)329-4254.

Water Resources Division

CENTRAL *(Colorado, Iowa, Kansas, Minnesota, Montana, Nebraska, New Mexico, North Dakota, Oklahoma, South Dakota, Texas, Wyoming)*—Regional Hydrologist, (MS 406), Denver Federal Center, Bldg. 25, Box 25046, Lakewood, CO 80225-0046. Phone: (303)236-5950, ext.0.

NORTHEAST *(Connecticut, Delaware, Illinois, Indiana, Kentucky, Maine, Maryland, Massachusetts, Michigan, New Hampshire, New Jersey, New York, Ohio, Pennsylvania, Rhode Island, Vermont, Virginia, West Virginia, Wisconsin)*—Regional Hydrologist, (MS 433), 433 National Center, Reston, VA 22092. Phone: (703)648-5813.

SOUTHEAST *(Alabama, Arkansas, Florida, Georgia, Louisiana, Mississippi, Missouri, North Carolina, Puerto Rico, South Carolina, Tennessee, Virgin Islands)*—Regional Hydrologist, Spalding Woods Office Park - Ste. 160, 3850 Holcomb Bridge Rd., Norcross, GA 30092-2202. Phone: (404)409-7701.

WESTERN *(Alaska, American Samoa, Arizona, California, Guam, Hawaii, Idaho, Nevada, Oregon, other Pacific Islands, Utah, Washington)*—Regional Hydrologist, (MS 470), 345 Middlefield Rd., Menlo Park, CA 94025-3591. Phone: (415)329-4414.

NATIONAL PARK SERVICE

For financial assistance information contact the State Historic Preservation Officer in your state, and the appropriate regional office for subgrant eligibility information, following.

15.904 thru 15.921 NATIONAL HEADQUARTERS

National Park Service—Professional Services, 1849 C St. NW, Washington, DC 20240. Phone: (202)208-3264.

REGIONAL OFFICES

ALASKA—2525 Gambell St., Anchorage, AK 99503-2892. Phone: (907)257-2690.

INTERMOUNTAIN—12795 W. Alameda Pkwy., Denver, CO 80225-0287. Phone: (303)969-2503.

MIDWEST—Professional Services and Legislation, 1709 Jackson St., Omaha, NE 68102. Phone: (402)221-3084.

NATIONAL CAPITAL—Finance Management Officer, 1100 Ohio Dr. SW, Washington, DC 20242. Phone: (202)619-7160.

NORTHEAST—U.S. Custom House, 200 Chestnut St. - 3rd fl., Philadelphia, PA 19106. Phone: (215)597-7013.

SOUTHEAST—Atlanta Federal Center - 1924 Building, 100 Alabama St. SW, Atlanta, GA 30303. Phone: (404)562-3100.

PACIFIC WEST—Resources, Stewardship and Partnership, 111 Jackson St. - Ste. 700, Oakland, CA 94607. Phone: (415)427-1321.

SERVICE CENTERS

Denver Service Center—P.O. Box 25287, Denver, CO 80225. Phone: (303)969-2100.

Harpers Ferry Center—Harpers Ferry, WV 25425-0050. Phone: (304)535-6211.

15.923 PTT Grants, NCPTT, 645 College Ave., Natchitoches, LA 71457. Phones: (318)356-7444; FAX (318)356-9119. **Internet:** e-mail, "ncptt@ncptt.nps.gov".

15.927 Listed under **15.904**.

DEPARTMENT OF JUSTICE

DRUG ENFORCEMENT ADMINISTRATION

16.001 thru 16.005

FIELD OFFICES (No phone numbers provided)

Atlanta—75 Spring St. SW - Rm.740, A53, Atlanta, GA 30303.

Boston—JFK Federal Bldg. - Rm.E-400, 15 Sudbury St., Boston, MA 02203-0402.

Caribbean—Metro Office Park - Bldg.17, Guayanabo, PR 00968.

Chicago—230 S. Dearborn St. - Ste. 1200, Chicago, IL 60604.

Dallas—10160 Technology Blvd., East Dallas, TX 75220-4343.

Denver—115 Inverness Dr. E., Englewood, CO 80112-5116.

Detroit—431 Howard St., Detroit, MI 48226.

El Paso—DEA/EPIC, SSG Sims St., El Paso, TX 79908-8098.

- 600 S. Mesa Hills Dr., El Paso, TX 79912.

Houston—1433 W. Loop South - Ste. 600, Houston, TX 77027-9506.

Los Angeles—Royal Federal Bldg. - 20th fl., 255 E. Temple St., Los Angeles, CA 90012.

Miami—8400 NW 53rd St., Miami, FL 33166.

Newark—80 Mulberry St. - 2nd fl., Newark, NJ 07102-4206.

New Orleans—Three Lakeway Center - Ste. 1800, 3838 N. Causeway Blvd., Metairie, LA 70002.

New York—99 10th Ave., New York, NY 10011.

Philadelphia—600 Arch St. - Rm.10224, Philadelphia, PA 19106.

Phoenix—3010 N. 2nd St. - Ste. 301, Phoenix, AZ 85012.

San Diego—4560 Viewridge Ave., San Diego, CA 92123-1672.

San Francisco—450 Golden Gate Ave., San Francisco, CA 94102.

Seattle—400 2nd Ave. W, Seattle, WA 98119-4140.

St. Louis—7911 Forsythe Blvd. - Ste. 500, St. Louis, MO 63105.

Washington, D.C.—801 K St. NW - Ste. 500, Washington, DC 20001.

16.001 thru 16.005 *(cont.)*

Laboratories

MID-ATLANTIC—460 New York Ave. NW, Washington, DC 20532-0001.

NORTH CENTRAL—536 S. Clark St. - Rm.800, Chicago, IL 60605,

NORTHEAST—99 Tenth Ave. - Rm.721, New York, NY 10011.

SOUTH CENTRAL—1880 Regal Row, Dallas, TX 75235.

SOUTHEAST—5205 NW 84th Ave., Miami, FL 33166.

SOUTHWEST—410 W.35th St., National City, CA 91950.

SPECIAL TESTING AND RESEARCH—3650 Concorde Pkwy. - Ste. 200, Chantilly, VA 20151.

WESTERN—390 Main St. - Rm.700, San Francisco, CA 94105.

Office of Training

Drug Enforcement Administration, FBI Academy, Quantico, VA 22134-1475.

CIVIL RIGHTS DIVISION

CRIMINAL SECTION

16.109 Contact local U.S. Attorney's Office, or FBI (addresses listed under **16.300**).

COMMUNITY RELATIONS SERVICE

16.200 REGIONAL OFFICES

REGION I *(Connecticut, Maine, Massachusetts, New Hampshire, Rhode Island, Vermont)*—408 Atlantic Ave. - Ste. 222, Boston, MA 02110. Phone: (617)424-5715.

REGION II *(New Jersey, New York, Puerto Rico, Virgin Islands)*—26 Federal Plaza - Rm.36-118, New York, NY 10278. Phone: (212)264-0700.

REGION III *(Delaware, District of Columbia, Maryland, Pennsylvania, Virginia, West Virginia)*—2nd and Chestnut St. - Rm.208, Philadelphia, PA 19106. Phone: (215)597-2344.

REGION IV *(Alabama, Florida, Georgia, Kentucky, Mississippi, North Carolina, South Carolina, Tennessee)*—75 Piedmont Ave. NE - Rm.900, Atlanta, GA 30303. Phone: (404)331-6883.

REGION V *(Illinois, Indiana, Michigan, Minnesota, Ohio, Wisconsin)*—55 W. Monroe St. - Rm.420, Chicago, IL 60603. Phone: (312)353-4391.

REGION VI *(Arkansas, Louisiana, New Mexico, Oklahoma, Texas)*—1420 Mockingbird Ln. - Ste. 250, Dallas, TX 75247. Phone: (214)655-8175.

REGION VII *(Iowa, Kansas, Missouri, Nebraska)*—1100 Main St. - Ste. 1320, Kansas City, MO 64105. Phone: (816)426-7434.

REGION VIII *(Colorado, Montana, North Dakota, South Dakota, Utah, Wyoming)*—1244 Speer Blvd. - Ste. 650, Denver, CO 80204-3584. Phone: (303)844-2973.

REGION IX *(Arizona, California, Guam, Hawaii, Nevada)*—888 S. Figueroa St. - Ste. 1880, Los Angeles, CA 90017. Phone: (213)894-2941.

REGION X *(Alaska, Idaho, Oregon, Washington)*—915 2nd Ave. - Rm.1808, Seattle, WA 98174. Phone: (206)220-6700.

FIELD OFFICES

Detroit—211 W. Fort St. - Rm.1404, Detroit, MI 48226. Phone: (313)226-4010.

Houston—515 Rusk Ave. - Rm.12605, Houston, TX 77002. Phone: (713)718-4861.

Miami—51 SW 1st Ave. - Rm.624, Miami, FL 33130. Phone: (305)536-5206.

San Francisco—120 Howard St. - Ste. 790, San Francisco, CA 94105. Phone: (415)744-6565.

FEDERAL BUREAU OF INVESTIGATION

16.300 thru 16.303

FIELD OFFICES (Special Agent in Charge)

REGION I *(Connecticut, Maine, Massachusetts, New Hampshire, Rhode Island, Vermont)*:

- Federal Office Bldg., 600 State St., New Haven, CT 06510-2020. Phones: (203)503-5000, 786-7000.
- 1 Center Plaza - Ste. 600, Boston, MA 02108-1801. Phones: (617)742-5533, 223-6000.

REGION II *(New Jersey, New York, Puerto Rico, Virgin Islands)*:

- One Gateway Center - 22nd fl., Newark, NJ 07102-9889. Phone: (973)792-3000.
- Foley Bldg., 200 McCarty Ave., Albany, NY 12209-2095. Phones: (518)465-7551, 431-7200.
- One FBI Plaza, Buffalo, NY 14202-2698. Phones: (716)856-7800, 843-4300.
- Javits Federal Office Bldg., 26 Federal Plaza, New York, NY 10278-0004. Phone: (212)384-1000.
- U.S. Federal Office Bldg. - Rm.526, 150 Carlos Chardon, Hato Rey, PR 00918-1716. Phones: (787)754-6000, -3292.

REGION III *(Delaware, District of Columbia, Maryland, Pennsylvania, Virginia, West Virginia)*:

- Washington Metropolitan Field Office, 601 4th St. NW, Washington, DC 20535-0002. Phone: (202)278-2000.
- 7142 Ambassador Rd., Baltimore, MD 21244-2754. Phones: (410)265-8080, 281-0198.
- Federal Office Bldg. - 8th fl., 600 Arch St., Philadelphia, PA 19106-1675. Phones: (215)418-4500, -4000.
- U.S. Post Office - Ste. 300, 700 Grant St., Pittsburgh, PA 15219-1906. Phones: (412)471-2000, 456-9100.
- 150 Corporate Blvd., Norfolk, VA 23502-4999. Phones: (757)455-0100, -0123.
- 111 Greencourt Rd., Richmond, VA 23228-4948. Phones: (804)261-1044, (700)923-2000.

REGION IV *(Alabama, Florida, Georgia, Kentucky, Mississippi, North Carolina, South Carolina, Tennessee)*:

- 2121 8th Ave. N. - Rm.1400, Birmingham, AL 35203-2396. Phones: FTS (205)715-0300; FAX (205)326-6166.
- St. Louis Centre - 3rd fl., 1 St. Louis St., Mobile, AL 36602-3930. Phones: (334)438-3674, (334)219-3555.
- 7820 Arlington Expressway - Ste. 200, Jacksonville, FL 32211-7499. Phones: (904)721-1211.
- 16320 NW 2nd Ave., North Miami Beach, FL 33169-6508. Phones: (305)944-9101, 787-6100.
- Federal Office Bldg. - Rm.610, 500 E. Zack St., Tampa, FL 33602-3917. Phones: (813)273-4566, 272-8000.

16.300 thru 16.303 *(cont.)*

- 2635 Century Pkwy. NE - Ste. 400, Atlanta, GA 30345-3112. Phones: (404)679-9000, -6100.
- Federal Office Bldg. - Ste. 500, 600 Martin Luther King Place, Louisville, KY 40202-2231. Phones: (502)583-3941.
- Federal Office Bldg. - Ste. 1553, 100 W. Capitol St., Jackson, MS 39269-1601. Phones: (601)948-5000, 360-7550.
- Wachovia Bldg. - Ste. 900, 400 S. Tyron, Charlotte, NC 28285-0001. Phone: (704)377-9200, 331-4500.
- 151 W. Park Blvd., Columbia, SC 29210-3857. Phones: (803)551-4200, 551-4209.
- 710 Locust St. - Ste. 600, Knoxville, TN 37902-2537. Phones: (865)544-0751, 544-3500.
- Eaglecrest Bldg. - Ste. 3000, 225 N. Humphreys Blvd., Memphis, TN 38120-2107. Phones: (901)747-4300, -9739.

REGION V *(Illinois, Indiana, Michigan, Minnesota, Ohio, Wisconsin)*:

- Dirksen Federal Office Bldg. - Rm.905, 219 S. Dearborn St., Chicago, IL 60604-1702. Phones: (312)431-1333, 786-2500.
- 400 W. Monroe St. - Ste. 400, Springfield, IL 62704-1800. Phones: (217)522-9675, 535-4400.
- Federal Office Bldg. - Rm.679, 575 N. Pennsylvania St., Indianapolis, IN 46204-1585. Phones: (317)639-3301, 321-6100.
- McNamara Federal Office Bldg. - 26th fl., 477 Michigan Ave., Detroit, MI 48226-2598. Phones: (313)965-2323, 237-4355.
- 111 Washington Ave. S. - Ste. 1100, Minneapolis, MN 55401-2176. Phones: (612)376-3200.
- Federal Office Bldg. - Rm.9000, 550 Main St., Cincinnati, OH 45202-8501. Phones: (513)421-4310, 562-5600.
- Federal Office Bldg. - Rm.3005, 1240 E. 9th St., Cleveland, OH 44199-9912. Phones: (216)522-1400, 622-6600.
- 330 E. Kilbourn Ave. - Ste. 600, Milwaukee, WI 53202-6627. Phones: (414)276-4684, 291-4899.

REGION VI *(Arkansas, Louisiana, New Mexico, Oklahoma, Texas)*:

- Two Financial Centre - Ste. 200, 10825 Financial Centre Pkwy., Little Rock, AR 72211-3552. Phones: (501)221-9100, 228-8400.
- 2901 Leon C. Simon Blvd., New Orleans, LA 70126-1061. Phones: (504)816-3000.
- 415 Silver Ave. SW - Ste. 300, Albuquerque, NM 87102. Phone: (505)224-2000.
- 3301 W. Memorial Rd., Oklahoma City, OK 73134. Phones: (405)290-7770, -3875.
- 1801 N. Lamar - Ste. 300, Dallas, TX 75202-1795. Phones: (214)720-2200, 922-7475.
- 600 S. Mesa Hills Dr. - Ste. 3000, El Paso, TX 79912-5533. Phone: (915)832-5000.
- 2500 E. T.C. Jester, Houston, TX 77008-1300. Phones: (713)693-5000, -3800.
- U.S. Post Office and Courthouse Bldg. - Ste. 200, 615 E. Houston St., San Antonio, TX 78205-9998. Phones: (210)225-6741, 978-5400.

REGION VII *(Iowa, Kansas, Missouri, Nebraska)*:

- U.S. Courthouse - Rm.300, 1300 Summit, Kansas City, MO 64105-1362. Phones: (816)221-6100, 512-8200.
- 2222 Market St. - Rm.2704, St. Louis, MO 63103-2516. Phones: (314)231-4324, 589-2500.
- Federal Office Bldg., 10755 Burt St., Omaha, NE 68114-2000. Phones: (402)493-8688, 492-3700.

REGION VIII *(Colorado, North Dakota, South Dakota, Utah, Wyoming)*:

- Federal Office Bldg. - Ste. 1823 (18th fl.), 1961 Stout St., Denver, CO 80294-1823. Phones: (303)629-7171, 628-3000.
- 257 Towers Bldg. - Ste. 1200, 257 E. 200 S., Salt Lake City, UT 84111-2048. Phones: (801)579-1400, -4400.

REGION IX *(American Samoa, Arizona, California, Guam, Hawaii, Nevada)*:

- Midtowne Business Centre II - Ste. 400, 201 E. Indianola Ave., Phoenix, AZ 85012-2080. Phones: (602)279-5511, 650-3300.
- Federal Office Bldg. - Ste. 1700, 11000 Wilshire Blvd., Los Angeles, CA 90024-3672. Phones: (858)565-1255, 514-5500.
- 4500 Orange Grove Ave., Sacramento, CA 95841-4205. Phones: (916)481-9110, 977-2200.
- Federal Office Bldg., 9797 Aero Dr., San Diego, CA 92123-1800. Phones: (619)565-1255, 514-5500.
- 450 Golden Gate Ave. - 13th fl., San Francisco, CA 94102-9523. Phones: (415)553-7400, -2000.
- Kalanianaole Federal Office Bldg. - Rm.4-230, 300 Ala Moana Blvd., Honolulu, HI 96850-0053. Phone: (808)566-4300.
- John Lawrence Bailey Bldg., 700 E. Charleston Blvd., Las Vegas, NV 89101-1545. Phones: (702)385-1281, (700)545-0110.

REGION X *(Alaska, Idaho, Oregon, Washington)*:

- 101 E. 6th Ave., Anchorage, AK 99501-2523. Phones: (907)258-5322, 276-4441.
- Crown Plaza Bldg. - Ste. 400, 1500 SW 1st Ave., Portland, OR 97201-5828. Phones: (503)224-4181, 552-5200.
- Federal Office Bldg. - Rm.710, 915 2nd Ave., Seattle, WA 98101. Phones: (206)262-2000, (700)391-8760.

Office of the Inspector General

FIELD INSTALLATIONS

Arizona—*Investigations,* 10 E. Broadway - Ste. 105, Tucson, AZ 85701. Phones: (520)670-5243; FAX (520)670-5246. *For mail:* Tucson, AZ 85702-0471.

California—*Investigations,* 321 S. Waterman Ave. - Rm.108, El Centro, CA 92243. Phones: (760)335-3549; FAX (760)335-3534.

- *Investigations,* 330 N. Brand St. - Ste. 655, Glendale, CA 91203. Phones: (818)543-1172; FAX (818)637-5082.
- 1200 Bayhill Dr. - Stes.220/201, San Bruno, CA 94066. Phones: *audits,* (650)876-9220; FAX (650)876-0902; *investigations,* (650)876-9058; FAX (650)876-9083.
- *Investigations,* 701 "B" St. - Ste. 560, San Diego, CA 92101. Phones: (619)557-5970; FAX(619)557-6518.

Colorado—*Investigations,* Plaza of the Rockies, 111 S. Tejon St. - Ste. 312, Colorado Springs, CO 80903. Phones: (719)635-2366; FAX (719)635-4769.

- *Audits,* The Chancery Bldg. - Ste. 1603, 1120 Lincoln St., Denver, CO 80203. Phones: (303)864-2000; FAX (303)864-2004.

District of Columbia—1425 New York Ave. NW - Stes.6100/7100, Washington, DC 20530. Phones: *audits,* (202)616-4688; FAX (202)616-4581; *investigations and fraud detection unit,* (202)616-4760; FAX (202)616-9881. *For mail(investigations)*: P.O. Box 27718, Washington, DC 20038-7718.

Florida—*Investigations,* 3800 Inverrary Blvd. - Ste. 312, Ft. Lauderdale, FL 33319. Phones: (954)535-2859; FAX (954)535-5436.

16.300 thru 16.303 *(cont.)*

Georgia—*Audits,* Russell Federal Bldg. - Ste. 1130, 75 Spring St., Atlanta, GA 30303. Phones: (404)331-5928; FAX (404)331-5046.

- *Investigations,* 60 Forsyth St. SW - Ste. 8M45, Atlanta, GA 30303. Phones: (404)562-1980; FAX (404)562-1960.

Illinois—Citicorp Center, 500 W. Madison Blvd. - Stes.3510/3510B, Chicago, IL 60661. Phones: *audits,* (312)353-1203; FAX (312)886-0513; *investigations,* (312)886-7050; FAX (312)886-7065. *For mail (investigations):* Chicago, IL 60690-1802.

Massachusetts—*Investigations,* 1 Courthouse Way - Rm.9200, Boston, MA 02210. Phones: (617)748-3218; FAX (617)748-3965. *For Mail*: Boston, MA 02106-2134.

New York—*Investigations,* JFK Airport, Bldg. 77 - Penthouse no. 2, N. Boundary Rd., Jamaica, NY 11430. Phones: FTS (718)553-7520; FAX (718)553-7533. *For mail*: JFK Airport, Jamaica, NY 11430-0999.

Pennsylvania—*Audits,* 701 Market St. - Ste. 201, Philadelphia, PA 19106. Phones: (215)580-2111; FAX (215)597-1348.

Texas—207 S. Houston St. - *(audits)* Rm.575 (Box 4), *(investigations)* Rm.551 (Box 5), Dallas, TX 75202-4724. Phones: *audits,* (214)655-5000; FAX (214)655-5025; *investigations,* (214)655-5076; FAX (214)655-5071.

- *Investigations,* 4050 Rio Bravo - Ste. 200, El Paso, TX 79902. Phones: (915)577-0102; FAX (915)577-9012.
- *Investigations,* Casey Federal Courthouse - Ste. 3307, 515 Rusk Ave., Houston, TX 77002. Phones: (713)718-4888; FAX (713)718-4706. *For mail:* P.O. Box 610071, Houston, TX 77208-9998.
- *Investigations,* Texas Commerce Center, Bentsen Tower - Ste. 510, 1701 W. Business Hwy.83, McAllen, TX 78501. Phones: (956)618-8145; FAX (956)618-8151.

Washington—*Investigations,* 620 Kirkland Way - Ste. 104, Kirkland, WA 98033-6021. Phones: (425)828-3998; FAX (425)827-2183.

NATIONAL INSTITUTE OF CORRECTIONS

16.601 thru 16.603

NIC Academy Division *or* Jails Division, 1960 Industrial Circle - Ste. A, Longmont, CO 80501. Phones: (303)682-0382, (800)995-6429; FAX (303)682-0469.

BUREAU OF JUSTICE ASSISTANCE

16.737 **G.R.E.A.T program regional offices:**

MIDWEST—La Crosse Police Dept., 400 La Crosse St., La Crosse, WI 54601. Phone: (608)789-8202.

NORTHEAST—Philadelphia Police Department, Community Relations Division, 1328 Race. St. - 2nd fl., Philadelphia, PA 19107. Phone: (215)686-1477.

NORTHWEST—Portland Police Bureau, 449 NE Emerson, Portland, OR 97211. Phone: (503)823-2111.

SOUTHEAST—Orange County Sheriff's Office, 2500 W. Colonial Dr. - 2nd fl., Orlando, FL 32804. Phone: (407)254-7369.

SOUTHWEST—Phoenix Police Dept., 620 W. Washington St., Phoenix, AZ 85003. Phone: (602)495-0432.

DEPARTMENT OF LABOR

BUREAU OF LABOR STATISTICS

17.002 thru 17.005 REGIONAL OFFICES

ATLANTA *(Alabama, Florida, Georgia, Kentucky, Mississippi, North Carolina, South Carolina, Tennessee)*—AFC - Rm.7T50, 61 Forsyth St. SW, Atlanta, GA 30303. Phone: (404)331-3446.

BOSTON/NEW YORK *(Connecticut, Maine, Massachusetts, New Hampshire, New York, Puerto Rico, Virgin Islands, Rhode Island, Vermont)*—JFK Federal Bldg. - E310, Boston, MA 02203. Phone: (617)565-2324.

- 201 Varick St. - Rm.808, New York, NY 10014-4811. Phone: (212)337-2420.

CHICAGO *Illinois, Indiana, Iowa, Michigan, Minnesota, Nebraska, North Dakota, Ohio, South Dakota, Wisconsin)*—Federal Office Bldg. - 9th fl., 230 S. Dearborn St., Chicago, IL 60604-1595. Phone: (312)353-7200, ext.229.

DALLAS/KANSAS CITY *(Arkansas, Colorado, Kansas, Louisiana, Missouri, Montana, New Mexico, Oklahoma, Texas, Utah, Wyoming)*—A. Maceo Federal Bldg. - Ste. 221, 525 Griffin St., Dallas, TX 75202-5028. Phone: (214)767-9379.

- City Center Square - Ste. 600, 1100 Main St., Kansas City, MO 64105-2112. Phone: (816)426-3176.

PHILADELPHIA *(Delaware, District of Columbia, Maryland, Pennsylvania, New Jersey, Virginia, West Virginia)*—The Curtis Center - Ste. 610 E., 170 S. Independence Mall W., Philadelphia, PA 19106-3305. Phone: (215)861-5603.

SAN FRANCISCO *(Alaska, American Samoa, Arizona, California, Guam, Hawaii, Idaho, Nevada, Oregon, Washington, Trust Territory of the Pacific Islands)*—71 Stevenson St. - 6th fl., San Francisco, CA 94105. Phone: (415)975-4403. *For mail:* San Francisco, CA 94119-3766.

EMPLOYEE BENEFITS SECURITY ADMINISTRATION

17.150 FIELD OFFICES

California—1055 E. Colorado Blvd. - Ste. 200, Pasadena, CA 91106. Phones: (626)229-1000; FAX (626)229-1098.

- 71 Stevenson St. - Ste. 915, San Francisco, CA 94105. Phones: (415)975-4600; FAX (415)975-4589.

District of Columbia—1335 East-West Hwy. - Ste. 200, Silver Spring, MD 20910-3225. Phones: (301)713-2000; FAX (301)713-2008.

Florida—Bldg. H - Site 104, 8040 Peters Rd., Plantation, FL 33324. Phones: (954)424-4022; FAX (954)424-0548.

Georgia—61 Forsyth St. SW - Ste. 7B54, Atlanta, GA 30303. Phones: (404)562-2156; FAX (404)562-2168.

Illinois—200 W. Adams St. - Ste. 1600, Chicago, IL 60606. Phones: (312)353-0900; FAX (312)353-1023.

Kentucky—1885 Dixie Hwy. - Ste. 210, Ft. Wright, KY 41011-2664. Phones: (859)578-4680; FAX (859)578-4688.

Massachusetts—JFK Bldg. - Rm.575, Boston, MA 02203. Phones: (617)565-9600; FAX (617)565-9666.

17.150 *(cont.)* **Michigan**—211 W. Fort St. - Ste. 1310, Detroit, MI 48226-3211. Phones: (313)226-7450; FAX (313)226-4257.

Missouri—1100 Main St. - Ste. 1200, Kansas City, MO 64105-5148. Phones: (816)426-5131; FAX (816)426-5511.

- Young Federal Bldg. - Rm.6310, 1222 Spruce St., St. Louis, MO 63101-2818. Phones: (314)539-2693; FAX (314)539-2697.

New York—33 Whitehall St. - Ste. 1200(12th fl.), New York, NY 10004. Phones: (212)607-8600; FAX (212)607-8681.

Pennsylvania—170 S. Independence Mall W. - Ste. 870 West, Philadelphia, PA 19106-3317. Phones: (215)861-5300; FAX (215)861-5347.

Texas—525 Griffin St. - Rm.900, Dallas, TX 75202-5025. Phones: (214)767-6831; FAX (214)767-1055.

Washington—1111 3rd Ave. - Ste. 860, Seattle, WA 98101-3212. Phones: (206)553-4244; FAX (206)553-0913.

EMPLOYMENT AND TRAINING ADMINISTRATION

BUREAU OF APPRENTICESHIP AND TRAINING (BAT)

17.201 REGIONAL OFFICES

Apprenticeship Training, Employer and Labor Services Director:

REGION I *(Connecticut, Maine, Massachusetts, New Hampshire, Rhode Island, Vermont)*—JFK Federal Bldg. - Rm.E-370, Boston, MA 02203. Phones: (617)565-2288; FAX (617)565-9171.

REGION II *(New Jersey, New York, Puerto Rico, Virgin Islands)*—201 Varick St. - Rm.602, New York, NY 10014. Phones: (212)337-2313; FAX (212)337-2317.

REGION III *(Delaware, Maryland, Pennsylvania, Virginia, West Virginia)*—3535 Market St. - Rm.13240, Philadelphia, PA 19104. Phones: (215)596-6417; FAX (215)596-0192.

REGION IV *(Alabama, Florida, Georgia, Kentucky, Mississippi, North Carolina, South Carolina, Tennessee)*—61 Forsyth St. NW - Rm.6T71, Atlanta, GA 30303. Phones: (404)562-2335; FAX (404)562-2329.

REGION V *(Illinois, Indiana, Michigan, Minnesota, Ohio, Wisconsin)*—230 S. Dearborn St. - Rm.708, Chicago, IL 60604. Phones: (312)353-7205; FAX (312)353-5506.

REGION VI *(Arkansas, Louisiana, New Mexico, Oklahoma, Texas)*—Federal Bldg. - Rm.311, 525 Griffin St. Dallas, TX 75202. Phones: (214)767-4993; FAX (214)767-4995.

REGION VII *(Iowa, Kansas, Missouri, Nebraska)*—1100 Main St. - Ste. 1040, Kansas City, MO 64105-2112. Phones: (816)426-3856; FAX (816)426-3664.

REGION VIII *(Colorado, Montana, North Dakota, South Dakota, Utah, Wyoming)*—U.S. Custom House - Rm.465, 721 19th St., Denver, CO 80202. Phones: (303)844-4791; FAX (303)844-4701.

REGION IX *(Arizona, California, Hawaii, Nevada)*—Federal Bldg. - Rm.815, 71 Stevenson St., San Francisco, CA 94105. Phones: (415)975-4007; FAX (415)975-4010.

REGION X *(Alaska, Idaho, Oregon, Washington)*—1111 3rd Ave. - Rm.925, Seattle, WA 98101-3212. Phones: (206)553-5286; FAX (206)553-1689.

17.202 thru 17.266 ETA REGIONAL OFFICES

Contact the nearest office of the state employment service in your area, or the appropriate regional office following:

REGION I *(Connecticut, Maine, Massachusetts, New Hampshire, Rhode Island, Vermont)*—JFK Federal Bldg. - Rm.E-350, Boston, MA 02203. Phones: (617)565-3630; FAX (617)565-2229.

REGION II *(Canal Zone, New Jersey, New York, Puerto Rico, Virgin Islands)*—201 Varick St. - Rm.755, New York, NY 10014. Phones: (212)337-2139; FAX (212)337-2144.

REGION III *(Delaware, District of Columbia, Maryland, Pennsylvania, Virginia, West Virginia)*—The Curtis Center- Ste. 825E, 170 S. Independence Mall West, Philadelphia, PA 19106-3315. Phones: (215)861-5205; FAX (215)861-5260.

REGION IV *(Alabama, Florida, Georgia, Kentucky, Mississippi, North Carolina, South Carolina, Tennessee)*—Atlanta Federal Center - Rm.6M12, 61 Forsyth St. SW, Atlanta, GA 30303. Phones: (404)562-2092; FAX (404)562-2149.

REGION V *(Arkansas, Colorado, Louisiana, Montana, New Mexico, North Dakota, Oklahoma, South Dakota, Texas, Utah, Wyoming)*—525 Griffin St. - Rm.317, Dallas, TX 75202. Phones: (214)767-8263; FAX (214)767-5113.

REGION VI *(Illinois, Indiana, Iowa, Kansas, Michigan, Minnesota, Missouri, Nebraska, Ohio, Wisconsin)*—230 S. Dearborn St. - Rm.628, Chicago, IL 60604. Phones: (312)353-0313; FAX (312)353-4474.

REGION VII *(Alaska, American Samoa, Arizona, California, Guam, Hawaii, Idaho, Micronesia, Nevada, Northern Mariana Islands, Oregon, Republic of Palau, Washington)*—71 Stevenson St. - Rm.830, San Francisco, CA 94119-3767. Phones: (415)975-4610; FAX (415)975-4612.

EMPLOYMENT STANDARDS ADMINISTRATION

OFFICE OF FEDERAL CONTRACT COMPLIANCE PROGRAMS

17.301 REGIONAL OFFICES

REGION I *(Connecticut, Maine, Massachusetts, New Hampshire, Rhode Island, Vermont)*—JFK Federal Bldg. - Rm.E-235, One Congress St., Boston, MA 02203. Phone: (617)565-2055.

REGION II *(New Jersey, New York, Puerto Rico, Virgin Islands)*—201 Varick St. - Rm.750, New York, NY 10014. Phone: (212)337-2007.

REGION III *(Delaware, District of Columbia, Maryland, Pennsylvania, Virginia, West Virginia)*—Curtis Center - Ste. 750W, 170 S. Independence Mall W., Philadelphia, PA 19106-3309 Phone: (215)861-5763.

REGION IV *(Alabama, Florida, Georgia, Kentucky, Mississippi, North Carolina, South Carolina, Tennessee)*—Atlanta Federal Center - Rm.7B75, 61 Forsyth St. SW, Atlanta, GA 30303. Phone: (404)562-2424.

REGION V *(Illinois, Indiana, Iowa, Kansas, Michigan, Minnesota, Missouri, Nebraska, Ohio, Wisconsin)*—Kluczynski Federal Bldg. - Rm.570, 230 S. Dearborn St., Chicago, IL 60604. Phone: (312)596-7010.

REGION VI *(Arkansas, Colorado, Louisiana, Montana, New Mexico, North Dakota, Oklahoma, South Dakota, Texas, Utah, Wyoming)*—Federal Bldg. - Ste. 840, 525 S. Griffin St., Dallas, TX 75202. Phone: (214)767-2804.

REGION IX *(Arizona, California, Guam, Hawaii, Nevada)*—71 Stevenson St. - Ste. 1700, San Francisco, CA 94105. Phone: (415)975-4720.

REGION X *(Alaska, Idaho, Oregon, Washington)*—1111 3rd Ave. - Ste. 745, Seattle, WA 98101. Phone: (206)553-7182.

17.301 (cont.)

DISTRICT AND AREA OFFICES

Alabama—Medical Forum Bldg. - Ste. 660, 950 22nd St. N., Birmingham, AL 35203. Phone: (205)731-0820.

Arizona—3221 N. 16th St. - Ste. 303, Phoenix, AZ 85016. Phone: (602)640-2960.

Arkansas—TCBY Tower - Ste. 735, 425 W. Capitol Ave., Little Rock, AR 72201. Phone: (501)324-5436.

California—Federal Bldg. - Ste. 8103, 11000 Wilshire Blvd., Los Angeles, CA 90024. Phone: (310)235-6800.

- 1301 Clay St. - Ste. 1080N, Oakland, CA 94612. Phone: (510)637-2938.
- 5675 Ruffin Rd. - Ste. 320, San Diego, CA 92123. Phone: (619)557-6489.
- 60 S. Market St. - Ste. 410, San Jose, CA 95113. Phone: (408)291-7384.
- 34 Civic Center Plaza - Ste. 406, P.O. Box 12800, Santa Ana, CA 92712. Phone: (714)836-2784.

Colorado—1244 Spee Blvd. - Rm.620, Denver, CO 80204-3584. Phone: (303)844-4481.

Connecticut—135 High St. - Rm.311, Hartford, CT 06103. Phone: (860)240-4277.

District of Columbia—Riddell Bldg. - Ste. 422, 1730 K St. NW, Washington, DC 20006. Phone: (202)254-2501.

Florida—1851 Executive Center Dr. - Ste. 200, Jacksonville, FL 32207. Phone: (904)232-3073.

- Brickell Plaza Federal Bldg. - Ste. 722, 909 SE 1st Ave., Miami, FL 33131. Phone: (305)536-5670.
- Commodore Bldg. - Ste. 160, 3444 McCrory Pl., Orlando, FL 32803. Phone: (407)648-6181.

Georgia—61 Forsyth St. - Rm.7B65, Atlanta, GA 30303. Phone: (404)562-2444.

Hawaii—300 Ala Moana Blvd. - Rm.7326, P.O. Box 50149, Honolulu, HI 96850. Phone: (808)541-2933.

Illinois—230 S. Dearborn St. - Rm.434, Chicago, IL 60604. Phone: (312)596-7046.

Indiana—429 N. Pennsylvania St. - Rm.308, Indianapolis, IN 46204. Phones: (317)226-5860.

Kentucky—Mazzoli Federal Bldg. - Rm.185, 600 Martin Luther King Place, Louisville, KY 40202. Phone: (502)582-6275.

Louisiana—701 Loyola Ave. - Rm.13029, New Orleans, LA 70113. Phone: (504)589-6575.

Maryland—Appraiser's Store Bldg. - Rm.202, 103 S. Gay St., Baltimore, MD 21202. Phone: (410)962-3572.

Massachusetts—JFK Federal Bldg. - Rm.E-235, Boston, MA 02203. Phone: (617)565-2055.

Michigan—McNamara Federal Bldg. - Rm.1320, 211 W. Fort St., Detroit, MI 48226. Phone: (313)226-3728.

- 50 Louis St. NW - 2nd fl.(NW-c/o), Ste. 300-HUD, Grand Rapids, MI 49503. Phone: (616)456-2144.

Minnesota—Bridgeplace Bldg. - Rm.102, 220 2nd St. S., Minneapolis, MN 55401. Phone: (612)370-3177.

Mississippi—Millsaps Bldg. - Ste. 700, 201 W. Capitol St., Jackson, MS 39201. Phone: (601)965-4668.

Missouri—1100 Main St. - Rm.860, Kansas City, MO 64105. Phone: (816)426-3860.

- 1222 Spruce St. - Rm.10207, St. Louis, MO 63103. Phone: (314)539-6394.

Nebraska—106 S. 15th St. - Rm.808, Omaha, NE 68116. Phone: (402)221-3381.

New Jersey—Bldg. 5 - Rm.203, 3131 Princeton Pike, Lawrenceville, NJ 08648. Phone: (609)989-2380.

- Diamond Head Bldg. - Rm.102, 200 Sheffield Dr., Mountainside, NJ 07092. Phone: (201)645-6104.

New Mexico—505 Marquette Ave. NW - Ste. 810, Albuquerque, NM 87102. Phone: (505)248-5015.

New York—O'Brien Federal Bldg. - Rm.740, 19 Aviation Rd., Albany, NY 12205. Phone: (518)435-0326.

- Six Fountain Plaza - Ste. 300, Buffalo. NY 14202. Phone: (716)551-5065.
- 26 Federal Plaza - Rm.36-116, New York, NY 10278. Phone: (212)264-7742.

North Carolina—Mart Office Bldg. - Rm.BB-401, 800 Briar Creek Rd., Charlotte, NC 28205. Phone: (704)344-6113.

- 300 Fayetteville Street Mall - Ste. 121, Raleigh, NC 27601. Phone: (919)856-4058.

Ohio—55 Rennaissance Center - Ste. 350, 1350 Euclid St. - Ste. 350, Cleveland, OH 44114. Phone: (216)522-7472.

- 200 N. High St. - Rm.409, Columbus, OH 43215. Phone: (614)469-5831.

Oklahoma—51 Yale Bldg. - Rm.304, 5110 S. Yale, Tulsa, OK 74135. Phone: (918)496-6772.

Oregon—Federal Office Bldg. - Ste. 1030, 1515 SW 5th Ave., Portland, OR 97201. Phone: (503)326-4112.

Pennsylvania—Nix Federal Bldg. - Rm.311, 9th and Market St., Philadelphia, PA 19107. Phone: (215)597-4122.

- Federal Bldg. - Rm.1132, 1000 Liberty Ave., Pittsburgh, PA 15222. Phone: (412)395-6330.

Puerto Rico—San Patricio Office Center - 4th fl., 7 Tabonuco St., Guaynabo, PR 00968. Phone: (787)775-1901.

South Carolina—Thurmond Federal Bldg. - Ste. 608, 1835 Assembly St., Columbia, SC 29201. Phone: (803)765-5244.

Tennessee—167 N. Main St. - Ste. 201, Memphis, TN 38103. Phone: (901)544-3458.

- 1321 Murfreesboro Rd., Ste. 301, Nashville, TN 37217. Phone: (615)781-5395.

Texas—Federal Office Bldg. - Rm.512, 525 Griffin St., Dallas, TX 75202. Phone: (214)767-2911.

- 2320 La Branch St. - Rm.1103, Houston, TX 77004. Phone: (713)718-3800.
- 800 Dolorosa St. - Rm.200, San Antonio, TX 78207. Phone: (210)472-5835.

Utah—Gateway Tower East - Ste. 1690, 10 E. South Temple, Salt Lake City, UT 84101. Phone: (801)524-4470.

Virginia—400 N. 8th St. - Rm.552, Richmond, VA 23240. Phone: (804)771-2136.

Washington—Federal Office Bldg. - Ste. 745, 1111 3rd Ave., Seattle, WA 98101. Phone: (206)553-7182.

Wisconsin—Federal Bldg. - Ste. 1115, 310 W. Wisconsin Ave., Milwaukee, WI 53203. Phone: (414)297-3821.

OFFICE OF WORKERS' COMPENSATION PROGRAMS

REGIONAL OFFICES

California—71 Stevenson St. - Ste. 1705, San Francisco, CA 94105. Phone: (415)975-4160.

Colorado—1801 California St. - Ste. 920, Denver, CO 80202-2614. Phone: (720)264-3160.

Florida—214 N. Hogan St. - Ste. 1026, Jacksonville, FL 32202. Phone: (904)357-4725.

17.301 (cont.)

Illinois—230 S. Dearborn St. - Rm.800, Chicago, IL 60604. Phone: (312)596-7131.

Massachusetts—JFK Federal Bldg. - Rm.E-260, Boston, MA 02203. Phone: (617)565-2130.

Missouri—City Center Square - Ste. 750, 1100 Main St., Kansas City, MO 64105. Phone: (816)426-2196.

New York—201 Varick St. - Rm.750, New York, NY 10014. Phone: (212)337-2033.

Pennsylvania—Curtis Center - Ste. 780 W., 170 S. Independence Mall W., Philadelphia, PA 19106-3313. Phone: (215)861-5406.

Texas—525 S. Griffin St. - Rm.407, Dallas, TX 75202. Phone: (214)767-4713.

Washington—1111 3rd Ave. - Ste. 615, Seattle, WA 98101-3212. Phone: (206)553-5508.

17.302 Longshore and Harbor Workers' Compensation

DISTRICT OFFICES

DISTRICT 1 *(Connecticut, Maine, Massachusetts, New Hampshire, Rhode Island, Vermont)*—JFK Federal Bldg. - Rm.E-260, Boston, MA 02203. Phone: (617)565-2103.

DISTRICT 2 *(New Jersey, New York, Puerto Rico, Virgin Islands)*—201 Varick St. - Rm.750, New York, NY 10014-0249. Phone: (212)337-2030.

DISTRICT 3 *(Delaware, Pennsylvania, West Virginia)*—Curtis Center - Ste. 790 W., 170 S. Independence Mall W., Philadelphia, PA 19106-3313. Phone: (215)861-5459.

DISTRICT 4 *(District of Columbia, Maryland)*—31 Hopkins Plaza - Rm.410-B, Baltimore, MD 21201. Phone: (410)962-3677.

DISTRICT 5 *(Virginia)*—200 Granby Mall - Rm.212, Norfolk, VA 23510. Phone: (757)441-3071.

DISTRICT 6 *(Alabama, Florida, Georgia, Kentucky, Mississippi, North Carolina, South Carolina, Tennessee)*—214 N. Hogan St. - Ste. 1040, Jacksonville, FL 32202. Phone: (904)357-4757.

DISTRICT 7 *(Arkansas, Louisiana)*—701 Loyola Ave. - Rm.13032, New Orleans, LA 70113. Phone: (504)589-2671.

DISTRICT 8 *(Oklahoma, New Mexico, Texas)*—8866 Gulf Freeway - Ste. 140, Houston, TX 77017. Phone: (713)943-1605.

DISTRICT 10 *(Illinois, Indiana, Iowa, Kansas, Michigan, Minnesota, Missouri, Nebraska, Ohio, Wisconsin)*—230 S. Dearborn St. - Rm.578, Chicago, IL 60604. Phone: (312)596-7153.

DISTRICT 13 *(Arizona, California-northern, Nevada)*—71 Stevenson St. - Rm.1705, San Francisco, CA 94119-3770. Phone: (415)975-4274.

DISTRICT 14 *(Alaska, Colorado, Idaho, Montana, Oregon, North Dakota, South Dakota, Utah, Washington, Wyoming)*—1111 3rd Ave. - Ste. 620, Seattle, WA 98101-3212. Phone: (206)553-4471.

DISTRICT 15 *(Hawaii, Pacific Area to 60 east longitude)*—300 Ala Moana Blvd. - Rm.5-135, P.O. Box 50209, Honolulu, HI 96850 *(via air mail)*. Phone: (808)541-1983.

DISTRICT 18 *(Southern California)*—401 E. Ocean Blvd. - Ste. 720, Long Beach, CA 90802. Phone: (562)980-3578.

17.303 and 17.306 Wage and Hour Division

REGIONAL OFFICES

MIDWEST—230 S. Dearborn St. - Rm.820, Chicago, IL 60604-1591. Phone: (312)596-7180.

NORTHEAST—The Curtis Center - Ste. 850 West, 170 Independence Mall W., Philadelphia, PA 19107-3317. Phone: (215)861-5800.

SOUTHEAST—Atlanta Federal Center - Rm.7M40, 61 Forsyth St. SW, Atlanta, GA 30303. Phone: (404)562-2202.

SOUTHWEST—Federal Bldg. - Rm.800, 525 S. Griffin St., Dallas, TX 75202-5007. Phone: (214)767-6895.

WESTERN—71 Stevenson St. - Ste. 930, San Francisco, CA 94105. Phone: (415)975-4510.

DISTRICT OFFICES

Alabama—Aronov Bldg. - Rm.708, 474 S. Court St., Montgomery, AL 36104-4158. Phone: (304)223-7641.

Arizona—3221 N. 16th St. - Ste. 301, Phoenix, AZ 85016-7161. Phone: (602)640-2990.

Arkansas—TCBY Tower - Ste. 725, 425 W. Capitol Ave., Little Rock, AR 72201. Phones: (501)324-5377.

California-Los Angelos—300 S. Glendale Ave. - Ste. 400, Glendale, CA 91205-1752. Phones: (213)894-6375.

- 2800 Cottage Way - Rm.W-1836, Sacramento, CA 95825. Phone: (916)978-6120.
- 5675 Ruffin Rd. - Ste. 320, San Diego, CA 92123-1362. Phone: (619)557-5606.
- 455 Market St. - Ste. 800, San Francisco, CA 94105. Phone: (415)744-5590.

Colorado—1999 Broadway - Ste. 2445, P.O. Drawer 3505, Denver, CO 80202. Phone: (720)264-3250.

Connecticut—135 High St. - Rm.310, Hartford, CT 06103-1595. Phone: (860)240-4160.

Florida—Federal Bldg. - Rm.408, 299 E. Broward Blvd., Ft. Lauderdale, FL 33301-1976. Phone: (954)356-6896.

- 3728 Phillips Hwy. - Ste. 219, Jacksonville, FL 32207. Phone: (904)232-2489.
- Sunset Center - Rm.255, 10300 SW Sunset Dr., Miami, FL 33173-3038. Phones: (305)598-6607; FAX (305)279-8393.
- Austin Laurel Bldg. - Ste. 300, 4905 W. Laurel Ave., Tampa, FL 33607-3838. Phone: (813)288-1242.

Georgia—Atlanta Federal Center - Rm.7M10, 61 Forsyth St. SW, Atlanta, GA 30303. Phone: (404)562-2201.

- Low Federal Bldg. Complex - Ste. B-210, 124 Barnard St., Savannah, GA 31401-3648. Phones: (912)652-4221, -4229.

Illinois—230 S. Dearborn - Rm.412, Chicago, IL 60604-1595. Phone: (312)596-7182.

- 509 W. Capitol Ave. - Ste. 205, Springfield, IL 62704-1929. Phone: (217)492-4060.

Indiana—429 N. Pennsylvania St. - Rm.403, Indianapolis, IN 46204-1873. Phone: (317)226-6801.

- River Glen Plaza - Ste. 160, 501 E. Monroe St., South Bend, IN 46601-1615. Phones:(219)236-8331, -8332.

Iowa—Federal Bldg. - Rm.643, 210 Walnut St., Des Moines, IA 50309. Phone: (515)284-4625.

Kansas—Gateway Tower II - Ste. 1010, 400 State Ave., Kansas City, KS 66101. Phone: (913)551-5721.

Kentucky—Snyder U.S. Courthouse and Custom House - Rm.31, 601 W. Broadway, Louisville, KY 40202-9570. Phone: (502)582-5226.

Louisiana—701 Loyola Ave. - Rm.13028, New Orleans, LA 70113-1931. Phone: (504)589-6171.

17.303 and 17.306 *(cont.)*

Maryland—207 Appraisers Stores Bldg., 103 S. Gay St., Baltimore, MD 21201-4061. Phone:(410)962-4984.

Massachusetts—Kennedy Federal Bldg. - Rm.525, Boston, MA 02203. Phone: (617)565-2066.

Michigan—211 Fort St. - Rm.1317, Detroit, MI 18226-2799. Phone: (313)226-7447.

- 2920 Fuller Ave. NE - Ste. 100, Grand Rapids, MI 49505-3409. Phone: (616)456-2004.

Minnesota—Midland Square - Ste. 920, 331 2nd Ave S., Minneapolis, MN 55401-2233. Phone: (612)370-3371.

Mississippi—One Jackson Place - Ste. 1020, 188 E. Capitol St., Jackson, MS 39201-2126. Phones: (601)965-4347, -4348.

Missouri—1222 Spruce St. - Rm.9102-B, St. Louis, MO 63103. Phones: (314)539-2706, -3014.

Nebraska—Federal Bldg. - Rm.715, 106 S. 15th St., Omaha, NE 68102. Phone: (402)221-4682.

New Hampshire—2 Wall St. - 1st fl., Manchester, NH 03101. Phones: (603)666-7716; FAX (603)666-7600.

New Jersey—Bldg. 5 - Rm.216, 3131 Princeton Pike, Lawrenceville, NJ 08648. Phones: (609)989-2247, -2368.

- 200 Sheffield St. - Ste. 102, Mountainside, NJ 07092. Phone: (973)645-2279.

New Mexico—Western Bank Bldg. - Ste. 840, 505 Marquette NW, Albuquerque, NM 87102-2160. Phone: (505)248-5115.

New York—O'Brien Federal Bldg. - Rm.822, Albany, NY 12207. Phone: (518)431-4279.

- 26 Federal Plaza - Rm.3700, New York, NY 10278. Phone: (212)264-8185.
- 1400 Old Country Rd. - Ste. 410, Westbury, NY 11590-5119. Phone: (516)338-1890.

North Carolina—800 Briar Creek Rd. - Ste. CC-412, Charlotte, NC 28205-6903. Phone: (704)344-6298.

- Somerset Park Bldg. - Ste. 260, 4407 Bland Rd., Raleigh, NC 27609-6296. Phones: (919)790-2741, -2742.

Ohio—525 Vine St. - Ste. 880, Cincinnati, OH 45202-3268. Phone: (513)684-2908.

- Federal Bldg. - Rm.817, 1240 E. 9th St., Cleveland, OH 44199-2054 Phones: (216)522-3892, -3893.
- 646 Federal Bldg., 200 N. High St., Columbus, OH 43215-2475. Phones: (614)469-5678; FAX (614)469-5428.

Oregon—1515 SW 5th Ave. - Ste. 1040, Portland, OR 97201-5445. Phone: (503)326-3057.

Pennsylvania—U.S. Customs House - Rm.400, 2nd and Chestnut St., Philadelphia, PA 19106. Phone: (215)597-4950.

- Federal Bldg. - Rm.313, 1000 Liberty Ave., Pittsburgh, PA 15222. Phone: (412)395-4996.
- Stegmaier Bldg. - Ste. 373-M, 7 N. Wilkes-Barre Blvd., Wilkes-Barre, PA 18702-3594. Phone: (570)826-6316.

Puerto Rico—San Patricio Office Center - 4th fl., 7 Tabonuco St., Guaynabo, PR 00968. Phone: (787)775-1924.

South Carolina—Federal Bldg. - Rm.1072, 1835 Assembly St., Columbia, SC 29201-9863. Phone: (803)765-5981.

Tennessee—Executive Plaza - Bldg.511, 1321 Murfreesboro Rd., Nashville, TN 37217-2626. Phones: (615)781-5343, -5345.

Texas—Smith Federal Bldg. - Rm.507, 525 S. Griffin St., Dallas, TX 75202-5007. Phone: (214)767-6294.

- South Bldg. - Ste. 202, 9990 Richmond Ave., Houston, TX 77042-4546. Phone: (713)339-5575.
- Northchase I Office Bldg. - Ste. 140, 10127 Morocco St., San Antonio, TX 78216. Phone: (210)308-4515.

Utah—10 E. South Temple - Ste. 1680, Salt Lake City, UT 84133. Phone: (801)524-5706.

Virginia—Federal Bldg. - Ste. 416, 400 N. 8th St., Richmond, VA 23240. Phone: (804)771-2995.

Washington—1111 3rd Ave. - Ste. 755, Seattle, WA 98101-3212. Phone: (206)553-4482.

West Virginia—500 Quarrier St. - Ste. 720, Charleston, WV 25301. Phone: (304)347-5206.

Wisconsin—740 Regent St. - Ste. 102, Madison, WI 53715. Phone: (608)264-5221.

17.307 Division of Coal Mine Workers' Compensation

DISTRICT OFFICES

Contact nearest Social Security office or appropriate CMWC office, following.

Colorado *(Western United States)*—1801 California St. - Ste. 925, Denver, CO 80202-2614. Phone: (720)264-3100.

Kentucky *(Kentucky)*—334 Main St. - 5th fl., Pikeville, KY 41501. Phone: (1-800-366-4599).

- *(Alabama, Florida, Georgia, Mississippi, North Carolina, South Carolina, Tennessee)*—402 Campbell Way, Spring St., Mt. Sterling, KY 40353. Phone: (1-800-366-4628).

Ohio *(Illinois, Indiana, Michigan, Minnesota, Ohio, Wisconsin)*—1160 Dublin Rd. - Ste. 300, Columbus, OH 43215. Phone: (1-800-347-3771).

Pennsylvania *(Connecticut, Delaware, District of Columbia, Maine, Massachusetts, New Hampshire, New Jersey, New York, Pennsylvania-eastern, Rhode Island, Vermont)*—S. Main Towers, 105 N. Main St. - Ste. 100, Wilkes-Barre, PA 18701. Phone: (1-800-347-3755).

- *(Maryland, Pennsylvania-western)*—Wellington Square - Ste. 405, 1225 S. Main St., Greensburg, PA 15601. Phone: (1-800-347-3753).
- *(Pennsylvania-central, Virginia)*—Penn Traffic Bldg. - 2nd fl., 319 Washington St., Johnstown, PA 15901. Phone: (1-800-347-3754).

West Virginia *(West Virginia-northern)*—Federal Bldg. - Ste. 3116, 425 Juliana St., Parkersburg, WV 26101. Phone: (1-800-347-3751).

- *(West Virginia-southern)*—Charleston Federal Center - Ste. 110, 500 Quarrier St., Charleston, WV 25301. Phone: (1-800-347-3749).

17.308 *Contact the nearest office of the state employment service in your area, or nearest Wage and Hour Division Office listed under* **17.303**.

OFFICE OF LABOR-MANAGEMENT STANDARDS

17.309 FIELD OFFICES

California—3660 Wilshire Blvd. - Ste. 708, Los Angeles, CA 90010-2713. Phone: (213)252-7508.

- 71 Stevenson Pl. - Ste. 725, San Francisco, CA 94105-2997. Phone: (415)975-4020.

17.309 (cont.) **Colorado**—1999 Broadway St. - Rm.2435, P.O. Box 46550, Denver, CO 80201-6550. Phone: (720)264-3231.

District of Columbia—Riddell Bldg. - Ste. 558, 1730 K St. NW, Washington, DC 20006. Phone: (202)254-6510.

Georgia—61 Forsyth St. SW - Rm.8B85, Atlanta, GA 30303-2219. Phone: (404)562-2083.

Illinois—Federal Office Bldg. - Ste. 774, 230 S. Dearborn St., Chicago, IL 60604-1505. Phone: (312)596-7160.

Louisiana—701 Loyola Ave. - Ste. 13009, New Orleans, LA 70113-1912. Phone: (504)589-6174.

Massachusetts—JFK Federal Bldg. - Rm.E-365, Boston, MA 02203-0002. Phone: (617)565-9880.

Michigan—211 W. Fort St. - Ste. 1313, Detroit, MI 48226-3237. Phone: (313)226-6200.

Missouri—1222 Spruce St. - Ste. 9.109E, St. Louis, MO 63103-2830. Phone: (314)539-2667.

New York—Federal Bldg. - Ste. 1310, 111 W. Huron St., Buffalo, NY 14202-2379. Phone: (716)551-4976.

- 201 Varick St. - Ste. 878,, New York, NY 10014-4811. Phone: (212)337-2580.

Ohio—525 Vine St. - Ste. 950, Cincinnati, OH 45202-3168. Phone: (513)684-6840.

- Federal Office Bldg. - Ste. 831, 1240 E. 9th St., Cleveland, OH 44199-2053. Phone: (216)522-3855.

Pennsylvania—The Curtis Center - Rm.760W, 170 S. Independence Mall West, Philadelphia, PA 19106-3310. Phone: (215)861-4818.

- Federal Office Bldg. - Ste. 801, 1000 Liberty Ave., Pittsburgh, PA 15222-4004. Phone: (412)395-6925.

Tennessee—233 Cumberland Bend Dr. - Ste. 110, Nashville, TN 37228-1809. Phone: (615)736-5906.

Texas—Maceo Smith Federal Bldg. - Ste. 300, 525 Griffin St., Dallas, TX 75202-5007. Phone: (214)767-6834.

Washington—Federal Office Bldg. - Ste. 605, 1111 3rd Ave., Seattle, WA 98101-3212. Phone: (206)553-5216.

Wisconsin—517 E. Wisconsin Ave. - Ste. 118, Milwaukee, WI 53202-4504. Phone: (414)297-1501.

OCCUPATIONAL SAFETY AND HEALTH ADMINISTRATION

17.502 thru 17.505 REGIONAL OFFICES

REGION I *(Connecticut, Maine, Massachusetts, New Hampshire, Rhode Island, Vermont)*—JFK Federal Bldg. - Low Rise Bldg. (Rm.E-340), Boston, MA 02114. Phone: (617)565-9860.

REGION II *(New Jersey, New York, Puerto Rico)*—201 Varick St. - Ste. 670, New York, NY 10014. Phone: (212)337-2378.

REGION III *(Delaware, District of Columbia, Maryland, Pennsylvania, Virginia, West Virginia)*—The Curtis Center - Ste. 740 West, 170 Independence Mall W., Philadelphia, PA 19106-3309. Phone: (215)861-4900.

REGION IV *(Alabama, Florida, Georgia, Kentucky, Mississippi, North Carolina, South Carolina, Tennessee)*—61 Forsyth St. SW - Rm.6T50, Atlanta, GA 30303. Phone: (404)562-2300.

REGION V *(Illinois, Indiana, Minnesota, Michigan, Ohio, Wisconsin)*—230 S. Dearborn St. - 32nd fl. (Rm.3244), Chicago, IL 60604. Phone: (312)353-2220.

REGION VI *(Arkansas, Louisiana, New Mexico, Oklahoma, Texas)*—525 Griffin Square Bldg. - Rm.602, Dallas, TX 75202. Phone: (214)767-4731.

REGION VII *(Iowa, Kansas, Missouri, Nebraska)*—City Center Square - Ste. 800, 1100 Main St., Kansas City, MO 64105. Phone: (816)426-5861.

REGION VIII *(Colorado, Montana, North Dakota, South Dakota, Utah, Wyoming)*—1999 Broadway St. - Rm.1690, Denver, CO 80202-5716. Phone: (720)264-6550.

REGION IX *(American Samoa, Arizona, California, Guam, Hawaii, Nevada, Trust Territory of the Pacific Islands)*—71 Stevenson St. - Rm.420, San Francisco, CA 94105. Phone: (415)975-4310.

REGION X *(Alaska, Idaho, Oregon, Washington)*—1111 3rd Ave. - Ste. 715, Seattle, WA 98101-3212. Phone: (206)553-5930.

AREA OFFICES

Alabama—Todd Mall, 2047 Canyon Rd., Birmingham, AL 35216-1981. Phone: (205)731-1534, ext.133.

- 3737 Government Blvd. - Ste. 100, Mobile, AL 36693-4309. Phone: (251)441-6131.

Alaska—301 W. Northern Lights Blvd. - Rm.407, Anchorage, AK 99503-7571. Phone: (907)271-5152.

Arizona—3221 N. 16th St. - Ste. 100, Phoenix, AZ 85016. Phone: (602)640-2007.

Arkansas—TCBY Bldg. - Ste. 450., 425 W. Capitol Ave., Little Rock, AR 72201. Phone: (501)324-6291.

California—Resource Center - Ste. 105, 101 El Camino Blvd., Sacramento, CA 95815. Phone: (916)566-7470.

- Resource Center, 5675 Ruffin Rd. - Ste. 330, San Diego, CA 92123. Phone: (619)557-5904.
- Resource Center, 71 Stevenson St. - Ste. 420, San Francisco, CA 94105. Phone: (415)975-4316.

Colorado—1391 Speer Blvd. - Ste. 210, Denver, CO 80204-2552. Phone: (303)844-5285.

- 7935 E. Prentice Ave. - Ste. 209, Englewood, CO 80111-2714. Phone: (303)843-4500.

Connecticut—Clark Bldg. - 4th fl., 1057 Broad St., Bridgeport, CT 06604. Phone: (203)579-5581.

- Federal Bldg. - Rm.613, 450 Main St., Hartford, CT 06103. Phone: (860)240-3152.

Delaware—Caleb Boggs Federal Bldg. - Rm.2209, 844 King St., Wilmington, DE 19801. Phone: (302)573-6518.

Florida—Bldg. H100, 8040 Peters Rd., Ft. Lauderdale, FL 33324. Phone: (954)424-0242.

- Ribault Bldg. - Ste. 227, 1851 Executive Center Dr., Jacksonville, FL 32207. Phone: (904)232-2895.
- 5807 Breckenridge Pkwy. - Ste. A, Tampa, FL 33610. Phone: (813)626-1177.

Georgia—450 Mall Blvd. - Ste. J, Savannah, GA 31406-1418. Phone: (912)652-4393.

- 2400 Herodian Way - Ste. 250, Smyrna, GA 30080-2968. Phone: (770)984-8700.
- La Vista Perimeter Office Park, Bldg. 7 - Ste. 110,, 2183 N. Lake Pkwy., Tucker, GA 30084-4154. Phone: (770)493-6644.

Hawaii—Resource Center - Ste. 5-146, 300 Ala Moana Blvd., Honolulu, HI 96850. Phone: (808)541-2685.

Idaho—1150 N. Curtis Rd. - Ste. 201, Boise, ID 83703. Phone: (208)321-2960.

17.502 thru 17.505 *(cont.)*

Illinois—1600 167th St. - Ste. 12, Calumet City, IL 60409. Phone: (708)891-3800.

- 701 Lee St. - Ste. 950, Des Plaines, IL 60016. Phone: (847)803-4800.
- 11 Executive Dr. - Ste. 11, Fairview Heights, IL 62208. Phone: (618)632-8612.
- 365 Smoke Tree Plaza, North Aurora, IL 60542. Phone: (630)896-8700.
- 2918 W. Willow Knolls Rd., Peoria, IL 61614. Phone: (309)671-7033.

Indiana—U.S. Post Office and Courthouse - Rm.423, 46 E. Ohio St., Indianapolis, IN 46204. Phone: (317)226-7290.

Iowa—210 Walnut St. - Rm.815, Des Moines, IA 50309. Phone: (515)284-4794.

Kansas—8600 Farley - Ste. 105, Overland Park, KS 66212-4677. Phone: (913)385-7380.

- 271 W. 3rd St. N. - Rm.400, Wichita, KS 67202. Phone: (316)269-6644.

Kentucky—Watts Federal Bldg. - Rm.108, 330 W. Broadway, Frankfort, KY 40601-1922. Phone: (502)227-7024.

Louisiana—9100 Bluebonnet Centre Blvd. - Ste. 201, Baton Rouge, LA 70809. Phone: (225)389-0474.

Maine—Muskie Federal Bldg. - Rm.G26, 40 Western Ave., Augusta, ME 04330. Phone: (207)626-9160.

- 202 Harlow St. - Rm.211, Bangor, ME 04401-4906. Phone: (207)941-8177.

Maryland—1099 Winterson Rd. - Ste. 140, Linthicum, MD 21090. Phones: (410)865-2055, -2056.

Massachusetts—639 Granite St. - 4th fl., Braintree, MA 02184. Phone: (617)565-6924.

- Valley Office Park - 1st fl., 13 Branch St., Methuen, MA 01844. Phone: (617)565-8110.
- 1441 Main St. - Rm.550, Springfield, MA 01103-1493. Phone: (413)785-0123.

Michigan—801 S. Waverly Rd. - Ste. 306, Lansing, MI 48917-4200. Phone: (517)327-0904.

Minnesota—330 S. 4th St. - Ste. 1205, Minneapolis, MN 55415. Phone: (612)664-5460.

Mississippi—3780 I-55N. - Ste. 210., Jackson, MS 39211-6323. Phone: (601)965-4606.

Missouri—6200 Connecticut Ave. - Ste. 100, Kansas City, MO 64120. Phone: (816)483-9531.

- 911 Washington Ave. - Rm.420, St. Louis, MO 63101. Phone: (314)425-4249.

Montana—2900 4th Ave. N. - Ste. 303, Billings, MT 59101. Phone: (406)247-7494.

Nebraska—Overland-Wolf Bldg. - Rm.100, 6910 Pacific St., Omaha, NE 68106. Phone: (402)221-3182.

Nevada—Federal Bldg. - Rm.204, Resource Center, 705 North Plaza, Carson City, NV 89701. Phone: (702)885-6963.

New Hampshire—55 Pleasant St. - Rm.3901, Concord, NH 03301. Phone: (603)225-1629.

New Jersey—Plaza 35 - Ste. 205, 1030 St. Georges Ave., Avenel, NJ 07001 Phone: (732)750-3270.

- 500 Rt. 17 S. - 2nd fl., Hasbrouck Heights, NJ 07604. Phone: (201)288-1700.
- Marlton Executive Park, South Bldg. 2 - Ste. 120, 701 Rt. 73, Marlton, NJ 08053. Phone: (856)757-5181.
- 299 Cherry Hill Rd.- Ste. 304, Parsippany, NJ 07054. Phone: (973)263-1003.

New Mexico—Western Bank Bldg. - Ste. 820, 505 Marquette Ave. NW, Albuquerque, NM 87102. Phone: (505)248-5302.

New York—Tomich Federal Bldg. - Ste. 300, 401 New Karner Rd., Albany, NY 12205-3809. Phone: (518)464-4338.

- 42-40 Bell Blvd., Bayside, NY 11361. Phone: (718)279-9060.
- 5360 Genessee St., Bowmansville, NY 14026. Phone: (716)684-3891.
- 201 Varick St. - Rm.905, New York, NY 10014. Phone: (212)620-3200.
- 3300 Vickery Rd., North Syracuse, NY 13212. Phone: (315)451-0808.
- 660 White Plains Rd. - 4th fl., Tarrytown, NY 10591-5107. Phone: (914)524-7510.
- 1400 Old Country Rd. - Ste. 208, Westbury, NY 11590. Phone: (516)334-3344.

North Carolina—Century Station, Federal Bldg. - Rm.438, 300 Fayetteville Mall, Raleigh, NC 27601-9998. Phone: (919)856-4770.

North Dakota—Federal Office Bldg., 1640 E. Capitol Ave., Bismarck, ND 58501. Phone: (701)250-4521.

Ohio—Federal Bldg. - Rm.4028, 36 Triangle Park Dr., Cincinnati, OH 45246. Phone: (513)841-4132.

- Federal Bldg. - Rm.899, 1240 E. 9th St., Cleveland, OH 44199. Phone: (216)522-3818.
- Federal Office Bldg. - Rm.620, 200 N. High St, Columbus, OH 43215. Phone: (614)469-5582.
- Ohio Bldg. - Ste. 600, 420 Madison Ave., Toledo, OH 43604. Phone: (419)259-7542.

Oklahoma—55 N. Robinson - Ste. 315, Oklahoma City, OK 73102. Phone: (405)278-9560.

Oregon—1220 SW 3rd St. - Rm.640, Portland, OR 97204. Phone: (503)326-2251.

Pennsylvania—850 N. 5th St., Allentown, PA 18102. Phone: (610)776-0592.

- 3939 W. Ridge Rd. - Ste. B-12, Erie, PA 16506. Phone: (814)833-5758.
- Progress Plaza, 49 N. Progress Ave., Harrisburg, PA 17109. Phone: (717)782-3902.
- U.S. Customs House - Rm.242, 2nd and Chestnut St., Philadelphia, PA 19106. Phone: (215)597-4955.
- Federal Bldg. - Rm.1428, 1000 Liberty Ave., Pittsburgh, PA 15522-4101. Phone: (412)395-4903.
- 7 N. Wilkes-Barre Blvd. - Ste. 410, Wilkes-Barre, PA 18702. Phone: (570)826-6538.

Puerto Rico—BBV Plaza Bldg. - Ste. 5B, 1510 F.D. Roosevelt Ave., Guaynabo, PR 00968. Phone: (787)277-1560.

Rhode Island—380 Westminster Mall - Rm.243, Providence, RI 02903. Phone: (401)528-4669.

South Carolina—1835 Assembly St. - Rm.1468, Columbia, SC 29201. Phone: (803)765-5904.

Tennessee—2002 Richard Jones Rd. - Ste. C-205, Nashville, TN 37215-2809. Phone: (615)781-5423.

Texas—903 San Jacinto Blvd. - Ste. 319, Austin, TX 78701. Phone: (512)916-5783.

- Wilson Plaza West - Ste. 700, 606 N. Carancahua, Corpus Christi, TX 78476. Phone: (361)888-3420.
- 8344 East R.L. Thornton Fwy. - Ste. 420, Dallas, TX 75228. Phone: (214)320-2400.
- 700 E. San Antonio - Rm.C-408, El Paso, TX 79901. Phone: (915)534-6251.
- North Star II - Ste. 302, 8713 Airport Fwy., Ft. Worth, TX 76180-7610. Phone: (817)428-2470.
- 17625 El Camino Real - Ste. 400, Houston, TX 77058. Phone: (281)286-0583.
- 507 N. Sam Houston Pkwy. E. - Ste. 400, Houston, TX 77060. Phone: (281)591-2438.
- Federal Bldg. - Rm.806, 1205 Texas Ave., Lubbock, TX 79401. Phone: (806)472-7681.

17.502 thru 17.505 *(cont.)*

Utah—1781 South 300 W., P.O. Box 65200, Salt Lake City, UT 84165-0200. Phone: (801)487-0521.

Virginia—200 Granby Mall - Rm.614, Norfolk, VA 23510. Phone: (757)441-3820.

Washington—505 106th Ave. NE - Ste. 302, Bellevue, WA 98004. Phone: (206)553-7520.

West Virginia—405 Capitol St. - Ste. 407, Charleston, WV 25301. Phone: (304)347-5937.

Wisconsin—1648 Tri Park Way, Appleton, WI 54914. Phone: (920)734-4521.

- 1310 W. Clairmont Ave., Eau Claire, WI 54701. Phone: (715)832-9019.
- 4802 E. Broadway, Madison, WI 53716. Phone: (608)441-5388.
- Reuss Bldg. - Ste. 1180, 310 Wisconsin Ave., Milwaukee, WI 53203. Phone: (414)297-3315.

MINE SAFETY AND HEALTH ADMINISTRATION

17.601 and 17.602 Coal Mine Safety and Health

DISTRICT OFFICES

DISTRICT NO. 1 *(Connecticut, Delaware, Maine, Massachusetts, New Hampshire, New Jersey, New York, Pennsylvania (counties east of and including Susquehanna, Sullivan, Columbia, Montour, Northumberland, Dauphin, York), Rhode Island, Vermont)*—Stegmaier Bldg. - Ste. 034, 7 N. Wilkes-Barre Blvd., Wilkes-Barre, PA 18702. Phone: (570)826-6321.

DISTRICT NO. 2 *(Pennsylvania counties west of and including Bradford, Lycoming, Union, Snyder, Juniata, Perry, Cumberland, Adams)*—Rural Rt.1 - Box 736, Hunter, PA 15639. Phone: (412)925-5150, ext.111.

DISTRICT NO. 3 *(Maryland, Ohio, West Virginia counties north of and including Jackson, Roane, Calhoun, Braxton, Randolph, Pendleton)*—5012 Mountaineer Mall, Morgantown, WV 26505. Phone: (304)291-4277.

DISTRICT NO. 4 *(West Virginia counties south of and including Mason, Putnam, Kanawha, Clay, Nicholas, Webster, Greenbrier, Pocahontas)*—100 Bluestone Rd., Mt. Hope, WV 25880. Phone: (304)877-3900, ext.125.

DISTRICT NO. 5 *(Virginia)*—P.O. Box 560, Norton, VA 24273. Phone: (540)679-0230.

DISTRICT NO. 6 *(Kentucky counties east of and including Mason, Robertson, Fleming, Rowan, Menifee, Morgan, Magoffin, Floyd, Pike, Letcher)*—159 N. Mayo Trail, Pikeville, KY 41501-3249. Phone: (606)432-0943, ext.116.

DISTRICT NO. 7 *(Alabama (counties north and east of, and including, Jackson, Marshall, Etowah, Cherokee), Georgia (counties north of, and including, Polk, Bartow, Cherokee, Forsyth, Hall, Jackson, Madison, Elbert), Kentucky (counties east of and including Boone, Grant, Scott, Woodford, Jessamine, Garrard, Lincoln, Pulaski, Clinton up to District 6 boundary), North Carolina, South Carolina, Tennessee)*—HC 66-Box 1699, Barbourville, KY 40906. Phone: (606)546-5123.

DISTRICT NO. 8 *(Illinois, Indiana, Iowa, Michigan, Minnesota, Missouri counties north of the Missouri River, Wisconsin)*—2300 Old Decker Rd. - Ste. 200, Vincennes, IN 47591. Phone: (812)882-7617.

DISTRICT NO. 9 *(All states west of the Mississippi River including Alaska and Hawaii, except Minnesota, Iowa and all counties of Missouri south of the Missouri River)*—Denver Federal Center, Denver, CO 80225-0367. Phone: (303)231-5458.

DISTRICT NO. 10 *(Kentucky counties west of and including Gallatin, Owen, Franklin, Anderson, Mercer, Boyle, Casey, Russell, Cumberland)*—100 YMCA Dr., Madisonville, KY 42431-9019. Phone: (270)821-4180.

DISTRICT NO. 11 *(Alabama and Georgia (counties south and west of the District 7 boundary) Florida, Mississippi, Puerto Rico, Virgin Islands)*—135 Gemini Circle - Ste. 213, Birmingham, AL 35209. Phone: (205)290-7300.

Metal and Nonmetal Mine Safety and Health

DISTRICT OFFICES

Alabama *(Southeastern: Alabama, Florida, Georgia, Kentucky, Mississippi, North Carolina, Puerto Rico, South Carolina, Tennessee, Virgin Islands)*—135 Gemini Circle - Ste. 212, Birmingham, AL 35209. Phone: (205)290-7294.

California *(Western: Alaska, California, Hawaii, Idaho, Nevada, Oregon, Washington)*—2060 Peabody Rd. - Ste. 610, Vacaville, CA 95687-6696. Phone: (707)447-9844.

Colorado *(Rocky Mountain: Arizona, Colorado, Kansas, Montana, Nebraska, North Dakota, South Dakota, Utah, Wyoming)*—Denver, CO 80225-0367. Phone: (303)231-5465.

Minnesota *(North Central: Illinois, Indiana, Iowa, Michigan, Minnesota, Ohio, Wisconsin)*—515 W. 1st St. - #333, Duluth, MN 55802-1302. Phone: (218)720-5448.

Pennsylvania *(Northeastern: Connecticut, Delaware, District of Columbia, Maine, Maryland, Massachusetts, New Hampshire, New Jersey, New York, Pennsylvania, Rhode Island, Vermont, Virginia, West Virginia)*—230 Executive Dr. - Ste. 2, Cranberry Township, PA 16066-6415. Phone: (724)772-2333.

Texas *(South Central: Arkansas, Louisiana, Missouri, New Mexico, Oklahoma, Texas)*—1100 Commerce St. - Rm.4C50, Dallas, TX 75242-0499. Phone: (214)767-8401.

TECHNICAL SUPPORT FIELD CENTERS

Pennsylvania—Safety and Health Technology Center, Cochrans Mill Rd., P.O. Box 18233, Pittsburgh, PA 15236. Phone: (412)386-6902.

West Virginia—Approval and Certification Center, Industrial Park Rd., Rural Rt. 1 - Box 251, Triadelphia, WV 26059. Phone: (304)547-2029.

National Mine Health and Safety Academy

1301 Airport Rd., Beaver, WV 25813-9426. Phone: (304)256-3200.

OFFICE OF THE SECRETARY, WOMEN'S BUREAU

17.700 REGIONAL OFFICES

REGION I *(Connecticut, Maine, Massachusetts, New Hampshire, Rhode Island, Vermont)*—JFK Federal Bldg. - Rm.E-270, One Congress St., Boston, MA 02114. Phones: (617)565-1988, 1-800-518-3585..

REGION II *(New Jersey, New York, Puerto Rico, Virgin Islands)*—201 Varick St. - Rm.601, New York, NY 10014. Phone: (212)337-2389.

REGION III *(Delaware, District of Columbia, Maryland, Pennsylvania, Virginia, West Virginia)*—The Curtis Center - Ste. 880 West, 170 S. Independence Mall W., Philadelphia, PA 19104. Phones: (215)861-4860, 1-800-379-9042.

REGION IV *(Alabama, Florida, Georgia, Kentucky, Mississippi, North Carolina, South Carolina, Tennessee)*—61 Forsyth St. SW - Ste. 7T95, Atlanta, GA 30367. Phones: (404)562-2336, 1-800-672-8356.

17.700 (cont.) **REGION V** *(Illinois, Indiana, Michigan, Minnesota, Ohio, Wisconsin)*—230 S. Dearborn St. - Rm.1022, Chicago, IL 60604. Phones: (312)353-6985, 1-800-648-8183.

REGION VI *(Arkansas, Louisiana, New Mexico, Oklahoma, Texas)*—Federal Bldg. - Ste. 735, 525 Griffin St., Dallas, TX 75202. Phones: (214)767-6985, 1-800-887-6794.

REGION VII *(Iowa, Kansas, Missouri, Nebraska)*—City Center City Square - Ste. 845, 1100 Main St., Kansas City, MO 64106. Phones: (816)426-6108, 1-800-252-4706.

REGION VIII *(Colorado, Montana, North Dakota, South Dakota, Utah, Wyoming)*—Federal Office Bldg. - Ste. 905, 1801 California St., Denver, CO 80202-2614. Phones: (303)844-1286, 1-800-299-0886.

REGION IX *(Arizona, California, Hawaii, Nevada)*—71 Stevenson St. - Rm.927, San Francisco, CA 94105. Phone: (415)975-4750.

REGION X *(Alaska, Idaho, Oregon, Washington)*—1111 3rd Ave. - Rm.925, Seattle, WA 98101-3211. Phones: (206)553-1534, 1-888-296-7011.

OFFICE OF THE ASSISTANT SECRETARY FOR VETERANS' EMPLOYMENT AND TRAINING

17.801 thru 17.807 REGIONAL AND STATE OFFICES

REGION I *(Connecticut, Maine, Massachusetts, New Hampshire, Rhode Island, Vermont, Virgin Islands)*—Connecticut Department of Labor Bldg., 200 Folly Brook Blvd., Wethersfield, CT 06109. Phone: (860)263-6490.

- JFK Federal Bldg. - Government Center (Rm.E-315), Boston, MA 02203. Phone: (617)565-2080.
- Hurley Bldg. - 2nd fl., ES Operations Section, 19 Staniford St., Boston, MA 02114. Phone: (617)626-6699.
- 5 Mollison Way, P.O. Box 3106, Lewiston, ME 04243. Phone: (207)753-9090.
- 143 N. Main St. - Rm.208, Concord, NH 03301. Phone: (603)225-1424.
- 57 Spruce St., Westerly, RI 02891. Phone: (401)528-5134.
- Post Office Bldg. - Rm.303, 87 State St., P.O. Box 603, Montpelier, VT 05602. Phone: (802)828-4441.

REGION II *(New Jersey, New York, Puerto Rico, Virgin Islands)*—Labor Bldg. - 11th fl. (CN058), Trenton, NJ 08625. Phone: (609)292-2930.

- Harriman State Campus - Bldg. 12 (Rm.518), Albany, NY 12240-0099. Phone: (518)457-7465.
- 201 Varick St. - Rm.766, New York, NY 10014. Phone: (212)337-2211.
- 198 Calle Guayama - 20th fl., Hato Rey, PR 00917. Phone: (787)754-5391.

REGION III *(Delaware, District of Columbia, Maryland, Pennsylvania, Virginia, West Virginia)*—500 C St. NW - Rm.108, Washington, DC 20001. Phone: (202)724-7005.

- 4425 N. Market St. - Rm.420, Wilmington, DE 19809-0828. Phone: (302)761-8138.
- 1100 N. Eutaw St. - Rm.210, Baltimore, MD 21201. Phone: (410)767-2110.
- Labor and Industry Bldg. - Rm.1108,, 7th and Forster St., Harrisburg, PA 17121. Phone: (717)787-5834.
- The Curtis Center - Ste. 770W, 170 S. Independence Mall West, Philadelphia, PA 19106. Phone: (215)861-5390.
- 703 E. Main St. - Rm.118, Richmond, VA 23219. Phone: (804)786-7269.

- Capitol Complex - Rm.204, 112 California Ave., Charleston, WV 25305-0112. Phone: (304)558-4001.

REGION IV *(Alabama, Florida, Georgia, Kentucky, Mississippi, North Carolina, South Carolina, Tennessee)*—649 Monroe St. - Rm.543, Montgomery, AL 36131-6300. Phone: (334)223-7677.

- Tallahassee, FL 32302-1527. Phone: (850)942-8800.
- Nunn Atlanta Federal Center - Rm.6-T85, 61 Forsyth St. SW, Atlanta, GA 30303. Phone: (404)562-2305.
- Sussex Place - Ste. 504, 148 International Blvd. NE, Atlanta, GA 30303-1751. Phone: (404)656-3127.
- c/o Department for Employment Services, 275 E. Main St., Frankfort, KY 40621-2339. Phone: (502)564-7062.
- 1520 W. Capitol St., Jackson, MS 39215-1699. Phone: (601)965-4204.
- P.O. Box 27625, Raleigh, NC 27611-7625. Phones: (919)733-7402, -7407.
- Columbia, SC 29202-1755. Phone: (803)765-5195.
- 915 8th Ave. N., Nashville, TN 37219-3795. Phone (615)736-7680.

REGION V *(Illinois, Indiana, Michigan, Minnesota, Ohio, Wisconsin)*—230 S. Dearborn - Rm.1064, Chicago, IL 60604. Phone: (312)353-0970.

- 401 S. State St. - 744 North, Chicago, IL 60605. Phone: (312)793-3433.
- 10 N. Senate Ave. - Rm.SE-103, Indianapolis, IN 46204. Phone: (317)232-6804.
- 7310 Woodward Ave. - Ste. 407, Detroit, MI 48202. Phone: (313)876-5613.
- 390 Robert St. N. - 1st fl., St. Paul, MN 55101. Phone: (651)296-3665.
- P.O. Box 1618, Columbus, OH 43216. Phone: (614)644-3688.
- Madison, WI 53708-8310. Phone: (608)266-3110.

REGION VI *(Arkansas, Louisiana, New Mexico, Oklahoma, Texas)*—P.O. Box 128, Little Rock, AR 72203. Phone: (501)682-3786.

- P.O. Box 94094, Rm.184, Baton Rouge, LA 70804-9094. Phone: (225)389-0339.
- P.O. Box 25085, Albuquerque, NM 87125-5085. Phone: (505)346-7502.
- 201 N. Lincoln Blvd., P.O. Box 52003, Oklahoma City, OK 73152-2003. Phone: (405)231-5088.
- P.O. Box 1468, Austin, TX 78767. Phone: (512)463-2814.
- 525 Griffin St. - Rm.858, Dallas, TX 75202. Phone: (214)767-4987.

REGION VII *(Iowa, Kansas, Missouri, Nebraska)*—150 Des Moines St., Des Moines, IA 50309-5563. Phone: (515)281-9061.

- 401 Topeka Blvd., Topeka, KS 66603-3182. Phone: (913)296-5032.
- 421 E. Dunklin St., Jefferson City, MO 65102-1087. Phone: (573)751-3921.
- City Center Square - Ste. 850, 1100 Main St., Kansas City, MO 64105-2112. Phone: (816)426-7151.
- 550 S. 16th St., P.O. Box 94600, Lincoln, NE 68508. Phone: (402)437-5289.

REGION VIII *(Colorado, Montana, North Dakota, South Dakota, Utah, Wyoming)*—1999 Broadway - Ste. 1730, Denver, CO 80202-2614. Phone: (303)844-1175.

- 2 Park Central - Ste. 400, 1515 Arapahoe St., Denver, CO 80202-2117. Phone: (303)844-2151.
- 1215 8th Ave., Helena, MT 59601-4144. Phone: (406)449-5431.
- 1000 E. Divide Ave., Bismarck, ND 58502-1632. Phone: (701)328-2865.
- 420 S. Roosevelt St., Aberdeen, SD 57402-4730. Phone: (605)626-2325.
- 140 E. 300 South, Salt Lake City, UT 84111-2333. Phone: (801)524-5703.
- 100 W. Midwest Ave., Casper, WY 82602-2760. Phone: (307)261-5454.

17.801 thru 17.807 *(cont.)* **REGION IX** *(Arizona, California, Hawaii, Nevada)*—1400 W. Washington St., P.O. Box 6123-SC760E, Phoenix, AZ 85005. Phone: (602)379-4961.

- 800 Capitol Mall - Rm.W-1142, P.O. Box 826880, Sacramento, CA 94280-0001. Phone: (916)654-8178.
- 71 Stevenson St. - Ste. 705, San Francisco, CA 94105. Phone: (415)975-4700.
- P.O. Box 3680, Honolulu, HI 96811. Phone: (808)522-8216.
- 1923 N. Carson St. - Rm.205, Carson City, NV 89702. Phone: (702)687-4632.

REGION X *(Alaska, Idaho, Oregon and Washington)*—1111 W. 8th St., Juneau, AK 99802-5509. Phone: (907)465-2723.

- P.O. Box 2697, Boise, ID 83701. Phone: (208)334-6163.
- 312 Employment Division Bldg. - Rm.108, 875 Union St. NE, Salem, OR 97311-0100. Phone: (503)947-1490.
- Olympia, WA 98507-0165. Phone: (360)438-4600.
- 1111 3rd Ave. - Ste. 900, Seattle, WA 98101-3212. Phone: (206)553-4831.

DEPARTMENT OF STATE

BUREAU OF EDUCATIONAL AND CULTURAL AFFAIRS

19.400 *Contact Fulbright program advisor at local college, or contact the Institute of International Education: 809 United Nations Plaza, New York, NY 10017, or via* ***Internet:*** *"www.iie.org".*

19.403 American Council of Young Political Leaders, 1612 K St. NW - Ste. 300, Washington, DC 20006. Phone: (202)857-0999.

19.410 *Young Professionals Component:*

CDS International, 330 7th Ave., New York, NY 10001. Phone: (212)497-3509.

Vocational Component:

Nacel/Open Door, 3410 Federal Dr. - Ste. 101, St. Paul, MN 55122. Phone: (651)686-0080.

19.430 ***International Education Training:***

NAFSA, Association of International Educators, 1307 New York Ave. NW - 8th fl., Washington, DC 20005-4701. Phones:(202)737-3699; FAX (202)737-3657.

Research: Institute of International Education, 809 United Nations Plaza, New York, NY 10017. Phone: (212)984-5331.

19.500 MEPI Regional Offices will open in Tunis, Tunisia and Abu Dhabi, UAE in summer 2004.

19.522 Office Director/MCE: (202)663-1075.

Refugee Children: (202)663-1713.

Refugee Women and GBV/NGO Liaison: (202)663-1481.

Office Director/PRP: (202)663-3954.

Program Officer, Policy Office: (202)663-3881, -3104.

DEPARTMENT OF TRANSPORTATION

FEDERAL AVIATION ADMINISTRATION

20.100 Aviation Information Distribution Program

REGIONAL OFFICES

Aviation Education:

ALASKA—(AHT-200/AAL-17), 222 W. 7th Ave., Box 14, Anchorage, AK 99513-7587. Phones: (202)267-3436, (907)271-5377.

CENTRAL—(ACE-4), 601 E. 12th St., Kansas City, M0 64106-2808. Phone: (816)329-2420.

EASTERN—(ACH-1), Technical Center, Atlantic City International Airport, Atlantic City, NJ 08405. Phone: (605)485-6515.

- (AEA-60), JFK International Airport, Federal Bldg. - Rm.111, Jamaica, NY 11430. Phone: (718)553-3363.

GREAT LAKES—(AGL-4), O'Hare Lake Office Center, 2300 E. Devon Ave., Des Plaines, IL 60018. Phone: (847)294-7106.

NEW ENGLAND—(ANE-40), 12 New England Executive Park, Burlington, MA 01803-5299. Phone: (781)238-7378.

NORTHWEST MOUNTAIN—(ANM-4CL), 1601 Lind Ave. SW, Renton, WA 98055-4056. Phone: (425)227-1725.

SOUTHERN—(ASO-1), 1701 Columbia Ave., P.O. Box 20636, Atlanta, GA 30320-0631. Phone: (425)227-1725.

SOUTHWEST—(AMC-3), Aeronautical Center, P.O. Box 25082, Oklahoma City, OK 73135. Phone: (405)954-5332.

- (ASW-18B), 2601 Meacham Blvd., Ft. Worth, TX 76137-4298. Phone: (817)222-5833.

WESTERN PACIFIC—(AWP-4), Worldway Postal Center, P.O. Box 92007, Los Angeles, CA 90009-2007. Phone:(310)725-3802.

20.106 REGIONAL OFFICES

Same addresses as **20.100**.

ALASKA—Phone: (907)271-5438.

CENTRAL—(ACE-600), Phone: (816)426-4698.

EASTERN—(AEA-600), Phone: (718)553-3331.

GREAT LAKES—(AGL-600), Phone: (847)294-7272.

NEW ENGLAND—(ANE-600), Phone: (617)238-7600.

NORTHWEST MOUNTAIN—(ANM-600), Phone: (206)227-2600.

SOUTHERN—(ASO-600), Phone: (404)305-6700.

SOUTHWEST—(ASW-600), Phone: (817)222-5600.

WESTERN PACIFIC—(AWP), Phone: (310)725-3600.

FEDERAL HIGHWAY ADMINISTRATION

20.205 thru 20.217 DIVISION OFFICES

Alabama—500 Eastern Blvd. - Ste. 200, Montgomery, AL 36117-2018. Phone: (334)223-7370.

Alaska—709 W. 9th St. - Rm.851, Juneau, AK 99802-1648. Phone: (907)586-7180.

Arizona—234 N. Central Ave. - Ste. 330, Phoenix, AZ 85004-2220. Phone: (602)379-3646.

Arkansas—700 W. Capitol Ave. - Rm.3130, Little Rock, AR 72201-3298. Phone: (501)324-5625.

California—980 9th St. - Ste. 400, Sacramento, CA 95814-2724. Phone: (916)498-5001.

Colorado—555 Zang St. - Rm.250, Lakewood, CO 80228-1097. Phone: (303)969-6730, ext.3.

Connecticut—628-2 Hebron Ave. - Ste. 303, Glastonbury, CT 06033-5007. Phone: (860)659-6703, ext.3009.

Delaware—300 S. New St. - Rm.2101, Dover, DE 19904-0726. Phone: (302)734-5323.

District of Columbia—Union Center Plaza - Ste. 750, 820 1st St. NE, Washington, DC 20002-4205. Phone: (202)523-0163.

Florida—227 N. Bronough St. - Rm.2015, Tallahassee, FL 32301-1330. Phone: (850)942-9650.

Georgia—61 Forsyth St. SW - Ste. 17T100, Atlanta, GA 30303-3104. Phone: (404)562-3630.

Hawaii—Kalanianaole Federal Bldg. - Rm.3-306, 300 Ala Moana Blvd., P.O. Box 50206, Honolulu, HI 96850-5000. Phone: (808)541-2700, ext.312.

Idaho—3050 Lakeharbor Lane - Ste. 126, Boise, ID 83703-6243. Phone: (208)334-9180.

Illinois—3250 Executive Park Dr., Springfield, IL 62703-4514. Phone: (217)492-4640.

Indiana—575 N. Pennsylvania St. - Rm.254, Indianapolis, IN 46204-1576. Phone: (317)226-7475.

Iowa—105 6th St., Ames, IA 50010-6337. Phone: (515)233-7300.

Kansas—3300 S. Topeka Blvd. - Ste. 1, Topeka, KS 66611-2237. Phone: (785)267-7281.

Kentucky—330 W. Broadway, Frankfort, KY 40601-1922. Phone: (502)223-6720.

Louisiana—5304 Flanders Dr. - Ste. A, Baton Rouge, LA 70808-4348. Phone: (225)757-7600.

Maine—Muskie Federal Bldg. - Rm.614, 40 Western Ave., Augusta, ME 04330-6394. Phone: (207)622-8487, ext.19.

Maryland—711 W. 40th St. - Ste. 220, Baltimore, MD 21211-2108. Phone: (410)962-4440.

Massachusetts—55 Broadway - 10th fl., Cambridge, MA 02142-1093. Phone: (617)494-3657.

Michigan—315 W. Allegan St. - Rm.207, Lansing, MI 48933-1528. Phone: (517)377-1844.

Minnesota—Galtier Plaza - Ste. 500 (Box 75), 380 Jackson St., St. Paul, MN 55101-2904. Phone: (651)291-6100.

Mississippi—666 North St. - Ste. 105, Jackson, MS 39202-3199. Phone: (601)965-4215.

Missouri—209 Adams St., Jefferson City, MO 65101-3203. Phone: (573)636-7104.

Montana—2880 Skyway Dr., Helena, MT 59602-1230. Phone: (406)449-5303, ext.235.

Nebraska—Federal Bldg. - Rm.220, 100 Centennial Mall N., Lincoln, NE 68508-3851. Phone: (402)437-5765.

Nevada—705 N. Plaza St. - Ste. 220, Carson City, NV 89701-0602. Phone: (775)687-1204.

New Hampshire—279 Pleasant St. Ste. 204, Concord, NH 03301-7502. Phone: (603)228-0417.

New Jersey—840 Bear Tavern Rd. - Ste. 310, West Trenton, NJ 08628-1019. Phone: (609)637-4200.

New Mexico—604 W. San Mateo Rd., Santa Fe, NM 87505-3920. Phone: (505)820-2021.

New York—O'Brien Federal Bldg. - Rm.719., Clinton Ave. and N. Pearl St., Albany, NY 12207. Phone: (518)431-4125.

North Carolina—310 New Bern Ave - Ste. 410, Raleigh, NC 27601-1441. Phone: (919)856-4346.

North Dakota—1471 Interstate Loop, Bismarck, ND 58501-0567. Phone: (701)250-4204.

Ohio—200 N. High St. - Rm.328, Columbus, OH 43215. Phone: (614)280-6896.

Oklahoma—300 N. Meridan - Ste. 105S, Oklahoma City, OK 73107-6560. Phone: (405)605-6011.

Oregon—The Equitable Center - Ste. 100, 530 Center St. NE, Salem, OR 97301-3740. Phone: (503)399-5749.

Pennsylvania—228 Walnut St. - Rm.558, Harrisburg, PA 17101-1720. Phone: (717)221-3461.

Puerto Rico—Degetau Federal Bldg. - Rm.210, 330 Carlos Chardon Ave., San Juan, PR 00916. Phone:(787)766-5600, ext.223.

Rhode Island—380 Westminster Mall - 5th fl., Providence, RI 02903-3246. Phone: (401)528-4560.

South Carolina—1835 Assembly St. - Ste. 1270, Columbia, SC 29201-2483. Phone: (803)765-5411.

South Dakota—116 E. Dakota Ave., Pierre, SD 57501-3110. Phone: (605)224-8033.

Tennessee—640 Grassmere Park Rd. - Ste. 112, Nashville, TN 37211-3658. Phone: (615)781-5770.

Texas—Federal Office Bldg. - Rm.826, 300 E. 8th St., Austin, TX 78701-3233. Phone: (512)536-5900.

Utah—2520 W. 4700 S. - Ste. 9A, Salt Lake City, UT 84118-1847. Phone: (801)963-0182.

Vermont—Federal Bldg., 87 State St., Montpelier, VT 05601-0568. Phone: (802)828-4423.

Virginia—400 N. 8th St. - Rm.750, P.O. Box 10249, Richmond, VA 23240-0249. Phone: (804)775-3320.

Washington—Evergreen Plaza, - Ste. 501, 711 S. Capitol Way, Olympia, WA 98501-1284. Phone: (360)753-9480.

West Virginia—Geary Plaza - Ste. 200, 700 Washington St. E., Charleston, WV 25301-1604. Phone: (304)347-5928.

Wisconsin—Highpoint Office Park, 567 D'Onofrio Dr., Madison, WI 53719-2814. Phone: (608)829-7500.

Wyoming—2617 E. Lincolnway - Ste. D, Cheyenne, WY 82001-5662. Phone: (307)772-2101, ext.40.

20.205 thru 20.217 *(cont.)*

Federal Lands Highway Division Offices

CENTRAL—555 Zang St., Lakewood, CO 80228-1010. Phone: (303)716-2000.

EASTERN—Loudoun Technical Center, 21400 Ridgetop Circle, Sterling, VA 20166-6511. Phone: (703)404-6201.

WESTERN—610 E. 5th St., Vancouver, WA 98661-3801. Phone: (360)619-7700.

FEDERAL MOTOR CARRIER SAFETY ADMINISTRATION

20.218

DIVISION OFFICES

(Other addresses same as **20.205**.)

Alabama—Phone: (334)223-7244.

Alaska—Historic Federal Bldg. - Rm.429, 605 W. 4th Ave., Anchorage, AK 99501. Phone: (907)271-4068.

Arizona—234 N. Central Ave. - Ste. 305, Phoenix, AZ 85004-2002. Phone: (602)379-6851.

Arkansas—Phone: (501)324-5050.

California—980 9th St., Sacramento, CA 95814-2724. Phone: (916)498-5050.

Colorado—555 Zang St. - Rm.264, Lakewood, CO 80228-1097. Phone: (303)969-6748.

Connecticut—Phone: (860)659-6700.

Delaware—Phone: (302)734-8173.

District of Columbia—Phone:(202)523-0178.

Florida—227 N. Bronough St. - Rm.2060, Tallahassee, FL 32301-1330. Phone: (850)942-9338.

Georgia—61 Forsyth St. SW - Ste. 17T85, Atlanta, GA 30303-3104. Phone: (404)562-3620.

Hawaii—Kalanianaole Federal Bldg. - Rm.3-243, 300 Ala Moana Blvd., P.O. Box 50206, Honolulu, HI 96850-5000. Phone: (808)541-2700.

Idaho—Phone: (208)334-1842.

Illinois—Phone: (217)492-4608.

Indiana—575 N. Pennsylvania St. - Rm.261, Indianapolis, IN 46204-1570. Phone: (317)226-7474.

Iowa—Phone: (515)233-7400.

Kansas—Phone: (785)267-7288.

Kentucky—Phone: (502)223-6779.

Louisiana—Phone: (225)757-7640.

Maine—Muskie Federal Bldg. - Rm.601, 40 Western Ave., Augusta, ME 04330-6394. Phone: (207)622-8358.

Maryland—711 W. 40th St. - Ste. 220, Baltimore, MD 21211-2100. Phone: (410)962-2889.

Massachusetts—55 Broadway - Rm.I-35, Cambridge, MA 02142-1093. Phone: (617)494-2770.

Michigan—315 W. Allegan St. - Rm.205, Lansing, MI 48933-1528. Phone: (517)377-1866.

Minnesota—Galtier Plaza - Box 75(Ste. 500), 175 E. 5th St., St. Paul, MN 55101-2904. Phone: (651)291-6150.

Mississippi—666 North St. - Ste. 103, Jackson, MS 39202-3199. Phone: (601)965-4219.

Missouri—Phone: (573)636-3246.

Montana—Phone: (406)449-4304.

Nebraska—Phone: (402)437-5986.

Nevada—Phone: (775)687-5335.

New Hampshire—Federal Bldg. - Rm.202, 279 Pleasant St., Concord NH 03301-7502. Phone: (603)228-3112.

New Jersey—Phone: (609)637-4222.

New Mexico—2400 Louisiana Blvd. NE - Ste. 520, AFC-5, Albuquerque, NM 87110. Phone: (505)346-7858.

New York—Phone: (518)431-4145.

North Carolina—310 New Bern Ave. - Ste. 468, Raleigh, NC 27601-1441. Phone: (919)856-4378.

North Dakota—Phone: (701)250-4346.

Ohio—Phone: (614)280-5657.

Oklahoma—300 N. Meridian - Ste. 106-S, Oklahoma City, OK 73107-6560. Phone: (405)605-6047.

Oregon—Phone: (503)399-5775.

Pennsylvania—228 Walnut St. - Rm.536, Harrisburg, PA 17101-1720. Phone: (717)221-4443.

Puerto Rico—US Courthouse and Federal Bldg. - Rm.329, Carlos Chardon St., Hato Rey, PR 00918. Phone: (787)766-5985.

Rhode Island—380 Westminster Mall - Rm.547, Providence, RI 02903-3246. Phone: (401)528-4578.

South Carolina—1835 Assembly St. - Ste. 1253, Columbia, SC 29201-2430. Phone: (803)765-5414.

South Dakota—Phone: (605)224-8202.

Tennessee—640 Grassmere Park Rd. - Ste. 111, Nashville, TN 37211. Phone: (615)781-5781.

Texas—Phone: (512)536-5980.

Utah—2520 W. 4700 S. - Ste. 9B, Salt Lake City, UT 84118-1847. Phone: (801)963-0096.

Vermont—87 State St. - Rm.216, Montpelier, VT 05602-2954. Phone: (802)828-4480.

Virginia—400 N. 8th St. - Rm.750, Richmond, VA 23240. Phone: (804)775-3322.

Washington—Phone: (360)753-9875.

West Virginia—700 Washington St. E. - Ste. 205, Charleston, WV 25301-1604. Phone: (304)347-5935.

Wisconsin—567 D'Onofrio Dr. - Ste. 101, Madison WI 53719-2814. Phone: (608)829-7534.

Wyoming—1916 Evans Ave., Cheyenne, WY 82001-3764. Phone: (307)772-2305.

20.219 Listed under **20.205**.

20.232 and 20.233 Listed under **20.218**.

FEDERAL RAILROAD ADMINISTRATION

20.303 REGIONAL OFFICES

Regional Director/Railroad Safety:

REGION I - Northeastern *(Connecticut, Maine, Massachusetts, New Hampshire, New Jersey, New York, Rhode Island, Vermont)*—55 Broadway - Rm.1077, Cambridge, MA 02142. Phone: (617)494-2302.

REGION II - Eastern *(Delaware, District of Columbia, Pennsylvania, Maryland, Virginia, West Virginia, Ohio)*—2 International Plaza - Ste. 550, Philadelphia, PA 19113. Phone: (610)521-8200.

REGION III - Southern *(Alabama, Florida, Georgia, Kentucky, Mississippi, North Carolina, South Carolina, Tennessee)*—Atlanta Federal Center - Ste. 16T20, 61 Forsyth St. SW, Atlanta, GA 30303-3104. Phone: (404)562-3800.

REGION IV - Central *(Illinois, Indiana, Michigan, Minnesota, Wisconsin)*—200 W. Adams St. - Ste. 310, Chicago, IL 60606. Phone: (312)353-6203.

REGION V - Southwestern *(Arkansas, Louisiana, New Mexico, Oklahoma, Texas)*—4100 International Plaza - Ste. 450, Ft. Worth, TX 76109. Phone: (817)862-2200.

REGION VI - Midwestern *(Colorado, Iowa, Kansas, Missouri, Nebraska)*—DOT Bldg. - Ste. 464, 901 Locust St., Kansas City, MO 64106-2095. Phone: (816)426-2497.

REGION VII - Western *(Arizona, California, Nevada, Utah)*—801 "I" St. - Ste. 466, Sacramento, CA 95814-2559. Phone: (916)498-6540.

REGION VIII - Northwestern *(Alaska, Idaho, Montana, North Dakota, Oregon, South Dakota, Washington, Wyoming)*—Murdock Executive Plaza - Ste. 650, 703 Broadway, Vancouver, WA 98660. Phone: (360)696-7536.

FEDERAL TRANSIT ADMINISTRATION

20.500 thru 20.518 REGIONAL OFFICES

REGION I *(Connecticut, Maine, Massachusetts, New Hampshire, Rhode Island, Vermont)*—c/o Volpe National, Transportation Systems Center, Kendall Square - Ste. 920, 55 Broadway, Cambridge, MA 02142-1093. Phone: (617)494-2055.

REGION II *(New Jersey, New York, Virgin Islands)*—Metropolitan Office - Ste. 429, One Bowling Green, New York, NY 10004-1415. Phone: (212)668-2170.

REGION III *(Delaware, District of Columbia, Maryland, Pennsylvania, Virginia, West Virginia)*—1760 Market St. - Ste. 500, Philadelphia, PA 19103-4124. Phone: (215)656-7100.

REGION IV *(Alabama, Florida, Georgia, Kentucky, Mississippi, North Carolina, Puerto Rico, South Carolina, Tennessee)*—61 Forsyth St. SW - Ste. 17T50, Atlanta, GA 30303-8917. Phone: (404)562-3000.

REGION V *(Illinois, Indiana, Michigan, Minnesota, Ohio, Wisconsin)*—200 W. Adams St. - Ste. 2410, Chicago, IL 60606-5232. Phone: (312)353-2789.

REGION VI *(Arkansas, Louisiana, New Mexico, Oklahoma, Texas)*—Lanham Federal Bldg. - Ste. 8A36, 819 Taylor St., Ft. Worth, TX 76102. Phone: (817)978-0550.

REGION VII *(Iowa, Kansas, Missouri, Nebraska)*—901 Locust St. - Rm.404, Kansas City, MO 64106. Phone: (816)329-3920.

REGION VIII *(Note: grant making activity for Arizona and Nevada falls under Region VIII) (Colorado, Montana, North Dakota, South Dakota, Utah, Wyoming)*—216 16th St. - Ste. 650, Denver, CO 80202-5120. Phone: (303)844-3242.

REGION IX *(American Samoa, Arizona, California, Guam, Hawaii, Nevada)*—201 Mission St. - Ste. 2210, San Francisco, CA 94105-1926. Phone: (415)744-3133.

REGION X *(Alaska, Idaho, Oregon, Washington)*—Jackson Federal Bldg. - Ste. 3142, 915 2nd Ave., Seattle, WA 98174-1002. Phone: (206)220-7954.

NATIONAL HIGHWAY TRAFFIC SAFETY ADMINISTRATION

20.600 thru 20.608 REGIONAL OFFICES

REGION I *(Connecticut, Maine, Massachusetts, New Hampshire, Rhode Island, Vermont)*—Transportation System Center, Kendall Square (Code 903), Cambridge, MA 02142. Phone: (617)494-3427.

REGION II *(New Jersey, New York, Puerto Rico, Virgin Islands)*—222 Mamaroneck Ave. - Ste. 204, White Plains, NY 10605. Phone: (914)682-6162.

REGION III *(Delaware, District of Columbia, Maryland, Pennsylvania, Virginia, West Virginia)*—Crescent Bldg. - Ste. 4000, 10 S. Howard St., Baltimore, MD 21201. Phone: (410)962-0077.

REGION IV *(Alabama, Florida, Georgia, Kentucky, Mississippi, North Carolina, South Carolina, Tennessee)*—61 Forsyth St. SW - Ste. 17T30, Atlanta, GA 30303-3104. Phone: (404)562-3739.

REGION V *(Illinois, Indiana, Michigan, Minnesota, Ohio, Wisconsin)*—19900 Governors Dr. - Ste. 201, Olympia Fields, IL 60461. Phone: (708)503-8822.

REGION VI *(Arkansas, Indian Nations, Louisiana, New Mexico, Oklahoma, Texas)*—819 Taylor St. - Rm.8A38, Ft. Worth, TX 76102-6177. Phone: (817)978-3653.

REGION VII *(Iowa, Kansas, Missouri, Nebraska)*—P.O. Box 412515, Kansas City, MO 64141. Phone: (816)822-7233.

REGION VIII *(Colorado, Montana, North Dakota, South Dakota, Utah, Wyoming)*—555 Zang St. - Rm.430, Denver, CO 80228. Phone: (303)969-6917.

REGION IX *(American Samoa, Arizona, California, Guam, Hawaii, Mariana Islands, Nevada)*—201 Mission St. - Ste. 2230, San Francisco, CA 94105. Phone: (415)744-3089.

REGION X *(Alaska, Idaho, Oregon, Washington)*—3140 Jackson Federal Bldg., 915 2nd Ave., Seattle, WA 98174. Phone: (206)220-7640.

RESEARCH AND SPECIAL PROGRAMS ADMINISTRATION

20.700 REGIONAL OFFICES

CENTRAL *(Illinois, Indiana, Iowa, Kansas, Michigan, Minnesota, Missouri, Nebraska, North Dakota, Ohio, South Dakota, Wisconsin)*—1900 Locust St. - Rm.462, Kansas City, MO 64106. Phones: (816)329-3800; FAX (816)329-3831.

EASTERN *(Connecticut, Delaware, District of Columbia, Maine, Maryland, Massachusetts, New Hampshire, New Jersey, New York, Pennsylvania, Rhode Island, Vermont, Virginia, West Virginia)*—400 7th St. SW - Rm.7130, Washington, DC 20590. Phones: (202)366-4580; FAX (202)366-3274.

SOUTHERN *(Alabama, Arkansas, Florida, Georgia, Kentucky, Mississippi, North Carolina, Puerto Rico, South Carolina, Tennessee)*—61 Forsyth St. - Ste. 16T15, Atlanta, GA 30303. Phones: (404)562-3530; FAX (404)562-3569.

20.700 (cont.) **SOUTHWEST** *(Arizona, Louisiana, New Mexico, Oklahoma, Texas)*—2320 La Branch - Rm.2100, Houston, TX 77004. Phones: (713)718-3746; FAX (713)718-3724.

WESTERN *(Alaska, California, Colorado, Hawaii, Idaho, Montana, Nevada, Oregon, Utah, Washington, Wyoming)*—Golden Hills Centre - Ste. A250, 12600 W. Colfax Ave., Lakewood, CO 80215. Phones: (303)231-5701; FAX (303)231-5711.

MARITIME ADMINISTRATION

20.801 and 20.802

REGIONAL OFFICES

CENTRAL (*Alabama, Arkansas, Colorado, Florida (western half), Louisiana, Mississippi, New Mexico, Oklahoma, Tennessee, Texas)*—501 Magazine St. - Rm.1223, New Orleans, LA 70130-3394. Phone: (504)589-2000.

GREAT LAKES (*Illinois, Indiana, Iowa, Kansas, Kentucky, Michigan, Minnesota, Missouri, Nebraska, New York (lake coastal area), North Dakota, Ohio, Pennsylvania (lake coastal area), South Dakota, West Virginia (western third), Wisconsin)*—2860 South River Road - Ste. 185, Des Plaines, IL 60018-2413. Phone: (847)298-4535.

NORTH ATLANTIC (*Connecticut, Delaware, Maine, Maryland, Massachusetts, New Hampshire, New Jersey, New York (except lake coastal area), Pennsylvania (except lake coastal area), Rhode Island, Vermont)*—26 Federal Plaza - Rm.3737, New York, NY 10278. Phone: (212)264-1300.

SOUTH ATLANTIC (*Florida (eastern half), Georgia, North Carolina, Puerto Rico, South Carolina, Virginia, West Virginia (eastern two-thirds)*—Bldg. 4D - Rm.211, 7737 Hampton Blvd., Norfolk, VA 23505. Phone: (757)441-6393.

WESTERN (*Alaska, Arizona, California, Hawaii, Idaho, Montana, Nevada, Oregon, Utah, Washington, Wyoming)*—201 Mission St. - Ste. 2200, San Francisco, CA 94105. Phone: (415)744-3125.

FIELD OFFICE

New York—U.S. Merchant Marine Academy, Kings Point, NY 11024-1699. Phone: (516)773-5000.

20.803 American War Risk Agency, 30 Broad St. - 7th fl., New York, NY 10004. Phone: (212)405-2814.

20.806 No field offices. Direct contact with HQ. See main entry. *Information for prospective students may be obtained from:*

- California Maritime Academy, Vallejo, CA 94591.
- Great Lakes Maritime Academy, Traverse City, MI 49684.
- Maine Maritime Academy, Castine, ME 04421.
- Massachusetts Maritime Academy, Buzzards Bay, MA 02532.
- State University of New York Maritime College, Ft. Schuyler, NY 10465.
- Texas State Maritime Program, Galveston, TX 77550.

20.807 thru 20.812 Listed under **20.801**.

OFFICE OF THE SECRETARY

20.900 Alaska Aviation Statistics Field Office, DOT, 801 B St. - Rm.506, Anchorage, AK 99501-23657. Phone: (907)271-5147.

DEPARTMENT OF THE TREASURY

INTERNAL REVENUE SERVICE

21.003 *Consult local phone directory under "U.S. Government - Internal Revenue Service."* Toll-free phones: Taxpayer Assistance Centers,(800)829-3676; Taxpayer Advocate's Help Line, (877)777-4778; hearing impaired, (800)829-4059.

21.004 *Contact:* District Director, Attn: Disclosure Officer, in local IRS offices or via **Internet:** "www.irs.gov/foia/article/0,,id=120681,00.html". *Consult local phone directory under "U.S. Government - Internal Revenue Service."*

APPALACHIAN REGIONAL COMMISSION

23.001 thru 23.011

STATE ALTERNATES OFFICES

Alabama—Director, Department of Economic and Community Affairs, 401 Adams Ave., Montgomery, AL 36104-5690. Phone: (334)242-8672.

Georgia—Director, Intergovernmental Relations, Office of the Governor, State Capital - Rm.131, Atlanta, GA 30334. Phone: (404)463-7775.

Kentucky—Community Holding Company, 220 Main St., P.O. Box 331, Inez, KY 41224. Phone: (606)298-3510.

Maryland—Director, Maryland Office of Planning, 301 W. Preston St. - Rm.1101, Baltimore, MD 21201. Phone: (410)767-4510.

Mississippi—Community Assistance, Mississippi Development Authority, Jackson, MS 39205-0849. Phone: (601)359-6622.

New York—Secretary of State, 41 State St., Albany, NY 12231. Phone: (518)486-9844.

North Carolina—Director, North Carolina Washington Office, 441 N. Capitol St. - Ste. 332, Washington DC 20001-1512. Phone: (202)624-5833.

Ohio—Director, Governor's Office of Appalachia, 77 S. High St. - 28th fl., Columbus, OH 43266-1001. Phone: (614)644-9228.

Pennsylvania—Deputy Secretary/Community Affairs and Development, Department of Community and Economic Development, Commonwealth Keystone Bldg. - 4th fl., 400 North St., Harrisburg, PA 17120. Phone: (717)787-3003.

South Carolina—Policy Advisor to the Governor, Office of the Governor, P.O. Box 12267, Columbia, SC 29211. Phone: (803)734-5166.

Tennessee—Commissioner, Department of Economic and Community Development, William R. Snodgrass Tennessee - 11th fl., 312 8th Ave. N., Nashville, TN 37243-0405. Phone: (615)741-1888.

Virginia—Department of Housing and Community Development, Jackson Center, 501 N. 2nd St., Richmond, VA 23219. Phone: (804)371-7002

West Virginia—Director/Community Development Division, West Virginia Development Office, State Capitol Complex - Bldg. 6 (Rm.553), Charleston, WV 25305. Phone: (304)558-4010.

OFFICE OF PERSONNEL MANAGEMENT

27.001 thru 27.006 *Contact should be made directly with personnel offices of federal agencies of interest, or through national job information sources listed under the Headquarters office.*

27.011 SERVICE CENTERS

REGION I *(Connecticut, Delaware, Maine, Maryland, Massachusetts, New Hampshire, New Jersey, New York, Pennsylvania, Rhode Island, Vermont)*—Green Federal Bldg. - Rm.3400, 600 Arch St., Philadelphia, PA 19106-1596. Phone: (215)597-7670.

(Puerto Rico)—Plaza Laz American Tower - Rm.1100, 525 Roosevelt Ave., Hato Rey, PR 00918. Phone: (809)766-5620.

REGION II *(Alabama, Arkansas, Mississippi, Tennessee)*—520 Wynn Dr. NW, Huntsville, AL 35816-3426. Phone: (205)837-1271.

(Florida, Georgia)—Russell Federal Bldg. - Ste. 956, 75 Spring St. SW, Atlanta, GA 30303-3109. Phone: (404)331-4588.

(North Carolina, South Carolina)—Somerset Park - Ste. 200, 4407 Bland Rd., Raleigh, NC 27609-6296. Phone: (919)790-2817.

(Virginia)—Federal Bldg. - Rm.500, 200 Granby St., Norfolk, VA 23510-1886. Phone: (804)441-3373.

REGION III *(Illinois)*—Kluzynski Federal Bldg. - DPN30-3, 230 S. Dearborn St., Chicago, IL 60604-1687. Phone: (312)353-6234.

(Indiana, Kentucky, Michigan, northern Ohio)—477 Michigan Ave. - Rm.594, Detroit, MI 48226-2574. Phone: (313)226-2095.

(Iowa, Kansas, Missouri, Nebraska)—Federal Bldg. - Rm.131, 601 E. 12th St., Kansas City, MO 64106-2826. Phone: (816)426-5706.

(Minnesota, North Dakota, South Dakota, Wisconsin)—Whipple Federal Bldg. - Rm.503, One Federal Dr., Ft. Snelling, MN 55111-4007. Phone: (612)725-3437.

(Ohio, Indiana, Kentucky, West Virginia)—U.S. Courthouse and Federal Bldg. - Rm.507, 200 W. 2nd St., Dayton, OH 45402-0001. Phone: (513)225-2576.

REGION IV *(Arizona, Colorado, Montana, New Mexico, Utah, Wyoming)*—12345 W. Alameda Pkwy. - Rm.316, P.O. Box 25167, Denver, CO 80225-0001. Phone: (303)969-6931.

(Arkansas, Louisiana, Nevada, Oklahoma, Texas)—8610 N. Broadway - Rm.305, San Antonio, TX 78217-0001. Phone: (210)805-2423.

REGION V *(California, Nevada)*—20 Howard St. - Rm.735, San Francisco, CA 94105-0001. Phone: (415)281-7074.

(Alaska, Hawaii (Honolulu and Island of Oahu), Pacific Overseas)—Federal Bldg., 300 Ala Moana Blvd., P.O. Box 50028, Honolulu, HI 96850-0001. Phone: (808)541-2795.

(Idaho, Oregon, Washington)—700 5th Ave. - Ste. 5950, Seattle, WA 98104-5012. Phone: (206)553-0870.

Students may obtain information from their college career guidance office, or via phone by contacting the *Career America Connection at (912)757-3000.* **Internet**: "www .opm.gov", under Presidential Management Intern Program. ID NUM = **27.013**

COMMISSION ON CIVIL RIGHTS

29.001 **REGIONAL OFFICES**

CENTRAL—Gateway Tower II - Ste. 908, 400 State Ave., Kansas City, KS 66101. Phones: (913)551-1400, TDD (913)551-1414.

EASTERN—624 9th St. NW - Ste. 500, Washington, DC 20425. Phones: (202)376-7533, TDD (202)376-8116.

MIDWESTERN—55 W. Monroe St. - Ste. 410, Chicago, IL 60603. Phones: (312)353-8311, TDD (312)353-8362.

ROCKY MOUNTAIN—1700 Broadway - Ste. 710, Denver, CO 80290. Phones: (303)866-1040, TDD (303)866-1049.

SOUTHERN—61 Alabama St. SW - Ste. 1840T, Atlanta, GA 30303. Phones: (404)562-7000, TDD (404)562-7004.

WESTERN—3660 Wilshire Blvd. - Ste. 810, Los Angeles, CA 90010. Phones: (213)894-3437, TDD (213)894-3435.

EQUAL EMPLOYMENT OPPORTUNITY COMMISSION

30.001 thru 30.011 **DISTRICT OFFICES**

Alabama—1130 22nd St. S. - Ste. 200, Birmingham, AL 35205-2397. Phone: (205)212-2100.

Arizona—Norwest Tower - Ste. 690, 3300 N. Central Ave., Phoenix, AZ 85012-2504. Phone: (602)640-5000.

California—255 E. Temple Ave. - 4th fl., Los Angeles, CA 90012. Phone: (213)894-5980.

- 350 Embarcadero - Ste. 500, San Francisco, CA 94105-1687. Phone: (415)625-5600.

Colorado—303 E. 17th Ave. - Ste. 510, Denver, CO 80203-9634. Phone: (303)866-1300.

District of Columbia—1801 L St. NW - Ste. 200, Washington, DC 20507. Phone: (202)275-7377.

Florida—One Biscayne Tower, 2 S. Biscayne Blvd. - Ste. 2700, Miami, FL 33131. Phone: (305)536-4491.

Georgia—100 Alabama St. - Ste. 4R30., Atlanta, GA 30303. Phone: (404)562-6930.

Illinois—500 W. Madison St. - Ste. 2800, Chicago, IL 60661. Phone: (312)353-2713.

Indiana—Federal Bldg. - Ste. 1900, 101 W. Ohio St., Indianapolis, IN 46204-4203. Phone: (317)226-7212.

Louisiana—701 Loyola Ave. - Ste. 600, New Orleans, LA 70113-9936. Phone: (504)589-2329.

Maryland—City Crescent Bldg. - 3rd fl., 10 S. Howard St., Baltimore, MD 21201. Phone: (410)962-3932.

Michigan—McNamara Federal Bldg. - Ste. 865, 477 Michigan Ave., Detroit, MI 48226-9704. Phone: (313)226-4600.

Missouri—1222 Spruce St. - Rm.8100, St. Louis, MO 63103. Phone: (314)539-7800.

30.001 thru 30.011 *(cont.)*

New York—33 Whitehall St. - 5th fl., New York, NY 10004-2112. Phone: (212)336-3620.

North Carolina—129 W. Trade St. - Ste. 400, Charlotte, NC 28202. Phone: (704)344-6682.

Ohio—Tower City, Skylight Office Tower - Ste. 850,, 1660 W. 2nd St., Cleveland, OH 44113-1454. Phone: (216)522-2001.

Pennsylvania—Bourse Bldg. - Ste. 400, 21 S. 5th St., Philadelphia, PA 19106-2515. Phone: (215)440-2623.

Tennessee—1407 Union Ave. - Ste. 621, Memphis, TN 38104. Phone: (901)544-0115.

Texas—207 S. Houston St. - 3rd fl., Dallas, TX 75202-4726. Phone: (214)253-2700.

- Leland Bldg. - 7th fl., 1919 Smith St., Houston, TX 77002. Phone: (713)209-3320.
- Mockingbird Plaza II - Ste. 200, 5410 Fredericksburg Rd., San Antonio, TX 78229-3555. Phone: (210)281-7600.

Washington—Federal Office Bldg. - Ste. 400, 909 1st Ave., Seattle, WA 98104-1061. Phone: (206)220-6883.

Wisconsin—Reuss Federal Plaza - Ste. 800, 310 W. Wisconsin Ave., Milwaukee, WI 53203-2292. Phone: (414)297-1111.

AREA OFFICES

Arkansas—820 Louisiana St. - Ste. 200, Little Rock, AR 72201. Phone: (501)324-5060.

California—410 B St. - Ste. 1550, San Diego, CA 92101. Phone: (619)557-7235.

Florida—501 E. Polk St. - Rm.1000, Tampa, FL 33602. Phone: (813)228-2310.

Kansas—400 State Ave. - Ste. 905, Kansas City, KS 66101. Phone: (913)551-5655.

Kentucky—U.S. Post Office and Courthouse - Rm.268, 600 Martin Luther King Jr. Place, Louisville, KY 40202. Phone: (502)582-6082.

Massachusetts—Kennedy Federal Bldg. - Rm.475, One Congress St., Boston, MA 02203-0506. Phone: (617)565-3200.

Minnesota—330 S. 2nd Ave. - Ste. 430, Minneapolis, MN 55401-2224. Phone: (612)335-4040.

Mississippi—100 W. Capitol St. - Ste. 207, Jackson, MS 39269. Phone: (601)965-4537.

New Jersey—One Newark Center - 21st fl., Newark, NJ 07102-5233. Phone: (973)645-6383.

New Mexico—505 Marquette Ave. NW - Ste. 900, Albuquerque, NM 87102-2189. Phone: (505)248-5201.

North Carolina—1309 Annapolis Dr., Raleigh, NC 27608-2129. Phone: (919)856-4064.

Ohio—Peck Federal Office Bldg. - Ste. 10-019, 550 Main St., Cincinnati, OH 45202-3122. Phone: (513)684-2851.

Oklahoma—Oklahoma Tower - Ste. 1350, 210 Park Ave., Oklahoma City, OK 73102-2265. Phone: (405)231-4911.

Pennsylvania—Federal Bldg. - Ste. 300, 1000 Liberty Ave., Pittsburgh, PA 15222-4187. Phone: (412)644-3444.

Puerto Rico—Plaza Las Americas - Ste. 120L, 525 F.D Rooseveldt Ave., San Juan PR 00918-8001. Phone: (787)771-1464.

Tennessee—50 Vantage Way - Ste. 202, Nashville, TN 37228. Phone: (615)736-5820.

Texas—300 E. Main St. - Ste. 500, El Paso, TX 79901. Phone: (915)534-6700.

Virginia—Federal Bldg. - Ste. 739, 200 Granby St., Norfolk, VA 23510. Phone: (757)441-3470.

- 830 E. Main St. - Ste. 600, Richmond, VA 23219. Phone: (804)771-2200.

LOCAL OFFICES

California—1265 W. Shaw Ave. - Ste. 103, Fresno, CA 93711. Phone: (559)487-5793.

- 1301 Clay St. - Ste. 1170-N, Oakland, CA 94612-5217. Phone: (510)637-3230.
- 96 N. 3rd St. - Ste. 200, San Jose, CA 95112. Phone: (408)291-7353.

Georgia—410 Mall Blvd. - Ste. G, Savannah, GA 31406-4821. Phone: (912)652-4234.

Hawaii—300 Ala Moana Blvd. - Ste. 7-127, P.O. Box 50082, Honolulu, HI 96850-0051. Phone: (808)541-3120.

New York—6 Fountain Plaza - Ste. 350, Buffalo, NY 14202. Phone: (716)551-4441.

North Carolina—2303 W. Meadowview Dr. - Ste. 201, Greensboro, NC 27407. Phone: (336)547-4188.

South Carolina—301 N. Main St. - Ste. 1402, Greenville, SC 29601. Phone: (803)241-4400.

FEDERAL COMMUNICATIONS COMMISSION

32.001 REGIONAL OFFICES

Regional Directors:

California—3777 Depot Rd. - Rm.420, Hayward, CA 94545-2756. Phone: (510)732-9046.

Illinois—Park Ridge Office Center - Rm.306, 1550 Northwest Hwy., Park Ridge, IL 60608-1460. Phone: (708)298-5405.

Missouri—Brywood Office Tower - Rm.320, 8800 E. 63rd St., Kansas City, MO 64133-4895. Phone: (816)353-9035.

DISTRICT OFFICES

Alaska—6721 Raspberry Rd., Anchorage, AK 99502-1896. Phone: (907)243-2153.

California—18000 Studebaker Rd. - Rm.660, Cerritos, CA 90701-3684. Phones: (310)809-2096, (310)865-0598.

- 3777 Depot Rd. - Rm.420, Hayward, CA 94545-2725. Phone: (510)732-9046.
- Interstate Office Park, 4542 Ruffner St. - Rm.370, San Diego, CA 92111-2216. Phone: (619)467-0549.

Colorado—165 S. Union Blvd. - Ste. 860, Lakewood, CO 80228-2213. Phones: (303)969-6497, 776-8026.

Florida—Rochester Bldg. - Rm.310, 8390 NW 53rd St., Miami, FL 33166-4668. Phone: (305)526-7420.

- 2203 N. Lois Ave. - Rm.1215, Tampa, FL 33607-2356. Phone: (813)348-1502.

Georgia—Koger Center-Gwinnett - Rm.320, 3575 Koger Blvd., Duluth, GA 30136-4958. Phone: (404)279-4621.

- Powder Springs, GA 30073-0085. Phones: (770)943-5420, 242-0165.

Hawaii—Waipahu, HI 96797-1030. Phone: (808)677-3318.

Illinois—Park Ridge Office Center - Rm.306, 1550 Northwest Hwy., Park Ridge, IL 60068-1460. Phones: (708)298-5401, -5402.

32.001 (cont.) **Louisiana**—800 W. Commerce St. - Rm.505, New Orleans, LA 70123-3333. Phone: (504)589-2095.

Maine—Belfast, ME 04915-0470. Phone: (207)338-4088.

Maryland—P.O. Box 250, Columbia, MD 21045-9998. Phone: (301)725-3474.

Massachusetts—One Batterymarch Park, Quincy, MA 02169-7495. Phone: (617)770-4023.

Michigan—P.O. Box 89, Allegan, MI 49010-9437. Phone: (616)673-2063.

- 24897 Hathaway St., Farmington Hills, MI 48335-1552. Phones: (810)471-5605; *recorded information,* 471-0052.

Minnesota—2025 Sloan Pl. - Ste. 31, Maplewood, MN 55117-2058. Phone: (612)774-5175.

Missouri—Brywood Office Tower - Rm.320, 8800 E. 63rd St., Kansas City, MO 64133-4895. Phone: (816)353-3773.

Nebraska—Grand Island, NE 68802-1588. Phone: (308)382-4296 (*recorded information at night*).

New York—1307 Federal Bldg., 111 W. Huron St., Buffalo, NY 14202-2398. Phone: *recorded information,* (716)551-4511.

- 201 Varick St., New York, NY 10014-4870. Phones: (212)620-3437, -3438, 660-3437; *recorded information,* (212)620-3435, 660-3436.

Oregon—1782 Federal Bldg., 1220 SW 3rd Ave., Portland, OR 97204-2898. Phones: (503)326-4114, -4115.

Puerto Rico—San Juan Field Office, Federal Bldg. - Rm.747, Hato Rey, PR 00918-1731. Phone: (809)766-5567.

Texas—Kingsville, TX 78363-0632. Phone: (512)592-2531.

Washington—11410 NE 122nd Way - Ste. 312, Kirkland, WA 98034-6927. Phone: (206)821-9037.

Equipment Construction and Installation Branch

3600 Hiram-Lithia Spring Rd. SW, P.O. Box 65, Powder Springs, GA 30073. Phone: (404)943-6425.

FOB Monitoring Assistance

Watch Officer, Signal Analysis Branch, Enforcement Division, 1919 M St. NW - Rm.749, Washington, DC 20554. Phone: (202)418-1180.

Field Operations Bureau

Chief, 1919 M St. NW - Rm.734, Washington, DC 20554-0001. Phone: (202)418-1100.

FEDERAL MARITIME COMMISSION

33.001 DISTRICT OFFICES

Los Angeles—Los Angeles Area Representative, U.S. Customs House Bldg. - Rm.320, 839 S. Beacon St., San Pedro, CA 90733-0230. Phones: (310)514-4905; FAX (310)514-3931.

Miami—South Florida Area Representative, Federal Maritime Commission, Hollywood, FL 33081-3609. Phones: (305)963-5362; FAX (305)963-5630.

New Orleans—New Orleans Area Representative, U.S. Customs House - Rm.309B, 423 Canal St., New Orleans, LA 70130. Phones: (504)589-6662; FAX (504)589-6663.

New York—New York Area Representative, JFK International Airport, Bldg. 75 - Rm.205-B, Jamaica, NY 11430. Phone: (718)553-2228; FAX (718)553-2229.

Seattle—Seattle Area Representative, c/o U.S. Customs, 7 S. Nevada St. - Ste. 100, Seattle, WA 98134. Phones: (206)553-0221; FAX (206)553-0222.

FEDERAL MEDIATION AND CONCILIATION SERVICE

34.001 REGIONAL OFFICES

MIDWESTERN—6161 Oak Tree Blvd. - Ste. 100, Independence, OH 44131. Phones: (216)522-4805; FAX (216)522-7541.

NORTHEASTERN—One Newark Center - 16th fl., Newark, NJ 17102. Phones: (973)645-2200; FAX (973)297-4860.

SOUTHERN—401 W. Peachtree St. NW - Ste. 472, Atlanta, GA 30308. Phones: (404)331-3995; FAX (404)331-4017.

UPPER MIDWESTERN—Broadway Place West - Ste. 3950, 1300 Godward St., Minneapolis, MN 55413. Phones: (612)370-3300; FAX (612)370-3104.

WESTERN—Westin Bldg. - Ste. 11000, 2001 6th Ave., Seattle, WA 98121. Phones: (206)553-5800: FAX (206)553-6653.

FEDERAL TRADE COMMISSION

36.001 REGIONAL OFFICES

California—10877 Wilshire Blvd. - Ste. 700, Los Angeles, CA 90024. Phone: (310)824-4343.

- 901 Market St. - Ste. 570, San Francisco, CA 94103. Phone: (415)848-5100.

Georgia—225 Peachtree St. NE - Ste. 1500, Atlanta, GA 30303. Phone: (404)656-1390.

Illinois—55 E. Monroe St. - Ste. 1860, Chicago, IL 60603-5713. Phone: (312)960-5634.

New York—One Bowling Green - Ste. 318, New York, NY 10004. Phone: (212)607-2829.

Ohio—Eaton Center - Ste. 200, 1111 Superior Ave., Cleveland, OH 44114-2507. Phone: (216)263-3455.

Texas—1999 Bryan St. - Ste. 2150, Dallas, TX 75201-6808. Phone: (214)979-9350.

Washington—915 2nd Ave. - Ste. 2896, Seattle, WA 98174. Phone: (206)220-6350.

GENERAL SERVICES ADMINISTRATION

39.002 Offices of Property Sales

NATIONAL CAPITOL REGION *(District of Columbia and the DC, Metropolitan area: In Maryland: Montgomery and Prince Georges counties. In Virginia: Arlington, Fairfax, Loudoun and Prince Williams counties)*—7th and D Sts. SW, Washington, DC 20407. Phone: (202)260-6438.

REGION I *(Connecticut, Illinois, Indiana, Maine, Massachusetts, Michigan, Minnesota, New Hampshire, New Jersey, New York, Ohio, Puerto Rico, Rhode Island, Vermont, Virgin Islands, Wisconsin)*—10 Causeway St., Boston, MA 02222. Phone:(617)565-5700.

REGION IV *(Alabama, Delaware, District of Columbia, Florida, Georgia, Kentucky, Maryland, Mississippi, North Carolina, Pennsylvania, South Carolina, Tennessee, Virginia, West Virginia)*—401 W. Peachtree St., Atlanta, GA 30365-2550. Phone: (404)331-5133.

REGION VII *(Arkansas, Colorado, Iowa, Kansas, Louisiana, Missouri, Montana, Nebraska, New Mexico, North Dakota, Oklahoma, South Dakota, Texas, Utah)*—819 Taylor St., Ft. Worth, TX 76102. Phone: (817)978-2331.

REGION IX *(American Samoa, Alaska, Arizona, California, Guam, Hawaii, Idaho, Oregon, Nevada, Trust Territory of the Pacific Islands, Washington)*—450 Golden Gate Ave. - 4th fl. E., San Francisco, CA 94102-3429. Phone: (415)522-3429.

39.003 Federal Supply Service/Property Management Offices

GREAT LAKES REGION *(Illinois, Indiana, Michigan, Minnesota, Ohio, Wisconsin)*—230 S. Dearborn St. - Rm.3430, (MS 34-6),Chicago, IL 60604-1696. Phone: (312)886-8996.

GREATER SOUTHWEST REGION *(Arkansas, Louisiana, New Mexico, Oklahoma, Texas)*—819 Taylor St. - Rm.3A05, Ft. Worth, TX 76102-6105. Phone: (817)978-3794.

HEARTLAND REGION *(Iowa, Kansas, Missouri, Nebraska)*—1500 E. Bannister Rd. - Rm.1102, Kansas City, MO 64131. Phone: (816)823-3700.

MID-ATLANTIC REGION *(Delaware, Maryland, Virginia, Pennsylvania, West Virginia (except those areas in the National Capital Region))*—Strawbridge's Bldg. - 10th fl., 20 N. 8th St., Philadelphia, PA 19107-3191. Phone: (215)446-5065.

NATIONAL CAPITAL REGION *(District of Columbia, the counties of Montgomery and Prince Georges in Maryland, the cities of Alexandria, Fairfax, and Falls Church and the counties of Arlington, Fairfax, Loudoun, and Prince William in Virginia)*—470 L'Enfant Plaza East SW - Ste. 8100, Washington, DC 20407. Phone: (202)619-8975.

- Central Office, GSA-FSS, 1901 S. Bell St. - Rm.804, Arlington, VA 22202. Phone: (703)605-5610.

NEW ENGLAND REGION *(Connecticut, Maine, Massachusetts, New Hampshire, Rhode Island, Vermont)*—O'Neill Jr. Federal Bldg. - Rm.347 (3rd fl.), 10 Causeway St., Boston, MA 02222. Phone: (617)565-7319.

NORTHEAST AND CARIBBEAN REGION *(New Jersey, New York, Puerto Rico, U.S. Virgin Islands)*—26 Federal Plaza - Rm.20-112, New York, NY 10278. Phone: (212)264-3300.

NORTHWEST/ARCTIC REGION *(Alaska, Idaho, Oregon, Washington)*—400 15th St. SW, Auburn, WA 98001-6599. Phone: (253)931-7934.

PACIFIC RIM REGION *(American Samoa, Arizona, California, Guam, Hawaii, Nevada, Northern Mariana Islands)*—450 Golden Gate Ave., San Francisco, CA 94102-3434. Phone: (415)522-3029.

ROCKY MOUNTAIN REGION *(Colorado, Montana, North Dakota, South Dakota, Utah, Wyoming)*—Denver Federal Center - Bldg. 41, P.O. Box 25506, Denver, CO 80225-0506. Phone: (303)236-7700.

SOUTHEAST SUNBELT REGION *(Alabama, Florida, Georgia, Kentucky, Mississippi, North Carolina, South Carolina, Tennessee)*—401 W. Peachtree St. - Rm.2600, Atlanta, GA 30365. Phone: (404)331-0040.

39.007 *Contact offices listed under* **39.003**, *or for DOD surplus property, contact:* Defense Reutilization and Marketing Service, National Sales Office, 74 Washington Ave. N, Battle Creek, MI 49017-3092. Phone: (no number provided). **Internet:** "www.gsa.gov".

GOVERNMENT PRINTING OFFICE

40.001 *No field offices. There are 1,270 depository libraries in the U.S., with GPO publications on file; consult local phone directory or local librarian for the nearest depository library.*

40.002 **GPO Bookstore** - Direct purchases of publications carried in stock may be made from the following GPO bookstores or via **Internet:** *(online bookstore,)* "www.bookstore.gpo.gov".

District of Columbia—Government Printing Office, 710 N. Capitol St. NW, Washington, DC 20401. Phone: (202)512-0132.

Maryland—Retail Sales Branch, 8660 Cherry Lane, Laurel, MD 20707. Phone: (301)953-7974.

LIBRARY OF CONGRESS

42.001 *There are 57 regional and 77 subregional libraries in the U.S. Each state has an agency that distributes talking book machines. Local public libraries have information available. Consult local phone directories. Otherwise, contact headquarters office.*

NATIONAL AERONAUTICS AND SPACE ADMINISTRATION

43.001 FIELD CENTERS

Education Officer:

Alabama—Marshall Space Flight Center, Huntsville, AL 35812.

California—Ames Research Center, Moffett Field, CA 94035.

- Dryden Flight Research Center, Edwards, CA 93523.

43.001 (cont.) **Florida**—John F. Kennedy Space Center, Kennedy Space Center, FL 32899.

Maryland—Goddard Space Flight Center, Greenbelt, MD 20771.

Mississippi—Stennis Space Center, Stennis Space Center, MS 39529.

Ohio—Glenn Research Center, 21000 Brookpark Rd., Cleveland, Ohio 44135.

Texas—Johnson Space Center, Houston, TX 77058.

Virginia—Langley Research Center, Langley Station, Hampton, VA 23365.

43.002 TECHNOLOGY UTILIZATION CENTERS

Technology Transfer Officer:

Alabama—Marshall Space Flight Center, (MS CD30), Marshall Space Flight Center, AL 35812. Phone: (205)544-4266.

California—Ames Research Center, (MS 202A-3), Moffett Field, CA 94035-1000. Phone: (650)604-1754.

- Dryden Flight Research Center, (MS 4839), Edwards, CA 93253-0273. Phone: (661)276-3689.
- NASA Management Office-JPL, (MS 301-350), 4800 Oak Grove Dr., Pasadena, CA 91109-8099. Phone: (818)354-3480.

District of Columbia—NASA Headquarters, Office of Exploration Systems, Washington, DC 20546-0001. Phone: (202)358-2320.

Florida—Kennedy Space Center, (MS YA-C1), Kennedy Space Center, FL 32899-0001. Phone: (407)867-6624.

Maryland—Goddard Space Flight Center, (MS 504), Greenbelt, MD 20771-0001. Phone: (301)286-5810.

Mississippi—Stennis Space Center, (MS JAOO), Stennis Space Center, MS 39529-6000. Phone: (601)688-1914.

Ohio—Glenn Research Center, (MS 3-7), 21000 Brookpark Rd., Cleveland, OH 44135. Phone: (216)433-5398.

Texas—Johnson Space Center, (MS HA), 2101 NASA Road 1, Houston, TX 77058-3696. Phone: (281)483-0474.

Virginia—Langley Research Center, (MS 118), 11 Langley Blvd., Hampton, VA 23681-0001. Phone: (757)864-6005.

REGIONAL TECHNOLOGY TRANSFER CENTERS

Persons or organizations desiring comprehensive technical information may contact the Central Network at (800)642-2872) or regional affiliates, following:

FAR WEST—3716 S. Hope St. - Ste. 200, Los Angeles, CA 90007-4344. Phone: (213)743-2353.

- Montana State University Techlink Center - Ste. A, 900 Technology Blvd., Bozeman, MT 59718. Phone: (406)994-7700.

MID-ATLANTIC—Technology Commercialization Center, Inc., 12050 Jefferson Ave. - Ste. 350, Newport News, VA 23606. Phone: (757)269-0025.

- Research Triangle Institute Center for Technology Applications, P.O. Box 12194, Research Triangle Park, NC 27709. Phone: (919)541-7205.

MID-CONTINENT—Texas Engineering Extension Service, Texas A and M University System, 301 Tarrow, College Station, TX 77843-8000. Phone: (979)845-8762.

MIDWEST—Great Lakes Industrial Technology Center, Battelle Memorial Institute, 25000 Great Northern Corporate Center - Ste. 260, Cleveland, OH 44070-5310. Phone: (440)734-0094.

NATIONAL RTTC—Wheeling Jesuit College, 316 Washington Ave., Wheeling, WV 26003. Phone: (800)678-6882.

NORTHEAST—Center for Technology Commercialization, Westborough, MA 01581. Phone: (508)870-0042.

SOUTHEAST—Georgia Tech Research Corp., Georgia Institute of Technology, Office of Sponsored Programs, Atlanta, GA 30332. Phone: (404)894-6786.

NATIONAL CREDIT UNION ADMINISTRATION

44.001 REGIONAL OFFICES

Arizona—1230 W. Washington St. - Ste. 301, Tempe, AZ 85281. Phone: (602)302-6000.

Georgia—7000 Central Pkwy. - Ste. 1600, Atlanta, GA 30328. Phone: (678)443-3000.

New York—9 Washington Square, Washington Ave. Extension, Albany, NY 12205. Phone: (518)862-7400.

Texas—4807 Spicewood Springs Rd. - Ste. 5200, Austin, TX 78759-8490. Phone: (512)342-5600.

Virginia—1775 Duke St. - Ste. 4206, Alexandria, VA 22314-3437. Phone: (703)519-6400.

Asset Management Assistance Center

4807 Spicewood Springs Rd. - Ste. 5100, Austin, TX 78759-8490. Phone: (512)231-7900.

NATIONAL LABOR RELATIONS BOARD

46.001 REGIONAL, SUBREGIONAL, AND RESIDENT OFFICES

Information Officer:

Alabama—Massey Bldg. - 3rd fl., 1900 3rd Ave., Birmingham, AL 35203-3502. Phone: (205)731-1492.

Alaska—Federal Office Bldg. - Ste. 21, 222 W. 7th Ave., Anchorage, AK 99513-3546. Phone: (907)271-5015.

Arizona—234 N. Central Ave. - Ste. 440, Phoenix, AZ 85004-2212. Phone: (602)379-3361.

Arkansas—425 W. Capitol St. - Ste. 375, Little Rock, AR 72201-3489. Phone: (501)324-6311.

California—888 Figueroa St. - 9th fl., Los Angeles, CA 90017-5455. Phone: (213)894-5200.

- 11150 W. Olympic Blvd. - Ste. 700, Los Angeles, CA 90064-1824. Phone: (310)575-7351.

46.001 *(cont.)*

- 1301 Day St. - Rm.300-N, Oakland, CA 94612-5211. Phone: (510)637-3000.
- 555 W. Beech St. - Ste. 418, San Diego, CA 92101-2939. Phone: (619)557-6184.
- 901 Market St. - Ste. 400, San Francisco, CA 94103-1735. Phone: (415)356-5130.

Colorado—North Tower - 7th fl., 600 17th St., Denver, CO 80202-5433. Phone: (303)844-3551.

Connecticut—One Commercial Plaza - 21st fl., Hartford, CT 06103-3503. Phone: (203)240-3522.

District of Columbia—1099 14th St. NW - Ste. 5530, Washington, DC 20570-0001. Phone: (202)208-3000.

Florida—550 Water St. - Rm.340, Jacksonville, FL 32202-5177. Phone: (904)232-3768.

- Federal Bldg. - Rm.1320, 51 SW 1st Ave., Miami, FL 33130-1608. Phone: (305)536-5391.
- 201 E. Kennedy Blvd. - Ste. 530, Tampa, FL 33602-5824. Phone: (813)228-2641.

Georgia—233 Peachtree St. NE - Ste. 1000, Atlanta, GA 30303-1504. Phone: (404)331-2896.

Hawaii—300 Ala Moana Blvd. - Rm.7318, Honolulu, HI 96850-4980. Phone: (808)541-2814.

Illinois—200 W. Adams St. - Ste. 800, Chicago, IL 60606-5208. Phone: (312)353-7570.

- 300 Hamilton Blvd. - Ste. 200, Peoria, IL 61602-1246. Phone: (309)671-7080.

Indiana—575 N. Pennsylvania St. - Rm.238, Indianapolis, IN 46204-1577. Phone: (317)226-7382.

Iowa—210 Walnut St. - Ste. 439, Des Moines, IA 50309-2103. Phone: (515)284-4391.

Kansas—8600 Farley St. - Ste. 100, Overland Park, KS 66212-4677. Phone: (913)967-3000.

Louisiana—1515 Poydras St. - Rm.610, New Orleans, LA 70112-3723. Phone: (504)589-6361.

Maryland—103 S. Gay St. - 8th fl., Baltimore, MD 21202-4061. Phone: (410)962-2822.

Massachusetts—10 Causeway, St. - 6th fl., Boston, MA 02222-1072. Phone: (617)565-6700.

Michigan—477 Michigan Ave. - Rm.300, Detroit, MI 48226-2569. Phone: (313)226-3200.

- 82 Ionia NW - Rm.330, Grand Rapids, MI 49503-3022. Phone: (616)456-2679.

Minnesota—330 2nd Ave. S. - Ste. 790, Minneapolis, MN 55401-2221. Phone: (612)348-1757.

Missouri—611 N. 10th St. - Ste. 400, St. Louis, MO 63101-1214. Phone: (314)425-4167.

Nevada—600 Las Vegas Blvd. S. - Ste. 400, Las Vegas, NV 89101-6637. Phone: (702)388-6416.

New Jersey—20 Washington Place - 5th fl., Newark, NJ 07102-3110. Phone: (973)645-2100.

New Mexico—505 Marquette Ave. NW - Rm.1820, Albuquerque, NM 87102-2181. Phone: (505)248-5125.

New York—Clinton Ave. at N. Pearl St. - Rm.342, Albany, NY 12207-2350. Phone: (518)431-4156.

- Jay St. and Myrtle Ave. - 10th fl., Brooklyn, NY 11201-4201. Phone: (718)330-7713.
- 111 W. Huron St. - Rm.901, Buffalo, NY 14202-2387. Phone: (716)551-4931.
- 26 Federal Plaza - Rm.3614, New York, NY 10278-0104. Phone: (212)264-0300.

North Carolina—4035 University Pkwy. - Ste. 200, Winston-Salem, NC 27106-3325. Phone: (919)631-5201.

Ohio—550 Main St. - Rm.3003, Cincinnati, OH 45202-3271. Phone: (513)684-3686.

- 1240 E. 9th St. - Rm.1695, Cleveland, OH 44199-2086. Phone: (216)522-3715.

Oklahoma—224 S. Boulder Ave. - Rm.318, Tulsa, OK 74103-4214. Phone: (918)581-7951.

Oregon—601 SW 2nd Ave. - Ste. 1910, Portland, OR 97204. Phone: (503)326-3085.

Pennsylvania—615 Chestnut St. - 7th fl., Philadelphia, PA 19016-4404. Phone: (215)597-7601.

- 1000 Liberty Ave. - Rm.1501, Pittsburgh, PA 15222-4173. Phone: (412)395-4400.

Puerto Rico—525 F.D. Roosevelt Ave. - Ste. 1002, Hato Rey, PR 00918-1002. Phone: (809)766-5347.

Tennessee—1407 Union Ave. - Ste. 800, Memphis, TN 38104-3627. Phone: (901)544-0018.

- 810 Broadway - Ste. 320., Nashville, TN 37203-3859. Phone: (615)736-5921.

Texas—700 E. San Antonio Ave. - Ste. C403, El Paso, TX 79901-7020. Phone: (915)534-6434.

- 819 Taylor St. - Rm.8-A-24, Ft. Worth, TX 76102-6178. Phone: (817)978-2921.
- 1919 Smith St. - Ste. 1545, Houston, TX 77002-2649. Phone: (713)209-4888.
- Travis Park Plaza Bldg. - Ste. 705, 711 Navarro St., San Antonio, TX 78205-1711. Phone: (210)472-6140.

Washington—915 2nd Ave. - Rm.2948, Seattle, WA 98174-1078. Phone: (206)220-6300.

Wisconsin—310 W. Wisconsin Ave. - Ste. 700, Milwaukee, WI 53203-2211. Phone: (414)297-3861.

RAILROAD RETIREMENT BOARD

57.001 REGIONAL OFFICES

Colorado—1999 Broadway - Ste. 3300 (Box 7), Denver CO 80202-5737. Phone: (303)844-0800.

Georgia—401 W. Peachtree St. - Ste. 1703, Atlanta, GA 30308-3519. Phone: (404)331-2691.

Pennsylvania—NIX Federal Bldg. - Ste. 304, 900 Market St., Philadelphia, PA 19107-4228. Phone: (215)597-2647.

SECURITIES AND EXCHANGE COMMISSION

58.001 REGIONAL OFFICES

California—5670 Wilshire Blvd. - 11th fl., Los Angeles, CA 90036-3648. Phone: (213)965-3998.

58.00 (cont.) **Colorado**—1801 California St. - Ste. 4800, Denver, CO 80202-2648. Phone: (303)844-1000.

Florida—801 Brickell Ave. - Ste. 1800, Miami, FL 33131. Phone: (305)982-6300.

Illinois—175 W. Jackson Blvd. - Ste. 900, Chicago, IL 60604. Phone: (312)353-7390.

New York—The Woolworth Bldg., 233 Broadway, New York, NY 10279. Phone: (646)428-1500.

DISTRICT OFFICES

California—44 Montgomery St. - Ste. 2600, San Francisco, CA 94104. Phone: (415)705-2500.

Georgia—3475 Lenox Rd. NE - Ste. 1000, Atlanta, GA 30326-1232. Phone: (404)842-7600.

Massachusetts—73 Tremont St., Boston, MA 02108-3912. Phone: (617)573-8900.

Pennsylvania—Mellon Independence Center, 701 Market St., Philadelphia, PA 19106-1532. Phone: (215)597-3100.

Texas—801 Cherry St. - Ste. 800, Ft. Worth, TX 76102. Phone: (817)978-6465.

Utah—15 W. South Temple St. - Ste. 1800, Salt Lake City, UT. 84101. Phone: (801)524-5796.

SMALL BUSINESS ADMINISTRATION

59.002 DISASTER AREA OFFICES

AREA 1 (Regions I and II)—130 S. Elmwood St., Buffalo, NY 14202-1192. Phone: (716)843-4100.

AREA 2 (Regions III, IV, and V)—One Baltimore Place - Ste. 300, Atlanta, GA 30308. Phone: (404)347-3771.

AREA 3 (Regions VI and VII)—14925 Kingsport Rd., Ft. Worth, TX 76155-2243. Phone: (817)868-2300.

AREA 4 (Regions VIII, IX, and X)—6501 Sylvan Rd., Citrus Heights, CA 95610. Phone: (916)735-1500.

59.005 thru 59.007 REGIONAL AND DISTRICT OFFICES

REGION I *(Connecticut, Maine, Massachusetts, New Hampshire, Rhode Island, Vermont)*—10 Causeway St. - Ste. 812, Boston, MA 02222. Phone: (617)565-8415.

Connecticut—Federal Bldg., 330 Main St. - 2nd fl., Hartford, CT 06106. Phone: (203)240-4700.

Maine—Federal Bldg. - Rm.512, 68 Sewall St., Augusta, ME 04330. Phone: (207)622-8274, ext.386.

Massachusetts—10 Causeway St. - Rm.265, Boston, MA 02222-1093. Phone: (617)565-5561.

- One Federal St. - Bldg.101-R, Springfield, MA 01105. Phone: (413)785-0484.

New Hampshire—55 Pleasant St. - Ste. 3101, Concord, NH 03301-1257. Phone: (603)225-1400.

Rhode Island—380 Westminster Mall - 5th fl., Providence, RI 02903. Phone: (401)528-4561.

Vermont—Federal Bldg. - Rm.205, 87 State St., Montpelier, VT 05602. Phone: (802)828-4422.

REGION II *(New Jersey, New York, Puerto Rico, Virgin Islands)*—26 Federal Plaza - Ste. 3108, New York, NY 10278. Phone: (212)264-1450.

New Jersey—2 Gateway Center - 15th fl., Newark, NJ 07102. Phone: (973)645-3680.

New York—Federal Bldg. - Rm.1311, 111 W. Huron St., Buffalo, NY 14202. Phone: (716)551-4305.

- 333 E. Water St. - 4th fl., Elmira, NY 14901. Phone: (607)734-1571.
- 35 Pinelawn Rd. - Ste. 207W, Melville, NY 11747. Phone: (516)454-0750.
- 26 Federal Plaza - Rm.31-00, New York, NY 10278. Phone: (212)264-1318.
- 100 State St. - Ste. 410, Rochester, NY 14614. Phone: (716)263-6700.
- 401 S. Salina St. - 5th fl., Syracuse, NY 13202. Phone: (315)471-9393.

Puerto Rico and U.S. Virgin Islands—Degatau Federal Bldg. - Ste. 201, 252 Ponce DeLeon Blvd., San Juan, PR 00918. Phone: (787)766-5002.

REGION III *(Delaware, District of Columbia, Maryland, Pennsylvania, Virginia, West Virginia)*—900 Market St. - 5th fl., Philadelphia, PA 19107. Phone: (215)580-2SBA.

Delaware Branch Office—1007 N. Orange St. - Ste. 1120, Wilmington, DE 19801. Phone: (302)573-6294.

District of Columbia—740 15th St. - 3rd fl., Washington, DC 20005. Phone: (202)272-0340.

Maryland—10 S. Howard St. - Ste. 6220, Baltimore, MD 21201-2565. Phone: (410)962-6195.

Pennsylvania—100 Chestnut St. - Rm.107, Harrisburg, PA 17101. Phone: (717)782-3840.

- 900 Market St. - 5th fl., Philadelphia, PA 19406. Phone: (215)580-2700.
- 411 7th Ave. - Ste. 1450, Pittsburgh, PA 15219. Phone: (412)395-6560.
- 7 N. Wilkes-Barre Blvd., Wilkes-Barre, PA 18702. Phone: (570)826-6497.

Virginia—400 N. 8th St. - Ste. 1150, Richmond, VA 23240-0126. Phone: (804)771-2400.

West Virginia—320 W. Pike St., Clarksburg, WV 26301. Phone: (304)623-5631.

REGION IV *(Alabama, Florida, Georgia, Kentucky, Mississippi, North Carolina, South Carolina, Tennessee)*—1720 Peachtree St. NW - Ste. 496, Atlanta, GA 30309-2482. Phone: (404)347-4999.

Alabama—801 Tom Martin Dr. - Ste. 201, Birmingham, AL 35203-2398. Phone: (205)290-7101.

Florida—7825 Baymeadows Way - Ste. 100-B, Jacksonville, FL 32256-7504. Phone: (904)443-1900.

- 100 S. Biscayne Blvd. - 7th fl., Miami FL 33131. Phone: (305)536-5521.

Georgia—233 Peachtree St., NE, Atlanta, GA 30303. Phone: (404)331-0100.

Kentucky—Federal Bldg. - Rm.188, 600 Martin Luther King Jr. Pl., Louisville, KY 40202. Phone: (502)582-5971.

Mississippi—2510 14th St. - Ste. 101, Gulfport, MS 39501. Phone: (228)863-4449.

- 210 E. Capital St. - 210E, Jackson, MS 39201. Phone: (601)965-4378.

North Carolina—6302 Fairview Rd. - Ste. 300, Charlotte, NC 28210-2227. Phone: (704)344-6563.

South Carolina—1835 Assembly St. - Rm.358, Columbia, SC 29201. Phone: (803)765-5377.

Tennessee—50 Vantage Way - Ste. 201, Nashville, TN 37228-1500. Phone: (615)736-5850.

59.005 thru 59.007 *(cont.)*

REGION V *(Illinois, Indiana, Michigan, Minnesota, Ohio, Wisconsin)*—Federal Bldg. - Ste. 1250, 500 W. Madison St., Chicago, IL 60661-2511. Phone: (312)353-4493.

Illinois—500 W. Madison St. - Rm.1250, Chicago, IL 60661-2511. Phone: (312)353-4508.

- 511 W. Capitol Ave. - Ste. 302, Springfield, IL 62704. Phone: (217)492-4416.

Indiana—429 N. Pennsylvania St. - Ste. 100, Indianapolis, IN 46204-1873. Phone: (317)226-7272.

Minnesota—100 N. 6th St. - Ste. 210C, Minneapolis, MN 55403-1563. Phone: (612)370-2306.

Michigan—477 Michigan Ave. - Rm.515, Detroit, MI 48226. Phone: (313)226-7204.

- 501 S. Front St., Marquette, MI 49885. Phone: (906)225-1108.

Ohio—1350 Euclid St. - Ste. 211, Cleveland, OH 44115. Phone: (216)522-4180.

- 525 Vine St. - Ste. 870, Cincinnati, OH 45202. Phone: (513)684-2814.
- 2 Nationwide Plaza - Ste. 1400, Columbus, OH 43215-2592. Phone: (614)469-6860.

Wisconsin—740 Regent St. - Ste. 100, Madison, WI 53715. Phone: (608)264-5263.

- 310 W. Wisconsin Ave. - Ste. 400, Milwaukee, WI 53202. Phone: (414)297-3941.

REGION VI *(Arkansas, Louisiana, New Mexico, Oklahoma, Texas)*—4300 Amon Carter Blvd. - Ste. 108, Ft. Worth, TX 76155. Phone: (817)684-5581.

Arkansas—2120 Riverfront Dr. - Ste. 100, Little Rock, AR 72202. Phone: (501)324-5871.

Louisiana—365 Canal St. - Ste. 2250, New Orleans, LA 70130. Phone: (504)589-6685.

New Mexico—625 Silver Ave. SW, - Ste. 320, Albuquerque, NM 87102. Phone: (505)346-7909.

Oklahoma—301 N. 6th St. - Ste. 116, Oklahoma City, OK 73102. Phone: (405)609-8000.

Texas—3649 Leopard St. - Ste. 411, Corpus Christi, TX 78408. Phone: (361)879-0017.

- 10737 Gateway West - Ste. 320, El Paso, TX 79935. Phone: (915)633-7001.
- 4300 Amon Center Blvd. - Ste. 114, Ft. Worth, TX 76155. Phone: (817)885-6500.
- Lower Rio Grande Valley District Office, 222 E. Van Buren St. - Rm.500, Harlingen, TX 78550. Phone: (956)427-8533.
- 8701 S. Gessner Dr. - Ste. 1200, Houston, TX 77074. Phone: (713)773-6500.
- 1205 Texas Ave. - Rm.408, Lubbock, TX 79401-2693. Phone: (806)472-7462.
- 7319 San Pedro Bldg.2 - Ste. 200, San Antonio, TX 78232. Phone: (210)403-5904.

REGION VII *(Iowa, Kansas, Missouri, Nebraska)*—323 W. 8th St. - Ste. 307, Kansas City, MO 64105-1500. Phone: (816)374-6380.

Iowa—215 4th Ave. SE - Ste. 200, Cedar Rapids, IA 52401-1806. Phone: (319)362-6405.

- New Federal Bldg. - Rm.749, 210 Walnut St., Des Moines, IA 50309. Phone: (515)284-4026.

Kansas—271 W. 3rd St. N. - Ste. 2500, Wichita, KS 67202. Phone: (316)269-6566.

Missouri—323 W. 8th St. - Ste. 501, Kansas City, MO 64105. Phone: (816)374-6708.

- 830 E. Primrose - Ste. 101, Springfield, MO 65807. Phone: (417)890-8501.
- 200 N. Broadway - Ste. 1500, St. Louis, MO 63102. Phone: (314)539-6600.

Nebraska—11145 Mill Valley Rd., Omaha, NE 68154. Phone: (402)221-4691.

REGION VIII *(Colorado, Montana, North Dakota, South Dakota, Utah, Wyoming)*—721 19th St. - Ste. 400, Denver, CO 80202-2599. Phone: (303)844-0500.

Colorado—721 19th St. - Rm.426, Denver, CO 80202-2599. Phone: (303)844-2607.

Montana—301 S. Park Ave. - Rm.334, Helena, MT 59626. Phone: (406)441-1081.

North Dakota—Federal Bldg. - Rm.219, 657 2nd Ave. N., Fargo, ND 58108-3086. Phone: (701)239-5131.

South Dakota—110 S. Phillips Ave. - Ste. 200, Sioux Falls, SD 57104-6727. Phone: (605)330-4243.

Utah—Federal Bldg. - Rm.2231, 125 S. State St., Salt Lake City, UT 84138-1195. Phone: (801)524-5804.

Wyoming—Federal Bldg. - Rm.4001, 100 E. "B" St., Casper, WY 82602-2839. Phone: (307)261-6500.

REGION IX *(Arizona, California, Hawaii, Nevada, Pacific Islands)*—330 N. Brand Blvd. - Ste. 1200, Glendale, CA 91203. Phone: (818)552-3436.

Arizona—2828 N. Central Ave. - Ste. 800, Phoenix, AZ 85004-1093. Phone: (602)745-7200.

California—2719 N. Air Fresno Dr. - Ste. 200, Fresno, CA 93727-1547. Phone: (559)487-5791.

- 330 N. Brand Blvd. - Ste. 1200, Glendale, CA 91203-2304. Phone: (818)552-3210.
- 650 Capital Mall - Ste. 7-5000, Sacramento, CA 95814. Phone: (916)930-3700.
- 500 W. C St. - Ste. 550, San Diego, CA 92101-3540. Phone: (619)557-7250.
- 455 Market St. - 6th fl., San Francisco, CA 94105. Phone: (415)744-6801.
- 200 W. Santa Ana Blvd. - Ste. 700, Santa Ana, CA 92701. Phone: (714)550-7420.

Hawaii—300 Ala Moana Blvd. - Rm.2-235, Honolulu, HI 96850-4981. Phone: (808)541-2990.

Guam—400 Route 8 - Ste. 302, Hagatna, GU 96910-2003. Phone: (671)471-7419.

Nevada—400 S. 4th St. - Ste. 250, Las Vegas, NV 89101. Phone: (702)388-6611.

REGION X *(Alaska, Idaho, Oregon, Washington)*—1200 6th Ave. - Ste. 1805, Seattle, WA 98101-1128. Phone: (206)553-5676.

Alaska—222 W. 8th Ave. - Rm.A36, Anchorage, AK 99513-7559. Phone: (907)271-4022.

Idaho—1020 Main St. - Ste. 290, Boise, ID 83702-5745. Phone: (208)334-1696.

Oregon—1515 SW 5th Ave. - Ste. 1050, Portland, OR 97201-5494. Phone: (503)326-2682.

Washington—1200 6th Ave. - Ste. 1700, Seattle, WA 98101-1128. Phone: (206)553-7310.

- 801 W. Riverside Ave. - Ste. 200., Spokane, WA 99201-0901. Phone: (509)353-2809.

59.008 Listed under **59.002**

59.009 thru 59.046 Listed under **59.005**

59.054 U.S Export Assistance Service Centers

California—3300 Irvine Ave. - #307, Newport Beach, CA 92660. Phone: (949)660-1688, ext.307.

Colorado—1625 Broadway Ave. - Ste. 680, Denver, CO 80202. Phone: (303)844-6622, ext.18.

Florida—5835 Blue Lagoon Dr. - Ste. 203, Miami, FL 33126. Phone: (305)526-7429, ext.21.

Georgia—75 5th St. NW - Ste. 1055, Atlanta, GA 30308. Phone: (404)897-6090.

Illinois—55 W. Monroe St. - Ste. 2440, Chicago, IL 60603. Phone: (312)353-8065.

Maryland—401 E. Pratt St. - Ste. 2432, Baltimore, MD 21202. Phone: (410)962-4539.

59.054 (cont.) **Massachusetts**—World Trade Center - Ste. 307, Boston, MA 02210. Phone: (617)424-5953.

Michigan—211 W. Fort St. - Ste. 1104, Detroit, MI 48226. Phone: (313)226-3670.

Minnesota—Plaza VSS Tower - Ste. 2240, 45 S. 7th St., Minneapolis, MN 55403. Phone: (612)348-1642.

Missouri—8235 Forsyth Blvd. - Ste. 520, St. Louis, MO 63105. Phone: (314)425-3304.

North Carolina—521 E. Morehead St. - Ste. 435, Charlotte, NC 28202. Phone: (704)333-2130.

Ohio—600 Superior Ave. - Ste. 700, Cleveland, OH 44114. Phone: (216)522-4731.

Oregon—One World Trade Center - Ste. 242, 121 SW Salmon St., Portland, OR 97204. Phone: (503)326-5498.

Pennsylvania—The Curtis Center - Ste. 580 W., 601 Walnut St., Philadelphia, PA 19106. Phone: (215)597-6101.

Texas—2000 E. Lamar Blvd. - Ste. 430, Arlington, TX 76006. Phone: (817)310-3749.

Washington—4th and Vine Blvd., 2601 4th Ave. - Ste. 320, Seattle, WA 98121. Phone: (206)553-0051.

DEPARTMENT OF VETERANS AFFAIRS

VETERANS HEALTH ADMINISTRATION

64.007 thru 64.026 VETERANS MEDICAL FACILITIES

Alabama—700 S. 19th St., Birmingham, AL 35233. Phone: (205)933-8101.

- 215 Perry Hill Rd., Montgomery, AL 36109-3798. Phone: (334)272-4670.
- Tuscaloosa, AL 35404. Phone: (205)554-2000.
- Tuskegee, AL 36083. Phone: (304)727-0550.

Alaska—Medical/Regional Office Center, 235 E. 8th Ave., Anchorage, AK 99508-2989. Phone: (907)257-4700.

Arizona—7th St. at Indian School Rd., Phoenix, AZ 85012. Phone: (602)277-5551.

- Prescott, AZ 86313-5000. Phone: (520)445-4860.
- Tucson, AZ 85723-0001. Phone: (520)792-1450.

Arkansas—Fayetteville, AR 72703. Phone: (501)443-4301.

- 300 E. Roosevelt Rd., Little Rock, AR 72205. Phone: (501)660-1202.

California—2615 E. Clinton Ave., Fresno, CA 93703-2223. Phone: (209)225-6100.

- Livermore, CA 94550. Phone: (510)447-2560.
- 11201 Benton St., Loma Linda, CA 90822-5201. Phone: (909)825-7084.
- 5901 E. 7th St., Long Beach, CA 90822-5201. Phone: (310)494-2611.
- 3801 Miranda Ave., Palo Alto, CA 94304-1207. Phone: (415)493-5000.
- 2800 Contra Costa Blvd., Pleasant Hill, CA 94523-3961. Phone: (510)372-2000.
- 3350 La Jolla Village Dr., San Diego, CA 92161-0001. Phone: (619)552-8585.
- 4150 Clement St., San Francisco, CA 94121-1598. Phone: (415)221-4810.
- Sepulveda, CA 91343-2099. Phone: (818)891-7711.

- 11301 Wilshire Blvd., West Los Angeles, CA 90073-1002. Phone: (310)478-3711.

Colorado—1055 Clermont St., Denver, CO 80220-0166. Phone: (303)399-8020.

- Ft. Lyon, CO 81038-5000. Phone: (719)384-3100.
- Grand Junction, CO 81501-6499. Phone: (303)242-0731.

Connecticut—55 Willard Ave., Newington, CT 06111. Phone: (860)666-6951.

- West Spring St., West Haven, CT 06516. Phone: (203)932-5711.

Delaware—1601 Kirkwood Hwy., Wilmington, DE 19805. Phone: (302)994-2511.

District of Columbia—50 Irving St. NW, Washington, DC 20422. Phone: (202)745-8000.

Florida—Bay Pines, FL 33744. Phone: (813)398-6661.

- Archer Rd., Gainesville, FL 32608-1197. Phone: (325)376-1611.
- Lake City, FL 32055-5898. Phone: (904)755-3016.
- 1201 NW 16th St., Miami, FL 33125. Phone: (305)324-4455.
- Bruce B. Downs Blvd., Tampa, FL 33612. Phone: (813)972-2000.
- West Palm Beach, FL 33420-3207. Phone: (561)882-6700.

Georgia—1670 Clairmont Rd., Atlanta, GA 30033. Phone: (404)321-6111.

- 2460 Wrightsboro Rd., Augusta, GA 30904-6285. Phone: (706)733-0188.
- 2460 Wrightsboro Rd., Dublin, GA 31021. Phone: (912)272-1210.

Idaho—5th and Fort St., Boise, ID 83702-4598. Phone: (208)336-5100.

Illinois—333 E. Huron St., Chicago, IL 60611. Phone: (312)943-6600.

- 820 S. Damen Ave., Chicago, IL 60612. Phone: (312)666-6500.
- Danville, IL 61832-5198. Phone: (217)442-8000.
- Hines, IL 60141-5000. Phone: (708)343-7200.
- 2401 W. Main St., Marion, IL 62959. Phone: (618)997-5311.
- North Chicago, IL 60064. Phone: (847)688-1900.

Indiana—1600 Randallia Dr., Ft. Wayne, IN 46805-5100. Phone: (219)426-5431.

- 1481 W. 10th St., Indianapolis, IN 46202-2884. Phone: (317)635-7401.
- 46952 E. 38th St., Marion, IN 46953-4589. Phone: (317)674-3321.

Iowa—30th and Euclid Ave., Des Moines, IA 50310-5774. Phone: (515)699-5999.

- Highway 6 W., Iowa City, IA 52246-2208. Phone: (319)338-0581.
- 1515 W. Pleasant St., Knoxville, IA 50138-3399. Phone: (515)842-3101.

Kansas—4201 S. 4th St. Traffic Way, Leavenworth, KS 66048. Phone: (913)682-2000.

- 2200 Gage Blvd., Topeka, KS 66622. Phone: (913)272-3111.
- 5500 E. Kellogg, Wichita, KS 67218. Phone: (316)685-2221.

Kentucky—Leestown Rd., Lexington, KY 40511-1093. Phone: (606)233-4511.

- 800 Zorn Ave., Louisville, KY 40206-1499. Phone: (502)895-3401.

Louisiana—Shreveport Hwy., Alexandria, LA 71301. Phone: (318)473-0010.

- 1601 Perdido St., New Orleans, LA 70146. Phone: (504)568-0811.
- 510 E. Stoner Ave., Shreveport, LA 71101-4295. Phone: (318)221-8411.

Maine—Rt. 17 E., Togus, ME 04330. Phone: (207)623-8411.

Maryland—Baltimore, Ft. Howard and Perry Point Divisions, 3900 Lock Raven Blvd., Baltimore, MD 21201. Phone: (410)605-7000.

Massachusetts—200 Spring Rd., Bedford, MA 01730. Phone: (617)275-7500.

- 150 S. Huntington Ave., Boston, MA 02130. Phone: (617)232-9500.
- 940 Belmont St., Brockton, MA 02401. Phone: (508)583-4500.

64.007 thru 64.026 *(cont.)*

- N. Main St., Northampton, MA 01060-1288. Phone: (413)584-4040.
- 1400 Veterans of Foreign Wars Pkwy., West Roxbury, MA 02401. Phone: (508)583-4500.

Michigan—2215 Fuller Rd., Ann Arbor, MI 48105-2300. Phone: (313)769-7100.

- 5500 Armstrong Rd., Battle Creek, MI 49016-0544. Phone: (616)966-5600.
- Detroit, MI 48201-1932. Phone: (313)576-1000.
- Iron Mountain, MI 49801. Phone: (906)779-3150.
- 1500 Weiss St., Saginaw, MI 48602-5298. Phone: (517)793-2340.

Minnesota—54th St. and 48th Ave. S., Minneapolis, MN 55417. Phone: (612)725-2000.

- 8th St., N. 44th Ave., St. Cloud, MN 56303. Phone: (612)252-1670.

Mississippi—Pass Rd., Biloxi, MS 39531. Phone: (601)388-5541.

- 1500 E. Woodrow Wilson Dr., Jackson, MS 39216. Phone: (601)362-4471.

Missouri—800 Stadium Rd., Columbia, MO 65201. Phone: (573)443-2511.

- 4801 Linwood Blvd., Kansas City, MO 64128. Phone: (816)861-4700.
- Hwy. 67 N., Poplar Bluff, MO 63901. Phone: (573)686-4151.
- Jefferson Barracks, St. Louis, MO 63125. Phone: (314)487-0400.
- 915 N. Grand Blvd., St. Louis, MO 63106. Phone: (314)652-4100.

Montana—William St. and Hwy. 12 W., Ft. Harrison, MT 59636-1500. Phone: (406)447-7900

- 210 S. Winchester, Miles City, MT 59301-4798. Phone: (406)232-3060.

Nebraska—2201 N. Broad Well, Grand Island, NE 68803-2153. Phone: (308)382-3660.

- 600 S. 70th St., Lincoln, NE 68510-2493. Phone: (402)489-3802.
- 4101 Woolworth Ave., Omaha, NE 68105-1873. Phone: (402)346-8800.

Nevada—1703 Charleston Blvd., Las Vegas, NV 89102-2395. Phone: (702)385-3700.

- 1000 Locust St., Reno, NV 89520-0111. Phone: (702)786-7200.

New Hampshire—718 Smyth Rd., Manchester, NH 02104. Phone: (603)624-4366.

New Jersey—Tremont Ave. and S. Center, East Orange, NJ 07018. Phone: (201)676-1000.

- Valley and Knollcroft Rd., Lyons, NJ 07939. Phone: (201)647-0180.

New Mexico—2100 Ridgecrest Dr. SE, Albuquerque, NM 87108-5138. Phone: (505)256-2843.

New York—113 Holland Ave., Albany, NY 12208. Phone: (518)462-3311.

- Redfield Pkwy., Batavia, NY 14020. Phone: (716)343-7500.
- Medical Center, Argonne Ave., Bath, NY 14810. Phone: (607)776-2111.
- 130 W. Kingsbridge Rd., Bronx, NY 10468. Phone: (718)584-9000.
- 800 Poly Pl., Brooklyn, NY 11209. Phone: (718)630-3521.
- 3495 Bailey Ave., Buffalo, NY 14215. Phone: (716)834-9200.
- Ft. Hill Ave., Canandaigua, NY 14424. Phone: (716)394-2000.
- Castle Point, NY 12511. Phone: (914)831-2000.
- Old Albany Post Rd., Montrose, NY 10548. Phone: (914)737-1216.
- 1st Ave. at E. 24th St., New York, NY 10010. Phone: (212)951-5959.
- Long Island-Middleville Rd., Northport, NY 11768. Phone: (516)261-4400.
- Irving Ave. at University Place, Syracuse, NY 13210. Phone: (315)477-7461.

North Carolina—Asheville, NC 28805. Phone: (704)299-7431.

- 508 Fulton St., Durham, NC 27705. Phone: (919)286-0411.

- 2300 Ramsey St., Fayetteville, NC 28301. Phone: (910)822-7059.
- 1601 Brenner Ave., Salisbury, NC 28144. Phone: (704)638-9000.

North Dakota—2101 Elm St., Fargo, ND 58102. Phone: (701)232-3241.

Ohio—17273 State Rt. 104, Chillicothe, OH 45601. Phone: (614)773-1141.

- 3200 Vine St., Cincinnati, OH 45220. Phone: (513)475-6300.
- 10701 East Blvd., Cleveland, OH 44106-3800. Phone: (216)791-3800.
- Medical Center Nursing Home and Domiciliary, 4100 W. 3rd St., Dayton, OH 45428. Phone: (513)262-2170.

Oklahoma—125 S. Main St., Muskogee, OK 74401. Phone: (918)683-3261.

- 921 NE 13th St., Oklahoma City, OK 73104. Phone: (405)270-0501.

Oregon—3710 SW U.S. Veterans Hospital Rd., Portland, OR 97207-1034. Phone: (503)220-8262.

- New Garden Valley Blvd., Roseburg, OR 97470-6153. Phone: (541)440-1000.
- Domiciliary, White City, OR 97503-3207. Phone: (541)826-2111.

Pennsylvania—Pleasant Valley Blvd., Altoona, PA 16602-4377. Phone: (814)943-8164.

- New Castle Rd., Butler, PA 16001-2480. Phone: (412)287-4781.
- Coatesville, PA 19320. Phone: (610)384-7711.
- 135 E. 38th St., Erie, PA 16504. Phone: (814)868-8661.
- S. Lincoln Ave., Lebanon, PA 17042. Phone: (717)272-6621.
- University and Woodland Ave., Philadelphia, PA 19104. Phone: (215)823-5800.
- Highland Dr., Pittsburgh, PA 15206. Phone: (412)363-4900.
- University Dr., Pittsburgh, PA 15240. Phone: (412)688-6000.
- 1111 East End Blvd., Wilkes-Barre, PA 18711-0026. Phone: (717)824-3521.

Puerto Rico—Barrio Monacillos, Rio Piedras, PR 00927-5800. Phone: (787)758-7575.

Rhode Island—380 Westminster Mall, Providence, RI 02908-4799. Phone: (401)273-7100.

South Carolina—109 Bee St., Charleston, SC 29401-5799. Phone: (803)577-5011.

- 1801 Assembly St., Columbia, SC 29201-1639. Phone: (803)776-4000.

South Dakota—I-90 and Hwy. 34, Ft. Meade, SD 57741. Phone: (605)745-2000.

- 5th St., Hot Springs, SD 57757. Phone: (605)745-2000.
- 2501 W. 22nd St., Sioux Falls, SD 57117. Phone: (605)336-3230.

Tennessee—1030 Jefferson Ave., Memphis, TN 38104-2193. Phone: (901)523-8990.

- Mountain Home, TN 37684. Phone: (423)926-1171.
- 3400 Lebanon Rd., Murfreesboro, TN 37129-1236. Phone: (615)893-1360.
- 1310 24th Ave. S., Nashville, TN 37212-2637. Phone: (615)327-4751.

Texas—6010 Amarillo Blvd. W., Amarillo, TX 79106. Phone: (806)355-9703.

- 2400 S. Gregg St., Big Spring, TX 79720. Phone: (915)263-7361.
- Sam Rayburn Memorial Veterans Center, Bonham, TX 75418. Phone: (903)583-2111.
- 4500 S. Lancaster Rd., Dallas, TX 75216. Phone: (214)376-5451.
- 5919 Brook Hollow Dr., El Paso, TX 79925. Phone: (915)564-6100.
- 2002 Holcombe Blvd., Houston, TX 77030. Phone: (713)479-1414.
- Memorial Blvd., Kerrville, TX 78028. Phone: (210)896-2020.
- 1016 Ward St., Marlin, TX 76661. Phone: (817)883-3511.
- 7400 Merton Minter Blvd., San Antonio, TX 78284. Phone: (210)617-5300.

64.007 thru 64.026 *(cont.)*

- 1901 S. 1st St., Temple, TX 76504. Phone: (817)778-4811.
- 4800 Memorial Dr., Waco, TX 76711. Phone: (817)752-6581.

Utah—500 Foothill Blvd., Salt Lake City, UT 84148-0001. Phone: (801)582-1565.

Vermont—White River Junction, VT 05001-0001. Phone: (802)295-9363.

Virginia—Emancipation Dr., Hampton, VA 23667. Phone: (804)722-9961.

- 1201 Broad Rock Rd., Richmond, VA 23249. Phone: (804)230-0001.
- 1970 Roanoke Blvd., Salem, VA 24153. Phone: (540)982-2463.

Washington—American Lake, WA 98493. Phone: (206)762-1010.

- 1660 S. Columbian Way, Seattle, WA 98108. Phone: (206)762-1010.
- North 4816 Assembly St., Spokane, WA 99205-6197. Phone: (509)328-4521.
- 77 Wainwright Dr., Walla Walla, WA 99362-3975. Phone: (509)525-5200.

West Virginia—200 Veterans Ave., Beckley, WV 25801. Phone: (304)255-2121.

- Milford and Chestnut St., Clarksburg, WV 26301. Phone: (304)623-3461.
- 1540 Spring Valley Dr., Huntington, WV 25704. Phone: (304)429-6741.
- Rt. 9, Martinsburg, WV 25401-9809. Phone: (304)263-0811.

Wisconsin—2500 Overlook Terrace, Madison, WI 53705. Phone: (608)256-1901.

- 5000 W. National Ave., Milwaukee, WI 53295. Phone: (414)384-2000.
- Tomah, WI 54660. Phone: (608)372-3971.

Wyoming—2360 W. Pershing Blvd., Cheyenne, WY 82001-5392. Phone: (307)778-7300.

- Fort Rd., Sheridan, WY 82801-8320. Phone: (307)672-1675.

VETERANS BENEFITS ADMINISTRATION

FIELD OFFICES

64.100 thru 64.128

Note: DVA provides toll-free phone service throughout the 50 states, Washington DC, and Puerto Rico: (800)827-1000.

Alabama—345 Perry Hill Rd., Montgomery, AL 36109-3798.

Alaska—2925 DeBarr Rd., Anchorage, AK 99508-2989.

Arizona—3225 N. Central Ave., Phoenix, AZ 85012-2405.

Arkansas—Ft. Roots - Bldg. 65, North Little Rock, AR 72115-1280.

California—Federal Bldg., 11000 Wilshire Blvd., Los Angeles, CA 90024-3602.

- Oakland Federal Bldg., 1301 Clay St., Oakland, CA 94612-5209.
- 8810 Rio San Diego Dr., San Diego, CA 92108-1508.

Colorado—155 Van Gordon St., Lakewood, CO 80228-1709.

Connecticut—450 Main St., Hartford, CT 06103-3077.

Delaware—1601 Kirkwood Hwy., Wilmington, DE 19805-4988.

District of Columbia—1120 Vermont Ave. NW, Washington, DC 20421-1111.

Florida—1833 Blvd. - Rm.3109, Jacksonville, FL 32206.

- Federal Bldg. - Rm.120, 51 SW 1st Ave., Miami, FL 33130.
- 5201 Raymond St. - Rm.1704, Orlando, FL 32806.
- 312 Kenmore Rd. - Rm.IG250, Pensacola, FL 32503-7492.
- 9500 Bay Pines Blvd., P.O. Box 1437, St. Petersburg, FL 33708.

Georgia—1700 Clairmont Rd., Decatur, GA 30033-4032.

Hawaii—PJKK Federal Bldg., 300 Ala Moana Blvd., P.O. Box 50188, Honolulu, HI 96850.

Idaho—805 W. Franklin St., Boise, ID 83702-5560.

Illinois—536 S. Clark St., P.O. Box 8136, Chicago, IL 60605-1523.

Indiana—575 N. Pennsylvania St., Indianapolis, IN 46204-1526.

Iowa—210 Walnut St. - Rm.1063, Des Moines, IA 50309-9825.

Kansas—5500 E. Kellogg, Wichita, KS 67218-1698.

Kentucky—545 S. 3rd St., Louisville, KY 40202-3835.

Louisiana—701 Loyola Ave. - Rm.4210, New Orleans, LA 70113-1912.

Maine—Bldg. 428 - Rm.103, 475 Stevens Ave., Portland, ME 04103.

- 1 VA Center, Togus, ME 04330-6795.

Maryland—Federal Bldg. - Rm.233, 31 Hopkins Plaza, Baltimore, MD 21201-0001.

Massachusetts—JFK Federal Bldg., Government Center - Rm.1265, Boston, MA 02203-0393.

Michigan—McNamara Federal Bldg. - Rm.1400, 477 Michigan Ave., Detroit, MI 48226-2591.

Minnesota—Federal Bldg., Ft. Snelling, St. Paul, MN 55111-4050.

Mississippi—1600 E. Woodrow Wilson Ave., Jackson, MS 39216-5102.

Missouri—601 E. 12th St. - Rm.120, Kansas City, MO 64106-0199.

- 400 S. 18th St., St. Louis, MO 63103-2676.

Montana—Williams St., Ft. Harrison, MT 59636-9999.

Nebraska—5631 S. 48th St., Lincoln, NE 68516-4198.

Nevada—1201 Terminal Way, Reno, NV 89520-0118.

New Hampshire—Cotton Federal Bldg., 275 Chestnut St., Manchester, NH 03101-2489.

New Jersey—20 Washington Pl., Newark, NJ 07102-3174.

New Mexico—Chavez Federal Bldg. and U.S. Courthouse, 500 Gold Ave. SW, Albuquerque, NM 87102-3118.

New York—O'Brien Federal Bldg., Clinton Ave. and N. Pearl St., Albany, NY 12207.

- Federal Bldg., 111 W. Huron St., Buffalo, NY 14202-2368.
- 245 W. Houston St., New York, NY 10014-4805.
- Federal Office Bldg. and Courthouse, 100 State St., Rochester, NY 14614. Phone: (800)827-0619.
- 344 W. Genesee St., Syracuse, NY 13202.

North Carolina—Federal Bldg., 251 N. Main St., Winston-Salem, NC 27155-1000.

North Dakota—2101 Elm St., Fargo, ND 58102-2417.

Ohio—801-B W. 8th St., Cincinnati, OH 45203-2001.

- 1240 E. 9th St., Cleveland, OH 44199-2001.
- Federal Bldg. - Rm.309, 200 N. High St., Columbus, OH 43215.

Oklahoma—Federal Bldg., 125 S. Main St., Muskogee, OK 74401-7025.

- 215 Dean A. McGee Ave. - Rm.276, Oklahoma City, OK 73102.

Oregon—Federal Bldg. - Rm.1217, 1220 SW 3rd Ave., Portland, OR 97204-2825.

Pennsylvania—5000 Wissahickon Ave., Philadelphia, PA 19101-8079.

- 1000 Liberty Ave., Pittsburgh, PA 15222-4004.
- 1111 East End Blvd., Wilkes-Barre, PA 18711.

Philippines—Manila Regional Office and Outpatient Clinic, FPO AP 96515-1100.

64.100 thru 64.128 *(cont.)*

Puerto Rico—U.S. Courthouse and Federal Bldg., Carlos E. Chardon St., Hato Rey, San Juan, PR 00936-4867. Phone: (809)766-5510.

Rhode Island—380 Westminster Mall, Providence, RI 02903-3246.

South Carolina—1801 Assembly St., Columbia, SC 29201-2495.

South Dakota—2501 W. 22nd St., Sioux Falls, SD 57117-5046.

Tennessee—U.S. Courthouse Federal Office Bldg., 110 9th Ave. S., Nashville, TN 37203-3817.

Texas—U.S. Courthouse and Federal Office Bldg., 1114 Commerce St., Dallas, TX 75242.

- 6900 Almeda Rd., Houston, TX 77030-4200.
- 4902 34th St. - Ste. 10 (Rm.134), Lubbock, TX 79410-0001.
- 3601 Bluemel Rd., San Antonio, TX 78229-2041.
- One Veteran Plaza, 701 Clay Ave., Waco, TX 76799-0001.

Utah—Federal Bldg., 125 S. State St., P.O. Box 11500, Salt Lake City, UT 84147-0500.

Vermont—215 Main St., White River Junction, VT 05009-0001.

Virginia—210 Franklin Rd. SW, Roanoke, VA 24011-2204.

Washington—Federal Bldg., 915 2nd Ave., Seattle, WA 98174-1060.

West Virginia—640 4th Ave., Huntington, WV 25701-1340.

Wisconsin—Bldg. 6, 5000 W. National Ave., Milwaukee, WI 53295-0006.

Wyoming—2360 E. Pershing Blvd., Cheyenne, WY 82001-5356.

NATIONAL CEMETERY ADMINISTRATION

64.201 AREA OFFICES

California—1301 Clay St. - 1230 North, Oakland, CA 94612-5209. Phone: (510)637-6270.

Colorado—P.O. Box 25126, Denver, CO 80225. Phone: (303)914-5700.

Georgia—1700 Clairmont Rd. - 4th fl., Decatur, GA 30333-4032. Phone: (404)929-5899.

Indiana—575 N. Pennsylvania St., Indianapolis, IN 46204. Phone: (317)226-0205.

Pennsylvania—5000 Wissahickon Ave., Philadelphia, PA 19144. Phone: (215)381-3787.

64.202 Memorial Programs Processing Sites

Kansas—Ft. Leavenworth National Cemetery, 395 Biddle Blvd., Ft. Leavenworth, KS 66027-2307. Phones: Toll free, 1-888-460-9709, (913)758-1805; FAX (913)758-1839.

Pennsylvania—Lebanon VA Medical Center - Bldg.27, 1700 S. Lincoln Ave., Lebanon, PA 17042. Phones: Toll free, 1-888-574-9107, (717)270-9424; FAX (717)270-9428.

Tennessee—Nashville Processing Site, 220 Athens Way - Ste. 102, Nashville, TN 37228-1346. Phones: Toll free, 1-888-367-1330, (615)736-2841, ext.228; FAX (615)736-2026.

Virginia—Logistics Management Service, 5105 Russell Rd., Quantico, VA 22134. Phone: (703)441-4014.

- 5109 Russell Road, Quantico, VA 22134. Phones: *Program Support Unit*, (202)501-3028; *Applicant Assistance Unit*, (202)501-3078; *Presidential Certificate Program*, (202)565-4259.

ENVIRONMENTAL PROTECTION AGENCY

66.001 Regional Grants Management Contacts

REGION I *(Connecticut, Maine, Massachusetts, New Hampshire, Rhode Island, Vermont)*—One Congress St. - Ste. 1100, (MC MGM), Boston, MA 02114-2023. Phones: (617)918-1972; FAX (617)918-1929.

REGION II *(New Jersey, New York, Puerto Rico, Virgin Islands)*—Grants Administration Branch, (OPM-GRA), 290 Broadway, New York, NY 10007-1866. Phones: (212)637-3402; FAX (212)637-3518.

REGION III *(Delaware, District of Columbia, Maryland, Pennsylvania, Virginia, West Virginia)*—Grants Management Section, Office of the Comptroller, (3PM70), 1650 Arch St., Philadelphia, PA 19103-2029. Phones: (215)814-5410; FAX (215)814-5271.

REGION IV *(Alabama, Florida, Georgia, Kentucky, Mississippi, North Carolina, South Carolina, Tennessee)*—Grants and Contracts Administration Section, Management Division, 61 Forsyth St. SW, Atlanta, GA 30303-8960. Phones: (404)562-8371; FAX (404)562-8370.

REGION V *(Illinois, Indiana, Michigan, Minnesota, Ohio, Wisconsin)*—Acquisition and Assistance Branch, (MC 10J), 77 W. Jackson Blvd., Chicago, IL 60604-3507. Phones: (312)886-2400; FAX (312)353-9096.

REGION VI *(Arkansas, Louisiana, New Mexico, Oklahoma, Texas)*—Grants Audit Section, (6M-PG), Management Division, First International Bldg., 1445 Ross Ave., Dallas, TX 75202-2733. Phones: (214)665-6510; FAX (214)665-7284.

REGION VII *(Iowa, Kansas, Missouri, Nebraska)*—Grants Administration Branch, 901 N. 5th St., Kansas City, KS 66101. Phones: (913)551-7346; FAX (913)551-7579.

REGION VIII *(Colorado, Montana, North Dakota, South Dakota, Utah, Wyoming)*—Grants Administration Branch, (8PM-GFM), 999 18th St. - Ste. 500, Denver, CO 80202-2466. Phones: (303)312-6305; FAX (303)312-6685.

REGION IX *(American Samoa, Arizona, California, Guam, Hawaii, Nevada, Trust Territories of Pacific Islands, Wake Island)*—Grants and Finance Branch, 75 Hawthorne St., San Francisco, CA 94105. Phones: (415)744-1693; FAX (415)744-1678.

REGION X *(Alaska, Idaho, Oregon, Washington)*—Grants Administration Unit, 1200 6th Ave., Seattle, WA 98101. Phones: (206)553-2722; FAX (206)553-4957.

Chemical Emergency Preparedness and Prevention Office (CEPP)

REGIONAL OFFICES

REGION I—One Congress St. - Ste. 1100, (MC SEP), Boston, MA 02114-2023. Phone: (617)918-1804.

REGION II—Bldg. 209, 2890 Woodbridge Ave., Edison, NJ 08837-3679. Phone: (732)906-6194.

REGION III—1650 Arch St., (MC 3HS33), Philadelphia, PA 19103. Phone: (215)814-3273.

REGION IV—Air Division - 12th fl., 61 Forsyth St. SW, Atlanta, GA 30303. Phone: (404)562-9085.

66.001 (cont.) **REGION V**—77 W. Jackson Blvd., (MC SC-6J), Chicago, IL 60604. Phone: (312)353-9045.

REGION VI—1445 Ross Ave., (MC 6SF-RO), Dallas, TX 75202-2733. Phone: (214)665-2270.

REGION VII—901 N. 5th St., (MC ATRDCRIB), Kansas City, KS 66101. Phone: (913)551-7540.

REGION VIII—One Denver Place, (MC EPR-SA), 999 18th St. - Ste. 300, Denver, CO 80202-2405. Phone: (303)312-6760.

REGION IX—75 Hawthorne St., (MC SFD 9-3), San Francisco, CA 94105. Phone: (415)972-3039.

REGION X—1200 6th Ave., (MC ECL-116), Seattle, WA 99101. Phone: (206)553-8414.

Municipal Solid Waste Primary Contacts

REGION I—One Congress St. - Ste. 1100, (MC SPP-SPP), Boston, MA 02114-2023. Phones: (617)918-1813; FAX (617)918-1810.

REGION II—290 Broadway, (MC 2DEPP-RPB), New York, NY 10007-1866. Phones: (212)637-4125; FAX (212)637-4437.

REGION III—1650 Arch St., (MC 3WC21/3HW60), Philadelphia, PA 19103. Phones: (215)814-3298; FAX (215)814-3163.

REGION IV—Atlanta Federal Center, (MC 4WD-RPB/RSS), 61 Forsyth St., Atlanta, GA 30303-3104. Phones: (404)562-8449; FAX (404)562-8439.

REGION V—77 W. Jackson Blvd., (MC DRP-8J), Chicago, IL 60604-3590. Phones: (312)886-0976; FAX (312)353-4788.

REGION VI—1445 Ross Ave., (MC 6PD-U), Dallas, TX 75202-2733. Phones: (214)665-6760; FAX (214)665-7263.

REGION VII—901 N. 5th St., (MC ARTD/SWPP), Kansas City, KS 66101. Phones: (913)551-7523; FAX (913)551-7947.

REGION VIII—999 18th St. - Ste. 500, (MC 8P-P3T), Denver, CO 80202-2466. Phones: (303)312-6099; FAX (303)312-6044.

REGION IX—75 Hawthorne St., (MC WST-7), San Francisco, CA 94105. Phones: (415)744-1284; FAX (415)744-1044.

REGION X—1200 6th Ave., (MC WCM-128), Seattle, WA 98101. Phones: (206)553-6117; FAX (206)553-8509.

Pollution Prevention Contacts

REGION I—JFK Federal Bldg. - Rm.2203 (SPN), Boston, MA 02203. Phones: (617)918-1817; FAX (617)918-4939.

REGION II—290 Broadway - 25th fl. (2-OPM-PPI), DEPP, New York, NY 10007-1866. Phones: (212)637-3742; FAX (212)637-3771.

REGION III—1650 Arch St. (3RA20), Philadelphia, PA 19103-2029. Phones: (215)814-2761; FAX (215)566-2782.

REGION IV—Air and Pesticide Center, 61 Forsyth St. SW, Atlanta, GA 30303. Phones: (404)562-9430; FAX (404)562-9066.

REGION V—Waste, Pesticide and Toxics Division, 77 W. Jackson Blvd. (DRP-8J), Chicago, IL 60604-3590. Phones: (312)353-4669; FAX (312)353-4788.

REGION VI—Compliance Assurance and Enforcement Division, 1445 Ross Ave. - Ste. 1200 (6EN-XP), Dallas, TX 75202. Phones: (214)665-2119; FAX (214)665-7446.

REGION VII—Air, RCRA and Toxics Division, 726 Minnesota Ave., (ARTD/TSPP), Kansas City, KS 66101. Phones: (913)551-7517; FAX (913)551-7065.

REGION VIII—Office of P2, State and Tribal Assistance, 999 18th St.- Ste. 500 (8P2-P2), Denver, CO 80202-2466. Phones: (303)312-6385; FAX (303)312-6339.

REGION IX—Waste Division, 75 Hawthorne St. (WST-1-1), San Francisco, CA 94105. Phones: (415)744-2192; FAX (415)744-1796.

REGION X—Office of Innovation, 1200 6th Ave., Seattle, WA 98101. Phones: (206)553-4072; FAX (206)553-6647.

RCRA and Superfund

REGION I—Office of Ecosystem Protection, (MC HHA) and/or Office of Site Remediation and Restoration, One Congress St., Boston, MA 02114-2023. Phones: (617)918-1501, -1201.

REGION II—Division of Environmental Planning and Protection, 26 Federal Plaza - Rm.1000 (2AWM-SW), New York, NY 10278. Phone: (212)637-3772.

- Emergency and Remedial Response Division, 290 Broadway, New York, NY 10007. Phones: (212)637-4390.

REGION III—Waste Chemical Management Division, 841 Chestnut Bldg. (3HWOO), Philadelphia, PA 19107. Phones: (215)814-2005.

- Hazardous Site Cleanup Division, 1650 Arch St., Philadelphia, PA 19106. Phone: (215)813-3143.

REGION IV—Waste Management Division, 61 Forsyth St., Atlanta, GA 30303. Phones: (404)562-8651.

REGION V—Waste, Pesticides and Toxics Division, 77 W. Jackson Blvd., Chicago, IL 60604-3507. Phones: (312)353-2024.

- Superfund Division, Metcalfe Federal Bldg., 77 W. Jackson Blvd., Chicago, IL 60604. Phone: (312)353-9773.

REGION VI—Multimedia Planning and Permitting Division and/or Superfund Division, Fountain Place - Ste. 1200, 1445 Ross Ave., Dallas, TX 75202-2733. Phones: (214)665-7200, -6701.

REGION VII—Air/RCRA Toxics Division and/or Superfund Division, 901 N. 5th St., Kansas City, KS 66101. Phones: (913)551-7020, -7664.

REGION VIII—Hazardous Waste Program, (MC 8P2-SA), Denver Place - Ste. 500, 999 18th St., Denver, CO 80202-2466. Phones: (303)312-7081.

- Office of Ecosystems Protection and Remediation, 999 18th St. - Ste. 500, Denver, CO 80202. Phone: (303)312-6598.

REGION IX—Waste Division and/or Hazardous Waste Management Division, 75 Hawthorne St., San Francisco, CA 94105. Phones: (415)744-2138, -1730.

REGION X—Office of Waste and Chemical Management and/or Office of Environmental Cleanup, 1200 6th Ave., Seattle, WA 98101. Phones: (206)553-4198, -7151.

66.032 Radon Regional Program Office Contacts

(No phone numbers provided.)

REGION I—JFK Federal Bldg. - Ste. 1100, One Congress St., (MC CPT), Boston, MA 02114-2023.

REGION II—290 Broadway - 28th fl., (MC R2DEPDIV), New York, NY 10007-1866.

REGION III—1650 Arch St., (MC 3AP23), Philadelphia, PA 19103-2029.

REGION IV—61 Forsyth St. SW, Atlanta, GA 30303-3104..

REGION V—77 W. Jackson Blvd., (MC AE-17J), Chicago, IL 60604-3590.

REGION VI—1445 Ross Ave., Dallas, TX 75202-2733.

REGION VII—901 N. 5th St., (MC ARTD/RALI), Kansas City, KS 66101.

REGION VIII—999 18th St. - Ste. 500, (MC 8P-AR), Denver, CO 80202-2466.

66.032 (cont.) **REGION IX**—75 Hawthorne St., (MC Air-6), San Francisco, CA 94105.

REGION X—1200 6th Ave., (MC OAQ-107), Seattle, WA 98101-9797.

66.033 thru 66.036 Listed under **66.001**.

66.110 One Congress St. - Ste. 1100, CPT, Boston, MA 02114. Phone: (617)918-1797.

66.111 EPA Region 7, 901 N 5th St., Kansas City, KS 66101. Phones: (913)551-7782, 7193; FAX (913)551-9782, -9193.

66.306 Listed under **66.001**.

Office of Enforcement and Compliance Assurance

66.310 Contact the EPA Regional Offices listed under **66.001** and the following telephone numbers:

REGION I—Phone: (617)918-1703.

REGION II—Phone: (212)637-3949.

REGION IV—Phone: (404)562-8425.

REGION V—Phone: (312)353-9681.

REGION VI—Phone: (214)665-6431.

REGION VII—Phone: (913)551-7381.

REGION VIII—Phone: (303)312-6974.

REGION IX—Phone: (415)947-4262.

REGION X—Phone: (206)553-8257.

66.418 thru 66.436 Listed under **66.001**.

66.437 USEPA Long Island Sound Office, Government Center - Ste. 6-5, 888 Washington Blvd., Stamford, CT 06904. Phones: (203)977-1541; FAX (203)977-1546.

66.439 Targeted Watershed Offices

REGION I—Phone: (617)918-1035, -1601.

REGION II—Phone: (212)637-3844.

REGION III—Phone: (215)814-2718.

REGION IV—Phone: (404)562-9351.

REGION V—Phone: (312)886-7742.

REGION VI—Phone: (214)665-6683.

REGION VII—Phone: (417)575-8028.

REGION VIII—Phone: (303)312-6215.

REGION IX—Phone: (415)972-3399.

REGION X—Phone: (206)553-1566.

66.454 Listed under **66.001**.

66.456 National Estuary Program Offices

REGION I—Water Quality Policy Division, Boston, MA 02114-2023. Phone: (617)918-1511.

REGION II—Environmental Planning and Protection Division, 290 Broadway, New York, NY 10007-1866. Phone: (212)637-3724.

REGION III—Environmental Services Division, 1650 Arch St., Philadelphia, PA 19103-2029. Phone: (215)814-2989.

REGION IV—Water Management Division, 61 Forsyth St. SW, Atlanta, GA 30303. Phone: (404)562-9345.

REGION VI—Water Quality Protection Division, 1445 Ross Ave., Dallas, TX 75202-2733. Phone: (214)655-7101.

REGION IX—Water Management Division, 75 Hawthorne St., San Francisco, CA 94105. Phone: (415)744-1860.

REGION X—Office of Ecosystems and Communities, 1200 6th Ave., Seattle, WA 98101. Phone: (206)553-4181.

66.458 and 66.460 Listed under **66.001**.

66.461 Wetland Program Offices

REGION I—One Congress St. - Ste. 100, (MC CSP), Boston, MA 02114. Phone: (617)918-1669.

REGION II—290 Broadway, New York, NY 10007. Phone: (212)637-3817.

REGION III—1650 Arch St., (MC 3EA30), Philadelphia, PA. 19103. Phone: (215)814-2715.

REGION IV—61 Forsyth St. SW, Atlanta, GA 30303. Phone: (404)562-9269.

REGION V—77 W. Jackson Blvd., (MC WW16J), Chicago, IL 60604. Phone: (312)886-0241.

REGION VI—1445 Ross Ave., (MC 6WQ-AT), Dallas, TX 75202. Phone: (214)665-7375.

REGION VII—901 N 5th St., Kansas City, KS 66101. Phone: (913)551-7297, -7542.

REGION VIII—999 18th St. - Ste. 300, Denver, CO 80202. Phone: (303)312-6235.

REGION IX—75 Hawthorne St., San Francisco, CA 94105. Phone: (415)972-3415, -3468.

REGION X—1200 6th Ave., Seattle, WA 98101. Phone: (206)553-6219.

66.463 *Use general addresses listed under* **66.001** or the Regional WCQA Coordinator shown via **Internet:** "http://epa.gov/owm/mab/indian/104coord.htm".

66.466 Chesapeake Bay Program Office, EPA, 410 Severn Ave. - Ste. 109, Annapolis, MD 21403. Phone: (410)267-5743.

66.467 thru 66.471 Listed under **66.001**.

66.472 Beach Monitoring

REGION I *(Connecticut, Maine, Massachusetts, New Hampshire, Rhode Island)*—One Congress St. - Ste. 1110, (CWQ), Boston, MA 02114-2023. Phones: (617)918-1626; FAX (617)918-1505.

REGION II *(New Jersey, New York, Puerto Rico, U.S. Virgin Islands)*—2890 Woodbridge Ave., (MS 220), Edison, NJ 08837-3679. Phones: (732)321-6797; FAX (732)321-6616.

REGION III *(Delaware, Maryland, Pennsylvania, Virginia)*—1650 Arch St., (3ES10), Philadelphia, PA 19103-2029. Phones: (215)814-5776; FAX (215)814-2729.

REGION IV *(Alabama, Florida, Georgia, Mississippi, North Carolina, South Carolina)*—61 Forsyth St. - 15th fl., Atlanta, GA 30303-3415. Phones: (404)562-9274; FAX (404)562-9224.

REGION V *(Illinois, Indiana, Michigan, Minnesota, Ohio, Wisconsin)*—77 W. Jackson Blvd., (WT-16J), Chicago, IL 60604-3507. Phones: (312)353-6704; FAX (312)886-0168.

66.472 *(cont.)* **REGION VI** *(Louisiana, Texas)*—1445 Ross Ave., (6WQ-EW), Dallas, TX 75202-2733. Phones: (214)665-7314; FAX (214)665-6689.

REGION IX *(American Samoa, California, Commonwealth of the Mariana Islands, Guam, Hawaii)*—75 Hawthorne St., (WtR-2), San Francisco, CA 94105. Phones: (415)744-1939; FAX (415)744-1078.

REGION X *(Alaska, Oregon, Washington)*—120 6th Ave., (OW-134), Seattle, WA 98101. Phones: (206)553-1646; FAX (206)553-0165.

66.474 Listed under **66.001**.

66.475 Contact the EPA Region 4 Office listed under **66.001**.

66.478 Listed under **66.001**.

66.479 Same as **66.461**.

66.480 Listed under **66.001**.

66.481 One Congress St. - Ste. 1100-CWN, Boston, MA 02114-2023. Phones: (617)918-1606; FAX (617)918-0606.

290 Broadway - 24th fl., New York, NY 10007-1866. Phones: (212)637-3779; FAX (212)637-3889.

66.509 thru 66.516 Listed under **66.001**.

66.600 Contact the EPA Region 2 and 9 Offices listed under **66.001**.

66.604 Environmental Justice

REGION I—One Congress St. - Ste. 1100 (RAA), Boston, MA 02203-0001. Phones: (617)918-1343, -1020.

REGION II—290 Broadway - 26th fl., New York, NY 10007. Phones: (212)637-5027, -3861.

REGION III—1650 Arch St. (3DA00), Philadelphia, PA 19103-2029. Phone: (215)814-2988.

REGION IV—61 Forsyth St., Atlanta, GA 30303-8960. Phones: (404)562-8407, -9650, -8316.

REGION V—77 W. Jackson Blvd. (DM7J), Chicago, IL 60604-3507. Phones: (312)353-1440, 886-5993.

REGION VI—Fountain Place - 13th fl., 1445 Ross Ave. (RA-D), Dallas, TX 75202-2733. Phones: (214)665-2713, -2209.

REGION VII—901 N. 5th St. (RGAD/ECO), Kansas City, KS 66101. Phones: (913)551-7649, -7058.

REGION VIII—999 18th St. - Ste. 300, (8ENF-EJ), Denver, CO 80202-2466. Phones: (303)312-6040, -6556.

REGION IX—75 Hawthorne St. (CMD -1), San Francisco, CA 94105. Phones: (415)972-3795, -3839.

REGION X—1200 6th Ave. (OMP-143), Seattle, WA 98101. Phones: (206)553-1107, -8580.

66.605 and 66.606 Listed under **66.001**.

66.611 thru 66.707 Listed under **66.001**.

66.708 **Pollution Prevention Information Network**

REGION I—One Congress St. - Ste. 1100(Rm.2203), (MC SPP), Boston, MA 02114-2023. Phones: (617)918-1814; FAX (617)918-1810.

REGION II—290 Broadway - 25th fl., (MC SPMMB), New York, NY 10007-1866. Phones: (212)637-3753; FAX (212)637-3771.

REGION III—1650 Arch St., (MC 3E100), Philadelphia, PA 19103-2029. Phones: (215)814-5415, -3299; FAX (215)814-3274.

REGION IV—Atlanta Federal Center, 61 Forsyth St. SW, Atlanta, GA 30303. Phones: (404)562-9028; FAX (404)562-9066.

REGION V—77 W. Jackson Blvd., (MC DW-8J), Chicago, IL 60604-3590. Phones: (312)866-4669; FAX (312)353-4788.

REGION VI—1445 Ross Ave. - Ste. 1200, (MC 6EN-XP), Dallas, TX 75202. Phones: (214)665-2119, -7261; FAX (214)665-7446.

REGION VII—901 N. 5th St., (MC ARTD/TSPP), Kansas City, KS 66101. Phones: (913)551-7097; FAX (913)551-7065.

REGION VIII—999 18th St. - Ste. 300, (MC 8P-P3T). Denver, CO 80202-2466. Phones: (303)312-6385; FAX (303)312-6044.

REGION IX—75 Hawthorne St., (MC WST-7), San Francisco, CA 94105. Phones: (415)972-3283, -3288; FAX (415)947-3530.

REGION X—1200 6th Ave., (MC 01-085), Seattle, WA 98101. Phones: (206)553-4072, -4803; FAX (206)553-8338.

66.709 Listed under **66.001**.

Pesticide Environmental Stewardship Program

66.714 Regional PESP Coordinator:

REGION I—One Congress St. - Ste. 1100 (CPT), Boston, MA 02114-2023. Phone: (617)918-1198.

REGION II—2890 Woodbridge Ave., (MS 500), Edison, NJ 08837-3679. Phone: (732)906-6183.

REGION III—1650 Arch St. (3WC32), Philadelphia, PA 19103-2029. Phone: (215)814-2129.

REGION IV—61 Forsyth St. SW, Atlanta, GA 30303-8960. Phone: (404)562-9014.

REGION V—77 W. Jackson Blvd. (DT-8J), Chicago, IL 60604-3507. Phone: (312)886-3572.

REGION VI—1445 Ross Ave. - Ste. 1200 (6PD-P), Dallas, TX 75202-2733. Phone: (214)665-7562.

REGION VII—901 N. 5th St. (WWPDPEST), Kansas City, KS 66101. Phone: (913)551-7137.

REGION VIII—999 18th St. - Ste. 300 (8P-P3T), Denver, CO 80202-2466. Phone: (303)312-6286.

REGION IX—75 Hawthorne St. (CMD-1), San Francisco, CA 94105. Phone: (415)947-4240.

REGION X—24106 N.Bunn Rd. (WSU-IAREC), Prosser, WA 99350. Phone: (509)786-9225.

66.715 and 66.716 Listed under **66.001**

66.717 Listed under **66.708**.

66.801 Listed under **66.001**.

66.802 Superfund Regional Administrators

REGION I—Office of Site Remediation and Restoration, One Congress St., (MC HBS), Boston, MA 02114-2023. Phones: Toll Free, 1-888-372-7341, (617)918-1421; FAX (617)918-1291.

REGION II—Grants and Contracts Management Branch, Office of Policy and Management, 290 Broadway - 27th fl., (MC 2 OPM-GCMB), New York, NY 10007-1866. Phones: (212)637-3420; FAX (212)637-3518.

REGION III—1650 Arch St., (MC 3HS52), Philadelphia, PA 19103. Phones: Toll Free, 1-800-553-2509, (215)814-5522; FAX (215)814-5518.

REGION IV—Waste Management Division, Program Services Branch, Atlanta Federal Center, 61 Forsyth St., (MC WDCSB), Atlanta, GA 30303. Phones: Toll Free, 1-800-564-7577, (404)562-8866(DB), -8867(RF); FAX (404)562-8842.

REGION V—Office of Public Affairs and Community Involvement Section (MC P-19J), Superfund Division and Contracts and Assistance Agreements Section (MC SM-5J), 77 W. Jackson Blvd., Chicago, IL 60604-3507. Phones: Toll Free, 1-800-621-8431, (312)353-1325, 886-6044; FAX (312)353-1155, 886-0186.

REGION VI—Wells Fargo Bank, Tower at Fountain Place - Ste. 1200, 1445 Ross Ave., (MC 6SF-PO), Dallas, TX 75202-2733. Phones: Toll Free, 1-800-533-3508, (214)665-8157, -8163; FAX (214)665-6660.

REGION VII—Office of External Programs, 901 N. 5th St., (MC PBAF), Kansas City, KS 66101. Phones: Toll Free, 1-800-223-0425, (913)551-7762; FAX (913)551-7066.

REGION VIII—Office of Communications and Public Involvement, 999 18th St. - Ste. 300, (MC 8EPR-PS), Denver, CO 80202-2466. Phones: Toll Free, 1-800-227-8917, (303)312-6696; FAX (303)312-6065.

REGION IX—Office of Community Involvement, 75 Hawthorne St., (MC SFD-3), San Francisco, CA 94105. Phones: Toll Free, 1-800-231-3075, (415)972-3237; FAX (415)947-3528.

REGION X—Community Involvement and Outreach Unit, 1200 6th Ave., (MC ECO-081), Seattle, WA 98101. Phones: Toll Free, 1-800-424-4372, (206)553-0247, -1237; FAX (206)553-2955.

HEADQUARTERS—Community Involvement and Outreach Branch, Ariel Rios Bldg., 1200 Pennsylvania Ave., NW, (MC 5204G), Washington DC 20460. Phones: (703)603-8889; FAX (703)603-9100.

66.804 and 66.805 Underground Storage Tank Regional Program Managers

REGION I—One Congress St. - Ste. 1100, Boston, MA 02114-2023. Phone: (617)918-1311.

REGION II—Water Compliance Branch (2DECA-WCB-GWCS), 290 Broadway, New York, NY 10007-1866. Phone: (212)637-4232.

REGION III—State Programs Branch (3WC21), 1650 Arch St., Philadelphia, PA 19103. Phone: (215)814-3231.

REGION IV—Atlanta Federal Center, 61 Forsyth St. SW, (MC GW-PB-15), Atlanta, GA 30303-3104. Phone: (404)562-9441.

REGION V—Underground Storage Tanks (DRU-7J), 77 W. Jackson Blvd., Chicago, IL 60604-3590. Phone: (312)886-6136.

REGION VI—1st Interstate Bank Tower - Ste. 1200. (6PD-U), 1445 Ross Ave., Dallas, TX 75202-2733. Phone: (214)665-6760.

REGION VII—901 N. 5th St., Kansas City, KS 66101. Phone: (913)551-7547.

REGION VIII—999 18th St. - Ste. 500 (8P2-W-GW), Denver, CO 80202-2466. Phone: (303)312-6137.

REGION IX—75 Hawthorne St. - 10th fl. (H-W-4), San Francisco, CA 94105. Phone: (415)744-2079.

REGION X—1200 6th Ave. (WD-133), Seattle, WA 98101. Phone: (206)553-1563.

66.806 Contact TAG coordinators listed under **66.802**.

66.808 and 66.809 Listed under **66.001**.

66.810 CEPP TECHNICAL ASSISTANCE

REGION I—One Congress St. - Ste. 1100, (MC SEP), Boston, MA 02114-2023. Phone: (617)918-1804.

REGION II—Bldg. 209, 2890 Woodbridge Ave., Edison, NJ 08837-3679. Phone: (732)906-6194.

REGION III—1650 Arch St., (MC 3HS33), Philadelphia, PA 19103. Phone: (215)814-3273.

REGION IV—Air Division - 12th fl., 61 Forsyth St. SW, Atlanta, GA 30303. Phone: (404)562-9085.

REGION V—77 W. Jackson Blvd., (MC SC-6J), Chicago, IL 60604. Phone: (312)353-9045.

REGION VI—1445 Ross Ave., (MC 6SF-RO), Dallas, TX 75202-2733. Phone: (214)665-2270.

REGION VII—901 5th St., (MC ATRDCRIB), Kansas City, KS 66101. Phone: (913)551-7540.

REGION VIII—One Denver Place - Ste. 300, 999 18th St., (MC EPR-SA), Denver, CO 80202-2405. Phone: (303)312-6760.

REGION IX—75 Hawthorne St., (MC SFD 9-3), San Francisco, CA 94105. Phone: (415)972-3039.

REGION X—1200 6th Ave., (MC ECL-116), Seattle, WA 98101. Phone: (206)553-8414.

66.812 Hazardous Waste Management for Tribes

REGION I—Phones: (617)918-1554; FAX (617)918-1505.

REGION II—Phones: (212)637-4099; FAX (212)637-4437.

REGION IV—Phones: (404)562-8457; FAX (404)562-8439.

REGION V—Phones: (312)353-1440; FAX (312)353-6519.

REGION VI—Phones: (214)665-7226, -7216; FAX (214)665-7263, -6762.

REGION VII—Phones: (913)551-7669; FAX (913)551-9669.

REGION VIII—Phones: (303)312-6149; FAX (303)312-6064.

REGION IX—Phones: (415)972-3378; FAX (415)947-3530.

REGION X—Phones: (206)553-6502; FAX (206)553-8509.

66.813 and 66.815 Listed under **66.001**.

66.816 Listed under **66.804** or via **Internet:** “http://www.epa.gov/OUST/regions/index.htm”.

OFFICE OF SOLID WASTE AND EMERGENCY RESPONSE

66.817 and 66.818 **Regional Brownfields Coordinator:**

REGION I—One Congress St. (HBT), Boston, MA 02114-2023. Phones: (617)918-1221; FAX (617)918-1291.

REGION II—290 Broadway - 18th fl., New York, NY 10007. Phones: (212)637-4314; FAX (212)637-4360.

REGION III—1650 Arch St., Philadelphia, PA 19103. Phones: (215)814-3129; FAX (215)814-5518.

REGION IV—Nunn Atlanta Federal Center, 61 Forsyth St., Atlanta, GA 30303. Phones: (404)562-8684; FAX (404)562-8566.

REGION V—77 W. Jackson Blvd., Chicago, IL 60604-3507. Phones: (312)886-7576; FAX (312)886-7190.

REGION VI—First Interstate Bank Tower at Fountain Place - Ste. 1200, 1445 Ross Avenue, Dallas, TX 75202-2733. Phones: (214)665-6737; FAX (214)665-6660.

REGION VII—901 N. 5th St., Kansas City, KS 66101. Phones: (913)551-7646, -7786; FAX (913)551-7063.

REGION VIII—999 18th St. - Ste. 300 (EPR), Denver, CO 80202-2406. Phones: (303)312-6803; FAX (303)312-6067.

REGION IX—75 Hawthorne St. (SFD-1-1), San Francisco, CA 94105. Phones: (415)972-3188; FAX (415)947-3528.

REGION X—1200 6th Ave., Seattle, WA 98101. Phones: (206)553-2100; FAX (206)553-0124.

American Indian Environmental Office

66.926 **Regional Indian Program Coordinator:**

REGION I—JFK Federal Bldg., One Congress St. - Ste. 1100, Boston, MA 02114-2023. Phone: (617)918-1672.

REGION II—26 Federal Plaza, New York, NY 10278. Phone: (212)637-3564.

REGION IV—345 Courtland St. NE, Atlanta, GA 30365. Phone: (404)562-9639.

REGION V—77 W. Jackson Blvd., Chicago, IL 60604-3507. Phone: (312)353-1394.

REGION VI—1445 Ross Ave.- Ste. 1200, Dallas, TX 75202-2733. Phone: (214)665-7454.

REGION VII—726 Minnesota Ave., Kansas City, KS 66101. Phone: (913)551-7539.

REGION VIII—999 18th St. - Ste. 500, Denver, CO 80202-2405. Phone: (303)312-6343.

REGION IX—75 Hawthorne St., San Francisco, CA 94105. Phone: (415)744-1607.

REGION X—1200 6th Ave., Seattle, WA 98101. Phone: (206)553-6200.

OFFICE OF POLICY, ECONOMICS AND INNOVATIONS

66.940 Listed under **66.001**.

OFFICE OF ENVIRONMENTAL EDUCATION

66.950 and 66.951 Listed under **66.001**.

COMMODITY FUTURES TRADING COMMISSION

78.004 **REGIONAL OFFICES**

CENTRAL—300 S. Riverside Plaza. - Ste. 1600 N., Chicago, IL 60606. Phone: (312)353-9000.

- 510 Grain Exchange Bldg., Minneapolis, MN 55415. Phone: (612)370-3255.

EASTERN—One World Trade Center - Ste. 3747, New York, NY 10048. Phone: (212)466-2071.

SOUTHWESTERN—4900 Main St. - Ste. 721, Kansas City, MO 64112. Phone: (816)931-7600.

WESTERN—10900 Wilshire Blvd. - Ste. 400, Los Angeles, CA 90024. Phone: (310)235-6783.

DEPARTMENT OF ENERGY

81.022 **FIELD OFFICES - OPERATIONS**

California—Oakland Operations Office, 1301 Clay St., Oakland, CA 94612-5208. Phone: (510)637-1802.

Colorado—Rocky Flats Office, Golden, CO 80402-0928. Phone: (303)966-7000.

Idaho—Idaho Operations Office, 850 Energy Dr., (MS 1221), Idaho Falls, ID 83401-1563. Phone: (208)526-0111.

Illinois—Chicago Operations Office, 9800 S. Cass Ave., Argonne, IL 60439-4899. Phone: (630)252-2001.

New Mexico—Albuquerque Operations Office, Albuquerque, NM 87185-5400. Phone: (505)845-6049.

Nevada—Nevada Operations Office, P.O. Box 98518, Las Vegas, NV 89193-8518. Phone: (702)295-1000.

Ohio—Miamisburg, OH 45343-0066. Phone: (937)865-4020.

Pennsylvania—National Energy Technology Laboratory, 626 Cochrans Mills Rd., P.O. Box 10940, Pittsburgh, PA 15236-0940. Phone: (412)386-6000.

South Carolina—Savannah River Operations Office, P.O. Box A, Aiken, SC 29801. Phone: (803)725-6211.

Tennessee—Oak Ridge Operations Office, P.O. Box 2001, Oak Ridge, TN 37831. Phone: (865)574-1000.

Washington—Richland Operations Office, 825 Jadwin Ave., P.O. Box 550, Richland, WA 99352. Phone: (509)376-7411.

West Virginia—National Energy Technology Laboratory, 3610 Collins Ferry Rd., Morgantown, WV 26507-0880. Phone: (304)285-4764.

OFFICE OF ENERGY EFFICIENCY AND RENEWABLE ENERGY

81.036 **REGIONAL OFFICES**

CENTRAL—1617 Cole Blvd., (MS 1521), Golden, CO 80401. Phone: (303)275-4785.

81.036 *(cont.)* **MID-ATLANTIC**—The Wanamaker Bldg. - Ste. 890 South, 100 Penn Square E., Philadelphia, PA 19107. Phone: (215)656-6954.

MIDWEST—One S. Whacker Dr. - Ste. 2380, Chicago, IL 60606-4616. Phone: (312)886-8588.

NORTHEAST—JFK Federal Bldg. - Rm.675, Boston, MA 02203. Phone: (617)565-9708.

SOUTHEAST—75 Spring St. SW - Ste. 200, Atlanta, GA 30303. Phone: (404)562-0599.

WESTERN—800 5th Ave. - Ste. 3950, Seattle, WA 98104-3122. Phone: (206)553-2875.

81.041 Listed under **81.022**.

81.042 *Contact may be made at the following phone numbers:*

CENTRAL—Phone: (303)275-4785.

MID-ATLANTIC—Phone: (215)656-6954.

MIDWEST—Phone: (312)886-8588.

NORTHEAST—Phone: (617)565-9708.

SOUTHEAST—Phone: (404)562-0599.

WESTERN—Phone: (206)553-2875.

81.049 Listed under **81.022**.

81.057 Project Office, National Energy Technology Laboratory, P.O. Box 10940, Pittsburgh, PA 15236. Phone: (412)386-4781.

81.065 Office of Repository Development, Las Vegas, NV. Phone: (702)794-1368.

81.079 Regional Biomass Energy Program Offices

GREAT LAKES—25 E. Wacker Dr., Chicago, IL 60601. Phone: (312)407-0177.

NORTHEAST—400 N. Capitol St. NW, Washington, DC 20001. Phone: (202)624-8454.

NORTHWEST—800 5th Ave. - Ste. 3950, Seattle, WA 98104. Phone: (206)553-2079.

SOUTHEAST—Southern States Energy Board, Norcross, GA 30092. Phone: (770)242-7712.

WESTERN—1200 N. St., Lincoln, NE 68508. Phone: (402)471-3218.

81.089 National Energy Technology Laboratory (MS 921-107)/ (FE-UPC/AD21), P.O. Box 10940, 626 Cochrans Mill Rd., Pittsburgh, PA 15276. Phone: (412)386-4524.

81.105 SUPPORT OFFICES

Colorado—DOE, Denver Regional Support Office, 1617 Cole Blvd. - Bldg.17-2, Golden, CO 80401. Phone: (303)275-4816.

- DOE, Golden Field Office, 1617 Cole Blvd, Golden, CO 80401. Phones: (303)275-4737; FAX (303)275-4788.

Georgia—DOE, 75 Spring St. SW - Ste. 200, Atlanta, GA 30303. Phone: (404)562-0556.

Illinois—DOE, One S. Wacker Dr. - Ste. 2380, Chicago, IL 60606-4616. Phone: (312)886-8571.

Massachusetts—DOE, JFK Federal Bldg. - Rm.675, Boston, MA 02203.Phone: (617)565-9700.

Pennsylvania—DOE, 1880 JFK Blvd. - 5th fl., Philadelphia, PA 19102. Phone: (215)656-6964.

Washington—DOE, 800 5th Ave. - Ste. 3950, Seattle, WA. 98104-3122. Phone: (206)553-1004.

81.106 Institutional Relations Manager, Area Office, DOE, Carlsbad, NM 88221-3090. Phone: (505)234-7335.

81.112 Listed under **81.022**.

81.114 Idaho Operations Office Program Manager: Phone: (208)526-4169

81.119 Listed under **81.022**.

81.121 Research and Development Division, Idaho Operations Office, 1955 Fremont Ave., Idaho Falls, ID 83401. Phone: (208)526-2176.

DEPARTMENT OF EDUCATION

84.007 REGIONAL ADMINISTRATORS/STUDENT FINANCIAL AID

Students should contact their educational institution. Educational institutions should contact:

REGION I—McCormack Post Office and Courthouse - Rm.502, 5 Post Office Square, (MS 01-0070), Boston, MA 02109. Phone: (617)223-9328.

REGION II—Institutional Review Branch, 75 Park Place - 12th fl., New York, NY 10007. Phone: (212)637-6423.

REGION III—3535 Market St. - Rm.16200, (MS 03-2080), Philadelphia, PA 19104. Phone: (215)596-1018.

REGION IV—P.O. Box 1692, Atlanta, GA 30301. Phone: (404)331-0556.

REGION V—401 S. State St. - Rm.700-D, (MS 05-4080), Chicago, IL 60605. Phone: (312)353-0375.

REGION VI—1200 Main Tower Bldg. - Rm.2150, (MS 06-5080), Dallas, TX 75202. Phone: (214)767-3811.

REGION VII—Institutional Review Branch, 10220 N. Executive Hills Blvd. - 9th fl., Kansas City, MO 64153. Phone: (816)880-4054.

REGION VIII—Institutional Review Branch, 1244 Speer Blvd. - Rm.322, Denver, CO 80204. Phone: (303)844-3676.

REGION IX—50 United Nations Plaza - Rm.227, (MS 09-8080), San Francisco, CA 94102-4987. Phone: (415)556-8382.

REGION X—1000 2nd Ave. - Rm.1200, Seattle, WA 98174-1099. Phone: (206)287-1770.

84.027 *Potential applicants should contact their state department of education.*

84.032 Listed under **84.007.** *(Each state with an operating guarantee agency maintains an office; obtain list from headquarters office.)*

84.033 thru 84.038 *Students should contact their educational institution. Public and private nonprofit organizations should contact grantee educational institutions. Educational institutions should contact the appropriate Regional Office, listed under* **84.007**.

84.042 and 84.047 SECRETARY'S REGIONAL REPRESENTATIVES

REGION I—McCormack Post Office and Courthouse - Rm.540, Boston, MA 02109. Phone: (617)223-9317.

REGION II—75 Park Place - 12th fl., New York, NY 10007. Phone: (212)637-6283.

REGION III—100 Penn Square E. - Ste. 505, Philadelphia, PA 19107. Phone: (215)656-6010.

84.042 and 84.047 (cont.) **REGION IV**—61 Forsyth St. SW - Rm.19T40, Atlanta, GA 30303. Phone: (404)562-6225.

REGION V—111 N. Canal St. - Rm.1094, Chicago, IL 60606. Phone: (312)553-8192.

REGION VI—1999 Bryan St. - Ste. 2700, Dallas, TX 75201-6817. Phone: (214)880-3011.

REGION VII—10220 N. Executive Hills Blvd. - Ste. 720, Kansas City, MO 64153-1367. Phone: (816)880-4000.

REGION VIII—Federal Regional Office Bldg. - Rm.310, 1244 Speer Blvd., Denver, CO 80204-3582. Phone: (303)844-3544.

REGION IX—50 United Nations Plaza - Rm.205, San Francisco, CA 94102-4987. Phone: (415)437-7520.

REGION X—915 2nd Ave. - Rm.3362, Seattle, WA 98174-1099. Phone: (206)220-7800.

84.063 Federal Student Aid Information Center. Phone: (800)433-3243. *Or, contact the director of student financial aid at the institution the student wishes to attend, high school guidance counselors, directors of state agencies, or regional office listed under* **84.007**.

84.069 *List of state student scholarship or assistance agencies available in the Regional Offices listed under* **84.007**. *Program administered from headquarters.*

84.126 thru 84.132 REGIONAL COMMISSIONERS/REHABILITATIVE SERVICES

REGION I—McCormack Post Office and Courthouse - Rm.232, Boston, MA 02109-4557. Phone: (617)223-4085.

REGION II—75 Park Place - 12th fl., New York, NY 10007. Phone: (212)264-4016.

REGION III—100 Penn Square E. - Ste. 512, Philadelphia, PA 19107. Phone: (215)656-8531.

REGION IV—61 Forsyth St. SW - Rm.18T91, Atlanta, GA 30303. Phone: (404)562-6330.

REGION V—10220 N. Executive Hills Blvd., Kansas City, MO 64153-1367. Phone: (816)880-4107.

REGION VI—1999 Bryan St. - Rm.2740, Dallas, TX 75202. Phone: (214)808-4927.

REGION VII—111 N. Canal St. - Ste. 510, Chicago, IL 60606. Phone: (816)880-4107.

REGION VIII—Harwood Center, 1999 Bryan St., Dallas, TX 75201-6817. Phone: (214)880-4927.

REGION IX—Federal Office Bldg. - Rm.215, 50 United Nations Plaza, San Francisco, CA 94102. Phone: (415)437-7840.

REGION X—915 2nd Ave. - Rm.2848, Seattle, WA 98174-1099. Phone: (206)220-7840.

84.145 FEDERAL REAL PROPERTY ASSISTANCE PROGRAM

REGIONAL OFFICES

EASTERN ZONE (Regions I, II, III, IV, V)—Director, Office of Administrator/Management Services, McCormack Post Office and Courthouse - Rm.536, Boston, MA 02109-4557. Phone: (617)223-9321.

WESTERN ZONE (Regions VI, VII, XIII, IX, X)—Director, Office of Administrator/Management Services, 400 Maryland Ave. SW - Rm.2C107, Washington, DC 20202. Phone: (202)401-0506.

84.161 and 84.169 Listed under **84.126**.

84.173 *Contact the state educational agency.*

84.177 thru 84.250 Listed under **84.126**.

84.256 Contact Pacific Resources for Education and Learning, Honolulu, HI. Phone: (no number provided).

84.263 thru 84.265 Listed under **84.126**.

84.268 Listed under **84.007**.

84.275 Listed under **84.126**.

84.315 Listed under **84.126**.

PENSION BENEFIT GUARANTY CORPORATION

86.001 *Contact the Employee Benefits Security Administration (Department of Labor) office listed under* **17.150**.

NATIONAL ARCHIVES AND RECORDS ADMINISTRATION

PRESIDENTIAL LIBRARIES

89.001 **Arkansas**—Clinton Presidential Material Project, 1000 Laharpe Blvd., Little Rock, AR 72201. Phone: (501)254-6866.

California—Ronald Reagan Library, 40 Presidential Dr., Simi Valley, CA 93065-0600. Phone: (800)410-8354.

District of Columbia—Presidential Materials Staff, 700 Pennsylvania Ave. NW, Washington DC 20408-0001. Phone: (202)501-5705.

Georgia—Jimmy Carter Library, 441 Freedom Pkwy., Atlanta, GA 30307-1498. Phone: (404)331-3942.

Iowa—Herbert Hoover Library, 210 Parkside Dr., West Branch, IA 52358-0488. Phone: (319)643-5301.

Kansas—Dwight D. Eisenhower Library, 200 SE 4th St., Abilene, KS 67410-2900. Phone: (785)263-4751.

Maryland—Nixon Presidential Materials Staff, National Archives at College Park, College Park, MD 20740-6001. Phone: (301)713-6950.

Massachusetts—John F. Kennedy Library, Columbia Point, Boston, MA 02125-3398. Phone: (617)929-4500.

Michigan—Gerald R. Ford Museum, 303 Pearl St. NW, Grand Rapids, MI 49504-5353. Phone (616)451-9263.

- Gerald R. Ford Library, 1000 Beal Ave., Ann Arbor, MI 48109-2114. Phone: (734)741-2218.

Missouri—Harry S. Truman Library, 500 W. U.S. Hwy. 24, Independence, MO 64050-1798. Phone: (816)833-1400.

89.001 (cont.) **New York**—Franklin D. Roosevelt Library, 511 Albany Post Rd., Hyde Park, NY 12538-1999. Phone: (914)229-8114.

Texas—Lyndon B. Johnson Library, 2313 Red River St., Austin, TX 78705-5702. Phone: (512)916-5137.

- George Bush Library, 1000 George Bush Dr. W., College Station, TX 77845. Phone: (409)260-9554.

OFFICE OF REGIONAL RECORDS SERVICES

CENTRAL PLAINS REGION—200 Space Center Dr., Lee's Summit, MO 64064-1182. Phones: (816)478-7079; FAX (816)478-7623.

- 2312 E. Bannister Rd., Kansas City, MO 64131-3011. Phones: (816)926-6920; FAX (816)926-6982. **Internet:** e-mail, "kansascity.archives@nara.gov".
- (Military Records) 9700 Page Ave., St. Louis, MO 63132-5100. Phones: (314)538-4247; FAX (314)538-4005. **Internet:** e-mail, "center@stlouis.nara.gov".
- (Civilian Records) 111 Winnebago St., St. Louis, MO 63118-4199. Phones: (314)425-5722; FAX (314)425-5719. **Internet:** e-mail, "center@cpr.nara.gov".

DISTRICT OF COLUMBIA—Washington National Records Center, Reference Service Branch, Washington, DC 20409-0002. Phone: (301)457-7000.

- Archives I - Research Room Support Branch, 700 Pennsylvania Ave. NW, Washington, DC 20408. Phone: (202)501-5403.

GREAT LAKES REGION—7358 S. Pulaski Rd., Chicago, IL 60629-5898. Phones: (773)581-9688; FAX (312)886-7883. **Internet:** e-mail, "chicago.archives@nara.gov".

- 3150 Springboro Rd., Dayton, OH 45439-1883. Phones: (937)225-2878; FAX (937)225-7236. **Internet:** e-mail, "center@dayton.nara.gov".

MARYLAND—Archives II - Research Room Support Branch, College Park, MD 20740-6001. Phone: (301)713-6800.

MID ATLANTIC REGION—900 Market St., Philadelphia, PA 19107-4292. Phones: (215)597-3000, -9752; FAX (215)597-2303. **Internet:** e-mail, "archives@philarch.nara.gov".

- 14700 Townsend Rd., Philadelphia, PA 19154-1096. Phones: (215)671-8005; FAX (215)671-8001.

NORTHEAST REGION—10 Conte Dr., Pittsfield, MA 01201-8230. Phones: (413)445-6885; FAX (413)445-7305.

- 380 Trapelo Rd., Waltham, MA 02154-6399. Phones: (617)647-8108; FAX (617)647-8008. **Internet:** e-mail, "waltham.archives@nara.gov".
- 201 Varick St., New York, NY 10014-4811. Phones: (212)337-1300; FAX (212)337-1306. **Internet:** e-mail, "newyork.archives@nara.gov".

PACIFIC REGION—654 W. 3rd Ave., Anchorage, AK 99501-2145. Phones: (907)271-2443; FAX (907)271-2442. **Internet:** e-mail, "alaska.archives@nara.gov".

- 24000 Avila Rd. - 1st fl. (east entrance), Laguna Niguel, CA 92607-6719. Phones: (949)360-2618; FAX (949)360-2624. **Internet:** e-mail, "laguna.archives@nara.gov".
- 1000 Commodore Dr., San Bruno, CA 94066-2350. Phones: (650)876-9249; FAX (650)876-9233. **Internet:** e-mail, "sanbruno.archives@nara.gov".

ROCKY MOUNTAIN REGION—Denver Federal Center - Bldg. 48, Denver, CO 80225-0307. Phones: (303)236-0801; FAX (303)236-9297. **Internet:** e-mail, "denver.archives@nara.gov".

SOUTHEAST REGION—1557 St. Joseph Ave., East Point, GA 30344-2593. Phones: (404)763-7438; FAX (404)763-7059. **Internet:** e-mail, "atlanta.archives@nara.gov".

SOUTHWEST REGION—Bldg. 1, 501 W. Felix St., Ft. Worth, TX 76115-3405. *For mail:*P.O. Box 6216, Ft. Worth, TX 76115-0216. Phones: (817)334-5736; FAX (817)334-5621. **Internet:** e-mail, "ftworth.archives@nara.gov".

DEPARTMENT OF HEALTH AND HUMAN SERVICES

OFFICE OF THE SECRETARY

93.001 HHS REGIONAL OFFICES

Regional Managers, Office for Civil Rights:

REGION I—JFK Federal Bldg. - Rm.1875, Boston, MA 02203. Phones: (617)565-1340; TDD (617)565-1343; FAX (617)565-3809.

REGION II—Javits Federal Bldg. - Ste. 3313, 26 Federal Plaza, New York, NY 10278. Phones: (212)264-3313; TDD (212)264-2355; FAX (212)264-3039.

REGION III—150 S. Independence Mall - Ste. 372, Philadelphia, PA 19106-3499. Phones: (215)861-4441; TDD (215)861-4440; FAX (215)861-4431.

REGION IV—61 Forsyth St. SW - Ste. 3B70, Atlanta, GA 30323. Phones: (404)562-7886; TDD (404)562-7884; FAX (404)562-7881.

REGION V—233 N. Michigan Ave. - Ste. 240, Chicago, IL 60601. Phones: (312)886-2359; TDD (312)353-5693; FAX (312)886-1807.

REGION VI—1301 Young St. - Ste. 1169, Dallas, TX 75202. Phones: (214)767-4056; TDD (214)767-8940; FAX (214)767-0432.

REGION VII—601 E. 12th St. - Rm.248, Kansas City, MO 64106. Phones: (816)426-7278; TDD (816)426-7065; FAX (816)426-3686.

REGION VIII—1961 Stout St. - Rm.1426, Denver, CO 80294. Phones: (303)844-2024; TDD (303)844-3439; FAX (303)844-2025.

REGION IX—50 United Nations Plaza - Rm.322, San Francisco, CA 94103. Phones: (415)437-8310; TDD (415)437-8311; FAX (415)437-8329.

REGION X—2201 6th Ave. - Ste. 900, Seattle, WA 98121. Phones: (206)615-2290; TDD (206)615-2296; FAX (206)615-2297.

ADMINISTRATION ON AGING

93.041 thru 93.053 REGIONAL OFFICES

Regional Administrator, Administration on Aging:

REGION I *(Connecticut, Maine, Massachusetts, New Hampshire, Rhode Island, Vermont)*—JFK Federal Bldg. - Rm.2100, Government Center, Boston, MA 02203. Phone: (617)565-1500.

REGION II *(New York, New Jersey, Puerto Rico, Virgin Islands)*—26 Federal Plaza - Rm.3835, New York, NY 10278. Phone: (212)264-4600.

REGION III *(Delaware, District of Columbia, Maryland, Pennsylvania, Virginia, West Virginia)*—Gateway Bldg. - Rm.11480, 3535 Market St., Philadelphia, PA 19104. Phone: (215)596-6492.

REGION IV *(Alabama, Florida, Georgia, Kentucky, Mississippi, North Carolina, South Carolina, Tennessee)*—101 Marietta Tower Bldg. - Ste. 1515, Atlanta, GA 30323. Phone: (404)331-2442.

93.041 thru 93.053 *(cont.)* **REGION V** *(Illinois, Indiana, Michigan, Minnesota, Ohio, Wisconsin)*—105 W. Adams - 23rd fl., Chicago, IL 60603. Phone: (312)353-5160.

REGION VI *(Arkansas, Louisiana, New Mexico, Oklahoma, Texas)*—1301 Young St. - Ste. 1124, Dallas, TX 75202. Phone: (214)767-3301.

REGION VII *(Iowa, Kansas, Missouri, Nebraska)*—601 E. 12th St. - Rm.210, Kansas City, MO 64106. Phone: (816)426-2821.

REGION VIII *(Colorado, Montana, North Dakota, South Dakota, Utah, Wyoming)*—Federal Bldg. - Rm.325, 1961 Stout St., Denver, CO 80294-3538. Phone: (303)844-3372.

REGION IX *(American Samoa, Arizona, California, Guam, Hawaii, Nevada, Northern Mariana Islands, Trust Territories of the Pacific Islands)*—Federal Office Bldg. - Rm.431, 50 United Nations Plaza, San Francisco, CA 94102. Phone: (415)437-8500.

REGION X *(Alaska, Idaho, Oregon, Washington)*—2201 6th Ave. - Rm.1208, Seattle, WA 98121. Phone: (206)615-2010.

93.066 Technical Information Management Section, CDC Procurement and Grants Office, 2920 Brandywine Rd., Atlanta, GA 30341. Phone: (770)488-2700.

93.067 Lead Contract Specialist, International Branch, 2920 Brandywine Rd., Atlanta, GA 30341. Phone: (770)488-2632.

FOOD AND DRUG ADMINISTRATION

93.103 DISTRICT OFFICES

No field offices. Direct contact with HQ concerning grants. See main entry. However, for general information concerning Food and Drug Administration activities contact the nearest district office, following:

California—1431 Harbor Bay Pkwy., Alameda, CA 94502-7070. Phone: (510)337-6783.

- 19900 McArthur Blvd. - Ste. 300, Irvine, CA 92715-2445. Phone: (714)798-7714.

Colorado—Denver Federal Center, 6th and Kipling St., Denver, CO 80225-0087. Phone: (303)236-3016.

Florida—7200 Lake Ellenor Dr. - Ste. 120, Orlando, FL 32809. Phone: (407)648-6995.

Georgia—60 8th St. NE, Atlanta, GA 30309. Phone: (404)347-4344.

Illinois—300 S. Riverside Plaza - Ste. 550 S., Chicago, IL 60606. Phone: (312)353-7379.

Kansas—11630 W. 80th St., Lenexa, KS 66285-5905. Phone: (913)752-2144.

Louisiana—4298 Elysian Fields Ave., New Orleans, LA 70122. Phone: (504)589-2401, ext.124.

Maryland—900 Madison Ave., Baltimore, MD 21201. Phone: (410)962-4012.

Massachusetts—One Montvale Ave. - 4th fl., Stoneham, MA 02180. Phone: (617)279-1675, ext.155.

Michigan—1560 E. Jefferson Ave., Detroit, MI 48207. Phone: (313)226-6260, ext.101.

Minnesota—240 Hennepin Ave., Minneapolis, MN 55401-1912. Phone: (612)334-4100, ext.121.

New Jersey—Waterview Corporate Center - 3rd fl., 10 Waterview Blvd., Parsippany, NJ 07054. Phone: (973)331-2901.

New York—850 3rd Ave., Brooklyn, NY 11232-1593. Phone: (718)340-7000, ext.5301.

- 599 Delaware Ave., Buffalo, NY 14202. Phone: (716)551-4461.

Ohio—1141 Central Pkwy., Cincinnati, OH 45202-1097. Phone: (513)684-3504.

Pennsylvania—U.S. Customhouse - Rm.900, 2nd & Chestnut St., Philadelphia, PA 19106. Phone: (215)597-4390, ext.4200.

Puerto Rico—466 Fernandez Juncos Ave., San Juan, PR 00901-3223. Phone: (787)729-6842.

Tennessee—297 Plus Park Blvd., Nashville, TN 37217. Phone: (615)781-5392, ext.128.

Texas—3310 Live Oak St., Dallas, TX 75204. Phone: (214)655-5315, ext.302.

Washington—Federal Office Bldg., 22201 23rd Dr. SE, Bothell, WA 98041-3012. Phone: (425)483-4950.

INDIAN HEALTH SERVICE

93.164 AREA OFFICES

Alaska Area *(Alaska)*—4141 Ambassador Dr., Anchorage, AK 99508-5928. Phone: (907)257-3686.

Arizona: Navajo Area *(Arizona, Colorado, New Mexico, Utah)*—Window Rock, AZ 86515-9020. Phone: (520)871-5811.

- **Phoenix Area** *(Arizona, Nevada, Utah)*—3738 N. 16th St. - Ste. A, Phoenix, AZ 85016-5981. Phone: (602)640-2052.
- **Tucson Area** *(Arizona)*—OHPRD, 7900 S. "J" Stock Rd., Tucson, AZ 85746-9352. Phone: (520)295-2406.

California Area *(California)*—1825 Bell St. - Ste. 200, Sacramento, CA 95825-1097. Phone: (916)566-7101.

Maryland: Headquarters Office—5600 Fishers Ln. - Rm.6-05, Rockville, MD 20857. Phone: (301)443-1083.

Minnesota: Bemidji Area *(Michigan, Minnesota, Wisconsin)*—127 Federal Bldg., Bemidji, MN 56601. Phone: (218)759-3412.

Montana: Billings Area *(Montana, Wyoming)*—2900 4th Genuire N. - P.O. Box 2143, Billings, MT 59103. Phone: (406)247-7107.

New Mexico: Albuquerque Area *(Colorado, New Mexico)*—505 Marquette NW - Ste. 1502, Albuquerque, NM 87102-2163. Phone: (505)248-4500.

- **Headquarters West Office**—5300 Homestead Rd. NE, Albuquerque, NM 87110. Phone: (505)248-4102.

Oklahoma: Oklahoma City Area *(Kansas, Oklahoma)*—5 Corporate Plaza, 3625 NW 56th St., Oklahoma City, OK 73112. Phone: (405)951-3768.

Oregon: Portland Area *(Idaho, Oregon, Washington)*—1220 SW 3rd Ave. - Rm.476, Portland, OR 97204-2892. Phone: (503)326-2020.

South Dakota: Aberdeen Area *(Iowa, Nebraska, North Dakota, South Dakota)*—Federal Bldg., 115 4th Ave. SE, Aberdeen, SD 57401. Phone: (605)226-7581.

Tennessee: Nashville Area *(Alabama, Arkansas, Connecticut, Delaware, Florida, Georgia, Illinois, Indiana, Kentucky, Louisiana, Maine, Maryland, Massachusetts, Mississippi, Missouri, New Hampshire, New Jersey, New York, North Carolina, Ohio, Pennsylvania, Rhode Island, South Carolina, Tennessee, Texas, Vermont, Virginia, West Virginia)*—711 Stewarts Ferry Pike, Nashville, TN 37214-2634. Phone: (615)736-2400.

93.217 Listed under **93.001**.

93.228 Listed under **93.164**.

93.260 Listed under **93.001**.

93.284 Listed under **93.164**.

93.441 Listed under **93.164**.

93.447 thru 93.449 Regional office information will be provided in the application packet, if applicable.

ADMINISTRATION FOR CHILDREN AND FAMILIES

93.550 thru 93.674 Regional Administrator, ACF, HHS Regional Office. *Use addresses listed under* **93.041**.

CENTERS FOR MEDICARE AND MEDICAID SERVICES

93.767 thru 93.778 Regional Administrator, CMS, HHS Regional Office. *Use addresses listed under* **93.041**.

93.779 thru 93.781 Same as **93.767**

93.782 *Contacts may be made at the following regional offices:*

- New York, NY. Phone: (212)264-3904.
- San Francisco, CA. Phone: (415)744-3598.

93.945 Listed under **93.041**.

93.971 and 93.972 Same as **93.164**.

93.982 Regional Director, FEMA Regional Office. *See addresses listed under* **97.017**.

CORPORATION FOR NATIONAL AND COMMUNITY SERVICE

94.002 thru 94.016

ATLANTIC CLUSTER OFFICES

CLUSTER DIRECTOR—801 Arch St. - Ste. 103, Philadelphia, PA 19107-2416. Phones: (215)597-9972; FAX (215)597-4933.

Connecticut—One Commercial Plaza - 21st fl., Hartford, CT 06103-3510. Phones: (860)240-3237; FAX (860)240-3238.

Delaware—*see* **Maryland**.

Maine—*see* **New Hampshire**.

Maryland—Fallon Federal Bldg. - Ste. 400B, 31 Hopkins Plaza, Baltimore, MD 21201-3418. Phones: (410)962-4443; FAX (410)962-3201.

Massachusetts—10 Causeway St. - Rm.473, Boston, MA 02222-1038. Phones: (617)565-7000; FAX (617)565-7011.

New Hampshire—1 Pillsbury St. - Ste. 201, Concord, NH 03301-3556. Phones: (603)225-1450; FAX (603)225-1459.

New Jersey—44 S. Clinton Ave. - Ste. 702, Trenton, NJ 08609-1507. Phones: (609)989-2243; FAX (609)989-2304.

New York—O'Brien Federal Bldg. - Rm.818, Clinton Ave. and Pearl St., Albany, NY 12207. Phones: (518)431-4150: FAX (518)431-4154.

Pennsylvania—Nix Federal Bldg. - Ste. 229, 900 Market St., Philadelphia, PA 19107. Phones: (215)597-2806; FAX (215)597-2807.

Puerto Rico - Virgin Islands—Federal Bldg. - Ste. 662, 150 Carlos Chardon Ave., Hato Rey, PR 00918-1737. Phones: (787)766-5314; FAX (787)766-5189.

Rhode Island—400 Westminster St. - Rm.203, Providence, RI 02903. Phones: (401)528-5424; FAX (401)528-5220.

Vermont—*See* **New Hampshire**.

NORTH CENTRAL CLUSTER OFFICES

CLUSTER DIRECTOR—77 W. Jackson Blvd. - Ste. 442, Chicago, IL 60604-3511. Phones: (312)353-7705; FAX (312)353-5343.

Illinois—77 W. Jackson Blvd. - Ste. 442, Chicago, IL 60604-3511. Phones: (312)353-3622; FAX (312)353-5343.

Indiana—46 E. Ohio St. - Rm.457, Indianapolis, IN 46204-1922. Phones: (317)226-6724; FAX (317)226-5437.

Iowa—Federal Bldg. - Rm.917, 210 Walnut St., Des Moines, IA 50309-2195. Phones: (515)284-4816; FAX (515)284-6640.

Michigan—211 W. Fort St. - Ste. 1408, Detroit, MI 48226-2799. Phones: (313)226-7848; FAX (313)226-2557.

Minnesota—431 S. 7th St. - Ste. 2480, Minneapolis, MN 55415-1854. Phones: (612)334-4083; FAX (612)334-4084.

Nebraska—Federal Bldg. - Rm.156, 100 Centennial Mall N., Lincoln, NE 68508-3896. Phones: (402)437-5493; FAX (402)437-5495.

North Dakota - South Dakota—Federal Bldg. - Rm.225, 225 S. Pierre St., Pierre, SD 57501-2452. Phones: (605)224-5996; FAX (605)224-9201.

Ohio—51 N. High St. - Ste. 451, Columbus, OH 43215. Phones: (614)469-7441; FAX (614)469-2125.

Wisconsin—Reuss Federal Plaza - Rm.1240, 310 W. Wisconsin Ave., Milwaukee, WI 53203-2211. Phones: (414)297-1118; FAX (414)297-1863.

PACIFIC CLUSTER OFFICES

CLUSTER DIRECTOR—P.O. Box 29996, Presidio of San Francisco, CA 94129-0996. Phones: (415)561-5960; FAX (415)561-5970.

Alaska—*See* **Washington**. Phones: (206)220-7736; FAX (206)553-4415.

California—11150 W. Olympia Blvd. - Ste. 170, Los Angeles, CA 90064. Phones: (310)235-7421; FAX (310)235-7422.

Hawaii, Guam, American Samoa—Federal Bldg. - Rm.6213, 300 Ala Moana Blvd., Honolulu, HI 96850-0001. Phones: (808)541-2832; FAX (808)541-3603.

Idaho—304 N. 8th St. - Rm.344, Boise, ID 83702-5835. Phones: (208)334-1707; FAX (208)334-1421.

Montana—Capitol One Center - Ste. 206, 208 N. Montana Ave. Helena, MT 59601-3837. Phones: (406)449-5404; FAX (406)449-5412.

Nevada—4600 Kietzke Ln. - Ste. E-141, Reno, NV 89502-5033. Phones: (702)784-5314; FAX (702)784-5026.

Oregon—2010 Lloyd Center, Portland, OR 97232. Phones: (503)231-2103; FAX (503)231-2106.

Utah—350 S. Main St. - Rm.504, Salt Lake City, UT 84101-2198. Phones: (801)524-5411; FAX (801)524-3599.

Washington—Jackson Federal Bldg. - Ste. 3190, 915 2nd Ave., Seattle, WA 98174-1103. Phones: (206)220-7745; FAX (206)553-4415.

Wyoming—Federal Bldg. - Rm.1110, 2120 Capitol Ave., Cheyenne, WY 82001-3649. Phones: (307)772-2385; FAX (307)772-2389.

94.002 thru 94.016 *(cont.)*

SOUTHERN CLUSTER OFFICES

CLUSTER DIRECTOR—60 Forsyth St. SW, - Ste. 3M40, Atlanta, GA 30323-2301. Phones: (404)562-4055; FAX (404)562-4071.

Alabama—Medical Forum - Ste. 428, 950 22nd St. N., Birmingham, AL 35203. Phones: (205)731-0027; FAX(205)731-0031.

District of Columbia—*See* **Virginia**.

Florida—3165 McCrory St. - Ste. 115, Orlando, FL 32803-3750. Phones: (407)648-6117; FAX (407)648-6116.

Georgia—75 Piedmont Ave. NE - Ste. 982, Atlanta, GA 30303-2587. Phones: (404)331-4646; FAX (404)331-2898.

Kentucky—Federal Bldg. - Rm.372-D, 600 Martin Luther King Place, Louisville, KY 40202-2230. Phones: (502)582-6384; FAX (502)582-6386.

Mississippi—100 W. Capitol St. - Rm.1005A, Jackson, MS 39269-1092. Phones: (601)965-5664; FAX (601)965-4617.

North Carolina—300 Fayetteville St. Mall - Rm.131, Raleigh, NC 27601-1739. Phones: (919)856-4731; FAX (919)856-4738.

South Carolina—1835 Assembly St. - Ste. 872, Columbia, SC 29201-2430. Phones: (803)765-5771; FAX (803)765-5777.

Tennessee—265 Cumberland Bend Dr., Nashville, TN 37228. Phones: (615)736-5561; FAX (615)736-7937.

Virginia—400 N. 8th St. - Ste. 446, P.O. Box 10066, Richmond, VA 23240-1832. Phones: (804)771-2197; FAX (804)771-2157.

West Virginia—10 Hale St. - Ste. 203, Charleston, WV 25301-1409. Phones: (304)347-5246; FAX (304)347-5464.

SOUTHWEST CLUSTER OFFICES

CLUSTER DIRECTOR—1999 Bryan St. - Rm.2050, Dallas, TX 75201. Phones: (214)880-7050; FAX (214)880-7074.

Arizona—522 N. Central - Rm.205A, Phoenix, AZ 85004-2190. Phones: (602)379-4825; FAX (602)379-4030.

Arkansas—Federal Bldg. - Rm.2506, 700 W. Capitol St., Little Rock, AR 72201. Phones: (501)324-5234; FAX (501)324-6949.

Colorado—999 18th St. - Ste. 1440 South, Denver, CO 80202. Phones: (303)312-7950; FAX (303)312-7954.

Kansas—444 SE Quincy - Rm.260, Topeka, KS 66683-3572. Phones: (785)295-2540; FAX (785)295-2596.

Louisiana—707 Florida St. - Ste. 316, Baton Rouge, LA 70801-1910. Phones: (504)389-0473; FAX (504)389-0510.

Missouri—801 Walnut St. - Ste. 504, Kansas City, MO 64106-2009. Phones: (816)347-6300; FAX (816)347-6305.

New Mexico—120 S. Federal Place - Rm.315, Santa Fe, NM 87501-2026. Phones: (505)988-6577; FAX (505)988-6661.

Oklahoma—215 Dean A. McGee - Ste. 324, Oklahoma City, OK 73102. Phones: (405)231-5201; FAX (405)231-4329.

Texas—903 San Jacinto St. - Ste. 130, Austin, TX 78701-3747. Phones: (512)916-5671; FAX (512)916-5806.

SOCIAL SECURITY ADMINISTRATION

96.001 thru 96.020 There are 1,296 district and branch SSA offices located in cities and towns throughout the U.S. Consult the local phone directory under "Social Security Administration" or "U.S. Government" or ask for address at local U.S. Post Office.

DEPARTMENT OF HOMELAND SECURITY

IMMIGRATION AND CUSTOMS ENFORCEMENT

97.009 DHS,ICE, OIA, PHAB Miami Office, 51 SW 1st Ave. - Rm.220, Miami, FL 33130. Phone:(305)536-4261.

97.010 FIELD OFFICES

Alabama—Mobile Border Patrol, P.O. Box 1526, Mobile, AL 36633. Phones: (334)441-6139.

- Mobile Port of Entry, P.O. Box 1526, Mobile, AL 36601. Phones: (334)441-5135.

Alaska—Anchorage District Office, 620 E. 10th Ave. - Ste. 102, Anchorage, AK 99501-3701. Phone: (907)271-3524.

- Anchorage International Airport, 4601 Satellite Dr., P.O. Box 19068, Anchorage, AK 99519-0688. Phone: (907)243-1400.
- Dutch Harbor Port of Entry, 2315 Airport Beach Rd. - Rm.205, P.O. Box 750, Dutch Harbor, AK 99692. Phone: (907)581-4114.
- Eagle Port of Entry, c/o Postmaster - Box 1, Eagle, AK 99738. Phone: (907)547-2211.
- Fairbanks Port of Entry, 6450 Old Airport Way, Fairbanks, AK 99709. Phone: (907)474-0307.
- Gambell Port of Entry, P.O. Box 1, Gambell, AK 99742. Phone: (907)985-5211.
- Dalton's Cache Port of Entry, Haines Hwy. - Mile 40, Haines, AK 99827-1509. Phone: (907)767-5580.
- Ketchikan Port of Entry, 111 Main St., Ketchikan, AK 99840. Phone: (907)225-2380.
- Alaska Marine Hwy. Terminal, Prince Rupert, BC Canada, c/o 111 Main St., Ketchikan, AK 99840. Phone: (604)624-3833.
- Nome Port of Entry, P.O. Box 281, Nome, AK 99762. Phone: (907)443-2065.
- Skagaway Port of Entry, Klondike Hwy. Border Station, Skagaway, AK 99840-0475. Phone: (907)983-3144.
- Turner Port of Entry, P.O. Box 1221, Tok, AK 99780. Phone: (907)774-2242.

Arizona—Ajo Border Patrol, 850 N. Tucson - Ajo Hwy. 86, P.O. Drawer J, Ajo/Highway, AZ 85321. Phone: (520)387-7002.

97.010 *(cont.)*

- Casa Grande Border Patrol, 396 Camino Mercado, Casa Grande, AZ 85222. Phone: (520)836-7812.
- Douglas Border Patrol, 1051 Lawrence St., P.O. Box 1175, Douglas, AZ 85608. Phone: (520)364-3991.
- Douglas Port of Entry, Pan American Ave. and 1st St., Douglas, AZ 85607. Phones: (520)364-5532, -6479.
- Eloy Processing Center, 4465 E. Hanna Rd. - Ste. 343, Eloy, AZ 85231. Phone: (520)466-2000.
- Florence Processing Center, 3250 N. Pinal Pkwy. Ave., Florence, AZ 85232. Phone: (520)868-5862.
- Lukeville Port of Entry, Highway 85, P.O. Box D, Lukeville, AZ 85341. Phone: (520)387-6047.
- Naco Border Patrol, 2136 Naco Hwy., Bisbee, AZ 85603. Phone: (520)432-5121.
- Naco Port of Entry, 106 "D" St., P.O. Box 277, Naco, AZ 85620. Phones: (520)432-3111, -2791.
- Nogales Border Patrol, 1500 W. La Quinta Rd., Nogales, AZ 85621. Phone: (520)377-6000.
- Phoenix Border Patrol, 3006 W. Claredon Ave., Phoenix, AZ 85017. Phone: (520)670-6865.
- Phoenix Sky Harbor Airport, P.O. Box 63673, Phoenix, AZ 85082-2673. Phones: (602)275-7745, -7763, -7785.
- Phoenix District Office, 2035 N. Central Ave., Phoenix, AZ 85004-1548. Phone: (602)514-7799.
- San Luis Port of Entry, Hwy. 95, P.O. Box 448, San Luis, AZ 85349. Phone: (520)627-3591.
- Sasabe Port of Entry, Federal Inspection Bldg., Sasabe, AZ 85633-0326. Phone: (520)823-4230.
- Sonoita Border Patrol, Hwy. 82 and 83, Sonoita, AZ 85637-0037. Phone: (520)455-5051.
- Tucson Border Patrol, 2010 Ajo Way, Tucson, AZ 85713. Phone: (520)670-6865.
- Tucson Border Patrol Sector Hdqtrs., 1970 W. Ajo Way, Tucson, AZ 85713. Phones: (520)670-6871, -6880.
- Wellton Border Patrol, 29820 Frontage Rd., P.O. Box 128, Wellton, AZ 85356. Phone: (520)785-9364.
- Willcox Border Patrol, 200 W. Downen St., Willcox, AZ 85644-0909. Phone: (520)384-2412.
- Yuma Border Patrol, 12122 S. Ave. A, Yuma, AZ 85366-2708. Phone: (520)726-8731.
- Yuma Border Patrol Sector Hdqtrs., 350 W. 1st St., Yuma, AZ 85366-2708. Phone: (520)782-9548.

Bahamas—Freeport Bahamas Sub-Office, P.O. Box F-2664, Freeport, Grand Bahama, BAHAMAS. Phone:(242)352-5586.

- Nassau, Bahamas Sub-Office, U.S. Immigration, Miami, FL 33159-9009. Phone: (242)377-7125.

California—Bakersfield Processing Center, 17635 Industrial Farm Rd., P.O. Box 81143, Bakersfield, CA 93380. Phone: (805)861-4465.

- Bakersfield Satellite Investigations, 800 Truxton Ave. - Rm.317, Bakersfield, CA 93301. Phone: (805)861-4478.
- Western Form Center, Bldg. 701 - Bay A, 5600 Rickenbacker Rd., Bell, CA 90201. Phone: (213)526-7404.

- Blythe Border Patrol, 16870 W. Hobsonway, P.O. Box 836, Blythe, CA 92226. Phone: (619)922-6715.
- Boulevard Border Patrol, 39701 Avenue de Robles Verde, P.O. Box 1320, Boulevard, CA 92005. Phone: (619)766-4542.
- Calexico Port of Entry, 200 E. 1st St., P.O. Box 1780, Calexico, CA 92231. Phones: (619)357-1189, -7968, -1143.
- Calexico East Port of Entry, 1699 E. Carr Rd., Calexico, CA 92231. Phone: (619)768-2450.
- Oxnard Border Patrol, 275 Skyway Dr., P.O. Box 88, Camarillo, CA 93011. Phone: (805)482-8997.
- Campo Border Patrol, 3 Forest Gate Rd., P.O. Box 68, Campo, CA 91906. Phone: (619)557-6144.
- Livermore Border Patrol Station and Sector Hdqtrs., 6102 9th St., Dublin, CA 94568. Phones: (925)828-3770, (925)828-0371.
- El Cajon Border Patrol, 225 Kenney St., El Cajon, CA 92020. Phone: (619)557-5072.
- El Centro Processing Center, 1115 N. Imperial Ave., El Centro, CA 92243-1739. Phone: (619)353-2170.
- El Centro Border Patrol Sector Hdqtrs., 1111 N. Imperial Ave., El Centro, CA 92243-1795. Phone: (619)352-3241.
- El Centro Border Patrol Station, 1081 N. Imperial Ave., El Centro, CA 92243. Phone: (760)353-0541.
- Fresno Border Patrol Station, 4367 N. Golden State Blvd., Fresno, CA 93722. Phone: (209)487-5506.
- Fresno Sub-Office, 865 Fulton Mall, Fresno, CA 93721-2816. Phone: (209)487-5126.
- Imperial Beach Border Patrol, 1802 Saturn Way, Imperial Beach Beach, CA 91933-0068. Phone: (619)662-7149.
- Indio Border Patrol, 45-620 Commerce St., Indio, CA 92201. Phone: (760)347-3658.
- Western Operations Region, 24000 Avila Rd., P.O. Box 30080, Laguna Niguel, CA 92607-0080. Phone: (714)643-4236.
- Long Beach Seaport Unit, 501 W. Ocean Blvd. - Ste. 6300, Long Beach, CA 90802. Phone: (310)980-3400.
- Los Angeles District Office, 300 N. Los Angeles St., Los Angeles, CA 90012. Phone: (213)894-4627.
- Los Angeles International Airport, Tom Bradley International Terminal - Lower Level, 380 Worldway, P.O. Box N-20, Los Angeles, CA 90045. Phones: (310)215-2104, ext.107; (310)215-2101, ext.103.
- Oakland International Airport, International Terminal, 1 Airport Dr., Oakland, CA 94621. Phone: (510)273-7390.
- Ontario Airport, 222 E. Airport Dr., Ontario, CA 91761. Phones: (909)395-8668, -8673.
- Riverside Border Patrol, 2060 Chicago Ave. - Ste. A2, Riverside, CA 92507. Phone: (909)686-4100.
- Sacramento Border Patrol Station, Bldg. 500 - Ste. 575, 7000 Franklin Blvd., Sacramento, CA 95823. Phone: (916)391-9087.
- Sacramento Sub-Office, 650 Capital Mall, Sacramento, CA 95814. Phone: (916)498-6460.
- Salinas Border Patrol, 1636 E. Alisal St., P.O. Box 218, Salinas, CA 93902. Phone: (408)754-0633.

97.010 *(cont.)*

- San Clemente Border Patrol, I-5 Northbound Traffic Checkpoint, P.O. Box 3188, San Clemente, CA 92674. Phone: (619)557-5272.
- San Diego District Office, 880 Front St. - Ste. 1234, San Diego, CA 92101-8834. Phone: (619)557-5645.
- Brown Field Border Patrol, 7560 Britannia St., San Diego, CA 92173. Phone: (619)661-3154.
- Ota Mesa Port of Entry, 2500 Paseo International, San Diego, CA 92143-9018. Phones: (619)661-3249, -3231.
- San Diego International Airport, Lindbergh Field Airport, 3665 N. Harbor Dr., San Diego, CA 92101. Phone: (619)298-2612.
- San Ysidro Port of Entry, 720 San Ysidro Blvd., San Diego, CA 92143-9018. Phones: (619)662-7314, -7240.
- San Francisco International Airport, Central Terminal - Lower Level, Customs Area, P.O. Box 280551, San Francisco, CA 94128. Phone: (415)876-2876.
- San Francisco District Office, 630 Sansome St., San Francisco, CA 94111-2280. Phone: (415)705-3102.
- San Jose International Airport, c/o P.O. Box 280551, Central Terminal - Lower Level, Customs Area, San Jose, CA 95110. Phone: (408)291-7209.
- San Jose Sub-Office, 280 S. 1st St. - Rm.1150, San Jose, CA 95113. Phone: (408)535-5174.
- San Luis Obispo Border Patrol Station, 1170 Calle Joaquin, P.O. Box 1486, San Luis Obispo, CA 93406. Phone: (805)543-9490.
- San Marcos Border Patrol, 126 S. Pacific, P.O. Box 5099, San Marcos, CA 92069. Phone: (619)557-5589.
- San Pedro Processing Center, Terminal Island, 2001 Seaside Ave., San Pedro, CA 90731. Phone: (310)732-0777.
- Stockton Border Patrol, P.O. Box 2047, Stockton, CA 95201. Phones: (209)946-6211, -6284.
- Tecate Port of Entry, Tecate, CA 92080-0219. Phone: (619)478-5029.
- Temecula Border Patrol, 43136 Rancho Way, P.O. Box 38, Temecula, CA 92593. Phone: (909)694-6871.
- Andrade Port of Entry, 235 Andrade Rd., Winterhaven, CA 92283. Phones: (619)572-5350, -5184.

Colorado—Denver District Office, Albrook Center, 4730 Paris St., Denver, CO 80239-2804. Phone: (303)371-6213.

- Grand Junction Port of Entry, 255 Main St., Grand Junction, CO 81501. Phone: (303)243-5141.
- Pueblo Port of Entry, P.O. Box 1879, Pueblo, CO 81002. Phone: (719)544-9369.

Connecticut—Hartford Sub-Office, Ribicoff Federal Bldg., 450 Main St., Hartford, CT 06103-3060. Phone: (203)240-3052.

District of Columbia—Dulles International Airport, P.O. Box 17775, Washington, DC 20041. Phone: (703)661-5100.

- INS Headquarters, 425 I St. NW, Washington, DC 20536. Phone: (202)514-4316.

Florida—Jacksonville Port of Entry, Federal Bldg - Rm.G-18, 400 W. Bay St., Jacksonville, FL 32202. Phone: (904)232-2164.

- Key West Port of Entry and Sub-Office, Federal Bldg. - Rm.201, 301 Simontown St., Key West, FL 33040. Phones: (305)293-9150, 296-2233. *For mail:*P.O. Box 86, Key West, FL 33041.
- Miami International Airport - Concourse E (3rd fl.), Miami, FL 33299-7895. Phones: (305)526-2612, -2626, -2851, -2930.

- Krome North Service Processing Center, Snapper Creek Station, 18201 SW 12th St., P.O. Box 160327, Miami, FL 33194. Phone: (305)552-1845.
- Miami District Office, 7880 Biscayne Blvd., Miami, FL 33138. Phone: (305)762-3405.
- Miami Border Patrol Sector Hdqtrs., 7201 Pembroke Rd., Pembroke Pines, FL 33023. Phone: (954)963-9807.
- West Palm Beach Port of Entry, 4 E. Port Rd. - Rm.410, Riviera Beach, FL 33419. Phone: (407)845-6898.
- West Palm Beach Sub-Office, 301 N. Broadway, Riviera Beach, FL 33404. Phone: (561)841-0498.
- Tampa Border Patrol, 1821B E. Sahlman Dr., Tampa, FL 33605. Phones: (813)228-2156, -2160.
- Orlando Border Patrol, Winter Park, FL 32790-0440. Phone: (407)648-6081.

Georgia—Atlanta District Office, 77 Forsyth St. SW, Atlanta, GA 30303-0253. Phone: (404)331-0253.

- Hartsfield International Airport Port of Entry, P.O. Box 45527, Atlanta, GA 30320. Phone: (404)763-7816.
- Savannah International Airport, 33 Bull St. - Ste. 505, Savannah, GA 31401. Phone: (912)652-4460.

Guam—Guam International Airport, Sirena Plaza - Ste. 100, 108 Hernan Cortez Ave., Agana, GU 96910. Phone: (671)642-7611.

Hawaii—Honolulu District Office, 595 Ala Moana Blvd., Honolulu, HI 96813. Phones: (808)532-3748, -3746.

- Honolulu International Airport, 300 Rodgers Blvd., Terminal Box 50, Honolulu, HI 96819. Phones: (808)861-8401, -8406, -8400, -8409.

Idaho—4620 Overland Rd. - Rm.108, Boise, ID 83705. Phone: (208)334-1822.

- Eastport Port of Entry, Hwy. 95, P.O. Box 8, Eastport, ID 83826. Phones: (208)267-2183, -3745.
- Porthill Port of Entry, P.O. Box 40, Porthill, ID 83853. Phone: (208)267-5309.

Illinois—Chicago District Office, 10 W. Jackson Blvd. - Ste. 600, Chicago, IL 60604. Phone: (312)385-1900.

Indiana—Indianapolis Sub-Office, Gateway Plaza - Rm.400, 950 N. Meridan St., Indianapolis, IN 46204. Phone: (217)226-6181.

Kansas—Garden City Port of Entry, 1404 E. Fulton, Box 1239, Garden City, KS 67846. Phone: (316)275-1054.

- Wichita Port of Entry, 625 N. Winterset, Wichita, KS 67212. Phone: (316)945-9741.

Kentucky—Louisville Sub-Office, Snyder Courthouse - Rm.604, 601 W. Broadway, Louisville, KY 40202. Phone: (502)582-6526.

Louisiana—Baton Rouge Border Patrol, 9522 Brookline Dr., P.O. Box 338, Baton Rouge, LA 70821. Phone: (504)389-0231.

- New Orleans International Airport, 900 Airline Hwy., Kenner, LA 70062. Phone: (504)589-3949.
- Lake Charles Border Patrol, P.O. Box 868, Lake Charles, LA 70601. Phone: (318)477-9245.
- New Orleans District Office, Postal Services Bldg. - Rm.T-8011, 701 Loyola Ave., New Orleans, LA 70113. Phone: (504)589-6521.
- New Orleans Border Patrol Sector Hdqtrs., 3819 Patterson Dr., P.O. Box 6218, New Orleans, LA 70174. Phone: (504)589-6107.
- Oakdale Processing Center, 207 E. 5th Ave., P.O. Box 5095, Oakdale, LA 71463. Phone: (318)335-0713.

97.010 *(cont.)*

Maine—Bangor Port of Entry, 267A Godfrey Blvd., Bangor, ME 04402-0677. Phone: (207)945-0334.

- Bar Harbor Port of Entry, Marine Atlantic Ferry Terminal, Eden St., Bar Harbor, ME 04609. Phone: (207)288-4675.
- Bridgewater Port of Entry, RFD Rt. 1 - Box 42, Boundary Line Rd., Bridgewater, ME 04735. Phone: (207)425-4502.
- Calais Border Patrol, One Main St., P.O. Box 245, Calais, ME 04619. Phone: (207)454-3613.
- Calais Port of Entry, Border Inspection Station, One Main St. - P.O. Drawer 421, Calais, ME 04619. Phone: (207)454-2546.
- Coburn Gore Port of Entry, Star Rt. 73, P.O. Box 35, Eustis, ME 04936. Phone: (207)297-2771.
- Ft. Fairfield Border Patrol, 205 Main St., P.O. Box 410, Ft. Fairfield, ME 04742. Phone: (207)472-5041.
- Ft. Fairfield Port of Entry, Rural Rt. 1 - Box 217, Ft. Fairfield, ME 04742. Phone: (207)473-7396.
- Ft. Kent Port of Entry, 98 W. Main St., Ft. Kent, ME 04743-1016. Phone: (207)834-3223.
- Houlton Border Patrol Sector Hdqtrs. and Border Station, Rt. 1 - Calais Rd., P.O. Box 706, Houlton, ME 04730. Phones: (207)532-9061, -6521, -6522 (24 hours).
- Houlton Port of Entry, Interstate 95, P.O. Box 189, Houlton, ME 04730. Phone: (207)532-2906.
- Jackman Border Patrol, Nickels Rd., P.O. Box 608, Jackman, ME 04945. Phone: (207)668-3151 (24 hours).
- Jackman Port of Entry, Star Rt. 76 - Box 629, Jackman, ME 04945. Phone: (207)668-3771.
- Limestone Port of Entry, R.F.D. 1, Box 258, Limestone, ME 04750-9729. Phone: (207)325-4760.
- Lubec Port of Entry, Federal Bldg., U.S. Post Office and Border Station, Washington St. and Campobello Bridge, Lubec, ME 04652. Phone: (207)733-4960.
- Madawaska Port of Entry, 2 Bridge St., Madawaska, ME 04756-1230. Phone: (207)728-4565.
- Vanceboro Port of Entry, USINS, Water St., P.O. Box C, Vanceboro, ME 04491. Phone: (207)788-7813.
- Van Buren Port of Entry, International Bridge, Bridge St., P.O. Box 116, Van Buren, ME 04785. Phones: (207)868-2202, -3900.
- Van Buren Border Patrol, Main St., P.O. Box 26, Van Buren, ME 04785. Phone: (207)868-3900.
- Hamlin Port of Entry, H.C. 62 - Box 63, Van Buren, ME 04785. Phone: (207)868-0966.

Maryland—Baltimore District Office, Fallen Federal Bldg., 31 Hopkins Plaza, Baltimore, MD 21201. Phone: (410)962-2010.

Massachusetts—Boston District Office, Kennedy Federal Bldg. - Rm.1700, Government Center, Boston, MA 02203. Phone: (617)565-4214.

- Boston Service Processing Center, 427 Commercial St., Boston, MA 02109. Phones: (617)223-3090, -3089, -3088.

Michigan—Algonac Port of Entry, 202 Fruit St., Algonac, MI 48001. Phone: (810)794-3321.

- District/Canada Tunnel, 150 E. Jefferson Ave., Detroit, MI 48226. Phone: (313)568-6019.

- Detroit International Bridge, 3033 Porter, Detroit, MI 48216. Phone: (313)963-4408.
- Detroit City Airport, 11499 Conner - Rm.138C, Detroit, MI 48213. Phone: (313)521-8430.
- Grand Rapids Border Patrol, 100 W. 7th St., Holland, MI 49422-1678. Phone: (616)392-4070.
- Port Huron Border Patrol, 2112 River Rd., Marysville, MI 48040. Phone: (810)364-6041.
- Port Huron Port of Entry, 2321 Pinegrove Ave., Port Huron, MI 48060. Phone: (810)942-0493.
- Detroit Metro Airport, International Terminal, Romulus, MI 48242. Phone: (313)955-6293.
- Sault Ste. Marie Port of Entry and Border Patrol, International Bridge Plaza, P.O. Box 141, Sault Ste. Marie, MI 49783. Phones: (906)632-3383, -8822.
- Trenton Border Patrol, 23100 W. Rd., P.O. Box 206, Trenton, MI 48183. Phone: (313)676-2972.

Minnesota—Baudette Port of Entry, International Bridge, P.O. Box 487, Baudette, MN 56623. Phone: (218)634-2661.

- St. Paul District Office, 2901 Metro Dr. - Ste. 100, Bloomington, MN 55425. Phone: (612)335-2211.
- Crane Lake Port of Entry, 7544 Gold Coast Rd., Crane Lake, MN 55725. Phone: (218)993-2321.
- Duluth Port of Entry and Border Patrol, U.S. Courthouse and Custom House, 114 Federal Bldg., 515 W. 1st St., Duluth, MN 55802. Phones: (218)720-5207, -5465.
- Ely Port of Entry, P.O. Box 28, Ely, MN 55731. Phone: (218)365-3262.
- Grand Marais Border Patrol, Hwy. 61 East - P.O. Box 685, Grand Marais, MN 55604. Phone: (218)387-1770.
- Grand Portage Port of Entry, Hwy. 61, Grand Portage, MN 55605. Phone: (218)475-2494.
- International Falls Border Patrol, 1412 Hwy. 11-71 West, International Falls, MN 56649. Phone: (218)283-2461.
- No.2 2nd Ave., International Falls, MN 56649-2328. Phone: (218)283-8611.
- Lancaster Port of Entry, Rt. 1 Box 138 - Hwy. 59, Lancaster, MN 56735. Phone: (218)762-4100.
- Noyes Port of Entry, Rural Rt. 1 - Box 110, Noyes, MN 56740. Phone: (218)823-6291.
- Pembina Border Patrol, Rural Rt. 1 - P.O. Box 106, Noyes, MN 56740. Phones: (218)823-6528, -6594.
- Pine Creek Port of Entry, Hwy. 89, Star Rt. 5, Roseau, MN 56751. Phone: (218)463-1952.
- Roseau Port of Entry, Rt. 1 Box 31 - Hwy. 310 N., Roseau, MN 56751. Phone: (218)463-2054.
- Warroad Port of Entry, H.C. 02, P.O. Box 245, Warroad, MN 56763. Phone: (218)386-1676.
- Warroad Border Patrol, P.O. Box 24, Hwy. 11, Warroad, MN 56763. Phone: (218)386-1802.

Mississippi—Gulfport Border Patrol, P.O. Box 4273, Gulfport, MS 39502. Phone: (228)863-3582.

- Gulfport Port of Entry, P.O. Box 1120, Gulfport, MS 39501. Phone: (601)864-3029.

Missouri—Kansas City District Office, 9747 N. Conant Ave., Kansas City, MO 64153. Phone: (816)891-0864.

97.010 (cont.)

- St. Louis Sub-Office, Young Federal Bldg. - Rm.100, 1222 Spruce St., St. Louis, MO 63103-2815. Phone: (314)539-2516.
- St. Louis International Airport, Lambert Field, P.O. Box 10406, St. Louis, MO 63145. Phone: (314)425-7179.

Montana—Piegan Port of Entry, P.O. Box 109, Babb, MT 59411. Phone: (406)732-9297.

- Chief Mountain Port of Entry, P.O. Box 376, Chief Mountain, MT 59411 via Babb, MT 59411. Phone: (406)732-4576.
- Billings Border Patrol, 2601 1st Ave. N., P.O. Box 2298, Billings, MT 59103. Phone: (406)247-7563.
- Del Bonita Port of Entry, Del Bonita Star Rt., Cut Bank, MT 59427. Phone: (406)336-2130.
- Eureka Border Patrol, Hwy. 93 (JB Shopping Center), P.O. Box 909, Eureka, MT 59917. Phone: (406)296-2938.
- Roosville Port of Entry, 8395 Hwy. 93 N., Eureka, MT 59917-9331. Phone: (406)889-3737.
- Havre Border Patrol Sector Hdqtrs., 2605 5th Ave. SE, P.O. Box 112, Havre, MT 59501. Phone: (406)265-6781.
- Wild Horse Port of Entry, Havre, MT 59501. Phone: (406)394-2371.
- Willow Creek Port of Entry, Simpson Rt., Havre, MT 59501. Phone: (406)398-5512.
- Havre Port of Entry, Simpson Rt., Willow Creek Station, Havre, MT 59501. Phone: (406)265-6781.
- Loring Port of Entry, Port of Morgan, HC82 - Box 9250, Loring, MT 59537-9600. Phone: (406)674-5248.
- Malta Border Patrol, P.O. Box 36, Malta, MT 59538. Phone: (406)654-2711.
- Opheim Port of Entry, P.O. Box 317, Opheim, MT 59250. Phone: (406)724-3212.
- Plentywood Border Patrol, P.O. Box 434, Plentywood, MT 59254. Phone: (406)765-1852.
- Raymond Border Patrol, P.O. Box 158, Raymond, MT 59256. Phone: (406)895-2620.
- Scobey Border Patrol, P.O. Box 820, Scobey, MT 59263. Phone: (406)487-2621.
- Scobey Port of Entry, P.O. Box 2300, Scobey, MT 59263. Phone: (406)783-5372.
- Shelby Border Patrol, 906 Oilfield Ave., P.O. Box 653, Shelby, MT 59474. Phone: (406)434-5588.
- Sweetgrass Port of Entry, P.O. Box 165 - Interstate 15, Sweetgrass, MT 59484. Phone: (406)335-2911.
- Whitetail Port of Entry, U.S. Border Inspection Station, P.O. Box 38, Whitetail, MT 59276. Phone: (406)779-3531.

Nebraska—Nebraska Service Center, 850 S. St., P.O. Box 82521, Lincoln, NE 68501-2521. Phone: (402)437-5464.

- Omaha District Office, 3736 S. 132nd St., Omaha, NE 68144. Phone: (402)697-9152.

Nevada—Boulder City Border Patrol, Boulder City, NV 89006-0928. Phone: (702)293-8507.

- Las Vegas Sub-Office, 3373 Pepper Lane, Las Vegas, NV 89120. Phone: (702)388-6640.
- Las Vegas Mecarren International Airport, 5757 Wayne Newton Blvd., Las Vegas, NV 89111. Phone: (702)388-6024.
- Reno Sub-Office, 1351 Corporate Blvd., Reno, NV 89502. Phone: (702)784-5186.

New Hampshire—Pittsburg Port of Entry, Rt. 3, P.O. Box 277, Pittsburg, NH 03592. Phone: (819)656-2261.

New Jersey—Newark District Office, Federal Bldg., 970 Broad St., Newark, NJ 07102. Phone: (201)645-2298.

- Newark International Airport, Terminal B (SAT 3), Newark, NJ 07114. Phone: (201)645-6589.

New Mexico—Alamagordo Border Patrol, 1997 Hwy. 54 S., Alamagordo, NM 88310-7377. Phone: (505)437-6960.

- Albuquerque Sub-Office, 517 Gold Ave. SW - Rm.1010, P.O. Box 567, Albuquerque, NM 87103. Phone: (505)248-7357.
- Columbus Port of Entry, Pershing Rd. - P.O. Box 307, Columbus, NM 88029. Phones: (505)531-2694, -2695, -2696.
- Deming Border Patrol, P.O. Box 230, Deming, NM 88031. Phone: (505)546-9036.
- Las Cruces Border Patrol, 3120 N. Main, Las Cruces, NM 88001. Phone: (505)527-6895.
- Las Cruces Patrol Training Center, 2320 Temple St., Las Cruces, NM 88001. Phone: (505)524-4730.
- Lordsburg Border Patrol, 441 Duncan Hwy., P.O. Box 459, Lordsburg, NM 88045. Phone: (505)542-3221.
- Truth or Consequences Border Patrol, P.O. Box 3310, Truth or Consequences, NM 87901. Phone: (505)744-5235.

New York—Albany Sub-Office, U.S. Post Office and Customhouse - Rm.220, 445 Broadway, Albany, NY 12207. Phone: (518)431-0339.

- Thousand Island Bridge and Cape Vincent Ports of Entry, 46735 U.S. Interstate Rt. 81, Alexandria Bay, NY 13607-9796. Phones: (315)482-2681, -2065, 654-2781, ext.8.
- Buffalo District Office, 130 Delaware Ave., Buffalo, NY 14202. Phone: (716)846-4741.
- Burke Border Patrol, Burke, NY 12917-0125. Phone: (518)483-5941.
- Champlain Port of Entry, Border Inspection Station, 234 W. Service Rd., Champlain, NY 12919. Phones: (518)298-3221, -8433, -2526.
- Champlain Border Patrol, P.O. Box 1228, Ridge Rd., Champlain, NY 12919. Phone: (518)298-2531.
- Chateaugay Port of Entry, Border Inspection Station, Star Rt. 374, Chateaugay, NY 12920. Phone: (518)497-6772.
- Trout River Port of Entry, Trout River, State Rt. 30, Via Constable, NY 12926. Phone: (518)483-5021.
- Ft. Covington Port of Entry, Border Inspection Station, Water St., Ft. Covington, NY 12937. Phone: (518)358-2231.
- Fulton Border Patrol Station, 215 S. 1st St. - Rm.228, Fulton, NY 13069-0070. Phone: (315)598-8510.
- Office of Inspector General, JFK Airport Station, P.O. Box 999, Jamaica, NY 11430. Phone: (718)553-7520.
- JFK International Airport, Bldg. 50 - International Arrivals, Jamaica, NY 11430. Phones: (718)553-1688, -1689.
- Lewiston Port of Entry, 1 Lewiston Queenston Bridge, Lewiston, NY 14092-1980. Phone: (716)285-1676.
- Mooers Port of Entry, Border Inspection Station, State Rt. 22, Mooers, NY 12958. Phone: (518)236-7116.

97.010
(cont.)

- New York District Office, 26 Federal Plaza, New York, NY 10278. Phone: (212)264-3911.
- Service Processing Center, 201 Varrick St. - 4th fl., New York, NY 10014. Phone: (212)620-3441.
- Niagara Falls Port of Entry, Rainbow Bridge, Niagara Falls, NY 14303. Phone: (716)282-3141.
- Niagara Falls Border Patrol, 1708 Lafayette Ave., Niagara Falls, NY 14305-0281. Phone: (716)285-6444.
- Ogdensburg Border Patrol, 127 N. Water St., Ogdensburg, NY 13669. Phones: (315)393-1150, -0100.
- Massena Port of Entry, P.O. Box 195, Roosevelt, NY 13683. Phones: (315)764-0310, -0677.
- Rouse Point Port of Entry, U.S. Rt. 9B, Rouse Point, NY 12979. Phone: (518)297-7521.
- Buffalo Border Patrol Sector Hdqtrs., 231 Grand Island Blvd., Tonawanda, NY 14150-6502. Phone: (716)551-4101.
- Watertown Border Patrol, Post Office Bldg., 153 Arsenal St., Watertown, NY 13601-0280. Phone: (315)482-7556.

North Carolina—Charlotte Sub-Office, 6 Woodlawn Green - Rm.138, Charlotte, NC 28217. Phone: (704)344-6313.

- Raleigh-Durham International Port of Entry, P.O. Box 80216, Raleigh, NC 27623. Phone: (919)840-5577.
- Wilmington Port of Entry, Lennon Federal Bldg. - Rm.105, 2 Princess St., Wilmington, NC 28401. Phone: (910)343-4876.

North Dakota—Ambrose Port of Entry, State Hwy 42, Rt. HC-1 - Box 202, Ambrose, ND 58833. Phone: (701)982-3211.

- Antler Port of Entry, Rural Rt. 1 - Box 7, Antler, ND 58711. Phone: (701)267-3321.
- Bottineau Border Patrol, P.O. Box 6, Bottineau, ND 58318. Phone: (701)228-3179.
- Carbury Port of Entry, Rural Rt. 1 - Souris, ND, Carbury, ND 58783. Phone: (701)228-2540.
- Dunseith Port of Entry, Rural Rt. 1 - Box 117, Dunseith, ND 58329. Phones: (701)263-4513, -4460.
- Northgate Port of Entry, Flaxton, ND 58737. Phone: (701)596-3805.
- Fortuna Port of Entry, Hwy. 85N - P.O. Box 37, Fortuna, ND 58844. Phone: (701)834-2493.
- Grand Forks Border Patrol Sector Hdqtrs., 2320 S. Washington St., Grand Forks, ND 52801. Phone: (701)775-6259. *For mail:* P.O. Box 12669, Grand Forks, ND 58208-2669.
- Grand Forks International Airport, Rural Rt. 2 - Box 72, 2787 Airport Dr., Hwy. 2 W., Grand Forks, ND 58203. Phone: (701)772-3301.
- Hannah Port of Entry, Hannah, ND 58239. Phone: (701)283-5271.
- Hansboro Port of Entry, Box 237, Hansboro, ND 58339. Phone: (701)266-5633.
- Maida Port of Entry, Hwy. 1, Maida, ND 58255. Phone: (701)256-5087.
- Neche Port of Entry, Hwy. 18, Neche, ND 58265. Phone: (701)886-7744.
- Noonan Port of Entry, Noonan, ND 58765. Phone: (701)926-5615.
- Pembina Port Of Entry, Rural Rt. 1 - P.O. Box 110, Noyes, Pembina, ND 58271. Phone: (701)825-6722.
- Portal Border Patrol, P.O. Box 298, Portal, ND 58772. Phone: (701)926-4111.
- Portal Port of Entry, P.O. Box 8, Portal, ND 58772. Phone: (701)926-4221.

- Sherwood Port of Entry, Rural Rt. 2 - Box 1D, Sherwood, ND 58782. Phone: (701)459-2250.
- St. John Port of Entry, Box 15 - Rt. 1, St. John, ND 58369. Phone: (701)447-3140.
- Sarles Port of Entry, P.O. Box 67 - Rt. 1, 6 miles from Village of Sarles, ND 58372. Phone: (701)697-5177.
- Walhalla Port of Entry, Rural Rt. 2 - Box 145, Walhalla, ND 58282-9459. Phone: (701)549-3233.

Ohio—Cleveland District Office, Celebreeze Federal Bldg. - Rm.1917, 1240 E. 9th St., Cleveland, OH 44199. Phone: (216)522-4766.

- Toledo Port of Entry, Federal Office Bldg. - Rm.713, 234 Summit St., Toledo, OH 43604-1536. Phone: (419)259-6474.

Oklahoma—Oklahoma Sub-Office, 4149 Highline Blvd. - Ste. 300, Oklahoma City, OK 73108. Phone: (405)231-5928.

Oregon—Astoria Port of Entry, P.O. Box 236, Astoria, OR 97103. Phone: (503)325-3054.

- Coos Bay Port of Entry, P.O. Box 209, Coos Bay, OR 97420. Phone: (503)242-4785.
- Portland District Office, 511 NW Broadway, Portland, OR 97209. Phone: (503)326-3962.
- Portland International Airport, P.O. Box 55067, Portland, OR 97238-5067. Phone(503)326-3409.
- Roseburg Border Patrol, 1036 SE Douglas, P.O. Box 1728, Roseburg, OR 97470. Phone: (503)440-4518.

Pennsylvania—Philadelphia District Office, 1600 Callowhill St., Philadelphia, PA 19130. Phone: (215)656-7150.

- Pittsburg Sub-Office, 2130 Federal Bldg., 1000 Liberty Ave., Pittsburgh, PA 15222. Phone; (412)385-4457.

Puerto Rico—Aquadilla Service Processing Center, P.O. Box 250480, Aquadilla, PR 00604-0408. Phones: (787)882-3565, -3567, -3568.

- Deferred Inspections, U.S. Federal Bldg. - Rm.380, Chardon St., Hato Rey, PR 00918. Phone: (809)766-5000.
- District Director's Office, New Federal Bldg. - 3rd fl., Carlos Chardon St., Hato Rey, PR 00918. Phone: (no number provided).
- San Juan International Airport, P.O. Box 37900, Isle Verde, PR 00937-0900. Phone: (809)253-4525.
- Mayaguez Port of Entry, Marina Station, Mayaguez, PR 00709-2990. Phone: (809)831-3440.
- Ponce Port of Entry, Playa Station, P.O. Box 173, Ponce, PR 00734-3173. Phone: (809)843-3220.
- San Juan District Office, P.O. Box 365068, San Juan, PR 00936. Phone: (787)766-5514.

Rhode Island—Providence Sub-Office, 200 Dyer St., Providence, RI 02903-3993. Phones: (401)528-5528, -5323.

South Carolina—Charleston Port of Entry, Federal Bldg. - Rm.110, 334 Meeting St., Charleston, SC 29403. Phone: (803)727-4421.

Tennessee—Memphis Sub-Office, 245 Wagner Place - Ste. 250, Memphis, TN 38103-3815. Phone: (901)544-4108.

Texas—Abilene Border Patrol, 555 Walnut St., Abilene, TX 79604-3076. Phone: (915)673-3010.

- Alpine Border Patrol, P.O. Box 958, Alpine, TX 79831. Phone: (915)837-3550.
- Amarillo Border Patrol, P.O. Box 2287, Amarillo, TX 79105. Phone: (806)324-2278.

97.010 ***(cont.)***

- Austin Sub-Office, 3708 S. 2nd St., P.O. Box 6496, Austin, TX 78704. Phones: (512)482-7901, -7904.
- Big Bend Park Border Patrol, P.O. Box 67, Big Bend, TX 79834. Phone: (915)477-2287.
- Brackettville Border Patrol, 802 W. Spring St., P.O. Box 216, Brackettville, TX 78832. Phone: (830)563-2477.
- Brownsville Port of Entry, 1500 E. Elizabeth St. - Rm.203, Brownsville, TX 78520. Phone: (210)546-1675.
- Brownsville International Airport, Brownsville, TX 78520. Phone: (210)542-8296.
- Brownsville Border Patrol, P.O. Box 5076, Brownsville, TX 78520. Phone: (956)542-3585.
- Carrizo Springs Border Patrol, Hwy. 85 E., P.O. Box 194, Carrizo Springs, TX 78834. Phone: (830)876-3557.
- Corpus Christi Border Patrol, 6809 Leopard St., P.O. Box 10344, Corpus Christi, TX 78460-0344. Phone: (512)289-0552.
- Comstock Border Patrol, Hwy. 85 E. - P.O. Box 700, Comstock, TX 78837. Phones: (915)292-4450, -4680.
- Cotulla Border Patrol, 692 N. Main, Cotulla, TX 78014. Phone: (830)879-3051.
- Dallas District Office, 8101 N. Stemmons Freeway, Dallas, TX 75247. Phone: (214)655-3011.
- Dallas/Ft. Worth Port of Entry, P.O. Box 610365, Dallas-Ft. Worth, TX 75261. Phone: (214)574-2141.
- Del Rio Border Patrol Sector Hdqtrs. and Border Station, Qualia Dr., Del Rio, TX 78841-2020. Phone: (210)703-2100.
- Amistad Dam Port of Entry, Del Rio, TX 78841-4060. Phone: (210)775-7213.
- Eagle Pass Port of Entry, International Bridge, P.O. Box 4280, Eagle Pass, TX 78852. Phones: (210)773-9205, -9206.
- El Paso District Office, 1545 Hawkins - Ste. 167, El Paso, TX 79925. Phones: (915)540-1700, -1701.
- Processing Center, 8915 Montana Ave., El Paso, TX 79925. Phone: (915)225-1941.
- Office of Inspector General, 3 Butterfield Trail Blvd. - Ste. 120, El Paso, TX 79906. Phone: (915)534-7370.
- El Paso Border Patrol Sector Hdqtrs., 8901 Montana Ave., P.O. Box 9578, El Paso, TX 79986. Phone: (915)834-8350.
- Intelligence Center, 11339 SSG Sims St., El Paso, TX 79908-8098. Phone: (915)760-2031.
- El Paso Port of Entry, Paso Del Norte Bridge, El Paso, TX 79901. Phone: (915)534-6767.
- Dallas Border Patrol, 2800 S. Pipeline Rd., Euless, TX 76040. Phone: (817)540-0150.
- Fabens Border Patrol and Port of Entry, 802 E. Main, P.O. Box 908, Fabens, TX 79838. Phones: (915)764-2417, -2419.
- Falfurrias Border Patrol, P.O. Box 479, Falfurrias, TX 78355. Phone: (512)325-5616.
- Ft. Hancock Border Patrol, P.O. Box 218, Ft. Hancock, TX 79839. Phone: (915)769-3978.
- Ft. Hancock Port of Entry, P.O. Box 235, Ft. Hancock, TX 79839. Phone: (915)769-3810.
- Ft. Stockton Border Patrol, P.O. Box 607, Ft. Stockton, TX 79735. Phone: (915)336-2468.

- Freer Border Patrol, P.O. Box "W", Freer, TX 78357. Phone: (512)394-7613.
- Galveston Port of Entry, P.O. Box 388, Galveston, TX 77550. Phone: (409)766-3581.
- Harlingen District Office, 2102 Teege Rd., Harlingen, TX 78550. Phone: (210)427-8691.
- Harlingen Border Patrol, 901 Rangerville Rd., P.O. Box 642, Harlingen, TX 78551. Phone: (956)427-8511.
- Hebbronville Border Patrol, 802 N. Sigrid St., Hebbronville, TX 78361. Phone: (512)527-3256.
- Pharr Port of Entry, 99105 Cage Blvd. - Ste. C, Pharr, TX 78557-9723. Phones: (956)783-4739, -4758.
- Hidalgo Port of Entry, International Bridge, Hidalgo, TX 78557-3019. Phones: (210)843-2201, -2202.
- Houston Intercontinental Airport, P.O. Box 60457, Houston, TX 77205. Phone: (713)233-3700.
- Kingsville Border Patrol, Navel Air Station - Bldg.3731, Kingsville, TX 78363. Phone: (512)592-3284.
- Laredo Border Patrol Sector Hdqtrs., 207 W. Del Mar Blvd., Laredo, TX 78041. Phone: (956)723-4367.
- Laredo South Border Patrol Station, Rural Rt. 3 - P.O. Box USBP-SLS/L, Laredo, TX 78043. Phone: (210)727-0644.
- Administrative Offices - Bldg. 2, 700 Zaragoza St., P.O. Box 179, Laredo, TX 78042-0179. Phone: (210)722-3283.
- Juarez-Lincoln International Bridge 2, Bldg. 3 - 700 Zaragoza St., Laredo, TX 78042. Phone: (512)722-5440.
- Gateway to the Americas International Bridge 1, 100 Convent St., Laredo, TX 78040. Phone: (210)722-2484.
- Llano Border Patrol, 211 E. Tarrant, P.O. Box 134, Llano, TX 78643. Phone: (915)247-4912.
- Los Ebanos Port of Entry, International Ferry, P.O. Box 399, Los Ebanos, TX 78565. Phone: (512)485-2721.
- Port Isabel Service Processing Center, Rt. 3 - Box 341, Los Fresnos, TX 78566. Phone: (210)548-2530.
- Port Isabel Border Patrol, Rt. 3 - Box 340, Los Fresnos, TX 78566. Phone: (956)233-9554.
- Port Isabel Port of Entry, Alien Processing Center (PIC), Rt. 3 - Box 341, Buena Vista Rd., Los Fresnos, TX 78566. Phone: (210)233-4431.
- Lubbock Border Patrol, 1205 Texas Ave., P.O. Box 1632, Lubbock, TX 79408. Phone: (806)742-7355.
- Marfa Border Patrol Sector Hdqtrs., 300 Madrid St., P.O. Box 1, Marfa, TX 79843. Phone: (915)729-4353.
- McAllen Border Patrol Sector Hdqtrs., 2301 S. Main St., McAllen, TX 78503. Phone: (210)686-5496. *For mail:* P.O. Box 1179, McAllen, TX 78502.
- McAllen Border Patrol, 4201 W. Military Hwy., McAllen, TX 78503. Phone: (210)618-8163.
- Mercedes Border Patrol, 623 International Blvd., P.O. Box 125, Mercedes, TX 78570. Phone: (956)968-0602.
- Midland Border Patrol Station, P.O. Box 60405, Midland, TX 79711. Phone: (915)561-8911.
- Presidio Border Patrol, P.O. Box 929, Presidio, TX 79845. Phone: (915)229-3330.

97.010 *(cont.)*

- Presidio Port of Entry, International Bridge, P.O. Box 937, Presidio, TX 79845. Phones: (915)229-3265, -3663.
- Port Arthur Port of Entry, 4550 Jimmy Johnson Blvd. - Ste. 3, Port Arthur, TX 77642. Phone: (409)727-3375.
- Port Arthur Port of Entry, 2875 75th St. - Rm.106, Port Arthur, TX 77640. Phone: (409)727-3375.
- Rio Grande City Border Patrol, 2230 E. Highway, P.O. Box 481, Rio Grande City, TX 78582. Phone: (956)487-2700.
- Rocksprings Border Patrol, 404 W. Austin, P.O. Box 576, Rocksprings, TX 78880. Phone: (830)683-2255.
- Falcon Heights Port of Entry, International Dam, P.O. Box 278, Roma, TX 78584. Phone: (210)848-5221.
- Rio Grande City Port of Entry, International Bridge, P.O. Box 278, Roma, TX 78584. Phones: (210)487-2200, 849-1676.
- San Angelo Border Patrol, P.O. Box 61106, San Angelo, TX 76906. Phone: (915)949-0139.
- San Antonio District Office, 8940 Four Winds Dr., San Antonio, TX 78239. Phone: (210)967-7109.
- San Antonio Border Patrol, 5000 N. Industrial Dr., San Antonio, TX 78268. Phone: (210)521-7926.
- San Antonio International Airport, 9800 Airport Blvd., Terminal 1, San Antonio, TX 78216. Phone: (210)826-6261.
- Sanderson Border Patrol, P.O. Box 628, Sanderson, TX 78268. Phone: (915)345-2972.
- Uvalde Border Patrol, Industrial Park #30, Uvalde, TX 78801. Phone: (830)278-7133.
- Van Horn Border Patrol, 700 NW Access Rd., P.O. Box 368, Van Horn, TX 79854. Phone: (915)283-2795.
- Progreso Port of Entry, International Bridge Rt. 2, Box 600, Westlaco, TX 78596. Phone: (210)565-6304.
- Zapata Border Patrol, Lot C-2015, U.S. Hwy. 83 S., Zapata, TX 78076-0685. Phone: (210)765-6395

Utah—5272 S. College Dr. - Ste. 100, Salt Lake City, UT 84123. Phone: (801)265-8807.

Vermont—Alburg Springs Port of Entry, Rural Rt. 2, Alburg, VT 05440. Phone: (802)796-3704.

- Alburg Port of Entry, U.S. Border Station, State Rt. 225, Alburg, VT 05440. Phone: (802)796-3703.
- Beebe Plain Port of Entry, Beebe Plain, VT 05823. Phone: (802)873-3151.
- Beecher Falls Border Patrol, P.O. Box 215, Beecher Falls, VT 05902. Phones: (802)266-3035 (24 hours).
- Beecher Falls Port of Entry, Border Inspection, Route 102, Beecher Falls VT 05902. Phone: (802)266-3320.
- Canaan Port of Entry, Border Inspection Station, State Rt. 114, P.O. Box 129, Canaan, VT 05903. Phone: (802)266-8994.
- Derby Line Port of Entry, Rt. 91 - P.O. Box 367, Derby Line, VT 05830. Phone: (802)873-3316.
- East Richford Port of Entry, RFD 1 - P.O. Box 1690, East Richford, VT 05476. Phone: (802)848-3001.
- West Berkshire Port of Entry, RFD 1 - Box 1110, Enosburg Falls, VT 05450. Phone: (802)933-2301.

- Morses Line Port of Entry, RFD 1, Morses Line, VT 05457. Phone: (802)285-2214.
- Newport Border Patrol, P.O. Box 815, Newport, VT 05855. Phone: (802)334-6722.
- North Troy Port of Entry, State Rt. 105, North Troy, VT 05859. Phone: (802)988-2633.
- Norton Port of Entry, Border Inspection Station, State Rt. 114, P.O. Box 117, Norton, VT 05907. Phone: (802)822-5222.
- Richford Border Patrol, Main St., P.O. Box 67, Richford, VT 05476. Phone: (802)848-7713.
- Pinnacle Port of Entry, R.D. 1 - Box 300, Richford, VT 05476. Phone: (802)848-3319.
- Richford Port of Entry, Border Inspection Station, RFD 1 - Box 40, Richford, VT 05476. Phone: (802)848-7766.
- Eastern Region Operations and Administrative Center, 70 Kimball Ave., South Burlington, VT 05403-6813. Phones: (802)660-5000, 660-1111.
- St. Albans Sub-Office, Federal Bldg., P.O. Box 328, St. Albans, VT 05478. Phone: (802)527-3191.
- Eastern Service Center, 75 Lower Welden St., St. Albans, VT 05479-0001. Phone: (802)527-3100.
- Swanton Border Patrol Sector Hdqtrs., Grand Ave., P.O. Box 705, Swanton, VT 05488. Phone: (802)868-3361.
- Highgate Springs Port of Entry, Border Inspection Station, U.S. Rt. 7, RFD Swanton, VT 05488. Phone: (802)868-3349.
- Swanton Border Patrol Station, Rt. 78 - P.O. Box 209, Swanton, VT 05488. Phones: (802)868-3229, -3320 (24 hours).
- Eastern Form Center, Williston, VT 05495-0567. Phone: (802)951-6225.

Virgin Islands—Charlotte Amalie, St. Thomas, VI Sub-Office, Nisky Center - 1st fl.(Ste. 1A), Charlotte Amalie, St. Thomas, VI 00801. Phone: (809)774-1390.

- Christiansted St. Croix Port of Entry, P.O. Box 1270 Kingshill, Christiansted, St. Croix, VI 00851. Phones: (809)778-6559, -6300.
- Cruz Bay Port of Entry, P.O. Box 450, Cruz Bay, St. John, VI 00831. Phone: (340)776-6390.

Virginia—Washington District Office, 4420 N. Fairfax Dr., Arlington, VA 22203. Phone: (202)307-1504.

- Norfolk Sub-Office, Norfolk Federal Bldg. - Rm.439, 200 Granby Mall, Norfolk, VA 23510-1882. Phone: (804)441-3095.

Washington—Bellingham Border Patrol, 2745 McLeod Rd., Bellingham, WA 98225. Phone: (360)733-8420. *For mail:*P.O. Box 31428, Bellingham, WA 98228-3428.

- Bellingham Border Port of Entry, 104 W. Magnolia and Cornall St. - Rm.207, P.O. Box 2055, Bellingham, WA 98227. Phones: (360)676-8411 (downtown), 734-3520 (airport).
- Blaine Border Patrol Sector Hdqtrs., 1590 H St., P.O. Box 3529, Blaine, WA 98231. Phones: (360)332-7707, -7919.
- Blaine Border Patrol, 1580 H St., P.O. Box 3529, Blaine, WA 98231. Phone: (360)332-4205.
- Pacific Hwy. Port of Entry, 9950 Pacific Hwy., Blaine, WA 98230. Phones: (360)332-6091, -7237.
- Blaine Port of Entry, Peace Arch POE, 100 Peace Portal Dr., Blaine, WA 98230. Phone: (360)332-8511.
- Colville Border Patrol, 209 E. Juniper Ave., P.O. Box 146, Colville, WA 99114. Phone: (509)684-6272.

97.010 ***(cont.)***

- Boundary Port of Entry, 5338 N. Port Juanita Rd., Colville, WA 99114. Phone: (509)732-4470.
- Ferry Port of Entry, 3559 Toroda Customs Bridge Rd., Curlew, WA 99118-9715. Phone: (509)779-4655 (Customs).
- Danville Port of Entry, 19130 N. Highway 21, Danville, WA 99121-9704. Phone: (509)779-4860.
- Friday Harbor Port of Entry, Staffed by Customs, 202 Front St. N., P.O. Box 1907, Friday Harbor, WA 98250. Phone: (206)378-2080.
- Laurier Port of Entry, Hwy. 395 - P.O. Box 40, Laurier, WA 99146. Phone: (509)684-2100.
- Longview Port of Entry, P.O. Box 1027, Longview, WA 98632. Phone: (206)423-5550.
- Nighthawk Port of Entry, Star Rt., Loomis, WA 98827. Phone: (509)476-2125.
- Lynden Border Patrol, 8334 Guide Meridian Rd., P.O. Box 708, Lynden, WA 98264. Phone: (360)354-4118.
- Lynden Port of Entry, 9949 Guide Meridian Rd., Lynden, WA 98264. Phone: (206)354-6661.
- Metaline Falls Port of Entry, P.O. Box 631, Metaline Falls, WA 99153. Phone: (509)446-2572.
- Frontier Port of Entry, 4939 Hwy. 25 N., Northport, WA 99157. Phone: (509)732-4418.
- Oroville Port of Entry, Rt. 1 - Box 130, Oroville, WA 98844. Phones: (509)476-2454, -3132.
- Oroville Border Patrol, 1105 Main St., P.O. Box 99, Oroville, WA 98844-9726. Phone: (509)476-3622.
- Vancouver-BC Canada, Point Roberts, WA 98281-0450. Phones: (604)278-3360, -3986, -2520.
- Port Angeles Border Patrol, 138 W. 1st St., Port Angeles, WA 98362. Phone: (360)452-5970.
- Port Townsend Port of Entry, Staffed by Customs, 1322 Washington, P.O. Box 951, Port Townsend, WA 98368-0004. Phone: (360)385-3777.
- Seattle District Office and Sea Inspections, 815 Airport Way S., Seattle, WA 98134. Phones: (206)553-1246, -0070.
- Seattle-Tacoma International Airport, S. 178 and Pacific Hwy., Seattle, WA 98158. Phones: (206)553-0466, -2299.
- Spokane Airport and Sub-Office, 691 U.S. Courthouse Bldg., Spokane, WA 99201. Phones: (509)353-2761, -4699.
- Spokane Border Patrol, N. 10710 Newport Hwy., Spokane, WA 99218. Phone: (no number provided).
- Sumas Port of Entry, 109 Cherry St., P.O. Box 99, Sumas, WA 98295. Phone: (360)988-4781.
- Tacoma Port of Entry, 3600 Port Tacoma Rd. - Ste. 303, P.O. Box 1296, Tacoma, WA 98401. Phone: (206)922-0848.
- Wenatchee Border Patrol, McQuaig Bldg., 93 Eastmont, P.O. Box 1825, Wenatchee, WA 98807. Phone: (509)884-8893.
- Yakima Port of Entry, 417 E. Chestnut, P.O. Box 49, Yakima, WA 98907. Phone: (509)575-5944.

Wisconsin—Federal Bldg. - Rm.186, 517 E. Wisconsin Ave., Milwaukee, WI 53202. Phone: (414)297-3161.

U.S. COAST GUARD

97.011 DISTRICT OFFICES

ATLANTIC *(Alabama, Arkansas, Colorado, Connecticut, Delaware, District of Columbia, Florida, Georgia, Illinois, Indiana, Iowa, Kansas, Kentucky, Louisiana, Maine, Maryland, Massachusetts, Michigan, Minnesota, Mississippi, Missouri, Nebraska, New Hampshire, New Jersey, New Mexico, New York, North Carolina, North Dakota, Ohio, Oklahoma, Panama Canal Zone, Pennsylvania, Puerto Rico, Rhode Island, South Carolina, South Dakota, Tennessee, Texas, Vermont, Virgin Islands, Virginia, West Virginia, Wisconsin, Wyoming)*—Commander (md), Maintenance and Logistics Command (Atlantic), 300 E. Main St. - Ste. 800, Norfolk, VA 23510. Phone: (757)628-4280.

PACIFIC *(Alaska, Arizona, California, Hawaii, Idaho, Montana, Nevada, Oregon, U.S. Pacific Island Possessions, Utah, Washington)*—Commander (md), Maintenance and Logistics Command (Pacific), Coast Guard Island, Bldg. 52, Alameda, CA 94501-5100. Phone: (510)437-3474.

97.014 District Bridge Administrator:

First Coast Guard District (obr), 408 Atlantic Ave., Boston, MA 02210-2209. Phones: (617)223-8364; FAX (617)223-8026.

- Battery Park Bldg. (obr), New York, NY 10004-5073. Phones: (212)668-7165; FAX (212)668-7967.

Western River Directorate (obr), 1222 Spruce St., St. Louis, MO 63103-2398. Phones: (314)539-3900; FAX (314)539-3755.

Fifth Coast Guard District (Aowb), Federal Bldg., 431 Crawford St., Portsmouth, VA 23704-5004. Phones: (757)398-6557; FAX (757)398-6334.

Seventh Coast District (oan), Brickell Plaza, 909 SE 1st Ave., Miami, FL 33130-3050. Phones: (305)415-6743; FAX (305)415-6757.

Eighth Coast Guard District (obc), Boggs Federal Bldg., 501 Magazine St., New Orleans, LA 70130-3396. Phones: (504)589-2965; FAX (504)589-3063.

Ninth Coast Guard District (obr), 1240 E. 9th St., Cleveland, OH 44199-2060. Phones: (216)902-6085; FAX (216)902-6088.

Eleventh Coast Guard District (oan-2), Bldg. 10 - Rm.50-6, Alameda, CA 94501-5100. Phones: (510)437-3514: FAX (510)437-5836.

Thirteenth Coast Guard District (ob), Federal Bldg., 915 2nd Ave., Seattle, WA 98174-1067. Phones: (206)220-7270; FAX (206)220-7285.

Fourteenth Coast Guard District (oan), Federal Bldg. - Rm.9139, 300 Ala Moana Blvd., Honolulu, HI 96850-4982. Phones: (808)541-2315; FAX (808)541-2318.

Seventeenth Coast Guard District (oan), Juneau, AK 99802-5517. Phones: (907)463-2268; FAX (907)463-2273.

UNITED STATES SECRET SERVICE

97.015 *Regional or local field offices are located in most state capitals and in some other cities. Consult local phone directory for addresses and phone numbers, or contact headquarters office directly (see main entry).*

FEDERAL EMERGENCY MANAGEMENT AGENCY

97.017 thru 97.070 REGIONAL OFFICES

REGION I—99 High St. - 6th fl., Boston, MA 02110. Phone: (617)223-9540.

REGION II—26 Federal Plaza - Rm.1307, New York, NY 10278-0002. Phone: (212)680-3600.

REGION III—615 Chestnut St., Philadelphia, PA 19106. Phone: (215)931-5608.

REGION IV—3003 Chamblee-Tucker Rd., Atlanta, GA 30341. Phone: (770)220-5200.

REGION V—536 S. Clark St., Chicago, IL 60605. Phone: (312)408-5500.

REGION VI—Federal Regional Center, 800 N. Loop 288, Denton, TX 76201-3698. Phone: (940)898-5399.

REGION VII—2323 Grand Blvd. - Ste. 900, Kansas City, MO 64108-2670. Phone: (816)283-7061.

REGION VIII—Federal Center - Bldg. 710, Denver, CO 80225-0267. Phone: (303)235-4800.

REGION IX—1111 Broadway - Ste. 1200, Oakland, CA 94607. Phone: (510)627-7100.

REGION X—Federal Regional Center, 130 - 228th St. SW, Bothell, WA 98021-9796. Phone: (425)487-4600.

AGENCY INDEX

NOTE: Entries cover administrative units and sub-units, referring to program numbers used in Parts II, III, and IV (explained in Part I under "Organization of the Federal Programs".)

MASTER INDEX

NOTES

Index entries refer to program numbers used in Part II. The program numbering system is explained on page 11.

- Italicized program *numbers* indicate programs that provide financial assistance. (Assistance classifications are explained on page 3.) Examples:

  ABANDONED MINE LAND RECLAMATION (AMLR) PROGRAM, *15.252*
  Women, Infants, and Children (WIC) Program, *10.557*

- Subject headings are in bold-face type. Examples:

  Adult education
  Wildlife, waterfowl

- Program titles are in capital letters. Bracketed agency identifiers are inserted when the title inadequately describes program focus. Examples:

  BUSINESS AND INDUSTRY LOANS [USDA], *10.768*

  GENERAL RESEARCH AND TECHNOLOGY ACTIVITY [HUD], *14.506*

- Also provided are (1) popular and abbreviated program titles, (2) government departments and independent agencies, (3) names of Acts, (4) section and title numbers of Acts when in general usage, and (5) entries with general references and cross-references to program activities and governmental sub-entities. Examples:

  (1) Age Search, 11.006
  VBOP (Veterans Business Outreach Centers), SBA, *59.044*

  (2) Department of Defense (DOD), 12.002 through 12.910
  Environmental Protection Agency (EPA), 66.001 through 66.952

  (3) AIDS Housing Opportunity Act, *14.241*

  (4) Section 22, Water Resources Development Act, 12.110
  Title I, ESEA, migrants, *84.011*

  (5) Acid precipitation research, NOAA, *11.432, 11.459*
  Brownfield projects, *see* Urban renewal
  National Institute on Drug Abuse (NIDA), NIH, 93.279

Remarks on using the index are offered in Part I in the section on "Obtaining Federal Assistance," under "STEP ONE: USE THE MASTER INDEX."